Effective Practices in Early Childhood Education

Building a Foundation

Sue Bredekamp

Early Childhood Education Consultant

PEARSON

Boston Columbus Indianapolis New York San Francisco
Upper Saddle River Amsterdam Cape Town Dubai London
Madrid Milan Munich Paris Montréal Toronto Delhi Mexico City
São Paulo Sydney Hong Kong Seoul Singapore Taipei Tokyo

Vice President and Editorial Director: Jeffery W. Johnston
Executive Editor: Julie Peters
Editorial Assistant: Pamela DiBerardino
Development Editor: Linda Bishop
Director of Marketing: Margaret Waples
Executive Product Marketing Manager: Chris Barry
Executive Field Marketing Manager: Krista Clark

Program Manager; Megan Moffo
Production Project Manager: Janet Domingo
Senior Art Director: Diane Lorenzo
Cover Art: iofoto/Shutterstock; Monkey Business/Fotolia; and Nenov Brothers Images/Shutterstock
Full-Service Project Management: Lumina Datamatics, Inc.
Composition: Lumina Datamatics, Inc.

Credits and acknowledgments for material borrowed from other sources and reproduced, with permission, in this textbook appear on the appropriate page within the text.

Every effort has been made to provide accurate and current Internet information in this book. However, the Internet and information posted on it are constantly changing, so it is inevitable that some of the Internet addresses listed in this textbook will change.

Library of Congress Cataloging-in-Publication Data
Bredekamp, Sue.
 Effective practices in early childhood education : building a foundation / Sue Bredekamp, Early Childhood Education Consultant. — Third edition.
    pages cm
Includes bibliographical references and index.
 ISBN 978-0-13-395670-2—ISBN 0-13-395670-9 1. Early childhood education—United States. 2. Child development—United States. I. Title.
LB1140.23.B72 2015
372.21—dc23

2015029580

10 9 8 7 6 5 4 3 2 1

PEARSON

Student Edition
ISBN 10:   0-13-395670-9
ISBN 13: 978-0-13-395670-2

Loose-Leaf Version
ISBN 10:   0-13-411549-X
ISBN 13: 978-0-13-411549-8

REVEL eBook
ISBN 10:   0-13-430324-5
ISBN 13: 978-0-13-430324-6

Dedication

To Joe Bredekamp, for a lifetime of love, friendship, wonderful memories, and tolerance of craziness, and to Darby whose unconditional love enriches our lives every day.

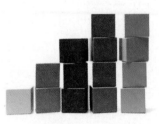

About the author

Dr. Sue Bredekamp is an early childhood education specialist from the Washington, D.C., area who serves as a consultant on developmentally appropriate practice, curriculum, teaching, and teacher education for state and national organizations such as NAEYC, Head Start, the Council for Professional Recognition, and Sesame Street. From 1981 to 1998, she was Director of Accreditation and Professional Development for NAEYC where she developed and directed their national accreditation system for early childhood centers and schools. Dr. Bredekamp is the editor of NAEYC's best-selling, highly influential publication, *Developmentally Appropriate Practice in Early Childhood Programs.*

Dr. Bredekamp is Chair of the Board of the HighScope Educational Research Foundation. She was a member of the National Research Council's (NRC) Committee on Early Childhood Mathematics, which produced a landmark report, *Mathematics in Early Childhood: Paths toward Excellence and Equity.* Dr. Bredekamp serves on several advisory boards and is a frequent keynote speaker and author of numerous books and articles related to standards for professional practice and teacher education. She has been a visiting lecturer at Macquarie University in Sydney, Australia; Monash University in Melbourne; University of Alaska; and University of Hawaii. She holds a PhD in Curriculum and Instruction from the University of Maryland. The McCormick Center for Early Childhood Leadership at National Louis University recognized Dr. Bredekamp with its Visionary Leadership Award in 2014. For 45 years, Dr. Bredekamp has worked for and with young children toward the goal of improving the quality and effectiveness of early childhood education programs.

About the contributor

Dr. Kathleen (Kate) Cranley Gallagher is an educational psychologist and scientist at Frank Porter Graham Child Development Institute at University of North Carolina at Chapel Hill. She is a Clinical Associate Professor in the School of Education at UNC, where she teaches undergraduate and graduate early childhood professionals. Dr. Gallagher has herself been an early childhood professional for over 30 years; she has taught in and administered diverse programs for children birth to 8 years of age, with and without disabilities. Dr. Gallagher's publications and applied work focus on developing, implementing and evaluating evidence-based interventions to support social-emotional well-being and development for young children, their families and early childhood professionals. Dr. Gallagher has served on state advisory panels, developing standards and assessments for early childhood education and health and is a founding member of the North Carolina Infant Mental Health Association. She developed *Be Well to Teach Well,* a program designed to support the well-being and of early childhood professionals. Dr. Gallagher is an accomplished teacher and frequently invited speaker nationally, and presented a keynote address at the *International Preschool Teachers' Conference* in Hangzhou, China as a guest of Zhejiang Normal University. She delivered a TEDx talk, entitled, *The Healthy Child: Assembly Required* in which Dr. Gallagher argued that the single most important feat of construction that our society undertakes is the assembly required to build physically, emotionally, cognitively, and socially healthy children. She lives in Carrboro, North Carolina, with her husband, John, and enjoys time with her two adult children, Jack and Bridget.

In the previous editions of this book, I described the challenge of my first day of teaching preschool in a child care center many years ago. It was the hardest job I have ever had, primarily because my bachelor's degree in English did not prepare me for it. I didn't know enough about child development, how and what to teach, how to communicate with families, how to positively guide children's behavior—the list goes on and on. Feeling completely incompetent, I seriously thought about not going back the next day. Then I realized that although I had a choice not to return, the children did not. They deserved a better teacher than I was at that time. As a result, I continued teaching, went back to school, and set out to learn as much as possible about child development and how best to teach young children. And I have been learning ever since. In short, my initial motivation in writing this book was a personal one—to help ensure that new teachers get off to a better start than I did and that the children do, too.

In the decades since I entered the early childhood profession, however, there has been an explosion of new knowledge and research, and a huge increase in public recognition and support for early education. A great many parents, policy makers, and researchers now consider early childhood programs essential for fostering school readiness and long-term success in life. Economists and business leaders consider high-quality child care and early education a necessary investment in the future of our country. Nobel Prize–winning economist James Heckman believes that investing in early education is a cost-effective strategy that will improve educational and health outcomes, strengthen the economy, help solve America's social problems, and produce a more capable, productive workforce.

But the power of early education depends on the quality of interactions teachers have with children, and the effectiveness of their instructional practices. To achieve their potential, children need and deserve highly competent, well-educated teachers. My goal in writing this book is to help all teachers, whether beginning or continuing their professional journeys, gain access to the exciting new knowledge about child development, engaging and challenging curriculum content, and effective ways of teaching. Today, our profession has a deep responsibility to meet the expectations of families, the general public, and policy makers and to fulfill the promise that has been made to children.

My hope is that every teacher embraces new knowledge as well as the enduring values of early childhood education, and encounters the sheer joy of teaching young children. Every child needs and deserves a highly qualified teacher from day one.

 # New to This Edition

This is the first edition of *Effective Practices in Early Childhood Education: Building a Foundation* offered in REVEL™.

REVEL™ is Pearson's newest way of delivering our respected content. Fully digital and highly engaging, REVEL offers an immersive learning experience designed for the way today's students read, think, and learn. Enlivening course content with media interactives and assessments, REVEL empowers educators to increase engagement with the course, and to better connect with students.

REVEL offers:

Dynamic content matched to the way today's students read, think, and learn

- **Integrated Videos and Interactive Media** Integrated within the narrative, videos empower students to engage with concepts and take an active role in learning. REVEL's unique presentation of media as an intrinsic part of course content brings the hallmark features of Pearson's bestselling titles to life.

- **Quizzing and Short-Answer Response Opportunities** Located throughout REVEL, quizzing affords students opportunities to check their understanding at regular intervals before moving on. Quizzes are in multiple-choice and short-answer response formats.

- **Chapter Quiz** "Demonstrate Your Learning" end-of-chapter multiple-choice questions allow students to check their understanding on chapter concepts.

Additional Significant Changes to this Edition

- A new feature, "Promoting Play," in every chapter addressing a different issue related to supporting children's learning through play or protecting children's right to play. See the Special Features page at the end of the Table of Contents for a list of all of the feature topics by chapter.

- Revised Chapter 3 with examination of current issues such as the Common Core State Standards and accountability through the lens of developmentally appropriate practice.

- New sections on the implications of the Common Core State Standards for curriculum and teaching in preschool through grade 3 in Chapter 10 on planning curriculum, Chapter 11 on assessment, Chapter 12 on language and literacy, and Chapter 13 on mathematics.

- Updated Chapter 1 with discussion of new policy initiatives, changing demographics, new research on the effectiveness of early education, and trends in the field.

- Updated Language Lenses on research-based classroom practices for effectively teaching dual language learners.

- New examples of developmentally appropriate use of digital media with children, teachers, and families throughout the text.

- Reorganized content by moving sections on developmentally appropriate learning environments, materials, and schedule to Chapter 3, Developmentally Appropriate Practice.

- Reorganized Chapter 10, Planning Effective Curriculum, to include discussion of Reggio Emilia.

- Updated research and new examples of effective practices for children with diverse abilities, particularly children with autism spectrum disorder.
- Expanded discussion of current research on brain development and executive function and implications for teaching.
- New artifacts and examples of children's work, especially from children in the primary grades.

Book Organization Reflects *Guidelines for Developmentally Appropriate Practice*

This book is designed to teach the concept of *developmentally appropriate practice* for students because an understanding of its principles is the foundation on which to build early childhood programs and schools for children from birth through age 8. Chapters are organized according to NAEYC's guidelines for developmentally appropriate practice, which I have coauthored for 30 years.

Part 1, Foundations of Early Childhood Education, describes the current profession and the issues and trends effecting it today (Chapter 1), the rich history from which developmentally appropriate practices evolved (Chapter 2), and an overview of its principles and guidelines, which are described in depth in later chapters (Chapter 3).

Part 2, Dimensions of Developmentally Appropriate Practice, includes chapters describing the key factors teachers must consider as they make professional decisions. Chapter 4 presents an overview of current knowledge about how all children develop and learn. Chapter 5 addresses the unique, individual differences among children, including children with diverse abilities. Chapter 6 discusses the critical role of social, cultural, and linguistic contexts on all children's development and learning and how teachers must embrace a diverse society to help every child succeed in school and life.

Part 3, Intentional Teaching: How to Teach, describes the role of the teacher in implementing developmentally appropriate practices. Each of the interconnected aspects of the teacher's role is addressed in separate chapters: building effective partnerships with families (Chapter 7), creating a caring community of learners and guiding young children (Chapter 8); teaching to enhance learning and development (Chapter 9); planning effective curriculum (Chapter 10); and assessing children's learning and development (Chapter 11).

Part 4, Implementing an Effective Curriculum: What to Teach, describes both *how* and *what to teach* children from birth through age 8 in language, literacy, the arts, mathematics, science, technology, social-emotional development, social studies, physical development, and health. Each chapter demonstrates how the continuum of children's development determines the appropriateness of curriculum content and intentional, effective teaching strategies for children of different ages.

Early childhood educators join this profession and stay in it because they believe their work can make a difference in the lives of children and their families. But to make a lasting difference, our practices must be effective—they must contribute to children's learning and development. This book reflects this core goal by building on the basic framework of developmentally appropriate practice while going beyond to emphasize intentional teaching, challenging and interesting curriculum, and evidence-based, effective practices for a new generation of early childhood educators. Each of these key themes is discussed on the following pages.

Intentional Teaching of Young Children

This text builds on the framework of developmentally appropriate practice emphasizing that effective teachers are intentional, thoughtful, and purposeful in everything they do.

Intentional teachers know not only what to do with children but also why they are doing it and can explain the rationale for the decisions they make to other teachers, administrators, and families. To help students understand this concept, **Becoming an Intentional Teacher** features reveal what teachers are thinking in classroom situations, *how* and *why* they select the strategies they do, and challenge students to reflect further on these scenarios.

Becoming an Intentional Teacher
Teaching in the "Zone"

Here's What Happened In my kindergarten, we are working on the basic mathematical number operations—adding and subtracting. In our classroom, children work in centers for part of the morning. Through assessments that I do during center time, I learned that Miguel can add two single-digit numbers on his own. I also learned that he is struggling with subtracting single-digit numbers, but is successful when I talk through the subtraction activities with him. I also observed that Miguel is able to subtract more successfully when the problem is applied, such as when he is playing cashier and giving "change" in our Home Improvement Store center. Miguel especially likes to play there because his Dad works in construction. I decided on a three-pronged approach to support his understanding and application of subtraction:

1) I set aside 5–10 minutes twice a week to work individually with Miguel. Using manipulatives, including an abacus and small counting trains. Miguel loves trains! During this time, I verbally support Miguel's grouping and counting, using short word problems and number cards.
2) I also intentionally join Miguel and other children in the Home Improvement Store at center time. I introduce the concept of "Supply Lists" to the center, using cards with pictures and labels of the different supplies. Children can add nuts, bolts, and tools to their baskets, according to the list, and return (subtract) things they no longer need for their building projects. As Miguel purchases and returns items for his building project, I support and make explicit his adding and subtracting, pointing out to Miguel how successfully he uses math for his project.
3) Finally, during the morning math challenge, I pair Miguel with a friend who understands subtraction concepts well, and is very verbal. I have them work together to solve the problem, explaining each of their steps.

After about two weeks of this more intensive approach, Miguel demonstrates ability to subtract single-digit numbers on his own, and begins to experiment with double-digit numbers. He insists on being the employee at checkout in the Home Improvement Store to showcase his adding and subtracting.

Here's What I Was Thinking As a kindergarten teacher, I know that understanding and applying these foundational mathematical concepts is essential for building children's later competence in math. I also understand that children learn best in the context of supportive relationships, and I structure interactions in my classroom to intentionally support each learner. I do this by: (1) assessing each child's level of independent performance on a skill, (2) assessing each child's level of supported (with help) performance on a skill, and (3) developing lessons that allow a child to practice in their supported level, until the child can do the skill independently. I then set the next higher level of skill as the child's goal skill.

Vygotsky used the term zone of proximal development (ZPD) to describe the child's skill level when supported by an adult or more experienced peer. He believed that by assessing only what a child knows, a teacher does not have information on how to support the child's progress. But by assessing a child's ZPD, I am able to structure for progressive development and learning.

Reflection How did this teacher use assessment to guide her intentional teaching? What other strategies could she have used to teach Miguel in his Zone of Proximal Development?

So we see that in meeting the children, Frida seamlessly draws on her knowledge of child development and learning, as well as her knowledge of them as individuals and members of cultural groups. Precisely because children are so different and their abilities vary so greatly, Frida will need to draw from a wide repertoire of teaching strategies to help them achieve developmentally appropriate goals.

So far we have described the areas of knowledge that teachers consider in making decisions about developmentally appropriate practice—what teachers need to know and think about. Now we turn to the work of the teachers—what do early childhood teachers do? What are the dimensions of practice that describe the teacher's role?

✓ **Check Your Understanding 3.3:** Developmentally Appropriate Decision Making

 The Complex Role of the Teacher

According to the NAEYC's (2009) guidelines for developmentally appropriate practice, the complex job of an early childhood teacher has five interrelated dimensions: (1) creating a caring community of learners, (2) teaching to enhance learning and development, (3) planning curriculum to achieve important goals, (4) assessing children's learning and development, and (5) establishing reciprocal relationships with families.

Effective teachers are informed decision makers who adapt for individual differences, including for children with disabilities and special needs. **Check Your Understanding** features engage students in assessing their own learning. Some questions involve critical thinking about a complex teaching situation or issue confronting the early childhood field. These quizzes appear only in REVEL™ and include feedback.

✓ Demonstrate Your Learning
Click here to assess how well you've learned the content in this chapter.

Readings and Websites

Carter, M., & Curtis, D. (2014). *Designs for living and learning: Transforming early childhood environments.* St. Paul, MN: Redleaf Press.

Copple, C., & Bredekamp, S. (Eds.). (2009). *Developmentally appropriate practice in early childhood programs serving children from birth through age 8* (3rd ed.). Washington, DC: National Association for the Education of Young Children.

Epstein, A. S. (2014). *The intentional teacher: Choosing the best strategies for young children's learning* (Rev. ed.). Washington, DC: National Association for the Education of Young Children.

ASCD Whole Child Initiative
This website provides resources promoting elementary education that supports all areas of children's development and learning.

National Association for the Education of Young Children
NAEYC's website has a special section on resources for developmentally appropriate practice and play, plus copies of all their position statements.

ZERO to THREE—National Center for Infants, Toddlers, and Families
This website provides resources and practical tips for working with infants, toddlers, and their families.

Intentional teachers must reflect and apply their knowledge using a broad repertoire of effective teaching strategies. **Demonstrate Your Learning** features at the end of each chapter require students to practice these skills. This end-of-chapter quiz appears only in REVEL™ and includes feedback.

Current Research on Effective Practices

In an era of Common Core State Standards and Early Learning standards, accountability, and rapid change in the field, the text makes research understandable and meaningful for students and illustrates the connections between child development, curriculum content, assessment, and intentional teaching.

What Works features present research-based practices in action, including descriptions of demonstrated effective practices such as teaching mathematics to dual language learners, father involvement, and using evidence-based curriculum to narrow the achievement gap.

Lens features present insights on culture, language, and including all children. These features discuss practice through diverse *lenses*, expanding the sources of information teachers use to make decisions and helping them look at questions or problems from broader perspectives. Widening the lens with which teachers view their practice is a strategy to move beyond the persistent educational tendency to dichotomize difficult or controversial issues into "either/or" choices, and move toward "both/and" thinking.

- Current research findings, such as effective strategies for teaching dual language learners or children with autism spectrum disorder, are brought to life and made meaningful by connections to classroom and community examples.
- The terms and definitions used in this text contribute to establishing a shared vocabulary for all of those in and entering the field.
- Approximately 40% of the references are from 2012 and beyond.

Connections between Curriculum and Child Development

Unlike many early childhood texts that focus on child development only, this text shows how child development and curriculum content knowledge are connected.

In the **Developmental Continuum** feature, the text provides an overview of the continuum of learning in the areas of language, literacy, mathematics, and cognitive, social, emotional, and physical development and describes how child development is linked to curriculum planning for children from birth through age 8.

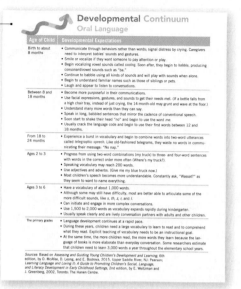

- Chapters 12 to 15 help early childhood teachers understand right from the start that there is content in the curriculum for young children. They describe the goals for young children's learning and development that predict success in school and life. Each of these chapters includes examples of effective strategies such as teaching children of diverse abilities in inclusive classrooms or ways to promote dual language learning.

A new feature, **Promoting Play**, presents new research on the important role of play in development and effective strategies to help children learn through play or protect their right to play. These features address play across the full age range, from birth through age 8. Discussions of play are also integrated in each chapter throughout this book as an effective means to support all domains of development and promote learning in all curriculum areas. Today many people are concerned about how the standards movement is negatively impacting play. We often hear statements such as "We can't let children play because we have to teach literacy," or "We don't have time for outdoor play in primary grades because we have to get children ready for standardized tests." Play should not be treated as a separate part of an early childhood program or day that can be cut if someone deems it unimportant. Therefore, you will find a discussion of play in every chapter of this book.

- The emphasis on implementing effective curriculum reflects current trends such as the goal of aligning prekindergarten and primary education, NAEYC accreditation and CAPE professional preparation standards, and enhanced expectations for teacher qualifications as described in the 2015 report, *Transforming the Workforce for Children Birth through Age 9: A Unifying Foundation* by the Institute of Medicine and the National Research Council.

Over more than four decades in early childhood education, I have had the privilege of working with and learning from countless friends, colleagues, teachers, and children. This book would not have been possible without the help and encouragement of the following people:

My deepest appreciation goes to Kathleen Cranley Gallagher, my collaborator on this edition, who revised Chapters 4, 5, 7, 8, 11, 14, and 15. Kate's vast experience with children, with and without disabilities, as well as her research on children's social-emotional development and mental health greatly inform this edition. Kate contributed research and effective practices on early intervention, teaching children with autism spectrum disorder, and other cutting-edge topics. Without Kate's help, I can't imagine completing this work in a timely fashion.

I especially wish to thank Carol Copple, with whom I have collaborated on *Developmentally Appropriate Practice in Early Childhood Programs* for several decades, and who contributed features as well as invaluable assistance in conceptualizing aspects of the book. Thanks also to Laura Colker for her overwhelming generosity, sharing of ideas, and gracious support.

I want to acknowledge Carol Brunson Day for teaching me so much about diversity, anti-bias education, and cultural influences on development. Her work contributed greatly to the Culture and Language Lens features and Chapter 6.

Thank you to Gail E. Joseph, who was especially helpful on the first edition, and many of her contributions are still present in Chapters 5 and 14 and the Including All Children lenses.

Thanks to my longtime friend Kay M. Albrecht, who contributed to Chapter 15 and provided numerous examples from her extensive classroom experience.

I wish to thank Linda Espinosa and Luis Hernandez for helping ensure that the book reflects the most current research and practical examples for teaching dual language learners.

Close colleagues whose wisdom and encouragement have educated and sustained me for decades include Marilyn Smith, J. D. Andrews, Barbara Willer, and Barbara Bowman. My deepest gratitude goes to Sharon Lynn Kagan for writing the foreword to this edition. The debt is never paid to the late Carol Seefeldt, who taught the first early childhood course I ever took and mentored me through my dissertation. I hope that my work continues to reflect her vision.

A sincere thank you and acknowledgment of support to Arlington Public Schools (APS) in Arlington, Virginia. Those assisting in the effort include: Arlington Public Schools administrative personnel Regina Van Horne, Lisa Stengle, and Linda Erdos; K. W. Barrett Elementary principal, Mr. Dan Redding; and K. W. Barrett instructional staff Joshua McLaughlin, Anastasia Erickson, Emily Sonenshine, Stephanie Shaefer, Judy Concha, Jennifer Flores, Elizabeth Jurkevics, and Richard Russey. Also, a big thanks to those students and their parents who allowed us to use the student artwork and artifacts found in this book.

I am also grateful to the many other schools, teachers, and administrators who welcomed me as an observer, shared examples, and contributed artifacts, including: Cathy Polanski, Second Grade, Arcola Elementary School; Hoaliku Drake Preschool, Kamehameha Schools Community-Based Early Childhood Education; the Center for Young Children at the University of Maryland; The Shoenbaum Family Center in Columbus, Ohio, including Anneliese Johnson; Wickliffe Progressive Community School and the Jentgen family; Linden, New Jersey, Public Schools; Far Hills Country Day School in Far Hills, New Jersey; the HighScope Demonstration Preschool in Ypsilanti, Michigan; and Easter Seals Blake Children's Achievement Center in Tucson, Arizona.

I continue to be indebted to Julie Peters, my editor at Pearson, for contributing her wealth of knowledge about early childhood teacher education, and her unwavering support for my work. I also wish to thank Linda Bishop for leading me through the development of an Interactive eText for the first time. Thanks also for the creative contributions to the first edition of Max Effenson Chuck and Kelly Villella Canton.

My life and work continue to be inspired by Patty Smith Hill, founder of NANE, whose vision for early childhood education laid the foundation for NAEYC's commitment to developmentally appropriate practice.

I would also like to thank the many reviewers who contributed to the development of this book. They are: Margaret Charlton, Tidewater Community College; Jody Eberly, The College of New Jersey; Amy Howell, Central Oregon Community College; Claire Lenz, St. Joseph's College; Marilyn Roseman, Mount Aloysius College; and Lois Silvernail, Spring Hill College.

Instructor Supplements

The following instructor tools supplement, support, and reinforce the content presented throughout the text. All supplements are available for download for instructors who adopt this text. Go to http://www.pearsonhighered.com, click "Educators," register for access, and download files. For more information, contact your Pearson representative.

- **Online Instructor's Manual** (013402687X). The *Instructor's Resource Manual* provides chapter-by-chapter tools to use in class. Lecture or discussion outlines, teaching strategies, in-class activities, student projects, key term definitions, and helpful resources will reinforce key concepts and applications and keep students engaged.
- **Online Test Bank** (0134026756). These multiple-choice and essay questions tied to each chapter provide instructors the opportunity to assess student understanding of the chapter content. An answer key is provided.
- **Online PowerPoint™ Slides** (0134026829). Each slide reinforces key concepts and big ideas presented throughout the text.
- **TestGen** (013402673X). This powerful test generator contains the same items that are in the Online Test Bank, but you may add or revise items. Assessments may be created for print or testing online. You install TestGen on your personal computer (Windows or Macintosh) and create your own tests for classroom testing and for other specialized delivery options, such as over a local area network or on the web.

The tests can be downloaded in the following formats:

TestGen Testbank file - PC • TestGen Testbank file - MAC • TestGen Testbank - **Blackboard 9** TIF • TestGen Testbank - **Blackboard CE/Vista (WebCT)** TIF • **Angel** Test Bank • **D2L** Test Bank • **Moodle** Test Bank • **Sakai** Test Bank

Like all Sue Bredekamp's work, *Effective Practices in Early Childhood Education: Building a Foundation* has become a landmark. Since its publication, it has been the major benchmark against which all volumes related to early childhood practice are measured, domestically and internationally. Indeed, it has been a driving force, not only guiding practice and scholarship, but also serving as a seminal vehicle to codify and chronicle the impact of history, the experiences of practitioners and leaders, and the impact of policy on the changing field of early education. In so doing, it has converted static assumptions and understandings about early childhood pedagogy into living, dynamic, and far more intentional practices.

Since its appearance, *Effective Practices* has been widely read and used to guide early childhood teacher preparation and practice. Its popularity has placed a special burden on the work; it, like the field, cannot remain stagnant or isolated from changes in the social context. Precisely because it is so well used and because the field is changing so rapidly, a new edition is necessary. Consider for example, the impact that the emergence of the K–12 Common Core has had on early education: whether one favors or disparages the Common Core ideologically, it is here to stay and is having profound impacts on American education generally, and American early education specifically. In addition, the revitalization of an emphasis on continuity and transition, emerging currently in the form of the "P–3 Movement," is altering the way early educators conceptualize and actualize the linkages between pre-primary and primary education. Within the birth to 5-year-old component of early childhood, a renewed emphasis on supporting the infrastructure through the Early Learning Challenge Fund, with its focus on Quality Rating and Improvement Systems, standards, and assessments, is precipitating dramatic changes in the way early childhood education services are being designed and delivered. Finally, new research related to the way children learn and process information is calling forth compelling pedagogical alignments that address the importance of dual language learners, executive functioning, early mathematics, and learning progressions.

With the early childhood field changing so rapidly, time-honored questions are being catapulted to new prominence, often begging for urgent response: What should be the balance between cognitive development and other domains historically important to early childhood? What should be the balance between a focus on learning processes and content? What should be the balance between teacher-guided, intentional pedagogy and child-guided experiential learning? Note that none of these questions is new and that each recognizes the critical importance of balance.

Indeed, the majesty of this volume is that it, too, understands and addresses the importance of the contemporary context and the balance in perspective and practice it demands. In this volume, Bredekamp takes a long-haul view; she renders solid definitions of the field, situating the reader firmly in reality, and provides one of the most thorough historical overviews available. But Bredekamp does not stop there, nor does she skirt the tough issues, the new research, or the new demands being placed on early educators. Rather, with clarity and grace, she systematically addresses them all, setting before the field a rich compendium of research, firsthand and extremely well-cultivated practice, and ever-wise counsel. Readers will be impressed by the currency, practicality, and clear intentionality of the volume, evoking the same from those who regard it with the care with which it was written.

Of particular importance in this ever-changing and increasingly connected world is the role of culture and language. Bredekamp addresses these issues with honesty and integrity, treating readers to a richly nuanced understanding of the important roles of each in the development of young children. Cautiously, she reminds us that the words "developmentally appropriate"—although bywords of the profession—must be deeply contextualized in order to be understood and mastered. Indeed, in discussing how to balance developmentally, individually, and contextually appropriate practices, Bredekamp brilliantly notes that "a child with a disability acts like a magnifying glass on the developmental appropriateness of an early childhood classroom." In turn, early educators must regard this seminal edition as the best possible lens through which to see and enlarge what matters most in our field; with wisdom and prescience, it sheds all the light necessary to advance our evolving, joyous profession and our critically important work on behalf of children, their families, and their countries.

Sharon Lynn Kagan, Ed.D.
Virginia and Leonard Marx Professor of Early Childhood and Family Policy,
Teachers College, Columbia University;
and Professor Adjunct, Yale University's Child Study Center

Brief Contents

Table of Contents

Part 4 Implementing an Effective Curriculum: What to Teach 378

Special Features

Tables—Effective Practices

Continuity and Change in Early Childhood Education

Learning Outcomes

After studying this chapter, you should be able to:

1.1 Define early childhood education.

1.2 Describe the career options of early childhood educators and the dimensions of intentional, effective teaching.

1.3 Explain high-quality early childhood education and how it is measured.

1.4 Report research about the positive effects of early childhood education.

1.5 Analyze the current trends affecting early childhood education.

© Kali9/E+/Getty Images

At Cresthaven Primary School, teachers, children, and family members of all generations are viewing children's work and sharing memories during the year-end celebration. This public school serves children from age 3 to grade 3, through a partnership with Reed Child Development Center nearby. The Reed Center provides state-funded preschool classrooms for 3- and 4-year-olds who will attend Cresthaven as well as before- and after-school care and child care for infants and toddlers.

The preschoolers are in awe of the "big school" where they will attend kindergarten and are excited to see their work displayed in the hallway. "Look, Mommy! Here's my painting of the yellow fish," cries 4-year-old Amber as she tugs on her mother's hand. "See where I wrote my name. And here's Brenda's picture. She's my new best friend." Amber's mother smiles and tries to read what her daughter wrote: "I lk fsh." The teacher, Ms. Engels, comes up and says, "Amber knows a lot about writing and letters. She can write her name, and she is starting to write the consonants she hears in words."

For several years, Cresthaven School has been involved with its neighbors in a community garden project. In each class, the teachers connect the larger curriculum—especially science and social studies goals—to aspects of the garden project. Six-year-old Sergio and his grandmother walk down the hall to find the list of all the meals the kindergartners prepared with the vegetables they harvested. He exclaims, "And tonight, we get to eat strawberries!" Meanwhile, first-grader Mathias quietly explains to some parents, "Me and my friends made this graph. It shows the vegetables the kids liked most." Third-grader Carola describes her class project to her father. "You'll like this, Dad. For social studies, we're figuring out where food comes from and why it costs so much."

The second-grade teacher, Ms. George, gets everyone's attention. "Our class is going to present their video of the garden project in 15 minutes." Seven-year-old Kelsey takes 75-year-old Mrs. Carrero by the hand and invites her to see the show. The children share most of the food raised in the garden with elderly neighbors such as Mrs. Carrero. "I'll show you the chapter book I can read, too," says Kelsey.

Four-year-old Cooper, who has autism, has been in Ms. Watson's class for 2 years. His mother comes up and quietly whispers to Ms. Watson, "I wanted you to know that Cooper got invited to Martie's birthday party. I never thought that would happen, but he's made more progress here than I ever imagined."

As she's leaving, Nicky's mom stops to thank Isela and Evan, who are finishing their first year of teaching 2-year-olds. They remember their struggles with Nicky's tantrums as he hugs his mom's leg and playfully peeks around at Evan. She says, "I know he is growing up and has to move to preschool, but we are really going to miss you two." ■

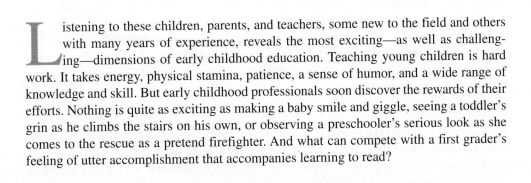

Listening to these children, parents, and teachers, some new to the field and others with many years of experience, reveals the most exciting—as well as challenging—dimensions of early childhood education. Teaching young children is hard work. It takes energy, physical stamina, patience, a sense of humor, and a wide range of knowledge and skill. But early childhood professionals soon discover the rewards of their efforts. Nothing is quite as exciting as making a baby smile and giggle, seeing a toddler's grin as he climbs the stairs on his own, or observing a preschooler's serious look as she comes to the rescue as a pretend firefighter. And what can compete with a first grader's feeling of utter accomplishment that accompanies learning to read?

Early childhood education is a rewarding profession for many reasons. We describe the diverse field of early childhood education and discuss its rewards in this chapter. We also discuss why early childhood education is a field on the rise and what the current trends are that present both challenges and opportunities. We also describe how, in a period of rapid change, the early childhood profession continues to be shaped by its enduring values. Above all, early childhood educators enter and stay in the field primarily for one reason—they know that their work makes a difference in the lives of children and families.

🏠 What Is Early Childhood Education?

early childhood education Education and child care services provided for children from birth through age 8.

Early childhood education is a highly diverse field that serves children from birth through age 8. During these years, children participate in many different kinds of care and education settings. Regardless of where they work or what their specific job titles are, however, early childhood teachers are **professionals**. This means that they make decisions based on a specialized body of knowledge, continue to learn throughout their careers, and are committed to providing the best care and education possible for every child. The opportunity to make a difference in this exciting field has never been greater.

professionals Members of an occupational group that make decisions based on a specialized body of knowledge, continue to learn throughout their careers, and are committed to meeting the needs of others.

Why Early Childhood Education Is a Field on the Rise

Early childhood education benefits greatly from increasing public recognition, respect, and funding. In fact, a bipartisan poll reported that 86% of American voters believe that "ensuring children get a strong start in life" should be a national priority, second only to increasing job opportunity and growing the economy (First Five Years Fund, 2014). A Gallup poll found that 70% of voters supported federal funding to make high-quality preschool programs available for all children (Jones, 2014). Although higher percentages of Democrats and Independents supported such funding, a majority of Republicans were also in favor.

Forty states—as diverse as Oklahoma, Georgia, New Mexico, New York, Illinois, Massachusetts, Tennessee, and Florida—provide funding for prekindergarten programs (Barnett, Carolan, Squires, & Brown, 2013). Continued funding even in challenging economic times reflects growing public recognition of the benefits of early education, especially for children at risk of later school failure, but also for middle-class children. A great many policy makers, parents, and researchers now consider early childhood programs essential for fostering school readiness and long-term success in life (Barnett, 2013a). Groups such as the prestigious Committee for Economic Development (2012) consider quality child care and early education a necessary investment in the future of our country. A powerful advocate for early education, Nobel Prize–winning economist James Heckman (2013) believes that investing in early education is a cost-effective strategy that will improve educational and health outcomes, strengthen the economy, help solve America's social problems, and produce a more capable, productive workforce.

Early education is also considered an effective crime-prevention strategy. A prestigious group of America's police officers and prosecutors call themselves, "the guy you pay later" because America's failure to pay for quality services for young children increases the costs of the criminal justice system (Fight Crime: Invest in Kids, 2014).

Several factors have contributed to the rise in status of early childhood education. These include an impressive body of research on the positive effects of early childhood programs and concerns about the persistent achievement gap in our schools. Next, we examine the overall landscape of the field, including the types of settings where children are served.

National Association for the Education of Young Children (NAEYC) The world's largest organization of early childhood educators, whose mission is to act on behalf of the needs and interests of children from birth through age 8. NAEYC establishes standards for teacher preparation and accreditation of early childhood programs.

The Landscape of Early Childhood Education

Although early childhood terminology is not uniform across diverse settings, throughout this text we will use vocabulary that is consistent with that used by the **National Association for the Education of Young Children (NAEYC)** and that we feel best represents the present and future of the field. NAEYC, headquartered in Washington, D.C., is the world's largest professional organization of early childhood educators. Founded in 1926, NAEYC's mission is to act on behalf of the needs, rights, and well-being of all young children from birth through age 8.

One way the association achieves its mission is by establishing standards for teacher preparation at the associate, baccalaureate, and graduate-degree levels (NAEYC, 2011b). NAEYC's standards have considerable influence in the field; it is likely that the course you are now taking is designed to meet the association's teacher education standards. NAEYC (2008b) also administers an accreditation system for high-quality children's programs and provides resources such as publications and conferences to support teachers' continuing professional development.

Given NAEYC's definition of the field—birth through age 8—early childhood teachers work with various groups:

1. *Infants and toddlers:* birth to 36 months
2. *Preschoolers:* 3- and 4-year-olds
3. *Kindergartners:* 5- and 6-year-olds
4. *Primary grades 1, 2, and 3:* 6-, 7-, and 8-year-olds.

Because early childhood is defined so broadly, the field encompasses child care centers and homes, preschools, kindergartens, and primary grade schools. Figure 1.1 provides an illustration of the various settings where young children are educated and cared for. Young children are always learning, and they always need loving care. Therefore, it is important *not* to distinguish child care from early education, but rather to ensure that all children have access to programs that are both caring and educational, regardless of the length of day or who provides the service.

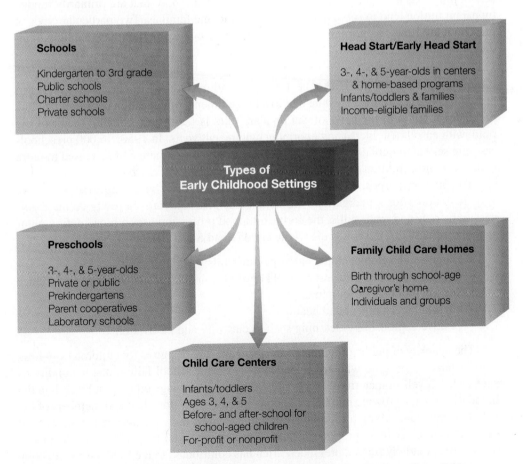

FIGURE 1.1 Types of Early Childhood Settings Early childhood education is a diverse field because young children's care and education occurs in a variety of settings as depicted here.

Child Care The term *child care* typically refers to care and education provided for young children during the hours that their parents are employed. To accommodate work schedules, child care is usually available for extended hours, such as from 7:00 A.M. to 6:00 P.M. In some settings, such as hospital-affiliated child care centers, care is offered for longer hours to accommodate evening, weekend, or even night-shift employment.

Child care is typically provided in two types of group programs: **child care centers** and **family child care homes**. In either setting, children's care may be privately funded by parent tuition or publicly subsidized for low-income families. Child care centers usually enroll children from infancy through preschool-age children, and many also offer before- and after-school care for primary grade children. In family child care homes, caregivers provide care in their own homes for a small group of children, often of varying ages. Family child care is the setting of choice for many parents of infants and toddlers because of its home-like atmosphere.

Preschool **Preschool** programs, as the name implies, serve 3- and 4-year-olds prior to their entrance into kindergarten. Preschool programs may be operated by community organizations or by churches, temples, or other faith-based organizations and also by **parent cooperatives**, which are run and partially staffed by groups of parents. Preschools often operate half-day, although extended hours—the school day—are becoming more common. Some colleges and universities operate **laboratory schools**, which usually serve children of students and faculty and also act as models for student teachers.

Preschools are called by various names, including *nursery schools* and *prekindergartens*. (To further complicate matters, child care centers are also called preschools.) Preschool programs are both privately and publicly funded. Those that are primarily funded by parent tuition tend to serve middle- or upper-income families. Two particular types of preschool are designed primarily for children from low-income families: public prekindergarten and Head Start.

Public Prekindergarten The term **prekindergarten (pre-K)** usually refers to preschools that are funded by state and local departments of education. Currently, public prekindergarten is in the news media regularly and is the fastest-growing sector of the field, with enrollment increasing enormously in recent years. In 1980, 96,000 preschoolers were served in public elementary schools; in 2012, enrollment had increased to more than 1.3 million children across 40 states (Barnett, Carolan, et al., 2013).

The primary purpose of prekindergarten is to improve **school readiness**; that is, to prepare children for kindergarten. Although some state officials narrowly define readiness as literacy and math skills, the early childhood profession uses a broad definition of school readiness that describes the whole child (Head Start, 2015):

- Language development and early literacy skills
- Cognitive development and general knowledge, including mathematics and science
- Social-emotional development
- Physical development and health
- Positive approaches to learning such as curiosity and motivation

The majority of public prekindergarten programs are designed for children from low-income families or those who are considered at risk for school failure due to conditions such as low levels of maternal education or speaking a language other than English in the home. However, a growing number of people, including the president and members of the U.S. Congress, are calling for funding of **universal voluntary prekindergarten**, the goal of which is to make these programs available to families of all income levels who choose to use them. Publicly funded prekindergarten has contributed to the field's growth; today the number of 4-year-olds in state pre-K programs exceeds the number enrolled in Head Start (Barnett, Carolan, et al., 2013).

child care center Group program that provides care and education for young children during the hours that their parents are employed.

family child care home Child care in which caregivers provide care in their own homes for a small group of children, often multi-age groups.

preschool Educational programs serving 3- and 4-year-olds delivered under various sponsorships.

parent cooperative Preschool program owned, operated, and partially staffed by parents.

laboratory school School operated by colleges and universities that usually serves children of students and faculty and also acts as a model of excellent education for student teachers.

prekindergarten (pre-K) Educational program serving 3- and 4-year-olds, usually in public schools.

school readiness Children's competencies related to success in kindergarten, including physical development, health, and well-being; social-emotional development and learning; cognitive development and general knowledge such as mathematics and science; positive approaches to learning such as curiosity and motivation; and language development and early literacy skills.

universal voluntary prekindergarten Publicly funded preschool, usually for 4-year-olds but sometimes 3-year-olds; available to any family that chooses to use it.

Early childhood education includes child care centers, preschools, prekindergartens, family child care homes, and schools. But every high-quality program provides both loving care and education for young children and support for their families.

Head Start **Head Start** is a federally funded, national program that promotes school readiness by enhancing the social and cognitive development of children ages 3, 4, and 5. Head Start provides educational, health, nutritional, social, and other services to the nation's poorest children and families whose incomes fall below the official poverty level (Head Start, 2013). Head Start's goal is to improve school readiness by supporting all areas of children's development and promoting the early reading and math skills needed for later success. In addition to these comprehensive services, parent involvement is a special focus of the program. Parents volunteer in the classroom and also serve in governance roles, with the goal of empowering families to move out of poverty. In fact, 23% of Head Start staff members are parents of current or former Head Start children (Head Start, 2013). Children with disabilities make up about 12% of Head Start's enrollment (Head Start, 2014b).

Head Start programs are quite diverse. Most Head Start children are served in classroom-based preschool programs, although in rural or remote areas, a home-based option is available. One of the smallest serves 30 children on the Havasupai reservation in the Grand Canyon, accessible only by helicopter or donkey, while the largest programs serve over 22,000 children in 400 centers across Los Angeles (Head Start, 2011a).

The families represent all the racial and cultural groups in the United States (Head Start, 2014b). About 43% of the children are White, 38% are Latino, and 29% are African American. A sizable number of families—almost 10%—report that their children are biracial or multiracial. In addition, the program has a special focus on serving American Indians, Alaska Natives, and migrant and seasonal workers. About 30% of the children speak a language other than English at home. Of these, 85% speak Spanish, but 140 other languages are spoken.

In response to brain research and concerns that age 4 or even age 3 is too late for services to be effective, the government launched **Early Head Start** in 1995. Early Head Start serves low-income pregnant mothers, infants, and toddlers and promotes healthy family functioning. As of 2012, there were more than 1,000 Early Head Start programs in all 50 states, the District of Columbia, and Puerto Rico (Head Start, 2014a). Research on Early Head Start (Vogel, Yange, Moiduddun, Kisker, & Carlson, 2010) demonstrates that it achieves its promise of lasting positive effects on children and families.

Head Start Federally funded, national program that promotes school readiness by enhancing the social and cognitive development of children ages 3, 4, and 5 through providing educational, health, nutritional, social, and other services to the nation's poorest children and families.

Early Head Start Federally funded program serving low-income pregnant mothers, infants, and toddlers that promotes healthy family functioning.

early childhood special education Services for children with disabilities or special needs who meet eligibility guidelines that are determined on a state-by-state basis according to the Individuals with Disabilities Education Act.

Individuals with Disabilities Education Act (IDEA) Federal law governing provision of services for children with disabilities and special needs.

early intervention Services for infants and toddlers who are at risk of developmental delay and their families.

inclusion Participation and services for children with disabilities and special needs in programs and settings where their typically developing peers are served.

Early Intervention and Early Childhood Special Education Early childhood special education serves children with disabilities or special needs who meet eligibility guidelines that are determined on a state-by-state basis, according to the **Individuals with Disabilities Education Act (IDEA)**. In addition to serving children with identified disabilities, some states provide **early intervention** services for infants and toddlers who are at risk of developmental delay and their families.

Federal legislation enacted during the past three decades has fundamentally changed the way in which early childhood services are organized and delivered to children with disabilities and special needs (Division for Early Childhood & NAEYC, 2009). These children, including children who are at risk for disabilities or who exhibit challenging behaviors, are far more likely to participate in a typical early childhood program than in the past. This trend, called **inclusion**, is defined and described in the *Including All Children: What Does Inclusion Mean?* feature.

All early childhood educators are likely to work with children with disabilities at some point in their careers. This inevitability broadens what teachers need to know right from the start, and requires that general early childhood teachers develop skills to collaborate with special educators.

Kindergarten and Primary Grades Most 5- through 8-year-old children attend public schools, although many attend secular or faith-based private schools funded

Including All Children

What Does Inclusion Mean?

Mark and Monique Berger operate a family child care program in their home. Their state permits group homes such as theirs to serve up to 12 children. The licensing agent informs them that they are required by law to serve children with disabilities and special needs. One mother, whose son Barry has cerebral palsy, has inquired about enrolling him in their program. Mark wants to be sure that they abide by the law, but Monique is a little unsure about what it means to include a child with a disability in her child care home.

Although full inclusion of children with disabilities in early childhood programs has been the law of the land for several years, Mark and Monique are not alone in being unsure about what it means. To help them and other professionals like them, the Division for Early Childhood of the Council for Exceptional Children and NAEYC (2009) jointly developed a statement defining early childhood inclusion:

Early childhood inclusion embodies the values, policies, and practices that support the right of every infant and young child and his or her family, regardless of ability, to participate in a broad range of activities and contexts as full members of families, communities, and society. The desired results of inclusive experiences for children with and without disabilities and their families include a sense of belonging and membership, positive social relationships and friendships, and development and learning to reach their full potential.

The statement describes the key features of high-quality inclusive programs, which are (1) access, (2) participation, and (3) supports.

A defining feature of high-quality early childhood inclusion is *access*, which means providing children with a wide range of learning opportunities, activities, and environments. In inclusive settings, adults also promote belonging, *participation*, and engagement of children with disabilities and their typically developing peers in a variety of intentional or purposeful ways.

Finally, an infrastructure of inclusion *supports* must be in place to ensure a foundation for the efforts of individuals and organizations that provide inclusive services to children and families. For example, Mark and Monique will need access to ongoing professional development and support to acquire the knowledge, skills, and dispositions required to effectively meet Barry's needs and contribute to his development. In addition, specialized services and therapies for Barry will need to be coordinated and integrated with the other activities they offer the children.

Source: Early childhood inclusion: A joint position statement of the Division for Early Childhood (DEC) and the National Association for the Education of Young Children (NAEYC), by Division for Early Childhood and National Association for the Education of Young Children, 2009, Chapel Hill: The University of North Carolina, FPG Child Development Institute, retrieved from http://community.fpg.unc.edu/resources/articles/files/EarlyChildhoodInclusion-04-2009.pdf.

by parent tuition. Typically considered the first year of formal schooling, **kindergarten** has traditionally been designed for 5-year-olds. States establish varying dates for the legal entrance age to kindergarten, but 40 states require that children who are entering kindergarten must have their fifth birthday before the end of September or earlier (Education Commission of the States, 2013). This means that today's kindergartens enroll many 6-year-olds. By contrast, in 1975, only nine states required that children be 5 by September (Colasanti, 2007)

First, second, and third grades are the **primary grade** years of school (6 through 8 years of age). These grades are especially important because during these grades, children are expected to acquire the fundamental abilities of reading and mathematics, along with the foundations of other academic disciplines including social studies, science, the creative arts, technology, and physical education. In first to third grade, children are learning to read; after that, they are expected to read to learn (Annie E. Casey Foundation, 2010). Therefore, if a good foundation is not laid during the primary years, children are likely to struggle in later years (U.S. Department of Health and Human Services, 2014).

Forty states and the District of Columbia permit funding of public **charter schools**. A charter school is a publicly funded school that is independently operated under a contract with the state or district. Typically, charter schools have greater flexibility than do regular public schools for meeting regulations, but they must also meet accountability standards. In school districts where charter schools are an option, parents have a choice of where to send their children. More than 2 million children attend charter schools and the percentage is increasing (National Center for Education Statistics, 2014a).

How Early Childhood Education Is Expanding

Participation in early childhood programs has increased steadily for many decades as more children participate in group programs at younger ages. In 1965, only 60% of 5-year-olds went to kindergarten, whereas today about 95% do (National Center for Education Statistics, 2014b). A similar but steeper growth trend is apparent for younger children. In 1960, only 10% of 3- and 4-year-olds were enrolled in any type of early childhood program. By 2012, 64% of 3- to 5-year-olds were enrolled in preprimary programs (National Center for Education Statistics, 2014b). Although the economic downturn has affected enrollment, all types of early childhood programs have seen growth over the years, including private preschools and child care centers, state-funded prekindergartens, preschool special education, and Head Start (Barnett, Carolan, Fitzgerald, & Squires, 2011; National Center for Education Statistics, 2014b).

Growth in Preschool Attendance Changes in preschool participation are apparent in the findings of the *Early Childhood Longitudinal Study, Birth Cohort* (Jacobson Chernoff, Flanagan, McPhee, & Park, 2007). The study revealed that preschool, rather than kindergarten, is now seen as the first year of school for children. The percentage of children who attend center-based preschools is approximately the same whether or not their mothers are employed. This finding indicates that the growth in preschool enrollment is related to increased demand for early education as much as increased need for child care (Barnett & Yarosz, 2007).

Child Care for Employed Families Expansion of the early childhood field is directly related to the demand for child care for employed families. Currently, 64% of women with children under age 6 are in the labor force (Bureau of Labor Statistics, 2014). Infant and toddler care is a particular need because 58% of mothers of children under age 1 are in the workforce. Almost 80% of school-agers need care for some hours of the day (Children's Defense Fund [CDF], 2011).

▶ **Classroom Connection**

This video defines inclusion as "belonging." How does inclusion benefit all children?

http://www.youtube.com/watch?v=n_qgW9FWEgQ

kindergarten Typically considered the first year of formal schooling; serves 5- and 6-year-olds.

primary grades First, second, and third grade; sometimes includes kindergarten.

charter schools Independently operated, publicly funded schools that have greater flexibility than regular schools in meeting regulations and achieving goals.

Recognizing how important good child care is to maintaining a productive workforce, some employers sponsor on-site child care centers or subsidize child care expenses as an employee benefit. Employers find that support for child care reduces absenteeism and turnover (National Child Care Information Center, n.d.).

In addition, the federal government provides child care assistance through **Temporary Assistance for Needy Families (TANF)**. The TANF program provides temporary financial aid but requires recipients to move into the labor force or schooling, further increasing the demand for child care. The **Child Care and Development Block Grants (CCDBG)** allocates funds to states for low-income working families to purchase their own child care. In 2014, Congress reauthorized the CCDBG for the first time since 1996, with significant bipartisan support. The new law significantly improved provisions designed to protect children's health and safety and improve the quality of care.

> **Temporary Assistance for Needy Families (TANF)**
> Federally funded program, more commonly known as Welfare to Work, that provides temporary financial aid but requires recipients to move into the labor force or schooling.
>
> **Child Care and Development Block Grants (CCDBG)** Federal funds allocated to states for low-income working families to purchase child care.

Access to Early Childhood Education

Despite the overall increase in the number of children attending preschool, access to programs varies considerably depending on family income and other factors. In fact, the children who are most likely to benefit from high-quality programs are the least likely to participate in them. Consider the following statistics:

- Young children who live in poverty are less likely to attend preschool than children from higher-income families.
- Head Start and state-funded prekindergarten programs increase the participation rates for low-income families, but insufficient slots are available to serve all the eligible children.
- Families with moderate incomes face the greatest hurdle because they are not eligible for subsidized programs and cannot afford private ones.
- Preschool participation varies considerably depending on the mother's education. About 75% of children whose mothers have a college education or higher participate in preschool, compared to 54% of those whose mothers are high school dropouts (National Center for Education Statistics, 2014b). Again, the children who need preschool the most—those whose mothers are less likely to provide educational experiences at home—are the least likely to get it.

How Early Childhood Education Is Changing

Recently, two enormous transformations in the United States have had significant impacts on early childhood education—changing demographics and economics. The nation is becoming increasingly diverse. At the same time, economic hardship and poverty—including homelessness—are affecting increasing numbers of families.

Changing Demographics The 2010 U.S. census revealed that the population is highly diverse, both racially and culturally. As illustrated in Figure 1.2, the racial and ethnic composition of the child population has changed dramatically since 1990. The white population of children declined from 60% to 53%. By 2018, the majority of young children will be children of color—members of groups currently identified as minorities (Annie E. Casey Foundation, 2014). In many school districts today, this is already the case (Ennis, Ríos-Vargas, & Albert, 2011).

The largest increase is among individuals who identify themselves as Hispanic or Latino. Between 2000 and 2010, the Hispanic population grew by 43%, accounting for over half of the total increase in the U.S. population (Ennis et al., 2011). Due to both higher birth rates and immigration, Latinos now constitute 24% of the nation's children

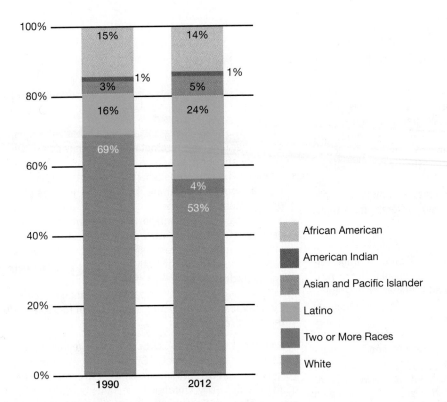

FIGURE 1.2 Child Population by Race and Ethnicity In the last two decades, the population of young children in the United States has become dramatically more ethnically and racially diverse.
Source: Annie E. Casey Foundation. (2014). *2014 Kids Count data book: State trends in child well-being.* Baltimore: Author. Retrieved November 16, 2014, from http://www.aecf.org/2014db

(Annie E. Casey Foundation, 2014). Many of these children are **dual language learners** because they are learning to speak two languages at the same time—their home language and English. These demographic shifts have important implications for early childhood educators as discussed in the feature *Language Lens: Preparing to Teach Dual Language Learners.*

dual language learners
Children who are learning to speak two languages at the same time—usually their home language and English.

Changing Economics The recent economic crisis led to millions of children and families falling into poverty, with potentially devastating impacts on children's health, development, and learning. Almost 25% of all children under 6 live in poverty, but African American and Latino children are about three times as likely to be poor as White, non-Hispanic children (CDF, 2014). Most alarming, in 2014, 2.5 million children, or nearly 1 in 30, experienced homelessness, an 8% increase in one year (National Center on Family Homelessness at American Institutes for Research, 2014). Children growing up in poverty are especially in need of high-quality early childhood experiences and good teachers.

Increased unemployment also negatively affects enrollments in early childhood programs as families struggle to pay for child care (NACCRRA, 2011). In some situations, families remove their children from preschool or child care centers because they can no longer afford or do not need these services. Some employers are less willing or able to subsidize child care as a benefit.

The effects of the economic downturn on children, families, and early childhood programs are real. However, increased funding for child care and early education at this difficult time in the nation's history is solid evidence of its broad support and the recognition of its value.

Language Lens
Preparing to Teach Dual Language Learners

Eight different languages are spoken among the children in Natalia's kindergarten class. Natalia and two of the children are the only ones whose first language is English. Natalia works hard to create a caring community where all the children comfortably experiment with learning English while also developing their home language. She strives to communicate with the parents by using translators. Last year, Natalia's class also included eight languages—but some of them were different from those spoken this year.

The number of languages represented in Natalia's classroom may seem extreme, but linguistic and cultural diversity is now the norm in our nation's schools. In the next 20 years, the biggest single child-related demographic change is predicted to be an increase in dual language learners. Most of these children speak Spanish as a home language, but many others speak Asian, Middle Eastern, and African languages. California, Florida, and Texas continue to have the largest percentages of Spanish-speaking families, but according to the last census, between 2000 and 2010, the Hispanic population grew in every region of the country.

In the past, most teachers could safely assume that they would never encounter a language other than English in their entire careers. Today, Natalia's experience or something like it is not so very rare. New teachers may find it beneficial to learn another language themselves, but learning eight languages is not a reasonable expectation. What can new and experienced teachers like Natalia do?

They can start by remembering some important principles about dual language learners:

- People who speak the same language, whether Spanish or another language, are not all alike—they come from a variety of countries and cultures.
- Learning two or more languages does not confuse children as some people think, but rather enhances brain development.
- Supporting home language development is essential because children can learn many skills in their home language and apply those skills as they learn English.
- Teachers need to intentionally teach English vocabulary and provide lots of opportunities for children to play together and practice their developing language skills.
- Communicating with families is essential regardless of the effort required.

The children of today must be prepared to function as citizens of a global society. Speaking two or more languages is an important skill for the 21st century. When children enter early childhood programs speaking a language other than English, the foundation is already there to build on.

Sources: The Hispanic population: 2010. 2010 Census Briefs, by S. R. Ennis, M. Ríos-Vargas, and N. G. Albert, 2011, U.S. Census Bureau, retrieved from http://www.census.gov/prod/cen2010/briefs/c2010br-04.pdf; *Pre-K-3rd: Challenging common myths about dual language learners, an update to the seminal 2008 report* by L. Espinosa, 2013, New York: Foundation for Child Development.

 Check Your Understanding 1.1: What Is Early Childhood Education?

Why Become an Early Childhood Educator?

Choosing to teach young children, like every career decision, involves weighing many factors. Prospective teachers need to be familiar with what the work entails and the possible career options. Most important, they need to determine whether the demands and rewards of their chosen profession are a good match with their own strengths, dispositions, and personal goals (Colker, 2008).

The Joys of Teaching Young Children

Working with children demands patience and the willingness to care for and about other people's children, even or especially the least lovable of those children. Teaching young children is truly rewarding work, even when it is most challenging (Colker, 2008). Each day brings new discoveries, accomplishments, and joys for children and teachers.

Picture a 4-year-old child. What are the first thoughts that come to mind? Is he or she curious? Eager to learn? Excellent early childhood teachers take advantage of young children's deep desire to actively engage with and make sense of the world around them. Recall the sense of satisfaction you felt when you mastered a difficult task such as learning to read or ride a bike. Children, too, gain great pleasure from the sense of mastery that comes from learning something new or overcoming an obstacle.

Another word that comes to mind when thinking of children is *fun*. Yes, early childhood programs prepare children for success in school, but they also provide them with joyful learning experiences every day of their young lives. Children should have fun in child care centers and homes, preschools, and schools. They love to joke, tease, and be silly; to sing, move, and dance; to play by themselves and with friends; to know that adults care for them; to wonder about and explore the natural world; and to generally enjoy living. When teachers create a safe and supportive place for children to experience the unique joys of childhood, children will thrive—and their teachers will also.

Intentional teachers are purposeful, but they are also playful. How can teachers keep the fun in childhood while helping children achieve important learning goals?

intentional teachers Teachers who have a purpose for the decisions they make and can explain that purpose to others.

Dimensions of Effective, Intentional Teaching

One overarching theme of this book is that effective early childhood practice requires teachers to be intentional in everything they do. **Intentional teachers** have a purpose for the decisions they make and can explain that purpose to others (Copple & Bredekamp, 2009; Epstein, 2014). However, we believe that intentional teaching involves much more. Intentional teaching is a multifaceted, multidimensional concept that conveys many of the personal and professional qualities of an early childhood educator. Consider how well your own aspirations and dispositions fit with our description of the dimensions of intentional teaching that appears in Figure 1.3.

For an example of intentional teaching, read the *Becoming an Intentional Teacher: Being Purposeful and Playful* feature. Now that we have described both the dedication and the delight that teaching young children entails, we turn to an overview of the job opportunities in the field.

Career Options for Early Childhood Educators

As the field of early education grows, so do the potential career options and opportunities for early childhood professionals. At the same time, however, the field is experiencing a shortage of qualified teachers (Whitebook, 2014). Even as a large percentage of the current teaching staff is nearing retirement, teacher qualification requirements are being raised in many sectors of the field.

Because the early childhood field is so diverse and covers such a broad age range, early childhood educators have many possible career choices. Careers tend to fall into two categories:

- Working *with* children involves daily interaction and direct responsibility for children's care and education and includes positions such as classroom teacher or family child care provider.
- Working *for* children involves work that supports children's development and education, whether in proximity to the children, such as being a child care center director, or at a further distance, such as being a teacher-education professor.

Over the course of their careers, many early childhood professionals move back and forth between these types of jobs. However, we believe that success in working *for* children is greater if an individual has actually worked *with* children. No one in the early

- **Caring and committed.** They recognize that developing a personal, positive, warm relationship with each child is the foundation for everything they do. Their commitment to children means putting children's needs before their own and recognizing that teaching young children is less a job than a calling.

- **Enthusiastic and engaged.** They genuinely enjoy being with young children however messy or challenging they may be, and share in the excitement of their discoveries. They become energetically and intensely involved in children's activity, whether it means getting down on the floor to play and talk with a baby or thinking through the solution to a problem with a kindergartner.

- **Curious and creative.** They are eager to learn, just as children are. Young children want to learn all sorts of things that teachers themselves may not know—what's inside a bug, why the sky is blue, how an airplane flies. Intentional teachers model an inquisitive attitude. They want to find out along with children, and they approach questions or problems in new, imaginative ways.

- **Respectful and responsive.** They value and treat children, families, and colleagues with dignity and esteem. They respond thoughtfully to diversity in all of its forms: language, culture, race/ethnicity, ability/disability, age, gender, and sexual orientation. They are open and accepting of perspectives that are different from their own.

- **Passionate and patient.** They bring into their work their own emotions and deep interests, such as a passion for music, painting, or poetry; a preference for belly laughs or quiet smiles. At the same time, they recognize that children have their own intense feelings that can spill over into anger, frustration, or fits of tears. Intentional teachers respond calmly and thoughtfully, without becoming upset or annoyed themselves.

- **Purposeful and playful.** They have important goals for children—to help them make friends, regulate their emotions, control their bodies, learn to read and write—and they plan carefully to help children achieve their goals. But along the way, they joke and laugh with children, accept silliness, encourage and support play, and make learning itself playful. A sense of humor is a necessity.

- **Focused and flexible.** They are like cameras that can scan the entire classroom and then narrow their attention to meet one child's need or respond to her question or idea. They can be teaching a reading lesson with a specific goal in mind and switch gears when a child starts talking about his brother's illness.

- **Aware and accountable.** They are self-aware, they reflect on and evaluate their own performance, and they strive to improve. But their judgments are not made in isolation; they compare their performance to a standard of excellence. Intentional teachers are willing to be accountable; they accept responsibility for their actions.

- **Informed and effective.** They know how children develop and learn; they know how to teach and what to teach. They use research-based teaching practices that lead to positive outcomes for children and help children make sense of the world around them. Intentional teachers also regularly check to see if what they are doing is actually working. Are children making progress toward developmentally appropriate goals?

- **Listening and learning.** They realize that the more they learn about children, the more they need to know. They understand that choosing to teach is choosing to be a lifelong learner. Intentional teachers learn from children every day; they listen to children, and they pay close attention to all of children's cues. They stay up to date about new knowledge and continue to grow as professionals.

FIGURE 1.3 Characteristics of Professional, Intentional Early Childhood Teachers Intentional teaching involves a wide range of personal and professional qualities such as those listed here.

childhood community can do his or her job well without knowing what life is like in an early childhood setting (Colker, 2008). This experience informs decisions at every level.

Working *with* Children Early childhood teachers are usually the first to admit that they aren't in this profession for the money. It is the satisfaction they get from working with children that is deeply rewarding. For many of them, the fact that they make an impact on the life of every child they encounter is a powerful incentive and the reason that, once they enter the field, they are there to stay (Colker, 2008).

Becoming an Intentional Teacher
Being Purposeful and Playful

Here's What Happened   It was the fifth straight day of rain facing my kindergarten children as they arrived at school on Friday. Some of them were already dragging their backpacks in apparent dread while others rambunctiously ran down the hallway as though they couldn't contain themselves another minute. The bell rang and the classroom door opened. The children stopped abruptly, almost stumbling over each other. Their eyes opened wide as if they thought elves had been at work overnight transforming the environment.

Laughing, I suggested they put away their things and come to the gathering area for morning meeting. We usually discuss the day's plans but today I gave some new directions. "Instead of our regular choice time in centers, we are going to divide into two groups and then switch group assignments later. Group 1 is going to use the obstacle courses we've set up here and in Mrs. D'Onofrio's room. Group 2 is going to go on a treasure hunt. Each group will have a map with clues in pictures and writing. You'll find answers to some of the clues in our classroom and some in hers. Her children will take turns switching rooms with us to look for clues. You'll divide up into teams to help each other find the treasure, but you'll want to be quiet deciphering your maps because you don't want to give away the clues to the other teams."

Here's What I Was Thinking   Our kindergarten curriculum is packed with learning goals based on the state standards. I always keep those goals in mind and have a purpose for everything I plan each day. After five straight days of rain, my fellow kindergarten teacher and I knew that we would have to adjust our regular plans. No outdoor play time again could only mean very distractible children whose attention spans would suffer greatly.

As kindergarten teachers, we know how much children need to play and how much their healthy development depends on it. That's why we thought of setting up the obstacle course. The course included a balance beam and narrow space to scoot through as well as objects to go over, around, and through. Each time children attempted the course, they were handed a different set of directions not only to use different muscles, but also to learn to read and follow directions. The children repeated the course several times as they practiced their developing skills.

We had different purposes for the treasure hunt. We still wanted children to be physically active, moving around the room. But we made the clues difficult to figure out, requiring kindergarten-level literacy skills. Having the children work in teams meant they had to use language, employ problem-solving skills, and cooperate. They also had to self-regulate so as not to give away their plans to other teams and to solve the puzzle.

At the end of the day, we'd all forgotten about the rain. Some of the children said it was the most fun they had ever had at school. It took a lot of work, but being playful *and* purposeful meant that we were able to accomplish curriculum goals and have a lot of fun as teachers, too.

Reflection   Feeling pressured to cover the curriculum, teachers may limit vitally important opportunities for children to play. What other ways do you think these teachers could have playfully but purposefully addressed their curriculum goals?

Early childhood teachers work with different age groups from infancy through primary grades in a wide range of settings. The qualifications and required certifications for specific jobs will vary, but a broad-based education in the field is necessary preparation. Following are some of the options and opportunities available for interesting and rewarding work:

- *Head Start* teachers can alter the life trajectory of young children and their families who are most in need. They help ensure that children from low-income families receive an excellent education and comprehensive health, nutrition, and other services.
- *Early Head Start* teachers intervene early with mothers and their babies to help set them on a course of healthy development.
- *Child care center* teachers provide loving care and education to children for extended periods of time each day, and help employed parents feel secure about their children's care so they can do their jobs. Careers in child care offer the option of teaching various age groups: infants and toddlers, preschoolers, and school-age children before and/or after school. Although teaching in child care pays less than does teaching in other settings, many teachers relish its flexible and creative environment. Conditions also vary by administrative agency; for example,

an employer-sponsored child care center may offer more benefits and higher compensation than a community-based one.

- Teachers in *family child care homes* literally open their doors to small groups of children from infancy through school age, providing a home-like atmosphere of care and education. Family child care means being your own boss, but requires administering a small business as well as caring for children.

- *Preschools* vary a great deal—public, private, faith-based, and so on—each with its own benefits that will appeal to different teachers' interests and match their goals. A public prekindergarten, for example, may provide better salaries, whereas a private one may be more flexible about curriculum and expectations for children.

- A teacher in a *parent cooperative preschool* has the opportunity to develop particularly close relationships with families but also needs the ability to work with parents as co-teachers, an acquired skill.

- Teachers in *public schools* have the option of teaching different age groups from kindergarten through primary grades. Schools are bureaucracies with regulations and an established curriculum and tests, but as professionals, teachers make hundreds of classroom decisions every day. Salaries and benefits in the public schools are the most secure of any sector in early childhood.

- *Early childhood special educators* and *early intervention specialists* are qualified individuals who work with children with special needs in various settings such as in school systems, Head Start, or child care. Inclusion of children with special needs means that early childhood special educators work closely with regular classroom teachers. In fact, in some states, the same teacher education program prepares teachers for certification in both fields simultaneously.

- *Mentor teacher* is an evolving career option for more experienced, outstanding professionals. It is helpful for new teachers to work with a mentor teacher to improve their skills or to get help for children with particular learning challenges. Mentor teachers are becoming more common in elementary schools, preschools, and child care programs.

- The need for *bilingual teachers* and those who are qualified to teach dual language learners is growing. As the population becomes ever more diverse, these qualifications will be useful in any early childhood setting.

Given the variety of careers available, early childhood teachers have many options. Even when an entire career is spent teaching the same age group in the same workplace, teachers will always encounter new challenges and new experiences. I once asked a former teacher who had taught for 40 years, "Didn't you ever get tired of teaching first grade?" She looked stunned and replied, "Never, because every group was different." Having been a child in her class at one time, I clearly understood what she meant—that every child is different and unique and that being a teacher never loses its fascination.

Working *for* Children At some point in their careers, all early childhood professionals should work with children in order to understand, firsthand, how educators help shape our young children. However, there are many opportunities for early childhood educators to pursue positions working *for* children. With additional education, specialized training, and experience, a background in early childhood can lead to positions such as these:

- *Director* of a child care center or preschool, or school principal (with additional course work in administration)
- *Curriculum developer* for an individual school, network of schools, or publisher
- *Home visitor* or *family services worker* in Head Start, Early Head Start, or another community agency
- *Policy staff* at local/state/federal agencies, associations, and organizations
- *College faculty* teaching teachers and/or conducting research
- *Writer/producer of resources for children* such as children's book author, technology developer, children's museum staff, or media performer

In previous sections, we discussed what it means to be a professional, intentional early childhood teacher. These definitions reflect the profession's core values and beliefs, a topic to which we turn next.

The Culture of Early Childhood Education

A key theme of this book is the important role that culture plays in development and learning. Broadly defined, **culture** is the rules and expectations for behavior of members of a group that are passed on from one generation to the next. These rules determine to a large extent what group members regard as important and what values shape their actions and judgments.

Like other professional groups, the early childhood profession has its own culture. This culture is transmitted both explicitly and implicitly from more experienced, competent members to new initiates in three ways: through formal education, through on-the-job experiences, and through mentoring in either setting. New teachers may become confused or flustered when the cultural rules transmitted in one setting, such as their college classroom, do not seem to match the expectations for behavior in another, such as their first teaching assignment.

Cultural groups define themselves in many ways, including through the language they use, how they identify themselves, the values they share, and their fundamental beliefs. We discuss these topics in the following sections.

Shared Vocabulary One aspect of early childhood culture is a shared vocabulary. Shared language facilitates communication and minimizes misunderstandings within groups. The profession gives particular meaning to terms like *developmentally appropriate*, *play*, *relationships*, *comprehensive services*, or *inclusion* (all of which are defined in this book). Their definitions are tailored to our profession and may not mirror how these words are used in other professions or everyday life.

An essential part of joining a profession is learning its language. For example, although the larger society uses the term *day care*, within the profession the accepted term is *child care*. We believe that saying *child care* is more respectful of children and a more accurate description of the setting and the job.

Shared Identity Most professionals feel a sense of belonging to their group. They identify themselves as members of the profession, whether it is as a doctor, a lawyer, or an accountant. In early childhood education, it is often harder to "name" ourselves. The profession itself does not have an agreed-on name (Goffin & Washington, 2007). Among the names it is known by are *early care and education*, *child care*, *early education*, and *early development and learning*. In this book, we refer to the field as *early childhood education*. We prefer this term because it contains the word *child*, which is an ever-present reminder of the primary focus of our work. We also believe that the term encompasses the key elements of caring, development, and learning.

Another challenge to establishing a clear identity is what to call the role itself. Infant/toddler teachers and teachers in center-based care are often called *caregivers*. In family child care, adults are called *providers*. But we embrace the term *teacher* because it is the broadest term, captures most of the job responsibilities, commands society's respect, and is after all what children usually call the adults who care for and educate them no matter what the setting.

Shared Values The early childhood profession is committed to a core set of values that is deeply rooted in the history of the field. NAEYC (2011a) articulates these core values in its code of ethical conduct:

We have made a commitment to:

- Appreciate childhood as a unique and valuable stage of the human life cycle
- Base our work on knowledge of how children develop and learn

culture The explicit and implicit values, beliefs, rules, and expectations for behavior of members of a group that are passed on from one generation to the next. These rules determine to a large extent what group members regard as important and what values shape their actions and judgments.

Early childhood educators are members of a profession that shares knowledge, values, and beliefs about children and their work. Meeting with more experienced teachers is one way of becoming a professional. Can you think of others?

- Appreciate and support the bond between the child and family
- Recognize that children are best understood and supported in the context of family, culture (including ethnicity), community, and society
- Respect the dignity, worth, and uniqueness of each individual (child, family member, and colleague)
- Respect diversity in children, families, and colleagues
- Recognize that children and adults achieve their full potential in the context of relationships that are based on trust and respect.

I often take informal polls of teachers during speeches at education conferences. A question I always ask is: "What are your values as an early childhood educator?" Most of the core values just listed are mentioned. Yet there is one that is always stated emphatically and is usually first—"play!" Early childhood professionals strongly value play as essential for children's development and learning. Because play is so important in early childhood, we will revisit the topic throughout this book. Political and economic forces threaten these values at times, but they nevertheless endure.

Shared Beliefs   Although early childhood culture shares many beliefs, a few dominate:

- The strong belief in the potential of all children, regardless of their life circumstances and individual abilities or disabilities.
- The belief in the power of **developmentally appropriate practice** to produce positive results for children. Developmentally appropriate practice is teaching that engages children's interests and adapts for their age, experience, and ability to help them meet challenging and achievable goals.
- The belief that early childhood teachers are professionals who make informed decisions about what is developmentally appropriate for each child in each situation.
- The fundamental belief in the potential of our work to make a real and lasting difference in the world.

developmentally appropriate practice Ways of teaching that engage children's interests and adapt for their age, experience, and ability, to help them meet challenging and achievable learning goals.

This is the final justification for joining the profession: the opportunity to make a contribution to children's lives. Many professions exist primarily to solve problems. Doctors and nurses treat illnesses. Firefighters put out fires and rescue people. Insurance agents help people recover from losses or catastrophes. The work of early childhood professionals, on the other hand, is to prevent problems from occurring. Our job is to set children on a positive course from the beginning. The proven effectiveness of early intervention when young children face difficulties creates room for optimism and hope.

✓ **Check Your Understanding 1.2:** Why Become an Early Childhood Educator?

Early Childhood Program Quality and Effectiveness

Growing attention to early education primarily results from impressive research demonstrating its effectiveness in improving outcomes for children. All of the research that has influenced policy, however, finds that the key ingredient in the effectiveness of early childhood education is the quality of the program for children. But what is quality?

Setting Standards for Quality

Earlier in this chapter, we described different types of early childhood programs. Various kinds of programs must meet different sets of standards, which are intended to determine the program's quality. Early childhood educators have been instrumental in setting standards for quality that, in addition to research, reflect the profession's core values and beliefs.

Child Care Licensing Standards Child care centers and, in some states, family child care homes, are regulated by each state's **child care licensing standards**. These set minimum requirements for a program to operate legally. Such standards usually establish a minimum number of teachers required per child (teacher/child ratios), teacher qualifications, and health and safety requirements.

These standards, designed to ensure children's protection, vary considerably from state to state. For example, one state requires a teacher for every four infants, whereas another permits a ratio of one to six. Child Care Aware® of America (2013) evaluates state licensing standards and monitoring of centers' compliance. They find that no states rank at the highest level, while 21 states rate a grade of D and 20 are failing to provide basic protection for children's health and safety and support for their development.

Because licensing standards vary and represent minimums, the quality of child care also varies considerably. Some licensed programs exceed the required standards, whereas others barely meet them (Child Care Aware® of America, 2013). To address this issue and help parents make informed decisions, many states now operate **quality rating and improvement systems (QRIS)**. These tiered systems rate program quality according to achievement of benchmarks beyond those required for minimal licensing, such as having more highly qualified teachers or better ratios (Mitchell, 2012). The state recognizes centers that meet higher standards with more stars and pay higher reimbursement rates for children served. In some states, achieving accreditation is the highest level. QRIS also helps families make informed decisions about choosing child care.

Accreditation Standards The early childhood profession under the leadership of NAEYC (2008) is committed to raising the overall quality of early education for all children. Toward this end, the association sets high-quality standards and administers a voluntary **accreditation system** for all types of early childhood centers and schools serving children from birth through kindergarten. The standards that programs must achieve to obtain accreditation are listed in Table 1.1. These standards apply to any early childhood

child care licensing standards Minimum requirements, legally established by each state, for a child care program to operate.

quality rating and improvement systems (QRIS) State-operated tiered systems that evaluate and rate the quality of child care programs according to achievement of benchmarks beyond those required for minimal licensing, such as having more highly qualified teachers or better ratios.

▶ **Classroom Connection**

The video outlines the high standards required of early childhood programs to become NAEYC accredited. The 10 program standards are the mark of quality and best practices for the field. Accreditation also assists families in choosing the best programs for their children.

http://www.youtube.com/watch?v=rhBBd9Tl4k4

accreditation system NAEYC's voluntary system for identifying high-quality early childhood centers and schools serving children from birth through kindergarten.

TABLE 1.1 NAEYC Early Childhood Program Standards

NAEYC's accreditation standards describe all the key elements of a high-quality early childhood program.

Standard	Standard Description
1. Relationships	The program promotes positive relationships among all children and adults to encourage each child's sense of individual worth and belonging as a part of a community and to foster each child's ability to contribute as a responsible community member.
2. Curriculum	The program implements a curriculum that is consistent with its goals for children and promotes learning and development in each of the following areas: social, emotional, physical, language, and cognitive.
3. Teaching	The program uses developmentally, culturally, and linguistically appropriate and effective teaching approaches that enhance each child's learning and development in the context of the program's curriculum goals. Teachers purposefully use multiple instructional approaches to optimize children's opportunities for learning.
4. Assessment of children's progress	The program is informed by ongoing systematic, formal, and informal assessment approaches to provide information on children's learning and development. These assessments occur within the context of reciprocal communications with families and with sensitivity to the cultural contexts in which children develop. Assessment results are used to benefit children by informing sound decisions about children, teaching, and program improvement.
5. Health	The program promotes the nutrition and health of children and protects children and staff from illness and injury.
6. Teachers	The program employs and supports a teaching staff that has the educational qualifications, knowledge, and professional commitment necessary to promote children's learning and development and to support families' diverse needs and interests.
7. Families	The program establishes and maintains collaborative relationships with each child's family to foster children's development in all settings. These relationships are sensitive to family composition, language, and culture.
8. Community relationships	The program establishes relationships with and uses the resources of the children's communities to support the achievement of program goals.
9. Physical environment	The program has a safe and healthful environment that provides appropriate and well-maintained indoor and outdoor physical environments. The environment includes facilities, equipment, and materials to facilitate child and staff learning and development.
10. Leadership and management	The program effectively implements policies, procedures, and systems that support stable staff and strong personnel, fiscal, and program management so all children, families, and staff have high-quality experiences.

Source: From *Overview of the NAEYC Early Childhood Program Standards*, 2008, by National Association for the Education of Young Children, Washington, DC, retrieved from http://www.naeyc.org/files/academy/file/OverviewStandards.pdf.

program regardless of length of day or sponsorship. NAEYC accreditation standards are designed to answer the question "What is high quality?"

To understand what we mean by *quality*, it is important to see the relationships among the standards rather than to see them as a discrete list. In the accreditation system, the primary focus is on *children* as described in the first five standards: relationships, curriculum, teaching, assessment of children's progress, and health. The other five standards address teachers, partnerships with families and communities, and administration, including the physical environment and leadership and management. Meeting these standards establishes a supportive context that makes it possible to achieve and maintain the quality of life for children described in the first five standards.

Head Start Program Performance Standards National standards that establish the level of quality of services provided by every Head Start program.

Head Start Standards Quality is also a critically important issue in Head Start, particularly so because it serves the nation's most vulnerable children. Head Start programs are regularly monitored for compliance with the national **Head Start Program Performance Standards** (Head Start, 2006). These standards are similar to accreditation standards, but they also address the comprehensive services that are part of Head Start's mandate.

Military Child Care Act The largest employer-sponsored child care system in the world is the U.S. military. Its voluntary workforce of men and women depends on the provision of high-quality child care. In 1989, Congress passed the Military Child Care Act to ensure consistently high standards of quality in these programs. The act required that centers seek NAEYC accreditation, and also included provisions for teacher training and a career ladder tying compensation to increased professional development. The Military Child Care Act resulted in significantly improved quality and learning outcomes for children that have been maintained for decades (Child Care Aware® of America, 2013; Neugebauer, 2011). In addition, the military child care system is now seen as a model for improving all child care systems (Whitebook, Phillips, & Howes, 2014).

Measuring Quality in Early Childhood Programs

The early childhood field defines quality as having two dimensions: structural and process (Minervino, 2013). **Structural quality** includes features such as maximum group sizes, teacher/child ratios, and teacher qualifications, which are relatively easy to quantify and measure. **Process quality**, on the other hand, refers to the quality of the relationships and interactions among teachers and children, and the appropriateness of the materials, learning experiences, and teaching strategies. These features are more difficult to evaluate, and yet they are the key aspects of the quality of children's experiences. They describe what life should be like for children in a program, how they should be treated, and how their learning and development should be promoted.

Structural quality and process quality are interconnected. For example, well-qualified teachers are needed to plan and implement an engaging curriculum and teach effectively. Similarly, positive relationships between teachers and children are more likely to be established when the size of the group and ratio of adults to children is relatively small. An age-appropriate, well-equipped, and organized environment is needed to protect children's health and safety and to promote active learning.

The most difficult challenge is determining how to measure compliance with quality standards. To see if a program is meeting requirements, it is relatively easy to examine transcripts of teachers or count the number of children in a group. But it is much harder—especially for an outside evaluator—to decide if teachers have positive relationships with each child and family or if they are using effective teaching strategies. These standards can be assessed only by directly observing what goes on in classrooms (FPG Child Development Institute, 2008).

To provide consistent ways of measuring quality, researchers have developed observation tools. The most widely used observational measure is the **Classroom Assessment Scoring System (CLASS)**, with versions for infants, toddlers, preschoolers and primary grades (Hamre, La Paro, Pianta, & Locasale-Crouch, 2014; La Paro, Hamre, & Pianta, 2012; Pianta, La Paro, & Hamre, 2008). The CLASS focuses on the quality of teachers' relationships with children and the instructional strategies they use to support children's learning. Research shows that how well classrooms and teachers score on these measures predicts how well children score on measures of language, literacy, mathematics, and social-emotional abilities (Curby, Brock, & Hamre, 2013; Downer et al., 2012). The CLASS has been adopted as a tool for monitoring quality in Head Start, state prekindergartens, and QRIS.

Another widely used program quality assessment is the **Early Childhood Environment Rating Scale (ECERS-3)** (Harms, Clifford, & Cryer, 2014) with versions for preschool, infant/toddler, family child care, and school-age programs. ECERS is used by many state QRIS systems.

The overall conclusion of all of the research on the effectiveness of early education is that what teachers actually do with children is the most important determinant of the quality of children's experiences and their learning outcomes. After decades of research on quality in early childhood programs, one thing we know for certain is that teachers matter. If children are to reach their full potentials, then professionals must also reach theirs.

structural quality Features of an early childhood program, such as maximum group sizes, teacher/child ratios, and teacher qualifications, that are relatively easy to quantify and measure.

process quality The quality of the relationships and interactions among teachers and children, and the appropriateness of the materials, learning experiences, and teaching strategies occurring in an early childhood program.

Classroom Assessment Scoring System (CLASS) Preschool and elementary classroom observational instrument that assesses the quality of teachers' relationships and interactions with children and the instructional strategies used to support children's learning.

Early Childhood Environment Rating Scale (ECERS-3) Observational instrument used to rate program quality on a 7-point scale from inadequate to excellent.

Measuring Effectiveness

As we have seen, program quality is usually defined and measured in terms of "inputs"—the environments children experience and their interactions with teachers. However, program effectiveness is usually defined in terms of "outcomes"—the effects of these experiences on children's development and learning. As a result, effectiveness is measured against specific, usually age- or grade-related goals. For preschoolers, the most common source of outcome goals are state **early learning standards**, which describe what children should know and be able to do before entering kindergarten (Scott-Little, 2011). All 50 states have comprehensive learning guidelines for preschool children, and 30 states have such goals for infants and toddlers (Barnett, Carolan, et al., 2013).

Head Start has established its own set of comprehensive goals for children—the Head Start Child Development and Early Learning Framework. Head Start programs are required by law to periodically assess children's progress toward the framework's goals.

State departments of education establish outcome standards for children in kindergarten and primary grades. Children's progress toward these goals is often measured by state-wide testing programs usually beginning at third grade, as we discuss later in this chapter.

 Check Your Understanding 1.3: Early Childhood Program Quality and Effectiveness

early learning standards
Describe what children should know and be able to do before entering kindergarten.

The Positive Effects of Early Childhood Education

We began this chapter by citing ways that early childhood is a field on the rise. The positive attention and support the field has garnered is to a large extent the result of an impressive body of research on the importance of the early years and the lasting benefits of early childhood programs.

Brain Research

Among the most exciting achievements in developmental psychology in the past century were new insights into how the brain grows and functions during the earliest years of life. Brain research, which had previously been confined to laboratories, is now reported regularly in popular newspapers and magazines. Technologies such as positron emission tomography (PET) scans and functional magnetic resonance imagery (fMRI) reveal the inner workings of babies' brains to policy makers, educators, and the public.

Major conclusions from brain research have significantly lifted the profile of early childhood education—and especially the importance of experiences in the first three years of life (Shonkoff, 2011; Shonkoff, Garner, & the Committee on Psychosocial Effects of Child and Family Health, 2012):

Brain research demonstrates the importance of early childhood education, especially for infants and toddlers.

© Carla Mestas/Pearson Education

1. Positive experiences in the early years—especially warm, responsive, caring, conversational relationships—literally grow babies' brains and lay the foundation for later learning.
2. Negative experiences such as prolonged stress, physical or sexual abuse, or exposure to violence can have dire and long-lasting effects on brain capabilities.
3. Early intervention including intensive early education and comprehensive support services for families—the earlier and more intensive, the better—can ameliorate the negative effects.

Dramatic evidence, along with powerful visual images of brain scans, has raised awareness of the vital importance of early experiences. For example, brain scans of maltreated children provide striking evidence of smaller brain volumes than those of children who have not suffered maltreatment, with more negative effects the earlier the abuse began and the longer it lasted (De Bellis et al., 1999). Findings such as these demonstrate the critical importance of early intervention.

Lasting Benefits of Early Childhood Education

A large body of research demonstrates that high-quality early childhood programs can have long-lasting positive consequences for children, especially children from economically disadvantaged backgrounds, and can be cost effective (Minervino, 2014; Yoshikawa et al., 2013). Three well-designed longitudinal studies—the Perry Preschool Project, the Abecedarian Early Childhood Intervention Project, and the Chicago Child-Parent Centers—followed children from early childhood into adulthood. The findings of these studies have been singularly influential with policy makers and are largely responsible for increased investments in early education such as President Obama's universal preschool initiative (Barnett, 2013b).

> ### ▶ Classroom Connection
>
> This video highlights brain research and the impact of quality early learning opportunities. Dr. Jack Shonkoff, founder of the Center for the Developing Child at Harvard University, presents the importance of positive early childhood experiences based on what scientists have learned by studying the brain.
>
> http://www.youtube.com/watch?v=tLiP4b-TPCA

The Perry Preschool Project   The Perry Preschool Project, which began in the early 1960s in Ypsilanti, Michigan, was one of the first studies to demonstrate the lasting effects of a high-quality preschool program on educational and economic outcomes. (Perry Preschool later became the HighScope Educational Research Foundation.) Researchers found that Perry Preschool graduates were less likely to be assigned to special education or be retained in grade and had better achievement test scores than children who did not attend preschool (Berrueta-Clement, Schweinhart, Barnett, Epstein, & Weikart, 1984). Preschool participation was also related to less involvement in delinquency and crime and a higher rate of high school graduation (Schweinhart, Barnes, & Weikart, 1993). At age 40, program participants were significantly more likely to have higher levels of education, be employed, earn higher wages, and own their own homes; they were less likely to be welfare dependent and had fewer arrests (Schweinhart et al., 2005).

These outcomes benefited not only the participants but the larger society as well. Economists estimated that for every dollar spent on the program, as much as $16 was returned on the original investment (Schweinhart et al., 2005). This means that Americans saved money in terms of the decreased costs of crime, special education, grade retention, and welfare payments, as well as increased taxes paid by those children who achieve in school and later earn higher incomes.

The Abecedarian Project   The University of North Carolina's Abecedarian Early Childhood Intervention Project demonstrated that intensive early intervention (five years of full-day, high-quality child care with parent involvement) can greatly enhance the development of children whose mothers have low income and education levels (Campbell et al., 2008). The Abecedarian program produced positive effects on achievement in reading and mathematics throughout elementary and high school. Children who participated were significantly less likely to be retained in grade or placed in special education, and they were more likely to attend 4-year colleges and to have skilled jobs. Access to free child care improved the mothers' long-term employment opportunities and earnings.

Chicago Child-Parent Centers   Perry Preschool and Abecedarian were relatively small-scale demonstration programs. A third longitudinal study of the Title I federally funded Chicago Child–Parent Centers reached similar positive conclusions with

> ### ▶ Classroom Connection
>
> This video describes the Chicago Child–Parent programs and cites the results of the studies conducted on the success of the program. Why has participating in this program resulted in lasting benefits for children and families?
>
> http://www.youtube.com/watch?v=ToCbcbpEfDw

a large-scale, public school program involving more than 1,500 children (Reynolds, Temple, Robertson, White, & Ou, 2011). Since 1985, the Chicago Child–Parent Centers (CPC) have provided preschool and kindergarten for children from low-income families and family support services with continued intervention in early elementary school.

Children who participated in CPC demonstrated higher school achievement, better social adjustment, less frequent grade retention, lower dropout rates, and lower rates of juvenile arrest. A follow-up study conducted 25 years later found strong positive effects into adulthood (Reynolds et al., 2011). Children who attended the program at age 3 attained better levels of education, income, job skills, and health insurance coverage, and lower rates of substance abuse, arrest, and imprisonment.

The Positive Effects of Prekindergarten, Head Start, and Child Care

As publicly funded prekindergarten programs have expanded, a great deal of research evaluating their effectiveness has become available. Numerous states across the country have found positive effects on children's readiness for school (Camilli, Vargas, Ryan, & Barnett, 2010; Minervino, 2014). For example, a longitudinal study of Michigan's prekindergarten program found that it decreased grade repetition and increased the number of children who passed the state's reading and mathematics tests and graduated from high school on time, and all these differences were greatest for children of color (Schweinhart, Xiang, Daniel-Echols, Browning, & Wakabayashi, 2012). Similar results were found in Virginia's state-funded prekindergartens (Huang, Invernizzi, & Drake, 2012). A study involving more than 60,000 children found that prekindergarten was related to improved literacy and less kindergarten retention. Results were most positive for Hispanic and African American students and also children with disabilities, and persisted through first grade.

Some of the strongest, most positive results were found in an evaluation of Tennessee's statewide prekindergarten program (Lipsey, Farran, Hofer, Bilbrey, & Dong, 2011). Children who attended prekindergarten improved on measures of literacy, language, and math between 37% and 176% more than did children who did not attend. The greatest gains were in language, which is very difficult to improve.

Most research demonstrates the value of preschool for children from low income families, but a growing body of research provides evidence of the positive effects of early education for *all* children. Read the *What Works: Increasing School Readiness for All Children* feature for an example.

Perhaps no other federally funded project has been as thoroughly studied as Head Start over the nearly 50 years of its existence. An overall conclusion that can be drawn is that Head Start has positive effects on children's overall development, health and dental care, and preparation for school, including improved literacy skills and social-emotional development (Barnett, 2008; Puma et al., 2005). Although there is evidence that Head Start needs to be improved and participation does not close the achievement gap between poor and middle-class children, it does narrow the gap. The effects are most positive for children who enter at age 3 and participate in full-day programs that include regular home visiting (Walters, 2014; Yoshikawa et al., 2013).

Child care research consistently finds that children who participate in high-quality programs demonstrate better language and mathematics ability and fewer behavior problems than do children in poor-quality care (Cost, Quality, and Child Care Outcomes Study Team, 1995; NICHD Early Child Care Research Network, 2002; Peisner-Feinberg et al., 1999). Positive effects are evident for all groups of children but are greater for children from lower-income families.

We could cite many other studies from states as diverse as New Jersey, Louisiana, Maryland, New Mexico, Massachusetts, and South Carolina that prove that high-quality early childhood programs can have positive short- and long-term consequences for young children. Research is also powerfully connected to another reason early childhood education is a field on the rise—the country's need to close the achievement gap, as addressed in the next section.

Social Justice and Closing the Achievement Gap

One of our nation's greatest challenges is addressing the persistent gap that exists between the school achievement of African American and Latino children and their white peers (Aud, Fox, & KewalRamani, 2010; Hemphill & Vanneman, 2011). Scholars tend to agree that these differences result primarily from the fact that race and ethnicity are strongly associated with **socioeconomic status (SES)** in the United States (National Center for Children in Poverty, 2014). For example, 42% of African American children and 35% of Latino children under the age of 5 are in the lowest socioeconomic level of U.S. citizens compared with 15% of white non-Hispanic children (CDF, 2014). And children of color are much more likely to live in conditions of extreme poverty (CDF, 2014). Achievement differences between racial and ethnic groups narrow considerably among children when they are from similar socioeconomic backgrounds (U.S. Department of Health and Human Services, 2014).

socioeconomic status (SES) Family income level.

As we have seen, the number of young children growing up poor in our country is increasing, with the largest growth in poverty among children under age 5 and children of color, which could further widen the achievement gap in the future. The achievement gap has profound consequences for our nation's future and its ability to compete in a global, highly technological society. Moreover, the potentially devastating effects on the life trajectories of individuals cannot be ignored.

What Works

Increasing School Readiness for All Children

As policy makers consider whether to increase funding for Head Start, public prekindergarten, or child care for needy families, they want to know whether these programs are effective. They want to know, "How well do early childhood programs prepare children for school?" and "Who should be eligible to attend?" A big issue is whether programs should be universal—that is, available to families of all income levels who choose to enroll their children—or targeted to low income families as Head Start is.

Oklahoma's state-funded prekindergarten has generated considerable attention. It is universal, based in the school system, and reaches a higher percentage of 4-year-olds than any other state pre-K program. Although most classes are located in public schools, some classes are located in Head Start and child care programs that meet the same standards for quality.

The Oklahoma program has high standards compared to other states, with lead teachers required to have a B.A. degree and be certified in early childhood education. Notably, prekindergarten teachers earn the same wages and benefits as other public school teachers. Student–teacher ratios are 10 to 1 and class sizes are limited to 20.

An evaluation of the program involving more than 3,000 children found strong positive effects for children from all income groups. All children's language and cognitive test scores improved, regardless of their economic status or ethnicity. The largest gains were for poor children of color, with Hispanic children making the most learning progress, followed by African Americans. But even though gains were somewhat higher for low-income children, gains for children in the higher income group were almost as large. A similar study comparing Tulsa's (Oklahoma) pre-K program and the Tulsa County Head Start program (which also receives state funds) found that both programs produce substantial improvements in early literacy and math.

It is increasingly clear that children from low-income families are not the only ones who need and can benefit from attending preschool. Research shows that many middle-income children are also behind their peers from the highest-earning families at kindergarten entry and they are less likely to have access to the kind of high-quality programs provided in Oklahoma.

Sources: The Effects of Oklahoma's Universal Pre-Kindergarten Program on Hispanic Children, by W. T. Gormley, 2008, Washington, DC: Center for Research on Children in the U.S. (CROCUS), Georgetown University, retrieved July 28, 2009, from http://www.crocus.georgetown.edu; "The Promise of Preschool: Why We Need Early Education for All," by W. S. Barnett and E. Frede, 2010, *American Educator, 34*(1), 21–29, 40.

Where the Gap Begins Differences in children's cognitive abilities are substantial at a very early age and widen over time (U.S. Department of Health and Human Services, 2014). By 18 months of age, SES differences in language development are evident, and by 24 months, economically disadvantaged children are as much as 6 months behind their more advantaged peers (Fernald, Marchman, & Weislader, 2013). At age 4, children who live below the poverty line may be 18 months below what is considered normal for their age group. In fact, inequity in socioeconomic status is the most important predictor of children's cognitive skills (Aud et al., 2010; McLoyd & Purtell, 2008).

To describe this discrepancy, a more accurate term than achievement gap is really *knowledge gap*. The differences in achievement are likely the result of differences in children's opportunities to gain knowledge from a variety of learning experiences. For example, children from higher-income families are much more likely to attend preschool.

Schools' Contributions to the Gap Children from low-income families not only enter kindergarten with fewer cognitive skills than their more affluent peers, but also are more likely to encounter poorer-quality elementary schools (Neuman, 2008). These schools are likely to have fewer resources and qualified teachers, more negative teacher attitudes, and poorer neighborhood or school conditions. As a result, the inequalities in cognitive abilities that are present even before kindergarten entry are not eliminated and often are magnified by their elementary school experience (Parkinson & Rowan, 2008).

One of the frequent criticisms of Head Start and prekindergarten is that the gains children make "fade-out" by later grades. These criticisms focus on standardized test scores rather than lasting social-emotional and meaningful life outcomes, and fail to take into account the quality of children's education in primary school (Barnett & Carolan, 2014). A more accurate term than *fade-out* is *convergence* (Yoshikawa et al., 2013). Children's achievement scores converge in the early grades because their school experiences do not build on preschool gains.

Children who begin school behind tend to stay behind. Although achievement has improved on average in the last few years, problems remain. By fourth grade, only 41% of public school students are proficient or above in mathematics and only 34% are proficient in reading (National Center for Education Statistics, 2013). Reading achievement at the end of first grade predicts reading skill at the end of fourth grade (Hernandez, 2011), which subsequently predicts high school graduation. Moreover, deep-seated inequities in communities and schools tend to increase rather than diminish these early achievement gaps over time. As one child advocacy group states, "Our children are not failing to learn. Our schools are failing to teach them effectively" (Foundation for Child Development, 2008, p. 4).

Early Education and Social Justice As we saw from research cited previously, these initial inequalities can be reduced. Children from low-income families who attend high-quality early childhood programs begin kindergarten with higher achievement, thus providing the potential to narrow the gap at the outset. This research, as well as studies on the effectiveness of services for children with special needs, proves that early intervention is less costly, more effective, and more humane than later remediation (Reynolds et al., 2011). Children living in poverty, however, are less likely to have access to high-quality programs.

Improving quality and increasing access to early childhood programs are important strategies for enhancing social justice in America and improving learning outcomes for all children. These goals can be addressed, however, only in the context of current trends in the field and the nation, which we discuss next.

✓ **Check Your Understanding 1.4:** Positive Effects of Early Childhood Education

Current Trends in Early Childhood Education

Early childhood education is literally a field in transition, experiencing rapid growth and widespread attention. Current trends affecting the field include major new policy initiatives at the federal and state level, more focus on standards and accountability resulting in increased emphasis on child assessment, calls for greater alignment across the full early childhood age span, increased teacher qualifications, expanding role of technology, and increased stress in the lives of children. These changes present new challenges, but also opportunities. In the sections that follow, we describe the potential benefits as well as the controversies of each trend. Even a cursory look at these trends reveals that they are interconnected.

New Federal and State Policy Initiatives

The first two decades of the 21st century have seen enormous growth in public support and funding for early education. The Obama administration proposed new investments to establish a continuum of high-quality early learning from birth to age 5 and to meet the following goals (Office of Early Learning, 2014):

- Provide access to high-quality infant and toddler care through Early Head Start–child care partnerships;
- Expand voluntary evidence-based home visiting to support our country's most vulnerable families; and
- Develop partnerships with states to provide voluntary, high-quality, full-day preschool for *all* 4-year-olds from families at or below 200 percent of the federal poverty line.

In response, a bipartisan group in Congress introduced the *Strong Start for America's Children Act* in 2014. The U.S. Department of Education distributed $1 billion in Early Learning Challenge Grants for statewide systems to improve the quality of early childhood programs and increase access for children who need them. Early Learning Challenge Grants support state efforts to build high-quality, accountable systems of early education; the grants call for states to use the same learning standards across all programs, measure children's learning outcomes, and improve professional development and compensation for teachers. As a result, the grants led states to develop or adopt kindergarten entry assessments (KEAs) to help teachers adapt instruction to individual children's needs. Preschool Development and Expansion Grants were also distributed to states to move the country forward in achieving universal prekindergarten.

Most public prekindergarten programs are not universal. Attendance is limited to children who qualify because they are from low-income families, are dual language learners, or have an identified disability. Proponents of universality cite research showing that middle-class children also benefit from prekindergarten, but the cost of high-quality programs is out of reach for most of these families (Burger, 2010; Yoshikawa et al., 2013). There is also evidence that academic and social skills of children from low-income families improve when they participate in mixed-income programs (Barnett & Frede, 2010; Schechter & Bye, 2007). In contrast, critics believe that limited funds should go to the neediest families (Fuller, 2007). Another concern is the competing need to fund services for infants and toddlers.

Expanding prekindergarten contributes to another trend: greater involvement of public schools in preschool education. In the past, young children rarely encountered a public school before kindergarten, but now the public education system is a major player in the early childhood landscape. As a

> ▶ **Classroom Connection**
>
> Watch this video from the National Institute for Early Education Research to learn about the research on effective teachers in high-quality preschool programs. How would this information be useful to advocate for universal prekindergarten?
>
> http://www.youtube.com/watch?v=or10f-YcM8Q

result, issues that have dominated K–12 education for some time now affect programs for younger children, such as more focus on standards and accountability.

Standards and Accountability

Since the 1990s, educational systems in the United States have emphasized learning standards—what children should know and be able to do at various ages. At the same time, a stronger emphasis on **accountability** has emerged, as seen in the Early Learning Challenge Grants. The concept is that schools and teachers, which receive public dollars, need to be held accountable for children's achieving learning standards. This leads to two related issues: (1) What are teachers to be held accountable for? and (2) How will it be measured?

Elementary and Secondary Education   Elementary and secondary education is primarily controlled and funded by state governments, which means that learning standards vary widely, with some states setting standards lower than others. The federal government provides support to states through the **Elementary and Secondary Education Act (ESEA)**. This law is periodically rewritten and therefore its requirements and funding are influenced by prevailing political trends. Since the 1990s, Congress has used the law as a lever to hold public schools accountable for eliminating the persistent gaps in achievement between different groups of children. Accountability is most often measured by test scores in core academic programs (reading and mathematics).

The law has also addressed the need for more highly qualified teachers to implement effective, **scientifically based instructional practices**, ways of teaching that research has demonstrated to improve learning outcomes. Emphasis on standards and accountability in elementary school has led to the development of learning standards for younger children and a stronger emphasis on early literacy and mathematics in Head Start and prekindergarten.

The Obama administration's Race to the Top initiative (which includes the Early Challenge Grants) was a recent approach to improving accountability and school reform. States competed for funding to adopt high standards that will prepare students to succeed

accountability The process of holding teachers, schools, or programs responsible for meeting a required level of performance.

Elementary and Secondary Education Act (ESEA) Law governing how the federal government distributes education funds to states and holds public schools accountable for the use of funding.

scientifically based instructional practices Curriculum and instructional practices that research has demonstrated improve learning outcomes.

Current trends in early childhood education include more focus on standards and accountability from prekindergarten through third grade. The overarching goal is to help children become more successful readers and writers.

in college and the workplace and compete in the global economy, ensure highly qualified teachers and principals, and turn around failing schools.

Common Core State Standards One problem with a large-scale accountability movement is the great variability among state content standards. To address this issue, in 2010, the Council of Chief State School Officers (CCSSO) and the National Governor's Association (NGA) released the **Common Core State Standards (CCSS)**, which are designed to establish a set of rigorous national standards in English language arts and mathematics for kindergarten through grade 12. The Common Core is intended to provide a consistent, clear understanding of what all students are expected to learn to be successful in college and careers, and for America to compete successfully in the global economy. As of 2014, 44 states and the District of Columbia officially adopted the Common Core, requiring much additional work to align curriculum and teaching practices, and create new assessments to measure achievement of the standards.

Although the Common Core began as a bipartisan effort, it has become politically controversial. A few governors who initially supported it withdrew their support. Some view it as a federal intrusion on state control of education because the federal government offered incentives to states to build systems around the CCSS. Others criticize the standards for being unachievable, narrowing the curriculum to two areas, and leading to overreliance on standardized tests for which students and teachers are not prepared.

Although the goals of increasing accountability and equity are worthy, the methods that have been used are highly controversial (Ravitch, 2013). Criticisms of the Common Core reflect broader concerns about the accountability movement in general. Some standards are actually unachievable for most children to meet even when they are in excellent schools (Graue, 2009). Although the standards do not apply to preschool, like many elementary school initiatives, they have a "push-down" impact on younger children.

Overemphasis on standardized test scores does tend to narrow the curriculum to what is tested, does not truly measure all of children's important capabilities, and punishes schools that need the most help. Regardless of the requirements of any specific piece of state or federal legislation, accountability is unlikely to go away in the future.

Higher Teacher Qualifications

Another related trend is to raise preschool teacher qualifications, with an emphasis on college degrees in early education or child development (Institute of Medicine [IOM] & National Research Council [NRC], 2015; Whitebook, Phillips, & Howes, 2014). Several research reviews have concluded that having bachelor's degree–level teachers with specialized preparation in early childhood education leads to better outcomes for young children (Minervino, 2014). Although some research has not found clear benefits of degrees (Walters, 2014), studies tend to support the fact that the more specialized education teachers have, the better it is for the children they teach.

Head Start's teacher qualifications have incrementally been raised over the years. For many years, teachers were required to have only a **Child Development Associate (CDA) credential**. This competency-based credential requires 120 clock hours of training (which may or may not be credit bearing) and 480 hours of experience with children, plus passing a written test and being observed working effectively with young children. The Head Start Act of 2009 requires that 50% of teachers hold a bachelor's degree with early childhood specialization. The program has exceeded this goal, with 66% of its preschool teachers holding a bachelor's degree or higher (Head Start, 2014c). Similarly, at least 50% of teacher assistants are required to have at least a CDA credential or be enrolled in a degree program. In addition, the CDA credential is the required qualification for teachers in Early Head Start.

Raising teacher qualifications has the potential to improve quality for children and also compensation and status for teachers. The biggest challenge is providing adequate funding to increase compensation commensurate with teacher qualifications, which, sadly, is far from the case (Whitebook, Phillips, & Howes, 2014).

Common Core State Standards Rigorous national standards in English language arts and mathematics for kindergarten through grade 12 developed by the Council of Chief State Officers (CCSSO) and the National Governor's Association (NGA).

Child Development Associate (CDA) credential National competency-based credential for entry-level early childhood educators.

An additional concern is the need to maintain a diverse workforce that reflects the population of children served. State prekindergarten programs have a larger percentage of teachers with bachelor's degrees than do Head Start or center-based programs. However, Head Start teachers are much more likely to reflect the cultural and linguistic diversity of the community (CLASP, 2011). For example, 30% of Head Start staff are proficient in a language other than English (Head Start, 2013).

Alignment of Services from Birth Through Age 8

A trend that is related to accountability and increased involvement of public schools in early education is the call for bridging the continuum of services for children from birth through third grade (Bornfreund, McCann, Williams, & Guernsey, 2014). Traditionally, preschool and K–3 have been two separate worlds with very little communication between them. **Alignment** means that curriculum at the preschool level would lay a foundation for the kindergarten curriculum, which could then more easily build on what children have learned. The idea is to ease transitions for students between schools and school levels and enhance continuity of learning while also respecting the needs of young children (Kauerz & Coffman, 2013).

Many early childhood educators are concerned that the push for alignment will narrow the curriculum to literacy and mathematics, apply learning standards intended for older children, and lead to inappropriate testing of young children (Graue, 2009; NAEYC, 2009). They are especially concerned that schools will eliminate valuable experiences such as play, the arts, and support for social-emotional development.

Advocates for Pre-K–3 alignment support better connected education for preschool and elementary children. They stress that alignment does not mean that preschool children should learn primary grade skills at an earlier age (Kauerz & Coffman, 2013; NAEYC, 2009). Rather, curriculum should reflect what children can and should learn at each age, and teachers should know how to help children make progress.

alignment Coordination of the curriculum from one level of education to the next in order to build on what children have already learned and to ease transitions for students between schools and school levels.

Advances in Technology

In no aspect of life is the speed of change as rapid as in the area of technology. In education, technology has a tremendous impact on how teachers teach and function in their work, but also on children's experiences at home and in school. Increasingly innovative uses of interactive media in all aspects of early education is a major trend. Given the demand for highly qualified teachers, online teacher preparation and professional development options are increasing rapidly.

As digital media such as handheld mobile devices and video games proliferate, so has the development of educational apps, the majority of which are targeted to preschoolers (Shuler, 2009; Thai, Lowenstein, Ching, & Rejeski, 2009). In their position statement on technology, NAEYC and the Fred Rogers Center for Early Learning and Children's Media (2012) acknowledge legitimate concerns about potential inappropriate uses of technology but also promote the almost unlimited creative ways that interactive media can support learning and development. The question is no longer whether young children should be exposed to digital media, but rather what is the quality of technological tools provided for them.

Stress in Children's Lives

The foregoing trends coupled with the economic downturn, increased violence in society, and other challenges facing families have all contributed to growing stress in the lives of young children (Almon & Miller, 2011). In turn, mounting stressors endanger children's long-term mental and physical health (Shonkoff et al., 2012). Teachers and parents are concerned about children's safety, while at the same time they feel pressured to prepare them for the academic rigors of school. These conditions conspire to threaten one of the most important and beneficial activities of childhood—play, as discussed in the feature *Promoting Play: Addressing Threats to Children's Play.*

Promoting Play

Addressing Threats to Children's Play

Pediatricians and psychologists agree that too many children today experience high levels of unrelenting stress. Factors such as poverty and violence are the primary sources, but stress affects the lives of all children to some extent. Teachers today report that more children are aggressive and disruptive as a result of stressful events. Increasing numbers of children, especially boys, are inaccurately diagnosed as hyperactive and needlessly medicated. Childhood obesity is also endemic.

Research demonstrates that exercise and child-initiated play are effective stress-relievers. Ironically, however, a survey of child care, preschool, and Head Start teachers found that they tend to limit children's opportunities for active play, especially outdoors, due to safety concerns and the need to prepare children academically for school. And children living in poverty are most likely to suffer because they have less access to safe outdoor play areas and programs feel extra pressure to focus on academic instruction to close the school readiness gap.

Part of the solution is that teachers, parents, and administrators need to understand that play and school readiness is not an *either/or* choice. The American Academy of Pediatrics emphasizes that play is essential for children's physical health, emotional and mental well-being, social relationships, and brain development and cognition. Vigorous play develops large motor skills, and can reduce obesity. In short, play contributes to all areas of development and learning.

In an attempt to get children ready for school and protect them from injury, early childhood programs may actually be contributing to children's stress by minimizing children's large muscle activity and child-initiated play time. Because children spend so much time in early childhood programs and school, it may be their only opportunity to have physical activity or outdoor play.

Early educators need to draw on the support of physicians and other experts to help educate parents and policy makers about the importance of play in children's lives and its essential role in helping children cope with stress and improve school success. They also need to advocate for funding to provide safe playgrounds and adequate spaces indoors and outdoors for active engagement. Play spaces and opportunities must be designed to protect children from injury, but protecting them from stress is equally important.

Sources: "Societal Values and Policies May Curtail Preschool Children's Physical Activity in Child Care Centers," by K. A. Copeland, S. N. Sherman, C. A. Kendeigh, H. J. Kalkwarf, & B. E. Saelens, 2012, *Pediatrics, 129*(2), retrieved from http://pediatrics.aappublications.org/content/early/2012/01/02/peds.2011-2102.full.pdf+html; "The Importance of Play in Promoting Healthy Child Development and Maintaining Strong Parent-Child Bond: Focus on Children in Poverty," by R. M. Milter, K. R. Ginsburg, & Council on Communications and Media Committee on Psychological Aspects of Child and Family Health, *Pediatrics, 129*(1), e204–e213, retrieved from http://www.pediatrics.aappublications.org.

Continuity and Change

One overarching trend always affecting education is continuity and change. As the field expands and changes occur in response to new political and economic realities, many longtime early childhood professionals are concerned that the fundamental values of the field will be lost. Development, including development of professions, is characterized by both continuity and change. In this book we describe how the fundamental values of early childhood education can be retained and enhanced (thus maintaining continuity with the important tenets of the past), while also presenting what is known from new research about effective teaching practices for *all* children. Some ways of thinking and practicing should be cherished and held onto, whereas others may need to be updated or abandoned.

Traditional Practices	Current Practices
• Processes of child development and learning	• *Both* how children learn *and* what they learn
• Inputs – standards such as licensing or accreditation that mandate what programs should do	• *Both* program standards *and* outcomes (early learning standards)
• Quality	• *Both* quality *and* accountability
• Activities	• *Both* coherent curriculum plans *and* links to learning goals
• Free play	• *Both* child-initiated, developmentally valuable play *and* playful learning
• Developmental appropriateness	• *Both* effectiveness *and* developmental appropriateness (Are children making progress from the experiences we deem appropriate?
• Observation of children	• *Both* observation *and* formal assessment of child outcomes
• Facilitating learning	• *Both* intentional teaching *and* positive, supportive relationships
• Development, not academics (viewing early childhood education as separate from primary grades)	• *Both* viewing learning and development as a continuum from birth to age 8 *and* alignment from pre-K to grade 3
• Typical, normative development	• *Both* adapting for individual variation of every child *and* intervention and adaption for children with disabilities and special needs, as well as children who are advanced

FIGURE 1.4 Continuity and Change in Early Childhood Education Early childhood education today builds on the enduring values of its past but also changes as we acquire new knowledge about children, families, and the contexts in which they live.

Resolving Contradictions Between Enduring Values and Current Trends We propose that the way to resolve potential contradictions that arise over difficult or controversial issues is to "widen the lens." Widening the lens is a metaphor for expanding the sources of information professionals use to make decisions; gaining insights from diverse perspectives including through the lenses of culture, language, and ability/disability; and looking at questions or problems from broader perspectives. Widening the lens is a strategy to move beyond the tendency to oversimplify complex educational issues into "either/or" choices and to move toward "both/and" thinking.

Embracing *Both/And* Thinking Widening the lens to consider diverse points of view—*both/and* thinking—is a constructive response to addressing both continuity and change in the field. Figure 1.4 illustrates how this process applies to the field today. The left side of the arrow describes traditional practices that have held sway in the past; the right side of the arrow illustrates how current views encompass these earlier approaches and extend beyond them, thus reflecting *both/and* thinking as well as continuity and change.

Throughout this text, we will revisit these issues as well as the profession's core values and demonstrate how new research can help teachers effectively put these values into practice. Chapters are devoted to each of the core values: child development and learning, relationships, families, communities, individuality, and cultural diversity. We discuss the overarching value of play in the context of all the key topics in this book.

We began by pointing out that early childhood education is a field on the rise. The profession is expanding, growing in status, and gaining support from policy makers and the general public. A huge body of research supports the importance of the work. It is indeed an exciting time to be an early childhood educator.

 Check Your Understanding 1.5: Current Trends in Early Childhood Education

Revisiting the Case Study

. . . Cresthaven Child Development Center

We began this chapter by peeking in and eavesdropping on the end-of-the-year event for Cresthaven Primary School and Reed Child Development Center. Now that we have seen the broader picture of the early childhood landscape, the teachers' thoughts and emotions become more meaningful. At this event, we saw the wide range of age groups that early childhood encompasses as well as some of the diverse settings. In addition, these teachers exemplify fundamentals of intentional teaching.

The collaborative partnership between the school and child care program supports alignment of curriculum from preschool through third grade, and eases transitions for children and families. The garden project is one example of how these teachers connect the curriculum to the larger community and provide children with meaningful, hands-on learning opportunities. Children, families, and teachers not only celebrated the good times they'd had, but children also demonstrated how much they'd learned through the displays of their work and through technology.

Across the classrooms, we saw the value of communication and responsive relationships among teachers and families. New teachers Isela and Evan have learned that early childhood education is hard work but have also begun to experience the rewards. Their patience and focus on intentional teaching is paying off for Nicky. Cooper's experience demonstrates the power of inclusion and how it benefits children with disabilities and their peers. At the end of the day, these teachers go home feeling good about what they've accomplished, but knowing that there is more to learn and new adventures awaiting them tomorrow. ■

 # Chapter Summary

- Early childhood education is a diverse field that covers the broad age range of birth through age 8. Teachers work in child care centers and homes, preschools, kindergartens, and primary grade schools.

- Becoming a professional, intentional early childhood teacher is a challenging and rewarding opportunity. Early childhood education is expanding and is a field on the rise, benefiting from growing public recognition and support. Many career options are available to work with children or work for children.

- Early childhood professionals are part of a cultural group that shares a vocabulary, an identity, values, and beliefs. These include emphasis on the uniqueness of early childhood, the value of play, the importance of relationships and a sense of community, valuing

and teaching each child as an individual, respecting linguistic and cultural diversity, and relationships with families.

- The early childhood profession sets high-quality standards for programs. The most important determinants of the quality of children's experiences and strongest predictors of positive outcomes are the social and instructional interactions that occur between teachers and children.

- Brain research demonstrates the importance of early experience to later development. A large body of evidence exists supporting the positive long-term and short-term consequences of high-quality early childhood programs.

- High-quality early education has an important role to play in improving children's school readiness and addressing social justice concerns about closing the achievement gap in our schools.

- New political and economic realities present challenges and opportunities for the field including the federal and state policy initiatives, universal prekindergarten movement, more focus on standards and accountability, increased teacher qualifications, calls for greater

alignment across the full early childhood age span, stress in children's lives, and advancing technology use by teachers and children.

- Early childhood education is a rewarding profession for many reasons, but above all, early childhood educators enter and stay in the field because they know that their work makes a difference in the lives of children and families.

Key Terms

- accountability
- accreditation system
- alignment
- charter schools
- Child Care and Development Block Grants (CCDBG)
- child care center
- child care licensing standards
- Child Development Associate (CDA) credential
- Classroom Assessment Scoring System (CLASS)
- Common Core state standards (CCSS)

- culture
- developmentally appropriate practice
- dual language learners
- early childhood education
- Early Childhood Environment Rating Scale (ECERS-3)
- early childhood special education
- Early Head Start
- early intervention
- early learning standards
- Elementary and Secondary Education Act (ESEA)

- family child care home
- Head Start
- Head Start Program Performance Standards
- inclusion
- Individuals with Disabilities Education Act (IDEA)
- intentional teachers
- kindergarten
- laboratory school
- National Association for the Education of Young Children (NAEYC)
- parent cooperative
- prekindergarten (pre-K)
- preschool

- primary grades
- process quality
- professionals
- quality rating and improvement systems (QRIS)
- school readiness
- scientifically based instructional practices
- socioeconomic status (SES)
- structural quality
- Temporary Assistance for Needy Families (TANF)
- universal voluntary prekindergarten

 Demonstrate Your Learning

Click here to assess how well you've learned the content in this chapter.

Readings and Websites

Chenfield, M. B. (2014). *Still teaching in the key of life: Joyful stories from early childhood settings.* Washington, DC: National Association for the Education of Young Children.

Feeney, S. (2012). *Professionalism in early childhood education: Doing our best for young children.* Upper Saddle River, NJ: Pearson.

Hyson, M., & Tomlinson, H. B. (2014). *The early years matter: Education, care and the well-being of children, birth to 8.* New York: Teachers College Press.

National Association for the Education of Young Children (NAEYC)

NAEYC's website has a wealth of resources on every aspect of early childhood education, including their publications, accreditation system, position statements on controversial topics, and public policy.

National Institute for Early Education Research (NIEER)

On this website, you will find summaries of research conducted by NIEER and other resources to learn about and advocate for high-quality, effective early childhood education for all young children.

National Resource Center for Health and Safety in Child Care and Early Education

This site provides access to child care licensing information for every state and resources for educators, families, and health professionals.

New America Foundation Early Education Initiative

The Early Education Initiative of New America Foundation, a nonpartisan organization that brings together diverse perspectives to address current issues, promotes a high-quality and continuous system of early care and education for all children, birth to age 8. Read their blog, EdCentral, to stay informed on the latest developments and research in the field.

2 Building on a Tradition of Excellence

Learning Outcomes

After studying this chapter, you should be able to:

2.1 Explain why it is important to learn from the past.

2.2 Describe how European educators influenced early education practices.

2.3 Describe the events and people that propelled the kindergarten, nursery school, and child care movements in the United States.

2.4 Explain the experiences and contributions of African Americans, Hispanic Americans, and Native Americans in the history of early childhood education.

2.5 Discuss the trends in early childhood history that came together to influence the launch of the national Head Start program and current trends in early childhood education.

Grant, Melinda, and Reece are enrolled in an introductory course in early childhood education. Their first assignment is to observe a preschool classroom. The professor says, "I want you to pretend that you are from another planet, or from such a remote part of the earth that you have never seen a preschool classroom before. Observe for one hour and write down exactly what you see. Don't try to guess what I want you to observe or second-guess yourself, just write what you see."

After completing their observations, Grant, Melinda, and Reece compare notes. Their lists are different in some respects but the following items appear on all three lists: child-sized furniture, one-inch cube blocks, and wooden parquetry blocks in various colors and shapes. They see groups of children building roads and towers with wooden blocks. Each classroom has a library area with picture books, alphabet books, and stories (each room even has a copy of *Goodnight Moon* on the bookrack). One class has sandpaper letters. There are also woodworking benches, sand tables, a posted recipe for cooking a snack, and dress-up clothes and props. In all three classes children are actively playing or working with teachers in small groups. One group had been to visit the firehouse (as evidenced by a chart on the wall recording children's remembrances) and there are firehats and hoses to play with. At snack time in one room, the children sing "Happy Birthday" to their friend.

During class, the professor asks each student to share one thing on his or her list and then for a show of hands to see who else had seen the same thing. There is remarkable uniformity among the observations. The professor explains, "What you observed are traces of the history of early childhood education. Your unfiltered observations are like the first steps archaeologists take in uncovering what has gone before. You may be surprised to find that all these things you observed can be traced back to specific people or events in the history of the field. They were put there and they remain there for a reason. First, we'll find out how they got there, and the rest of this course will help you understand why they are still there or how practices have changed in the intervening years." ■

Early childhood educators tend to like stories. We love sharing stories about the enchanting things that young children say and do. We listen to parents' stories about their children. And we exchange stories about our teaching—sometimes when we have a bad day, and almost always when we have a very good day. Those good days usually involve seeing an exciting example of a child's developmental progress.

Stories—that is what *history* is. The goal of this chapter, then, is to tell the story of early childhood education. We begin by describing how studying history is relevant. Next, we describe how the concept of childhood has changed over the course of history. Finally, we tell several stories about major historical movements and how they influence early childhood education practice today. Parts of these stories occurred simultaneously and overlap. **Click here** to review the major events in early childhood education.

Learning from the Past

Early childhood education is a field with a long and rich history going back to ancient times. Its history differs from that of education for older children, which has been considered a public responsibility for more than a century. By contrast, young children's care and education are so closely tied to families that private and public support for early childhood

Traces of the history of the field of early childhood education can be found in any preschool classroom today. What in this classroom environment might have been present in a pre-school 80 years ago? Why do you think it is still being used?

care and education is a very recent phenomenon. In addition, early childhood education is a more interdisciplinary field than is elementary education, with historical influences coming from not only child development and education but also from medicine, psychology, sociology, and other areas. As a result, many historical paths have converged to lead the field to where it is today.

Why History Is Relevant

The history of early childhood education, especially during the past 150 years, reveals that the past and the present are inexorably linked. Most of the current issues and controversies have been visited in some form in the past. For example, even all those years ago, teachers grappled with questions such as these: What environments and materials should be provided? What are the goals for children's learning and development? How should children be taught? What is the role of the teacher? How should parents be involved? Who is qualified to be a teacher? All of these issues have dominated debates about early education since its inception, and continue to do so.

Rather than assuming that these issues are being encountered for the first time, understanding how they have been resolved in the past can inform current discussions. One reason this is so important is that "the solution to every problem contains the seeds of a new problem" (Bredekamp & Glowacki, 1996). For example, early in the 20th century, advocates fought for kindergarten to be part of public schools. Succeeding in doing so eventually meant that kindergarten teachers were able to earn public school salaries and that services became available for all children. But this solution also created a new problem—kindergartens became, and still are, more like first grades than like preschools in curriculum expectations and teaching methods. Today's advocates for public prekindergarten need to be aware of this history as they pursue their goals.

Consider how this phenomenon may be evident in your own life. A problem that many college students face is the high cost of tuition. Students solve this problem in different ways—taking out loans, working full time or part time while going to school, or choosing less expensive schools. But each of these solutions can lead to new challenges. The loans need to be repaid; a full-time job delays graduation; the accessible schools may not meet the students' needs. In turn, each of these "problems" leads to a subsequent solution, and the process begins anew.

The idea that solving problems creates new challenges can be discouraging; however, it need not be. As long as we are working on solving new problems or challenges, we are making progress. History is composed of such progress in spurts as well as in setbacks. As you reflect on early childhood history you will encounter many example of solutions creating new challenges.

Avoid Getting Stuck in the Past Just as it is true that we continue to confront questions and challenges similar to those faced by our forebears, it is equally true that responses to these issues need to reflect current knowledge. As we will see, many of the principles and values that guide the field today are remarkably consistent with earlier views (Copple & Bredekamp, 2009). There are also essential differences based on newer research, theories, and realities. Getting stuck in the past can lead to defending past practices simply because we have always done it that way. Knowing why it was "done that way," however, can lead to changing it for the better.

Aspire to Make a Difference for Children History is not just the story of events, but the stories of people. The history of early childhood education is replete with inspiring stories of women and men who devoted themselves to improving the lives of children and families. Many "dauntless women" (Snyder, 1972) contributed in countless ways to early childhood education at a time when women's opportunities for higher education and careers were severely restricted. Similarly, men have been at the forefront of building the profession even though children were considered the purview of women.

The stories of these pioneers of early childhood education, who were forward looking in both their thinking and their deeds, serve as inspiration and motivation for current and future professionals. Learning about their lives, the obstacles they faced in their work, and the brilliance of their minds sets a high standard for the rest of us.

Advocate for Change Understanding the paths history has taken is important if early childhood educators are to be successful in improving services in the future. Even a brief summary of historical underpinnings reveals that change is a constant. For example, at times, services for children have been a priority while at other times (regularly, in fact), the services are threatened. The Head Start program is a case in point. In the mid-1960s, Head Start was launched to great fanfare as a means to end poverty in this country, an impossibly unrealistic goal. But over the years, the program has fallen prey to changing public attitudes and funding priorities.

Throughout these years, some advocates have set idealistic goals, which can be inspiring; yet history has taught us that unrealistic goals doom a program to failure. In the intervening years, advocates have made it plain that Head Start plays a key role in empowering low income families to improve their lives and in preparing their children for success in school. However, Head Start is not a cure for the ills of poverty, nor is it an inoculation against poor school experiences that might follow. To be most effective, advocates for improving Head Start and other early childhood programs and services should use the lessons of successful efforts in the past.

Examining the history of childhood education reveals that there have been significant changes—transformations, actually—in how children are viewed. In the sections that follow, we examine the changing view of childhood and its effect on children's lives.

The Changing View of Children

Different periods of history have had differing perspectives on children and the idea of childhood itself (Aries, 1962). These perspectives matter because they have direct implications for how children are treated and what kinds of education they are provided. Different eras in history have tended to view children as miniature adults, born in sin, blank slates, innocent, economic valuables, competent, and as citizens with rights. At different times, one or the other of these perspectives has tended to prevail. To some extent, all of these views of children persist to this day. In the sections that follow, each of the perspectives of childhood just mentioned is described, along with the potential positive and negative consequences for children's lives.

Children as Miniature Adults From the Middle Ages to about the 17th century in Western Europe, children were basically seen as adults on a smaller scale (Aries, 1962). Children dressed like adults, did adult-like work, and even played the same games. In fact, it wasn't until the 15th and 16th centuries that children appeared in paintings wearing specialized children's clothing.

In the 18th century, discovery of smallpox inoculation and better conditions in general reduced the death rate among children, which likely contributed to changes in the idea of childhood (Aries, 1962). Previously, the extremely high infant mortality rate motivated families to produce a large number of children to ensure the survival of a few. Families depended on their children to provide labor to support the family. As children's survival became less precarious, so too did their value as individuals and the image attached to them.

Centuries ago, children were viewed as "miniature adults." Children today are once again dressing like adults, playing adult-type games, and being exposed to adult images through the media at younger and younger ages.

© Robin Laurance/Alamy

Today, the image of children as miniature adults is apparent once again in the clothes children wear and the images they are exposed to through the media. Primary-grade girls dress like teenagers or young adults. Concern exists that they are too sexy too soon (Levin & Kilbourne, 2008). Preschoolers engage in team sports previously reserved for older children. Children's toys have been replaced by adult-like video games and digital devices.

Children in Need of Redemption

The image of the child during the 1300s to 1800s was shaped by the religious belief that children were born in sin and needed redemption. Misbehavior of any kind was considered sinful and punished harshly.

Schools in Europe and America in the 18th and 19th centuries were based on this image of children. Children learned to read from the Bible, recited memorized passages, and were often beaten or ridiculed for errors. Many people today continue to believe that severe punishment is necessary to shape children's moral character.

Children as Blank Slates

English philosopher John Locke (1632–1704) countered the religious argument that children are born with a predetermined sinful nature. Instead, he believed that children are born as *tabula rasa*, blank slates. What gets written on the slates is determined by their experiences in the environment. Locke's view was a step forward because it rejected the notion of inherent sinfulness and strongly emphasized the importance and value of education.

Locke was accurate in assuming that environmental experiences play a major role in children's learning; however, he did not see individual differences in children or how they actively shape their own experiences. Nevertheless, Locke's image of children as blank slates persists. Many schools today still operate on the notion that children are empty vessels that need to be filled, rather than active participants in the process of education.

Children as Innocents

In contrast to Locke's theory as well as the notion of children as sinners in need of redemption, French philosopher Jean-Jacques Rousseau (1712–1778) introduced the Romantic image of the child as innocent. Rousseau's novel *Emile* promoted the idea that children are born good rather than evil, and that they have inherent abilities upon which to build (Wolfe, 2000). He thought education should build on children's natural goodness.

Rousseau believed that it is important to observe children. He was among the first to propose the concept of stages of development. He believed that children should not be rushed through stages, nor that one stage was simply preparation for another, a concept that continues to influence practice 150 years later.

Rousseau's image of childhood was a radical departure from the views of his day. Although he did not put these ideas into practice, they influenced many thinkers who followed and continue to have an influence today. Early childhood education has a strong tradition of focusing on the positive in children to develop individual potential.

Children's Economic Value

At various points in history, children's value has been calculated in response to a number of factors. Even today, some consider children to be their parents' property. They were, and still are in some communities, economically necessary to contribute work to the sustenance and care of the family; this includes taking care of other children and parents in old age. In the 19th and early 20th centuries, however, child labor laws limited children's potential economic contributions to family well-being. As children's economic contributions diminished, they began to take on more intrinsic emotional value in the family. For example, insurance companies compensated parents for a child's death or injury not only because of the costs involved and the potential income lost, but also as an attempt to compensate for the emotional loss (Zellizer, 1981).

competent child The image of children as active players in their own development and learning.

The Competent Child

Scientific study of children beginning in the 20th century led to an alternative view of childhood—the **competent child**—the idea that children are active players in their own development and learning. The more researchers learned about children's competencies beginning at birth, the less plausible it became to see them as blank slates. Brain research in recent decades has further reinforced this image of children's innate competence.

The image of the competent child has had a major impact on early childhood practices and the larger culture. But negative consequences can emanate as well. Producers of videotapes and television and computer programs claim that they can teach a baby to read or produce a future Einstein. In addition, the image of the competent child has contributed to the trend to hurry young children through childhood toward expectations or experiences more appropriate for older children or adults (Elkind, 2007; Levin & Kilbourne, 2008).

The Child as a Citizen with Rights The image of the child throughout history has come almost full circle in its relation to adults. But rather than seeing children as small-scale adults, a present-day development is to view children as citizens who have rights just as adults do (Hall & Rudkin, 2011). In a democratic society, rights are implemented as laws such as those that protect children from abuse or prosecution as adults. Similarly, toys and products used by children must meet safety regulations.

Internationally, the image of a child with rights has gained widespread attention. In 1989, the United Nations Convention on the Rights of the Child (http://www.unicef.org/crc) went into effect. It has been ratified by every developed country in the world except Somalia and the United States. The declaration calls for protection of all children from physical, mental, and sexual abuse. One provision states that, although parents have primary responsibility for children's upbringing, states should provide appropriate assistance and support for child care programs. This is one of several provisions that have been politically controversial in this country. Although the United States has not endorsed the UN Convention, its existence promotes an image of the child with rights.

Images of Childhood Today Elements of all of these images of childhood are present in children's lives today and influence how they are treated. Although our country tends to see children as innocents in need of protection by parents and the government, we also propel them into adult experiences at young ages. Our schools swing back and forth, between taking an approach that children are empty vessels, and viewing them as competent contributors to their own learning. On the one hand, children are highly valued, and on the other hand, they are abused and neglected. As we have seen throughout history, the prevailing image of children impacts their lives in many ways. One example is the role of play, which is described in the feature *Promoting Play: The Image of the Child and the Role of Play*.

As we explore the evolution of early childhood practice in the sections that follow, it will become apparent which of these images has had the greater influence on the field. We can only present highlights of the rich history of the field here; for a more complete picture, **click here** to consult the timeline of major events.

 Check Your Understanding 2.1: Learning from the Past

European Influences on American Early Childhood Education

Like much of American history, early education was strongly influenced by Western European ideas. Although European ideas were not the only, nor necessarily the best, educational concepts in the world, current practices in the United States strongly reflect these early influences. Later in this chapter, we consider early childhood history through a wider lens.

Rousseau's belief in the inherent goodness and potential of children had a strong impact on the educational ideas and practices that followed. Two other thinkers who shared similar views are Comenius and Pestalozzi. Unlike Rousseau, both created schools that implemented their vision.

Promoting Play

The Image of the Child and the Role of Play

Children always play. However, many factors influence how they play and the materials they play with. To some extent, children's play reflects the prevailing image of the child. For example, when children were considered miniature adults, there was little difference between their play pastimes and those of their elders. Adults and children played with hoops and danced the same dances. When children were thought to be born in sin, Puritanical adults frowned on play as idleness and thought children's time should be spent in Bible study or productive work.

The view that children are innocents who are inherently good meant greater freedom for children to play in less restricted, more creative ways. The late 19th and early 20th centuries saw changes in children's play as living conditions improved. When child labor laws went into effect, children enjoyed more time for free play unsupervised by adults. Children created their "toys" from real objects, such as bats out of sticks. Boys and girls played make-believe, often outdoors. Boys tended to engage in informal ball games, and girls enacted housekeeping scenarios with dolls and pretend, rather than manufactured, props.

As scientific study of child development expanded in the later 20th century, the image of the "competent child" had a significant impact on children's play. Whereas previously toys such as balls, dolls, blocks, and cards were relatively open-ended and primarily designed for fun, "educational toys" began to flood the market. Middle-class parents purchased toys to teach rather than entertain their children.

And children's free time became much more structured with formal dance or music lessons and participation on sports teams at younger ages.

The recent image of children as citizens with rights is a noteworthy development relevant to play. Article 31 of the United Nations Convention on the Rights of the Child affirms that governments recognize the right to "engage in play and recreational activities appropriate to the age of the child."

Although play is influenced by adults' image of the child, children always exercise a certain amount of control over play, or the activity isn't play at all. And their play is often based on their image of adults. As a result, children prefer toys and play themes that are connected to the adult world. For instance, when horses were the primary mode of transportation, children played with hobby horses or stick horses. Subsequently, these were replaced by cars, and then airplanes, and eventually spaceships.

The U.S. culture now seems to have come full circle. In many respects children are once again seen as miniature adults. They dress like adults, play with adult-like toys (Barbies instead of baby dolls), and desire the same exact "toys" as adults—video games, cell phones, and iPads.

Sources: *Centuries of Childhood: A Social History of Family Life*, by P. Aries, 1962, New York: Vintage Books; *Play and Child Development*, 4th edition, by J. L. Frost, S. C. Wortham, and S. Reifel, 2012, Upper Saddle River, NJ: Pearson; United Nations Convention on the Rights of the Child, 1989, retrieved from http://www.ohchr.org/en/professionalinterest/pages/crc.aspx.

John Amos Comenius

John Amos Comenius (Jan Komensky in his native Czech) (1592–1670) was a minister who wrote about educational reform and directed a school where he could put his ideas into practice. He believed in three key ideas (Wolfe, 2000): (1) Teaching methods needed to be radically changed from punitive approaches to make learning easier, deeper, and more pleasant; (2) teachers should engage children with nature and follow their lead; and (3) children should learn in their own language, rather than in Latin.

To accomplish his last goal, Comenius wrote a new kind of book, *Orbis Pictus*, or "the world in pictures." Popular for the next 200 years, this was the first children's picture book or illustrated textbook ever published. It was organized around topics of interest such as birds and plants and included pictures with labels attached. Comenius also wrote the first illustrated alphabet book to teach children to read in their own languages.

Some of the educational ideas that Comenius practiced in his school were radical for his time but sound familiar today. For example, he thought the early years were an extremely important foundation for later learning. He believed that children learn through their senses and need to be active, and he felt that children's interests and firsthand experiences promote learning and memory. Comenius believed that children are born in the image of God, and was vehemently opposed to physical punishment (Wolfe, 2000). Like Rousseau, he identified developmental stages.

Comenius's ideas have endured for centuries. For example, in the 1990s Eastern European countries that had been under Communist dictatorship moved toward democracy. One strategy was to reform previously rigid educational systems. With the help of American philanthropy, the International Step by Step Association (http://www.issa.nl) was founded to develop Head Start–like preschool programs. There was some concern that these "American" ideas—such as child-centered education—would be culturally inappropriate. However, these concerns underestimated the lasting reverence for native son Komensky (Comenius)—who is, after all, the forerunner of much of American early childhood education.

First created more than 400 years ago, picture books remain one of the most popular, valuable, and engaging learning materials in early childhood programs and homes.

Johann Pestalozzi

Johann Pestalozzi (1746–1827) was a Swiss educator who, like Comenius, founded his own school and trained the teachers. He believed that all children—including children who lived in poverty—could benefit from education (Nourot, 2005). The field's current views of best practice are remarkably consistent with many of Pestalozzi's ideas about teaching and learning.

Learning and Teaching in Pestalozzi's School Pestalozzi (1894/2007) described his philosophy in a book titled *How Gertrude Teaches Her Children*. He believed that teachers must study child development. He thought that learning proceeds through stages, with children needing to master skills and knowledge before moving on to the next stage (Wolfe, 2000). Pestalozzi promoted what came to be called the "whole child" point of view—that children's physical, emotional, social, moral, and intellectual development are integrated. He called these "the hand, heart, and head."

Other important ideas of Pestalozzi included the notion that children need to discover ideas for themselves through their own activity—a precursor of Piaget's theory of **constructivism**. He rejected punishment and threats and felt that children are motivated to learn by their interests. Like many early theorists, Pestalozzi viewed development as a natural unfolding or blossoming from within, with teachers acting as gardeners who nurture the process rather than direct it. Although this view is simpler than our understanding of development today, it persisted well into the 20th century.

constructivism Learning theory derived from the work of Jean Piaget, which assumes that children actively build their knowledge from firsthand experiences in stimulating environments.

Impact of Pestalozzi's Work Pestalozzi's ideas directly influenced schools for young children in the 19th century. Particularly influential was his notion of object lessons—learning from direct observation and sensory experience in the natural world—that begin with the here and now and move beyond (Wolfe, 2000).

A well-known school influenced by Pestalozzi was founded by Robert Owen (1771–1858) as part of his idealized community in Scotland, New Lanark. Owen spread his ideas to America by founding a similar model community in New Harmony, Indiana. Although his experiment did not survive long, the school provided care and education for hundreds of children, from infancy to age 10, whose parents worked in the mills—one of the earliest examples of a child care center.

▶ Classroom Connection

This video clearly depicts the materials Froebel developed for use in the first kindergartens. How did Froebel's educational philosophy influence early childhood today, and which materials are still popular toys for children?

https://www.youtube.com/watch?v=LNBzmCKLNdU

Friedrich Froebel

Friedrich Froebel (1782–1852) built on Pestalozzi's ideas but extended them to develop educational materials. His view of development as a process of natural unfolding is evident in the name of his school, a "garden for children." Froebel is well known as the "father of the kindergarten."

Froebel believed in the innate goodness and capacities of children, and saw God's image in them. Like Pestalozzi, he believed that education should be based on children's interests and their active involvement, and that teachers need to understand children's development by directly observing their actions (Giardiello, 2014).

He described stages of development that are similar to those Piaget articulated in the 20th century. He saw infancy (birth to 3 years) as focused on the family and the infant's relationship with the mother. He wrote *Mother Play and Nursery Songs* to assist mothers in their interactions with very young children—something most mothers today take for granted. Froebel's second stage (ages 3 to 7), for which he developed his kindergarten materials, was the focus of most of his work. The third stage (ages 7 to 10) focused on more formal school instruction.

Froebel's Kindergarten   Froebel's metaphor of the children's garden was more than poetry. He strongly believed that children's learning is a process of unfolding from within. He also believed that learning would occur on the child's own timetable and not until the child was ready. Froebel's kindergarten emphasized children's free play, singing, and movement (Nourot, 2005). The materials he developed, which were called **Froebel's occupations and gifts**, were used to guide and structure children's play. As a result, Froebel's view of "free" play was not as free as some interpret today.

The role of the teacher in Froebel's kindergarten was to be like a gardener. Teachers were to observe, nurture, and help but not interfere with the natural growth of the child. They needed to be aware of children's development, however, so they could provide a new challenge as children engaged with the gifts and occupations.

Froebel's occupations and gifts Invented by Froebel for kindergartners, occupations were planned experiences designed to train children's eye–hand coordination and mental activity, and gifts were concrete materials, many of which influenced later toy development.

Froebel's Gifts and Occupations   Froebel's gifts were concrete materials for children to manipulate in specific ways. The first gift was a box of six wooden balls in the colors of the spectrum—red, orange, yellow, green, blue, and violet—plus corresponding strings. Each child could use these materials in many creative ways, but Froebel and his teachers identified more than 100 games to play with this one gift and accompanying songs and rhymes (Elkind, 2015).

Another gift was a cube that could be divided into eight smaller cubes and put back together to form a whole. Children could play many games with this gift, but it also promoted basic math concepts related to number and geometry. Froebel also invented parquetry blocks—a set of flat, colored, wooden shapes that could be put together to form various designs. Other gifts included sticks and rings made of wire and natural materials such as seeds and pebbles. The same or similar materials are prevalent in early childhood classrooms today, where children use them in creative ways, and also to learn mathematics and science.

In contrast to the gifts, occupations were planned experiences designed to train children's eye–hand coordination and mental activity (Wolfe, 2000). The occupations included activities such as drawing on grid paper, lacing paper strips, weaving mats, folding and cutting paper into designs, constructing with sticks, or making models from cardboard.

Froebel believed that the use of the gifts and occupations engaged children in symbolically representing objects and events in the real world—such as creating a model or drawing a picture of a building. The importance of representation, which Froebel presaged, is now supported by research.

Impact of Froebel's Work Froebel's work had a major impact on education in the United States, leading directly to a large-scale kindergarten movement here. Several teachers and teacher educators who studied Froebel's methods in Europe—"kindergartners" as they were called—transplanted his ideas to this country.

Kindergartens today bear less and less resemblance to Froebel's "children's garden"; today they have become more like formal first grades (Strauss, 2014). However, many of his basic ideas are still evident in preschool and child care programs. His gifts and occupations were clearly the prototypes for many of the toys and materials, such as one-inch cube and parquetry blocks, that are pervasive in preschool classrooms. Common activities—constructing models or using natural materials in art and projects—also mirror some of his occupations.

Froebel's work had a significant impact on the development of American kindergartens, which we return to later in this chapter. First, we visit another European educator who lived a century later than Froebel, but whose work also stands out for its contributions to the field—Maria Montessori.

Maria Montessori

Maria Montessori (1870–1952) was a major figure in the history of early childhood education. A brilliant woman, she was Italy's first female physician. She was nominated for the Nobel Peace Prize, and her face graced the 1,000 lira note until Italy abandoned the lira for the euro. Montessori was, and probably always will be, the only early childhood educator whose face adorned a currency.

History of the Montessori Method Montessori's contributions grew out of her work with poor children in the slums of Rome. The prevailing opinion was that these children were mentally deficient. However, Montessori believed that what appeared to be mental retardation was not biologically based, but rather caused by the lack of stimulation in their environments.

In 1907, she started a program for children, ages 4 through 7, called *Casa dei Bambini* (Children's House), and developed a highly successful approach to teaching the children, which revealed that they were not mentally disabled at all. Montessori demonstrated that educating needy children is a less costly and more effective strategy than waiting until they create problems for society. This is the same justification that was used to launch Head Start, and it is still the core rationale for much of the current investment in early education.

Key Elements of the Montessori Method The Montessori method includes several basic elements. In the sections that follow, we briefly describe Montessori's views about children and learning, the environment, and the teacher's role.

Image of Children: The Absorbent Mind Like other key figures in early childhood history, Montessori (1909/1964) believed that children develop naturally in an organized environment. Her image of the child is the **absorbent mind**—actively learning from sensory experiences. She also believed that children from 4 to 7 years old are internally motivated to interact with the world, and do not need external encouragement or rewards.

Where Montessori deviated greatly from others in the field was in her opinion of play. Montessori dismissed play as a waste of children's time (Wolfe, 2000). She also minimized the value of social interaction for children's learning. As evidence, children each had an individual small mat to work on and not be disturbed by others.

absorbent mind Maria Montessori's image of the child as actively learning from sensory experiences.

A Prepared Learning Environment

Montessori believed that poor children deserve high-quality experiences. She thought that children need an orderly environment that supports their ability to work on and complete tasks independently. Accordingly, she designed classroom environments and materials that demonstrate respect for children. Montessori innovations included child-sized tables and other furnishings, and materials arranged on open shelves for easy access by children.

To facilitate learning and prevent wasted time, she developed educational materials for children to use in prescribed ways. Montessori designed self-correcting learning materials for children, many of which are still commonly used. For example, she created puzzles with little knobs attached to each piece, for very young children to practice the pincer grasp used for writing; and to practice fine motor skills, she invented a cloth board with buttons and buttonholes. Montessori emphasized that there was one right way to use each of her materials. She did not consider her materials to be toys; instead, she viewed them as educational tools. Children were also taught practical life skills such as washing a table and sweeping a floor.

Montessori's belief in sensory learning extended to academic areas as well, specifically writing, reading, and mathematics (Montessori, 1912/1964). For example, she created sandpaper alphabets so that children could feel the shapes of the letters as a first step toward writing. She thought children should learn to write as a strategy to teach reading. This was an innovative concept for its time (when promoting reading at an early age was not accepted by her peers in early education), and also presaged later understandings of the strong connection between writing and reading in becoming literate.

Montessori classrooms are specially designed environments in which children learn by interacting with the materials. What skills might children acquire by working with the Montessori materials depicted here?

▶ Classroom Connection

This video shows the arrangement and the materials found in a typical Montessori classroom. As you watch, reflect on the key elements of the Montessori Method, how the materials themselves promote learning, and the role of the teacher in a Montessori classroom.

The Teacher's Role Montessori's view of the teacher's role is to prepare the environment, observe children, and demonstrate materials, but not to interfere with their natural exploration. Although teachers' interactions with children are very intentional in the Montessori method, much of the learning is assumed to occur as children interact with materials. The teacher presents brief individual or small-group lessons, but most of the day children choose their activities. Their choices have limits, however, because the adults arrange those choices.

Impact of Montessori's Work From 1910 to 1920, interest in Montessori's approach gained popularity in the United States; several elements of her approach remain widely accepted. However, overall interest in her methods soon faded here, primarily due to her unwillingness to adapt to new knowledge and her rejection of key elements of American philosophy, such as the importance of play. Maria Montessori's lasting contribution to the field was her development of Montessori materials and her impact on the organization of environments.

Not until the 1950s was interest in Montessori revived in the United States. In contrast to Montessori's original intent to serve poor children, Montessori schools in the United States tended to be private, serving a more affluent population. In recent years, however, the approach has been embraced by some magnet and charter public schools. A study of a public Montessori school in Milwaukee found that the approach contributed positively to 5-year-olds' literacy, math, and social skills (Lillard, 2005) and to creativity and social skills at age 12 (Lillard & Else-Quest, 2006). With its emphasis on individualized instruction, the Montessori approach also has been found to be effective in improving the school readiness of Latino prekindergartners (Ansari & Winsler, 2014). Interestingly, the founders of Google, Larry Page and Sergey Brin, attribute their success to the self-motivation they gained from attending Montessori preschool (http://msr.org/google-founders-pay-homage-to-dr-maria-montessori/).

 Check Your Understanding 2.2: European Influences on American Early Childhood Education

Early Childhood Movements in the United States

The following sections present three interwoven stories of early childhood education in America—the kindergarten movement, progressive education, and the nursery school movement. These stories are described separately but, in reality, they happened simultaneously and were inextricably connected. A parallel story—the child care movement—was also occurring, but played out differently as you will read later in this section.

The Kindergarten Movement

The United States provided fertile ground for the growth of Froebel's "children's gardens." In the sections that follow, we describe how the movement began and spread widely and its lasting impact.

Early Days of the Kindergarten Movement
The earliest leaders in the kindergarten movement transplanted Froebel's ideas directly. The first kindergarten in the United States was founded by Margarethe Schurz (1833–1876) in Wisconsin in 1856 (Snyder, 1972). Schurz had studied with Froebel and, upon immigrating to the United States, started a German-speaking school to teach her own and neighbors' children. Later, Schurz met Elizabeth Palmer Peabody (1804–1894), and their encounter was the impetus for the American kindergarten movement.

Elizabeth Peabody was part of a well-known family of social reformers. Her sister, Mary, was married to Horace Mann, considered to be the father of public education in the United States. In Boston, Elizabeth Peabody organized the first English-speaking kindergarten in 1860, and soon after wrote the first American kindergarten textbook for teachers (Cantor, 2013). She understood that teachers needed to be trained in Froebel's philosophy to ensure the quality and integrity of the expanding kindergarten movement. She also traveled widely and became an outspoken advocate for the cause, inspiring new generations of leaders, the most influential of whom was Susan Blow.

Susan Blow's Leadership
Susan Blow (1843–1916) was the major voice in expanding the kindergarten movement and in fighting to keep it true to Froebel's original vision. Inspired by Elizabeth Peabody's promotion of kindergarten, Blow visited Froebelian kindergartens in the United States and Germany and became the leading interpreter of the approach at home.

Founding Public Kindergarten In 1873, with the support of William Harris, a reform-minded school superintendent in St. Louis, Blow founded the first public school kindergarten (Snyder, 1972) in response to Harris's concern that schooling did not begin until age 7. Blow was ambivalent about connecting kindergarten to public school, fearing that "the formality of the grades would seize kindergarten in its grip" (Snyder, 1972, p. 66). Nevertheless, she worked with Harris and launched more than 50 kindergarten classrooms. Teacher training was an essential part of her strategy, with teachers working with children in the mornings and attending lectures in the afternoons on topics such as the correct use of Froebel's gifts and occupations—a combination of theory and practicum that continues to this day in teacher education.

Upon Harris's departure from his post, a new school administration was less supportive of Blow's cause and threatened her ideal vision of kindergarten. Subsequently, Blow turned her energy from developing and spreading Froebelian kindergarten ideals to defending them (Snyder, 1972). Blow promoted a rigid application of Froebel's methods (such as using the gifts in narrowly prescribed ways), which was actually antithetical to his vision of kindergarten.

Founding the International Kindergarten Union In 1892, Blow convened a group of ardent kindergartners from throughout the country and formed the International Kindergarten Union (IKU). (Much later the IKU became the Association for Childhood Education International.) The original mission of the IKU was not just to disseminate information but also to protect the integrity of Froebelian kindergartens. Within two decades, this mission was to come into direct conflict with winds of change that were occurring in the wider educational world, emanating from the progressive education movement, described in the next section.

Progressive Education

The **progressive education movement** was a major effort to reform schooling at all levels to make it more democratic. Its tenets were in direct contrast to the prevailing practices in schools of the time, which emphasized rote memorization, strict conformity, and harsh discipline. The traditional curriculum was limited to the "3 Rs": reading, writing, and arithmetic.

The story of the progressive education movement in the United States is integrally connected to the story of the nursery school movement (or preschool, as we now call it). Many principles of developmentally appropriate practice are derived directly from the work of early progressive leaders. Although differences exist between the earlier ideas and current views, the commonalities between the two visions—progressive education and developmentally appropriate practice—are striking. The following sections present the contributions of John Dewey.

John Dewey John Dewey (1859–1952) was a professor of philosophy first at the University of Chicago and then for 47 years at Teachers College, Columbia University, in New York City. While in Chicago, John and his wife, Alice Chapman Dewey (d. 1927), founded the University of Chicago Laboratory School to implement their philosophy of a humane approach to education. Alice taught at the school, prepared the curriculum, and served as principal. The school, which they ran from 1893 to 1903, became a laboratory for developing and trying out their approach.

Principles of Progressive Education Dewey (1916) believed that the purpose of education is to ensure the effective functioning of a democratic society. He believed that the traditional approach to schooling could not produce citizen decision makers. He was concerned that in a democratic society, it is "impossible to foretell definitely what civilization will be twenty years from now" (Dewey, 1929, p. 6). Therefore, it is important to teach children to take initiative and use judgment. Dewey (1929) articulated his philosophy in *My Pedagogic Creed*. Let's take a look at some of the principles of progressive education, as described by Dewey in that document.

What Education Is "Education is the process of living and not preparation for future living" (Dewey, 1929, p. 7). This famous quote of Dewey summarizes his definition of education and continues to influence early childhood education.

Dewey was a prolific writer whose words still inspire. The titles of his books alone convey his basic ideas about education: *Democracy and Education, Education and*

progressive education movement Major effort to reform schooling in the early 20th century to make it more democratic and responsive to children's needs. This movement was highly influential on early childhood education and later ideas about developmentally appropriate practice.

Experience, The School and Society, Freedom and Culture, and *The Child and the Curriculum.* In Dewey's mind, schooling could not be separated from the larger needs of democratic society, and children, rather than subject matter, needed to be at the center of the curriculum.

What the School Is Dewey (1900) believed that the school should function as a community. The teacher's role is to be a member of the community. Teachers should not directly impose discipline, but rather influence and assist children as they work together.

According to Dewey, teachers and parents should learn from each other—an accepted idea today, but radical for his time. In his school, parents and teachers met regularly to discuss topics such as why children should or should not learn to read at an early age—again, an issue that many educators and parents debate today (Wolfe, 2000).

What the Curriculum Is Dewey believed that subject matter—reading, writing, geography, history, science—should be introduced to children in ways that they can understand and that involve them in social interaction. He introduced the idea of **integrated curriculum**, now a staple of early childhood education, which addresses learning goals across multiple subjects at the same time. For example, children might learn economics, history, geography, and other subjects by studying the workers in their neighborhood. A tenet of Dewey's philosophy is that teachers should find ways to integrate traditional curriculum into topics of interest to children, such as building a model of the neighborhood. Dewey also brought expressive and constructive activities into the classroom such as cooking, sewing, and woodworking. He felt academic skills should grow out of these activities.

> **integrated curriculum**
> Learning plan that addresses goals across multiple areas of the curriculum at the same time.

What Teaching Should Be Dewey (1929) believed that the traditional emphasis on children as passive learners was a "waste of time." He strongly emphasized the importance of teachers observing children and building on their interests. In progressive schools, the role of teachers is to guide or facilitate learning based on what they know about children and to choose the right problems and questions to further children's learning. For example, teachers don't simply teach geography as adults know it; rather, they teach the geography concepts and topics that the child is interested in and capable of learning. This approach, called the **child-centered curriculum**, has been falsely interpreted over the years to mean that children determine the curriculum (Bredekamp & Copple, 1997). Although teachers build curriculum from children's experiences and interests, Dewey felt strongly that teachers needed to know *both* what children are interested in *and* the content that children needed to learn. This *both/and* thinking principle in progressive education has often been lost in translation.

> **▶ Classroom Connection**
>
> This video shows how an integrated curriculum can be used effectively in the classroom. As you watch, consider the ways in which key elements of John Dewey's educational approach have influenced early childhood education and continue to be implemented today.

The Impact of Progressive Education on Schooling Although progressive education has often been misinterpreted and periodically comes under attack by proponents of more traditional practices, its contributions to American education are profound. Lois Meek Stoltz (1977), the first president of NAEYC and a contemporary of Dewey, eloquently captured the impact:

> **child-centered curriculum**
> John Dewey's idea that curriculum should reflect the concepts and topics that the child is interested in and capable of learning.

> I think it is very difficult for people of this generation to realize, or even picture, what the public schools were like in the early 1900s. Children were in their seats all day long. When they rose, they rose to count, "1, 2, 3," they then turned, marched, and went to the cloakroom. Then they did the same thing when they marched out of the school and when they marched in. Everybody read out of the same book at the same time. There was very little consideration for individual differences. (p. 103)

Earlier in this chapter, we talked about how solutions to problems contain the seeds of new problems. Progressive education was a case in point. Giving children more freedom meant that some people interpreted this as chaos, creating a backlash or a new problem.

And yet, as Stoltz points out, the efforts overall led to real change in schools—and that change is progress.

Although he was a philosophy professor, Dewey was strongly influenced by the trend in his day toward more scientific approaches in education. This trend, called the *child study movement*, is described in the next section.

The Child Study Movement   As far back as Pestalozzi, educators understood that teaching should be based on direct study of children. Beginning in the late 19th century, G. Stanley Hall (1844–1924) launched the **child study movement**. Hall was interested in understanding individual differences in children through direct observation.

Hall's students went on to develop systematic scientific approaches to studying child development. Arnold Gesell (1880–1961) is famed for launching a child study laboratory at Yale University called the Gesell Institute. There he observed large samples of children and derived age-related norms for children's growth and development such as by what age children should take their first steps or speak their first words. These norms were considered "universal" and have been widely influential. However, in the late 20th century, Gesell's age-related norms were criticized for understating individual differences and not using diverse samples of children.

Hall was a strong critic of Froebelian kindergarten. He thought that its rigid methodology lacked a scientific basis. Thus, the child study movement played an important role in bringing about changes in the kindergarten movement, and it also contributed in large measure to the growing nursery school movement. We tell this story in the section that follows.

The Nursery School Movement

Dewey's laboratory school and his emphasis on child observation reflected his understanding of the need to base education on the study of children. Similarly, other universities launched lab schools to train teachers and study children. Many of these schools served children younger than kindergarten age, and were called **nursery schools**, based on their philosophy of nurturing development. Laboratory schools were established for the purposes of research and demonstration of teaching methods, rather than to serve parents or neglected children (Hewes & the NAEYC Organizational History and Archives Committee, 2001). As a result, many of these programs served middle- and upper-class children of faculty or community members.

The nursery school movement eventually launched the wider field of early childhood education. It grew out of the kindergarten and child study movements through the leadership of two women whose contributions to early childhood education are unparalleled: Patty Smith Hill, founder of NAEYC, and Lucy Sprague Mitchell, founder of Bank Street College. Every early childhood educator should know the stories of these women and their contemporaries, who played seminal roles in laying the foundation of early childhood education as we know it today. We who follow are their direct descendents.

Patty Smith Hill   Patty Smith Hill's life story parallels the early history of early childhood education, with each phase of her life connected to important developments in the field. She was a joyful child, teacher of young children, creator of resources for children, teacher educator, and national leader.

Hill's Early Life Experiences   Patty Smith Hill (1868–1946) had an idyllic childhood. Her

---

child study movement Early 20th century effort to scientifically observe and systematically document children's individual development under the leadership of G. Stanley Hall and Arnold Gesell.

nursery schools Schools serving children younger than kindergarten age; out-of-date term for preschool or prekindergarten.

Early leaders of the nursery school movement in the United States, such as Patty Smith Hill, saw the value of pretend play for children's development. The need to defend children's right to play continues to this day.

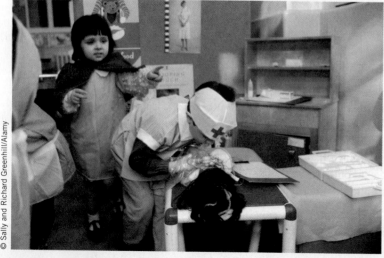

© Sally and Richard Greenhill/Alamy

father believed that girls should be educated, a radical idea at the time. Her mother was a progressive thinker who had secretly, and also illegally, taught enslaved people to read, write, and calculate (Wolfe, 2000). Furthermore, Hill's mother believed that play was essential to childhood.

Work as a Kindergarten Teacher By the 1880s, the kindergarten movement was underway and Anna Bryan launched a teacher training program in Louisville, Kentucky, where Patty Hill became one of the first students (Snyder, 1972). Hill started her own kindergarten where she encouraged creative uses for Froebel's gifts as toys, and constructive materials such as blocks and clay. Her kindergarten evidenced her belief in the value of children's play as a way to learn.

In 1896, Hill and Bryan were among a group of influential kindergarten educators who attended one of G. Stanley Hall's lectures on new knowledge and insights gained from the systematic study of children's development. Hall's severe criticism of the Froebelian approach as unscientific outraged the attendees, all of whom stormed out of the meeting—with the exception of Hill and Bryan (Hewes, 1976). They stayed and continued to study with Hall, and they developed a new curriculum for teaching young children.

In 1903, Louisville's kindergartens became part of the public schools. Hill was excited about the potential benefits, but feared that key kindergarten practices, including parent education, would be lost (Snyder, 1972). Hill's vision for kindergarten included three purposes: (1) to meet the needs of 4 to 6 year olds, (2) to lay the foundation for the first-grade curriculum while ensuring the right of kindergarten children to develop at their own level, and (3) to connect the child's experiences at home and school, building on what children learn there (Hill, 1926/1987). This vision of kindergarten, especially the role of parents, was not just ahead of Hill's time, but one to aspire to today.

Creator of Resources for Children Hill developed resources for children, including a set of lumberlike wooden blocks from which children could build structures large enough for them to play in. She and her musician sister, Mildred, wrote songs for children, using music as a teaching tool. Their most famous song is "Happy Birthday," although few people know its composers.

Hill also wrote many poems about children's interests as well as books to help children learn to read. Much like her mother, Hill was concerned about racial inequality. In the early 1940s, she worked for months on a set of readers showing African American children, but she despaired when no publisher would consider them (Hewes, 1976). She believed that respectful images would help resolve racial prejudices.

Hill's Work as a Teacher Educator In 1905, Hill joined the faculty of Teachers College in New York, where she stayed for 30 years and was considered a master teacher (Snyder, 1972). She focused her work in the community school, which served poor children, as opposed to the campus lab school, which served well-off children of faculty.

The Dean of Teachers College, James Earl Russell, was famous for bringing together divergent points of view (Snyder, 1972). One of his provocative ideas was to bring Susan Blow to coteach a course on kindergarten methods with Hill. Among the topics they debated were opposing views of work and play. Although students loved their lively debates, eventually it became clear that Hill's point of view was carrying the day (Snyder, 1972).

Hill's Contributions as a National Leader Hill was active in the IKU and served as its president. However, her more liberal ideas about kindergarten methods, including her promotion of play and creativity, came into conflict with others' more rigid interpretations of Froebel's ideas.

In 1904, the IKU formed the Committee of Nineteen, a group with varying perspectives on kindergarten practice, to resolve disputes on topics such as the role of play and the curriculum (Wolfe, 2000). Each year the committee issued a report, and disagreements became more apparent over time. By 1909, differences could not be resolved and three reports were produced: one by Blow, another one by Hill, and a compromise report by Lucy Wheelock (Snyder, 1972). Hill's report was to become the vision for early childhood practice as we know it today. Nevertheless, the process of debating conflicting points of view, which she embraced, continues to be an essential part of the work of early childhood educators (Bredekamp, 2001).

Founder of NAEYC As nursery schools began to proliferate in the 1920s, Hill was concerned about the lack of standards and curriculum and the threat of unqualified people taking leadership positions (Hewes, 1976). In 1926, she formed the National Committee on Nursery Schools, which became the National Association for Nursery Education (NANE). The committee included Lois Meek Stoltz, Arnold Gesell, and Abigail Eliot. Stoltz became the first president.

In the 1960s, NANE changed its name to NAEYC, the National Association for the Education of Young Children. Hill was its first member, and her views dominated the work of the nursery school movement during its early years. NANE's first publication in 1929 was *Minimum Essentials for Nursery School Education*. In this tradition, NAEYC has been involved in setting standards ever since (Bredekamp, 2001).

We have chosen to tell the story of Patty Smith Hill in such detail because she lived so many of the historical events that helped define present-day early childhood education. In the next section, we share the story of one of her close colleagues working in progressive education, Caroline Pratt.

Caroline Pratt
Caroline Pratt (1867–1954) attended the kindergarten education program at Teachers College. Like Hill, Pratt rejected the Froebelian approach. She believed that it was far too structured and did not allow children to play freely or experiment with materials.

Pratt's Educational Philosophy Pratt focused her energies on studying children directly. Her motto, as well as the title of the book for which she is best known, was "I learn from children" (Pratt, 1948). She became intrigued by the potential of engaging children with open-ended play equipment and materials.

Like others in the progressive education movement, Pratt looked to education to transform society and worked in settlement houses with poor children. She set up classrooms with her own hand-made blocks and toys, crayons, and paper and observed children's play. Based on her observations, Pratt realized the benefits for children of firsthand experiences and self-directed plans, field trips and pretend play, letting children find answers to their own questions, the relationship of play and intelligence, and the need to nurture children's play (Wolfe, 2000). Pratt also saw an active role for teachers in supporting children's play. These conclusions have all been supported by empirical research in the intervening years.

Caroline Pratt's invention of wooden unit blocks was a major contribution that countless children have enjoyed and benefited from ever since. Research continues to uncover new and lasting learning benefits of block play.

© Benjamin LaFramboise/Pearson Education

Inventor of Unit Blocks Pratt's most lasting contribution is undoubtedly her design of wooden unit blocks. She admired Hill's blocks but found them difficult for younger children to manipulate. She wanted blocks that would allow children to openly express their ideas about the world. Her blocks are made of natural hardwood, in various three-dimensional shapes, and mathematically precise because each block is a fraction or multiple of the standard unit. For example, the standard unit block is one-half of the next size block, one-quarter of the size after that, and so forth. What Pratt intuitively believed about the value of these tools for children's learning has been proven true by

What Works

Developing Mathematical Skills with Unit Blocks

Terence and Sam are building tracks for their subway train. "It isn't finished," Terence says. "Let's make the dark part where it's got a roof [the underground]." He starts to lay blocks along the side and then a roof.

"Wait, that's not going to work," Sam worries. "The subway cars can't get in. We need to make it higher for them."

After some trial and error, the boys use taller blocks for the tunnel sides, add a roof and run the train underneath, shouting, "Yay, we did it!"

The wooden unit blocks Terence and Sam are using are among the most popular and highly regarded play and learning materials for young children. In the early 1900s, when teacher Caroline Pratt designed these blocks—called *unit blocks* because each block is a fraction or multiple of the standard unit—she was most interested in providing open-ended tools to promote children's creative play. But many learning possibilities emerged. As children built with the blocks, they developed their fine motor skills; measured blocks and classified them by size and shape; explored symmetry, balance, and stability; discovered the mathematical relationships among the blocks (e.g., two small blocks equal one longer block); engaged in pretend play; worked and solved problems together; and did many other things that would contribute to their development and give them hours of pleasure.

Today, researchers agree that unit blocks are indeed valuable learning materials. Because of the spatial and mathematical relationships that exist between the types of unit blocks,

researchers studying children's math development and learning have been particularly interested in the effects of block play. Young children's spontaneous activities with blocks do in fact include mathematical play and exploration of spatial relationships. Research suggests that benefits from block play persist over the years.

Evidence also indicates that teachers make a difference in the complexity level of children's constructions and the outcomes of their block play. Children's block structures are more complex when teachers talk with children during their play, saying, for example, "What would happen if . . .?" or "Sometimes people use a block to join a structure. . . ." And children are especially likely to develop math concepts in block play if teachers introduce math vocabulary and engage children in mathematical thinking related to their play. For example, the teacher might comment, "For your wall you have the blocks standing on their thin edge," or "Hmm, you've run out of the long blocks for your road. What can you do ... and how many will you need?" When teachers give voice to thought and extend children's thinking, they enhance the learning potential of an already valuable and much-loved learning material—unit blocks.

Source: Based on *Mathematics Learning in Early Childhood: Paths toward Excellence and Equity*, edited by C. T. Cross, T. A. Woods, and H. Schweingruber, Committee on Early Childhood Mathematics, and National Research Council, 2009, Washington, DC: National Academies Press.

---

research. For a summary of these benefits of block play, read the feature *What Works: Developing Mathematical Skills with Unit Blocks* feature.

Pratt created wooden people representing families and community workers to add a pretend element to the block play. She also designed large hollow wooden blocks to encourage large muscle play and for outdoor use. For more than a century, millions of children have enjoyed and learned from these wonderful, creative materials. However, because she did not patent them, Pratt never benefited financially.

One of Pratt's closest colleagues was Lucy Sprague Mitchell. Mitchell's enormous contributions to the field are described in the next section.

Lucy Sprague Mitchell Lucy Sprague Mitchell (1878–1967) has been identified as a major link between Dewey's progressive education movement of the early 20th century and NAEYC's current concept of high-quality, developmentally appropriate education (Field & Baumi, 2014; Greenberg, 1987). Indeed, her life spanned the period from the beginning of John Dewey's work to the birth of Head Start in 1965. In the sections that follow, we describe her early life, her educational experiments and ideas about curriculum, and the important role of Bank Street College, which she founded.

Mitchell's Early Years Lucy Sprague Mitchell was a brilliant woman who studied at Teachers College with John Dewey and Edward Thorndike, the father of educational measurement and statistical research. Her life's work drew on both of these influences—a progressive philosophy combined with research-based practice.

The Bureau of Educational Experiments In 1916, using inherited funds, Mitchell launched the Bureau of Educational Experiments (BEE) to teach teachers and conduct research. The goals of the Bureau of Educational Experiments (Wolfe, 2000) were to:

- Focus on child development rather than learning specific curriculum
- Take a whole-child approach to learning and development
- Observe how children's development is stimulated by experiences and activities
- Focus on scientific measurement of stages of development and establishing norms (representing the influence of Arnold Gesell as well as Thorndike).

Bank Street College When the bureau moved to 69 Bank Street in New York City, its name was changed to Bank Street College of Education. A graduate program in teacher education, Bank Street College played essential roles in the history of early childhood education and continues to do so. We can only mention a few here.

Most notably, Mitchell's educational philosophy emphasized children's firsthand experiences and play. Her ideas came to be called the **Bank Street approach**, later called the Developmental-Interaction approach to more accurately describe its tenets. In this model, children's experiences in the "here and now" provide the launching pad for their learning (Mitchell & David, 1992). These experiences, such as the field trips or projects described earlier, gradually widen children's horizons beyond the here and now. The concept is that curriculum should be based on individual children's development, and that learning occurs through interaction with the environment and other people (Biber, 1977; Shapiro & Nager, 1999). The Bank Street approach has been widely influential in early childhood curriculum development, especially in teaching social studies.

One element of the Bank Street approach that has sometimes been underemphasized is the role of the teacher. In Mitchell's words, "We were looking at children learning, and *intentionally* facilitating the process every day" (Greenberg, 1987, p. 75). Read the feature *Becoming an Intentional Teacher: Expanding Children's Experience* for an example of the teacher's role in the Bank Street approach.

The Writer's Workshops for Children's Authors Mitchell herself was a prolific writer and authored a series of children's books. She created a writer's workshop in 1937 for authors of children's books at Bank Street, which offered scholarships to ensure racial and socioeconomic diversity. The writer's laboratory was established to help authors better understand children's development and interests, and to promote their use of the rhythms and rhymes of language that are so important and enjoyable for children (Wolfe, 2000). Among the best-known writers who participated in the workshop were Margaret Wise Brown and Ruth Krauss. Brown's books *Goodnight Moon* and *The Runaway Bunny* remain classics, as does *The Carrot Seed* by Krauss.

Near the end of her life, Mitchell was instrumental in numerous national efforts to expand early childhood education beyond laboratory schools and use it for true social reform (Field & Baumi, 2014). She lived to see the Bank Street approach used as the model for the Head Start program. Head Start is also known for its emphasis on parent involvement, which was another part of the nursery school movement, described in the next section.

Parent Cooperative Preschools As early as 1916, parents organized to start their own nursery schools. In these programs, which are called *parent cooperatives* or *co-ops*, the parents "own" and administer the program. They hire a teacher and take turns volunteering in the classroom as a second staff member. Most parent co-ops throughout the 20th century used a play-based, progressive education–influenced approach.

The number of parent cooperative nursery schools grew rapidly in the 1950s and 1960s, and through the leadership of Katherine Whiteside Taylor, an association was

---

Bank Street approach
Originating with Lucy Sprague Mitchell at Bank Street College and later called the Developmental-Interaction approach, a curriculum framework based on individual children's development, emphasizing that learning begins in children's experiences in the immediate environment (here and now).

Becoming an Intentional Teacher

Expanding Children's Experience

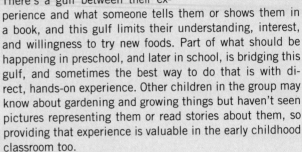

Here's What Happened   The preschool I work in uses the Bank Street curriculum approach. I was planning to do some cooking with my 4-year-old class, so I wanted them to learn more about where foods come from. In our urban neighborhood, most children have limited experience with growing things; however, there is a community garden that a few of the families participate in, and those children are involved with planting, watching things grow, and eating the produce. In talking with the "garden families" to find out what they grow and what the children do in the garden, I found that the parents were eager to send in a tomato or zucchini from their gardens for the class to see and taste. We did that first, and then made a trip to the garden. After the trip, I encouraged the children to draw and write about what they had seen, and I brought in library books like *The Carrot Seed* (Krauss, 1945) and *Whose Garden Is It?* (Hoberman, 2004) to share with them.

Here's What I Was Thinking   When children have little experience with growing things, they eat fruits, vegetables, and other foods without understanding where they come from. Even if an adult tells them, "Tomatoes come from the ground," it doesn't compute. There's a gulf between their experience and what someone tells them or shows them in a book, and this gulf limits their understanding, interest, and willingness to try new foods. Part of what should be happening in preschool, and later in school, is bridging this gulf, and sometimes the best way to do that is with direct, hands-on experience. Other children in the group may know about gardening and growing things but haven't seen pictures representing them or read stories about them, so providing that experience is valuable in the early childhood classroom too.

Reflection   Many public school kindergartens today are given a curriculum that prescribes certain topics of study such as weather or animals. If you were a teacher in such a situation, how could you apply the principles of the Bank Street approach to make the experiences more meaningful?

formed, Parent Cooperative Preschools International (http://www.preschools.coop). In recent years, the number of parent cooperative preschools has declined due to the increase of mothers in the workforce. Nevertheless, the movement reinforced the integral role of parents in early childhood education.

In the previous sections, we discussed the interconnected stories of the kindergarten, progressive education, and nursery school movements. Many more outstanding leaders contributed to these efforts than we can describe briefly. **Click here** to review the timeline of major events in early childhood history to fill in the chronology. Consider this chronological review as you read about the history of child care in the United States, which followed a different path from that of kindergarten and preschool.

The Child Care Movement

Kindergartens and preschools grew out of child study, were focused on middle-class children, and were associated with education and development. By contrast, child care grew out of social welfare efforts for poor families and focused on the need to support working parents. Consequently, child care became associated with physical care rather than education.

In the later part of the 20th century and into the 21st century, these differences have become less distinct. However, these histories still play out in public policy and attitudes. For example, federal child care funding is part of public assistance for needy families, whereas prekindergarten support comes from state education agencies. In the sections that follow, we describe some of the key events and people involved in the history of the child care movement.

McMillan Sisters Margaret McMillan (1860–1931) and Rachel McMillan (1859–1917) worked to improve the lives of young children in London and North America during the early 20th century. The purpose of their work was to offer children a temporary alternative to the dreadful living conditions in the London slums, which severely damaged the health of most poor children. Accordingly, they set up a health clinic, a nursery school (they coined the phrase) for children under age 5, and teacher training.

The McMillan sisters developed a model open-air nursery that was unique in emphasizing outdoor play, nutritious food, cleanliness, and rest to promote healthy development. The program was also educational. These centers for working families were called **day nurseries**—the forerunner of present-day child care centers.

The McMillan sisters' work was influential in the United States. Several Americans studied with them in England, including Abigail Eliot (1892–1992), who subsequently imported many of their ideas and founded one of the first nursery schools in the United States in 1922.

As always happens, events in the larger context had a major impact on early childhood education and particularly on the history of child care. These included the Great Depression and World War II.

Works Progress Administration Nurseries

During the Great Depression of the 1930s, the Works Progress Administration (WPA) was established to address the high unemployment rate (25%) and to build needed public works throughout the country. One of the WPA programs established in 1933 was the Federal Emergency Relief Nursery Schools. The purpose of the **WPA nurseries**, which were open from 9 A.M. to 5 P.M., was to support the economy by providing jobs for those who worked on the site and child care to families seeking work (Nourot, 2005). Like the day nurseries of the McMillan sisters, WPA centers focused on promoting physical care and healthy living habits (Nourot, 2005). But in contrast to the McMillan sisters' vision, most WPA centers did not emphasize education.

The WPA nurseries had both positive and negative effects on early childhood education. Because day nurseries served children from poor families, the idea of expanding nursery education to all children was born (Nourot, 2005). However, the rapid expansion of WPA nursery schools meant that teachers were hired with minimal training. This cycle of expanding services without attention to ensuring qualified staff has plagued the child care field throughout its existence. As the Depression ended, so too did the WPA nursery schools. But a major national crisis—World War II—followed shortly, leading to another important chapter in the history of child care.

The Lanham Act

World War II necessitated full deployment of not only men into the armed services but also women into the workplace to replace the men and support industry. This massive workforce shift required immediate child care assistance, which the federal government provided in the form of the **Lanham Act**. This legislation funded emergency work-site child care centers, which operated for 10 to 12 hours per day.

One of the most famous centers was located at the Kaiser Shipbuilding company in Oregon (MacKenzie, 2011). Kaiser was the largest of the Lanham Act centers, operating 24 hours a day all year long. Lois Meek Stoltz was the director, and the manager was Jimmy Hymes, who later became a professor and president of NAEYC (Anderson, 2013). The program, still considered a model, provided health services and nutritious meals for children and mothers, parent education, teacher training, and a play-based educational experience for children.

As happened with the WPA nurseries, the Lanham Act centers ended along with the war. Child care was no longer supported because mothers left the workforce as fathers reentered it. These high-quality centers remain an ideal for working families; yet it wasn't until the 1980s that employer-sponsored child care again became a major sector of the early childhood field.

The stories related thus far of the kindergarten, nursery school, and child care movements were lived and recorded by members of the majority group—white, European Americans. However, various groups of Americans were also part of these stories and have made significant contributions to the history of early childhood education, which we discuss in the next section.

day nurseries Programs designed to serve working families in the late 19th and early 20th centuries; the forerunner of present-day child care centers.

WPA nurseries Federal emergency relief nursery schools, funded by the Works Progress Administration (WPA) during the Great Depression, designed to support the economy by providing jobs for those who worked on the site and child care services to families seeking work.

Lanham Act Federal legislation to provide emergency child care and other services for families employed in the war effort during World War II.

 Check Your Understanding 2.3: Early Childhood Movements in the United States

A Wider View of Early Childhood History

History is written by those who gain the largest amount of power. It is important to note that the previous discussion is dominated by white European Americans because they were the individuals with the most power in the society, and their work is most often included in the "official" written history of the field. At the same time, however, parallel stories were occurring among the many groups that populated the United States. That history is less well known primarily because historical sources are scarce, but also because there is a strong oral rather than written tradition in these communities (Simpson, n.d.).

These stories deserve our attention and respect because they also have made the field of early childhood education what is it today. Here we briefly describe historical events and contributions from the perspective of African Americans, Native Americans, and Hispanic Americans. It is essential to point out that there is huge diversity within these population groups. In fact, they are hardly groups at all except as designated by the United States Census Bureau. To further understand history from an even wider view, read the accompanying *Culture Lens: Early Childhood Education through the Lens of Non-Western Culture* feature.

Culture Lens

Early Childhood Education through the Lens of Non-Western Culture

Ideas from non-Western, alternative histories have much to offer early childhood education practices. One contemporary scholar who has written of diverse cultural approaches to educating children is Timothy Reagan (2005). He studies views from Africa, the Aztecs, North American Indians, the Rom, Chinese Confucians, Indian Hindus and Buddhists, and Islamic traditions.

Consider the African culture in which child-rearing practices and education are based on African people's view of the relationship between the physical and spiritual reality (Mbiti, 1992). They believe that understanding children requires understanding their spiritual purpose. Before a child is born, the child is a complete spirit—in some traditions, the child is an ancestor returning. At birth, children are celebrated and the community is expected to make room for this child's purpose in the community. Because the spirit has come home to a community, not just to a biological set of parents, it becomes a community responsibility to take care of this child (Bunseki Fu-Kiai & Lukondo-Wamba, 1988; Some, 1999).

According to Dr. Itihari Toure (C. B. Day, personal communication, December 2008):

The view of the spirit returning for the sake of the community also informs the responsibilities for the child. Child rearing is a collective process and children in different traditions not only have specific family responsibilities but partake in various community traditions as they must retain and transmit the values of the specific community. Biological parents and community members take care of all children. Exposure to various crafts and skills needed for the community to thrive, songs and dances that represent various stages of life, and the countless stories that recall the history of the people are part of the child-rearing experience.... When children engage in formal schooling, the motivation is not based on personal achievement alone; there is a desire to bring pride and regard to the community through the personal achievement. This perception of purpose and success comes from a consistent socialization about the value of one's family and community interdependent with the value of oneself. It is often referred to as *Ubunutu* (I am because we are; we are because I am).

Understanding how other cultures rear children brings to light a very important consideration for all educators: Every child is a product of his or her own history. Knowing that other cultures rear their children according to non-Western beliefs deepens and broadens the possibilities for educating children to their full potential, in ways that may resonate with their own historical and cultural realities.

Sources: Kindezi: The Kongo Art of Babysitting, by K. K. Bunseki Fu-Kiai and A. M. Lukondo-Wamba, 1988, New York: Vantage Press; *African Religions and Philosophy*, 2nd edition, by J. Mbiti, 1992, Portsmouth, NH: Heinemann; *Non-Western Educational Traditions: Indigenous Approaches to Education Thought and Practice*, 3rd edition, by T. Reagan, 2005, Mahwah, NJ: Lawrence Erlbaum Associates; *Welcoming Spirit Home: Ancient African Teachings to Celebrate Children and Community*, by S. Some, 1999, Novato, CA: New World Library.

African Americans in Early Childhood History

Throughout U.S. history, African Americans have been denied power beginning with slavery, when it was illegal to teach enslaved people to read and write, much less attend school. Once schooling became available, it was legally segregated by race until the 1954 Supreme Court's *Brown v. Board of Education* decision banned the practice. But even after desegregation became the law of the land, equal rights and equal educational opportunity for all racial groups were still denied.

Over the centuries of enslavement, a few formal, mostly religious schools provided education for African American children (Cunningham & Osborn, 1979). By the 1830s, however, such schools were prohibited. Educating enslaved people was a clandestine and dangerous operation, requiring courage on the part of teachers as well as students. We saw earlier how Patty Smith Hill's mother was one of those who took that risk and what its effects were on her daughter's life choices thereafter.

African American Kindergartens and Teacher Training
After the Civil War, education became the vehicle for advancement of African Americans, propelled by national leaders such as Mary McLeod Bethune (1875–1955), who founded Bethune-Cookman College in 1904, and became an effective voice for civil rights and equal educational opportunity. Between 1865 and 1890, prominent African American institutions of higher education were founded such as Howard University (1867), Hampton University (1868), Tuskegee University (1881), and Spelman College (1881). These and other historically black colleges and universities (HBCUs) made important contributions to the study of child development, then usually housed in Home Economics departments (Cunningham & Osborn, 1979).

Early childhood education was seen as an important foundation for future advancement. Many HBCUs operated teacher education programs and laboratory schools (Osborn, 1991). These programs reflected the prevailing philosophies of Pestalozzi, Froebel, and later Dewey and G. Stanley Hall. By 1873, Hampton Institute (now University) in Virginia had a kindergarten teacher-training program and a children's school that was influenced by Montessori's ideas about children learning practical skills (Cunningham & Osborn, 1979). Tuskegee in Alabama offered training for parents in child-rearing methods. In the early 1900s, Howard University in Washington, D.C., awarded degrees in kindergarten education, and Atlanta University operated a Froebelian kindergarten and an elementary and high school for African American students (J. E. Hale, personal communication, February 2009).

The National Association of Colored Women (NACW) was founded in 1896. Its first president, Mary Church Terrell (1863–1954), was the daughter of enslaved parents and one of the first African American women to earn a college degree and later a master's. She was a strong supporter of early education. Under her leadership, the NACW helped establish kindergartens for African American children throughout the country (Cunningham & Osborn, 1979).

Historically Black Colleges and Universities have played important roles in the study of child development and the education of future generations of teachers. Although not well-known, the contributions of African American early childhood educators have been significant in the field's history.

African Americans and the Nursery School Movement
In 1927, five years after Abigail Eliot started the first nursery school in the United States, Dorothy Howard founded the "first Black nursery school" in Washington, D.C., to serve professional families. She operated the school for more than 50 years (Simpson, n.d., p. 262). Spelman College in Atlanta opened the first laboratory school in an African American college in 1930, under the direction of Pearlie Reed (Cunningham & Osborn, 1979). This school used the "whole-child" philosophy of the larger nursery school movement. Still in operation, the school is named for

Marian Wright Edelman, founder and president of the Children's Defense Fund, the nation's premier children's advocacy organization (http://www.spelman.edu).

From 1929 to 1969, Oneida Cockrell (1900–1970) directed the Rosenwald-Garden Apartment Nursery School and Kindergarten in Chicago (Simpson, 2012). This program became a model for children's centers in urban apartment dwellings, and also served children with disabilities early on. Cockrell participated in the White House Conference on Children and Youth in 1950. Cockrell also taught at the University of Chicago laboratory school.

Spelman College produced many future early childhood luminaries. Its first graduate student, Ida Jones Curry, became head of teacher training at Hampton Institute in 1932 (Cunningham & Osborn, 1979). Curry worked with the McMillan sisters for a time in London and was a leader in NANE.

Among Curry's students at Hampton was Evangeline Ward (1920–1985), who made significant contributions to the field (Simpson & McConnell-Farmer, 2013). Ward was president of NAEYC from 1970 to 1974, and not only was she the first African American president of the organization but also the only president ever to serve two terms. In the mid-1970s, Ward (1977) was the first to take on the challenge of developing a code of ethics for the profession. She was also the first executive director of the Child Development Associate (CDA) national credentialing program.

Many other African American early childhood leaders played major roles in the field's history. Space does not permit citing all of their accomplishments. At a time when their educational opportunity was severely limited, these professionals overcame huge obstacles to earn doctoral degrees at major national and international universities, to educate and mentor future generations of teachers, and to voluntarily serve in professional organizations. The harvest of their work is still being reaped, but was essential as the field expanded tremendously.

Native American Early Childhood History

The native population of this country is highly diverse within and among various tribes—each with its own cultural traditions, identity, and languages—and encompassing American Indians, Alaskan Natives, Native Hawaiians, and Pacific Islanders. Today, almost half of Native Americans live in urban areas rather than on reservations. However, the history of oppression, broken treaties, and removal from native lands has had a uniformly devastating impact on our indigenous population.

Schooling for Indian Children Historically, education was part of the government's strategy of oppression and control. For example, in the 19th century, children were often removed from the reservation to attend boarding schools in which they were not allowed to wear native dress, speak their language, or practice their cultural traditions (Wortham, 2002). Schools were also established on reservations but controlled by the Bureau of Indian Affairs with the goal of assimilating native peoples into the larger society and thus suppressing their cultural identity (Wortham, 2002). Surprisingly, one exception was William N. Hailmann, Superintendent of Indian Schools both on and off reservations from 1894 to 1898, who tried to implement Froebel's ideas and methods and introduced kindergarten teacher training (Lascarides & Hinitz, 2000).

In 1928, a government investigation resulted in the Meriam Report, which concluded that previous policies toward Indians had been detrimental to their health, social, and economic well-being. The report led to a shift in Indian education toward more progressive practices—connecting education to family and the values of the community, and to relevant skills and knowledge (Lascarides & Hinitz, 2000). However, schooling continued to be mostly segregated and inferior.

Federal legislation between 1965 and 1978 brought about significant change in the education of Indian children. Funds became available to public schools to better meet their needs and to provide bilingual education, enabling transmission of the culture and preservation of the languages, many of which were becoming extinct. In 1972, the Office of Indian Education of the U.S. Department of Education was established. Regulations began to require that parents and tribal leaders be involved in setting policies.

American Indian/Alaska Native Head Start

Head Start had a major impact on Native communities, bringing more emphasis on early education and comprehensive services. For example, Head Start played a significant role in ensuring that Indian children with disabilities receive intervention (T. Dobrec, personal communication, August 2, 2011). Dr. James Wilson, an Ogalala Sioux, worked with tribal leaders to get them to accept programs on reservations (T. Dobrec, personal communication, August 2, 2011).

Today, American Indian/Alaska Native Head Start programs are located in 26 states (Marks & Graham, 2004). Promoting home language and cultural identity are key goals of families and tribal leaders. Some, like the Cherokee nation, are committed to tribal language preservation, and many Pueblos have teachers who are fluent in the tribal language. But generally, language preservation is a challenge because in many situations, only a few tribal elders still speak the language, and there is no written form. Head Start and foundations such as Kellogg have been instrumental in expanding teacher preparation by providing grants to tribal colleges.

Native American Early Childhood Leaders

The field and Native American children and families have benefited from the contributions of many key leaders. One who was particularly important in higher education was Alice Paul (1930–2005). A lifelong educator in Tucson, she was the first Tohono O'odham woman to receive a Ph.D. from the University of Arizona. She served on the faculty of the University of Arizona from 1986 through 1999 and became head of Teaching and Teacher Education. Paul helped create the Tohono O'odham Community College and served on the Board of NAEYC in the 1990s.

Winona Sample (1917–2008), another important role model and national leader, was involved with Head Start from its beginning. Born on the Redlake Chippewa reservation in Minnesota, Sample had to go away to school like many Indian children. She became director of a large Head Start program and eventually head of Indian Health Services for the state of California. She, too, served on the NAEYC Board. In her own words, "The highlight of my life was being selected as the vice chair of the International Year of the Child (1979–1980)" (Neugebauer, 1995, p. 57).

Helen Scheirbeck (1935–2010) has been described as one of the 20th century's most significant American Indian leaders. She was an untiring advocate for American Indian civil rights, Indian children and families, Indian control of their own education, and the sovereignty of her Lumbee Tribe of North Carolina. She served as director of the Office of Indian Education, where she led efforts to pass the Indian Education Act of 1975. She was the head of the Indian Head Start Program beginning in 1991. Notably, Scheirbeck was a member of the first Board of Trustees of the Smithsonian's National Museum of the American Indian in Washington, D.C., for which she planned museum exhibitions, cultural arts programs, and educational materials.

Latino Early Childhood History

As with African Americans and Native Americans, the history of early education among Latinos has involved social injustices and shifting political winds. We use the term *Latino* to describe a highly diverse population with countries of origin including Mexico, Puerto Rico, Cuba, and various Latin and South American nations. Despite recent controversies surrounding immigration, most Latinos in the United States are American citizens and were born here.

In this brief overview of history from a Latino perspective, we address the two most significant influences: bilingual education in the K–12 sector, and the history of dual language programming in preschool and Head Start. Of course, the topic of bilingual education is relevant to hundreds of language groups in this country, but we discuss it here because the Spanish-speaking population of children is by far the largest group. Only Mexico has a larger population of Spanish speakers than the United States (Rumbaut, 2006). Also the issue of bilingual education is central to the history of early education from a Latino perspective.

American schools have always served large numbers of children who speak a language other than English at home. Every early childhood teacher needs to know and use effective strategies to teach dual language learners.

K–12 Bilingual Education Perhaps because the United States has always been a nation of immigrants, bilingual education has always been an issue. As far back as the colonial era, German, French, and Scandinavian immigrants provided bilingual schools (Cerda & Hernandez, 2006). In the 1870s, William Harris, the Superintendent of Schools in St. Louis who helped Susan Blow found the first public kindergarten, also founded the first kindergarten taught in German to help immigrant children get a "head start" on their education (Cerda & Hernandez, 2006). By the 1920s, however, most bilingual schools were abolished and children were expected to learn only English.

Modern bilingual programs began in the 1960s. The first two-way immersion program (taught in both Spanish and English) was established in Miami in 1963. Several important court cases in the 1970s, such as the *Lau vs. Nichols* decision in California and *Aspira vs. the City of New York* on behalf of Puerto Rican children, established that meeting linguistic and cultural needs, including providing bilingual education, was essential for children to have equal educational opportunity.

The federal government has played an important albeit changing policy-setting role in this history. Consider how names have changed in the U.S. Department of Education over time. In 1973, the Office of Bilingual Education was established to implement the first national Bilingual Education Act. From 1980 to 1995, the agency was called Office of Bilingual Education and Minority Languages Affairs (OBEMLA). Eugene Garcia, a highly respected scholar and advocate for early childhood education, was a director of the agency. Another important early childhood advocate, Delia Pompa, also led the agency and is now an executive at National Council of La Raza. OBEMLA's mission included helping school districts serve "limited English proficient" children (sadly called LEPs) and administering provisions in the Elementary and Secondary Education Act that included serving preschool children.

In the 1990s, bilingual programs came under attack as not effective and voters succeeded in banning them in California, Massachusetts, and Arizona. Emblematic of this political shift, OBEMLA was renamed the Office of English Language Acquisition. Many more states now have English-only laws for K–12 schools. These laws have not yet been applied to preschool programs but certainly have an effect on how and by whom children are taught. Despite research in support of dual language programs, strong public sentiment against them prevails. In the words of Antonia Lopez, Early Childhood Director at the National Council of La Raza: "The history of Latinos in early childhood education is tied into the history of not being seen as fully fledged Americans" (A. Lopez, personal communication, March 30, 2012).

Preschool Level A slightly brighter picture of Latino history has prevailed at the preschool level, with Head Start leading the way from its earliest days in support of children and families who speak languages other than English. In 1972, *The Head Start Program Performance Standards* required that programs help each child build cultural identity and that staff speak the primary language of the children and are knowledgeable about their culture. As part of the *Strategy for Spanish-Speaking Children* in the 1970s, Head Start funded development and dissemination of four Bilingual and Bicultural Curriculum

Models. These models provided an important foundation on which subsequent curricula and professional development have been built.

In 1982, the Child Development Associate (CDA) Credential Bilingual Specialization was established for candidates who have a working knowledge of two languages and to provide more well-prepared staff to work with dual language learners. In 1991, *Multicultural Principles for Head Start Programs* were developed by a cadre of professionals such as Yolanda Garcia, who provided training on the four multicultural curricula. In 1996, they were incorporated into the revision of the *Head Start Program Performance Standards*. For decades, Head Start has served migrant and seasonal workers, most of whom now are Spanish-speaking, which has stimulated much of the Bureau's work on linguistically and culturally responsive resources.

Despite these positive contributions to the field, historically, Latino children have been underrepresented in Head Start. The prevailing view has been that Latino families have a cultural preference for in-home care rather than formal programs for their children. This view, which is not supported by research, masked the reality that Latino families did not have adequate access to programs in their communities, nor were all programs culturally and linguistically responsive (M. Lopez, personal communication, January 26, 2012). However, the expansion of Head Start and increase in Early Head Start programs led to its population now being one-third Hispanic. In 2009, Yvette Sanchez Fuentes became the first Latina director of the Office of Head Start.

Latina Early Childhood Leadership   As we have seen throughout this chapter, history is primarily the story of how people impact organizations. The efforts of a small but committed group of leaders brought about real change within the early childhood establishment. Leaders such as Antonia Lopez, Amie Beckett, Mary Margarita Contie, Lily Wong Fillmore, Lourdes Diaz Soto, and Marlene Zepeda launched the Early Childhood Interest Group of the National Association of Bilingual Education. A handful of people attended its first meeting, but before long, more than 400 people flocked to their sessions (A. Lopez, personal communication, March 30, 2012). These advocates were joined by many others, including Governing Board member Rebeca Barrera, to influence policy within NAEYC. As a result, in 1995, the association adopted a position statement, *Responding to Linguistic and Cultural Diversity,* and also significantly revised its position statement on developmentally appropriate practice to reflect their input.

In widening the lens on the history of early childhood education to include the perspective of African Americans, Native Americans, and Latino Americans, it is apparent that Head Start has played a key role in providing services for these populations of children and families. We conclude by describing how Head Start wound all the various strands of early childhood history together.

 Check Your Understanding 2.4: A Wider View of Early Childhood History

 Bringing the Stories Together

The separate stories described previously continue to influence early education today. For example, we struggle with the large gap between preschool practices and what follows in kindergarten and primary grades. Similarly, child care and preschool continue to be divided in terms of standards, funding, and populations they serve. But over time, the stories began to converge, most notably in the national Head Start program and, more recently, in the prekindergarten movement.

The Story of Head Start

The harvest of the work of diverse leaders in the past is still being reaped, but was essential as the field expanded exponentially with the launch of Head Start in the mid-1960s, which brought together the strands of early childhood history (Hinitz, 2014). The Civil Rights movement of the 1960s brought about real change in virtually every aspect of society. Early childhood education was no exception. In response to the call for equal opportunity in this country, President Lyndon Johnson launched the War on Poverty. One of the cornerstones of this effort, and the only one that still exists, was the Head Start program. Head Start represents a coming together of the nursery school movement, which had previously served middle-class families, and the child care movement, which originated to serve the indigent and working poor. The following sections describe how the key elements of Head Start reflect the lessons learned from early childhood history.

▶ **Classroom Connection**

This video shows a quality Head Start program. How does Head Start today reflect the lessons learned from early childhood history?

A Comprehensive Program Just like Patty Smith Hill, Maria Montessori, the McMillan sisters, and so many others, the framers of Head Start believed in serving the whole child. Early childhood education has long been a multidisciplinary field. Head Start reflects this history as a comprehensive program providing health, mental health, social services, and parent involvement in addition to education.

Head Start was also a pioneer in fully including children with disabilities, who must constitute 10% of the population served. This mandate harkens back to the lessons learned from Montessori about the benefits of early intervention. Early education for all children with disabilities is a relatively recent phenomenon. For an overview of its history, see the lens on *Including All Children: Early Childhood Special Education in Historical Perspective*.

Including All Children
Early Childhood Special Education in Historical Perspective

When I first met my neighbor Clark—a large, friendly man about my age—I was struck by his delightful sense of humor and learned of his love of fishing and television. Even a brief encounter with Clark revealed that he had an intellectual disability, but spending time with him was always great fun. One day, while reading a book on my porch, I spied Clark watching me. When I asked him to join me, he replied, "I'd like to read a book." An older neighbor who'd known Clark since he was a child later explained, "Clark started school like all the other kids, back in the mid-1950s, but after a few days, they sent him home. They said, 'It didn't work out.'" Clark never returned to school.

If Clark had been born today, he would probably be diagnosed as having mild intellectual disability. His life experience would have been quite different due to major changes in special education services. In the latter part of the 20th century, parents of children with disabilities who were unable to obtain services formed organizations such as the Association for Retarded Children (ARC) and United Cerebral Palsy and also started preschools for the children. With the advocacy of parents, special educators, and other professionals, public laws began to change. In 1972, the government mandated that 10% of Head Start's student population be children with special needs.

By far the most important event in the history of special education was the passage of Public Law 94-142, the Education for All Handicapped Children Act of 1975, which in 1990 was renamed the Individuals with Disabilities Education Act (IDEA). This law established standards for how public schools must serve children with disabilities, from ages 3 to 21. A few years later, Public Law 99-457 extended services to children from birth to 3 years of age with emphasis on the role of families in early intervention. In addition, the Americans with Disabilities Act (ADA) of 1990 requires that programs be accessible for persons with disabilities, and prohibits child care centers from discriminating on the basis of disability

Early childhood special education today is the result of an amalgamation of traditional K–12 special education, regular early childhood education, and compensatory education including federal programs such as Head Start that were originally designed to "compensate" for areas of need in children's lives. The history of special education goes back to well before Maria Montessori demonstrated the power of early intervention to change children's lives. It is the story of many people working together to make a difference on behalf of children like Clark.

An Educational Program   The educational model for the Head Start program is the nursery school, specifically the Bank Street model (Shapiro & Nager, 1999). Over the years, Head Start's educational program has changed as new knowledge has emerged. But its core is developmentally appropriate practice, with its foundation going as far back as Comenius and Pestalozzi.

Because it was based on the laboratory nursery school model, many Head Start programs were and still are half-day. This is changing as more families need full-day child care, but Head Start has yet to completely merge the child care and nursery school threads of the field.

The rapid launch and expansion of Head Start meant that, like the WPA and Lanham Act centers, a large workforce was needed on short notice. As a result, minimal training was required for teachers. In recent years, the program has raised qualifications significantly but compensation remains a challenge.

A Parent Involvement Program   A core component of Head Start's mission is parent involvement. Here we see the influence of Lucy Sprague Mitchell and Jimmy Hymes, and the parent cooperative movement. In Head Start, however, parents are not only involved in the classroom; they are also part of the governance of the program, acting in major decision-making roles.

As part of the War on Poverty, Head Start's mandate included hiring parents as teachers and in other positions. At times, as many as one-third of the staff have been parents in the program. As in the case of WPA nurseries, however, hiring parents has presented the challenges of ensuring that the teachers are professionally qualified and has created the need for a professional development system.

The National Laboratory   An important part of Head Start's mission is to act as the national laboratory for the field. In this role, Head Start has funded seminal research and contributed to the development of curriculum and teacher training models. Head Start programs also partner with universities on research projects. In this capacity, Head Start has supplanted the child study laboratory schools of the early 20th century.

Head Start programs are locally administered and controlled. But Head Start has maintained its integrity and consistency despite its national scope because every grantee must meet the Head Start Program Performance Standards. These standards address, at least for Head Start, the recurring questions that confront the early childhood field.

The Prekindergarten Story

Leaders such as Susan Blow and Patty Smith Hill were deeply concerned about the potential negative consequences of public school involvement in kindergarten and nursery school. Some of their deepest fears have come to pass. With kindergarten an integral part of the public school system, much of the child development focus they espoused has been lost. Similarly, with the movement toward universal, voluntary preschool and more states providing funding for pre-K programs, the rigid dividing line between preschool and public education no longer exists.

On the other hand, bringing the nursery/kindergarten movements together with public education has contributed to more children having access to early education. This story is only beginning; the consequences have yet to be revealed. However, if Pre-K–3rd grade curriculum were aligned in a developmentally appropriate way and comprehensive services offered for all children from birth through age 8, all the stories could be brought together in the best possible way.

Building on a Tradition of Excellence

The fundamental questions that have faced the field since its inception continue to dominate the conversation: How is quality defined in programs for children? What should be the qualifications for teachers and how should they be prepared? What are the goals for children's learning and development? What should be the content of the curriculum and how should it be taught?

Looking back through history, we find that many ideas are revisited: stages of development, active learning, children's interests, sensory learning, positive guidance, image of the child, the teachers' role, and the role of materials and environments. But differences emerge as well. Today we view the teacher's role as more intentional than our predecessors did, and we no longer see children's development as a natural unfolding. Instead, we better understand the interaction of environment and biology. In addition, developmental stages are not rigid as previously assumed. Standards and approaches need to be flexible and changing—based on new knowledge—unlike Maria Montessori and Susan Blow, who refused to change their views.

The most basic history lessons that early childhood teachers should never forget include these:

- We all need to learn from children, as did all of the historical figures discussed in this chapter and as Caroline Pratt wisely put it.
- We need to draw on science and the wisdom of experience, as Patty Smith Hill and Lucy Sprague Mitchell modeled for us.
- And, as Patty Smith Hill believed, it is always valuable to listen to opposing points of view and to learn from them.

 Check Your Understanding 2.5: Bringing the Stories Together

Revisiting the Case Study

. . . the Preschool Classroom

Take a moment to revisit the classroom observations of the college students in the opening vignette of this chapter. The traces of early childhood history should now be apparent. The students saw Comenius's picture books and alphabet books, evidence of Froebel's gifts in the wooden cube and parquetry blocks, and the legacy of Maria Montessori in the child-sized furniture and sandpaper letters. They also observed children's active play with Caroline Pratt's unit blocks and Patty Smith Hill's beloved dramatic play. Their firehouse field trips are reminiscent of John Dewey's call for active learning and integrated curriculum as well as Lucy Sprague Mitchell's Bank Street approach. The woodworking tables and cooking are more evidence of Dewey's influence. Finally, the students saw the lasting contribution of Lucy Sprague Mitchell's writer's workshops in Margaret Wise Brown's *Goodnight Moon* and the enduring joy of singing Patty Smith Hill's "Happy Birthday" on one child's most special day. ■

2 Chapter Summary

- Studying history is valuable because it helps people understand current issues, avoid getting stuck in the past, aspire to make a difference for children, and advocate for change.

- Different periods of history have had different perspectives on children and childhood, which have implications for how children are treated and what kinds of education they are provided.

- Early education in the United States was strongly influenced by Western European ideas, such as those of Comenius, Pestalozzi, Froebel, and Montessori. Although European ideas are not the only, or necessarily the best, educational concepts in the world, current practices strongly reflect these early influences.

- The kindergarten movement in the United States was based directly on the work of Froebel and led by Elizabeth Peabody, Susan Blow, and others who spread his ideas widely through teacher training and founding the International Kindergarten Union.

- The progressive education movement led by John Dewey had a profound impact on education in the United States, especially early childhood education, whose principles of developmentally appropriate practice are congruent with progressive ideas.

- The nursery school movement, which grew out of the child study movement, eventually launched the wider field of early childhood education through the leadership of Patty Smith Hill and Lucy Sprague Mitchell, among many others.

- The child care movement grew out of social welfare efforts for low-income families, focused on the need to support working parents, and became associated with physical care rather than education, although this division is changing.

- African Americans, Native Americans, and Latino Americans played significant roles in the history of early childhood education, although their contributions are not well documented.

- The launch of Head Start in the mid-1960s brought together the various strands of early childhood history, which are reflected in its comprehensive services, developmentally appropriate educational program, parent involvement, and its role as a national laboratory.

Key Terms

- absorbent mind
- Bank Street approach
- child-centered curriculum
- child study movement
- competent child
- constructivism
- day nurseries
- Froebel's occupations and gifts
- integrated curriculum
- Lanham Act
- nursery schools
- progressive education movement
- WPA nurseries

 Demonstrate Your Learning

Click here to assess how well you've learned the content in this chapter.

Readings and Websites

Hinitz, B. F. (2013). History of early childhood education in multicultural perspective. In J. L. Roopnarine & J. E. Johnson (Eds.), *Approaches to early childhood education* (6th ed., pp. 3–24). Upper Saddle River, NJ: Pearson.

Wortham, S. (2002). *Childhood: 1892–2002*. Wheaton, MD: Association for Childhood Education International.

American Montessori Society

Check this website for information about the history of Montessori and also its present-day practices, professional development opportunities, and other resources.

Association for Childhood Education International

Originally the IKU, ACEI now provides a global community of advocates for children from birth through early adolescence.

Office of Head Start

The website provides many valuable resources for all aspects of Head Start programming, which are also useful for any early childhood program, and the list of Head Start Program Performance Standards.

3 Understanding and Applying Developmentally Appropriate Practice

Learning Outcomes

After studying this chapter, you should be able to:

3.1 Define developmentally appropriate practice.

3.2 Identify the behaviors of intentional teachers.

3.3 Describe how teachers make decisions about developmentally appropriate practices.

3.4 Identify the key roles of early childhood teachers.

3.5 Apply principles of developmentally appropriate practice in planning learning environments and daily schedules.

3.6 Discuss research about developmentally appropriate practices.

Today is Olivia's first day of preschool at the elementary school that her older brothers also attend. They have been teasing her about how hard school is, and she is a little fearful as well as excited. She hesitantly enters the building clutching the postcard her teacher sent her to welcome her to school. Aware that several of the newly enrolled children and their families speak Spanish at home, Olivia's teacher, Mr. Washington, has arranged for a translator to be present this morning. He has also learned a few key phrases in Spanish himself, including how to say, "I'm sorry, I don't speak Spanish, but Ms. Lopez is here to help."

When Olivia's grandmother arrives at the classroom door, Mr. Washington greets her in Spanish and pulls the translator into the conversation. Olivia's brothers and mother speak English but her grandmother speaks only Spanish. Then Mr. Washington stoops down to Olivia's eye level and greets her warmly with a smile, "I'm so happy that you are here, Olivia. We're going to have lots of fun playing, listening to stories, and making friends." Mr. Washington offers his hand to Olivia and escorts her to a cubby with her name on it where she can store her belongings. He asks, "Would it be okay if I took a picture of you? We will print it and put it next to your name. Later we can display a photo of your whole family on the wall with the other children's families." She shyly smiles for the camera and then asks to see herself.

"Now we're going to have some quiet play time while the children are arriving and then we'll eat breakfast together. Your grandmother says that you like to do puzzles, so I'll show you where we keep them," Mr. Washington says. Olivia's eyes sparkle as she spies all the materials in the room, alighting on the iPad that two children are using to listen to a song in Spanish. She is especially delighted by the dress-up clothes, the painting easel, and the sand table. She feels good already because her teacher is so nice and she likes the chairs and tables that are just her size. The puzzles are ones that she can put together all by herself, too. Olivia is already feeling comfortable at school on her first day because her teacher understands and engages in developmentally appropriate practice. ■

Throughout this book and throughout your studies and work as an early childhood educator, you will hear the term *developmentally appropriate practice*. In this chapter we discuss the evolution of this concept and examine how it is used in the classroom. We also discuss the concept of becoming an intentional teacher. Next, we address the question of how to decide what is developmentally appropriate and the multi-faceted role of the early childhood teacher. We apply this decision-making process to how teachers plan appropriate learning environments and daily schedules for children. Finally, we briefly describe the research base for developmentally appropriate practice.

The concepts addressed in this chapter are part of the foundational knowledge of early childhood education. These topics provide a basic framework for organizing much of your beginning knowledge. A large body of literature exists about child development and its application to early childhood practice (see Berk, 2012; Kostelnik, Soderman, Whiren, & Rupiper, 2014). This chapter considers some of this literature, as well as the definition, principles, and guidelines for developmentally appropriate practice as described by the National Association for the Education of Young Children (NAEYC, 2009).

What Is Developmentally Appropriate Practice?

Over time, the phrase *developmentally appropriate practice* (often abbreviated as DAP) has been defined and used in different ways. Its definition has evolved as new research and knowledge have become available.

developmentally appropriate practice is teaching that is attuned to children's ages, experience, abilities, and interests and that helps them attain challenging and achievable goals. The foundations of developmentally appropriate practice, as it is defined today, lie in the history of early childhood education. Most fundamental is the premise that teaching young children should be based on what is known about how they develop and learn optimally.

Within the field of developmental psychology, the concept of *developmentally appropriate* has been widely used for more than a century and refers to age-related and individual human variation. Early childhood educators have long used the phrase *developmentally appropriate* to describe high-quality environments, materials, learning experiences, or expectations for children of varying ages.

developmentally appropriate practice (DAP) Ways of teaching that engage children's interests and adapt for their age, experience, and ability to help them meet challenging and achievable learning goals.

NAEYC'S Position Statement on Developmentally Appropriate Practice

The concept of developmentally appropriate practice gained widespread recognition and influence in the mid-1980s when NAEYC published position statements on developmentally appropriate practice (Bredekamp, 1987). A **position statement** is a document that articulates a research-based stance that an organization is taking in response to an issue or a problem. Based on new research, emerging controversies, and the changing contexts in which early childhood education occurs, NAEYC revised its statement on developmentally appropriate practice in the mid-1990s (Bredekamp & Copple, 1997) and again in 2009 (NAEYC, 2009).

position statement A document that articulates a stance, usually research based, that an organization is taking in response to an issue or a problem.

NAEYC's 2009 position statement describes principles and guidelines for teaching young children from birth through age 8. NAEYC also presents recommended practices for different age groups: infants and toddlers, preschoolers, kindergartners, and children in the primary grades (Copple, Bredekamp, Korelek, & Charner, 2013a, 2013b, 2014a, 2014b). The position statement is widely used as a summary of the field's best thinking, a defense of its valued practices, and an advocacy tool for improving programs for young children.

The position statement serves several purposes. Originally NAEYC sought to clarify the term to help professionals consistently interpret its standards for early childhood program accreditation. A second purpose that continues to be an issue was to address the issue of age-appropriateness of expectations for children, as well as curriculum and teaching practices. In addition, the 1997 revision brought more attention to the critical role of culture and language in development, the inclusion of children with disabilities, and the teacher's role as intentional decision maker (Bredekamp, 1997a, 1997b). The 2009 statement continues these emphases and also responds to current issues such as addressing the achievement gap and alignment from pre-K to grade 3.

▶ **Classroom Connection**

In this video, Sue Bredekamp discusses the achievement gap within the framework of developmentally appropriate practice. How do you think we can teach most effectively when children come to school with very different levels of vocabulary or mathematics skills?

Current Issues in Developmentally Appropriate Practice

The early childhood profession continues to raise concerns about what is developmentally appropriate as new issues arise in the lives of children. Three issues are currently under serious debate: push-down curriculum, Common Core State Standards, and appropriate practice in the digital age.

In developmentally appropriate classrooms, teachers get to know each child as an individual and build a positive relationship. What is this teacher doing to "meet children where they are" as individuals?

Push-down Curriculum Perhaps the most important motivation for defining developmentally appropriate practice over the years has been to counter the trend toward **push-down curriculum**, in which content that was previously taught in first grade is being taught in kindergarten or even preschool. This was one of the original motivations for writing developmentally appropriate practice. However, the problem is even more urgent today because the trend toward increased academic focus in kindergarten has accelerated (Bassok & Rorem, 2014). For example, in 1998, about one-third of kindergarten teachers believed that most children should learn to read in kindergarten. By 2005, 65% of teachers held this expectation (Bassok & Rorem, 2014).

> **push-down curriculum** Content previously taught in a higher grade in school being expected to be learned in an earlier grade

Not surprisingly, these increased academic expectations led to changes in the curriculum. Time devoted to literacy in kindergarten has increased by 25% and social studies, science, music, art, and physical education have decreased (Bassok & Rorem, 2014). Increased academic demands have resulted in many teachers using practices such as worksheets and whole-group, didactic instruction that are not developmentally appropriate (Strauss, 2014). A related trend is that young children no longer are given time or materials to play in school (Alliance for Childhood, 2010; Squires, 2014). As a result, increasing numbers of children are experiencing stress, being judged not ready for kindergarten, or struggling and failing in their earliest school experience (Almon & Miller, 2011; Bassok & Reardon, 2013).

Push-down curriculum has been a trend for decades and is often attributed to the accountability movement, whereby teachers are held responsible if children fail to achieve certain standards. This trend was propelled by No Child Left Behind legislation in the early 1990s. More recently, a particularly troublesome trend is the requirement in many states that children read by the end of third grade or be held back. This requirement puts additional pressure on teachers in the earlier grades, thus pushing down curriculum even more.

Common Core State Standards   Another controversial issue is the impact on curriculum and teaching, and especially on children, of the *Common Core State Standards* (CCSS) (Common Core State Standards Initiative, 2011a, 2011b). The Common Core establishes national standards in English Language Arts and Mathematics in kindergarten through grade 12 that were initially adopted by 45 states but subsequently became politically controversial. Some early childhood educators have expressed deep concern that the Common Core standards themselves are not achievable for most children in K–3, that they will lead to developmentally inappropriate teaching practices, and that they will narrow the curriculum further to the two subject areas (Defending the Early Years, 2014; Miller & Carlsson-Paige, 2013).

NAEYC (2012) charges the field to approach the CCSS with caution but also to see it as an opportunity. Many of the standards call for the kind of higher-order thinking and problem solving that developmentally appropriate practices promote, and they should not automatically lead to bad teaching. The fact is that Common Core establishes standards for what children should know and be able to do, but does not address how teachers should teach. These words appear in the English Language Arts standards: "The use of play with young children is not specified in the Standards, but it is welcome as a valuable activity in its own right and as a way to help students meet the expectations in this document" (Common Core State Standards Initiative, 2011a, p. 6).

Nevertheless, some of the standards will be unattainable by many children in kindergarten through grade 3, especially those children who have not had enriching prior experiences. Therefore, it is important that early childhood educators remain vigilant as the Common Core is implemented and children's learning is assessed. Standards themselves are periodically reviewed and if they are found to not be achievable for the majority of children (that is, are developmentally inappropriate), then they should be revised.

Appropriate Practice in the Digital Age   A third issue that is often discussed in the context of developmentally appropriate practice is technology. Some early educators are troubled by the fact that children spend too much time engaged with "screens," which takes away time from important activities such as play, outdoor time, conversations with other children and adults, and other joyful childhood experiences (Campaign for Commercial-Free Childhood & Alliance for Childhood, 2012). The fact is that from 2011 to 2013, the number of children under age 8 using mobile devices doubled, and the average amount of time children spent on digital media tripled (Common Sense Media, 2013). A related concern is the quality and value of the content that is provided via digital devices.

On the other hand, technology and interactive media permeate children's lives and have demonstrated great potential to support young children's learning (Donohue, 2015). Rather than simply "protecting" children from technology by limiting screen time, educators have a responsibility to promote the effective integration of high-quality, developmentally appropriate media (Donohue, 2015; Rogow, 2015). Lisa Guernsey (2014), a national expert on children's media, advises that the most important considerations are the quality and appropriateness of the content on the screen, the context within which it is used (how long, under what supervision), and the age and characteristics of individual children.

The joint position statement on technology in early childhood programs by NAEYC and the Fred Rogers Center for Early Learning and Children's Media (2012) is an excellent guide for decision making in the digital age. The fundamental principle is that "Technology and interactive media are tools that can promote effective learning and development, within the framework of developmentally appropriate practice"(p. 5). In short, interactive media require many professional decisions on the part of early childhood teachers and media developers to ensure that they are of the highest quality and are used appropriately and effectively.

Undoubtedly other issues will arise as they have in the past. Over the years, the position statement has generated controversies, including questions about whether the recommended practices apply equally well to diverse groups of children (e.g., Dahlberg, Moss, & Pence, 2007; Graue & Delaney, 2011; Woodhead, 2006). In turn, new research

Promoting Play

Does Developmentally Appropriate Practice = Play?

For many early childhood educators, *play* is synonymous with *developmentally appropriate practice*. There are many reasons why this is true. The primary reason is that a vast amount of research demonstrates that play is critical to healthy development and learning in the early years. To be developmentally appropriate, teaching practices *must* reflect what is known about how children develop and learn most effectively. Therefore, play *must* be an integral component of a developmentally appropriate program for young children.

But play is complex. There are many types of play that have different benefits for children and children play differently depending on their age, level of development, and experience. Observe how babies play and you will notice that they tend to play with objects and explore the world using their senses—especially touch and taste. As toddlers gain mobility, their play involves their whole bodies with running and climbing among their favorite activities. They begin to play more with toys, and occasionally with or near one other child. The preschool years are prime time for play, with children engaging in virtually every type of play both alone and with friends such as block building, table toys, pretend, or rough-and-tumble play. Primary-grade children continue to need lots of play, including active outdoor free play, games with rules, and dramatization.

Children's play also varies with their individual interests and prior experiences. Girls and boys often gravitate toward different types of play despite the efforts of teachers and parents to discourage gender stereotyping. Some children prefer solitary play while others take the lead in organizing a small group to build a fort or set up an airport.

Finally, children play the culture in which they live. Play is a natural context for children to practice adult roles, and they mimic the activities, behaviors, and language of the adults and older children in their cultural group. For example, in a highly technological society such as ours, children play with digital tools as well as the typical tools of daily life such as cars or microwaves.

Like all other aspects of development and learning, play varies in predictable ways by children's ages, individual characteristics, and the social and cultural contexts in which they live. To fully benefit children, teachers must intentionally promote children's play and use it to help children reach challenging and achievable goals. Developmentally appropriate practice is more than play, but play is developmentally appropriate.

and critiques will continue to stimulate productive discussions among early childhood educators about what is best for young children.

Developmentally Appropriate Practice in the Classroom

Developmentally appropriate practice begins with early childhood educators' knowledge of how children learn and develop. Its ultimate goal is to promote the development and enhance the learning of each individual child served. "Developmentally appropriate practice" is used by some as a shorthand term for the value of play or letting children be children, not pushing them to grow up too soon. Play is an integral component of developmentally appropriate practice; however, it is only one facet. To better understand how play relates to developmentally appropriate practice, read the feature entitled *Promoting Play: Does Developmentally Appropriate Practice = Play?*

The term, developmentally appropriate practice, is used within the early childhood profession to describe the complex work of the early childhood teacher. Knowing how children learn and develop is essential for teachers of young children. The more they know about and are sensitive to the way children think and learn, the more effective their teaching and the more satisfying their work. To successfully engage in developmentally appropriate practice (Copple, Bredekamp, Koralek, & Charner, 2013b), teachers need to:

- Meet children where they are, as individuals and as a group.
- Use a variety of intentional strategies to help each child attain challenging and achievable goals that contribute to his or her ongoing development and learning.

Meet Children Where They Are   Knowing what children, within a given age range, are generally capable of and how they learn provides teachers with a starting point for planning and organizing a program. But such a broad picture is not enough. Teachers must go beyond what is "typical"; they must recognize that they will have little success if they try to teach everyone the same way. They must also recognize that if their expectations are too high, children become frustrated; if their expectations are too low, their students will become bored. In either case—teaching only what is "typical" or having unrealistic expectations—children will fail to make learning progress.

Good teachers continually observe children's engagement with materials, activities, and people in order to learn about each child's abilities, interests, and needs. Based on this information, they plan curriculum and adapt their teaching strategies to help children make continued progress. Meeting children where they are might look something like this:

> Nathan knows only a few letters, he does not sit still during story time, and he is significantly behind on many of the kindergarten literacy goals. His teacher knows, however, that all kinds of transportation vehicles fascinate him. On a class visit to the library, she helps Nathan locate several information books on transportation to read with him and have him take home. He especially likes one book about all kinds of trucks. To interest Nathan in learning letters and words, his teacher prints the names of the different trucks on cards for him to match with the pictures. Soon, Nathan is drawing pictures of the trucks and trying to write the words himself.
>
> Four-year-old Jamal speaks Arabic at home and is learning English at school. His teacher often reads to him in a small group, with other children whose home language is not English, using books with limited vocabulary and clear correspondence between the pictures and words. She also uses other cues to aid his understanding. For instance, she uses real objects as props when she introduces new words such as the kinds of food that the *Very Hungry Caterpillar* (Carle, 1969) is eating. She stays in close contact with his parents, communicating through a translator, to learn about the competencies he demonstrates at home, and she encourages the family to talk and read with him in their own language.

These examples demonstrate how teachers meet children where they are by assessing what they already know as well as learning about their interests. At the same time, teachers keep in mind the teaching goals.

▶ Classroom Connection

As you watch this video, identify the challenging goals that the teacher has for the children and how she intentionally uses play to help them achieve those goals.

Help Children Reach Challenging and Achievable Goals
Meeting learners where they are is important, but it is just the beginning. As illustrated in the preceding examples, learning is most effective when materials or experiences not only build on what children already know and on what they can do, but also require them to stretch toward new skills and understandings.

Developmentally appropriate goals for a given group of children need to be realistic and attainable for most children within the age range of the group. However, developmentally appropriate practice does not mean making things easier for children. Instead, goals must be challenging but not so difficult that children are unable to achieve them. Further, children need to have plenty of opportunities to practice their newly acquired skills to the point of mastery. Young children often initiate such practice on their own, such as when they repeatedly count the steps they climb or try time and again to balance on one foot.

Once new skills have been mastered, children need new challenges to continue to learn. These new challenges should provide children with a reasonable stretch that is "just achievable." For example, consider a group of kindergartners learning to play catch. If the teacher consistently throws the ball way over children's heads, they will soon give up in frustration. But if she makes the task too easy—rolling the ball on the ground—most 5-year-olds would quickly grow bored and call it "baby stuff." Instead, a teacher who is taking into account what is developmentally appropriate will provide just the right amount of challenge. One child will need the ball thrown right into her extended arms, while another who has had more practice will joyfully leap to catch it over her head.

Teaching in a developmentally appropriate way brings together meeting the learner where he or she is and helping children achieve goals. Teachers keep the curriculum's learning goals in mind as they determine where children are and what the next steps forward are. What is challenging and achievable varies from one child to the next, depending on each child's level of development; prior experiences, knowledge, and skills; and the context within which the learning takes place.

To be developmentally appropriate, teaching practices must be effective—they must *contribute* to children's ongoing development and learning. That is, if children are not learning and progressing toward important outcomes, then the practices and experiences in the program are not developmentally appropriate. To ensure their practices are in fact effective and developmentally appropriate, teachers need to be intentional in everything they do.

 Check Your Understanding 3.1: What Is Developmentally Appropriate Practice?

Intentional Teaching

To be effective in their work, teachers cannot leave important aspects of children's development and learning to chance. In everything early childhood teachers do—from organizing

Developmentally appropriate teaching practices must be effective. Intentional teachers don't simply assume that play is developmentally appropriate. They support children's play so that it benefits children's development as much as possible.

intentional teachers Teachers who have a purpose for the decisions they make and can explain that purpose to others.

the environment to planning the curriculum to choosing specific teaching strategies or adapting their plans for individual children—effective teachers are **intentional teachers**. Intentional teachers have a purpose for their actions; they make decisions for a reason. The intentional teacher plans carefully in advance, but also has enough knowledge to make thoughtful decisions throughout the day, even during the unplanned, spontaneous "teachable moments" that inevitably arise.

Purposeful Planning

Intentional teaching and developmentally appropriate practice go hand in hand. Sometimes in early childhood classrooms where children spend significant periods of time in exploration, play, and activities they choose and pursue independently, uninformed observers may think that the situation is "anything goes." However, if the child is in a program that truly is developmentally appropriate, teachers' intentionality undergirds the entire program and all of the experiences provided. The teacher carefully organizes the environment and selects and arranges the materials to promote children's active engagement, both mental and physical.

In planning the learning experiences, the intentional teacher thinks carefully about what will foster children's enthusiasm for learning and enable them to reach important goals in all areas of their development and learning. She regularly observes and assesses children and then uses the information gleaned to gauge her interactions with the children, both individually and in small groups, to promote ongoing learning and enable children to master new challenges.

▶ **Classroom Connection**

Observe how the teachers in this video engage the children in playful activities that are fun but also thoughtfully planned to meet learning goals.

Understand and Explain Practices

Intentional teachers are able to explain the rationale for their practices to administrators, other teachers, and family members. Intentional teachers are also alert to the need to modify plans, recognizing that there will be times when what they have planned doesn't work out. Perhaps the children master a skill sooner than expected and lose interest in the activity; conversely, a task may be beyond the children's current abilities and they become confused or discouraged. In either case, an intentional teacher will have planned for such possibilities and be prepared to modify the learning experience or shift to another strategy that will be more effective in achieving the goal. Consider the following examples of practices, which are generally thought to be developmentally appropriate, and light of the additional criteria of intentionality and effectiveness:

Tiana Carstairs teaches 4-year-olds. Each day she reads a different Big Book (an oversize picture book with limited text per page) to the class. The children enjoy the readings and respond readily to Tiana's questions about the letters in print or sounds they hear. She also points out concepts of print by tracking the words on the page left to right and noting how to turn the pages. An observer in Tiana's class would probably view her practice as developmentally appropriate. What the casual observer would miss, however, is that 14 of the 16 children have mastered the print concepts that Tiana continues to teach. In addition, 4 children already know all the letters.

Rather than use this same teaching strategy every day without reflection, Tiana should regularly assess children's learning so that she continually adds challenge as children achieve new goals. Although the children enjoy the Big Book readings, the limited vocabulary contained in the books is not helping them learn new words. Tiana needs to be more intentional about building vocabulary in this group of children who are already significantly behind in language development. She needs to employ effective practices such as reading more complex stories and information books in small groups and engaging children in conversations about the readings.

Jana Baker teaches in a full-day kindergarten. She believes strongly in the value of play for children's learning and development, and she has been able to preserve time and materials for play in her classroom. In the early days of Jana's career, when

Becoming an Intentional Teacher
Expanding Thinking and Communication Skills

Here's What Happened After the 45-minute learning center time in my preschool classroom, I asked each child to tell what he or she had done. A few children just pointed to where they had gone or ran back over there to show me. I thought of these children as the "Pointers." A few others verbally identified the center they had played in, saying something like, "I was in the block area" or just "Blocks." I'll call them the "Namers." Other children—the "Detailers"—said more about what they had done and who they played with, though their descriptions were often unclear to anyone who hadn't been there ("I tried to get it to stay, but it fell"). There were variations, but basically the children fell into these three groups.

After a few days, I began asking children to reflect in small groups and added some more challenge. For example, with children who were Pointers, I had a photo of each center, and I asked the child to find the center where they had worked. Then I said, "Ah, you were building in the block area." I repeated the name of the center several times.

With the Namers, I asked them to tell me what they did in the center they identified. Sometimes I asked a question such as, "What were you building today?" and if I got no response, I added, "Were you building a road, or something else?" I would also say things like "Hmm, let's see, what was I doing? I took my sick puppy to Mark and Bobbie's veterinarian's office."

With the Detailers, I used a variety of methods. Sometimes I paired two children who responded at similar levels and had them tell each other what they had done that day. Often children would ask each other questions like, "What fell? What were you trying to build?"

Here's What I Was Thinking I decided to start this routine—asking the children what they had done in the centers—for two reasons. First, it helps develop their ability to reflect, to think about the past rather than the present. At their age, children are increasing in their capacity to think back (or forward to the future) if they are encouraged to do so. They're very interested in their own activities, so they are motivated, and this is a good way to extend their oral language and communication skills.

I started wherever each individual child was and tried to help each one go a little farther. Sometimes I tried using a visual support like the photos to see if that would help stimulate more language. I also modeled both the language—for instance, by repeating the center names—and the practice of thinking back and reflecting on what one has done.

Having pairs of children talk to each other is useful because children want their peers to understand them and will try hard to get their message across. I also model talking and asking questions, and the children pick it up and do it themselves. Gradually the more verbal children who at first give a lot of disjointed details get better at giving a coherent account of their activities.

Reflection Are there other intentional teaching strategies this teacher could use to achieve her goals? What other skills might these experiences help children develop?

---

parents or principals questioned her, she defended play by simply stating that it is developmentally appropriate. But as pressures increased for literacy instruction in kindergarten, Jana found herself thinking more critically about her practice. She observed that during choice time, children's play had become repetitive. Boys built the same roads and towers in the block area. Few children engaged in dramatic play, and those who did pretended to be characters they had seen on TV or in video games. Other children wandered from one activity to another without engagement or sustained interest.

Jana realized that she didn't know enough about play; she couldn't explain clearly why it was valuable for children and didn't know how to enhance children's involvement. After attending workshops and reading professional journals, Jana became aware that there were many missed opportunities for learning in her classroom. She learned ways to help children engage in mature, sustained, sociodramatic play that builds social and emotional skills and language. She introduced board games to help children learn mathematics while cooperating and having fun.

Jana began to see that choice time provided many opportunities for her to engage in one-on-one, extended conversations with children or to build writing, reading, and math into their play. In short, Jana became intentional in her interactions with children during play and in the kind of play experiences she provided. As a result, play became a more effective teaching and learning experience for the children in her kindergarten.

As we can see in the previous scenarios, intentional teachers continually reflect on their own decisions and gather evidence of how well children are doing. They may discuss their practices with colleagues and children's families. They modify their practices when these are not benefiting children. Read the feature titled *Becoming an Intentional Teacher: Expanding Thinking and Communication Skills* for an example of a teacher's actions and the thinking behind them.

Intentional teaching requires constant decision making. Next we describe what teachers need to consider when making good decisions.

 Check Your Understanding 3.2: Intentional Teaching

Developmentally Appropriate Decision Making

Teachers of young children make hundreds of decisions every day: which book to read to what size group, which questions to ask when, how to intervene with a child who is struggling to enter a play situation, and so forth. They must be able to negotiate difficult situations, such as what to do when a child shares a confidential family secret, how much support to give two boys who are trying to fairly divide the blocks, and what intervention to try with a first grader who is significantly behind in reading development. The list goes on and on. Day after day and hour after hour, teachers are called on to determine what is developmentally appropriate.

In many cases, decisions are the result of careful advance consideration and planning. For example, teachers must consider what kinds of learning experiences will help the group achieve important learning goals. These decisions include planning curriculum so that the learning goals established for the group are achievable and challenging for the children. For instance, although the school district prekindergarten curriculum calls for teaching the alphabet, Ms. Jonas determines which children in her class have not yet achieved this goal and which children have already mastered the alphabet. The curriculum plan as written may be appropriate for many children in the former group, but the latter group can connect letters and sounds and use recognizable letters in their own writing.

Other decisions include setting up the physical environment, which materials to place where, how to schedule the day, or how to group children for various learning experiences. Ms. Jonas ensures that the alphabet is displayed at children's eye level as a model for children's writing, and that magnetic letters and alphabet puzzles are available for children to manipulate in their work and play. She organizes the daily schedule to ensure that children have ample time to write on their own and, during the day, she works in small groups with children who need extra help.

Some situations require teachers to make immediate decisions. For instance, suppose a dump truck pulls up outside the preschool window. The teacher may decide to interrupt his prior plans and follow the children's interest by taking them outside to observe the truck unloading the gravel for a new driveway. Or he may see that most of the children are engrossed in learning centers and decide not to interrupt. Likewise, if the story a teacher is reading to a group doesn't hold the children's interest, she can readily switch gears and select another book or engage children in an active song.

Primary-grade teachers must make numerous short- and long-term decisions as they support children's learning, particularly each child's reading progress. Some teaching decisions have lasting consequences for individual children. For example, identifying a child for special education services or determining a plan to work with a child who is extremely aggressive and disruptive has far-reaching consequences. When making such a decision, the teacher needs to take into consideration many sources of information, observations over time, and the diverse perspectives of family members and other professionals such as special educators or social workers.

Make Informed Decisions

Large or small, all decisions that teachers make should be informed decisions. NAEYC (2009) identifies three fundamental considerations that guide teachers in making decisions about what is developmentally appropriate for children:

1. *Consider what is known about development and learning of children within a given age range.* Having knowledge of age-related human characteristics allows teachers to make general predictions within an age range about what materials, interactions, and experiences will be safe, interesting, challenging, and within reach for children, and thus likely to best promote their learning and development. This dimension is sometimes called **age appropriate**.
2. *Consider what is known about each child as an individual.* Gathering information about the strengths, interests, and needs of each individual child in the group enables teachers to adapt and be responsive to that individual variation.
3. *Consider what is known about the social and cultural contexts in which children live.* Learning about the values, expectations, and behavioral and linguistic conventions that shape children's lives at home and in their communities allows teachers to create learning environments and experiences that are meaningful, relevant, and respectful of all children and their families.

age appropriate Age-related human characteristics that allow teachers to make general predictions within an age range about what materials, interactions, and experiences will be safe, interesting, challenging, and within reach for children and, thus, likely to best promote their learning and development.

Considering all this information is important because it reflects what we know about how children develop. At each age, they share characteristics with other people within that age range but also develop as individuals and as members of cultural groups whose values and beliefs shape how their development occurs. Figure 3.1 depicts this model of child development.

In each of these three areas, the knowledge to be considered is substantial and changes over time. Intentional teachers make sure to stay informed both through ongoing professional development, which includes gaining information from new research, and through those avenues that will provide necessary information about the children they teach, their families, and their communities. Let's examine each of these areas more closely and see what each contributes to the decisions teachers make.

Consider What Is Known about Child Development and Learning

During early childhood, it is possible to make relatively accurate predictions about children's capabilities based on age ranges. Babies need constant care and careful

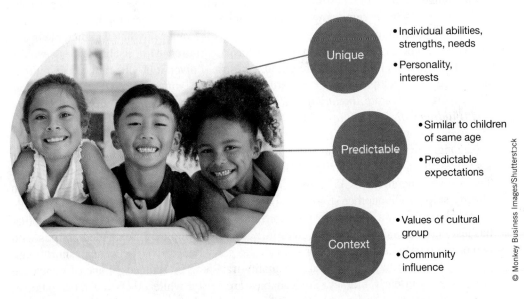

FIGURE 3.1 Model of Child Development This model illustrates the three core considerations of developmentally appropriate practice—child development in general, individual variation, and social and cultural contexts.

▶ **Classroom Connection**

As you watch this video, observe the diverse ways that children play in early childhood programs and listen as Dr. Jeffrey Trawick-Smith describes what we know from child development research about the important benefits of play.

https://www.youtube.com/
watch?v=vnH4Ijen7OI

supervision because they put everything in their mouths. Two-year-olds who have mastered walking waste no time in running headlong into furniture and walls. Preschoolers are fairly good communicators but need help to keep expanding their vocabulary. Primary-grade children are reasonably independent learners when motivated by the topic or activity.

Adults—especially parents, family members, and teachers—consider what is developmentally appropriate every day without necessarily recognizing it. For instance, when selecting a toy for 2-year-old Hudson, his aunt chooses a schoolhouse with a handle for carrying. The toy has a label that indicates there are no small parts that can be swallowed. She determines that the toy is manageable for most toddlers whose fine motor skills are limited, so they are unlikely to become frustrated. Because the toy is age appropriate, it should hold Hudson's interest. Like most 2-year-olds, Hudson is beginning to engage in pretend play and also loves to carry his toys around with him. At other times, adults fail to recognize what is inappropriate as when competitive soccer leagues for 4-year-olds are organized.

Some characteristics that young children typically demonstrate are common knowledge. For example, when a young panda cub makes his media debut, reporters observe that he behaves "like a toddler." Readers immediately get the picture even without the description—"He squirmed in the arms of his keepers, climbed and tumbled over a rock pile, and walked through a small stream. He also showed a penchant for putting things in his mouth" (Barker, 2005).

Knowing age-related characteristics helps guide teachers' expectations of children's behavior and abilities, the organization of the environment, and the materials provided. They also guide teachers' planning and affect their interactions with children. One example of age-appropriate interaction is how parents, teachers, grandparents, friends, older children, and even strangers talk to babies differently from how they do to each other. All over the world, people speak to babies in a high-pitched, repetitive voice, called *motherese* or *parentese,* which infants consistently prefer hearing (Matychuk, 2005). Hearing the exaggerated sounds of *parentese* apparently makes it easier for babies to learn the sounds of their own language and is emotionally engaging.

Consider What Is Individually Appropriate One of the most basic principles of child development is that there are individual differences. In fact, children demonstrate a wide range of variability across every area of development—physical, cognitive, social, and emotional—while remaining within the range of "typical" development.

The development of some children falls beyond the range of what's predictable in one aspect or another. For example, in some respects, children with disabilities or developmental delays and children who are gifted add further diversity to the range of individual differences. A developmentally appropriate program accommodates individual variation. The expert lens feature, *Including All Children: Developmentally Appropriate Practice and Children with Disabilities,* illustrates this point.

Averages or norms never tell more than a small part of the story. Far more informative is the range; that is, the large variation of growth or performance across different individuals within the age (Copple & Bredekamp, 2006). Picture a group of 4-year-old children. They range in height from 35 to 46 inches, and in weight from 30 to 55 pounds. One can already skip, while another still takes the stairs two feet at a time. One can read, while another knows only a few letters. One converses fluently in two languages, while another has just mastered talking in complete sentences. One will play for extended periods with two or more friends, while another struggles to play cooperatively for even a short time.

Children also have individual personality traits and preferences, some of which are obvious even in early infancy. Some babies are feisty, while others are more passive. Some children stand back and watch for quite a while before attempting something new, and some plunge right in. Some children talk nonstop, while others cannot be enticed to speak up. One preschooler rides a tricycle with abandon, while another prefers to sit

Including All Children
Developmentally Appropriate Practice and Children with Disabilities

People sometimes wonder if developmentally appropriate practices are effective for children with disabilities. The fact is that the basic elements of developmentally appropriate practice are necessary for inclusion to succeed. Consider the following example:

Isaac is 4 years old and has a diagnosis of autism. He is sitting on a brightly colored carpet square between two of his preschool peers at circle time. His teacher is reading a book the class made called *Friends, Friends, Who Do You See?* It is adapted from *Brown Bear, Brown Bear* (Martin, 1996), but features pictures of the children in the class paired with their names. Isaac loves the book, and reads along with the teacher. As the teacher reads each child's name in the story, he or she stands up and moves. After the story, it is time for singing. Isaac knows this because circle time happens in a similar routine each day.

The teacher pulls out the "song chart" featuring the pictures and titles of eight different songs. One song is about a train. Isaac loves trains and seems eager to hear the new song. He points to the "Trains on the track." The teacher helps Isaac remove the song card. Isaac holds the card while the children sing. Then Isaac makes the sign for "play" with his hands. The teacher says, "Yes, Isaac, it is time for centers." She lets Isaac choose a center first because she knows it is hard for him to wait. Isaac brings the teacher the song card and then points to the picture of the water table. His teacher models, "I want to play at the. . . ." Isaac says, "Water table." His teacher, proud of his increasing verbal skills, gives him a hug and says, "Off you go to the water table." When Isaac's mother picks him up from school, his teacher describes how often he used his words and which friends he played with during center time.

By contrast, when children with disabilities are included in programs that are *not* developmentally appropriate, it becomes difficult for the child with special needs—indeed, for all of the children—to make meaningful progress. Compare this child's experience to Isaac's:

Tara, also a 4-year-old with autism, is sitting next to her teacher at circle time. The teacher is reading from a small-sized book, and many of the children cannot see the pictures very well, including Tara. Circle time has been in progress for over 20 minutes and many of the children are getting restless. Tara begins rocking back and forth and looking at the door. Without warning, the teacher stops reading the book and tells the children to stand up for a finger play. Tara bolts from the circle and runs to the water table. She begins splashing and yelling. The teacher stops and asks Tara to return to circle. When Tara does not return on her own volition, the assistant teacher physically moves her back to the circle, and a 10-minute struggle ensues. When Tara's father comes to pick her up, the teacher describes "her bad day" and asks him to talk to Tara about listening at school.

A child with a disability acts like a magnifying glass on the developmental appropriateness of an early childhood program. As is clear from Isaac's case and by contrast Tara's experience, developmentally appropriate practice provides the necessary foundation for his successful inclusion in the program. But individually appropriate adaptations are also essential for children with disabilities and other special needs.

---

quietly with a puzzle or pegboard. A second grader loves to read and spends all of her free time with a book, while another struggles with reading but looks forward to math because it's her best subject.

The term **individually appropriate** refers to teachers using what they know about the personality, strengths, interests, and abilities of each individual child in the group to adapt for and be responsive to individual variation. Consider, for instance, two tricycle riders: The fearless rider may need more careful supervision to prevent injury, while the warier child may need extra encouragement and support to develop his large motor skills. Similarly, some children will need enriched experiences to accelerate their language development, while a few may need individual support to continue to build on their precocious reading ability. A withdrawn, timid child may need a great deal of emotional support to cope with life's challenges, while another needs help controlling aggression to make friends.

With the individual differences that exist, teachers clearly cannot expect all children in a group to learn the same thing in the same way at the same time. Even when the teacher introduces a concept or reads a book to a whole group, each child will take away something different from the learning experience. Therefore, to help children progress,

individually appropriate
Information about the strengths, interests, abilities, and needs of each individual child in the group that enables teachers to adapt to and be responsive to individual variation.

Because children's needs, interests, and abilities differ as they grow and change, a developmentally appropriate environment for babies and toddlers looks very different from one for preschoolers or primary grade children.

teachers must continually keep track of what children know and are able to do, what they are struggling with, and what is engaging their interest and meets their needs.

Consider Children's Social and Cultural Contexts

All learning and development occur in and are influenced by social and cultural contexts (Bronfenbrenner, 2004). In fact, *appropriate behavior* is always culturally defined. The cultural contexts a child grows up in begin with the family and extend to include the cultural group or groups with which the family identifies. **Culture** refers to the behaviors, values, and beliefs that a group shares and passes on from one generation to the next. Because children share their cultural context with members of their group, cultural differences are differences between groups rather than individuals. Therefore, cultural variation needs to be considered as well as individual variation in deciding what is developmentally appropriate.

Children learn the values, beliefs, expectations, and habitual patterns of behavior of the social and cultural contexts in their lives. Cultural groups, for example, have characteristic ways of showing respect; there may be different rules for how to properly greet an older or younger person, a friend, or a stranger. Attitudes about time and personal space vary among cultures, as do the ways to take care of a baby and dress for different occasions. In fact, most of our experiences are filtered through the lenses of our cultural group. We typically learn cultural rules very early and very deeply, so they are not part of our conscious thought.

Social contexts of young children's lives differ in ways such as these: Is the child growing up in a large family, or a family of one or two children? In a single-parent family, a two-parent family, with same-sex parents, or in a household that includes extended family members? In an urban, suburban, or rural setting? Has the child been in group care from a young age, or is this the first time in a group program? What social and economic resources are available to the family? All of these situations frame the social context and impact children's lives in unique ways.

For young children, what makes sense and how they respond to new experiences are fundamentally shaped by the social and cultural contexts to which they have become accustomed. To ensure that learning experiences are meaningful, relevant, and respectful to children and their families—that is, for those experiences to be **culturally appropriate** or *culturally responsive*—teachers must have some knowledge of the social and cultural contexts in which children live. Such knowledge helps teachers build on children's prior experiences and learning so they can help children progress.

All young children must adjust when they move from the security and familiarity of their homes into schools or early childhood programs. The challenge is greatest, however, for children whose cultural experiences at home differ sharply from those predominating at the school or program. For these children, the transition can be confusing and frightening. Consider a Native American child, whose culture expects children to quietly listen and observe adults, entering a classroom where the teacher expects everyone to speak up. Think of how you feel, at least for a moment, when people around you are speaking a language you don't understand. Even as adults with all of our coping mechanisms intact, we tend to feel uncertain, ignorant, and uncomfortable in environments different from those to which we are accustomed. (Are they talking about us?)

For teachers, being responsive to all social and cultural variation can be challenging. Our own cultural experience is so integral to us that we are rarely aware of it. If we are in the position of power as a teacher, we must be especially careful to be aware of and respectful toward those whose cultural backgrounds and accepted rules for behavior may be different from ours. Most important, we must be careful not to assume that our own cultural perspective is superior and make negative judgments based on our cultural variations. An example illustrates the potentially damaging result of such judgments:

> A European American teacher is employed in a school serving a predominantly African American community. One of her principal teaching strategies is questioning. But she finds that her questions are often met with blank stares or disdain from the children and she assumes they don't know the answers. She doesn't realize that within their cultural community, people rarely ask questions that they already know the answers to.

To better accommodate the realities of cultural and linguistic diversity in schools and early childhood programs, teachers today need to work at being especially sensitive and responsive to the perspectives of children and their families that may be different from their own. To broaden your own perspective, read the *Culture Lens: The Role of Culture in Development* feature.

culture The explicit and implicit values, beliefs, rules, and expectations for behavior of members of a group that are passed on from one generation to the next.

culturally appropriate Applying knowledge of the social and cultural contexts in which children live, which helps teachers build on children's prior knowledge and make experiences meaningful and responsive.

Consider All You Know When Making Decisions

The three considerations that teachers must take into account when making decisions—knowledge about children's learning and development, information about individual children, and information about the social and cultural contexts of children's lives—

Culture Lens

The Role of Culture in Development

Take a moment to think about what you understand about culture. Do you tend to think about culture only as characteristic of children and families who are "culturally different"? Does the concept of culture apply only to some children? Actually, it is important to remember that *every* child is socialized in a cultural group, and the most important elements influencing children's development are really aspects of their cultural experiences that are often the hardest to observe.

What people sometimes think of as "cultural" are the products that culture produces, such as dress or holiday celebrations. These are the surface features of culture. But culture produces more indiscernible behaviors and attitudes that emerge from the same set of rules as the surface features of culture. These deep structural aspects of culture act as much more powerful influences on children's development than the surface features do. For example, if the cultural group believes that women should not be seen by men except for those in the immediate family, a woman's mode of dress will reflect this value. At the same time, this cultural belief will have much farther reaching effects on her behavior and life choices than simply how she dresses. Consider an example in an early childhood classroom:

It is circle time in kindergarten and the children are supposed to bring an object from home that has writing on it. Most of the children eagerly seek their turn, waving their hands widely, and showing off how well they can read the words. Jai has brought something but is not eager to share. The teacher assumes that he can't read the words. So, she doesn't call on him.

As in all developmental domains, culture influences the expression of emotions. Although emotions such as fear, anger, and happiness are part of human interaction in all cultural groups, variations emerge in the way they are expressed. Jai, who is from India, is from a cultural group that avoids drawing too much attention to individuals or expressing emotions too openly. Children from other, more individualistic cultures such as the United States' are generally encouraged to express their feelings openly. These cultural differences account for Jai's behavior and that of the other children in his class more than their reading abilities do.

Cultural differences do not mean that one way is right and the others wrong. They simply demonstrate that there is a wide variety of developmental patterns that can be explained best by understanding the cultural context in which development occurs.

should not be viewed in isolation. All three considerations, in fact, interact with and influence each other; they are always intertwined in shaping children's development and behavior. For example, children all over the world follow a similar developmental pattern when learning language. They all progress from cooing, to babbling, to one-word utterances, to telegraphic speech ("Daddy up"), to short sentences, and finally to more complex sentences. However, a wide range of individual variation exists in language acquisition of children who are roughly the same age, because of differences in language experience as well as developmental variation. At age 3, Joey speaks in three-word utterances, whereas his same-age cousin, Michael, expounds in paragraphs. Finally, each child speaks the language, including the dialect, of his or her own cultural group. Six-year-old Amelia speaks English to her mother and Spanish to her father. All of these factors influence children's language development and how teachers think about supporting it optimally for all children.

Now let's look at how the meshing of the three considerations plays out in the decisions of one primary grade teacher:

> Frida Lopez has 22 children in her first-grade class. Her first challenge each year is to get to know the children well. She meets with their families, engages in one-on-one conversations with children, observes their behavior and skills throughout the day, and sets up specific tasks to evaluate their skills such as literacy tasks or solving math problems with counters.
>
> As she gets to know her students, she regularly assesses their abilities and interests in relation to what she knows from her study of child development, the curriculum goals, and her experiences teaching other 6- and 7-year-olds. She finds that a few children exceed her expectations in reading or social skills, whereas others are significantly behind their peers in some areas. Each child has a unique personality and profile of abilities, and Frida becomes more aware of these.
>
> Neela has Down syndrome, and Frida has already met with her parents and the team of special education professionals who create and implement an individualized educational plan for her. After a few weeks, Frida becomes concerned that another child, Almonzo, might have an undiagnosed language delay. In the case of the six children whose home languages are not ones Frida knows, she recognizes that she must take extra steps to find out about them. Using community volunteers and, in one case, a paid translator, Frida connects with the families of her students to build relationships and to learn what capabilities the children exhibit in their homes and communities.

So we see that in meeting the children, Frida seamlessly draws on her knowledge of child development and learning, as well as her knowledge of them as individuals and members of cultural groups. Precisely because children are so different and their abilities vary so greatly, Frida will need to draw from a wide repertoire of teaching strategies to help them achieve developmentally appropriate goals.

So far we have described the areas of knowledge that teachers consider in making decisions about developmentally appropriate practice—what teachers need to know and think about. Now we turn to the work of the teachers—what do early childhood teachers do? What are the dimensions of practice that describe the teacher's role?

 Check Your Understanding 3.3: Developmentally Appropriate Decision Making

 The Complex Role of the Teacher

According to the NAEYC's (2009) guidelines for developmentally appropriate practice, the complex job of an early childhood teacher has five interrelated dimensions: (1) creating a caring community of learners, (2) teaching to enhance learning and development, (3) planning curriculum to achieve important goals, (4) assessing children's learning and development, and (5) establishing reciprocal relationships with families.

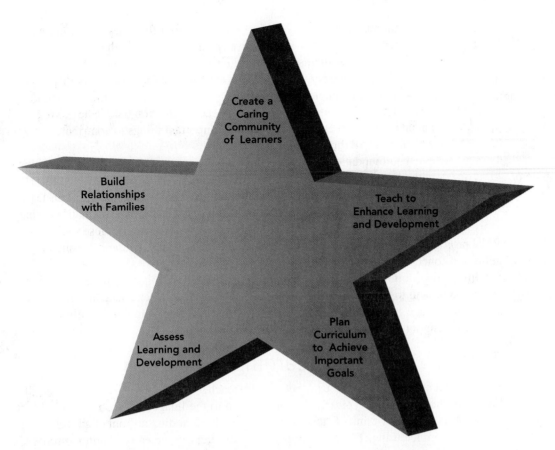

FIGURE 3.2 Mariner's Star: The Complex Role of the Teacher The image of the Mariner's Star illustrates how the teacher's many roles are integrally connected.

Source: Adapted from *Basics of Developmentally Appropriate Practice: An Introduction for Teachers of Children 3 to 6*, by C. Copple and S. Bredekamp, 2006, p. 24, Washington, DC: NAEYC. Reprinted with permission from the National Association for the Education of Young Children.

One way to remember these dimensions is to visualize the five points of a star, as depicted in Figure 3.2. Each of the five points is necessary for the star to be complete, and they are all interrelated—take one away and the figure is no longer a star.

It may be helpful, in fact, to think of it as a "mariner's star." Seafaring people use the stars to guide their way, but without considerable knowledge of the stars' positioning and their relation to navigation, mindlessly following a star won't lead to a destination. So it is with the mariner's star of early childhood teaching. Each of the star's points links to a set of guidelines that represent a large body of knowledge about early childhood education. Just as the stars guide seafaring people, the mariner's star helps guide teachers' professional behavior; but without that strong foundation of knowledge, the guidelines themselves have little meaning.

In the following sections, we introduce each aspect of the teacher's role in accordance with NAEYC's guidelines for developmentally appropriate practice. Each of these aspects of the teacher's role is described in later chapters.

Create a Caring Community of Learners

An early childhood setting—whether it serves infants and toddlers, preschoolers, kindergartners, or second graders—needs to be a caring community of learners. The term **caring community of learners** incorporates several key ideas that characterize early childhood education: (1) Children's care and education are equally important; (2) children learn through positive relationships with adults and other children; and (3) the learning context matters—the indoor and outdoor environments, how the environments are organized, and the materials and equipment they contain.

caring community of learners
A group or classroom in which children and adults engage in warm, positive relationships, treat each other with respect, and learn from and with each other.

▶ **Classroom Connection**

Listen as these primary-grade children describe what it means to be part of a caring community of learners. What other ways do you think a caring school community benefits children?

https://www.youtube.com/watch?v=zjrl2HqCTuA

Children learn when they feel safe and cared for. They thrive in an environment in which they see positive images that reflect their own identity, such as photos of themselves and their families; where they see their own contributions to the community; and when they see their own work displayed. They also see examples throughout the community that reinforce their cultural identity. The messages are clear to each child: You belong here. We care about and support each other. You have important things to contribute to this group. You will thrive here.

The foundation of young children's learning is in positive relationships with other people who are responsive to them. At the same time, the early childhood setting is a learning community where adults and children learn with and from each other. Each child's thinking can build on or challenge that of another. When Josué tells Willa she can't be the doctor because she's a girl, Willa promptly informs him, "I go to Dr. Ashai and she's a lady, so there." Josué has to adjust his concept of *doctor* to include women as well as men.

In a caring community, children acquire the ability to regulate their own emotions and behavior and to make friends. Teachers actively teach children social and emotional skills and engage in individualized interventions for children who persistently demonstrate challenging behaviors such as aggression.

Teach to Enhance Learning and Development

Teaching seems the most obvious aspect of the teacher's role, but it isn't simple at all. Early childhood teachers typically do not conform to the images that come to mind for many adults when they think of "teaching"—the teacher standing in front of a blackboard or at a podium lecturing. Teaching simply looks different in the early childhood setting, and it takes many forms.

Effective early childhood teachers know the children in their group very well. They thoughtfully plan the learning experiences and environment with these children in mind while also keeping in mind the learning goals. They use a variety of teaching strategies to help each child develop and learn. And they guide young children to become socially responsible, self-regulating, contributing members of the community.

Intentional teachers use every possible opportunity to promote children's learning, including preplanned small group lessons, and conversations throughout the day.

Teachers also use various learning contexts such as teacher-guided group work, including large-group and small-group preplanned experiences, and periods of play and engagement in which children primarily guide their own activity with the support of teachers (Epstein, 2014; Pianta, Barnett, Burchinal, & Thornburg, 2009). Teachers use various ways of grouping children for learning; they may gather a reading group of similar ability level or organize a group of children with different language abilities to work together on a project. Teachers' behavior needs to vary with the setting as well. In addition, routines such as eating meals and transitioning from one place or activity to another are all potentially valuable learning contexts if teachers use these activities as opportunities for one-on-one conversations with children or to reinforce a learning goal through singing a song or reciting a poem.

Plan Curriculum to Achieve Important Goals

If developmentally appropriate practice tends to focus on the *how* of teaching, then curriculum is the *what*—the content that children are expected to learn. **Curriculum** is a written plan that describes the knowledge and skills to be taught in the educational program and the learning experiences through which teaching takes place (Copple & Bredekamp, 2006, p. 61).

Currently, there is increased demand for **scientifically based curriculum** that is based on research about important learning goals that predict later achievement, the sequences in which concepts and skills build on each other, and the teaching strategies that have proven effective. Whatever the process through which a curriculum is selected, developed, or planned, to be effective it must be implemented with attention to individual differences and cultural variation among children (NAEYC & National Association of Early Childhood Specialists in State Departments of Education [NAECS/SDE], 2003).

Good curriculum, whether published resources used in school districts or teacher developed, offers teachers flexibility and ways of adapting, often providing many more suggested activities or materials than teachers could possibly use. Thus, they have many further decisions to make. Teachers need to be very familiar with the curriculum plan, especially the key learning and development outcomes for children—that is, what children should know and be able to do as a result of their participation in this program.

curriculum A written plan that describes the goals for children's learning and development, and the learning experiences, materials, and teaching strategies that are used to help children achieve those goals.

scientifically based curriculum Derives from research evidence about what kinds of learning outcomes relate to later achievement, and what types of teaching and learning experiences help children acquire those outcomes. Such a curriculum has been evaluated and its effectiveness demonstrated.

Assess Children's Development and Learning

In the current era of educational accountability, assessment is often a controversial topic. However, it is an integral component of developmentally appropriate practice. **Assessment** is the process of observing and documenting the work children do and how they do it as the basis for a variety of educational decisions. Assessment is important because teachers must draw on assessment information about individual children in an ongoing, systematic process to understand children's learning and development.

Children, especially very young children, are moving targets. What they can't do today, they can do tomorrow. What they didn't know or understand yesterday may gradually become clear, or they may have an "Aha!" moment of recognition. Their development may follow a predictable though somewhat slower trajectory in one area, or they may be in need of intervention for a serious developmental delay. To address any of these situations, teachers must use appropriate, accurate tools to assess children.

Each decision that teachers make about children has consequences. The more important and lasting the consequence, the more vital it is that the decision is based on multiple sources of information, including information from parents.

assessment The ongoing process of gathering evidence of children's learning and development, and then organizing and interpreting the information to make informed decisions about instructional practice.

Build Relationships with Families and Communities

Young children do not come with résumés; they come with families. NAEYC (2009) guidelines emphasize the importance of teachers and administrators developing **reciprocal relationships** with children's families. *Reciprocal* refers to a two-way relationship,

reciprocal relationship A two-way relationship in which information and power are shared evenly.

© Ariel Skelley/Blend Images/Getty Images

Developmentally appropriate practices are respectful of children's cultural and linguistic backgrounds. Intentional teachers build two-way, reciprocal relationships with families to get to know children as individuals and to understand their cultural context.

in which information and power are shared evenly. Such a relationship is based on mutual respect, trust, cooperation, and shared responsibility. A reciprocal relationship requires regular open communication and a willingness to negotiate differences toward shared goals.

We've already seen that in order to teach young children effectively, teachers must get to know each child well. The younger the child, the more teachers must rely on family members as key informants about the child's competencies, interests, needs, and cultural experiences. Young children's competencies are not always apparent, especially if they have been acquired in a cultural context that is different from that of the teacher. For example, a child may know colors and basic shapes and be able to count up to 20 in Russian, yet demonstrate none of this knowledge in English at school. Through a relationship with the parents, however, this teacher can ascertain that she needs to help the child learn the English words for concepts he already knows, rather than teach these concepts. This allows both the teacher and child the opportunity to use what he already knows and move on to other important concepts more efficiently.

The Teacher's Role in Context

In each aspect of their work, whether creating a caring community, teaching, planning curriculum, assessing, or working with families, teachers must draw on a broad base of information to make useful decisions. The following example illustrates how the five dimensions of the teacher's role come together during a memorable experience for a beginning teacher:

Scotty's teacher, Gina, believes him to be the "bad boy" in his preschool class. Gina feels she is constantly correcting what he has done wrong. One day, a fight breaks out in the block corner and a chorus of voices arises, shouting, "Scotty did it!" Gina sighs, not surprised by these events, until she remembers that Scotty isn't there that day. She realizes that her focus on Scotty's misdeeds has made him the "bad boy" in everyone's eyes.

Her realization forces Gina to reflect on her own and Scotty's behavior. She realizes that she doesn't really know Scotty, and spends time systematically observing him. Soon she discovers strengths she can help him build on, such as his exceptional fine motor skills, and comes to see that there is much Scotty can do well. She gives him opportunities to use these skills (she allows him to cut up the oranges for snack under her supervision), and finally catches him doing something right for a change. Gina also meets with Scotty's mother so that together they can begin to focus on his positive behavior rather than his missteps. Gradually, Gina notices that Scotty's behavior improves. As a result, both Gina and Scotty's mother begin to enjoy him more. With more support and a sense of accomplishment, he makes friends with several other children.

Scotty's teacher wasn't named Gina. I was actually his teacher, and I learned a lot about developmentally appropriate practice from this firsthand experience. In making professional decisions, teachers should always consider strategies to broaden their own perspective, as illustrated by Scotty's situation. They need to take into consideration as many points of view as possible—to "widen the lens" with which they see children, their families, and the educational process.

Widening the Lens: Moving from *Either/Or* to *Both/And* Thinking

Questions of educational practices in the United States are often dichotomized as either/or choices (Bishop-Josef & Zigler, 2011; Zigler, Gilliam, & Barnett, 2011). Is phonics *or* vocabulary more important in learning to read? Should preschool stress social-emotional development *or* cognitive development? Should early childhood programs provide child-initiated *or* teacher-directed experiences? These either/or choices oversimplify the complex processes of becoming literate or developing the whole child. Either/or thinking assumes that there is one right answer to a complex question. Instead, children would be better served and educators more effective if the questions were addressed with *both/and* thinking. Both/and thinking rejects simplistic answers to complex questions and requires diverse perspectives and several possible answers to be considered.

To avoid either/or thinking, it is useful to use the analogy of *widening the lens*. Think of yourself as holding a camera and altering the view by adjusting the lens. Depending on how you adjust the lens, your view and, therefore, your perspective changes. You might zoom in on one child's expression, or you might zoom out to see the whole room arrangement. If you use a video camera, you could gain more information about the context, perhaps including the child's friends, extended family, or community. In fact, to engage in developmentally appropriate decision making, teachers must indeed widen their views. Just as the camera lens adjusts to display different views, teachers allow their minds to expand and accommodate several ideas at once.

As we have discussed, children of similar ages are *both* alike *and* different. Likewise, children of the same cultural group share some characteristics but not all. When you widen the lens, you will find that your view broadens and you can incorporate more information. As a result, you are less likely to get stuck in either/or thinking. When you widen the lens through which you look at children, the curriculum, teaching practices, assessment, and families—all aspects of your work—you begin to recognize the complexity and interrelationships among the principles that guide early childhood practice.

When teachers are willing to look beyond the view they have held, they enhance their effectiveness in their work with children and families. Consider the following example that demonstrates the power of widening the lens:

Ms. Grantham is the director of a Head Start program. Several parents complain to her that they aren't seeing worksheets or similar products showing their children's learning coming home in the backpacks or displayed in the classroom. Her program doesn't use worksheets because their philosophy of developmentally appropriate practice is based on children's active engagement. Ms. Grantham believes that worksheets are just busy work for children and don't really teach them anything.

At first, she thinks that the parents are just uninformed about good early childhood education. But she asks a few more questions to better understand their perspective. Ms. Grantham comes to see that both she and the parents want the children to succeed—in the wider view, they are in agreement. And what the families are asking for is evidence that the children are in fact learning and on track to succeed in school.

Reflecting on the parents' legitimate desire, Mrs. Grantham realizes that she could do a much better job of sharing with the families concrete samples of the children's work that show what they are learning and how they are thinking. She explains that worksheets are not effective because instead of active learning, they simply call for right answers ("circle the 4") and busy work like coloring. Worksheets are more like testing than learning. She begins to collect portfolios of children's drawings and writing, transcripts of their language, and photos of their project work and meets with families regularly. She displays the children's work, describes what they have learned and will be learning next, and what she and the teachers are doing to help build the children's skills and knowledge. Along with the children, Mrs. Grantham develops a class website through which they communicate to families about their work in progress.

Now it's your turn. What do you see when you widen your lens? Try to think of several examples where widening the lens would help you be a better teacher or improve your relationships with family members, college professors, or work colleagues. For an example of the effectiveness of *both/and* practices, read the feature, *What Works: How Both Teacher-Directed and Child-Initiated Experiences Promote Learning*.

 Check Your Understanding 3.4: The Complex Role of the Early Childhood Teacher

What Works

How *Both* Teacher-Directed *and* Child-Initiated Experiences Promote Learning

One issue that is too often presented as a dichotomy in discussions of developmentally appropriate practice is teacher-directed vs. child-initiated experiences. As we have seen, both are important components of intentional teaching. Considerable research supports this finding, including data from the influential, longitudinal study of the Chicago Child-Parent Centers. These centers provided preschool and kindergarten for children from low-income families with extensive parent involvement that continued into early elementary school. Strong positive effects on participating children's school achievement and life outcomes were found 25 years later.

To delve deeper into what accounted for the lasting effects, researchers analyzed the curriculum and teaching practices that teachers reported using most often. This analysis involved more than 900 children in 20 centers. The researchers found that children whose teachers used a *blend* of teacher-directed and child-initiated activities were more likely to be ready for kindergarten, have higher reading achievement in third and eighth grades, and avoid being retained in grade. Moreover, they found that teaching practices that emphasized *only* teacher-directed *or* child-initiated activities were less related to children's school success over time.

One interesting pattern they found was that child-initiated teaching in the early years was more associated with high school *completion by age 22 than approaches that were low in both teacher directedness and child initiation (that is, a low degree of intentionality among teachers), and those that were overly teacher-directed.*

The researchers concluded that this *both/and* approach to early childhood teaching—intentionally providing teacher-initiated and child-initiated learning experiences—along with a high degree of parent involvement accounted for the long-term benefits of the Chicago Child-Parent Centers.

Source: "More Than Teacher Directed or Child Initiated: Preschool Curriculum Type, Parent Involvement, and Children's Outcomes in the Child-Parent Centers," by E. Graue, M. A. Clements, A. J. Reynolds, and M. D. Niles, 2004, *Education Policy Analysis Archives, 12,* retrieved from http://epaa.asu.edu/ojs/article/viewFile/227/353.

Developmentally Appropriate Learning Environments

How the learning environment and children's daily schedules are organized are the most obvious indicators of whether a program is developmentally appropriate. The environment should be rich in equipment and materials that are safe, healthy, interesting, and engaging for the age group of children for which it is designed. Because children's needs and abilities predictably vary by age, to be developmentally appropriate, environments should look different for infants, toddlers, preschoolers, or school-age children.

▶ Classroom Connection

This video takes you on a tour of a developmentally appropriate preschool environment. Notice how the furnishings, toys, and space are organized to allow for children's independent use while also encouraging them to stretch their abilities.

Organize the Physical Space

Environments send messages, often subtle or even subconscious, about how to behave or which behaviors are acceptable. Libraries convey the message that soft voices and quiet reading are expected. Open spaces and playgrounds invite children to run and chase one another around. With the knowledge that environments send messages, teachers need to consciously think about the messages they want their classroom environments to send to children.

The classroom needs to be accessible to all children, including children with disabilities, and organized so that children can interact positively, function as independently as possible, and learn decision-making skills. For example, teachers should make sure there is enough space for active play that is protected from traffic. They should also make sure to provide enough age-appropriate materials and duplicates of popular toys so children do not always have to share, which can lead to frustration and, ultimately, conflict.

A developmentally appropriate preschool or kindergarten environment should be organized into separate **learning centers**, which are defined areas of the classroom that have a particular purpose and that contain relevant furnishings and materials. Learning centers in a preschool typically include a library area, blocks, dramatic play, writing center, art center, manipulative toys near tables, and a group meeting area. Learning centers enable children to focus their attention, promote small-group interaction, and require children to make choices and experience the consequences of those choices. Figure 3.3 depicts a room arrangement for a preschool or kindergarten classroom that is organized with these guidelines in mind:

learning centers Defined areas of the classroom that have a particular purpose and that contain relevant furnishings and materials.

- Allow children to independently choose their own activities for part of each day.
- Establish clear boundaries between learning centers by using furniture, floor coverings (carpet, tile), or shelves that help limit the number of children who work or play in each area at one time.
- Locate quiet areas, such as the book, art, writing, and computer centers, next to each other, separated from noisier and more active centers such as blocks, dramatic play, or woodworking.
- Provide easily supervised places for children to be alone or with a friend.
- Locate messy activities such as sand and water play and art projects near a source of water for easy access and cleanup.
- Provide a comfortable meeting space for the whole group to engage in music, movement, book reading, and other large-group activities. Designate seating arrangements so children are not crowded or distracted by toys within reach.
- Eliminate unnecessary clutter, which can distract and agitate some children.
- Avoid large open spaces or corridors that invite children to run.

An environment for babies and toddlers, on the other hand, should be more individualized with large areas for active play and separate spaces for sleeping, feeding, and diapering. There should be carpeting for crawlers and soft furniture for children to snuggle with a teacher while looking at a book or pull themselves up on.

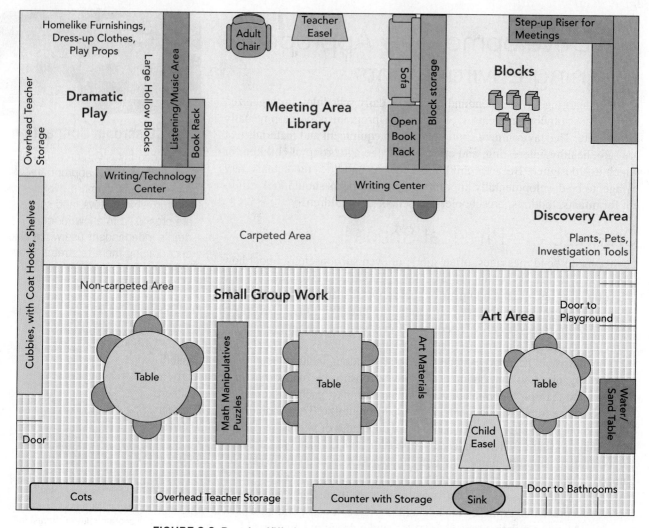

FIGURE 3.3 Preschool/Kindergarten Classroom Arrangement A developmentally appropriate environment for preschoolers or kindergarteners is organized into learning centers that support child-guided and teacher-guided experiences.

A classroom for primary-grade children would have tables or desks arranged in clusters so children can face each other and work collaboratively. Primary-grade children should take an active role in designing the environment. Learning centers in a primary-grade school are more closely linked to curriculum areas such as a reading corner or a science observation area. Spaces for individual or small group work are also needed as well as a whole class meeting area.

Organize the Day

Another way for teachers to ensure developmentally appropriate learning experiences for children is to carefully plan how time is used. If the schedule is not carefully planned with children's developmental needs in mind, learning opportunities will be missed or children's valuable time will be wasted. Many of the difficulties that children exhibit in school are related to how the day is organized. Teachers can alleviate these difficulties by providing a consistent, predictable routine that children can rely on. At the same time, teachers need to be flexible so they can easily change plans in response to children's interests or to unanticipated events.

Young children are often thought to have short attention spans; however, the amount of time they engage in small-group activities that they have chosen is often considerably longer than adults would expect. Children's attention during activities that involve the whole group, such as story reading or morning meetings, is usually more limited and

Approximate Times (vary by program or school schedule)	Activity
15 to 30 minutes 8:00–8:30	**Arrival:** Teachers greet children and families. Children store belongings, wash hands, find a quiet activity such as looking at books or drawing, or eat breakfast.
15 to 20 minutes 8:30–8:50	**Morning meeting:** Teachers and children gather in whole group to plan for the day and encourage a sense of community and belonging in the group. They share music and movement.
60 to 75 minutes 9:00–10:15	**Center time and small groups:** Children play and work in learning centers that the teacher has prepared. Teachers observe and interact one on one with children and also work with small groups on projects, book reading, and playing a math game. Children clean up and wash hands.
15 minutes 10:15–10:30	**Morning snack time:** Teachers sit with children, engage in conversation, and model mealtime behavior. Children serve themselves.
15-20 minutes 10:30–10:45	**Group time:** Children share/revisit experiences of the morning. Teachers lead music, movement, and read and discuss a book.
30 to 45 minutes 10:45–11:30	**Outdoor play:** Teachers supervise children at play and as they make nature discoveries; they interact with them one on one or in small groups.
10 to 15 minute 11:30–11:45	**Half-day program, group meeting:** Teacher and children reflect on the day and plan for tomorrow. **Full-day program, group meeting:** Do a calming activity, prepare for lunch.
30 to 45 minutes 11:45–12:30	**Lunch:** Teachers sit with children, engage in conversation, and model mealtime behavior. Children serve themselves.
60 to 90 minutes (varies with age and needs of children) 12:30–2:00	**Full-day program, group meeting, nap, or rest time:** Teachers help children relax. They also supervise and provide quiet activities for those who do not sleep.
15 to 30 minutes 2:00–2:30	**Afternoon snack and activities:** Children have an afternoon snack and engage in quiet activities such as putting puzzles together, book reading, drawing, or writing.
45 to 60 minutes 2:30–3:30	**Full-day program:** Children engage in outdoor play or large muscle experiences indoors. **Children continue projects from morning and/or make different choices or play outdoors:** Continue projects from morning and/or make different choices, or outdoor play.
10 to 15 minutes 3:15–3:30	**Group time:** Reflect on the day and plan for tomorrow.
60 to 90 minutes 3:30–4:30/5:30	**Full-day program center time:** Children play, continue projects from morning, and/or make different choices.

FIGURE 3.4 Sample Daily Preschool/Kindergarten Schedule Young children need a predictable daily schedule designed to meet their developmental needs, but they also need flexibility.

Source: Based on *The Creative Curriculum for Preschool*, 5th ed., by D. T. Dodge, L. J. Colker, and C. Heroman, 2010, Washington, DC: Teaching Strategies.

difficult to maintain because there are so many distractions. So time should be planned accordingly. Figure 3.4 provides an example of a daily schedule for a preschool or kindergarten classroom.

Ideally, in an effective classroom, the schedule for the day is posted so that children can predict what will happen throughout the day. At times, the schedule will change for planned or spontaneous events, such as a celebration or finding a bird's nest on the playground. But for the most part, a regular schedule allows children to thrive in predictable environments. If the schedule has to be changed, teachers need to inform the children in advance. The daily schedule should be based on the following guidelines:

- Plan for a balance of learning experiences: large group, small group, and individualized; child initiated and teacher initiated; active and quiet; indoor and outdoor.
- Allow 60 to 75 minutes for learning-center time so children can become deeply engaged in play and projects. In a full-day program, allow at least 1 hour in the morning and another in the afternoon.
- Limit whole-group meeting times to 10 to 20 minutes (allowing more time as children get older) and give opportunities for children to be actively engaged during these experiences.

 Check Your Understanding 3.5: Developmentally Appropriate Learning Environments

Research on Developmentally Appropriate Practice

The basic research question regarding any educational practice is this: Does it work? Is this educational practice effective in helping children achieve important learning outcomes? Because developmentally appropriate practice involves many different teaching behaviors and aspects of classroom organization, research on the broad construct of developmentally appropriate practice is difficult to conduct. However, subsequent chapters present the research base for each dimension of the teacher's role and area of the curriculum.

Research Reviews

Well-grounded research about learning and development is the foundation for NAEYC's work on developmentally appropriate practice and provides solid guidance for early childhood educators. This knowledge is summarized in major scientific reports such as *Eager to Learn: Educating Our Preschoolers* (Bowman, Donovan, & Burns, 2001), *From Neurons to Neighborhoods: The Science of Early Childhood Development* (Shonkoff & Phillips, 2000), *Handbook of Early Childhood Education* (Pianta, Barnett, Justice, & Sheridan, 2012), and *Handbook of Child Development and Early Education* (Barbarin & Wasik, 2009).

A vast amount of evidence demonstrates the lasting positive effects of high-quality early childhood programs (see Diamond, Justice, Siegler, & Snyder, 2013; Weiland & Yoshikawa, 2013; Yoshikawa et al., 2013). Although the studies reviewed were not designed to evaluate developmentally appropriate practice per se, the practices employed in effective programs are consistent with NAEYC's guidelines. One large-scale review identified the key components of effective early childhood education as "stimulating and supportive interactions between teachers and children that support learning *and* are emotionally supportive, and effective use of curricula" (Yoshikawa et al., 2013, p. 10). That review found the most benefit from *developmentally focused curricula*, meaning curricula that are not intended to be completely comprehensive, but rather that focus on a developmental area such as social skills or an academic topic such as mathematics or literacy.

One review of research identifies the key components of effective early childhood education as a blend of "explicit instruction, sensitive and warm interactions, responsive feedback, and verbal engagement or stimulation intentionally directed to ensure children's learning while embedding these interactions in a classroom environment that is not overly structured or regimented" (Pianta, Barnett, Burchinal, & Thornburg, 2009, p. 50). They point out that this type of teaching is also related to children's achievement in K–12.

The Oklahoma universal prekindergarten program, which is the largest state-funded voluntary pre-K program in the country, found substantial improvements in school readiness for children from all racial and ethnic groups. The largest gains, however, were for Hispanic children and boys. When the children were followed through third grade, the most lasting benefits were found in mathematics (Hill, Gormley, Adelstein, & Willemin, 2012). Similarly, a large-scale effort to address inequity in the quality of education in the Abbott School District in New Jersey focused on providing excellent prekindergarten programs for low-income children. The children who participated made strong gains in language, literacy, and math at kindergarten entry that persisted into second grade. Researchers followed the children through fifth grade and found that the program helped close the achievement gap, and fewer children were assignment to special education or retained in grade (Barnett, Jung, Youn, & Frede, 2013).

Research on Elements of Developmentally Appropriate Practice

Some studies examined effects of developmentally appropriate practice in preschool or kindergarten compared to "inappropriate" practices. These studies typically have defined appropriate classrooms as those characterized by child-initiated activity, active learning, problem solving, and positive, warm relationships between teachers and children. On the other hand, inappropriate classrooms are characterized by didactic lessons, heavy reliance on whole-group instruction, and emphasis on seatwork and rote learning. Much of the feedback in such classrooms tends to be teachers' correcting of children rather than expanding on their thinking and understanding.

Several studies compare the effects of such practices on children's social or emotional outcomes. For example, studies relating teaching practice to stress behaviors in children found significantly fewer stress-related behaviors in preschool and kindergarten children in more developmentally appropriate classrooms compared to children in less appropriate classrooms (Honig, 2010; Miller & Almon, 2009; Shanker, 2012). Children in less appropriate classrooms have also been found to score lower on measures of motivation (Stipek, 2011).

Over the years, a number of observational measures have been used to evaluate the quality of early childhood classrooms and the effects on children's outcomes. These tools, such as the CLASS and ECERS-R, are based on the same principles of child development and learning as developmentally appropriate practice. Children enrolled in classrooms that score higher on these measures are more likely to demonstrate positive outcomes including language, early literacy, mathematics, and social and cognitive skills (Bryant, 2010; Pianta et al., 2009).

Effects of Positive Teacher–Child Interactions A large body of research supports the efficacy of one of the key aspects of developmentally appropriate practice—warm, responsive relationships between teachers and children (Diamond et al., 2013). In observing numerous preschool and kindergarten classrooms, Stipek (2011) found that positive affect among teachers and children seemed to go along with developmentally appropriate practice, whereas negative affect was more likely to be found in classrooms using more inappropriate practices.

Observational research in preschool and primary classrooms has also found that positive, warm relationships with teachers that are developmentally appropriate promote academic success, social competence, and fewer behavior problems (Hamre & Pianta, 2005, 2007, 2010; Mashburn et al., 2008). Research following children from infancy to age 4 in child care programs also found that high-quality, developmentally

Developmentally appropriate classrooms function as caring communities of learners where each child is valued, and families are welcomed.

appropriate experiences and interactions with teachers contribute positively to children's development (NICHD Early Child Care Research Network, 2003).

Effects of Teaching Practices

In the last decade, more research has increasingly become available on the effectiveness of developmentally appropriate teaching strategies. A large number of studies using the CLASS have found that teachers' scores on instructional climate (which measures the quality of their language modeling, concept development, and feedback that engages children's higher-order thinking) predict children's language, literacy, and mathematics ability and their on-task behavior (Mashburn et al., 2008; Rimm-Kaufman, La Paro, Downer, & Pianta, 2005).

The Boston public schools are engaged in a highly successful early childhood initiative to close the achievement gap by instituting high-quality prekindergarten programs that are NAEYC accredited and use the same developmentally appropriate mathematics and literacy curricula with professional development for teachers. A rigorous evaluation found substantial gains in language, literacy, mathematics, and executive function for all groups of children, but the largest gains were for Hispanic children (Weiland & Yoshikawa, 2013).

A large-scale observational study in England (Sammons et al., 2008) used an expanded version of the ECERS that incorporated curriculum content items. The study found that by age 5, children who attended developmentally appropriate, high-quality programs scored better on measures of early literacy, math, reasoning, and social-emotional skills. This study also found that the most effective preschools provided both teacher-initiated small group work and child-initiated play activities that were supported by teachers (Sylva, Melhuish, Sammons, Siraj-Blatchford, & Taggart, 2004). A similar balance of child-directed, free-choice activity and teacher-directed group activities was found to improve low-income children's language development in U.S. preschools (Fuligni, Howes, Huang, Hong, & Lara-Cinisomo, 2012).

A classic, longitudinal study compared the effects of the HighScope curriculum or child-centered nursery school experience with a highly scripted, teacher-directed curriculum called Direct Instruction (Schweinhart, Weikart, & Larner, 1986). The HighScope curriculum is a blended approach incorporating child-centered, active learning and intentional teaching. A longitudinal follow-up study (Schweinhart & Weikart, 1997) found that at age 23, the Direct Instruction group had three times as many felony arrests per person, especially those involving property crimes, while 47% of the Direct Instruction group exhibited emotional problems during their schooling, as compared to only 6% in the other groups. Researchers attributed these results to the emphasis on planning, social reasoning, and other social objectives in the developmentally appropriate HighScope and nursery school curricula, but not in the Direct Instruction curriculum.

A more recent study demonstrated the effectiveness of building on a developmentally appropriate framework such as HighScope with additional research-based teaching strategies (Bierman et al., 2008), such as those we describe in this book. This Head Start intervention program involved brief lessons on literacy and social skills, hands-on activities, and specific teaching strategies designed to promote children's social-emotional competencies, language development, and emergent literacy skills. Materials were also provided to parents to enhance children's development at home. The program significantly improved children's vocabulary, emergent literacy, emotional understanding, social problem solving, social behavior, and learning engagement.

The Future of Developmentally Appropriate Practice

One of the most important functions of NAEYC's work on developmentally appropriate practice has been to further discussion and debate in the field about teaching practices. Given the history of the field, it is likely that this topic will continue to be debated. What aspects are most likely to continue to provoke thought? Undoubtedly the realities of diversity and changing cultural contexts in our country will continue to raise questions about what is culturally responsive as well as developmentally appropriate. Increased demands for accountability and the challenge to close the achievement gap raise the stakes over which practices can be successfully defended (Bassok & Rorem, 2014; Graue, 2009). Likewise, debates about curriculum have been a constant and will continue in the future, but are likely to be driven more by research than in the past.

The word *appropriate* is a culturally laden term and thus will continue to provoke controversy. Similarly, it is difficult to counteract the tendency of teachers and other professionals to emphasize "typical development" over individual differences and cultural variations (Graue, Kroeger, & Brown, 2003). After all, the first can be learned by reading books and journals, whereas the latter two require ongoing assessment of children, building relationships with families, and reflecting on how our own cultural perspectives influence our judgments and behavior.

To be developmentally appropriate, practices must contribute to children's learning and development. Therefore, this book focuses on recommended teaching practices, which must be responsive to children's individual development and cultural variation to be deemed appropriate. At the same time, we also focus on whether those practices help children achieve important learning goals. By definition, developmentally appropriate practices should be effective practices. To be effective, teachers must know children, they must know *how* to teach, and they must know *what* to teach. Each of these areas of knowledge must be informed by research. The following equation describes these components of effective, research-based practice.

Effective Practice = Knowing Children + Knowing How to Teach + Knowing What to Teach

Ultimately, the truest measure of developmentally appropriate practice is seeing children joyfully, physically, and intellectually engaged in meaningful learning about their world and everyone and everything in it (Copple & Bredekamp, 2009).

✓ **Check Your Understanding 3.6:** Research on Developmentally Appropriate Practice

Revisiting the Case Study

. . . Mr. Washington's Classroom

At the beginning of this chapter we met Olivia, who was somewhat timidly experiencing school for the first time. Having explored the basic premises of developmentally appropriate practice, we can now see Olivia's experience with a more informed eye. Her classroom, with its *age-appropriate* materials, furnishings, and environment, not only made Olivia feel comfortable but also encouraged her involvement. Furthermore, her teacher, Mr. Washington, drew on his knowledge of how children develop and learn by working to establish a warm, positive relationship with Olivia right from the start. He also provided Olivia with a learning experience that would build on what she was already able to do, such as her proficiency with puzzles.

At the same time, Mr. Washington demonstrated the importance of paying attention to what is *individually appropriate*. He made Olivia feel welcome by sending her a personal postcard, speaking with her at eye level, designating her cubby with her name and photo, and piquing Olivia's interest in puzzles. Finally, Mr. Washington was *culturally appropriate*—sensitive to the cultural context in which Olivia lives—using his own language attempts and a skilled translator to communicate with and reassure Olivia's grandmother. He also plans to display a family photo so Olivia's identity will be honored. In so doing, he demonstrated that he values and respects Olivia's family, their language, and cultural background. Taken together, the actions in that brief scenario demonstrate the teacher's broad base of knowledge and bode well for Olivia's successful transition to school. ∎

3 Chapter Summary

- Developmentally appropriate practice is teaching that is attuned to children's ages, experience, abilities, and interests, and that helps them attain challenging and achievable goals.

- Intentional teachers have a purpose for everything that they do, are thoughtful and prepared, and can explain their decisions and actions to other teachers, administrators, or parents.

- Decisions about developmentally appropriate practice are based on knowledge of child development and learning (what is age appropriate), knowledge about children as individuals, and knowledge of the social and cultural contexts in which children live (what is culturally appropriate).

- The role of the early childhood teacher has five interrelated dimensions: (1) creating a caring community of learners, (2) teaching to enhance learning and development, (3) planning curriculum to meet important goals, (4) assessing children's learning and development, and (5) establishing reciprocal relationships with families.

- "Widening the lens" is a metaphor to help teachers remember to consider diverse perspectives and move beyond *either/or* thinking to *both/and* thinking when solving problems or making decisions about practice.

- How the learning environment and children's daily schedules are organized are the most obvious indicators of whether a program is developmentally appropriate and therefore, they should look different for infants, toddlers, preschoolers, and school-age children because abilities and needs predictably vary by children's ages.

- Well-grounded research about learning and development is the basis for NAEYC's position statements on developmentally appropriate practice and provides solid guidance for early childhood educators.

Key Terms

- age appropriate
- assessment
- caring community of learners
- culturally appropriate
- culture
- curriculum
- developmentally appropriate practice (DAP)
- individually appropriate
- intentional teachers
- learning centers
- position statement
- push-down curriculum
- reciprocal relationships
- scientifically based curriculum

 Demonstrate Your Learning

Click here to assess how well you've learned the content in this chapter.

Readings and Websites

Carter, M., & Curtis, D. (2014). *Designs for living and learning: Transforming early childhood environments.* St. Paul, MN: Redleaf Press.

Copple, C., & Bredekamp, S. (Eds.). (2009). *Developmentally appropriate practice in early childhood programs serving children from birth through age 8* (3rd ed.). Washington, DC: National Association for the Education of Young Children.

Epstein, A. S. (2014). *The intentional teacher: Choosing the best strategies for young children's learning* (Rev. ed.). Washington, DC: National Association for the Education of Young Children.

ASCD Whole Child Initiative

This website provides resources promoting elementary education that supports all areas of children's development and learning.

National Association for the Education of Young Children

NAEYC's website has a special section on resources for developmentally appropriate practice and play, plus copies of all their position statements.

ZERO to THREE—National Center for Infants, Toddlers, and Families

This website provides resources and practical tips for working with infants, toddlers, and their families.

Applying What We Know about Children's Learning and Development

Learning Outcomes

After studying this chapter, you should be able to:

4.1 Distinguish the meanings of development and learning and describe the relationship between the two.

4.2 Discuss how knowledge of brain development in early childhood informs teaching practice.

4.3 Identify key components of developmental theories (Erikson, Maslow, Piaget, Vygotsky, and Bronfenbrenner) and apply them to early childhood practice.

4.4 Identify key components of learning theories (Behaviorism and Social Cognitive theories) and apply them to early childhood practice.

4.5 Explain the role of play in children's development and learning, and describe ways teachers can support play in early childhood settings.

4.6 Apply theories of development and learning to early childhood practice.

Yvonne Donati is a prekindergarten teacher in an inclusive public school. One of her goals is to create a caring community in which her energetic youngsters learn how to get along and work together. Yvonne's approach to guiding children's behavior is to engage the children in lively discussions of the classroom rules and how to solve conflicts that arise with their classmates.

In planning curriculum, Yvonne draws on the children's interests to integrate literacy instruction with science study of plants or animals, and children often work on small-group projects such as making a terrarium. She and the children have large-group meetings and she sometimes reads to the whole group, but she keeps these periods brief. She tries to find ways to make sure the children are physically active such as doing motions to songs or fingerplays. She also actively engages children's minds, as when she gives clues for the children to guess what object is hidden in a paper bag or has them take turns figuring out what a new word means in a story.

When children encounter challenges in their play, Yvonne helps them to come up with their own solutions rather than solving the problem for them. She asks probing questions: "Why do you think your tomato plant didn't grow tall?" "Let's compare your plant and Juana's—why is hers taller?"

Because some children in Yvonne's class have identified disabilities, she regularly meets with the special education team and cooperates in implementing the children's individualized education programs (IEPs). Maya has severe behavior problems, and the team works together to plan and implement a positive behavior support program to reinforce her desirable behaviors. After a few weeks of systematically working with Maya, Yvonne observes that the new strategy is working and Maya is less aggressive.

After a month of school, Yvonne observes that every day the block area is dominated by boys, while girls prefer the dramatic play center. She isn't sure if this is just reflecting typical gender differences or if there is another reason. Yvonne knows from studying the importance of play that children benefit from both block building and pretend play and that the benefits differ. She contemplates assigning children to areas, but then she designs an experiment. One week she closes the dramatic play center, and the next week she closes the block center, observing and recording children's behavior. Yvonne finds that without the availability of the dramatic play center, girls freely enter the block area; some boys play with them while others go elsewhere. On the other hand, when the block center is closed, the girls continue to play in the dramatic center, but the boys seem at loose ends and do not choose pretend play. Based on the results of her experiment, Yvonne institutes a play planning session each morning to make sure that girls have block-building opportunities. She also adds themes and props, such as creating a car wash, to interest more boys in pretend play. ■

This brief visit to Yvonne's classroom reveals several things about her approach to teaching. Although Yvonne may not be fully aware of it, the decisions she makes, like those of every teacher, actually reflect various theories of how children learn and develop. The purpose of this chapter is to help you understand and apply the prevailing theories of child development and learning. At times, beginning as well as experienced teachers wonder why theories matter or what relevance theories have to their work.

We begin by describing how theories of child development and learning are most useful in informing and influencing practice. Next, we describe research on brain development and its implications. Then, we discuss all the major theories and how they apply to early childhood practice. Next, we explain the critically important role of children's play, which is supported by the key developmental theories. We conclude the chapter with a summary of the main principles of child development and learning derived from research and theory that guide early childhood practice.

Understanding Development and Learning

Intentional, effective teaching requires that teachers understand how children think and learn, and how best to support their healthy development at various ages in all areas—physical, social, emotional, and cognitive. Both development and learning are complicated processes requiring that teachers not only study research and theory but also study children themselves.

What Is Development?

If you spend any time with early childhood educators, you are likely to hear that it is important for teachers to understand child development. This is true. But what do they need to know about development and why is it important? To answer these questions, we must first define terms. **Development** refers to age-related change that results from an interaction between biological maturation and physical and/or social experience.

Development occurs as children grow, adapt, and change in response to various experiences. Consider how language develops. Biology plays a role, with babies all over the world producing similar sounds at about the same age. But language development requires more than maturation. Babies need social interaction with adults and older children who talk to them. As they grow physically and are able to get around on their own, infants and toddlers encounter more examples of language interaction, and their speech starts to take off around age 2 (just as their legs do).

Domains of Development   Different areas of human functioning, including physical, cognitive, social, and emotional, are often described as **domains of development**. **Physical development** refers to biological growth and acquisition of fine motor skills, such as drawing, and gross motor skills, such as running. **Cognitive development** is a broad term encompassing thinking, intelligence, and language abilities. **Social development** refers to interpersonal relationships such as the ability to make friends, cooperate, and resolve conflicts. **Emotional development** is the ability to regulate and appropriately express feelings.

Discussions of child development inevitably address these domains as if they were separate. In reality, of course, human development does not occur in different categories. Our brains do *not* have separate compartments for cognition or social development. Aspects of development are inextricably linked, which is one reason we often talk about social-emotional development as though it were a single construct. Domains of development are an artifact of how researchers study development, rather than how development actually occurs. The integrated nature of development requires that teachers maintain their awareness of the *whole child* at all times.

Recently, researchers and educators have begun to focus less on skills related to specific domains and more on abilities that cut across traditionally defined developmental domains, such as executive function and self-regulation (Jones & Bailey, 2014), which we discuss later in this chapter. Bolstered by new findings from brain research, we now know that such broad **domain-general processes** strongly predict children's success in school and life. For example, Galinsky (2010) identifies seven essential life skills that every child needs: focus and self-control, perspective taking, communicating, making connections, critical thinking, taking on challenges, and self-directed engaged learning. A similar list is promoted by the Partnership for 21st Century Learning (n.d.): critical thinking, communication, collaboration, and creativity. Another way of describing these skills is children's approaches to learning—motivation, interest, persistence, curiosity, engagement, and enthusiasm

development Age-related change that results from an interaction between biological maturation and physical and/or social experience; development occurs as children grow, adapt, and change in response to various experiences.

domains of development Areas of human development and functioning that include cognitive, social, emotional, and physical.

physical development Biological growth and acquisition of fine motor and gross motor skills.

cognitive development Thinking, intelligence, and language abilities.

social development The ability to establish positive relationships with adults and peers, make friends, cooperate, and resolve conflicts.

emotional development The ability to regulate and appropriately express feelings.

domain-general processes Broad abilities that cut across traditionally defined developmental domains.

(Hyson, 2012). These lists of goals are overlapping and consistent, and they demonstrate the connection between development and learning, which we define in the next section.

What Is Learning?

Learning is a change in knowledge or skill that results from experience or instruction. Learning and development are not the same things, although they affect each other. Learning is a similar, though not identical, process whether a person is 3 years old or 33. For example, for a first grader, learning to read isn't completely different from the way it is for an older person.

Because experience plays a role in both development and learning, there is a close connection between these processes, especially in the early years of life when children are growing and changing so rapidly. Sometimes development leads to learning (Piaget, 1952). For example, when a baby develops the ability to grasp objects and begins to put them in her mouth, she learns a lot about the objects in her world. Some are hard, others soft; some taste good, others don't. In this case, her development fosters her learning. Children's developmental level can also put limitations on what they are capable of learning. For example, preschoolers can do some abstract thinking, but they won't fully understand complex, abstract concepts such as chronological time until they are older.

Learning also drives development. As children participate in the activities of their cultural groups and come to understand more complex concepts, their cognitive development is affected (Rogoff, 2012; Vygotsky, 1978). What children learn at home and in their cultural community powerfully affects their development. Consider the developmental differences between a 5-year-old child in America, whose primary "job" is to attend kindergarten, and a 5-year-old in rural Africa, whose primary responsibility is to transport water for the family.

During early childhood, children's development and learning are closely connected. Right from the start, babies put things in their mouths, which teaches them about objects in the world—how they feel and what they do.

learning A change in knowledge or skill that results from experience or instruction.

The Role of Theory

Centuries ago, human beings thought that the world was flat. No one wanted to venture too far out onto the sea for fear of falling off the edge. Slowly, more people traveled farther from shore, and others observed that the tops of arriving ships appeared first and then gradually the rest. If the earth were flat, the entire ship would appear at once. These observations and experiences led to the conclusion that the earth is not flat, but is actually a sphere.

This simple example illustrates the power of theories. A **theory** is an explanation of how information and observations are organized and relate to one another. As we can see, theories are important because they affect how people think and behave. In education, theories of learning and development affect how people treat children, how they structure environments, and how they teach.

theory An explanation of how information and observations are organized and relate to one another.

The Relationship between Theory, Research, and Practice

Where do theories come from? Theories usually evolve from research, which can take the form of systematic observations over time or scientifically controlled experiments. In fact, a theory derives from a **hypothesis**, which is a tentative explanation for a phenomenon. The more research is available to support the "truth" of a theory, the more useful the theory becomes in guiding practice. Yvonne had a theory about why girls and boys play differently. She tested and then revised her theory by conducting an informal research study.

When research findings contradict earlier conclusions, theories evolve, are discarded, or are replaced with new ones. In the early part of the 20th century, the prevailing theory of child development was **maturationist**. According to this theory, derived from research by Arnold Gesell (1940; Ames & Ilg, 1979), the sequence of changes in abilities and behavior is largely predetermined by children's biological growth processes rather than by their experiences or learning.

hypothesis An assumption about or tentative explanation of a phenomenon.

maturationist Theory of development that assumes that the sequence of changes in abilities and behavior is largely predetermined by children's biological growth processes rather than by their experiences or learning.

Culture Lens
The Effect of Culture on Research and Theory

An especially important consideration in evaluating theories is the cultural background of the children and families who participated in the research. For decades, one theory of how parental child rearing affects preschool children's development has been assumed to apply to all children and families (Baumrind, 1971). The theory identifies three parenting styles:

- **Authoritative.** Loving, nurturing, involved, and sensitive parents who explain their reasons for discipline have children who are motivated to learn and are well adjusted socially and emotionally.
- **Authoritarian.** Restrictive, punishing, rejecting, and controlling parents have children who lack initiative and are inhibited.
- **Permissive.** Parents who are warm and accepting of children but minimally involved and laissez-faire about discipline have children with the lowest levels of motivation and achievement.

Authoritative parenting is found to be the most effective style of child rearing. Most research on the theory, however, has been conducted with Caucasian middle-class families. More recent research with Head Start families (McWayne, Owsianik, Green, & Fantuzzo, 2008) using culturally familiar language and behaviors identified similar but not identical types of parenting:

- **Active-responsive** (e.g., tell child "I'm proud" when he tries to be good).
- **Active-restrictive** (e.g., I spank the child when she is disobedient).
- **Passive-permissive** (e.g., tell child "I'll punish," but don't).

Research with low-income, urban, African American families found no relationships between these different parenting styles and preschool children's social-emotional skills. What might account for these contradictory findings between diverse cultural groups? When children grow up in poverty-stricken, dangerous communities and face possible discrimination and prejudice, parents' priorities reflect these conditions. They may express their love by focusing on survival skills and making sure that their children behave maturely and competently in situations where people are biased against them. With these goals in mind, the effectiveness of restrictive parenting makes more sense.

In addition, compared to Caucasian middle-class families, African American child rearing tends to be spread among a number of people in the extended family and community. The mother may be relatively passive and permissive, for example, whereas others in the child's circle such as a grandmother or aunt may be more restrictive or actively responsive.

What can we conclude from revisiting a widely accepted child development theory like Baumrind's parenting framework? **Research that leads to a new theory needs to be conducted with diverse populations of children and families.** Otherwise, the theory simply can't be said to apply to them. In addition, research needs to be interpreted through a wide lens that considers the social and cultural contexts in which children live—in this case, the realities of life for low-income, urban, African American families.

Sources: "Current Patterns of Parental Authority," by D. Baumrind, 1971, *Developmental Psychology, 4,* 1–103; "Parenting Behaviors and Preschool Children's Social and Emotional Skills: A Question of the Consequential Validity of Traditional Parenting Constructs for Low-Income African Americans," by C. M. McWayne, M. Owsianik, L. E. Green, and J. W. Fantuzzo, 2008, *Early Childhood Research Quarterly, 23,* 173–192.

Maturation theory led to the notion that teachers needed to wait until children were ready for experiences to be effective. Because it was assumed that children were not ready to read until first grade, few literacy experiences were provided in preschool or kindergarten. Research in the intervening years demonstrated that differences in children's abilities are heavily influenced by their experiences (Sameroff, 2009; Tierney & Nelson, 2009). As a result, maturationist theory has been displaced by other theories. Nevertheless, maturationist theory continues to influence some practices such as kindergarten "redshirting"—holding children out of kindergarten until they are a year older and presumably more ready to learn.

Theories can also drive the way research is conducted and findings are interpreted. For example, if a theory is assumed to be universally true for all children, then research that supports the theory is assumed to apply to all children. Even if the research has been conducted only with white, middle-class children, the findings are applied to children of color or children of different socioeconomic, linguistic, or cultural backgrounds. Understanding the role of culture in development and learning requires that theory and research be more cautiously interpreted through these lenses. Therefore, despite the frequent claim that theories are "universal" and apply equally well to all children, they need to be evaluated from a broader perspective, as described in the *Culture Lens: The Effect of Culture on Research and Theory* feature.

Why Study Child Development and Learning?

Understanding theories of learning and development is particularly important for early childhood teachers for several reasons. During the first eight years of life, children grow and change more rapidly than at any other period of the life span. As a result, development and learning are more closely connected in early childhood, making the developmental accomplishments and learning that take place at this point critically important foundations for what follows.

Understanding child development and learning helps teachers in many ways, including:

- Setting and evaluating goals that are achievable for most children within a given age range and that also challenge children to go on learning
- Accurately interpreting children's behavior as predictable for their age or in need of intervention
- Knowing predictable sequences of development and learning to plan curriculum and adapt teaching to accommodate where individual children are in the sequence
- Predicting the kinds of topics and experiences that will be interesting and meaningful to children of different ages
- Understanding how children's social and cultural contexts affect their learning and development
- Using information about typical and atypical development to identify and diagnose potential disabilities or developmental delays in children, as well as to determine if children's development is advanced

In previous sections, we defined and described the relationships between development and learning, and between theory, research, and practice. Teachers have much to learn about these topics, but we begin with the most current area of new knowledge, brain development.

✓ **Check Your Understanding 4.1:** Understanding Development and Learning

 # Brain Development and Implications for Practice

Some of the most exciting discoveries about human development ever made have occurred in the past 30 years as advanced technologies have enabled scientists to directly study how the brain grows and changes. Tools such as positron emission tomography (PET) scans and functional magnetic resonance imagery (fMRI) open windows into how the brain functions when people perform different tasks and how the brains of children and adults compare (Fusaro & Nelson, 2009). An explosion of brain research has captured the imagination of the general public and policy makers, in addition to educators and parents.

A major conclusion of this research is that brain development results from an interaction between what is happening in children's minds and their experiences in the world (Center on the Developing Child at Harvard University, 2010). In other words, experiences, both positive and negative affect brain development, and brain growth and change affect learning.

How the Brain Promotes Learning

The brain is the most complex of human organisms, the most important to overall functioning, yet we know the least about it. But we are learning more.

The Physical Brain   The brain is composed of a massive number of nerve cells, or **neurons**, that receive information through the senses or from other neurons and then communicate information back to other parts of the body (Fusaro & Nelson, 2009). One

neurons Nerve cells in the brain that receive information through the senses or from other neurons, and then communicate information back to other parts of the body.

connection might alert the baby to look at a human face; another might signal a smile in response to mommy's face. These connections that carry information between neurons are called **synapses**.

In utero, the baby's brain undergoes astonishing growth. Neurons are produced at a rapid rate, and they migrate (or move) to the places in the brain where they will develop and be used. They also begin the process of differentiation—specialization for particular functions. The processes of neuron production, migration, and differentiation are mostly directed by genes. However, they are also affected by maternal health, nutrition, and environmental risks such as alcohol or drug use.

The adult brain has about 100 billion neurons, about the same number that babies have at birth. The major difference between the newborn brain and adult brain, however, is the intricate network of connections (synapses) between the neurons, the brain's wiring system (Fusaro & Nelson, 2009). During the first 2 to 3 years of life, babies' brains overproduce synapses, going from about 2,500 at birth to 15,000—many more than adults have. After that, the brain starts **pruning** unnecessary or unused synapses. Throughout life, new synapses are formed and others are pruned away.

Pruning is important because it contributes to efficient brain operation, aids learning and memory, and increases the brain's flexibility, actions that neuroscientists term *plasticity*. **Plasticity** is the brain's ability to develop and change in response to experiences. After pruning, fewer and stronger connections among brain cells strengthen those that remain. This process is similar to pruning a bush that has grown too large; cutting off unneeded branches strengthens those that remain and may mean more blossoms in the future.

The Role of Experience in Brain Development

During early childhood—a period of rapid brain growth—the brain is most receptive and responsive to experience (Center on the Developing Child at Harvard University, 2010). Children's relationships with the family and community impact brain development and influence how well the neurological system works. Both positive and negative experiences modify the brain architecture, with the most emotionally intense and most meaningful experiences having the greatest effects (Levitt, 2008). For these reasons, highly stressful experiences during early childhood can have lasting negative consequences (Center on the Developing Child at Harvard University, 2010).

Although too little stimulation can lead to poor outcomes, exposing young children to overstimulating environments is not supported by brain research (Thompson, 2008). Babies and toddlers in particular become stressed when they are overstimulated. They either tune out (usually by going to sleep) or act out (usually by crying). Either way, they aren't learning.

Brain research indicates that the years up to age 10 are the prime time for learning. Instead of critical periods, researchers use the term **windows of opportunity** to suggest that there are times in life when the brain is most open to certain types of experiences. One such example is language development, as described in the feature *What Works: Exposing Babies to Different Languages*.

Young children's brains are much more active, connected, and flexible than are adults' (Thompson, 2008). However, this does not mean, as some people have concluded, that the first few years of life are such a critical period that after age 3 or 5, the window for learning closes. On the contrary, brains remain flexible throughout life, as demonstrated when an 80-year-old learns to knit or a 58-year-old learns Italian.

Implications for Children

Fostering optimal early brain development is essential for positive outcomes for children. Reviews of brain research (Fusaro & Nelson, 2009; Tierney & Nelson, 2009) conclude that:

- The brain's most significant development occurs before birth, placing great importance on prenatal care.
- Early experiences change and organize the physical structure of the brain.

---

synapses Connections in the brain that carry information between neurons.

pruning The process whereby the brain eliminates unnecessary or unused synapses, which contributes to efficient brain operation, aids learning and memory, and increases the brain's flexibility.

plasticity The brain's ability to develop and change in response to experiences.

▶ **Classroom Connection**

Watch this video to learn more about how the young child's experiences and interactions influence the architecture and health of the developing brain.

https://www.youtube.com/watch?v=m_5u8-QSh6A

windows of opportunity Periods of time during which human brains are particularly susceptible and responsive to certain types of experience.

What Works

Exposing Babies to Different Languages

One of the conclusions from research on brain development is that there are windows of opportunity during which human brains are particularly susceptible and responsive to certain types of experiences. One of those windows relates to language development among very young children.

Patricia Kuhl is a leading authority on speech development. She has conducted numerous studies with very young infants to test babies' ability to discriminate the sounds of diverse languages. Using MEG (magnetic) technology to view stimulation of different areas of the brain, Kuhl and colleagues found that the auditory (hearing) and motor areas of the brain were activated when hearing speech syllables of any language, including those they had never heard. This means that American babies reacted when new sounds were introduced, whether in English, Spanish, or other languages. Kuhl next investigated what would happen after babies were a little older and had more experience hearing the language around them. At 11 months of age, babies showed more auditory reaction to syllables from their own language, and more motor reaction to syllables from another language. This suggests that by 11 months, babies already know the sounds from their own language, and that they are attempting to understand and make the sounds from their nonnative language. Apparently, long before babies can talk, the brain is practicing the sounds, especially those of their native language.

This research supports the value of intensive social interaction for learning language for infants, for building the brain's capacity to learn and use language. Previously, Kuhl and others have found that if children are introduced to a second language before 7 years of age, they are able to speak it like a native—that is, without an accent. After about age 10, however, people who learn another language are never able to speak it like a native speaker. Contrary to this finding, most "foreign" language instruction in U.S. schools doesn't occur until high school, long after this window of opportunity has closed, making learning a new language more difficult.

What brain research tells us is that when babies are born, a great deal of neurological capacity is in place. But during the first few years of life, the brain changes in major ways in response to experience—the brain learns, especially from human interaction. Which leads to another conclusion: The brain—and the baby, of course—learn best from interaction with people.

Source: "Infants' Brain Responses to Speech Suggest Analysis by Synthesis," by P. K. Kuhl, R. R. Ramirez, A. Bosseler, J. L. Lin, and T. Imada, 2014, *Proceedings of the National Academies of Sciences, 111*(31), 11238–11245.

- Different parts of the brain are more responsive to experiences at different times. There are windows of opportunity for particular types of learning.
- Neglect, abuse, and stress pose serious threats to healthy brain development. Prevention and early intervention become even more important in light of the potentially lasting negative consequences for brain development.
- Brains develop best when children experience loving relationships, play, opportunities to explore their world, interesting and engaging things to learn about, and healthy, safe environments.
- Brain development is integrated; as children get older, the areas within the brain become better connected.

During preschool and the primary grades, considerable growth and change take place in the frontal lobes of the brain, the areas that are responsible for regulating thought and action (Obradović, Portilla, & Boyce, 2012). As a result, the following skills improve considerably during these years: attention, impulse control, planning, reasoning, problem solving, and memory.

Implications for Practice

Brain research has electrified public interest in early childhood education. Nevertheless, neuroscience provides clearer guidance about the kinds of experiences that harm development, such as prolonged stress, rather than those that enrich it (Center on the Developing Child at Harvard University, 2010). Learning to handle the typical stresses of childhood is a normal part of growing up, such as when children go to the doctor or start a new

toxic stress Children's experience of intense, frequent, and/or prolonged anxiety such as abuse, neglect, violence, or economic deprivation without adult support to help them cope.

school. At other times, children may experience more long-lasting stressful experiences, such as an injury or death in the family, which are difficult but tolerable as long as a caring adult is there for support. The biggest threat to children's developing brains is **toxic stress**, which occurs when children experience intense, frequent, and/or prolonged anxiety such as abuse, neglect, violence, or economic deprivation without adult support to help them cope (Shonkoff, Garner, & the Committee on Psychological Aspects of Child and Family Health, 2012). Such prolonged stress can impair brain growth and have lasting negative consequences for physical and mental health.

Threats to brain development reinforce the need to prevent child abuse and neglect and to eliminate risk factors such as poor nutrition and exposure to toxic substances. Likewise, evidence from brain research supports the need for Head Start–like comprehensive family services to minimize stress and trauma in children's lives and improve the mental and physical health of caregivers.

At least at the present time, brain research is not precise enough to provide guidance about specific ways to optimize development (Center on the Developing Child at Harvard University, 2010). In general, it validates the importance of positive relationships with parents and teachers. And because the areas of the brain that contribute to social-emotional and cognitive development are connected, early childhood programs should focus on both (Thompson, 2008).

However, we have much less knowledge of specific curricula, products, or teaching practices that enhance brain development; therefore, teachers should be wary of products that claim to be based on brain research (Center on the Developing Child at Harvard University, 2010). It appears that the best course is to use educational practices that have been shown to be effective. Neuroscience is most useful when coupled with the larger body of knowledge about theories of development and learning, which we describe in the sections that follow.

 Check Your Understanding 4.2: Brain Development and Implications for Practice

 # Child Development Theories

In this section, we present the theories of child development that are influential in early childhood education today. One of the most debated aspects of human development has been whether biology or experience (nature or nurture) plays the bigger role in explaining individual differences. Some theories place greater emphasis on inborn, biologically driven changes, whereas others consider the environment to be the primary influence. Most of the prominent theories, however, reflect the prevailing view that human development is a product of *both* biology/heredity *and* environment/experiences.

Multiple theories exist because of the various dimensions of development, such as social, emotional, and cognitive. The work of Erik Erikson and Abraham Maslow, which we describe in the sections that follow, has been influential in guiding practice in social and emotional development and motivation to learn. We follow with a description of two developmental theories that explain how children develop cognitive skills, Piaget's Cognitive Developmental Theory and Vygotsky's Sociocultural Theory. The section closes with a comprehensive theory of human development that explains how characteristics of the individual child and the settings interact, Bronfenbrenner's Bio-Ecological Systems theory.

Erikson's Psychosocial Theory of Human Development

Psychologist Erik Erikson (1902–1994) was influenced by cultural anthropologists and came to see the importance of culture and social experience in shaping development.

TABLE 4.1 Erikson's Stages of Personal and Social Development

Approximate Age	Stage	Lessons Learned from Life's Challenges
Infants Birth to 1 year	Trust vs. mistrust	Gaining feelings of security and positive attachment, learning to trust other people to meet needs as well as exert some control over environment
Toddlers 1 to 3 years	Autonomy vs. doubt	Becoming aware of increasing competence, strong will to practice new skills without restriction, and growing sense of self as individual
Preschoolers 3 to 5 years	Initiative vs. guilt	Becoming more purposeful in initiating play with other children and toys, increasing power and ability to act without taking too many risks
Elementary School-age 6 to 12 years	Industry vs. inferiority	Becoming confident in school work, mastering challenging tasks, and acting responsibly
Adolescence 10 to 20 years	Identity vs. role confusion	Finding sense of self and building relationships with peers
Young adulthood	Intimacy vs. isolation	Building close relationships with sexual partners, friends, and colleagues, beginning career
Middle adulthood	Generativity vs. self-absorption	Gaining satisfaction from life's work and contributing to larger society, nurturing next generations and caring for others
Late adulthood	Integrity vs. despair	Reflecting on life with contentment, engaging in rewarding activities, coping with loss and end of life challenges

Source: Based on *Child Development and Education* (5th ed.) by T. M. McDevitt and J. E. Ormrod, 2013, Upper Saddle River, NJ: Pearson.

Based on extensive investigations conducted with his wife, Joan, Erikson published his seminal book, *Childhood and Society* (1950/1963).

He proposed an eight-stage theory of personal and social development in which at each stage of life an individual confronts a major challenge or "crisis." Successful negotiation of the crisis requires achieving a balance between two possible extremes. If crises are not resolved positively at particular points in the life span, Erikson postulated that later problems will ensue. Table 4.1 provides an overview of Erikson's eight stages, the typical crisis, and successful resolution.

Stages of Personal and Social Development in Early Childhood

Erikson hypothesized the following four stages of psychological and social development in the lives of children. He assumed that mothers and other family members are the principal actors in children's lives during the first three stages. However, children today participate in out-of-home child care from birth. Therefore, teachers also play significant roles in helping young children negotiate these critical life events. Following are examples of how features of Erikson's stages can be seen in young children's behaviors and relationships.

Stage 1: Trust versus mistrust (birth to 18 months). Eight-month-old Martin is standing up in his crib sobbing and bouncing on his chubby legs. His family child care provider, Joanne, comes in and soothingly says, "I can tell you are wet and hungry. Let's change your diaper now." Martin sighs as she picks him up lovingly. Joanne knows Martin well enough to interpret his cries and respond accordingly; in turn, Martin is comforted by the fact that when he cries, Joanne is there for him.

The major task of infants and their caregivers is to develop a sense of trust in the world, a feeling that their needs for food and love will be met. Babies' trust develops through responsive relationships with caregivers. If adults are inconsistent or rejecting, the baby learns that the world is an untrustworthy place and that he has little power to influence what happens to him.

Stage 2: Autonomy versus doubt (18 months to 3 years). Belinda is 22 months old. She has been in the same child care center with the same primary caregiver, Sandy, since she was 5 months old. She and Sandy have a warm, loving relationship. But lately, Belinda has begun to resist just about everything Sandy wants her to do. As soon as Sandy finishes dressing her, Belinda starts pulling off her shoes or shirt. She yells, "I want red shirt." Sandy calmly says, "Okay, you can choose. Do you want your red shirt or your yellow one (the one she is already wearing)?" Belinda pumps up her chest and says, "Yellow one."

Belinda's behavior may seem like a step backward toward infancy, but actually it is evidence of her advancing development. By 18 months, most babies are mobile and are soon able to communicate their wants and needs in words. They begin to separate from primary caregivers, try to do things for themselves, and assert their autonomy with statements like "Me do it!" or "Mine." This desire to break away from caregivers is sometimes called the "terrible twos" because it can lead to power struggles. One minute the child wants to hold onto the adult, and the next minute she wants to push away. But becoming a more autonomous human being is a major task of growing up. If adults are too harsh or restrictive with children at this age, children can feel powerless and doubt their own competence. One effective strategy is giving a toddler a manageable amount of power, such as Sandy did by offering a choice of two shirts.

Stage 3: Initiative versus guilt (3 to 6 years). Donald teaches 4-year-olds. He loves this age group because he finds that most 4-year-olds can do many things on their own, while at the same time expressing their unbridled joy at every new accomplishment. He sets up his classroom and daily schedule to allow for as much choice as possible, while also being available to assist children during these periods of child-initiated activity. Dorcas especially needs his help because her parents have been somewhat overprotective and she is hesitant to try new experiences.

The preschool and kindergarten years are marked for most children by an increasing sense of their own abilities, especially improved motor skills and exploding language capacity. This sense of confidence, at times unwarranted, leads children to initiate their own activities. When children's initiatives are regularly punished or thwarted, they may begin to feel guilty and withdraw. The resolution for negotiating this stage is making sure that encouraging children's initiative and risk-taking is balanced by ensuring their safety.

Stage 4: Industry versus inferiority (6 to 12 years). Melodie's second-grade class is working in small groups on subtraction problems. One group works feverishly, arguing over the correct answers and giving each other high fives when they figure them out. Another group of children is quieter, appearing frustrated and unsure. Looking over at the others, Max says, "We're the dumb group. We'll never do good in math."

During the elementary school years, children's spheres expand, and the opinions of teachers and peers become more important and parents' less so. School work becomes a major part of children's lives, and they begin to find satisfaction in achievement and in mastering new skills. They also begin to compare themselves to others and are more capable of judging their own performances. When children's accomplishments are not up to their standards, they may develop a sense of inferiority.

Erikson emphasized that development does not end during childhood but continues throughout the life span. Adults—students, teachers, and parents—will see themselves in the later stages (see Table 4.1). Understanding the struggles of the later stages—identity versus role confusion, intimacy versus isolation, generativity versus self-absorption, and integrity versus despair—can provide teachers with insight into the behavior of adolescents (who may be parents) and other adults, including parents and colleagues. However, the first four stages are most relevant to the work of early childhood educators.

Implications for Teaching

Erikson's theory has important implications for the social-emotional climates of early childhood programs, as we can see from visiting the

Love and Learn Child Care Center. In this center, babies and toddlers have primary care-givers who stay with them for 2 or 3 years so teachers get to know them well and can provide consistent, responsive care. The preschool and kindergarten classes are structured with extended periods of time for children to initiate their own activities within the op-tions that the teacher provides. Teachers encourage children to voice their opinions and ideas. The after-school program provides time, space, and materials for primary-grade children to pursue and master hobbies and interests such as photography, computers, painting, sports, and writing stories.

In this book, we advocate a *both/and* approach to many questions regarding early childhood practice. Erikson's theory is an example of this approach because each of the crises that children must negotiate is resolved by achieving a balance between the two poles. Trust is essential, for example, but children also need to develop a healthy sense of caution when interacting with strangers. Similarly, preschool children's initiative should be encouraged, but they also need to learn limits.

Erikson's theory emphasizes the role of the sociocultural context on children's per-sonal and social development, but parts of his theory assume particular cultural perspec-tives. For example, his emphasis on the singular role of the mother during the first three stages doesn't reflect the value that some cultural groups place on multiple caregivers (see the *Culture Lens* feature on page 104).

Maslow's Self-Actualization Theory

Abraham Maslow (1908–1970) was part of a group of psychologists, called humanists, who studied healthy personality development rather than mental illness, as psychologists had done previously. Maslow (1954) developed **self-actualization theory**, which identi-fies a hierarchy of needs, as depicted in Figure 4.1, that motivate people's behavior and goals that are necessary for healthy personality development.

self-actualization theory Maslow's view that behavior and learning are motivated by a hierarchy of needs.

Hierarchy of Human Needs Maslow's hierarchy is a pyramid depicting the relationship between needs and goals. The bottom two layers represent the basic physical needs required to sustain life, such as food, water, and shelter, and the fundamental psychological needs for safety and security. Maslow postulated that unless these needs are met, humans cannot move up the hierarchy to achieve the next goals: love and a sense of belonging and then self-esteem. The top of the pyramid represents self-actualization, which is achievement of life's goals in many individual forms. Goals that contribute to self-actualization are things that make life meaningful and satisfying. Maslow speculated that self-actu-alization is not achieved by everyone, although most people strive for it.

Implications for Practice Maslow's theory is useful as a framework for understanding how people are motivated. If children are hungry, it follows that they cannot focus their attention on any-thing else. Similarly, if children are frightened or emotionally in-secure, they cannot learn effectively. Meeting children's basic physical needs as well as their need for psychological safety and emotional security is at the heart of good early childhood practice. Consider free school lunch programs and state li-censing standards that set requirements for operating a child care center—these mandates are designed to protect chil-dren's health, safety, and security.

Effective early childhood programs go beyond meeting children's basic needs, however. Their goals include estab-lishing positive, affectionate relationships among children and adults (the need for love and belonging) and building children's competence in all areas and, therefore, their self-esteem. Meeting children's needs and helping them achieve

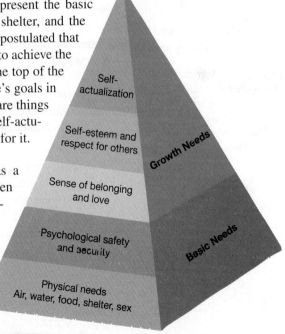

FIGURE 4.1 Maslow's Hierarchy of Needs Maslow's Hierarchy of Human Needs graphically depicts how successful relationships, positive self-esteem, and learning depend on a strong foundation of physical safety and security.

Source: Maslow, A., *Motivation and personality.* © 2013. Reprinted and electronically reproduced by permission of Pearson Education, Inc., Upper Saddle River, NJ.

these goals contributes to life satisfaction and successful learning. Although children will not reach the pinnacle of Maslow's hierarchy—self-actualization—the foundations are laid during those early years. Adults might want to consider that a career teaching young children can be a self-actualizing experience, especially for those who find this work meaningful, playful, rewarding, and contributing to a better world.

The theories of both Erikson and Maslow apply primarily to social and personality development and the motivation to learn. Next, we turn to two theorists—Piaget and Vygotsky—whose work applies primarily to cognitive development. Because all domains of development are so integrally connected, however, these theories also have implications for social-emotional development.

Piaget and Cognitive Developmental Theory

The cognitive-developmental theory of Jean Piaget (1896–1980) has had enormous impact on early childhood education. Although parts of his theory—particularly the stages of cognitive development—have been criticized, he remains a towering and influential figure decades after his death.

Swiss-born, Piaget spent the greater part of his life observing and listening to children of various ages, beginning with detailed observations of his own children as infants. Piaget's wife, Valentine, did most of the minute-by-minute, day-by-day observing and recording of the children's behavior beginning at birth using the only tools available at the time, pen and paper (Gopnik, Meltzoff, & Kuhl, 1999).

Several aspects of Piaget's theory readily apply to education. The following sections present key concepts for teachers: constructivism, the process of learning (adaptation), types of knowledge, and the general idea of stages of cognitive development.

constructivism Learning theory derived from the work of Jean Piaget; assumes that children actively build their knowledge from firsthand experiences in stimulating environments.

Constructivist Learning Theory
Piaget's relatively complex theory can be summed up in a simple sentence: *Children think differently from adults.* Einstein called this discovery by Piaget "so simple that only a genius could have thought of it" (Papert, 1999). Piaget believed that children's minds are not empty vessels to be filled with knowledge by adults; instead, children actively make sense of their experiences by building or constructing their own knowledge. Piaget's theory of how children learn is called **constructivism.**

From his own perspective as a scientist, Piaget viewed children as little scientists who hypothesize about how the world works, and continually test and refine their own theories (Piaget, 1955). The following example illustrates how Piaget (1930) did his work and how a young child thinks:

> *Piaget:* Where does the wind come from?
> *Ost (age 4):* From outside.
> *Piaget:* How is it made outside?
> *Ost:* By the motor cars.
> *Piaget:* What else can make the wind?
> *Ost:* Bicycles, trams, carts, dust.
> *Piaget:* What else?
> *Ost:* When you blow, when you sweep. (p. 35)

This dialogue demonstrates Piaget's idea that children develop their own theories of how the world works. With their experiences, children test their theories and eventually either strengthen, change, or discard them.

How Development Occurs: The Process of Adaptation
One way we can tell that children construct their own knowledge is that they come up with their own ideas about or explanations for events. This is one reason why young children can be so enchanting. Five-year-old Pearson arrives at kindergarten one morning and proudly announces to his teacher, "I know what A + A is—B!" Pearson hasn't discovered algebra, but he does apply what he has learned about how numbers work (1 + 1 = 2) to the alphabet.

As young children play and interact with objects and other people, they construct their own understanding about the world, such as what a crayon can do and how paper is used.

However mistaken Pearson is at this point, he is clearly thinking and trying to connect what he is learning to what he already knows.

Piaget believed that all children, like Pearson, have an inborn ability to organize and make sense of their experiences. Piaget coined the term **scheme** or **schema** for the organizing structures people use to think or guide behavior. Schemes develop and change with experience. Toddler Veronica has a big German shepherd dog named Darby. When Veronica meets the Labrador next door, she calls him Darby, too. Her mom responds, "He's a doggie, but his name isn't Darby. It's Milo." Then, Veronica sees a pony at the petting zoo and exclaims with glee, "Doggie!" But when she goes to pet the pony, she realizes he is much taller than either Darby or Milo. Again, her mother clarifies: "No, he has four legs like Darby and Milo, but he's a pony, not a doggie."

After many such experiences, Veronica changes her scheme for dogs (including the fact that dogs are not all the same) and another scheme for ponies. This process of changing schemes in response to experiences is called **adaptation**, and occurs in two ways: through assimilation and accommodation. **Assimilation** occurs when new information or experience is understood in connection with an existing scheme. Veronica assimilated her experience with Milo into her scheme for dogs.

By contrast, if the new information doesn't fit within an existing scheme, the child must modify that scheme or construct a new one, a process called **accommodation**. In Veronica's case, the pony couldn't be assimilated into her doggie scheme, so a new scheme for pony had to be created. As Veronica gets older and has many more experiences, she will create different schemes to organize this basic information. Pony will be connected with the general scheme of animals, as well as the narrower scheme of animals you can ride.

When Veronica touched the pony and her mother gave her new information, she experienced **disequilibrium**, which is an imbalance in thinking that occurs when new information or physical experience cannot be understood in terms of what is already known (i.e., cannot be assimilated). Piaget believed that human beings seek equilibrium—we want the world to make sense, so we try to restore balance by creating new schemes or adapting existing ones, the process of **equilibration**.

Piaget theorized that learning depends on this process of adapting schemes through assimilation and accommodation in order to achieve equilibrium. He also believed that

scheme or **schema** The organization of mental structures people use to think or guide behavior; the structures develop and change with experience.

adaptation The mental process of altering concepts (schemes) in response to experience, which occurs in two ways: through assimilation and accommodation.

assimilation When new information or experience is understood in connection with existing knowledge (schemes).

accommodation When new information or experience doesn't fit within an existing concept (scheme), the child must modify it or construct a new scheme.

disequilibrium An imbalance in thinking that occurs when new information or physical experience cannot be understood in terms of what is already known (cannot be assimilated).

equilibration The process whereby humans try to make sense of new experiences by creating new concepts (schemes) or adapting existing ones.

to change schemes, or accommodate, children need hands-on physical experience (they need to act on objects) and social interaction with peers and adults who help clarify their thinking. In the case of Veronica, her pony scheme was constructed through her real-life encounter at the zoo as well as her conversations with her mother.

Types of Knowledge Another important point of Piaget's theory is that there are different kinds of knowledge. Piaget believed that children's minds develop as the result of interactions between experience and biology. But the process is not identical for every type of learning. In fact, Piaget (1952) identified three types of knowledge—physical, logico-mathematical, and social-conventional—each acquired in different ways.

physical knowledge Understanding how objects move and function in space and how the physical world works.

- **Physical knowledge** is understanding how objects move and function in space—how the physical world works. Two-year-old Evan loves to watch the rubber ball roll down the ramp, and repeats the action over and over. Then he tries using a rubber block. Even though the block is soft like the ball, it doesn't cooperate. Evan's hands-on experience with the ball and block adds to his knowledge of how different objects function in the physical world.

logico-mathematical knowledge The relationships that are constructed in our minds between objects or concepts.

- **Logico-mathematical knowledge** is the relationships that are constructed in our minds between objects or concepts. Unlike physical knowledge, logico-mathematical knowledge is not directly observable. While playing with his ramp, Evan sees that Delia has two small balls and he has one big one. He decides that he wants a second ball. The idea that two balls are more than one ball is an example of logico-mathematical knowledge. Evan created the relationship between the objects in his mind; it does not exist otherwise. He could just as easily have focused on the relationship of size instead of quantity and decided to keep the big ball.

social-conventional knowledge The culturally agreed-on names and symbols that need to be transmitted to the learner directly.

- **Social-conventional knowledge** is the culturally agreed-on names and symbols that need to be transmitted to the learner directly. For example, the letters of the alphabet, number names, and the meaning of the colors on the stoplight are all arbitrary. This kind of knowledge can't be reinvented by every learner. Usually, children learn these symbols by repeated exposure (hearing and seeing them frequently) or being directly taught.

A challenge for teachers is that different types of knowledge require different types of teaching and learning. Just because social-conventional knowledge is most efficiently learned through instruction does not mean that other types of knowledge can be easily acquired this way. Complex concepts such as counting, which is logico-mathematical knowledge, require much deeper understanding than simply reciting the number names. At the same time, children can't learn to count if they don't know the number sequence, just as they can't learn to read if they don't know the alphabet. Therefore, in constructing their understanding of concepts, children often draw on all three kinds of knowledge.

Cognition and Biology: Stages of Cognitive Development Piaget believed that biology plays a key role in cognitive development, with specific cognitive abilities changing in significant ways as children get older. His theory identifies four stages of cognition, as listed in Table 4.2. Piaget theorized that although the ages were approximate, the order of the stages is fixed and that every child goes through each stage.

Sensorimotor Stage (Birth to Age 2) During the years from birth to about age 2, children learn about the world through a combination of their sensory abilities—sight, hearing, taste, touch, smell—and their motor skills. Newborn and young infants rely on reflexes such as sucking and grasping to build schemes. When baby Sonia grasps her rattle and brings it to her mouth, she finds out lots of things about the rattle—it makes a noise she likes, and it feels hard and cold. Another characteristic of the sensorimotor period is that babies lack **object permanence**, which means that when an object is no longer in their sight, it ceases to exist for them. For example, if Mommy hides the favorite rattle under a blanket, Sonia won't look for it. Then when the blanket is removed, Sonia will inevitably be surprised to find the rattle there.

object permanence A concept that babies lack early in the period of sensorimotor development, so that when an object is no longer in their sight, it ceases to exist for them.

TABLE 4.2 Piaget's Stages of Cognitive Development

Stage	Approximate Age	Characteristics
Sensorimotor	Birth to 2 years	Learns through senses and physical movement, gradually moving from reflexes to conscious activity.
Preoperational	2 to 7 years	Develops ability to learn through symbols—language and mental representations of thoughts; thinking is controlled more by perceptions than logic.
Concrete operational	7 to 11 years	Able to think and solve problems more logically, through concrete experience; abstract thinking is limited.
Formal operational	11 years to adulthood	Can think and solve problems abstractly, using symbolic thought and systematic experimentation.

Source: Based on *Educational Psychology: Theory and Practice*, 11th edition, by R. Slavin, 2015, Upper Saddle River, NJ: Pearson.

As children get older and are able to move on their own, crawling and toddling, they use more conscious movements to find out how things work. But their learning occurs through their actions; they don't yet think or plan in advance. Consider 18-month-old Ronde, who stacks his blocks in front of the cabinet door. When he opens the door, the blocks fall over, much to his surprise and dismay. Nevertheless, Ronde keeps stacking and knocking over the blocks, not realizing that if he moved the toys before opening the door, they wouldn't fall down.

Very young children also tend to see everything from their own point of view, what Piaget called **egocentrism**. Their experiences, such as shaking the rattle or making milk flow by sucking, convince them that they are the center of their world and can cause events to happen.

egocentrism The process whereby very young children tend to see everything from their own intellectual and emotional point of view.

By about age 2, young children begin to be able to use symbols such as words, instead of relying on actions and objects to learn about the world, and they move into Piaget's second stage of cognitive development—preoperational.

Preoperational Stage (Ages 2 to 7) Several major cognitive developments occur during this stage. First, children's language development explodes, which provides symbols that enable children to think (that is, hold a mental representation) of an object or event. Ronde can now picture the door knocking down his blocks and, therefore, thinks ahead to building in a safer place. As a result of this new thinking ability, children are less dependent on sensorimotor learning, although active learning is still most effective.

Piaget did many classic experiments with preoperational children, trying to gauge their ability to solve various prearranged tasks. What he concluded from these studies is that preoperational children rely on their perceptions or intuitions about solutions rather than on logic. For example, at snack time, 4-year-olds Isela and Ruth each have one graham cracker. Isela breaks hers into four pieces and tells Ruth, "Look! I have more crackers than you do!" Nothing her teacher says will convince Ruth that they have the same amount. Ruth is not content until the teacher resignedly breaks her cracker into four pieces as well.

From his observations, Piaget concluded that there are several specific limitations to the thinking of preoperational children. Ruth and Isela's situation demonstrates that they were unable to conserve quantity. **Conservation** is the concept that the quantity of objects or liquids does not change just because their physical appearance is transformed. If Ruth had a tall glass of milk and her teacher poured the milk into a short fat one, no doubt she would think that she had less milk and feel cheated once more. Ruth is unable to reverse the operation of pouring the milk in her mind and figure out that the amount has not changed. The same phenomenon—judging by appearances rather than logic—is observed when preschool children are presented with two equal rows of checkers. After one row is spread out and appears longer, even though no checkers have been added or removed, preoperational children will assume that the spread-out row has more checkers.

conservation The understanding that the quantity of objects stays the same regardless of changes in appearance.

Preoperational children also continue to be egocentric—interpreting the world from their own point of view, though less so over time. During a visit to the Gettysburg battlefield, 3-year-old Ryan declares to his Nana, "I was too little to fight in the battle. I had to stay in the van."

Concrete Operational Stage (Ages 7 to 11) During the elementary school years, children's thinking becomes more logical, and they are able to solve problems mentally and reverse operations. They are no longer fooled by a conservation problem. Children are capable of carrying out mental actions. Piaget used the word *concrete* to refer to this stage of cognition because this age group is not yet capable of thinking about and fully comprehending complex, abstract concepts such as historical time or death. Instead, they are most successful at solving problems they can directly experience. Piaget believed that abstract reasoning is not possible until the stage of formal observations in adolescence and adulthood, and that some people never reach this stage of cognitive development.

Criticisms of Piaget's Theory Piaget's theory was first widely disseminated in the United States in the 1970s and had a major impact on views of how children learn and appropriate ways to teach. Parents, toy manufacturers, and publishers were also influenced by Piaget's ideas about the competence of children, leading to an explosion in educational products for babies.

Piaget's stage theory emphasized the limitations of children's thinking at each stage, leading some educators to focus more on what children were *not* able to do rather than on their developing competencies. Preschool classrooms provided an interesting environment for children to "discover," with little interaction with adults to support expanding children's thinking. And most educators assumed that mathematics and literacy, which are based on understanding symbols, were too abstract for preoperational children and, therefore, not taught until children were older.

In recent decades, researchers and educators have challenged some of the fundamental tenets of Piagetian theory. Researchers have found that Piaget overestimated the role of biologically based stages and discovery in children's development and underestimated the role of the environment and teaching. For example, researchers have found that Piaget underestimated children's abilities to think in more complex ways (Case & Okamoto, 1996; Gelman, 2000; Gelman & Baillargeon, 1983; Mix, Huttenlocher, & Levine, 2002). Using carefully designed experiments, researchers have found that infants have object permanence much younger than Piaget theorized. With support, children can begin to understand the perspectives of other people at a much younger age than Piaget assumed. In addition, the inability to conserve quantity does not interfere with some preschool children's learning basic mathematics concepts, as Piaget assumed (Clements & Sarama, 2009).

Researchers today agree that a major, though gradual, transformation occurs in children's cognitive abilities around kindergarten age, known as the **5- to 7-year shift** (Berk, 2006; Sameroff & McDonough, 1994). Children don't pass through sharply drawn stages; rather, their brain development and experiences contribute to their expanded memory and more logical reasoning (Bauer, 2009; Ornstein, Coffman, & Grammer, 2009).

5- to 7-year shift Major transition in cognitive abilities that gradually occurs between 5 and 7 years of age, resulting in increased ability to think logically, self-regulate, and solve problems.

Contributions of Piagetian Theory to Practice Despite the criticisms of Piagetian theory, the contributions of his work are enormous. Visit any good-quality early childhood program and you will see evidence of these contributions. Children are actively engaged in learning—not sitting still and listening to a teacher talk most of the time. There are concrete learning materials, and children have time to use them on their own. The environment itself is designed to promote learning. While Piaget underestimated infant and toddler understanding, he was the first to suggest—correctly—that infants have an active intellectual life. Knowledge of the sensorimotor state of development literally launched the industry of toys and equipment for babies—mobiles over cribs, noise-making toys that babies control, and board books.

Piaget changed the way we view young children and how they learn. Piaget believed that children developed understanding by interacting with objects and people in the environment. He relied on observing and interviewing to understand what children thought. However, he overestimated the role of exploration and discovery in children's cognitive development and underestimated the important role of the teacher. Piaget also thought cognitive development was essentially the same across cultures. Lev Vygotsky, a Russian psychologist, studied Piaget's theory and expanded our understanding of children's development in important ways.

▶ Classroom Connection

See constructivism in action in this primary school classroom. Observe how the teacher supports children as they construct their own knowledge. He asks questions and encourages experimentation. How do you think questioning supports children's scientific understanding better than just telling them the information?

Vygotsky and Sociocultural Theory

Lev Vygotsky (1896–1934) was born in Russia the same year as Piaget. Although he died young, he was a prolific writer, and after his death his theories were further developed and disseminated by his students. Because his work was not translated into English until 1962, it was unknown in the West until long after his death. The Stalinist regime also suppressed his work in his native country.

Vygotsky's **sociocultural theory** is based on his belief that children learn from social interaction within a cultural context. He emphasized that *what* children learn is determined by the culture in which they grow up, such as an urban child learning to negotiate dangerous street crossings, or a rural child learning to milk a cow. In recent years, Vygotsky's views on learning and teaching have become more influential than Piaget's, although the theories are actually complementary (Copple & Bredekamp, 2009).

sociocultural theory
Vygotsky's theory that children learn from social interaction within a cultural context.

Vygotsky's Theory of How Development Occurs Among developmental theorists, Vygotsky provided the greatest amount of guidance for educators (Stetsenko & Vianna, 2009). He viewed development as a continuous process driven by learning. At particular ages, the primary learning task differs. Babies learn through their senses and by manipulating objects (similar to Piaget's view). Relationships with adults, who talk and play with babies and often use objects when doing so, drive learning during the first 2 years of life.

From ages 2 to 5, children's development is dominated by their perceptions and reactions. They pay attention to what is interesting and meaningful to them, rather than to what adults prefer. They act and react without prior thinking or reflecting on past actions. For example, when Ms. Broyles says, "It's time to go outside, so put away your toys and get your coats," most 3- and 4-year-olds will run to the door. Much to Ms. Broyles's dismay, they still have this reaction after weeks of school. Vygotsky believed that a major goal of preschool is to help children move from such reactive thinking to the ability to think *before* they act (Bodrova & Leong, 2012b).

During the preschool years, children need to acquire cognitive and social-emotional competencies that shape their minds for all further learning—language, memory, focused attention, and self-regulation (Bodrova & Leong, 2012b). If these important foundations are in place, in the primary grades children acquire the ability to "learn on demand," as Vygotsky called it. They are more likely to cooperate with the school's agenda—learning to read, calculate, and follow group rules—even when they would rather be doing something else.

According to Vygotsky, cognitive development involves the zone of proximal development, scaffolding, social construction of knowledge, language and other symbol systems, self-regulation, and play. These concepts, discussed in the sections that follow, have important implications for practice.

Zone of Proximal Development Twenty-month-old Ave is trying desperately to get on the pony riding toy. Her teacher, Khari, observes that she is about to cry in frustration. He could pick her up and put her on it, but instead he gently lifts her leg so that she

Becoming an Intentional Teacher
Teaching in the "Zone"

Here's What Happened In my kindergarten, we are working on the basic mathematical number operations—adding and subtracting. In our classroom, children work in centers for part of the morning. Through assessments that I do during center time, I learned that Miguel can add two single-digit numbers on his own. I also learned that he is struggling with subtracting single-digit numbers, but is successful when I talk through the subtraction activities with him. I also observed that Miguel is able to subtract more successfully when the problem is applied, such as when he is playing cashier and giving "change" in our Home Improvement Store center. Miguel especially likes to play there because his Dad works in construction. I decided on a three-pronged approach to support his understanding and application of subtraction:

1) I set aside 5–10 minutes twice a week to work individually with Miguel. Using manipulatives, including an abacus and small counting trains. Miguel loves trains! During this time, I verbally support Miguel's grouping and counting, using short word problems and number cards.
2) I also intentionally join Miguel and other children in the Home Improvement Store at center time. I introduce the concept of "Supply Lists" to the center, using cards with pictures and labels of the different supplies. Children can add nuts, bolts, and tools to their baskets, according to the list, and return (subtract) things they no longer need for their building projects. As Miguel purchases and returns items for his building project, I support and make explicit his adding and subtracting, pointing out to Miguel how successfully he uses math for his project.
3) Finally, during the morning math challenge, I pair Miguel with a friend who understands subtraction concepts well, and is very verbal. I have them work together

to solve the problem, explaining each of their steps.

After about two weeks of this more intensive approach, Miguel demonstrates ability to subtract single-digit numbers on his own, and begins to experiment with double-digit numbers. He insists on being the employee at checkout in the Home Improvement Store to showcase his adding and subtracting.

Here's What I Was Thinking As a kindergarten teacher, I know that understanding and applying these foundational mathematical concepts is essential for building children's later competence in math. I also understand that children learn best in the context of supportive relationships, and I structure interactions in my classroom to intentionally support each learner. I do this by: (1) assessing each child's level of independent performance on a skill, (2) assessing each child's level of supported (with help) performance on a skill, and (3) developing lessons that allow a child to practice in their supported level, until the child can do the skill independently. I then set the next higher level of skill as the child's goal skill.

Vygotsky used the term zone of proximal development (ZPD) to describe the child's skill level when supported by an adult or more experienced peer. He believed that by assessing only what a child knows, a teacher does not have information on how to support the child's progress. But by assessing a child's ZPD, I am able to structure for progressive development and learning.

Reflection How did this teacher use assessment to guide her intentional teaching? What other strategies could she have used to teach Miguel in his Zone of Proximal Development?

---

zone of proximal development (ZPD) The distance between the actual developmental level an individual has achieved (her independent level of problem solving) and the level of potential development she could achieve with adult guidance or through collaboration with other children.

scaffolding The assistance, guidance, and direction teachers provide children to help them accomplish a task or learn a skill (within their ZPD) that they could not achieve on their own.

gets over the last hurdle herself. Ave gives him a big smile as she pushes off with her feet and makes a circle around the room.

By giving Ave "a leg up," Khari helped her accomplish a goal that she couldn't do on her own, but could achieve with his assistance. Vygotsky (1978) identified this as the **zone of proximal development (ZPD)**—the distance between the actual developmental level an individual has achieved (their independent level of problem solving) and the level of potential development they could achieve with adult guidance or through collaboration with other children. The assistance, guidance, and direction teachers provide children in their ZPD is called **scaffolding**. To gain deeper understanding of how children learn in their ZPD, read the feature *Becoming an Intentional Teacher: Teaching in the "Zone."*

Social Construction of Knowledge Scaffolding does not mean that teachers control or shape learning, as behaviorists believe (see p. 124). Instead, children learn by solving problems collaboratively with the teacher's support or by working with peers, which is called **co-construction**, or social construction of knowledge.

Seven-year-olds Lucrezia and Gloria are drawing a map of their school. Lucrezia is working on the classrooms and Gloria is drawing the entrance area, lunchroom, and offices. They have the following exchange:

Lucrezia: You are making them too big. There won't be room for my part.
Gloria: Well, they are bigger. See all the stuff we have to put in.
Lucrezia: But the lunchroom is the biggest. How can we make this work?

Each girl has a different perspective on the problem. As they continue to work on it, they try different solutions, none of them satisfactory to both. Finally, they determine the following:

Gloria: We need to figure out how to measure the rooms.
Lucrezia: My brother showed me on the GPS that one inch means one mile. We need to figure out something like that.

They then proceed to address the new problems of finding a way to measure the school and creating a scale for their map.

In this example, peers work collaboratively to construct understanding. They challenge each other's ideas and alter their perspectives as a result. Lucrezia, the more accomplished peer, introduces some cultural knowledge—what she has learned about a GPS. In other situations, the teacher plays the role of provocateur, challenging the children's thinking and thus, promoting their learning.

Language and Thought Because Vygotsky (1962) believed that learning depends on interaction with other people, he also believed that speech is the most important tool for learning. Babies begin by communicating through gestures, as when they learn that holding up their arms means "pick me up." Then they connect sounds and words with their meanings; saying "Da Da" gets a different result from saying "Ma Ma." Language growth during the preschool years enables children to learn through conversation. Speech gradually becomes internalized and used for thinking.

Think of a situation, such as learning a psychology concept or solving a mathematics problem, which you didn't really understand until you talked about it with someone else or at least stated your ideas out loud. According to Vygotsky, articulating an idea is necessary for real understanding. He described the relationship between language and thought as moving from interpersonal (between people) to intrapersonal (inside the child). Learning begins in conversation between people and then becomes part of an individual's thinking.

Interpersonal understanding or socially constructed knowledge is turned into intrapersonal knowledge through **private speech** (Vygotsky, 1962). For preschool children, private speech can look like thinking out loud. As 3½-year-old Ivor stands in front of the easel contemplating the next color to use, thick paint starts running down the paper. Ivor says, "Whoa, don't do that. I'm gonna get you with my brush," and proceeds to do so. By age 6 or 7, private speech becomes silent and is used for thinking and problem solving.

To summarize, children first use language for conversation. Then, through the vehicle of private speech, they literally use language to talk to themselves and to control their own behavior—that is, for self-regulation (Bailey & Brookes, 2012).

Self-Regulation Vygotsky considered the development of self-regulation the primary task of the years before formal school entry. **Self-regulation** is the ability to adapt or control behavior, emotions, and thinking according to the demands of the situation (Bodrova & Leong, 2012b). Preschool children's self-regulation ability, more so than their intelligence or family background, predicts their academic success in the early grades (Blair & Razza, 2007; McClelland, Acock, & Morrison, 2006). By contrast, early problems in self-regulation are strongly related to later problems in school and life (Calkins & Williford, 2009). Teachers or parents may understand self-regulation as "the

co-construction Children learning by solving problems collaboratively with the teacher's support or by working with peers; also called *social construction of knowledge.*

private speech The process whereby interpersonal understanding or socially constructed knowledge is turned into intrapersonal knowledge (thinking aloud becomes thinking to oneself).

self-regulation The ability to adapt or control behavior, emotions, and thinking according to the demands of the situation.

Effective teachers draw on all the relevant theories to support children's learning progress. What strategies do you think this teacher is using to help this young girl accomplish a new skill?

capacity to control one's impulses both to stop doing something that is unnecessary (even if one wants to continue doing it), and to start doing something that is needed (even if one does not want to do it)" (Boyd, Barnett, Bodrova, Leong, & Gomby, 2005, p. 4). This is why self-regulation is so strongly related to success. Every day preschool teachers require children to stop playing (which they usually want to continue) and start cleaning up (which they don't want to do). Similarly, children in primary grades must attend to the reading lesson when they would rather go outside for recess.

The activities of the prefrontal cortex region of the brain that allow us to self-regulate—to manage our emotions, focus and shift attention, and regulate behavior to meet our goals—are known as **executive functions** (EF) (Jones & Bailey, 2014; Obradović, Portilla, & Boyce, 2012). They are some of the most important skills for learning and development (Galinsky, 2010; Gilpin, Boxmeyer, DeCaro, & Lochman, 2014). Children who have ADHD typically have developmental delays in their executive functions. They are often impulsive, and have trouble paying attention. They also may have difficulty with working memory, the brain ability that allows us to remember information in the short term and use the information to understand and solve problems. While some children are identified with ADHD in preschool, children are typically diagnosed in early elementary school, when the demands of formal schooling highlight children's EF skills of attention and regulation.

Teachers can support EF in development of children with ADHD in several ways (Murphy, 2014). To help children focus better, teachers can break instructions and tasks into structured pieces, give individualized instructions, and check for understanding of instructions. Teachers can help children regulate their own behavior by providing positive reinforcement for positive behavior, and by avoiding negative feedback, which can lead to poor self-image in children with ADHD. Many children with ADHD take medication to help them attend and regulate in the school setting; however, research suggests that the supports families and teachers can provide may help as much as medication in helping children experience school success.

Children with ADHD benefit from an environment that allows for play and exercise. Recent research has examined the role of physical activity in children's attention and EF. Physical exercise enhances sustained

executive function The ability to control emotions, focus attention, plan and think ahead, and monitor cognitive processes.

▶ **Classroom Connection**

In this video, learn more about how executive function develops, why it is important, and how adults can support its development in early childhood.

https://www.youtube.com /watch?v=efCq_vHUMqs

Promoting Play

Incorporating Playful Exercise into the Curriculum

Tamara has 22 children in her combined kindergarten-first grade class. She enjoys their energy and enthusiasm, but has noticed that several children have been struggling with maintaining attention during math and literacy work blocks. A few children have even started to act silly when they are supposed to be working. Two of the children who struggle with attention, Mabel and Nassim, have diagnoses of ADHD. Tamara knows that they are intelligent, but sees that they are falling into patterns of not finishing their work. Mabel is acting a bit anxious, possibly in response to frequent redirection and reminders. Nassim's disruptive behavior is escalating during large group activities, and he is wandering during center time and teasing his classmates. Tamara consults with her co-teacher and the school resource teacher, and together they come up with a plan that will support Mabel, Nassim, and all of the children in the class.

Before implementing any changes in the classroom, Tamara, her co-teacher, and the resource teacher take turns observing the children during the course of classroom routines and activities. They notice that children are more attentive after morning recess, lunchtime recess, and physical education. Conversely, they notice that before recess and lunch, the children have the most difficulty attending, following directions, and working independently. Although Tamara and colleagues cannot add more recess time to the children's day, they decide to: (1) introduce physical activities into large group time, (2) shift activities in the daily schedule, (3) introduce an exercise area at center time, and (4) adjust learning environments for children who need more activity.

First, Tamara shifts the most demanding aspects of the daily schedule. She starts the day with a large group activity that ends in a "dance time"—the children pick the music and they spread out across the room—and dance playfully. Children may move as they wish or follow a leader. Literacy block follows, and Tamara ensures that Mabel and Nassim complete their most demanding tasks at the beginning of the literacy block. Tamara schedules other demanding lessons such as math and science after morning and lunch recess.

Next, Tamara and her co-teacher arrange for a movement center, and choose animals for the first theme. Using cue cards and a flip-video camera, children in the center tape each other moving like animals. The teachers plan themes for future movement centers, including yoga, calisthenics, and dance party. They discuss how to introduce rules for this center and monitor for safety, and include the children in thinking of fun ways to move in the center.

Finally, Tamara makes accommodations for Mabel and Nassim, observing any other children who might benefit. Because she knows that children with ADHD often benefit from being able to move while learning, Tamara arranges for Mabel and Nassim to stand while doing work, if they choose. She provides "fidget toys" for them to hold during large group time, and identifies special classroom jobs for them to move and help during the day.

Tamara knows that she can't let children play all day, but by thinking about playful movement and exercise in her daily routines and curriculum, Tamara and her co-teacher witness dramatic increases in engagement and attention for Mabel, Nassim, and the entire class.

attention in preschoolers (Palmer, Miller, & Robinson, 2013) and EF in elementary school children with ADHD (Gapin & Etnier, 2010). In the feature *Promoting Play: Incorporating Playful Exercise into the Curriculum,* you can learn how one teacher integrates playful movement to support all the children in her classroom, including children with ADHD.

Play and Vygotsky's Theory   According to Vygotsky (1978), make-believe play is the *leading activity* in children's development from about ages 2 through 5. Play creates a zone of proximal development in which a child behaves "as though he were a head taller than himself" (Vygotsky, 1978, p. 102). When children pretend to be adults—parents, teachers, or workers, as they often do—they use more sophisticated language than usual and model grown-up behavior.

▶ Classroom Connection

Observe these two instances of sociodramatic play in a preschool classroom. What are some things you notice about the children's play? How might the different theorists view the learning and development supported in the context of the children's dramatic and block play?

Pretend play in small groups is especially valuable for promoting self-regulation because it is the one activity that requires children to regulate their own behavior, be regulated by others, and regulate others all within the same context (Bodrova & Leong, 2007; Boyd et al., 2005). Picture 5-year-olds playing restaurant. Each child, whether playing customer, waiter, or cook, has an assigned role and must stick to the script. The customer can't say, "Can I take your order?" That's the waiter's role. If the customer begins serving the food, the play breaks down. The waiter says, "You can't do that. You have to sit down, look at the menu, and eat." The rules have to be renegotiated. The customer may say, "Okay, but I get to be the waiter next." So we see that the customer has to regulate herself (stay in her role and follow the rules), be regulated by others (the waiter), and regulate others (place her order so the waiter can do his job).

As is evident in the foregoing example, sociodramatic play promotes children's ability to take another person's perspective (Vygotsky, 1977). Assuming a pretend role—being another person for a while—helps children move to another perspective and then back to their own. This ability to take another's perspective—to go beyond egocentrism—is necessary in school where children need to see the perspectives of teachers and other children.

Elena Bodrova, who studied with Vygotsky's students, and her colleague Deborah Leong developed a Vygotskian curriculum model, *Tools of the Mind* (Bodrova & Leong, 2007, 2012b). The model focuses on teachers building self-regulation in children through mature sociodramatic play.

Implications for Practice   Vygotsky's sociocultural theory has many implications for early childhood practice. Teaching in the zone of proximal development requires that children experience a challenging curriculum—not content that is meant for older children, but content that moves them ahead in thinking and problem solving.

Similarly, the role of the teacher becomes more important than ever, not as controller of the classroom, but as a collaborator with children. Teachers need to scaffold children's learning and set up situations where groups of children work together to solve problems and have the freedom to think out loud. During preschool and kindergarten, teachers need to intentionally support mature sociodramatic play to promote self-regulation, a topic we will return to later in this chapter.

Major contributions of Vygotsky's theory were his emphasis on (1) the role of adults in children's development, and (2) the transmission of cultural understandings as a part of children's development. We'll next consider a model that expands theory to a systems level, in which children develop in the context of many environments and interactions over time.

Bronfenbrenner's Ecological Systems Theory of Development

ecological systems theory
Bronfenbrenner's theory that describes the diverse, interactive contexts that influence children's development over time.

One of the most useful theories for understanding the interactive influence of social and cultural contexts on human development is the ecological systems model proposed by psychologist Urie Bronfenbrenner (1917–2005). Figure 4.2 illustrates **Bronfenbrenner's ecological systems theory** (Bronfenbrenner, 1979, 2004), which describes the diverse, interactive contexts that influence children's development over time.

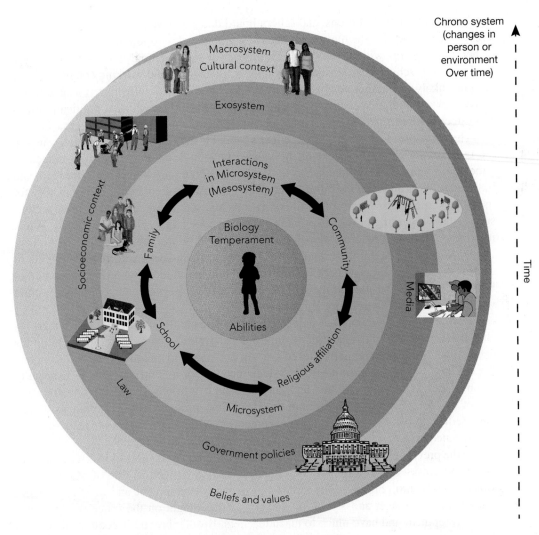

FIGURE 4.2 Model of Bronfenbrenner's Ecological Systems Theory
Source: McDevitt, Teresa M., Ormrod, Jeanne Ellis, *Child Development and Education*, 5th Ed., © 2013. Reprinted and electronically reproduced by permission of Pearson Education, Inc., Upper Saddle River, NJ

At the center of the model is the individual whose development is influenced by their own biological factors, social interaction, and experiences in a variety of contexts. The environments, or systems, surrounding an individual from birth and beyond plays significant interactive roles in a child's development. The systems in which the child directly participates on a regular basis are known as **microsystems**, and include the family, child care, school, and faith-based settings. The child's daily interactions, which Bronfenbrenner called **proximal processes** (Bronfenbrenner & Morris, 2006) have the most impact on a child's development, due to their frequent, ongoing nature, often over extended periods of time. Thought of as "drivers" of development, proximal processes include the physical care children receive, daily conversations with parents and teachers, and playground interactions with peers.

The next level of system that impacts a child's life is the **mesosystem**, which refers to the interaction of different microsystems in a child's life. Parent-teacher interactions, including conferences, phone calls, home visits, and back-to-school nights are examples of a mesosystem—where the child's microsystems of home and school come together—and interact and influence each other. Bronfenbrenner believed that the strength of these mesosystems—the degree to which the systems worked together—is important for supporting the child's positive development.

The **exosystem** consists of systems that affect the child's microsystems, but in which the child doesn't directly participate. This includes parents' employment, child care

microsystem System in which the child directly participates on a regular basis and include the family, child care, school and faith-based settings.

proximal processes Interactions in the context of daily living that have the most impact on a child's development, due to their frequent, ongoing nature, often over extended periods of time.

mesosystem Interaction of different microsystems in a child's life.

exosystem Systems that affect the child's microsystems, but that the child doesn't directly participate in, including economic, media, education, health, legal and political entities that directly affect a person or circumstance in the child's microsystem.

regulations, religious traditions, and school board decisions. When a teacher experiences stress in her home life, she may carry that stress into the classroom, impacting the quality of her relationships with students and the impact of her teaching. On the other hand, a teacher whose school board institutes policies that support good working conditions may be more likely to interact positively with children and provide effective instruction. An exosystem can include economic, media, education, health, legal, and political entities that directly effect a person or circumstance in the child's microsystem.

The outermost level of Bronfenbrenner's model is the **macrosystem**, which refers to the overarching cultural context of the values, beliefs, laws, and policies of a society. American society, for example, is strongly influenced not only by values of freedom and individual rights and responsibilities, but also by the value of collective responsibility for its neediest members. As a result, our institutions and social policies reflect these values, such as laws regarding provision of public assistance for families living in poverty. While it may not seem that macrosystems effect a child's daily life, they can exert a powerful influence over time. Bronfenbrenner uses the term **chronosystem** to refer to effects of circumstances over time. According to Bronfenbrenner, children who experience homelessness for a short period of time will likely suffer fewer negative outcomes than a child who is homeless for their entire childhood.

Bronfenbrenner's theory has helped educators and child development researchers realize the importance of considering the multiple, complex systems that impact children's development. Bronfenbrenner believed that society needs to attend carefully to supporting children by supporting all of the systems needed for a child to develop. Especially committed to supporting children and families who live in poverty, Bronfenbrenner was one of the key conceptual founders of the Head Start program. The comprehensive services (education, health, and family engagement) that are the hallmark of Head Start can be attributed, in part, to the influence of Bronfenbrenner's thinking.

In the previous sections we described the developmental theories of Erikson, Maslow, Piaget, Vygotsky and Bronfenbrenner. Erikson's work, as well as that of Maslow, provides insights into children's social and personality development and their motivation. The theories of Piaget and Vygotsky cast considerable light on the processes of cognitive development and have much to teach teachers. Bronfenbrenner's ecological systems theory attempts to connect children's social and cognitive development with the many influential systems that are involved in children's development. In the next section, we turn to descriptions of the most influential theories of learning.

 Check Your Understanding 4.3: Child Development Theories

 # Learning Theories

In contrast to developmental theories, which are linked to age-related changes in children, learning theories are assumed to apply in the same way regardless of the age of the learner. In the following sections, we describe the work of two major learning theorists: B. F. Skinner and Albert Bandura. (Another learning theory is Howard Gardner's multiple intelligences theory, which we discuss in the chapter on individual differences.)

B. F. Skinner and Behaviorism

One of the most influential learning theories of the last half century is **behaviorism** or **behavioral learning**. According to this theory, learning is reflected in changes in behavior that are controlled by the consequences, either positive or negative, that follow the behavior. Using pleasant or unpleasant consequences to control behavior is called **operant conditioning**.

Psychologist B. F. Skinner (1904–1980) developed the theory of operant conditioning through systematic experiments. Skinner discovered that he could train rats to press a lever by rewarding them with food. From experiments with animals and people,

macrosystem System that includes the overarching cultural context of the values, beliefs, laws, and policies of a society

chronosystem System that refers to effects of circumstances over time.

behaviorism or **behavioral learning** Theory that learning is a change in behavior that is controlled by the consequences, either positive or negative, that follow the behavior.

operant conditioning The process of using pleasant or unpleasant consequences to control behavior.

Skinner developed the core principles of operant conditioning, an example of which follows:

> During center time in her prekindergarten, teacher Nessa Stokes observes as Jemma struggles to print her name next to her artwork. As Jemma tires and looks as though she will give up, Nessa says, "You've almost got it, Jemma, J-E-M—two more letters and you will have written your name!" Jemma smiles proudly and continues her task. Nessa is reassured that her encouraging praise will keep Jemma working on a task that is difficult.
>
> Nessa also understands how technology can provide reinforcement to keep children motivated on difficult learning tasks. In the Tech Center, three children gather around a math game on the computer that has the boys distinguishing "more" and "less" in groups of dinosaurs. "More!" shouts Jessica, and Brian presses the button that indicates there are more dinosaurs in the new array than the previous. With the correct answer button pressed, the dinosaurs break out into a dance on the screen, leaving the children laughing. "Let's try the next one—a harder one" says Azim. "They get even funnier with harder ones." Nessa smiles, as in this activity she witnesses children cooperating, learning important math concepts, and getting positively reinforced for practicing their skills and also doing progressively more difficult math problems.

Although Nessa's actions in this brief scenario may seem relatively simple, she is in fact implementing several key principles of operant conditioning.

Operant Conditioning The most important principle of operant conditioning is that behavior changes as a result of its immediate **consequences**. Positive consequences strengthen the frequency of specific behaviors; unpleasant consequences decrease the frequency. **Reinforcers** are consequences that increase or strengthen behaviors. There are two kinds of reinforcers: positive and negative.

Positive reinforcement is a reward or pleasant consequence that follows a behavior, causing that behavior to be repeated. In the previous example, Nessa reinforced or rewarded Jemma's writing efforts with a smile and positive words of encouragement. As a result, Jemma kept working at a difficult task. While Jessica, Brian, and Azim were sufficiently reinforced by the dancing dinosaur math game, she knows to monitor their engagement in the activity to keep the learning and interactions positive and productive.

Negative reinforcement also increases the frequency of a desired behavior, but in a different way. A negative reinforcer is an unpleasant consequence that is *avoided* if the person performs a behavior more frequently. For example, an annoying bell or buzzer—a negative reinforcer—signals when the seat belt is still unfastened after a car is started. To avoid the sound, most people fasten the seat belt as soon as they can. If Nessa had observed the children arguing over the computer game, she may have pointed out that they would lose computer time if they did not find a way to cooperate. Azim may have responded, "Let's take turns pressing the button, Brian." In this circumstance, negative reinforcement would have changed the children's behavior in positive ways.

Negative reinforcement is sometimes confused with, but is not the same thing as, **punishment**. Punishment is an unpleasant consequence that stops or *decreases* the frequency of a behavior. Many people, teachers as well as parents, think punishments are effective in changing behavior and use them often. However, the problem with punishment is that it may temporarily stop an undesirable behavior, but it does not teach the child what to do instead. As a result, repeated punishment soon becomes ineffective in changing behavior. For example, in Tiffany's first-grade classroom, when children misbehave they get a red card and their name goes on the board, while those who behave well get a green card. But day after day, the same children get the red card. Receiving the card—a punishment—does not improve their behavior.

Teachers need to understand that punishment only decreases an undesirable behavior temporarily. To increase a desired behavior, reinforcement is needed. In fact, in some cases, punishment actually serves as a negative reinforcer and increases the behavior. Consider the situation where a first-grade teacher decides to punish a disruptive child by

consequences Principle of operant conditioning that behavior changes as a result of what occurs immediately afterward.

reinforcer Consequence—either positive or negative—that increases or strengthens a behavior.

positive reinforcement A reward or pleasant consequence that follows a behavior, causing that behavior to be repeated.

negative reinforcement An unpleasant consequence that is avoided if the person performs a desired behavior more frequently.

punishment An unpleasant consequence that stops or decreases the frequency of a behavior.

When teachers use positive reinforcement such as smiling or commenting on what a child is doing well, children are more likely to continue to stay engaged in learning.

making him miss recess. If the child wants to avoid recess because he doesn't get chosen for a team or is bullied, then removing him from recess is not a punishment but a reward and, thus, will have the opposite effect from the one the teacher intended. When reinforcers are removed, the conditioned behavior diminishes and eventually disappears, a process called **extinction**.

extinction The process whereby a conditioned behavior diminishes and eventually disappears when reinforcers are removed.

What to Reinforce: Shaping Behavior

Most human behavior is complex, much more so than that of the hungry rats Skinner studied. Children learn to take turns, follow classroom rules, or ride a bike over time and after many tries, some successful and others not. It would be impossible to wait to reinforce a highly complex behavior until a child performed it well. What if a kindergarten teacher only reinforced a child's writing when the letters were formed perfectly on the line? Many children would give up. Instead, an effective teacher recognizes the child's attempts, each step on the way to mastering writing the letters correctly. Teaching a new skill or behavior by rewarding each step toward the goal is called **shaping**.

shaping Teaching a new skill or behavior by rewarding each step or successive approximation toward the goal.

successive approximations Behaviors that are reinforced (shaped) that are not the actual desired behaviors, but each approximate behavior that is closer to the goal.

Shaping requires the teacher to carefully observe the **successive approximations**—not the actual desired behaviors, but each approximate behavior that is closer to the goal. For example, when 3-year-old Lola's scribbles begin to look like (approximate) a circle or straight line, her family child care provider Titia says, "Oh, look, Lola, you made an O like in your name." Lola didn't intend to draw an O, but it is likely that Titia's praise will result in Lola producing pages of O's to get more of Titia's positive attention.

Implications of Behaviorism for Practice

Research supports the effectiveness of principles of behaviorism, especially for children with special needs (Division for Early Childhood of the Council for Exceptional Children, 2014). Some disabilities, such as cerebral palsy or Down syndrome, affect children's ability to perform functional behaviors (e.g., eating or dressing) that typically developing children learn relatively easily through imitation and repetition. Children with autism benefit from behavioral techniques to support learning social communication skills (Wong et al., 2014). In these situations, using behavioral learning techniques can be effective, as Yvonne learned in the opening vignette of this chapter. For another example of the application of behavioral principles,

Including All Children
Teaching Self-Help and Social Skills to Children with Disabilities

Children with disabilities may have difficulty making friends and being accepted by other children in the group. Peer rejection is harmful for every child, but especially painful for children with disabilities, who face multiple developmental challenges. And many parents of children with disabilities want most of all for their children to have friends and be treated like their typically developing peers. To achieve these goals, children with special needs often need adults—teachers and parents—to intervene, as the following example illustrates.

Tommy is a 5-year-old child with Down syndrome. He has attended preschool for the past 2 years and is now in kindergarten. Tommy's social relationships with the other children have been generally positive, especially with several children from his preschool. Recently, however, both Tommy's parents and teachers have noticed that other classmates have begun to tease him, and former playmates are less interested in including him in their play unless he takes on the role of the baby. In fact, one playmate says, "Tommy still wets his pants, so he has to be the baby."

Tommy's teacher, Ms. Wasky, was trained in early childhood education and has little experience in or knowledge about special education. She strives to provide interesting learning experiences that keep children engaged. She believes strongly in activating children's intrinsic motivation to learn rather than using external reinforcements like stickers or happy faces. She talks with the children and encourages them to include Tommy. Under Ms. Wasky's supervision, a few children grudgingly let Tommy join them, but then they ignore him. She is concerned that Tommy's social development is regressing.

Ms. Wasky and Tommy's parents discuss ways to help him become more accepted by his peers.

The parents and teacher believe that Tommy is physically capable of self-toileting and, in fact, the pediatrician agrees. All adults involved want to allow Tommy to achieve this important developmental task on his own terms rather than rely too heavily on external reinforcement.

The dilemma they confront is weighing the risk of waiting longer while Tommy continues to be rejected by his peers against the risk of Tommy possibly becoming dependent on extrinsic reinforcement. Their growing concern about the social costs of peer rejection or infantilization of Tommy leads them to decide on a behavioral intervention. Tommy's teacher and parents, in consultation with the special education team members, decide to initiate a behavioral intervention that uses operant conditioning. They begin with concrete reinforcers for appropriate toileting behavior (in this case, stickers that Tommy selected). Eventually the reinforcement shifts to tokens that Tommy can trade for extra time on the computer or other experiences he especially likes.

As a result of this intervention, Tommy becomes more aware of and gradually learns to anticipate and respond appropriately to his toileting needs. As a result of this explicit teaching strategy, Tommy not only experiences the intrinsic satisfaction of controlling his own toileting practices, but this functional achievement also significantly contributes to an improvement in his social status in the classroom. No longer is he relegated to the role of the baby on every occasion.

Source: Adapted from "Developmentally Appropriate Practice: The Early Childhood Teacher as Decision-Maker," by S. Bredekamp, 1997, p. 48, in *Developmentally Appropriate Practice in Early Childhood Programs,* revised edition, edited by S. Bredekamp and C. Copple, Washington, DC: NAEYC. Reprinted with permission from the National Association for the Education of Young Children.

read the feature *Including All Children: Teaching Self-Help and Social Skills to Children with Disabilities.*

Behaviorism is a learning theory, not a theory of development. Therefore, the principles apply regardless of the age of the learner. However, as the name implies, the effectiveness of behaviorism is *limited* to teaching or changing observable behaviors. Even with this limitation, the important thing to remember is that behaviorism can be highly effective. At times, the wrong behaviors get reinforced, such as when an aggressive child gets what he wants by bullying.

Behaviorism, as epitomized by Skinner's work, is often pitted against developmental theories and teaching approaches. This is usually because behaviorism is connected to specific instructional practices, such as when teachers tell children facts and reward their correct answers. Another strong criticism of behaviorism is that overreliance on external rewards undermines children's internal motivation (Kohn, 2014; Reineke, Sonsteng, & Gartrell, 2008).

For example, paying children to read books may make them less motivated to read on their own when the payment isn't available.

But effective teaching is not an *either/or* choice between constructivism and behaviorism. These theories each apply best to different phenomena. Behaviorism may work to change observable behaviors, but it does not explain, nor is it effective in influencing the less visible but essential processes of thinking, concept development, and problem solving. To explain this kind of learning, we must look to the theories of Piaget or Vygotsky, as described earlier. Building on the work of behaviorists and bridging the gap between behaviorism and cognitive theory is the work of Albert Bandura, described in the next section.

Albert Bandura and Social Cognitive Theory

social cognitive theory
Bandura's theory that people can learn efficiently from observing the consequences of another person's behavior.

Developed by psychologist Albert Bandura (born in 1925), **social cognitive theory** (also called *social learning theory*) is both a behavioral and cognitive theory and therefore serves as a bridge between those two views of learning. Whereas Skinner's work emphasized that a person's behavior needs to be directly reinforced to change, Bandura demonstrated that people can learn more efficiently from observing the consequences of another person's behavior. This theory has important implications for classroom teaching.

Bandura theorized that observational learning depends on learners having an image in their mind of the behavior they observed and its consequences—a memory of an event captured in pictures and/or words. This theory explains an important way that children learn—they observe and then model the behaviors they observe. Bandura's emphasis on the importance of a mental image adds a cognitive dimension to the learning theory and separates it from Skinnerian behaviorism.

To test his hypothesis that children would model observed behaviors, Bandura (1973) conducted hundreds of studies. In now famous research, he filmed situations in which an adult or another child were complimented or rewarded for beating up a plastic inflated clown "Bobo." Then, given the opportunity, kindergarten children who watched the demonstration not only beat up Bobo but also used the exact motions and expressions, "Sockeroo!"

modeling Teacher showing children a skill or desirable way of behaving or speaking; also children imitating the behavior of others.

Modeling and Observational Learning The basic principles of social cognitive theory are (1) children learn by **modeling**—that is, imitating the behavior of

According to Bandura, children learn from watching what other children do and the consequences that follow. What do you think the teacher should do if one of the children is hurting other people?

others—and (2) they can learn vicariously. **Vicarious learning** is based on observing the effects of other people's behavior rather than experiencing the rewards or punishments directly. Consider the following example of modeling:

> Mr. Evans's group of 3-year-olds is getting louder and louder as they boisterously encourage each other to jump up and down and scream at the top of their lungs. Wanting to scream himself, Mr. Evans chooses instead to tiptoe around the group, take Bettina by the hand, and whisper softly to follow him. One by one, the children stop their jumping and begin imitating Mr. Evans's toe walking. Gradually, their voices quiet, in hopes of getting a turn to be the teacher's partner.

The children in Mr. Evans's group observed his behavior and saw that Bettina gained his favor by following his lead. According to Bandura (1986), observational learning has four phases:

1. *Attention.* The first step in observational learning is paying attention. Children pay attention to role models who are interesting, novel, or seemingly powerful. This is why action figures on television garner a lot of children's attention. Teachers use many fun and interesting ways to get and hold children's attention, such as talking through a puppet, having them guess what is hidden in a bag, or simply being excited themselves. Mr. Evans surprised the children with the novel behavior of walking on his tiptoes.
2. *Retention.* During this phase of the process, the teacher models the behavior and gives children a chance to practice it. Mr. Evans's goal was to get the children to lower their voices, so he modeled whispering and got the children talking softly.
3. *Reproduction.* The next step is for children to try to reproduce the behavior on their own. Mr. Evans and Bettina step aside from the group and observe as the other children take their turns whispering and tiptoeing.
4. *Motivation.* Observational learning works because children find that they will be rewarded in some way for imitating the desired behaviors. Such motivation can be based on something that happened in the past or is promised in the future. Or, as in Mr. Evans's class, the potential reward can be vicarious. Seeing Bettina rewarded with the teacher's positive attention encouraged the others to follow her lead.

Self-Regulated Learning Bandura's theory goes even further as a cognitive theory in his concept of **self-regulated learning**. Bandura (1997) postulated that people learn not only by modeling the behavior of others, but also by observing and evaluating their own. Self-regulated learning requires that individuals have internalized standards and that they have the ability to reflect on their own performances and to reward or punish themselves. Bandura's emphasis on self-regulation is similar to Vygotsky's. Both theories view self-regulation as essential for cognitive and social-emotional development.

These high-level cognitive abilities are developing in preschoolers but are further along in most primary-grade children. Teachers can promote self-regulated learning by engaging children in setting goals, evaluating their own performances, and celebrating their successes. For example, Ms. Ross's first-graders do a lot of writing. Periodically she sits down with one child to discuss various pieces of work. The child chooses a few to scan into the computer and preserve in a portfolio. When parents come for a conference, the children talk about why they chose this special piece of work.

Children in the primary grades become capable of setting standards for their own behavior and comparing their performance to that of others. Eight-year-old Melissa is unhappy with herself because she watched TV last night instead of studying, and today she got a failing grade in science.

We have now described the major theories that explain how children develop and learn. Table 4.3 summarizes the theories and their implications for effective teaching. In the following section, we discuss how play contributes to all areas of children's lives.

✓ **Check Your Understanding 4.4:** Learning Theories

vicarious learning Learning by observing the effects of other people's behavior, rather than experiencing rewards or punishments directly.

self-regulated learning Bandura's theory that people not only learn by modeling the behavior of others, but by observing and evaluating their own.

TABLE 4.3 Comparing Theories of Child Development

Theorist and Theory	Summation of Theory	Implications for Practice
Erik Erikson: Stages of Personal and Social Development	Through a hypothesis of four stages of psychological and social development in the lives of children, Erikson identifies how children might typically negotiate personal challenges and resolve them dependent on their age and stage of development.	Erikson's theory emphasizes the role of the sociocultural context on children's personal and social lives. Erikson provides useful observations of developmental patterns so teachers can anticipate and respond to children's needs appropriately.
Abraham Maslow: Self-Actualization Theory	Maslow identified a hierarchy of needs that motivate people's behavior and their ability to reach a hierarchy of personal goals. Maslow pointed out that if basic needs are not met, it is not possible for people to actualize personal satisfaction and succeed at a higher level of growth and learning.	The foundations for self-actualization of goals are laid early in life. Teachers may need to ensure that basic needs—food, water, shelter, safety, and security—are met to assist in helping children to develop a sense of community and belonging, self-esteem, and respect for others.
Jean Piaget: Cognitive Theory	According to Piaget, children learn by constructing their own understanding based on their direct experiences with people and objects. Piaget identified four age-related stages of cognitive development that describe how cognitive abilities change as children get older.	From birth, children are viewed as competent actors in constructing their own understanding. Teachers need to provide an enriching environment and hands-on materials for children to explore and investigate. Teachers facilitate children's engagement in projects.
Lev Vygotsky: Sociocultural Theory	Vygotsky described learning as the result of social interaction within a cultural context. He identified the zone of proximal development (ZPD)—the distance between the actual developmental level a child has achieved (their independent level of problem solving) and the level of potential development they could achieve with adult guidance or through collaboration with other children. The support teachers provide children is called scaffolding.	What children learn is determined by the needs of the culture in which they live. Children learn by solving problems collaboratively with the teacher's support or by working with peers, which is called co-construction or social construction of knowledge. Teachers use many strategies to scaffold learning—gradually providing less assistance as children become more capable of performing on their own. Play is essential for children's development of self-regulation.
Urie Bronfenbrenner: Ecological Model	Bronfenbrenner proposed that the child develops in interaction with many environmental systems—some in which the child doesn't even participate. Family life, parents' employment, state laws, and national culture all influence how each child develops. The most important influences on development, though, are the proximal processes, or daily routines, that children experience in their microsystems of family, school, and community.	Children do best when connections in the mesosystem are strong—when family, child care, and school communicate and work collaboratively to support children's development. The quality of children's daily experiences, though, is most important for development. Teachers emphasize building strong relationships with children and family members—strengthening the child's daily experiences in childcare and school, as well as collaborating with the family to help the child develop and learn.
B. F. Skinner: Behaviorism	Skinner developed the theory of operant conditioning that defines learning as a change in behavior that is controlled by the consequences that follow the behavior. Positive consequences strengthen the frequency of specific behaviors; unpleasant consequences decrease the frequency. Punishment temporarily stops a behavior but does not teach a new one.	Teachers use reinforcement to increase children's positive behavior and decrease their challenging behavior. They use shaping to teach a new, complex skill or behavior by rewarding each step—successive approximation—toward the desired goal.
Albert Bandura: Social Cognitive Theory	Bridging behaviorism and cognitive theory, Bandura demonstrated that people can learn more efficiently from observing the consequences of another person's behavior rather than having to directly experience them. Children learn by modeling the behavior of others. They also learn vicariously, whether the behavior of other people is rewarded or punished.	Teachers model and demonstrate the kinds of behaviors they want children to perform. They draw children's attention to other children's behavior and its positive consequences. Children are motivated to perform behavior that they see rewarded in other people.

The Role of Play in Development and Learning

Psychologists and educators have studied children's play for a very long time. Despite the large body of research supporting its benefits, however, child-initiated play is becoming less valued and is disappearing from children's lives today (Alliance for Childhood, 2010; Hirsh-Pasek, Golinkoff, Berk, & Singer, 2009; Zigler & Bishop-Josef, 2004). Many factors conspire against play: television and digital media, lack of safe playgrounds, overemphasis on direct teaching of literacy and mathematics, and highly structured activities or lessons such as sports or ballet (Elkind, 2008; Hirsh-Pasek et al., 2009).

Early childhood educators deeply value play. But to use play effectively in teaching children, and to advocate for its value, it is important to be clear about what types of play matter and why it is worth defending. In the sections that follow, we describe what play is, how it develops, and how it benefits children.

Types of Play

Play is complex and difficult to define because there are different kinds of play: play with toys, movement play, rough-and-tumble play, make-believe play, and play with games and computers. Most often, *play* is defined as activity that is freely chosen, initiated and controlled by children, and enjoyable. Despite the lack of definitional clarity, most people would say, "You know it when you see it." And more important, children know when they are playing.

Different types of play have different benefits for children. Definitions for different types of play follow:

- *Functional play.* Children play with and manipulate objects, such as when a baby shakes a rattle or a toddler bangs a drum.
- *Constructive play.* Children use toys or objects to create something new, such as making a puppet from a sock, a design on a computer screen, or a castle out of Legos.
- *Symbolic play.* Children use one thing to represent or stand for another. Pretend play is a form of symbolic play. A stick becomes a magic wand. A piece of cloth becomes a veil or a cape.
- *Games with rules.* Children follow prescribed rules for playing together toward a common goal. Games include simple ones such as *Candyland* or *Chutes and Ladders*, as well as complex ones such as chess or baseball.

Piaget related types of play to stages of development (Johnson, Christie, & Wardle, 2005). He theorized that functional play dominates the sensorimotor stage (birth to 2 years) and that the preoperational stage (2 to 7 years) is characterized by symbolic and constructive play. Children in the concrete operational stage (7 to 11 years) tend to play games with rules. Children's pretend play becomes more complex over time, especially if people play with them and provide props. The following sections describe this sequence.

Functional Play   Babies and toddlers engage in functional play, focusing on objects and then on the people who use the objects with them. Toddlers enjoy repetition and practice as they play—for example, when they bang a toy hammer over and over.

If parents or teachers pretend with young children during functional play, toddlers will begin to pretend, too. Ms. Morgan sits next to 2-year-old Hester, picks up a cup, and pretends to drink. "This is delicious tea," she says. Soon Hester takes a cup and says, "Yum." This type of pretense is the foundation for later symbolic play.

Constructive Play   Constructive play begins as functional play and becomes more symbolic as children use objects to create new ones. For example, children act out pretend roles during block building. Constructive play aids logico-mathematical learning and can be as basic as a 2-year-old stacking three blocks or as complex as a second grader building a model airplane.

symbolic representation The process of mentally using one thing to stand for something else.

Symbolic Play

Play helps build **symbolic representation**—using one thing to mean something else—such as when letters are used to represent sounds or number symbols represent quantities. At first, toddlers use real objects or toys in their pretend play, such as picking up the cup and pretending to drink. If adults encourage this type of play, children use other objects in their play. They might pretend that a block is a cup. Finally, children who have lots of experience with pretend play no longer need an object to pretend, using their hands to represent drinking from a cup or stomping their feet and saying, "I'm an elephant." This type of play helps children move from thought that is linked to physical actions to the ability to use words and other symbols to represent concepts (Piaget, 1962; Vygotsky, 1962).

By the time most children turn 4 years old, they begin to develop more complex play with roles and symbolic uses of props. Many preschool- and even kindergarten-age children, however, still play at the toddler level. Bodrova and Leong (2012b) define this kind of repetitive, unimaginative play as "immature play" to distinguish it from the "mature play" that is expected of 4- and 5-year-olds. Mature play promotes self-regulation, executive function, and other skills (Diamond & Lee, 2011).

Games with Rules

As children move into primary grades, they spend less time in pretend play and more time playing games with rules (e.g., sports and board or computer games). Games, including well-designed digital games, can build turn-taking skill, delay of gratification, problem-solving, strategizing, and motivation to learn (Lieberman, 2006).

Games require children to follow the established rules; they rarely get a chance to discuss, negotiate, or change the rules—which would contribute to the development of social competence and self-regulation (Bodrova & Leong, 2012a). When pretend play is replaced by sports or other organized activities during the preschool years, these important foundational skills might not develop fully (Bodrova & Leong, 2012a).

© Benjamin LaFramboise/Pearson Education

Vygotsky saw play as the leading activity of the preschool years. Socio-dramatic play—when children dress up and play parts in a scenario—builds many skills such as language and self-regulation.

The Benefits of Play

Research demonstrates that play contributes to language development, self-regulation, attention, creativity, problem solving, and social and emotional skills (Berk, Mann, & Ogan, 2006; Bodrova & Leong, 2012b; Diamond & Lee, 2011). Play has been found to help prepare children for school (Frost, Wortham, & Reifel, 2012). Research also links play to children's literacy and mathematics skills (Ginsburg, 2006; Zigler, Singer, & Bishop-Josef, 2004).

Children's play can be enhanced through adult intervention, as in the *Tools of the Mind* curriculum described previously. Sara Smilansky (1968), an Israeli psychologist, conducted seminal studies of play among children living in poverty. She found that they did not engage in the same kind of mature sociodramatic play favored by their middle-class peers and were behind in other areas as well. Smilansky trained children to play in more complex ways—using modeling and other techniques—which significantly improved their language and social and cognitive development, findings that have been replicated with other populations (Smilansky & Shefatya, 1990).

> **▶ Classroom Connection**
>
> Children love to play and so do animals. Learn more in this video about how play is hard-wired into our brains and why it is important for development.
>
> https://www.youtube.com/watch?v=4Z_hMYGAQ6k

Play and Motivation

Although it is very important for children's development, play is not the only way that children learn, as we have seen from examining several different theories. If so, why is it so important for teachers to defend and use play as a major context for teaching and learning? One reason is that preschool children themselves are intrinsically motivated to play. Play is so enjoyable for children that teachers don't need to coerce or cajole them to participate (Bredekamp, 2004).

In one study (Wiltz & Klein, 2001), preschoolers were asked what they like to do at school. Ninety-eight percent of the children said play was their favorite activity. When asked what they did not like about school, nearly a third of the children said meanness by teachers or peers, and others did not like naptime and time-out. But many also disliked circle time, especially in poorer-quality programs where it lasted 30 to 40 minutes and involved repetition of calendar, letters, and numbers. Even in high-quality classrooms where circle time was more interesting and engaging, many children reported disliking it primarily because it takes too long. As one little boy, Don, said, "Well, I don't really like . . . you know, like sit in circle and listen . . . I don't like that part [because] I think it's too long for me. I'd rather be playing" (Wiltz & Klein, 2001, p. 225).

 Check Your Understanding 4.5: The Role of Play in Development and Learning

Connecting Theory and Practice

Too often, teachers think that theories of child development and learning have little relevance to their daily work with children, but the opposite is true. Theory and practice are, or should be, integrally connected. We conclude the chapter with an overview of the research-based and theory-derived principles that are the basis for developmentally appropriate practice.

Looking across theories and research, teachers can become confused. As we have seen, theories explain different aspects of children's learning or development, and at times they may seem contradictory. How can teachers make sense of diverse theories? To address these questions, we provide a framework for thinking holistically about development and learning.

NAEYC (2009) summarizes the research and theory undergirding developmentally appropriate practice in a list of principles. Although these principles do not cover everything teachers need to know about development and learning, they highlight some of the key concepts that have implications for practice. In Table 4.4 the principles are listed and illustrated with a few examples.

TABLE 4.4 Principles of Development and Learning to Guide Practice

Principle of Development and Learning	Implications for Practice	Example
Principle 1: Domains of children's development—physical, social, emotional, and cognitive—are closely related. Development in one domain influences and is influenced by development in other domains.	Curriculum should be comprehensive, addressing development and learning of the whole child.	During a project on animals, 4-year-olds learn science concepts about animals' natural environments, use language and literacy to tell and illustrate stories about their favorite animals, and act out those animals' movements.
Principle 2: Many aspects of children's learning and development follow well-documented sequences, with later abilities, skills, and knowledge building on those already acquired.	Teachers need to know the predictable, but not rigid, sequences of development and learning so they can assess children accurately and plan for children's continued progress.	Ms. Rodriguez is familiar with the scope and sequence in the first-grade reading curriculum, so she adjusts her expectations and work with children individually and in small groups at their various levels of reading ability.
Principle 3: Development and learning proceed at varying rates from child to child, as well as at uneven rates across different areas of a child's individual functioning.	Teachers need to get to know each child well, regularly observing and assessing each child's abilities, skills, knowledge, and dispositions.	Josh is 3 years old and very verbal, while Jon, also 3, seldom speaks. Jon has excellent fine motor skills that Josh lacks. Their teacher pairs them to play with interlocking blocks, where they practice and improve their language and motor skills.
Principle 4: Development and learning result from a dynamic and continuous interaction of biological maturation and experience.	Teachers recognize that although there are inborn individual differences and limits on children's learning based on maturation, experience plays a large role in children's development. Teachers know the benefits of early intervention for preventing later problems.	Kindergarten teachers explain to parents that the "gift of time"—holding children out of school until they are older—is not a good policy because children will benefit more from the experience of attending school rather than simply waiting to mature.
Principle 5: Early experiences have both cumulative and delayed effects on individual children's development. Optimal periods exist for certain types of development and learning.	Teachers need to know research on the short- and long-term effects of early experience.	In her family childcare home, Mrs. Pickett rarely uses TV because too much exposure can harm children's long-term attention spans and doesn't build language the way real conversation does.
Principle 6: Development proceeds toward greater complexity, self-regulation, and symbolic or representational capacities.	Teachers add greater complexity to learning experiences over time. Teachers engage children in conversations about thinking and problem solving.	Because young children often "think out loud," preschool teachers don't expect silent classrooms. They organize activities for children that encourage conversation.
Principle 7: Children develop best when they have secure, consistent relationships with responsive adults and opportunities for positive relationships with peers.	Teachers develop a warm, positive, trusting relationship with each child. Teachers protect the physical health and safety of each child.	At the beginning of the school year, Ms. Vargas conducts a home visit or meets with parents to get to know each child and family. She takes time to talk with each child every day.
Principle 8: Development and learning occur in and are influenced by social and cultural contexts.	Teachers recognize that children's competence acquired in their home culture may not be apparent in the school culture, and know that what is meaningful to children varies, depending on their culture and language.	Concerned about Marta's language development, Ms. Kamp works with a Spanish bilingual teacher, Ms. Gonzales, to obtain an accurate assessment of Marta's vocabulary and grammar in her home language.
Principle 9: Always mentally active in seeking to understand the world around them, children learn in a variety of ways; a wide range of teaching strategies and interactions are effective in supporting all of these kinds of learning.	Teachers use a variety of teaching strategies—both teacher-guided and child-guided—to meet the needs of individual children. Teachers use a variety of learning contexts—large group, small group, and individual, carefully considering each child's unique learning needs.	Ms. Hayes demonstrates and instructs the children in how to move the images on the computer screen for a new math program. The children take turns experimenting with the program, with Ms. Hayes close by to provide assistance as needed.

(Continued)

TABLE 4.4 Principles of Development and Learning to Guide Practice *(Continued)*

Principle of Development and Learning	Implications for Practice	Example
Principle 10: Play is an important vehicle for developing self-regulation as well as promoting language, cognition, and social competence.	Teachers purposefully plan time and materials for children's educationally valuable play. Teachers observe children at play and interact constructively with them.	Ms. Phillips models customer behavior in the grocery store center in her kindergarten, while children engage in counting money, reading labels, making lists, and using vocabulary as they play.
Principle 11: Development and learning advance when children are challenged to achieve at a level just beyond their current mastery, and also when they have many opportunities to practice newly acquired skills.	Teachers provide children with experiences at which they can be successful as well as providing them with some experiences that are at the "just achievable" level of challenge to stretch their learning and development.	Mr. Durkin observes that many children are interested in writing only their own names. He suggests that friends write each other's names and provides name cards as models.
Principle 12: Children's experiences shape their motivation and approaches to learning, such as persistence, initiative, and flexibility; in turn, these dispositions and behaviors affect their learning and development.	Teachers draw on and cultivate children's interests to get their attention and keep them engaged in learning. Teachers encourage positive approaches to learning such as curiosity and creativity.	Ms. Elias's kindergartners show little interest in the required reading workbooks. She encourages the children act out the stories, make up songs, and write their own stories—experiences that encourage engagement with the literature.

Source: Based on *Developmentally Appropriate Practice in Early Childhood Programs Serving Children from Birth through Age 8,* revised edition, edited by C. Copple & S. Bredekamp, 2009, Washington, DC: National Association for the Education of Young Children.

In promulgating this list of principles, NAEYC (Copple & Bredekamp, 2009, pp. 10–11) offers several caveats. First, while the list is comprehensive, it is not exhaustive; other principles could be added. In addition, just as all domains of development and learning are interconnected, so too are the principles. For instance, cultural and individual variations are addressed in separate principles, and yet they play a role in all of the other principles. In other words, decisions about applying any given principle should consider children as individuals and as members of cultural groups. Despite these limitations, the principles reflect a solid base of research to guide teachers' decision making.

 Check Your Understanding 4.6: Connecting Theory and Practice

Revisiting the Case Study

. . . Ms. Donati's Classroom

We began this chapter by visiting Yvonne Donati's classroom. Having examined various theories of learning and their applications, we can see her practices in a clearer light. Yvonne operates from a constructivist perspective. She sees children as active learners and structures her classroom and plans curriculum accordingly. Yvonne also implements sociocultural theory as she scaffolds children's learning in the zone of proximal development through appropriately timed prompts, questions, and assistance. She applies brain research, building positive relationships, and research on play.

Although Yvonne's teaching practices primarily reflect cognitive theories, she also applies principles of operant conditioning—reinforcements to increase positive behaviors. Yvonne discovers that behavioral principles can be particularly effective under certain circumstances, such as when she applies them for a limited period of time in working with Maya's special need.

Finally, Yvonne does some theory building of her own by testing her hypotheses about children's play with an informal research study. Theories are born, grow, or die from research that often begins in informal observations of children such as Yvonne's. ■

4   Chapter Summary

- Development is age-related change that occurs as the result of an interaction between biological maturation and physical and/or social experience. Learning is a change in knowledge or skill that results from experience or instruction.

- A theory is an explanation of how information and observations are organized and relate to one another. Theories are important because they affect how people think and behave. In education, theories of learning and development affect how teachers treat children, how they structure environments, and how they teach.

- Early experiences change and organize the physical structure of the brain. Neglect, abuse, and stress pose serious threats to healthy brain development. High-quality, developmentally appropriate early childhood education can contribute to healthy brain development.

- The most influential theories of social-emotional development are Erikson's psychosocial theory and

Maslow's hierarchy of needs. The most prominent theories of cognitive development are Piaget's theory of constructivism and Vygotsky's sociocultural theory. A theory for understanding the interactive influence of social and cultural contexts on human development is Bronfenbrenner's ecological systems model.

- The most prominent learning theories are B. F. Skinner's theory of behaviorism and Albert Bandura's social cognitive theory.

- Research demonstrates that play contributes to language development, self-regulation, attention, creativity, problem solving, social and emotional skills, and literacy and mathematics skills.

- Effective early childhood education is based on knowledge of child development and learning. NAEYC summarizes the key concepts of that knowledge base in 12 principles that can be used to guide practice.

Key Terms

- accommodation
- adaptation
- assimilation
- behaviorism or behavioral learning
- chronosystem
- cognitive development
- co-construction
- consequences
- conservation
- constructivism
- development
- domains of development
- domain-general processes
- disequilibrium
- ecological systems theory

- egocentrism
- equilibration
- emotional development
- executive function
- exosystem
- extinction
- 5- to 7-year shift
- hypothesis
- learning
- logico-mathematical knowledge
- macrosystem
- maturationist
- mesosystem
- microsystem
- modeling
- negative reinforcement

- neurons
- object permanence
- operant conditioning
- physical development
- physical knowledge
- plasticity
- positive reinforcement
- private speech
- proximal processes
- pruning
- punishment
- reinforcer
- scaffolding
- scheme or schema
- self-actualization theory
- self-regulated learning
- self-regulation

- shaping
- social cognitive theory
- social-conventional knowledge
- social development
- sociocultural theory
- successive approximations
- symbolic representation
- synapses
- theory
- toxic stress
- vicarious learning
- windows of opportunity
- zone of proximal development (ZPD)

Demonstrate Your Learning

Click here to assess how well you've learned the content in this chapter.

Readings and Websites

Copple, C. (Ed.). (2012). Growing minds: Building strong cognitive foundations in early childhood. Washington, DC: NAEYC.

Mooney, C. G. (2013). *Theories of childhood: An introduction to Dewey, Montessori, Erikson, Piaget, and Vygotsky* (2nd ed.). St. Paul, MN: Redleaf Press.

Nell, M. L., Drew, W. F., & Bush, D. E. (2013). *From play to practice: Connecting teachers' play to children's learning*. Washington, DC: NAEYC.

Mind in the Making website

Ellen Galinsky's book, *Mind in the making: The seven essential life skills every child needs*, and website of the same name, provide a useful description for families and teachers of how to support children developing life skills that are essential for healthy development and learning and success in life, including executive function and self-regulation.

Center on the Developing Child at Harvard University

This website has rich resources about brain development and explains how early relationships and experiences shape the brain and behavior of the child. There are several videos and powerpoints to use for teaching adults about the importance of healthy brain development, as well as activities to use with children and families.

ZERO to THREE

Explore this website for information on the development of infants and toddlers. You'll also find information for supporting brain development and young children's mental health, and resources for teachers and families.

National Association for the Education of Young Children (NAEYC)

The NAEYC website has a section dedicated to *Play and Learning* including research, books and teaching resources. Information on gender in play, how to choose toys, and how to support play at different ages is included.

5 Adapting for Individual Differences

Learning Outcomes

After studying this chapter, you should be able to:

5.1 Identify the kinds and sources of individual differences among children.

5.2 Describe what teachers need to know about variation among children, and identify ways to accommodate individual differences.

5.3 Restate Gardner's Theory of Multiple Intelligences, and discuss its implications for teaching practices.

5.4 Compare ways of differentiating instruction to adapt for individual differences in ability, interest, and personality among children.

5.5 Explain practices that are required by law for children with disabilities and special needs.

5.6 Apply your knowledge of effective practices for teaching children with special needs to teaching all children.

© Kali9/E+/Getty Images

Lindsay Creighton is ready for open house night. When Shira arrives with her mom in tow, she greets Lindsay with an exuberant hug and turns to see Rohan coming down the hall. "Rohan! It's the open house!" Rohan clings to his father's leg. He is painfully shy and seems unnerved by Shira's enthusiastic greeting. His father says, "Go play with Shira." But Rohan retreats and shakes his head "no."

The next to arrive are Cal and his grandmother. "Cal!" screams Shira, and the two embrace. Cal runs by his grandmother on his way to play, and she speaks sternly to him in Chinese. He stops running. Slowly he moves to the block corner with Shira. When she hands him a pink car, Cal sighs, "This is for girls. I need a boy car."

Carter and his parents arrive. Shira says hello to Carter, but then speaks to his parents, "Carter can play if he wants." Carter flaps his arms and repeats a favorite phrase from a children's movie. He moves closer to Shira and grabs her cheeks. His parents intervene and say, "Too close, Carter." Behind Carter and his parents are the twins, Alice and Alexandra. Shira's mom, Beth, greets them, "Hello, Alice. Hello, Alex." Alice rolls her eyes and says, "You got us mixed up again!" Beth apologizes, but the twins' mom says, "Even I get them mixed up sometimes, until they are in a place like this. Just watch. Alice will try to take over, and Alex will stay in a quiet corner until the open house is over." Ruby is the last to arrive. Her father immediately asks Lindsay if any of the food has nuts. When Lindsay says, "No, I made sure," he still asks to see the ingredient labels due to Ruby's severe allergy.

Later, Lindsay reflects on the evening. Although the children are all about the same age, they are so different. She marvels at the fact that even the identical twins have such different personalities. She wonders if Rohan's shyness is exacerbated by his father's insistence on participation. And what about Shira—how did she get to be such a social butterfly? Is it in her genes, or did her parents cultivate that, too?

Lindsay's thoughts turn to Carter, who has autism. She considers how well his parents coordinate with his teacher and other specialists to reinforce what he's learning in school. Lindsay also thinks of 5-year-old Cal, living with his grandmother after his mother's parental rights were revoked as a result of neglect. How is it that he is such a positive and vivacious boy given all he has had to deal with in his young life? Lindsay smiles when she thinks about Cal wanting a "boy car." How and when do these gender stereotypes crystallize?

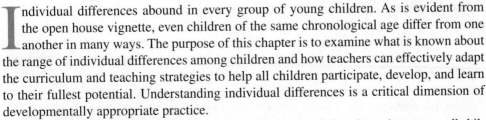

Finally, her thoughts turn to the challenges she faces. How will she be able to meet the needs of these children? How will she provide experiences that challenge Shira and Cal but don't overwhelm Carter? How will she make Rohan and Alex feel at ease in social situations? And how will she create a strong sense of belonging and friendship among these children? ∎

Individual differences abound in every group of young children. As is evident from the open house vignette, even children of the same chronological age differ from one another in many ways. The purpose of this chapter is to examine what is known about the range of individual differences among children and how teachers can effectively adapt the curriculum and teaching strategies to help all children participate, develop, and learn to their fullest potential. Understanding individual differences is a critical dimension of developmentally appropriate practice.

We begin with a discussion of the range of individual variation that exists among all children and some of the origins of these differences. Next we describe Howard Gardner's theory of multiple intelligences, which is a useful framework for thinking about individual children's strengths, needs, interests, and abilities. Then we discuss differentiating instruction and present a framework for responding to the diverse learning needs of all children. We conclude with a discussion of effective practices for teaching children with disabilities and special needs.

🏠 The Importance of Individual Differences

Anyone who has been a parent or a teacher is aware of the fact that every child is unique. Even people who do not have parenting or teaching experience have been children themselves and know that we are all different. Try to remember your earliest school experience and picture the children in your class. Were all the boys or girls alike? Did everyone enjoy and excel at the same activities? Did all of your classmates learn at the same pace and in the same way? Was anyone exactly like you? Of course, the answer to all of these questions is "No."

Acknowledging the uniqueness of each child is only the beginning. Effective early childhood teachers understand typical and atypical child development; they also understand the importance of knowing each child as an individual. They use this knowledge to plan and adapt curriculum and to help each child meet important learning goals (NAEYC, 2009).

Why Pay Attention to Individual Differences?

One of the most well-known facts about child development is that there is a wide range of individual variation (Shonkoff & Phillips, 2000). But what does "wide range" mean and what are the implications for teachers? The concept of a range of variation is based on an average; for example, we might say that, on average, men are 5′ 10″ tall. This average was calculated based on the heights of a huge number of men. When we consider their heights individually, however, they may range from 4′ 8″ to 7′ 1″. Now, consider a range of variation in relation to children's development. On virtually every characteristic we could measure—saying first words, balancing on one foot, knowing the alphabet—the pace and timing of children's performance vary. The average age at which most children master a skill, for example, doesn't tell us much without knowing the range, which gives us a far clearer picture of reality.

In general, teachers need to be cautious about focusing too much on averages. Many aspects of schooling, including the graded structure and power of standardized tests, tend to reflect the assumption that all children will achieve certain skills and knowledge at the same time. As a result, the tendency is for schools to ignore the range of variation and to try to teach all children the same way.

But if we want every child to achieve the same goals, we must treat them and teach them as individuals. Acknowledging that individual differences exist does not mean lowering expectations for some children. In fact, high expectations for children's learning are necessary if they are to succeed. In the sections that follow, we describe some important aspects of variation among children. But first we discuss theories about the origin of individual differences—the question of nature versus nurture.

Where Do Individual Differences Come From?

One of the most enduring debates in psychology is the degree to which development is the product of biology (nature) or environment (nurture). The question is often framed as whether nature or nurture is more influential in determining who we become as individuals. Although we know that physical characteristics are inherited, the genetic markers are less clear when it comes to an individual's behavior, intelligence, and personality. Consider the twins in Lindsay Creighton's classroom at the beginning of this chapter. Is Alice more outgoing and Alex more cautious because these personality traits are not part of the genetic pattern they share? Or does this difference result because their parents encouraged the girls in different ways?

The Influence of Biology on Development In the past, some psychologists (Jensen, 1980) proposed that people behave as they do because of inborn characteristics. This belief emphasizes the influence of **nature**, the hereditary or genetic

nature The hereditary or genetic contributions to human development.

contributions to human development. Whether we are male or female, have freckles, black hair, or a certain type of personality can be influenced by genetic factors.

Nature also refers to the biological and neurological drivers of development. For example, physical growth and advances in motor skills for most humans develop in a predictable sequence. Newborn reflexes soon give rise to voluntary movements and the development of abilities such as rolling over, crawling, walking, and running. Similarly, language development has a biological component. The fact that most infants, regardless of culture, begin to coo and babble at approximately the same ages provides strong evidence that nature indeed affects development.

Every class of young children is made up of unique individuals. Intentional teachers must find ways to meet the needs of every child while also challenging each one to make continued learning progress.

© Christopher Futcher/E+/Getty Images

Whereas some aspects of nature influence a similar course of development for most children, genetics also affects individual differences. For example, most children take their first steps by about 1 year of age, but there is a wide range of variation among individuals. David took his first steps at 7 months; his brother Jeffrey wasn't mobile until 18 months.

The Role of the Environment Although biology influences individual differences, some scientists (Skinner, 1953, 1968) believe that people behave in certain ways more as a result of their experiences in the environment or because they are taught to do so. This belief stresses the influence of **nurture** on human behavior.

Heredity may play a role in influencing personality traits, but according to the nurture perspective, environmental factors ultimately determine who we become. Parents' discipline methods, for example, might have more influence on their children's behavior than the parents' genetic contributions. Other dimensions of the environment also influence children's development, such as the family's economic resources, the quality of their child care setting, the number of siblings in the home, and the safety of the community.

nurture Environmental factors and experiences that influence human development and behavior.

The Transactional Relationship between Nature and Nurture Although the nature versus nurture debate continues, the current thinking is that "nature and nurture are partners in how developing people interact with the surrounding environment" (Shonkoff & Phillips, 2000, p. 39). The **transactional theory of development** (Sameroff, 2009) explains that development is the result of *both* biology *and* experience and the ways in which they influence each other.

transactional theory of development Theory that development is the result of both biology and experience and how they influence each other.

To illustrate how nature and nurture interact, consider the following examples. Myra, a highly verbal and inquisitive 6-year-old, seems to inspire her teacher to engage her in intellectually stimulating projects, such as finding out what causes earthquakes, which in turn further Myra's already accelerated development and learning. By contrast, Alyssa, who is deaf, is withdrawn and rarely joins in activities even though her teacher uses sign language. Alyssa's lack of responsiveness may provoke her teacher to initiate communication with her less often.

Both biology and experience play critical, interrelated roles in children's development. Therefore, the kinds of experiences children have become vitally important. As the Center on the Developing Child at Harvard University (2010) reports, "Experiences children have early in life—and the environments in which they have them—shape their developing brain architecture and strongly affect whether they grow up to be healthy, productive members of society" (p. 1).

> ▶ **Classroom Connection**
>
> Understand more about how biology and environment interact to influence how individuals develop in different ways in this video "What is Nature vs. Nurture?" What does the presenter say about the importance of environments for how young children develop? What can teachers do to provide positive environments?
>
> https://www.youtube.com/watch?v=P-D33oWiOEg

How Experience Affects Outcomes for Children: Risk or Resilience

According to the transactional theory of development, children's experiences impact their overall development. Accumulation of certain kinds of experiences can place children at risk for negative outcomes. Similarly, if children have repeated positive experiences, their development is likely to be enhanced.

Understanding Risk Factors Risk factors are inherited or experiential conditions that potentially contribute to negative outcomes for children (Huffman et al., 2001). Among the most frequently identified risk factors are living in poverty, living with a single parent, low education level of parents, disability, and child abuse (Moore, 2006). The concept of risk factors has led to the use of the term *children at risk* of school failure.

> **risk factors** Inherited or experiential conditions that potentially contribute to poor developmental outcomes for children, such as peer rejection, academic failure, juvenile delinquency, and school expulsion.

When risk factors multiply in children's lives, they produce a growing number of poor developmental outcomes (Burchinal & Willoughby, 2013). That is, the more risk factors children have, the more likely they are to experience developmental delays and social or health problems. These conditions, in turn, can lead to a host of poor outcomes such as peer rejection, academic failure, dropping out of school, mental health disorders, or criminal behavior.

Promoting Resilience Research on children with multiple risk factors demonstrates that exposure to risk and adversity does not necessarily result in negative outcomes for some children (Center on the Developing Child at Harvard University, 2010). Positive, supportive experiences can mediate risk and help children become resilient (Masten & Powell, 2003). Resilience refers to a child's ability to overcome, adapt to, or minimize the damaging effects of adversity (Werner & Smith, 2001).

> **resilience** A child's ability to overcome, adapt to, or minimize the damaging effects of adversity.
>
> **protective factors** Mechanisms, both inherited and experiential, that may minimize the potentially negative effects for children living in identified high-risk situations.

Mechanisms—called **protective factors**—exist that may minimize the potentially negative effects for children living in identified high-risk situations. Like risk factors, protective factors are both inherited (nature) and experiential (nurture). A continuous, positive parent-child relationship has been found to be one of the most important contributors to the development of resilience (Thompson & Goodman, 2009). Other protective factors include a variety of external social supports such as extended family, membership in a church or spiritual group, and close friends and neighbors.

Children's inherent characteristics also contribute to resilience. For example, resilient children often possess temperaments in infancy that elicit positive responses from their caregivers (Shonkoff & Phillips, 2000). For example, Stefano is a happy, easily soothed baby who draws positive attention from everyone. Timothy, on the other hand, cries all night and doesn't nurse readily. His mother begins to feel inadequate and has difficulty attaching to him.

In short, risk and resilience are not the result of either biology or environment alone. Rather, the interactions between children's biological makeup and their experiences contribute to the wide variation among children and families (Gest & Davidson, 2011). Teachers must remember that a child's genetic inheritance or environmental circumstances should never limit their expectations of children. In fact, one of the most important sources of resilience in children is positive relationships with teachers (Hamre & Pianta, 2010; Howes & Ritchie, 2002; Sabol & Pianta, 2013).

✔ **Check Your Understanding 5.1:** The Importance of Individual Differences

⬆ What We Know About Individual Differences

Children whose development is well within the typical range differ from one another in many ways. Gender is a key area where biology and environment interact to influence development, as described in the next section.

Gender Differences

"Is it a boy or a girl?" seems to be the first question asked about a new baby. From the first moments of life, and even prenatally, powerful assumptions are made about children on the basis of their sex. These assumptions are soon influenced by experience. When 3-year-old Lucienne receives a soccer ball and goal, she insists that she cannot play with them because "It's for boys." Her belief was reinforced by the fact that the packaging showed two boys playing soccer. Indeed, stereotypes about girls and boys are durable and pervasive, which raises questions about what the actual differences are, if any, in the development and characteristics of boys and girls.

Physical Development There is little evidence of gender differences in most domains of development and learning. In some domains, however, the characteristics of females and males have been found to differ. Physically, for example, females are typically more mature at birth, and males are more likely to be miscarried, die in infancy, or develop hereditary diseases (Jacklin, 1989). On average, females also reach developmental milestones, such as talking earlier, than do males (Bukatko & Daehler, 2003). Current research is beginning to reveal some sex differences in brain structure, but much remains to be learned before definite conclusions can be drawn (Woolfolk & Perry, 2015).

Cognitive Skills Although there are no significant gender-based differences in overall intelligence, tests of cognitive abilities find some specific differences between girls and boys. Notably, boys demonstrate a slight but consistent advantage in the domain of visual-spatial rotation (Woolfolk & Perry, 2015), the ability to visualize and mentally transform or rotate figures or objects. While this ability is related to success in other mathematics areas, evidence suggests that early experience and attitudes toward mathematics may play a more important role in mathematical learning (Krinzinger, Wood, & Willmes, 2012).

Some evidence suggests, however, that gender differences in visual-spatial ability are to some extent a product of children's experience (Clements & Sarama, 2008). For example, during the preschool years, boys tend to spend more time than girls do involved in the kinds of activities that build visual-spatial skills: building with blocks, playing with Legos, and putting puzzles together. When girls engage in such play and teachers make the experience meaningful, such as talking with them about what they are doing or reading a story about shapes, girls perform as well as boys on these visual-spatial tasks (Casey, Erkut, Ceder, & Young, 2008).

Social Behavior Popular culture suggests that vast differences exist in social behavior between females and males; however, scientific research suggests that few broad gender differences exist in the area of social behaviors (Eliot, 2009). There are, however, subtle differences. Girls engage in more imaginary play than boys do, while boys tend to play in slightly larger groups and their play generally takes up more space (Woolfolk & Perry, 2015). Girls tend to form more intimate play and friendships (Dolgin & Kim, 1994), whereas boys' friendships are more geared toward a mutual interest in activities (Erwin, 1998). And even as early as 2 years of age, girls talk more about emotion than boys do (Cervantes & Callanan, 1998).

Perhaps the most notable gender difference is that boys are more overtly aggressive than girls beginning in the preschool years. Possibly as a result of male hormones, boys are also more physically active and more likely to engage in rough-and-tumble play (Woolfolk & Perry, 2015). They display more physical aggression, try to dominate peers, and subsequently display more antisocial behaviors than females (Woolfolk & Perry, 2015).

Although it is tempting to think these gender differences are innate, the reality is more complicated. Current thinking is that sex differences in social behaviors are heavily influenced by the situation (Zakriski, Wright, & Underwood, 2005). Because boys and girls are often observed playing with their same-sex peers, differences between the sexes can appear to be greater than they really are and similarities less obvious (Maccoby, 2002). For example, preschooler Leo gets into frequent fights with his peers and appears to be more aggressive than Johanna. But this difference might have more to do with Leo's rough-and-tumble play than any innate tendency to aggressive behavior.

In addition, gender differences in aggression are largely a function of where the behavior occurs and how aggression is defined. The largest gender differences are found in less structured, natural environments such as on the playground. However, when aggression consists of attempts to hurt another person through manipulation, gossip, or exclusion from a social group, it is called *relational aggression*. When we consider relational aggression, girls are more aggressive than boys starting in the preschool years (Burr, Ostrov, Jansen, Cullerton-Sen, & Crick, 2005; Crick, Casas, & Mosher, 1997). If Johanna were to be picked on as often as Leo is, she might be perceived as being aggressive, too. There is also the possibility that Johanna would react differently from Leo. Rather than using physical aggression, she would probably resort to relational aggression, such as name-calling or saying, "I won't be your friend."

Gender-Related Expectations   Although gender is a biological trait, much gender-related behavior is learned. From very early ages, children receive messages about what is expected of girls and boys that influence their behavior. By preschool age, children are beginning to firmly establish their gender identity, although they may still think that changing their clothes or activity can affect it. Sex-role stereotyping can play a powerful role in the classroom.

Among the individual differences that have the greatest significance for teachers are variations in cognitive development and abilities, social and emotional development (including temperament), approaches to learning, physical development, and interests. These topics are discussed briefly in the sections that follow.

Cognitive Development and Abilities

A major contributor to individual differences is variation in language development. Consider the fact that although, on average, babies say their first word at 11 months, the range is from 8 to 14 months (Hart & Risley, 1999). In addition, although the average age at which half of what children say is understandable is 19 months, the range is from 15 to 30 months (Hart & Risley, 1999), making teaching toddlers a challenging task indeed.

As children get older, variation only increases. Observations of 2-year-olds demonstrate that, on average, children produce 134 different words per hour, but the range is from 18 to 286 words (Hart & Risley, 1999). Such wide variation makes it challenging for teachers and parents to determine whether a child's development is just at the slow end of the range or is actually delayed.

By the time children reach kindergarten, their language, literacy, and mathematics abilities vary widely, and the achievement gap is already apparent (Hart & Risley, 2003; West, Denton, & Germino-Hausken, 2000). However, it is important to remember our earlier caution about averages when thinking about a large group of individuals such as children from low-income families. A wide range of variation exists within this group as well; although many children will be far behind, others will not. A large national study found that although Head Start children on average score below national norms, especially in vocabulary, the top one-quarter of the children scored at national averages on letter recognition and writing skills (Tarullo, Aikens, Moiduddin, & West, 2010).

Emotional and Social Development

Social skills and emotional self-regulation are among the most important skills for success in school and life. Positive social skills include the ability to make friends, join in play, and comfort other children in distress (Bowman, Donovan, & Burns, 2001). Children who have poor social skills are more likely to be angry and to argue and fight or withdraw from others.

Individual differences in social and emotional development are often related to temperament, and can often be observed when children are infants and toddlers. **Temperament** refers to individual differences in reactivity and self-regulation as shown in children's emotions, activity level, and attention (Rothbart, 2011). While temperament has genetic and biological roots, research has shown that warm relationships with family members and teachers help all children develop positive social skills, regardless of their temperament type (Bates, 2012; Stright, Gallagher, & Kelley, 2008). One important aspect of temperament is how children react to new situations and people. Recall the twins, Alexandra and Alice, in the chapter-opening vignette. Alice confidently joins in and becomes the life of the party, whereas Alex is fearful and inhibited in the new situation.

> **temperament** The pattern of arousal and emotionality that is characteristic of an individual.

Some studies have shown that children with certain temperament characteristics struggle in school (Gartstein, Putnam, & Rothbart, 2012); however, warm and responsive relationships with caregivers help children to be successful in academics and social relationships (Bates, 2012; Rudasill, Gallagher & White, 2010). Teachers who learn about and understand their children's different temperaments will learn how to adapt the learning setting to meet children's individual needs (Bates, 2012). Instead of assuming that a shy child has poor social skills or that an outgoing, energetic child is too aggressive or out of control, teachers should adapt to each child's needs. Alex's teacher will need to help her feel comfortable in new surroundings and teach her skills for making new friends (Gallagher, 2013). Alice's teacher may need provide gentle guidance for following structured routines, redirecting her energy, and paying attention when needed. Temperament is one dimension of a larger topic, approaches to learning, which is discussed next.

Approaches to Learning

Early childhood educators are becoming increasingly aware that children's *approaches to learning* are critically important determinants of their success in school (Fantuzzo, Perry, & McDermott, 2004; Hyson, 2008). **Approaches to learning** are "behaviors, tendencies or typical patterns that children use in learning situations" (Hyson, 2008, p. 10). These include both how children feel about learning—their level of enthusiasm, interest, and motivation—and how children engage with learning. Do they pay attention? Do they persist when tasks are challenging or frustrating? If one solution doesn't work out, are they flexible and creative in trying something new?

> **approaches to learning** Behaviors, tendencies, or typical patterns that children use in learning situations that include both how they feel about learning—their level of enthusiasm, interest, and motivation—and how they engage with learning.

As with all other aspects of learning and development, there are individual differences in children's approaches to learning, which vary depending on the situation. For example, 7-year-old Wes enjoys taking things apart and putting them together; he will persist for hours working on his simple machines project for science. But during reading class, Wes loses interest and his attention wanders; his reading progress suffers. In response, his teacher brings in several books on machines and Wes's enthusiasm for reading improves.

> There are individual differences in children's approaches to learning. As you can see, this child hesitates to join in play, while others may be enthusiastic and engaged right from the start.

Even a brief visit to a classroom during choice time reveals the diversity of children's approaches to learning. Dontrelle can play with Legos for an hour. Ivy loves music, especially songs with movements, but wanders from one area to another, never alighting on one activity. Becca prefers painting but is perfectly happy if it is not available. The challenge for teachers is to foster children's positive approaches to learning and build on their strengths to help them acquire new abilities.

Physical Development

Children of the same chronological age vary considerably in height and weight. Teachers sometimes inaccurately judge children's maturity based on their physical characteristics. For example, boys who are small for their age may be thought to be less mature than taller boys and inaccurately judged as not ready for kindergarten. At the same time, taller children, girls as well as boys, are often assumed to be older and more capable than they are.

Physical development is largely determined by biology; however, experience also plays a role in how physical skills and abilities develop, as when childhood malnutrition or chronic illness stunts growth. On average, girls develop fine motor skills earlier than boys do, but cultural expectations for girls' behavior may contribute to these differences (Woolfolk & Perry, 2015). Girls, for instance, may be given dolls to dress with miniature clothes and shoes that require fine motor skills, and they may be encouraged by teachers or parents to play in a more restricted way than boys. Similarly, because boys may be less adept with pencils or unable to sit still for group time, teachers might think they are less competent. Just as teachers must understand each child's temperament, they must also come to understand each child's physical skills and capabilities in order to provide a wide range of learning opportunities to find the best match.

Seeing Each Child as an Individual

There is a scene in the movie *Mary Poppins* when Ms. Poppins meets her charges, Jane and Michael, for the first time. The star nanny pulls out her "magical measuring tape." The special tape measurer allows her to instantaneously surmise important and unique information about the children that helps her to plan how she will best care for them. While this type of measuring tape does not exist in reality, it illustrates a necessary first step in working with children: getting to know them.

For teachers to build positive relationships and teach effectively, they need to understand children's preferences, interests, background, and culture. For children, this information is most often accessed by carefully and purposefully observing what they do, and by speaking with parents and other caregivers. The task of knowing children involves observing and assessing on a regular basis.

Some teachers find it helpful for parents to complete surveys about their child. Items on these surveys include family members; pets; fears; favorite foods, toys, or activities; how to tell when their child is upset; or what other special needs a child may have. With this information, teachers can help ensure that children are motivated to get involved, that the content of conversations and level of instruction are relevant, and that they communicate respect for children's families and cultural background.

As we have seen in previous sections, individual differences result from both heredity and experience. A key determinant of children's experience is their culture. For example, cultural groups differ in their views about appropriate behavior for males and females. Cultural differences and individual differences are not the same thing, but they are connected. The *Culture Lens* feature will help you understand the relationship between individual and cultural differences, and respond effectively.

The connection between interests and abilities is the foundation of an important theory relevant to individual differences in human beings. This theory of multiple intelligences is described in the section that follows.

This All About Me interview helps the teacher get to know each child in her class.

All About Me

Name Molly

When I grow up, I want to be a vet

A food I really don't like is peas

A food I love is watermelen

My favorite animal is a dog and a lion

My favorite sport is soccer

When nobody is around I like to have a playdate

My favorite place to be is home and the beach

The things I like to make are freind ship bracks

The thing I like best about school is monky bars freinds and studying animals

Culture Lens
Responding to Cultural and Individual Differences

Early childhood teachers must respond to both individual differences in children and to cultural differences. Why both? When teachers respond to the individual child, aren't they also responding to the cultural child? The answer is yes and no.

Every child is unique and develops an individual personality as a result of her or his personal history. At the same time, everyone develops some behaviors that are shared with members of his or her cultural group. Because culture is a group characteristic, the rules of a culture are shared by group members and are not unique to individuals. When teachers think of children only as individuals, they risk missing important information about what children have learned about group expectations. Consider this example:

> Edwin comes in from outdoor play crying; he is soaked and covered with sand and mud. His teacher, Ms. Amos, starts to undress him to help him get cleaned up and he cries harder. When she tries to help him remove his shoes, he forcefully pulls away. Ms. Amos knows him to be stubborn and tries to coax him into letting her help and consoles him while attempting to undress him, but to no avail. What his teacher doesn't know is that in Edwin's cultural group, you don't get your school clothes dirty, boys don't cry, and boys dress and undress themselves in private.

Had this teacher known more about Edwin's cultural group, she could have responded in a more appropriate way. She might have offered him a change of clothes and let him go to a private place to change himself. On the other hand, what teachers know about group differences when blindly applied to all individuals in a cultural group may be equally inappropriate because individuals within groups differ from one another.

After the incident with Edwin, Ms. Amos decides to learn more about his background. She talks to colleagues and becomes a more careful observer of Edwin and his family, as well as of other children from his cultural group. One day Edwin's cousin Sammy comes in soaked and covered with mud. Ms. Amos decides not to help him clean up, but offers him a change of clothes. When he takes the clean clothes, returns to the playground, and throws them in the sandbox, his teacher is stunned because she expected him to go in the bathroom and change. Sammy, however, was not at all upset by the wet clothes and enjoyed acting contrary to expectations.

So why did the two boys—both from the same cultural group—behave so differently? Because culture is learned; it can be well learned by some people in the group and less well learned by others. Some families are tradition oriented, others less so. Further, even though families and individuals learn the cultural rules, some people conform to what they have learned, while others don't.

Thus, members of a cultural group will behave differently depending on how deeply embedded they are within the core of a culture. Thinking about differences in behavior in this way helps teachers understand why, for instance, all Japanese people don't always "act Japanese." And it helps teachers avoid stereotyping groups and applying untested assumptions about individuals.

An important thing to remember is that knowing who children are as members of cultural groups provides more information than simply knowing them as individuals. But the most important point is that children are both individuals and cultural beings at the same time and in the same place.

 Check Your Understanding 5.2: What We Know about Individual Differences

Multiple Intelligences: A Theory of Individual Differences

A useful framework for thinking about individual differences among children is the **theory of multiple intelligences** developed by Howard Gardner (2004). Rather than thinking about intelligence as one score that can be measured by an intelligence test, Gardner identified eight different intelligences, which are listed and described in Table 5.1. Gardner believes that people have different profiles of strengths and weaknesses among these intelligences. His theory challenges teachers to think of the many different ways children are intelligent and can demonstrate their competence.

Gardner (2004) points out that traditional schooling typically focuses on only two of the intelligences: logical/mathematical and linguistic. Consider the fact that college entrance

theory of multiple intelligences Theory developed by Howard Gardner that identifies eight different intelligences as opposed to a single score on an intelligence test; this theory is useful for thinking about variation among children and teaching to their strengths.

TABLE 5.1 Gardner's Theory of Multiple Intelligences

Intelligence	Definition	Children's Possible Interests in School and Later Life
Logical/mathematical	Ability to reason, analyze, solve logical problems	Earth, space, and physical sciences; mathematics; computers
Linguistic	Ability to communicate; sensitivity to words and functions of language	Reading, writing, teaching, public speaking
Musical	Ability to produce and appreciate music	Singing, playing instruments, composing, listening to music
Naturalist	Sensitivity to the natural world, plants, animals	Outdoor play, nature, biology, environmental science, gardening
Spatial	Ability to perceive the visual-spatial world	Visual arts, photography, architecture, graphic design
Bodily/kinesthetic	Ability to control body movements and objects	Dancing, physical education, sports, movement exploration
Interpersonal	Sensitivity to the feelings and desires of others	Making friends, collaborative learning, social studies
Intrapersonal	Awareness of own feelings and strengths	Keeping a diary, reading, writing poetry, meditation

Sources: Based on Gardner (2004, 2006).

exams result in scores for math and verbal ability. When educators test only children's verbal and math abilities, as is often the case, they miss children's strengths in other important areas such as sociability or psychomotor skills. Gardner also believes that attention to the full range of children's capabilities could help more children succeed in school, thus narrowing the achievement gap for children from low-income families and children of color.

What are the implications of Gardner's theory for teachers? Consider the following example of teaching with multiple intelligences in mind. Hanita Blume teaches a mixed-age group of 4- and 5-year-olds. One of the primary goals of the math curriculum is to develop children's concept of number, which includes counting and beginning operations such as adding and subtracting. The range of ages and experiences among children within her group affects their levels of math ability. She takes these differences into account as well as the fact that each of these children has different capabilities and interests.

Hanita does not try to evaluate individual children's "intelligences." Instead, she plans a variety of learning opportunities to draw on children's strengths and interests to help them all achieve the math goals. Following are some of the learning experiences she provides relevant to each of the multiple intelligences:

- *Logical/mathematical.* Hanita engages children in solving real-world problems with numbers, such as "We have nine children and only five chairs. How many more chairs do we need?"
- *Linguistic.* Hanita reads a counting book in small groups and engages children in counting the objects on each page.
- *Musical.* In large and small groups, Hanita sings counting songs and does fingerplays such as *Five Little Monkeys* to engage children in counting forward and backward.
- *Naturalist.* During outdoor play time, Hanita works with children to make collections of natural objects such as leaves or stones. Children place the objects in categories (large or small, according to color), count the number in each category, and determine which has more or fewer.
- *Spatial.* Hanita provides many different kinds of blocks and small manipulative toys for children to count and categorize, and talks with them, supplying the counting words for those who need the help.
- *Bodily/kinesthetic.* Hanita engages children in using their bodies to learn the counting sequence and concept of number. Children stomp their feet or clap their hands three times, four times, and so on.
- *Interpersonal.* Hanita organizes small cooperative groups of children to work on math games such as *Chutes and Ladders*; children roll the die, read the number of dots, and count the number of spaces. There is no competition.

- *Intrapersonal.* Hanita works one-on-one with some children in tasks such as calculating attendance, and then asks them to reflect on what they know about counting.

As we can conclude from the example of Hanita's classroom, seeing children as individuals with multiple intelligences does not mean that every child must be taught differently. Instead, individual variation among children requires using various teaching practices to be responsive to the abilities of all learners, including children whose development is well above the typical range, as discussed next.

Gifted and Talented Children

A small percentage of children may display highly specialized talents at a young age. Gardner's theory of multiple intelligences is helpful in adapting instruction for these children. What is giftedness? The National Association for Gifted Children (2010) defines it as: "Individuals who demonstrate outstanding levels of aptitude or competence in one or more domains." However, there is no universally accepted definition; giftedness, intelligence, and talent may look different in different contexts and cultures (Heward, 2014). Traditionally, giftedness was determined by a high IQ score, but today broader conceptions are used to identify a child as gifted and talented. A child may be gifted in music, drama, or sports, for instance.

One way to identify young gifted children is to focus on a range of behaviors and characteristics that occur in daily activities as well as in school (Heward, 2014). Some common abilities of gifted young children include (National Association for Gifted Children, 2008):

- Curiosity and thoughtful questions about many things
- Solving problems in unique ways and using prior knowledge in new contexts
- Sustained attention span, willingness to persist on challenging tasks, and good memory
- Especially original imagination, wit, and humor
- Keen observation skills and rapid mastery of new learning
- Desire to work independently and take initiative
- Talent in making up stories and reading

However determined, for their talents to flourish, gifted children need challenging educational experiences and individualized instruction (Coleman & Johnsen, 2011; National Association for Gifted Children, 2010). When interesting, engaging experiences are provided for all children, the needs of gifted children are more likely to be met in a regular classroom.

For example, Melvin's second-grade teacher, Ms. Dell, thinks he is "very precocious." He reads well above grade level and has a large vocabulary. One day he announces to her that his brother is funny. She asks, "How so?" and he answers, "You know, strange, odd, peculiar." Melvin exhibits an intense curiosity, asking high-level questions such as, "Where does gasoline come from?" Ms. Dell modifies the curriculum to challenge him. She sets up a time for Melvin to read to preschoolers. She orders *National Geographic* to satisfy his voracious curiosity about geography. She is also patient with Melvin's persistent questioning that would bother most other adults.

Ms. Dell understands the importance of recognizing early signs of giftedness in young children—particularly in children like Melvin from low-income families who are more often considered at risk than gifted—and nurturing the gift so that it may flourish. She also understands that gifted children's development can be uneven, in that they may have great strengths in many areas but still be at age level or below in others. For example, cognitively gifted children may be very good at articulating school rules and the reasons behind them but at the same time be less able to follow rules in action. A gifted child may also stand out from peers as different and may struggle to make friends.

✓ **Check Your Understanding 5.3:** Multiple Intelligences: A Theory of Individual Differences

Responsive Education for All Learners

In this section, we first describe how intentional teachers adapt their teaching practices in response to individual variation among all children. Then we describe a specific framework for systematically addressing the needs of all learners—Response to Intervention.

Differentiating Instruction

differentiated instruction
The creation of multiple paths so that children of different abilities, interests, and learning needs experience equally appropriate ways to achieve important learning goals.

In every classroom, teachers need to differentiate instruction so that they support the engagement, interest, full participation, and success of every child (Tomlinson, 2014). **Differentiated instruction** refers to creating multiple paths so that children of different abilities, interests, and learning needs experience equally appropriate ways to achieve important learning goals. *Equally appropriate* does not mean the same or uniform. Nor does differentiated instruction mean that children receive their own assignments or that they receive a private, one-on-one lesson. Rather, it means that teachers provide interrelated learning opportunities that help facilitate children's mastery of new skills and content knowledge.

▶ **Classroom Connection**

In this video, the teacher implements a math lesson that takes the form of a game with dominos. How is this game an example of differentiated instruction?

Differentiated instruction is a cyclical process that is illustrated in Figure 5.1. First, teachers must get to know each child in the classroom. They must also know the curriculum. Both of these components influence how teachers plan and differentiate instruction. Planning must take into account the learning environment and materials, the content, the teaching strategies, and the products that demonstrate what children have learned (Tomlinson, 2014), each of which is described next.

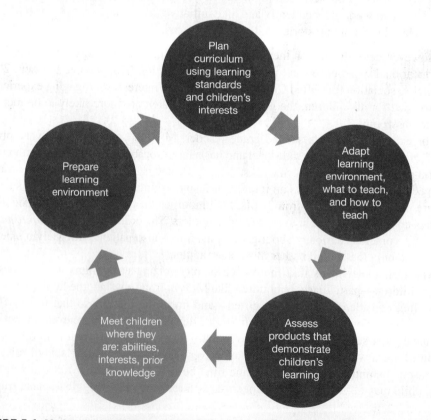

FIGURE 5.1 Model of Differentiated Instruction As illustrated here, differentiated instruction is a cyclical process that enables teachers to meet the needs and support the learning of each individual child.

Plan the Environment The environment refers to the overall look and feel of the classroom. A differentiated environment provides various spaces throughout the classroom for learning to occur. For example, soft, cozy spaces allow some children to work alone. Other spaces are designed for intrapersonal learners to work together in small groups. A differentiated environment also provides a variety of materials. For example, a reading center includes books at different levels on various topics for children. A writing center might have sandpaper letters or plastic magnetic letters for tactile learners. Children who learn best while moving may have places to stand and work at tables.

Differentiate Content Differentiating the content involves meeting children where they are and focusing instruction on what they need to learn next. For example, a child who knows letters can begin to map letter sounds to the alphabet and is also ready to receive instruction on blending letters to make sounds. A child who is skilled at decoding words can focus on fluency and comprehension.

Adapt Teaching Strategies Strategies are the ways teachers provide specific content instruction. The intentional teacher considers the child's abilities and interests when planning content instruction. For example, when teaching science, the teacher provides hands-on tools for children to observe, measure, and record their observations. A computer program or mobile app is motivating for many children. Other examples include providing information books for linguistic learners and cooperative learning activities for the intrapersonal learners.

Assess Learning Products The product that results from differentiated instruction is the demonstration of learning. When content and processes are differentiated for children, the products they produce will be different, too. Consider Josh Peters, a kindergarten teacher in an inclusive classroom. As he is reading a story, he stops occasionally to ask questions. The purpose of asking questions is so the children can demonstrate what they have learned (the product). He asks some children to recall the events of the story and others to predict what will happen next. One child may even be asked to simply point to an illustration of a character in the story. Josh takes each child's level of literacy into account and targets their engagement to successful participation and extending learning.

Response to Intervention (RTI)
A three-tiered framework intended to prevent learning delays in primary grades from becoming learning disabilities.

Response to Intervention

As we have seen, every early childhood classroom is composed of diverse learners—children of widely varying abilities and interests. Although every classroom teacher is responsible for differentiating instruction for the children in her class, in recent years, greater emphasis has been placed on preventing learning problems and intervening earlier for *all* children, rather than waiting until a child falls too far behind or is labeled as having a learning disability. To accomplish this goal, one frequently used approach is **Response to Intervention (RTI)**, a three-tiered, comprehensive framework for bridging assessment and instruction that is intended to prevent school failure, especially in the areas of reading and mathematics (Allington, 2009; National Center on Response to Intervention, 2010; National Professional Development Center on Inclusion [NPDCI], 2012). Figure 5.2 depicts the three-tiered RTI framework for early childhood.

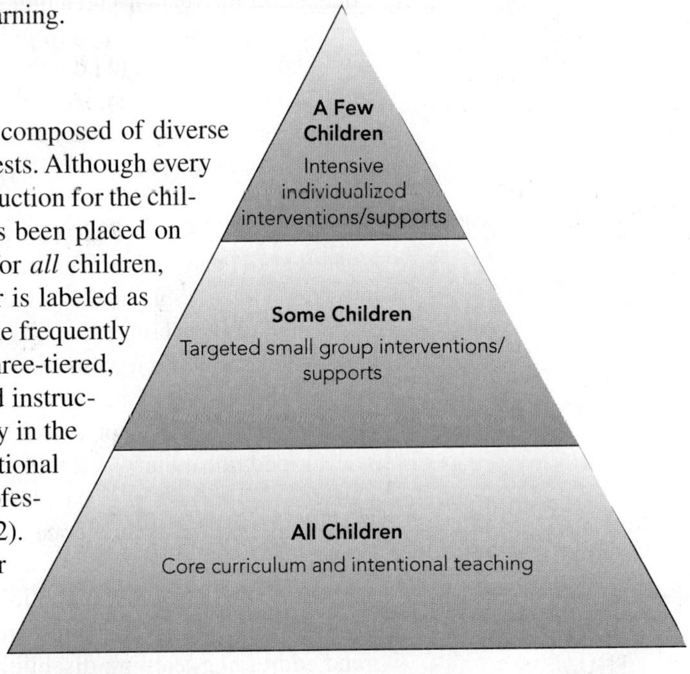

Response to Intervention is *not* a special education framework or approach; when well implemented, it yields effective results for children with and without disabilities as well as dual language learners. Compared to differentiated instruction, RTI is a more systemic approach that is implemented by a program

A Few Children
Intensive individualized interventions/supports

Some Children
Targeted small group interventions/supports

All Children
Core curriculum and intentional teaching

FIGURE 5.2 Response to Intervention (RTI) in Early Childhood

Source: National Professional Development Center on Inclusion, 2012, *Response to intervention (RTI) in early childhood: Building consensus on defining features*, Chapel Hill: The University of North Carolina, FPG Child Development Institute, Author. Reprinted with permission.

or school system. It requires collaborative participation by teachers, administrators, specialists, and families.

The three tiers of the RTI framework are:

1. Research-based curriculum, differentiated instruction, and ongoing assessment for all children (typically meets the needs of 80% of the children).

   Tier 1 of the framework provides a foundation of high-quality education for all children, including a comprehensive, evidence-based curriculum and intentional teaching. Tier 1 involves universal screening, assessment, and monitoring of children's progress to obtain information about each child and to determine whether a child would benefit from additional support.

2. Screening for learning difficulties, focused instruction, and ongoing progress monitoring for those who are not making expected learning progress (approximately 15% of children).

   Tier 2 provides developmentally appropriate, large- and small-group interventions for children who need more focused learning experiences. For example, some children may need regularly scheduled small-group reading to improve vocabulary and other literacy skills. To complement the more explicit activities and build on children's strengths and interests, teachers also embed learning opportunities in daily activities and routines. With these children, teachers monitor their learning progress more frequently and use the information to guide instruction.

3. Intensive instructional intervention for those children who need it (approximately 5%).

   Tier 3 focuses on the approximately 5% of children who do not make expected progress via the Tier 1 and Tier 2 interventions. At Tier 3, children receive intensive, individualized interventions. These include effective strategies to scaffold children's learning such as prompting and modeling (described later in this chapter). Progress monitoring and collaborative problem solving continue to guide decisions about the child.

Although it is a general-education model, RTI can bridge the gap between general and special education by ensuring that children with special needs fully access and participate in the regular curriculum. This framework looks at all students with the goal of preventing learning delays from becoming learning disabilities (Coleman, Roth, & West, 2009). It is important to note that children with already identified disabilities are expected to be found at all three tiers of the model. For children who show signs of struggling, this framework provides additional supports such as more focused time, content, scaffolding, and/or one-on-one attention.

Benefits of RTI   RTI is a framework that applies to all children. It is very important that RTI tiers are not misinterpreted or misused to categorize or label children. In reality, the tiers are flexible, and individual children move between them based on ongoing assessment of their progress.

Successful implementation of RTI depends on accurate, ongoing assessment of children, which can be challenging for teachers of dual language learners. An English language learner or a child who speaks a variation of English may have a well-developed vocabulary and understand many concepts, but may not be well understood at school (Espinosa, 2010a). In such a situation, it can be difficult to accurately assess either the child's competence or his or her needs, as illustrated in the *Language Lens* feature.

The value of such prevention/intervention models is becoming more widely recognized. A growing body of research demonstrates the effectiveness of RTI in preventing and addressing learning disabilities (Coleman et al., 2009). As of 2004, the Individuals with Disabilities Education Act (IDEA) permits schools to use special education funds for RTI, which may reduce the number of children who are identified for special education. Nevertheless, there will always be a small percentage of children with identified disabilities and special needs, a topic we discuss next.

Language Lens

Accurate Assessment of Linguistically Diverse Children

Accurately assessing the abilities of children who speak a home language other than English or whose cultural background varies from the majority of children and teachers can be a challenging task. Cultural and linguistic diversity are *not* learning delays or disabilities. However, cultural and linguistic diversity can have a significant impact on identification and diagnosis of children's special needs, as the following example illustrates:

The student body of Rosa Parks Elementary School is about 30% Latino, 30% European American, and 40% African American. Scott James is an African American first-grade teacher. The school's speech therapist, Tess Brooks, is a white, European American. Scott meets with Tess because he is concerned about two students, Reynoldo and Patrizia, who are behind in reading. Both children speak Spanish at home but speak both English and Spanish at school. Reynoldo is quite verbal; Patrizia hardly speaks at all. Scott thinks that Reynoldo's reading problem is related to a language delay but, because Scott doesn't speak Spanish, he can't be sure. However, the other children, even the Spanish-speaking children, don't seem to understand Reynoldo, either. As for Patrizia, Scott thinks she may have an undiagnosed hearing loss.

Scott's bigger concern is that the screening tools aren't very accurate for assessing language delays in Spanish, and Tess shares his concern. She thinks the best strategy is to get more information from Reynoldo's family about his communication at home. Using an interpreter, Tess and Scott meet with Reynoldo's mother. She is clearly alarmed. She tells the translator that these teachers think Reynoldo is stupid because he doesn't

speak English, but she knows that there is nothing wrong with her son.

Scott privately meets with Patrizia's grandmother, again using a translator. Her reaction is different from Reynoldo's mother's reaction: "I've been worried, too, because she hardly talks at home either. But I understand her when she talks, and so does her brother."

In these situations, Scott and Tess must walk a fine line. They can easily make a mistake. In this case, Reynoldo's speech problems were real and not a product of learning a second language. Without an accurate assessment of the problem, Reynoldo did not receive therapy and his language delay worsened. Patrizia, on the other hand, did not have a hearing loss. What her grandmother and Scott thought was a language delay was actually shyness.

When assessment tools aren't sensitive to language differences, or when professionals do not understand a child's language, they can inaccurately diagnose a delay. In this case, a child may be mislabeled as "delayed," which can negatively affect teachers' and parents' expectations for him. On the other hand, if professionals assume that a language difference is the only cause, they can miss a real problem. The latter error has lasting consequences because the child may not receive needed intervention services.

Source: Based on *Cross-Cultural Considerations in Early Childhood Special Education* (Technical Report #14), by T. Bennett et al., 2001, Urbana-Champaign, IL: University of Illinois, Culturally and Linguistically Appropriate Services (CLAS), retrieved December 15, 2011, from. http://clas.uiuc.edu/techreport/tech14.html#4b.

 Check Your Understanding 5.4: Responsive Education for All Learners

 # Individual Differences in Ability

For several reasons, all teachers must be prepared to work with children who have special needs. First, federal laws require that children with special needs be included in classrooms and programs where their typically developing peers are found, and that their learning progress be reported for accountability purposes. Second, effective practices exist that can positively alter the course of children's development and their success in life. Third, many of the strategies proven effective for children with special needs can be equally effective in addressing the individual variation among typically developing children. In short, early childhood educators who are familiar with the expertise of early childhood special education can be more effective teachers of all children.

To understand how to work with children with special needs, we next address the language of special education. In the sections following, we introduce principles that teachers should know about children with disabilities, describe the laws regulating special education, and the benefits of serving children with disabilities in settings with their typically developing peers.

The Language of Early Childhood Special Education

One of the challenges for generalist early childhood educators is learning special education terminology. Because each field tends to have its own vocabulary, communicating effectively across these related fields requires a common vocabulary.

Defining Terms **Children with special needs** is a broad term used to describe children who may have multiple risk factors, specialized health care needs (such as asthma), mental or emotional health concerns, severe allergies, or physical and/or cognitive disabilities. The more specific term **children with disabilities** refers to children who have been identified as having a specific category of disability, such as autism or cerebral palsy. However, the terms *children with special needs* and *children with disabilities* are often used interchangeably.

Another all-encompassing, though less frequently used, term is **exceptional children**. This term is used to communicate inclusion of gifted and talented children as well as children whose development is below the expected range. In fact, the professional association for special education professionals is called the **Council for Exceptional Children (CEC)**. Early childhood special education professionals are members of the **Division for Early Childhood (DEC)** of the Council for Exceptional Children. Table 5.2 lists and defines some of the most common categories of exceptionality.

Using Person-First Language A standard for professionals who work with individuals with special needs is that they use what is called **person-first language**. Person-first language recognizes that a child is a child first, whether or not he or she has a disability. Consider the difference between describing 4-year-old Zain as "a special needs child" and describing him as "a child with special needs." The former phrase emphasizes

children with special needs A broad term used to describe children who may have multiple risk factors, specialized health care needs, mental or emotional health concerns, severe allergies, or physical and/or cognitive disabilities.

children with disabilities Children who have been identified as having a specific category of disability, such as autism or cerebral palsy.

exceptional children An all-encompassing term used to communicate inclusion of gifted and talented children as well as children whose development is below the expected range.

Council for Exceptional Children (CEC) The national professional association for special educators.

Division for Early Childhood (DEC) Subdivision of the Council for Exceptional Children that is the national professional organization for early childhood special educators and early intervention specialists.

TABLE 5.2 Some Types of Exceptionality

Category	Definition
Attention deficit/hyperactivity disorder (ADHD)	Diagnosis describing children who display a pattern of severe inattentive, hyperactive, and/or impulsive behavior that interferes with the child's learning.
Autism spectrum disorder (ASD)	Condition in which child has impairments in social communication and interactions, and demonstrates restricted, repetitive patterns of behavior and interests.
Down syndrome (DS)	Condition in which extra genetic material causes the child to exhibit developmental delays and/or intellectual disability. Children with DS tend to share physical features such as a flat facial profile, an upward slant to the eyes, small ears, a single crease across the center of the palms, and an enlarged tongue.
Cerebral palsy (CP)	A neurological disorder that appears in infancy or early childhood and permanently affects the child's body movement, motor development, and muscle coordination.
Deafness and hearing impairment	A condition in which hearing is impaired, either permanently or temporarily, and negatively impacts a child's academic performance. Deafness is a severe hearing impairment that prevents a child from hearing and processing language and other sounds.
Visually impaired or blind	Condition describing loss or partial loss of vision.
Intellectual disability	Disability in which the child has limitations both in cognitive functioning and in social and adaptive behavior.
Developmental delay	Diagnosis describing a child whose development is behind expectations for his or her age group as measured by appropriate diagnostic instruments and procedures. Occurs in one or more areas of development: physical, cognitive, communication, social, emotional, or adaptive.
Gifted	Term applied to children with outstanding talent who perform or show potential for performing at remarkably high levels of accomplishment when compared with others of their age, experience, or environment.

the disability, whereas the latter communicates that Zain is first and foremost a child, whose special needs are only part of his identity.

By contrast, placing the adjective first modifies the entire noun to which it is referring; this can place undue emphasis on inability. For example, if you hear a traffic reporter describe a "disabled car," you think of a car that cannot be driven at all. Compare this to what you may think when you hear "a car with a flat tire." For similar reasons, we refer to a "child with Down syndrome" or "a child with autism," instead of saying a "Down's child" or "an autistic." A fundamental tenet of inclusion is that children are children regardless of disability status, and the use of person-first language reflects this principle.

Admittedly, using person-first language can sometimes feel cumbersome. But language matters. How we describe people and conditions communicates our attitudes about them. Currently, person-first terms begin with the word individuals, thus emphasizing the uniqueness of each person regardless of an identified disability.

> **person-first language**
> Language that recognizes that a child is a child first, whether or not he or she has a disability (e.g., saying "child with special needs" as opposed to "special needs child").

What Teachers Should Know about Children with Disabilities

Children with disabilities display a variation in skills beyond what is considered typical; as a result, in many instances, these children qualify for special education services. These services are provided by professionals and therapists who have specialized knowledge about childhood disabilities and disorders. Therefore, it is neither necessary nor reasonable for early childhood educators to know everything about every disorder that might affect a child. Yet, they do need to understand several key principles about children's disabilities (Wolery & Wilbers, 1994):

1. *Children with disabilities are diverse and distinct from one another.* All children have unique skills, interests, dislikes, and talents. Therefore, it is essential that teachers recognize each child as a distinctive individual. Children with disabilities share similarities with other children, but they may need more specialized and/or individualized instruction and care than children without special needs. However, it is vitally important for teachers to remember that no child is defined by their disability; children are diverse in countless ways including culturally, linguistically, and socioeconomically.
2. *Some children may have more than one disability.* For example, a child with a hearing impairment may also have low vision or a seizure disorder. Moreover, children may develop additional disabilities as a result of their primary disability. For example, a child with a visual impairment may not be able to explore his environment and may develop motor or cognitive delays. Early identification and effective intervention can sometimes prevent secondary disabilities.
3. *A diagnosis rarely leads to specific educational interventions.* Educational practices and therapies, such as speech and language therapy, are not selected by the diagnosis. The selected interventions need to align with the child's current skills and abilities, family concerns, needs and resources, and what works best for the child. Teachers should not assume that a particular diagnosis will automatically respond to a specific intervention (Wolery & Wilbers, 1994).

Seeing Children with Disabilities as Individuals: The Case of Autism

Even with the same diagnosis, a great deal of individual variability exists, as in the case of autism spectrum disorder (ASD), one of the fastest-growing serious developmental disabilities in the United States today. The Centers for Disease Control and Prevention (2014a) estimates that 1 out of every 68 children has been identified with ASD, and boys are five times as likely as girls to receive the diagnosis. Thus, early childhood teachers will likely encounter a child with autism at some point in their careers.

Autism spectrum disorder (ASD), also known as autism, is a diagnosis associated with impairments in social interaction and communication and restricted, repetitive behaviors

> **autism spectrum disorder (ASD)** complex developmental disabilities that impact the normal development of the brain processes related to social interaction and communication skills.

Inclusion means that every teacher must be prepared to work with children with disabilities and special needs in the regular classroom. The first step is for teachers to remember that children with disabilities are children first and, like every child, they are unique.

(American Psychiatric Association, 2013). The first signs of autism often appear between 2 and 3 years of age. Young children with autism often have delays in language and communication, including nonverbal communication such as pointing and gesturing. They may display repetitive motor behaviors, and are often inflexible in their routines and play. For example, a child with autism may have a severe emotional reaction to a change in schedule or inability to find a favorite toy. The thinking and learning abilities of children with autism can vary—from gifted to a more significant intellectual disability. Consider the following examples:

> Jeffrey is two and a half years old with a head of curly brown hair. He does not talk yet, but if he wants something he will pull an adult by the hand to what he wants. Sometimes it is easy for his teacher to guess what he wants, but lately he has started crying, screaming, and falling on the ground if she is not able to get him what he wants right away. He spends most of his time wandering around the classroom holding his favorite toy. When another child or teacher tries to play near him, he will quickly leave the area. He will often cry when changing from one activity to another, and once he starts crying it is very difficult to calm him down. Other children and teachers are starting to avoid interacting with him, afraid it may trigger his crying.

> Nathan is 3 years old and can climb higher and faster than most other 3-year-olds. He has known his letters and numbers since age 2 and can read a variety of words and phrases. He cannot, however, consistently answer simple questions from adults, interact with children his own age, or tolerate changes to his routine. His parents are extremely concerned because they have been asked to stop bringing him to music lessons at the local community center. They were also told to find a "more appropriate" placement than the local co-op preschool. His grandparents wonder if there is anything "really wrong" with him or if his parents are simply overindulgent.

> Cherish is 30 months old and has beautiful blue eyes. Her parents report that she used to walk around the house, point to objects, label them, and laugh. She does not do that anymore. In fact, these days she rarely speaks except to request certain apps or preferred foods. She rarely looks at people or things, unless she can find something that is spinning, and then she is mesmerized by it. Her parents cannot remember the last time that they heard her laugh.

These children are some of the characteristics of ASD. Each child is a reminder that ASD is a spectrum disorder, which means that children who receive this diagnosis differ dramatically in their abilities, preferences, needs, and areas of delay. As Jeffery, Nathan, and Cherish remind us, there is no "typical" child with ASD. Every child and family brings a unique set of strengths and challenges that must be considered when planning an educational program. Early identification and intervention for children with ASD can dramatically improve educational outcomes (Dawson et al., 2010).

Often, the first adults to notice some of the early signs of autism are teachers and caregivers. It can sometimes be difficult for caregivers to articulate developmental concerns when autism is the question, because many of the behaviors associated with ASD can seemingly be explained by other factors such as "He just needs to be disciplined," "He is just like his father," or "It is a phase he or she is going through." As a result, teachers are often the first to recognize that a child's behavior may be a red flag for a more serious developmental delay and may need to recommend to the family to take action by seeking out a trained professional in this area who can help. Red flags for autism in early childhood (http://www.autismspeaks.org) include:

- No big smiles or other warm, joyful expressions by 6 months or thereafter
- No back-and-forth sharing of sounds, smiles, or other facial expressions by 9 months or thereafter
- No babbling by 12 months
- No back-and-forth gestures, such as pointing, showing, reaching, or waving, by 12 months
- No words by 16 months
- No two-word meaningful phrases by 24 months
- Any loss of speech or babbling or social skills at any age

The foundation of any program for a child with autism should be the practices that are important for all children, including supportive, caring adults, activities that promote high levels of active engagement, and meaningful interactions with peers. While a common goal is for all children to have opportunities to interact successfully with children and adults, children with autism may require special supports and strategies to be successful in social interactions. Fortunately, researchers have identified many practices that work well for supporting learning and social development for children with autism; some of these practices are described later in this chapter (Wong et al., 2014). One of the most valuable of these strategies is using pretend play to engage children with autism, as described in the feature, *Promoting Play: Supporting Pretend Play for Children with Disabilities*.

In addition to understanding how to work effectively with children with special needs, all teachers must be familiar with special education laws. These laws are discussed in the next section.

What Teachers Should Know about Legal Requirements for Children with Disabilities

Federal laws govern how special education services are delivered in the United States. First, we describe the legislation generally. Then we discuss in more detail the requirements for individualized planning for children with special needs.

The Individuals with Disabilities Education Act Many children with disabilities are eligible for early intervention and early childhood special education services. Both early intervention (EI) and early childhood special education (ECSE) are regulated under the Individuals with Disabilities Education Act (IDEA), formerly the Education of the Handicapped Act. IDEA was designed to provide protections for children to ensure their right to a **free appropriate public education (FAPE)**. The principle of the law is that children with disabilities should not be denied the same opportunities offered to everyone else. To receive specially designed instruction, at no cost to parents, to meet the unique needs of a child with a disability, children must meet **eligibility guidelines** according to IDEA. These guidelines are determined on a state-by-state basis.

free appropriate public education (FAPE) Education for children with disabilities that is required by IDEA, so that children with disabilities are not denied the same opportunities offered to everyone else.

eligibility guidelines Guidelines established on a state-by-state basis according to IDEA that determine whether children may receive special education services.

Promoting Play

Supporting Pretend Play for Children with Disabilities

Play is an important learning activity for all children, and an important context for teachers to observe what and how children are learning. Pretend play skills are associated with later language and social skills, self-regulation, and even reading skills. Children with disabilities, and especially children with autism, often have difficulty engaging in social and pretend play. Since pretend play is an important context for learning and development, teachers should carefully plan and support play activities and opportunities for children with disabilities.

Pretend play skills are excellent functional goals for children with disabilities: children learn to play with peers in a natural setting, and can learn important cognitive and motor skills embedded in the context of play. Furthermore, teachers can learn about children's skill strengths and challenges by watching children play.

Teachers can support growth in children's pretend play by modeling (showing how) and prompting children to engage in more sophisticated levels of pretend play. At the most basic level, children engage in *functional play with some pretense*, in which a child might pretend to pour milk into a cup and drink it. At the next level, *substitution*, the child uses an object in some symbolic manner, such as using a block as a pretend cell phone. Teachers can support children in using *sequences of pretend play* and add *vocalization*. As an example, Adele enjoys playing with dolls, and her teacher, Alec, has noticed that she uses the toy spoon to feed the doll. Alec takes the opportunity to encourage a higher level of pretend play, and uses a small block as a bottle to "feed the baby" (substitution). He then encourages Adele to feed the baby, offering the block "bottle," saying, "It's your turn to feed the baby." As Adele's play becomes more sophisticated, Alec can continue to add more play sequences with the baby doll and include Adele's peers in the pretend play.

Sources: "Teaching Pretend Play to Children with Disabilities: A Review of the Literature," by E. E. Barton and M. Wolery, 2008, *Topics in Early Childhood Special Education, 28*, 109–125; and "Children's Play: Where We Have Been and Where We Could Go," by K. Lifter, E. J. Mason, and E. E. Barton, 2011, *Journal of Early Intervention, 33*, 281–297.

Part B of IDEA is a federal program that provides funds to states and local school districts to support education for children with disabilities from ages 3 to 21. The most relevant part of the law for early childhood teachers is Section 619 of Part B (also known as Early Childhood Special Education), which applies specifically to preschoolers with disabilities. To meet all children's individual needs, the law requires that a team of educators and family members create an individualized education plan for each student.

Part C (Early Intervention) provides funds for states to provide services for infants and toddlers who have disabilities or developmental delays. Some states provide early intervention services for infants and toddlers who are *at risk* of developmental delay and their families. Early Intervention services are discussed in more detail later in the chapter.

individualized education program (IEP) A written plan designed to meet the unique needs of a child with a disability or special need; it is developed, reviewed, and revised by an IEP team during meetings for each child who is eligible for special education services.

Individualized Education Programs When a child meets the disability requirements of the law and is identified as needing special education and related services, school districts are obligated to prepare and implement an **individualized education program (IEP)**, which is designed to meet the unique needs of the child. The IEP is a written plan for services that is developed, reviewed, and revised by an IEP team. **Click here** to see a sample IEP. An IEP must contain the following information:

1. A statement of the child's present levels of academic achievement and functional performance

2. A statement of measurable annual goals, including academic and functional goals designed to:
   - Meet the child's needs that result from the child's disability to enable the child to be involved in and make progress in the general education curriculum
   - Meet each of the child's other educational needs that result from the child's disability
3. A description of benchmarks or short-term objectives
4. A description of:
   - How the child's progress toward meeting the annual goals will be measured
   - When periodic reports on the progress the child is making toward meeting the annual goals (such as through the use of quarterly or other periodic reports, concurrent with the issuance of report cards) will be provided
5. A statement of the special education and related services and supplementary aids and services, based on peer-reviewed research to the extent practicable, to be provided to the child, or on behalf of the child
6. A statement of any individually appropriate accommodations that are necessary to measure the academic achievement and functional performance of the child on state- and district-wide assessments

The IEP Team The IEP is developed by a team that consists of educators, therapists and medical professionals, and family. By law, the team members must include:

- The child's parent(s) or guardian(s)
- The child's early childhood teacher
- The child's early childhood special education teacher
- A representative of the community program who has certain specific knowledge and qualifications
- An individual who can interpret the instructional implications of evaluation results (this may be one of the other listed members, such as an occupational therapist or speech language pathologist)
- Other individuals, who are chosen at the discretion of the parent or the agency, who have knowledge or special expertise regarding the child, including related services personnel such as the speech language pathologist or physical therapist, as appropriate

© Suzanne Clouzeau/Pearson Education

A universal design element, such as this automatic sink, eliminates a barrier for children who might have difficulty operating the handles while also achieving the goal of teaching proper hand washing to all children.

Early Intervention for Infants and Toddlers Children from birth to 3 years old who have a developmental delay, a diagnosed condition, or, in some states, who are identified as at risk for developing a developmental delay may qualify for early intervention (EI) services. These children will have an **individualized family service plan (IFSP)**. An IFSP documents and guides the early intervention process for children with disabilities and their families. The IFSP contains information about the services necessary to support a child's development and enhance the family's capacity to facilitate the child's development. Some parents learn that their child has a disability before or immediately after birth, and the hospital may initiate EI soon after. For other children, delays or disabilities emerge later. In these cases, a parent, other family member, pediatrician, teacher, child care provider, or family friend initially may raise concerns about the child's development.

> **individualized family service plan (IFSP)** Documents and guides the early intervention process for children with disabilities from birth to age 3 and their families; contains information about the services necessary to facilitate a child's development and enhance the family's capacity to facilitate the child's development.

Children with developmental delays enter EI services following diagnostic testing or developmental evaluation administered in partnership with the family by a team of specialists. Through the IFSP process, family members and service providers work as a team to plan, implement, and evaluate services tailored to the family's unique concerns, priorities, and resources.

According to IDEA, the IFSP, like the IEP, is a written plan that must contain specific information, including:

1. The child's present levels of physical, cognitive, communication, social or emotional, and adaptive development
2. The family's resources, priorities, and concerns relating to enhancing the development of the child with a disability
3. The major outcomes to be achieved for the child and the family; the criteria, procedures, and timelines used to determine progress; and whether modifications or revisions of the outcomes or services are necessary
4. Specific early intervention services necessary to meet the unique needs of the child and the family, including the frequency, intensity, and the method of delivery
5. The environments in which services will be provided, including justification of the extent, if any, to which the services will not be provided in a *natural environment*. The *natural environment* refers to settings that are natural or normal for the child's same-age peers without disabilities
6. The projected dates for initiation of services and their anticipated duration
7. The name of the service provider who will be responsible for implementing the plan and coordinating with other agencies and persons
8. Steps to support the child's transition to preschool or other appropriate services

Differences between IFSPs and IEPs Unlike the IEP, the IFSP (Bruder, 2001):

▶ Classroom Connection

In this video, a parent describes her experience with early intervention and early childhood special education services. In what ways have these services helped her daughter and supported her family?

- Revolves around the family, because the family is the constant in a child's life
- Includes outcomes for the family, as opposed to focusing only on the child
- Includes activities involving multiple agencies to integrate all services into one plan
- Names a service coordinator to help the family during the development, implementation, and evaluation of the IFSP
- Involves the notion of natural environments, which create opportunities for learning interventions in everyday routines and activities, rather than only in formal, contrived environments

The laws that dictate services for children with disabilities and special needs reflect research demonstrating the benefits of such services for children with special needs and the larger society. The laws also reflect underlying values about what life should be like for all children. However, laws and procedures related to services can be confusing for families. Community organizations, schools, and teachers are responsible for understanding and communicating to families how educational systems work for children with special needs.

Embracing Natural Learning Environments and Inclusion

One of the primary goals of federal laws governing services for children with disabilities is to make sure that these children lead lives that are as similar as possible to those of children who do not have disabilities. To achieve this goal, professionals need to understand the rationale and embrace the values that led to the law being passed in the first place.

Benefits of Natural Learning Environments Part C requires that EI services be embedded in everyday routines and activities, and occur in the children's **natural learning environments**. Settings where infants, toddlers, and their families would be spending time if the child did not have a disability, natural learning environments can be child care centers, parks, a neighbor's house, or the zoo. Natural learning environments are important because for young children, learning occurs most effectively in the contexts where children will need to use the new skill (Dunst, 2011; Dunst, Hamby, Trivette, Raab, & Bruder, 2000).

So, what is *not* a natural environment? Places children go because they have a disability, such as hospitals, clinics, and therapy offices, are not optimal places for children to learn new skills. Young children, especially those under age 3, do not easily learn a skill in one setting and transfer it to another. Furthermore, just because a setting is natural does not insure that a child with a disability will be able to access and benefit from what the environment offers. Teachers can use principles of universal design to plan for curriculum, assessment, and environmental adaptations to accommodate the individual needs of all learners (http://ectacenter.org/topics/atech/udl.asp). Learn more about how early childhood teachers can use materials and technology to accommodate the individual needs of all learners in the feature *What Works: Principles of Universal Design.*

natural learning environments
Settings that are natural or normal for the child's same-age peers without disabilities such as child care centers, parks, a neighbor's house, or the zoo, as opposed to hospitals, clinics, and therapy offices.

Benefits of Inclusion Inclusion is based on the same principle as natural learning environments—that children with disabilities need to be with their peers without disabilities. Although most images of inclusion involve school settings such as preschool or public schools, inclusion is also important in home and community environments such as parks, recreation, and faith settings.

Inclusion requires more than just access to settings; children need to participate as fully as possible and receive the supports they and their teachers need to ensure they make progress toward important learning goals (Division for Early Childhood [DEC] & National Association for the Education of Young Children [NAEYC], 2009). Successful inclusion means that *all* children in the classroom participate, learn, and thrive. Many, but not all, children with special needs will need individualized instruction to achieve positive learning and developmental outcomes in inclusive programs. But it is also important to cultivate a culture of inclusion that provides children with and without disabilities a sense of belonging and membership in the peer group (DEC & NAEYC, 2009).

It is important for teachers to understand that inclusion benefits all of society, in addition to the children with disabilities. Children with disabilities

Intentional teachers foster friendships between children with special needs and their typically developing peers. What are some ways teachers can build positive relationships among children in inclusive classrooms?

© Fotosearch/Getty Images

What Works

Principles of Universal Design

Universal design is the creation of products and environments that are accessible to all people—individuals with and without disabilities. Obvious examples of universal design are sidewalk curb cuts and ramps that are essential for people in wheelchairs. However, ramps also benefit travelers with roller-bag luggage, parents with strollers, elderly people, and even toddlers who haven't mastered steps. Examples abound in today's world, including Velcro, automatic doors, nonslip surfaces, closed captioning, and signs with universally recognizable symbols.

Planning environments based on principles of universal design from the beginning prevents the need to modify at a later time. Successful inclusion in early childhood programs requires three major components: access to the learning environment and curriculum, participation in activities and routines, and adequate support for teachers—all of which are facilitated by attention to universal design. Intentional planning and implementation of universal design enables teachers to promote development and differentiate instruction for every child. Following are examples of practices based on universal design principles:

- Provide toys and learning materials that have a variety of textures, scents, and sounds, as well as visual stimuli. For example, an assortment of balls of different colors, sizes, and textures (squishy, soft, or rubbery) facilitate engagement for children with sensory impairments. Some balls make noise or light up as they roll or bounce, providing extra cues for children with special

needs and also making the toys more interesting for all children.

- Blocks are an excellent example of universal design because there is no right or wrong way to play with them. Wooden unit blocks come in various shapes and sizes, enabling children to engage with them in multiple ways. Blocks that have textured sides and make noise add additional sensory clues as well as challenges for children.
- Colorful, magnetic plastic blocks or table toys can be stacked and rearranged easily without frustrating children who have physical or sensory disabilities. Originally invented by Maria Montessori, puzzle pieces with knobs enable children with visual impairments to use their sense of touch to successfully play with others.
- Books with easy-to-turn pages, and various sizes of pictures and text, facilitate children's independent literacy learning. Those with textures, cutouts, and sound effects engage children's interests. Sturdy board books make page-turning easier. Books on iPad or audiotape help children with hearing disabilities participate in the language and literacy curriculum.

Sources: Based on "Learning Materials for Children of All Abilities: Begin with Universal Design," by K. Haugen, 2005, *Exchange, 161* (January/February), 45–47; and *About UDL: What Is Universal Design for Learning*, National Center on Universal Design for Learning, retrieved September 22, 2012, from http://www.cast.org/udl.

---

universal design The creation of products and environments that are accessible to all people—individuals with and without disabilities.

develop opportunities to share in the daily life of their community, and they do as well or better than children in specialized programs, particularly with respect to social development (NPDCI, 2007). Children without disabilities benefit by developing positive attitudes toward individuals with diverse abilities. Families of children with and without disabilities benefit from developing strong, supportive relationships that enhance the quality of life. In the sections that follow, we describe what teachers need to do for children with special needs if inclusion is to be effective.

 Check Your Understanding 5.5: Individual Differences in Ability

Effective Practices for Children with Diverse Abilities

The purpose of inclusion is to ensure that the individual needs of all children are being met in shared settings. However, identifying what practices are best for children of varying abilities may be challenging for an early childhood teacher. The Division for Early Childhood (2014) has established a set of recommended practices designed to improve outcomes for children with disabilities, birth to 5 years of age. They include practices associated with assessment, environment, family, instruction, interaction, teaming and collaboration, and transitions. All professionals who work with children with disabilities should be familiar with and adhere to this set of recommended practices.

Children with disabilities often require environments that are "organized and adjusted to minimize the effects of their disabilities and to promote learning of a broad range of skills" (Wolery, Strain, & Bailey, 1992, p. 95). They also may need specialized instruction, as with Tier 3 interventions in RTI (NPDCI, 2009). Such **specialized instruction** involves teachers matching an individual child's goals and objectives with appropriate teaching methods and materials. In addition, teachers need to decide what amount of assistance each child with special needs requires, provide the assistance, and then determine whether the instruction was effective. Most often, a team of specialists is available to help the early childhood teacher achieve these goals. Three types of practices that early childhood teachers can employ to support children with special needs are described below: team collaboration, assessment, and planning and implementing individualized strategies.

> **specialized instruction**
> Involves teachers matching an individual child's goals and objectives with appropriate teaching methods and materials, deciding what amount of assistance each child with special needs requires, providing the assistance, and then determining whether the instruction was effective.

Work on a Team

Working collaboratively with a team is critical to the success of including young children with special needs in the classroom. Each member of the team has different expertise in areas such as early childhood, special education, motor development, and communication development. Additionally, all members possess specific knowledge about the particular child. The child's family plays an important role in the collaborative team. They (1) provide information about their child's strengths and needs, (2) help assess functional skills and develop the IFSP or IEP with the team, (3) implement intervention strategies at home and in the community, and (4) provide critical information about the effectiveness of interventions.

At the IEP or IFSP team meeting, professionals and family members collaborate to (1) identify and prioritize individualized goals, (2) determine if modifications to the environment or curriculum are needed, (3) design specialized instructional strategies, and (4) monitor the child's progress toward the goals. Teamwork and collaboration goes beyond team meetings. Many people, including family members, teacher assistants, and community partners, work to facilitate children's learning beyond the classroom, into home and community settings.

Assess Young Children of Diverse Abilities

The effectiveness of individualized instruction for children with disabilities depends in large part on accurately assessing their needs and progress. Throughout this book we address the topic of assessment as related to all children. In this section, we discuss types of assessment that are used in order to best accommodate children with special needs. Screening, diagnostic, and eligibility assessments, are used by specialists to determine whether the child has a developmental delay or disability and is eligible for services. Curriculum-based assessment and routines-based assessment are the most appropriate and useful to early childhood teachers for planning what children with special needs should be learning.

Curriculum-Based Assessments Curriculum-based assessments trace a child's progress along a continuum of functional skills within a developmentally sequenced curriculum organized by developmental domain. **Functional skills** are those that are useful and meaningful to children in their everyday lives. For example, it is generally useful for children to learn to use the toilet, feed themselves, communicate and play with peers, and count objects. A **developmental domain** is an area of development such as fine and gross motor skills, cognitive abilities, self-help capabilities, and social and communication skills. Curriculum-based assessments serve to link assessment, intervention, and evaluation, as the following example illustrates:

> **functional skills** Skills that are useful to children in their everyday lives.
>
> **developmental domain** An area of development such as fine and gross motor skills, cognitive abilities, self-help capabilities, and social and communication skills.

Corwin (age 3½) has experienced an eligibility evaluation for special education based on a recommendation from his pediatrician. According to the multidisciplinary team, he qualifies for early childhood special education because he has a moderate communication and social skills delay. Consequently, Corwin's parents are referred to the local preschool special education program near their house. After his parents observe the inclusive program, they enroll Corwin. During his first week at school, Corwin's teachers use a published curriculum-based measure to identify his needs and develop functional goals and objectives for his IEP. Test items list functional skills in predictable developmental sequence. The assessment is conducted within the context of the preschool routines and activities.

When Taiya Stoner, Corwin's teacher, observes him independently perform items that are on the test, these tasks are noted as "mastered" and listed as his current levels of performance on his IEP. For example, Corwin mastered one goal—uses simple problem-solving strategies—because he said "NO!" when a child took his crayon. Behaviors he had difficulty displaying or did not display over the course of a few observations, such as initiating play activities with another child, were considered targets for intervention and added as goals for his IEP. After his teachers and therapists provide instruction to Corwin on the identified goals, they administer the assessment again to determine whether their guidance was effective and to establish new goals for Corwin.

In this example, all of the steps of the linked system are in place. First, the teachers use the assessment to determine what the child needs to learn and then they teach the skills identified. Finally, the team reassesses, using the same tool to determine whether Corwin is making progress.

Routines-Based Assessment Another approach for determining goals for a child is called *routines-based assessment*, which is used to determine which functional skills a child should be taught. In a routines-based assessment, those who know the child well (e.g., family members, teachers) describe how their child participates in the typical routines of daily living (McWilliam, 2010). For example, Gwynneth's kindergarten teacher, Tamara Calhoun, is asked by the special education teacher to complete a routines-based assessment of Gwynneth's performance throughout the day in order to identify some functional learning goals for her. Tamara lists classroom activities in chronological order, such as arrival, circle time, centers, clean up, snack, and so on. She then observes Gwynneth's behavior during these routines and sets goals to work on with her, such as "Gwynneth will get off bus; walk to the classroom with group; put coat and backpack in cubby." Using routines-based assessment at home, her parents' list includes typical daily routines such as wake up, eat breakfast, and get dressed.

To ensure accurate information as well as follow-through, parents of children with special needs must participate in the assessment process. After the team gathers information to determine the child's functional goals, the next step is to plan for individualized instruction.

Plan Individualized Instructional Strategies

Every early childhood teacher needs a repertoire of teaching strategies to be effective with all children. Sometimes, however, in order to learn new skills, children with special needs require more explicit teaching than do typically developing children. In these instances, teachers use strategies that are carefully planned and implemented more frequently throughout the day. Individualizing instruction involves identifying specific goals, creating learning opportunities, providing teacher support, reinforcing children's learning, and monitoring their progress.

Identify Goals for Children Either of the assessment approaches described previously can be used to determine learning goals. The ECSE teacher on the team can help write objectives that are functional and generative. **Generative skills** are those that can be used across settings, people, events, and objects. For example, one of the skills identified for Damon is "uses two fingers to pick up objects." To be generative, Damon needs to learn to use the skill across settings such as during mealtime to pick up Cheerios, or in the bath to pick up the soap. He also needs to use the skill across objects, such as crayons or beads, and under various conditions, such as when the items are mushy or hard. If an identified skill is too limited, such as "uses a finger and thumb grasp to put beads into a bottle," it is difficult to create enough learning opportunities to be effective and the skill is less likely to be useful in different situations.

> **generative skills** Skills that can be used across settings, people, events, and objects.

Create Learning Opportunities Effective teachers create learning opportunities in daily routines and activities that provide the child with multiple tools for learning a new skill (McWilliam, 2010). These opportunities may be more focused but are not essentially different from those provided for every child. One strategy is to introduce unexpected events, as when the teacher says or does something that the child does not anticipate. These events may be funny or interesting things the adult says. For example, when teaching 6-year-old Miguel to use prepositions, his teacher walks over to where he is sitting and sits backwards next to him. Then she asks, "Miguel, where are you?" Miguel, giggling, says, "Right here." His teacher says "Right where? Are you *behind* me or *in front* of me?"

Use Helping Strategies To help children learn skills, teachers use helping strategies called **prompts**. These are gestural, model, physical, pictorial, or verbal supports that help children use a specific skill (Neitzel & Wolery, 2009; Sandall & Schwartz, 2008):

> **prompts** Gestural, model, physical, pictorial, or verbal clues that elicit responses from children to assist them in using a specific skill.

- *Gestural prompts.* Movements that teachers use to let children know what behavior is expected. For example, when the teacher wants Julia to ask for more raisins, she waits and looks expectantly at Julia until Julia says, "I want more raisins."
- *Model prompts.* Involves the teacher saying or doing the behavior he wants the child to do. The teacher says "please" and "thank you" when he passes food during lunchtime.

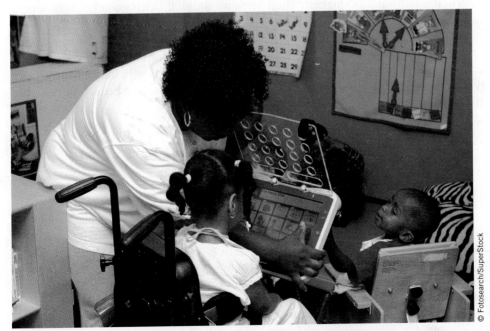

All children have different abilities and interests that teachers can use to help them meet learning goals. With minor adaptations, this teacher provides support for every child to learn early literacy skills.

- *Physical prompts.* Gentle touching and guiding of children by the teacher to help the children accomplish a skill. When teaching Larisha to wash her hands, the teacher places her hands over Larisha's hands and helps her to turn on the faucet, get soap, rub her hands together, dry her hands, and turn off the faucet with the towel.
- *Pictorial prompts.* Visual cues that help children accomplish a skill. To help Owen play independently at center time, his teacher places pictures of each center on a piece of construction paper, and Owen refers to a picture when he moves to another activity area.
- *Verbal prompts.* Teacher language strategies that help children accomplish a skill. When it is time for Dushawn to come to the group for story time, his teacher gives him a verbal prompt: "Dushawn, please come sit on your carpet square next to me." This may be enough for Dushawn to learn that he is expected to join the group.

Reinforce Children's Learning   When children receive positive reinforcement following performance of a new skill, they are more likely to try the new skill again. In educational settings, positive reinforcement can be very simple and natural. **Naturally occurring reinforcers** are consequences that are likely to occur *whenever* the child performs the skill and are therefore highly effective. For example, when Raven puts on her coat independently, the teacher says, "Raven, you zipped up your coat all by yourself. Now you can go outside to play." Some examples of naturally occurring reinforcers include the child using the paint after making a request to do so; playing with friends after asking to join the group; and being acknowledged by a teacher for trying hard at a difficult task.

naturally occurring reinforcers
Consequences that are likely to occur *whenever* the child performs the skill and are, therefore, highly effective.

Monitor Progress   The effectiveness of instruction depends on the team monitoring the child's progress to determine if the child has met a goal and is ready to move on to learning a new skill, or if the IEP needs modification. Information about children's progress can be collected in many ways. One data collection system used by many teachers is to observe and document the child's learning using a checklist of skills or a rating scale of the child's performance. A rating scale allows the teacher to indicate the level of a child's skill along a continuum. For example, the lowest level might be "child refuses to perform the skill" and the highest "child performs the skill independently," with several steps in between.

States must also monitor Early Childhood Outcomes (ECO) for children who receive services for special needs, whether through Part C (Early Intervention) or Part B (Preschool). They must report the percentage of infants and toddlers with Individualized Family Service Plans (IFSPs) or preschool children with Individualized Education Programs (IEPs) who demonstrate improved:

a. Positive social-emotional skills (including social relationships)
b. Acquisition and use of knowledge and skills (including early language/communication [and early literacy for preschoolers])
c. Use of appropriate behavior to meet needs

Because these outcomes apply to all children, they can help professionals and families communicate effectively regarding children's goal progress and needs (http://ectacenter.org/eco/pages/faqs.asp).

All early childhood teachers need to learn how to teach children with special needs in inclusive settings. In addition, when general early childhood educators learn some of the important skills of early childhood special education, they can apply these skills to teaching all children. Read the *Becoming an Intentional Teacher: Individualizing Group Time* feature for an example of applying this special education knowledge with typically developing children.

Becoming an Intentional Teacher

Individualizing Group Time

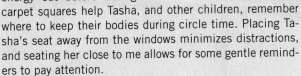

Here's What Happened Halfway through the kindergarten year, there was a child in my class, Tasha, who continued to have difficulty with large-group instruction times. She would touch the other children, sometimes even leaning her whole body against them and touching their hair or faces. She was easily distracted and stood up to look out the windows several times during story time. She also would leave circle time before it finished and wander around.

So, here is what I did. I gave each child a carpet square to use during circle time, placing Tasha farthest away from the window but closest to me. I started circle time with an active movement song. When the children sat down, I gave Tasha a card to hold that had pictures of the expected behaviors when sitting in a large group (keep feet and hands to self; look and listen to the action; raise a quiet hand to ask a question). Tasha and I had made the card together. She drew the pictures and I wrote the words for each reminder. I also used Tasha's favorite puppet, Whiskers, to greet and excuse children at circle time.

Here's What I Was Thinking Tasha has difficulty attending in large groups and is easily distracted. Young children in general can have difficulty remembering expected behaviors and directions. I also realized that Tasha wasn't as motivated as other children were to listen and participate at circle time. At first, I thought that perhaps I should let Tasha wander when she didn't want to be at circle time. But she is already 6 years old and, although she has some difficulties with attention, her parents and I

believe that she can be successful at circle time. Starting with an active song helps get some energy out before sitting. The carpet squares help Tasha, and other children, remember where to keep their bodies during circle time. Placing Tasha's seat away from the windows minimizes distractions, and seating her close to me allows for some gentle reminders to pay attention.

I wasn't completely sure that I should single Tasha out by giving her a "reminder card," but then I figured Tasha was already being singled out by her peers as the one who always disrupted their story. I could explain to the children that everyone in the class has their individual needs met—for example, children with allergies, special diets, adaptive pencils, and so on. The reminder card is helping Tasha remember what we all are supposed to be doing at group time. The card also keeps Tasha's hands busy, making it less likely that she will touch her peers. Beginning and ending circle time with Whiskers, the cat puppet, motivates Tasha to come to circle right away and stay through the end. These easy-to-implement modifications help Tasha to learn more and spend more time with her peers.

Reflection Even though all children are not alike, teaching in whole group can be an efficient and effective strategy at times. Do you think it's fair that some children are treated differently during group times? What other strategies could the teacher use to engage all the children fully?

Having explored the topic of individual differences among typically developing children as well as children with special needs, we now see that teachers can draw on a large body of effective practices to achieve their goals for all children. Successful inclusion of children with disabilities and special needs involves much more than the children's presence in the classroom. Teachers need to get to know all of the children and continually assess their learning and development. They must plan and implement individualized instructional strategies. Most important, teachers must create a classroom climate in which every child is valued and fully included.

 Check Your Understanding 5.6: Effective Practices for Children with Diverse Abilities

Revisiting the Case Study

. . . Ms. Creighton's Classroom

At the beginning of this chapter, we met some of the children in Lindsay Creighton's preschool class and wondered how she could possibly meet the needs of these diverse children. Now that we have explored the topic of adapting for individual differences, we can see how Lindsay successfully teaches all of the children.

Lindsay's study of child development helps her to understand that children's personalities and behaviors are the result of an interaction between their genetic makeup and their experiences in the environment. Therefore, she is aware of how important her work is in helping them achieve their full potential. Lindsay has high goals for each child's learning. But she realizes that because children are unique, she needs to use differentiated instruction to help them achieve the goals.

For Cal, whose grandmother does not speak English, Lindsay works with a translator as well as a team that includes a social worker. Lindsay recognizes that Rohan and Ruby, who both seem painfully shy, are also very different. They each have different interests and abilities. Because Rohan likes quiet activities and playing with one other child, Lindsay encourages him in that direction and he gradually becomes more confident. Ruby is hesitant until she is assured that Lindsay will protect her from an allergic reaction. The other children soon become comfortable with that fact as they say, "Ruby's body was born not liking peanuts." They all embrace the need to protect Ruby's health.

Although at first Lindsay and the other children mix up the twins, Alex and Alice, they soon become aware that each is an individual. Lindsay focuses on working with each girl separately and engaging them in different activities so their uniqueness becomes evident to all. Carter's needs are more severe and specific. Working as a member of his IEP team and supported by his parents, Lindsay becomes more confident in her ability to teach Carter and to help him achieve his individualized goals.

After several months of working with this class, Lindsay decides that adapting for individual variation is the most interesting part of her work. At first, she was concerned when confronted with such diversity. But now, she finds that children's individuality is what makes her days most interesting and unpredictable. As she expands her repertoire of skills for working with diverse children, she finds that seeing individual children's progress is richly rewarding. ■

5 Chapter Summary

- Children differ from one another in many ways, including rate and timing of cognitive and language development, social skills and temperament, and interests. The transactional theory of development explains that development is influenced by *both* biology *and* experience, and how they interact with each other.

- Effective early childhood teachers understand the importance of knowing each child as an individual. One of the most useful frameworks for thinking about the variation among children is Gardner's theory of multiple intelligences.

- *Differentiating instruction* means to create multiple paths so that children of different abilities, interests, or learning needs experience equally appropriate ways to achieve important learning goals.

- All teachers need to be prepared to work with children who have special learning and developmental needs because federal law requires it, effective practices exist to alter the course of children's learning, and many of these practices can be used with typically developing children.

- Specialized instruction involves teachers matching an individual child's goals with appropriate teaching methods and materials, deciding what amount of assistance is needed by the child, providing the assistance, and determining whether the instruction was effective. Of equal importance to specialized instruction is cultivating a culture of inclusion, which provides children with disabilities with a sense of belonging and membership in the peer group.

Key Terms

- approaches to learning
- autism spectrum disorder (ASD)
- children with disabilities
- children with special needs
- Council for Exceptional Children (CEC)
- developmental domain
- differentiated instruction
- Division for Early Childhood (DEC)
- eligibility guidelines
- exceptional children
- free appropriate public education (FAPE)
- functional skills
- generative skills
- individualized education program (IEP)
- individualized family service plan (IFSP)
- natural learning environments
- naturally occurring reinforcers
- nature
- nurture
- person-first language
- prompts
- protective factors
- resilience
- Response to Intervention (RTI)
- risk factors
- specialized instruction
- temperament
- theory of multiple intelligences
- transactional theory of development
- universal deign

 Demonstrate Your Learning

Click here to assess how well you've learned the content in this chapter.

Readings and Websites

Division for Early Childhood of the Council for Exceptional Children. (2014). *DEC Recommended practices in early intervention/early childhood special education.* Available on DEC website.

Gadzikowski, A. (2013). *Challenging exceptionally bright children in early childhood classrooms.* St. Paul, MN: Redleaf Press.

Sandall, S., & Schwartz, I. (2008). *Building blocks for successful early childhood programs: Strategies for including all children* (2nd ed.). Baltimore: Paul II. Brookes.

Center for Response to Intervention in Early Children

Visit this website for more information and resources on differentiating instruction for young learners.

Division for Early Childhood (DEC) of the Council for Exceptional Children

On the DEC website, you can find numerous resources, and can also download and read *DEC Recommended*

practices in early intervention/early childhood special education.

Early Childhood Technical Assistance Center (ECTA)

This website at FPG Child Development Institute offers resources about early childhood outcomes, universal design, Response to Intervention, early intervention, Preschool 619 services, and a variety of other topics.

National Professional Development Center on Inclusion

At this website at FPG Child Development Institute, you will find research and resources for supporting the inclusion of children with disabilities in settings with peers.

Project Zero

View the Project Zero website at Harvard University to learn more about application and research studies related to multiple intelligences and learning.

6 Embracing a Culturally and Linguistically Diverse World

Learning Outcomes

After studying this chapter, you should be able to:

6.1 Define culture and explain how cultural contexts influence children's learning and development.

6.2 Describe how the rules for behavior differ among various cultural groups and how they are similar.

6.3 Describe how your own cultural background influences your thinking and behavior.

6.4 Analyze why teachers need to understand and be sensitive to children's linguistic and cultural diversity.

6.5 Discuss effective cross-cultural communication strategies.

6.6 Apply principles of culturally responsive, developmentally appropriate practices.

With her newly achieved associate's degree in early childhood education, Stacey Griffin is excited about her first job as a teacher of 18- to 30-month-old children in a child care center. Even though the center is located in a neighborhood close to where Stacey grew up, the population of the area has changed considerably in recent years. An influx of immigrants from Latin America is apparent in the number of families with young children who have displaced the elderly, white, European American, long-term residents, as well as in the goods available and language spoken in local markets. Despite these changes, Stacey feels confident that she knows enough about child development and early childhood practice to be a good teacher.

By the end of the first month, however, Stacey is feeling frustrated and less sure of herself. In the mornings, most of the families arrive late. They continue to carry their children into the classroom even though Stacey has informed them (gently, she thinks) that the children are capable of walking on their own and need to practice their developing motor skills. Similarly, she disapproves of the parents' continuing to spoon-feed the children rather than giving them finger food that they can manage on their own.

Mrs. Arguenta is unhappy that Stacey isn't cooperating in toilet training 18-month-old Ilsia. Stacey thinks Ilsia is too young because she can't verbalize her need to use the potty. Mrs. Arguenta says that Ilsia is already using the potty at home and wants Ilsia to be dry. To make matters worse, Mrs. Arguenta sends Ilsia to child care wearing her best clothes and buckle shoes. Stacey thinks toddlers need to move about in comfort and should go barefoot to help them with their walking. Besides, the floor is carpeted.

Stacey tries to build a relationship with Mrs. Arguenta. She asks Mrs. Arguenta to call her Stacey instead of Miss Griffin, but Mrs. Arguenta ignores this friendly overture. Every time Stacey tries to meet with her to discuss Ilsia, Mrs. Arguenta is late or doesn't come. One day, Mrs. Arguenta sends Ilsia's 10-year-old sister to pick her up, which is a violation of center policies. Stacey can't understand why Mrs. Arguenta and the other families are being so difficult when she works so hard to communicate with them. ■

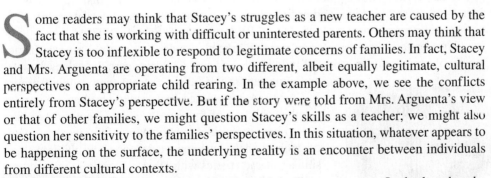

Some readers may think that Stacey's struggles as a new teacher are caused by the fact that she is working with difficult or uninterested parents. Others may think that Stacey is too inflexible to respond to legitimate concerns of families. In fact, Stacey and Mrs. Arguenta are operating from two different, albeit equally legitimate, cultural perspectives on appropriate child rearing. In the example above, we see the conflicts entirely from Stacey's perspective. But if the story were told from Mrs. Arguenta's view or that of other families, we might question Stacey's skills as a teacher; we might also question her sensitivity to the families' perspectives. In this situation, whatever appears to be happening on the surface, the underlying reality is an encounter between individuals from different cultural contexts.

The United States is becoming an increasingly diverse country. In the last decade, the number of white students in public schools decreased from 60% to 52%, and the Hispanic population of students increased from 17% to 24% (National Center for Education Statistics, 2014c). Most early childhood programs serve children from diverse linguistic and cultural groups or will do so in the future. Therefore, it is essential for teachers to understand and embrace the realities of a culturally and linguistically diverse world.

But culture and its influences are subtle. Moreover, the majority cultural group of the United States—predominantly individuals of Anglo-European descent—tends to define culture and linguistic diversity as issues or challenges to be dealt with or solved. In fact, the word *diverse* means different, which raises the question, "Different from what?" The implication is that people whose cultural identity is not white European American or who are not native speakers of English are different from the norm.

In this book, we talk about the realities of culture and language because these forces influence the learning and development of all children. At the same time, we use the verb *embrace* when discussing culture and language to create a classroom climate that is culturally and linguistically supportive and responsive for *all* children. We believe that such a perspective is a precursor to helping all children achieve their full potentials.

In this chapter, we define the term *culture* and identify the basic principles of the role of culture in development and learning. We also describe a framework for thinking about contrasting cultural beliefs, values, and practices. We discuss effective teaching and learning strategies for working with all children, beginning with awareness of one's own cultural perspective.

Understanding Cultural Diversity

The United States has always been a nation of immigrants, its diversity being a hallmark of American society. Recent waves of immigration and higher birth rates among certain groups have made the nation even more diverse. The U.S. Census Bureau projects that by 2020, approximately 51% of the children in the United States will be Latino, Asian, or African American/African (Child Trends, 2014), and 26% of children will be Hispanic. In many parts of the country, the majority of children are members of a so-called "minority" group. In the future, the concepts of majority and minority status are likely to become confusing if not meaningless.

Given the diversity of children and families served in programs, as well as changing demographics, every teacher will work with diverse groups of children and families. Even if differences are not outwardly apparent, individuals differ from one another in many ways: religion, national heritage, language, traditions, and many more. Therefore, all teachers must be committed to making it part of their ongoing education to learn about the diverse populations of their classrooms.

culture Explicit and implicit values, beliefs, and patterns of behavior that are passed on from generation to generation; customs, rituals, ways of interacting and communicating, and expectations for behaviors, roles, and relationships that are shared by members of a group.

The population of young children in the United States is becoming ever more diverse. Effective teachers embrace the realities of cultural and linguistic diversity to help all children reach their full potentials.

What Is Culture?

Culture refers to explicit and implicit values, beliefs, and patterns of behavior that are passed on from generation to generation (National Association for the Education of Young Children [NAEYC], 2009). Culture encompasses customs, rituals, ways of interacting and communicating, and expectations for behaviors, roles, and relationships that are shared by members of a group (Olsen, Bhattacharya, & Scharf, 2007).

To understand the concept of culture, it is crucial to understand that culture is a characteristic of *groups*, not an aspect of individual variation. Children learn the values, beliefs, and expectations for behavior from their cultural group. In Chapter 4, we learned how young children are similar to other children of the same age. In Chapter 5, we discussed how each child is unique and different from every other child. In this chapter, we describe how children share similar characteristics with other children of their cultural group. Although each of these three chapters focuses on a distinct principle of development, it is important to recognize that these principles are interrelated. All three of the following statements are equally true:

© Zuma Press, Inc/Alamy

- Every child is like all other children in some ways.
- Every child is like some other children in some ways (those who are members of the same cultural group).
- Every child is like no other child.

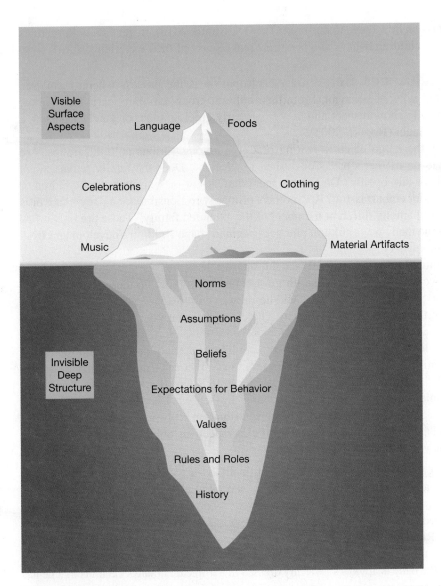

FIGURE 6.1 Model of Culture The complexity of culture is like an iceberg—the visible elements are only a small part while the deeper structures truly influence behavior and decisions.

Sometimes discussions of culture are limited, focusing on superficial characteristics such as those that can be observed. For example, we judge cultural origin based on the clothing that people wear, the holidays they celebrate, the accents with which they speak, or the music they enjoy. Although these external cues reveal something about children and their families, they neglect or ignore the deeper structures of culture—the values and rules—that truly influence behavior and decisions. Figure 6.1 illustrates the reality of culture, in which the surface characteristics are only the "tip of the iceberg" while the fundamental elements tend to be invisible.

The Role of Culture in Development

Why is culture so relevant for early childhood educators? The simplest answer to this question is that culture shapes and influences every child's development and learning (Bronfenbrenner, 1979, 2004; Trawick-Smith, 2013). In fact, all aspects of human life are touched and affected by people's cultural contexts. This includes how people communicate, think, behave, solve problems, and organize communities and governments (Lynch, 2011).

Although the biological factors that influence maturation are similar for all human beings, culture has a huge influence on how children experience their growth and development—on how they are nurtured (Trawick-Smith, 2013). In general, cultural rules influence how children behave and how they make sense of their experiences.

acculturation The process whereby children learn expected rules of behavior.

Culture Influences Behavior

Acculturation is the process whereby children learn expected rules of behavior. From their cultural group, children learn such critical lessons as how to show respect and how to properly greet an older or younger person, a friend, or a stranger (Rogoff, 2003).

Consider the range of child-rearing practices among various cultural groups. Are babies carried on mother's backs or pushed in strollers? Does the family remain silent during meals or talk openly? Do parents feel comfortable playing with their children or find this behavior embarrassing? Are mothers primarily responsible for a baby's care or is that care shared among different members of the extended family? These are only a few examples of the many ways cultural practices begin to shape children's development from the earliest moments of life.

Some cultural rules are explicitly taught, such as "hold the fork in your right hand and the knife in your left," or vice versa. In most countries, mixing up these rules would be of little consequence. By contrast, in Middle Eastern cultures, people eat with their right hand and use their left hand for toileting. Therefore, offering your left hand to someone is interpreted as a grave insult.

Children learn many cultural rules from adults or other children through modeling. From observation, children learn when to smile or look someone in the eye (Gonzalez-Mena, 2008). They also learn when to speak up and when to listen (Ramsey, 2004). They learn whether people shake hands or bow in greeting. In fact, what is considered *appropriate* behavior, thinking, or problem solving in a given situation is always culturally determined (Lynch, 2011). Consider how different cultural perspectives on appropriate child rearing come into play in the following situation:

> Patty Briggs is so excited because she has finally been approved to adopt a child from Costa Rica. She is prepared to stay there for several weeks to get to know her little boy, who is 12 months old, and for his foster family to get to know her. Even though Patty has studied child development and taken care of many young children, after a few days in Costa Rica, she starts to feel uncertain. Whenever she puts the baby down to crawl on the floor, the foster mother frowns and immediately picks him up. Patty is concerned because the baby is always so warmly dressed in a tropical climate. She finds that he has diaper rash and wants to remove some of his warm clothing to help him heal. However, it's clear that the foster mother thinks he will get cold and become ill. During the time that Patty is in Costa Rica, she respects the foster mother's mode of caring for the baby, but also treats his diaper rash. After the adoption, she sends photos of him to his foster family to reassure them that he is well cared for. (P. Briggs, personal communication, 1990)

Culture Creates Meaning

Cultural rules determine the meaning attached to particular behaviors. Therefore, teachers need to be aware of how different experiences can carry different meanings for children. Consider the example of physical touch. Touch is an important aspect of human behavior, but different cultural groups attach different interpretations to the same kinds of touch (Lynch, 2011). In the United States, it is not unusual for opposite-sex couples to hold hands or lock arms as outward signs of affection. In other parts of the world, these behaviors between men and women might not be tolerated. Similarly, in some countries, members of the same sex walk arm in arm as a sign of friendship, but in the United States, same-sex public displays of affection are interpreted as a sign of sexual orientation. Accordingly, we see that the same behavior—holding hands or taking someone's arm—means something different, depending on the cultural context.

How does this concept affect teachers and children? When the same behaviors mean different things or different behaviors mean the same thing, mixed messages can result, as occurred in Stacey's classroom at the beginning of this chapter. Stacey thinks that using one's first name signals a positive relationship, whereas Mrs. Arguenta interprets it as a sign of disrespect.

How Culture Functions: Principles to Keep in Mind

As you continue your professional journey, you will probably find that the more you learn about culture, the more you need to know. This is not a comfortable position for most educators. While you may think that you should know all the answers, this is not realistic; the most effective stance is to acknowledge what you don't know and remain open to new learning. This will serve you well throughout your teaching career and in all areas of your professional journey.

In the meantime, it is useful to understand several key principles about how culture affects human development. These principles are listed and briefly described here (Day, 2006; Hanson, 2011):

1. *Everyone is rooted in one or more cultural groups.* This first principle is the foundation of all understanding about culture (Head Start, 2010b). Accepting this principle requires going beyond respecting diversity to deeper understanding; it requires that European American teachers reject the tendency to see white, European American children as exhibiting *ordinary* behaviors, while thinking about children of other ethnic ancestries as exhibiting *cultural* behaviors (Day, 2006; Head Start, 2010b). Members of the majority cultural group in any country tend to have more difficulty recognizing that their cultural background influences their thinking and behavior.

2. *Cultures are dynamic.* Culture is not a fixed, static entity. Because it is born of traditions and historical experiences, intervening events can affect and change cultural rules. When groups immigrate, they take aspects of their culture with them; however, as they interact with members of other cultural groups, they may change. Similarly, the cultural traditions in the country of origin may diverge as a result of differing circumstances.

   New information and changing political situations may also challenge cultural assumptions, such as appropriate roles for men and women. In the 1960s, for instance, the women's movement and other political events led to rapid shifts in expectations for women and men in America. Similarly, female candidates for president and vice president of the United States altered perceptions about women as leaders, especially for young girls.

   Because culture is dynamic, teachers need to be careful not to make assumptions about students' and families' behaviors based on outdated information or even prior experience with members of a particular group. A teacher might assume, for example, that European American parents reject gender stereotyping, but change that assumption when several families send in princess costumes for their daughters to play with.

3. *Culture, language, ethnicity, and race are aspects of experience that influence people's beliefs and values.* Culture is only one determinant, albeit a strong one, of people's values, beliefs, and behaviors. **Ethnicity** refers to the shared characteristics and experiences of a group of people, such as nationality, race, history, religion, and language. Ethnicity is usually connected to the geographic origin of a group, as with Greek or Chinese people. Additional factors, including socioeconomic status, education, occupation, ability/disability, sexual orientation, personality, and events in the larger society influence how people behave and how groups function (Lynch, 2011).

   All of these factors interact to influence the values and behavior of various groups and of individuals within groups. History in particular plays a key role. For example, the history of slavery, racism, and discrimination in the United States and other countries has had a significant, differential effect on people's lives and opportunities and continues to do so. Racism persists as new groups become its target, including Arabic people and immigrants from Spanish-speaking countries. In addition, gay and lesbian people have been and continue to be discriminated against. Although considerable progress has been made toward equality of all groups of Americans, the struggle continues.

ethnicity The shared characteristics and experiences of a group of people, such as nationality, race, history, religion, and language.

© Explorer/Science Source/Photo Researchers, Inc.

Individual children within the same cultural group can be as different from each other as they are from those in other groups. In what ways might these children be similar to each other? How might they differ?

▶ **Classroom Connection**

This video describes how experts currently define culture. What are some of the ways that defining culture is a complex task?

4. *Differences within a cultural group may be as great as, or greater than, differences between cultural groups.* Assuming that children who share the same culture or language are all alike is like assuming that all 3-year-olds are alike. Although there are some similarities, there are many differences in their skills, abilities, and behaviors. Likewise, children from the same cultural group share some attitudes, beliefs, and values, but there are many that they do not share. Children from one cultural group are both alike and different from children of another. African American children growing up in low-income, urban areas will share some but not all of the culturally determined behaviors of African American children whose families have been middle-class professionals for generations. Therefore, it is vitally important not to stereotype individuals who are members of particular groups even while learning some of the common practices, values, or beliefs of those groups.

5. *Culture is defined in terms of differences among groups and is complicated by issues of power and status.* Think for a minute about words like *mainstream, dominant, majority,* and *minority.* In the United States, each of these words is used to describe group differences in relationship to white European Americans. But to members of other cultural groups such as Latinos, Native Americans, or African Americans, European Americans are the diverse group. When one group, such as European Americans, becomes the reference point against which other groups are compared, that group is the one with the most power and privilege in the society (Delpit, 2006; Lynch & Hanson, 2011).

The practices of the cultural group that has the greatest power and status become the standard or norm against which other behaviors are judged (Lynch & Hanson, 2011). Cultural groups that have less status and power are perceived as deficient in some way (Delpit, 2006). Understanding how issues of power and privilege affect relationships and communication among cultural groups is critically important.

The election of President Barack Obama was hailed as a significant indicator of the nation's progress toward racial equality. Although that historical event did not negate the continued reality of racism and discrimination in many people's lives, it did challenge implicit assumptions about power and status in the society—not only for African Americans and other people of color, but for European Americans as well. There can be no question that, to some extent, the face of power was changed.

Relationship of Race and Culture An overview of the principles just discussed reveals that there is a complex relationship between race, ethnicity, and culture that knowledgeable teachers need to understand. Because race is a sensitive topic in the United States, the words *culture* and *race* are sometimes inaccurately used synonymously, but they are not the same thing (Wardle, 2008b).

Scientists argue that a person's race cannot be determined by examining her or his biological makeup (Wardle, 2008a, 2008b). Nevertheless, race is associated with a person's biology and is determined by who their parents are, whereas culture is learned. As evidenced by how census data are collected, racial classifications are complex and, for the most part, politically determined (Banks, 2012). For example, the same person might be considered racially black in the United States, colored in South Africa, and brown in Brazil. Moreover, according to the 2010 U.S. Census, almost 5% of children are multiracial, mostly likely an underestimate.

Teachers need to understand that although a very limited number of racial categories, such as Asian or Caucasian, are identified based on skin color and other physical characteristics, hundreds of cultural/ethnic groups exist. Asian peoples include Chinese, Japanese, Koreans, Vietnamese, Hmong, and many others, some of which have been historical enemies (Wardle, 2008a). Similarly, Hispanic is not an actual racial, cultural, or even linguistic group, despite its designation as such by census takers. The term *Latino/a* is currently used to refer to people of Mexican, Cuban, Puerto Rican, South or Central American, or other Spanish culture or origin (Derman-Sparks & Edwards, 2010). Given these complex realities, the increasing diversity of immigrants, and the growing number of biracial and multiracial children, it is essential that teachers not make assumptions about children and families' racial and cultural identities (Wardle, 2008a).

The most useful strategy is for responsive teachers to create a classroom climate in which it is safe to talk about and notice racial and cultural differences (Derman-Sparks & Edwards, 2010). Reading books such as *Colors around Me* (Church, 1997) or *Shades of People* (Rotner & Kelly, 2010) can start a conversation about how people with different shades of black skin are a part of the same race because their ancestors originally came from Africa.

In the previous sections, we described principles for understanding culture and how they interrelate. In the next section, we discuss similarities and differences among diverse cultures and how they govern various cultural groups' thinking and behavior.

✓ **Check Your Understanding 6.1:** Understanding Cultural Diversity

A Framework for Thinking About Culture

To help you understand the role of culture in the lives of children and families, and your own life, we examine a framework for thinking about values, beliefs, and practices among various cultural groups. In using this framework, it is important that you develop an awareness of similarities and differences among groups (Lynch, 2011).

Different cultural groups have different sets of values and beliefs, but beyond that, they have different ways of connecting with each other and functioning as a group. In some cultural groups, individual members put their needs first before those of the group; other cultures are group-oriented, putting the group's needs before their own individual needs. This framework classifies cultural groups in terms of two general orientations: (1) individualistic and (2) interdependent (Gonzalez-Mena, 2008).

Individualistic Cultural Orientation

The values of **individualistic cultural groups** include focusing on the needs of the individual, independence, self-expression, and personal property and choice. In individualistic cultures, the primary goal is individual achievement and fulfillment. These cultures emphasize the rights of the individual over the rights of the group. With its history of individual rights and focus on personal achievement, this is the dominant cultural orientation in the United States.

individualistic cultural groups
Cultural groups that focus on the needs of the individual, independence, self-expression, and personal property and choice.

Picture an individualistic-oriented classroom. All of the children have their own cubbies marked with their names in which to store their belongings. Developing independence in children is an important goal. The children's individual work is displayed and carefully identified. Children are praised for their achievements and graded in comparison to one another. When parents visit, they look carefully to find their child's contribution. The focus on individual children and their accomplishments is evident.

Interdependent Cultural Orientation

interdependent cultural groups
Cultural groups that focus on
the needs of the group rather
than those of the individual,
also called collectivist.

By contrast, **interdependent cultural groups** focus on the needs of the group rather than on those of the individual. These cultural groups, also called *collectivist*, value interdependence, cooperation and mutual assistance, shared property, and social responsibility. Interdependent cultures stress respect for tradition and authority over the rights of the individual. Among cultural groups that exhibit an interdependent orientation are Latinos, Asians, and people in West African and Middle Eastern countries. Because the United States is a nation of immigrants, many cultural groups within this country, as well as Native Americans and African Americans, are oriented more toward interdependence than individualism (Hanson, 2011).

In an interdependent-oriented classroom, individual children do not draw attention to themselves. Children readily share their possessions with each other. Group work is displayed. A colorful mural representing the contributions of scores of children adorns the entrance to the school. These two classrooms are described in overly simplistic terms. Most classrooms would evidence both cultural orientations because, in reality, they are not polar opposites but rather points on a continuum.

Continuum of Common Cultural Values

Instead of classifying cultural groups as *either* individualistic *or interdependent*, a more useful strategy is to think of values that are common across all cultural groups as varying along a continuum. Such a continuum is depicted in Figure 6.2.

Individuals within cultural groups vary all along the continuum; families are more or less inclusive, just as they are more or less traditional rather than either traditional or not. In addition, the ends of the continuum can be seen from a *both/and* perspective. For example, in the United States, schools and society emphasize *both* individual achievement *and* cooperation, working together to solve problems, and taking care of those in need.

Consider how misunderstandings can occur when teachers and family members operate from different points on the interdependent and individualist continuum, as in the following example:

▶ **Classroom Connection**

This video provides some specific examples of the continuum of cultural values and its impact on children's behavior. How could teachers use this information to teach more effectively?

Mr. Wu is late for a team meeting to discuss his son's IEP. The disabilities coordinator, Ms. Armstrong, impatiently taps her foot, repeatedly looks at her watch, and gets more and more irritated as minutes tick by. Ms. Garcia, the classroom teacher, seems less concerned. When Mr. Wu arrives, he doesn't apologize for being late, but he does tell Ms. Garcia that his mother is taking care of his son and she has questions to ask about her grandson. Ms. Garcia understands that Mr. Wu's respect for his mother took precedence over arriving at the meeting on time.

When the meeting ends, Ms. Garcia reviews her notes with Ms. Armstrong. She politely states, "I could see that you were concerned about the meeting running overtime. I know that you are very busy, but I believe that Mr. Wu did not intend to inconvenience us by being late. His greatest priority was to show respect for his mother, and I'm glad he consulted her because with her input we can do a better job of helping her grandson." In this way, Ms. Garcia did not tell Ms. Armstrong that her cultural views are wrong; instead, she clarified her own cultural views and those of Mr. Wu.

Applying the Continuum in Practice

Conceptualizing variations in cultural values along a continuum helps teachers in several ways: (1) It reduces the tendency to stereotype groups; (2) it reduces the likelihood that differences will be categorized as right or wrong, that is, an *us versus them* mentality; and (3) it has the potential to increase understanding and communication among teachers and families who may differ in their perspectives (Lynch, 2011).

Interdependent Orientation	Individualistic Orientation
Families value the welfare of the group—the extended family—over the achievements of individual members.	Families value the welfare of the nuclear family and its individual members.
Contributions to the community are valued.	Individual accomplishments are valued.
Respect for elders, traditions, and the past is a strong focus.	The future, youth, and technological advances are valued.
Respect for adult authority is expected; teacher-child relationships are formal.	Relationships with adults are relatively informal; children are encouraged to engage in conversation with teachers.
Time is flexible; people are more important than time.	Time is valuable; schedules are important. Being late or wasting time is considered disrespectful.
Extended families—grandparents, aunts, uncles, older siblings—care for and help raise children.	The nuclear family is primarily responsible for childrearing and may live far away from relatives.
Calling attention to oneself—standing out from the group—may be seen as selfish and rejection of family. Cooperation is valued.	Children's individual achievement and self-esteem are highly valued. Competition is encouraged.
Children are expected to contribute to the family functioning.	Children are expected to achieve on their own.
Children are encouraged to help each other, older ones help younger.	Children are encouraged to do things for themselves such as toileting, feeding, dressing at an early age.
Activity focuses on relationships, not objects; babies are carried and children engage in daily routines with family members.	Activities often focus on objects; children play on floor and with own toys and materials.
Ownership is shared.	Individual ownership is valued.
Children share family and community spaces, activities, and events.	Children have their own separate spaces (for example, their own rooms) and child-centered activities.
Gender and age determine rights and roles.	Individual freedom and rights are highly valued.

FIGURE 6.2 Continuum of Cultural Values

Source: Based on "Perspectives in Childrearing Values," by J. Bromer, K. Modigliani, and C. Callahan, no date, The Family Child Care Accreditation Project, Boston, MA: Wheelock College; and "Developing Cross-Cultural Competence," by E. W. Lynch, 2011, in *Developing Cross-Cultural Competence: A Guide for Working with Children and Their Families*, 4th edition, edited by E. W. Lynch and M. J. Hanson, Baltimore: Paul H. Brookes.

Ultimately, cultures may tend toward one end of the continuum or the other, but the values of most people fall somewhere in between. All cultures value families, for instance, but they define family membership differently. Similarly, rigidly categorizing groups is likely to lead to inaccurate assumptions. For example, Japanese cultural values are typically viewed as traditional (on the interdependent end of the continuum) and yet Japan readily embraces new technologies.

Following is an example of what might happen during an encounter between members of individualist and interdependent cultural groups:

To help children feel comfortable in their new surroundings, kindergarten teacher Alisha Watson created a bulletin board to display photos of children's families so that there would be something familiar to the children in the room. She asked for children to bring in pictures of themselves with their siblings and parents, and couldn't understand why some of the families never responded to her request. She thought perhaps families didn't have cameras or didn't want to participate in school activities. In frustration, she finally gave up the idea of the family bulletin board. Alisha never imagined that some parents weren't comfortable limiting the photo to just the immediate family. To many of them the extended family, which includes neighbors and friends, is what matters. One mother was upset that grandparents would not be included, but didn't want to alienate the new teacher.

As we can see, Alisha's concept of "family" represents a more individualistic orientation than that of many families in her classroom. Alisha could have avoided the problem by respecting the families' own definitions of their members.

The continuum of cultural values (Lynch, 2011) is intended to help you concentrate on common values—how cultural groups are similar as well as different. At the same time, effectively working across cultural groups requires looking inward and analyzing your own cultural perspective, as we describe next.

 Check Your Understanding 6.2: A Framework for Thinking about Culture

Understanding Your Own Cultural Perspective

As you read about interdependent and individualistic cultural values, how did you feel? Did you identify with one end of the continuum or the other? Did you find yourself judging people whose values and practices reflect the other extreme?

Teachers, like all human beings, view the world through their own cultural lenses. To be effective, you will need to overcome any potential biases about children's behavior in order to establish positive relationships, build on their prior knowledge and current levels of ability, and to help children make sense of their experiences. The first step in accomplishing this goal is to examine your own cultural perspective. Figure 6.3 will help you focus your reflections.

Become Aware of Your Own Cultural Experiences

Begin by reflecting on the origins of your family. Here are some questions to stimulate these reflections (Lynch, 2011):

FIGURE 6.3 Reflecting on Your Own Cultural Experiences

Source: Based on *Revisiting and updating the multicultural principles for Head Start programs serving children ages birth to five,* Office of Head Start, 2010, Washington, DC, retrieved from http://eclkc.ohs.acf.hhs.gov/hslc/tta-system/cultural-linguistic.

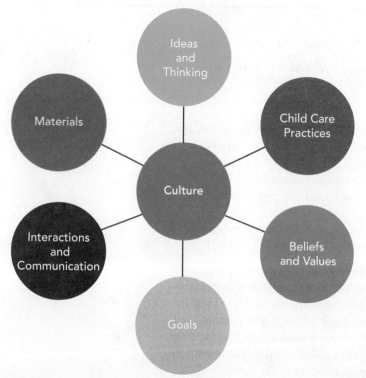

- What stories have you heard about your ancestors or relatives living in other parts of the world?
- How do you identify yourself culturally? Do you feel a connection to your cultural background?
- Do you or does anyone in your family speak a language other than English? What language(s) do you speak?
- Are there rituals, traditions, or holidays that reflect your family's heritage?
- How does your family express affection or disapproval?
- How do your family members communicate? Are they more likely to listen and think before speaking, or do they jump into conversation eagerly, even talking over one another?
- Can you think of advice or sayings that guided behavior in your family?

Questions like these help you become aware of how your own values, beliefs, and practices affect your behavior. Now think about how your cultural perspective affects your views of appropriate child-rearing practices. Ask yourself the following questions and compare your answers with those of colleagues:

- What are your thoughts regarding infant feeding practices? Should the goal be for children to learn as toddlers how to independently feed themselves? Or do you believe that adults should feed babies as long as possible?
- What do you think are appropriate discipline techniques? Should children be given time-outs, spanked, or lose privileges when they misbehave? Should parents explain their reasoning to children?
- Should young children be directed by adults and their movements controlled? Or should they be allowed to explore and make choices?
- What behaviors are acceptable for girls? For boys?
- How should children behave around adults?

Finally, examine how your cultural beliefs and biases affect your behavior and emotions. Reflect on these questions:

- Have you ever felt uncomfortable or surprised in another part of the United States or in another country? What was the situation? Perhaps you felt that people invaded your personal space? Or weren't respectful of your possessions?
- Have you ever felt awkward or embarrassed by something you said or did when you were traveling or among another cultural group? Did you think about why you might have felt that way?
- Have you ever done or said something that was culturally inappropriate? For example, did you fail to offer an appropriate greeting? Did your behavior embarrass or offend other people?

Finding yourself in another group and experiencing what it feels like not to be certain of the rules is an excellent way to gain deeper understanding of your cultural views and those of other groups. I (the author) have had many such experiences when speaking about early childhood education throughout the United States and in other countries. I remember specifically telling a story about the struggles I encountered during my early days of teaching. I often said, "I knew that I was smart, but I also knew that I didn't know enough about teaching young children and I had a lot to learn." Much to my surprise (and subsequent embarrassment), I later learned that some audiences were so stunned to hear me call myself smart that they couldn't hear anything else I said! Pointing out individual achievement even with self-deprecating humor is simply not considered appropriate behavior in many groups.

A part of reflecting on your own cultural experience includes comparing your perspective with that of other people. Therefore, the next step is to learn about other cultural groups and how your views and behaviors compare and contrast with theirs.

Learn about the Perspectives of Various Cultural Groups

To fully understand your own cultural perspectives, it is useful to learn as much as possible about how various groups think and respond to different situations and events. This knowledge will help overcome the tendency to impose your values and beliefs on the children that you teach and their families. To learn more about the values of various cultural groups:

- Read widely about children and families of diverse cultures and backgrounds.
- Seek out and read what has been written about diversity by researchers and theorists from a wide variety of cultural backgrounds.
- Identify key informants—family members, community elders, neighborhood leaders—who are willing to talk openly with you about their beliefs, values, and practices. To get as much accurate information as possible and to avoid stereotyping, don't rely on one person to be your cultural translator.

- Read books and magazines, watch movies, or search websites produced by members of diverse cultural groups.
- If possible, immerse yourself in another culture and experience the discomfort of not knowing exactly what to say or how to behave.
- Most important of all, observe carefully and listen closely to learn how various cultural groups communicate and nurture their young.

Learning generalities about cultural groups is a useful starting point, but it can easily lead to stereotyping—making assumptions that all children who appear part of a group share similar backgrounds. For example, a Cuban American father was dismayed to learn that his daughter's teacher kept telling her what she knew about the young girl's "Hispanic" culture and how the teacher was being responsive to it. None of the teacher's accommodations were meaningful to the little girl, whose family had lived in Minnesota for three generations.

Now that we have discussed the complex concept of culture and identified several key principles that describe how culture functions in children's development, consider how this knowledge can be applied to the classroom. How will this knowledge inform your teaching?

 Check Your Understanding 6.3: Understanding Your Own Cultural Perspective

Teaching in a Culturally and Linguistically Diverse World

Imagine it is the first day of school. Parents who are dropping off their children are using various dialects and languages that you don't recognize. Some of the children are crying and clinging to their parent, while others, it is clear, have been told that crying is not allowed, so they are standing with quivering chins trying to hold it together. You are making the rounds, introducing yourself to the children, trying to get them excited about the day and the upcoming year.

You may have been through this before, as a student teacher working in a culturally diverse classroom, but every year the dynamic and the ethnic mix change. It will be up to you to find a way to communicate with dual language learners, to be sensitive to the fact that the English language has many idioms that may be foreign to children who are mastering English, and to be sensitive to each child's home life, whether they live with their parents and siblings, or their extended family, or are from a single-parent home. The key is to learn as much as you can about each of the children, to get to know their families, and to always be culturally and linguistically responsive in the classroom.

Why Does Culture Matter to Teachers?

Children from diverse language and cultural groups and those from low-income families (who are disproportionately linguistically and culturally diverse) are the very children who are not being well served in our nation's schools. In fact, federal education policy is often designed to hold schools accountable for educating every child and to close the achievement gap between groups of children.

The underlying causes and remedies for the achievement gap are complex, but part of the solution must be to recognize and build on the competencies that children bring from prior experiences (Oertwig, Gillanders, & Ritchie, 2014). To do so requires that teachers acquire cultural understanding. Without such knowledge, at least three problems can occur: (1) teachers can misunderstand children, (2) teachers can inaccurately assess children's competence, and (3) teachers can plan incorrectly to promote children's learning (Barbarin, 2011; Bowman, Donovan, & Burns, 2001).

Misunderstanding Children Failing to understand the influence of children's backgrounds on their development can lead to misunderstanding and miscommunication about children and their families, as the following example illustrates (based on Zepeda, Rothstein-Fisch, Gonzalez-Mena, & Trumbull, 2006):

> In Carey Foster's Head Start class, she tries to promote children's self-concepts and self-esteem by having them make "All About Me" books at the beginning of the year. The children draw pictures and Carey writes down what they say about themselves.
>
> Four-year-old Antonia Rodriguez dictates, "My brothers are big and strong and help me and my mother."
>
> Carey says, "But this book isn't about your brothers. It's about you. Let's say you have brown eyes and you can write your name."
>
> Antonia doesn't respond. She feels unsure because she is proud of how her family helps each other, but her teacher doesn't seem to care about that. During the parent open house, Carey proudly displays Antonia's book for her mother, who doesn't look impressed. Carey doesn't realize that Antonia's mother thinks her daughter is becoming conceited and selfish in this school.

Carey's classroom activity was at odds with the interdependence valued by Antonia's family. Most likely, this situation would have turned out better if Carey had been sensitive to Antonia's discomfort initially. Instead of taking over for Antonia, Carey could have said, "Tell me more about your family." Listening would have helped Carey better understand the values of Antonia's family.

One area where cultural groups often differ is how they approach discipline. If teachers are unaware of these differences, they may be ineffective in guiding children's behavior. Furthermore, their methods may prove to be counterproductive. For example, time-out—removing children from the group for misbehavior for a period of time—is a discipline strategy that is widely used by parents and teachers. In general, the strategy is not effective, because it simply stops the children's negative behavior temporarily without teaching children what to do instead. Nevertheless, some teachers continue to use time-out. Let's consider time-out from a cultural perspective in the following example:

> Mark Temple is a new teacher who is struggling to control his first-grade class for reading instruction. His school is in a close-in suburb of a major city, and some people call it the "little United Nations" because it serves so many cultural groups. Today, Mark is reading a story to the group and Yao cannot keep still. He touches and sits very close to the other children, who pull away and are distracted by his behavior. After several warnings, Mark puts Yao in time-out for the duration of the story. Mark notices that Yao is sitting very quietly with his head bowed and a dejected look on his face, trying hard not to cry. Mark assumes that Yao is sorry for disrupting story time and that the time-out was effective.
>
> Mark's interpretation of Yao's response to his time-out, however, is uninformed. Mark's ignorance of Yao's Chinese cultural values causes him to misunderstand Yao's behavior. Yao loves school and is excited by the opportunity to sit close to the other children. Being assigned to time-out means being isolated from the group where he feels most comfortable and happy. Yao feels ashamed and guilty, not because he didn't follow the rules, but because he has been separated from the others. Yao is humiliated because he thinks that the group has rejected him. Mark also fails to recognize that Yao's desire to belong is a strength that he can build on to engage Yao positively in the group.

Inaccurate Assessment of Children Ignorance of children's culturally determined behavior can lead teachers to make inaccurate assessments of children's competence and ability. Language barriers can also lead to incorrect assessments of children's abilities. Cultural and linguistic differences can lead to errors in identifying and serving children with disabilities.

Assessing the learning of English language learners or children who speak a variation of English requires special tools and expertise. Too many English language learners are judged to be language delayed when they are actually demonstrating typical second language development (Paradis, Genesee, & Crago, 2011). No assumptions about children's competence should be based on measures in a language in which children are not fluent (Barrueco, Lopez, Ong, & Lozano, 2012). An English language learner or a child who speaks a variation of English may have a well-developed vocabulary and understand many concepts, but may not be well understood at school (Espinosa, 2010a).

One of the biggest mistakes that educators and the general public make is to equate cultural differences with disabilities. The fact is that children with disabilities cross all cultural groups. Likewise, cultural and linguistic diversity impact all dimensions of special education services.

In a classroom of diverse learners, teachers may have a difficult time identifying students who have special needs. In addition, diagnosis and intervention planning for children with disabilities is a challenge when the child is of a different culture or language group than the professionals (Hanson & Lynch, 2004). Read the *Including All Children: Diversity and Disability* feature for an example of these challenges.

Including All Children

Cultural Diversity and Diverse Ability

Effective early intervention practices are supposed to be *family centered*, involving families both in decision making and in implementation. However, cultural differences can complicate communication and understanding between families and professionals. These differences can become a challenge in planning intervention strategies for children with disabilities, as the following example illustrates:

Little Sparrow is a 3-year-old Native American child who was born with Down syndrome. Her family believes that such births are natural and that Little Sparrow's contributions to the community are important, however small. The community's goal is to maintain harmony among everyone. Little Sparrow is enrolled in Head Start on the reservation. Head Start program standards require that they provide early intervention services for children with disabilities. The teachers are members of the tribe, but they must work with the disabilities coordinator, who is not. Together, they help Little Sparrow improve her functional skills such as feeding and toileting, and she is making progress at school.

The disabilities coordinator meets with the family to ensure that they will follow up on the effective strategies at home. But the family seems nonresponsive. They can't understand why the school is so concerned about changing Little Sparrow when they love her just the way she is. And they don't want to single her out for special attention among the other children, which could upset the harmonious relationships in their community.

In this example, we see how a family's cultural perspective can be at odds with professional views. The professionals' intervention goals may not emphasize what is valued by the family, or the intervention may emphasize what they do not value. Such conflicting goals need to be negotiated if children's best interests are to be served.

In the case of Little Sparrow, the teachers worked with the disabilities coordinator to relinquish control of the situation and meet with elders in the community. They described their goals and how they thought that supporting Little Sparrow to do more would benefit everyone, actually bringing more harmony to the group. The elders decided that help for Little Sparrow would be shared by many adults and children in the tribe, and that in turn the little girl would help the others as best she could.

Sources: Based on *Understanding Families: Approaches to Diversity, Disability, and Risk*, by M. J. Hanson and E. W. Lynch, 2004, Baltimore: Paul H. Brookes; and "Cross-Cultural Conceptions of Child-Rearing: Implications for Reviewing/Evaluating Intervention Practices," by J. T. McCollum, T. Yates, M. Ostrosky, and J. Halle, 2001, Chap. 4 in *Cross-Cultural Considerations in Early Childhood Special Education* (Technical Report #14), by T. Bennett et al., 2001, Urbana-Champaign, IL: University of Illinois, Culturally and Linguistically Appropriate Services (CLAS), retrieved December 15, 2011, from http://clas.uiuc.edu/techreport/tech14.html#4b.

Failure to Promote Children's Achievement Misunderstanding and inaccurate assessment of children's competence can lead to ineffective teaching that does not meet the needs of all students. If children's competence is acquired in a context that does not match that of the teacher or school, several potential problems can arise. Teachers can negatively judge children on the basis of their culturally influenced behaviors. Without accurate assessment, teachers' expectations for children's learning can be too low.

If teachers do not recognize what students already know—what they have learned from prior experiences—teachers cannot build on it (Oertwig, Gillanders, & Ritchie, 2014). For example, many early childhood programs encourage and expect children to speak up and share stories of their own experience or background. Yet this may not be a task that all students can do. Consider, for instance, that among many Native American tribes, children are expected to listen to older adults rather than speak themselves (Paradis, Genesee, & Crago, 2011).

If teachers do not understand these diverse communication styles, they may have trouble assessing what children already know. For example, researchers working with Inuit people in northern Canada (Native Canadians, called First Nations) assumed that children's language development was delayed because they spoke little in interactions with teachers. But in a play situation with interesting objects and toys and other children with whom they were comfortable, the children's vocabulary and grammar were far more complex than what they used with teachers (Paradis, Genesee, & Crago, 2011).

As we stated earlier, different cultural groups often make different meanings from the same experience. If new learning is to be meaningful, teachers must help children make connections between what they know and are able to do at home and in their community and what is expected in school. Meaningful learning is more likely when teachers focus on the learning goal rather than on the specific means to the goal. For example, if the goal of a first-grade science curriculum is for children to understand life cycles, studying buffalo, which may be familiar to Native American children in the West, is as effective as learning about cows would be for children in the Midwest.

Misunderstandings, the roots of which are cultural in many cases, can have dire consequences. For example, cultural studies of African American children, boys in particular, find that on average they tend to be more physically active and emotive than their European American peers (Woolfolk & Perry, 2012). Teachers may incorrectly judge this exuberance as aggression. As a result, the very behavior that is rewarded and expected in their community may be censored by their teachers in school (Barbarin, 2011). When such negative responses persist, children may become discouraged and, perhaps, more disruptive (Ritchie & Gutman, 2014). African American boys are disproportionately represented in special education and more likely to be expelled, even in preschool. The civil rights division of the U.S. Department of Education (2014) found that African American children represent 18% of preschool enrollment, but 42% of students had been suspended once, and 48% of the students were suspended more than once. To better understand this disturbing phenomenon, read the feature, *Promoting Play: African American Children and Play.*

In the previous sections, we saw how teachers' lack of cultural understanding can lead to several errors in supporting children's learning and development. In the next section, we focus on the realities of linguistic diversity and its interaction with culture in children's development and learning.

Embracing Linguistic Diversity

The primary goal of this chapter is to encourage you to embrace the realities of cultural and linguistic diversity. Although we have focused much attention on culture, language and culture are inextricably linked (Hamayan, Genesee, & Cloud, 2013). Language is the lens through which children make sense of the world, and it is a major vehicle for

Promoting Play

African American Children and Play

Early childhood educators consider pretend play to be an integral part of developmentally appropriate practice and beneficial for children's development and learning. However, there are individual and cultural differences in how children play as well as how teachers view children's play that have important consequences for children, as revealed by recent research.

This study compared a large group of racially mixed preschoolers' pretend play and their adjustment (self-regulation and cognitive flexibility) as evaluated by outside observers in a laboratory setting with teachers' reports of children's social and educational adjustment. Teachers rated children's school readiness, peer relationships, and amount of teacher–child conflict.

The main finding of the study was that preschoolers' race affected how teachers viewed their play and how they rated their adjustment in the classroom, even after accounting for differences in individual children's age, IQ, family income, and gender. Moreover, even when the teacher and child were the same race, and the teacher and child knew each other for the same length of time, these different evaluations of children based on their race held true. For Black preschoolers, teachers evaluated their imaginative and expressive pretend play and rated them as less prepared for school, less

accepted by their peers, and more prone to teacher-child conflict. On the other hand, comparable levels of imagination and expression in pretend play resulted in positive ratings of these same characteristics for non-Black children.

Children in all racial groups—Hispanic, Black, White, and bi/multiracial—played similarly in imaginative and expressive ways. But Black children's pretend play skills were evaluated negatively by teachers, while non-Black children with similar play behaviors were evaluated positively. Teachers also rated Black children who demonstrated more negative play behaviors as less prepared for school, less accepted by other children, and involved in more teacher-child conflict than non-Black children whose play behaviors were equally negative.

This study raises significant concerns about teacher bias regarding the play of young African American children. Black children who are imaginative and expressive may be judged and treated differently in early childhood programs. Teachers need to become self-aware about the way they view children based on race and how those judgments can have lasting negative effects for children.

Source: "Through Race-Colored Glasses: Preschoolers' Pretend Play and Teachers' Ratings of Preschooler Adjustment," by T. M. Yates and A. K. Marcelo, 2014, *Early Childhood Research Quarterly, 29*, 1–11.

► **Classroom Connection**

This video describes the relationship between language and culture. Note the important ways that teachers can help dual language learners become bicultural to be successful in school.

transmitting culture. Dual language learners are learning not only two languages, but also two cultures. Children must learn how to use each language in culturally meaningful and appropriate ways (Hamayan, Genesee, & Cloud, 2013).

If a concept does not exist in a culture, there is no need for a word to represent that concept. Consider a language without a word for *privacy*. What would that tell you about the culture's values? Most likely, the cultural group places greater value on the needs and rights of the group than on those of the individual. Also, personal space and private ownership may be less important.

How words are defined and used also reflects cultural differences. For example, in Italian, the verb *discutere* can mean "to discuss" but can also mean "to argue." Picture a group of Italians or Italian Americans all talking at once, with raised voices and many gestures. Arguing is just another form of discussion and is much less threatening than in societies where English is spoken and where *arguing* has negative connotations.

Similarly, some languages may have many words to distinguish subtle variations in meaning that are important to the group. A large vocabulary for types of snow and ice is essential in the Arctic, but unnecessary in more temperate climates. What if English only had one word for *blue*? How could we communicate clearly without words like *turquoise*, *navy*, or *periwinkle*? The inextricable link between language and culture means that one cannot be embraced without also embracing the other. Language is also strongly connected to emotions. Words can trigger strong emotions in some cultures and not in others. For example, in Arab cultures the word *crusade* carries a negative connotation dating back to the Middle Ages, while in the United States we regularly have positive crusades to collect money for charity or fight disease.

The United States has always been a country in which many people are bilingual or multilingual. With increasing numbers of children speaking a language other than English at home, opportunity exists to help these children become bilingual. To do so, it is important that teachers support children's development and maintenance of their home language while helping them acquire proficiency in English. In short, these children are **dual language learners**—learning two languages at once. In fact, many children are **multi-language learners** who are learning more than two languages.

> **dual language learners** Children who are learning to speak two languages at the same time—usually their home language and English.

> **multi-language learners** Children who are learning more than two languages.

All children in our society need to acquire English, but they can become proficient without giving up their home language (Espinosa, 2010c; Tabors, 2008). The key is for teachers to support continued development of the home language and to inform parents that if they encourage their children to speak English both in the home and at school at a very early age, their children may lose their home language. Home language loss can harm children's long-term academic achievement (Espinosa, 2010c; Slavin & Cheung, 2005). In addition, if parents do not speak English well and their children lose the home language, serious communication and relationship problems between parents and children are likely to occur (Espinosa, 2010c; Wong Filmore, 1991). Therefore, teachers should encourage families to speak to children in whatever language the parent is most proficient, usually their native tongue, to support children's educational achievement.

In the previous sections, we discussed how educational systems often misunderstand, inaccurately assess, and fail to serve culturally and linguistically diverse children. One key to avoiding these pitfalls is for teachers to become more culturally competent, as we discuss in the next section.

✓ **Check Your Understanding 6.4:** Teaching in a Culturally and Linguistically Diverse World

Cultural Competence: The Key to Effective Teaching

To accommodate diverse learners, teachers must integrate students' diverse backgrounds into the curriculum. A particular kind of ability is required to successfully use this type of effective practice in the classroom: cultural competence. Conflict may arise in situations where families and teachers do not have an inherent understanding of each other. Consider the following example:

> Decatur Elementary School, which serves a wide range of cultural groups, has a lending library to encourage primary-grade children to read at home. After a few weeks, the library is bare because the families don't return the books. The European American teachers make insistent pleas for return of the books. The children begin to feel that their teachers are accusing them of stealing. But the children and their families don't understand; they assumed the books were meant for all the children in the neighborhood.

To resolve a conflict such as this, teachers must be well versed in effective cross-cultural communication. To provide the best education for all children, teachers need to become *culturally competent*.

cultural competence The ability to work effectively across cultural groups.

Cultural competence is the ability to work effectively across cultural groups (Olsen et al., 2007, p. 2) and to work respectfully with those who are different from oneself. Cultural competence is not a set of skills but is instead a way of being—an openness to continual learning (Olsen et al., 2007). Although various characteristics demonstrate cultural competence, several are particularly applicable to teachers in diverse classrooms (Lynch, 2011; Lynch & Hanson, 2011). Some characteristics of cultural competence follow, along with the ways they apply to the teachers at Decatur Elementary School and the lending library situation:

- *An awareness of their own cultural perspectives.* Teachers reflect on their own feelings about losing the books. They are mystified and a little upset. They invested time and money in the library and can't understand why it failed.
- *Appreciation and respect for individuals from other cultures.* Teachers do not pre-judge children and families by their standards, realizing that more interdependent cultural groups view ownership of materials differently than do individualistic ones.
- *A belief that cross-cultural interactions should be viewed as learning opportunities rather than challenges.* Teachers decide to find out what might have caused the misunderstanding, rather than giving up in frustration.
- *An ability to identify and use cultural resources.* Teachers seek the advice of leaders in the community to help them understand what happened.
- *An appreciation for the integrity and value of all cultures.* Teachers realize that sharing the books more widely is a valuable although different way of achieving their goal of making reading material available to children.
- *Willingness to continue to try to understand other people's perspectives.* Teachers decide to talk regularly with older children, family, and community members to discuss school happenings.
- *Flexibility and a sense of humor.* Teachers look back and laugh at how naïve their expectations were and how rigid their reactions.
- *Comfort with uncertainty.* The main lesson the teachers learn is that they aren't going to be right all the time; there are no simple answers to complex situations.

This list of competencies is prerequisite for becoming a truly successful teacher. Encompassing all of these characteristics and behaviors is an attitude of *cultural humility*—the stance that one can "expect to be surprised, to be wrong, and (the need) to ask for help" (Sparrow, 2011, p. 14). Cultural humility assumes that one can never fully comprehend the perspective of another human being and requires the ability to put aside feelings of superiority and the tendency to judge.

Cross-Cultural Communication

The foundation of cultural competence is the ability to communicate effectively with members of diverse cultural groups (Lynch, 2011). To foster good communication, teachers must develop an understanding of how various cultural groups use verbal and nonverbal means of communicating. These communication styles are another example of a cultural continuum such as those described earlier in the chapter. In this case, the continuum extends from high-context cultures to low-context cultures.

▶ Classroom Connection

In this video, experts describe intercultural communication. Why are such communication skills important and what strategies can teachers use to foster cross-cultural communication in the classroom?

high-context culture Culture in which communication relies less on words and more on contextual cues, such as facial expressions, gestures, or other physical clues, to convey meaning.

High-Context and Low-Context Cultures Awareness of different communication styles will help you better appreciate the competence of children whose cultural background is different from your own and avoid misunderstandings in communicating with parents.

Communication among those in **high-context cultures** relies less on words and more on contextual cues such as facial expressions, gestures, or other physical clues to convey meaning (Lynch, 2011). Examples of groups that are more attuned to nonverbal messages include Asian, American Indian, African American, Arab, and Latino groups.

In contrast, **low-context cultures** focus on direct, logical, precise verbal communication (Lynch, 2011). Low-context cultural groups include European Americans, Germans, and Scandinavians. Members of low-context cultures often become impatient if the speaker does not come to the point quickly or the communication is not direct (Lynch, 2011). Similarly, low-context communicators may be confused when they miss the meaning of gestures or unstated emotions.

Culturally competent teachers are able to work effectively across cultural groups. What knowledge and skills do teachers need to be culturally competent?

low-context culture Culture that focuses on direct, logical, precise verbal communication.

Effective communication across these styles can be challenging. Shirley Brice Heath (1983, 1989) was one of the first to describe the consequences when children of high-context backgrounds encounter low-context schools. Her research identified situations such as the typical sharing time (show-and-tell), during which the teacher asks children what they did over the weekend. A low-context girl might chronologically describe events: "I went to my brother's soccer game. Then we went to McDonald's. Then my grandma came for dinner." This recitation meets the teacher's expectations of a clear, precise account. On the other hand, a high-context girl uses a more narrative, episodic style, which assumes that the listener can fill in the context. "My brother sang a funny song. Here's how it goes." When the child begins to sing, the teacher grows impatient, thinks the little girl's description doesn't make sense, and asks her to sit down. Think of the conflicting messages these children receive about the value of their experiences and their communication.

Difficulty communicating between low-context and high-context groups is not limited to teachers and children. Adults are even more steeped in their culture's ways of behaving than children are. Imagine the difficulties that can arise when a high-context teacher attempts to talk to a low-context parent about a child's behavior problem. Or think of involving a high-context parent in creating an IEP for a child with a disability, which requires very accurate communication.

Verbal and Nonverbal Communication A general description of high- and low-context communication styles only begins to describe the complexity of cross-cultural communication. Virtually every aspect of nonverbal communication can be misinterpreted. Of greater concern is that the failure to understand and respect cultural rules of behavior can offend and insult the very people with whom you are trying to communicate.

A number of nonverbal cues can lead to misunderstandings between people from different cultures. For example, allowing or not allowing for personal space, when and why we smile, when we make eye contact or touch, and how we use silence and view time are all culturally relevant (Gonzalez-Mena, 2008). We have already discussed some of these, but a few others may be surprising. Consider smiling. Most of us assume that smiling is a universal, human way of communicating—and it is. But like other behaviors, it can mean different things to different cultural groups. Russians, for example, smile when they are happy, not just to be friendly (Gonzalez-Mena, 2008). This could account for why Russians are often depicted in American movies as unusually dour. Some Asian groups, on the other hand, smile more often than Americans, even when embarrassed or unhappy (Gonzalez-Mena, 2008).

Silence can communicate volumes, but it is also interpreted through a cultural lens. Some Asian groups pause before speaking as a respectful sign that they are really listening (Gonzalez-Mena, 2008). Some European Americans may interpret such periods of silence to mean that the other person isn't listening or doesn't have anything to say.

A full discussion of the typical ways of communicating among various cultural groups is beyond the scope of this book. Consult the resources listed at the end of this chapter to learn more about the practices, beliefs, values, and communication styles of various groups. As you encounter diverse, changing groups of children, you will need to continually update your knowledge to improve communication and avoid misunderstandings with children and parents. And, most of all, remember not to stereotype individuals based on such general descriptions of cultural expectations.

In the previous sections, we discussed the importance of becoming culturally competent. In the upcoming sections, we discuss how the curriculum for children should be culturally responsive. We also look at what kinds of practices are effective for teaching diverse learners.

✔ **Check Your Understanding 6.5:** Cultural Competence: The Key to Effective Teaching

 # Effective Practices for Diverse Learners

Every group of children is diverse on every conceivable dimension of development and learning, including their various cultural backgrounds and languages. It is important to remember that when we speak about teaching diverse learners, we really mean *all* learners. In the following sections, we discuss culturally and linguistically responsive teaching strategies, and anti-bias educational goals.

Culturally Responsive Teaching

Effective practices for working with culturally and linguistically diverse children are best practices for every child. For example, research on human learning demonstrates the critical importance of building on prior knowledge, which is naturally one of the most important principles of culturally responsive teaching (Espinosa, 2010b). The challenge for teachers is to uncover children's culturally acquired prior knowledge and then use effective strategies to build on it. Read the *What Works: Making Education Culturally Compatible* feature for a description of such research-based practices.

Linguistically Responsive Teaching

Too often, educational discussions tend to lump children into categories such as "low income" or "children with special needs." This also happens frequently with dual language learners, despite the fact that there is great diversity among these children. Consider these 6-year-olds:

> Rosalinda's father and mother are well educated and speak both English and Spanish fluently. Her parents have read and spoken to her in both languages since birth. The family lives in an upper-middle-class community and they travel to Argentina at least once a year to visit her grandparents.
>
> Manuel lives with his parents, four siblings, and other extended family members. They speak only Spanish at home. His family is very loving and they tell wonderful long stories but they have few books in their home. They cannot return to the family's native country because of the political situation and also because they do not have the financial resources.

▶ Classroom Connection

In this video clip, two teachers plan a science lesson of sorting the different properties of rocks. Listen as the teachers describe some effective teaching practices for linguistically and culturally diverse learners.

Clearly, Rosalinda's and Manuel's language learning experiences are different in many ways, including the language(s) spoken at home, the ages when they are introduced to English, the family's resources, and their verbal and written proficiency in either or both languages. In addition to primary and secondary language development, Rosalinda's and Manuel's capacities and interests differ in countless ways. For example, she loves to sing and paint, and her best subject is mathematics. Manuel loves soccer and animals, and his teacher soon discovers that he has great aptitude for reading. They and their families need to be treated as individuals with diverse strengths and needs.

What Works

Making Education Culturally Compatible

A body of research demonstrates that taking children's cultural backgrounds into consideration in curriculum and teaching is related to positive learning outcomes for students across age groups. These studies were conducted with elementary school children across many cultural groups: Puerto Ricans, African Americans, Native Hawaiians, Native American Indians, Mexican immigrants, Appalachian urban immigrant whites, Southeast Asian newcomers, Eskimos or Aleuts, and European American gifted and talented children. Based on this research, six key principles of effective practice for culturally diverse learners were gleaned that are also congruent with several aspects of NAEYC's position on developmentally appropriate practices:

1. Teachers and students work together toward a common goal. Teachers participate with children in activity such as a nature walk near the school.
2. Teachers incorporate language and literacy learning throughout the day and in all areas of the curriculum. For example, children talk, read, and write about the life cycles of the animals they observe on their walk.
3. Teachers make learning meaningful by connecting school learning to children's lives. The conversation begins with what children already know about animals.
4. Teachers have high expectations for children, challenging their learning, and focusing on complex thinking. Teachers pose problems for children to think about, such as what would happen if the trees were cut down.
5. Teachers and children engage in instructional conversations, discussing the content they are learning. Children are grouped by interest, talk with each other, and meet with the teacher to discuss and share what they have learned and identify new questions.
6. Teachers model language and actions, such as carefully handling a pet, so that children can learn through observation.
7. Teachers provide opportunities for child-initiated learning. Children generate learning topics or brainstorm solutions to problems.

Sources: "From High Chair to High School: Research-Based Principles for Teaching Complex Thinking," by R. Tharp and S. Entz, 2012, in C. Copple (Ed.), *Growing minds: Building strong cognitive foundations in early childhood*, edited by C. Copple, pp. 131–136, Washington, DC: National Association for the Education of Young Children; "Research to Practice. Joint Productive Activity: Collaboration That Builds New Understandings," by L. A. Yamauchi and R. H. Kuwahara, 2008, *Young Children, 63*(6), 34–38.

Following are some effective, research-based practices that help dual language learners achieve at high levels in English (Alanis, 2013; California Department of Education Child Development Division, 2008; Magruder, Hayslip, Espinosa, & Matera, 2013):

- Directly instruct children on English vocabulary and certain aspects of literacy, such as pointing to objects or pictures as you say the word ("This book is about a bird. See the bird. Say bird."). Model the language for children, describing what the child is doing ("You put on your coat") or what you're doing ("I'm getting the red paint for you").
- Give lots of opportunities for children to practice the new language, such as during play and small-group times that require them to speak (rather than just point) to take a turn
- Pair children with English-speaking peers for several activities. For example, ask a question in whole group and have children turn to a buddy to talk it over ("What do you plan to do outside today?").
- Support continued development in the home language, including teaching in that language as much as possible (at least learning key words and phrases), using qualified teachers, family members, or volunteers from the community who fluently speak the home language.
- Collaborate with families to plan curriculum reflecting children's cultural backgrounds and language(s), such as rhymes, song, and books children can identify with to help them connect what they already know to what is taught at school.
- Frequently review skills and concepts, do repeated reading.
- Draw attention to similarities between English words and the word in the home language, called *cognates* (mucho/much).

Dual language learners are individuals. They need differentiated instruction to develop their English skills, to maintain and further develop their home language, and achieve in school. Today's vast array of digital tools make individualizing instruction for multi-language learners much easier than in the past, as described in the feature *Language Lens: Using Technology to Teach Dual Language Learners*.

Awareness and responsiveness to all forms of diversity must be integrated across all areas of curriculum and teachers' relationships with children to ensure that all children succeed in school. But more than that, schools have a responsibility to provide today's children with the skills to function in a complex, global society. In short, they benefit from an anti-bias education, which we describe in the next section.

Anti-Bias Education

anti-bias education Learning experiences and teaching strategies that are specifically designed not only to prepare all children for life in a culturally rich society, but also to counter the stereotyping of diverse groups, and to guard against expressions of bias.

The early childhood field has embraced the concept of an anti-bias education. **Anti-bias education** includes learning experiences and teaching strategies that are specifically designed not only to prepare all children for life in a culturally rich society but also to counter the stereotyping of diverse groups and to guard against expressions of bias (Derman-Sparks & Edwards, 2010). In this section, we discuss goals of culturally responsive, anti-bias education and ways of helping children achieve those goals. The overarching goal of anti-bias education is to help all children reach their full potential. To do so, anti-bias education focuses on four core goals for children (Derman-Sparks & Edwards, 2010; Teaching Tolerance, 2012):

1. *Identity.* Teachers foster and support children's self-awareness, confidence, and pride in their family and own identity.

Language Lens

Using Technology to Teach Dual Language Learners

With growing numbers of dual and multi-language learners in our classrooms, all teachers need to be prepared to support English language acquisition while also promoting continued home language development. Using technology exponentially increases teachers' options to achieve these goals, as these examples illustrate:

Yao is a Chinese speaker who doesn't talk at all in preschool. He is isolated from the other children who won't play with him. His teacher knows that without social interaction, his English skills won't develop. She loans his family an iPad and with the help of a translator shows him a digital storytelling app to create a story about his family with photos and narration in both English and Chinese. When he shares the story with the other children, they realize that Yao has an interesting life and several of them decide to use the app to create stories about themselves.

Kara's kindergarten includes speakers of four different home languages, some of whom are newly arrived immigrants. She relies on technology to create an accessible environment for all the children as they acquire sufficient English to navigate the school. Kara posts pictures and labels in various languages (in some cases with phonetic spellings) to help children learn routines and safety precautions. On the Internet she finds images, songs, and stories that accurately depict children's homelands, and uses these to spark conversations among small groups of children. She teaches all the children to use iTranslate on classroom tablets to aid communication and support burgeoning friendships. The class uses Skype to communicate with children's relatives in other parts of the country or world. Within a few weeks, all the children, including native English speakers, enjoy helping each other explore different languages and learn together.

Children all over the world speak multiple languages. The opportunity to become bilingual or multilingual awaits every child in America if schools take advantage of young children's inborn ability to learn language and the affordable, technological resources now available.

Sources: Digital Story Helps Dual Language Learner Connect with Classmates, by D. Bates, no date, Washington, DC: National Association for the Education of Young Children, retrieved August 27, 2014, from http://www.naeyc.org/technology/digital-story-helps-dual-language-learner; "Using Technology as a Teaching Tool for Dual Language Learners in Preschool through Grade 3," by K. N. Nemeth and F. S. Simon, 2013, *Young Children*, 68(1), 48–52.

2. *Diversity.* Teachers assist children to experience and value human diversity, and use accurate language for differences.
3. *Justice.* Teachers help children recognize unfairness, stereotypes, and biases (negative expressions toward groups) and their harmful impact on people.
4. *Action.* Teachers help children to stand up, alone or with others, to counteract unfairness, prejudice, and/or discrimination against others.

Curriculum and teaching practices to help children achieve these goals need to be developmentally appropriate; that is, within the range of what is understandable and achievable for children. Let's look more closely at each of these goals.

Goal 1: Foster Children's Positive Identity within Their Own Group

One of your goals as a teacher working with young children is to foster a positive sense of identity and help them develop a sense of self-worth. **Identity** refers to the characteristics that individuals recognize as constituting a sense of self and belonging to a group. Consider how important your own name is—it represents you and is a strong part of your identity. Teachers need to ensure that children's names are spelled and, most important, pronounced correctly. Because membership in a cultural/ethnic group has such a strong influence on identity, it is important for teachers to be aware of and support children's connection to their group. Fostering children's identity may also involve their bicultural and/or biracial identity; it should not be assumed that these children or their families identify themselves with any particular ethnic, cultural, or racial group (Wardle, 2014).

In classrooms with children from multiple cultural or ethnic groups, teachers sometimes try to minimize the differences among students instead of acknowledging them. In an effort to discourage prejudice in the classroom, they may state proudly, "We don't see differences among children. We're color-blind here." Such statements deny the reality that children plainly see and experience (Killen, 2012). Teachers may think that talking about differences draws unnecessary attention to them and leads to prejudices. But this attitude, although well intentioned, actually has the opposite effect by denying vitally important aspects of children's identity (Derman-Sparks & Edwards, 2010). Consider how you would feel if your significant other said, "I don't notice that you are a woman (or a man)."

One question European American teachers often ask is, "But what if all the children in the class are white?" This question itself reveals the confusion that exists between race and culture in our society because "white" is not a cultural group, and white-skinned people are members of many different cultural groups. In addition, close examination of this question reveals the perspective, discussed earlier in this chapter, that the white, majority group somehow doesn't have a culture (Derman-Sparks & Ramsey, 2011). Thus, it is important to help all children become aware of similarities and differences between themselves and others. Society sends countless messages about the superiority of white European Americans. Therefore, in supporting a positive sense of identity among these children, teachers must avoid contributing to feelings of entitlement and superiority to others who are not of the majority culture.

To foster positive identity, teachers must make an effort to ensure that the learning environment is welcoming to *every* child and reflects the identities and cultures of every child in the class. They can use photos or drawings of children with family members and audiotapes and videos of family member's voices and activities, as well as books, music, and other materials that reflect children's cultural identity in a positive way.

identity The collection of characteristics that individuals recognize as constituting their sense of self and belonging to a group.

Culturally responsive curriculum and teaching promotes children's positive sense of their own identity, valuing of diversity, and critical thinking about stereotyping and bias.

© David Kostelnik/Pearson Education

Goal 2: Experience and Value Human Diversity Just as it is important to have a strong sense of self, it is important to value diversity in others. Related goals are the ability to respectfully ask about and comfortably adapt to differences (Derman-Sparks & Edwards, 2010). The following sections describe how teachers can help children acquire the knowledge and disposition to learn about the similarities and differences among people.

Help Children Learn about Differences As our nation's history demonstrates, just exposing children to people of different races, cultures, abilities, or backgrounds is not sufficient to help them learn to value diversity. In fact, simple exposure can actually exacerbate negative reactions (Derman-Sparks & Edwards, 2010).

Research on inclusion of children with disabilities, for example, finds that teachers need to work with all of the children to help a child with special needs be accepted and included in the group (Sandall & Schwartz, 2008). Preschoolers may think that if they talk to or play with a child in a wheelchair, they won't be able to walk, either. Teachers need to actively support positive interactions among children and intervene when negative reactions occur. Teachers shouldn't deny differences with statements such as "He's just like you." Instead, an honest explanation is best: "You and Justin both like to move around the classroom and playground. You walk and run, while Justin uses his wheelchair to get where he wants to go."

Similarly, teachers should not admonish children for noticing differences. A teacher who says "It isn't nice to ask questions about other people" leaves a child without the correct information she or he needs. A child might ask, "Why is Derrick's skin darker than Deion's?" A more helpful explanation might be, "Children usually look like their parents, and Derrick's parents also have dark skin."

Likewise, dismissing children's anxieties or fears about differences may lead to avoidance or contribute to the development of prejudices. Consider the situation where 5-year-old Ariel says, "I don't like Mashiko because she don't speak English." Her teacher responds, "Oh, yes, you do. We're all friends here." Such a patronizing comment may lead Ariel to avoid or dislike Mashiko even more. Instead, the teacher might say, "Mashiko can speak Japanese and she's learning English. Maybe you can help her. And she can teach you some words in her language."

Avoid Tourist Curriculum In helping children to understand and value diversity, teachers need to avoid the "tourist curriculum." A **tourist curriculum** (Derman-Sparks & Edwards, 2010) is one in which a culture is visited as though it were an exotic destination where people dress, talk, dance, and eat differently before returning to the "normal" place where we all live. Here are some signs of a tourist curriculum (Derman-Sparks & Edwards, 2010):

- Trivializing by organizing activities around food or holidays
- Tokenism, such as having only one book about any cultural group
- Disconnecting diversity from the rest of the curriculum, such as having a one-week unit on a different culture or only discussing diversity on Martin Luther King Day
- Stereotyping groups, such as using Native American images only from the past or wearing traditional dress
- Misrepresenting groups such as using only books about Africa to teach about African Americans

tourist curriculum An approach in which a culture is visited as though it were an exotic destination where people dress, talk, dance, and eat differently before returning to the "normal" place where we all live.

Integrate Diversity into the Curriculum Developing relationships with people from diverse cultural groups and engaging in authentic experiences is the best way to help children experience and value diversity. Such opportunities also help children to understand that their perspective on the world is not necessarily the only or the best, but simply different. It is also important for children to understand that there are many languages in the world and no language is better than others. Regardless of the composition of their class or school, children today are exposed to diversity through the media—for example, seeing an African American president on television or listening to a Latino news anchor. Their wider community may also be more diverse than the immediate neighborhood and serve as a source of study.

Cultural diversity can also be integrated throughout the curriculum. One way to help children experience and learn to value diversity is to teach overriding concepts that cut across cultural groups—we all need shelter, nourishment, friends, families, and exercise, but we meet these needs in various ways. In the primary grades, children begin to study history and the lives of people in their communities and beyond. Through oral histories and reading biographies and autobiographies, children can learn about their own ethnic group and others.

Building each child's positive identity and helping them appreciate and value diversity lays the foundation for them to think critically about fair treatment of all people. This is the third goal of culturally responsive teaching.

Linguistically responsive teaching provides the opportunity for all children to become bilingual if schools take advantage of children's innate ability to learn language and the affordable, technological resources now available.

Goal 3: Foster Critical Thinking about Justice and Fairness We live in a society in which great strides toward tolerance, understanding, and acceptance have been made; yet racism, classism, sexism, homophobia, ageism, and other negative expressions of bias and forms of discrimination persist. As a result, children will often experience these biases and at times express them. **Biases** are negative feelings and expressions toward groups or individuals. Understanding bias means recognizing that differences are not problematic, but negative reactions to differences are.

bias Negative feelings and expressions toward groups or individuals.

Countering bias and stereotypes is an area in which teachers must be ever vigilant. To achieve this goal, teachers must review books, videos, games, toys, and other curriculum materials to ensure that they do not perpetuate negative images of any group of people. Teachers must also pay attention to toys or materials that children bring from home.

In addition, teachers need to work with children to establish expectations for behavior that prohibit expressions of bias toward other people to ensure that race, gender, age, sexual orientation, appearance, and ability are never the subject of teasing or ridicule. This is an area where teachers must have a zero tolerance policy. They should intervene immediately when such behavior occurs, reminding children of the rules for how children are treated in the classroom. They also need to offer comfort to the child who is the target of biased behavior: "Yolanda, it was unfair and unkind for Caleb to say you can't play because you have brown skin. Caleb, remember that we treat people fairly in this school."

Following are three important considerations when handling discriminatory or biased behaviors (Derman-Sparks & Edwards, 2010):

1. *Don't ignore.* Teachers need to address any signs of bias head on. Ignoring discriminatory behaviors implies that they are acceptable. Consequently, the victim feels unsafe and the perpetrator feels supported, the opposite of what is desirable. For example, Ms. Eli is busy helping her first graders with math problems—when she hears Jasmine tell Hiroke that he has funny eyes. Ms. Eli contemplates saying nothing. Instead, she quietly says to Jasmine, "Everyone's looks are unique and different. Please remember that negative comments about people's appearance are hurtful and we don't allow that here."

2. *Don't excuse.* Sometimes teachers will avoid an uncomfortable situation by saying things like "He didn't really mean it." Excusing expressions of bias teaches one child that the behavior is okay and the victim of that behavior that he or she will not be protected. Instead, the teacher could have said, "Calling other people names

hurts them, but it also makes you look mean and not very smart. If you have bad feelings about someone's behavior, we need to learn better ways for you to express them."

3. *Don't be afraid to intervene.* Fear and ignorance are among the biggest impediments to confronting and eliminating discrimination in our society. Teachers may be afraid that they will say the wrong thing to children, or that parents will be upset if they talk about race, culture, language, or socioeconomic conditions. However, unless they are part of the solution to addressing bias and discrimination in society, teachers must accept the responsibility for being part of the problem. For example, two children in Mr. Pinto's second-grade class are living in a homeless shelter. The children are teased for coming to school each day wearing the same clothes. Mr. Pinto privately arranges for them to receive clothing donations. He also talks with the teasers about their feelings, and finds out that some of the most verbal children are actually afraid of losing their homes, too.

Goal 4: Take Action to Address Bias and Discrimination

Goal 4 builds on Goal 3. As children develop, they become more aware of others' feelings and ever more sensitive to the concept of fairness. How often have you heard a 4- or 5-year-old say, "That's not fair" in defense of their own rights? With teacher modeling and supports as described in the previous section, children begin to care about others who are treated unfairly and to do something about it, including telling an adult. This work is essential to address the epidemic of bullying in schools.

In kindergarten and primary grades, children can problem-solve together ways to take action to address situations in the school or community. For example, one school in Washington, D.C., is having a lengthy discussion about the name of the local football team, the *Redskins*. Children's positions on changing the name tend to represent their parents' point of view; some think the name is offensive to Native Americans, while others think it is a tradition that honors them. The children read books about the history of Native Americans and current articles about why various people think the name should be changed. The children even explore what it feels like to be called, "Whiteskin," "Blackskin," "Brownskin," or "Yellowskin." After much study, the class takes a vote on whether the name should be changed, with 15 *yes* votes and 6 voting *no*. Those who vote for changing the name decide to write letters to the team owner and the local newspaper advocating for a change. They also work together to think of alternative names to suggest.

The goals of anti-bias education do not need to be addressed as separate subject areas or topics of study. Instead, these goals should be integrated throughout the learning environment and curriculum and in all aspects of teachers' interactions with children and their families.

As we saw in the chapter-opening scenario, contradictions may arise because what professionals think is good for children and what families believe and value might be very different. Finding a middle ground that balances what professionals consider developmentally appropriate practice with what families consider culturally appropriate is paramount to effective teaching.

Developmentally Appropriate and Culturally Responsive Practices

In this section, we address the sometimes controversial topic of the congruence of developmentally appropriate and culturally appropriate practices (Bredekamp & Copple, 1997; Mallory & New, 1994; NAEYC, 2009). Just as we are all products of our cultural upbringings, we are also products of our cultural environments, such as our schools, summer programs we might have attended, and jobs we have held. Professional organizations, including schools and child care programs, also have their own cultures.

When the culture—especially the rules for behavior—of the school or child care center is similar to that of children's families, their adaptation and ability to make sense of experiences is greatly eased. These children implicitly know much of what is expected even though they need to learn specific information such as the classroom routines.

On the other hand, when there are cultural differences between the rules imposed at school and those imposed at home, children have greater difficulty adjusting. Not only do they have to learn the curriculum, but they also have to learn the implicit rules of discourse, such as "Respond promptly" or "Even though the teacher knows the answer, he will still expect you to answer the question."

For culturally diverse children to be successful in school, teachers must explicitly teach the rules of behavior that children of the majority culture already know. Lisa Delpit (2006), an African American education professor and recipient of a MacArthur "genius" award, eloquently describes how the school culture is the "culture of power,"

© Christopher Futcher/Vetta/Getty Imagesv

When there are cultural differences between what the school defines as developmentally appropriate and the expectations of the family, children are likely to have greater difficulty adjusting.

and children who have access to its rules are more likely to succeed and gain access to the power in society. Delpit further describes how constructivist teaching, such as the developmentally appropriate practices advocated by NAEYC (2009), may leave children of diverse cultural perspectives at a disadvantage. In her view, constructivism and other progressive education approaches reflect the dominant European American cultural perspective. For children of other cultural backgrounds, success in school may depend on their ability to become *bicultural*, that is, to learn the rules of the school culture while holding on to the rules of the home culture.

Like Delpit, many early childhood educators have questioned the cultural appropriateness of developmentally appropriate practice (Dahlberg, Moss, & Pence, 2007; Gonzalez-Mena, 2008; Graue & Delaney, 2011; Mallory & New, 1994; Sanders, Diehl, & Kyler, 2007). Let's think about this question in terms of what we've learned so far about culture.

The Culture of Early Childhood Education: Revisited Previously we presented a framework contrasting individualistic and interdependent cultures. Even a cursory examination of NAEYC's guidelines for developmentally appropriate practice (NAEYC, 2009) or the association's accreditation standards (NAEYC, 2007) reveals the degree to which these documents reflect the individualistic cultural orientation. Goals such as promoting independence, self-concept and self-esteem, exploration, verbal communication, and child-initiated activity permeate the standards. Overall, a "child-centered" philosophy underlies the approach.

A clear example of this orientation is the role of play in early childhood education (Zepeda et al., 2006). Children are encouraged to play and explore the environment and materials, and to play with and talk to adults. On the other hand, in interdependent cultural groups, learning is directed by adults and depends more on observation of adults than on play, discovery, and child-chosen activity (Zepeda et al., 2006). In these cultures, objects such as toys are less important than social interaction, and play occurs mostly with siblings and other children. Consider that children from these diverse cultural orientations might gravitate toward peers in a free-flowing preschool classroom, instead of making independent choices of materials as expected by the teacher.

Another standard focuses on the importance of warm, nurturing relationships among teachers and children (NAEYC, 2008a, 2009). But the definition of "nurturing" behavior is also culturally influenced. For example, white European Americans might think that African American parents and teachers are harsh in the way they talk to or discipline their children (Hale, 1994). This "harshness" may reflect the need to help children of color navigate in a society that is often hostile to them (Killen, 2012).

Consequently, those who observe this dynamic without this shared cultural perspective may not appreciate the love that is being conveyed. Similarly, African American teachers and parents may value children learning academics more than playing in preschool because they know these skills are essential for their children to succeed in school (Sanders et al., 2007).

To further illustrate how culturally determined our view of "best practice" is, consider a recent effort by Chinese researchers (Li, Hu, Pan, Qin, & Fan, 2013) to adapt a widely used American measure of high quality, the *Early Childhood Environment Rating Scale* (Harms, Clifford, & Cryer, 2005). The researchers found that the tool did not adequately reflect their Asian collectivist culture, especially in terms of their emphasis on group activities and whole-group instruction. They found it necessary to develop items measuring the quality of whole-group teaching, which they subsequently found to be highly related to children's learning outcomes. Another difference was in the way quality outdoor play is defined. Such play is far more restricted in their programs, perhaps due to overprotection by parents because most children are the only child in the family.

The point of this discussion is to acknowledge that the prevailing standards for good practice in early childhood education described throughout this book and taught in most teacher education courses reflect the dominant culture of society. At the same time, these standards require that programs be responsive to cultural and linguistic diversity. Given the diversity of children and families served today, teachers must help children to become **bicultural**, capable of operating successfully in both their home environment and the culture of the larger world. Accomplishing this goal requires teachers to resolve some of the inevitable contradictions that arise between what is considered developmentally appropriate and what is culturally appropriate.

bicultural Capable of operating successfully in both the home environment and the dominant culture of the larger world.

Resolving Contradictions

As you have seen, when you are caring for and educating other people's children, you are being relied on to do so in a way that adheres to other people's beliefs and values. In the case of infants and toddlers, for example, how feeding, sleeping, dressing, and toileting are handled is not consistent across cultures. Likewise, with preschoolers and elementary-grade children, teachers and families may disagree fundamentally on appropriate discipline as well as how and what children should be learning. Resolving these differences is an important part of working with children and families. Read the *Becoming an Intentional Teacher: Responding to Cultural Differences* feature for an example of how one teacher finds the balance between her ideas and family perspectives.

Professionals tend to think they know the right answers to situations that arise in the classroom. Yet in most situations, no one right answer exists. It is true that some practices, such as spanking children, are prohibited by law and others by licensing standards. In these cases, no compromise is possible. But more often, *both/and* solutions are more useful than *either/or* choices when such contradictions occur, as illustrated in the following real-life example (adapted from Bredekamp, 1997a, p. 47):

> Antonia Lopez was director of a program for Mexican American children and families in California. One of the program's primary objectives was to promote cultural congruity. As a relatively interdependent cultural group, Mexican Americans value cooperation over competition, and this value was encouraged in the program. Another accepted cultural practice is the giving of gifts to express respect and appreciation.
>
> During the year, an uncomfortable situation arose. Parents began giving teachers gifts, and over time the gifts became more elaborate. The gift-giving escalated into a competition to see who could give the best gift, a direct contradiction of the program's goals. To resolve this dilemma, Antonia and her staff established two rules for dealing with the situation:
>
> Rule 1) You can't accept the gifts.
> Rule 2) You can't reject the gifts.

Becoming an Intentional Teacher
Responding to Cultural Differences

Here's What Happened Before the new group of 3-year-olds started in the fall, I let all of the families know that the children were welcome to bring from home any kind of "comfort object" they would like. Emma brought her favorite bear, Cookie. When she went to get him from her cubby at naptime, Cookie was gone, and when she searched for Cookie, she found Linh curled up and ready for her nap, holding the bear. I explained to Linh that the bear was Emma's and gently took him from her and returned him to Emma. After this sequence of events repeated itself for several days, I talked to Linh's mother, Mrs. Pham, and asked for her help in getting her daughter to leave Emma's bear alone. Although she understands English fairly well, she looked at me with total incomprehension at this request. During the next few weeks, I talked with a few Vietnamese people who had lived in the community for a while. From our discussions, I saw the part of the picture I had been missing. In the Vietnamese and most other Asian cultures, the idea of individual ownership is not as important as shared ownership and enjoyment of objects.

I went back to Linh's mom to give her a sense of how Emma's experiences were different from Linh's. I also talked with Emma's mom about Linh's perspective. At her mother's encouragement, Linh brought in a toy animal that she and her siblings play with at home. After a few weeks, Linh and Emma sometimes would have their animals play together in the dramatic play area.

Here's What I Was Thinking Getting the information from members of the Vietnamese community was very helpful, as was my own research about "interdependent" cultures. Maybe I could have gotten to this eventually by talking with Linh's mother, but because I didn't understand the basis of her response, I didn't want to risk offending her as a result of my own ignorance. Once I had some understanding of interdependent and individualistic cultural values, I could talk with Mrs. Pham and see if we were communicating clearly. I felt it was important to go beyond just resolving the immediate conflict between the girls.

I think it is important for the families as well as the children to learn about the differences in cultural values and practices. After all, the Vietnamese children will experience the values predominant in European American culture throughout their lives in the United States, and ultimately the goal is for them to become sufficiently "bicultural" so that they can manage well in both worlds. At the same time, I was impressed with the way the Vietnamese children get along and share toys, which is a goal we have for all 3-year-olds. And the families who are natives to our area need to understand the new people who are joining our community, too. In fact, because Linh and Emma are so young, I thought their families might gain more cultural knowledge from this situation than they would.

Reflection Rethink this situation from the perspective of a teacher whose own cultural values are interdependent. What might she have been thinking and what would she have done?

With these rules in place, the staff had to arrive at an alternative solution. They agreed that rather than teachers' accepting gifts for themselves, gifts would be accepted on behalf of the school. Depending on the gift, it was shared by all the children, or displayed in a place of honor for everyone to appreciate. Soon families' gift-giving became less competitive and moved toward the goal of making the program a better place for everyone.

When teachers and families disagree on what is best for children, remembering Antonia's rules may be a good strategy. If teachers cannot accept the family's position for some reason, but they also cannot reject it, then they will have to work toward an alternative solution—one that might better serve everyone's interests.

Although it is true that all children are born ready to learn, it is equally true that their learning takes place within social and cultural contexts. Just as our cultural backgrounds influence our own development, behavior, and learning, developing an understanding of the role of each child's culture should influence what and how we teach young children. Although overall learning goals may be more or less the same across cultures, different teaching strategies may be required to help children achieve those goals.

To build successful relationships with children, you will need to take into account and learn about each child's cultural worlds because their experiences and home language are integral components of their identity. As a teacher, you will need to demonstrate respect and support for children's language and culture. You must also help children make sense of their new experiences in school by making connections to their prior knowledge and experiences obtained in their own cultural contexts. Culturally and linguistically appropriate ways of teaching are not "add-ons"; they are integral dimensions of developmentally appropriate practice.

 Check Your Understanding 6.6: Effective Practices for Diverse Learners

Revisiting the Case Study

... Ms. Griffin's Classroom

At the beginning of this chapter, we saw how Stacey struggled in her relationship with families during her first year of teaching. Now that we have explored the many ways culture influences thinking and behavior, we can revisit Stacey's situation and see how it could be improved for everyone involved.

Rather than giving up in frustration, Stacey attends a professional conference and takes workshops on cultural and linguistic diversity. This motivates her to do some reading and talking with the more experienced staff members at her center. These experiences cause Stacey to reexamine some of her prior assumptions and, in turn, change some of the ways she teaches.

Her first step is to alter her daily schedule so the beginning of the day is an informal time for her to talk and play with small groups or individual children. Before she calls for a group gathering to sing or tell the children the plans for the day, Stacey waits for all of the children to arrive. This schedule means that she is no longer frustrated if parents bring their children late.

Stacey reflects on the disagreements she has been having with families over carrying and dressing their children. She recognizes that these differences are quite minor. Consequently, she decides not to interfere with close family relationships by imposing her views of what is best for children's development.

Stacey explains to families that she doesn't always have time to feed each child individually, so at times she gives them finger food. In response to parents' concerns, however, she promises that she will help feed the children as much as possible. In general, she finds that once their families leave for the day, the children tend to model each other. In some ways, they function more independently, such as when they attempt self-help skills. In other ways, they function interdependently by helping each other often and waiting till Stacey tells them what to do.

In her conflict with Mrs. Arguenta, Stacey realizes that Mrs. Arguenta was showing respect by refusing to call her by her first name. Stacey comes to see that Mrs. Arguenta has a legitimate point of view about teaching Ilsia to use the toilet. She tries using the skills she learned for resolving conflict. She agrees to try Mrs. Arguenta's strategies, while Mrs. Arguenta agrees that they may not be entirely successful because Stacey has a group of children to supervise.

Finally, Stacey realizes that Mrs. Arguenta sent Ilsia's 10-year-old sister to pick her up because within their cultural group, older children naturally look after their younger siblings. Stacey respectfully explains to Mrs. Arguenta that because of licensing laws, the center can only release a child to an adult. This is an issue where compromise is not possible. Mrs. Arguenta presents a list of adult family members who have permission to pick up Ilsia.

As we see from the encounter between Stacey and Mrs. Arguenta, cultural competence and cross-cultural communication are key elements of effective practice in early childhood education. ■

6 Chapter Summary

- Culture can be defined as the values, beliefs, and patterns of behavior, both explicit and implicit, that are passed on from generation to generation. All learning and development occur in and are influenced by social and cultural contexts.

- A framework for studying culture is to understand that the beliefs, values, and behaviors that characterize cultural groups vary along a continuum from individualistic to interdependent.

- Teachers need to become aware of their own cultural perspectives as the first step toward becoming culturally competent.

- Knowledge of culture is important because without it, teachers can misunderstand children, inaccurately assess children's competence, and/or fail to promote children's learning.

- Cultural competence is the ability to work and communicate effectively, both verbally and nonverbally, with members of various cultural groups.

- Culturally responsive learning goals for children are to foster and support children's development and sense of identity within their own cultural group, to assist children to experience and value diversity, to foster children's critical thinking, and to counter stereotypes and biases (negative expressions toward groups).

- Given the diversity of children and families served today, teachers must help children to become bicultural, capable of operating successfully in both their home environment and the larger world. Helping children become bicultural requires teachers to resolve some of the inevitable contradictions that arise between what is considered developmentally appropriate and what is culturally appropriate.

Key Terms

- acculturation
- anti-bias education
- bias
- bicultural
- culture
- cultural competence
- dual language learners
- multi-language learners
- ethnicity
- high-context culture
- identity
- individualistic cultural groups
- interdependent cultural groups
- low-context culture
- tourist curriculum

 **Demonstrate Your Learning**

Click here to assess how well you've learned the content in this chapter.

Readings and Websites

Derman-Sparks, L., & Edwards, J. O. (2010). *Anti-bias education for young children and ourselves*. Washington, DC: NAEYC.

Lynch, E. W., & Hanson, M. J. (Eds.). (2011). *Developing cross-cultural competence: A guide for working with children and their families* (4th ed.). Baltimore: Paul H. Brookes.

National Black Child Development Institute. (2013). *Being Black is not a risk factor: A strengths-based look at the state of the Black child*. Washington, DC: National

Black Child Development Institute. Retrieved from http://www.nbcdi.org/resource.

Nemeth, K. N. (2012). *Basics of supporting dual language learners: An introduction for educators of children from birth through age 8*. Washington, DC: National Association for the Education of Young Children.

Souto-Manning, M. (2013). *Multicultural teaching in the early childhood classroom: Approaches, strategies and tools preschool–2nd grade*. New York: Teachers College Press.

Head Start National Center on Cultural and Linguistic Responsiveness

This federally funded center provides online practical resources to guide programs serving culturally and linguistically diverse children and families, including materials in Spanish and other languages.

Multicultural Children's Literature

A number of sites offer multicultural children's books, but searching for one that has "multiculturalchildrenslit" in the online address will lead you to a site with a large selection of books representing many diverse groups and in many languages.

Teaching Tolerance: A Project of the Southern Poverty Law Center

This website has a wealth of classroom resources including sample lessons designed for different age groups on all aspects of diversity and anti-bias education.

7 Building Effective Partnerships with Families

Learning Outcomes

After studying this chapter, you should be able to:

7.1 Distinguish characteristics of contemporary families and describe the role of families in their children's development, including how social, economic, and cultural contexts affect family functioning.

7.2 Discuss how reciprocal relationships develop with families and apply principles of family-centered practice.

7.3 Explain effective strategies for maintaining two-way communication with families.

7.4 Elaborate on how teachers can productively involve families in their children's care and education.

7.5 Apply what you have learned about families to build partnerships that achieve both teachers' and parents' goals for children.

Vilma Suarez has worked as a toddler teacher in an Early Head Start center for 3 years. She loves her job, but her days can be exhausting. Today was one of those days. Before the children even arrived, Vilma had a meeting with the early intervention team to discuss Aiya's individualized family service plan (IFSP). Aiya is deaf, and the team wants Vilma to begin signing with her. Aiya's mother is silent throughout the meeting. She is a new immigrant and feels threatened by this powerful group of professionals. Vilma is patiently working to gain her trust, beginning with being available to talk about other things besides Aiya's hearing impairment.

When Mrs. Vacaro drops 2-year-old Tomas off, he sobs and clings to her, and Mrs. Vacaro is clearly torn about leaving him. Vilma speaks softly to Tomas and gets his attention with his favorite stacking toy. Finally, Mrs. Vacaro is able to pry him loose and reluctantly departs. Vilma tries to call and text her during the day to reassure her, but Mrs. Vacaro attends school and must have turned off the sound on her phone.

The assistant teacher supervises the children's naptime while Vilma conducts a parent conference. The conference is difficult because she has to talk to Mr. Henderson about his son's out-of-control biting. Mr. Henderson angrily says, "Just smack him. That's what I do." Vilma realizes that this situation will have to be negotiated carefully.

At 5:00 p.m., when Mrs. Vacaro comes in clearly dreading the worst, Vilma greets her with the news that Tomas had great fun today playing with his friends, ate well, and even said two new words. As Vilma reassures her about how well Tomas is doing, Mrs. Vacaro sighs and fights back tears. She stoops to cuddle Tomas, and Vilma turns to talk with Marcy's grandmother and David's father, who have just arrived.

During her bus ride home, Vilma reflects on her day. She remembers that when she began her career, she was excited about working with very young children. Because she has three children of her own and helped parent her younger siblings, she felt confident working with babies and toddlers and was relieved to have a job where she didn't have to work with adults. Vilma shakes her head, remembering how naïve she was. She now knows that working with children is only one part of her job. Working with their families is the bigger challenge. But doing so is also very rewarding. She understands that by learning from and with families, her contributions to children's lives will last long after they leave her classroom. ■

Whatever your age, if someone asked you to picture the most important people in your life, images of your family members would likely come to mind. Perhaps you would picture the people you grew up with, or your spouse/partner and children. Some of you might picture both your nuclear family of parents and siblings and your extended family of cousins, aunts, uncles, and grandparents. Families play essential roles in every aspect of human development through the life span. During early childhood, however, families are the primary context for children's development and learning, with child care and early education settings playing a secondary, albeit critically important, role. Given that these two contexts—families and early childhood programs—are the two main environments in which children develop and learn, it is essential for teachers and parents to work in concert if children are to develop to their fullest potential.

Because young children are inherently connected to their families, early childhood teachers work with children *and* families. The younger the child, the stronger the connection to family and, therefore, the closer the relationship between teacher and parent must be. Most early childhood educators enter the field because of their interest in teaching young children; initially, they may not grasp the importance of developing skills to work with families. In fact, teachers report that working with families is among the areas where they feel least prepared and need the most help (Early & Winton, 2001). Throughout this book, we use the terms *families* and *parents* to mean those people who are primarily responsible for the children you teach, whoever they are—parents, stepparents, grandparents, guardians, foster families, or other household members.

This chapter describes how teachers establish reciprocal relationships with families. We begin by painting a picture of today's families, their exquisite diversity, and the challenges they face in providing for their children. Next, we describe the principles of family-centered practice as well as the nature of productive, reciprocal partnerships between teachers and families. We describe effective strategies for communicating with families and involving them in their children's education. We also acknowledge that some strategies are not effective in all situations; relationships with families are not always smooth. Therefore, the chapter provides a framework for building partnerships that is effective in resolving the inevitable conflicts that arise when working with families.

Today's Families

One can hardly read a newspaper or watch a television program today without hearing dire warnings about the state of the American family and the myriad threats it faces. Although it is true that families in the 21st century confront many challenges, it is equally true that the family is and has always been a dynamic, resilient, and effective institution for nurturing and acculturating each new generation.

What is a family? This may seem like a fairly easy question to answer, but it is not. Each of you, no doubt, has your own definition of family based on your own experiences. Throughout your career as a teacher, you will work with children who experience a wide range of family configurations, as discussed next.

Families today come in all shapes and sizes. How would you describe the membership in your family? How does it compare with the family your parents or grandparents grew up in?

Welcoming Diverse Families

Louise's child care class consists of fifteen 3- to 5-year-olds. Four of the children live with their biological mothers and fathers; Blake and Debra are only children, Madeline is the youngest of four, and Stephen is the eldest of three. Five children live with their mothers only, but among them Joseph and Lauren are in shared custody arrangements and split days of the week living with their fathers. Both Joseph and Lauren have stepmothers as well as stepsiblings. Lauren also has a baby half-brother. Of the other three children who live with their mothers, Marin doesn't know her father at all, and Jackson has infrequent contact with his biological father. Jeanine's mom is serving in the military overseas. Marta lives with her two dads, and Logan lives with his two moms. Kim lives with his parents and siblings and also his paternal grandparents, aunt, and one cousin. David has lived with his grandmother and two brothers since his mother died, and his father is in prison. The diverse family configurations represented in Louise's class are typical of America today: two-parent, single-parent, families of divorce, blended/stepfamilies, LGBT (lesbian/gay/bisexual/transgender) families, and extended families.

Despite statistics and experience to the contrary, many people still think of the family as consisting of two first-time married parents and their biological or adopted children, known as the nuclear family. In looking at how children grow up today, however, as depicted in Figure 7.1, we see that about two-thirds (64%) of *all* children live with two married parents, but considerable variation exists among these families. About 1 in 8 of these children lives in a family with a stepparent or adoptive parent (Kreider & Ellis, 2011). Mother-only families account for 24%, and 4% of children live with their fathers only (Child Trends, 2014a). Another 4% of children live with neither parent but rather with other family members, usually grandparents, or nonrelatives.

A significant trend is the difference in children's living arrangements by race and ethnicity (Children's Defense Fund [CDF], 2011). More than half of African American children live with their mothers only, as do about 28% of Latino children (Child Trends, 2014a). By contrast, 15% of white children and only 11% of Asian children live in mother-only households. In addition, more than twice as many African American children (6%) as white children do not live with either parent (Child Trends, 2014a).

Increasing numbers of children live in extended families, which are defined as a family unit where two or more generations of close family relatives live together in one household. Here again we see racial and ethnic diversity, with about 9% of white, 17% of African American, and 14% of Latino children living with at least one grandparent (Ellis & Simmons, 2014).

Families form and re-form over time. At various times, children may live with only one or even no parents because of divorce, separation, remarriage, death, or other circumstances. In early childhood programs, conversations and curriculum often focus on children's families, but because families today are so diverse, teachers need to be careful not to make assumptions.

Contrary to popular belief, there has never been a "typical" or "traditional" family structure in America (Welch, 2011). Various factors contribute to changing family structures over time. For example, until quite recently in history, women died in childbirth at alarming rates, and men also died young in wars or of disease. Therefore, although divorce was less common, many children grew up in single-parent families or blended families. Consider for a moment your own experiences of family, and those of your parents and grandparents. While some grow up in a "traditional" nuclear family with married parents of different sexes, many children grow up in single-parent, grandparent, or same-sex parent households.

FIGURE 7.1 Living Arrangements for All Children
Today, children's living arrangements vary widely depending on their family backgrounds, circumstances, and configurations.

Source: Family Structure, Child Trends Data Bank, from Child Trends, 2014, retrieved from http://www.childtrendsdatabank.org.

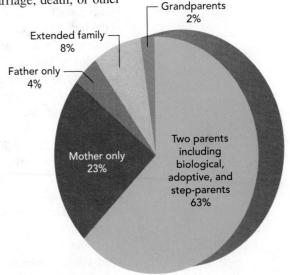

Grandparents 2%

Extended family 8%

Father only 4%

Mother only 23%

Two parents including biological, adoptive, and step-parents 63%

Regardless of your own family experiences or values, as a teacher you will encounter many different family configurations. The likelihood of successfully working with families will increase if you accept the following assumptions:

- Families are diverse in many ways: composition, culture, religion, economic status, work, mobility, and sexual orientation.
- Families are not good or bad; they are different and unique.
- Families, with rare exceptions, want the best for their children, regardless of the difficult circumstances they may be trying to overcome.
- All families have strengths and resources, hopes and dreams for their children, just as all families face challenges.
- It is not your right to pass judgment on families. You do not need to agree with families at all times, but you cannot reject a child's family and at the same time successfully care for and educate the child.

The more you know about the intricacies of family functioning, the more likely you will be able to put the above assumptions into practice. In the next section, we describe the theoretical perspectives that help explain how families function and change.

Family Dynamics

Joelynn and Jeff Robeson already have 18-month-old twins when their third child, Eric, is born with spina bifida, a physical disability that requires repeated hospitalizations and considerable care. Just when Joelynn and Jeff are beginning to adjust to the strain on their marriage of caring for three young children, including one with special needs, the factory where Jeff works closes down and he loses his job. Suffering from depression and alcohol abuse, Jeff leaves Joelynn without child support, forcing her to seek public assistance. After a while, however, the rules for continuing on public assistance require Joelynn to work full time, and she must leave her three young children in the care of her sister, who also has two preschool-age children. Joelynn suffers from the stresses of caring for her children and supporting them on her minimum wage salary.

As is true for every family, the development of each member of the Robeson family is affected by many different factors, both internal and external to the family. Two theoretical perspectives are helpful for thinking about families: Bronfenbrenner's ecological theory of human development and family systems theory. Each of these frameworks helps explain the complex interactions known as family dynamics.

Bronfenbrenner's Ecological Model of Human Development As we learned in Chapter 4, ecological theory is a useful model for understanding the influence of social and cultural contexts on human development (Bronfenbrenner & Morris, 2006), and especially the important influence of family. At the center of Bronfenbrenner's model is the individual child, whose development is influenced by biology, and by the proximal processes of daily interactions in the family microsystem. In the Robeson family, Eric's disability at birth is a biological contributor to his development, but other variables also contribute to his development and mediate his disability. For example, Eric's personal characteristics, such as his above-average intelligence and his lively personality, attract the positive attention of everyone he meets.

In the Robeson family, Eric was born into a family that was already caring for very young twins. His siblings' existence was part of the context into which he was born, but his birth and his disability dramatically changed the family's context. As a result, Eric's aunt provided child care; this event occurs within the microsystem in which experiences interact and affect each other. The interactions that Eric has with his parents, siblings, and extended family—proximal processes, or daily routines—bear the most influence on his development.

Other aspects of the systems surrounding Eric also matter for his development. Interactions between his family and his aunt, doctors, and early intervention professionals represent the mesosystems—the interactions among Eric's microsystems. For the Robeson family, the exosystem includes economic factors beyond their control that seriously affected the family. Jeff's unemployment led to the family's requiring public assistance. The laws governing eligibility for public support necessitated Joelynn's employment and the children's enrollment in child care.

Consider how changes in various elements of the exosystem could alter outcomes for the Robeson family and their children, especially Eric. With Jeff out of work and Joelynn working for minimum wage, the family's income is below poverty level, making them eligible for Early Head Start. This federal program provides child care for children from birth to age 3, early intervention services for Eric, and family support. The early intervention team helps Joelynn learn how to support Eric's development at home. They put Jeff in touch with mental health counselors to help him deal with his depression, and they also connect him to Alcoholics Anonymous and career retraining. Through the counseling offered by Early Head Start, Jeff gets a maintenance job while he attends computer school. Joelynn begins training as a nurse's aide, inspired by her newfound abilities to care for Eric's health. The twins thrive in the social atmosphere at the child care center. The family reunites, and its emotional as well as financial security improves. The changes in Eric's family will have lasting benefits for his development as well.

When aspects of the child and family systems provide substantive supports outside of their home life, families have what they need to have positive interactions inside their home—and children benefit. Now that you have seen how various ecological systems interact to influence the family and children's development, we focus on family systems theory, which explains more about the internal workings of family dynamics.

Family Systems Theory Understanding family dynamics is an important aspect of working with children of any age, but of young children in particular because they don't always have the language to describe their emotions and needs. Rodney may be angry because his father was just deployed, which makes his mother sad and nervous and his big sister silent. To describe how this one event impacts the entire family, **family systems theory** views family members as interconnected parts, with each member influencing the others in predictable and recurring ways (Welch, 2011). Family systems theory focuses on explaining family behavior—that is, why individual family members behave as they do in relation to one another and to those outside the family. Understanding how families function as systems can help teachers serve diverse children and build family partnerships more effectively.

Family systems theory describes some common characteristics of families, including boundaries, roles, rules, hierarchy, climate, and equilibrium (Christian, 2006). Each of these characteristics can be described on a continuum. For example, all families have rules regarding the acceptable behavior of members; some families operate according to strict and inflexible rules, whereas others have few rules or apply rules inconsistently. Table 7.1 presents characteristics of family systems, what they mean, and implications for effective teaching practice. Because each dimension of family functioning is particularly influenced by the cultural beliefs and practices of the family and community, teachers need to view family variability on these dimensions as differences rather than positives or negatives (Christian, 2006).

In the previous sections, we have seen how families influence and are influenced by social, cultural, and political contexts. We have also seen how different families' characteristics influence their behavior toward their children and in relation to teachers and school. In the next section, we describe some of the challenges confronting America's families today.

family systems theory Views family members as interconnected parts, with each member influencing the others in predictable and recurring ways.

Family Circumstances and Challenges

Families today face many challenges in providing the best care and education for their children. We regularly hear dire predictions about children *at risk*. This term is widely used, typically to refer to children who have characteristics (such as a disability) or life circumstances (such as poverty) that increase the likelihood that they will experience

TABLE 7.1 Characteristics of Family Systems

Dimension	Explanation	Implication and Example
Boundaries	Limitations on what or who is considered in or out of the family. Some families are open to new people and new ideas, whereas others tend to be more closed and restrictive. Families at one extreme may share too much information about the private workings of the family, whereas extremely closed families may conceal information such as domestic violence or substance abuse.	Respecting a family's boundaries is an important skill of effective early childhood professionals. When the Robeson family enrolled in the Early Head Start program, the staff found that Joelynn was open to sharing her problems and seeking help, but Jeff at first felt the program was too intrusive into his personal business.
Roles	In every family, individual members have roles—the parts that individuals typically play in relation to others. Most of us readily remember our role in the family. Were you the baby, the peacemaker, or the rescuer?	These roles have powerful lasting effects on development that are often played out in school as well. For example, 7-year-old Deon's parents have addiction problems. From a young age, he has felt responsible for taking care of them and his younger sister. Deon's teacher values his serious attitude toward his work, but wishes that he didn't worry so much about his parents and could be more carefree.
Rules	The standards or traditions that dictate correct behavior in various situations and how we relate to one another. Defining and passing on rules for behavior is the major function of cultural groups; therefore, rules are, by definition, culturally determined.	Differences in teachers' and parents' expectations about rules often require negotiation. Deon's parents think he should act like a man and contribute to the family rather than play outside or spend time with friends.
Hierarchy	The decision making, control, and power within the family, who is in charge, and how power is distributed and used. Like rules, hierarchy is strongly influenced by culture. In some families, parents share responsibility equitably; in others, hierarchy is determined by gender, with fathers and mothers making decisions about different aspects of parenting. In some groups, power is vested in elders. Hierarchies change over time.	Teachers need to be aware of family hierarchy because so many interactions involve decisions, and effective family partnerships and family-centered practice require the sharing of power. In the Robeson family, Jeff was the one in charge during the early years of the marriage, but when he lost his job, power shifted to Joelynn as the breadwinner and single parent. Power shifts can also occur when a military parent is deployed.
Climate	The emotional and physical environment in which a child grows up. Emotionally close families can compensate to some extent for threatening physical environments.	The classroom climate needs to be emotionally safe and secure for all children. The Robeson family lived in a physically safe neighborhood, but the tensions between the parents created a hostile emotional climate in the home for a time.
Equilibrium	The sense of balance or consistency that family members experience. Growth and change, both positive and negative, are inevitable aspects of human development, but too much inconsistency creates confusion and resentment.	Teachers can help work with families during times of change to maintain stability and consistency. For example, at the Early Head Start center, the Robeson twins were kept in the same class with the same teachers for 2 years during the period of upheaval in their family. Then the staff worked with the Head Start program to transition the twins smoothly to preschool.

Source: Based on "Understanding Families: Applying Family Systems Theory to Early Childhood Practice," by L. G. Christian, 2006, *Young Children, 61*(1), 12–20.

negative developmental and learning outcomes, such as dropping out of school. However, the term "at risk" has no consistent definition and often tends to stigmatize children, families, and/or communities by oversimplifying the strengths and challenges of children and families with a label that does not help address their needs (Moore, 2006).

Because families are the most critical setting for children's development, risk factors affecting families, such as poverty, single parenthood, and low levels of parental education (which tend to co-occur), are found to be related to poor outcomes for children. Other factors that place families at risk include family dysfunction, abuse, parental mental illness, substance abuse, and illness (U.S. Department of Health and Human Services, n.d.). Community risk factors create challenges for families as well; these include poverty, crime, unemployment, and high levels of teen parenthood.

Challenges for Families

The largest risk factor for poor child outcomes is poverty, which the federal government defines as less than $22,050 per year for a family of four. Because research shows that almost twice this income is required to adequately cover expenses, the National Center for Children in Poverty (2014) estimates that almost 45% of children live in low-income families. In 2012, almost 25% of children under the age of 6 were living in poverty or extreme poverty (less than half the poverty level)—an increase of 33% in the first decade of the 21st century (Children's Defense Fund [CDF], 2014). Growing up in poverty is related to many negative outcomes for children, including increased likelihood of abuse, neglect, school failure, delinquency, and violence.

Child poverty continues to grow despite the fact that most poor children live in working families (CDF, 2014). Moreover, a disproportionate number of children of color live in poverty (CDF, 2014). Compared to 12% of white children, 40% of African American, 34% of Hispanic, and 37% of American Indian children under age 5 are poor (CDF, 2014).

Children living in poverty are at risk for poor physical and dental health, more likely to experience hunger and malnutrition, and less likely to have access to health care (CDF, 2014). African American children are more than twice as likely as white children not to have medical insurance. In addition, homelessness is on the rise; in fact, families with children, including many preschoolers, are the fastest growing group of homeless people (CDF, 2014).

Cumulative risk factors increase the likelihood of poor outcomes for children. Poverty coupled with other factors such as low level of parent education (less than high school), single-parent family, or teen parent multiplies risk. Economic stress also affects two-parent families. Almost 60% of mothers of children under age 5 are in the workforce, which adds the cost of child care for many financially strapped families.

> **▶ Classroom Connection**
>
> Watch this video about the Campsey family, and analyze how family experiences, in this case the birth of a child with disabilities, can change family dynamics and circumstances in challenging ways.
>
> http://www.youtube.com/watch?v=exaWw4hPzwE&index=34&list=PLK1JOJxrAG2E-BE-CoAk15nr190X3Sw8Zl

© Carla Mestas/Pearson Education

Programs such as Head Start and Early Head Start serve our nation's neediest families. Early childhood teachers work closely with families and can be resources to help strengthen and build resilience in families facing challenges.

Resilient Families Despite difficult family circumstances and challenges, it is important to note that poverty, neglect, and discrimination do not necessarily set children up for failure. Families' assets or strengths—their protective factors—can counter the potential negative effects of risks (Cabrera, 2013). Although public attention tends to focus on all that is wrong with the American family, compelling evidence exists that many families—including those living in the most difficult circumstances—have inner strengths that counter risk factors and predict positive results for children (Iruka, 2013).

Contemporary families have high levels of important family strengths: closeness, concern, caring, and interaction (Moore, Chalk, Scarpa, & Vandivere, 2002). Moreover, a positive, caring relationship with a parent can mitigate many risk factors (Bandy & Moore, 2008). Similarly, ongoing positive relationships with other adults, especially caregivers and teachers, are important protective factors (Driscoll, Wang, Mashburn, & Pianta, 2011).

Child Trends (2007) finds that about 10% of children growing up in two-parent, low-conflict families have problems, whereas 20% of all other children experience problems. Their conclusion is somewhat contrary to the popular images of at-risk children and families today: Most kids do fine. Some children with highly stable families will have problems; more children whose families experience several risk factors will struggle. The takeaway message with regard to risk and protective factors is that there are no guarantees. Poor outcomes are not inevitable for children placed at risk, just as low risk is not a guarantee of success in life. Given the critical role of families in children's development and learning, the simple conclusion is that anything we can do to strengthen families is a good idea (Child Trends, 2007). Later in this chapter, we discuss family-centered practice, which includes research-based, effective strategies to support families.

Because they work directly with families as well as children, early childhood educators have the opportunity as well as the responsibility to strengthen families. In the next section, we address ways teachers can build reciprocal relationships with families toward the goal of achieving better outcomes for all children.

✓ **Check Your Understanding 7.1:** Today's Families

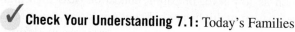

Reciprocal Relationships with Families

In her book on partnerships with parents, Janis Keyser (2006, p. xi) describes her development as an early childhood professional as progressing through three stages of relationship with parents: save the child, save the parents, and draw on parents' expertise. These stages are identical to my own experience and that of many other early childhood teachers.

Like many others in the early childhood profession, Keyser chose this field because of her love of children. In the earliest days of her practice, when she encountered a child whose needs were great, she entered the first stage: "save the child." Inevitably there would be several children whom she thought if only she could save them from their parents, their lives would be better. She quickly realized the futility of this approach and moved on to the next stage of her development, which she calls "save the parents." Realizing that it would be impossible to save all of the children from their parents, she determined to fix the parents. She thought that if she taught them everything early childhood professionals know, they would become better parents. Soon, however, she realized that this notion fails to recognize that families bring **funds of knowledge**—experiences, traditions, goals, resources, and rich culture to their roles. In fact, she concluded that families add unique value to the knowledge of early childhood teachers (Gonzalez, Moll, & Amanti, 2005; Iruka, 2013). In the final stage of development in her relationships with families, she rejected both goals of saving children and saving parents in favor of drawing on parents' expertise to work in partnerships with them in ways that are in the children's best interests.

funds of knowledge Experiences, traditions, goals, resources, and rich culture that families bring to their roles.

Keyser's story about her own development as a teacher mirrors how the profession's views of parent-teacher relationships have evolved over time (Powell & Gerde, 2006; Powell & O'Leary, 2009). In the past, and even today in some educational settings, teachers thought that they could care for and educate children almost in spite of their parents. Today, however, the prevailing view of effective practice requires reciprocal relationships and partnerships between teachers and families (Olsen & Fuller, 2012; Iruka, 2013). **Reciprocal relationships** are two-way relationships in which information and power are shared. Before describing the elements of effective partnerships, it is important to clarify the distinct roles of teachers and parents in the lives of young children.

> **reciprocal relationships**
> Two-way relationships in which information and power are shared; based on mutual respect, trust, cooperation, and shared responsibility.

Roles of Teachers and Parents

One of the challenges to building effective partnerships for early childhood teachers is that the younger the child in their care, the more blurred the lines become between families and teachers. Nevertheless, there are definite distinctions between the roles of parent and teacher. Children's relationships with their family members often last a lifetime. They view their children's development and learning more emotionally. Their relationships are often intense, and culturally embedded. While family members are considered children's "first teacher," they typically have no training in how to care for and educate their child. While teachers' relationships with children are very important for their learning and development they typically have short-term relationships with children and find it easier to be objective. Furthermore, teachers benefit from formal education related to supporting children's learning and development. These distinctions help explain why both perspectives are essential in providing high-quality care and education for each child (Baker & Manfredi-Pettit, 2004).

Understanding these different but complementary roles reminds teachers of the important boundaries between their roles and those of parents. Children benefit greatly from the lasting unconditional love of at least one adult, usually a parent (Brazelton & Greenspan, 2000). At the same time, children benefit from the more objective view that

Young children are integrally connected to their families. Effective early childhood programs depend on positive relationships between teachers and parents.

teachers can bring when they evaluate the children's needs and strengths. To help all of their students, teachers can draw on their experience from observing many children's development and knowing how to effectively support children's social and academic development in group situations such as that of the school or child care center. By contrast, parents are the most knowledgeable sources of information about their child's development and experience in settings outside the school. Moreover, parents are the most accurate, key informants about children's cultural and linguistic backgrounds. Once teachers are clear about what they and parents bring to the table, the opportunity exists to build reciprocal relationships with families.

Family-Centered Practice

Reciprocal relationships can develop only in an atmosphere of mutual respect, trust, cooperation, and shared responsibility. These are the elements of what is now called *family-centered care* or *family-centered practice* (Child Welfare Information Gateway, 2014).

family-centered practice
Providing resources and supports to families that promote children's development and learning and, at the same time, strengthen the competency of families in their role.

Family-centered practice is a term that originated in the early childhood special education community. According to special educators, family-centered practice provides to families the resources and supports that promote children's development and learning and, at the same time, strengthen the competence of families in their roles and improve family well-being (Dunst, 2011). Professionals may provide parent education to support parents' competence, confidence, and enjoyment of interactions with their child. To achieve these goals, professionals must actively involve families, be responsive to their requests, and treat them with dignity and respect.

Considerable research documents the benefits of family-centered practice for children and families, especially for children with disabilities and special needs (Trivette, Dunst, & Hamby, 2010). The *Including All Children* feature demonstrates the value of family-centered practice for children and their families. Although family-centered practices have been at the heart of early childhood special education, they are also now recognized as essential elements of all high-quality early childhood programs (NAEYC, 2014).

Family-centered practice is interpreted slightly differently by general educators than by special educators because the needs of the families they work with are different, and because of the child's specific needs. For general educators, family-centered practice focuses on building partnerships with families. These partnerships are characterized by several key principles: mutual respect and trust; regular, frequent two-way communication; collaboration, shared decision making, and shared power; and negotiation of conflicts toward win-win solutions (Bredekamp, 1997a, 1997b). When working with families who are racial and ethnic minorities, Iruka (2013) suggests that professionals employ a bi-directional approach, which integrates the families' culture and perspectives, and capitalize on a strengths-based approach. What this means for teachers is that efforts to increase family engagement should include extensive, meaningful input from families on their family traditions, interaction preferences, and individual needs.

Mutual trust and respect develop gradually after numerous interactions. Although teachers and parents may initially disagree on certain issues, the goal is to recognize and respect one another's knowledge and expertise (Keyser, 2006). If parents feel respected, they are more likely to share information that teachers need to know.

Differences of opinion and goals are inevitable when working with other people's children. If mutual trust and respect are to be maintained and parents are to continue to be empowered, such conflicts must be negotiated toward win-win solutions (discussed later in this chapter). There are instances, however, when negotiation is not an option, such as in cases of suspected child abuse or neglect. Policies regarding teachers' responsibilities for reporting child abuse should be clearly communicated to families as well as teachers (National Research Council [NRC], 2014).

Including All Children

Family-Centered Practice

Teachers' skill in using family-centered practices is essential to the success of programs for children with special needs. Family-centered practices reflect the belief that the more time, energy, knowledge, and skills families have, the more likely the child's development will thrive, as we see in the following example.

Jennifer, the family service worker from the Beginnings Child Development Center, works with Carolyn and Bill's son Ben. Three-year-old Ben is diagnosed with language and social skills delays and also demonstrates challenging behaviors. Jennifer alternates her visits between Ben's preschool classroom and family home. She visits Ben's home in the evening so Bill and Carolyn can both be there. When she arrives, Jennifer spies Ben behind a chair, kneels down, and pulls some cars and race track pieces out of her bag. As Ben comes closer, Jennifer suggests to Bill that he might enjoy playing with his son. Bill moves to the floor and begins assembling the pieces. Jennifer models how to provide a choice for Ben to get him to use his words. With a toy in each hand, Jennifer brings them close to her face, and asks, "Ben, do you want the bus or the car?" Ben reaches for the bus, and Jennifer responds, "I want the . . ." and looks at expectantly. Ben points and says, "Bus." Jennifer smiles and gives him the bus. She turns to Bill and asks, "Want to try?" She moves to let Bill play with Ben.

Jennifer's tablet rings, and she answers a video call from Ben's teacher, Rashida, who would like to join Jennifer in her home visit, but must be home in the evening. She—and Ben's family—are happy to meet using Skype, and share successes and ideas for Ben's progress. Rashida has posted a video of Ben and another child playing at the sand table together on their secure school website. She plays the video for Bill and Carolyn, highlighting Ben's cooperative play, as the other child and Ben take turns pouring sand into a bucket, and laughing together when they dump it out. Rashida points out how well Ben's social skills and friendships have developed,

and they chat about some ideas for having successful play dates with a friend outside of school. Before she hangs up, Rashida tells them to look out for a surprise text the next day.

Carolyn notices Ben enjoying the cars and comments on how he is using more words. Jennifer shows Carolyn how she can use a paper towel roll to make a "track" for small cars. Carolyn loves the idea and decides to tape the track to the side of the refrigerator. "This way, he can play and we can talk while I am making dinner." Jennifer is pleased because she knows dinnertime has been very stressful for Ben's family. Jennifer will check back in a couple of days to see how the new ideas are working. As she packs to go, Jennifer gives Bill information about the "dads' support group" he is interested in and gives Carolyn a list of respite care providers.

The next day, Bill and Carolyn are surprised when they see that Ben used a tablet at school to take a picture of the big sand structure with cars around it. With Rashida's help, Ben sent the picture and a voice message "big garage" via text message. Since they cannot visit Ben's school often, Bill and Carolyn find these text messages and Skype visits very valuable for keeping in touch with Ben's teacher. That day, Ben comes home from school with a printed picture of his "big garage," and they hang it on the refrigerator next to his tube track.

Although Jennifer spends only a little time interacting directly with Ben during this visit, she provides supports to his family that will enable them to be true partners in Ben's development and learning. She provides opportunities for teacher–parent connections using technology, and connects family members with resources such as support groups. Jennifer coaches the family on how to use learning strategies used in Ben's therapy sessions and preschool activities. Thus, by partnering with Ben's family and classroom teacher, Jennifer supports important relationships that will benefit Ben far beyond the one hour of her visit.

Collaboration, shared decision making, and shared power can be difficult to negotiate for inexperienced teachers. Many early childhood educators fail to grasp the extent of their actual and perceived power in relationships with families. In addition, cultural differences may be a complicating factor in supporting family engagement in school community and activities. The *Culture Lens* feature describes research that sheds light on how Latino mothers may view engagement in their child's education differently than mothers of other cultures—and how building on cultural strengths can support the family and child in the educational process.

Culture Lens

Developing Partnerships with Latino Families

Teachers are sometimes frustrated when families don't participate in the parent involvement activities offered. Some families don't attend back-to-school night, rarely return paperwork, or fail to volunteer for school activities. Research shows that children develop and learn best when families are engaged in their children's education. Developing productive relationships and partnerships with families can be challenging. Just as with children, a teacher cannot assume a "one-size-fits-all" approach toward building family partnerships. When families' culture and language are different from the school culture, it can be even more challenging.

Families' cultural perspective impacts how they engage in the school community, and in their children's educational activities. Taking a perspective of capitalizing on family strengths and funds of knowledge, Manica Ramos interviewed immigrant Latino mothers about how culture impacted their involvement in their preschool-aged children's education. Ramos found that Latino mothers were very invested in their children's education, and that they expressed this investment in ways that were similar to and different from non-Latino families. For example, Latino mothers in Ramos's study reported attending student–teacher conferences and reading to their children, similar to school expectations. However, they also discussed forms of involvement in their children's education that were more culturally specific to Latino families,

including *sacrificios* (sacrifices), *consejos* (advice), and *apoyo* (moral support).

Most mothers shared that they believed in making sacrifices (*sacrificios*) to support their children's education and took great pride in working hard to support their children's education. They described how they gave advice (*consejos*) to their children to support their education, which for these Latino mothers included academic and social education. Finally, they described how they saw their role related to supporting their children's motivation to learn, morale and confidence, and respect (*respeto*) related to learning.

Ramos translated her findings to important implications for teachers working with immigrant families and non–European American families, in addition to Latino families. She recommends that teachers learn about the family cultures of the children in the classroom and school—from the families themselves. Ramos encourages teachers to think creatively about what constitutes family engagement opportunities, and consult with families on how they would like to be engaged. To understand different family values and beliefs, Ramos recommends visiting families regularly in their homes to develop warm and productive relationships.

Source: The Strengths of Latina Mothers in Supporting their Children's Education: A Cultural Perspective, by M. Ramos, 2014, Bethesda, MD: Child Trends, retrieved November 1, 2014, from http://www.childtrends.org.

If you, like many of your colleagues, think early childhood education involves just working with children, you might feel intimidated by the idea of developing reciprocal relationships with families. In the next section, we address the fundamental skill of two-way communication with families.

 Check Your Understanding 7.2: Reciprocal Relationships with Families

 # Communication with Families

Building relationships with families requires effective communication—one of the biggest challenges teachers face. Before we describe positive ways of communicating with families, we begin with considering some of the most common barriers to effective communication.

Barriers to Effective Communication

Effective communication between teachers and families means more than sharing information; it means developing shared understanding about who the child is, each party's goals, and how to achieve them. Early childhood education covers a broad age span—from birth through age 8. During the earliest years, children are most likely to be served in some form of child care while parents work. At the other end of the age continuum, children are in school and perhaps child care for part of the day. In each of these situations, communication problems can arise.

Communication Problems in Child Care Settings In child care programs for infants, toddlers, and young preschoolers, deep emotions can consume parents as they leave their children in someone else's care, which can create tension with teachers. Following are examples of typical situations that arise over the care of young children and the feelings they may generate in parents:

- *Competition.* Parents may feel jealous if the child becomes attached to another adult. Three-year-old Madison has been in child care for 1 month. Her mother feels conflicted about it and threatened by the growing relationship between Madison and her teacher. She tells her husband, "I'm afraid Madison loves her teacher more than me. When I left the center, Madison called her teacher 'Mommy' and I cried all the way to work."

- *Guilt and loss.* At times, parents feel a sense of loss over missed experiences. Jacob is 11 months old. His mother is torn between her desire to spend more time with him and her rewarding but demanding career. She worked very hard to earn her law degree, and her job is stressful. At the same time, she feels guilty about neglecting Jacob. She thinks, "I'm going to miss seeing my baby's first steps."

- *Differing child-rearing goals.* Disagreements between parents and teachers, both large and small, are inevitable. Tawanna, who is 4½ years old, enrolled in a new center recently, and her father has concerns about the informality and lack of emphasis on academic skills. He tells his wife, "I don't like Tawanna getting dirty at school. And I want her to learn to read to be ready for school, but they say that's not important yet. And they let the children call them by their first names in that school. I want Tawanna to learn good manners."

- *Power struggles.* Parents may feel that they are losing control over their child's upbringing. Sonya is turning 6, a milestone event in her family. Her grandmother is incensed, however, because she wants to hold a party at school, and the teachers won't let her control it. She tells her friend, "They say I can't send cupcakes for Sonya's birthday because they're not healthy food, but she wants cupcakes and so do I."

Infant/toddler teachers sometimes find that parents may feel threatened or unsure about sharing their child's care with another person. How can this teacher build a positive relationship that will benefit the baby and the family?

These parents' feelings illustrate that sharing their children with other adults is difficult and can be threatening to the close parent–child relationship. When other people have considerable influence over their children's lives, parents can feel powerless.

Communication Problems in School   Schools and parents can encounter a number of obstacles in their efforts to communicate. Following are examples of some common barriers to communication:

- *Confusion about regulations and policies.* Parents may lack the information they need about the school's goals, procedures, and policies. For example, Summit School has a policy that parents need to be alerted in the middle of first grade about whether their children's reading is below grade level so that an intervention plan can be set up. Shelley's mother becomes very anxious: "It's only January, and the teacher thinks that Shelley will have to stay back in first grade because she's not reading at grade level. I don't want my little girl to flunk, but what can I do?"
- *Lack of flexibility.* The school may not be sensitive to parents' individual needs and concerns. Mr. Jenkins is a concerned father who wants to be involved in his children's education, but he is frustrated: "That school always has meetings and events during the day, but I can't take off work."
- *Lack of attention to individual children.* At times, parents' concerns arise from fears that teachers don't really know and understand their children. Parents may feel that teachers' expectations for their children are too low because of the child's socioeconomic status, disability, or race, as in these examples:
  - Seven-year-old Abigail has Down syndrome. Her two mothers believe that the teachers don't think Abigail can learn, so they don't teach her anything.
  - Ms. Rice tells her mother, "I think that teacher is racist. She assigned all the black boys to the lowest reading group."

Communication problems can arise when parents don't understand how the school functions and how they can influence decisions. They may feel powerless to alter a policy or the teacher's perceptions about their child. Teachers may think they provide adequate information, but if the parent doesn't understand the message, considerable anxiety and confusion may result for the parents and the child as well.

At other times, power struggles can ensue due to conflicting goals. Some families have very high expectations for their children's success in school, so they may pressure teachers and children to ensure academic achievement. The term *helicopter parent* describes parents who "hover over" their children and try to control everything in their lives. Some parents will come forward and complain often, whereas others are too intimidated to voice even the gentlest concerns.

To address these communication problems openly and honestly, teachers can use a variety of strategies, discussed next, that will benefit both the child and the family.

Effective Communication Strategies

Communication is the basis of all relationships. Positive relationships begin when parents feel welcome in the school.

A Welcoming Environment   On entering a school or child care center, parents can usually tell how welcome they are. The environment communicates messages about whether families are expected to be regular participants, infrequent guests, or simple agents of transmittal. Is there a sign greeting children and families? Do teachers greet them at the door? Is there an area where they can gather and visit with each other? Are there adult-sized chairs? Is there a bulletin board stocked with current information? Can parents easily find their children's work and space for their belongings?

The physical environment plays an important role in welcoming families. However, face-to-face communication between teachers and parents is more important.

Types of Messages Substantive communication is possible and more effective when it is built on a strong base of casual, routine conversation. Think of the messages that teachers need to send to parents as basically two kinds: tennis balls and slippery eggs (NAEYC, 1998).

Picture yourself tossing a tennis ball back and forth from hand to hand. **Tennis ball messages** are easily "tossed" and easily received. These messages help form the foundation of a relationship. Tennis ball messages constitute the everyday chitchat between teachers and parents. This kind of back-and-forth communication helps each party in the relationship to learn and become comfortable with the other's style.

> *Teacher:* Hello, Mr. Watkins, it's good to see Neil back at school today. I hope your family enjoyed the visit with his grandparents.
>
> *Parent:* We had a great time. They live so far away that Neil only sees them a few times a year. They had to leave this morning, so we are all a little down.

Now picture yourself tossing a slippery egg to another person. You would hold the egg carefully and toss it very gingerly, assuming that the other person is prepared to catch it with equal care. If the egg were tossed carelessly or too abruptly, a mess would result. The same is true of **slippery egg messages**. They are more difficult to toss and catch, and must be tossed gently to be sure that the catcher receives the communication as intended (NAEYC, 1998). Even the best of relationships requires slippery egg messages at times. Some relationships seem to consist almost entirely of slippery egg communications. How these messages are sent—the style of communication—determines how well they are received, as we see in the next section.

Communication Styles There are at least three styles of communication: passive, aggressive, and assertive (NAEYC, 1998). **Passive communication** is sensitive to the

▶ **Classroom Connection**

This video shows the start of the school day in a typical preschool classroom. As you watch, reflect on how these teachers use everyday conversations to build positive, reciprocal relationships with families and help children transition from home to school.

tennis ball messages
Communications that are easily "tossed" and easily received and that help form the foundation of a relationship; they constitute the everyday chitchat between teachers and parents.

slippery egg messages
Communications that are difficult to "toss" (send) and "catch" (receive), and must be expressed gently to be sure that the "catcher" receives the communication as intended.

passive communication
Speaking in a way that is sensitive to the listener's feelings, but so vague that the message is easily misunderstood.

Reciprocal relationships with parents begin in everyday chit chat—casual conversation about children that builds trust and respect.

aggressive communication
Speaking the truth in a hurtful way.

assertive communication
Telling the truth in a thoughtful and considerate way; considered the most effective form of communication.

listener's feelings, but so vague that the message is easily misunderstood. The listener becomes confused about expectations and loses trust. **Aggressive communication** is truthful, but the delivery is hurtful. The listener feels angry and resentful, and the relationship is damaged. **Assertive communication**—telling the truth in a thoughtful and considerate way—is the most effective form of communication (NAEYC, 1998). Assertive communication strengthens relationships and increases the likelihood of successfully resolving problems.

The goal in sending a slippery egg message—the kind that is difficult to send as well as to receive—is to use assertive communication. Compared to passive or aggressive styles of communication, assertive communication succeeds in delivering the difficult message while also maintaining and perhaps deepening the relationship.

Following is an example of these three communication styles in action. First-grade teacher Julia Sykes is concerned that one of her students, DeShawn Jameson, is not making progress in reading. Julia sets up a meeting with DeShawn's mother to discuss the problem. They chat comfortably for a few minutes, but Ms. Jameson is clearly nervous, anticipating bad news. Here are three ways that Julia might present the situation:

- *Passive communication.* "I know you are worried about how DeShawn is doing in school, and so am I. All the children take time to get settled and he'll come around as soon as he's ready." With such a passive statement, Julia demonstrates caring for the parent and child, but fails to convey the seriousness of the situation. Ms. Jameson is confused and a little angry because she doesn't understand why she took off work for this meeting.
- *Aggressive communication.* "We've got a problem with DeShawn. He is so far behind in reading, he'll probably have to repeat first grade." Julia dreaded delivering this bad news, so she blurted it out with little concern for Ms. Jameson's feelings. Ms. Jameson immediately becomes defensive: "What do you mean? Why aren't you teaching him right?"
- *Assertive communication.* "Ms. Jameson, during the first three months of school, I've found that DeShawn isn't making the reading progress that he should be. We don't expect all the children to learn to read at the same time. But I'm concerned that if he falls further behind, he will really have a hard time catching up. What I'd like to do is have a reading specialist evaluate him to see if he would benefit from tutoring, which is provided free by the school. I wanted you to come in today so we could talk about how DeShawn is doing at home and what options we have to help him." In this communication, Julia conveys caring for DeShawn and his mother, but she also tells the truth—that there is a problem and there are possible solutions to work on together.

Assertive communication is often effective when the teacher is working with challenging situations and distraught or angry parents. As the *Becoming an Intentional Teacher* feature reveals, it is important to be open and really listen to parents' concerns and complaints. Teachers use many different vehicles to accomplish clear, honest, regular communication. In the sections that follow, we describe some of these strategies.

Informal Communication   In programs for infants and toddlers, families and teachers must communicate daily, both morning and evening, to ensure that children receive optimum care. Morning drop-off and afternoon pickup times are good for engaging in the kind of chitchat, or tennis ball back-and-forth, communication that builds relationships between teachers and parents.

For example, "How are you this morning, Ms. Kelly? I can see that Monique doesn't look too happy. Is there something I should know to help her get settled?"

Two-year-old Monique's mom might say, "She wouldn't eat her breakfast and I had to leave or I'd be late for work." "No problem. We'll feed her here, and don't worry or you'll be late," the teacher replies.

Becoming an Intentional Teacher
Responding to Parents: Welcoming "Complainers"

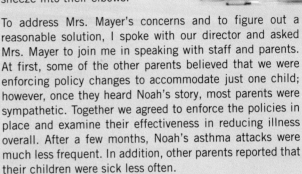

Here's What Happened I taught 3- and 4-year-olds in an NAEYC-accredited child care center. Our program was well known in the community as a high-quality center. I taught there for 10 years and we enjoyed good relationships with our families. One mother, Mrs. Mayer, became a constant complainer, however, when her little boy, Noah, kept getting sick. I knew that Noah had asthma, so I wasn't surprised when he missed days at the center. I was surprised, however, by how much Mrs. Mayer blamed me for Noah's repeated illnesses. At first, I tried to explain to her that increased illness is not unusual for children when they are in group care. When my explanation met with resistance, I started to become defensive. I assured Mrs. Mayer that our program was licensed and accredited, which means that we meet all required health standards.

One day, when Noah returned after an absence, his mother looked particularly weary. I asked my assistant teacher to take over the group while I spoke with Mrs. Mayer privately. She explained that she had spent the night with Noah in the emergency room. As we talked, I realized that due to Noah's chronic illness, colds and other seemingly innocuous childhood sicknesses are life-threatening experiences. I gave Mrs. Mayer a copy of our center's health policy handbook and asked her to review it and give me feedback. We set up a time to meet again.

Mrs. Mayer came back to me 2 days later with suggestions for ways we could focus everyone's attention on illness prevention. For example, to accommodate parents so they wouldn't have to miss school or work, we often allowed sick children to attend the center when perhaps they should have stayed home. We had a policy that required children to remain home when ill. When children arrived at school with symptoms of illness, our policy said we should take the child's temperature and exclude children who had a fever. We also had a policy that stated if children were heavily sneezing and coughing, or required one-on-one care for their symptoms, that they should not attend the program until their symptoms remitted. And though our program worked hard to teach and attend to staff and child handwashing, we didn't teach them to cough or sneeze into their elbows.

To address Mrs. Mayer's concerns and to figure out a reasonable solution, I spoke with our director and asked Mrs. Mayer to join me in speaking with staff and parents. At first, some of the other parents believed that we were enforcing policy changes to accommodate just one child; however, once they heard Noah's story, most parents were sympathetic. Together we agreed to enforce the policies in place and examine their effectiveness in reducing illness overall. After a few months, Noah's asthma attacks were much less frequent. In addition, other parents reported that their children were sick less often.

Here's What I Was Thinking Months before school begins, I work hard to build a relationship with my children's families. I make home visits, hold open houses, and write letters or e-mails to families to introduce myself and the school—everything I can think of. When Mrs. Mayer began to complain about Noah's getting sick at school, I wondered if she was just a negative person or if she should find another program. As I spoke more with her, I came to realize that her complaints were evidence of her commitment as a parent. In meeting with Mrs. Mayer, I learned that her experience as the parent of a chronically ill child provided valuable knowledge and a perspective that could help our program be better. I realized that it wouldn't work if I was the only one who changed health procedures, so I had to get the other parents and staff involved. The outcome was improved health for all the children and for the teachers, too.

Reflection What issues or situations in child care programs or schools might parents frequently complain about? In the above situation, the teacher almost automatically felt defensive and initially attributed blame to the "complaining" parent. How do you think you would feel if the same parent consistently complained about your teaching? What could you do in response?

In another circumstance, Ms. Kelly looks distraught and responds, "Monique's father left last night and I've been up all night crying."

Here is an entirely different situation, calling for an entirely different response. "I can see you are upset. I'll take Monique now so you can go to work and I'll call to let you know how she's doing. If you would like, we can talk privately later."

Moments of informal conversation are so important for building trust and mutual respect. At the same time, teachers need to make sure that children are supervised during these conversations, and that it is clear who is responsible for this duty. Any confidential conversation should be scheduled for another time.

Following are strategies for ensuring that messages are delivered:

- *Information logs.* Daily messages must be relayed about children's eating, sleeping, toileting, signs of change in mood, and changes in developmental status. For example, last night baby Maggie stood up and tried to climb out of her crib—a first in her skill achievement. When her dad drops her off at child care, he needs to let the staff know about Maggie's new skill so they can take steps to prevent accidents and ensure her safety. Given that several different people are responsible for Maggie's care throughout the day, the staff keep written logs about each child's needs and development, and pass them along to each other.
- *Daily notes "About My Day."* This message delivery system is important for all young children, but it is essential for babies and toddlers. Very young children can't communicate for themselves to families and teachers, so daily communication can't be left to chance conversations. Written notes, text messages, or e-mails that take little time to complete are essential. Ms. Evans sends a message to 2½-year-old Gabriel's mother: *Gabriel had a hard time waking up from nap this afternoon. He doesn't seem to be sick, but didn't eat as much as usual.*
- *Daily chitchat.* For teachers and parents of preschoolers, regular communication—the daily chitchat—is still important for building and maintaining the relationship. Teachers need to know about events at home that may affect a child, and parents love to hear about interesting or funny things their children have said or done. Teachers should be very careful to keep this informal conversation light and save talking about more difficult issues until private, scheduled times.
- *Weekly updates.* For preschoolers and older children, regular reporting of activities, such as the topic of study or upcoming events, is sufficient. Technology such as classroom websites or blogs greatly increases the opportunities for family communication and involvement.

Children's learning and development is supported best when schools and families work together. Traditional parent meetings can be combined with the latest technology to achieve goals of both teachers and families. For example, in the Promoting Play feature, *Get Outside and Play*, a primary-school teacher enlists families' support in promoting active play to improve her young students' health and learning.

Use Technology Technology has transformed all communication in the 21st century. Parents are more accessible than ever because of handheld mobile devices. Individual e-mails, texts, or voice-mail messages can be used to share information about a child's daily activity or progress. Teachers, along with children, can create and maintain a classroom or school website where they post photos and samples of children's work. The potential is limited only by their imaginations and the technological resources available. Kaldor (2015) recommends many ways that teachers can use technology to strengthen relationships with families and increase family engagement in the school community, such as:

- Use video e-introduction before the school year begins. By posting on YouTube or a secure website, and e-mailing the link, children and family members can see the classroom and learn about their child's teacher.
- Use video from the classroom to demonstrate daily routines, and tips for transitions and guiding children's positive behavior.
- Use the Message from Me online feature. Children can use tablets and cameras to take photos or videos of classroom activities and send with an audio message to their family.
- Create e-books to share with families. Children can use photos, text, and audio recordings to document classroom experiences and produce e-books that can be shared online or printed, and read at home with family.
- Use messaging technology, such as instant message, Twitter, or WhatsApp to send messages and images (photos or videos) of special happenings during the school day.

Promoting Play

Get Outside and Play!

With the demands of the elementary curriculum and restrictions on recess in her school district, Lucia is concerned that her students are not getting enough active play time during the day. During the day at school, children have recess for only 20 minutes after lunch.

Realizing that she cannot take on the full responsibility of her students' health, Lucia enlists families as partners to support children's active play. Lucia holds a Get Active parent meeting. Because many of her students' families work evening shifts at the local restaurants, Lucia videotapes the meeting for those who cannot attend and posts it on a secure YouTube site. Using resources from the Centers for Disease Control and the Internet, Lucia illustrates for families the importance of active play for children's health, development, and learning. She explains the research that children need 60 minutes or more of daily, active play, and they discuss many ways children could reach that goal.

Families brainstorm and generate many ideas for active play, including turning on music and dancing in the home, making an obstacle course in the house or backyard, sport activities, and going to the neighborhood playground with an older sibling. After generating many ideas, Lucia turns their attention to safety, and they discuss bicycle and scooter safety (including helmets), supervision, and following safety rules. Lucia shares resources for limiting screen time, and explains how adults' modeling of activity is also important for children. The evening ends with a healthy snack, while families share their plans for building more active play in every day. Following the encouragement of families, Lucia agrees to send text messages several times a week, reminding them to support their child's active play and sharing some good ideas of how to do so.

Arguing that technology devices should be used responsibly and respectfully, Kaldor (2015) provides guidelines for how to do a BYOD (Bring Your Own Device) Night. Rather than leaving devices behind, families bring their devices and learn how to connect with their child's classroom and school, and see demonstrations of children's technology use in the classroom. Families learn how to respect boundaries around technological communication, and sign a digital contract.

Families may turn to early childhood professionals to learn about using technology with their children. Teachers can provide important information regarding how children use technology and how much they use it. Children under 3 years old should have few, short periods of screen time, combined with lively interaction with family members (Lerner & Barr, 2014). Early Connections (http://www.commonsensemedia.org/educators/early-connections) provides guidelines and ideas for families to use technology to enhance social relationships and learning.

Technology can make communication with families much more efficient. For example, listservs can be used to inform parents of logistical information such as reminders about school closings. Technology also addresses the challenge presented by the fact that many children go back and forth between the homes of divorced parents or extended family (Mitchell, Foulger, & Wetzel, 2009). However, it is also important to recognize limitations of technology. For example, sensitive information should typically not be shared by text or e-mail—telephone conversations or in-person meetings are much better for discussing behavior concerns and for problem solving (Kaldor, 2015). Teachers should set clear boundaries on communicating with families, and families' preferences for communication should be respected. For example, teachers may not be willing to answer e-mails in the evening while they are with family, but will answer the next day. These boundaries and expectations should be clearly stated in the digital contract.

Formal parent-teacher conferences are important times to communicate about children's progress and potential problems. But for conferences to be effective, teachers need to make parents as comfortable as possible and listen as much as they talk.

Websites need to be password secured to limit access. Interactive sites are labor intensive, needing to be checked and responded to regularly and monitored for inappropriate content. Some families might not have access to the Internet. For families that do not speak or read English, teachers should be prepared to enlist the assistance of a bilingual colleague or an online translator application (Nemeth, 2015). Finally, e-mail and especially texting may foster the use of incorrect grammar and spelling. Teachers should always be accurate in written communication, electronic or otherwise.

Conferencing   In addition to their everyday, routine communication with families, teachers and parents need to meet for more formal regular conferences. Traditionally, the purpose of parent-teacher conferences has been for teachers to report on children's progress. These conferences are usually a one-way communication, with teachers providing information to parents, who serve as the passive audience. With one-way communications, however, parents might feel as though the teachers are issuing a report card on their parenting.

More effective conferences promote two-way communication (Hanhan & Kartoshkina, 2012). Teachers not only provide parents with information about their child's progress but also listen to what parents say about their child's development and learning. In this setting, parents and teachers have a conversation and ask as well as answer questions.

Because families have diverse needs and schedules, arranging conference times can be tricky. Consider Noreen Hayes, a kindergarten teacher in a large, urban school district. Three months into the school year, she is preparing for her first set of formal family conferences. Because many of the families work two jobs or odd hours, she is concerned that scheduling conferences will be difficult. To ease the stress for families, she offers a full week of times for them to sign up, including early morning, evening, and weekend hours. To make sure she can accommodate these families, she arranges for community volunteers to provide babysitting and translation services as needed. She also arranges for snacks to be available for parents arriving after work. She organizes the seating arrangement with adult-sized chairs comfortably facing each other. Before conferences, she carefully collects samples of drawings, writing, and photos of projects and other work to share with each child's parents. Consider this scenario:

When Jillian's mother arrives, looking nervous, Noreen offers her coffee. After they are comfortable, Noreen begins by saying, "Jillian is such a curious little girl. Every day, her questions keep me on my toes. Last week, before we visited the aquarium, she wanted to know how the fish breathe."

Jillian's mother smiles and says, "She drives us crazy with her why, why, why."

"Let me show you some of the things she's been learning," Noreen replies, "and how she's discovering ways to get answers to her questions."

When Noreen describes some of the literacy goals, Jillian's mother says, "Oh, I know. At home she is always rhyming words and retelling me the stories you read."

Noreen makes a note about what she's learned from this parent because Jillian has not yet demonstrated these skills at school.

As children get older, three-way conferencing becomes more possible and desirable. Kia is a third grader whose parents are surprised to find that during the "parent–teacher" conference, their role is primarily to observe while Kia and her teacher, Mr. Colbert, have a conversation about her work. Kia reports on how well she thinks she's doing and sets a goal for next term: to read 8 chapter books. He then asks what she wants to be when she grows up. "A chef!" she replies. He asks her to pretend she is interviewing for a job and convince him that she would make a good chef. Kia proceeds to describe how she helps her mom cook, reads cookbooks, and makes up her own recipes—exhibiting her language and literacy skills, general knowledge, and reasoning ability as well as her confidence and competence. Kia's parents watch in wonder as their usually soft-spoken and shy daughter becomes increasingly animated. Privately, her Dad questions Mr. Colbert about whether reading 8 books will be too hard for her. "Trust her," replies Mr. Colbert.

▶ Classroom Connection

In this video, observe how the teacher shares information with Kayla's mother and learns some new ways to work with Kayla in the classroom.

These two examples include many key points to keep in mind when preparing and conducting conferences with families. Table 7.2 summarizes principles for planning and conducting family conferences. Formal conferences take considerable time to plan and carry out effectively. This time is well spent, however, when it is used to build partnerships and solve problems.

Home Visiting In **home visiting**, a teacher goes to the child's home on a regular basis to exchange information with parents. Home visiting has a long tradition in early childhood education. Since its inception, Head Start has required regular home visits. The large majority (71%) of Early Head Start programs combine home visiting with center-based child care (Cohen, Vogel, & the Baby FACES Team, 2011). In addition, the model early childhood programs that demonstrated lasting effects, such as the Perry Preschool Project and the Abecedarian Project, included weekly home visits. Two types of home visiting exist—teacher home visits and home-based programs.

home visiting Visits made by a teacher to the child's home on a regular basis to exchange information with parents.

Teacher Home Visits Home visits are an excellent way for every teacher to establish more comfortable relationships with families, and children usually love the idea of their teacher visiting them at home. Conferences are typically held at school or in the child care center—on the teacher's turf. As a result, a disproportionate amount of power is attributed to the professionals, putting parents at somewhat of a disadvantage. Home visits by teachers can be effective in creating a more reciprocal relationship and enhancing children's learning. Even middle schools are now discovering the power of home visiting to increase student achievement and motivation. Following are some guidelines for successful home visits:

- *Be available for a home visit.* Let families know that you would like to visit the children at home to make them more comfortable with you and to learn more about their interests. Do not be offended if families decline the opportunity.
- *Set a time for the visit and stick to it.* Visits should last from 15 to 30 minutes.
- *Reassure families in advance about the visit's purpose.* Families need to know that you do not expect them to entertain you, feed you, or clean up for your visit. Nevertheless, teachers should be respectful of diverse cultural perspectives; for example, some cultural groups would be hurt or insulted if a guest refused food.

TABLE 7.2 Planning and Conducting Family Conferences

Principles of Effective Conferences	Strategies for Implementing Conferences
Prepare families in advance.	Notify families in writing about the purpose of the conference. Ask families to think about what goals they have for the conference and for their children, what information they want to share, and what questions they want to ask.
Schedule the conferences at times convenient for parents as well as teachers.	Accommodate parents' work schedules as much as possible. Set a specific time limit for the conference, 20 to 30 minutes, so parents can plan accordingly.
Provide appropriate space for the conference.	The space should be private to ensure confidential conversations. The furniture arrangement should communicate openness and comfort; use adult-sized chairs around a table or in front of a desk. There should be no physical barrier between teachers and families, such as a desk that sets up an artificial power relationship.
Collect children's portfolios or samples of their work.	Use examples of children's work as a springboard for discussion. Involve children themselves in this process.
Plan the conference agenda.	Make sure to include time to talk about children's progress and ask questions of each other.
Always begin on a positive note.	Begin your discussion about the child by sharing a specific comment about the child's strengths, interests, or abilities. An anxious parent can then relax, become less defensive, and be more able to listen and talk freely.
Plan in advance how to deliver a slippery egg message.	When you have difficult information or a problem about the child to discuss, think in advance how you would phrase the concern and what suggestions or solutions you would offer. "Four-year-olds are just learning how to make friends. I have observed that Kenny often plays alone, and sometimes when he tries to join in, he gets aggressive. I thought maybe he could bring something interesting from home to get the other children's attention in a positive way. I'm also going to give him some phrases to say when he wants to play. I wondered if he has had any difficulty like this at home or in the neighborhood, or if you have any ideas for me to help Kenny make friends."
Give and receive information about children's progress.	Use open-ended questions as much as possible. Two-way communication, shared power, and collaborative decision making build true partnerships with families. "Reshia loves the construction center and is learning words for all the tools and equipment. What does she like to talk about at home?"
Set goals together for next steps.	Strive to identify a common goal and create a plan to work together. "I hear you saying that you want Garrett to learn to use the toilet on his own as soon as possible, before the new baby is born. That's a goal we share. But he hasn't shown any interest at the center yet. What's he doing at home? Maybe we could try to be consistent in how we work with him."

Source: Based on *Families, Schools, and Communities: Building Partnerships for Educating Children*, 3rd edition, by C. Barbour, N. H. Barbour, and P. A. Scully, 2005, Upper Saddle River, NJ: Merrill/Pearson; and *From Parents to Partners: Building a Family-Centered Early Childhood Program*, by J. Keyser, 2006, St. Paul, MN: Redleaf Press.

- *Include the child in the visit.* Ask children to share something they like to do at home or in the community.
- *If you take a photo, ask permission first, and perhaps pose the family together at the front door to protect their privacy.* Use a digital camera so the family can see the photo that you will display at school.

Home-Based Programs Child development programs based on visits to families—**home-based programs**—are designed to support parents in the parenting role, fully involve them in their children's education, and help them achieve their own life goals (Council for Professional Recognition, 2012). In recent years, research demonstrating the lasting benefits of home-visiting programs for expectant and new parents, infants, and toddlers has led to significant expansion and increases in funding. In 2010, states invested $1.4 billion in home-visiting programs (Pew Center on the States, 2010a). Home-visiting

home-based programs
Programs based on visits to families designed to support parents in the parenting role, involve them in their children's education, and help them achieve their own life goals.

programs enhance mother and child health, strengthen parenting skills, reduce child abuse, increase children's achievement, and have lasting economic benefits for parents by decreasing unemployment and welfare dependence (Pew Center on the States, 2010b).

The most effective home visiting programs employ qualified early childhood professionals who actively engage parents with their children. Parents stay in close proximity to the child and home visitor, interact and play with their child, and learn how to use daily activities of life to promote children's development (Roggman, 2011).

Meeting on Neutral Ground In recent years, teacher home visits have become more challenging for several reasons. They are time consuming, and union contracts may discourage them. Because children do not live in self-contained communities and take transportation to school, home visits become logistically difficult. Teachers may feel unsafe visiting communities where there have been incidents involving violence or drugs. Likewise, some families may be uncomfortable about teachers' visiting for reasons of poverty or differences in language and cultural background.

Given that home visiting and conferencing at school can be threatening or difficult, some teachers find that meeting families on neutral ground such as a local coffee shop or fast-food restaurant may be the best strategy (Powell, 2013). Talking in a less formal setting over a cup of coffee, parents and teachers may be more relaxed and able to work out solutions to difficult problems.

Early childhood education is most effective when there is regular two-way communication between families and teachers. Truly effective programs go beyond communication to active engagement of families in their children's education, a topic addressed in the next section.

✓ **Check Your Understanding 7.3:** Communication with Families

 # Family Engagement in Programs and Schools

More than 40 years of research confirms that family engagement has a positive impact on children's achievement in school (Powell, 2013; Sheldon, 2009). The benefits are so well established that they are written into public law. For example, the Head Start program requires parent involvement at all levels, from classroom interaction with children to representation on policy-making boards. Special education laws also dictate specific roles for families as decision makers about services for their children. In the sections that follow, we examine research on the benefits of family involvement and then describe ways to engage families meaningfully in their children's education.

Benefits of Family Involvement

A thorough review of research (Sheldon, 2009) summarizes the impact of family involvement on children's achievement in school. The more frequently and actively families are engaged, the more likely children are to:

- Earn higher grades and score better on achievement tests
- Perform better in reading and mathematics
- Be promoted
- Have better school attendance
- Have fewer behavior problems, better social skills, and adapt well to school
- Benefit from long-term positive consequences such as completing high school and seeking postsecondary education

Further, engaging families can reduce family risk, increase resilience, and be an especially effective deterrent to child abuse (Lim, 2012). Research shows that children prosper when families of all income and education levels and of diverse cultural backgrounds support their children's learning at home (Cowan, Cowan, Pruett, Pruett, & Wong, 2009; Halgunseth, Peterson, Stark, & Moodie, 2009).

Family involvement in school has the greatest benefit for children at risk of school failure (Dearing, Kreider, Simpkins, & Weiss, 2007). When low-income families become more involved in school from kindergarten to fifth grade, children's literacy performance increases significantly (Dearing et al., 2007). Typically there is an achievement gap in literacy performance between children of more- and less-educated mothers, but this gap is nonexistent when family involvement levels are high (Dearing et al., 2007). However, white, middle-class families are more likely to be involved in school and to be better informed about how to help their children at home (Swick, Head-Reeves, & Barbarin, 2006). Therefore, schools need to make extra effort to involve all families because this would be an effective way to address the achievement gap between children of color growing up in poverty and their more affluent, white peers.

Opportunities for Meaningful Family Engagement

As we have seen, the benefits of family involvement for children's success in school and life are well documented (Epstein et al., 2009; Halgunseth et al., 2009; Powell, 2013). In addition, family engagement has significant benefits for schools, including increased job satisfaction among teachers and principals, despite the necessary additional work (Lim, 2012). Some effective strategies for engaging families in centers and schools are described in Table 7.3.

Meaningful family engagement requires effort on the part of teachers and parents. For instance, volunteering is one of the most common ways of involving parents. Sometimes, however, volunteers are used only to wipe tables, clean playgrounds, or bake cookies for bake sales. These may be necessary tasks, but more meaningful opportunities are available. If the school prepares parents in advance, classroom volunteers can provide

TABLE 7.3 Strategies for Engaging Families

Type of Engagement	Effective Strategies
Positive Relationships between Teachers and Families	Teachers focus on family strengths as opposed to deficits. Relationships between teachers and families are characterized by mutual trust, respect, and power sharing.
Two-Way Communication	Teachers and families use informal and formal—face-to-face, written, and technological—ways to communicate frequently about children's progress and experiences in school and at home.
Learning in School and at Home	Teachers and parents share information about ways to promote and extend children's learning at home and effective parenting practices. Teachers learn about families' cultural values and childrearing practices.
Home-School Connections	Schools provide a welcoming environment for all families. Families observe and participate in the life of the classroom by volunteering, or sharing a skill or cultural experience. Teachers conduct home visits.
Decision Making and Advocacy	Families participate in decisions affecting their children and assume leadership and policy-making roles in the school. Families act as advocates to improve children's educational and life experiences.
Collaboration between Schools, Families, and Communities	Schools connect families to community resources, services, and social networks. Schools provide services to families and community.

Sources: Based on *The Head Start Parent, Family, and Community Engagement Framework: Promoting Family Engagement and School Readiness from Prenatal to Age 8*, by Office of Head Start, 2011, Washington, DC; and *PTA National Standards for Family-School Partnerships: An Implementation Guide*, by National Parent Teacher Association, 2009, Alexandria, VA.

one-on-one conversation or small-group reading for young children. If families engage in such learning experiences with children at school, they are more likely to do these things at home with their children.

Too often, "parent" involvement is based on the assumption that the engaged parent will be the mother. However, there are distinct benefits to fathers' engagement in children's education (Minnesota Fathers & Families Network, 2013). To learn more about involving fathers, read the *What Works: Father-Friendly Practices* feature.

What Works

Father-Friendly Practices

Fathers play a critical role in the healthy development of young children. When fathers are involved in their children's education, children of all ages perform better academically, demonstrate more empathy, and exhibit healthier behavior. Although mothers as well as fathers have close emotional bonds with their children, in general fathers tend to interact physically, and mothers are more verbally soothing. For example, fathers are more likely to engage children in risk-taking and rough-and-tumble play. Perhaps this is why research finds that children who have involved fathers demonstrate greater curiosity, problem-solving ability, social skills, and confidence. Regrettably, fathers, especially those from low-income backgrounds, are much less likely to be involved in schools than are mothers and therefore need more targeted encouragement.

A main barrier to fathers' involvement is time and work schedules that conflict with school hours. But subtle barriers can be even more powerful. Fathers may perceive that involvement in school is not part of their role, but rather the mothers' job. They may feel awkward and unwelcome entering a female-dominated environment. Female teachers may hesitate to encourage father participation for fear their actions will be misinterpreted. Because a large number of children do not live with their fathers, programs are often hesitant to promote father involvement for fear of harming children's self-esteem or offending single mothers and lesbian mothers. In addition, programs may be legitimately concerned about perpetuating gender stereotyping or disrespecting cultural groups for whom the *machismo* role of fathers is particularly important.

Although these barriers are justifiable, they need not be insurmountable. Research shows that the following *father-friendly practices* not only increase father involvement in schools but also improve family functioning and relationships and outcomes for children:

- Make father involvement a priority by designating a male teacher, administrator, community leader, or parent volunteer to organize a father initiative. Fathers are more likely to participate when they see other men doing so.
- Be clear that your definition of "father" includes non-resident fathers as well as father figures such as grandfathers, uncles,

older siblings, foster fathers, or mother's boyfriends.
- Create a father-friendly school environment. Greet fathers with a sign, "Dads Welcome Here!" Post pictures of positive images of diverse men engaged in various occupations and activities with and without children.
- Invite fathers explicitly and personally to participate in school so they know they are welcome and expected. Often fathers don't feel that invitations to "parents" apply to them.
- Provide opportunities related to fathers' interests and skills such as sports or afterschool tutoring in science or math. Draw on fathers' real interests—such as woodworking or motorcycles—even if the activity may seem to reflect a stereotype of male abilities.
- Provide fathers-only events (such as discussion groups) or father–child experiences such as a Father's Breakfast or playground repair day—not only on Father's Day.
- Be sensitive to fathers' literacy levels. For example, provide wordless picture books so fathers who do not feel comfortable reading can talk about the pictures with children.
- Be responsive to cultural values. For example, Hispanic groups value *familismo* (relationships and distinct gender roles) and *respeto* (respect for elders and extended family).
- Be flexible and schedule events around fathers' schedules as much as possible.
- Provide bigger chairs!

Most important is to focus on fathers' strengths. Too often, fathers are portrayed in a negative light as absent or irresponsible. Every father has unique strengths and abilities. Engaged fathers are likely to be major contributors to the well-being of all children, schools, and communities.

Sources: Based on "Fathering, Schools, and Schooling: What Fathers Contribute and Why It Is Important" by C. B. Hennon, G. Palm, and G. Olsen, 2012, in *Home and School Relations: Teachers and Parents Working Together*, 4th edition, edited by G. Olsen and M. L. Fuller, pp. 284–323, Upper Saddle River, NJ: Pearson; and *Dad Stats*, by National Responsible Fatherhood Clearinghouse, retrieved January 4, 2011, from http://fatherhood.gov/library/dad-stats#Research.

Community Partnerships

As we see in Table 7.3, one effective form of family engagement is community collaboration. Just as partnerships between teachers and families contribute to positive outcomes for children, early childhood programs and schools function most effectively when they build reciprocal partnerships in the broader community (NAEYC, 2008c). For example, a Head Start program, with its comprehensive services for families, may serve as a focal point for positive change in a poverty-stricken community. Likewise, a community organization might adopt a neighborhood school, clean up and equip its playground, or provide literacy volunteers and other services that improve school performance.

Teachers, especially beginning teachers, may feel overwhelmed by the idea of building partnerships with communities in addition to carrying out their other responsibilities. However, community linkages can enhance their work and make it more effective. All communities have unique individuals with talents to share. A local orchestra might have musicians who are willing to visit and perform for the children. Artists of all kinds can enrich children's experiences with demonstrations and skill instruction. Doctors, nurses, dentists, or hygienists can demonstrate healthy practices for children. One preschool has an annual Truck Touch as a community experience and fund-raiser in which the nearby International Harvester company lends giant tractor trailers for the children to see and explore under careful supervision. The Truck Touch is open to all children in the community for free, and an accompanying snack bar raises funds for the preschool's library.

Schools can also inform families about child-related events or activities in the community such as concerts, puppet shows, museum exhibits, storytelling, and the like. Connecting families, including siblings, through such community events can help create a network of family support, which is especially helpful for single or teen parents. Such a network can serve as a protective factor for families in communities at risk (Bryant, Maxwell, & Burchinal, 1999).

In addition, teachers can use knowledge of the community in planning curriculum. For example, a town has an ongoing project to clean up the environment around a creek area that was once a beaver dam. Each class in the local primary school takes on an aspect of the project and expands its study of ecology over several years. When early childhood programs fully integrate into the community by inviting participation and by taking advantage of what the community has to offer, positive outcomes result for everyone involved.

Throughout this chapter, we have discussed the importance of relationships with families. In the next section, we provide a conceptual framework—a "how to" guide—for building partnerships with families and describe specific skills for negotiating conflicts.

✓ **Check Your Understanding 7.4:** Family Engagement in Programs and Schools

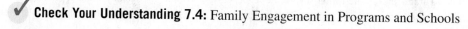

A Framework for Building Partnerships with Families

Denyce Lyons is nearing the end of her first year teaching 4-year-olds in Head Start. She has enjoyed the children, but continues to struggle at times in her relationships with parents. Now she's facing one of the biggest challenges of the year. The program where Denyce works traditionally holds a graduation ceremony, complete with caps, gowns, and diplomas and lengthy performances by the children to mark the year's end. Denyce feels strongly that such programs are not developmentally appropriate. She also thinks they are a waste of time and money that could be used more effectively. When she announces that there will be no graduation ceremony this year, several parents become very angry and go to the director, who threatens to fire Denyce if she doesn't change her mind. Such drastic breakdowns in relationships between teachers and families are all too common in programs for young children. In this section, we present a framework for building effective partnerships with families. This framework is designed to prevent crises such as Denyce's and to address them when they do arise.

Effective partnerships with families involve four key strategies: clarity about preferences, ability to communicate, ability to negotiate, and willingness to learn and change (NAEYC, 1998). Figure 7.2 presents this partnership model visually. Each of these building blocks of partnership is described in the sections that follow and then used to address Denyce's graduation ceremony dilemma.

Clarify Preferences

Teachers and families have preferences about all aspects of children's learning and development. Sometimes these preferences are shared. For example, most people prefer that children dress warmly in cold weather. However, in other cases, parents and teachers may have conflicting preferences in their child-rearing practices or educational goals. Areas where teacher and family preferences may be strong and at odds include napping, snacking and meal structure, tasks children should do for themselves, learning to use the toilet and bathroom habits, talking and listening, cleanliness, discipline techniques, roles of girls and boys, and traditions and holidays. There are various sources and reasons for these different preferences:

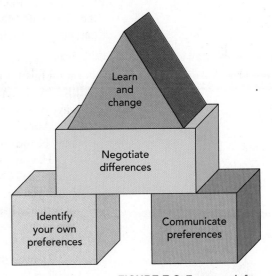

FIGURE 7.2 Framework for Partnerships with Families Effective partnerships with families involve four key strategies that connect to and build on each other as depicted in this framework.

- Cultural backgrounds
- Personal experiences as members of families both as children and as parents
- Outside influences such as information gained from the media
- Education and training

Teachers as well as parents are influenced by all of these factors. To understand and negotiate these differences, teachers must clarify their preferences and reflect on the sources of their beliefs. Is a strong preference for children learning to feed themselves at an early age the result of studying child development or being the mother of five children? Does a teacher believe that children should take turns based on research about social skills or a cultural judgment about good manners?

Revisiting the Head Start graduation dilemma presented earlier, Denyce needs to reflect on why she feels so strongly about preschool graduation ceremonies. She recalls that one of her professors at the community college stated unequivocally that requiring preschoolers to perform for adults is not developmentally appropriate. Denyce reasons that such events are inappropriate because they last too long, straining children's attention spans and self-control. She also objects to a few children being singled out for "star" treatment. She thinks that valuable class time is spent unproductively in rehearsals and teaching children how to march in line. Upon reflection, Denyce believes that the money spent on props such as caps and gowns would be better used to buy books or other educational materials for the school. Denyce also recognizes that she is worried that the children will misbehave and she will be judged a poor teacher. On closer analysis, Denyce has to admit to herself that she thinks graduating from preschool is not much of an accomplishment and the ceremonial trappings should be saved for greater achievements such as high school graduation.

Communicate Preferences

The next step in building partnerships is communicating with families about preferences. In situations such as Denyce's where a difference of opinion exists, clear and honest communication is vital. Denyce needs to begin by listening to parents' preferences for holding a graduation ceremony. She does this by organizing a meeting to which she invites

> ▶ **Classroom Connection**
>
> In this video, learn how these teachers build productive partnerships with diverse children and families.
>
> http://www.youtube.com/watch?v=vNdwJTKuHDw

the disgruntled families. Rather than beginning with her viewpoint, Denyce encourages parents to air their concerns:

> "We've always had graduations here. My two older kids have their diplomas and I want this for Dedra, too," says one mother.

> "We want to have this big party so we can let the kids know how proud we are," says one of the fathers.

> After several parents express their feelings, a grandmother sighs and says, "This may be the only graduation I get to go to. My other grandkids dropped out of school."

> Having listened carefully and respectfully to each one's concerns, Denyce states her interpretation of what the parents have said. "I think you want me to understand how much you value your children's accomplishments in Head Start, and how important this experience has been for the children and for you. I can tell from your comments that you really value education, and it sounds like you think it's a really important thing to celebrate." Several parents nod, and agree that Denyce's summary reflects their feelings.

> Denyce then explains her own concerns about the graduation. "I value learning, too, but I am concerned that spending time getting ready for the ceremony will take away time that the children could be learning skills they'll need in kindergarten. I also think that the money we spend could be used for classroom supplies such as books that would last longer."

This opportunity to communicate identifies differences in the parents' and Denyce's perspectives. If Denyce continues to insist she is right, the parents will probably feel disrespected and lose power in the relationship. The children will see their parents' anger at the teacher. If the parents "win" and the director forces Denyce to hold graduation, she will do so begrudgingly and the children will sense her lack of commitment. In both cases, whether teachers win and parents lose or parents win and teachers lose, the real losers are the children. The next step to build and maintain a partnership is to negotiate the conflict toward a win-win solution (Fisher, Ury, & Patton, 2011).

Negotiate Successfully

Collaborating and sharing power with families requires negotiation skills. There are certain characteristics of power relationships that determine successful or unsuccessful negotiations. Figure 7.3 illustrates these characteristics and shows that neither exercising power

No Power or Avoidance	Shared Power or Negotiation	Power or Fighting
Characterized by:	Characterized by:	Characterized by:
Walking away	Talking about the problem	Put downs
Giving up	Communicating	Threats
Holding in feelings and opinions	Seeking solutions	Punishment
Changing the subject		Arbitrary action
Gets these results:	Gets these results:	Gets these results:
Problem is still there	Both sides can win	One winner
No one is satisfied	Real solutions	Doubts and fears
Ongoing discomfort	All are satisfied	Revenge

FIGURE 7.3 Understanding Shared Power Understanding power relationships is essential for successful collaboration and negotiation of differences.

Source: Reprinted with permission from the National Association for the Education of Young Children (NAEYC). www.naeyc.org.

unilaterally nor avoiding a power struggle results in a positive outcome. Shared power requires win-win negotiation.

The Five-Step Negotiation Process Successful negotiations that result in a win-win solution to a conflict involve several steps (Fisher et al., 2011). Figure 7.4 depicts the five-step negotiation process, which is described next and illustrated using the conflict over the graduation.

Step 1: Express preferences, interests, and concerns. As a teacher, when you are expressing preferences, you will find it useful to focus on what you value rather than taking a rigid position. Denyce might have stated her strongly held position: "I'm against graduations for young children because they're developmentally inappropriate." Instead, Denyce expressed her preferred value for her students: "I would like to use the money for classroom materials and I don't want to take time away from teaching." Similarly, the families made their interests known by pointing out that they value education and that graduation marks an important milestone in their children's lives.

Step 2: Find common ground. Successful negotiation requires compromise. Sometimes people view compromise as a loss, a sign of weakness, or as giving in. Compromise is actually an effective strategy for achieving a win-win negotiated solution to a conflict. To achieve a satisfactory compromise, parties need to identify their common ground: their fundamental agreements, as well as the areas where they disagree. Denyce and the parents agree on the value of education and their desire to communicate their pride in the children. The areas they don't agree on are wearing caps and gowns and allowing time for rehearsals and a ceremony.

Step 3: Identify areas of flexibility. The next step in the negotiation process is to identify areas of potential flexibility. These might include ways of varying timing, frequency,

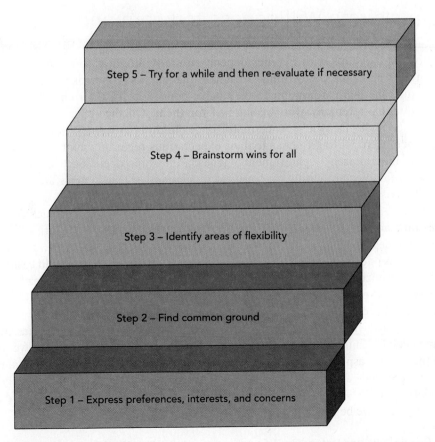

FIGURE 7.4 Five-Step Negotiation Process This 5-step negotiation process is designed to ensure a win-win resolution to the inevitable conflicts that arise between teachers and families.

or quantity. For example, the time designated for preparing for graduation and for the performance are negotiable areas. In addition, the amount of money available and how it is used are areas that could be flexibly negotiated. The parents' expectations of the ceremony could also be negotiable.

Step 4: Brainstorm wins for all. Having identified areas of flexibility, Denyce and the parents can brainstorm possible solutions that would be agreeable to all concerned. One possible solution is having a party for everyone, during which the children sing some of the songs and recite some of the poems they have learned this year. Other possibilities include using the money that would have been spent on caps and gowns to buy books for the center and creating "diplomas" on the computer rather than buying them. Other suggestions are that parents provide refreshments and that all of the children wear white shirts during the party.

Step 5: Try for a while and then reevaluate if necessary. Negotiated solutions should be tried and evaluated to make sure that all parties are satisfied. During and after the "graduation" party, Denyce talked with the parents to get their reactions. Some of the parents still missed the caps and gowns, but they were pleased when the children took such interest and pride in the new books. Several parents thought the program was actually more fun because it was less rehearsed and funnier than in previous years. One parent pointed out that he was glad that there weren't any stars of the show and all the children performed the same thing. Perhaps because the program was only 15 minutes long, none of the children misbehaved and all seemed to enjoy themselves, including Denyce. Because some parents didn't like the white shirts and wanted their children to dress up in their best clothes, Denyce agreed to try that idea next year.

The final building block of successful partnerships is the willingness to learn and change, described next.

Demonstrate Willingness to Learn and Change

We can see from the negotiation between Denyce and the parents in her classroom that effective partnerships with families depend on the willingness to learn and change. In Denyce's case, she was willing to listen to the parents' concerns respectfully and, as a result, she learned how much they value education for their children and why the graduation ceremony was meaningful for them. On the other hand, the families learned about Denyce's concerns for their children's readiness for kindergarten and, hence, were willing to change their expectations regarding appropriate ways to celebrate the children's achievements. True partnerships occur only when teachers as well as families are willing to learn from one another and to grow and change as a result.

The five-step negotiation process outlined here does not involve a quick fix; it requires time and respect for the other parties' interests, strengths, and abilities. Win-win negotiation depends on appreciating the importance of everyone's interests, particularly parents' perceptions about what is important for their children. Denyce could easily have erred by trivializing the parents' desire to see their children "graduate." Instead, she accurately perceived that graduation represented an underlying value of education rather than the actual ceremony.

As we have seen, teaching young children requires working with families, which requires good communication and negotiation skills. Throughout this chapter, we examined the various aspects of building effective partnerships with families and communities. These include establishing reciprocal relationships, communicating effectively, and negotiating conflicts. We conclude with a return visit to Vilma Suarez's Early Head Start program where we began.

 Check Your Understanding 7.5: A Framework for Building Partnerships with Families

Revisiting the Case Study

. . . Ms. Suarez's Classroom

Now that we have explored the many ways in which teachers build effective partnerships with families, we can see how well Vilma Suarez fulfills this important responsibility. She plays a key role in implementing Aiya's IFSP plan, but she also respects and supports Aiya's mother and works to gain her trust. She helps Tomas and Mrs. Vacaro through difficult daily transitions and takes time to communicate with her throughout the day.

Her biggest challenge will be resolving the conflict with Mr. Henderson over his son's biting. She needs to employ all of her skills of effective communication and negotiation. She begins by saying, "Mr. Henderson, I know how upsetting it is when children bite, but the law prohibits hitting children at the center. I would like to talk with you about other ways we can work together on this problem." Thus begins the complex negotiation process that Vilma knows from experience may take one meeting or many.

As the families arrive the next morning, Vilma notices that Mrs. Vacaro is even more anxious than she was the night before when she picked up Tomas. Feeling that she has gained Mrs. Vacaro's trust over the many months they have known each other, Vilma carefully asks, "Is everything all right?" Mrs. Vacaro's eyes well up and she whispers, "I'm pregnant again, and I don't have health insurance."

Vilma calmly replies, "Tomas will make a wonderful brother. He's so loving. I'm sure you're feeling a lot of stress. But our Early Head Start program can help you. With your permission, I'll check with the director during the day about the resources we have to offer you and the help we can find in the community. If you have time, we can meet this evening or I'll phone you at home." Mrs. Vacaro exhales with relief and promises to check back at the end of the day. She calls goodbye to Tomas, who is already eating his breakfast with the other children. ■

7 Chapter Summary

- Families are diverse in many ways: composition, culture, religion, economic status, work, mobility, and sexual orientation.

- Along with reciprocal relationships and partnerships between teachers and families, family-centered practice is characterized by several key principles: mutual respect and trust; regular, frequent two-way communication; collaboration, shared decision making, and shared power; and negotiation of conflicts toward win-win situations.

- Effective two-way communication is the basis for positive relationships with families. Communication strategies include teachers' creating a welcoming

environment; informal conversation; sharing important information on a daily and/or weekly basis, depending on the age of the child; using an assertive communication style, especially when discussing delicate issues; conferencing; home visiting; and using technology.

- More than 40 years of research confirms that family engagement in schools and early childhood programs has a positive impact on children's success in school and life.

- Effective partnerships with families involve four key strategies: clarity about preferences, ability to communicate, ability to negotiate, and willingness to change and learn.

Key Terms

- aggressive communication
- assertive communication
- family-centered practice
- family systems theory
- funds of knowledge
- home-based programs
- home visiting
- passive communication
- reciprocal relationships
- slippery egg messages
- tennis ball messages

 Demonstrate Your Learning

Click here to assess how well you've learned the content in this chapter.

Readings and Websites

Ernst, J. D. (2014). The welcoming classroom: *Building strong home-school connections for early learning*. Lewisville, NC: Gryphon House.

Gonzalez-Mena, J. (2014). *50 strategies for communicating and working with diverse families* (3rd ed.). Upper Saddle River, NJ: Pearson.

Schweikert, G. (2011). *Partnering with families: Winning ways for early childhood professionals*. St. Paul, MN: Redleaf Press.

Harvard Family Research Project

This website has information and strategies for involving families in children's learning and development.

National Center on Parent, Family, and Community Engagement

A center of Office of Head Start, the NCPFCE website has many resources for engaging families in their children's learning, engaging fathers, safety and health, and learning games.

National Coalition for Parent Involvement in Education

This website offers resources and guidance for developing partnerships with families and offers resources for families, educators, and administrators. The NCPIE also provides resources for families and professionals related to disabilities.

CONNECT Module 4: Family-Professional Partnerships

This web-based module, from FPG Child Development Institute, offers learning opportunities and strategies for building partnerships with families, including videos, handouts, and activities.

National Black Child Development Institute (NBCDI)

Among a variety of helpful resources for engaging with families of color, the NBCDI website offers a Classroom Family Engagement Rubric that teachers can use to identify their strengths and needs related to engaging families around children's learning and development.

Common Sense Education

On this website, Common Sense Media offers "Early Connections: A Parent Education Toolkit for Early Childhood Providers." Teachers can share materials with families to build partnerships and support family activities around children's learning.

8

Creating a Caring Community of Learners: Guiding Young Children

Learning Outcomes

After studying this chapter, you should be able to:

8.1 Explain the value of a caring community of learners and how the Teaching Pyramid model helps teachers create such a classroom community.

8.2 Review ways teachers can build positive relationships with young children.

8.3 Discuss how teachers can organize daily routines and experiences to support children's positive behavior and learning, and prevent behavior problems.

8.4 Outline strategies for how teachers can effectively guide children's behavior toward the goal of promoting positive social-emotional development in each child.

8.5 Describe individualized interventions that can be used with children who exhibit persistent challenging behaviors.

8.6 Apply the Teaching Pyramid model to specific situations such as teaching boys, addressing biting and alleviating bullying.

© Jamie Grill/Getty Images

Today is the first day of school for Sue Brady, a teacher of 20 four-year-olds in a child care center. She and her co-teacher, Elly Donahue, are both inexperienced teachers responsible for a group of children for the first time. Sue and Elly spent the last week preparing their classroom. They are a little worried that there are not enough toys to keep children's interest and have requested more from the director. The room has a sink, but it is located in the pathway from the front door to the closet so it is not possible to put the paint easels near it. There is no book rack, and the books are stacked on an open shelf near the blocks. There is one large open area with a rug that they plan to use for group time and block building next to a table for toys. Tables are lined up along the far side of the room.

As soon as the children begin to arrive, things go wrong. Playtime becomes disorganized and the children dump materials all over the floor rather than use them constructively. The teachers give so much attention to the children who are out of control that they neglect the others who are behaving well, such as Edie, who is absorbed in her painting. Over the course of the day, the teachers' voices become louder as they try to restore order while the noise level in the room becomes almost unbearable. No one cooperates during cleanup time.

At lunch, Ricky blows milk at his friends through his straw and the others soon emulate his skill. Sue asks Paula and Aimee, "Would you like to go outside now?" and they simply say, "No," leaving her unsure about what to do since she can't leave them alone inside. On the playground, Booth punches Elijah hard in the stomach, seemingly for no reason. Furious but feeling totally incompetent, Sue grabs Booth by the arms and repeatedly says, "Say you're sorry!" while Booth just smirks and Elijah cries loudly. Both teachers can't wait for naptime, but when they turn out the lights, the ensuing chaos becomes overwhelming. Children refuse to stay on their cots, grab toys off the shelves, talk loudly, and make it impossible for even the most exhausted to sleep. Sue will remember this day vividly because it is one of the longest days of her life, and unfortunately the next day will be all too similar. ■

This glimpse into Sue's classroom is not a fictional account. It is actually what happened to me on my first day of teaching many years ago. I learned very quickly that teaching young children is hard work. I also discovered that there was a lot more that I needed to know to become an effective teacher.

The goal of this chapter is to help ensure that you and the children you teach do not experience days like the one described above. This chapter describes research-based practices—ways of creating a caring community of learners—that make teaching young children more effective and enjoyable. To help you learn how to promote children's social competence and address challenging behaviors, we will describe a conceptual framework—the Teaching Pyramid (Center on the Social and Emotional Foundations of Early Learning, n.d.; Fox, Carta, Strain, Dunlap, & Hemmeter, 2009). Applying this framework will help you create a caring community of learners in which young children thrive. Using these research-based, positive guidance strategies will not prevent all of the challenges you face as a teacher, but it will help you become more effective in your work with all children.

A Caring Community of Learners: The Teaching Pyramid Model

A **caring community of learners** is a group or classroom in which children and adults engage in warm, positive relationships; treat each other with respect; and learn from and with each other. The late Jim Greenman (2005a), one of the foremost experts on children's environments, described early childhood programs as "caring spaces, learning places." This phrase is apt because it emphasizes a fundamental principle of early childhood education: children's care and education are interrelated.

Wherever children are served, they are always learning and being cared for. In other words, *both/and* thinking is required. Effective early childhood programs provide *both* nurturing, responsive relationships *and* stimulating, interesting educational experiences. If children's needs for either care or learning are neglected, the program will be ineffective.

The Value of a Caring Community of Learners

Children learn and develop best in the context of a caring community of learners. Research provides strong evidence that this is the case. One tool for evaluating the quality and effectiveness of early childhood programs is the *Classroom Assessment Scoring System* (CLASS), which assesses the social-emotional climate and the instructional climate of preschool or primary-grade classrooms through detailed observations of teachers' behaviors (Pianta, La Paro, & Hamre, 2008). Research using the CLASS has found that high-quality emotional and instructional classroom climates uniquely predict children's academic achievement and improve social and emotional outcomes (Curby, Brock, & Hamre, 2013). Teachers who provide high-quality emotional support are aware of and respond to children's individual needs, rarely display intense negative emotion, and engage in positive, respectful interactions with children (Hamre, 2014). This chapter is dedicated to providing information for how teachers can provide classroom climates that support children's emotional and social development.

Equally important, if not more so, is that the emotional climate *not* be negative—that there is little or no aggression or hostility among children and teachers (Hamre, 2014). Most of us have observed classrooms or been students in them in which it is obvious which children are the "bad kids." They may be sitting at a desk by themselves or their names may be the ones you hear over and over. They may be waving their hands in the air while the teacher continues to ignore them. Young children are very perceptive. They know whether teachers like them and which kids are the favorites (Janson & King, 2010). Imagine figuring out within a few days after school starts that your teacher doesn't like you very much and facing 9 months of being in that person's control with no choice to stay home or switch to another teacher. Children soon begin to act the way they are perceived and live up to low or negative expectations.

Building a caring community of learners requires effort on the part of teachers and children, but the effort pays off in short- and long-term benefits. In the present, the classroom will be a more harmonious, pleasant environment in which children are more likely to learn successfully. In addition, experiencing a caring community helps achieve three essential, long-term goals for children:

1. To develop positive social skills and emotional self-regulation, which are essential tasks during the first 5 to 8 years of life
2. To prevent future social and behavioral difficulties, which is more efficient, effective, and humane than later remediation
3. To build a foundation of learning for later success in school and in life.

Develop Social Skills and Self-Regulation A major developmental accomplishment of the first 5 years of life is the development of self-regulation in all spheres of behavior. This process begins early as babies learn to regulate their sleeping, crying, and other behavior patterns, and expands during the preschool years to more complex self-regulation. During these years children develop the ability to control emotions, to learn to delay gratification, and to build relationships with other people—all key factors essential for healthy development (Riley, San Juan, Klinkner, & Ramminger, 2008).

Children's ability to regulate their emotional responses is associated with successful learning and social relationships (Zins, Bloodworth, Weissberg & Walberg, 2007). Children who regulate their emotions can work collaboratively, play with others, seek help, and offer help to others. Children who have difficulty regulating their emotions exhibit more frustration in school and often have trouble focusing their attention, completing tasks and working with other children (Raver, Garner, & Smith-Donald, 2007). Because learning to regulate one's emotions involves acquiring a complex set of skills, children need support from adults in order to be successful.

Other important goals of the early years are the development of self-concept and self-esteem. **Self-concept**, which forms rapidly during the preschool years, refers to children's stable perceptions about themselves despite variations in their behavior. Children's **self-esteem**, or perception of their own worth, is also in its formative stages during these years and can be fragile. Similarly, children gradually acquire a sense of **efficacy**, a belief in their own ability to accomplish what they set out to do. Positive self-concept, self-esteem, and feelings of efficacy don't develop by people telling children how special and talented they are, but rather as children take initiative and master challenges with a lot of adult encouragement (Galinsky, 2010).

self-concept Children's stable perceptions about themselves despite variations in their behavior.

self-esteem Children's perception of their own worth.

efficacy Children's belief in their own ability to accomplish what they set out to do.

Prevent Social and Behavioral Difficulties Teachers today report a larger percentage of children who exhibit extremely challenging behaviors, such as excessive aggression, anger, and hostility (Kaiser & Rasminsky, 2017). These children take up most of the teacher's attention, yet fail to improve. In worst case scenarios, some children may be expelled from child care or preschool, experiencing failure before their educational experiences have even begun (Gilliam, 2008). During the last few decades, since federal laws began requiring child care programs and schools to fully include children with disabilities and special needs, the number of children with challenging behaviors may have increased. Some disabilities such as attention deficit/hyperactivity disorder (ADHD) or autism may adversely affect children's social behavior (Lieber, 2009). To successfully teach in these increasingly complex classrooms, teachers must have knowledge of effective, research-based early intervention strategies before they encounter these difficult situations. Children who exhibit persistent challenging behaviors are those most in need of good teaching.

Building positive social skills and healthy emotional relationships during the early years is more effective than trying to remedy problems later. Research demonstrates that preschool children who lack self-regulation and/or fail to develop positive relationships with peers are likely to encounter significant difficulties in school and in life (Diamond, 2012; Moffitt et al., 2011). Children who don't acquire minimal social competence and thus are unable to make friends are at significant risk of dropping out of school, becoming delinquent, or experiencing mental health problems in adolescence or adulthood (Ladd, Herald, & Andrews, 2006; Moffitt et al., 2011).

Even when children are 3 or 4 years old, it is possible to observe which children are socially isolated and do not make friends easily. Even adults sometimes find these children difficult to interact with, and may want to avoid them. Yet teachers must recognize that socially isolated children need

Teachers today report that more children are exhibiting challenging behaviors than in the past. Why might this be true? What might account for this perception?

© Carla Mestas/Pearson Education

their help the most. With systematic support and intentional teaching, teachers can promote children's development of social competence.

If children's problems are ignored or set aside because teachers hope "they'll grow out of it," the problems only get worse as children get older. Teachers can instead adopt a proactive approach, such as this one:

> Preschool teacher Karen Hagey observed that every time 3½-year-old Marcus tried to push his way into the block corner, the other children shouted, "Get out, Marcus! You can't play." She thought about forcing the children to accept Marcus, but realized that they would resent him and he would be humiliated by her interference. Instead, Karen quietly coached Marcus on strategies for entering play: "Let's sit next to Jason and see if you and I can build a tall tower." Marcus's tower soon eclipsed that of his peers, who started to pay attention to his skill. After a few days of this kind of assistance from Karen, Marcus entered the play area more calmly and Jason said, "Hey, Marcus, help me make my building as tall as me."

Promote Academic Success Social-emotional competence is clearly linked to academic success throughout all the years of school (Durlak, Weissberg, Dymnicki, Taylor, & Schellinger, 2011). Children in preschool and the primary grades perform better on measures of academic achievement, language, and social-emotional development when they have positive, sensitive, trusting relationships with their teachers (Hamre, 2014). Relationships with teachers predict children's later relationships with their peers, behavior problems, school satisfaction, and learning (Diamond, 2012; Howes & Ritchie, 2002).

Vygotsky's theory of learning as a social construction of knowledge emphasizes that much of our understanding occurs as we talk with and listen to other people's ideas. This give and take of conversation and debate with other people plays a major role in learning. Promoting social construction of knowledge requires that children learn not just as individuals but also in the context of small and large groups—as part of a community of learners. We now have a large body of research to guide teachers in this important work.

The Teaching Pyramid Model

The Center on the Social and Emotional Foundations for Early Learning (http://www. vanderbilt.edu/csefel) disseminates resources to teachers that translate research on social-emotional development into best practice. The center developed a model—the *Teaching Pyramid*—for promoting social competence and preventing challenging behavior in young children, which is depicted in Figure 8.1. **Challenging behavior** is defined as "any behavior that interferes with children's learning, development, and success at play; is harmful to the child, other children, or adults; and/or puts a child at high risk for later social problems or school failure" (Kaiser & Rasminsky, 2017).

Pyramid Components The Teaching Pyramid is composed of four parts: (1) positive relationships with children, (2) high-quality supportive environments, (3) social and emotional teaching strategies, and (4) intensive individualized interventions. The base of the pyramid is the largest portion because it represents the foundation of positive relationships on which everything else depends. Each subsequent topic on the pyramid builds on the ones below, and represents a proportionately smaller amount of teachers' time and effort. This model indicates that if teachers effectively provide these supports, children will learn social competence, their positive behaviors will increase and challenging behaviors will diminish.

When teachers encounter children who exhibit negative behaviors such as aggression or hostility, their first inclination is to try to "fix" that child. As teachers, we naturally assume that if we could just quickly change that child's behavior, everything would be well and our job would be so much easier. The truth is that there are no quick fixes; in fact, the more effective strategy is not to try to fix the child at first. It is always more difficult to change another person's behavior, even if that person is only 3 years old, than to change our own behavior.

The Teaching Pyramid turns our prior assumptions on their head. Rather than trying to change children first, we begin by changing ourselves—that is, we examine our

challenging behavior Any behavior that interferes with children's learning, development, and success at play; is harmful to the child, other children, or adults; or puts a child at high risk for later social problems or school failure.

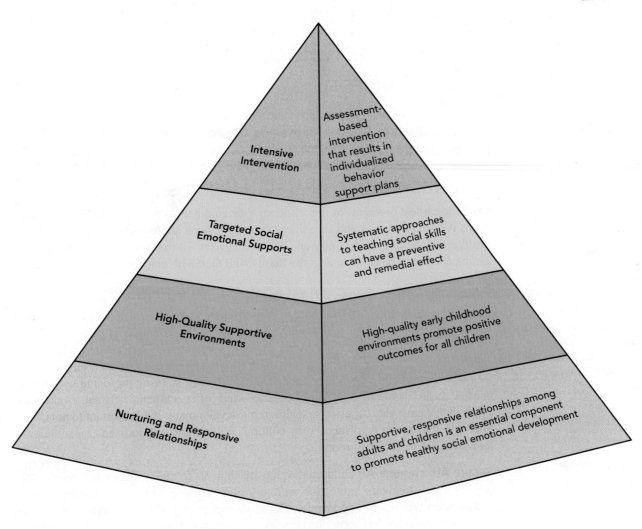

FIGURE 8.1 Teaching Pyramid Model for Promoting Children's Social and Emotional Competence The Teaching Pyramid is a research-based, effective framework to help teachers support children's social-emotional learning and reduce challenging behaviors in the classroom.

Source: From *Promoting Social and Emotional Competence in Infants and Young Children.* The Center on the Social and Emotional Foundations for Early Learning, http://csefel.vanderbilt.edu. Reprinted by permission.

behavior in order to focus on establishing a positive relationship with each child. We recognize that more difficult children will take more effort, but we also acknowledge that the effort will pay off greatly. Next, we evaluate teaching environments and routines and determine what changes need to be made to support children's positive behavior. How can we support routines that help children do their best? How can we teach social skills and emotional self-regulation? By asking these questions and exploring solutions, we attempt to directly address individual children's challenging behaviors.

The Pyramid's Effectiveness Research demonstrates that when teachers consistently apply the strategies described in the Pyramid Model, positive social interactions among children increase and behavior problems decrease (Hemmeter, Snyder, Fox, & Algina, 2011). Research suggests that fewer than 4% of children require the more intensive level of interventions (Fox, Dunlap, Hemmeter, Joseph, & Strain, 2003). In a group of 20 children, that equates to only one child. In a center serving 100 children, about 4 children might require this level of intensive assistance. In the following sections, we discuss each level of the Teaching Pyramid and provide examples of effective teaching practices.

✓ **Check Your Understanding 8.1:** A Caring Community of Learners: The Teaching Pyramid Model

Positive Relationships with Children

A key premise of the Teaching Pyramid is that the most fundamental way to promote healthy development and learning in young children is for teachers to build and sustain positive relationships with children.

The Importance of Relationships

From the earliest moments of life, children's development—who they become—is influenced by the nurturance and care that they receive from adults—first their parents, then members of the extended family and other caregivers. In the next sections, we describe the importance of relationships in the family, and then with teachers and other children.

Family Relationships: Attachment Theory Decades of research on mother-child interactions support the concept that children's ability to learn depends on their developing trusting relationships with caregivers—what is called **attachment theory** (Bowlby, 1969/2000). Much of the research was conducted by Mary Ainsworth and her colleagues (1978). They observed how young children interacted with their mothers when they were brought into a novel or strange situation (such as being presented with new or unusual materials to explore). They identified kinds of attachments between mothers and children that have varying effects on children's development. It is important to note, however, that attachment is influenced by cultural contexts and will look and mean different things to diverse cultural groups.

Secure Attachment All children develop attachments to their primary caregivers. They rely on their caregivers' protection and nurturing and base their understanding of relationships on their early experiences. Based on the quality of care infants receive from caregivers, they develop secure or insecure attachments. According to attachment theory (Ainsworth et al., 1978; Bowlby, 1969/2000; Scroufe, 1996), when children's caregivers are responsive and sensitive to their needs, children develop **secure attachment relationships**. Securely attached children rely on their caregivers for support, yet comfortably explore their surroundings. Children who are securely attached to their caregivers have a strong foundation not only for building relationships with other people, but also for learning (Watson, 2003). They see their caregivers as trustworthy and, in turn, see themselves as competent and worthy of attention.

What does secure attachment look like? Consider Matthew, a 2½-year-old who enjoys a warm, loving relationship with his mother. When his mother enrolls him in a child care center, she stays with him for almost an hour while he becomes acclimated. At first he clings to her leg and eyes the toys and other children. Gradually, however, he ventures a few steps toward an enticing ramp that the other kids are sliding down, but quickly runs back to his mother. After a few more attempts, he hesitantly joins in the fun by rolling a ball down the incline, all the while seeking regular eye contact with his mother. After a while, he begins to explore the classroom, occasionally returning to her side for reassurance. Matthew relies on his mother as a **secure base** from which to explore his new environment. During the next few days, his mother stays with him for shorter periods of time, until one day he joyfully waves goodbye to her at the door. He no longer needs her actual presence as a physical base from which to explore because he has internalized the sense of trust and confidence that she provides. Teachers can help children make such transitions from the secure attachments of home to child care settings. Read the *Becoming an Intentional Teacher: Easing Separation Woes* feature for a classroom example.

Insecure Attachment By contrast, some children grow up in families that, for a variety of reasons, are unable or unwilling to provide reasonably consistent, sensitive, responsive

attachment theory The theory that children's ability to learn depends on their developing trusting relationships with caregivers.

secure attachment relationship A responsive and sensitive relationship with caregivers that allows children to venture forth and comfortably explore and learn about the world.

secure base An attachment figure (mother or caregiver) who serves as an anchor for children to rely on and from which children can safely venture out and explore.

Becoming an Intentional Teacher

Easing Separation Woes

Here's What Happened A month before a new group of 1- and 2-year-olds entered our child care center, I contacted the families to learn about the daily routines at home. I encouraged the parents to have the child bring a favorite blanket or toy to the center. I also asked if there were snapshots of family members or maybe a pet that they could share so I could make a little photo book for each child. I suggested to parents that, if possible with their work schedules, children stay for a shorter time for a few days rather than a full day.

On the first day, Sasha's mom whispered to me that she was going to sneak out so her 2-year-old son wouldn't get upset at seeing her go. I told her I thought it would help Sasha if she said goodbye and told him when she would be back.

Here's What I Was Thinking From 10 months to about 2 years of age, the typically developing child learns that separations from parents are not permanent and begins to cope with short periods of time apart. The child's increasing representational abilities—remembering people and situations—help this understanding to develop. Thus, bringing a favorite toy or photo from home often provides comfort and reminds the child that home is still a part of his day. Transitioning to the program with a shorter day also allows children to hold on to the idea that a parent is coming back and then gradually extend that to a longer period of time.

Parents sometimes want to leave without saying goodbye, and that's understandable. They think the child will be less upset, and that this may be less stressful for teachers. However, sneaking away actually creates mistrust in children; it sends the message that the child cannot rely on the parent. One- and 2-year-olds fare better when a parent tells them, "I'm leaving now and I'll be back after you eat lunch." I try to reassure the parents, and tell them not to worry or feel guilty if their child is crying and having difficulty with the separation for a while. It means their child feels a bond and is learning to cope with strong emotions. During the day, I also try to call or text parents to ease their anxiety.

Reflection More than one-third of mothers of Head Start children report symptoms of depression, including 9% who are severely depressed (Malone, Hulsey, Aikens, West, & Tarullo, 2010). How might the teacher or child react differently in this situation if the mother is depressed and the mother–child attachment appears to be less secure? What might a teacher do to support this parent?

care. Mothers or other caregivers may be depressed, ill, or stressed by economic or other conditions that lead them to be neglectful, punitive, or hostile to their young children. Some children grow up in very difficult circumstances in which they may have been abused, neglected, or exposed to drugs and violence. Children growing up in such an environment may be unable to trust caregivers to keep them safe, and as a result, they develop poor social skills. Such *insecurely attached* children may often have difficulty developing positive social relationships and may exhibit disruptive behavior in child care centers or schools (Ainsworth et al., 1978).

Various patterns of insecure attachment exist, depending on children's experiences, which are related to different patterns of behavior (Ainsworth et al., 1978; Bowlby, 1969/2000). Children who have experienced rejection and insensitivity from adult caregivers may demonstrate **insecure-avoidant attachment**. These children tend to turn away from or avoid adults and do not seek their comfort; in fact, they may become hostile in order to avoid rejection before it occurs.

Other insecurely attached children who have experienced confusing and inconsistent nurturing from adults are said to be experiencing **insecure-ambivalent/resistant attachment**. Because they are unsure whether adults will be there for them, these children may appear to seek comfort but then reject it when it is offered. They may be irritable and fussy, easily frustrated, and difficult to manage in a group.

In more extreme circumstances, when children have experienced neglect, abuse, or violence in the home, they may exhibit **disorganized/disoriented attachment** (Main & Solomon, 1990). Because their past experiences with adults have left them without secure attachments, they have not developed useful strategies for seeking comfort or attention or for handling difficulties. Their behavior can be very unpredictable and confusing to teachers and negatively affect the children's ability to learn.

insecure-avoidant attachment Rejection and insensitivity from adult caregivers that causes children to turn away from or avoid adults and not seek their comfort.

insecure-ambivalent/resistant attachment Children's inability to trust adults to keep them safe due to neglect, abuse, or other difficult circumstances that results in a lack of social competence.

disorganized/disoriented attachment Seen in children who lack secure attachments with adults due to having experienced neglect, abuse, or violence in the home, who have not developed useful strategies for seeking comfort or attention or handling difficulties.

▶ **Classroom Connection**

How does the teacher in this video foster a warm, caring relationship with the infants and toddlers in her care?

Attachment to Teachers Although earlier attachment studies focused on mother–child attachment, current research also applies the theory to teacher–child relationships (Hamre, 2014; Howes & Ritchie, 2002). This research demonstrates that across the full age span of infancy through the primary grades, a caring, sensitive relationship with a teacher is related to positive social and academic development. For example, in one study, first graders who were at high risk for school failure but who had emotionally supportive teachers had achievement scores and relationships with teachers comparable to those of children who were not at risk (Hamre & Pianta, 2005). By contrast, children whose teachers were not emotionally supportive had lower achievement and more conflict with their teachers and peers. Other studies demonstrate that when teachers have positive relationships with children and are sensitive to their needs, children develop better self-regulation and social skills (Johnson, Seidenfeld, Izard, & Kobak, 2013; Williford, Vick Whittaker, Vitiello, & Downer, 2013).

In addition, attachment relationships with parents may not predict attachment relationships with teachers (Howes & Ritchie, 2002). Just as a child who is securely attached to parents may be insecurely attached to teachers, a child who is insecurely attached to parents may develop a secure attachment to a teacher. In this way, teachers know that they can make a positive difference for all children, even those who have troubled family relationships.

Although building relationships with insecurely attached children can be challenging for teachers, these children are most in need of such support if they are to succeed in school and life. Research shows that teachers have more conflict in their relationships with children with behavior challenges, with boys, and with children of color (Gallagher, Kainz, White, & Vernon-Feagans, 2013). Most likely related to this research finding is the fact that: (1) although African American children make up only 18% of preschoolers, they account for 48% of multiple pre-K suspensions; and (2) more than 75% of preschool suspensions are boys (U.S. Department of Education Office of Civil Rights, 2014).

Responsive teachers observe children carefully and notice when children need extra attention or support, and children respond by growing in their social and academic competence (Hamre, 2014). Although the attachment literature tends to focus on individual relationships between parents or teachers and children, it does not focus on children's roles as members of groups, which we discuss next.

Relationships with Other Children Across the age span of birth through age 8, teachers create a caring community by promoting positive interactions among young children (National Association for the Education of Young Children [NAEYC], 2008c, 2009). Such a community is essential not only for social-emotional development but for learning in every area. Teaching that supports children's peer relationships depends, in part, on the age of the children served.

Infants and Toddlers Building relationships with babies and toddlers takes time, sensitive touch, talking, and playful learning experiences (Raikes & Edwards, 2009). Teachers create a climate of respect by listening and responding to babies' verbal and nonverbal cues, such as their cries or coos, their facial expressions, and body movements. These behaviors send signals about the baby's wants and needs, such as "I'm hungry" or "I'm bored and want to do something else." When adults respond appropriately to their cues, babies begin to develop a sense of trust and efficacy.

Teachers also model the kind of warmth and caring that they want children to develop. Even very young infants and toddlers demonstrate empathic behaviors toward their peers (Raikes & Edwards, 2009). Teachers can promote empathy by labeling children's feelings and helping them comfort one another—for instance, "Claudia is crying because she dropped her binky. Let's help her." Finally, teachers can engage in conversations with infants and toddlers that focus on discussions of their peers. They can point out to Felix that Anna chose the same color for her painting, and that Amir is waiting for them to finish painting for his turn. To Amir, the teacher can say, "Look, Felix and Anna are painting with green, I wonder what color you will choose when it is your turn."

Preschoolers and School-Age Children As children get older, their understanding of relationships and need of friendship increases. Teachers set the tone for a harmonious classroom by organizing cooperative learning experiences so that children can play and work together on projects or in small groups. In preschool and even more so in the primary grades, achieving a harmonious classroom involves the entire group working together (Durlak et al., 2011). To foster such harmony, encouraging children to talk about potential or actual social problems, offer solutions, and reflect on the outcomes during class meetings can be effective (Vance, 2013). In the *Promoting Play: All Can Play* feature, learn how Tasha creates a context for children to build a strong community.

Promoting Play

All Can Play

Tasha teaches in a combined kindergarten–first grade classroom in a diverse, urban school. Her students enjoy periods of intensive learning balanced with rambunctious dramatic play over the course of their daily routines and lessons. An intentional teacher, Tasha has mindfully prepared the classroom and schedule to meet children's group and individual needs. She includes the children in planning and enforcing class rules, and teaches emotional literacy and social skills as part of her curriculum. So Tasha is surprised when she realizes that a group of older children—mostly first graders—has created a sort of "members-only club" in the class. They have rules for participation and dictate who can play and who cannot. They give out-of-school privileges to their "members" such as play and party invitations.

Because the "club" children (who call themselves the Dinosaur Kings) are not visibly mean to other children, Tasha initially just observes their interactions. Eventually, however, she notices that their exclusion of peers has been somewhat systematic. In addition to excluding younger children from their activities, they have prohibited membership to several other first graders: Thu, a recent immigrant who speaks little English; Alphonse, a boy with intellectual disabilities; and Rita, a shy child who wears the same clothing almost every day.

Tasha shares her concerns with a colleague, who recommends reading Vivian Paley's classic book, *You*

Can't Say You Can't Play (1992). In Paley's book, she describes her journey with kindergarten and elementary-school children in learning how to create a classroom community that espouses inclusion. Using stories and daily group discussion, Paley leads the children to view inclusion as social justice, and exclusion as unacceptable. Like Paley, Tasha begins to use morning meeting as a time to teach children about inclusion and differences, and supports excluded children to advocate for themselves. Children bring daily stories of their playground interactions to the group, and no child (even the excluders) is shamed for their perspective. Because Tasha has developed positive relationships with all children in her group, the children feel safe sharing their stories.

Eventually, Tasha's group reaches the same decision as Paley's children did: "You can't say you can't play" becomes a classroom rule. To support this rule, Tasha is available to help children join group activities, and to provide ideas for how play and cooperative activities can go well, even if one or more children struggle. Before children head to the free choice activities each day, Tasha has the children proactively plan for how their chosen activities can be expanded to include peers. Her perspective is, "not IF, but HOW" when she thinks about including children who want to play.

Reference: You Can't Say You Can't Play, by V. Paley, 1992, Cambridge, MA: Harvard University Press.

Beyond focusing on children's social "skills," teachers also need to promote positive interactions among children and be attentive to supporting children's close, reciprocal friendships (Gallagher, 2013). Teachers can identify potential friends for children, and arrange for them to work together on a project or be placed at the same table. Teachers can make cooperative games part of their learning centers, and assign classroom duties to pairs of children. They can include families in their planning, and suggest play dates or shared activities after school. Teachers can make a point of communicating with parents about relationships among children as they emerge, and share photos or stories of children sharing each other's company.

Children need to share space and activities with all of the children in their group; however, only a few of the children may actually be chosen as friends. Friends are a type of relationship that is special and intimate—and chosen by the child. There is a current trend in early childhood to refer to all children in a group as "friends" and to call and refer to children as "friends" (as when a teacher says, "Your friend is waiting for her turn." However, teachers should be mindful of the use of the word "friend." While all children can play, only children can choose with whom to be friends.

Teachers play an important role in children's relationship development at all ages, and they can play an essential role in making sure that children develop friendships (Gallagher, 2013; Gallagher & Sylvester, 2009). Friendships are a specific and complex type of relationship and are important for lifelong health and well-being. When children are mutual friends, they share interests and affection for each other. When teachers learn how important friendships are for children's well-being, they can use the Teaching Pyramid to organize classroom environments, routines, and experiences to support children's friendship development (Gallagher, 2013). A teacher can pair preschoolers with similar interests. She can teach them how to enter group activities by observing and commenting on the play. Elementary-school teachers can use board games (with some adult guidance) and playing games that require teamwork. American classrooms often emphasize the importance of independence, but children fare much better, socially and academically, when we shift our attention to relationships and interdependence in the classroom.

Effective Strategies to Build Positive Relationships

Teachers who have positive relationships with children are significantly more likely to influence their behavior because children pay more attention to responsive, caring adults (Fox et al., 2003). In addition, caring relationships help children develop positive self-concept, confidence, and a sense of safety, which in turn reduces the incidence of

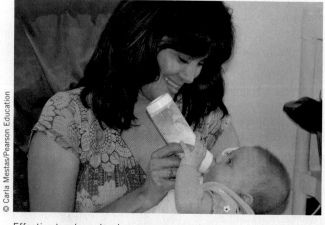

Effective teachers develop warm, responsive, positive relationships with each child. From infancy through primary grades, the quality of teacher–child relationships is related to positive learning and developmental outcomes for children.

challenging behavior. In fact, "the time spent building a strong relationship is probably less than the time required to implement more elaborate and time-consuming strategies" to address challenging behaviors (Fox et al., 2003, p. 49).

A sage piece of advice comes from Kaiser and Rasminsky (2017): "Start fresh every day." This seems simple, but sometimes teachers find themselves storing up grievances against children for past transgressions, creating resentment in both parties. One proven effective strategy is called "banking time" (Driscoll & Pianta, 2010). Just as saving money for unexpected expenses helps in an emergency, taking 5 to 15 minutes a week to focus individually on each child—playing with them or talking about something interesting unrelated to academics or the child's behavior—can pay dividends in building a relationship.

An important but often overlooked aspect of creating a caring community of learners is the health and well-being of the leaders of the classroom—the teachers. Just as healthy parents raise healthy children, well teachers create and support a high-quality social-emotional climate. Teachers who experience more work stress have more conflict in their relationships with children (Whitaker et al., 2014). In order to calmly and effectively respond to the demands and stresses of working daily and intensively with young children and their families, effective early childhood teachers find it necessary to practice self-care. Teachers can do this by taking care of their physical health (eating well, sleeping, and exercising) as well as making sure to stay socially connected. Friendships are important for teachers, too. Some teachers find that practicing **mindfulness**, or noticing present moments without judgment, helps them to regulate their emotions and respond to stressful situations more effectively (Jennings, 2014).

mindfulness The practice of purposefully and nonjudgmentally noticing sensations (bodily, mentally, emotionally) in the present moment.

That said, the effectiveness of any strategy will vary with individual children. For this reason, it is important for teachers to have a large repertoire of strategies to use as they build relationships with each child. Table 8.1 describes a caring community from the points of view of both of the children and the teachers.

TABLE 8.1 What a Caring Community Looks Like

To create a true caring community of learners, teachers need to consider the child's point of view as well as their own, as described in this table.

From a Child's Point of View	From a Teacher's Point of View
My teacher cares about me, really listens to me, and likes me.	Shows respect and warmth to all children through physical affection, using a soothing tone of voice, smiles, and laughter. Listens carefully to children's feelings and ideas with attention and respect.
My teacher knows me well—my abilities, strengths, interests, and needs.	Engages in individual conversations with children throughout the day. Gets to know children by carefully observing them and developing a relationship with their families.
I feel safe, secure, and happy.	Holds a child's hand, smiles, or pats a child lightly on the shoulder.
I'm not scared, no one bullies me.	Is sure to protect every child and has zero tolerance for bullying.
I feel like I belong. My identity, language, and culture are valued.	Greets children personally each day when they arrive, calls each child by his or her name, and talks with children at their eye level. Learns key phrases in the child's home language.
I feel proud of my family and they are welcome in my school.	Greets families warmly. Displays family photos. Conducts home visits or, if parents prefer, meets privately with them at a comfortable site such as a library or local community center.
I have friends.	Helps children who are isolated or lonely connect with at least one other child.
I am challenged and I am learning.	Expects children to succeed, acknowledges effort and accomplishments with nods, smiles, hugs, high-fives, or thumbs-up.
My teacher still likes me even if I don't always remember the rules or if I sometimes do the wrong thing.	Acknowledges and supports children's positive behavior, especially those children who tend to demonstrate challenging behavior. Takes time to nurture individual relationships each day.
I experience joy.	Begins each day anew, genuinely enjoys children, and delights in their accomplishments.

Source: Based on *Inventory of Practices for Promoting Children's Social-Emotional Competence,* by the Center on the Social and Emotional Foundations for Early Learning and WestEd San Marcos, 2011, retrieved from http://cainclusion.org/camap/pdfs/CACSEFEL/InventoryOfPractice_AUG11.pdf.

Human relationships are complex, two-way interactions, and children's behavior influences adults' reactions and behaviors just as much as adults influence children. Therefore, it is important for teachers to spend time reflecting on the basis for their expectations and judgments about children's behavior.

Personal, Family, and Cultural Views of Children's Behavior Each of us has her own views about the acceptability of specific behaviors in children based on personal, family, and cultural experiences (Kaiser & Rasminsky, 2017). For example, some adults welcome children's exuberance, whereas others see rambunctious play as misbehavior. Some children are hypersensitive to touch. With 3-year-old Shisuko, pats or hugs would not be welcome, but sitting nearby and talking quietly would. Relationship building, like all other aspects of teaching, requires individualizing.

Because what is considered acceptable behavior in one family, community, or cultural group may be frowned on or prohibited in another (Kaiser & Rasminsky, 2017), teachers should help children learn the kinds of behaviors that predict success in school. In doing so, they can help young children learn that there are different rules of behavior for different environments. Children make these distinctions all the time. Early on, they learn that what is accepted and safe behavior in their own home is not acceptable behavior in the neighborhood. Read the *Culture Lens: Helping Children Adapt to School* feature for an example of what teachers can do to help children feel comfortable at school.

Culture Lens

Helping Each Child Adapt to School

Children from diverse cultural backgrounds may face challenges adapting to unfamiliar environments, and school can be the most daunting. On the first morning of kindergarten, Miguel Hernandez sets in motion a plan to build a sense of community among the children. His class includes children from many different countries and cultural backgrounds. Miguel greets the children, most of whom arrived by bus, at the door. He hasn't had a chance to meet their families.

He begins the day with a morning meeting and wants the children to introduce themselves. Quickly, however, he changes his plan. In gathering the group and observing them, he realizes how uncomfortable and awkward many of the children would feel if he asked them to speak up in the group. Instead, he introduces himself and reassures them by talking briefly about what will happen today and what they can expect.

Even though Miguel has lived and worked in many different contexts in his life, he remembers vividly his first day of kindergarten. His mother had given him some last-minute instructions so that he would be successful in school. She told him to do three things: stand tall, show respect to his teacher, and speak only in English. When he arrived at school, the teacher said, "Look at me. Now what's your name?" He was nervous and confused then because he wanted to do what the teacher had told him, but he also wanted to follow his mother's instructions.

He knew that looking into the teacher's eyes would be disrespectful, and he was unsure of how to say his name in English. On his first day of school, differing cultural expectations clashed and he was caught in the middle.

Fortunately for the children in Miguel's class, he knows not to make assumptions and is sensitive to their needs. He will continue to work toward his goal—to create a caring community of learners—but he also knows that to achieve it, he will have to learn as much as possible about the children's families, their values, and their behavioral repertoires. Although it would have been better for this to happen before the first day, he will find ways to talk with families to discover areas where school and home expectations might differ. Once these are revealed, he will be able to propose some options to make things easier for each child and to offer a chance to talk about the differences. For example, "At home you remove your shoes before entering the house. At school we keep shoes on."

Teachers can use the same principle when problems arise over differing expectations about appropriate behavior, which may be more sensitive to discuss with parents, such as the use of profanity. Children may hear and use language at home that is prohibited at school. Helping children adapt to the expectations of school without criticizing their family or community can be a tricky balancing act for teachers, but is likely to be in the child's best interest.

Examine Your Own Attitudes toward Challenging Behavior An essential part of your development as a teacher is to examine your own attitudes toward children's challenging behavior. These attitudes are based in your own upbringing, your personal values, your cultural practices, and many other aspects of your prior experiences. Which behaviors do you find most unacceptable? Which behaviors "push your buttons"? Spitting, hitting, name-calling, bullying? Are they equally unacceptable? Do you see challenging behavior as characteristic of the child or something that is learned?

It is also important for you to consider your personal beliefs about the causes of specific types of unacceptable child behavior. Do you attribute motives to certain children but not to others? Do you find yourself thinking that a particularly aggressive child is mean-spirited, or do you think that she wants your attention and is willing to get it any way she can?

Mistaken Behavior, Not Misbehavior Considering the causes for children's behavior is an important part of the reflection process. Dan Gartrell (2011), an expert on guiding children's behavior, prefers the term **mistaken behavior** to *misbehavior*. Young children are still learning acceptable behavior and are bound to make mistakes, just as they make mistakes when learning to tie their shoes or write their names. We not only tolerate, but we expect mistaken behavior as part of the learning process. Why, then, are we so much less tolerant of mistakes in children's social behavior?

mistaken behavior Alternative term for children's misbehavior, recognizing the fact that young children are still learning acceptable behavior and that they are bound to make mistakes.

Some aspects of children's behavior that disturb adults are actually reflections of children's typical development. For example, toddlers come to love and overuse the word *no* and may accompany their insistent "No!" with temper tantrums. These behaviors demonstrate children's growing independence from adults, their beginning knowledge of the power of language, and frustration over not being able to do everything they would like. Most of the time, children grow out of these oppositional behaviors if given appropriate support and nurturance.

Behavior Is Functional All behavior is a form of communication; it serves a function (Kaiser & Rasminsky, 2017). Teachers need to understand that even challenging behaviors—those behaviors that are potentially harmful in the short or long term—are conveying some type of message. Experts who study children's behavior have found that most challenging behavior serves one of three functions: It helps children get something, avoid something, or change the level of stimulation (Kaiser & Rasminsky, 2017). For example, Brian wants Tonia's truck, so he pushes her down. Tray doesn't want to clean up, so he throws the toys at Emma. Lala is bored waiting in line for the bathroom, so she pinches Mona. As undesirable as these behaviors may be, to effectively handle the children's frustration, the teacher must determine what each behavior is conveying and provide the appropriate support and guidance.

If teachers think about children's challenging behavior as either a mistake on the path to learning or a message they are trying to send, it is likely that their attitudes toward challenging behaviors will change. Instead of blaming children or rejecting them, teachers are more likely to embrace these challenges as problems to solve. Of course, the most effective strategy is to prevent problems in the first place, which is the second step on the Teaching Pyramid.

✓ **Check Your Understanding 8.2:** Positive Relationships with Children

⬆ High-Quality Supportive Environments

The quality of the learning environment is also very important in creating a caring community of learners and enabling children to do their best. Teachers' work begins before they meet the children in their group. The physical environment, the schedule including

Environments send messages to children about what behavior is acceptable and what is valued. What messages does this classroom environment send to children?

use of routines and transitions, and curriculum plan are all important factors in promoting children's positive outcomes, preventing negative behaviors, and creating a caring community. As discussed in Chapter 3, the arrangement of the physical space and materials provides the framework to support children's positive behavior. When the classroom is well organized and predictable, children's behavior reflects that. In addition, the classroom literally communicates to children what is acceptable. In a wide open space, children may become boisterous or unruly as compared to a quiet, cozy nook where they are more likely to calmly peruse a book.

To ensure the best possible outcomes, teachers need to plan engaging daily routines with smooth transitions. Teachers can establish clear expectations for classroom behavior and make sure supports are in place so that children can develop warm relationships, demonstrate their best behavior, and engage productively in learning.

Ensure Smooth Transitions

Young children's care and education involves numerous changes in activity and relocation of their physical space. They move from group time to learning centers, eat regularly, wash their hands, use the bathroom, take naps, and go outdoors and return. Primary-grade children move between special classes such as music, art, or physical education in addition to lunch and recess, or switch subject matter teachers. Each of these situations involves transitions.

transitions Changes from one activity or place to another.

Transitions are the changes from one activity or place to another. Although inevitable, transitions can be difficult for young children who are not particularly good at waiting or who do not adapt well to change. Children who exhibit challenging behaviors tend to display oppositional behavior during transitions. Following are principles to keep in mind to ease transitions:

- Prepare ahead of time for the next activity so children do not spend excessive amounts of time waiting. For instance, have several children setting up for snack while the others are cleaning up centers so the transition to snack time is smooth.
- Give children a 5-minute warning before a transition happens, such as "Five more minutes till cleanup time." Point out the numbers on a digital clock (which becomes a math/addition learning experience) or the hands of the clock to help children grasp the concept of 5 minutes.
- For those children who have particular difficulty with transitions, give them an individual warning and explanation of what is to come, or perhaps a pictorial cue.
- Make transitions learning experiences by singing songs, reciting rhymes or poems, counting steps, following the leader's motions, doing movement exercises, or following specific directions such as "If your name starts with a K, get your coat."
- Minimize the number of transitions between activities and the amount of time children spend in transitions.

▶ **Classroom Connection**

Teachers often struggle with guiding children's behavior during the difficult transition to naptime. What effective strategies does this teacher use to ease the transition and turn a daily routine into a learning opportunity?

Use Engaging Routines

The early childhood day is governed by routines of daily living, which, if planned well, can provide children with excellent learning experiences. A large-scale study of 652 prekindergartens in 11 states found that, on average, children spent more than one-third of their time in routines and transitions, but during 87% of that time they were waiting idly and/or uninvolved in any learning activity (Early et al., 2010). These regular, informal moments of the day provide valuable learning opportunities that should not be wasted.

Routines—snacks and mealtimes, cleaning up, washing hands, dressing for out-doors—all provide opportunities for children to practice newly acquired skills and to engage in conversation essential for developing language. In addition, teachers can use routines as times for individual interactions such as sitting and talking with children during snacks and meals.

Teachers should establish routines that allow children to do as much as possible for themselves. When adults do things for children that they can already do themselves, they rob children of important learning experiences. Routines such as dressing or cleaning up also provide many chances for children to practice fine motor skills as well as cognitive abilities such as categorization (for example, the long blocks go together and the short blocks go together).

Establish Clear, Consistent, Fair Rules for Behavior

Just as children thrive in predictable physical and temporal environments, they also thrive when the expectations for behavior are clear and predictable. Therefore, it is essential that teachers involve children early on in establishing clear rules, limits, and consequences for behavior. It is equally important that teachers consistently and fairly enforce these rules in order for children to feel safe and secure.

In establishing classroom rules or *guidelines* for behavior, as Gartrell (2011) calls them, teachers need to engage children in discussing and enforcing a manageable number (three to six) of positively stated classroom rules. These discussions should take place during times of calm and quiet reflection. Some teachers may be tempted to focus children's attention on what not to do—don't hit, or don't throw toys. However, a more effective approach is to positively state what children should do. Virtually all situations can be covered by these three rules:

1. We take care of ourselves.
2. We take care of other people.
3. We take care of our school.

When we say "Don't run" to young children, their brains might process only the word *run*; they don't process the prohibition. Therefore, it is always more effective to state expectations clearly and positively: "Keep the food on the table" or "Walk inside." It is also important to provide reasons for the expected behavior: "If you run, someone might get knocked over."

Support Children to Do Their Best

Earlier, we identified several reasons why children behave as they do: to get something, to avoid something, or to change the level of stimulation. When it comes to "getting something," the object of desire is usually the teacher's attention. Children are willing to do almost anything to attract adults' attention, and they tend not to discriminate between positive and negative attention. To guide children toward using positive strategies to attract attention, teachers must keep in mind that because they have the power to control only their own behavior, they can determine which behaviors of children they give attention to and when. Teachers can ignore mistaken behavior, redirect behavior, and give positive feedback and encouragement.

Ignore When Appropriate   Behaviors that are not reinforced will be extinguished or eliminated. If the reinforcement that children are seeking is the teacher's attention—and they are behaving inappropriately to receive that attention—then ignoring the inappropriate behavior can be an effective way of extinguishing it. When teachers react to these behaviors, they continue.

Consider, for example, 3½-year-old Curt, who has daily temper tantrums and lies on the floor kicking and screaming. His teacher, Janine, knows that he is too old for this behavior and believes that it is a cry for her attention. She decides to ignore the tantrums by physically removing herself to the other side of the room, but as soon as Curt tires from his explosion and quiets, she returns and invites him to sit by her and read a story. It takes several days during which she has to remind the other children not to pay attention to Curt during these episodes, but gradually Curt's tantrums disappear.

To be effective, teachers must be careful to give more attention to children's positive behaviors than to their negative ones. Teachers can identify a select few negative behaviors to ignore and also identify prosocial or positive behaviors to acknowledge that are the opposite of the ones they are trying to ignore. It may also be necessary to teach the other children to ignore a peer's undesirable behavior since the child may desire the attention of his or her peers as well as the teacher's.

redirection Drawing a child's attention or behavior toward a more desirable alternative than the one on which the child is currently focusing.

Redirect Behavior Another strategy for supporting children to do their best is **redirection**, which is the drawing of a child's attention or behavior toward a more desirable alternative. Redirection is especially effective with very young children whose attention is easily distracted. For instance, 18-month-old Jamie appears ready to bite Erika because she has the toy train he covets. His teacher has anticipated this situation and heads it off by offering him an identical engine and turning his attention toward her and away from where Erika is playing.

Redirecting children toward more productive activities is a useful strategy for toddlers who have yet to learn language or other problem-solving strategies and for children who are wandering or withdrawn. As children get older and become more competent problem solvers, adults should rely less on redirection and more on intentionally teaching children to get along with others. Because adults won't always be available to redirect behavior, it is important to use this strategy sparingly.

▶ **Classroom Connection**

Redirection is a powerful tool for guiding young children's behavior. This video, designed for parents, explains why and how to use redirection.

http://www.youtube.com/watch?v=kROuuaLM15g

Give Positive Feedback and Encouragement One of the most powerful ways teachers have for supporting children's prosocial behavior is to give positive attention when children behave in desirable ways. When teachers use positive feedback and encouragement related to children's appropriate behavior, children feel supported and are more likely to continue to behave acceptably.

If a teacher wants a behavior to continue, it is necessary to provide positive feedback or encouragement. It is important for teachers not to give empty praise such as "Good girl" or "Nice job," but rather to enthusiastically encourage and describe the desired behavior or acknowledge the effort. "Heath, thank you for telling me why you were angry," says his teacher, Jane. "Next time, I'll make sure you get a turn on the balance beam." At times, encouragement will be nonverbal, offering a child a smile, a nod, or a thumbs-up for an achievement.

Intentional teachers encourage young children's positive behavior. Sometimes, just a smile or nod is enough to communicate that you noticed a child's effort or success.

For positive feedback and encouragement to be effective, teachers need to recognize that there are individual differences in the forms of acknowledgment that children find positive. Communicating with families about what kinds of feedback work for their children may be necessary. One might prefer to sit by the teacher, while another prefers to be given a task to do. When teachers frequently give positive support for appropriate behavior, children will often pick up on their lead, giving positive feedback to each other. Repeating words she has heard her teacher use, 5-year-old Karena says to her friend Darla, "Thanks for helping me clean up this mess. I'll help you next time."

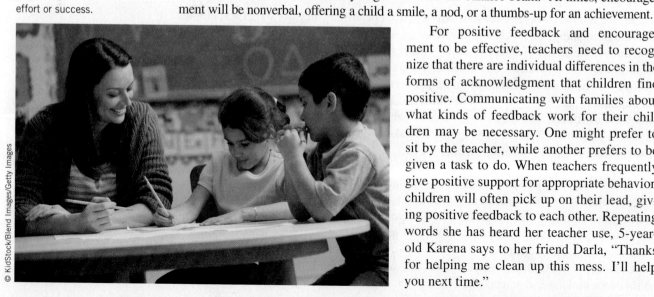

© KidStock/Blend Images/Getty Images

Let's think about how a teacher might use all of these ways of supporting children to do their best when confronted with a challenging situation. Andy picks his nose and it definitely irritates his teacher. She finds this behavior disgusting, but realizes after reflection that she overreacts every time he does it, and the frequency of the behavior is actually increasing, especially during snack times. She decides to encourage more appropriate behavior by giving him his own box of tissues and reminding him in advance how to use them. At first, Andy's nose picking increases, but his teacher decides to ignore it. Instead, when he does anything with the tissue box, even if he simply picks it up, she gives him attention and encouragement. She also gives him positive attention unrelated to the negative behavior: "Andy, thanks for helping me bring the tricycles inside." Over time, his teacher finds much to enjoy in Andy and the nose picking becomes a rare event.

As we have seen, there are many effective strategies teachers can use to support children to do their best and prevent problem behaviors. In addition to preventing negative behaviors, however, adults have key roles to play in teaching children appropriate behavior, which we examine next.

 Check Your Understanding 8.3: High-Quality Supportive Environments

Teaching Social-Emotional Competence and Guiding Behavior

Children aren't born with the ability to get along well with other people and regulate their own strong emotions. These social and emotional skills are learned gradually over the first years of life, and they are among the most important accomplishments of children's lives.

Guiding children to function well in a caring community of learners, however, depends on three key aspects of teaching practice: fostering emotional literacy, teaching social skills, and teaching conflict negotiation. Before addressing each of these dimensions of teaching practice, it is important to clarify the distinction between guidance and punishment.

Guidance and Punishment

When children display unacceptable or inappropriate behavior, which is a natural part of growing up, adults' automatic response is often to discipline them. Consider that the word *discipline* means "to learn." Often when teachers and adults discipline, however, they do so not to teach, but rather to punish. However, children do not learn positive behaviors from punishment. Although punishment may stop a negative behavior temporarily, it does not teach the child what to do instead. Consequently, teachers may find that using the same punishment repeatedly with a child (which they often do) doesn't deter the negative behavior.

One discipline strategy teachers and parents too often use is time-out. **Time-out** is removing a child to a specified chair or area of the room for a period of time following an unacceptable behavior. Many adults think that time-out is a good way to get children to stop their unacceptable behavior. Removing a child from a situation for a period of time, however, can be a form of punishment and, if so, it is unlikely that the child is reflecting on righteousness in this situation. Time-out does not teach the child what to do instead of the negative behavior and, in fact, may achieve the child's purpose by removing him from the situation he sought to avoid, such as helping to clean up. On the other hand, occasionally giving children a brief time away to calm down *before* negative behavior escalates may be helpful, if the child feels supported by the teacher in this situation and if the child's culture does not consider isolation from the group as humiliation (Kaiser & Rasminsky, 2017).

Guidance is the process of teaching children the life skills they need to function productively. Instead of punishments, children need adults to actively teach them

time-out Removing a child to a specified chair or area of the room for a period of time following an unacceptable behavior.

guidance The process of teaching children the life skills they need to function productively with other children.

positive behaviors to replace negative, ineffective behaviors. Children must be taught important life skills, such as appropriate expression of negative emotions, getting along with others, and conflict resolution, using a variety of developmentally appropriate learning experiences and teaching strategies. In the busy classroom atmosphere, teachers often guide children's behavior very publicly, calling attention to children who struggle more with self-regulation. For Micah, hearing that the teacher "likes the way" other children are sitting, and hearing his name called out by the teacher, "We're waiting for you, Micah," convinces Micah over time that he is not very good at keeping up with the demands of school.

Sometimes teachers adopt shortcut techniques that seem to simplify child guidance in the classroom, such as the often used "Traffic Light" technique. In this method, each child has three cards, a green (for positive behavior), yellow (for a "warning") and red (for challenging behavior). The teacher assigns colors to individual children, based on their behavior, often publicly displaying children's traffic light status. For children who struggle, and whose cards are often yellow or red, this technique can bring shame and frustration. Sadly for those children, there's no card for trying hard. The Traffic Light behavior control method is frequently used school- or district-wide, which is surprising given that it is not an effective strategy for teaching children positive behavior. The same children receive a red card repeatedly and, as is true of punishment in general, their behavior often worsens. In the next sections, you'll learn strategies for supporting children's positive behavior and responding to their challenging behavior in respectful ways.

Teach Emotional Literacy and Social Skills

When children grapple over a toy, hit, or bite, teachers often suggest, "Use your words." This is an effective strategy if, and only if, children have the vocabulary to describe their emotions and the language proficiency to articulate their wants and needs. **Emotional literacy** is "the ability to identify, understand, and respond to emotions in oneself and others in a healthy manner" (Joseph, Strain, & Ostrosky, 2006). Children who have a strong foundation in emotional literacy are more likely to tolerate frustration and to fight less, and are less lonely and impulsive. They also are more focused and have greater academic achievement. Developing a vocabulary for expressing feelings is an essential aspect of emotional literacy because the larger a child's emotional vocabulary, the finer the distinctions she can make when expressing her feelings to other people (Kusché & Greenberg, 2012).

emotional literacy Children's ability to identify their own and others' emotions and to express emotions in a healthy way.

Think about the number of words you know related to feeling bad: *angry, mad, furious, upset, anxious, unhappy, distraught, disturbed, disappointed, depressed, disgusted, dismayed, frustrated*—we could empty a thesaurus. The same could be said for other emotional states. Being frustrated, however, is not the same as being furious. Children's behavior may be communicating frustration or fury and, without knowing which, we may be more or less effective in helping them.

An important aspect of emotional literacy is being able to reflect on one's own emotions. Read the *What Works: Teaching Emotional Literacy* feature for examples of effective strategies to promote emotional literacy in young children.

> ### ▶ Classroom Connection
>
> In this video, the teacher and occupational therapist work together to support a preschooler with autism play in block play with peers. Why might this strategy be more beneficial than removing the child for a therapy session?
>
> https://www.youtube.com/watch?v=jHD7uEra-Kc&list=PL818D7E62353903B4&index=15

Just as children need adults to teach them how to regulate and express emotions constructively, children need adults to explicitly teach them social skills such as cooperation, social problem solving, and interacting with peers. In addition, children with disabilities may need particular help from adults in forming friendships with typically developing peers (Joseph & Strain, 2003a, 2003b).

One important decision facing teachers is when to teach social skills. Some moments in time are more effective than others to teach social skills. Teachers often try to teach problem solving in the middle of a crisis situation, when intervention is least effective. Read the *Including All Children: When to Teach Social and Emotional Skills* feature to learn timely ways to teach social skills.

What Works

Teaching Emotional Literacy

Teaching emotional literacy is a proven strategy for promoting children's self-regulation and social skills and preventing challenging behavior. Here are some research-based ways teachers can help children become more emotionally literate.

- Express your own feelings. "I'm frustrated because this is the third time I tried to open the paint jar and it's stuck. I'm going to take a deep breath and then try again."
- Label children's feelings and your own emotions. "You look disappointed that Micah didn't come to school today. I miss him, too."
- Help children talk about their own and others' emotions and discuss acceptable ways of expressing strong feelings. "I think you and Rashid are angry because you both want to paint. Can you ask how much longer it will be before you can have a turn at the easel?"
- Use or adapt songs and rhymes, games, and stories that introduce and expand feeling words. "If you're happy and you know it, clap your hands. If you're excited and you know it, jump up high. If you're frustrated and you know it, take a breath."
- Narrate and describe ongoing interactions to help children develop vocabulary related to prosocial behaviors. "Gregory and Keisha, you are working so well together at the computer. You look pleased and proud of the book you've created."
- Draw children's attention to the feelings or experiences of others, at times using pictures or photos of people's faces. "Look at this face. Can you tell how this person feels?"
- Help children develop empathy by reminding them of their own similar feelings or experiences. "You know what it feels like when someone says you can't play."

- Model caring, positive regard for others. When a child is sick, have children make cards or send e-mails.

Emotional literacy helps children calm down when they are feeling very strong emotions. Teachers can use an emotion thermometer to help children monitor their own feelings. The children decorate the thermometer with pictures of feeling faces from "happy" and "relaxed" in the blue, cool section of the thermometer all the way up to "angry" or "stressed out" in the red, hot section of the thermometer. The teacher then asks children to describe a recent conflict and together they retrace the steps that led to the angry outburst. Then the teacher discusses with the child the thoughts, actions, and words that the child can use to reduce her anger.

As the teacher retraces the steps of the angry outburst, the children identify the time or situation that began the episode. This is marked as the "Danger Point" on the thermometer. Once children have established their danger points, they name the zone, such as "Think Calm Thoughts," "Cool Down," or "Code Red." Then, the teacher and children can use this code word as a signal that anger or stress has reached the threshold. This in turn can trigger the use of a calming strategy such as taking three deep breaths or visualizing happy and calming places.

Sources: Based on *Fostering Emotional Literacy in Young Children: Labeling Emotions* (What Works Brief 21), by G. Joseph, P. Strain, and M. M. Ostrosky, 2006, Urbana-Champaign, IL: Center on the Social and Emotional Foundations for Early Learning; and *Fostering Social and Emotional Competence: Implementing Dina Dinosaur's Social Skills and Problem Solving Curriculum in Inclusive Early Childhood Programs*, by G. E. Joseph, C. Webster-Stratton, and M. Reid, 2006.

Conflict Resolution

Organizing the environment and routines, and establishing classroom expectations and structure around respect will prevent much classroom conflict. However, conflict is an inevitable part of social interaction, especially with young children who are just developing their ability to get along with other people. In fact, episodes of conflict should be considered learning opportunities. Teaching children specific steps in conflict resolution before problems occur and trusting them to solve their own problems are important steps in children's social-emotional development.

During conflicts between students, when teachers remain calm and in control of their own emotions, children feel assured and safe. It is important to acknowledge children's strong feelings and help them learn to describe their feelings and perceptions of the conflict to each other. Rather than asking a question that children will not be able to answer such as "How do you think that made him feel?" ask the child, "What happened? How do you feel?" Like adults, children experiencing strong negative emotions are less able to "use their words" or use perspective-taking to think about how other children

▶ Classroom Connection

Young children often need guidance and support to learn how to get along with other people. What are some of the strategies the teacher in this video uses to help the children resolve their conflict and avoid future conflicts?

Including All Children

When to Teach Social and Emotional Skills

The figure below illustrates the cycle of challenging behavior as it typically occurs in early childhood settings. It depicts the point at which teachers are most effective in supporting children's social-emotional development and in preventing challenging behaviors. Consider how the cycle unfolds in the following scenario.

At choice time, Jessie moves to the block corner, sits down, and begins constructing a boat with the unit blocks. He is serious about his project, but calm and content. His teacher, Sarah, looks around the room and notices that all of the children are happily playing and learning. A few minutes pass and more children are now in the block corner. There are fewer blocks to go around, and it is getting crowded. Still, Jessie is busy concentrating and enjoying his creation.

Fifteen minutes later, Jessie has an idea and searches for the Y-shaped block. He sees a child using it and demands it with angry words, but the other boy continues to claim it.

Sarah hears a scream and rushes to see what happened. Jessie has attacked the boy with the Y-shaped block, who is badly hurt and cries loudly.

At precisely this point—marked by the red arrow—many teachers try to teach Jessie a social skills lesson. For example, teachers might say any of the following: "Use your words!" "Hitting is not okay." "We share our toys." "Say you're sorry!" "You need to calm down. Go to the thinking chair."

It is true that preschoolers need to use words to resolve conflict, to understand that aggression is not okay, to share materials, to know how and when to use an apology, and how to regulate their emotions. However, teaching these skills is ineffective if teachers try to do so at the wrong time. The crisis moment (red arrow) is not a teachable moment for several reasons: (1) The challenging behavior has already occurred. (2) The child who engages in aggression is likely to be upset and agitated and not responsive to a lesson highlighting his or her mistakes. (3) The time and attention the teacher spends trying to teach the child what to do instead (even if it is negative attention) may serve to reinforce the challenging behavior. (4) If the teacher uses these crisis moments only as times to teach social-emotional skills, the child will never receive enough positive learning and practice opportunities to effectively alter his or her behavior.

The most effective teachable moments happen *before* problems occur, when the teacher and children are calm and engaged in appropriate behavior—green arrows. At these times, teachers can build positive relationships and teach key social-emotional skills, such as identifying emotions and resolving conflict.

Source: Based on "'You Got It!' Teaching Social and Emotional Skills," by L. Fox & R. H. Lentini, 2006, *Young Children, 61*(6), 36–42. Based on information from the National Association for the Education of Young Children (NAEYC), http://www.naeyc.org.

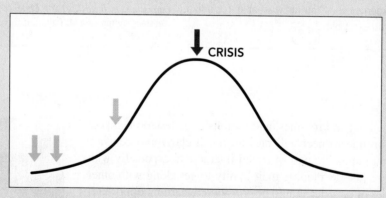

Cycle of Challenging Behavior

feel. Think about the last time you were very angry, and how effectively you were able to describe your feelings or consider the other person's perspective. By giving each child the opportunity to offer solutions to the conflict and by offering their own only if needed, teachers help children become better negotiators and communicators. Table 8.2 describes strategies for teaching conflict resolution.

Helping children learn conflict negotiation skills takes time and practice. Sometimes a conflict does not warrant a full-scale negotiation because one child is not as vested in the

TABLE 8.2 Strategies for Teaching Conflict Resolution

Effective strategies exist for teaching children to solve their own conflicts, as illustrated here in the examples.

Strategy	Example
Acknowledge, accept, and validate all children's feelings and perceptions of the conflict.	Use "I messages"—sentences that describe your own observations or perceptions about a situation, such as "Katie, I think you are angry because Ally took the blocks you wanted."
Help children verbalize feelings and desires to each other and listen to one another. Use *active listening*, which reflects what you are hearing so the child can agree or disagree.	The teacher says, "Katie, it sounds like you wanted all the big blocks for your bridge." Katie responds, "No, I just want the two biggest and Ally took them."
Clarify and state the problem.	"Katie and Ally, you both want the two biggest blocks."
Give children the opportunity to suggest solutions.	The teacher says, "How could we solve this problem?" Katie says, "I get to have the blocks because I was here first." Ally says, "You have been playing with them the whole time. I want a turn." Katie replies, "I could play with them today and you can have them next week." Ally ponders for a while and says, "Okay, but only if you promise."
Propose solutions when children do not have ideas or if their ideas are too extreme or punitive.	"Next week seems like a long time away," the teacher says. "Maybe tomorrow would be a fairer solution."
Uphold the value of mutual agreement and give children the opportunity to reject proposed solutions. That is, both parties in the conflict must mutually agree on the solution. When both children lose interest in the conflict, do not pursue it.	"Do you both agree that tomorrow Ally can have the two biggest blocks? If so, we'll write it down so we remember."
Help children recognize their responsibility in a conflict situation.	"Ally, I know you wanted the blocks, but Katie got angry when you took them without asking."
Help children repair the relationships, but do not force children to be insincere.	"Ally, you usually like to build with Katie. And I know Katie is your friend."
Encourage children to resolve their conflict by themselves.	"Katie, I know that you and Ally built a hospital together last week so I think you can solve this problem together."

Sources: Based on Guidance Matters, by D. Gartrell, 2006, in *Beyond the Journal: Young Children on the Web*, retrieved from https://www.naeyc.org/files/yc/file/200603/GuidanceBTJ.pdf; *Moral Classrooms, Moral Children: Creating a Constructivist Atmosphere in Early Education*, 2nd edition, by R. DeVries and B. Zan, 2012, New York: Teachers College Press; and *Conflict Resolution in Early Childhood: Helping Children Understand and Resolve Conflicts*, by E. Wheeler, 2004, Upper Saddle River, NJ: Pearson.

issue. But equipping all children with conflict negotiation skills helps ensure that rules are fairly and equitably applied and that the classroom is truly a caring community of learners.

Applying the first three parts of the Teaching Pyramid—establishing positive relationships, organizing high-quality supportive environments, and teaching social and emotional skills and positively guiding behavior—will go a long way toward creating a caring community of learners. Nevertheless, a few children will require more individualized interventions to successfully navigate the classroom and learn optimally, as we discuss next.

 Check Your Understanding 8.4: Teaching Social-Emotional Competence and Guiding Behavior

Intensive Individualized Interventions

individualized intervention
A systematically planned and implemented set of actions designed to alter the course of a child's development or learning.

In most classrooms, it is likely that there will be a few children who demonstrate persistent challenging behaviors. To effectively reach these students, it may be necessary to use **individualized intervention**, which is a systematically planned and implemented set of actions designed to alter the course of a child's development or learning.

Research demonstrates that **positive behavior support (PBS)** is a highly effective, humane intervention approach for working with children with severe and persistent challenging behaviors (Fox et al., 2009; Kaiser & Rasminsky, 2017). Positive behavior support is a method of identifying the causes and functions of problem behaviors in order to develop support strategies that prevent such behaviors and teach new, more appropriate skills. In the following sections, we identify and describe challenging behaviors and then explain each of the elements of positive behavior support.

Understand Challenging Behaviors

Conflicts are inevitable when children are together in group situations. Effective teachers do not solve problems for children. They teach children the skills they need to resolve their own conflicts.

positive behavior support (PBS) A method of identifying the causes and functions of problem behaviors in order to develop support strategies that prevent challenging behaviors and teach new, more appropriate skills.

A formal definition of *challenging behaviors* is "behaviors that are dangerous, disruptive, or disgusting; cause injury to the child or others; damage the physical environment; interfere with learning; or cause the child to be isolated from peers" (Neilsen, Olive, Donovan, & McEvoy, 1999). However, each of us defines *challenging behaviors* according to our own values, experiences, and cultural perspectives. Strain and Hemmeter (1999) take a more pragmatic view in their definition: "Challenging behavior is any behavior that is disturbing to you and you wish to see stopped"(p. 17).

Strain and Hemmeter (1999) also offer some practical advice for anyone working with children with challenging behaviors (and that's everyone who works with children!). They advise early childhood professionals to become more "comfortable" with challenging behavior; they emphasize how important it is to recognize that when stressed, embarrassed, disturbed, or feeling hopeless, it is difficult to be effective. They suggest that teachers need to acknowledge these feelings and serve as mutual support for each other. Then, if a child loses control and a teacher begins to feel herself losing control as a result, she can seek help from a colleague. These researchers (Strain & Hemmeter, 1999) also suggest that teachers avoid blaming parents or other uncontrollable events, and focus on small successes. For example, instead of lamenting that Andy picks his nose, celebrate that he picked his nose only once today instead of 10 times.

Positive behavior support involves several steps. The first, and perhaps most important, is determining the function of the child's behavior.

Assess and Address the Function of the Child's Behavior

functional assessment or **functional analysis** The process of determining why a child is behaving a certain way, based on the principle that all behavior serves a function or purpose.

Functional assessment, also called **functional analysis**, is the process of determining why a child is behaving in a certain way. "Any challenging behavior that persists over time is 'working' for the child" (Strain & Hemmeter 1999, p. 19) and is an attempt to communicate a message such as "You're asking me to do something that is too difficult" (e.g., when a teacher expects preschoolers to sit still for a 30-minute group time) or "I'm bored; pay attention to me."

Acknowledging that children's behavior serves a function and communicates a message helps teachers focus on teaching alternative ways of interacting with other people. Remember Tray, who didn't want to clean up and threw the toys at Emma? If his teacher puts him in time-out, Tray will most likely throw toys again tomorrow because he succeeded in avoiding cleanup time.

Functional assessment is a process of systematic observation and documentation of children's behavior over time involving three steps that are easily remembered using the letters A, B, C (Kaiser & Rasminsky, 2017):

- *A* = *Antecedents*. This step is observing what usually occurs before the negative behavior or what conditions trigger the behavior, such as a whole-group time.

© Bill Aron/PhotoEdit, Inc.

- *B = Behavior.* During this step, teachers systematically document what the behavior is and how frequently it occurs.
- *C = Consequences.* During the third step, the teacher or child care provider attempts to determine the function the behavior serves; that is, what does the child get, avoid, and/or change as a result of the behavior?

Identify Antecedents Assessing the antecedents (A) of the behavior requires a teacher to carefully observe to determine the conditions or situations that most often trigger the behavior. By identifying key triggers, the teacher can change the conditions to prevent the behavior or redirect the child before the occasion arises. For example, observing that Lala's behavior usually deteriorates during transitions, such as when she pinched Mona while standing in line, her teacher uses a rhyming game to keep her engaged.

Document Behavior The next step is documenting the behavior (B). In using functional assessment, it is important to carefully define and count the frequency (how often) of the behavior to be changed. For example, in the midst of working with a particularly disturbing behavior such as spitting or biting, sometimes teachers lament, "He spits constantly," or "He bites all the time." In fact, a child could not spit or bite "all the time"; even the most avid spitter or biter must come up for air occasionally. Systematic observation and recording of the actual number of unacceptable behaviors is required for successful intervention. In doing so, Andy's teacher finds that he picks his nose 10 times a day and sets out to intervene to decrease this behavior.

Observe Consequences Objectively observing the consequences (C) of the behavior is essential to form a hypothesis about the function of the child's behavior. What usually happens after the behavior occurs? Does Hans get the Legos after pushing Natasha away from the table? Does Manny avoid reading group because he cries and insists he has a stomachache?

Once antecedents, behavior, and consequences are documented, teachers can assess possible functions that the behavior is serving. What does the child appear to be getting or avoiding? Children most often exhibit challenging behavior to get attention from adults or peers. At times, however, a child wants *power*, the ability to control what is happening to him or others. This may be the case for a child who is experiencing some kind of disruption that is beyond his power to control, such as his parents' divorce or an abusive relationship. Avoiding power struggles with children is always advisable. Adults often lose, and there is nothing scarier to a child than having too much power. If a child is trying to get power, it is best to give him choices and power over manageable things, such as what book to read or who to play with and where.

Objective documentation describes behaviors without adding judgmental comments. Using a form such as the one shown in Figure 8.2 facilitates a teacher's objective documentation of an ABC analysis. With children whose challenging behaviors are severe and persistent, it is especially important to involve a team of people in the process of functional assessment and developing a plan.

Team with Families and Professionals to Implement Individualized Plans

Too often teachers, especially new teachers, feel alone and helpless when confronted by children who display challenging behaviors. They can find strength and knowledge in a team for several reasons. Children benefit from consistent, clear messages about expectations for their behavior from the significant adults in their lives. Teachers and parents need support to both endure and transform children's challenging behavior. Finally, some children have problems that are more serious and need the support of a mental health specialist. While this can be difficult for family members to understand and accept, addressing serious problems early on prevents much more serious difficulties later (Center on the Developing Child, Harvard University, http://developingchild.harvard.edu/resources/briefs/inbrief).

Child's Name	Duncan	Date:	9/25	
Time & Activity	**Antecedent**	**Behavior**	**Consequences**	**Perceived Function**
9:00 Arrival	Duncan arrives and refuses to take off his coat. The teacher tells him he can't play unless he takes off his coat.	Duncan yells, "No! I won't."	The teacher offers Duncan the container of race cars. He takes off his coat and begins to play.	Gets to play with his favorite toy.
10:30 Clean-up	The teacher announces that it is time to clean up for lunch.	Duncan falls to the floor and starts crying.	The teacher says, "Duncan, why don't you help me set the table."	Avoids cleanup time and gets to set the table, which he enjoys.
11:00 Circle time	The teacher tells the children it is time for class meeting. The teacher walks toward Duncan.	Duncan starts crying and says, "No! I don't want to!"	The teacher says, "Duncan, everyone has to sit down for meeting time. Go to time-out." Duncan sits in a chair away from the rest of the children.	Avoids meeting time and looks out the window at the construction going on.

FIGURE 8.2 Functional Assessment for 4-Year-Old Duncan A form such as this is useful in conducting a functional assessment of a child's behavior—the first step in implementing a positive behavior support plan.

Source: Based on *Challenging Behavior in Young Children: Understanding, Preventing, and Responding Effectively,* 3rd edition, by B. Kaiser and J. S. Rasminsky, 2017, Upper Saddle River, NJ: Pearson.

Although it can be difficult to get some parents involved, intervention is more likely to be successful if family members are engaged. Understanding how children behave at home and communicating to parents how their children behave in school is an essential part of the process.

Creating and implementing individualized intervention plans require the expertise of professionals beyond classroom teachers. Early childhood special educators, mental health professionals, social workers, and therapists play key roles in developing the plan. Every state has such resources available to families and child care programs through its public school system and is required by law to provide this assistance to children with disabilities and special needs.

Use Positive Behavior Support

behavior intervention plan
Describes the strategies adults will use to prevent a child's negative behavior and to teach more acceptable behavior.

Once a team has been established and a functional assessment completed, the next step is to develop and implement a **behavior intervention plan**, which describes the behavior to be changed and the strategies adults will use to prevent the negative behavior and to teach more acceptable behavior. For example, once a teacher better understands what triggers the behavior, she can prevent or redirect the child before events escalate. In addition, understanding the consequences of a behavior enables the teacher to ensure that the behavior is not effective in achieving its goals.

replacement behaviors
Desirable prosocial behaviors that replace problem behaviors.

Although one goal of the behavior plan is to diminish negative behaviors, a more important goal is to teach **replacement behaviors**, which are the prosocial behaviors you want the child to exhibit instead of the problem behaviors. To replace negative, challenging behaviors with prosocial behavior, teachers can use the teaching strategies described previously in this chapter as well as more explicit instruction and reinforcement of acceptable alternatives. Replacement skills should be taught throughout the day, particularly during times when the problem behavior is not occurring.

The last stage of the behavior plan is to carefully monitor and document the child's progress and make adjustments as needed. Teachers should not become discouraged if results are not immediately positive. The fact is that when interventions are first initiated, children's behavior often gets worse before it improves. As a result, teachers or parents often abandon the intervention too soon. Teachers and team members must continue to observe children's behavior over time and change strategies that are not successful.

Working with children with challenging behaviors can be a humbling experience, but the ultimate result can be tremendously rewarding for everyone involved, particularly the child. In the following sections, we demonstrate how to apply the Teaching Pyramid in specific circumstances that teachers are likely to encounter in practice.

✓ **Check Your Understanding 8.5:** Intensive Individualized Interventions

Applying the Teaching Pyramid Model

Using the Teaching Pyramid to guide teaching practice every day will improve the quality of the educational experience for all children and teachers. In this section we illustrate how the Teaching Pyramid can be used to teach more effectively in commonly encountered situations—teaching boys, working with children who bite, and preventing and responding to bullying.

Apply the Pyramid Model to Teaching Boys

Darlene is the sole kindergarten teacher in a group of 23, 15 of whom are boys. During center time, a fight breaks out in the block corner. When Darlene tries to intervene, Jamie screams at her, "You're stupid!" and the other four boys cover their ears and laugh. For 20 minutes at a time, four of the girls happily play in the grocery store Darlene has set up, but Darryl and Jason rush in and knock over the food stands as they race with the shopping carts. At story time, a group of boys start tickling each other or pushing one another over while Darlene tries to read. Despite years of experience as a teacher, Darlene finds herself struggling to control her emotions, speaking harshly to the boys, and putting them in time-out repeatedly—but to no avail.

Perhaps fearing the label of *gender biased*, many educators avoid discussing boys' behavior in the classroom. However, many teachers, who are often female themselves, may find active, energetic boys difficult to manage. Denying this fact does not help teachers any more than it helps boys function more successfully in school. One could speculate that increasing the presence of male teachers in early education might alleviate the problem because males might be more understanding and tolerant of boys' typical behavior. However, as of 2012, fewer than 6% of child care teachers and 2% of prekindergarten and kindergarten teachers were male (MenTeach, 2012).

We realize that addressing the behavior of boys as a group runs the risk of stereotyping. Of course, all boys are not alike, any more than all girls are alike. Most boys do not exhibit challenging behaviors and many girls do. However, there are some observable gender differences in the behavior of young children. Boys are more likely than girls to engage in off-task behavior, rough-and-tumble play, and physical aggression, whereas girls are more often verbally aggressive during conflicts (Sprung, Froschl, & Gropper, 2010).

Boys are described as socially immature and developmentally young more often than girls are. As a result, boys are more likely to be held back in preschool or kindergarten. In addition, boys are disproportionately labeled as having ADHD, are assigned to special education, and/or are expelled from school, especially African American boys (Barbarin, 2013; King & Janson, 2010; U.S. Department of Education Office of Civil Rights, 2014). In fact, there is some evidence that African American boys are more often stigmatized as troublemakers and singled out for harsh punishment (Barbarin, 2013).

While prekindergarten teachers are likely to describe African American and Latino boys as socially competent as white boys, by the time they reach second grade, teachers describe them as less socially and academically competent. Do boys' social-emotional skills decrease during this time? Not likely, but the contexts of early elementary classrooms and expectations may be a poor match for the strengths of boys of color (Barbarin et al., 2013).

In the sections that follow, we discuss strategies from the Teaching Pyramid model to build positive, encouraging relationships with boys; rethink the environment and routines to prevent boys' challenging behaviors; and adapt teaching and intervention strategies for boys.

Build Positive Relationships with Boys   All children need nurturing to thrive. This statement is no less true for boys than for girls. Because girls tend to be more verbal, less active, and more comfortable with emotional expression, teachers may find it easier to establish warm, positive relationships with them. Boys need physical affection, kind words, and emotional support just as much as girls do. However, preschool boys may be more likely to demonstrate warmth by jostling a teachers' leg or climbing over her back than curling in her lap—behaviors that some female teachers may misinterpret. And primary-grade boys may feel the need to demonstrate their "manliness" even if it manifests as emotional withdrawal.

Relationships enable teachers to get to know boys as individuals and to learn their abilities and interests, whether insects or robots. This information is especially important for teachers to use in planning the environment and activities to prevent problem behaviors in boys.

Rethink the Environment for Boys   The following classroom modifications, based on research and observations of the activity level of boys, are designed to prevent problems and support boys to do their best (Barbarin, 2011; King & Gartrell, 2004; King & Janson, 2010):

Effective teachers can apply the Teaching Pyramid to help active boys succeed in school and prevent challenging behaviors. These same strategies will work with girls as well.

1. Increase indoor and outdoor large-motor and whole-body experiences such as allowing rough-and-tumble play, and regularly alternating active and quiet learning experiences.

© David Kostelnik/Pearson Education

2. Provide opportunities for children to communicate and interact through movement rather than rewarding only verbal communication.
3. Add sensory exploration and experimentation, such as digging a garden or science investigation both indoors and outdoors.
4. Provide active experiences and technology that uses larger muscles as an alternative to quiet seatwork requiring fine motor skill and focusing on handwriting.
5. Enlarge and enrich construction and block building areas with props such as hard hats, and add a woodworking center with real tools, lumber, and safety goggles.
6. Increase variety by adding novel dramatic play experiences such as space travel and boating.
7. Use materials such as books, comic books, and games on topics of interest to boys such as sports, dinosaurs, or space travel, and those that include male role models.

Rethinking the environment with boys in mind will go a long way toward preventing many of the challenging behaviors of boys, especially those that result from their trying to change the level of stimulation. Boys who are engaged in stimulating activities

TABLE 8.3 Effective Teaching and Intervention Strategies for Boys

These teaching strategies and examples support positive behavior and school success in boys, but are also effective for girls.

What Works	What Doesn't Work
Speaking privately before or after a difficult situation or conflict arises	Publicly shaming, humiliating, or embarrassing a boy
Observing carefully and downplaying a conflict before it happens ("Rodney didn't mean to knock over your building. It was an accident.")	Waiting until a situation escalates out of control
Providing a space for "time away" where a child can calm down before a situation escalates	Separating the boy from the group by putting the child's desk in a corner or frequently using time-out
Reflecting on your own behavior and how it may be perceived by the boy and the other children	Stigmatizing to the point that the other children in the group can readily identify the "bad boy" or the troublemaker
Appealing to boys' sense of justice and fair play	Issuing threats that create a power struggle
Following through with logical consequences ("If you throw the sand, you have to leave the sand table.")	Inflicting harsh discipline or punishment ("If you throw the sand, you can't go out to recess.")
Offering boys' choices to help them feel in control	Attempting to overly control boys' impulses
Teaching boys to think before they act and offering them alternatives to physical aggression.	Waiting until boys behave impulsively and punishing them afterwards
Allowing for movement during all learning activities: fidget toys for group time, standing to do writing and fine motor activities.	Punishing boys for fidgeting or requiring them to sit "criss-cross applesauce" for more than a few minutes.
Encouraging boys to move without disturbing other children; teaching all children to have a little extra "body space" in group activities, lines, and circle time.	Publicly chastising boys for touching others, bumping in line or getting too close to peers.

Sources: Based on "Guidance with Boys," by M. King with D. Gartrell, in *The Power of Guidance: Teaching Social-Emotional Skills in Early Childhood Classrooms,* edited by D. Gartrell, 2004, Clifton Park, NY: Delmar Learning; *Supporting Boys' Learning: Strategies for Teacher Practice, Pre-K–Grade3,* by B. Sprung, M. Froschl, & N. Gropper, 2010, New York: Teachers College Press; and *Wired to Move: Facts and Strategies for Nurturing Boys in an Early Childhood Setting,* by R. H. Morhard, 2013, Lewisville, NC: Gryphon House.

are less likely to be bored and uninvolved and, thus, less disruptive. The next two levels of the Teaching Pyramid—teaching social and emotional skills, and individualized interventions—should also be adapted to ensure successful experiences for boys.

Adapt Teaching and Intervention Strategies for Boys   The Teaching Pyramid strategies described earlier apply to all children; however, researchers who study boys' behavior in school offer several adaptations to increase the likelihood of their success (Barbarin, 2013; Gartrell, 2011; King & Janson, 2010; Sprung et al., 2010). These suggestions are based on the fact that boys tend to have a strong sense of justice and fair play and may feel humiliated or unfairly treated by a teacher. With boys, what teachers *don't* do may be more important than what they do. Table 8.3 lists effective as well as ineffective teaching and intervention strategies for boys. It is important to note that these strategies are important for working with boys and girls.

With these adaptations for boys in mind, kindergarten teacher Darlene rethinks her classroom environment:

Darlene realizes that with so many boys trying to build, the construction area is too small. By removing some of the puzzles and other table toys that are not used, she creates more space for building. She also obtains additional blocks from one of the other kindergartens where they are not being used. Darlene teaches prosocial behaviors and steps to conflict resolution. "If someone takes the block you're using, Jake, what could you say to him?" When Jake and the other boys suggest silly things like "Tell him he's a butthead," Darlene laughs with them. She calmly says, "That sounds funny now, but I don't think Marco will laugh. What else could you say?"

Darlene also finds the boys are interested in playing ambulance, so she transforms the grocery store into a hospital, which the girls enjoy as well. Instead of reading to the whole group, which invites the boys to act up, Darlene, in smaller groups of eight, reads more books with male characters to actively involve all of the children in talking about the story or acting it out.

Having applied the Teaching Pyramid to working with boys, in the next section we demonstrate its applicability to one of the most common but challenging behaviors teachers confront that cuts across gender lines—biting.

Apply the Pyramid Model to Address Biting

Experienced teachers of toddlers tend to think of dealing with biting as one of the occupational hazards of group care for this age group. Biting is viewed as an aspect of typical development in all children, like separation anxiety or oppositional behavior. Nevertheless, biting is a very emotional experience for the biter, the victim, their parents, and their teachers (Greenman, Stonehouse, & Schweikert, 2007). Parents of children who are bitten often become very upset and demand better supervision of their children. Parents of biters may feel they are somehow responsible and fear that if the situation continues, the child care center will demand they remove their child.

As we learned from the Teaching Pyramid, teachers in groups where biting occurs need to assume responsibility for the safety and nurturance of all of the children while also taking steps to prevent biting, teach alternative behaviors, and intervene when it persists. Biting is not a behavior to ignore; once biting starts in a group of toddlers, others may imitate the behavior, leading to an epidemic of biting that is very hard to control. Biting, like other challenging behaviors, serves a function. There are actually two kinds of biting. The first is a communication strategy, which usually responds to prevention strategies. The second occurs when a child persists in using biting because biting is successful in getting the child what she wants. The persistent form of biting requires systematic intervention.

Prevent Biting Applying the levels of the Teaching Pyramid to biting begins with making sure that toddlers feel nurtured, loved, and cared for. Having close relationships with very young children and their families enables caregivers to be aware of situations that may contribute to biting, such as the stress of a new baby or divorce, or a developmental transition such as beginning to eat solid food. Children tend to treat others the way they are treated. Therefore, it is important for caregivers to speak softly and be gentle and kind.

One theory relates biting to children's sensory and oral development (Ramming, Kyger, & Thompson, 2006). During the earliest years of life, "the mouth is the quickest route for providing sensory information to the brain" and children are literally hungry to experience and make sense of their world (Ramming et al., 2006, p. 21). The hypothesis is that biting may occur because the foods children are offered do not meet their needs for tactile stimulation and do not sufficiently stimulate their senses.

To prevent this type of biting, researchers recommend that caregivers offer toddlers foods with a variety of textures, tastes, and temperatures to suck, gum, munch, or crunch and chew (Ramming et al., 2006). Of course, caregivers must supervise children while the children are eating and make sure foods are the right size to prevent choking. Varying the textures and types of foods, as well as when children are fed, is found to be effective in reducing biting in child care settings (Ramming et al., 2006).

Most biting is preventable if children are closely supervised. When child care groups are too large (as happens when licensing standards are weak), or classrooms are very small, it is more difficult to prevent biting. In such cases, teachers should separate the large group into smaller groups as much as possible, especially if there is a second adult. In a smaller group, a child is less likely to bite when a peer invades his space. The teacher also has more opportunity to play and talk with children and redirect those who frequently have conflicts.

One of the best ways to prevent biting is to minimize frustration. Programs need to provide enough developmentally appropriate toys so children do not fight over them and do not become frustrated if the toy requires skills they do not yet have. For example, large cardboard blocks are lightweight and easily moved by toddlers, whereas smaller toys may be too difficult to manipulate.

Teach Alternatives to Biting   Because most children who bite are under the age of 3 and have not yet developed language, biting is often used as a powerful form of communication. The biter may be saying, "You are too close to me," "I want that toy," or "I'm tired." Biting may occur as a self-defense mechanism by the child who feels threatened.

Biting may occur more frequently when children are feeling stress due to changes in their development or the environment, or lack of attention from caregivers (Greenman et al., 2007). When children are undergoing periods of rapid development, such as when they first learn to walk or talk, they can easily become frustrated if their emerging skills do not match their desires for locomotion or communication (Greenman et al., 2007). Some toddlers begin to bite when their family (often at the recommendation of the pediatrician) weans them from their pacifier. Others begin biting after the birth of a sibling. It is common to see biting among children who develop language more slowly than their peers; it must be very frustrating to want to communicate, but unable to generate the words. Initially, biting may relieve the stress or enable the child to get what she wants.

An important dimension of responding to biting is to teach children how to express their feelings and desires. In working with very young children who are just learning language, it is important to give them the words, or use signs or visual images to support their communication. Teachers should model specific language: "Say 'I want it,'" rather than an unhelpful phrase, such as "Use your words."

It is very important that teachers and families respond to this biting in ways that do not escalate the biting behavior. This is difficult, because biting is seen as a dangerous behavior; a bite that breaks the skin of the victim can have serious health consequences. But biting needs only a little reinforcement to become a big problem. When a bite occurs, the victim should quietly and quickly be attended to and comforted. The biter should be quickly and quietly redirected to an activity. Remembering that there often was a perceived offense that preceded the bite ("You're too close to me" or "You took my toy"), direct the offender to another activity (not the toy he was trying to get) with a reminder such as "We need to be gentle." When a teacher or parent exclaims, "No, we don't bite our friends" or placing the child in a time-out, it is practically guaranteeing a repeat of the behavior.

Teachers can be very helpful in sharing this information and strategy with parents. Once a child has bit another, it is a good idea to increase the level of prevention. Teachers should observe when and under what circumstances the toddler tends to bite, and increase teacher presence during those times. Many teachers find it helpful to use books with children about biting (and hitting)—but not close to the time the biting has occurred.

Intervene with Persistent Biters   If biting persists over time, or if children continue to bite beyond the toddler years, then the behavior is working for them in some way. In this situation, caregivers need to apply the fourth level of the pyramid and use functional assessment to determine what conditions tend to trigger the behavior and what function biting is serving for the child. Then a behavior plan can be implemented involving parents and other staff members to eliminate the biting and replace it with more socially acceptable behaviors.

We have seen how the Teaching Pyramid relates to addressing the common phenomenon of biting among young children in groups. In the final section, we apply the framework to one of the most disturbing and potentially destructive of all challenging behaviors—bullying.

Apply the Pyramid Model to Alleviate Bullying

bullying Occurs when a person repeatedly commits aggressive acts that intend to harm, and an imbalance of power makes it hard for the victim to defend himself or herself.

Tragic events such as high school shootings and teen suicides have drawn public attention to an age-old societal problem—bullying. **Bullying** occurs when a person repeatedly commits aggressive acts that intend to harm, and an imbalance of power makes it hard for the victim to defend himself or herself (Kaiser & Rasminsky, 2017). Despite media attention that would suggest the contrary, bullying among children in the United States is not epidemic and is harmful for both bully and bullied (Temkin, 2014). In recent years, school personnel and mental health experts have become much more attuned to the long-term damage that bullying can inflict on bullies and their victims, as well as on the bystanders who may assist or incite bullying behavior.

Every teacher needs to be alert to the existence of bullying, take steps to prevent it, and intervene immediately when bullying occurs. Although bullying usually begins to appear during the primary grades of school, there is evidence that the roots of bullying behavior are evident during preschool. However, little research has addressed bullying with young children (Lawner & Terzian, 2013). Earlier in this chapter, we cautioned teachers to be alert for children who are socially isolated or neglected by peers, as these children may be more likely to bully or be bullied.

Prevent Bullying

Bullying is a learned behavior, and can be minimized and prevented (Kaiser & Rasminsky, 2017). As with other, less volatile aspects of challenging behavior, solutions to bullying can be found in the framework of the Teaching Pyramid, beginning with the foundation level of relationships.

Research suggests that programs using a whole-school awareness approach that involves teachers, administrators, children, counselors, and families, have the most impact in reducing bullying and its effects in school settings (Lawner & Terzian, 2013). The goal is to prevent bullying by restructuring the environment so that there are fewer opportunities for bullying to occur, more reinforcement of positive behavior, and assurance of protection for all children.

Intervene in Bullying

Research on specific programs targeting bullying in early childhood suggests that no quick-fix curriculum can be used to solve the problem (Lawner & Terzian, 2013). Preventing and addressing bullying relies on establishing the high-quality environment and supports that have been addressed throughout the chapter. Responding to bullying would be an example of the more intensive strategies discussed

Children who need intensive, individualized intervention for persistent, challenging behaviors benefit from a team approach. In these situations, it is essential to involve not only teachers and other professionals but family members as well.

earlier. Among the most important and effective tools teachers, families, and schools can use are (Kaiser & Rasminsky, 2017):

- A school-wide commitment to Positive Behavior Support
- Integrating anti-bullying content into the curriculum, including the important roles that bystanders play
- Sensitive, responsive, and involved relationships with children
- Clear rules about unacceptable behavior
- Close monitoring and supervision, including secluded areas where bullying is likely to occur
- Modeling the positive use of power and problem-solving techniques
- A cooperative classroom climate—what we call a caring community of learners

Regular class meetings are an effective strategy to involve children in setting limits and establishing clear rules: Don't bully other children, help children who are bullied, and include children who are left out (Kaiser & Rasminsky, 2017). Children can discuss and analyze complex topics such as empathy, peer pressure, courage, and the difference between teasing and bullying.

Children also need to learn the difference between *tattling*, the purpose of which is to get someone in trouble, and *telling* to get someone out of trouble, which is necessary when bullying is observed or experienced. Useful strategies include helping children report where they don't feel safe and, in primary grades, providing a box for anonymous reporting of bullying. Meeting times can then be used to discuss prosocial skills such as cooperation and to practice responses.

In this chapter, we discussed the importance of creating a caring community of learners, as well as strategies for positively guiding children's behavior and promoting their social and emotional development. With this information in mind, we return to Sue and Elly's classroom, where we began this chapter.

 Check Your Understanding 8.6: Applying the Teaching Pyramid Model

Revisiting the Case Study

... Ms. Brady and Ms. Donahue's Classroom

At the beginning of this chapter, Sue, Elly, and the children in their classroom were having a very bad day. The director of their program worked with them to help them learn about the Teaching Pyramid— encouraging them to start with the foundation of their classroom and integrate practices that supported creating a caring community of learners. Let's revisit their classroom now that these two teachers have begun to implement many of these research-based strategies.

The day begins with Sue and Elly greeting each child individually and talking briefly with their family members. The two teachers have been doing home visits and making phone calls to parents so that they could get to know the children and their interests much better. In addition, they have put practices into place that support building warm, nurturing relationships with each child in the class (level 1 of the pyramid). They make sure to touch base with each child every day, even if for only a moment. They create a safe environment for children by arriving each day rested, healthy, and mindful that their interactions with children are important for children's well-being.

They reorganize their classroom to support positive behavior by making signs, labeling bins, organizing shelves, and designating specific areas where materials belong. They also create learning centers where children can comfortably work and play. They've been holding group meetings each morning to talk with children about the class routines and making choices during Center Time, and the children are playing more productively.

Sue and Elly also remember to use calm and quiet voices themselves at all times; when they really want to be heard, they whisper. The noise level is now much more tolerable. When it's time to go outside, they offer Aimee and Paula the choice of what they'd like to carry. The teachers focus a lot of attention on transitions, such as preparing for naptime and cleanup because these are times when children have struggled in the past. They now give warnings before transitions and assign children different responsibilities at cleanup time. At naptime, they play soothing music, turn out the lights, and rub the backs of children who are slow to relax. These changes to the environment and adult–child interactions have made a world of difference for the teachers and children because they are preventing many problems and helping children to do their best (level 2).

Sue and Elly also teach social skills and emotional self-regulation to all the children. For those children who need extra help, however, they use more individualized instruction. For example, Ricky so wants to have friends that he will do anything to get the children's attention. Sue and Elly coach him in acceptable ways to play with others and strategies for joining in a group. Ricky likes Aimee, and she has a calming effect on him, so the teachers encourage the two of them to play together. They also suggest to his mother that he bring something interesting from home to gain attention from the other children in a positive way (level 3).

Having attended to the first three levels of the Teaching Pyramid, Sue and Elly have solved almost all of their behavior challenges. However, Booth's physical aggression and unprovoked attacks continue to be a serious problem. The director is aware of the federally funded early intervention services provided by the state. She contacts the school district, which coordinates mental health consultation to child care centers. The director and Sue initiate a meeting with a consultant and Booth's family to develop an individualized intervention plan (level 4). Sue and Elly are pleased to see that the consultant uses strategies that include the Teaching Pyramid ones that they have become familiar with. The consultant helps them to organize their interactions to support Booth. Sue and Elly now realize that although there are no quick fixes to children's challenging behavior, there are many effective ways to create a caring community of learners. ■

8 Chapter Summary

- A caring community of learners is a group or classroom in which children and adults engage in warm, positive relationships; treat each other with respect; and learn from and with each other.

- Teachers have a significant role to play in promoting children's social competence, helping them acquire emotional and cognitive self-regulation and preventing later difficulties.

- The Teaching Pyramid is a research-based framework for promoting social competence and addressing children's challenging behaviors.

- The foundation level of the Teaching Pyramid is teachers' positive relationships with children. Young

children learn best when they experience warm, positive, responsive relationships with adults—parents, teachers, and caregivers.

- Level 2 of the pyramid describes high-quality supportive environments that help promote positive outcomes for children and prevent challenging behaviors, including the physical space and organizing routines and schedules. A critical aspect of high-quality supportive environments is how teachers support children's engagement in play and learning.

- Level 3 of the pyramid describes positive ways to guide children's behavior and effective strategies such as teaching emotional literacy, social skills, and conflict negotiation.

- Level 4 describes intensive individualized interventions to address persistent, severe, challenging behaviors. Intervention includes functional assessment, a team approach involving families and specialists, and a behavior plan that includes teaching replacement skills.

- The Teaching Pyramid can be applied to more effectively teach in many diverse situations including teaching boys, addressing biting, and alleviating bullying.

Key Terms

- attachment theory
- behavior intervention plan
- bullying
- caring community of learners
- challenging behavior
- disorganized/disoriented attachment

- efficacy
- emotional literacy
- functional assessment or functional analysis
- guidance
- individualized intervention
- insecure-ambivalent/ resistant attachment

- insecure-avoidant attachment
- learning centers
- mindfulness
- mistaken behavior
- positive behavior support (PBS)
- redirection
- replacement behaviors

- secure attachment relationship
- secure base
- self-concept
- self-esteem
- time-out
- transitions

 Demonstrate Your Learning

Click here to assess how well you've learned the content in this chapter.

Readings and Websites

Bruce, N., & Cairone, K. B. (2011). *Socially strong, emotionally secure: 50 activities to promote resilience in young children*. Silver Spring, MD: Gryphon House.

Forrester, M. M., & Albrecht, K. M. (2014). *SET for life: An early childhood teacher's guide to supporting strong emotional foundations and successful social relationships*. Houston, TX: Innovations in ECE Press.

Kaiser, B., & Rasminsky, J. S. (2017). *Challenging behavior in young children: Understanding, preventing, and responding effectively* (4th ed.). Upper Saddle River, NJ: Pearson.

Morhard, R. H. (2013). *Wired to move: Facts and strategies for nurturing boys in an early childhood setting*. Lewisville, NC: Gryphon House.

Friendship Resources and Websites

Resources to support friendships among children can be found on several websites:

1. Center on Social Emotional Foundations for Early Learning (CSEFEL) has "Superfriend" social stories (Super Friend) and booklists (Being a Friend).

2. Bucketfillers has a story and resources related to friendship and kindness.

3. The Head Start Center for Inclusion has a Friendship Kit that includes activities and printable resources.

Collaborative for Academic, Social, and Emotional Learning

This website offers research and resources for supporting social and emotional learning for children in elementary school.

Devereux Center for Resilient Children

This website offers resources for supporting children's social development and building resilience, and for the social-emotional well-being of the adults who care for them.

Center on the Social and Emotional Foundations of Early Learning

This website offers a variety of resources for supporting children's positive behavior and relationships.

9

Teaching to Enhance Learning and Development

Learning Outcomes

After studying this chapter, you should be able to:

9.1 Discuss ways in which teaching is both a science and an art.

9.2 Identify effective teaching strategies for helping children achieve learning and developmental goals.

9.3 Explain how specific strategies are effective for connecting teaching with broad learning goals such as helping children make meaning, develop concepts, and acquire higher-order thinking skills.

9.4 Demonstrate how effective teachers use grouping as an instructional approach.

9.5 Analyze how teachers use play as a context for teaching and learning.

9.6 Evaluate the most effective uses of digital media for teaching young children.

Sally Hanson is a kindergarten teacher in a large, urban school district. Her class of 23 children includes several children whose home language is not English and two children with IEPs. Some of the children have been in child care since they were infants, but five did not attend any early childhood program before entering school. The children's skills and abilities are at different levels. In short, Sally's class is typical, with a wide range of individual variation in the children's development and learning and in their preparedness to tackle the demands of the curriculum.

Sally's school district uses the Common Core English language arts standards. Among the goals for kindergartners are: "with prompting and support, ask and answer questions about key features in a text; retell familiar stories; and identify characters, settings, and major events." Children also need to "know all upper- and lowercase letters, and use a combination of drawing, dictating, and writing to express an opinion about a topic or a book they are reading, e.g., *My favorite book is . . . "* (Common Core State Standards Initiative, 2011a).

Sally has been teaching for many years and was concerned at first that the Common Core standards were not developmentally appropriate for kindergarten. As she began working with the standards, she found that most of the children were capable of achieving the standards through a combination of her integrated curriculum and diverse teaching strategies.

When the children arrive each morning, they immediately go to the library area and choose a book to look at or read, depending on their skills. Children often choose to revisit books that Sally has read previously to the group. Elena has only recently arrived from Guatemala and speaks little English. Sally kneels next to her and offers an e-book that has print and audio versions of the same story in both Spanish and English. Soon they are joined by the other children whose home language is Spanish. Sally then encourages Lucy, who has Down syndrome, to find the book that Sally made for her with photos and words about her family. Sally says, "Lucy, I see you found the *L* in your name."

Logan's reading skills are advanced. He picks up a book that he hasn't seen before and begins to decode it himself along with his friend Gabe. When they finish, Sally asks, "Logan, why did you pick this book?" Logan explains, "It's about pirates and the story was scary." She turns to Gabe and says, "I haven't read this book yet, can you tell me what happened in the story?"

Marguerite is still working on identifying letters. She has a long name, struggles to remember the order of the letters, and usually forgets the *E* in the middle. Sally gives her a name card with the middle *E* written in red to draw her attention to the correct order of the letters. With this assistance and reminder, Marguerite spells her name correctly. Some children are not interested in reading, so Sally directs them to their journals to begin drawing and writing about the books they read yesterday. A few children need more direct instruction and practice in writing letters. "Tommy, when you write your *T*, make a straight line down. That's right." Pointing to the left side of the paper, Sally says, "Now begin on the left and draw a shorter line across the top." Because Amanda needs practice on letters but is easily distracted, Sally suggests several letter-learning apps on the tablet. Sally sits with the children, offering assistance as needed and using strategies adapted to each child's skill level. ■

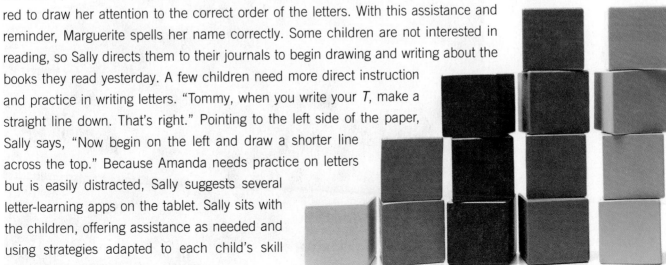

As we see in Sally's interactions with each child in her classroom, the early childhood teacher's role is complex. Engaging in developmentally appropriate practice involves knowing the learner, knowing what to teach, and knowing how to teach. Teachers are always teaching *something* to *someone*. In this chapter, we focus on knowing *how to teach* to help children reach challenging and achievable learning goals. Becoming an intentional teacher requires an understanding of the range of effective teaching strategies and how and when they are most useful (Ritchie & Willer, 2008c; NAEYC, 2009). Armed with this knowledge, teachers can intentionally choose the strategies that work best with each learner or group of learners in a given situation.

Because many teaching behaviors in early childhood classrooms are subtle or take place in the context of play or child-initiated learning, the novice may be uncertain of what "effective teaching" entails and how to do it. Without knowledge of research-based teaching practices, inexperienced or ill-informed teachers may be too passive and miss important opportunities to promote children's learning. On the other hand, they may err in assuming that the only time they are "teaching" is when they are talking. The fact is that good teaching is a complex interplay of both science and art.

Teaching: Both a Science and an Art

pedagogy What a teacher says or does that engages children and contributes to their learning and development.

effective teaching The use of approaches that are proven to be successful based on scientific evidence and that have a high probability of enhancing children's learning and development.

This chapter is about teaching—also known as **pedagogy**—which is what a teacher says or does that engages children and contributes to their learning and development. In this book, we emphasize **effective teaching**, which is the use of an approach that has proven to be successful based on research evidence and that has a high probability of enhancing student achievement (Reutzel, 2013). Using knowledge of research to inform planning and decisions about practice is essential to becoming an intentional teacher.

© David Kostelnik/Pearson Education

Intentional teachers use research-based teaching strategies, and they get to know each child to provide just the right kind and amount of assistance.

The Science of Teaching

Since the 1990s and in response to federal laws, the emphasis in education has been on scientifically based practice (McCardle & Chhabra, 2004). Such practice is informed by at least three areas of research: the science of child development, including neuroscience; cognitive science, or the study of how people learn; and research on effective instructional strategies and contexts.

Scientific Research   Research is used to answer two sets of questions: (1) What skills and abilities predict children's later outcomes in important areas like reading, writing, and mathematics? and (2) What teaching behaviors, curriculum, and other educational interventions contribute to or inhibit gains in children's skills and abilities in these areas? Reviews of research by experts, such as the National Reading Panel (National Institute of Child Health and Human Development [NICHD], 2000), the National Early Literacy Panel (2008), and the National Committee on Early Childhood Mathematics (National Research Council [NRC], 2009) have been particularly influential.

Classroom Research   Although debate is ongoing about various aspects of practice, the strong consensus is that the daily interaction among teachers and children is the most important determinant of the quality and effectiveness of programs from infancy through primary grades (Hamre, Hatfield, Pianta, & Jamil, 2014; Hamre & Pianta, 2007, 2010; Ritchie & Willer, 2008b, 2008c). Regardless of the specific curriculum used or the materials in the environment, everything that happens in the classroom is influenced by the teacher's interactions with children.

This conclusion is supported by several large-scale studies of prekindergarten, kindergarten, and primary-grade classrooms that used a teacher observation tool called the *Classroom Assessment Scoring System* (CLASS) (Early et al., 2010; Hamre & Pianta, 2010). The CLASS assesses three dimensions of classroom quality: emotional climate, classroom organization, and instructional climate (Pianta, La Paro, & Hamre, 2008).

> ▶ **Classroom Connection**
>
> In this video well-known researchers describe and illustrate the many studies that demonstrate the effectiveness of positive teacher–child interactions for children's development and learning.
>
> http://www.youtube.com/watch?v=2HwODbxOmJQ

Emotional Climate   A high score on emotional climate on the CLASS means that teachers are sensitive and responsive and have positive relationships with children. In classrooms where teachers score high on emotional climate, children's language improves and they have fewer behavior problems in preschool, kindergarten, and primary grades (Hamre et al., 2014; Pianta et al., 2008).

Classroom Organization   In well-organized classrooms, teachers use positive strategies to guide children's behavior. They are well prepared in advance and manage time productively, maximizing opportunities for learning. For example, they don't waste children's time during routines or transitions. Teachers who score high on classroom organization also use a variety of materials, teaching strategies, and learning formats to engage children and activate their interest.

Instructional Climate   The CLASS instructional climate score indicates how well teachers use a variety of teaching strategies to promote children's concept development and higher-order thinking. The classroom's instructional climate has been found to be the strongest and most consistent predictor of children's learning over time (Hamre et al., 2014; Hamre & Pianta, 2010). Researchers have found that children gain more from a learning experience when a teacher interacts with them in an intentional way or when the teacher has prepared the environment and supports children's learning during play and other child-initiated activity (Sammons et al., 2008).

Research Results   Large-scale studies conducted by the National Center on Early Development and Learning (NCEDL) (Early et al., 2005, 2010) found that, on average, the emotional climate of classrooms rated around 5 on a 7-point scale, which indicates that they are generally positive, supportive environments for children. However, researchers also found poor-quality instructional climates in the early childhood classrooms studied, with an average score of about 2 on the 7-point scale. Teachers in these classrooms either provided very little instruction at all or tended to rely on worksheets or whole-group repetitive lessons.

The study also examined how children spend their time in prekindergarten. Almost 30% of children's time is spent in free choice and about 37% engaged with a teacher-assigned activity (Early et al., 2010). However, observers found that no specific learning activity occurred during 19% of free choice time, 23% of teacher-assigned time, and 87% of meal and routine time (Early et al., 2010). Therefore, almost half of preschool children's day did not involve experiences to promote their social or academic learning. The researchers concluded that most of these classrooms were pleasant places in which there were many missed opportunities for learning. Moreover, classrooms with higher percentages of Latino and African American children were less educationally stimulating.

In recent years, Head Start has used the CLASS to improve the quality of teaching and evaluate the effectiveness of its programs. In 2013, the national average scores were: 5.99 for Emotional Climate, 5.63 for Classroom Organization, and 2.72 for Instructional Climate. Despite the fact that Instructional Climate scores continue to trail the other dimensions of quality, Head Start's scores are higher than most typical early childhood programs.

These studies provide a window through which we can assess the quality of teaching practices occurring in early childhood classrooms today. Similar results were found for primary-grade classrooms as well (Hamre & Pianta, 2010). In Chapter 8, we described how you as a teacher can provide a positive emotional climate in your classroom. The goal of this chapter is to prepare you to create an effective instructional climate to help all children achieve their learning potential.

The Limits of Research Early childhood education has a large and growing research base to guide practice. Where research evidence is strong, teachers have a professional responsibility to adhere to its guidance. However, research on effective teaching is an evolving science. Although a great deal of work has been done, we still need answers to questions about which practices work best with which learners.

With classrooms increasingly serving children with diverse language and cultural backgrounds, teachers need to adapt for individual variation of all kinds. Consequently, valid research is not always available to guide practice. In these instances, teachers need to supplement the evidence base with practical wisdom and information obtained from families (Buysse & Wesley, 2006). Even when research is available, applying evidence-based practice in unique classroom situations with diverse groups of children requires considerable skill. Teachers need to respond to situations as they happen, which often requires creativity—more art than science.

The Art of Teaching

Although effective teaching is informed and guided by research, teaching is also an art in that it requires vision, creativity, and decision making. What makes good science is controlling as many variables as possible to be able to determine cause and effect. But in classrooms, there are simply too many variables to control. Effective teaching requires creatively adapting to individual children and to the situations that arise (Beneke & Ostrosky, 2013; Gadzikowski, 2013b).

Consider the following analogy, comparing the work of a painter to the work of a teacher: Skilled painters are knowledgeable about theories of art, composition, color, and perspective. But each artist, like each teacher, applies her or his knowledge in creative ways. One of the painter's most powerful tools is the use of color, and knowledge of how the myriad colors in nature can be created by mixing a few basic colors. For example, given the three primary colors—red, yellow, and blue—a skilled painter can create virtually every color of the spectrum. Think of those basic colors as the basic strategies from which teachers create innumerable variations in interactions with individual children and groups. If we add to the color wheel the many gradations of gray—ranging between white and black—and mix these with our primary colors, we have an almost infinite variety of options from which to "color" the world of experiences for children.

We begin our exploration of the science and art of teaching by examining research-based teaching strategies. This discussion will demonstrate how art and science can coexist to create an enriching classroom filled with color, creativity, and a variety of options for teachers as well as children.

Effective teaching is both an art and a science. Intentional teachers ensure that children's experiences in the classroom are as creative and colorful as the world around them.

✔ **Check Your Understanding 9.1:** Teaching: Both an Art and a Science

🔺 A Repertoire of Effective Teaching Strategies

The most effective teachers have a large repertoire of teaching strategies that they use as situations present themselves. Teachers must first become familiar with the many options. In practice, there is no one teaching strategy that will address all situations.

Children's development and learning are complex processes. Therefore, the more strategies teachers know how to use, the more ways they will be able to meet the needs of diverse learners. Throughout your career as a teacher, you will continue to add to and refine your repertoire of effective teaching tools.

What Are Teaching Strategies?

A **teaching strategy** is a behavior or activity that a teacher deliberately selects and flexibly applies to help students construct meaning (Mehigan, 2005, p. 557). Applying teaching strategies demands conscious thought and flexible decision making, which are the essence of intentional teaching. Earlier, for example, we saw how Sally Hanson encouraged some of the children to practice their writing but also demonstrated how to write a letter for those who needed more help.

Because the processes of teaching and learning are linked, the most effective teaching strategies parallel learning strategies. A **learning strategy** refers to how children construct meaning in every context or situation. As later examples illustrate, some of the most effective teaching strategies are designed to develop students' own learning strategies.

teaching strategy A behavior or activity that a teacher deliberately selects and flexibly applies to help students construct meaning.

learning strategy How children construct meaning in any context or situation.

Strategies as Tools Education is often plagued by *either/or* debates that pit one practice against another, or that dichotomize complex decisions into either/or choices, such as "Which is better, direct instruction or active learning?" As teaching becomes more scientific, we realize that these are the wrong questions. Asking which teaching technique is best is like asking whether a hammer is better than pliers. The answer, of course, depends on what the carpenter needs to do. In teaching, as in carpentry, the selection of tools depends on what the teacher is trying to accomplish and with which child; there is no one best teaching practice (NRC, 2000).

The Right Tools You may have heard the statement—in fact, I've written it myself— that young children are not miniature adults and do not think and learn the way adults or older children do. Although this statement is essentially true, it is equally true that some practices that are inappropriate for young children, such as listening in a whole group for an extended period of time, are not effective for older students, either (Dean, Hubbell, Pitler, & Stone, 2012; NAEYC, 2009).

In fact, many of the most effective teaching practices for young children—such as connecting new learning to what students already know and can do—are also effective with college students. The particular strategies teachers use to help children build on prior learning will vary with the age and ability of the learner (that is, if the strategies are developmentally appropriate). All of these strategies can be used in the context of teacher-initiated or child-initiated experiences, which we discuss next.

Teacher-Initiated and Child-Initiated Experiences

Early childhood practices are often described as either teacher-initiated or child-initiated experiences. However, both contexts are effective for learning and should be used concurrently depending on the teachers' goals (Graue, Clements, Reynolds, & Niles, 2004; Hong & Diamond, 2012). During **teacher-initiated experiences**, teachers take the lead by providing explicit information and modeling or demonstrating skills. Teacher-initiated learning experiences are determined by the teacher's goals and direction, but children should be actively engaged (Epstein, 2014). Under these conditions, focused, teacher-guided instruction can contribute significantly to children's learning (Hamre & Pianta, 2010; Hong & Diamond, 2012).

By contrast, during **child-initiated experiences**, children acquire knowledge and skills through their own exploration and interactions with objects and other children (Epstein, 2014). Child-initiated experiences grow out of children's interests. However, teachers organize the environment and materials and provide the learning opportunities from which children make choices (Epstein, 2014). Teachers observe children during child-initiated activities and interact with them to support their continued learning and development. During child-initiated experiences, teachers as well as children should be actively involved.

Using an Array of Teaching Strategies

Many different strategies are effective in supporting children's learning and development. Understanding when and how to apply each strategy gives teachers the tools necessary to be thoughtful, purposeful, and intentional (Bowman, Donovan, & Burns, 2001; Copple & Bredekamp, 2009; Epstein, 2014).

Note, however, that in practice, strategies are used in combination. Observe a skilled teacher at work and you will find it almost impossible to isolate an example of a teaching strategy, even explicit instruction, that doesn't also include some other strategy such as encouragement, modeling, or questioning. For example, a preschool teacher may acknowledge a child's accomplishment by saying, "Luca, you found the two shapes that match." Then she immediately provides specific information, "They have eight sides and they are called octagons," while quickly adding challenge to the task, "Can you find another octagon in our room?"

One particularly effective strategy, which is called *scaffolding*, draws on many different strategies at once; therefore, we discuss it following our description of the individual strategies. In the sections that follow, we define and give examples of a variety of teaching strategies, which are listed in Table 9.1.

Acknowledging and Encouraging Acknowledging is the positive attention a teacher gives to a child that tells the child that the teacher noticed what the child did. Teachers often use this strategy without conscious awareness. Acknowledging is particularly effective in keeping children engaged in desirable behaviors. For example, after observing 3-year-old Keily while she serves as the snack helper, her teacher says, "I see you gave each person a napkin, Keily. Now we're ready for our snack." Noting 2-year-old Bailey's empathic behavior, her teacher says, "Thank you, Bailey, for sitting with Kayla. She was sad that her

TABLE 9.1 Effective Teaching Strategies

Effective teachers have a large repertoire of teaching strategies to use depending on their goals for children, as described and illustrated in this table.

Teaching Strategy	Definition	Most Effective Uses
Acknowledging and encouraging	Giving positive verbal or nonverbal attention that promotes a child's persistence and effort	Teachers influence children to stay engaged; demonstrate desired behaviors; and help children master skills, complete tasks, and solve complex problems.
Giving quality feedback	Providing specific information on a child's performance or responding to questions and comments	Teachers expand learning and understanding (how children come to solve a problem) rather than focusing only on the correct answer or end product.
Modeling	Displaying or showing children a skill or desirable way of behaving or speaking	Teachers portray positive social skills and self-regulation. Teachers model language—repeating and extending children's verbal responses, describing their own and children's actions, and using advanced vocabulary.
Demonstrating	Showing the correct way to perform a skill or procedure while children observe the outcome	Teachers teach skills that require particular steps in a certain order.
Giving cues, hints, and offering assistance	Reminding children of what they already know and can do, and helping them to use that knowledge for new learning	Teachers help children build on prior knowledge to gain new skills and understanding.
Creating and adding challenges	Making learning situations harder by generating a problem, or adding difficulty to a task so that it is a bit beyond what children have already mastered	Teachers add challenges to interest children and motivate them to learn, but not so much that they become frustrated or repeatedly fail. Children continue to make learning and developmental progress.
Questioning	Eliciting different types of responses and promoting different types of thinking	Teachers ask open-ended questions that require children to analyze information or engage in higher-order thinking.
Co-constructing	Thinking with different points of view; working collaboratively to solve a problem or clarify a concept	Teachers and children think and talk together during a joint activity such as a project, and both parties learn from the exchange.
Giving direct or explicit instruction	Explicitly giving directions for completing a task; providing facts, verbal labels, or other specific information; or providing instructions for a child's action or behavior	Teachers transmit knowledge that can be learned only from one person telling another, that is, social-conventional or procedural knowledge.
Scaffolding—using the above strategies in combination	Supporting children's ability to accomplish learning tasks that they could not otherwise accomplish independently; using strategies such as cues, hints, assistance, questions, and so on to help children work "on the edge" of their current level of competence.	Teachers adapt instruction for individual children of different skill levels, cultural backgrounds, personalities, and talents toward new, achievable goals. Teachers help children acquire the skills to eventually achieve the same task independently.

Sources: Based on *Basics of Developmentally Appropriate Practice: An Introduction for Teachers of Children 3 to 6,* by C. Copple and S. Bredekamp, 2006, Washington, DC: NAEYC; and *Developmentally Appropriate Practice in Early Childhood Programs Serving Children from Birth through Age 8,* revised edition, edited by C. Copple and S. Bredekamp, 2009, Washington, DC: NAEYC.

© Bill Aron/PhotoEdit, Inc.

Positive feedback provides children with specific information and helps focus their attention. Back-and-forth exchanges in small groups help everyone learn more.

encouragement Verbal comments or nonverbal signs such as pats or high fives that promote the child's persistence and effort.

feedback loop Back-and-forth communication between a teacher and a child or small group of children in an effort to reach deeper understanding.

mommy left." By understanding the power of their acknowledgment of children's competence and performance, teachers are able to influence children to demonstrate desired behaviors.

Encouragement can be conveyed through verbal comments or nonverbal signs such as pats or high fives that promote the child's persistence and effort. Although encouragement doesn't directly enhance a child's understanding or skill, it is most valuable in helping children realize that effort is necessary for mastering skills, completing tasks, and solving complex problems. For example, second-grader Jushawn struggles with writing a funny story about his dog. His teacher encourages him to persist by making comments such as "I really laughed when you told me how he spilled his food." When Jushawn finishes, she points out, "You worked hard writing your story and I enjoyed reading it, and I laughed again at your dog's antics."

Giving Quality Feedback

Feedback, in which teachers provide specific information on a child's performance or respond to questions, helps focus the child's attention on the process of learning. Effective feedback helps children expand their learning and understanding, rather than focusing on correct answers (Pianta et al., 2008). Research finds that such instructional feedback helps improve literacy and language in preschool and kindergarten children (Howes et al., 2008) and helps close the achievement gap for children in first grade and up (Hamre & Pianta, 2001, 2005).

Effective feedback often involves back-and-forth exchanges between teachers and students. This exchange is called a **feedback loop** and involves a teacher and a child or small group of children communicating in an effort to reach deeper understanding. Consider the following example of a feedback loop that occurred in a preschool class where the teacher and children were discussing a book about shadows:

Teacher points to a picture in book: What do you think made this shadow?
Various children call out: An animal. A dog. A cat.
Teacher: Kami, why do you think it's a cat?
Kami: The tail.
Teacher: What makes you think that it's a cat's tail?
Kami: Well, it looks like a long tail.
Connor: But dogs have tails, too. It could be a wolf.
Teacher to class: What do you notice about the tail?
Kami: It's a cat's tail. It's skinny, and it has a curl on the end.
Teacher: Oh, so you're sure it's a cat. Let's find out.

Modeling

modeling Showing children a skill or desirable way of behaving or speaking.

Teachers are especially powerful models for children with whom they have built positive relationships. **Modeling** is a technique teachers use to show children a skill or desirable way of behaving or speaking.

Language modeling is among the most effective instructional strategies teachers can use. A large body of research demonstrates that teacher's language modeling strongly predicts children's achievement in all areas of learning and development (Beck, McKeown, & Kucan, 2013; Neuman & Wright, 2013). Effective *language modeling* includes:

- Engaging children in frequent, extended one-on-one conversations—called "serve and return" as in a tennis game, where teachers and children take turns speaking in response to what the other has said
- Listening carefully, waiting for a response, minimizing questions, and gauging comments to children's remarks

- Using open-ended questions to stimulate and extend discussions, such as "What do you think will happen if . . . ? Why do you think that?" and "How did that happen?"
- Repeating and expanding on what children say
- Using new and advanced words that children may not know or use in everyday speech
- Supporting children's conversations with each other

Adult–child language interactions are especially important because the most competent language user in the classroom is the teacher. One of the most effective strategies for developing young children's language is to engage them in conversations during their play without being too intrusive (Dickinson, 2011; Meacham, Vukelich, Han, & Buell, 2014). In the following example, preschool teacher Ms. Lawry models language with children who are pretending to cook in the dramatic play center:

Child: Here's your dinner. It's hot.
Ms. Lawry: Thank you. This soup must be boiling hot. I think I can see steam rising up. I'll just sip it slowly. I don't want it to scald me.
Child: Huh? Scald?
Ms. Lawry: Yes. I don't want it to burn my lips.

During this pretend scenario, the teacher modeled advanced vocabulary words like *boiling*, *rising*, *sip*, *steam*, and *scald*, and introduced some science concepts at the same time. In some respect, teachers are always engaged in modeling because children pay attention to what teachers do as much as to what they say.

Demonstrating   An effective strategy for teaching skills that require performing particular steps in a certain order is **demonstrating**. When teachers show the correct way to perform a skill or procedure, children are able to observe the outcome. Similar to modeling, demonstrating is more formal and directive, with the adult drawing children's attention to the correct steps necessary to complete a task, as in the following examples:

> Irene demonstrates for her 3-year-olds how to wash their hands thoroughly to prevent the spread of infection. As she washes her own hands, she says, "See? Now I'm drying my hands with the paper towel. Before I throw the towel away, I use it to turn off the faucet. That way, my hands stay really clean. Now you try it."

> In the art area, kindergarten teacher Max introduces potter's clay to the group. As he demonstrates, he says, "Watch how I pinch off a little piece of clay and use a small amount of water to make the little piece stick to the bigger piece."

Children often learn by observing not only adults but also more accomplished peers performing tasks. Such learning has been called **apprenticeship**, and researchers have observed it across cultural groups (Rogoff, 1990, 2003). When young children watch others perform basic skills of living such as dressing, feeding, or tying shoes, they gradually learn how to accomplish these skills themselves. For demonstrating to be effective, children's observations must be followed by opportunities for them to practice the skills themselves with adult guidance and support.

Giving Cues, Hints, and Assistance   Giving *cues* or *hints* are ways of reminding children what they already know and helping them use that knowledge to build new skills. For example, when a child is reading and is stuck on a word, the teacher may say, "That word has 'ch' at the beginning like another one you know." In this case, the teacher is cueing the beginning reader to compare the new word to one she already knows.

Other common teaching strategies fall in the general category of **facilitating** or **supporting** learning. When teachers *facilitate*, they provide short-term, temporary assistance to help a child achieve the next level of functioning, such as when the teacher gently holds a preschooler's hand as he walks across the balance beam. When teachers *support* learning, they provide a more fixed-form of assistance such as providing a word wall (displaying frequently used words) for kindergartners to refer to as they work in their

demonstrating Showing the correct way to perform a skill or procedure while children observe the outcome.

apprenticeship The process of children learning by observing adults and more accomplished peers performing tasks and by practicing the skills themselves with adult guidance and support.

facilitating Providing short-term, temporary assistance to help a child achieve the next level of functioning.

supporting Providing assistance that helps the child to accomplish a difficult task by making it easier.

© Goodluz/Shutterstock

Effective teachers have a large repertoire of strategies to use in different situations. When there is a specific skill that children need to learn, a teacher may intentionally demonstrate it for children.

journals. In both facilitating and supporting learning, the teacher provides assistance that helps the child to accomplish a difficult task by making it easier.

Creating and Adding Challenges

Although cues, hints, and other assistance make children's learning tasks easier, effective teachers also intentionally make learning situations harder at times by creating challenge, generating a problem, or adding difficulty to a task so that it is a bit beyond what children have already mastered. For example, Hiroki is especially adept at doing puzzles and quickly completes all that are available in his preschool classroom. His teacher, Keith, brings in an alphabet puzzle with 26 pieces, one for every letter, challenging Hiroki's skill with puzzles to help him learn the alphabet.

In her second-grade classroom, Catarina determines that although most of the children are reading at or below grade level, two of them are much more advanced. She provides fourth- and fifth-grade-level reading materials to ensure that they are challenged to continue their reading growth. In addition, she adapts her writing assignments to add challenge. For example, if the other children's assignment is to describe their own experiences over the weekend, to add challenge for the more advanced children, Catarina asks them to write a different ending for a story they've read, requiring higher-level comprehension and analysis.

questioning Eliciting different types of responses and promoting different types of thinking.

open-ended questions Questions that require children to analyze information in some way and that have many possible answers.

closed questions Lower-level questions that have one right answer and usually require children to recall information or facts.

Questioning   One of the most frequently used teaching strategies, **questioning** is used to elicit different types of responses and to promote different types of thinking. Research on questioning finds that higher-level, **open-ended questions**—those that require children to analyze information in some way—are more effective learning tools than lower-level questions are (Gonzalez et al., 2014; Meacham et al., 2014). Lower-level or **closed questions** have one right answer, usually requiring children to recall information or facts. Closed questions, which are often the type used on tests, may reveal what a child knows, but they do not propel further learning. Open-ended questions, on the other hand, have many possible answers. Indeed, a truly open-ended question is one for which the teacher does not have an answer in mind.

To understand how different types of questions elicit different types of responses, compare the following two questions, asked after a reading of Beatrix Potter's *The Tale of Peter Rabbit*:

> *Question 1:* Where did Peter Rabbit get lost?
> *Question 2:* How would you feel if you were lost like Peter?

Question 1 has one right answer—Mr. McGregor's garden. This question offers little opportunity to generate further conversation. Conversely, question 2 would most likely evoke many different responses from children with various adjectives describing feelings—*scared, nervous, afraid, unhappy, sad, tired,* or *hungry*—as well as opportunities for follow-up questions that would extend the conversation. For example, "What would you do?" or "How could you get help?" would elicit a host of responses. Even more beneficial, the open-ended questions would enable children to connect the story to their own experience beyond the classroom, making the reading even more meaningful.

Questions That Promote Problem Solving   Teachers often use questions as ways to cue or prompt children to take the next step in solving a problem or performing a skill. In addition, they may use questions to remind children of what they already know before introducing new information, as well as to focus their attention and thinking in advance.

In the following example, before reading *Caps for Sale*, by E. Slobodkina, to a group of preschoolers, Carol holds up the book cover and begins a conversation with a question:

Teacher: What do you see in this picture?
Mark: A man with lotsa hats on his head.
Tory: He looks funny. The hats are all different colors.
Teacher: So you think this will be a funny story, Tory?
Tory: I don't know. How can those hats stay on his head? I bet they fall off.
Teacher: Let's read the story and find out.

By asking questions before she reads the book to the children, Carol engages their interest. As soon as Carol begins reading, the children are observing and analyzing the pictures and making predictions about the story. After the story, Carol and the children will discuss whether their predictions were correct.

Quality of Questioning Research on questioning demonstrates its effectiveness as a teaching strategy. However, research also finds that although questions are by far the most frequent verbal interaction among teachers and children, teachers most often ask low-level questions (Justice, Mashburn, Hamre, & Pianta, 2008; Meacham et al., 2014). One observational study of preschool classrooms in England (Sylva, Melhuish, Sammons, Siraj-Blatchford, & Taggart, 2010) found that even in good programs, only about 5% of teachers' questions were open ended. More than 34% of their questions were closed (one-right-answer, low-level questions), and more than 60% were related to controlling behavior and not directly related to pedagogy.

Despite the scarcity of open-ended questions, however, when open-ended questions were asked, they provoked rich conversations and thoughtful speculation and extended children's imaginations. The researchers concluded that given their potential effectiveness, increasing the use of open-ended questions could greatly improve outcomes for children, especially children who are at risk of school failure (Sylva et al., 2010).

Wait Time An important aspect of questioning is **wait time**, the length of time that a teacher waits for a response after asking a question. Research reveals that when teachers pause or wait briefly—about 5 seconds—for responses from children, it increases the frequency and depth of children's responses (Cohrssen, Church, & Tayler, 2014; Tharp & Entz, 2012;).

wait time The length of time that a teacher waits for a response after asking a question or responding to a comment.

As you see in this situation, activities such as a digital table provide rich opportunities for children and teachers to talk and think together—what is called co-construction.

Wait time is especially valuable for young children who are just beginning to master verbal communication and also for children who are learning a second language (Espinosa, 2010c).

Wait time also helps extend conversations with children and among groups of children. Sometimes, when children do not immediately respond to adult questions or comments, adults might impatiently talk for them or over them. For teachers who are patient and recognize the beauty of wait time, however, it becomes a highly useful strategy to add to their repertoire.

Co-Constructing Learning and Understanding   One of the most important ways children learn is by constructing their own understanding of concepts as they actively try to make sense of their experiences. The process of co-construction often happens when children work collaboratively with teachers and/or other children on a joint project or activity (Tharp & Entz, 2012). This strategy of working collaboratively to solve a problem or clarify a concept is called **co-construction**, because both parties in the task think and talk together and each learns from it. The value of this strategy was demonstrated in a large-scale observational study in England. The researchers found that in the most effective classrooms, teachers encouraged co-construction during children's play activities, which they called *sustained shared thinking* (Sylva et al., 2010), as in this example:

> Four-year-old James is watching various objects floating in the water table. "Look at the toys. The blocks are sinking. I don't like that." he observes. Modeling curiosity and extending the interaction, his teacher says, "Why do you think they're sinking?" James responds, "Because they're too big." The teacher picks up a bigger block and shows the children how two blocks compare in size. Another child, Kathy, says, "That's going to sink too." When the block floats, the children look astonished. The teacher asks "Why do you think that happened?" and the children begin to share many different explanations.

This process of co-construction, or sustained shared thinking, proved to be so predictive of positive outcomes for young children that the researchers concluded that it is a prerequisite of effective preschool education. Co-construction is also one of the most frequently used strategies in the schools in Reggio Emilia, Italy. Although open-ended questioning is one way to initiate co-construction during children's play, teachers need to sustain the back-and-forth conversation and think along with the children to help them construct their understanding of new concepts.

Giving Direct or Explicit Instruction   **Direct instruction** occurs when a teacher gives explicit directions for completing a task; provides facts, verbal labels, or other specific information; or provides instructions for a child's action or behavior. Direct or explicit instruction is used for transmitting knowledge that can be learned only from one person telling another the culturally agreed-on labels for objects, events, and experiences, which is called *social-conventional knowledge*. For example, the days of the week, letters, or punctuation symbols have conventionally agreed-on names that children learn more easily and efficiently through direct instruction. Writing a question mark on chart paper, first-grade teacher Lydia uses direct instruction when she points out, "This is a question mark, and we write it at the end of a sentence that is asking a question or making a request."

Teachers also use direct instruction during child-initiated activities and when working with small groups. For example, when working with a group of 4-year-olds building with blocks, the teacher points to a block and says, "This rounded block is called a cylinder. You used four cylinder blocks to hold up your bridge."

Uses and Misuses of Direct Instruction   Direct instruction can be the most efficient and effective way of conveying information and introducing new concepts, procedures, or vocabulary. Like every other strategy, however, it should not be overused. Studies of children's experiences in the primary grades have found that direct instruction in the whole

co-construction Teaching strategy that involves thinking and working collaboratively to solve a problem.

direct instruction Explicitly giving directions for completing a task; providing facts, verbal labels, or other specific information; or providing instructions for a child's action or behavior.

group is the most frequently used teaching strategy (NICHD Early Child Care Research Network, 2002, 2003). In addition, whole-group, direct teaching is used much more often in kindergarten than in preschool (Hamre & Pianta, 2007; Oertwig & Holland, 2014).

Direct instruction is the easiest and most efficient way to present new knowledge, such as agreed-on names for tools, and some skills, such as tying shoes. However, this type of instruction is only one part of helping children learn concepts. For example, children can learn aspects of mathematical computation through direct instruction, but they need many additional experiences to understand the complex concepts of number and operations.

Although the list of teaching strategies presented so far is not exhaustive, it provides a basic overview of options teachers can use to become intentional, effective teachers. Next, we turn to a particularly effective teaching strategy, scaffolding, that draws on the strengths of several different strategies at once.

► **Classroom Connection**

This video shows teachers using a variety of strategies to guide children's learning about different kinds of birds. How do these intentional teachers artfully scaffold children's learning?

The Power of Scaffolding: An Integrated Approach

We have now discussed a number of effective strategies that will help you create an effective classroom. Yet how do you best guide children of different skill levels, cultural backgrounds, personalities, and talents toward new, achievable goals? Scaffolding is the most effective teaching strategy for such a challenging task.

What Is Scaffolding? **Scaffolding** is a metaphor for a series of teacher behaviors that support children's ability to accomplish learning tasks or solve a problem that they could not otherwise accomplish independently (Wood, Bruner, & Ross, 1976). This strategy not only allows children to progress toward challenging goals but also gives them the skills to eventually achieve the same task on their own. Scaffolding may be such an effective teaching practice because it actually draws on the strengths of many of the other teaching strategies all at once.

Literally, scaffolding is a temporary structure, usually an elevated platform, that builders or painters stand on to reach otherwise inaccessible parts of a building. Like the painter's platform, the scaffold used in the classroom is the right amount of teacher support for the learner to achieve a task or accomplish an objective that would be beyond his or her reach without the assistance.

Scaffolding assists a child to work in his or her *zone of proximal development*—the area just beyond a child's current level of understanding or ability to achieve (Vygotsky, 1978). What makes scaffolding effective is that it presents learners with just the right amount of challenge—enough so they don't give up or fail, but not so much that they aren't solving the problem themselves (Clark & Graves, 2005). Scaffolding also gives children the opportunity to practice skills they couldn't do on their own. Despite the demonstrated effectiveness of scaffolding as a teaching strategy, it is used all too seldom. In the NCEDL prekindergarten study, teachers supported children's learning by scaffolding less than 10% of the time (Early et al., 2010).

scaffolding Using a variety of strategies to support children's ability to accomplish learning tasks that they could not otherwise accomplish independently.

The Teacher's Role The process of scaffolding, which is depicted in Figure 9.1, begins with the teacher having responsibility for the learning and gradually releasing more and more of it to the learner until the child is capable of assuming full responsibility for the task. At that point, a new zone of proximal development is created, and a new challenge can be presented, starting the process once again. Alternatively, scaffolding may occur in a situation where a child is close to mastering a task and therefore the teacher provides just a little assistance. For example, 7-year-old Barry loves jigsaw puzzles but he is working on a very difficult one. He has completed the outside border

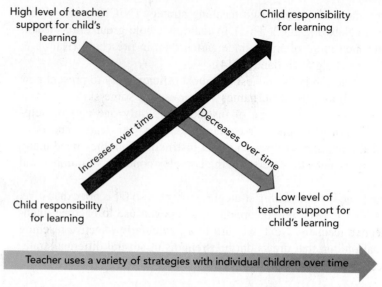

FIGURE 9.1 **Scaffolding in Action** Scaffolding involves using multiple teaching strategies to assist children to move from learning with assistance to learning on their own.

but he is struggling with the middle. His family child care provider suggests that he put all the pieces that are the same color together and match the colors first, and then try to match the shapes. He finds this suggestion works well and is able to complete the puzzle on his own.

The process of scaffolding comes to life in the following example, in which Ms. Riley, a kindergarten teacher, gradually releases responsibility for learning to the students as she teaches writing and social studies content.

> During morning meeting, after a visit to the classroom by a local dentist, Ms. Riley leads a discussion of what the children learned. Ms. Riley writes their ideas on chart paper as they watch. Then she suggests that the children write thank-you notes and models for them how to begin a letter. "Dear Dr. Martinez," she writes, pointing out how she uses capital letters for the dentist's name and a period after "Dr." During choice time, children visit the writing center and work on writing their thank-you letters. Ms. Riley sits down with a small group. She prompts their memories about the visit. They were impressed by the big brush and set of teeth and the kinds of food, such as apples, that help clean teeth. Ms. Riley places the chart the children dictated where they can see it for reference. With Ms. Riley's help, the children take turns copying some of the words on the chart. She is available as they use their own invented spelling to sound out the words they want to write. Occasionally she draws attention to the correct spelling of Dr. Martinez's name. Gradually, the children take more responsibility, creating drawings to include in their letters. On their own, some children make a chart with pictures and words of how to brush teeth, which they post in the bathroom.

Intentional teachers use scaffolding and the other teaching strategies described previously to teach all children. However, additional specific adaptations and modifications may be necessary to help children with disabilities make progress toward their individualized learning goals. The *Including All Children* feature provides examples of research-based strategies for teaching children with autism spectrum disorders. These adaptations are helpful for working with children with other disabilities, any child who is not making expected progress, and for dual language learners as well.

In the previous sections, we described an array of research-based effective strategies. In the following section, we illustrate how intentional teachers apply these strategies in practice to help individual children reach developmentally appropriate goals.

Including All Children

Project DATA: A High-Quality Comprehensive Early Intervention Program for Children with Autism Spectrum Disorders

The need for a high-quality early childhood educational experience is a need shared by all children, regardless of whether they have an identified disability. Recommended practices for early childhood environments highlight the importance of the physical aspects of a learning environment, including the availability of developmentally appropriate materials, the use of a consistent schedule of routines, and the availability of responsive adults and peers. Because children with autism spectrum disorder (ASD) are children first, it follows that the components of high-quality early education for all children are necessary but may not be sufficient in an environment for children with ASD. The important role early childhood educators play in providing the necessary supports for children with ASD to participate in general early childhood activities makes them critical members of the educational team.

An example of a program that integrates the components of a high-quality early childhood educational program with other specialized techniques is called Project DATA (Developmentally Appropriate Treatment for Autism). A unique feature of this model is the central role of an integrated early childhood program. The core element of the model is the classroom experience. The goal is for every child with ASD to have opportunities to interact successfully with typically developing children. To make the interactions successful, they may need to be planned and supported systematically. This component is not just about being with other children; it is about interacting with and developing relationships among all children.

In addition to a high-quality environment, other elements should be included to provide opportunities for the children with ASD to interact successfully with their peers.

To achieve this, toddlers and preschoolers in Project DATA attend an integrated classroom as part of their comprehensive educational program. The model incorporates the following elements into early childhood environment.

- Structuring the classroom environment to promote independence, participation, and successful interactions with typically developing peers. This can be accomplished by providing visual cues (i.e., signs or pictures) about what the expectations are for a routine or activity.
- Developing a consistent schedule and following it. It is helpful to display the schedule in a child-friendly manner (pictures or line drawings).
- Creating the need to communicate with adults and peers. This element includes such strategies as "forgetting" important components of an activity so that children need to comment to continue the activity.
- Using preferred materials and activities to promote engagement. For a child with ASD, this could mean incorporating unexpected materials in an activity such as toy cars or trains in the art area for painting.
- Providing embedded and explicit instruction on valued skills. Children with ASD need to know very clearly what we are trying to teach them. Showing and role playing how to do something can be effective strategies.
- Providing frequent reinforcement and developing effective motivation systems. Encouraging children with ASD to participate in difficult activities or routines can be a challenge; incorporating praise and using preferred materials can help increase the child's motivation to stay engaged long enough for learning to occur.

Many recommendations are available regarding the best way to support the development of a young child with ASD, some of which are based on sound research and others that are not. Project DATA is an effective program, based on Division for Early Childhood (DEC) recommended practices, that includes extended, intensive instruction for children, strong supports for families, transition planning as children move to the next setting, and collaboration and coordination with team members.

Sources: Based on "Getting a Good Start: Effective Practices in Early Intervention" by I. Schwartz & B. McBride, 2008, in *Educating Learners on the Autism Spectrum: Translating Theory into Meaningful Practice*, edited by K. D. Buron and P. Wolfberg, pp. 66–91, Kansas City, KS: Autism Asperger Publishing Company; and "Project DATA for Toddlers: An Inclusive Approach to Very Young Children with Autism Spectrum Disorder" by G. L. Boulware, I. S. Schwartz, S. Sandall, and B. J. McBride, 2006, *Topics in Early Childhood Special Education*, 26(2), 94–105.

✓ **Check Your Understanding 9.2:** A Repertoire of Effective Teaching Strategies

Connecting Teaching Strategies and Learning Goals

As you are starting to see, various teaching strategies accommodate different types of knowledge and different ways of learning. Teachers, therefore, must always be open to different ways of teaching. In the volume *Eager to Learn: Educating Our Preschoolers* (Bowman et al., 2001), experts reviewed the research on young children's cognitive development and its implications for teaching. They identified three key principles of early childhood teaching and learning:

1. Effective teachers make learning meaningful by building on what children already know and can do.
2. Effective teachers develop children's conceptual understanding by teaching topics in depth, using many examples, and making connections to children's everyday experiences. For example, learning knowledge and skills (such as identifying letters and numbers) must be framed within the larger, key concepts involved in each domain of learning (such as the written language system in literacy or the concept of quantity in mathematics).
3. Effective teachers promote children's higher-level thinking and problem solving. They encourage development of children's metacognitive skills such as reflecting, predicting, questioning, and hypothesizing.

The above three principles of learning apply to people of all ages (NRC, 2000). Consider what these three principles mean to you as a college student or as a professional who is expanding your knowledge of teaching.

Reflect on Your Own Learning

During the course of your schooling and from your work experiences, you have probably identified subjects that you are more interested in than others and that you are likely to pursue as a major or minor. Whenever you take an additional course in your major or in an area you have studied thoroughly before, it becomes easier for you to understand and learn the material because you already know a great deal about the subject. In short, you begin by activating your prior knowledge by connecting new learning to what you already know. An additional advantage to you as a learner is that in your preferred subject area, you are gradually building conceptual frameworks, or mental models, to which you can integrate new information, thereby deepening your understanding.

conceptual frameworks
Mental models that connect new learning to prior knowledge, enhance memory, and deepen understanding.

These types of **conceptual frameworks** serve as memory aids when you need to recall something you've learned or apply knowledge to a new situation. In fact, the more you know about a topic, the more necessary these mental models become in helping you organize, retrieve, and use your knowledge. Finally, when you have that level of understanding, you can begin to analyze your thinking, engaging in metacognitive strategies such as reflecting on what you know and don't know, and apply your knowledge to solve new problems.

By contrast, consider some of the general electives you were required to take. You might have very little prior knowledge about those subjects—and perhaps even less interest. If you are like many other students, you may resort to memorizing the facts for a test without developing a deep understanding. Without a mental framework of concepts to which you can connect and, therefore, retain new information, you soon forget everything you have "learned." In addition, you cannot engage metacognitively in this subject area because you don't know enough about what you know to reflect on it, analyze it, make predictions about it, or evaluate your own thinking in regard to it.

Now that we have introduced teaching strategies and discussed the importance of accommodating each child's needs, we will show how teachers can use these strategies to make learning meaningful for children, to help them develop conceptual understanding, and to build higher-level thinking and problem-solving skills.

Strategies That Make Learning Meaningful

According to the principles identified previously, effective teaching draws out and builds on children's preexisting understandings (Bowman et al., 2001; NRC, 2000). Several strategies are effective in activating and building on children's prior knowledge, including cueing, questioning, and using some form of advance organizer (Ausubel, 1978; Cameron & Morrison, 2011).

Cues and Questions   A straightforward way of activating children's prior knowledge is to provide cues that will spark a connection (Dean et al., 2012). Another strategy is to ask questions. For example, before reading *Caps for Sale*, Carol continues to engage children's prior knowledge to help make the story meaningful:

> *Teacher:* Our story is called Caps for Sale: *A Tale of a Peddler, Some Monkeys, and Their Monkey Business.* You already know what caps are, don't you Jason?
> *Jason:* Yeah. I wore a baseball cap to school today.
> *Teacher:* That's right. It's a kind of hat.

[Pressing on with more pointed questions, the teacher continues:]

> *Teacher:* What do you think the author means when he says the story is about "monkey business"? Have you ever heard that before?
> *Marly:* When my grandma babysits us, she always tells my mommy that she won't allow any monkey business, but she is smiling when she says it.
> *Teacher:* So what is Marly's grandma talking about, do you think?
> *Ricardo:* I guess she means she won't let anybody act silly.

Prior to reading the story, the teacher used cues and questions to tap into what the children already know and understand. As she reads the story, she connects the antics of the monkeys to children's ideas and effectively builds on their prior knowledge.

Advance Organizers   Another way teachers help children build on their background knowledge to engage new learning is to use advance organizers. **Advance organizers** are used before introducing new information and serve as a bridge between what the student already knows and the new learning (Ausubel, 1978; Dean et al., 2012). A widely used advance organizer strategy is known as **K-W-L** (Ogle, 1986), an example of which appears as Figure 9.2. In using K-W-L, teachers first ask children what they already *know* (K) about the topic of study. Then they ask children what they *want* (W) to know or what questions they have about the topic. One early childhood educator uses the "W" to stand for "What I wonder about . . ." (McDermott, 2012). After the study is complete, these responses are compared to the answers children provide to the third question, "What did you *learn* (L)"? Sometimes teachers use a K-W-H-L chart, with H standing for "How will I find information?" In other words, which resources, web pages, books, observations, or people will I consult?

K-W-L is a useful strategy to build reading comprehension or to organize learning about a science or social studies topic. Consider the following example:

> In his second-grade classroom, Mr. Ivey uses K-W-L to launch a study on wolves with a small group of children:

> *Mr. Ivey:* Today we're going to read a book about wolves. What do you already know (K) about wolves?

Children's responses include these: They live in the forest. They kill other animals. They are scary.

> *Mr. Ivey:* What do you want to find out about wolves? (W)

The children raise many questions: What do they eat? Where do they sleep? Do they sleep all winter like bears? How big do they grow? How do they take care of their babies? Mr. Ivey writes each question on chart paper.

advance organizers Ways of introducing new information that serve as a bridge between what the student already knows and the new learning.

K-W-L An advance organizer strategy in which teachers ask children what they already know (K) about the topic of study, what they want (W) to know, and then what they learned (L).

K	W	L
What do I <u>know</u>	What do I <u>want</u> to find our?	What did I <u>learn?</u>
Eggs are white. my mommy cooks eggs. I like eggs sometimes but not when the yellow part is runny. We get eggs at the store. We play with egg cartons. Chickens lay eggs. A robin made a nest with eggs in it. Birds hatch out of eggs.	Why do animals lay eggs? What other animals come from eggs? Do butterflies lay eggs? How long does a chicken have to sit on an egg to make it crack open with a little chick inside? How do you cook eggs? What shape is the egg? Are eggs good for you?	Eggs come out of a chicken's behind. It pops out of the bird. You have to wash your hands after holding or touching an egg. Eggs are oval like a head. Eggs are white, oval, hard outside. Cracked eggs are yellow and wet inside. If you drop eggs, they break. Birds lay them in the nest & sit on them to keep them warm. A chick comes from eggs. Eggs come from crocodiles, fish, and turtles. Snakes and frogs lay eggs. Cats don't lay eggs. I like to eat eggs. I can share them with my family. You can crack thm to make scrambled eggs

FIGURE 9.2 Example of K-W-L Chart This K-W-L chart from an egg-hatching project reminds children of their prior knowledge and encourages them to reflect on what they have learned.

Mr. Ivey: Let's read this book and afterward we'll write down what we've learned.

Following the reading, the children have learned many facts about wolves, but they still don't know if they hibernate.

Mr. Ivey: How could you find out if wolves hibernate?
Melinda: We could Google it or we could e-mail the zookeeper.

This process of building on prior knowledge is easier when teachers and children share a common language and similar cultural background. When children's prior knowledge is acquired in a language and/or cultural context that is different from that of the teacher, the task of building on the children's prior knowledge becomes more difficult but no less important. Teachers of dual language learners must become aware of children's abilities and how to build on them.

Cueing, questioning, and using advance organizers are all effective approaches to activate children's prior knowledge, which, in turn, enhances their understanding and retention of what they learn (Bransford, Brown, & Cocking, 2000). Next, we identify some strategies for building concept development.

Strategies That Develop Concepts

The second principle of teaching and learning emphasizes the need for children to learn topics in depth rather than amassing a large number of unrelated facts. Such understanding is enhanced when children's factual knowledge is organized into conceptual frameworks with many examples and apparent connections. To help children build conceptual frameworks, teachers can engage them in classification and representation activities.

Classify and Identify Similarities and Differences Teachers can help children build concepts by engaging them in forming **classification systems** that identify similarities and differences or compare and contrast objects and ideas (Dean et al., 2012). These cognitive activities begin early for young children.

> **classification systems** Systems teachers use to help children build concepts by identifying similarities and differences or by comparing and contrasting objects and ideas.

When interacting with babies, adults continually use comparative language: "Look how big you are! You're bigger than the teddy bear now, but Scruffy is the biggest." Likewise, children learn many mathematical concepts through building classification systems. With her group of 2- and 3-year-olds, Jeanne helps the children learn the concept of the number *2* by matching pairs of shoes and socks. They soon apply this new concept to their body parts, singing a song while pointing out their two feet, two hands, two legs, two ears, and on and on.

Create Graphic Representations "A picture is worth a thousand words" may be a hackneyed cliché, but when it comes to developing children's conceptual understanding, the phrase is true. In fact, it is also true for college students. You've probably experienced seemingly endless pages of text or hours of lecture that become clear to you only after you've seen a chart, graph, or Venn diagram. This teaching strategy, called **graphic representation**, is the process of depicting thoughts and ideas through drawing, modeling, or using other media.

> **graphic representation** The process of depicting thoughts and ideas through drawing, modeling, or other media.

Teachers can use representation is many ways. For instance, when learning about "quantity," first graders create a graph showing their preference: basketball or soccer. The higher bar, soccer, is the one with "more" votes, providing a visual representation of the concept for the children. They then create a graph comparing the votes of boys and girls.

Teachers' use of graphic representations is an effective way to teach concepts and to engage children. Another powerful use of representation is to engage children in creating their own representations. This activity is a defining characteristic of the Reggio Emilia approach and one of their many contributions to the knowledge base of early childhood.

Loris Malaguzzi (1998) described the purpose of representation as clarifying children's understanding. George Forman, one of the earliest disseminators of the Reggio approach in America, described children's use of graphic representation in Reggio as "not learning to draw, but drawing to learn" (Forman, 1994). Reggio educators (Edwards, Gandini, & Forman, 2012) view graphic representation as a communication tool that is simpler and clearer than words and, therefore, an invaluable way to help children clarify and extend their thinking—that is, deepen their conceptual understanding. Because children are trying to communicate with others through their drawings, clay models, or other representations, they often pause to clarify their ideas before putting them down on paper and making them visible to other people. Important thinking is going on at such moments.

One example of how representation reveals and challenges a child's thinking is related to a study of rain (from the Hundred Languages of Children exhibit, Commune of Reggio Emilia, Italy, cited in Landry & Forman, 1999). After many days of rain, teachers asked children, "Where do you think rain comes from?" Children expressed various theories, such as "the Lord makes the rain." But Simone, age 5½, explained, "The sun heats the rain that has fallen and that's how it goes away afterwards. It goes back into the clouds and then it starts to rain again." From her explanation, it seems that Simone has a good understanding of the rain cycle.

After writing down (representing) children's theories in words, their teacher asked them to draw pictures of where the rain comes from. Simone's detailed drawing included pipes or tubes going up from the ground to the sky to convey the water. Thus, when asked to represent her theory, the child had to further elaborate on it. By engaging children in graphic representation of their theories, the teacher got a much clearer picture of Simone's understanding—somewhat different from her seemingly accurate verbal representation. Additionally, other children might challenge her theory—"Look outside, I don't see any pipes"—causing her to reflect on and probably rethink her ideas.

Strategies That Promote Higher-Level Thinking and Problem Solving

metacognitive activities Activities that engage children in thinking and reflecting about their own learning.

Strategies that are effective in building higher-level thinking and problem solving are those that integrate teaching of metacognitive skills. **Metacognitive activities** engage children in thinking and reflecting about their own learning. Early childhood education has a long tradition of incorporating these strategies in effective ways (Copple, Sigel, & Saunders, 1984; Hohmann & Weikart, 2002). We next describe three strategies that not only engage children's metacognition but also contribute to their achievement in school and life.

planning Requires children to make intentional choices and encourages them to identify their goals, consider the options for achieving them, make predictions, and anticipate consequences; helps build children's higher-level thinking and problem solving.

Planning and Reflection   Many early childhood programs offer children choices during center time, but planning is more than making choices. **Planning** requires children to make intentional choices and encourages them to identify their goals, consider the options for achieving them, make predictions, and anticipate consequences (Epstein, 2012).

Reflection is remembering with analysis, which is more than just memory and recall of events (Epstein, 2012). Teachers help children go beyond remembering what they did to becoming aware of what they learned, what was interesting, how they felt about the experience, and what they can do to build on and extend the experience. Planning and reflection promote intentionality and metacognition among teachers as well as children.

reflection Teaching strategy in which teachers help children go beyond remembering what they did to becoming aware of what they learned, what was interesting, how they felt about the experience, and what they can do to build on and extend the experience.

Reciprocal Teaching   One of the best-researched strategies available to primary grade teachers is reciprocal teaching (Palincsar & Brown, 1984). **Reciprocal teaching** involves teachers working with groups of children to enhance their reading comprehension (Oczkus, 2010). The learning strategies that children develop make them better readers but can also be applied to other areas of the curriculum such as social studies or science. For an example of this effective practice in action, read the feature titled *What Works: Reciprocal Teaching.*

reciprocal teaching A strategy that promotes' children's reading comprehension and higher-order thinking by engaging them in summarizing, questioning, clarifying, and predicting.

Generate and Test Hypotheses   Tisha, a second grader, stares up at the sky for a long time and announces, "I think we're going to have a bad storm. It was hot but now it's cold, and see those cumulus clouds." Impressed, her grandma asks her where she learned all that. "We're studying weather all year in my class. We go outside every day."

At least once a week, Tisha's class looks at the weather map online, discusses what has been happening during the last 24 hours, and then goes outside and observes the sky in the morning and again in the afternoon. The children make predictions about what they think will happen before the next school day, explaining the reasoning behind their predictions. The next morning, they discuss their hypotheses and the extent to which they were correct. If their predictions were accurate, they identify the observations that were the most helpful. If their predictions were not accurate, they try to figure out what they missed or misunderstood (adapted from Marzano, Pickering, & Pollock, 2001, p. 103).

hypothesis generating and testing Applying previously acquired knowledge to a new situation by making a prediction and then observing and reflecting on the outcome.

In the above scenario, Tisha's teacher uses a strategy that draws on children's metacognitive abilities. **Hypothesis generating and testing** is the strategy of applying previously acquired knowledge to a new situation by making a prediction and then observing and reflecting on the outcome. Using this strategy, learners activate prior knowledge, gather new information, and expand and deepen their understanding of concepts. The greatest benefit of hypothesis testing comes when learners explain their thinking, which deepens understanding (Dean et al., 2012).

What Works

Reciprocal Teaching

Reciprocal teaching engages children in summarizing, questioning, clarifying, and predicting—all metacognitive strategies and higher-level thinking skills. Reciprocal teaching is also a good example of scaffolding because, at first, the teacher models the use of effective strategies, such as summarizing a passage that is read and asking questions, and then she gradually turns over those tasks to individual children, as seen in the example that follows.

Ms. Leon, a second-grade teacher, works with five children as they read the tale *The Emperor's New Clothes*. Having previously modeled the strategies of summarizing, questioning, clarifying, and predicting, Ms. Leon chooses a student leader to take on these tasks with the group.

Summarizing After the children silently read a short passage, she asks Christopher, acting as the student leader, to summarize what they read. Christopher says, "The emperor is like the king of the country. He's kind of ugly but he always wants to look good by getting new clothes." Ms. Leon gives cues to help Christopher elaborate on the story, "What did the emperor do to get new clothes?" "Oh, yeah, he hired some tailors," Christopher says.

Questioning Next, the student leader asks the other children some questions to identify important information in the passage.

Christopher asks, "Were those guys really tailors?" The other children try to answer the question based on their recollection of what they read.

Clarifying Then, the student leader tries to clarify confusing parts in the passage or asks the other children for clarification. "How did the tailors trick the emperor?" Ermalinda answers, "They weren't really tailors, and they just pretended to sew new clothes to cheat the emperor."

Predicting The student leader asks the other children to predict what will happen in the next section, "What do you think will happen when the emperor walks down the street in his underwear?"

From this brief example, we see that reciprocal teaching engages children in assuming the role of teacher and involves them in higher-level thinking processes and metacognitive strategies.

Source: Based on *Reciprocal Teaching at Work: Powerful Strategies and Lessons for Improving Reading Comprehension* (2nd ed.), by L. D. Oczkus, 2010, Newark, DE: International Reading Association.

Hypothesis testing is used in science curricula because it actively engages children in applying the **scientific method**: Begin with a hypothesis, test it with an experiment, make observations and gather data, and then confirm or disconfirm the initial hypothesis. However, hypothesis testing is not exclusively used for science; in fact, it is used in all kinds of problem-solving situations, such as those encountered in mathematics or social studies or when negotiating social problems among peers. Consider how hypothesis testing is used in the following example:

scientific method Method of beginning with a hypothesis, testing it with an experiment, making observations and gathering data, and then confirming or disconfirming the initial hypothesis.

A small group of preschoolers wants to construct model cars to use on the race track they have built. Their teacher asks them to hypothesize about what kinds of materials they could use to get the wheels to turn, and the children offer suggestions:

Mary: Straws with buttons glued on the ends.
Damon: Donuts. (Several children laugh.)
Teacher: Why do you think donuts wouldn't work?
Gina: We'd eat them before we finished the car!
Damon: But maybe something like a donut because a wheel needs to have a hole in the middle.

Damon and his friend Jaleel search for objects among the collage art materials that might work to test their hypothesis, while Mary and her friend glue the buttons. Later the teacher and children describe what happened with their experiments and whether their hypotheses were accurate. The girls admit that although the buttons are round, the glue makes them stationary and, therefore, not very good wheels.

In the previous sections, we described an array of teaching strategies and how teachers apply them to make learning meaningful for children, to help them learn concepts, and to engage them in higher-level thinking. To be an effective teacher, you will need to have all of these strategies in your repertoire and know when and how to use them.

✓ **Check Your Understanding 9.3:** Connecting Teaching Strategies and Learning Goals

Grouping as an Instructional Approach

In Chapter 8, we described how the environment influences children's behavior and helps teachers create caring communities. At the same time, the environment provides a powerful context for learning. Environments communicate messages to children about what kind of learning is valued and what their role is in the process. For example, a classroom with rows of individual desks and the teacher's desk in the front sends the message that children work only as individuals and teachers control the dissemination of knowledge.

On the other hand, a classroom with tables that encourage groups of children to work together, an open space for class meetings and discussions, and learning centers for children to choose where they will work and play sends an entirely different message. In the latter environment, the expectation is clear that the teacher and children will work together in various learning contexts.

The Learning Environment

Appropriate learning environments for children will vary depending on the age of the children, the time of the year, and the topic of study. Child-centered environments are organized so that many materials are accessible to children. In preschools, children have access to blocks, dramatic play props, puzzles and other manipulative toys, art materials, and books. In primary-grade classrooms, children might have books to read, science tools to explore and investigate, math games, computer centers, and other learning materials. Table 9.2 lists the types of centers available in a challenging, engaging preschool and kindergarten learning environments and materials that they might include.

Learning in the Whole Group Whole group, which is also called *circle time* or *class meeting time,* provides a valuable context for class discussions, music and movement, planning for the day or for special experiences such as visitors or field trips, and for children to share their experiences and ideas. Whole group is a time to build a sense of community and shared purpose.

Children benefit most from whole group time when a teacher uses it to orient them to upcoming activity that will occur during center time or projects. One research study found that, although rarely done, when preschool teachers model or demonstrate an activity in advance and explain the rationale for it, children's general knowledge, mathematics, literacy, vocabulary, and self-regulation significantly improved (Cameron & Morrison, 2011).

Research with preschoolers demonstrates that during large-group times, teachers' explanations and use of challenging vocabulary is related to improving learning outcomes for children (Dickinson, 2001), as in this example:

> Prior to a visit by a local police officer, Margo gathers her whole class of preschoolers on the rug. She explains, "Officer Gardner is coming tomorrow. She will be wearing her uniform and her badge that identify her to everyone as a police officer. She wants to tell you some ways to stay safe because keeping people safe is the main job of the police. I'll write on our chart some questions you want to ask her." During this brief introduction, Margo provided the children with a concise explanation of what to expect. She also clarified the meanings of the vocabulary she used, such as *uniform, badge,* and *identify.*

Teachers may also engage the whole group in discussion, using questions to prompt and sustain the interaction. For example, a teacher might have her third-grade children

TABLE 9.2 Learning Centers and Suggested Materials

Developmentally appropriate learning environments include a wide variety of materials organized in centers to promote child-chosen experiences as well as small- and large-group instruction.

Learning Center	Examples of Materials
Library area	Culturally and linguistically appropriate books and literacy materials of all kinds (storybooks, information, poetry, wordless, leveled readers), listening center with earphones and CDs, puppets and puppet theater, flannel board
Writing center	All types of paper, envelopes, blank notebooks and journals, variety of pencils, pens, markers, word walls, letter stamps, alphabet cards, computers with writing software and Internet, mobile digital devices
Mathematics	Variety of objects to count, sort, and order (buttons, bottle caps), manipulatives (peg boards, Legos), tangrams, pattern blocks, number cards, interlocking cubes, attribute games, cuisinare rods, graphing mats, dice, card and board games, puzzles, gaming apps
Science	Plants, pets, fish tank, natural objects (shells, rocks, leaves, soil), tools for investigating and recording (magnifying glasses, stethoscope, magnets, funnels, lenses, balance scales, journals, clipboards)
Music and movement	Musical recordings from diverse cultural groups for listening and dancing, rhythm instruments, picture songbooks, props for movement (scarves, flags, streamers), CD player and headsets
Art	Many different kinds of paper; large variety and many colors of crayons, markers, pencils, chalks, and paint; easel; clay, playdough, and tools for sculpting; scissors, paste, glue, collage materials; construction materials (foam pieces, wood scraps, wire, pipe cleaners, recyclable materials); water and sand table; art and photograph books from diverse cultural groups, posters, light table, overhead or LCD projector
Dramatic play	Dress-up clothes, mirrors, home-like materials reflecting children's cultures, child-sized furniture, phone, empty food containers, cookbooks, junk mail, calendars, culturally sensitive dolls and accessories, props for pretending various occupations or settings such as store, restaurant or doctor's office, cash registers, measuring cups and spoons, store coupons, magazines, books, paper; open-ended materials (large pieces of fabric, cardboard boxes)
Blocks	Unit blocks, large hollow blocks, props (people and animal figures, transportation vehicles, dress-up clothes), open-ended materials (cardboard boxes, plastic tubing), literacy materials (writing tools and paper, signs, books about transportation and architecture)
Technology	Computers, digital media (iPad, tablets, smartphone), printers, Web cam, digital camera, scanners, digital microscope, whiteboard

Sources: Based on "Teaching in the Kindergarten Year," by C. Heroman and C. Copple, 2006, in *K Today: Teaching and Learning in the Kindergarten Year,* edited by D. F. Gullo, Washington, DC: NAEYC; *and The Right Stuff for Children Birth through Age 8: Selecting Play Materials to Support Development,* by M. B. Bronson, 1995, Washington, DC: NAEYC.

working in small groups on an investigation of batteries and electricity. Each group will share their theories about how electricity works with the rest of the class.

In general, the younger the child, the shorter the length of time she or he should spend in whole-group experience. Young children are easily distracted, and the context is less effective if overused (Montie, Xiang, & Schweinhart, 2006). Nevertheless, if children are actively engaged in a large group, mentally and/or physically, this setting can be an effective learning context where children have the opportunity to express themselves, to hear the opinions of others, and to feel part of the larger learning community. The important caveat is that teachers need to take their cue from the children. If interest wanes during whole group, it is best to bring the group time to a close and move on to another activity setting or actively engage all the children in singing or movement.

Learning in Small Groups Small groups, usually composed of four to six children, are especially valuable learning contexts for two reasons. First, they provide the opportunity for more focused attention and individualized

▶ Classroom Connection

Watch this video to see how a first-grade teacher effectively uses grouping and various instructional strategies to teach important content and skills. What do you observe about the children's engagement in each context? What are the benefits for children's learning of using different ways of grouping for instruction?

http://mediaplayer.pearsoncmg. com/_blue-top_640x360_ccv2/ab/ streaming/myeducationlab/WSO_ Vignettes/G1_Dana-Surveys.mp4 instruction from the teacher. Teachers can give children immediate, high-quality feedback and also evaluate their performance more accurately (Abou-Sayed, 2011). Second, small groups give children the opportunity to interact with and learn from peers and also engage in hands-on experiences (Wasik, 2008). Teachers also use small groups for a focused learning experience such as introducing a new skill or concept.

Small groups are highly effective for learning vocabulary, literacy, and mathematics (Dickinson & Smith, 1993; Morrow & Smith, 1990; NRC, 2009). Reading a story to a small group makes it easier for teachers to engage children in conversation before, during, and after reading, which has been found to be especially beneficial for building vocabulary and other literacy skills (Gonzalez et al., 2014; Whitehurst & Lonigan, 1998). Despite a great deal of research supporting the positive effects of small group instruction, only 6% of preschoolers' day is spent in small group interaction (Early et al., 2005).

One of the greatest benefits of small-group interaction is the back-and-forth exchanges among children, which can scaffold children's learning just as teacher interactions can. Small groups also provide the opportunity for active engagement in the learning experience. Without such active involvement, the benefit of small groups goes unrealized. Children should have the opportunity to participate in more than one small group each day, depending on the instructional goals, and should work with peers of varying ability levels (Bates, 2013). For an example of grouping as an instructional strategy, read the feature titled *Becoming an Intentional Teacher: Working in Small Groups*.

Becoming an Intentional Teacher

Working in Small Groups

Here's What Happened   With my kindergarten class, I decided to play a marble game to engage them in thinking about measurement and also the processes of predicting, observing, and recording results. After explaining the game, I organized children into groups of three or four. Each had a hollow piece of plumbing pipe and a marble. With one end of the pipe on the ground, a child held the other end. Each group dropped a marble down the pipe to see how far it would travel out the other end. After the initial try, the children held the pipe at different angles to see if the angle affected the distance the marble traveled. The children recorded how far the marble went in an initial try and then tried to get it to roll farther based on where they were holding the other end of the pipe. I asked each group questions as the game proceeded to engage them in thinking about and predicting what would happen.

Here's What I Was Thinking   I planned the marble game as a small-group activity for several reasons. Small groups of children are better than large groups for focusing their attention on an idea. When each child can participate more actively in investigating, predicting, and recording measurements, they care more about the outcome—in this case, making the marble go farther than it has before. They pay attention to what affects the distance it rolls, and they are motivated to work out a way to measure if they've succeeded in improving their previous results. Small groups allow the children to participate and, at the same time, allow me to observe what each child does and does not understand and engage each child in the learning experience at his or her own level.

I typically put together these small groups during center time. I invited a group of children to work with me; if there was something else the children really wanted to do instead, I allowed them to choose. It was rare, however, for them to pass up this opportunity—they loved the extra interaction of small groups, and I worked hard to make these experiences engaging.

I formed groups that were mixed with respect to the children's developmental levels, or what I thought their ability would be on this task. I thought that five children were starting to grasp the general idea of standard units in measurement—a big breakthrough that many children don't make until age 7 or 8. I dispersed those children among the five groups I worked with. I encouraged these five children to explain their ideas to the others because it helps them get a firmer understanding of the concepts. And the exposure the less advanced children get gives them a new idea to chew on.

Reflection   A large body of research supports the benefits of teaching children in small groups, yet most teachers rarely use this approach. Why do you think this is so? What conditions might make teachers more likely to decrease time spent in whole-group instruction and increase small-group experiences for children?

Source: Based on *The Young Child and Mathematics*, by J. V. Copley, 2000, pp. 103–104, Washington, DC: NAEYC.

Teaching in Learning Centers Effective early childhood classrooms provide an extended period of time, from 45 to 90 minutes, for children to engage in child-initiated experiences in learning centers (Epstein, 2013; Sylva et al., 2010). These defined areas of the classroom have particular purposes. The library area promotes book reading and listening. A block area provides for building, pretending, and learning mathematics concepts. Art and writing centers promote creative expression, symbolic representation, and development of fine-motor skills. Manipulative toys such as peg boards, beads, and Legos offer opportunities to practice fine-motor skills and solve problems. The dramatic play area promotes symbolic pretend play, self-regulation, and language interaction.

During learning center time, children have opportunities to plan, initiate, and make choices and to practice their developing skills, which is essential for mastery. Learning centers provide natural laboratories for children to work out social problems with other children and to practice their language. Center time also promotes decision-making skills because children make choices about how they will spend their time, what they will do, and with whom they will play.

Effective teachers use center time to engage children in one-on-one, extended conversations (Dickinson, 2011). During this period in which children are engaged with various tasks, such as writing, doing a puzzle, or pouring water, teachers are available to scaffold individual children's learning as needed. Finally, center time also provides an

Language Lens

Teachable Moments with Dual Language Learners

For children who are learning English, every moment in the classroom is a teaching and learning opportunity. They may be wearing winter clothes for the first time, riding a school bus, and meeting people who do not look or sound like them. Learning a new language takes time, effort, and intentional teaching. Teachers need to take advantage of every teachable moment. Here are some points for teachers to keep in mind:

- As a role model of the language, speak slowly but not loudly, simplifying your vocabulary and sentence structure as you might for a younger child. Over time, work toward more challenging vocabulary, sentences, and short conversation.
- Use your body and facial expressions to communicate. For instance, to emphasize words like *under, through, around,* or *on top,* play with children around a table to physically demonstrate these words and concepts.
- Use repetition. Be as clear as possible in pronunciation and diction, which may mean opening the mouth wider because children look for facial clues.
- Use large-group time to engage children in the joy of group movement and exercise, singing and choral repetition, preparing children in advance for upcoming activities.
- Use small-group time, which is especially effective for dual language learners because it allows for active participation, individual attention, and experiences with objects. For example, if children are learning about vegetables, have real broccoli, carrots, and squash for them to see, touch, and taste.

- Use small groups of children with the same home language to introduce new concepts in the home language first.
- Vary the composition of groups, at times bringing together learners who speak the same language and, at other times, children from two or more language groups.
- Provide a visually rich environment with pictures and words in multiple languages.
- Organize centers with language learning in mind, including spaces for individuals such as a listening center with tapes in the home language, tablets or smartphones with translation apps, or a computer with programs in both languages.
- Provide private, quiet spaces for children to de-stress—being surrounded by an unfamiliar language for long periods of time can be overwhelming for anyone.
- Outdoor playtime is a great venue for children to learn new English words for physical actions and social interactions. Create games that repeat words like *run, kick, walk, jump, throw over,* or *throw under.* Making friends and playing together motivate children to learn a new language.
- Give special attention to particular sounds that may not exist in the child's home language. For some Spanish-speaking children, it may be the /ch/ or /sh/ or /w/ pronunciations; for some Asian children, it may be the /r/ or /th/ sounds.
- Encourage children's efforts at speaking the new language; avoid correcting children by simply rephrasing and repeating.

excellent opportunity for teachers to observe and assess children's developing capabilities in various contexts.

All of the grouping approaches described previously—the arrangement of the learning environment and materials, centers, large group, small groups, and individual activities—provide excellent opportunities for teachers to support dual language learners. Read the *Language Lens: Teachable Moments with Dual Language Learners* feature for suggested strategies.

In the previous sections, we described the various contexts commonly found in early childhood classrooms: whole group, small group, and learning centers. Center time is an excellent opportunity for children to engage in their favorite activity—play (Wiltz & Klein, 2001). Play is also a highly effective context for learning and teaching, as described next.

 Check Your Understanding 9.4: Grouping as an Instructional Strategy

 # Play as a Context for Learning

The word *play* is used to describe different types of activities, including constructive play and games with rules as well as pretend play. In the previous discussion of learning centers, we saw how teachers' behaviors support learning during various forms of play. In this section, we explore teachers' roles during sociodramatic play, a particularly effective form of play for developing children's self-regulation, problem-solving, and language and literacy skills (Bodrova & Leong, 2007; Diamond & Lee, 2011; Smilansky & Shefatya, 1990).

Rarely is play thought of as a teaching strategy. Researchers define play as child-initiated experience, and, in fact, children themselves see play as something they control (Singer, Golinkoff, & Hirsh-Pasek, 2006; Sutton-Smith, 1980). Nevertheless, decades of research on play demonstrates that teachers have important roles in children's play and they can help play achieve its full potential as an effective learning experience for children (Singer et al., 2006; Zigler, Singer, & Bishop-Josef, 2004). The key is not to take over or turn play into a formal lesson.

During sociodramatic play, children pretend, create a theme, use props, develop roles, and follow rules related to the roles. Moreover, sociodramatic play involves language interaction (Bodrova & Leong, 2007), as we see in this example:

> In her Head Start classroom, Marita Lewis sets up a grocery store with food boxes, plastic fruit and vegetables, shopping carts, a cash register, and check-out counter. She adds paper and pencils for writing shopping lists, play money, and paper receipts. As 4-year-old Carey pushes her cart up to the counter, the "cashier" Angela, her classmate, asks, "Paper or plastic?" After Carey selects, "Paper," Angela, continues to recite the script of a cashier to the best of her recollection, "Credit card or money?" Meanwhile, sitting nearby, Marita is approached by LaToya who needs help writing her shopping list. She wants to add bananas. Marita says, "BBBBananas" drawing out the /b/ sound at the beginning of the word. "What letter does it start with?" "B!" shouts LaToya, who quickly starts to write a *B* on her list.

Teachers' Involvement during Play

Research reveals that teachers play a variety of roles during children's play that can be placed on a continuum from minimal to maximum teacher involvement (Jones & Reynolds, 2011). Figure 9.3 depicts the continuum of teacher roles in play (Johnson, Christie, & Wardle, 2005). As the figure illustrates, the effective *facilitating* roles are the ones in the middle of the continuum.

The two extremes of teacher behavior, either *uninvolved* or *overly directive*, have a negative effect on play. If teachers are uninvolved and ignore children during play, using playtime

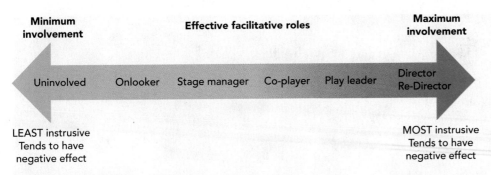

FIGURE 9.3 Continuum of Teacher Roles in Play Teachers can use various strategies to support children's play—from minimal to maximum involvement—as depicted on this continuum.

Source: From Johnson, James E.; Christie, James F.; Wardle, Francis. *Play, Development and Early Education,* 1st Ed., © 2005. Reprinted and electronically reproduced by permission of Pearson Education, Inc., Upper Saddle River, New Jersey.

to do paperwork or housekeeping tasks, children's pretend play tends to become simplistic, repetitive, and raucous, featuring themes like monsters and superheroes (Johnson et al., 2005). In these situations, the play often turns into a disciplinary situation with the teacher only stepping in to police behavior. Consequently, the learning potential of play is lost.

At the other end of the continuum, teachers are ineffective if they take too much control of children's play, either by trying to direct what children do from the sidelines or by redirecting the play away from what the children are doing toward the teacher's goal. Situations where teachers are maximally involved cease to be child-initiated play, and most of the time, children will simply withdraw mentally from the pretend scenario or leave the scene entirely.

So we see that using play as a context for teaching and learning requires teachers to walk a fine line between doing too little and doing too much. Next, we discuss several effective roles of teachers during play.

Teachers' Role during Play

The four roles in the midrange of the continuum are onlooker, stage manager, co-player, and play leader. These roles are all effective in helping children get involved and stay engaged in play situations. In each of these roles, the teacher becomes more involved in the play scene. At the same time, the teacher adapts her role as the children play, depending on their interests and needs.

Onlooker In the **onlooker** role, teachers act as the audience for children's play. They position themselves nearby, acknowledging and encouraging children's play by nodding, smiling, or making positive comments. The onlooker role lets children know that play is valued and important, and encourages them to persist. In the onlooker role, teachers observe and assess children's competencies exhibited during their play interactions. Based on these observations, the teacher intentionally decides whether and how to become more involved in the play (Jones & Reynolds, 2011).

onlooker Teachers act as the audience for children's play.

Stage Manager As the name implies, **stage managers** do not actively enter the play; they instead set the stage by providing the props and theme. They are also available to respond to children's requests for materials or assistance. In the grocery store play described previously, Marita acted as a stage manager, having prepared the setting, which encouraged children's involvement. Stage managers scaffold children's learning, as when Marita helped LaToya with her shopping list. Teachers as stage managers also make suggestions to help extend the play. For example, if LaToya began to lose interest, Marita might ask, "What else do you need for your dinner tonight?"

stage manager Teachers set the stage for children's play by providing the props and theme and being available to respond to children's requests.

Co-Player As **co-players**, teachers actually join in and take an active role in the play. Co-players are equal play partners with children, but it is best if teachers take the

co-player Teachers actually join in and take an active role in children's play.

Play is a valuable context for children's learning. But children don't automatically play productively. How can teachers support play to benefit children without taking over?

subordinate role in the drama, such as the patient in the doctor's office or the passenger on the airplane, leaving the prime roles of doctor or pilot for the children. As a co-player, the teacher is careful to let the children take the lead. This role provides ample opportunity, however, for the teacher to model play skills, including pretending with objects and roles, turn-taking, ways to enter an ongoing scene, and vocabulary (Johnson et al., 2005, p. 272). Consider how the teacher accomplishes all of these goals in the following play situation:

> In Sascha Britt's preschool classroom, the children are playing pet store as part of their study of domestic animals. Sascha arrives cradling a stuffed dog and says, "I just got a brand new puppy. I don't know what I'm going to need to take care of him. Can you help me?" The children scramble about looking for supplies on the shelves of their store. Martha says, "He'll be hungry. Here's some dog food." Dominic chimes in, "He has to take walks. You better get him a leash." "I think he needs a nice soft bed," says Emory, who looks around but can't find anything to fit the bill. Instead, he picks up the pillow off the doll bed and hands it to his teacher. Sascha replies, "I'm glad I came to this store. You have lots of supplies. How much will this cost?"

Play Leader   This role involves teachers' direct participation in children's play, but exerts more influence than the co-player's role. As the **play leader**, the teacher deliberately attempts to enrich and extend the play episode, suggesting a theme and introducing new props or plot elements. Teachers become play leaders when children have difficulty beginning sociodramatic play or when play breaks down:

play leader Teachers participate in children's play; includes making deliberate attempts to enrich and extend the play episode.

> After several days playing in the grocery store, the children's play becomes repetitive and fewer children choose to play there. To spark some interest, Marita puts herself in the role of store manager.
>
> *Marita:* This store is losing business. I think it needs some new attractions for shoppers. What if we reduce the prices on everything and have a sale?
> *Josh:* We'll have to change all the signs.
> *Marita:* What else could we do to get more customers?
> *Toby:* We could put in a McDonald's like they have at the mall.

The children quickly embrace Toby's idea. Josh starts to draw a big "M" for the McDonald's sign, while other children start gathering props for the food. Toby's suggestion leads to many changes in the dramatic play episode with new roles such as cook that extend the play over several days.

Because sociodramatic play is such an effective learning context, teachers need to be aware of and use the full range of roles and strategies available to them in supporting children's make-believe play. Although some educators believe that pretend play comes naturally to children and that adults are not needed, this is a misperception. In fact, children who are skilled "players" during preschool most likely had parents or caregivers who played with them beginning as babies and toddlers (Elias & Berk, 2002).

Today's teachers report that many children, often children from low-income backgrounds but also their middle-class peers, are unskilled at pretend play when they come to early childhood programs. Their play tends to be repetitive and immature. In situations such as these, teachers in the role of stage manager can coach children from the sidelines to improve play behaviors or, as co-players or leaders, they can model and scaffold appropriate play behavior.

Research demonstrates that participation in sociodramatic play has positive effects on children's language, social, and cognitive development (Barnett et al., 2008; Bodrova & Leong, 2007; Diamond, 2012). To be effective, however, teachers must be intentional in their role in children's play. Play has a long tradition in early childhood programs as well as a thorough, although sometimes contradictory, research base. In the next section, we discuss a more recent educational phenomenon, digital media in schools and child care centers.

▶ **Classroom Connection**

The children in this video are pretending to run a restaurant. What roles does the teacher play in the restaurant scenario? How does she support children's engagement in sociodramatic play?

 Check Your Understanding 9.5: Play as a Context for Learning

 # Teaching with Digital Media

At a very young age, most children today are expert users of every type of technological device and application—digital media, smartphones, touch tablets and apps, e-books, social networking, whiteboards, video games, computers, Internet, digital cameras, and video camcorders. As these words are written, new and emerging technologies are being developed at lightning speed.

Research on Digital Media

Digital media is ubiquitous in children's lives. A survey by Common Sense Media (2013) found that increasing numbers of children are using mobile devices at younger and younger ages, and for longer periods of time. In 2013, about 80% of children used a mobile device for playing games or apps compared to 38% just two years before, and 38% of children under 2 used them (Common Sense Media, 2013). More than 75% of all children under age 8 have access to smartphones or tablets at home.

Although a digital divide and an "app gap" continue to exist, access is increasing for lower-income families (Common Sense Media, 2013). Within 2 years among lower-income families, smartphone ownership went from 27% to 51%, and tablet ownership increased from 2% to 20%. Despite this increase, the gaps remain large. For example, although 20% of lower-income children have a tablet device at home, 63% of higher-income children do. And about one-third of lower-income parents have downloaded educational apps compared to 75% in higher-income families. Lack of technological opportunity is one more potential contributor to the achievement gap, leaving large numbers of children unprepared for success (NAEYC & Fred Rogers Center on Early Learning and Children's Media, 2012).

Although we know that young children spend a considerable amount of time using mobile devices, research on the effects on their development is relatively slim. One study examined preschoolers' use of iPads and three types of apps—*gaming* apps that children often enjoy and master quickly, *creating* apps with which children can build or draw something, and *e-books* (Cohen Group, 2011). The researchers found that children embraced the apps that share characteristics with all effective early childhood experiences: learning by doing, building on interests and prior skills, self-pacing, and offering "a no-fail environment and endless possibilities and outcomes" (Cohen Group, 2011, p. 2).

Although research on the effects and benefits of mobile digital media is limited, studies on the use of desktop computers demonstrate that they can be highly effective in promoting children's learning as long as software is developmentally appropriate and children are in control (NRC, 2009; Sarama & Clements, 2002, 2004). Unlike adults, who tend to work at computers in isolation, preschool and primary-grade children willingly seek peer involvement and conversation if the software is engaging and interactive. Placing two seats in front of a computer or having two or more children share a tablet encourages interaction.

Using technology in early childhood programs is not without controversy. Much of the criticism focuses on the negative effects of passive television viewing; promotion of violence, sexuality, and commercialism; and the importance of limiting children's screen time for their physical health and overall development (Levin, 2013). The debate becomes complicated, however, because all "screens" are not equal (Kleeman, 2010; Lerner & Barr, 2014). Television often becomes background noise that harms language development and social interaction (Lerner & Barr, 2014). The quality of television content also matters. Nevertheless, decades of evidence exists demonstrating the educational benefits of programs such as *Sesame Street* and *Super Why!* (Linebarger, McMenamin, & Wainwright, n.d.; Wainwright, 2006).

Using Technology and Digital Media to Teach

Digital media, mobile devices, and Web 2.0 tools for education, communication, social networking, and user-generated content have transformed every aspect of children's lives, including how teachers use technology in the classroom and how teacher education is delivered. The early childhood technology market is vast and growing, with tens of thousands of apps available. Of the 100 top-selling education apps in Apple's iTunes App store, almost three quarters are aimed at preschoolers and primary-grade children (Shuler, 2012).

Bombarded by an ever-changing technological landscape, teachers must make informed decisions about effective uses of technology and also teach children to be critical thinkers and consumers of media. NAEYC and the Fred Rogers Center for Early Learning and Children's Media (2012) take the position that "technology and interactive media are learning tools that, when used in intentional and developmentally appropriate ways and in conjunction with other traditional tools and materials, can support the development and learning of young children"(p. 1). (This statement focuses on interactive media, not television.)

In the past, conversations have focused on how much time children should spend with screens, which remains a critical issue. But the NAEYC–Fred Rogers Center position raises the most challenging question for early educators: What is developmentally appropriate digital media, and how can it contribute to children's learning? Research by the RAND Corporation (Daugherty, Dossani, Johnson, & Wright, 2014) identifies these considerations:

- Technology use should be well integrated into the larger curriculum.
- Most of the time, children should use technology in collaboration with peers and/or adults.
- Apps and other software should be engaging and interactive, but also have clear educational goals that are achievable by children in the targeted age group.

- Devices should be sturdy, and easy for children to operate and manipulate; for example, tablets can be adapted and help develop fine-motor skills.
- Digital media should promote active experiences rather than sedentary activity.

Mobile devices have the potential advantage of being incorporated into children's active play. Read the feature *Promoting Play: Teaching and Learning through Transmedia Play* for some examples.

Promoting Play

Teaching and Learning through Transmedia Play

Early childhood professionals sometimes view technology and play as an either/or choice. They are concerned that mobile digital devices take valuable time away from children's self-initiated, social play. One solution that addresses both children's need to learn through play and their motivation to engage with the newest technologies is transmedia play. *Transmedia* simply means "across media." Thinking creatively across digital media tools and applications and how they can be integrated in a play-rich curriculum leads to exciting, new possibilities, as in the following example.

With funding from the U.S. Department of Education's Ready to Learn initiative, the Early Learning Collaborative of the Hispanic Information Television Network (HITN) launched an initiative for 3- to 5-year-old children to help prepare them for success in school and later life. The Collaborative developed research-based digital media applications, known as the Pocoyo® PlaySet™, in collaboration with Zinkia Entertainment. Pocoyo is a delightful little character who, along with his friends, teaches English language vocabulary while having fun adventures. Each PlaySet is presented as a playground with lots of options for playful engagement, organized around a theme to help children learn concepts as well as target vocabulary words. PlaySets are designed to meet Head Start Learning Outcomes and Common Core State Standards. They focus on English language development, early literacy, and math skills in an integrated curriculum approach.

One English language development theme, *Things That Go*, teaches vocabulary related to transportation and also positional words to describe objects (above, under, behind). Children also learn to compare and sort objects by attributes (which

objects go together). Another English language development theme is *Grow It!* which teaches target vocabulary and science concepts related to plants and food.

The Playgrounds are transmedia because they combine interactive games, songs, and bilingual story books in engaging instructional applications. Both native English speakers and dual language learners enjoy playing and learning with Pocoyo and acting out Pocoyo's adventures. The Early Learning Collaborative also distributes educational materials to parents, teachers, and other adults to interact with the child around the PlaySet content.

Transmedia initiatives for primary-grade children often build off storytelling applications. These go beyond traditional reading experiences in the early grades to creating stories using various forms of digital media and engaging children in writing and telling their own stories.

Playing with interactive media is now a major activity in the lives of young children. What's important is to ensure that such experiences maintain the benefits of open-ended play while achieving the potential of the latest technologies to expand children's worlds and their learning.

Sources: T is for Transmedia: Learning through Transmedia Play, by B. Herr-Stephenson, M. Alper, E. Reilly, and H. Jenkins, 2013, Los Angeles and New York: USC Annenberg Innovation Lab and The Joan Ganz Cooney Center at Sesame Workshop, retrieved October 1, 2014, from http://www.annenberglab.com/viewresearch/46; "Initiative," by HITN Early Learning Collaborative, 2014, retrieved November 15, 2014, from http://earlylearningcollaborative.org/products/.

▶ **Classroom Connection**

As you watch this video, reflect on the many ways first-grade teacher Eric Crouch, uses digital media in his classroom. What appear to be the benefits for children's learning of integrating technology in curriculum and instruction?

https://www.youtube.com/watch?v=IzSNdxsfkOQ

Effective teachers integrate interactive media into curriculum and instruction throughout the day. For example, children can use e-books independently and do online research for projects or research on topics of study. Teachers as well as children use digital cameras regularly to document children's progress and products. Children can use a program to create their own story by clicking on the characters and events of their choosing. In addition, the Internet allows communication with other children or adults, such as favorite authors, in other cities, states, or countries. Through technology, a second-grade class can take an electronic field trip and regularly monitor the growth of the baby panda at the National Zoo via the zoo's website. In turn, during an actual field trip to the zoo, children can use a mobile device to view the native environments of pandas in China and access information about other species of bears.

Numerous digital media resources are available that make learning meaningful, promote concept development, and engage children in higher-level thinking and problem solving. For example, the International Children's Digital Library (http://www.childrenslibrary.org) provides access to children's books in diverse languages including Spanish, Arabic, Swahili, Chinese, Thai, Farsi, and many more. The digital format makes it possible for books to be projected onto large screens for whole-group reading or by an individual child to build on home language and culture. Imagine the pride on children's faces upon seeing their home language shown so much respect.

Other software is designed primarily for children to practice basic skills such as phonics or counting. A teacher might introduce a concept like rhyming in whole-group time, and then during center time, the children can play a rhyming game on a tablet or laptop. Choosing appropriate digital media is like choosing books or any other educational resource. Educators making decisions about technology need to carefully evaluate the philosophy and purpose as well as the developmental, individual, and cultural appropriateness of the resource. For example, providing bilingual software may be an excellent decision.

assistive technology A piece of equipment or product that is used to increase, maintain, or improve the functional capabilities of individuals with disabilities.

Use of assistive technology may be part of a child's IEP. Well-designed assistive technology can be valuable for children with and without disabilities.

Just as digital media has created limitless options for social interaction and information dissemination, the use of technology in classrooms has endless possibilities. These possibilities are achieved, however, only if intentional teachers make good choices about developmentally appropriate interactive media and teach children how to use these resources well. Interactions with media should be playful and creative, promoting exploration, problem-solving, pretend, physical activity as with Wii or Kinect, and social interaction. The key is for children and teachers to jointly engage with media. All experts in children's digital media agree on one major criterion—to the extent possible, children themselves should be in control of the medium (Donohue, 2015). The most innovative and effective technological devices and apps empower children to take charge of their learning (Bailey & Blagojevic, 2015).

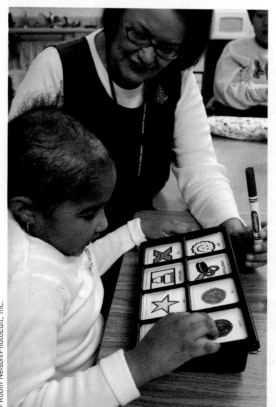

Assistive Technology for Children with Diverse Abilities

One of the most valuable uses of technology is that it can empower children with disabilities to participate more fully and successfully in inclusive classrooms. The Individuals with Disabilities Education Act (IDEA) defines **assistive technology** as "any item, piece of equipment, or product system whether acquired commercially off the shelf, modified, or customized, that is used to increase, maintain, or improve functional capabilities of individuals with disabilities."

Assistive technology incorporates a wide range of options designed for many different purposes, offering various benefits to children with special needs. Technology can be essential for successful inclusion by not only ensuring children access to a setting, but facilitating their participation and providing the supports they need (DEC & NAEYC, 2009).

For example, a child with cerebral palsy can use a device that supports him to stand at an easel or another device to help him grip a pencil. A girl with attention deficit disorder can use headphones at a computer to decrease distractions from the classroom. Assistive technologies such as these help children to function independently and support their inclusion in classrooms with their peers (Hooper & Umansky, 2010). Such technology is valuable for children without disabilities as well.

Many assistive technology devices are available, ranging from low-tech toys to complex communication systems (Heward, 2013). Children who lack the physical ability to write can use voice-activated computer software to express their ideas and feelings. Children who cannot speak can use communication boards that they touch with a hand, foot, or other body part to activate a voice that speaks for them. The options are considerable, depending on the creativity of individuals and the resources available.

If appropriate, the use of assistive technology will be part of a child's individual education plan (IEP). Teachers working in inclusive settings need to be prepared to use whatever technology is required to successfully include children with disabilities and special needs and help them achieve individualized learning goals.

 Check Your Understanding 9.6: Teaching with Digital Media

Revisiting the Case Study

. . . Ms. Hanson's Classroom

In this chapter, we provided a conceptual framework that enables teachers to build a repertoire of effective teaching strategies. We also cited research demonstrating that current practices in preschool and primary-grade classrooms could be improved to reflect what is known about effective teaching. At the outset, we visited Sally Hanson's kindergarten class, where she used various strategies to help the children achieve literacy goals. Having now explored the array of effective strategies that make up a teacher's repertoire, we can analyze what Sally was doing and why.

Sally's goal was for all of the children to make progress on some of the Common Core standards. Because the children have differing skill levels and prior knowledge, however, she adapted her teaching to match their needs. She used *encouragement, cueing,* and *questioning* as needed for different children. She provided *scaffolding* for Elena and Lucy, adapting her instruction to help them do tasks that they could not do independently. Homemade books and posted words helped several children to function with less of her direct support. Sally provided a more fixed form of *support* for Marguerite to focus her attention on the order of the letters in her name. Sally *activated prior knowledge* for Logan and Gabe and *added challenge* to extend their learning. She used *direct instruction* with Tommy, who was struggling to form the letter *T*. Any one of these strategies would have been less effective if used with every child.

Intentional teachers know the children in their classroom as well as their curriculum goals. They flexibly draw on their professional knowledge of teaching strategies to effectively promote children's learning and development. ■

9 Chapter Summary

- Effective teaching is a science, informed and guided by research. Teaching, however, is also an art because it requires vision, creativity, and decision making.

- The most effective teachers have a large repertoire of research-based teaching strategies, including acknowledging and encouraging, giving quality feedback, modeling, demonstrating, giving cues and hints, adding challenge, questioning, co-constructing learning, giving direct instruction, and scaffolding.

- Children learn best when teaching strategies build on their prior knowledge (make learning meaningful), build conceptual understanding, and promote higher-order thinking and problem solving.

- An intellectually engaging learning environment provides various contexts that offer different opportunities for learning and types of teacher–child interactions: individual interactions, whole-group meetings, small groups, center choice time, and opportunities for play.

- Teachers use play as a teaching strategy by taking on various roles—onlooker, stage manager, co-player, and play leader—to help children get involved and stay engaged in play situations.

- Digital media can be effective in supporting all children's learning and development. Assistive technology can enable children with and without disabilities to participate more fully and successfully in inclusive classrooms.

Key Terms

- acknowledging
- advance organizers
- apprenticeship
- assistive technology
- child-initiated experiences
- classification systems
- closed questions
- co-construction
- conceptual frameworks
- co-player
- demonstrating
- direct instruction
- encouragement
- effective teaching
- facilitating
- feedback loop
- graphic representation
- hypothesis generating and testing
- K-W-L
- learning strategy
- metacognitive activities
- modeling
- onlooker
- open-ended questions
- pedagogy
- planning
- play leader
- questioning
- reciprocal teaching
- reflection
- scaffolding
- scientific method
- stage manager
- supporting
- teacher-initiated experiences
- teaching strategy
- wait time

Demonstrate Your Learning

Click here to assess how well you've learned the content in this chapter.

Readings and Websites

Dombro, A. L., Jablon, J., & Stetson, C. (2011). *Powerful interactions: How to connect with children to extend their learning*. Washington, DC: National Association for the Education of Young Children.

Donohue, C. (Ed.). (2015). *Technology and digital media in the early years: Tools for teaching and learning*. New York: Routledge.

Epstein, A. S. (2014). *The intentional teacher: Choosing the best strategies for young children's learning* (Rev. ed.). Washington, DC: National Association for the Education of Young Children.

Jacobs, G., & Crowley, K. (2014). *Supporting students, meeting standards: Best practices for engaged learning in first, second, and third grades*. Washington, DC: National Association for the Education of Young Children.

Children's Technology Review

Edited by Dr. Warren Buckleitner, an expert on early education and technology, CTR is both a website and an annual e-book publication that provides detailed reviews of thousands of apps as well as reviews of new technological devices and their utility for young children.

Common Sense Media

Go to this website and click on "Best Apps and Games" for up-to-date reviews of apps by age group. The criteria these experts use to rate apps are useful lenses for teachers to use in selecting apps on their own. The organization also conducts and disseminates research on educational media.

National Center for Quality Teaching and Learning

Sponsored by the Office of Head Star, this Center's website provides videos of effective instructional practices, Webinars, written resources, and a library of visual supports and classroom activity suggestions based on the latest research.

TEC Center at Erikson Institute

On Erikson's Technology in Early Childhood website, you will find videos, webinars, and other resources on the most effective, current practices for using technology to teach young children.

10 Planning Effective Curriculum

Learning Outcomes

After studying this chapter, you should be able to:

10.1 Define curriculum.

10.2 Describe the components of an effective curriculum.

10.3 Explain how standards influence curriculum planning.

10.4 Evaluate how various approaches to curriculum planning engage children's interest and promote their learning.

10.5 Compare the focus and goals of various comprehensive curriculum models.

10.6 Apply content standards and child development knowledge to planning effective curriculum.

This is an exciting week at Ross Elementary School, a public school serving prekindergarten through fifth-grade students. All the classes are engaged in a school-wide project called *Career Explorations: What Do I Want to Be When I Grow Up?* The project is designed to help children achieve the following goals: learn about a variety of careers and occupations; build their self-concepts about the world of work; understand that what they are studying now is preparing them for their future careers; connect character and careers; and set high expectations and goals for themselves.

To begin the project, parents and community members are invited to spend about 30 minutes in each of the classrooms explaining their work. The younger children eagerly await their visits with a police officer, doctor, and veterinarian. The primary-grade classes are thrilled to meet a real pilot. Among their other visitors are a librarian, chef, author, and artist/illustrator. Prior to the visits, teachers prepare the students by asking them to come up with six good questions for the experts. Plus, the children ask the expert how they use what they learned in school in their job or in their everyday life—whether science, social studies, math, or any other subject. Most visitors are asked, "Why did you choose this job?" and "What is the best part of it?" Their answers cause the children to reflect on the type of character needed to perform each job and whether they are suited for it. For example, 5-year-old Maisie changes her mind about being a veterinarian when she realizes that the vet may be there when the dogs die. She decides to be an author instead.

Beyond the presentations by parents and community volunteers, children explore the world of potential careers via technology. Working in class sessions with their teachers or using individual time to explore on computers or tablets, they visit an interactive career website that has information, games, and apps related to about 100 different career options. For example, *Kids Search* allows them to click on their interests, such as sports, computers, and traveling, or their favorite school subject, perhaps music or geography, and learn how it applies to real jobs. The older children seek out the section devoted to unusual occupations such as aerial cinematographer, digital artist, forensic crime scene investigator, toy designer, highway worker, landscaper, language translator, or marine animal trainer. As children became more interested, they conduct more research and connect via e-mail with other career experts such as zookeeper, Army captain, scientist, secret service agent, inventor, professional soccer player, and even an astronaut.

After the information-gathering portion of the project, children create posters and write essays and poems addressing the question, *What do I want to be when I grow up?* that are displayed in the school hallway. There's also a career dress-up and hat day where everyone dresses as their favorite job. The project culminates with a poster and essay contest, voted on by the children in each class. The majority vote for the astronaut as favorite poster, which appears in Figure 10.1. ■

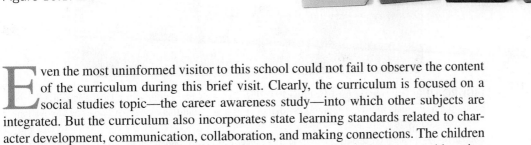

Even the most uninformed visitor to this school could not fail to observe the content of the curriculum during this brief visit. Clearly, the curriculum is focused on a social studies topic—the career awareness study—into which other subjects are integrated. But the curriculum also incorporates state learning standards related to character development, communication, collaboration, and making connections. The children are speaking and listening, and reading and writing about a topic of interest and learning

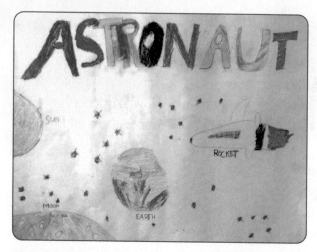

FIGURE 10.1 Career Awareness Poster The school-wide career awareness project engaged children's interests while also addressing several state learning standards.

new vocabulary words and concepts. Skills such as using technology, planning, and researching are also addressed. The theme is literally "played out" on dress-up day, where children use the language they are learning as well as their social skills. The curriculum is so rich and engaging that there are very few discipline problems; the school hums with children's happy voices, smiles, and laughter.

The goal of this chapter is to help you understand the complexity of planning effective curriculum and the intentional teacher's roles in working with curriculum. We begin by defining the term *curriculum* and describe ways of organizing curriculum plans. We discuss the early childhood profession's indicators of effective curriculum and the role of standards. Next, we describe some frequently used curriculum models. Finally, we present a model for planning curriculum that demonstrates the connection between discipline-based content and child development knowledge.

Defining Curriculum

Curriculum is usually thought of as the "what"—the content that children are learning—while teaching is the "how." In early childhood education, it is especially difficult to separate curriculum from teaching. There is no one agreed-on understanding of curriculum that is a comfortable fit for this diverse field. In this chapter, however, we present our vision of early childhood curriculum and its contributions to children's learning.

We begin by illustrating the relationship of curriculum to other aspects of the complex role of the teacher. Figure 10.2 is a visual representation of the elements of

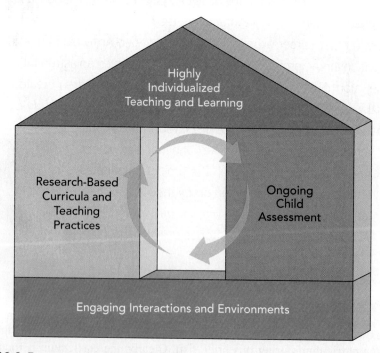

FIGURE 10.2 Framework for Effective Practice Choosing and implementing a strong curriculum is one of the four pillars of effective practice—depicted as a house in this model developed by The National Center on Quality Teaching and Learning.

Source: National Center on Quality Teaching and Learning, 2011, U.S. Department of Health and Human Services, Administration for Children and Families, Office of Head Start. http://eclkc.ohs.acf.hhs.gov/hslc.

everyday practice that foster children's learning and development, depicted as a house (National Center on Quality Teaching and Learning [NCQTL], 2011). The foundation of the building is engaging interactions with children that build positive relationships and create a caring community. The two pillars that support the structure are (1) choosing and implementing a strong curriculum, and (2) using regular assessment of children's skills. Each of these pillars supports the roof—individualized teaching strategies that ensure each child's progress.

Although in reality these structural components of practice are integrally connected, in this book we address each in a separate chapter. In Chapter 8, we describe the foundation of a caring community; Chapter 9 presents evidence-based teaching strategies; Chapter 11 discusses ongoing assessment of child progress; and in this chapter we describe curriculum content and planning.

What Is Curriculum?

Curriculum is a written plan that describes the goals for children's learning and development and the learning experiences, materials, and teaching strategies that are used to help children achieve those goals (NCQTL, 2011). The goals include the knowledge, skills, and dispositions (or attitudes and approaches toward learning) that we want children to achieve.

Curriculum content—*what* children are learning about—is vitally important. One of the strongest predictors of preschool children's later academic success is their general understanding of the world—what's happening in nature and what people do and say (Grissmer, Grimm, Aiyer, Murrah, & Steele, 2010). The achievement gap in our schools is now widely understood to be a knowledge gap that must be addressed if all children are to reach their full potential (Christodoulou, 2014). Moreover, young children *want* to learn. They are curious about their world and everyone and everything in it. As 4-year-old Ryan said when asked what he likes about preschool, "I learn stuff!"

The word *curriculum* is often used in relation to various models, approaches, or frameworks. Because these general terms are sometimes used interchangeably, we provide definitions and examples of each in the next sections.

> **curriculum** A written plan that describes the goals for children's learning and development, and the learning experiences, materials, and teaching strategies that are used to help children achieve those goals.

Curriculum Models, Approaches, and Frameworks

A **curriculum model** is a research-based, idealized version of what and how teaching and learning should occur. Widely used early childhood curriculum models include the High-Scope Curriculum, Creative Curriculum, Montessori method, and Bank Street, which are based on theories of child development and learning. To ensure **fidelity**, that is, faithful implementation of the curriculum model, developers typically provide professional development for teachers in how to implement the model.

A **curriculum approach** describes the main elements or direction of a program (Roopnarine & Johnson, 2013) and is less detailed than a model. For example, Reggio Emilia educators purposely call their work the Reggio Emilia *approach* and reject the word *model*. They do not see their work as a model to be imitated or adopted, but rather as a set of principles to be applied in various contexts with diverse children, families, and teachers (Edwards, Gandini, & Forman, 2012). Similarly, the project approach (discussed later in the chapter) is not a curriculum, but a method of engaging children with curriculum content.

Curriculum is sometimes defined as a framework; however, a **curriculum framework** is more precisely defined as a guide for designing or choosing a curriculum. For example, most state departments of education write curriculum frameworks that influence or determine which commercial curriculum packages school districts purchase. A state reading framework would include ways of grouping for and differentiating instruction and how much time should be devoted to language arts. A published curriculum that did not address the standards would not be used in that state.

> **curriculum model** A research-based, idealized version of what and how teaching and learning should occur.
>
> **fidelity** Faithful implementation of a curriculum model.
>
> **curriculum approach** Describes the main elements or direction of a program; is less detailed than a curriculum model.
>
> **curriculum framework** A guide for designing or choosing a curriculum.

Written Curriculum Plans

Different types of written plans can be used to guide instruction and meet the needs of specific groups of children. These include research-based curricula, teacher-developed and locally developed plans, and published curriculum resources.

Research-Based Curriculum   Current trends place increasing emphasis on formal, research-based curriculum in early childhood education. In an effort to increase accountability, federal laws require that public schools as well as Head Start programs use scientifically based curriculum. **Scientifically based curriculum**, also called *research-based*, derives from research evidence about what kinds of learning outcomes relate to later achievement and what types of teaching and learning experiences help children achieve those outcomes (National Institute for Literacy, n.d.).

scientifically based curriculum Derives from research evidence about what kinds of learning outcomes relate to later achievement and what types of teaching and learning experiences help children acquire those outcomes; also called research-based.

validated curriculum Curriculum that has been evaluated and its effectiveness demonstrated.

Validated curriculum is scientifically based curriculum that has been evaluated and has demonstrated its effectiveness in producing desired learning outcomes. A growing number of validated early literacy, mathematics, and social-emotional curricula have been developed for preschool and primary grades (Institute of Education Sciences, 2009). Despite the current emphasis on research-based curriculum, the early childhood field has a long history and comfort with teacher-developed and locally developed plans.

Teacher-Developed Plans   Because teachers know individual children best and are most familiar with the context in which children live, teachers often prepare their own curriculum plans. For example, Dominique and Tami teach a group of 2-year-olds. Their child care center has goals for the children such as fostering their language and helping them learn about the physical world. Each week, Dominique and Tami meet to prepare written plans that help them think in advance about their goals and the kinds of experiences and materials they need to prepare. Such advance planning frees them to focus their attention on the children. This week, the group is exploring water by playing in the water table, splashing in a wading pool outside, and blowing bubbles. Tami suggests putting ice cubes in the water table to encourage new words like *freezing*, *melting*, and *floating*. Dominique thinks of adding food coloring to create more interest and challenge.

Locally Developed Plans   In other cases, an agency such as a child care program or a school district develops a written plan. In these situations, a curriculum specialist or team of teachers develops a plan that is designed to achieve the program's goals for children. For example, Frankie Sanders's job is education leader for a chain of employer-supported child care centers. To ensure consistency across the 10 centers in the agency and meet the parents' goal that their children will be prepared for kindergarten, she develops, with input from the teachers, the curriculum based on the state early learning standards. The teachers will use the plan flexibly, but its existence helps keep them focused on important goals for children and prevents missed opportunities for learning.

Curriculum for very young children is often developed by teachers. Even for toddlers, having a curriculum plan helps teachers prepare engaging learning opportunities.

Published Curriculum   In the primary grades, more than 80% of teachers use some form of published curriculum (Shanahan, 2006). These decisions may be made at the state, district, or school level. In such situations, a committee, which usually includes teachers, reviews the available options and makes a decision about which curriculum resource to adopt. Periodically, state departments of education review new editions of primary-grade curricula in subject areas such as reading, mathematics, and science and identify a list of approved programs from which schools may choose.

The universal pre-K movement has led to greater involvement of public schools in preschool as well as calls for alignment of pre-K with K–12 curricula. As a result, all major publishers of K–12 curricula now publish curricula for 3- and 4-year-olds (Goffin & Washington, 2007). The greater availability of published curricula for preschoolers adds another factor to the curriculum decision-making process at that level (National Center on Quality Teaching and Learning, 2014).

Written curriculum plans, including those that are commercially published and used in primary grades, are by no means uniform. Some curricula provide an organizing structure and require a lot of initiative on the part of the teacher and children. Others provide goals, suggested activities to help children achieve those goals, and recommended teaching strategies. Usually, curriculum packages include teacher's guides with many options for learning experiences, strategies, and resources, from which teachers choose those that fit their goals for children. In other cases, the curriculum is more prescriptive, and less choice is available or expected (Beatty, 2011).

Advantages of Written Curriculum Plans Whereas critics of written plans believe that they limit teachers' creativity, decision making, and responsiveness to individual children, this is not necessarily true. One advantage of written curriculum plans is that they can be evaluated. Written plans make it possible for administrators, teachers, families, funders (such as taxpayers, families, or contributors), evaluators, and other interested parties to review, debate, and potentially revise the program's goals, expectations, and learning opportunities for children. Written plans can also be evaluated for their responsiveness to cultural and linguistic diversity and to community values.

Putting expectations for children in writing also means that teachers can evaluate whether they are developmentally appropriate. For instance, if the kindergarten curriculum calls for all children to learn to read, teachers who know the children can determine that this expectation is too high for most, but may be appropriate for some.

The Teacher's Role

Among teachers' most important responsibilities is planning and implementing intentional curriculum. With increasing calls for accountability and rising expectations, providing teachers with thoughtfully planned, research-based curriculum resources can free them to focus on adapting their teaching for individual children's abilities, needs, and interests. Instead of using all of their time preparing lessons and locating related resources, teachers can instead spend their valuable time observing and assessing children's learning and adapting their teaching. In cases such as these, the written plan serves as a scaffold for teachers, providing them with the support they need to go beyond and do more on their own (Kauffman, Johnson, Kardos, Liu, & Peske, 2002).

Curriculum plans do not take the place of teacher creativity or decision making. Early childhood leaders frequently use pejorative terms such as "curriculum in a box" or "canned curriculum" to describe any published curriculum resource (Frede & Ackerman, 2006; Jones & Nimmo, 1994). These terms imply that such products are by definition less desirable than teacher's "homemade" curriculum. Terms like "canned," "in-a-box," and "homemade" are analogous to food preparation. There was a time when all food preparation was from scratch, and the only good cooking was completely homemade. Some people still look back on this time with nostalgia. But in an age of microwave and prepared foods, even the best cooks don't make everything from scratch, such as homemade pasta. The analogy is offered not to justify commercial curricula, but to acknowledge that good teachers can produce high-quality educational experiences using either emergent curriculum or published curriculum resources. Similarly, published curriculum does not automatically produce poor teaching.

Research shows that no curriculum is teacher proof, and that teachers' qualifications as well as how they teach content matter (National Center for Children in Poverty [NCCP], 2007). Teacher-proof curriculum is the concept that curriculum can be designed to control for variations in teacher behaviors and professional preparation. The concept is talked about a lot, but it is a myth. There is no such thing as teacher-proof curriculum. Teachers matter, regardless of the type of curriculum they are given.

Rather than dichotomize curriculum as *either* completely teacher-planned and emerging from children's interests *or* commercially published and scripted, consider a more complex range of curriculum options. Table 10.1 describes a continuum of types of curricula available and the impact on the teacher's role. The primary-grade examples illustrate various approaches to teaching reading (Commeyras, 2007).

In Table 10.1, we suggest a way of conceptualizing curriculum plans while at the same time thinking about the teacher's role in relation to those plans. Two basic points should be clear: (1) in some cases, curriculum is developed very close to the classroom and is highly open-ended, flexible, and responsive to individual children. Teachers plan instruction to fit the needs of individual children and the class as a whole, responding and adapting to children's interests, motivation, and understanding. (2) In other cases, curriculum is developed at a distance from the classroom and is highly prescribed. Teachers pace instruction to ensure the curriculum scope and sequence is covered so that children are exposed to and learn concepts that prepare them for formal assessment and learning goals and expectations. In reality, curriculum is usually somewhere in between these two extremes.

TABLE 10.1 Continuum of Curriculum Approaches and the Teacher's Role

Rather than dichotomize curriculum as *either* emergent or scripted, this table describes a continuum of types of curriculum and the impact on teachers' roles.

Type of Preschool Curriculum	Type of Primary-Grade Curriculum	Teacher's Role in Curriculum Implementation (in collaboration with other teachers and families)
Emergent curriculum, e.g., Reggio Emilia approach, or curriculum based on children's interests	A teacher-developed literacy lesson	Identify developmental and learning goals. Know hierarchy of skills and knowledge in each curriculum area. Observe and assess children's interests and progress. Prepare the environment and obtain resources. Plan interest-based curriculum to help children achieve goals. Adapt teaching to help individuals make progress.
Curriculum model with linked assessment tools and professional development, e.g., Creative Curriculum, HighScope, Tools of the Mind	A guided reading lesson using leveled readers as defined by Fountas & Pinnell (1996).	Observe and assess children's interests and progress. Prepare the environment and plan learning experiences within the suggested framework. Use intentional teacher-guided and child-guided strategies. Adapt teaching to help individual children make progress toward identified goals.
Published curriculum with Teacher's Guide, e.g., Pearson's Opening World of Learning (OWL) or DLM Early Childhood Express	A basal reading program from a major publisher, e.g., Scott Foresman	Observe and assess children's interests and progress. Reference Teacher's Guide to identify scope and sequence. Make decisions about how to use or adapt suggested learning plans. Adapt teaching, including suggested scripts or prompts to help individuals make progress.
Prescribed/scripted curriculum, e.g., Open Court or Direct Instruction	A scripted lesson from Reading Mastery (formerly DISTAR)	Implement prescribed curriculum closely to ensure fidelity to program. Use program's assessment tools to track children's progress. Maintain children's attention through positive responses. Remain sensitive to children's responses and plan for needs. Adapt teaching to help children make progress.

Becoming an Intentional Teacher
Shaping Curriculum to Connect with Children's Needs and Interests

Here's What Happened I've been teaching first grade for 4 years now, and this year the district adopted a K–2 curriculum. It isn't bad, but I believe it's far more effective when used with flexibility and a close eye on what the children need and are ready for. Consequently, I made quite a few changes. My principal has agreed to my modifications as long as I can make a good case for them.

Last month we were working on measurement, and the kids wanted to measure their bean plants. Some of the plants were growing like gangbusters and others were not. We made a chart of the plants' heights, and the kids wanted to know why the plants varied so much in size. This seemed like the perfect time to get into the unit on plant growth, so I moved this lesson up in the curriculum sequence. We did several experiments on the effects of water and light, giving the children more experiences in measurement and recording results.

Here's What I Was Thinking When I switch the order of the curriculum plan, there's always a good reason. As in this case, I like to capitalize on what the children are engaged in right then and make the learning more meaningful, as I hoped to do with the bean plants. Some areas of the curriculum, such as phonological awareness or number, have a learning path that is sequenced, with one concept or skill building on another. For other things in the curriculum, the order doesn't matter so much. Before changing the order of topics substantially, I have to think about this. I have to consider whether the change would affect the way the children's learning proceeds and whether there are any related skills where the learning path would be negatively affected.

Besides changing the order of lessons in the packaged curriculum, I sometimes adjust the pace. I may see that we need a detour or to slow down to work on a skill the children must master before going on. In other cases, some children may be ready for more challenge and I want to keep them engaged. Sometimes it's just a few children who need these kinds of adaptations; sometimes it's the class as a whole.

Reflection In what other ways might this teacher adapt the curriculum plan for the group as a whole? What could the teacher do if a few children showed no interest in this topic? What problems might arise when a teacher changes the order or pace of a school-wide curriculum?

The complexity of the roles of teachers is only alluded to in Table 10.1. Nevertheless, even this cursory description reveals the relationship of curriculum and teaching. At one extreme, teachers have huge responsibilities and are expected to create almost everything while at the same time ensuring that children achieve important learning outcomes. At the other extreme, teachers' expertise is underestimated and undervalued, especially if principals or supervisors do not permit them to deviate from a prescribed script, a growing concern of early educators.

Regardless of the type of curriculum used by a program or school, teachers need to apply their professional expertise. For this reason, all along the continuum, we acknowledge that teachers must observe and assess children and adapt their teaching to help individuals make progress. That adaptation may take many forms, such as adjusting student groupings, daily schedules, the nature of teacher-child interactions, or the amount and kind of scaffolding provided. The feature *Becoming an Intentional Teacher: Shaping Curriculum to Connect with Children's Needs and Interests* describes one teacher's thinking as she uses the curriculum as a springboard to adapt plans for individual children. In general, curriculum should be selected or developed using the criteria that we describe in the next section.

✓ **Check Your Understanding 10.1:** Defining Curriculum

Components of Effective Curriculum

Now that we have established a common vocabulary with which to discuss curriculum, we turn to a discussion of indicators of effective curriculum. According to the position statement on curriculum, assessment, and program evaluation of NAEYC and the

National Association of Early Childhood Specialists in State Departments of Education (NAECS-SDE) (2003), programs should implement curriculum that is "thoughtfully planned; challenging, engaging, and developmentally appropriate; culturally and linguistically responsive; comprehensive and likely to promote positive outcomes for all young children" (p. 1). These guidelines set a high standard.

With the proliferation of options available today, making decisions about which curriculum to choose can be daunting. To assist with this task and to help professionals evaluate whether a specific curriculum is effective, the Office of Head Start (National Center on Quality Teaching and Learning, 2014) developed a consumers' guide. The evaluation criteria used in the guide are congruent with the NAEYC and NAECS-SDE (2003) position statement. Listed in Table 10.2, the criteria apply to planning, developing, and implementing effective curriculum.

In evaluating effective curriculum, it is important to consider the challenge of providing culturally and linguistically responsive curriculum. Several different curriculum

TABLE 10.2 Components of Effective Curriculum

The Head Start Bureau's standards for effective curriculum are congruent with the position statements of major early childhood organizations.

Component	Key Considerations
Based on current knowledge of child development	Are essential principles of how children develop and learn reflected in the curriculum philosophy and planned experiences?
Is evidence based	Has the curriculum been rigorously evaluated? Is there evidence of its effectiveness with diverse groups of children—in terms of ethnicity/race, language, and socioeconomic background?
Shows positive effects on child outcomes	Do children who experience the curriculum demonstrate positive learning and developmental outcomes
Is comprehensive across learning domains	Does the curriculum address "the whole child"—all domains of development (cognitive, social, emotional, and physical)—and all content areas such as literacy, mathematics, science, social studies, health and physical education, and the arts?
Covers learning domains in depth	Is there an organized scope and sequence in each of the learning domains that describes progressive steps and individual learning experiences? Does the curriculum build on prior learning and experiences?
Clearly defines specific developmentally appropriate, learning goals	Does the written plan address important goals such as the standards of the disciplines (mathematics or literacy)? Are the goals reasonable expectations for most children within the age range for which the curriculum is designed?
Includes well-designed learning experiences	Does the curriculum provide opportunities for children to be active and engaged both mentally and physically?
Emphasizes responsive teaching	Do learning experiences include both child-focused exploration and investigation and teacher-guided instruction? Is curriculum responsive to children's interests? Does it promote positive interactions among teachers and children?
Supports individualized instruction	Is the curriculum flexible enough for teachers to adapt to individual variation in children? Can the curriculum be adapted for children with special needs?
Is culturally and linguistically appropriate	Does the curriculum promote positive images of children's cultural identities and home languages and also recognize and build on their competence?
Includes ongoing assessment tools and strategies aligned with goals and activities	Is there support for teachers to analyze and use assessment results to adapt and individualize instruction, and help children to make continued progress?
Provides professional development	Are there initial and ongoing professional learning opportunities to ensure that teachers implement the curriculum with fidelity?
Supports family involvement	Are materials and strategies provided for families to extend children's learning at home?

Source: Based on *Preschool Curriculum Consumer Report,* by National Center on Quality Teaching and Learning, 2014, Washington, DC: U.S. Department of Health and Human Services, Office of Head Start, retrieved January 8, 2015, from http://eclkc.ohs.acf.hhs.gov/hslc/tta-system/teaching/practice/docs/curriculum-consumer-report.pdf.

Language Lens
Curriculum Approaches for Dual Language Learners

Schools today serve increasing numbers of dual language learners, with most speaking Spanish as a home language. Many of these children are growing up in homes below the poverty level and need excellent educational experiences to help close the achievement gap (Reardon, 2011). The following are brief descriptions of commonly used approaches for educating dual language learners:

- *English immersion.* All the instruction is in English throughout the child's school career. Students may receive assistance from specialists in English as a second language, but the classroom teacher uses English only.
- *English-Plus-Spanish.* Programs use English and Spanish in a wide range of formal and informal teaching and learning experiences. For example, instruction might be English, but teachers use Spanish to explain, clarify, or ask questions to assess children's understanding. Teacher–child conversations occur in both English and Spanish. Sometimes children are taught academic subjects in Spanish until their English is sufficiently developed.
- *Two-way dual immersion approach.* In these programs, half of the instruction takes place in English and the other half occurs in the second language, usually Spanish, but perhaps a Native American language or other language such as Mandarin. The goal is for *all* the children to become bilingual and biliterate and achieve academic standards.

Consider each of these approaches and how they might affect Antonia Zapeda, who is starting kindergarten:

Antonia's family came to the United States from Mexico 1 year ago and want very much for their children to succeed in school, but they are struggling to learn English themselves. Antonia's language development in Spanish is advanced; however, she tends to be shy in new situations, relying on her brothers to pave the way for her.

Put yourself in Antonia's shoes as she encounters school for the first time. What would her experience be like? How would she feel about her home language and family?

What will she be learning? How successful will she be in mastering curriculum content? The school district's curriculum approach for dual language learners like Antonia is likely to have a significant impact on her later success in school and life, depending on the type of approach used. For example, in an English immersion situation, she is likely to struggle both emotionally and academically despite her competence and knowledge in her home language. In fact, research finds that English immersion is not an effective approach. An English-Plus-Spanish program would be much more likely to build her confidence, competence, and English proficiency.

By contrast, consider what Antonia's experience might be like in a *two-way dual language* program:

In the morning, Ms. Cafritz does all of the teaching in English, and in the afternoon, Mr. Jimenez teaches in Spanish, or vice versa. All of Antonia's friends at school are learning both English and Spanish. Her new best friend, Joy, speaks English at home and has trouble with some of the sounds in Spanish, so Antonia helps her when they are on the playground. They laugh together about how funny each other sounds. During Spanish instruction time, Antonia knows most of the answers to the teacher's questions and often speaks up, while Joy listens more. After several months, Antonia becomes more confident in English, mixing languages on the playground with her friends but trying to answer the teacher's questions in English. Her parents are proud when she begins to read in English as well as Spanish. They are impressed that she is learning so many new Spanish words while also learning English.

In your career as a teacher, you are likely to work in situations with different policies regarding dual language learners. As you do, remember Antonia. Be intentional in your approach, considering children's best interests and respecting the languages and cultures of the families.

Source: Based on *Challenging Common Myths about Young English Language Learners: An Update to the Seminal 2008 Report,* by L. Espinosa, 2013, New York: Foundation for Child Development.

approaches are used to accommodate dual language learners (Espinosa, 2013). Read the *Language Lens: Curriculum Approaches for Dual Language Learners* feature and consider the potential strengths and weaknesses of each approach.

This brief examination of indicators of effective curriculum demonstrates the role of standards on current thinking about curriculum. The connections between learning standards and curriculum are becoming increasingly important and powerful in education, as we discuss in the next section.

 Check Your Understanding 10.2: Indicators of Effective Curriculum

The Role of Standards in Curriculum

One of the most influential trends in education today is the standards movement. By the beginning of the 21st century, each of the discipline-based content organizations had developed standards for what students should know and be able to do at various grade levels, which in turn influenced the content of state standards. Also highly significant was the development of K–12 Common Core standards for English language arts (reading, writing, speaking, and listening) and mathematics (Common Core State Standards Initiative, 2011a, 2011b). This initiative is designed to prepare all students for college and careers by bringing greater consistency and higher expectations to school curriculum across the country. By 2015, 44 states and the District of Columbia adopted the Common Core as the framework for their school standards.

learning standards Expectations for student learning.

content standards Describe what students should know and/or be able to do within a particular discipline such as math or science.

performance standards Describe the knowledge or skill that students should acquire by a particular point in their schooling, usually tied to grade or age level; also known as *benchmarks*.

What Are Standards?

Every state has standards for K–12 schools, 49 states have developed early learning standards for preschool, and many even have infant/toddler standards (Barnett, 2010). To understand the relevance and impact of the standards movement, it is important to understand the language of standards.

- **Learning standards** are expectations for student learning.
- **Content standards** describe what students should know and/or be able to do within a particular discipline such as math or science.
- **Performance standards**, or *benchmarks*, describe the knowledge or skill that students should acquire by a particular point in their schooling, usually tied to grade or age level.

How Do Standards Affect Curriculum?

A major portion of the day in primary grades is devoted to reading and writing instruction using published curriculum. Intentional teachers know that regardless of the source of the curriculum, their role is to adapt the plan for individual children.

Standards are not curriculum; nevertheless, they have a powerful influence over curriculum development. Today, curriculum is usually designed for the express purpose of helping children achieve standards (Rose, 2010). Similarly, assessment of learning is linked to achieving standards (Gewertz, 2014). Ideally, the goals of a curriculum include, but are not necessarily limited to, the relevant early learning standards (Bredekamp, 2009). As teachers implement curriculum, they should regularly assess children's learning and adapt the curriculum and their teaching to ensure that children make progress toward the standards. In such a scenario, standards *guide* but do not determine or standardize the curriculum (Bredekamp, 2009).

Because curriculum is influenced by standards, it is essential that standards be comprehensive and developmentally appropriate. Yet this may not be the case; an evaluation of state early learning standards found uneven attention to all areas of child development and learning (Scott-Little, 2011). For example, although every state addresses the areas of language and cognition, less consistent attention is paid to social-emotional development, physical health and development, and approaches toward learning such as curiosity and persistence. In some cases, standards may underestimate children's competence, such as the standard of counting only to 10 in kindergarten (National Research Council [NRC], 2009). In others, they overestimate it, such as expecting 4-year-olds to segment or blend phonemes, a task more appropriate for late kindergarten or first grade (Neuman & Roskos, 2005).

Alignment of Standards and Curriculum across Age Groups

A major trend in education is the move to align standards and curriculum from birth through age 8 and beyond. **Alignment** means that standards and curriculum are designed to progress as children get older so that they acquire the foundations of skills and knowledge to continue to achieve (Kauerz & Coffman, 2013). Alignment also reflects the fact that many curriculum areas such as mathematics are sequential, with later understandings built on earlier ones. Further, if done well, alignment should support developmentally appropriate practice because the expectations for an older age group may not be appropriate for younger children.

alignment Standards and curriculum progress as children get older so that they acquire the foundations of skills and knowledge to continue to achieve.

Even with alignment, in each of the broad age periods of early childhood—infants/toddlers, 3- through 5-year-olds, and primary grades—standards and the curriculum take a different form with different emphases. The NAEYC and NAECS/SDE (2003) position statement on curriculum, assessment, and evaluation describes how the *focus* of curriculum changes at each period of the early childhood age continuum.

Curriculum for Infants and Toddlers

A thoughtfully planned, challenging, and engaging curriculum for infants and toddlers focuses on, but is not limited to (Copple, Bredekamp, Koralek, & Charner, 2013a):

- Relationships that promote a sense of identity, security, and social interaction
- Language development
- Exploration of the physical world and play

Most states now have early learning guidelines for infants and toddlers. These standards are usually organized around developmental domains and by age spans such as young infants (0 to 8 months), mobile infants (about 6 to 18 months), and toddlers (16 to 36 months). In addition to developmental domains such as physical and social, the guidelines may include precursors of learning in subject areas such as literacy, science, and mathematics. An added feature of guidelines for very young children is that they usually include suggestions for what adults can do to promote children's ongoing progress, as illustrated in Figure 10.3, from Oklahoma's early learning guidelines for infants and toddlers.

Effective curriculum for babies and toddlers is highly individualized and responsive to children's needs and interests, while also extending their language and learning (Gonzalez-Mena & Eyer, 2014). High-quality programs for babies and toddlers use an **emergent curriculum** process, in which learning experiences are responsive to children's interests (Lally, Mangione, & Greenwald, 2006). Guidelines such as the one depicted in Figure 10.3 can assist teachers as they observe children, assess their capacities, and respond by enriching and extending the play or by adding novelty and complexity.

emergent curriculum Curriculum that develops in an educational environment in response to children's interests and needs rather than according to predeveloped plans.

Curriculum for Preschoolers

Thoughtfully planned curriculum for 3- through 5-year-olds addresses the development of the whole child, including physical well-being and motor development, social and emotional development, approaches to learning such as curiosity and persistence, language development, and cognition and general knowledge (NAEYC & NAECS/SDE, 2003). At the same time, the curriculum builds knowledge and skill in literacy, mathematics, science, social studies, and the visual and performing arts.

In preschool, integration across subject-matter areas is the primary planning strategy, although at times the curriculum will focus on one area such as math or early literacy (NAEYC, 2009). Play and projects are particularly valuable ways of bringing curriculum content to this age group. In fact, research shows that in content-rich classrooms with engaging social studies and science, children play in more complex and high-level ways (Nayfeld, Brenneman, & Gelman, 2009).

Standard—Pre-Writing: The child will explore different tools that will lead to making random marks, scribbles, and pictures

Young Infant: 0–8 months

The Baby Might: Begin to develop eye-hand coordination and intentional hand control.

The Baby Might for Example:	**The Teacher Can:**
Reach, grasp, and put objects in his/her mouth	Allow infant to grasp finger or other object while holding, feeding, or playing.
	Provide infant safe items, including color contrasting and assorted shapes and sizes, for the child to practice grasping, reaching, releasing, and grasping again. (For example: rattles, teething rings, etc.)
Bring hands together to middle of body, hold toys with both hands or pass objects from one hand to the other.	Place objects near infant, giving the infant opportunity to reach with either hand or both.

FIGURE 10.3 Example of Early Learning Guideline for Infants and Toddlers—Pre-Writing
Many states now have early learning guidelines for babies and toddlers which can be helpful if they are developmentally appropriate.

Source: From *Oklahoma Early Learning Guidelines for Infants, Toddlers, and Twos: Ages 0 through 36 Months,* no date, by Oklahoma Department of Human Services and Oklahoma Child Care Services, retrieved January 13, 2015, from http://www.okdhs.org/nr/rdonlyres/dcbc98d7-48b3-42c3-befe-c4abe6f486ac/0/1023_oklahomaearlylearningguide_occs036mo_04012011.pdf.

Almost every state has early learning standards for preschoolers, and most of these are based on the Head Start Child Development and Early Learning Framework (Head Start, 2010a), which is depicted in Figure 10.4. In addition to all the areas of development and learning listed the figure, the Head Start framework addresses English language development for dual language learners.

Each of the broad goals in the Head Start framework include examples of benchmarks that describe widely held expectations for children's development and learning. For example, a curriculum designed to help children achieve the early literacy goals would provide materials, time, and opportunities to engage in writing. For example, a preschool science curriculum about eggs hatching provides ample opportunities for children to draw and write in their journals about their observations of an incubator and chicks. An egg-hatching project also addresses one of the science standards: "Observes, describes, and discusses living things and natural processes" (Head Start, 2010a, p. 18). These are a few examples of how curriculum is designed to help children meet learning standards and how standards guide curriculum development.

Curriculum in Kindergarten and the Primary Grades In primary school, the curriculum focus shifts to knowledge and skills in the subject-matter areas. These include language, literacy, mathematics, science, social studies, health, physical education, and the visual and performing arts. Goals should continue to address the importance of social-emotional development and approaches to learning including motivation, curiosity, creativity, and initiative. Other essential non-content goals include self-regulation

▶ **Classroom Connection**

This video shows a first-grade classroom completing lessons from the English Language Arts curriculum. As you watch, think about what teachers do during the planning phase to present a coherent, organized curriculum. Consider the impact that standards have on the curriculum and other aspects of their teaching and children's learning experiences.

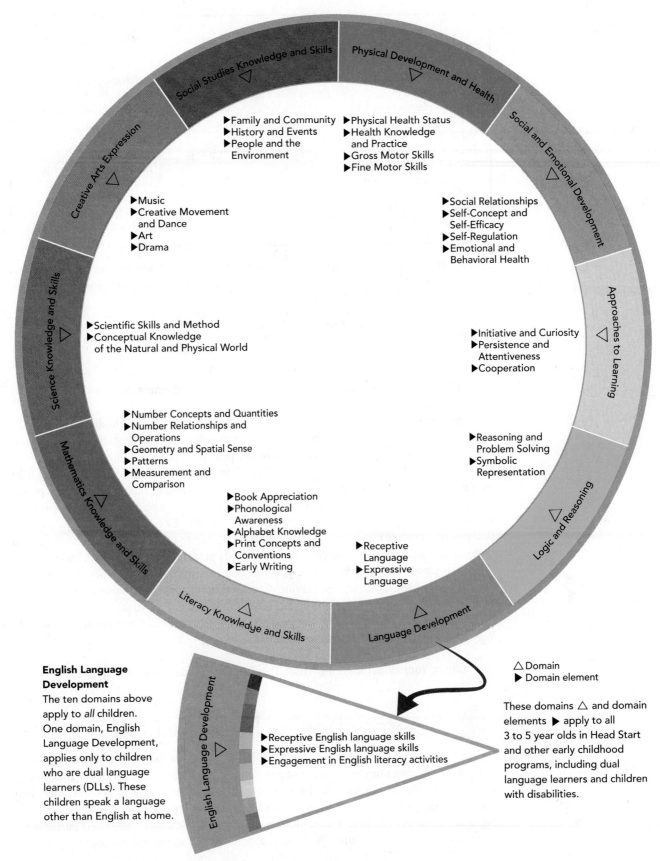

FIGURE 10.4 Head Start Child Development and Early Learning Framework The development and learning goals articulated in the Head Start Framework are congruent with preschool learning standards in many states.

Source: Head Start Child Development and Early Learning Framework: Promoting Positive Outcomes in Early Childhood Programs Serving Children 3–5 Years Old, Head Start, 2010, Washington, DC: U.S. Department of Health and Human Services.

Kindergartners	Grade 1 Students	Grade 2 Students
Use a combination of drawing, dictating, and writing to compose opinion pieces in which they tell a reader the topic or the name of the book they are writing about and state an opinion or preference about the topic or book (e.g., *My favorite book is . . .*).	Write opinion pieces in which they introduce the topic or name the book they are writing about, state an opinion, supply a reason for the opinion, and provide some sense of closure.	Write opinion pieces in which they introduce the topic or book they are writing about, state an opinion, supply reasons that support the opinion, use linking words (e.g., *because, and, also*) to connect opinion and reasons, and provide a concluding statement or section.

FIGURE 10.5 Example of Common Core English Language Arts Standard Common Core State Standards are not a curriculum. They are designed to promote consistent, high learning standards across states and alignment across grade levels.

Source: Common Core Standards for English Language Arts, by Common Core State Standards Initiative, 2011, Washington, DC: Council for Chief State School Officers and National Governors Association, retrieved January 13, 2015, from http://www.commoncorestandards.org. © Copyright 2010. National Governors Association Center for Best Practices and Council of Chief State School Officers. All rights reserved.

and executive function abilities such as problem solving, planning, focused attention, and persistence.

Challenging and engaging curriculum for this age group helps children develop and use oral and written language, mathematical and scientific thinking, and investigation skills across the disciplines. Curriculum in the primary grades should help children develop a sense of their own competence and confidence—Erikson's notion of mastery. The overarching goal of the primary grades, however, is learning to read. As described previously, many states now use the Common Core standards. Figure 10.5 is a Common Core writing standard for kindergarten through second grade. Consider how this standard is designed to promote alignment of curriculum across grade levels and how these standards build on the infant/toddler and preschool standards presented in Figures 10.3 and 10.4.

During your career as a teacher, you will confront many decisions about curriculum that will be related to standards. Having discussed indicators of effective curriculum and the role of standards, we now turn to a discussion of general approaches to planning curriculum. These approaches share the goal of making curriculum meaningful and interesting to children and, therefore, more effective.

 Check Your Understanding 10.3: The Role of Standards in Curriculum

 ## Approaches to Planning Curriculum

A plan helps guide teachers in making decisions about what, when, and how to teach. In other words, curriculum is not a set of random activities that children might find enjoyable; instead, the activities must be connected in a coherent way to content goals and teaching strategies (NAEYC & NAECS/SDE, 2003). There are several ways of organizing a coherent curriculum. These include emergent curriculum, integrated curriculum, thematic curriculum, webbing, the project approach, and scope and sequence.

Emergent Curriculum

Early childhood education has a strong tradition of emergent curriculum. According to this perspective, the focus should be on children, not on curriculum. Emergent curriculum is "what happens in an educational environment, not what is rationally planned to happen but what actually takes place" (Jones & Nimmo, 1994, p. 12). Advocates of emergent curriculum believe that children's interests and needs, rather than a predetermined plan, should determine what goes on in a classroom. They assume that a written curriculum plan may be too rigid to be responsive to children's individual and cultural variation.

Although emergent curriculum places considerable emphasis on following children's interests, it does not mean that nothing is planned and that everything emerges solely from the children. Elizabeth Jones, one of the foremost proponents of emergent curriculum, describes it as a *planning process* in which teachers work from children's interests, creating webs of possibilities that become tentative plans for experiences (Jones & Nimmo, 1994). What follows depends on children's responses, with the teacher observing what happens and evaluating and adjusting the plans as needed:

> Monday morning in John and Bettina's preschool class begins with a class meeting in which children talk about their weekend experiences.
>
> *Courtney:* "My dad took me and my cousins to a museum and we saw dinosaur bones. They were humongous."
>
> *Shauntae:* "I went there. My mom only came up to the dinosaur's knee."

Within a broad topic of study such as transportation, teachers build children's language and other skills. This child learns accurate terms for vehicles and motions in the context of an exciting real-life experience.

The discussion continues, with children becoming more animated by the minute. John and Bettina look at each other and smile. Their plan was to introduce a discussion about families. They don't think that dinosaurs are the best topic of study because young children can't grasp concepts of historical time and extinction. At the same time, the teachers recognize that young children are drawn to dinosaurs because they are "manageable monsters." They decide that with this much enthusiasm generated, following the children's interest could open up new possibilities.

> *Bettina:* "It looks like you want to learn more about dinosaurs. Let's start by thinking about everything we already know and writing down what we want to find out."

Later, Bettina and John meet to map out how a study of dinosaurs can help them meet the goals of their original plan. They decide that it will be a novel way to help children learn math concepts, including classification and measurement, and some of the "big ideas" in science such as change and living/nonliving things.

One of the goals of this chapter is to address the tendency in the field to view emergent curriculum and written curriculum as complete opposites. To be effective, curriculum planning needs to be intentional while at the same time responsive to children's interests and needs. In other words, goal-directed written curriculum must be flexible and adapt to children's interests and needs, and emergent curriculum must use children's interests to help them achieve important learning goals. Whichever approach a program chooses, to be effective, children's learning must benefit. One way to help children achieve important goals while also responding to their interests is to use an integrated curriculum, defined next.

▶ Classroom Connection

In this video, a preschool teacher's personal experience propels an in-depth curriculum study on the hospital. What do you observe about the teacher's planning and role in the study? How do children's interests and curiosity influence the decisions and what learning goals are being addressed?

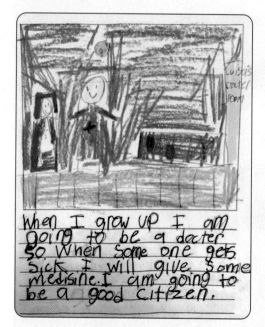

When I grow up I am going to be a dacter so when some one gets sick I will give some medisine. I am going to be a good citizen.

FIGURE 10.6 First-grader's Career Awareness Poster
This first-grader's career awareness poster illustrates how the project addressed several learning standards at the same time, including social studies, literacy, and art.

integrated curriculum
Addresses learning goals across multiple areas of curriculum at the same time.

thematic curriculum Way of integrating curriculum in which a broad topic of interest or a "big idea" provides the basis for making connections across learning goals.

Integrated Curriculum

A curriculum can be focused on one subject area such as mathematics or science, or it can be comprehensive, addressing all learning goals for a specified age or grade level. It may also focus on various developmental domains such as cognitive, physical, language, and social-emotional. **Integrated curriculum** addresses learning goals across multiple areas of curriculum at the same time (Fantuzzo, Gadsden, & McDermott, 2010). For example, it might address literacy and social-emotional goals within a single experience or lesson, such as when a preschool teacher reads books about feelings or making friends. A third-grade reading curriculum can include biographies of historical figures such as Harriet Tubman or Abraham Lincoln. In this way, children acquire knowledge of both history and literacy in the same experience.

Integrated curriculum is useful for several reasons. First, it helps address the challenge of covering many learning goals in a limited period of instructional time. Recall our visit to Ross Elementary School in the opening vignette of this chapter. The school-wide project integrated various subject areas such as social studies and literacy. The children engaged in reading and writing about a topic of interest—what they want to be when they grow up. At the same time, the children learned concepts about the world of work and the relevance of education, symbolic representation, and technological skills. Figure 10.6 shows how a first grader's career awareness poster demonstrates her achievement of these goals.

Integrated curriculum helps children make connections between skills and knowledge in various domains and decreases wasted time when no learning occurs. Integrated curriculum is usually organized around a topic of study or theme, which we discuss next.

Thematic Curriculum

Another advantage of integrated curriculum is that curriculum can be organized around topics (also called *units*) that children find interesting or engaging. This type of integrated curriculum is called a **thematic curriculum**, in which a broad topic of interest or a "big idea" provides the basis for making connections across learning goals. The life cycle of birds, for example, can be the organizing structure for several weeks or longer.

Thematic curriculum not only motivates children but also builds deeper conceptual understanding (Bransford, Brown, & Cocking, 2000). For example, a predictable interest of preschool children—building with blocks—provides a basis for integrating curriculum around the theme of construction. Children's interest in building structures becomes a vehicle for teaching concepts of physical science, such as how buildings stand up or how roofs are constructed to make enclosed spaces (Chalufour & Worth, 2004). A construction study helps children understand math concepts such as counting, measuring, and classification, which they will need when they decide how to balance a skyscraper. Children also learn vocabulary words related to building. Books, such as *Alphabet under Construction* by D. Fleming (2006), can bring in literacy skills. A neighborhood walk to see architecture, historical structures, or civic buildings addresses social studies standards.

For thematic curriculum to be effective, however, it is important that teachers select truly "big" ideas—concepts that are rich enough to be studied in depth and lead to new learning. Consider the difference between a unit on teddy bears and one on living bears—there is no comparison in terms of the concepts that can be explored. Yet children love teddy bears, so a teacher might be tempted to pursue that interest despite its shallow nature. How then do teachers decide whether a topic is sufficiently rich to pursue? One strategy is to use webbing, discussed next.

Webbing

In Chapter 9, we discussed teaching strategies that build children's understanding. These included using advance organizers and graphic representations such as K-W-L. **Webbing** is another example of a graphic organizer and also an effective planning tool that teachers use to organize curriculum content. For an example of a planning web based on a concept that children are learning, see the photo on page 338. Webbing serves many valuable functions in early childhood curriculum. It helps teachers organize their planning and acts as a conceptual organizer for children's thinking and learning. Webbing graphically represents the connections children make among facts and larger concepts.

webbing A planning tool that teachers and children create together to organize curriculum content.

Webbing is a useful tool for all of the ways of organizing curriculum discussed thus far: emergent, integrated, and thematic. But it is particularly valuable as a core component of the project approach, a topic to which we turn next.

The Project Approach

Engaging children in projects or investigations, a concept going as far back as John Dewey and an integral part of the Bank Street approach, continues to be one of the most popular activities among early childhood teachers and children (Helm, 2014; Helm & Katz, 2010). A **project** is an in-depth investigation of a topic worth learning more about, usually involving a small group but occasionally the whole class. The key feature of a project is that it is a research effort focused on finding answers to questions posed by the children, the teacher, or the teacher working with the children (Katz & Chard, 2000).

project An in-depth investigation of a topic worth learning more about, usually involving a small group, but occasionally the whole class.

Benefits of Projects The **project approach** is not a curriculum; rather it is a way of engaging children's minds with curriculum content and processes (Helm & Katz, 2010). In the project approach, teachers guide children through in-depth studies of real-world topics of interest to children. When teachers implement the project approach well, children can be highly motivated, feel actively involved in their own learning, and produce high-quality work (Helm, Beneke, & Steinheimer, 2007).

project approach Strategy for conceptually organizing curriculum by engaging children in in-depth investigation of a topic, focused on finding answers to questions posed by the children, the teacher, or the teacher working with children.

Well-planned and implemented projects engage children's interests and eagerness to learn, focus their attention, and are lots of fun. More important than simple enjoyment is the fact that projects or investigations are effective ways of integrating curriculum content and promoting children's understanding and thinking. Consider the following example of a project that integrates social studies and other areas of the curriculum, shared by Gail Joseph:

> One morning at the Active Learning Center, the organic milk delivery service mistakenly left chocolate milk. Before she notices, the teacher, Diane, asks Lamont and Sara to bring it to the kitchen because they have the "milk deliverer" job today. Lamont and Sara shriek as they carefully lift a glass bottle filled with chocolate milk out of the box. They head for the classroom to find Diane, but along the way they tell each child in the class about the yummy mistake, "We got chocolate. It's brown!"
>
> By the time they reach Diane, there is a line of children asking if they can have the chocolate milk with their snack. After Diane agrees, a more dedicated line of inquiry ensues. "Who left this for us?" "How do they make it brown?" "Does it cost more money?" "Can we have it again?" Diane sees that the milk mistake has the potential for an interesting project.
>
> At group time, Diane asks the children to list what they know about chocolate milk and what else they want to find out. She records their ideas on chart paper. During the next 2 weeks, the children learn a lot about chocolate milk. They write stories about the "chocolate mistake" in the writing center. They write letters to the milkman, thanking him for the mistake. They examine the price list to compare the cost of chocolate and plain milk. They make chocolate milk and graph how many children like chocolate versus plain milk (a skewed distribution for sure!).

The project approach is an excellent way to engage children's interest while meeting learning goals. Projects have three phases: cultivating children's interest, preparing for and conducting the investigation, and a culminating event.

The milk investigation goes into greater depth when the children take a field trip to the dairy and learn about "organic" milk, and why people might prefer it to nonorganic. They observe dairy cows and see milking machines. The children also learn how the milk is transported to the customers and why they use glass bottles. On the trip, they discover that the empty bottles are recycled, which prompts one of the children to propose a "recycler" job in the classroom. The children learn that not all people drink milk and the reasons why. They learn why regular milk is healthier than chocolate.

During the last week, the children decide to have a "chocolate milk celebration" with their families. They make invitations, propose and vote on the menu, and help develop displays documenting their field trip and what they've learned. They also offer a book signing for the class book they title *The Chocolate Mistake.*

At the end of the project, Diane revisits the chart created a few weeks ago and asks the children what they have learned. It is clear that they thoroughly enjoyed the project and learned a lot about chocolate milk. But they learned much more about social studies, including concepts about culture, health, community, the environment, diverse beliefs, production of goods and services, and economics, and they also engaged in reading, writing, mathematics, and science.

Phases of a Project   The previous example illustrates the phases of a project:

- *Phase 1: Beginning a project.* The beginning phase occurs when a possible topic emerges either from the children's interest or from an idea initiated by the teacher. During this phase, the class might create a K-W-L list or web of what they know and what they want to find out. At this stage in a project, the teacher needs to decide whether the topic is appropriate, practical, and consistent with the goals of the curriculum (Helm & Katz, 2010). In the scenario above, Diane recognizes that the children are very interested in the chocolate milk, although the interest was a fortuitous mistake. Other ways to discover or cultivate children's interest could be through bringing something into the classroom, such as a hen that a teacher brought in, or through a story. The key is to notice what children are interested in and to follow it. The next step is to develop a web of children's thoughts and questions about the topic.

- *Phase 2: Developing a project.* In this phase, children begin to think about and engage in an investigation of the topic. The questions children want answered should be broad enough to allow for substantive research. They might take a field trip as Diane's class did when they went to the dairy, hear from visiting experts to learn more about the topic, or conduct experiments.
- *Phase 3: A culminating event.* An event can be arranged that involves communicating, sharing, and presenting the work of the project to others. Diane's class held a chocolate milk celebration to share with their families all they had learned.

The project approach draws on and cultivates children's interests as it builds their motivation to learn. But more important, it engages children in thinking and problem solving, finding answers to their questions, and building content knowledge and skills. Research on the project approach finds that although it is challenging to implement, it is most effective when teachers have content knowledge themselves (David, 2008).

In previous sections, we described several well-known approaches to organizing curriculum content in early childhood settings. Next, we turn to a different approach, organizing curriculum sequentially.

Scope and Sequence

In recent years, research on early learning has provided greater insight about which skills are foundational in content areas such as reading and mathematics (National Council of Teachers of Mathematics, 2000, 2006; National Early Literacy Panel, 2008; National Institute of Child Health and Human Development, 2000; NRC, 2009). This knowledge is useful in developing the *scope* and *sequence* of a curriculum, especially in areas where sequential learning is particularly important. In mathematics, for example, children need to have a basic understanding about number before they can tackle number operations such as adding and subtracting. **Scope** refers to the particular focus of the curriculum at a given point in time; that is, how much of a larger content area will be addressed. **Sequence**, as the word implies, is the order in which knowledge and skills will be taught.

Scope and sequence are familiar terms in elementary education, where the curriculum is more closely linked to teachers' guides and textbook series for children, but is relatively new in the preschool world. Scope and sequence curriculum provides teachers with guidance about what to teach and when. For example, learning to read involves many different abilities that children acquire over time. A primary-grade reading curriculum identifies the expectations for children's reading achievement at each age level (the scope of what is to be learned) and suggests an order in which reading skills should be taught as well. However, because children's acquisition of skills and knowledge does not occur in a predetermined order and because many skills are acquired simultaneously, curriculum sequences should not be applied rigidly.

In the previous sections, we described several ways of planning curriculum: emergent, thematic, integrated, webbing, the project approach, and scope and sequence. Earlier, we described types of plans, from teacher developed to commercially published. All of these curriculum approaches can be used from preschool through primary grades. For example, although a second-grade teacher is highly likely to use a published reading program with a predetermined scope and sequence, she may also use an integrated science curriculum and the project approach to teaching social studies.

Having defined curriculum and explored indicators of effective curriculum, next we go deeper into the concept of curriculum models. In the following section, we describe well-known, though somewhat different, models of early childhood curriculum.

scope The particular focus of the curriculum at a given point in time; that is, how much of a larger content area will be taught.

sequence The order in which knowledge and skills will be taught.

✔ **Check Your Understanding 10.4:** Approaches to Planning Curriculum

Research-Based Early Childhood Curricula

Effective early childhood curriculum focuses on both the process of teaching and the content of what children are learning. Two types of early childhood curricula exist: (1) comprehensive models that address the whole child, and (2) focused curricula that target a content area such as science or a developmental domain such as social-emotional.

Comprehensive Curriculum

Several research-based comprehensive curriculum models are widely used—HighScope, Creative Curriculum, Core Knowledge, and Tools of the Mind. HighScope and Creative are the most widely used curriculum models in Head Start and public prekindergarten programs (Zill, Sorongon, Kim, Clark, & Woolverton, 2006). In this section, we discuss the key components of each of these models.

HighScope Curriculum
The HighScope curriculum was first developed by David Weikart and his colleagues, who launched the Perry Preschool Project in the early 1960s. HighScope is a *validated curriculum* because research has demonstrated that using it has lasting positive effects on children's long-term success in school and in life (Schweinhart, Barnes, & Weikart, 1993; Schweinhart et al., 2005; Schweinhart, Weikart, & Larner, 1986). An evaluation of the Georgia universal prekindergarten program found that the HighScope curriculum positively predicted children's language, literacy, math, and social skills in kindergarten (Henry et al., 2004).

> ▶ **Classroom Connection**
>
> Watch this video to see how teachers use the plan-do-review process, an essential element of the HighScope Curriculum that contributes to its effectiveness.
>
> http://www.youtube.com/watch?v=8X6ncsGkAxA&list=PL3176BCD80C15A22F

The HighScope curriculum reflects current research and provides guidance for teachers' scaffolding learning based on a constructivist view of child development (Epstein & Hohmann, 2012). The curriculum emphasizes that children need to be engaged in active learning—direct, hands-on experience with people, objects, events, and ideas. Teachers and children play an active role in the HighScope curriculum, functioning as partners in learning.

A key element of HighScope's curriculum is the *plan-do-review process* that begins with a small-group time during which children plan what they want to do during work time—that is, the area they plan to visit, the materials they will use, and the peers they will play with. The children then have a work time of about an hour for carrying out their plans. Following this period is another small-group time for children to review and recall with the teacher and the other children what they have done and learned. The HighScope curriculum is effective because it intentionally promotes use of higher-order thinking skills and executive function (Heckman, Pinto, & Savelyev, 2013). Many early childhood programs offer children choices during play time, but planning is more than making choices.

The content of the HighScope preschool curriculum consists of a set of 58 key developmental indicators that describe goals across 10 child-development areas. For example, there are two key indicators for the goal area "Approaches to Learning": (1) making and expressing choices, plans, and decisions, and (2) solving problems encountered in play. The key developmental indicators provide a framework for teachers to use as they plan activities and observe children's progress.

An online assessment system, the COR Advantage (Epstein, Marshall, & Gainsley, 2014), is available and is a key to effective implementation. It is an 8-point rating scale that can be used by any program serving infants through kindergarten. HighScope also provides a specific literacy component; a mathematics-focused curriculum, *Numbers Plus*; and an infant/toddler curriculum (Post, Hohmann, & Epstein, 2011). The HighScope Educational Research Foundation assumes that teachers need professional development to implement the curriculum at a high level.

Promoting Play

Involving Children in Planning Their Play

When children engage in planning, they use their minds actively. As they work out what they will do, children become initiators, problem solvers, and artists who make things happen and create meaning for themselves and others. To help children develop the ability to plan, consider the following strategies.

Make Planning a Regular Part of the Day If tasks that require planning become a routine classroom activity, children are more likely to improve their planning skills. To encourage children to plan tasks and events, it is useful to have a designated planning time, such as just before center time. You can plan with children in small groups, pairs, or individually, making sure each child gets to express his or her intentions. Children benefit from planning in small groups because the thoughts and elaborations of others often spark their own ideas. For example, notice how the teacher is talking with a group of 4- and 5-year-olds about what they will do during center time:

Jason: I'm going to make a race track in the block area.
Teacher: You made a track yesterday that stretched all the way to the bookshelf.
Mike: Me and him made it together. Today we're gonna make a longer one.
Teacher: It sounds like Jason and Mike are planning to work together today.
Darya: I'm going to work together, too.
Teacher: Who are you planning to work with?
Darya: With Mei Lin.
Mei Lin: Let's fill all the jars with water and make them sing.
Darya: First let's make the water orange. I'll mix the watercolors while you get the jars.
Teacher: Let me know when the jars are ready to sing. I want to hear them.

Encourage Children to Elaborate on Their Plans For inexperienced planners, try simple follow-up questions: "What will you need to do that?" Sometimes a comment about what the child is doing elicits more details than a question would. When the teacher observed 4-year-old Mitch's behavior, she said, "You're barking like a dog," to which Mitch replied, "I'm a lost dog and I want you to find me."

In your eagerness to assist younger children, don't overlook opportunities to promote older children's progress as planners as well. Encourage them to give specifics about where they will work, the materials they intend to use, the sequence of their activities, and the outcomes they expect to achieve. When Rachel announces she is going to draw the family dog, her teacher says, "I wonder how you're going to show the puppies growing inside Daisy." This comment encourages Rachel to consider such issues as size and spatial relationships as she plans her drawing.

Write Down Children's Plans Written plans communicate that children's ideas are valuable. Take dictation when children describe what they will do and how they will go about it. Encourage older 4-year-olds and kindergarten children to begin writing their own ideas. Documenting children's work through writing, drawing, and photography—which children and teachers can be involved in—helps young learners become more conscious of the process and value of planning. Children can also look back to their documented plans as they reflect on their experiences and compare their intentions with the actual outcomes.

Source: Based on "How Planning and Reflection Develop Young Children's Thinking Skills," by A. S. Epstein, 2003, *Young Children, 58*(5), pp. 28–36.

Play is an integral component of the HighScope curriculum. But what sets HighScope's approach apart, and what has been emulated by many other programs, is its emphasis on children planning their play. To see an example of this effective practice in action, read the feature titled *Promoting Play: Involving Children in Planning Their Play.*

Creative Curriculum   *Creative Curriculum System for Preschool*, developed by Diane Trister Dodge and her colleagues (2010), is a comprehensive curriculum addressing all areas of child development as well as literacy and mathematics. Revised in 2010, the curriculum identifies intentional teaching strategies and learning sequences, provides guidance for book discussions, and suggestions for "mighty minutes"—ways to support learning during transitions and routines. It includes integrated topics of study such as clothing, building, trees, and recycling. Creative Curriculum's goals are described in a developmental continuum that guides teachers' observations and assessment of children's progress and their planning, called GOLD™.

Creative Curriculum strongly emphasizes the learning environment, children's play, and child-initiated activity. The learning environment is the organizing framework of the curriculum. Teachers use children's involvement in centers in the classroom, including blocks, dramatic play, toys and games, art, library, discovery (science center), sand and water, music and movement, cooking, computers, and outdoors, to foster development and learning (Dodge et al., 2010).

The Creative Curriculum has evolved over the years, drawing on the work of several learning theorists, including Maslow, Erikson, Piaget, Vygotsky, and Gardner. These influences have contributed to the teacher's role as observing, reflecting, and responding to children in their environment in order to facilitate and scaffold their development and learning. The Creative Curriculum has a program for infants, toddlers, and twos (Dodge et al., 2010). Materials are available in English and Spanish.

Both HighScope and Creative Curriculum are child-centered curriculum models that focus on the goals as well as the process of how children learn and develop, reflecting a constructivist theoretical perspective. HighScope's distinguishing characteristic is the plan-do-review learning process, whereas Creative Curriculum emanates from the learning environment. Another approach to curriculum development focuses on content: what children should know and be able to do. This is the key component of the Core Knowledge curriculum.

Core Knowledge   In 1986, E. D. Hirsch Jr., professor at the University of Virginia, founded the Core Knowledge Foundation, a nonprofit organization that promotes greater excellence and fairness in education. The concept is based on the fact that successful education systems in other countries tend to teach a common core of knowledge to all children. The premise of Core Knowledge is that equal educational opportunity can be guaranteed for every child, including children from low-income families, only by explicitly identifying the competencies and knowledge that all children should acquire (Hirsch & Wiggins, 2009). Hirsch believes that the achievement gap in American schools is actually a result of inequity in exposure to curriculum content. This belief led the Core Knowledge Foundation to develop a curriculum sequence for prekindergarten through eighth grade.

The Core Knowledge preschool sequence (Core Knowledge Foundation, 2013) is designed to be a coherent, content- and language-rich curriculum that offers a progression of skills and knowledge across all areas of development as well as mathematical reasoning and number sense, orientation in time and space, scientific reasoning and the physical world, music, and visual arts.

These areas of skill and knowledge are similar to those included in the other curriculum models described previously. However, the Core Knowledge preschool sequence differs from those approaches in at least two ways:

- *Specificity regarding content.* The preschool sequence identifies specific experiences, knowledge, and skills for all children, including particular stories, fables, legends, nonfiction books, songs, rhymes, and poems. A month-by-month planning guide promotes the concept of a sequence of knowledge and competencies building on one another. Although the program is flexible, it does establish expectations that all the content and language should be incorporated in order to prepare children for the next level of curriculum.

- *Lack of specificity regarding pedagogy.* The Core Knowledge preschool sequence specifies *what* to teach, not *how* to teach. It does not advocate any particular approach, but rather a wide range of strategies that includes teacher-directed large- and small-group experiences as well as children's play and discovery learning.

Tools of the Mind Based on Vygotsky's sociocultural theory of learning, the Tools of the Mind curriculum is designed for preschool through second grade (Bodrova & Leong, 2007). The comprehensive curriculum provides teachers with ideas and strategies to support children's development of executive function, self-regulation, and academic skills. The curriculum emphasizes the teacher's role in scaffolding children's learning along with child-directed experiences and teacher-supported socio-dramatic play. Teachers engage in ongoing assessment of children's development to provide individualized scaffolding in which they increase or decrease their level of support depending on the degree to which children independently perform specific skills (Blair & Raver, 2014). The curriculum is designed to achieve two main, interrelated goals:

1. Development of foundational cognitive abilities that include self-regulation of behavior, emotions, and cognition; memory; and focused attention (Blair & Raver, 2014; Diamond & Lee, 2011).
2. Learning academic skills aligned with the Common Core standards, such as literacy, mathematics, and science (Blair & Raver, 2014).

The central element of Tools of the Mind is using high-level, mature socio-dramatic play to develop children's self-regulation. Such mature play includes a theme, roles with rules, language, and symbolic props such as using a rhythm stick standing for a magic wand.

To make play a more effective learning experience, teachers engage children in play planning before and even during the play. Children produce their own play plans, which include written and graphic descriptions of what the child intends to do during the play. By writing and/or drawing their plans, the children's writing abilities improve over time, a process called *scaffolded writing.* Children state their plans verbally, and the teacher draws lines on the paper for each spoken word. This serves as a short-term memory scaffold as children write and draw their plans. Over time, teachers help children make more complex plans, encouraging two or more children to plan together to build friendships and collaborative learning.

To enhance the quality of the play, teachers also provide children with relevant experiences that will inform their play. For example, a trip to the firehouse helps children learn about the roles and scenarios that occur there. But teachers do not leave the learning to chance. They ask the firefighters and other workers to demonstrate for children what they actually say before and after the fire bell goes off. Such experiences expand children's vocabulary and use of complex language, which they then practice during play.

One of the key aspects of Tools of the Mind is that it is based on the assumption that if children lack underlying cognitive skills such as self-regulation, trying to teach them academic skills is more difficult and inefficient. As a result, activities in Tools of the Mind promote these abilities simultaneously. Teachers organize the classroom routines to eliminate or minimize situations that tend to interfere with the development of self-regulation, such as long periods of whole-group instruction or lengthy waits for a turn.

Teachers embed self-regulation practice in all activities. For example, a preschool teacher might use props to scaffold children's practice of conversation turn-taking. After the teacher explains what to do with the props, Kesharia holds a cardboard ear to prompt her to listen, while Ashanti holds a cardboard mouth assigning him the role of speaker. Then, they switch roles.

Considerable research has been conducted on the effectiveness of Tools of the Mind. Read the *What Works: Using Tools of the Mind to Close the Achievement Gap* feature to learn the results of a rigorous evaluation of the curriculum and its lasting impact on kindergarten children's self-regulation and academic skills.

What Works

Using *Tools of the Mind* to Close the Achievement Gap

The Tools of the Mind curriculum is based on the premise that developing young children's executive functions—flexible thinking, focused attention, and working memory—and self-regulation of emotions and behavior is the key to their later academic success and social competence. Neuroscientists and child development researchers are finding strong support for the effectiveness of the curriculum in achieving this objective.

A well-designed evaluation study involving 29 schools, 79 kindergarten classrooms, and 759 children compared the impact of Tools of the Mind to the traditional curriculum. What was unique about this study was that it not only assessed children's executive function abilities and academic skills, but it also tested saliva samples to compare children's stress levels.

At every grade level, Tools of the Mind has the same overarching goals, but the teaching strategies and learning activities vary by age group. At the kindergarten level, children meet with teachers to create and implement weekly learning goals and plans. Instead of the strong emphasis on sociodramatic play that occurs in preschool, Tools of the Mind kindergartens use dramatization. Children "play out" the stories that they are learning to read, beginning with fairy tales and moving to chapter books, rather than pretending about everyday experiences. This intentional pretend play develops language, vocabulary, reading, and creativity. By contrast, the traditional, academically focused kindergarten classrooms typically allow only 10 to 15 minutes of play during free choice time and have no materials to support pretend play or connect it to literacy learning.

Another major difference between Tools of the Mind classrooms and the traditional kindergartens is the emphasis on peer interaction and teacher scaffolding to support higher-order thinking and promote social competence and intrinsic motivation. Children talk with teachers, question, and reflect on their own understanding. Mistakes become learning opportunities.

The study found that children in Tools of the Mind classrooms performed better on neurologically based executive function tasks such as focusing attention, ignoring distractions, and working memory. Children's reading, vocabulary, and mathematics also improved at the end of kindergarten and even better reading and vocabulary results were achieved in first grade. Significantly, these differences were greater in schools serving children in poverty.

One of the most encouraging aspects of the study is the neurobiological findings. Children in the Tools of the Mind kindergartens demonstrated lower levels of stress. Given the heightened academic demands of kindergarten resulting in increased stress for all children coupled with the toxic stress associated with poverty, lowering stress is essential. Children cannot learn effectively if they are anxious, worried, or unable to focus. This study demonstrates that through teacher-scaffolded support of executive function and self-regulation, Tools of the Mind can benefit children in high-poverty schools academically, physically, and emotionally, and has the potential to close the achievement gap.

Source: "Closing the Achievement Gap through Modification of Neurocognitive and Neuroendocrine Function: Results from a Cluster Randomized Controlled Trial of an Innovative Approach to the Education of Children in Kindergarten," by C. Blair and C. C. Raver, 2014, *PLoS ONE, 9*(11), e112393, doi:10.1371/journal.pone.0112393.

Focused Curriculum

The four curricula described previously are comprehensive, addressing the learning and development of the "whole child." Historically, in early childhood education, comprehensive curriculum has been essentially the only approach. Recently, however, there has been an explosion in curriculum development among researchers as well as publishers, much of which focuses on a single area such as literacy, mathematics, or social-emotional development. Perhaps because these curricula are targeted to relatively specific goals, several have been found to be more effective in improving children's outcomes than comprehensive approaches (Yoshikawa et al., 2013).

For example, in an effort to improve the quality and consistency of preschool classrooms, one large urban school district implemented a literacy curriculum, *Opening the World of Learning* (OWL) (Schickedanz & Dickinson, 2012), and a mathematics curriculum, *Building Blocks* (Clements & Sarama, 2007a), system-wide. An evaluation of the program found significant positive effects on children's literacy, language, early math, and executive function abilities (Weiland & Yoshikawa, 2011). The researchers concluded that using a uniform curriculum and intentional teaching strategies with professional development for teachers made the difference. The effects on executive function were especially important because these abilities are vital for later success.

Similarly, one study (Wilson, Dickinson, & Rowe, 2013) found that the OWL curriculum produced large improvements in literacy and language outcomes for all children but especially for dual language learners. These children performed nearly as well or better than native speakers at kindergarten entry, and reached national norms on standardized tests. Dual language learners in OWL classrooms performed better on expressive and receptive vocabulary than those who did not experience the curriculum.

The Reggio Emilia Approach

The internationally known schools of Reggio Emilia, Italy, have been called "the place theory and practice touch like the magic moment when night becomes day" (quoted in Bredekamp, 2008b, p. 49). Since the approach was first introduced in the United States, it has inspired teachers throughout the country and made major contributions to the knowledge base (Baldini, Cavallini, Moss, & Vecchi, 2012; Edwards, Gandini, & Forman, 2012).

The Schools of Reggio Emilia, Italy The city-run preschools and infant/toddler centers serving children from birth through age 6 originated as a movement among parents following World War II. Founder Loris Malaguzzi was inspired by the parents and committed himself to the continued evolution of the schools until his death in 1994.

Malaguzzi used the metaphor "the hundred languages of children" to connote the complex elements of the approach. First and foremost, the metaphor communicates the inherent genius of every child. Secondly, the "hundred languages" stand for the processes of children's learning as well as how they demonstrate it. In addition, "languages" are various forms of media—drawing, sculpting, writing, photography, video, music, dance, words, numbers, and so on—that are used to promote and display children's understanding of the world. By focusing attention on what children are capable of doing, the Reggio approach has made young children's amazing competence visible to the world.

The Reggio Emilia approach is not a curriculum, nor is it a model. It draws on several theories in an integrated fashion, but also goes beyond them. For example, a visitor to the schools would see evidence of Vygotskian sociocultural theory in the collaborative project work among small groups of children and also in the co-construction of knowledge between teachers and children. In addition, teachers and peers place themselves in zones of proximal development, continually scaffolding each other's learning. Teachers often act as provocateurs for children, deliberately creating what Piaget termed *disequilibrium*, to drive children's learning.

Principles and Values of the Reggio Emilia Approach The Reggio Emilia approach is based on a set of core values and principles (Gandini, 2008). However, the complexity and uniqueness of the approach cannot be reduced to a list of principles. Anyone attempting to implement a Reggio-inspired program should devote considerable study to the intricacies of its cultural origins and theoretical underpinnings (Rinaldi, 2006; Vecchi, 2010). A brief summary of its core components follows.

The Image of the Child The foundation of the Reggio Emilia approach is the *image of the child* as rich in potential, strong, and powerful with rights as a citizen and contributing member of the community. In Reggio, children with special rights (what Americans call *children with special needs*) are given precedence in school enrollment.

Children's Relationships and Interactions Malaguzzi (1993) called the approach "an education based on relationships." Teachers stay with the same group of children for 3 years and focus on reciprocal relationships among children (often in small groups) and the community.

The Reggio Emilia approach has inspired schools in the United States to rethink the environment and children's representational ability. What does this Reggio-inspired learning environment communicate about and to children?

© Erika Landorf-Kelly/Pearson Education

The Role of Parents Malaguzzi often said that the school has three protagonists without which schools do not exist: children, teachers, and parents. The active participation of parents is essential to the operation of the schools; parents are deeply involved in the learning activities of the children.

The Role of Space: An Amiable School The environments convey the message that "this is a place where adults have thought about the quality and the instructive power of space" (Gandini, 2008, p. 25). Americans are struck by the aesthetic beauty of the schools, but each element is designed for a purpose, such as to promote small-group interaction or display evidence of the process of children's learning.

Teachers and Children as Partners in Learning Although highly knowledgeable, teachers do not consider themselves experts who impart knowledge, but rather partners with children in the journey of discovery. They act as a resource to children, asking provocative questions, exploring children's thoughts and hypotheses, and learning along with them.

Curriculum as a Process of Inviting and Sustaining Learning There is no preset curriculum in Reggio schools. Teachers prepare a declaration of intent about possible learning experiences they will offer to children, but the curriculum emerges from children's interests in topics or questions and their desire to find out more or to solve a problem. However, teachers do have goals and plan in advance for possible directions the work will take. They listen carefully to children and regularly meet to discuss how to further children's involvement and deepen their understanding.

The Many Languages of Children Each school has a special teacher, called an *atelierista*, who is knowledgeable about the visual arts and works closely with the other teachers and children. Each preschool has an *atelier*, a specially equipped studio that contains a wide range of materials and resources that are used by children to represent their ideas and thinking and in projects.

In the United States, the Reggio Emilia approach is sometimes described as an art program. However, the Italians see the children's work as symbolic representation that is an integral part of learning. When children represent the same concept using different media, their understanding deepens. For example, drawing a horse in two dimensions conveys a partial concept of the animal. Constructing a three-dimensional model of a horse in clay requires thinking about how the horse stands up and how it runs.

Learning through Projects Short- and long-term projects are a major teaching and learning strategy in Reggio schools. Facilitated by teachers, children work in small groups on a topic or a problem of interest to them. Ideas for projects, great and small, grow out of children's experiences or chance encounters. An invitation from the town to design a theater curtain for the opera house led to a lengthy project that included generating artistic designs, making computer models, painting large murals, and exploring cloth production. The project culminated in a celebratory unveiling (Vecchi, 2002).

The Power of Documentation The growth in children's thinking that occurs through project work is captured in one of the most compelling and unique aspects of the approach: documentation. As a project proceeds, teachers and the *atelierista* carefully arrange and display transcripts of children's discussions, photographs of them at work, and representations of their thinking and learning in various media (drawings, sculptures, and constructions). These documentations can be interpreted as assessments, but they are more like records of the processes of learning and problem solving in groups of children. What goes on in children's minds cannot be seen, but documentation *makes learning visible* (Reggio Children & Project Zero, 2001). Documentation powerfully communicates the competence of children to parents, community members, and policy makers. Teachers use documentation to help children revisit their experiences, remember and analyze their thinking, and deepen their understanding.

Finally, play is a vital part of Reggio schools, although most written accounts or presentations about Reggio in the United States fail to talk about play. One must observe in the schools to see that play is as important to the Reggio Emilia approach as it is to developmentally appropriate practice.

The Influence of the Reggio Emilia Approach One of the most important contributions of Reggio Emilia is the deeper understanding of how *representation* not only reflects what children know and can do but also changes it (Vecchi, 2010). Other practices that have expanded theoretical understandings are the role projects and documentation can play in higher-order thinking and memory, and the effectiveness of collaboration and co-construction as teaching and learning strategies. Although these practices are not entirely new to the United States, the quality of implementation in Reggio is beyond what is usually seen here, with few exceptions.

The Reggio Emilia approach is deeply rooted in the sociocultural context of its region and town in Italy. Therefore, it cannot be successfully imitated in a different cultural milieu. Instead, many American educators learn from and with Reggio educators, and are inspired by the possibilities inherent in their work (Biddle & White, 2010; Scheinfeld, Haigh, & Scheinfeld, 2008).

> **▶ Classroom Connection**
>
> As you watch these children and teachers in a Reggio-inspired primary school, reflect on how curriculum planning and implementation occurs and how the principles of the Reggio approach are demonstrated.
>
> https://www.youtube.com/watch?v=kPmuYVn6AOg

Research on Preschool Curriculum

The irony of mandates for research-based curriculum is that there is a limited body of well-designed research on the comparative effectiveness of preschool curricula. However, as we see from the studies cited previously, this situation is changing (Bierman, 2011; Fantuzzo et al., 2010; Yoshikawa et al., 2013). In the last decade, expansion of publicly funded preschool has increased demand for accountability and newly developed curriculum. As a result, research has increased as well.

In the past, much of existing research compared the effectiveness of teacher-directed instruction and more child-initiated, play-oriented approaches to curriculum. In fact, these studies were more about particular teaching strategies than evaluations of curricula.

The federal government funded a large-scale study to evaluate the effectiveness of various preschool curricula (Preschool Curriculum Evaluation Research Consortium, 2008). After 6 years of work, however, this large-scale study raised more questions than it answered. The results demonstrated that children make learning gains in most well-designed curriculum approaches; however, there are very few significant differences *between* the curricula. Several lessons can be drawn from the mixed results of curriculum research to date. Ample evidence exists that a well-planned, research-based curriculum is an essential element of an effective early childhood program (Bierman, 2011; Bowman, Donovan, & Burns, 2001; Landry, 2005). The bottom line is that to be most effective, teachers need *both* good curriculum knowledge *and* understanding of child development (Cunningham & Davidson, 2007; Siraj-Blatchford, Muttock, Sylva, Gilden, & Bell, 2003). Teachers who have this knowledge possess the fundamental resources for planning and implementing an effective curriculum, which is described in the next section.

✓ **Check Your Understanding 10.5:** Research-based Curriculum

⬆ A Model for Planning Effective Curriculum

In this section, we present a general model for planning effective curriculum that applies across the full age range of early childhood as well as in diverse settings. This model for developing and planning curriculum is shown in Figure 10.7 (Bredekamp & Rosegrant,

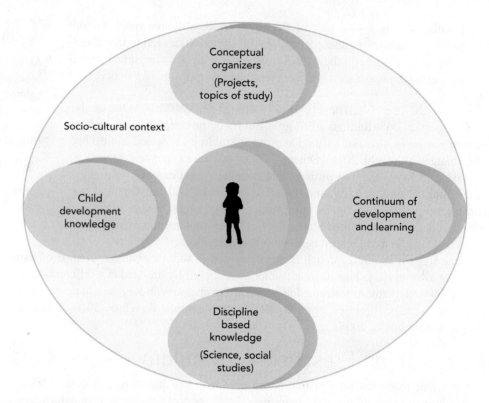

FIGURE 10.7 Child-Centered Curriculum Planning Model   This model depicts the major sources of knowledge that must be considered in planning an effective, child-centered curriculum.

Source: Based on "Reaching Individual Potentials through Transformational Curriculum," by T. Rosegrant and S. Bredekamp, 1992, pp. 66–73, in *Reaching Potentials: Appropriate Curriculum and Assessment for Young Children, Vol. 1,* edited by S. Bredekamp and T. Rosegrant, Washington, DC: NAEYC. Reprinted with permission from the National Association for the Education of Young Children (NAEYC). www.naeyc.org

1995; Rosegrant & Bredekamp, 1992). In the sections that follow, we briefly describe the sources of knowledge that are brought together in a coherent curriculum, and then we provide examples of applying the planning model in action. All good early childhood curriculum needs to focus first on children, as we discuss next.

The Child in the Sociocultural Context

Early childhood curriculum is often called *child centered*; accordingly, this model places the child at the center of curriculum planning. In a child-centered curriculum, learning is an interactive process—children change from exposure to the curriculum, and the curriculum changes in response to the learner's progress. Teachers involve children in planning by determining what they already know, as well as what they want and need to know. As curriculum is implemented, teachers continually assess children's abilities and interests and adapt the curriculum and teaching in response.

However, children do not grow and learn in isolation; in early childhood classrooms, children are part of a group. The group, in turn, exists in a larger context of a program or school, a community, state, and nation. Therefore, the model situates the child in a sociocultural context that influences what is included in the curriculum (Bronfenbrenner & Morris, 2006).

The cultural values of families and the community always influence curriculum decisions. For example, a faith-based private school may include religious study in its curriculum, whereas a public school may avoid reference to religious activity of any kind. Similarly, if the program serves a cultural community that values interdependence over independence, a focus on the individual child at the center of the curriculum may not be appropriate. Most likely, families would prefer a model with children as part of a cultural group as its focus.

In this model of curriculum planning, culture is not viewed as a separate source of curriculum, but rather as the context within which all curriculum decisions are made. Therefore, culture influences all of the aspects of curriculum planning, as we describe in the sections that follow on each dimension of the model.

Sources of Curriculum

As illustrated in Figure 10.7, curriculum planning draws on four sources:

1. *The content of the disciplines.* Much of the curriculum comes directly from the subject-matter disciplines: what children need to know and be able to do in science, mathematics, language arts, health, social studies, and the arts. Such content gives curriculum intellectual integrity; that is, it teaches accurate information about how the world works and how to obtain new knowledge. However, the content of the disciplines can be abstract and removed from children's direct experiences. Therefore, early childhood curriculum needs to be conceptually organized.

2. *Conceptual organizers.* We have already discussed several approaches to conceptually organizing curriculum. **Conceptual organizers** make content knowledge more meaningful, interesting, and understandable for young children. For example, children can learn key scientific concepts by planting a garden or studying the effects of light on shadows.

3. *Child development knowledge.* Knowledge of how young children develop and learn is critical in planning curriculum that will reach all children. Research on children's cognitive, language, social, emotional, and physical development allows teachers to anticipate whether curriculum goals will be achievable and challenging (that is, developmentally appropriate).

4. *Developmental/learning continuum.* A **developmental continuum** is a predictable, but not rigid, sequence of typical developmental accomplishments within age ranges (McAfee & Leong, 2011). A **learning continuum** (also called a **learning trajectory** or **learning path**) is similar to a developmental continuum but focuses on sequences of knowledge or skill in a content area such as mathematics or physical education, with each level more sophisticated than the last (Clements & Sarama, 2009; Sarama & Clements, 2009). (The terms *developmental continuum* and *learning trajectory* are often used interchangeably.) Research-based developmental and learning continua are the basis for planning the scope and sequence of a curriculum. Teachers use a continuum of development and learning in a curriculum area to determine when, where, and how to provide individual instruction and scaffolding.

conceptual organizer Ways of organizing curriculum, such as the project approach, that make content knowledge more meaningful, interesting, and understandable for children.

developmental continuum A predictable but not rigid sequence of typical developmental accomplishments within age ranges.

learning continuum, learning trajectory, or learning path Similar to a developmental continuum, but focuses on sequences of knowledge or skill in a content area.

This model illustrates how both content knowledge and child development knowledge must be considered in planning effective early childhood curriculum. If state learning standards are well done, they should play a role in guiding discipline content and the developmental/learning continua. The goal of this curriculum planning model is for early childhood programs from birth through age 8 to teach the *whole child*—the thinking, feeling, moving, expressing, creating, problem-solving, interacting human being.

Applying the Curriculum Model in Practice

In the following example, we see teachers putting the planning model into practice.

Jamie, who is hearing-impaired, is a 4-year-old in Kathleen and Cheryl's classroom. Before school started, Kathleen took a brief course in American Sign Language to ensure that she could communicate with him and to teach the other children some essential signs.

On the first day of school during morning meeting, the children become fascinated by Jamie and Kathleen's ability to talk with their hands and want to learn signs themselves. Jamie begins to feel comfortable and make friends. Kathleen and Cheryl soon observe the children's general fascination with the power of communicating with hands and launch a curriculum project about hands.

© Huntstock/Getty Images

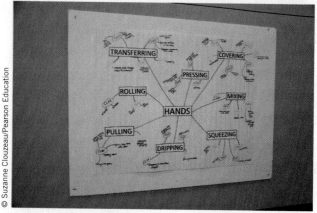

© Suzanne Clouzeau/Pearson Education

Intentional teachers can use children's interests to plan curriculum that meets many learning goals. One child's use of American Sign Language can lead to a project about hands as evident in this preschool concept web.

The project begins with the children generating a concept web about all the things that they do with their hands using materials such as sand and clay—squeezing, covering, pressing, and transferring (see photo on this page). The concept web introduces many new vocabulary words, as well as new signs to practice with Jamie. The teachers decide to set up two play areas to extend the interest in hands. One is a clothing store that includes props such as gloves and mittens of various colors and fabrics, as well as clothing that requires zipping, buttoning, or other fine-motor skills. They also set up the woodworking table for carpentry, which requires eye-hand coordination skills as well as creativity.

Angelique: I'm going to visit my grandma in Alaska, so I need a heavy coat and warm gloves.
Mitchell, the store manager: What kind?
Angelique, pointing to her hands: I want pink ones.
Mitchell sorts through his boxes and replies: We got red, green, and blue gloves. I got pink mittens. They'll be warm.
Angelique: No, they won't. Gloves are better. I'll look online.

Overhearing their conversation, Kathleen raises the question at group time—which is warmer, gloves or mittens? The children vote and make a graph of their answers. Most choose gloves. They begin an experiment to see which is actually warmer and explore the larger question of how people stay warm.

In large group, the children also enjoy fingerplays and songs such as "Where Is Thumbkin?" and "I Have a Family in My Hand." At small group time, Cheryl reads *The Mitten* to four children. Kathleen plays a math game with several others, challenging them to find everything in the classroom that comes in pairs like hands. After looking everywhere and feeling stumped, Ross shouts with glee, "Ear lobes!"

Over time, the study expands to investigate the type of jobs that require working with hands, some requiring strength and others finesse, such as musicians, painters, computer scientists, and many others.

This glimpse into Kathleen and Cheryl's classroom finds happy children, laughing and playing together. What is not immediately apparent, however, is the planning that has gone into the curriculum. To begin, the teachers identified the topic of hands as a conceptual organizer for several reasons. They had observed how much interest the children showed in Jamie's capacity to communicate with his hands and how they could do it, too. Thus, Jamie became a leader in the study. Also the teachers could predict that preschoolers are generally interested in their own bodies and mastering new skills, in this case zipping, tying, or keyboarding.

Next, the teachers considered how well the topic promotes child development. They agreed that it would provide opportunities to build cognitive processes such as matching, describing, organizing, and categorizing by size, color, and function (dress-up, carpentry, inclement weather). The topic promotes physical development such as practicing fine-motor skills and eye-hand coordination. The clothing store and other activities such as modelling with clay encourage social interaction and turn-taking as well as language development.

As for content knowledge, the study supported children's learning in every discipline area listed below.

Mathematics: counting by ones and twos; ordering by size (hands are different sizes); learning about patterns and relationships (clothing designs are in patterns; hands have similarities and differences)

Science: learning technology about tools and materials we use with our hands; physical properties (some gloves are water repellant, others are not); learning about body warmth

Language and literacy: vocabulary (nouns such as *fist, tight, loose,* and verbs such as *transfer, squeeze, grab, pinch*); books, songs, and fingerplays; nonverbal communication using gestures, body language, and signing

Social studies: economics of buying and selling clothing; cultural differences related to when and what kind of clothing to wear or what jobs people do

Health: gloves and clothing for protecting hands from injury and weather

The final element of the curriculum model is that teachers need to know the continuum of development and learning in each area so they can adapt the curriculum to accommodate individual differences in children. Although we raise this issue at the end of the chapter, it is the most important aspect of implementing an effective curriculum.

▶ **Classroom Connection**

As you observe this preschool classroom in Hawaii, note how all the elements of the child-centered curriculum planning model are used during their in-depth study of birds.

Adapting for Individual Differences

One important criterion in planning curriculum for every age group is the need to adapt for individual differences in children, including children with special needs. The *Including All Children: Individualized Education Plans: Meeting Individual Children's Needs* feature illustrates how a teacher uses her general curriculum goals as a framework.

Including All Children
Individualized Education Plans: Meeting Children's Individual Needs

In Kiara's Head Start classroom of 14 three-year olds, three of the children, Nikki, Devren, and Theo, have individualized education programs (IEPs). Once a month, Kiara meets with the children's IEP team to brainstorm ideas for addressing their individual goals in the context of the general curriculum and daily routines. First, the team considers the current IEP objectives for each child:

- *Nikki:* Improve fine motor skills such as holding writing instruments and cutting; identify colors and shapes; demonstrate one-to-one correspondence.
- *Devren:* Make requests; initiate interactions with his peers; watch, listen, and participate in large-group settings.
- *Theo:* Ask for help when needed; label objects; share toys and materials.

During the meeting, the team considers these individual goals along with the curriculum plan for the entire class, which at the moment is a unit on transportation. With this approach, the children with special needs do not need to be segregated from their peers for one-on-one direct instruction, and they have many opportunities to learn and practice skills. Because the curriculum topic is interesting and motivating for young children,

learning occurs more quickly for children with special needs.

To ensure sufficient practice opportunities throughout the day, Kiara prepares an activity matrix (page 340) that describes the opportunities to embed the children's learning goals in the daily schedule and lesson plans.

Classroom teachers and early childhood special educators can collaborate to create fun, meaningful curriculum that provides powerful motivation for children, both with and without special needs, to practice important skills throughout their day.

Effective curriculum planning involves several key steps, whether curriculum is locally developed or purchased. Curriculum should be selected or developed using the NAEYC key indicators. If teachers use a published program, they need to use it flexibly and adapt it in response to children's cues and information obtained from ongoing assessment. Similarly, if teachers develop their own curriculum plans, they need to ensure that those plans reflect the most current knowledge from the disciplines as well as research on child development and learning.

	Nikki	**Devren**	**Theo**
Arrival	Have Nikki "sign in" for the day holding an adaptive marker.	Have Devren be the greeter and ask children if they would like to sign in.	Have Theo be in charge of the dry erase markers for sign-in time so that he has opportunities to share.
Breakfast	Nikki will be the helper and set out plates and utensils at each place mat. She will help "take orders" by making a mark on her paper for each child who wants milk.	Serve some of Devren's favorite foods at mealtime to encourage him to verbalize his requests.	Provide Theo's favorite snack (crackers) inside a jar with a lid and wait for a request for help to open and provide the snack. Put the lid back on when done so that Theo will ask for help again.
Group time	Have Nikki hand out colored bus circle time props (she waits for peer to request a specific color). Sing modified version of "Wheels on the Bus," i.e., "The red bus goes . . ."	Have Devren collect circle time props, initiating to each peer, "___, please hand me your bus."	Have Theo label the color pattern of the bus props the children use: red, green, blue.
Free choice/ centers	Provide colored train tickets to correspond with colored train car. Ask Nikki to identify the colors of both.	Devren can be the engineer and request tickets from peers. At art, keep glitter in sight but out of reach and have Devren request to use it.	Have train engineer clothes available for dramatic play. Prompt Theo to ask for help with dressing.
Outdoor play	Take colored sidewalk chalk outside. Have Nikki draw and identify chalk colors.	Put teeter-totter and Sit and Spin (Devren's favorites) outside to increase initiations with peers.	Make a scavenger hunt of transportation objects outside. Have Theo label the items as he finds them.
Small group/ tables	Make trains out of shapes. Have Nikki identify different shapes.	Put peer in charge of highly preferred art material. Devren has to initiate with a peer to make a request.	Close lid on glue after each use. Prompt Theo to ask for help.
Story	Ask questions about the colors and shapes in the book.	Let Devren sit close to teacher and hold favorite item during story to increase engagement.	Ask object identification questions after reading the story to Theo.
Departure	Have children identify a shape and color before leaving to get their coats.	Have children identify a shape and color before leaving to get their coats.	Have children identify a shape and color before leaving to get their coats.

Teachers must take into account that children vary enormously on practically every dimension of development and learning. These differences are manifest in rates of development; prior experiences, which greatly influence learning; diverse cultural and linguistic backgrounds; and the existence of specific abilities and disabilities.

Understanding students' diverse needs is critical in implementing curriculum and adapting for individual variation. Regardless of the type of curriculum used, teachers need to apply their professional expertise. Adaptation may take many forms, such as adjusting the groupings, the time schedule, the nature of teacher-child interactions, or the amount and kind of scaffolding provided.

 Check Your Understanding 10.6: A Model for Planning Curriculum

Revisiting the Case Study

. . . Ross Elementary School

In this chapter, we described indicators of effective curriculum and provided a model for planning curriculum that draws on both content knowledge and knowledge of child development, while also placing children at the center of the planning process. At the outset, we saw a career awareness project involving all the children from pre-K to fifth grade. Now we can revisit the school and think about the project in relation to what we have learned about curriculum.

To implement the principles of effective curriculum, the teachers had thoughtfully planned what they wanted children to think about and learn during this study, and also considered the relevant learning standards. Although it was a school-wide project, the activities varied by grade level to be developmentally appropriate and connected to children's predictable interests.

Children were active and engaged as they interacted with the visiting experts, drew pictures for their posters, and wrote essays and poems. They used various forms of technology for research and to communicate with other experts. The project addressed several state learning goals including English language arts and social studies. But children also learned about other disciplines, new concepts, and vocabulary in their discussions with professionals—such as how they use math and science in their work. The study drew on children's interests, connected what they are learning in school to the real world, and motivated them to continue learning. This activity illustrates integrated curriculum in action, with children's experiences contributing to different areas of their development and learning at the same time.

With regard to the planning model used in this classroom, the curriculum is based in the discipline of social studies, but content is made accessible to children through a topic that fascinates them: their own lives and future careers. At the same time, children are learning the key concepts and tools of inquiry used by researchers. For example, they investigate using the Internet and interview experts. They enhance their language and literacy as they learn new words and concepts related to the occupations they are studying.

Child development knowledge is reflected in providing developmentally appropriate experiences, including play and book reading. At the same time, teachers assess each child's progress in relation to learning goals, and support their developing abilities, as when they evaluate their writing, observe their symbolic representation ability in drawings, and listen when they engage in conversation with experts and peers. As this school-wide project demonstrates, effective early childhood curriculum is not only motivating and engaging but also intellectually challenging for children and teachers. ■

10 Chapter Summary

- Curriculum is a written plan that describes the goals for children's learning and development, and the learning experiences, materials, and teaching strategies that are used to help children achieve those goals.

- Scientifically based curriculum derives from research evidence about what kinds of learning outcomes relate to later achievement and what types of teaching and learning experiences help children acquire those outcomes. Scientifically based curriculum has been evaluated, and it has demonstrated its effectiveness.

- Effective curriculum is thoughtfully planned; challenging, engaging, and developmentally appropriate; culturally and linguistically responsive; comprehensive; and likely to promote positive outcomes for all young children.

- Learning standards define what is to be taught and what kind of performance is expected. Standards provide guidance to curriculum developers and teachers about what and when to teach particular content.

- Effective approaches to planning early childhood curriculum include emergent curriculum, integrated curriculum, thematic curriculum, webbing, the project approach, and scope and sequence.

- Curriculum models are idealized versions of what and how teaching and learning should occur. Frequently used early childhood curriculum models include HighScope, Creative Curriculum, Core Knowledge, and Tools of the Mind. The Reggio Emilia Approach is a comprehensive approach to early childhood education and curriculum that has inspired programs throughout the world.

- A child-centered model of curriculum planning draws on content knowledge, conceptual organizers, knowledge of child development, and developmental and learning continua. All four dimensions of the model are influenced by sociocultural contexts.

Key Terms

- alignment
- conceptual organizers
- content standards
- curriculum
- curriculum approach
- curriculum framework

- curriculum model
- developmental continuum
- emergent curriculum
- fidelity
- integrated curriculum

- learning continuum, learning trajectory, or learning path
- learning standards
- performance standards
- project
- project approach

- scientifically based curriculum
- scope
- sequence
- thematic curriculum
- validated curriculum
- webbing

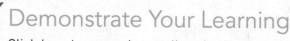

✓ Demonstrate Your Learning

Click here to assess how well you've learned the content in this chapter.

Readings and Websites

Helm, J. H. (2014). *Becoming young thinkers: Deep project work in the classroom.* New York: Teachers College Press.

Jacobs, G., & Crowley, K. (2014). *Supporting students, meeting standards: Best practices for engaged learning in first, second, and third grade.* Washington, DC: National Association for the Education of Young Children.

National Center on Quality Teaching and Learning. (2014). *Preschool curriculum consumer report.* Washington, DC: U.S. Department of Health and Human Services, Office of Head Start. Available online.

Wien, C. A. (2014). *The power of emergent curriculum: Stories from early childhood settings.* Washington, DC: National Association for the Education of Young Children.

Common Core State Standards Initiative

On this website, you will find complete copies of the Common Core standards, information about state adoption, answers to frequently asked questions and responses to commonly-held myths about the initiative.

Edutopia

Sponsored by the George Lucas Educational Foundation, Edutopia's website contains innovative resources to implement project-based learning, social and emotional learning, comprehensive assessment, integrated curriculum, and effective use of technology.

Project Approach

Visit this website, directed by Sylvia Chard, to find a wealth of resources for using the project approach including rich project examples for pre-K to grade 12, and downloadable study guides.

11 Assessing Children's Learning and Development

Learning Outcomes

After studying this chapter, you should be able to:

11.1 Define assessment literacy, and identify the terms teachers must know and use to become assessment literate.

11.2 Identify purposes for assessing young children.

11.3 Describe the most important indicators of effective assessment.

11.4 Apply effective strategies for gathering and recording evidence to support teaching, and children's learning and development.

11.5 Explain features of standardized testing, and evaluate its appropriate and inappropriate uses.

First-grade teacher Bonnie Kinsela begins every day with group meeting. She reads a story and calls on children to check their understanding of the story. Then she and her students discuss their day. Today, Bonnie makes short notes and a few checkmarks on her clipboard as the children transition to their literacy centers. She notes that Alexi and Nassim are able to answer questions about key details in the story. This is one of the Common Core standards, and Alexi and Nassim have not previously demonstrated this ability. She is pleased, and wonders if this is because they followed this particular story or if their listening comprehension has improved. She makes a note to observe this skill again.

Literacy block follows. Bonnie finds herself intensely engaged in a cycle of assessment and instruction, working with some children individually and others in small groups. Bonnie takes notes about each child as she observes one group writing a play. She uses her iPad to take photos of an in-progress poem that Ariana is writing and uploads it to the online assessment site. She'll use this example for Ariana's portfolio and share it at the next Professional Learning Community (PLC) meeting. The kindergarten teachers requested some examples of the kinds of creative writing the first graders are doing to help them adapt some experiences for their writing centers.

Approaching the listening center, Bonnie notices that Bella and Cal are arguing over the headphones. Cal becomes angry, unplugs the headphones and raises them over his head, about to throw them. He then lowers them and looks to Bonnie for assistance. She draws the children's attention to the visual schedule in the center and helps them plan when each has a turn. Both children calm down. Bonnie is grateful that their school district has integrated social-emotional assessment scales into ongoing assessment tools. Cal has made great progress in developing emotion regulation. The assessment scale has helped Bonnie understand the gains he has made, and how he can continue to grow in this regard. She jots a note that Cal looked for help in this situation and will enter this into his assessment profile later.

After listening to two groups in guided reading, Bonnie calls Devin and Egan over for reading. Devin has a diagnosis of autism spectrum disorder (ASD) and has an IEP to help meet his educational needs. Devin sounds out words and reads aloud well; however, he has trouble comprehending meaning in the text. Egan is his best friend, and Devin listens well and follows Egan's lead for reading time. Devin's annual IEP review meeting is approaching, and Bonnie wants to make certain that she has data that represents Devin's literacy progress and ongoing needs. Last week, she used a standardized tool to assess Devin's reading comprehension, but now she wants to assess his supported level of comprehension. She suspects that Devin will demonstrate better comprehension when reading high interest content with a supportive peer. Using her iPad, Connie tapes the session to share a clip with his parents before the IEP meeting. The boys have a great interactive reading session, and Devin demonstrates higher level skills than on the standardized measure. Both are valuable data, but Bonnie is pleased that she is able to show the higher edges of Devin's ability.

Over the course of the literacy block, children engage in rhyming games at the writing center. Although their interactions are sometimes silly, and need a bit of redirection to complete their work, Bonnie observes that the children produce some high-level rhyme and rhythmic patterns. Her poetry unit is scheduled for later in the year, but it seems as though the children's interest is peaked now. Bonnie decides to modify her teaching plan to capitalize on children's interests. ■

Bonnie's school is in their second year using the Common Core to guide instruction. This means making sure that all her first graders meet literacy standards for reading, writing, and language. Sometimes the work related to tracking and addressing the standards can seem overwhelming. However, Bonnie also finds that the structure helps her to ensure that she is addressing all of the important literacy needs of first graders.

Accurate assessment of children's learning and development is a vital component of effective practice in early childhood education. The profession has a long history of studying children, and observation of young children is essential to providing developmentally appropriate practice (Reifel, 2011). To a large extent, early childhood education has grown because research based on assessments of children's learning has found that high-quality programs have positive, lasting effects on children's development. The closely related field of early intervention is steeped in the necessity for and value of assessment for educating children with special needs. Recently, the school accountability movement and federal policies have placed considerable emphasis on testing in the early years of school to ensure that all children achieve reading and mathematics skills.

The goal of this chapter is to prepare you to achieve the most important purpose of assessment: to improve children's learning and development. If children are to benefit fully from early childhood programs, intentional teachers must know why, what, and how to assess. Like many other areas of education, assessment has its own—sometimes bewildering—vocabulary and jargon. We begin by helping you learn the language of assessment. Then we discuss four fundamental purposes of assessment and connect these to various tools and procedures. We present indicators of effective assessment. The chapter concludes with a discussion of appropriate and inappropriate uses of standardized tests and of program evaluation and accountability.

Learning the Language of Assessment

assessment The ongoing process of gathering evidence of children's learning and development for informed decisions about instructional practice.

evidence An outward sign or indication of children's learning, such as their response to a question or their solution to a problem.

formative assessment The process of gathering information about children and using it to plan effective and individualized instruction.

summative assessment Assessing student learning at the end of an educational experience to evaluate the effectiveness of the experience.

evaluation The process of making a judgment about assessment results; frequently considered the last step in assessment.

The first step in understanding and using assessment appropriately and accurately is for teachers to acquire the vocabulary of assessment. As teachers become more experienced in using various assessment methods and tools, their knowledge of assessment—their *assessment literacy*—grows and deepens. Broadly defined, **assessment** is the ongoing process of gathering evidence of children's learning and development, then organizing and interpreting the information in order to make informed decisions about instructional practice (McAfee, Leong, & Bodrova, 2015). **Evidence** is an outward sign or indication of children's learning, such as their response to a question or their solution to a problem (McAfee et al., 2015). Therefore, assessment involves using multiple sources of evidence systematically collected over time from which professionals make judgments about specific actions to take on behalf of children.

Each of the many different types of assessment has various implications for how and when it is conducted. We begin by describing assessment in its broadest terms—formative and summative—and then describe more specific types of assessments.

Formative and Summative Assessment

Formative assessment is the process of gathering information about children and using it to plan effective and individualized instruction (Riley-Ayers, 2014). The information obtained from formative assessment helps *form* the next steps in the teaching and learning process. In practice, formative assessment is so closely linked to teaching and curriculum that teachers may not even recognize it as assessment.

At the end of an educational experience, student progress is assessed using a **summative assessment**, which *sums up* or evaluates the effectiveness of an experience after it concludes. **Evaluation** is the process of making a judgment about assessment results and is frequently considered the last step in assessment (McAfee et al., 2015).

In a college English course, for example, the instructor's feedback on student essays is formative assessment, whereas the final exam is summative. Similarly, in a preschool or primary classroom, summative assessment may occur at the end of the year, when teachers compare their observations of children's progress to those they conducted when the school year began.

Informal and Formal Assessments

Assessments are often identified as informal or formal. **Informal assessment** refers to information that is gathered for teachers' use to make everyday classroom decisions or adjustments to teaching (McAfee et al., 2015). For instance, while reading a storybook to her preschool class, Abby Cosgrove observes that some children are listening intently while others are clearly uninterested and not following the story. She uses this informal observation of children's cues to quickly adapt her behavior. "This is a very long story," she says. "I will finish reading it during choice time if you want to hear the rest. Right now, let's all reach for the sky . . . turn around . . . touch the ground . . . and sit down." As Abby slowly gives each direction, all of the children become engaged in the physical movement and return their attention to her. "Now who has a song for us to sing?" In this example, Abby used her informal assessment of the children to adapt her teaching and engage them in the learning process.

A **formal assessment** is an assessment that follows a specific procedure and uses a specially designed instrument or tool. Teachers often use such assessments to report results to others. Formal assessments include structured child observations or assessments that produce specific scores. Formal assessment, in contrast to informal assessment, is also used to describe any method of gathering information that is standardized, a topic discussed later in this chapter.

Observation

Observation of children's behavior and development is the most important and frequently used assessment strategy. Observation can be used for both formative and summative evaluation, informal or formal. Teachers observe informally on a daily basis as part of the instructional process, and they also assess children formally using rigorously designed observational tools.

One type of formative assessment is **curriculum-embedded assessment**, which is based on teacher observation that is integrated into the curriculum and not conducted as a separate procedure. The teacher assesses the children while teaching using the classroom activity itself—for example, when a teacher listens to children describe their reasoning or watches them write. A similar formative assessment strategy is **play-based assessment**, in which the context for observing and interacting with children is the children's play.

Performance Assessment

Performance assessment, also known as **authentic assessment**, is used to determine what children know and can do from their demonstration of a skill or their creation of a product. Consider, for instance, how figure skaters are judged on the basis of their skating *performance*, not on whether they can draw a skating maneuver or write a description of how to do a triple axel.

For children, authentic assessment engages them in tasks that occur in real-life contexts, whether in the classroom or on the playground, or in situations as close as possible to that context. For example, to assess children's reading ability, a teacher listens

---

informal assessment
Gathering information for teacher's use to make everyday classroom decisions or adjustments to teaching.

> ▶ **Classroom Connection**
>
> How does this teacher use observation as a source of informal assessment in her classroom? What are some of the benefits of this type of observation?
>
> http://www.youtube.com/watch?v=RyQpNhaWzOc

formal assessment
Assessment that follows a specific procedure and uses a specially designed instrument or tool.

curriculum-embedded assessment Formative assessment that is integrated into the curriculum; this assessment does not occur as a separate procedure.

Accurate assessment is essential for effective practice. Intentional teachers observe children and gather information about their learning and development to plan curriculum and adapt their teaching.

© Monashee Frantz/OJO Images/Getty Images

play-based assessment
Similar to curriculum-embedded assessment, but the context for observing and interacting with children is the children's play.

performance assessment or **authentic assessment** Determines what children know and can do from their demonstration of a skill or their creation of a product.

to them read aloud rather than giving them a multiple-choice test. Assessments such as this, which call for a child to produce a response rather than select from a list of possible responses, are also called **alternative assessments** (Gullo, 2006).

Dynamic Assessment

Based on Vygotsky's concept of the zone of proximal development, **dynamic assessment** analyzes a child's performance not just in terms of what the child can do independently, as most assessment procedures require, but what the child can do with the assistance of a teacher or peer (McAfee et al., 2015). A teacher may provide prompts, cues, hints, or questions that elicit a child's response. Analyzing the amount and kind of assistance the child needs to perform a task provides information about the child's current level of understanding and skill and also guides the next steps in teaching (McAfee et al., 2015).

Standardized Testing

Many people hear the word *assessment* and automatically think of testing. **Standardized assessment** refers to the assessment of all children, using the same procedures and performing the same task under the same conditions. The thought behind standardizing procedures is that it leads to less biased and more objective results.

Although assessment is sometimes used as a synonym for testing, testing is only one part of the larger concept of assessment. **Testing** is a systematic procedure for evaluating a child's behavior and knowledge, which results in the assignment of a score (McAfee et al., 2015). Therefore, a test is a snapshot of a child's performance or knowledge that is administered to an individual or group under controlled conditions. Some tests are teacher developed, whereas others are developed by test publishing companies. Some, but not all, commercially published tests are standardized.

alternative assessments
Assessments that call for a child to produce a response rather than select from a list of possible responses.

dynamic assessment
Analyzes a child's performance not just in terms of what the child can do independently, but what the child can do with the assistance of a teacher or peer.

standardized assessment
Assessment of all children using the same procedures and performing the same task under the same conditions.

testing A systematic procedure for evaluating a child's behavior and knowledge that is then assigned a score.

standardized testing Uses prescribed methods for administering and scoring.

reliability The extent to which the results obtained from a test are accurate and consistent over time.

validity The degree to which an instrument measures what it purports to measure.

Standardized testing uses prescribed methods for administering and scoring and needs to meet technical standards for educational and psychological testing (American Educational Research Association, American Psychological Association & National Council on Measurement in Education, 2014). These standards are designed to ensure that tests have high levels of reliability and validity.

Reliability Reliability is the extent to which the results obtained from a test are accurate and consistent over time. A test is said to be reliable if the tool is likely to get the same or similar results when used by different people or on different days. To understand the concept of reliability, consider an example unrelated to education: measuring cooking ingredients. If a recipe calls for 1 cup of flour, even a beginning cook would reach for a standard, 8-ounce measuring cup. If one cook used a demitasse cup, another chose a giant-size coffee mug, and another filled a tea cup half full, the final results would vary considerably. The standard measuring cup, therefore, is reliable, whereas the other cup selections are not.

Validity Validity means that the instrument measures what it purports to measure. For example, a test designed to measure children's physical skills should not depend on children's ability to understand verbal directions; in such a case, the test is really a measure of the children's language.

In revisiting our cooking example, suppose we are trying to measure volume. There are a number of ways to measure volume, such as using a liquid measuring cup or an 8-ounce standard cup, which would yield an equally accurate amount of flour for a recipe. However, if we tried to measure flour with a yardstick, which is for measuring length, the results would be not only messy but also inaccurate and, therefore, lacking validity. If a standardized test lacks reliability or validity, the results it yields are meaningless.

Types of Standardized Tests

In addition to reliability and validity, standardized tests involve one of two ways of scoring. They may be either norm referenced or criterion referenced.

Criterion-Referenced Tests

Criterion-referenced tests compare a person's score to a predetermined level of performance. They are designed to measure how well an individual has learned a specific body of knowledge and skills (FairTest, 2007). Third-grade standardized achievement tests administered by state departments of education are criterion-referenced tests. The criterion for passing is a preset number of correct answers, which presumably represents how much a child has learned. Similarly, the SAT test is a criterion-referenced test, with different colleges setting the cut-off score, or criterion, needed for admission.

criterion-referenced tests Tests that compare a person's score to a predetermined level of performance.

Norm-Referenced Tests

By contrast, **norm-referenced tests** compare an individual's score to that of other test takers—who knows the most and who the least? Scores are reported by percentage rank, with half scoring above and half scoring below the midpoint or average (FairTest, 2007). Many school-administered tests are norm referenced. For example, screening or diagnostic tests used in the process of identifying children's special needs compare children's scores to that of other children to determine if their development is within the typical, or "normal," range.

norm-referenced tests Tests that compare an individual's score to that of other test takers.

Norm-referenced tests are developed by giving the tests to large numbers of children and comparing their scores. These tests result in a distribution of scores that look like a bell or **normal curve**, with most people scoring at the midrange and fewer scoring at the higher and lower ends. For example, on a hypothetical vocabulary test of 4-year-olds, most children's vocabulary might average about 1,200 words, whereas some know as many as 2,500 and others know as few as 400.

normal curve A distribution of scores that looks like a bell shape, with most people scoring at the midrange and fewer scoring at the higher and lower ends.

In administering a norm-referenced test, it is essential to know the characteristics of the group used to develop the norms—that is, the *norming group*. In the vocabulary test example, the norming group is the thousands of 4-year-olds whose vocabularies were measured. If a norm-referenced test is used, the administrator needs to consider the composition of the norming group in terms of gender, ethnicity, age, socioeconomic background, culture, language, and inclusion of children with disabilities. If the norming group differs a great deal from the group of children with whom the test will be used, the results may not be accurate or reliable. For example, if a vocabulary test designed to identify language delays were given to a child who is learning English, the result might indicate a learning problem where none actually exists.

The language of assessment is complex. In practice, terminology is often misused or used inconsistently. Teachers need to be clear about the concepts underlying the words; they need to become assessment literate. Now that we have established a common vocabulary with which to discuss assessment, in the next section we describe fundamental purposes of assessment.

 Check Your Understanding 11.1: Learning the Language of Assessment

Purposes of Assessment: Why Assess?

Before engaging in any form of assessment, teachers need to ask, "What is the purpose of the assessment?" The answer to this question determines all aspects of how the assessment will be conducted, including:

- Who is to be assessed
- What is to be measured and with what tool

Intentional, effective teaching begins with observing and getting to know each child.

• Who will conduct the assessment and when
• What technical requirements are needed for the assessment
• How the results will be interpreted and used.

In early childhood programs, the four basic purposes of assessment are (1) to improve teaching and learning, (2) to identify children with special learning or developmental needs, (3) to evaluate programs, and (4) to demonstrate accountability (National Research Council [NRC], 2008). First, we discuss these purposes and then we give examples of informal and formal assessments related to them.

Assessing to Improve Teaching and Learning

Effective teaching cannot occur without ongoing assessment. The first step in developmentally appropriate practice—*meeting the learner* or monitoring children's progress—requires assessment. Consider the following examples of how teachers use the information they gather to make decisions about curriculum planning and teaching:

In David Billings's preschool, a curriculum goal is for children to distinguish beginning and ending sounds in words. David first introduced these skills using poems and songs during whole-group time. But when he finds that a few children can't pick out the rhyming sounds, he plans to work with them in a small group, playing rhyming games and reading rhyming books.

Margie Wasky regularly monitors whether her second graders comprehend what they read. She discovers a few children who read very fast but can't accurately answer questions about the passages they read. She has these children read aloud to each other in pairs, and finds that reading more slowly with expression to a partner improves their understanding of what they've read.

FIGURE 11.1 Cycle of Assessment, Teaching, and Curriculum Effective curriculum and teaching depend on systematic, ongoing assessment as depicted in this cycle.

In these examples, we see that planning and adapting curriculum and teaching practices requires ongoing assessment. These teachers assessed children's learning by observing and documenting and then reflecting on and interpreting the information. They then adapted their teaching and planned curriculum accordingly. Although we address teaching, curriculum, and assessment in separate chapters in this book, in reality they are integrally connected. What happens in one area influences and is influenced by what happens in the others, as depicted in Figure 11.1.

Many schools now use systematic, ongoing assessment as an integral part of three-tiered-models of instruction such as Response to Intervention (RTI), which we describe in Chapter 5. In this framework, children's learning is assessed regularly and teaching adapted accordingly. Based on assessment data, some children receive more individualized instruction in reading and mathematics

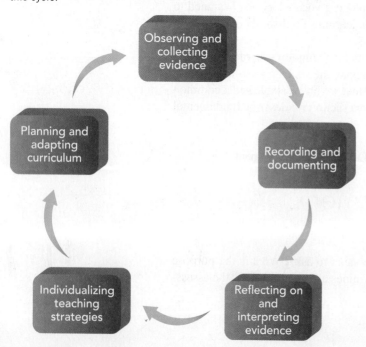

or other areas; a few children receive highly individualized interventions (National Center on Response to Intervention, 2010).

Teachers are the primary assessors as well as the primary audiences for classroom assessment. In early childhood, much classroom assessment is informal and performance based, relying heavily on teacher observations. Because everyday decisions are not high stakes, and easily corrected, classroom assessment does not need to meet technical standards for reliability and validity. For instance, if participation in the small group doesn't help Jamal's rhyming, David begins working with him one-on-one and also gives his mother some ideas to try at home.

Nevertheless, teacher observations and judgments can be unreliable, invalid, or biased. This is why teachers need to use many sources of information. They should observe children in different situations over time, rather than base their conclusions about children's ability on one encounter. Intentional teaching depends on accurate assessment tools, which we discuss later in this chapter.

Identifying Children with Special Learning or Developmental Needs

This purpose of assessment encompasses routine checks for vision, hearing, and immunization to ensure healthy development as well as identification of physical, cognitive, or emotional disabilities. Regular health checks by physicians beginning at birth may also uncover possible disabilities or special needs. Vision and hearing problems, if undetected, can have long-term consequences for children's learning, so early health screenings are essential for every child.

Because the benefits of early intervention are well established, professionals have an ethical as well as a legal responsibility to accurately identify young children with special needs and help them access appropriate services (Division for Early Childhood [DEC], 2014). These decisions have lasting consequences for individual children; therefore, the instruments used need to meet high standards of reliability and validity (McAfee et al., 2015). Screening and diagnostic tests are used as part of a two-step process of identifying children who may have disabilities or special learning or developmental needs.

Screening Screening tests, also called *developmental screening*, are administered to all children, usually in preschool or kindergarten, as the first step in a process to determine which children are at risk of a possible disability or learning problem. Teachers or other professionals administer these brief tests, which include general items on motor development, perception, language, and cognitive development. A screening test is like the toy screen used in a sandbox; most of the grains of sand will pass through readily, but a few will be left for closer inspection. In many preschools and child care programs, screening is a well-established rite of fall.

The process is not foolproof, and some children may have problems that go undetected. Therefore, teachers and families play a critical role in contributing information to the screening and identification process. Information on a child's functioning should be drawn from multiple sources, and include family members in the screening process (DEC, 2014). As teachers assess children's progress on a daily basis, they may obtain information that raises concerns that formal screening may confirm or deny. Those few children who do not pass the initial screening may or may not have a more serious condition; to make this determination, diagnostic testing is required (DEC, 2014).

Diagnostic Testing Diagnostic tests are designed to gather information to identify the specific learning or developmental delays a child may have and to plan educational interventions. The second part of the two-step process is a complete diagnostic evaluation designed to identify the child's areas of need and strength, to prepare individualized goals, and to plan activities and supports. Multiple sources of information are used, such

screening tests Tests administered to all children, usually in preschool or kindergarten, as the first step in a process to determine which children are at risk of a possible disability or learning problem; also called *developmental screening*.

diagnostic tests Tests designed to identify the specific learning or developmental problems a child has and to plan interventions; must be administered by specially trained professionals.

One of the most important purposes of assessment is screening and identification of children with special needs. To ensure accurate identification, valid and reliable measures must be used along with information from parents and teachers.

program evaluation The process of gathering information about a program's quality and effectiveness.

accountability The process of holding teachers, schools, or programs responsible for meeting a required level of performance.

as medical evaluations, standardized tests, and teacher and parent observations in authentic contexts. The Division for Early Childhood (2014) recommends that assessment for children with disabilities include input from the family and address children's interests, needs, and personal characteristics in addition to intellectual and ability testing. Furthermore, testing should be done in the child's dominant language, and should consider other cultural factors. Diagnostic tests require specialized training to administer and interpret and, therefore, are given by special educators, school psychologists, speech pathologists, or therapists.

For the first two purposes of assessment—to support learning and to identify children with special needs—the target of assessment is the individual child. Next we turn to assessment purposes, for which information is gathered on groups of children.

Evaluating Program Quality

Program evaluation is the process of gathering information about the quality of the classroom and its effects to determine whether the program is achieving its goals and objectives. Observational instruments that are often used to evaluate the quality of children's experiences are the Early Childhood Environment Rating Scales for infants, toddlers, preschoolers, and school-agers (Harms, Clifford, & Cryer, 2014) and the Classroom Assessment Scoring System for preschool through primary grades (Pianta, La Paro, & Hamre, 2008). These tools are frequently used to evaluate the quality of programs as part of state Quality Rating and Improvement Systems and in Head Start and public prekindergarten.

Some types of program evaluation such as licensing or accreditation may not require information about children's performance. Increasingly, however, program evaluation includes data on child outcomes—how well the group of children as a whole is achieving the goals of the program. The results of assessment for program evaluation are usually *aggregated*; that is, they are combined and reported as total scores for the group rather than scores attached to individual children.

The audience for program evaluation data is usually policy makers or funders who want to know if a program represents a cost-effective use of public or private dollars. Although stakeholders need accurate program evaluation data for future decision making, the stakes for such assessment are not as high as for accountability assessment.

Assessing for Accountability

Closely related to program evaluation, assessment for accountability is, by definition, high-stakes testing. **Accountability** is "holding teachers, schools, or programs responsible for meeting a required level of performance" (McAfee et al., 2015). Accountability requirements often specify what children should know and be able to do based on state learning standards. The audiences for accountability data include federal, state, and local policy makers; parents; and the general tax-paying public.

As we discussed earlier, the stakes attached to accountability testing are high. By the same token, holding schools accountable can lead to more attention being focused on the children who need it and on improvements in teaching and learning (Au, 2007). The standards for accuracy of accountability testing must be extremely rigorous because scores are attached to individuals—children and teachers—rather than a group or program (NRC, 2008).

TABLE 11.1 Matching Purpose and Types of Assessment

Each type of assessment has specific purposes. To yield accurate results, assessment tools must be used for the purposes for which they were developed.

Purpose	Types of Assessment	
	Formal	Informal
To monitor children's progress and make decisions about teaching and learning	Published, validated observation tools and rating scales; criterion-referenced achievement tests	Observation; interviews, analysis of work samples; teacher-made tests and procedures
To identify children who may have special needs	Developmental screening tests to be followed by diagnostic evaluation for those identified; norm-referenced standardized tests with high reliability and validity	Structured observation of behavior and performance by teachers; information from parents
Program evaluation	Validated observational measures of classroom quality and teacher-child interactions; criterion-referenced tests for samples of children keyed to program goals	Surveys of children, teachers, and parents; data collected by teachers from informal classroom assessments including observations, performance assessments, and portfolios
Accountability	Criterion-referenced standardized achievement tests	Data collected by teachers from informal classroom assessments including observations, performance assessments, and portfolios

Source: Adapted from "Reaching Potentials through Appropriate Assessment," by T. W. Hills, 1992, pp. 43–63, in *Reaching Potentials: Appropriate Curriculum and Assessment for Young Children, Vol. 1,* edited by S. Bredekamp and T. Rosegrant, Washington, DC: NAEYC. Reprinted with permission from the National Association for the Education of Young Children.

Connecting Purposes and Types of Assessment

As we have seen, each of the four purposes of assessment demands various types of tools and procedures. Given that all effective assessment decisions require multiple sources of information, teachers need to know which kinds of assessment are most effective for which purposes. Table 11.1 provides examples of formal and informal assessment tools appropriate for each of the four purposes.

Using assessment tools for the right purpose is essential. However, other important indicators of effective assessment exist and are described in the next section.

 Check Your Understanding 11.2: Purposes of Assessment: Why Assess?

 Indicators of Effective Assessment

According to the NAEYC and the National Association of Early Childhood Specialists in State Departments of Education (NAECS-SDE) (2003), ethical, appropriate, valid, and reliable assessment is a central part of early childhood education. These professional associations call for assessment methods that are "developmentally appropriate, culturally and linguistically responsive, tied to children's daily activities, supported by professional development for teachers, inclusive of families, and connected to beneficial purposes" (NAEYC & NAECS-SDE, 2003, p. 2). The ultimate goal of all early childhood assessment should be to benefit children by making sound decisions about teaching and learning, providing access to intervention services, or improving the quality of the program.

Early childhood professional organizations have established guidelines for effective assessment and evaluation (DEC, 2014; NAEYC & NAECS-SDE, 2003). Key indicators of effective assessment practices are described in Table 11.2. To implement these

TABLE 11.2 Effective Assessment Practices

Due to the power of assessment results to effect children's lives, assessment practices must meet high, professional standards, as described in this table.

Indicators	Key Considerations
Ethical principles guide assessment practices.	Children should never be denied opportunities or services on the basis of assessment findings. Decisions should never be made on the basis of a single assessment or test score. Assessment findings should remain confidential.
Assessment instruments are used for their intended purposes.	Using a measure for a different purpose inevitably invalidates the results. For example, a developmental screening test should be used as the first step in an identification process, not as a measure of kindergarten readiness.
Assessments are appropriate for the ages and other characteristics of children being assessed.	Assessments should be used with groups of children who are similar to the group with which the measure was validated in terms of age, culture, home language, socioeconomic status, and abilities and disabilities.
Assessment instruments comply with professional criteria for quality.	Test development must meet technical guidelines for reliability and validity.
What is assessed is developmentally and educationally significant.	Because assessment takes up considerable time and resources, it should address the important learning goals and standards that are emphasized in the curriculum.
Assessment evidence is used to understand and improve learning.	Good assessment teaches teachers about children. That knowledge needs to be put to use in individualizing instruction or adapting curriculum, or else both teachers' and children's time and effort are wasted.
Assessment evidence is gathered in realistic settings and situations that reflect children's actual performance.	This indicator calls for authentic performance assessment based on the results of teachers' observations of children in context, interviews, and on collections of children's work.
Assessments use multiple sources of evidence gathered over time.	Repeated, systematic observation, documentation, and other forms of criterion- or performance-based assessment are needed to accurately assess young children.
Screening is always linked to follow-up.	When screening or informal assessment indicates a possible problem, referral to specialists for diagnostic assessment follows. Labeling a child as having a disability is never made on the basis of a brief screening or one-time assessment.
Use of individually administered, norm-referenced tests is limited.	Formal, standardized, and norm-referenced tests are potentially beneficial as part of the process of identification and diagnosis of special needs.
Professionals and families are knowledgeable about assessment.	Teachers as well as families need to see assessment as a tool to improve outcomes for children. Parents are not simply audiences for assessment information; they are also important sources of information about children's capabilities at home and in the community that must be considered in the assessment process.

Source: Early Childhood Curriculum, Assessment, and Program Evaluation: Building an Effective, Accountable System in Programs for Children Birth through Age 8. Joint Position Statement, by National Association for the Education of Young Children and National Association of Early Childhood Specialists in State Departments of Education, 2003, Washington, DC: NAEYC. Reprinted with permission from the National Association for the Education of Young Children (NAEYC). www.naeyc.org.

assessment practices, teachers need to understand the implications for assessing very young children, English language learners, and children with special needs, discussed in the sections that follow.

Developmentally Appropriate Assessment

Most parents, grandparents, and teachers would agree with the statement "Young children are not good test takers." But why is this statement a truism? Sound assessment of young children is difficult for several reasons: (1) the nature of typical child development, (2) children's sensitivity to context, and (3) their lack of motivation, as well as (4) their inability to perform many of the tasks required by traditional assessments (McAfee et al., 2015). For assessment to be developmentally appropriate, each of these factors must be taken into consideration.

The Nature of Child Development Many of the characteristics of young children make it difficult to obtain trustworthy assessment information. Children's development is rapid, uneven, and embedded in their own cultural and linguistic contexts (McDevitt & Ormrod, 2013). For example, 2½-year-old Brian barely said a word at child care, and then one day he got so excited about the new set of trucks that he couldn't stop talking. Four-year-old Wyatt spent all day showing off how he could balance on one foot, but when his aunt arrived to pick him up, he refused to demonstrate this newly acquired skill.

Young children's development and learning is marked by spurts and plateaus (McAfee et al., 2015). For months, 6-year-old Aura struggled during language arts period. Then in March, she seemed to have an "ah-ha" moment. She stopped guessing at words she didn't know and began really reading for the first time. At times, children's development may even go backward. Three-year-old Jacob seemed to have thoroughly mastered the potty until his baby sister was born, and then he started having accidents every day.

Children's progress is also uneven across different developmental areas. Five-year-old Claudio has the vocabulary of an 8-year-old and can read at the second-grade level, but he struggles to regulate his emotions and is aggressive when frustrated. If only Claudio's reading skills were assessed, we would have a skewed picture of his school performance.

Language development is also a work in progress during early childhood. Most types of assessment require that children understand directions, know particular vocabulary words, or be understood by an adult, perhaps even a relative stranger. Limited language skills can easily interfere with obtaining an accurate picture of children's competence. Accurate assessment of children who are learning two languages raises an additional set of concerns, which are addressed later in this chapter.

Children's Sensitivity to Context The context where an assessment takes place, either informal or formal, can affect children's performance. Context includes the physical setting, whether in the classroom, home, or on the playground, and the social setting: one on one, small group, or whole group. A familiar context can serve to make children comfortable and relaxed and more likely to perform naturally and do their best.

A strange or unfamiliar context, either in terms of the place or the people, can be distracting or even stressful. Consider Hugo, who is a relatively fearless 5-year-old. Because Hugo usually charges into new situations head first, his mother wasn't concerned about taking him to the community center for kindergarten readiness testing. But Hugo became so interested in seeing the other children and examining the lines on the floor of the basketball court that he didn't attend at all to the tasks the kindergarten teacher asked of him.

Context influences not only children's attention to the assessment task but also their actual performance. Young children behave differently at home than at family child care, the child care center, or school. Five-year-old Dolly goes to gymnastics with her mom and can do backflips and cartwheels, but when her teacher at school asks her to skip, Dolly says, "I don't know how." Perhaps Dolly didn't demonstrate her advanced physical skills at school because she didn't want to be different from the other children, but maybe she just wasn't interested in skipping. Motivation, as well as context, is a big factor in obtaining accurate assessment of young children.

The Role of Motivation Assessment is "an adult's agenda" in which young children have little interest (Hills, 1992). Children are most likely to be motivated in situations that appeal to their interests and cultivate their curiosity, that offer choices of activities and materials, and that provide active involvement with other people. Many formal assessment procedures do not allow for any of these conditions. Young children are not interested in being assessed. They may be removed from the usual activity setting, and their movement, talk, and expression of feelings may be restricted (Hills, 1992).

As children get older, they can reflect more on their performance and competence and can be encouraged to do their best in an assessment situation (Hills, 1992). For some children, demonstrating their competence will become intrinsically motivating. In general, however, assessment results will be more accurate if children's interests are taken into consideration. For example, second-grader Laticia loves stories about horses and reads these stories with more expression than she does other books.

A final developmental constraint on assessment is children's ability to perform the tasks required. Group-administered, paper-and-pencil tests are especially challenging for children before third grade (NAEYC & NAECS/SDE, 2003). They may not be able to follow the directions and may not understand why the teacher can't help today. Some children may not have the fine-motor skill to fill in the bubble carefully or may generally operate at a slower pace than the others.

Characteristics of Developmentally Appropriate Assessment Even a cursory discussion of typical child development characteristics leads to the conclusion that the younger the child, the more difficult it is to obtain accurate assessment (Mindes & Jung, 2015). Therefore, assessment can be considered developmentally appropriate when it:

- draws on multiple sources of evidence, especially observations by teachers and parents who can observe children's performance in various contexts over time.
- occurs in a variety of situations representing children's typical range of activities, in the regular classroom or at home.
- makes children feel comfortable, which means that they are assessed by familiar adults, or that parents or other known adults can stay with them.
- accommodates children's rapid developmental changes. This doesn't mean that assessment consumes other important teaching and learning experiences, but rather that it occurs frequently but is embedded in children's ongoing experiences.
- engages children's interest and is within their range of ability. For example, instead of requiring a child to circle the picture of four kittens, the item requires the child to count four toy plastic kittens, one for each of her friends.

Culturally and Linguistically Responsive Assessment

Developmentally appropriate assessment must be culturally and linguistically responsive (Ritchie & Willer, 2008a). One of the biggest challenges is serving the needs of dual language learners because, to some extent, all assessments of children are fundamentally measures of language ability (Espinosa, 2010a). Children's ability to demonstrate their learning depends a great deal on their language capacity, both to understand the demands of the task and to respond either to a teacher's question or a written test. Although the role of language in assessment is relevant for all children, it is of special concern for children whose home language is not English.

In many instances, the only way to get a fully accurate picture of children's learning is to assess them in their home language. But even if valid and reliable assessment tools were available in multiple languages, which they are not, such assessments are not a foolproof solution. All languages,

Accurate assessment of children whose home language is not English is difficult. Standardized tests are often not reliable. How can teachers get accurate information about the abilities of English language learners?

© John Lund/Marc Romanelli/Blend Images/Getty Images

including English, have dialects, so translations do not always solve the problem. A child from Mexico and one from Peru may not understand the same Spanish translation of a test. Nonetheless, children should be assessed in their dominant language (usually home language for young children) and in other languages they are learning, Often their language competence is found in the combination of their capacity in each language (Atkins-Burnett, Bandel, & Aikens, 2012; DEC, 2014).

Determining whether a child is sufficiently proficient in English for accurate testing is also difficult. Academic language used in schools is quite different from the conversational language children use on a daily basis. Linguists estimate that it takes 4 to 7 years to acquire proficiency in academic English (Garcia, 2005). A child may speak English well on the playground or in casual conversation, yet struggle with the language of an assessment. Because of this, it is especially important to include families in assessment of dual language learners. Some research suggests that parents are often more reliable reporters of their children's vocabulary learning than are teachers (Vagh, Pan, & Marcella-Martinez, 2009). The importance of linguistically appropriate assessment is illustrated in the *Language Lens: Involving Parents in Assessment of Dual Language Learners* feature.

Language Lens

Involving Parents in Assessment of Dual Language Learners

The only way to obtain an accurate, meaningful assessment of dual language learners' competence is to draw on many different sources of information. Teachers' observations and conversations with children are invaluable, but information gleaned from families is essential in determining dual language learners' proficiency in each language.

Most parents are good judges of their children's language ability, but many teachers are unsure of how to efficiently obtain the needed information. Following are interview questions for teachers to ask of parents to effectively involve parents in assessing their child's language. The interview would need to be conducted in the parents' home language or translated for them. Here are some of the important questions to include:

1. What name do you use for your child? How did you decide to give your child this name? Does this name have a particular meaning or translation?
2. What language(s) do you use to talk to your child? Who else does your child spend time with and what language do they use?
3. Tell me your opinion about how well your child speaks each language. (The same questions would be asked about the home language and English.)
   (0) My child cannot speak (e.g., Spanish, Tagalog, etc.), has a few words or phrases, but cannot produce sentences (e.g., "I want cookies"). My child understands only a few words.
   (1) My child cannot speak _____, has a few words or phrases, but understands the general idea of what is being said.
   (2) My child has limited proficiency in _____ with grammatical errors, has limited vocabulary,

but understands the general idea of what is being said.
   (3) My child has good proficiency in _____ with some grammatical errors, has some social and school vocabulary, and understands most of what is said.
   (4) My child has native-like proficiency in _____ with few grammatical errors, has good vocabulary, and understands most of what is said.
4. How much does your child use each language?
   (0) Never speaks (e.g., Spanish, Tagalog, English, etc.), never hears it.
   (1) Never speaks _____, hears it very little.
   (2) Speaks _____ a little, hears it sometimes.
   (3) Speaks _____ sometimes, hears it most of the time.
   (4) Speaks _____ all of the time, hears it all of the time.

Of course, there is much more teachers need to learn from parents about their children, such as their interests, routines, cultural preferences, and much more. But conducting an interview such as one described here, whether during a home visit before the school year begins or in writing, is an essential first step in getting to know a child who is learning more than one language and becoming the best possible teacher for that child.

Source: Based on "How Can Teachers and Parents Help Young Children Become (and Stay) Bilingual" by P. O. Tabors and L. M. López, 2005, pp. 14–16, and "Assessment of English Language Learners: Challenges and Strategies" by V. F. Gutiérrez-Clellen, 2005, pp. 47–51, both in *Head Start Bulletin: English Language Learners, Vol. 78*, Washington, DC: Head Start Bureau, Administration on Children, Youth and Families, U.S. Department of Health and Human Services.

Accurate assessment of dual language learners poses difficult challenges for teachers and educational leaders (Atkins-Burnett et al., 2012). Children's language and prior knowledge are closely tied to their culture, yet assessment materials do not take into account culturally influenced variations in knowledge and skills. For example, a language assessment may ask children to identify items that are unique to U.S. culture, such as a hamburger. Inclusion of many such culturally biased items in a measure biases the outcome for individual children and misrepresents their abilities. High-stakes standardized testing is particularly problematic, as the following examples demonstrate.

Children's learning is a product of their experiences, which occur in cultural contexts. For example, a standardized test asks where to find a lion, and 4-year-old Omari replies, "In the park." His answer, accurate in his native Kenya, is marked incorrect because the correct answer in the test manual is "in the zoo." Such cultural influences exist within the United States as well. Consider a test item that asks children to point to a picture of a *swamp*. Imagine the blank stares of children living in New York City or rural Nebraska when presented with such a request, compared to the nodding heads of those from parts of Florida or Louisiana. Omari's experience and its consequences are powerful reminders not only of the importance of using linguistically appropriate assessment tools but also the risks of high-stakes testing.

Individually Appropriate Assessment for Children with Special Needs

Young children with disabilities or special needs face a lifetime of being assessed. Federal laws govern how, when, and under what conditions children with disabilities are to be assessed and how assessment information should be used by teachers in implementing individualized education plans and individualized family service plans. Furthermore, the Council for Exceptional Children's Division for Early Childhood (2014) has established recommended practices for screening, establishing eligibility for special education services, individualized planning, monitoring child progress, and assessing child outcomes for reporting. Ensuring that assessments are *individually appropriate* for all children may require accommodations or modifications to the tools or procedures used.

accommodations Changes in assessment procedures, materials, or setting to eliminate barriers related to the child's disability that might keep children from demonstrating their full capabilities.

Accommodations are changes in assessment procedures, materials, or setting to eliminate barriers related to the child's disability that might keep children from demonstrating their full capabilities (Pretzel, Hiemenz, & Kahng, 2009). Assessments for children with disabilities should take child's age and developmental level into account (DEC, 2014). A child with a physical disability might be allowed to answer questions verbally rather than in writing. A child with attention deficit/hyperactivity disorder (ADHD) might be given more time or allowed to take a test in a separate place away from distractions.

modifications Changes in an assessment that alter what the assessment measures or what the results mean.

Modifications are changes in the assessment that alter what the assessment measures or what the results mean (Pretzel et al., 2009). For example, rather than asking Jade, a child with special needs, to point to pictures of objects to measure her receptive vocabulary, her teacher talks with Jade as she plays with real toys and makes notes of which ones Jade names correctly.

The process of identifying children for special education services requires the use of many different sources of information, including standardized, norm-referenced tests. Even with these various sources, however, the wide use of standardized tests with children who have special needs is fraught with problems (Macy & Bagnato, 2010). Because standardized tests are based on norms of typically developing children, the results are often not relevant or useful to the goals for a child who has a disability. It is important to use tools that are very sensitive to identify children's progress, as changes are sometimes small (DEC, 2014). Moreover, considerations needed to make assessment developmentally appropriate and authentic are even more important for children with special needs, such as learning about their functioning in multiple environments, including home, school, child care, and community (DEC, 2014).

Early childhood special educators strongly advocate a play-based approach to assessment that focuses on children's **functional skills**, the essential abilities needed to fulfill goals parents have for their children such as communicating, making friends, and learning self-help skills (Macy & Bagnato, 2010). As described earlier in this chapter, play-based assessment involves systematic observation of children's behavior and skills in the context of their play. The feature titled *Including All Children: Individually Appropriate Assessment Practices* discusses assessment practices for children with special needs.

functional skills The essential abilities needed to fulfill goals parents have for their children, such as communicating, making friends, and learning self-help skills.

Including All Children
Individually Appropriate Assessment Practices

Individually appropriate assessment of young children with special needs requires that professionals and family members work together and respectfully share useful information. In the following contrasting scenarios, we see how important individually appropriate assessment practices are for children as well as their families:

The O'Briens' 4-year-old son, Dan, has been diagnosed as having developmental delays in language, cognitive, and social development. During a conference with his teacher, Ms. Blako, about Dan's progress, Mrs. O'Brien becomes increasingly discouraged as she is told, once more, what her child cannot do and that he is functioning at the 24-month level on a norm-referenced test. Ms. Blako explains that they will continue to work with Dan on colors, writing his first name, and counting to 20. Mr. O'Brien is frustrated because these are the same skills Dan has been working on all year. Mrs. O'Brien is concerned that Dan still isn't potty trained and doesn't seem to have friends. Ms. Blako smiles and suggests some good books on toilet training. The O'Briens leave feeling belittled, apprehensive, and concerned about Dan's remaining preschool year and pending transition to kindergarten.

In contrast, consider the conference between Larisha's mother, Tina, and the preschool teacher, Stephanie. Larisha, who has cerebral palsy, attends an inclusive preschool. The meeting is attended not only by Tina and Stephanie but also the physical therapist, speech-language pathologist, and psychologist, who all know Larisha and her family well. The purpose of the conference is to discuss what Larisha does well at home and at school and to establish new goals for her. Stephanie shares the results of her observations of physical, language, social, and emotional skills that Larisha displayed during the last several months. Tina shares what she has observed Larisha doing at home. The team agrees that Larisha is showing impressive growth and is making progress toward full participation

in all aspects of the preschool day. They identify target skills in functional and pre-academic areas to work on with her over the next few months:

1. In the morning, sign in by writing her initials on the attendance board, and put her things in her cubbie.
2. Initiate play with peers, not just her cousins at home.
3. Watch, listen, and participate in small- and large-group times, including singing songs and answering questions about stories and lessons. Larisha can sit in a supportive chair to stabilize her trunk (rather than on the carpet).
4. Pedal and steer a tricycle. The physical therapist agrees to modify the trike so Larisha can reach the pedals and grasp the handles better.
5. Recognize when she needs to use the restroom, notify the teacher, and complete toileting activities independently. Stephanie will provide information for how to work on this at home as well.

Tina says that her number-one priority is for Larisha to have friends, and the team agrees to include this as an area of focus. Tina leaves the conference feeling heard, valued, and inspired about Larisha's progress and her future skill development.

The difference between these two assessment scenarios is profound. Dan's parents were passive recipients of information. Dan's assessment focused solely on traditional academics rather than his overall development. This led to underestimating his skills as well as to setting goals that are of questionable value to his family.

In sharp contrast, Larisha's family is part of the team, providing valuable information about her development. Her teacher uses observational assessment, focusing on skills in all developmental domains—the skills that Larisha needs to function well in the classroom, on the playground, or at home. Both her teacher and her mother can use the assessment information to identify goals for Larisha's further development.

With increased demands for demonstrating program effectiveness and accountability, teachers must be knowledgeable consumers of assessment information. It is usually the classroom teacher who must explain the results of testing to parents or children, and teachers themselves most often feel the pressure of testing and assessment. Nevertheless, teachers' most important use of assessment is to improve learning outcomes for children, as discussed next.

✔ **Check Your Understanding 11.3:** Indicators of Effective Assessment

Observation and Recording to Improve Learning

Like every other aspect of intentional teaching, assessment engages teachers in professional decision making. They must decide what evidence is important to collect, as well as how and when to gather information. The process of gathering evidence of children's learning is also called *documenting* and involves two kinds of decisions: (1) how to gather information about children, and (2) how to record the findings (McAfee et al., 2015). Thinking of these processes separately opens up more options for assessment, or more "windows" into children's learning (McAfee et al., 2015).

Observation is the most frequently used method of gathering information. However, there are many ways of recording findings from observation—among them, *anecdotal records*, *checklists*, or *rating scales*—that increase teachers' options for learning about children. In the sections that follow, we describe ways teachers can observe and collect information about children, and then we describe various ways to record or document the information for later reflection and analysis.

Observing and Gathering Evidence

The most effective classroom assessment procedures need to be part of every teacher's repertoire. These include systematic observation, eliciting responses from children, collecting work products, and gathering information from family members and other adults (McAfee et al., 2015). We begin with observation, which is the foundation of effective, developmentally appropriate practice (Copple & Bredekamp, 2009).

Keen observation skills are the most important assessment tool a teacher can develop and use. Effective teaching requires positive relationships and building on children's prior learning. Therefore, teachers must know as much as possible about children's strengths, needs, interests, temperament, typical behavior, and much more. Careful observation is the best way to get to know individual children, especially infants, toddlers, and young preschoolers who have limited ability to create products and communicate verbally. During preschool, kindergarten, and the primary grades, teachers continue to regularly observe children's interests, interactions, and performance of tasks to assess their skills and understanding as part of an overall assessment plan (Mindes & Jung, 2015). Since play is so central to young children's experiences, it is also an important context for assessing children's interests, interactions, and skills. In the feature *Promoting Play: Play as an Assessment Context*, read how one teacher uses play to assess and document children's progress, and applies the information to inform her teaching.

Accurate, objective observation can be quite difficult. Consider the fact that eyewitness accounts of events tend to vary considerably. Likewise, even everyday experiences may be described differently by different participants. For instance, a teenager's view of a holiday gathering she didn't want to attend would be quite different from her grandmother's, who savored seeing the whole family together. Similarly, if two teachers observe the same preschooler's boisterous behavior, one might see happiness where the other sees rowdiness.

Promoting Play

Play as an Assessment Context

Adele understands that schools have increased expectations of kindergarteners' academic performance over the years. But her professional education convinced her that much of young children's learning happens in the context of play. Adele uses intentional, short periods of direct instruction, and includes longer periods of supported and free play for children to learn and practice. However, Adele also knows that play is where children's learning and development is demonstrated, and she takes full advantage of play as an assessment context. Because she often uses the project approach, Adele engages children in the assessment process as well.

All of Adele's centers are stocked with reading and writing materials and appropriate learning equipment. Children are encouraged to experiment and imagine. Problem solving and socio-dramatic play are valued equally. As part of their "Food" study, children play and demonstrate learning in a grocery store center. Food items are sorted and priced, and children add and subtract pennies to spend their grocery money and fulfill their planned grocery lists. At the garden center, children plant different seeds and nurture their growth. They compare different types of plants as they grow, writing descriptions and recording plant growth. They use a classroom iPad to take photos and record oral descriptions of

their garden progress. Children compare how carrots grow in soil that is fed different ways. They have conversations about the weather, pretending to be farmers, and consult a website called "Old Farmer's Almanac for Kids."

Everywhere in Adele's classroom, children are engaged, exploring, and producing products that provide evidence of powerful learning. For each project, children create vocabulary lists that they use in their writing, and they work together to produce a class book. The book becomes part of their classroom library.

Adele uses video, audiotape, photographs, and paper products to document children's learning. After collecting artifacts, she consults her online assessment tool, identifies the area of evidence, and rates the products according to proficiency. She meets with each child every two weeks for portfolio review, and helps children to set learning goals for the upcoming weeks. Children's learning goals are posted on the online assessment tool, which parents can access. Using play as a context for learning and assessment keeps Adele focused on children's development, while also addressing learning standards. All the while, children are motivated to learn and to take responsibility for their learning.

Learn to Observe Systematic observation means that teachers focus their attention on individual children or groups, watch what children do as they work and play together, and listen carefully as they speak. Table 11.3 lists the important skills of systematic observation that every effective teacher needs and why.

At times, teachers stand back and observe children as they engage in the ongoing life of the classroom or on the playground. Who does Marcus play with and for how long? Does he play alone or with a friend? At other times, teachers arrange specific tasks or activities and observe children's performance. First-grade teacher Ms. Victor adds frequently used words to the "word wall" each week and observes which children refer to them as they are writing. In most situations, teachers are participant-observers who converse with children, listen carefully, and assess while they teach individuals as well as small and large groups.

Observation is most effective if teachers think in advance about what they want to observe while remaining flexible to observe events as they proceed. Janice planned to observe the babies in her care during feeding time to see how their fine-motor skills

TABLE 11.3 Learning to Observe

Effective teachers must be skilled observers in order to assess children's learning and development accurately, as described in this table.

Effective Observation Practice	Explanation
1. Describe behavior objectively and avoid judgmental labels	An objective statement ("During clean-up time, David ran from one center to another for 10 minutes making siren sounds") provides specific information that can be interpreted more accurately as more evidence is gathered. A judgmental statement ("David is hyperactive") may be meaningless or inaccurate, and can lead to false assumptions and ineffective interactions with a child.
2. Observe in different contexts	Children's behavior varies depending on the context, their engagement, and interest. David loves center time and will engage with table toys for extended periods of time, but often acts out during cleanup. Observing his behavior in only one context would be misleading.
3. Observe at different times of the day	Children's behavior and learning are affected by many variables such as fatigue, hunger, boredom, exhilaration, fear, and anxiety. Accurate interpretation of behavior and effective teaching depends on having the most complete information.
4. Observe children as individuals and in groups	Children learn and display their learning, both as individuals and as members of groups. Obtaining the most complete picture of a child's abilities, such as their language, social skills, and problem solving, requires observing their interactions with other children.
5. Plan to observe each child during a given time period each week	Teachers' time is limited by many conflicting demands. Too often, some children receive most of the teachers' attention while others are overlooked. To guard against this natural tendency, teachers need to set aside specific times weekly to systematically observe each child, if only for 10 minutes.
6. Devise a system for recording information that works for you	Every system for observing and recording assessment evidence places demands on teachers' time and energy. Teachers need to experiment with and adopt strategies that work for them whether using sticky notes, strategically placed clipboards, iPads, laptops, digital cameras, or handheld devices.
7. Be aware of and avoid individual and cultural biases	The same behavior may be interpreted differently depending on a teacher's personal or cultural perspective. Such bias can never be completely eliminated but requires that teachers become self-aware and strive for understanding of others' points of view.
8. Gather information from other teachers and parents	The eye of the beholder always influences what is observed and how it is interpreted. The best way to avoid misinterpretation and inaccurate conclusions is to gather information from as many people as possible who interact with children in various contexts. Parents and other family members are essential informants about what children know and are able to do outside of school.

▶ Classroom Connection

The teacher in this video uses observation regularly and intentionally to learn about the children in her class. How might her observations influence her assessments of the children's learning progress and her planning for future instruction?

were developing. She observed that two of the 13-month-olds, Josie and Ana, could pick up the cereal on the highchair tray. However, 15-month-old Tania became frustrated and started to cry. Janice watched to see whether and how soon Tania would calm herself before she had to intervene. In this case, an observation of fine-motor skill turned into an observation of emotional self-regulation, an example of the kind of shift that occurs constantly in early childhood programs.

Elicit Responses from Children Aspects of children's learning and development that cannot be directly observed, such as their conceptual understanding or reasoning, can be elicited from children through questioning, conversation, or other informal teacher–child interactions. Eliciting children's responses—drawing out their ideas or reflections—is an efficient way of gathering information; this way, teachers do not have to wait for behaviors or responses to occur spontaneously (McAfee et al., 2015).

Teachers can have interviews and conferences to elicit children's ideas, problem-solving strategies, and feelings (McAfee et al., 2015). **Interviews** usually involve the teacher asking predetermined questions that are designed to reveal what children understand. For example, rather than asking a closed question such as "How many is 9 + 5?" the teacher might ask, "How would you figure out what 9 + 5 is?" Such an open-ended question is valuable because it requires an extended response that reveals more about children's thinking and understanding.

Conferences engage children in reflecting on their own work. Second-grade teacher Ernestine Cunningham holds regular writing conferences with her students to discuss the child's writing samples and identify ways to edit or improve them.

Observing children's behavior is important but it doesn't reveal what children are thinking. To find out more, intentional teachers interview individuals or conference with small groups of children.

Small-group discussions provide opportunities to elicit children's thinking in collaboration with other children. At the end of each science unit, rather than giving a multiple-choice test to see what facts children remember, third-grade teacher Devon Kerns meets with small groups of children and asks them to discuss the phenomenon they have been studying. During one such discussion, Mr. Kerns begins this way: "We've been learning about sinking and floating. So why don't giant ships weighing several tons sink?" The children's responses reveal varying degrees of understanding of the concept of displacement. Barry stays silent until the end when he admits, "I think there's something magic going on."

interviews Teacher-created, predetermined questions that are designed to reveal what children understand.

Collect Work Products Much of children's work and play produces a product such as a drawing, a painting, a construction in a particular medium, a piece of writing, a dramatic performance, or speaking in a group. These products, if systematically collected over time, provide evidence of changes in children's development and learning. Examples of individual work might be one child's journal or an art project.

Teachers may also collect or evaluate the work of a group, such as a mural, or a compilation of children's observations from a field trip, such as a PowerPoint presentation with digital photos. Portfolio assessment, which is discussed later in the chapter, is one strategy for systematically collecting and analyzing children's work samples.

Gather Information from Family Members Parents are often thought of as the audience for assessment information, passively receiving report cards or listening attentively during parent–teacher conferences. However, teachers must not only *give* information *to* parents, they must *get* information *from* parents as well. Parents can provide insights about children's behavior and capabilities outside the school or child care center. They can also serve as key informants about children's culture and language. Family involvement is so necessary to valid assessment of children with disabilities and special needs that it is legally required (DEC, 2014).

Each of these methods of gathering assessment information has advantages and disadvantages, which are summarized in Table 11.4.

Effective assessment systems—those that provide valid, reliable, and useful information for decision making—use all the ways of gathering evidence discussed in previous sections. Intentional teachers regularly gather evidence and then use it to inform their teaching decisions about individual children. In the feature *Becoming an Intentional Teacher: Using Assessment to Inform Teaching*, we see this process in action for one teacher.

Recording What Children Know and Can Do

Observation, eliciting children's responses, collecting work samples, and other authentic assessment procedures are generally informal and, therefore, not subject to the technical requirements of standardized testing. Nevertheless, for informal assessment results to

TABLE 11.4 Methods of Gathering Assessment Information: Advantages and Disadvantages

Teachers can gather assessment information in several ways, but they should consider the advantages and disadvantages of each method.

Method	Advantages	Disadvantages
Observation	• Truly authentic assessment • Best way to obtain information about children's behavior • Can observe without interfering with the ongoing activities in the classroom • Can see children's performance in relevant context (play, routines, group projects, outdoors)	• Time consuming • Children's thinking and/or problem solving cannot be directly observed • Can distract teachers from interacting with children • Can be affected by individual and cultural biases
Eliciting Responses from Children (interviews, conferences, and discussions)	• Saves time • Provides insight into children's thinking and learning that cannot be directly observed • Engages children in thinking and reflecting about their own learning—important meta-cognitive processes that contribute to further development • Demonstrates a child's ability in interaction with other children and adults	• If children do not respond, teachers may inaccurately assume that they don't know the answer • Wording of questions may influence the child's response • Cultural or emotional factors such as lack of self-confidence may inhibit child's response
Collecting Work Products	• Gathered over time • Provide multiple sources of information • Can be used to evaluate children's progress and analyze where help is needed • Concretely demonstrate children's progress to parents and to children themselves	• Teachers may not be sure which products to keep, how many to save, and how to evaluate them • Organization and storage can be difficult
Information from Family Members	• Provide insight into children's cultural and linguistic backgrounds • Describe children's abilities in familiar context • Required for children with disabilities and special needs	• May be intimidating or threatening to families • Language and/or cultural differences may create communication barriers • May not be reliable

Source: Based on *Assessing and Guiding Young Children's Development and Learning* 6th edition, by O. McAfee , D. Leong, and E. Bodrova, 2015, Upper Saddle River, NJ: Pearson; and *Observing Development of the Young Child*, 8th edition, by J. J. Beaty, 2013, Upper Saddle River, NJ: Pearson.

be accurate and useful, they need to be as objective and nonbiased as possible. Various methods of documenting assessment are designed to increase the likelihood of gathering reliable and valid information. We turn now to a description of the most commonly used methods of documentation. These methods include descriptive records, frequency counts, checklists, rating scales and rubrics, and portfolios.

Descriptive Records *Narratives* are stories in which the narrator stands outside the experience and describes the people, situation, and events that occur. The same is true of narrative approaches to observation. **Narrative records** are teachers' attempts to record detailed descriptions of children in a situation or event that is the focus of the observation (McAfee et al., 2015). It is important for narrative records to focus on the observed behavior rather than implying judgment. "Kery kicked over Stan's building, threw the sand toys on the floor, and pushed Mimi down" is much more informative and useful later than "Kery was disruptive at school today."

Teachers use various methods of collecting anecdotal records for later reflection and analysis. They may take brief notes while observing children in action or as soon as possible, adding more detail later. After documenting their observations, teachers reflect on

narrative records Teachers' attempts to record detailed descriptions of children in a situation or event that is the focus of the observation.

Becoming an Intentional Teacher

Using Assessment to Inform Teaching

Here's What Happened Four-year-old Moses is a gentle boy who plays alone and rarely speaks up. I made a point of observing Moses with other children during center time and when we were doing things that interested him. I also spoke with his mother.

One morning, I observed Moses in the block corner with two other boys for 7 minutes. Buddy and Eugene were building a house and kept up a running conversation about what they were doing. Buddy: "This is the bathroom right here. This is the bathtub and toilet." Eugene, picking up a block: "This is the frigerator." Moses sat silently right next to them, frowning, and watching every move they made. After 6 minutes, Moses went to the shelf, picked up three plastic people, and said, "This is fun, too." Buddy grabbed the people from Moses's hands, put them in the house, and said, "This is my family, my mommy and daddy." Frowning, Moses quietly sat down and continued to observe. He then picked up the bin of plastic people figures and went to the table to play with them alone.

Here's What I Was Thinking Before I can take action to help a child, I need to know as much as possible about the child's skills, abilities, and needs. That's where assessment comes in. Maybe Moses did not successfully join the play because he was intimidated by Buddy, in which case I would focus attention on helping him become more comfortable expressing himself. Or maybe he was behind in language and vocabulary development, so I should work on that. Observing him in different situations was the key. I also needed to ask Moses open-ended questions about how he felt about the experience. It could have been that his sad face and frown meant that he longed to join in the play, or he could have been patiently but unhappily waiting a turn to play alone with the blocks.

From my observations and conversations with Moses's family, I now have a working hypothesis. It seems likely that not participating in cooperative play is related to his limited vocabulary and lack of experience interacting with other children because he is an only child. To help Moses with both of these issues, I will set up situations to encourage his ease when talking with others. I will also plan some activities that work directly on his social skills. This observation also gave me insights into Buddy's and Eugene's behaviors, and I plan to work with them on their skills at making friends.

Reflection How else might the teacher have interpreted her observations of Moses's behavior during the play sequence? What other tools could she use to assess his social skills and then plan accordingly?

and interpret their records and plan how to improve teaching and learning. Anecdotal records should include the date and time of observation, names of children observed, location of the incident such as lunch table or hallway, and what the children said and actually did (Mindes & Jung, 2015). Figure 11.2 presents contrasting examples of anecdotal records about the same situation. A teacher would have difficulty interpreting the first example because it is too general and judgmental to be helpful. By contrast, the second example lends itself to deeper reflection and more effective intervention.

Here are some types of narrative records:

- A **running record** is a chronological record, much like a diary, of an individual child's behavior that helps teachers better understand that behavior (Wortham & Hardin, 2015). The diary format allows the teacher to compare and analyze a child's behavior and development over time. Ms. Dollan worries about Jennifer's shyness and is concerned that it is interfering with her ability to become involved and learn in kindergarten. She keeps a running record for 1 week, noting as many of Jennifer's social interactions as she can observe. At the end of the week, Ms. Dollan is surprised to find that Jennifer engages much more than she thought; Jennifer just tends to wait and observe before she gets involved.

  running record A chronological record, like a diary, of an individual child's behavior that helps teachers better understand that behavior.

- **Anecdotal records** are short descriptions of incidents, or anecdotes, involving one or more children (McAfee et al., 2015). "Monday 5/8—When I read *Hansel and Gretel* to 5 children, Sam (a child with special needs) sat up front and counted the pebbles on the page. He kept his eyes glued to the story for 15 minutes. He frowned when the children were lost and smiled at the ending. He picked up the book on his own afterward." When his teacher, Joanne, reflects on her anecdotal record about Sam, she realizes that previously she underestimated Sam's attention span. Sam's attention during whole

  anecdotal records Short descriptions written by teachers and based on observations of incidents, or anecdotes, involving one or more children.

Example 1

Child's Name: Ledo
Date: July 15, 2013
Setting: Classroom
Activity: Reading Group
Book: Frog and Toad Are Friends. He is really struggling to read this book. It's Level 2 – he's way behind. No fluency, Loses attention.

Example 2

Child's Name: Ledo
Date: July 15, 2013
Setting: Reading Group with Moria and Devonne
Activity: Frog and Toad Are Friends – 2 pages each Ledo got excited that it's a Frog and Toad book – he likes these characters. He stopped at p.1 – no picture clue for him. First word – Spring, he used structure and visual cues. He made 15 errors on the page. Self-corrected 5 times. When turned page and saw picture of Toad Knocking – went back and changed (smiled) his expression – "I got that right."

FIGURE 11.2 Contrasting Examples of Anecdotal Records Compare these examples of anecdotal records. Which one provides more useful information for the teacher?

group wanders, but she had never assessed it in the small-group context before. Joanne is looking forward to sharing this newly found strength with Sam's dad.

- *Videotapes*, *audiotapes*, and *digital photography* are tools for capturing ongoing streams of behavior or performances that are difficult to document in writing. Doreen videotaped a small group of 5-year-olds as they discussed how they would build a replica of the zoo's panda house in their classroom. When she played back the tape with the children, she discovered that the group really listened to each other's ideas, abandoned some, and agreed on others, which she later helped them implement.

The benefits of such detailed observations are that they are open-ended and flexible and provide a wealth of information. Children can be assessed in the context of regular classroom routines and activities so their behavior is most natural and authentic. The primary disadvantage of narrative records, on the other hand, is that they are time consuming to both record and interpret. However, using technology can increase the ease of collecting and evaluating narrative data. Other assessment tools and methods are available that essentially count or tally what is observed.

frequency counts Method used by teachers to keep track of how often a behavior occurs.

Frequency Counts In some cases, teachers need to know how often a behavior occurs—the *frequency*—and/or how long it lasts—the *duration*. For example, to intervene with a child who hits, teachers begin by keeping track of how often the negative behavior occurs. Then, once an intervention plan is in place, they can use a frequency count to evaluate its effectiveness.

Teachers use **frequency counts**, also called event sampling, to tally each time a specific behavior occurs. The teacher simply makes a mark whenever a child demonstrates a behavior or participates in an activity, as shown in Figure 11.3. For example, the teacher was concerned about Avery's continued crying after several weeks of school, but her mother dismissed it as a phase. Based on the frequency count, the teacher decided to keep more detailed narrative records of the

Child's Name: Avery Lucas
Date: 10/1 to 10/4
Time: 9.00 to 10:30
Setting: Classroom
Behavior: Crying

Date	Frequency	Day Total
9/21	⊪⊪ /	6
9/22	///	3
9/23	⊪⊪	5
9/24	⊪⊪	5
Total		19

FIGURE 11.3 Sample Frequency Count Chart
A frequency count chart such as this is simple to use and can provide teachers with helpful information about children's behavior.
Source: McAfee, Oralie; Leong, Deborah J.; and Bodrova, *Assessing and Guiding Young Children's Development and Learning*, 8th ed., © 2015. Reprinted and electronically reproduced by permission of Pearson Education, Inc., Upper Saddle River, New Jersey.

child's behavior and convinced Avery's mother to work with her to ease her adjustment to school.

Frequency counts serve a valuable but limited function. They are easy to use and help teachers quickly gather general information about children's participation and experience. However, they do not provide contextual information about what occurs before and after a specific behavior. For that evidence, teachers need to supplement frequency tallies with narrative records or checklists, addressed next.

Checklists One of the most commonly used recording methods, **checklists**, are practical and versatile tools for gathering assessment information about almost any aspect of children's behavior, skills, or attitudes (McAfee et al., 2015). They can be based on learning standards in literacy or mathematics, or on sequences of development such as physical or social skills. Some checklists are designed by teachers; others are commercially published.

Some checklists require marking only "yes" or "no" as to whether a child engages in a behavior (such as "Follows two directions"). Other, more open-ended checklists require the teacher to make a judgment of the degree to which a child has mastered a skill. Teachers may make notes while observing children and then use those notes to complete the checklist at a later time. One of the strengths of checklists is that they focus teachers' observations; in effect, checklists tell teachers what to look for and which skills are important. Checklists can provide data that can be analyzed and compared over time and also aggregated for a group of children. Their limitation is that no checklist can adequately capture the complexity of an individual child's competence.

Rating Scales and Rubrics *Rating scales* and *rubrics* record teachers' judgments about how a child's performance compares to that of peers or to a predetermined standard (McAfee et al., 2015). Ratings should be based on sound assessment evidence collected over time. **Rating scales** require the assessor to evaluate an individual on a characteristic and then rank the individual's ability on a continuum from low to high frequency or quality (McAfee et al., 2015). For example, a frequency scale might rate whether a child performs a skill "usually," "sometimes," "seldom," or "never." A scale designed to rate the quality of a child's performance might be "exceeds standard," "meets standard," or "making progress toward standard."

Rubrics are descriptive rating scales that include clear descriptions of each point on the scale or guidelines for making judgments about a rating (McAfee et al., 2015). Figure 11.4 shows a sample rubric of the geometry item from *COR-Advantage*, the revised Child Observation Record, developed by the HighScope Educational Research Foundation (Epstein, Marshall, & Gainsley, 2014). *COR-Advantage* articulates 8 levels of development or learning because it is designed for children from infancy through age 5. Note that in this instrument, all 8 levels of the rubric are described. This specificity helps teachers make more accurate ratings and increases reliability between teachers. The tool also includes additional descriptions of what behaviors to observe as well as examples of anecdotal observations that would lead teachers to make their ratings.

Rating scales and rubrics are relatively quick and systematic ways of keeping track of children's progress, and they assist teachers by focusing their observations and evidence collections. Rubrics are more reliable than rating scales because the guidelines for rating are explicit, which helps teachers make more accurate judgments. Rating scales and rubrics also help teachers identify where children are in relation to program objectives, and help guide curriculum planning and teaching. Some commercially published authentic assessment tools that use rating scales and/or rubrics have been validated (i.e., they meet standards for reliability and validity).

Portfolios **Portfolios** are systematic and organized collections of children's work and demonstrations of their progress relevant to the goals of the curriculum (Mindes & Jung, 2015). Portfolios have several benefits. They focus on how individual children

checklists Practical and versatile tools for gathering assessment information about children's behavior, skills, or attitudes.

rating scales Method of recording teacher's judgments about how a child's performance compares to that of peers or to a predetermined standard.

rubrics Descriptive rating scales that detail the qualities related to each rank on the scale; includes clear descriptions of each point on the scale or guidelines for making judgments about a rating.

portfolios Systematic and organized collections of children's work and demonstrations of their progress relevant to the goals of the curriculum.

Geometry: Shapes and Spatial Awareness

Level 0	Level 1	Level 2	Level 3	Level 4	Level 5	Level 6	Level 7
Child tracks a moving object.	Child fits an object into an opening that is the correct size.	Child moves him- or herself or objects in response to a simple position or direction word.	Child recognizes and names two-dimensional shapes (circle, triangle, square, rectangle).	Child transforms (composes or decomposes) shapes and identifies the resulting shape(s).	Child describes what makes a shape a shape (identifies shape attributes).	Child names a three-dimensional shape (cube, cylinder, pyramid).	Child describes three-dimensional shapes to compare their similarities and differences.

FIGURE 11.4 Rubric Example from COR-Advantage Rubrics are valuable assessment tools because having specific descriptions for each point on the scale helps teachers make more accurate and reliable ratings.
Source: "Geometry: Shapes and Spatial Relations" by A. S. Epstein, B. Marshall, and S. Gainsley, © 2014, in *COR Advantage 1.5 Scoring Guide*, Ypsilanti, MI: HighScope Press, pp. 50–51. Used with permission.

change over time, rather than comparing children to each other. Teachers create portfolios to document how well children are learning the content of the curriculum. In addition, portfolios provide concrete and meaningful information about children's progress to share with parents, other teachers, administrators, specialists, and even the general public (Gullo, 2006).

The materials contained in a portfolio provide teachers and children with the opportunity to reflect together on children's progress, as evident in Figure 11.5. Most teachers involve children in selecting work to be included in a portfolio. This requires children to think about which of their products are worth keeping and evaluate the quality of their own performances.

The contents of portfolios can vary, but they need to be consistent among children in a group. Generally, portfolios include dated samples of children's work representing at least the beginning, middle, and end of a school year. These samples should include teacher notes about context or children's verbal comments made about the work. A portfolio may also include anecdotal or other narrative records plus observational checklists related to curriculum goals. One widely used, validated portfolio assessment system that includes all these elements is the Work Sampling System, designed for children from preschool to grade 6 (Meisels, Marsden, Jablon, & Dichtelmiller, 2013).

FIGURE 11.5 Sample Contents of a Second-Grade Child's Portfolio The contents of a child's portfolio serve as important evidence of children's learning over time.

Your Child's Portfolio

In your child's Portfolio, you will find . . .

✓ Best read book orally recorded with written reflection (child selected)
✓ Writing piece with written reflection (child selected)
✓ Math piece with written reflection (child selected)
✓ Sample of best handwriting
✓ Strengths and goals (teacher and child selected)
✓ Math reflection
✓ School, family, and friends reflection
✓ Field trip reflection

Documentation as Dynamic Assessment

Earlier in this chapter, we defined documenting as the process of collecting and recording evidence about children's learning and development. The word *documentation* is often used to refer to the recorded evidence that is then analyzed and interpreted. However, the influence of the Reggio Emilia approach on early childhood practice (Edwards, Gandini, & Forman, 2011) created a new, expanded definition of documentation.

Teachers can assess children's learning by documenting a project or activity through note-taking, photography, audiotaping, videotaping, and collecting samples of student work. Through the children's verbal expression, writing, drawing, and construction, researchers and teachers are able to see what the children understand and how they convey their ideas and knowledge.

From carefully studying the children's work and tapes of their discussions, teachers are able to see what misconceptions and areas of incomplete knowledge the children have, as well as in their writing, communication skills, and pictorial representation. This information guides their planning of what additional experiences and instruction to provide next. Characteristics that make documentation a unique assessment tool include the following (Helm, Beneke, & Steinheimer, 2007; Reggio Children & Project Zero, 2001):

- Involves teachers intensely observing and recording, using all forms of technology and displaying children's processes of thinking and problem solving as they work together on projects.
- Captures the collaborative interaction that occurs among teachers and children and depicts the process of learning rather than any one product.
- Encourages children to revisit and remember their experiences as they examine the documentation, which extends and deepens their learning.
- Draws parents into the life of the school through compelling, visual evidence of their children's competence.
- Serves as research on children's thinking and learning processes that contributes to teachers' professional development.
- Provides evidence of children's competencies that cannot be measured on more formal tests, such as their ability to collaborate with other children.

As we saw with ways of gathering assessment information, every method teachers use to record assessment information has strengths but also limitations, which are described in Table 11.5.

Effective solutions to these challenges are now available through the use of technology. To learn more about these powerful assessment resources, read the *What Works: Using Technology to Assess Learning* feature.

▶ **Classroom Connection**

Observe how teachers in this Reggio-inspired classroom use documentation as evidence of learning and development in children's portfolios. How do teachers then use this information to inform the curriculum? What are some strengths of using this approach?

Interpreting and Using Evidence to Improve Teaching and Learning

So far we have described two major steps in classroom assessment: (1) gathering evidence of children's development and learning, and (2) recording the findings. The next step is interpreting and using the evidence to plan curriculum or adapt teaching strategies.

Accurate interpretation and effective use of assessment evidence depend on how well teachers know what children should accomplish at developmental junctures and when those junctures occur. This means that every teacher needs to be familiar with the continuum of development and expected learning sequences relevant to the age range he or she teaches. Given the wide range of individual variation, in fact, early childhood teachers should be familiar with the full range of development from birth through age 8.

A **developmental continuum** is a predictable, but not rigid, sequence of typical accomplishments within age ranges that is used to plan curriculum. A developmental continuum is an effective assessment tool because it helps teachers to focus attention on what is important to assess—what children can do—and to identify goals for continued progress (McAfee et al., 2015; McDevitt & Ormrod, 2013). When teachers are familiar with predictable sequences of learning and development, they can use these to assess where children are in the sequence and adjust their teaching to help them progress.

developmental continuum
A predictable, but not rigid, sequence of typical accomplishments within age ranges that is used to plan curriculum; also an effective assessment tool used to focus teacher attention on what is important to assess—what children can do—and to identify goals for continued progress.

TABLE 11.5 Methods of Recording Assessment Information: Advantages and Disadvantages

Teachers need to use various ways of recording assessment information but they should consider the advantages and disadvantages of each, as described in this table.

Method	Advantages	Disadvantages
Descriptive records (narrative, running, anecdotal)	• Provide rich, detailed information about children's behavior in context • Can be objective • May assess individuals or groups	• Time-consuming and difficult to record streams of behavior • May be judgmental • May be difficult to interpret
Frequency counts (event sampling)	• More objective because focuses on specific behavior • Document how often behavior occurs • Show change in behavior over time • Not time-consuming • Efficient	• No description or information about behavior and context • May lead to biased view of child because often focuses on one negative behavior
Checklists	• Efficient way of gathering information • Helps teachers know what to observe • Can be completed quickly and easily • Data can be analyzed and compared over time • Can be scored for individuals and groups	• No information provided about context • Can't capture the complexity of a child's performance • Provide limited guidance for teachers' decisions
Rating scales and rubrics	• Focus teachers' observations on specific goals • Help teachers understand development and learning progressions • Relatively quick and easy to use • Can assist curriculum planning and teaching • Data can be analyzed and compared over time • Can be scored for individuals and groups	• Limited information about context • Ratings may not be reliable across teachers or children • Scores can oversimplify complex behavior and ability
Portfolios	• Demonstrate an individual child's progress over a long period of time • Include multiple sources of information (photos, videos, work samples, teacher's and parents' observations) • Can be passed along to next teacher (with parents' permission)	• Difficult to organize, store, and access easily • Teachers may not be sure which products to keep, how many to save, and how to evaluate them
Documentation as dynamic assessment	• Makes learning visible to children, teachers, and families • Uses multiple sources of information (videos, audio recording, photos, observations, work samples) • Displays children's thinking and problem solving as they work together on projects • Helps teachers assess children's understanding and misconceptions • Illustrates both individual and group learning	• Time-consuming to collect information and create display panels • Requires large amount of space • Does not identify their individual child's work, which may frustrate parents

Sources: Based on *Assessing and Guiding Young Children's Development and Learning,* 6th edition, by O. McAfee, D. J. Leong, and E. Bodrova, 2015, Upper Saddle River, NJ: Pearson; and *Observing Development of the Young Child,* 8th edition, by J. J. Beaty, 2013, Upper Saddle River, NJ: Pearson.

Learning standards set curriculum goals for what a child should know and be able to do. They also guide the development of assessments. Effective teachers interpret and use the assessment information they have gathered and recorded in relation to learning standards. For instance, Micah observes that at the midpoint of the year, most of the children in his preschool class can recognize the first letter in their names and maybe one other letter. Is this good or bad? Unless Micah is familiar with early learning standards in the area of literacy, he can't make a judgment about whether his children are achieving at an acceptable rate. Similarly, four of the children in Micah's class do not speak in complete

What Works

Using Technology to Assess Learning

Teachers can be overwhelmed at the prospect of recording their observations, keeping track of all the data they collect about children's progress, and compiling portfolios of children's work. Fortunately, technology including smartphones, digital cameras, tablets, and laptops is now available that can minimize these disadvantages and support teachers to reliably assess and document children's learning.

One such example is the 36-item online *COR-Advantage*, an authentic assessment tool for evaluating the development and learning of children from birth through age 5, developed by the HighScope Educational Research Foundation (Epstein, Marshall, & Gainsley, 2014). This system enables teachers to use the Internet and a smartphone or tablet to record and store anecdotal records and to generate scores, charts, and graphs of children's progress, and narrative reports for individuals and for the group. The data can be aggregated to meet reporting requirements of school districts or Head Start. Children's files can be easily updated with new information. Scanned artwork, photographs, sample writing, or video clips may also be included. Families can access their child's online community, view uploaded attachments, and participate in the assessment process.

Similarly, the *Creative Curriculum System* for birth through kindergarten includes an authentic observation assessment that is also available online, *Teaching Strategies GOLD*. Teachers observe and document children's learning and development and upload evidence to an online portfolio. Using this evidence, they rate children's progress on a continuum of 38 objectives for learning and development. Children's individual portfolios can be shared with families, and with therapists and school districts for children who receive special educational services (with the family's permission, of course). The online system also offers a process to ensure that results are reliable among different observers. *Teaching Strategies GOLD* is aligned with the Creative Curriculum, allowing teachers to access teaching strategies connected to the items they assess.

Wireless Generation is an educational technology company that is best known for innovative use of handheld devices to assess children's learning during classroom interactions. Its *mCLASS: Circle* assessment for 3- to 5-year-olds includes note-taking tools and observational checklists to monitor social and emotional development. The system also provides brief tasks to measure critical skills for early literacy, such as phonological awareness and letter knowledge as well as mathematics. The data is synced to the Web and provides analysis and reports to help teachers identify areas of concern or strength for each child. For K–3 and up, the company offers similar software on handheld devices that assess children's literacy and math skills.

Many educational software companies provide electronic portfolios that can be used to create, preserve, and store children's work using digital technology. With smartphones and tablets that allow teachers to photograph, scan, and record video and audio products, the possibilities for storing work samples and performances are almost endless. The long-term storage capabilities make it possible to continue to track children's progress across grades and to produce a permanent record for children's families.

These and other technology-based assessment systems help teachers assess and are designed to be closely connected to curriculum. They provide suggestions for individual and group learning experiences and intentional teaching strategies. Thus, technology not only lightens the time-consuming demands of gathering assessment information but also links results to improving teaching and curriculum planning. With the speed of technology advancement, we can hardly imagine what solutions lay in the future.

---

sentences. Because Micah is familiar with the developmental continuum of language, he realizes these children are significantly behind their peers in language. He adds book reading and additional one-on-one conversation time to his teaching plan, continues to observe and record their language, and seeks out the speech pathologist to consider systematic evaluations.

Effective assessment systems—those that provide valid, reliable, and useful information for decision making—gather evidence from many sources. An example of such a system designed for children from birth to 3½ years of age, a notoriously difficult age group to accurately access, is the Ounce Scale (Meisels, Marsden, Dombro, Weston, & Jewkes, 2003). The tool includes an Observation Record, an album for gathering the family's responses, and Developmental Profiles and Standards to use in completing the observation and analyzing the evidence.

The role of authentic assessment in effective practice for children from birth to age 8 is now widely accepted. At the same time, educational policy and practice in elementary schools has become increasingly dominated by standardized testing, a controversial topic that is discussed next.

 Check Your Understanding 11.4: Observation and Recording to Improve Learning

Standardized Testing of Young Children

Anyone who has attended school in the United States in the past half century is intimately familiar with the regular rituals of standardized testing. We have all taken some form of state-mandated achievement test at some time in our educational careers. Most of us took the SAT or ACT to get into college. In many states, passing standardized tests is required to become a certified teacher. Despite educators' concerns and increasing doubts expressed by the general public, standardized testing is inescapable in today's political climate. Therefore, teachers must be more knowledgeable than ever about the content that will be tested as well as the appropriate and inappropriate uses of standardized tests.

Types of Standardized Tests

There are many types of standardized tests. Most standardized tests can be categorized as achievement tests, aptitude or ability tests, readiness tests, or screening and diagnostic tests (McAfee et al., 2015).

achievement tests Tests designed to measure what children have learned in general or in a content area such as reading or mathematics.

Achievement Tests One of the most familiar types of standardized tests are **achievement tests** such as the SAT, the Iowa Test of Basic Skills, or the California Achievement Test. Achievement tests are designed to measure what children have learned in general or in a content area such as reading or mathematics. The test items are a sample of the curriculum content, and children's responses are an indication of what they have learned. Recent examples of achievement tests are those administered to meet federal requirements or state learning standards.

readiness tests Achievement tests administered to children at entry to kindergarten.

Readiness Tests School **readiness tests** are typically administered before entrance to kindergarten (Snow, 2011). Some norm-referenced readiness tests are considered aptitude tests because they purport to predict whether children are sufficiently developed to benefit from kindergarten instruction. These tests are especially problematic because the younger the child, the more difficult it is to obtain an accurate assessment of what she or he has learned, much less what the child is capable of learning in the future (NAEYC & NAECS-SDE, 2003).

The fact is that children's scores on readiness tests actually reflect their past experiences and opportunities to learn and, hence, are more accurately categorized as achievement tests (Snow, 2011). The use of readiness tests to keep children out of kindergarten is considered inappropriate by NAEYC and other early childhood professional organizations because it denies children what they need most: the opportunity to attend school (Snow, 2011).

aptitude tests Tests designed to measure children's potential for learning in the future.

Aptitude or Ability Tests **Aptitude tests** are presumably designed to measure not what children have already learned, but their potential for learning in the future (McAfee et al., 2015). Consequently, scores on aptitude tests are intended to predict future performance. As such, they are sometimes used to identify children for gifted and talented programs. One example is a career aptitude test used to determine if an individual's abilities are a good match to learn the skills required of a job, such as piloting an airplane.

In education, intelligence or IQ tests such as the Stanford-Binet or the McCarthy Scales of Children's Abilities are aptitude tests. Such tests are controversial because children's scores will naturally be influenced by their prior experience. If children do not perform well on such tests, it may be because they have not had the opportunity to learn rather than because they are incapable of learning. Before addressing the controversies and concerns about standardized testing, it is important to recognize the benefits and well-intended purposes for using standardized tests.

Appropriate Uses of Standardized Testing

Standardized tests are not inherently good or evil. Although some published tests do not meet technical requirements for reliability and validity, many

Portfolios are a valuable alternative to standardized testing for evaluating children's learning. Parents can see authentic evidence of children's progress, and children themselves can feel proud of their accomplishments.

utility Used to benefit children.

others are technically sound. As described earlier in this chapter, standardized tests have particular characteristics and specific purposes for which they have been developed. When used for these purposes, they can have **utility**; that is, they can be used to benefit children. The most positive uses of standardized tests are: (1) to help identify and diagnose children with special needs, (2) to serve as a source of information for assessing children for instruction, and (3) to provide information for program evaluation and accountability. Tests are also used for research purposes.

Standardized testing has appropriate uses as long as the instruments are technically sound, used for the purposes for which they were designed, used to benefit children, and used in conjunction with other sources for decision making. Throughout your career as a teacher, you will face decisions about using standardized tests. Although there are appropriate uses for standardized testing, there are controversies and concerns that surround their use, which we discuss next.

Concerns about Standardized Testing

High-stakes testing refers to the use of standardized test scores to make decisions that have potential long-term consequences for individual children, teachers, or schools. Today's school accountability movement has increased the amount of high-stakes testing. Test results can lead to children being retained in grade, a decision with lifelong consequences. School districts use children's test scores in teacher performance evaluations and even for decisions about teacher pay. Schools are ranked on websites according to test scores. When the stakes surrounding testing become so high, unintended consequences may result, such as narrowing the curriculum to teach only what is tested, or even cheating by giving children assistance or changing the conditions under which a test is administered (Au, 2007; Meisels, 2007).

High-stakes accountability testing can have adverse consequences for teaching practices in primary grades that trickle down into kindergarten and preschool. Among the major concerns about standardized testing are potential for bias and negative effects on curriculum and teaching.

high-stakes testing
Using standardized test scores to make decisions about individual children, teachers, or schools that have potential long-term consequences.

Bias in Standardized Tests One of the biggest fallacies of standardized tests is that they are completely fair and objective (Horton & Bowman, 2002; Santos, 2004). Although objectivity is the intent behind standardization, that goal has not been reached. The only truly objective part of standardized tests is the scoring, often done by machine (FairTest, 2006). The choice of test content, wording of items, and determination of the correct answer is decided by human beings who have their own subjective perspectives (FairTest, 2006). As a result, it is virtually impossible to develop a truly objective test, free of all cultural and other forms of bias.

Negative Effects on Curriculum and Teaching   The power of paper-and-pencil, multiple-choice tests to drive what happens in schools is well documented (Ravitch, 2010). Although testing was a controversial issue before federal laws such as No Child Left Behind and Race to the Top were introduced, since these policies went into effect, schools report narrowing of the curriculum to put more focus on the content that is being tested, especially reading and math. This means that other areas of the curriculum such as physical education, the arts, and even academic subjects such as social studies are sacrificed. Some schools have even taken away recess to allow more time for reading practice.

Another negative effect of standardized testing is on instruction itself. Because multiple-choice tests tend to measure basic skills and factual knowledge, instructional practices are adversely affected (Ravitch, 2010). Instead of using effective teaching practices that emphasize learning as a socially constructed process, direct instruction on the basic skills that will be tested takes precedence in many classrooms. The "one right answer" format fails to reveal children's true competence. Consider 4-year-old Lulu's experience during such a test (G. Joseph, personal communication, June 2011):

> *Tester:* "What do you do when you're cold?"
> *Lulu:* "I start to shiver" [which is not the "correct answer" in the test booklet].
> *Tester:* "What else do you do?"
> *Lulu:* "The hair on my neck starts to stand up."
> *Tester, in somewhat frustrated voice:* "What do you do if you *don't* want to be cold?"
> *Lulu, with a slightly disdainful look:* "I put a coat on" [which is seemingly the only "correct" answer to the question].

Without the extended conversation, the tester would judge Lulu to be incorrect and her rich language expression would have been missed.

Perhaps the biggest problem with large-scale standardized testing for accountability is that it often fails to achieve its well-intended purpose, which is to improve learning outcomes for individual children (Ravitch, 2010). Test scores become available *after* children have moved on from the classroom that is being evaluated. More important, the results of such tests are not useful for informing curriculum and teaching. A single score in no way describes the complexity of children's achievement, as the following example demonstrates.

A study that analyzed the results of children who failed the state fourth-grade reading test shows the ineffectiveness of large-scale testing in improving teaching (Valencia & Buly, 2004). The researchers wanted to understand why these children were experiencing reading difficulty. Among the students in their study, they identified six very different clusters of reading problems. For example, one group of children could read fast, but didn't understand what they read. Another group of children had good comprehension skills but slow decoding ability, which interfered with their comprehending what they read. In addition, the researchers found considerable variance among individual children that would call for different kinds of reading support. Some of the children failed the test by only one or two points. Fewer than 10% of the children were identified as "disabled" readers. These few children are what we picture when we hear that large numbers of children failed the state tests.

As the researchers concluded, the standardized test score alone does not begin to describe the complexity and diversity of the reading difficulties children face. Neither is it useful in helping teachers address children's individual problems. Although their conclusion could extend to other areas of the curriculum as well, it is particularly ironic here, since improving reading achievement is the primary goal of so many accountability efforts.

Currently, the Common Core State Standards and the Kindergarten Entry Assessments standards are generating the most heated discussion and controversy related to assessment for children, teachers, schools, and districts. These issues are described in the sections that follow.

Assessment and the Common Core

The Common Core State Standards (CCSS) have changed the landscape of child assessment—directly in kindergarten and higher grades, and indirectly in preschool. States are simultaneously interpreting the standards for curriculum while attempting to assess what children are learning and how well teachers and schools are teaching. In order to manage the large task of integrating standards, and aligning curriculum and assessment, states have formed consortia to establish guidelines and develop products. Two such consortia are the Smarter Balanced Assessment Consortium (http://www.smarterbalanced.org) and the Partnership for Assessment of Readiness for College and Careers (PARCC) (http://www.parcconline.org). Both groups developed assessment approaches aligned to the CCSS in English language arts and mathematics. The groups differ in how technology is used to achieve their assessment goals. While PARCC uses computerized assessments, Smarter Balanced uses computer adaptive assessment with which it is possible to individualize a student's questions.

Because the Common Core standards focus on higher-level competencies such as problem solving, analyzing, and interpreting evidence, the assessments differ from other large-scale testing efforts that rely on machine-scored, low-level multiple-choice questions. For example, Common Core assessments require written responses to open-ended questions and keyboard skills.

Many are uncomfortable with several aspects of the assessments, including the increased difficulty and developmental appropriateness of the grade-level content, the new types of testing needed, new testing formats, and the difficult task of scheduling test administration. Some states are developing formative assessments for K–3, in an effort to be more developmentally appropriate. However, the ultimate test will be whether CCSS and its aligned curricula and assessments are able to enhance learning for *all* children.

Kindergarten Entry Assessment

While early childhood teachers are being trained to be keen observers and skilled at formative assessment, many states and school districts are developing and using Kindergarten Entry Assessments (KEAs). The U.S. Department of Education's Race to the Top—Early Learning Challenge grants (RttT-ELC) stimulated this trend. The goals for KEAs as part of this federal grant program include the following (Scott-Little, Bruner, Schultz, & Maxwell, 2013):

- Assess the extent to which the state's children are "ready" for formal schooling.
- Identify and target populations of children that require extra educational effort.
- Guide kindergarten teachers in their efforts to support children's development and learning.
- Inform and engage parents in their children's development and learning.
- Provide information about needed professional development for teachers.

The Early Learning Challenge grants emphasize that KEAs are not designed or intended to function as high-stakes assessment and should adhere to the NRC's recommendations on assessment in early childhood (NRC, 2008). NAEYC (Snow, 2011) echoes these recommendations and asserts that KEAs can have value for identifying children with special educational needs and targeting effective interventions, but cautions that the tools used must have strong psychometrics (reliability and validity) and be administered in ways consistent with developmentally appropriate practice.

For dual language learners, assessments should be culturally appropriate, include the child's family in the process, and be administered by someone who has linguistic and cultural competence that aligns with the child's experience (Espinosa & Garcia, 2012). Although these standards may be difficult to achieve, they are necessary conditions to increase the validity of assessment for dual language learners. Used properly, KEAs could prove to be a valuable tool for states and school districts in determining what supports are needed for early childhood programs and for teachers in planning the kindergarten curriculum and adapting for individual children.

Despite the challenges and controversies surrounding testing of young children, accurate assessment of young children's development and learning is an essential component of developmentally appropriate practice. Intentional teachers use the effective assessment strategies described in this chapter to meet children where they are in order to plan curriculum and adapt their teaching to help children achieve challenging goals.

 Check Your Understanding 11.5: Standardized Testing of Young Children

Revisiting the Case Study

. . . Ms. Kinsela's Classroom

At the outset of this chapter, we met a first-grade teacher, Bonnie Kinsela. During the course of a two-hour literacy block, Bonnie's work demonstrates the positive power of informal as well as formal, authentic assessment to improve teaching and learning outcomes for young children. Bonnie smoothly embeds assessment in her curriculum and teaching as she helps children to document their work. She uses technology to keep track of her observations, narrative records, ratings of children's performance, and portfolios. The children in her classroom clearly benefit from their district's emphasis on using assessment to support the progress of all children.

Bonnie's experiences expanded her thinking about assessment. She knows the benefits of using standardized measures for screening and diagnosing children's special needs, and for documenting IEP progress. At the same time, she realizes that using observation and other tools to formally and informally assess children's learning and development provides her with essential information to make good decisions about her teaching. Most important, she now believes that assessment is not an add-on to her job, but rather an integral aspect of her role as an intentional teacher. Using assessment wisely and accurately is essential if children are to benefit from their school experiences.

Assessing children's progress on specific literacy goals helps Bonnie see the need to adapt and individualize her teaching. The families she works with are integrally involved in the assessment process, examining online portfolios, sharing anecdotes, and marveling at their own children's competence. In Bonnie's program, assessment meets the ultimate test—it benefits children and their families. ■

Chapter Summary

- Assessment literacy is teachers' understanding and using the vocabulary of assessment and testing.
- Assessment is the ongoing process of gathering evidence of children's learning and development, and then organizing and interpreting that information in order to make informed decisions about instructional practice.
- Early childhood programs have four basic purposes for assessment: (1) to inform teaching and promote

learning, (2) to identify children with special learning or developmental needs, (3) to evaluate programs, and (4) to demonstrate accountability.

- Indicators of effective assessment include (1) using multiple sources of evidence; (2) using assessments only for the purpose for which they are reliable and valid; and (3) considering what is developmentally appropriate, culturally and linguistically responsive, and individually appropriate for all children, including children with special needs.

- The most effective methods for collecting evidence to improve learning and development are observing children's behavior and performance, eliciting responses from children, collecting work products, and gathering information from family members.

- Accurate interpretation and effective use of assessment evidence depend on teachers' knowing what and when children should be accomplishing certain developmental tasks and learning skills.

- Benefits of standardized tests include: (1) they help to identify and diagnose children with special needs, (2) they serve as a source of information for assessing children for instruction, and (3) they are one source of information for program evaluation and accountability.

- High-stakes accountability testing can have adverse consequences for teaching practices in primary grades that trickle down into kindergarten and preschool, including biased results and negative effects on curriculum and teaching.

Key Terms

- accommodations
- accountability
- achievement tests
- alternative assessments
- anecdotal records
- aptitude tests
- assessment
- authentic assessment
- checklists
- criterion-referenced tests
- curriculum-embedded assessment

- developmental continuum
- diagnostic tests
- dynamic assessment
- evaluation
- evidence
- formal assessment
- formative assessment
- frequency counts
- functional skills
- high-stakes testing

- informal assessment
- interviews
- modifications
- narrative records
- normal curve
- norm-referenced tests
- performance assessment
- play-based assessment
- portfolios
- program evaluation
- rating scales

- readiness tests
- reliability
- rubrics
- running record
- screening tests
- standardized assessment
- standardized testing
- summative assessment
- testing
- utility
- validity

 Demonstrate Your Learning

Click here to assess how well you've learned the content in this chapter.

Readings and Websites

Curtis, D., & Carter, M. (2013). *The art of awareness: How observation can transform your teaching* (2nd ed.). St. Paul, MN: Redleaf Press.

McAfee, O., Leong, D., & Bodrova, E. (2015). *Assessing and guiding young children's development and learning* (6th ed.). Upper Saddle River, NJ: Pearson.

Center on Enhancing Early Learning Outcomes (CEELO)

This website has many resources on assessment to support children's learning, including products developed to support states' efforts.

Early Learning Challenge Collaborative

This website has valuable information about Kindergarten Entry Assessments and discussion points for using with colleagues and families.

Smarter Balanced Assessment Consortium and Partnership for Assessment of Readiness for College and Careers

These websites describe states' efforts to collaborate on the development and implementation of state-level assessments designed to measure students' progress on meeting Common Core State Standards.

12 Teaching Children to Communicate: Language, Literacy, and the Arts

Learning Outcomes

After studying this chapter, you should be able to:

12.1 Describe the continuum of language development from birth to age 8.

12.2 Identify effective strategies teachers can use to promote children's language learning.

12.3 Explain how children acquire a second language and describe effective strategies for teaching dual language learners.

12.4 Analyze effective teaching strategies to promote key early literacy skills that predict later success in reading.

12.5 Discuss the components of effective literacy instruction in the primary grades and the impact of Common Core English Language Arts standards.

12.6 Demonstrate how children learn to communicate through the visual arts, music, movement, dance, and drama, and effective strategies for engaging children in arts education.

Thurgood Marshall Early Learning Center is a public school, serving prekindergarten through second grade. In April, the whole school faculty plans to focus on art appreciation and communication. Each class takes a field trip to the local art museum. In preparation, the kindergarteners take a virtual tour on the museum's website and identify pictures they'd like to see on their visit. The teacher, Ms. Barker, prints copies of the favorites to focus the children's attention. Each group of four children chooses one painting, such as one depicting bright sunflowers by Vincent Van Gogh. Meeting with children in small groups, Ms. Barker stimulates their conversations with open-ended questions such as "What do you see in this painting? What do you think the artist was feeling/ thinking?"

After their discussions, each group tries its hand at producing paintings on the same theme as the artist. Using their own attempts at spelling, children write about or dictate to the teacher descriptions of their paintings and how they compare to the original: "I painted yellow flowers, too, but mine are little," explains Elijah.

Before the visit, the teacher projects paintings by each of the artists on the interactive whiteboard for the whole group to compare subjects, styles, and colors. At the gallery, the groups look carefully for their "own" painting, and the teacher asks if they are surprised by what they see.

Bruce [upon encountering the Van Gogh]: It looks rough!

Ms. Barker: How a painting feels is called texture. The painter used thick layers of paint.

Marion [pointing to the copy in his hand]: But here it looks smooth.

Ms. Barker [reinforces the new word]: That's true. The texture of the copy isn't rough. It's smooth.

Tallulah: The sunflowers are so yellow. They almost hurt my eyes.

Ms. Barker: The color in the painting is brighter and more intense than in the copy.

After the trip, children discuss and write about what they observed, and do more painting. Their paintings and the words they use to describe them are far more detailed than before their visit. The field trip stimulated a new interest which leads to playing *Museum Mix-Up* on the iPad, a game developed by the Fred Rogers Center to help children discover great works of art.

Similar experiences occur in other classes, and the teachers set up an art gallery in the hallway. Children display their paintings next to the posters of the great artists' works that inspired them. In the first and second grades, the teachers and children do Internet research, read short biographies of some of the famous artists, and write summaries to display on the gallery walls. The first graders are surprised to learn that many famous artists painted outside. The teachers set up easels outside so children can paint the views from their school. Their vocabulary for colors expands as they try to mix new variations to match what they see, such as *lavender, chartreuse,* or *magenta.*

The art study lasts several weeks, during which children increase their language and literacy skills. They sharpen their observation skills, learn descriptive vocabulary, and broaden their understanding of how art is used for communication and expression. ■

In this chapter, we address fundamental areas of the early childhood curriculum: language and literacy development. Speaking and understanding, reading, and writing are the foundation of all other learning in school and essential for success in life. Also in this chapter, we address the arts, a content area that, in contrast to literacy, is often seen as expendable. Today's emphasis on reading and test scores now drives the curriculum to a large extent. Some schools have eliminated the arts altogether; others use them only as a reward for good behavior. This chapter views the arts as an essential means of communication for young children and demonstrates their connection to other areas of communication: language and reading. Although we focus on the integration of the arts, we also believe in art for art's sake, especially for young children for whom art experiences contribute to development in so many ways.

First, we address the all-important area of language development—how both first and second language develops and ways teachers can scaffold children's language learning. Next, we discuss the foundations of literacy from birth through age 5, as well as the key components of reading instruction in the primary grades. We then turn to the creative arts, describing goals for art education and teaching strategies to enhance children's enjoyment and engagement in the arts.

Children's Language Development

After 3 months of separation, 4-year-old Liam is excited to see his Nana. He talks and talks as she tries to quiet him for bedtime. Finally, in exasperation, he says to her, "But I have so many words for you, and they never get tired."

Seeing their language skills blossom is one of the most delightful aspects of teaching young children. Perhaps the most important task of the first 5 years of life is development of language because it supports learning in so many other areas. Language is a strong predictor of later success in learning to read and write (National Institute of Child Health and Human Development [NICHD], 2000; Neuman & Wright, 2013). Likewise, children who are skilled communicators demonstrate better social competence and emotional self-regulation.

The Critical Importance of Language Development

Because children seem to learn language naturally, adults often assume that it is simply the product of maturation, like learning to walk. But it is not. Biology primes humans for language, but the language children speak is learned over many years through verbal interaction with adults and other children (Neuman & Wright, 2013). By the time they reach preschool, children are experienced users of language. However, the amount and type of language they use may differ from the language used in the school because children's speech is acquired in the context of their home and cultural and linguistic community.

Language learning is far from complete when children enter kindergarten or even finish elementary school. Human beings learn language throughout school and life. Undoubtedly, as a college student, you continually add new words to your vocabulary. As a teacher working with a diverse population of children and their families, you will find that your vocabulary will continue to expand.

Types of Language

receptive language The ability to understand what is being said.

There are basically two types of language: receptive and expressive. **Receptive language** is the ability to understand what is being said. **Expressive language** is the ability to communicate through use and knowledge of spoken language. Receptive language skills—listening and understanding—develop earlier than the expressive abilities of speaking and communicating. At any point in time, children understand more words and more advanced sentence structures than they use.

expressive language The ability to communicate; use and knowledge of spoken language.

Vocabulary   **Vocabulary** is a combination of receptive and expressive language—that is, the number of words a person knows and uses when listening or speaking (Snow, Burns, & Griffin, 1998). An important goal of all teaching is to increase both the quantity and quality of children's receptive and expressive vocabulary. It is not enough that children speak a lot. We must pay attention to the range of words they understand and use—the use of pronouns, prepositions, adverbs and adjectives, and other parts of speech (Snow et al., 1998).

Vocabulary words are the labels children use for concepts they are learning, as well as for those they already know and understand. Consequently, the more limited the vocabulary, the more limited the child's understanding of the world is (Neuman & Wright, 2013). A child who knows the words *mail*, *stamp*, *envelope*, *address*, *package*, and *delivery* has a more refined concept of the postal system than a child who refers to all of those concepts as *mail*.

vocabulary A combination of receptive and expressive language; the number of words a person knows and uses when listening or speaking.

Grammar   Another important element of language development is the complexity of sentence structure children use, referred to as **syntax** or grammar. As children become more skilled users of language, their syntax becomes more complex. For example, a toddler may say, "Me go" to indicate he wants to play outside. But a preschooler will use a more conventional sentence structure such as "I wanna go to the playground and climb the ladder swing."

A related goal is for children to begin to acquire **script language**—the typical ways that people communicate in different settings. For example, what the doctor says is different from what the grocery clerk says. Similarly, the way one talks at school is different from the way one talks at home or on the playground. Learning the language of school, what is called **academic discourse**, is important for school success, and it is not an automatic process. For example, if you have ever seen children "play school," you have seen how they rehearse the script that teachers use (and it is not always comfortable for adults to watch their behavior played back for them).

syntax Grammar and sentence structure.

script language The typical ways that people communicate in different contexts or settings.

academic discourse The language of school, which is important for school success.

Language Differences in Children

During the preschool years, language develops far more rapidly than at any other time, but there are enormous individual differences (Hart & Risley, 1999). Of particular concern is that differences in children's language abilities exist between socioeconomic groups as early as 18 months of age (Hart & Risley, 2003). Recent research finds that not only does the size of very young children's vocabularies differ, but also how quickly they process and respond to language (Fernald, Marchman, & Weisleder, 2013). These differences become greater over time and contribute to the persistent achievement gap in our country (Neuman & Wright, 2013). Therefore, programs serving children from low-income families and children from diverse linguistic and cultural backgrounds must take on the challenge of accelerating children's language progress.

Children's language development affects all areas of their learning as well as their social-emotional development. Intentional teachers use every opportunity to help children learn language.

Effects of Early Language Experience
A classic study of early language acquisition found that socioeconomic background was a major factor affecting young children's language development (Hart & Risley, 1995). The researchers videotaped language interactions between

parents of different income levels and their children from infancy to age 3. The study found that, over the course of a year, children of parents who were professionals were exposed to more than 11 million words. In contrast, children whose families were receiving public assistance were exposed to only 3 million words.

Researchers estimated that during the first 4 years of a child's life, an average child in a professional family would have accumulated experience with almost 50 million words, whereas an average child living in poverty would have been exposed to 13 million words (Hart & Risley, 1995). Consequently, children's vocabulary growth reflected their experience. By age 4, children from more affluent homes had vocabularies approximately three times as large as those of children living in poverty.

It is important to note that Hart and Risley (1995) found economic advantage to be the *only* factor related to language differences. Race/ethnicity, gender, or birth order of the child made no difference. The researchers also cautioned about negatively judging the parents, who are coping with the many stresses of poverty:

> Particularly striking among the welfare parents was their resilience and persistence in the face of repeated defeats and humiliations, their joy in playing with their children, and their desire that their children do well in school. They could spend an hour on a bus holding a feverish child and wait longer than that in a public health clinic. But these parents did not talk to their children very much. (Hart & Risley, 1995, pp. 69–70)

The large vocabulary difference between income groups has come to be called "The 30 million word gap" (Hart & Risley, 2003). Public recognition of this disparity helped propel the White House to convene a summit called "Bridging the Word Gap" in 2014 and to propose increased investments in early education.

Recently, concerns have been raised about the interpretation of these findings. Researchers at the White House summit emphasized that just increasing the number of words children hear is not enough; more important is the complexity and variety of words that children learn (Quenqua, 2014). Additionally, the Hart and Risley study involved a small number of families. SES may no longer be as influential a factor because many of today's economically advantaged parents spend more time on handheld devices than in conversation with their children. Nevertheless, an achievement gap persists, and children's language capacity is a contributing factor.

To address this gap in children's language development, teachers must first understand how language typically develops. Teachers must also be aware that many types of disability affect communication; some individual children will need access to assistive technology—called *augmented communication devices* and/or sign language.

Developmental Continuum: Oral Language

Language development follows a relatively predictable sequence, but there are individual differences that are well within the range of normal (Hart & Risley, 1999). In addition, as we saw in research cited earlier, if children have many opportunities to speak and be spoken to, they are likely to develop richer, more complex language. The *Developmental Continuum: Oral Language* feature provides an overview of the typical progression of language development and how children of different ages communicate.

Impact of Common Core Speaking and Listening Standards

The Developmental Continuum provided here describes widely held expectations for typical language development. However, the K–3 Common Core Speaking and Listening standards (2011a) establish specific expectations by grade level. For example, kindergartners need to participate in collaborative conversations in small and large groups and confirm their understanding of a read-aloud book by asking and answering questions. Standards at each grade level build on earlier abilities and become progressively more

Developmental Continuum
Oral Language

Age of Child	Developmental Expectations
Birth to about 8 months	• Communicate through behaviors rather than words; signal distress by crying. Caregivers need to interpret babies' sounds and gestures. • Smile or vocalize if they want someone to pay attention or play. • Begin vocalizing vowel sounds called **cooing**. Soon after, they begin to **babble**, producing consonant/vowel sounds such as "ba." • Continue to babble using all kinds of sounds and will play with sounds when alone. • Begin to understand familiar names such as those of siblings or pets. • Laugh and appear to listen to conversations.
Between 8 and 18 months	• Become more purposeful in their communications. • Use facial expressions, gestures, and sounds to get their needs met. (If a bottle falls from a high chair tray, instead of just crying, the 14-month-old may grunt and wave at the floor.) • Understand many more words than they can say. • Speak in long, babbled sentences that mirror the cadence of conventional speech. • Soon start to shake their head "no" and begin to use the word *me*. • Usually crack the language code and begin to use their first words between 12 and 18 months.
From 18 to 24 months	• Experience a burst in vocabulary and begin to combine words into two-word utterances called **telegraphic speech**. Like old-fashioned telegrams, they waste no words in communicating their message: "No nap."
Ages 2 to 3	• Progress from using two-word combinations (my truck) to three- and four-word sentences with words in the correct order more often (Where's my truck?). • Speaking vocabulary may reach 200 words. • Use adjectives and adverbs. (Give me my blue truck now.) • Most children's speech becomes more understandable. Constantly ask, "Wassat?" as they seem to want to name everything.
Ages 3 to 6	• Have a vocabulary of about 1,000 words. • Although some may still have difficulty, most are better able to articulate some of the more difficult sounds, like *s, th, z, r,* and *l.* • Can initiate and engage in more complex conversations. • Use 1,500 to 2,000 words as vocabulary expands rapidly during kindergarten. • Usually speak clearly and are lively conversation partners with adults and other children.
The primary grades	• Language development continues at a rapid pace. • During these years, children need a large vocabulary to learn to read and to comprehend what they read. Explicit teaching of vocabulary needs to be an instructional goal. • At the same time, the more children read, the more words they learn because the language of books is more elaborate than everyday conversation. Some researchers estimate that children need to learn 3,000 words a year throughout the elementary school years.

Sources: Based on *Assessing and Guiding Young Children's Development and Learning*, 6th edition, by O. McAfee, D. Leong, and E. Bodrova, 2015, Upper Saddle River, NJ: Pearson; *Learning Language and Loving It: A Guide to Promoting Children's Social, Language, and Literacy Development in Early Childhood Settings*, 2nd edition, by E. Weitzman and J. Greenberg, 2002, Toronto: The Hanen Centre.

cooing Vocalizing vowel sounds.

babble Producing consonant/vowel sounds such as "ba ba."

telegraphic speech Combining words into two-word utterances.

challenging. For example, kindergartners need to have back-and-forth conversations; first graders' conversations need to build on what the other person says through questions and comments; and second graders need to have multiple exchanges that link what they say to the other person's comments. Obviously, these standards directly affect how teachers teach. Teachers have to move beyond "yes or no" questions to provoking more intellectually engaging, stimulating conversations among children.

In the previous sections, we described the critically important role of early experience to language development and expectations across the period from birth to age 8. Next, we describe what adults can do to help develop children's communication skills.

 Check Your Understanding 12.1: Children's Language Development

Scaffolding Children's Language Development

Public reports about the "30 million word gap" have garnered considerable media attention that can lead to inaccurate information about how to help children develop language. As we've seen, it isn't just the quantity of words that children hear, it is the quality and complexity of their language experience. Children learn language and expand their vocabulary from their interactions with more competent speakers. However, effective teaching strategies differ based on the age of the children. Next we discuss developmentally appropriate ways of promoting language in each age group.

▶ Classroom Connection

Watch this video and listen to the teacher as she takes time to have a conversation with a toddler during play to develop a warm relationship with the child and expand his language.

http://www.youtube.com/watch?v=ZUajb1Ll2qQ&list=PLoYCO2fwBJJpPrly7mLNSWnOPoSKdMk-R

Supporting Language Development in Babies and Toddlers

Depicting language development as a progression may imply that it happens automatically. Although very young children learn to talk without formal instruction, adults play a critical role in supporting that process.

Talk to Babies and Toddlers The role of conversational partner is especially important for teachers working with babies and toddlers because the first 3 years of life are prime time for developing language. Nevertheless, some teachers and parents of very young children persist in the view that there is no reason to talk to children who can't talk back. The opposite is true. From the earliest moments of life, babies are trying to communicate. Teachers need to talk as if the child can talk back and respond to almost any attempt to communicate.

If you are like most adults, your interaction with a baby may sound like a high-pitched voice saying this: "Hi, baby. How are you this morning, baby, baby?" You pause. The infant moves his mouth, waves his arms, or just looks at you intently. And now you say, "Oh, you had a good sleep, did you? Are you ready to have some fun today?" When the baby gurgles, you say, "You are ready, aren't you? Jesse's ready, ready to play!"

parentese The high-pitched tone of voice adults and even children tend to use naturally with babies; also called *motherese.*

Adults (and even older children) talk to babies differently than they do to each other. The high-pitched tone of voice that adults tend to use naturally with babies is called **parentese** *or motherese*, and researchers have observed its use around the world (Rivera-Gaxiola, Silva-Pereyra, & Kuhl, 2008). What's more, they know that babies like it. Infants consistently prefer hearing parentese to adult conversation. In laboratory studies, they show this preference by turning their heads one way to trigger a tape of parentese more often than they turn it the other way to hear a tape of adult-to-adult conversation.

Effective communication begins as babies pay attention and respond. When the child initiates, teachers need to respond enthusiastically and then wait for a response. They interpret what babies are trying to communicate and expand on the message with words.

Teachers shouldn't pressure young children to talk. Communication needs to be meaningful; it should not test children with obvious questions such as "What are you doing?" or direct them with comments like "Put the car on the road" (Greenberg & Weitzman, 2014). Instead, the teacher might say, "Your car is going fast." If the comment sparks the child's interest, the child might respond, "Fast." Then it's the teacher's turn: "You're making the car go very fast."

Describe Their Experiences

One of the most effective ways of building language in babies and toddlers is to use **play-by-play language** or *running commentary* during routines and social interactions with babies and toddlers. Think of watching a sporting event on TV. A play-by-play announcer describes the action even though you're seeing it before you. This sort of commentary connects actions and objects with words and familiarizes babies with the cadences of speech. Here's an example of play-by-play during a typical routine, with the words tied to each action: "Let's change your diaper now. I need to pick you up. You're such a big boy. Let's lie down on the changing table. You can hold your horsie. We need to take off these wet pants" and on and on.

Finally, to promote language in babies and toddlers, two very important points must be kept in mind. First, children need a lot of opportunities to play with different kinds of toys, to touch real objects, and to move around. Think of the many different words a child could learn from playing in water, eating applesauce, climbing on a low ramp, rolling a ball, or looking at a cardboard book. Secondly, in each of these situations, teachers need to supply the words. While children play on a ramp, the teacher can introduce the words *slide, roll, climb, fast, shiny, push,* and many more.

As children's understanding and language use improves, teachers need to adapt their language by using longer, more complex comments and more sophisticated vocabulary. Many of these same strategies apply to promoting language with preschoolers, discussed next.

Infants and toddlers are learning language and also literacy skills from birth. What do you think this child is learning from examining a cardboard book?

play-by-play language Language that describes what is happening during routines and social interactions with babies and toddlers; also called *running commentary*.

© Jules Selmes/Pearson Education

Scaffolding Preschoolers' Language Development

Research demonstrates that several strategies are particularly effective in promoting preschooler's language acquisition (Dickinson, 2011; Neuman & Wright, 2013). These strategies include modeling language, conversation, listening, decontextualized speech, and intentional teaching of new words.

Model Language and Complex Vocabulary Teachers do a lot of talking and are important role models for children. Therefore, they need to use standard grammatical speech. They also need to recognize that many of the grammatical errors children make, such as *I goed to the store* or *three sheeps,* show their efforts to learn a language rule. As they learn the rule, like using *s* to indicate plural, they overgeneralize it. Instead of pointing out the mistake, a more effective approach is to pick up on what the child says and say it correctly. A child might say, "I gots two foots," to which the teacher replies, "Yes, you have two feet so you need two socks."

Similarly, if children speak a dialect or vernacular version of English, teachers should not correct or prohibit their speech. Doing so tells children that the speech of their family and their cultural group is inferior. This negative message may inhibit children's attempts to communicate. A more effective alternative is to help children see that there are different ways to say the same thing. For example, a child might say, "He ain't got no shoes." Rather than correcting the double negative, the teacher could say, "Yes. He doesn't have any shoes. He's barefoot." Especially as children get older, the teacher should intentionally draw their attention to the fact that there are different ways to say the same thing.

Engage in One-to-One Conversation

One of the most effective strategies for promoting children's language development is engaging them in one-to-one conversations (Dickinson, 2011; Neuman & Wright, 2013). When children are served in groups, the task of supporting each child's language acquisition and understanding what they are trying to say can be daunting. Too often, the children whose language is most advanced are spoken to more often. This leads to a vicious cycle where those children who are lagging behind get less language interaction than they need, while those who need less actually get more (Bredekamp, 2002).

Extend Conversation

One of the best ways to build children's vocabulary is to increase the amount of talk in the classroom and to intentionally extend conversations. **Extended discourse** occurs when adults talk with children in ways that build on and expand what the children say (Dickinson & Tabors, 2001). Researcher David Dickinson encourages teachers to "strive for five," that is, five back-and-forth exchanges during a conversation with a child. In short, teachers need to use fewer conversation closers and more conversation stretchers, as described in Table 12.1.

extended discourse Talking with children in ways that build on and expand what they say.

Build Listening Comprehension

Conversation involves turn-taking. One person speaks and the other person listens. Listening is critical to understanding what is said. In addition, listening comprehension prepares young children for later reading comprehension (Jalongo, 2008). As important as listening is, most teachers do not treat it as a skill to be taught. When adults tell children to "Listen," they often mean "Behave" or "Do as I say." No wonder children often tune out the word.

Young children need to listen in order to learn; therefore, they need to learn to listen (Jalongo, 2008). Because teachers or parents tell children, "Be quiet, sit still, and listen," listening may seem to be a passive activity. However, effective listening is an active process. **Listening** is "the process of taking in information through the sense of hearing and making meaning from what was heard" (Jalongo, 2008, p. 12).

listening The process of taking in information through the sense of hearing and making meaning from what is heard.

To promote listening and understanding, teachers should model good listening for children. They can use the conversation stretchers and avoid the conversation closers, listed in Table 12.1 and depicted in the following example:

> Ms. Abell's kindergarten class gathers around her for meeting time. The children become excited when they spy the "mystery box," which signals that they are going to play one of their favorite games.
>
> *Ms. Abell, putting her hand inside the box:* I'm touching something that is hard and has points on one end.
> *The children take turns guessing:* A pencil. . . . A knife. . . . A carrot.
> *Ms. Abell:* Listen to my clue. I said points.
> *Ashley:* I know. It's scissors. (The other children nod and agree.)
> *Ms. Abell, feeling in the box:* "That's close, but it has four points, called prongs."
>
> Because *prongs* is a new word for them, the children need other clues. Ms. Abell says, "Who can remember all the clues?" After Dorsey lists the clues so far, Ms. Abell adds another one: "You use it at lunchtime." Soon, Robin figures out that the mystery item is a fork.

This game is only one of the ways in which Ms. Abell promotes listening skills. During center time, a group plays a matching sounds Lotto game. Two children from Cambodia

TABLE 12.1 Improving Teacher–Child Conversations

The examples in this table help teachers become more aware of how they can encourage and extend conversations with children or unwittingly close off communication.

AVOID Conversation Closers—Types of Teacher Talk That Cut Off Conversation with Individual Children

Conversation Closers	Examples
Answering own questions—talking for children or over children	Teacher speaking without waiting for a reply: "How did you like our trip to the firehouse, Jack? I bet you liked hearing the fire bell. I saw you looking at the pole. That was neat."
Moralizing	Jack: "I wanna ring that bell." Teacher: "You can't ring the bell. It's not allowed."
Using empty praise or phrases	Teacher: "That's nice, Jack." "Good boy."
Time-passing remarks	Jack: "Can we drive the truck?" Teacher: "We'll be going pretty soon."
Focusing on safety and rules	Jack: "Look, I found a caterpillar." Teacher: "You'll have to wash your hands now."

INCREASE Conversation Stretchers—Types of Teacher Talk That Extend One-to-One Conversation and Contribute to More Turn-Taking

Conversation Stretchers	Examples
Focusing on and adding details	"The firefighter's boots are tall. Let's see how big they are compared to your shoes, Jack. They're gigantic. Why do you think they have these handles?"
Expanding and asking questions	"It sounds like you want to build a firehouse out of your blocks with a pole. What materials will you need?"
Repeating important words	"Here's the fire extinguisher. We have a fire extinguisher like this at school. Who remembers where we keep the extinguisher?"
Sharing own experiences	"When I was on my way to school, I heard an ambulance siren. It startled me."
Explaining terms	"A false alarm. *False* means it is not real. So a false alarm means there isn't a real fire."
Wondering aloud	"I wonder what it would be like to work in a fire station. . . ."
Using wait time	Give plenty of time (5 to 10 seconds) for children to respond, especially less verbal children. The other children and you will learn that waiting for a less verbal child can sometimes yield keen insights.

Source: Based on *Oral Language and Early Literacy in Preschool: Talking, Reading, and Writing,* 2nd edition, by K. A. Roskos, P. O. Tabors, & L. A. Lenhart, 2009, Newark, DE: International Reading Association; *Learning Language and Loving It: A Guide to Promoting Children's Social, Language, and Literacy Development in Early Childhood Settings,* 2nd edition, by E. Weitzman and J. Greenberg, 2002, Toronto: The Hanen Centre.

listen to a story on tape in their home language. Ms. Abell sets up a treasure hunt where children must listen and follow a series of directions to find the surprise.

Use Decontextualized Speech

One of the most effective ways to expand children's language is to use **decontextualized speech**. This is talk about events, experiences, or people that are beyond the here and now or that inhabit children's imaginations. Such interaction requires children and adults to use more complex and varied vocabulary in explanations, descriptions, dialogue, and pretend talk.

decontextualized speech Talk about events, experiences, or people that are beyond the here and now or that inhabit children's imaginations.

Decontextualized speech can be complicated because the speaker and the listener can't rely on cues from the context to understand the communication. When children talk about the here and now, the context permits using words like *this, that, there, here,* and *it.* These are words that children already know. Such conversation doesn't require or challenge them to use more descriptive language to be understood.

Furthermore, decontextualized speech is valuable preparation for reading (Snow et al., 1998). In spoken communication, lots of cues such as gestures, facial expressions, physical space, and objects are available. If someone says, "Take your seat," the listener quickly understands that he is being told to sit down. But if the same sentence appears in writing, the reader would have to figure out whether it means *sit in a chair* or *pick up a cushion*. This is just one example of the important connection between speaking and reading.

Teach New and Rare Words

Four-year-old Liam has a new baby brother named Ryan. Liam decides that the baby should be named Nathan, after his best friend at preschool. The first few days after Ryan comes home from the hospital, Liam persists in calling him Nathan. His parents don't correct him, but they keep calling the baby *Ryan*. Sitting next to his mom and Ryan on the couch one day, Liam thoughtfully says, "We can call him Rynathan. That will be a compromise."

Liam's advanced vocabulary, which also includes words such as *actually, amazing, entertaining,* and *nocturnal,* did not develop by chance. His parents and teachers talk with him, use these words regularly, and explain and show what they mean.

Learning new words occurs through repeated exposure to the words in a context where the meaning becomes clear. Liam's parents undoubtedly negotiate with him rather than get into power struggles. For example, if he wants to watch TV and his mother wants him to go outside, she might say, "Let's compromise. You can go outside while it's still light, and we'll tape the program so you can watch it later." After hearing and using this word several times, Liam begins to use it himself.

rare words Multisyllable words that are not typically part of a young child's vocabulary.

Teachers need to use explicit instruction to expand children's vocabulary, and should intentionally introduce new and **rare words**—multisyllable, sophisticated words that are not typically part of a child's vocabulary (Collins, 2012; Neuman & Wright, 2013). For example, in *The Tale of Peter Rabbit*, Peter's coat gets caught in the fence and the birds *implore* him to *exert* himself. Before reading the book, the teacher introduces these words with simple definitions, "*Implore* means to ask someone to do something you really want them to do" and "*Exert* means to try really hard." During the reading, she pauses at the sentence to ask the children what it means. Then later she reinforces the learning by using the new words repeatedly, sometimes jokingly, "I implore you to get your coats on," and encouraging children to use them.

Effective teachers read to children in small groups. In a group of five or six, children can see the pictures, ask questions, and talk about the story before, during, and after the reading.

Use Interactive Book Reading

One of the most effective ways to promote children's language and increase their vocabulary is to engage in interactive book reading (McGee, 2013). In many classrooms, storybook reading is the favorite activity of teachers as well as children. However, teachers usually read books only to the whole group (Dickinson, 2011). At times, reading is seen as entertainment only; at other times, teachers use it as a transition activity, with children taking turns to go wash their hands while the teacher reads. These practices are missed opportunities for learning. Instead, interactive book reading can serve many valuable purposes for individual children, as we see in the following example (based on Connect Module 1—Embedded Interventions, http://www.community.fpg.unc.edu/connect-modules/learners/module-1):

Four-year-old Tristan eagerly joins a group of friends in his Head Start classroom during choice time. At least 10% of Head Start children have identified disabilities, and like the majority of those children, Tristan has a speech and language delay. His teacher, Ms. Freedman, uses interactive book reading to

© Dean Mitchell/Vetta/Getty Images

help meet Tristan's speech therapy goals and also build all the children's language development. As she reads a book specially made by Tristan's therapist to a small group of five children, all the children respond to the language prompts. The children love it when Ms. Freedman passes around a mirror and they see how to put their lips together to make the /M/, /B/, /P/ sounds. In this inclusive classroom, Tristan receives peer support to improve his speech articulation, and the other children serve as language models for him.

Reading in Small Groups Research shows that book reading is most effective when it occurs in groups of four to six children (Karweit & Wasik, 1996; Morrow, 1988). The power of reading is not in the book alone, but in the conversation about the book among teachers and children before, during, and after reading (Gonzalez et al., 2014). This type of interaction is more likely to occur in a small group than in the whole group or even in a one-on-one reading situation (Bates, 2013; McGee, 2013). Reading in small

dialogic reading Interactive, shared picture book reading during which the adult and the child gradually switch roles so that the child learns to become the storyteller with the assistance of the adult, who plays the role of active listener and questioner.

What Works

Dialogic Reading

Dialogic Reading is interactive, shared picture book reading that enhances children's language and literacy skills, according to the What Works Clearinghouse at the U.S. Department of Education. During the shared reading practice, the adult and child gradually switch roles so that the child learns to become the storyteller with the assistance of the adult, who plays the role of active listener and questioner.

Teachers can use dialogic reading with children individually or in small groups. While reading books with the children, the teacher uses five types of prompts or questioning strategies to stimulate children's language interaction. A handy mnemonic device to remember the prompts is the word *CROWD*. The table below lists the prompts with examples of questions from a reading of *The Tale of Peter Rabbit*, by Beatrix Potter.

The CROWD prompts are used by the adult in a reading technique called PEER:

Prompts the child to say something about the book.
Evaluates (listens to) the child's response to decide how to respond.
Expands the child's response.
Repeats the prompt.

As the child becomes increasingly familiar with a book, the adult reads less, listens more, and gradually uses more high-level prompts to encourage the child to go beyond naming objects in the pictures to thinking about what is happening in the pictures and how this relates to the child's own experiences.

Research on dialogic reading demonstrates that it enhances the language skills of children from middle- and upper-income families more than typical picture book reading alone. More important, studies conducted with children from low-income families found substantial positive changes in the development of children's language.

Prompt	Description	Example
Completion prompt	Child completes an incomplete sentence.	Teacher: "Peter Rabbit got stuck in _____."
Recall questions	Teacher asks questions about the book the child has read.	Teacher: "What did Peter lose in the garden?"
Open-ended questions	Teacher encourages child to tell what is happening in a picture.	Showing the picture of Peter caught and the birds flapping their wings, the teacher asks: "How are the birds helping Peter?"
Wh- questions	Teacher asks *Wh-* questions about the pictures in books. These questions help children think about a character's motives or feelings.	Teacher: "Why do you think Peter went in the garden even though his mother told him not to?"
Distancing questions	Teacher relates pictures and words in the book to children's own experiences outside of the book.	Teacher: "Have you ever been scared like Peter? What happened? What did you do?"

Source: Based on *Dialogic Reading* (What Works Clearinghouse Intervention Report), by Institute of Education Sciences, 2007, Washington, DC: U.S. Department of Education, retrieved February 20, 2012, from http://www.eric.ed.gov/ERICDocs/data/ericdocs2sql/content_storage_01/0000019b/80/29/e1/30.pdf.

completion prompt A prompt that requires the child to verbally complete the end of a sentence.

recall questions Questions asked by the teacher about a book to see what children remember.

open-ended questions Questions asked by the teacher that encourage a child to tell what is happening in a picture.

Wh- **questions** Questions that begin with "Why" or "What" to get children thinking about characters' motives or feelings.

distancing questions Questions that relate pictures and words in the book to children's own experiences beyond the book.

narrative A story with a beginning, middle, and end; characters; dialogue; and a plot with a problem to solve or a dilemma to be resolved.

predictable books Books with controlled vocabulary using parallel text structures that become familiar to children.

groups and rereading the same book are especially effective strategies for dual language learners and children from low-income families (McGee, 2013; Schickedanz & Collins 2013).

Small groups make it possible for each child to see the pictures, follow the print, participate in a discussion, and comprehend the story better. Small-group reading makes it more feasible for teachers to interact with children before, during, and after reading. This is particularly valuable when the book has a complex narrative and rare words. A **narrative** is a story with a beginning, middle, and end; characters; dialogue; and a plot with a problem to solve or a dilemma to be resolved. Interactive, shared book reading is a highly effective strategy for expanding children's language and listening comprehension. To learn more about this research-based practice, read the *What Works: Dialogic Reading* feature.

Reading to the Whole Group The effectiveness of small-group reading does not mean that teachers should never read to the whole group. If the book is relatively short and involves children's active participation and *predictable* text, whole-group reading may be the best choice. **Predictable books** use parallel text structures that become familiar to children, such as those in Bill Martin's *Brown Bear, Brown Bear* or Dr. Seuss's *Hop on Pop*. The whole group can chime in during Eric Carle's *The Very Hungry Caterpillar* with predictable text such as "But he was still hungry."

Throughout the first five years of life, children develop language and early literacy skills simultaneously, and the two are interrelated (Dickinson, 2011; Shanahan & Lonigan, 2013). Reading to children enhances their language because the structures and words used in books are more complex than those used in everyday speech. Knowing more words, in turn, helps children make sense of print and find what they read more meaningful and interesting. Talking with children about what is read further boosts vocabulary and comprehension. But what about children who don't speak the language of the classroom? Next, we discuss the timely topic of learning in two languages.

✓ **Check Your Understanding 12.2:** Scaffolding Children's Language Development

dual language learning Simultaneously learning two languages: the home or first language as well as English or another second language.

 # Dual Language Learning

Consider these two phrases: *English language learners* and *dual language learners*. The first communicates that the focus is on children learning English. In contrast, **dual language learning** conveys that children are learning two languages—their home or first language as well as English or another second language. Effective teachers understand the process by which children acquire a second language and how best to support children as they learn two languages (Espinosa, 2013).

How Children Learn a Second Language

Acquiring two or more languages is a complex process that doesn't happen as easily for young children as some people think. Generally, children take one of two paths to becoming bilingual—either simultaneous or sequential (Genesee, Paradis, & Crago, 2011). When children learn two languages at the same time during the earliest years of life—**simultaneous acquisition**—their dual language development is similar to that of monolingual children, those who are learning only one language. All over the world, children grow up in homes learning multiple languages from birth. Sometimes one language will become more dominant depending on the context. Similarly, it is normal for vocabulary development in each language to be uneven (Espinosa, 2013).

simultaneous acquisition Learning two languages at the same time during the earliest years of life.

By contrast, many children, especially in the United States, are **sequential language learners**. They learn a second language *after* their first language is relatively well established (Espinosa, 2013). Learning two languages sequentially is a more complicated, highly individual process that varies with children's personality, experience, and other factors but tends to follow a relatively predictable pattern, described in the next section.

sequential language learning Learning a second language *after* the first language is relatively well established.

Developmental Continuum: Dual Language Acquisition

The sequence of second language acquisition is described in the feature *Developmental Continuum: Second Language Learning.* The length of time individual children spend at each level varies, and unlike learning their home language, learning a second language is a conscious process that requires effort.

Young children who are learning a new language will often alternate between the two languages even within the same sentence. When children understand and use elements of both their home language or dialect and English, they **code switch**, also called language mixing. Teachers aren't always sure what to do about it. Code switching is a well-developed skill in most bilingual, bicultural individuals, and it contributes to their ability to think and analyze complex problems and express emotions (Garcia, 2005). To learn more about this skill and how teachers should respond to it, read the *Culture Lens: Understanding and Responding to Code Switching* feature (see page 393).

code switch The ability to understand and use both the mainstream version of English and the home dialect or language.

Teaching Dual Language Learners

Several myths about teaching dual language learners continue to persist despite research to the contrary. Some of the most common myths are that children must learn one language before they can learn another, that learning a second language delays or interferes with learning the first, or that learning more than one language harms brain functioning (Espinosa, 2013). In fact, learning two languages does not confuse or overwhelm children, nor does it delay their English acquisition.

Research demonstrates that beginning at birth, all children have the capacity to learn any of the world's languages and the younger the child's brain, the greater its capacity to learn more than one language (Rivera-Gaxiola, Silva-Pereyra, & Kuhl, 2008). Moreover, bilingualism in children from ages 4 to 8 has long-term positive effects on cognitive development and executive function, including the ability to think flexibly and solve problems that require taking different perspectives (Rodriguez, Carrasquillo, & Lee, 2014). This may be because bilingualism regularly requires children to mentally shift between two language systems.

Some non-English-speaking parents are so concerned that their children learn English that they avoid speaking their native language and want early childhood programs to do the same. In these cases, teachers need to help parents understand that it is important for children to have a strong foundation in their home language. Maintaining and developing the home language is vital for nurturing family relationships and cultural values (Rodriguez et al., 2014).

As for school achievement, the more words and concepts children know in their first language, the more likely that knowledge will transfer as children become proficient in English (Espinosa, 2013). Learning to read is also more effective when instruction occurs in the home language (Cheung & Slavin, 2012). Children who receive content instruction in their home language perform better academically later in school than those enrolled in programs designed primarily to teach them English (Rodriguez, Carrasquillo, & Lee, 2014; Thomas & Collier, n.d.).

The reality of so many dual language learners in today's classrooms means that teachers have a special responsibility to help children make progress in understanding and speaking *both* English *and* their home language. A growing body of research finds that

Developmental Continuum
Second Language Learning

Stage	Description	How Teachers Can Help
Stage 1: Home Language Use The child speaks the home language only.	Even though other people are speaking English, children may not realize or understand that the two languages differ. At first, they try to use their home language, but soon learn that this isn't working. At some point, this becomes frustrating and they stop trying, leading to the second stage.	Teachers provide cues to help children make sense of words by pointing to and labeling objects. At lunchtime, Rachel sits with a group of Spanish-speaking 4-year-olds. As they eat, she labels the utensils and food, speaking slowly and distinctly. "Spoon," she says as she picks up her own. "Here's your spoon for your soup," as she guides Carlos to follow her directions.
Stage 2: Nonverbal, Observational Period After children stop trying to speak in their first language, they enter a period where they do not talk at all, but rather listen and observe.	This period can last for a long time or can be relatively brief, depending on the individual. This stage is sometimes called the silent period, but a better name is the nonverbal period. Silent implies that no communication occurs. Actually, during this period, children are learning a lot about the new language by listening and observing, but they are not verbal themselves. Children may not be talking, but that does not mean they are not communicating.	Teachers should not force nonverbal children to speak. Instead of talking, children may try to communicate nonverbally to get help from adults or other children. They may point to the object they want or smile when their request is granted. Gradually, they begin to rehearse the new language by speaking some words quietly to themselves or playing with the sounds. A child says, "Paint paper" and the teacher interprets whether the child wants to paint or to take her picture home.
Stage 3: Telegraphic and Formulaic Speech Children have a small, working vocabulary in the second language and begin to use it out loud.	Children speak in one- or two-word utterances and repeat routine phrases without understanding what they mean. At story time, Carlos automatically says, "It's circle time" because he has heard these words in this context many times.	Teachers give simple choices that require "yes" or "no" or one-word responses, such as "Do you want to play with blocks or paint?" Children can also answer simple *who*, *what*, or *where* questions.
Stage 4: Productive Language Children begin producing the new language. This stage can take 1 to 2 years, during which children gradually produce longer sentences.	Listening comprehension improves as receptive language increases. Children use the social language of the classroom or playground, such as "My turn now" or "Be my friend." They begin to apply the grammar rules of the new language, but not consistently. Children are better able to participate in academic learning.	Rather than correcting "errors," teachers strive for communication. Carlos might say, "I like my school big" rather than "I like my big school." His teacher responds, "I'm glad you like our big school." Teachers ask *how* and *why* questions that require short responses: "How did your shoes get wet?"
Stage 5: Fluent Second-Language Production Moving from emergent to fluent language production can take 1 to 2 years.	Children can understand what is said in the classroom and begin to understand written communications.	Teachers use open-ended questions that engage children in producing more complex sentences. Second language learners will probably need extra help in the early grades, where the curriculum focuses on learning to read. Teaching reading in the home language is most effective.

Stage	Description	How Teachers Can Help
Stage 6: Advanced Language Proficiency	Children have developed understanding of specialized, content-related vocabulary. It can take from 5 to 7 years for children to master this level of cognitively demanding language.	Teachers intentionally teach the vocabulary and language skills required for academic achievement in school. For example, mathematics requires knowing words like *addend* or *double-digit multiplication* that are not used in everyday speech.

Sources: Based on *Getting It Right for Young Children from Diverse Backgrounds: Applying Research to Improve Practice*, by L. M. Espinosa, 2010, Upper Saddle River, NJ: Pearson; *Oral Language and Early Literacy in Preschool: Talking, Reading, and Writing*. 2nd edition, by K. A. Roskos, P. O. Tabors, and L. A. Lenhart, 2009, Newark, DE: International Reading Association.

Culture Lens

Understanding and Responding to Code Switching

Code switching is the ability to understand and use both the commonly accepted version of English and the home language or dialect. When children are learning a second language, they often code switch, usually beginning a sentence in one language and then switching to the other as in: "I drew a picture de mi madre" or "Mi mano es dirty." Code switching is not limited to children. In fact, bilingual people of all ages alternate between languages depending on the setting and the topic of conversation. Many bilingual individuals find that they can best express their feelings and personal thoughts in their native language.

In the past, it was assumed that code switching meant that children were confused or incompetent. But now we know that the opposite is true: children are able to separate the languages in their brains and apply the different rules of grammar of each language. Code switching is actually a sign of children's growing communicative competence. They are using all they know to communicate as clearly as they can.

So what should teachers do about code switching? First, they should expect code switching as a normal aspect of dual language learning. The most important thing is *not* to correct children when they mix languages. Correcting children's language attempts sends a signal that they've done something wrong. They may stop trying to communicate in order to avoid making the "mistake" of code switching.

Instead of focusing on children's "errors," teachers should focus on understanding the child's message. They should view code switching as a strength. As always, teachers should be good language models themselves, using the same strategies that promote language learning in all children: listening and responding in a meaningful way, using real objects and nonverbal cues, intentionally teaching new words, and extending conversations with questions and ideas.

Sometimes bilingual teachers think that they can support dual language learning by alternating languages themselves. Again, the opposite is true. Children's brains will automatically listen and respond to the language they know best and tune out the other one. To promote dual language development, bilingual teachers can read books in each language but should do so at separate times.

Encouraging children to code switch and responding positively honors the language system that they already possess and helps them adapt to different communication requirements in different situations. And it also respects and supports their cultural identity because language and culture are inextricably linked. Teachers should always create a warm, positive classroom climate in which children feel safe to express themselves. Capable code switchers acquire the ability to think about their own use of language, which serves them well in other learning situations and has long-lasting positive effects on language, cognition, and social development.

Source: Code Switching: Why It Matters and How to Respond, by National Center on Cultural and Linguistic Responsiveness, no date, Washington, DC: U.S. Department of Health and Human Services, Office of Head Start. Retrieved January 26, 2015, from http://eclkc.ohs.acf.hhs.gov/hslc/tta-system/cultural-linguistic /fcp/docs/code-switching.pdf.

Language Lens

Teaching Dual Language Learners

Of 16 children in Pedro Cordero's Head Start classroom, 12 speak Spanish as their home language. Pedro intentionally uses both English and Spanish to support explicit goals for children in each language. During conversations with individual children, he often speaks Spanish, finding that it helps him get to know the children and build positive relationships with them. During more formal gatherings such as story time or small-group activities, he often speaks English. But he connects new words to real objects or pictures, and he checks children's understanding regularly. Pedro's assistant teacher speaks only English; she and the English-speaking children provide language models for the dual language learners.

In many states in the United States today, the type of teaching Pedro does would be prohibited by law in K–12 public schools. In the belief that bilingual education prevents learning English and hurts academic success, some states have adopted "English-only" laws.

But what does research say about English-only teaching and children's success in school? Many studies now support the long-term benefits of bilingualism. One large-scale study of 345 Spanish-speaking children in 161 prekindergarten programs found that when teachers spoke some Spanish, Spanish-speaking children demonstrated better social skills than children whose teachers spoke only English. In addition, children whose teachers spoke some Spanish were less likely to be victims of aggression, bullying, or teasing, and their teachers were more likely to have a positive relationship with them. The amount of Spanish that teachers spoke was significantly related to teachers' ratings of children's assertiveness, attention and task persistence, and ability to get along with other children. On the other hand, the more English interactions children had, the more likely they were to

have behavior and learning problems and become easily frustrated.

An important—and seemingly contradictory—finding was that the amount of Spanish spoken in the classroom was not related to a child's English proficiency. In the study, teachers spoke Spanish with Spanish-speaking children only 20% of the time. When speaking directly to Spanish-speaking children, teachers who spoke some Spanish still used English two-thirds of the time. When speaking to a group, teachers tended to use English. When teachers spoke Spanish, however, they had more elaborate conversations with children, a key finding considering the research on the value of extended conversations for vocabulary development.

The researchers concluded that English-only teaching of young children may contribute to the achievement gap rather than help close it. Numerous other studies confirm that compared to children in bilingual programs, children in English immersion programs are more likely to have low reading and math achievement in fifth grade and to eventually drop out of school. From the perspective of research, the Spanish-speaking children as well as the English-speaking children in Pedro Cordero's Head Start class should benefit from his approach to teaching.

Sources: Based on "Spanish Speaking Children's Social and Language Development in Pre-Kindergarten Classrooms," by F. Chang, G. Crawford, D. Early, and D. Bryant, 2007, *Journal of Early Education and Development*, 18(2), 243–269; "A National Study of School Effectiveness for Language Minority Students' Long-Term Academic Achievement," by W. P. Thomas & V. P. Collier, no date, Center for Research on Education, Diversity, and Excellence, retrieved from http://www.usc.edu/dept/education/CMMR/CollierThomasExReport.pdf.

supporting their home language has distinct benefits for children, as discussed in the *Language Lens: Teaching Dual Language Learners* feature.

In the previous sections, we described how children learn both their first and second languages and ways to promote language development from birth through primary grades. Next we turn to the related topic of how children become literate.

 Check Your Understanding 12.3: Dual Language Learning

 # Early Literacy: Birth through Age 5

Young children begin the process of learning to read and write long before they enter formal school. Decades of research shows that children who enter kindergarten with specific kinds of knowledge and skill are more likely to become successful readers and writers (National Early Literacy Panel [NELP], 2008; Shanahan & Lonigan, 2013).

Developmental Continuum: Early Literacy Learning

Some of the widely held expectations for children's literacy development from birth through age 5 are presented in the *Developmental Continuum: Early Literacy* feature. Accomplishing these goals assumes that children have had good learning opportunities. Individual children's progress will vary, depending on their prior experiences with written language and other factors.

Teachers need to be intentional in promoting children's language and literacy learning. This means that they thoughtfully plan and prepare in advance but are also playful (Roskos, Tabors, & Lenhart, 2009). Children need to playfully explore and engage in activities involving reading, writing, and learning letters and sounds. These opportunities are more likely to occur in a literacy-rich environment.

▶ **Classroom Connection**

In this video you will see many examples of how a print-rich environment can contribute to children's early literacy learning. However, children do not learn automatically. What should an intentional teacher do to ensure that children learn optimally in such an environment?

Literacy-Rich Environments

Some children grow up in homes where they observe family members reading books and magazines, writing lists, browsing the Internet, or answering e-mail. But access to literacy and technology is unequal in our society. Affluent American children may have as many books in their bedrooms as poor children have in their entire neighborhoods (Neuman & Celano, 2002).

From their environment, children learn whether literacy is valued and important. Therefore, every classroom needs to be rich in literacy-enhancing materials and experiences (Roskos & Neuman, 2011). To picture a literacy-rich environment, consider the following example:

A look into Ms. DeSoto's preschool room reveals the many ways she creates an environment that communicates the value of literacy to children and teaches them important skills. In strategic places, she posts signs, labels, and other print materials that have real purposes, such as the names of today's helpers, classroom attendance, message boxes, menus, and directions. But she is careful not to clutter the classroom because too much print on the walls becomes as meaningless to children as wallpaper. Instead, she engages children in creating and using the print and calls children's attention to it as when she points to the written schedule on the wall and says, "Let's look at the schedule and see what we will do after lunch."

One of the children's favorite spots is the cozy, well-lit library area with its comfortable, child-size furniture and pictures of favorite story characters. Books are attractively displayed on open shelves, accessible to children and inviting their interest, much as bookstores do when they attractively display covers of new titles. The classroom library is well stocked with at least five books per child, with two to three per child on display at one time. The collection includes culturally and developmentally appropriate storybooks, information books, wordless picture books, and poetry. There are also iPads with e-books and apps in multiple languages.

Ms. DeSoto places books and writing tools in centers where they are relevant, such as a book on construction in the block area and paper and markers to make signs. Even a casual observer notices that books are in children's hands throughout the day, not just in the teacher's hands during story time. Shelves are stocked with games, toys, and equipment that promote knowledge of letters and sounds such as alphabet blocks, magnetic letters, and an alphabet puzzle. Handheld digital devices are available with apps for children to practice letters and phonological awareness as well as more sophisticated apps with which children practice writing and creating their own stories.

Developmental Continuum
Early Literacy

Age Range	Widely Held Expectations
Most babies (about 6 to 12 months)	• Play with books, so books should be sturdy cardboard • Put them in their mouths, chew them • Open and close them • Bang on them • Look at the pictures briefly • May look at the book with an adult for a short time
Most toddlers (about 12 to 24 months)	• Love to look at the same book again and again • Point out pictures to the adult and label pictures with names • Like to turn the pages (though not in order) • Sit for a few minutes to look at a book • Pretend to read by turning the pages and babbling • Connect the pictures to real objects (point out a doll after seeing the picture of a doll) • Take books off the shelf • Like books with textures or sounds
Most 2-year-olds	• Recognize favorite books by their cover • Listen to short stories and enjoy book-reading routines, such as lap book reading • Label objects pictured in books • Begin to pay attention to print, especially the first letter of their name. • Play with sounds and enjoy rhymes and songs • Scribble and gradually produce increasingly controlled scribbles with some letter-like forms (circles and lines)
Most 3- and 4-year-olds	• Enjoy listening to and talking about age-appropriate story books and information books • Understand that print carries a message • Can follow the sequence of events in a story and answer questions that demonstrate listening comprehension • Pretend to read and attempt to write • Recognize familiar labels and environmental print (signs for stores, street signs). • Understand concepts of print and directionality (English is read left-to-right and top-to-bottom) • Attend to chunks of sound in spoken language, identify rhymes and alliteration (silly Susie), clap syllables • Recognize many letters, especially those in meaningful words • Make some letter-sound matches (as when attempting to write words) • Use known letters and letter-like symbols to represent written language

Sources: Based on *Learning to Read and Write: Developmentally Appropriate Practices for Young Children: A Joint Position Statement,* by the International Reading Association and National Association for the Education of Young Children, 1998, Washington, DC: NAEYC; and *Preventing Reading Difficulties in Young Children,* edited by C. E. Snow, M. S. Burns, and P. Griffin, 1998, Washington, DC: National Academies Press.

Early Literacy from Birth to Kindergarten

Early literacy is the knowledge and skills that are the forerunners of conventional reading and writing. Research demonstrates that specific early literacy skills predict later success in learning to read and write (Shanahan & Lonigan, 2013). These **predictors** do not guarantee success, but they do increase the likelihood of success. More important, without these abilities upon entrance to kindergarten, children are more likely to encounter difficulties in learning to read (Snow et al., 1998).

Research-based early literacy skills include phonological awareness, alphabet knowledge, print awareness, and oral language (NELP, 2008). Other important skills that contribute to later reading include writing (specifically, name writing), listening comprehension, and motivation to read. In the following sections, we define and describe each of these skills and effective ways teachers promote children's literacy learning. (In the previous sections, we described numerous strategies for building vocabulary.)

Phonological Awareness and Letter Knowledge Written language is a symbol system—a code that children need to learn. This code may seem abstract and beyond young children's capacity. However, children are constantly exposed to abstract symbols, including *walk/don't walk* symbols, computer icons, pictures to signify male and female restrooms—the list is endless.

Precisely because written language is a complex symbol system, children need practice playing with it over many years to become proficient users (Yopp & Yopp, 2009). At preschool, the two important skills for learning the code are phonological awareness and learning the alphabet (Shanahan & Lonigan, 2013).

Understanding Phonological Awareness **Phonological awareness** is the consciousness that the stream of spoken language is made up of smaller units or chunks of sound (Schickedanz & Collins, 2013). Phonological awareness develops along a continuum, from recognizing the larger units of sound, such as **rhymes** (two words ending with the same sound) and **alliteration** (two words beginning with the same sound), to the smaller units such as syllables. A more complex level of phonological awareness involves awareness of parts of syllables.

The most difficult level is **phonemic awareness**, or recognizing that spoken words are made up of individual sounds called **phonemes**. English has approximately 44 phonemes that are represented by the 26 letters of the alphabet either alone or in combination. The letter *m* stands for a sound, while the letters *th* stand for another sound. The word *bat* is made up of three phonemes: /b/, /a/, and /t/. If one phoneme is changed—using /m/ instead of /b/—the meaning of the word is changed. Phonemes are important to later reading because written language represents these sounds.

Teaching Phonological Awareness As with virtually every other early literacy skill, children do not automatically acquire phonological awareness. Teachers need to intentionally plan experiences that help children make progress on the phonological awareness continuum, beginning with the bigger chunks of speech (words) and eventually moving to the smallest ones (individual phonemes). Some preschool teachers provide limited experiences or continue rhyming activities, although children have acquired this skill rather than moving

Literacy-rich environments help children experience the pleasure and power of reading and writing. In classrooms such as this one, children use print for real purposes. What would children learn about literacy in this environment?

early literacy Skills and knowledge that come before and lead up to (forerunners) conventional reading and writing.

predictors Set of early literacy skills and knowledge that increase the likelihood of later success in learning to read and write.

phonological awareness Consciousness that the stream of spoken language is made up of smaller units or chunks of sound.

rhymes Two words ending with the same sound.

alliteration Two words beginning with the same sound.

phonemic awareness Recognizing that spoken words are made up of individual sounds that can be manipulated.

phonemes The individual sounds of spoken language; changing one in a word changes the meaning of the word.

Knowing the alphabet is one of the best predictors of later success in learning to read. What are some developmentally appropriate ways to teach letters to young children?

alphabetic principle The understanding that there is a systematic relationship between letters and sounds, and that all spoken sounds and words can be represented by a limited set of agreed-on symbols called *letters*.

print awareness Beginning knowledge about written language.

on to more complex abilities (Pelatti, Piasta, Justice, & O'Connell, 2014). But these activities need to be fun and playful to ensure children's participation, motivation, and interest (Yopp & Yopp, 2009).

Learning the Alphabet The ability to read and write depends on mastering the **alphabetic principle**, the understanding that there is a systematic relationship between letters and sounds, and that all spoken language can be represented by a set of agreed-on symbols called *letters* (Adams, 1990). Children will not master the alphabetic principle in preschool, but knowing the alphabet at kindergarten entry is the strongest predictor of success in reading during first grade (Jones, Clark, & Reutzel, 2012). *Knowing letters* means remembering their shapes, names, and sounds (Stahl, 2014). Because the names of many letters mirror the sounds they represent, learning letter names is an important skill.

Teaching the Alphabet Katya, age 2½, and her dad drive to Kmart to buy some clothes. Her dad points to the large sign and says, "Look, Katya, there's your K." Katya wonders, "This is my store. Why are these people here?"

Like many children her age, Katya has discovered her letter and she feels personal ownership. But how did this important discovery occur? As her father demonstrated, Katya's parents helped her learn the first letter in her name. As with phonological awareness, children need adult support to learn the alphabet.

The alphabet is a set of arbitrary symbols with preset names that require instruction. Teaching the alphabet is necessary, but how it is taught is also important. Because adults clearly value this skill, most children are motivated to learn the letters. However, teachers need to make learning the alphabet meaningful. Teaching one letter a week or teaching letters without any connection to sounds and words is not effective (Jones, Clark, & Reutzel, 2012). Letters are not "equal." Some letters, such as *M* and *S*, are easily mastered because the letter name and sound are very similar; while others such as *Y* and *C* are much more difficult. Focusing on a letter a week gives too much time to some and not enough to others; it also doesn't help children compare and see relationships among letters.

As Katya did, children first focus on the letters in their own names. If they frequently see their name in writing, at some point between about 18 months and age 3, they will identify the first letter as their own. A child may be affronted if someone else claims the letter, too. Toddlers love to sing the alphabet song, play with alphabet blocks, and look at alphabet books.

In the classroom, letters should be where children can see, touch, and manipulate them, such as magnetic or sandpaper letters (Neuman, Copple, & Bredekamp, 2000). Name writing is an important ability that helps build all other early literacy skills (Puranik & Lonigan, 2012). Children need to see uppercase as well as lowercase letters and different fonts of the same letter. This way, children learn the "essence" of the letter symbol rather than only one representation of it. For a description of how to effectively teach the letters and sounds, read the *Becoming an Intentional Teacher* feature.

Print Awareness **Print awareness** is beginning knowledge about written language. Various purposes of print include communication, expression, explanation, direction, and

Becoming an Intentional Teacher

Teaching the Alphabet and Phonological Awareness

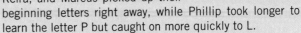

Here's What Happened   I teach 4-year-olds in a Head Start program. Our literacy goals include alphabet knowledge, phonological awareness, print concepts, early writing, and book appreciation. Most of my children have had limited exposure to books in their homes so I take every opportunity to integrate literacy learning throughout the day. Fortunately, our program is well equipped with both traditional reading and writing materials, and various digital devices including touch-screen tablets and an interactive whiteboard.

At the beginning of the year, I found that most children could identify only one or two letters. I began to set aside a short time each day (a total of about 10 minutes) to focus on teaching letters and phonological awareness together, in large- or small-group activities. For example, during morning meeting, I may use the interactive whiteboard to introduce a new letter—perhaps the beginning letter of a child's name or a special day such as Valentine's. The children can trace letters and move images around on the whiteboard. We also play active games like making the letter in the air or with our bodies. Another activity is for children to go on a hunt to find the letter in the classroom or in a book, or to find an object that begins with the letter.

The children especially enjoy focusing on how their mouth feels when they form letter sounds, which inevitably makes them laugh. I also demonstrate both the uppercase and lowercase versions of a letter, starting with those that look most alike and later moving on to the more difficult ones.

At the end of a week, we review the letters and sounds we've learned. Children may also independently practice their letter skills on the tablets, which I've loaded with educational apps for basic skills such as *Elmo Loves ABC* and others that promote vocabulary, writing, and comprehension. I also have Spanish language apps so that children can learn these skills in Spanish, which will later to transfer to English.

I find that children's writing is especially effective in building their letter-sound knowledge and motivation to learn letters. Working in small groups primarily, we begin with the letters in children's names. Falicia, Bode, Keira, and Marcus picked up their beginning letters right away, while Phillip took longer to learn the letter P but caught on more quickly to L.

Here's What I Was Thinking   Previously, I thought that learning the alphabet was a relatively easy skill that children would pick up from reading books and seeing print in the classroom. But after I systematically assessed children's letter knowledge, I realized that I needed to explicitly teach letter-sound relationships—always in a fun and engaging way—as well as embed letter-sound learning in read-alouds, writing, and other literacy experiences. Given the children's lack of prior alphabet knowledge, I found that they needed repeated opportunities to play with and practice letters and sounds.

Integrating digital media was highly motivating for the children and me. My two biggest challenges have been to identify high-quality apps and to find time to scaffold individual children's engagement. But almost all the parents have smartphones and many have tablets, so I recommended some free apps for children to practice with at home or in the car. And I talked to parents about how they could play along with their child.

Reflection   This teacher intentionally used whole-group, small-group, and individual instruction as well as print and digital media to promote literacy skills. She provided more complex experiences as children mastered new ones. What other ways could she have taught letter-sound relationships, language, and early literacy?

Source: "Research into Practice: New Insights about Letter Learning," by K. A. D. Stahl, 2014, *The Reading Teacher, 68*(4), 261–265; "Enhancing Alphabet Knowledge Instruction: Research Implications and Practical Strategies for Early Childhood Educators," by C. D. Jones, S. K. Clark, & D. R. Reutzel, 2012, *TEaL Faculty Publications*, Paper 404, retrieved from http://digitalcommons.usu.edu/teal_facpub/404.

information. Concepts and abilities related to print awareness include (Schickedanz & Collins, 2013):

- Understanding that print performs a variety of functions and purposes
- Recognizing print in the environment (such as in signs or labels)
- Knowing that print, not pictures, carries the message in the story
- Understanding the concept of *word*—that is, that specific clusters of letters on the page with spaces between them represent the words said by the reader
- Realizing that print represents speech or thought that is written down
- Realizing that print in English is read left to right, top to bottom

The skills listed above—also called **concepts of print** *or print conventions*—are important elements of literacy learning (Schickedanz & Collins, 2013). These developmentally appropriate outcomes are challenging but achievable for preschool children if they have good teaching and planned learning experiences.

concepts of print Beginning understandings about the forms and functions of written language, such as that words carry messages.

Early Writing

Encouraging young children to write is an effective way to help them learn to read (Schickedanz & Collins, 2013). Research demonstrates that talking, reading, and writing are developing simultaneously, and that progress in one area supports learning in the others (NELP, 2008; Snow et al., 1998).

Continuum of Early Writing   As children try to write on their own, the writing process promotes print awareness as well as many other early literacy skills (Schickedanz & Collins, 2013). Children's writing is another area that tends to follow a developmental progression, as described in the continuum on page 396 and depicted in the examples in Figure 12.1. At first, they do not distinguish drawing and writing. But over time they learn the difference and will label scribbles that are indistinguishable to adults as one or the other. Pointing to an elongated scribble, 4-year-old Chris identifies it as his name (see Figure 12.1a).

Gradually children's scribbles become more deliberate and controlled. Between the ages of 3 and 4, children incorporate letter-like shapes or symbols (circles and straight lines) and random strings of letters (see Figure 12.1b). Often children begin to identify sounds within words, and 4-year-olds begin to use *invented spelling*, at least with initial consonants in English. Spanish-speaking children tend to use vowels first (Snow et al., 1998). Typically, the first recognizable word children produce is their name (see Figure 12.1c).

Temporary **invented spelling**, also called *developmental* or *phonetic spelling*, represents children's initial attempts to associate sounds with letters, as when a 4-year-old writes "Mk" for "Mike." This process of trying to figure out how to write words is an important step on the way to learning conventional spelling. Observing and talking with children as they produce these spellings enables teachers to monitor children's understanding of letter-sound relationships. For example, 6-year-old Katie writes: "Good moraning. We are going to be bise [busy]. We are genu go to the postofs [post office]."

Using invented spelling does not interfere with learning conventional spelling. In fact, the opposite is true. Invented spelling actually accelerates children's later development of phonemic awareness and conventional spelling when it is taught in the primary grades (Snow et al., 1998). With practice and support, primary-grade children's writing becomes more conventional as in the example of a first grader's writing and drawing in Figure 12.1d.

invented spelling Developmental or phonetic spelling that represents children's initial attempts to associate sounds with letters.

Teaching Early Writing Skills   When children see adults writing, they want to write, too. To encourage and scaffold writing, teachers need to reinforce children's sense of competence (Graham & Harris, 2013). Curriculum should expose children to various types of writing. A cooking project requires them to attend to a recipe. Science experiments require data collection. Children's desire to protect a block structure motivates them to write a sign.

It is important that teachers not focus too much attention on children's handwriting because that approach is likely to be less meaningful and potentially frustrating for children. Teachers and parents should not be alarmed when children reverse letters or even write words as if in mirror-image. These "errors" are normal at this age (Schickedanz & Collins, 2013). If children persist in writing letters backwards, however, teachers scaffold correct production. For example, 4½-year-old Franklin tends to write his name backwards. Mr. Gandini notices that he starts writing on the right-hand side of the page and usually runs out of room, so he continues toward the left. He simply says, "Franklin, why don't you start your name up here in the left-hand corner of your paper, the way I write people's names on their paintings. Then you have plenty of space."

Book Appreciation and Motivation to Read

Children who are motivated to read show interest in books and reading, connect reading events to real life, and experience the pleasure and power of reading (Neuman et al., 2000). All children can come to appreciate books and find that reading is enjoyable, especially if they are exposed to books at a very early age.

Reading with Babies and Toddlers   Earlier in this chapter, we described how interactive book reading facilitates language development. Reading aloud is especially valuable for promoting children's literacy skills and motivation to read. Like so many other aspects of teaching, appropriate use of books varies with the age of the child.

FIGURE 12.1 Progression of Child's Writing These figures illustrate the typical progression of children's writing skills—from scribbles, to letter-like forms, to recognizable letters and words, and then to complete sentences.
(a) Scribble-writing
(b) Letter-like forms
(c) Prekindergarten name writing
(d) First grader drawing and writing

Babies and toddlers explore and "play" with books. This is why publishers sell board books and cloth books that can stand up to the onslaught of a baby's interest. Teachers should sit with a child on their laps or close by a few children to feel an affectionate connection. They shouldn't expect children to sit still nor should they try to read a book word for word or beginning to end. Instead they should describe what they're doing—"I'm going to open the book. Now let's turn the page," and use simple words to talk about the pictures: "The fish is swimming. Splish, splash." Exploring books with babies and toddlers builds their interest and enjoyment, which is further developed during the preschool years.

Reading Aloud with Preschoolers One of the most important goals of all early literacy experience is to get children excited about books and eager to learn how to read. In fact, young children who love books ask for them to be read over and over, memorize them, and proudly announce that they are reading. For a variety of reasons, however, not every child has these wonderful early experiences with books. Therefore, preschool teachers must actively make reading pleasurable and fun, and build children's appreciation for books and motivation to become literate. To build children's motivation to read, effective teachers (based on Head Start, 2003):

- Hold children on their laps or snuggle with them in small groups so their children can see and touch the book, helping to develop positive feelings about reading.
- Hold the book and turn the pages so children can always see the pictures.
- Read with expression and enthusiasm, using different voices for characters in the story. Overdramatizing distracts children from attending to the book.
- Occasionally pause to build suspense, to ask children to predict what will happen next, or to increase their interest ("Uh, oh. Here comes the big bad wolf!"). They pause briefly to clarify the meaning of an unknown word if it is crucial to understanding the story.
- Make sure that books reflect children's culture, home language, and identity.
- Plan times during the day when children select their own books to look at alone or with a friend. They allow children to take books home or to receive books to keep.
- Read to children several times a day, every day, expressively and enthusiastically.
- Read favorite books repeatedly when requested. Talk with children about their favorite books and authors, and encourage children to write or e-mail them and use the Internet to get more information about authors' lives and work.

For nearly every child, the process of learning to read becomes difficult at some point, whether in first grade, when decoding becomes the focus of instruction, or in third grade, when comprehension takes center stage (Snow et al., 1998). Children who are motivated to read are more likely to persist when they encounter these challenges. Motivation is also important because the more a child reads, the better reader he or she becomes (Snow et al., 1998; Stanovich, 1986). Children who like reading and, therefore, choose to read are almost always good readers.

Literacy and Background Knowledge Early literacy experiences are now a key part of every good early childhood program but they should not become the whole curriculum. Because the curriculum lends itself to integration, many teaching strategies are effective for multiple goals. For example, book reading promotes listening and understanding, vocabulary development, phonological awareness, alphabet knowledge, print awareness, knowledge in a subject area such as science, and even social problem-solving skills. Learning curriculum content builds all-important **background knowledge**, concepts, and basic information about how the world works (Neuman, Roskos, Wright, & Lenhart, 2007).

background knowledge
Concepts and basic information about how the world works that is essential for reading comprehension.

Background knowledge is essential for reading comprehension. Information books are especially valuable sources of such knowledge. As a result, the Common Core standards call for a 50-50 balance between fiction and nonfiction reading in kindergarten. Information books are more cognitively challenging than stories. However, teachers tend to talk less when reading them, which is a missed opportunity to enhance their value (Price, Bradley, & Smith, 2012). Exposure to information books and academic vocabulary in the early years helps prepares children for the texts they will later encounter in elementary school.

Play and Literacy Children's play provides an excellent and highly motivating context to learn literacy and language. Various types of play can be employed to help children develop these important skills. Read the feature *Promoting Play: How Play Supports Language and Literacy Development* for some examples.

Promoting Play

How Play Supports Language and Literacy Development

Next year, Ms. Keegan's preschoolers will attend kindergartens in which the curriculum is designed to meet Common Core standards. She knows how important it is to prepare them for the rigorous expectations. But she also understands the value of play for children's development and learning and provides various types of play to help meet her language and literacy goals.

To build children's speaking and listening skills, she uses several strategies. She identifies a theme or project that children are interested in and key vocabulary words that are connected to the topic. She intentionally teaches new words, frequently repeats them, and engages children in extended conversations using the words. Much of this "instruction" happens during their play, as we see in the following example.

After a visit to the local airport, Ms. Keegan's preschool class wants to take an airplane ride. She helps them set up an airport and airplane that includes lots of literacy opportunities: a computer to make plane reservations; paper and markers to write tickets, baggage tags, and signs for departures and arrivals; and magazines and iPads to read on the plane. They organize chairs into the two aisles of the plane and choose roles. Two children are the pilots, three are the flight attendants, one is the ticket agent, another is the baggage handler, and the rest are passengers. In preparation, one group writes tickets while another sets up a beverage cart.

As the plane loads, Grayson, the flight attendant, greets each passenger with a "Welcome aboard" and tells the assembled group to fasten their seat belts. The pilots announce that the plane is going to Disneyland. Most children get deep into the scenario and stay with it for 20 minutes or more. The play is repeated for several days, with children exchanging roles and practicing the language of air travel.

After a few days, Ms. Keegan invites a real pilot to visit. She explains her job and introduces new words. She also describes how pilots read and write every day. After the visit, children consult Google maps and other geography apps to identify and practice writing flight plans.

One of the defining characteristics of sophisticated socio-dramatic play is the use of language. During such play, children try to imitate adults, and their language becomes more complex and sophisticated. Similarly, when children play out roles in pretend contexts, they adapt their speech style and employ the familiar scripts common to those settings. For instance, the airport, office, and restaurant are different contexts, each with its own vocabulary and script.

To stimulate language, teachers may need to take a role in play to get it going or to extend it to include more language. For instance, Ms. Keegan might arrive at the airport and say, "I almost missed the plane. Can you tell me what to do in case of emergency? How does the oxygen mask work?" Play provides many opportunities to practice such verbal interaction with other children and occasionally with adults.

Ms. Keegan used play to support children's use of sophisticated language and extended conversations. The play also provided many opportunities for the children to express their ideas and extend their knowledge of letter-sound relationships through writing.

Sources: "Learning through Play," by L. M. Morrow, S. B. Berkule, A. L. Mendelsohn, A. L. Healey, and C. B. Cates, 2013, in D. R. Reutzel (Ed.), *Handbook of Research-Based Practice in Early Education*, pp. 100–118, New York: Guilford Press; *All about Words: Increasing Vocabulary in the Common Core Classroom, PreK–2*, by S. B. Neuman and T. S. Wright, 2013, New York: Teachers College Press.

The predictors described in the previous sections are the forerunners of successful reading and writing. We now turn to the topic of the formal teaching of reading in the primary grades.

 Check Your Understanding 12.4: Early Literacy Birth through Age 5

Literacy in the Primary Grades

In this section, we introduce some of the key terms and issues in teaching reading. We revisit the reading and writing developmental continuum. Then, we describe the components of an evidence-based reading program and the importance of digital literacy. We conclude with a discussion of the impact of the Common Core English Language Arts (ELA) standards.

Learning to Read

Conventional reading is reading in which the reader gains meaning from unfamiliar text. This is what we think of when we talk about being literate—the ability to read without conscious effort, the way adults and older children read. English is an alphabetic language, as are Spanish and many other languages. In these languages, we translate or **encode** speech sounds into symbols—the letters of the alphabet—to create writing. Reading requires the ability to **decode**—that is, to figure out what those symbols represent.

Basically, reading involves two processes:

1. **Word identification**: the process of decoding unfamiliar words and recognizing high-frequency (both regularly and irregularly spelled) words by sight, such as *the*, *with*, *that*, *house*, *dog*.
2. **Comprehension**: the ability to understand what is read and to interpret and analyze the author's meaning.

For many decades, there have been heated debates about which of these processes is more important and needs more attention when teaching beginning reading. Today, researchers agree that effective reading instruction helps children master the alphabetic principle and acquire meaning from text—what is called a **balanced approach** (International Reading Association [IRA] & National Association for the Education of Young Children [NAEYC], 1998; Kim, 2008; Snow et al., 1998). Such an approach is more likely to be meaningful and motivating for children and, therefore, more likely to help them become successful readers.

Learning to read is an example of a *both/and*, not an *either/or* choice—both decoding and comprehension are required. Teachers need to realize that it is impossible to understand what you cannot decode, but it is possible to decode what you cannot understand. Those of us who have never studied physics, for example, would probably be able to "read" (that is, decode) the words in a physics textbook, but would have no idea what we've read.

Sidebar glossary

conventional reading Reading in which the reader gains meaning from unfamiliar text.

encode Translating speech sounds into symbols—the letters of the alphabet—to create writing.

decode The ability to figure out what written symbols—letters of the alphabet—represent.

word identification The process of decoding unfamiliar words and recognizing high-frequency (both regularly and irregularly spelled) words by sight.

comprehension The ability to understand what is read and to interpret and analyze the author's meaning; the ability to make sense of what is read.

balanced approach Effective reading instruction that helps children master the alphabetic principle *and* acquire meaning from text.

Developmental Continuum: Literacy in Kindergarten and Primary Grades

The *Developmental Continuum: Literacy in Kindergarten and Primary Grades* feature describes reading and writing expectations for this age group. Being familiar with such a continuum is useful for teachers because it identifies the goals for literacy instruction at each age level and helps them assess children's progress toward those goals (McAfee, Leong, & Bodrova, 2015).

Children's progress along the continuum depends to a large extent on their earlier experience. Children will arrive at kindergarten and first grade with very different abilities. Some will already be reading; others may know only a few letters. Therefore, teachers must adapt their instruction to start where children are and help them make continuing progress.

Evidence-Based Reading Instruction

Given the current understanding of research, the National Reading Panel identified five components of an evidence-based reading program that are now widely used in planning and evaluating curriculum (NICHD, 2000).

▶ Classroom Connection

Observe the many ways the teacher in this video effectively uses learning centers to implement a research-based, balanced approach to teaching reading with her primary-grade students. What do you observe about the children's developing skills, understanding, and motivation to learn?

Developmental Continuum
Literacy in Kindergarten and Primary Grades

Age/Grade Level	Widely Held Expectations
Most kindergartners	• Enjoy being read to, retell stories and what they've learned from information books • Experiment with and use early literacy skills • Respond to open-ended questions that require inferences about a story and connections to events beyond the story • Begin to track print when listening to book • Use language to describe and explain what is read • Recognize and name all upper- and lowercase letters automatically and makes most letter-sound matches • Demonstrate phonemic awareness, blend and segment syllables in words, and blend and segment onsets and rimes • Write letters and high-frequency words • Recognize some words by sight, including common ones (a, the, me, you, is) • Use phonemic awareness and letter knowledge to write with invented spelling • May read emergent literacy texts conventionally by the end of kindergarten
Most first graders	• Make the transition from experimental to "real" or conventional reading • Read aloud accurately and with reasonable fluency texts appropriate for beginning grade 1 • Use letter-sound associations, word parts, and context to identify new words • Use strategies when comprehension breaks down (picture and context clues, rereading, predicting, questioning) • Use reading and writing for various purposes on their own initiative ("I want to write a Valentine for my mom.") • Sound out and represent all substantial sounds when spelling a word • Identify an increasing number of words by sight, including common irregularly spelled words, such as *said*, *where*, and *two* • Write various kinds of texts about meaningful topics (journals, stories) • Use some punctuations and capitalization correctly
Most second graders	• Read more fluently and write various text forms using simple and more complex sentences • Use word identification strategies to figure out unknown words • Use strategies to aid comprehension more efficiently, such as rereading, questioning, using context • Read with greater fluency • Identify an increasing number of words by sight • Write about a range of topics for different audiences • Use common letter patterns to spell words • Punctuate basic sentences correctly and proofread their writing • Read daily and use reading to get information on topics of study

(Continued)

Age/Grade Level	Widely Held Expectations
Most third graders	• Read fluently and enjoy reading • Extend and refine their reading and writing for various purposes and audiences • Use a range of strategies to make meaning from unfamiliar text • Use word identification strategies appropriately and automatically when encountering unknown words • Recognize and discuss elements of different text structures • Write expressively in various forms such as stories, reports, and letters • Use a rich vocabulary and complex sentence structure • Revise and edit their writing during and after composing • Spell words correctly in final drafts

Sources: Based on *Learning to Read and Write: Developmentally Appropriate Practices for Young Children: A Joint Position Statement*, by the International Reading Association and National Association for the Education of Young Children, 1998, Washington, DC: NAEYC; *Preventing Reading Difficulties in Young Children*, edited by C. E. Snow, M. S. Burns, and P. Griffin, 1998, Washington, DC: National Academies Press.

Each of these components—phonemic awareness, phonics, fluency, vocabulary, and comprehension—is described in the sections that follow.

Phonemic Awareness Phonemic awareness is one of the strongest predictors of success in reading (Strickland & Schickedanz, 2009). Without it, later instruction in phonics doesn't make sense. However, although research has found that phonemic awareness is absolutely necessary for success in reading, it is not by itself sufficient; there is much more to beginning reading than the spoken sounds of words (NICHD, 2000).

phonics A system of teaching the correspondences between letters or groups of letters and the sounds they represent.

Phonics Phonics is a system of teaching the correspondences between letters or groups of letters and the sounds they represent. Although the use of phonics to teach reading has been hotly debated, the value of phonics has long been established as a necessary component in an effective, research-based program (Chall, 1967; Strickland, 2011). The major issue concerning phonics instruction is not whether to teach phonics and other skills such as spelling, but how to teach them in engaging ways that support children's continued reading development as well as their motivation to read. Whereas some children need extensive help with phonics, other children do not (Strickland, 2011).

fluency Rapid, efficient, and accurate word recognition skills that permit the reader to comprehend the meaning of text.

Fluency Fluency refers to rapid, efficient, and accurate word recognition skills that permit the reader to comprehend the meaning of text (Rasinski, 2009). Fluency is first apparent when children are able to read out loud quickly, accurately, and with appropriate expression. This ability then leads to their ability to comprehend what they read silently.

Fluency is like the bridge between phonics and comprehension (Rasinski, 2009). If children's decoding skills are inadequate, they must slowly sound out and stumble over each word. By the time they've reached the end of the sentence, they've forgotten the words they've read and, as a result, the sentence doesn't make sense. Fluency requires practice and careful matching of texts to children's approximate reading ability.

How do children become fluent readers? One way is for teachers to read aloud to children, modeling the elements of fluent reading (Pikulski & Chard, 2005). Fluency requires practice. Another way is for children to read short passages to each other in pairs. Even after children in the primary grades become fairly competent readers, teachers should continue to read to them, using more sophisticated chapter books than students can read independently.

Vocabulary As described earlier, vocabulary knowledge is perhaps the strongest predictor of reading comprehension (NICHD, 2000). Children who understand and use more words to begin with are more likely to recognize these words in print. When they encounter unknown words in their reading, they can figure them out based on what they already know (Snow et al., 1998).

Because children in the primary grades need to grow their vocabularies by about 3,000 words per year, they need to learn about 15 words per day (Beck, McKeown, & Kucan, 2013). Consequently, vocabulary instruction needs to be intentional and explicit during these years, especially for children who are behind in vocabulary development at school entry (Neuman & Wright, 2013).

Reading Comprehension *Reading comprehension* is the construction of meaning from unfamiliar text—the ability to make sense of what is read. A prerequisite for high levels of reading achievement is a rich amount of background and content knowledge. The content that children learn in social studies, science, and other areas provides essential background knowledge to comprehend what they read. For this reason, children need a great deal of experience with information (nonfiction) texts in the primary grades (Duke, 2014).

A solid base of knowledge is essential for becoming a skilled reader and succeeding in school (NICHD, 2000). By third grade, the curriculum shifts from a focus on learning to read to an expectation that children read to learn, as they encounter increasingly more complex textbooks. In fact, the fourth-grade reading slump that typically occurs in American schools may be caused in part by children's lack of content knowledge from which to make sense of more challenging texts (Duke, 2014; Hirsch, 2007).

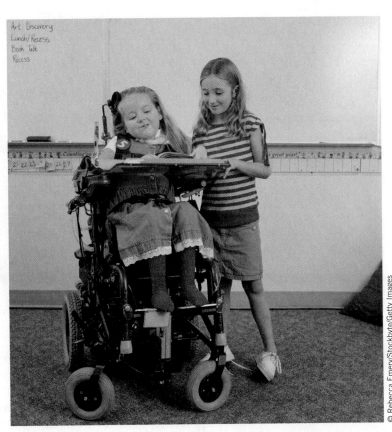

Reading information books in primary grades serves the dual purpose of helping build word identification skills and background knowledge. Both are needed for reading comprehension.

Digital Literacy

In 2015, the International Reading Association officially changed its name to the International Literacy Association (ILA) to reflect the fact that reading is only part of literacy today. Children of every age must learn to use technology and digital media to enhance all their communication skills—reading, writing, speaking, and listening. Across the curriculum, they need to seek information online and connect that knowledge with what they learn offline. Children also need to learn the strengths and limitations of various technological tools and media, and choose those that are suited to their communication goals.

Life in our technological society, requires more than reading; it requires **digital literacy**, the ability to locate, understand, interpret, and evaluate information from multimedia, digital sources (Labbo & Nogueron-Liu, 2013). One of the biggest challenges teachers face, however, is deciding among the vast number of educational apps and games that purport to teach children to read. A survey (Guernsey, Levine, Chiong, & Severns, 2012) of the most popular ones found that despite lofty claims, more than half focused on very basic skills—letters, sounds, phonics, and word identification. Only about 10% addressed higher-level abilities such as vocabulary, comprehension, and storytelling.

digital literacy The ability to obtain, use, interpret, and evaluate information available through multimedia, digital sources.

© Hero Images/Getty Images

Digital literacy is essential today as children must learn to find, use, interpret, and critically evaluate information from print and nonprint sources.

Impact of the Common Core State Standards

In the past, reading instruction in kindergarten and the primary grades focused on such basic skills as phonics and word identification. Concerns about uneven, low educational standards and poor academic achievement in many states led to the Common Core State Standards initiative (2011a). Common Core standards are designed to ensure that all children are prepared for college and careers in reading, writing, speaking, listening, and language, and they significantly raise the bar across all grades.

The Common Core English Language Arts (ELA) standards begin at kindergarten, but because they are so rigorous, they have had a significant impact on prekindergarten as well. Many early childhood educators are seriously concerned that the standards are developmentally inappropriate and that implementing them is harming children (Carlson-Paige, McLaughlin, & Almon, 2014). Most worrisome is the expectation that kindergartners should "Read emergent-reader texts with purpose an understanding." Common Core includes examples of what is meant by *emergent-reader* story books such as *Are You My Mother?* by P. D. Eastman and *Green Eggs and Ham* by Dr. Seuss, and information books such as *My Five Senses* by Aliki.

To help children achieve the overarching goals of comprehension, critical thinking, communication, and creativity, the ELA arts standards (Common Core State Standards Initiative, 2015a) emphasize the following:

- *Complexity.* Students are expected to comprehend complex texts and learn academic vocabulary that is used in a variety of content areas such as science or social studies.
- *Evidence.* Students are required to provide evidence—gleaned from literature and information books—to support their opinions and conclusions, both verbally and in their writing. For example, instead of simply asking children if they liked the story or how it made them feel, the teacher would ask, "What in the story made you feel (that emotion)?"
- *Background knowledge.* To build content knowledge, the K–third-grade standards call for a 50-50 balance between fiction and nonfiction books.

Common Core also stresses that literacy involves using, communicating, interpreting, and evaluating digital media sources. For example, Common Core assessments are delivered on computers or tablets requiring students to have technological aptitude and keyboard skills.

The Common Core standards have become a political hot button. Abolishing them has become part of presidential candidates' platforms as well as parents' and some teachers' agendas. Whether the Common Core is implemented or changed drastically, it has had a significant impact on the way that literacy is defined and the expectations for teaching and learning.

In previous sections, we discussed the development and learning of verbal and written communication skills. In the final sections, we address another dimension of human communication—the creative arts.

✓ **Check Your Understanding 12.5:** Literacy in the Primary Grades

Communicating Through the Arts

We began this chapter with a visit to a primary school where teachers used children's art production and appreciation to teach language, reading, and writing. In previous sections, we focused on two dimensions of communication: language and literacy. Although it is true that speaking, listening, reading, and writing skills are essential for school success, they are not the only ways of communicating and learning, as is clear from Gardner's theory of multiple intelligences.

Young children, who tend to be less inhibited than older children and adults, use their entire bodies to express their ideas and emotions. If encouraged and provided a range of interesting materials, they can be incredibly creative in representing their world through traditional and digital media. Children's enjoyment and accomplishment in the creative arts depend, in part, on teachers providing adequate materials, time, and instruction in specific art techniques.

The Value of Creative Arts

The creative arts include visual arts, music, movement, dance, and drama. *National Core Arts Standards* for pre-K through grade 12 now exist that address all these areas plus media arts (National Coalition for Core Arts Standards, 2014). The overarching goals of the standards are that children create art; perform, present, and produce art; respond to art (interpret, evaluate, and find meaning in it); and connect art to their lives and the larger culture. The media arts standards address how all forms of art are created and presented using technology and digital media. The Core Arts standards are designed to align with the Common Core and also elevate the value and importance of the arts in education.

Each type of creative art supports children's imaginative thinking and expression of their ideas and emotions (Isenberg & Jalongo, 2013). Participation in the arts achieves several goals for children: enhanced cognitive development, promotion of symbolic representation, support for creativity, and engagement of children from all cultural and linguistic backgrounds.

As we saw in the case study at the opening of this chapter, the arts also provide an excellent basis for integrating curriculum. In fact, one study of an arts-enriched integrated curriculum in a preschool serving low-income children found that engaging children in music, creative movement, and visual arts improved their school readiness skills (Brown, Benedett, & Armistead, 2010). And a large body of research demonstrates that involvement in the arts enhances development and learning throughout schooling (Munsen, 2013; Ruppert, 2006). Such research contradicts the tendency today to minimize the arts in order to spend more time supposedly preparing children for academic success.

Creative Arts and Cognitive Development The creative arts contribute to children's development in many ways. Engaging in the arts helps children reflect on their own thinking, which becomes more complex as a result. The following example illustrates this relationship between the arts and cognition:

> Karen Spitzer's kindergarten class is involved in a yearlong study of plants and growing things. In the early days of spring, the children become very excited by the flowers bursting forth on the grounds surrounding their rural school. Karen guides the children to observe several types of roses closely. The children take sketch pads outside and draw the roses, and also take digital photos. When they return to the classroom, Karen reads an information book about flowers and projects their photos on the whiteboard. Then, she instructs them to "Use your poet's eyes (It's like . . .) instead of your scientist's eyes (I see and I describe specifically)." The children write short poems or sentences about how the flowers make them feel. Next, they create

pictures using various media such as tempera paint, watercolors, colored pencils, and chalk. Then, the children examine and critique each other's pictures:

Kehembe: I wanted my roses to be pink, but they look too red.
Chrystal: Yeah. Maybe you could add more white next time.
Tyree: Why don't you try the chalks? They come in more shades than the watercolors. Or try the paints because they're easier to mix colors.

The next day, Karen brings in a dozen roses. She places them in water near the art area and then gives each child one to hold.

Karen: Now look very carefully at your flower and compare it to your picture. What do you see?
Chrystal: Ouch! I forgot about the thorns. I'm going to put some in my painting.
Kehembe: My rose isn't just one color. Even though it's mostly light pink, there's white and some darker pink, too. And the stem is way longer than I thought.
Tyree: I'm going to try making a rose from wire and colored tissue paper so it will look more like a real one, not flat like my drawing and the photos.

Karen also projects different images of artists' depictions of flowers. The ensuing class discussion leads the children to conclude that there isn't a "right" way to represent an object—every artist has their own interpretation. In this example, many important things are going on. Children are having fun creating art. But even more important, they are developing key abilities: *symbolic representation* and *visual literacy* (discussed later in this chapter), which support language and literacy as well as thinking in all areas.

symbolic representation The process of mentally using one thing to stand for something else.

Symbolic Representation
Symbolic representation is the process of mentally using one thing to stand for something else. When children engage in the visual arts, they are using various media to represent their concepts of the real world (Thompson, 2013). Language is a representation of objects, experiences, feelings, and concepts. For example, in English we use the word *chair* to represent an object with four legs that we sit on. Other languages use a different word to stand for the same object. Written language is also an example of symbolic representation. The letters of the alphabet are symbols to represent the sounds of the spoken language. Developing symbolic representation is essential to speaking and reading.

Consider how Karen Spitzer, in the previous example, uses the arts to build symbolic representation in her kindergartners. The children represented the flowers in their initial drawings, in verbal descriptions, and in writing, and they read about them in books. Using different media, such as paint and sculpture tools, they again represented the roses. Then they observed real roses closely and discussed their pictures, reflecting on each other's representations. Finally, they were able to add more realistic detail, representing their more accurate concepts of a rose. The processes that Karen used with her class promoted their creativity, artistic ability, and symbolic representation skills. The activities were part of a science unit that also integrated language and literacy skills.

Supporting Creativity
Individuals are *creative* when they take existing objects or ideas and combine them in different ways for new purposes. Creative individuals use their ever-growing body of knowledge to generate new and useful solutions to everyday challenges (Isenberg & Jalongo, 2013). Therefore, creativity applies not only to the arts but to all aspects of children's experience.

To support children's involvement in the creative arts, effective teachers need to understand their role. Teachers can err in doing either too little or too much (Isenberg & Jalongo, 2013). Some teachers are too passive, providing no help with art techniques. They merely provide materials and stand back. The commonly heard phrase "It's not the product, it's the process" relates to this view of creativity. The assumption is that whatever children produce is unimportant compared to their creative use of materials.

▶ **Classroom Connection**

Watch this video to see how the visual arts promote symbolic representation, creativity, appreciation for the beauty of nature, observation skills, and content learning in an integrated curriculum study about birds.

By contrast, some teachers are too controlling, overemphasizing the finished product. These teachers may assume that parents want children to color within predrawn lines or produce art that conforms to adult-made models. Envision a classroom wall decorated with a series of rabbits that look like they came off an assembly line. The rabbit ears and other parts were obviously cut out by the teacher.

Cultural differences also exist in how adults view and support children's creativity. For example, one study found that Chinese American parents and teachers believe that children need formal art instruction first and then creativity will follow, while European Americans tend to assume

Working with diverse media helps build children's symbolic representation ability. What abilities do you think children gain by working on a group art project?

that children's creativity will emerge naturally (Huntsinger, Jose, Krieg, & Luo, 2011). In this study, Chinese American children's drawing skills from age 5 to 9 were more mature and creative than those of the European American children who had received less instruction.

The best approach is for teachers and children to value *both* the process *and* the product. Teachers need to understand that the process of producing art is more satisfying and educationally valuable if children have been taught some techniques (Thompson, 2013). Children will enjoy the art more and become less frustrated. At the same time, they will feel prouder about the products they themselves produce.

Teachers can also encourage creativity and learning through the arts by introducing children to excellent examples of art. As the teachers from the Thurgood Marshall School did at the beginning of the chapter, they can involve children in noticing, thinking about, and discussing the work of other artists. Then, to promote discussion, effective teachers use open-ended questions, which invite children to observe, critique, evaluate, and develop their own aesthetic preferences.

Engage Every Child All areas of the arts can involve and engage diverse groups of children. It is always important to adapt materials and experiences to ensure that children with disabilities can fully engage in the creative arts.

Art, music, and movement are areas where dual language learners can be included without needing to rely on their English language skills. All children can enjoy learning a song in either English or another language. In addition, when singing, there is a clearer distinction between each word than in speaking. With her 3-year-olds, Derry sings, "Head, shoulders, knees, and toes . . . and eyes, and ears, and a mouth and nose," touching each body part as she sings. Such a rhyme or song helps dual language learners by connecting physical movements with words.

Every cultural group has its tradition of artistic expression. Consider origami in Asian cultures or African masks. Teachers can involve families by inviting them to share creative art from their own culture and families. Exploring children's cultural diversity should not be limited to examining such artifacts, but including them is important.

Even at an early age, some children will say, "I can't draw." They've already learned that the broader culture values particular ways of representing the world. Digital media is a great way to motivate reluctant artists as well as those who happily embrace their creative selves. Engaging art production apps abound, such as *MoMA Art Lab* from New York's Museum of Modern Art.

In the following discussion, we describe and give examples of effective teaching strategies in each area—visual arts, music, movement, dance, and drama.

Visual Arts

The **visual arts** are creative processes and products that involve drawing, painting, sculpting with clay, or making models of objects using a variety of materials. Art experiences allow children to convey their ideas, feelings, and knowledge in visual forms. Individually and in groups, children use materials such as crayons, markers, paint, playdough, clay, wire, found objects, glue, tape, and paper, along with tools such as scissors, brushes, rolling pins, and cookie cutters. Developing an appreciation for and an aesthetic awareness of art is another important element. Including art forms, materials, and techniques from children's home cultures can increase their motivation and interest in art.

Developmental Continuum: Artistic Development The arts are part of the curriculum and, therefore, are influenced by children's development just like literacy or mathematics. To plan and implement a challenging and achievable arts curriculum, teachers need to understand the typical course of children's artistic development. As with other developmental areas, children pass through several stages as they progress in drawing and painting. However, children's progress is not as tightly linked to age as assumed in the past; instead it is strongly influenced by their experiences with various media and adult scaffolding (Thompson, 2013). Depicted in Figure 12.2, the progression of drawing is similar to early writing development.

When young children begin to draw, they first make random scribbles, lines, zigzags, and circles that may cover the whole paper (see Figure 12.2a). As they gain experience, children begin to produce shapes such as crosses, squares, and rectangles. Then they combine shapes, making sun-like objects using circles and lines. Soon children make figures that look like humans beginning as stick figures that gradually get more features, animals, houses, and trees (see Figures 12.2b & 12.2c).

With experience and adult scaffolding, children's artwork becomes more and more representational over time. They talk the process they used and what the product represents (Epstein, 2007). Increasingly, they plan what to create and decide which materials and techniques they will need and their work becomes more sophisticated, as we see in a first grader's action-packed firefighter scene in Figure 12.2d.

Understanding the typical sequence of children's artistic development helps teachers know what kinds of materials and experiences will be safe, interesting, achievable, and challenging for each age group; that is, what art is developmentally appropriate. For example, with a group of toddlers, it is unrealistic to expect representational drawing, but teachers can expect preschoolers to increasingly present more recognizable objects in their work, especially if the teachers provide scaffolding, as Karen Spitzer did in the earlier example of drawing flowers.

Artistic skills are related to physical development. When finger painting or sculpting with wire, playdough, or clay, children use their senses, explore the properties of the materials, build fine-motor skills, and practice eye-hand coordination. Children build the same muscles and skills they need for writing. Fine-motor skills are a strong predictor of later achievement because they enable children to have more diverse and challenging experiences that promote their cognitive development (Grissmer, Grimm, Aiyer, Murrah, & Steele, 2010).

Scaffold Artistic Development and Learning Many people think that creativity is inborn. Actually, children's ability to be creative depends in large part on their skills in producing art. Children who lack the skills to model with clay, for instance, may continue to roll clay into balls or make "snakes," but they won't advance to sculpting objects. Soon they may lose interest in working with clay altogether.

When teachers provide adequate materials, time, instruction in specific techniques, and assistance when needed, children's skills continue to develop (Thompson, 2013). For example, after observing the art center in her kindergarten, Lara Mann sees that Duane has a tendency to use too much water, sopping the paper that he inevitably wads up and

September 3,

This is how I draw my family on the first day of Pre-K

(a)

A L L I I N   October 3,

This is how I draw my family.

brother Brandon   Dad   mom   me

(b)

(c)

(d)

FIGURE 12.2 Progression of Child's Drawing These figures illustrate the typical progression of children's drawing from scribbles to stick figures, to more detailed and recognizable representations.
(a) Family drawing scribble
(b) Stick figure family
(c) 5-year-old's drawing "Mommy and me"
(d) Second grader's drawing

tosses away. With a little instruction in how to use watercolors effectively, Duane produces a painting he wants to take home.

Specific art skills that can be taught can be as simple as tapping the paint on the side of the can to get a more controlled stroke, as complex as using potter's clay to make elaborate and durable sculptures. Effective teachers encourage children by making positive, specific comments rather than by giving compliments. Instead of saying, "What a beautiful picture," they say, "I see you've made a pattern—two red stripes, two blue stripes, two red stripes, two blue stripes." The following example illustrates how important teacher scaffolding can be to maintaining children's enjoyment of art:

Three-year-old Emily, budding artist, loves to paint. She often spends long periods of time at the easel, layering colors of thick paint until her paper is wet through. After weeks of this activity, she tells her teacher, Lelia, that she doesn't want to paint anymore. When Lelia asks why, Emily says, "It always comes out brown." At this point, Emily's teacher has a choice. She can smile and ignore Emily's problem, or she can see the situation as a teachable moment.

Lelia begins by asking: Emily, let's think about why your pictures turn brown. What color do you put on first?

Emily: I like red best. And I like blue and yellow, too.

Lelia: Those are all pretty colors. Let's mix them together and see what color we get.

As Lelia and Emily mix the colors, Emily's eyes get very wide.

Emily: It makes brown! Let's try it again.

After they mix the color brown over and over, Lelia asks, "What could you do next time you paint a picture so it won't come out brown?" With such minimal assistance, Lelia supports Emily to find the solution of separating colors on her paper instead of continually painting over the same spot and renews Emily's enthusiasm for painting.

To effectively support children's artistic development and creativity, teachers need to organize the environment to provide sufficient space and materials for messy activity, cleanup, and storage of children's work and work-in-progress. Also critically important is for teachers to treat children's work with respect. To do so, teachers display children's work with their permission. They can also mat or frame selected works for each child to display and keep. Teachers encourage children to take art home to share with families. In preschool and in kindergarten and the primary grades, children can evaluate their own artwork and decide which products they judge worthy of keeping. Digital cameras and scanning extend the life of children's creations.

visual literacy Ability to create visual messages and to interpret messages contained in visual communications.

Intentional teachers use the visual arts to promote creativity, symbolic representation, visual literacy, and much more. Creative arts should be an integral part of the early childhood curriculum.

Promote Visual Literacy

All of the experiences described previously contribute to the development of children's visual literacy. **Visual literacy** is the "ability to create visual messages and to 'read' messages contained in visual communications; to perceive, understand, interpret, and evaluate the visual environment" (Johnson, 2008, p. 74). To build children's visual literacy experiences, teachers engage them in talking about art, extending their thinking about art, and reflecting on art (Johnson, 2008). These processes are similar to the connections that exist among speaking, reading, and writing.

Teachers engage children in talking about their art by commenting on colors, textures, techniques, and patterns. They also lead children through thinking and problem solving by asking open-ended questions such as "What materials did you use to make this flower sculpture?" and "How can you make a door in your house structure? What will you need? What could you do first?"

As in the case study that opened this chapter, teachers can help children observe, compare, and respond to the properties of artistic works. With a teacher's guidance, children can discuss the artist's use of color, shape, line, pattern, texture, and more. Typical comments might include "Look at the big blocks of color in

the Mondrian painting." "Look very closely. Can you see how the people in this picture by Seurat are painted with tiny dots of color?" "See how the Romare Bearden picture is a collage like we make." To bring art closer to children's firsthand experience, local artists can share and discuss a work-in-progress or display their work in the classroom.

Music, Movement, and Dance

On the first day of school for her preschool class, Yasmine gathers the children on the rug and begins to sing a simple song with corresponding hand gestures: "Open, shut them. Open, shut them. Give a little clap. Open, shut them. Open, shut them. Put them in your lap. Creep them, creep them. Creep them, creep them, right up to your chin. Open wide your little mouth . . . but do not let them in!" The children are enchanted and their attention is fully engaged. They beg for her to do it again. Many of them begin following her movements and mimicking the words immediately. Right from the start, the children learn that music will be a fun and active part of every day in Yasmine's room.

Developmentally appropriate music and movement experiences involve creating, performing (singing, making and moving to music), listening and responding, and connecting music and movement to interests, ideas, and knowledge (National Coalition for Core Arts Standards, 2014). Music and movement should be a primary focus of the curriculum and should also be used to accomplish other learning goals. Every day, teachers can provide opportunities for children to sing favorite songs, learn new ones, and make up their own. Children should also use simple rhythm instruments to create music or to accompany live or recorded music.

Music in the Lives of Young Children Children's experiences and connections with music begin at birth, when they are comforted by lullabies or the soft humming of their mothers' voices. Some families make music an integral part of their lives. By the time they reach the toddler years, many children have favorite songs and musical pieces. They listen attentively, sing along with a familiar chorus, move to the music, and begin making their own music by shaking a tambourine or banging on a pot or drum. As language skills develop, toddlers begin making up their own songs. If they have had many opportunities to listen to and talk about music, they can identify the sounds made by specific instruments such as a trumpet, drum, or violin.

Music experiences play an important role in children's lives. Music and dance influence children's identities, connect them to their cultural group and the larger society, help them experience and express emotions and ideas, and support their learning across the curriculum. Moreover, music and dance can be lots of fun.

Every cultural group and family has a musical tradition. As communities connect within a broader culture, these musical traditions are shared and influence each other. Rock and roll began as a blending of several musical forms, including the blues and gospel. This is what makes music a part of children's identities and why it is important to incorporate the music of children's cultures and home languages into the curriculum. If children don't know the songs, they can sing along with a recorded version of a song, such as "Abiyoyo," until everyone learns the words. An iPod can be loaded with literally hundreds of selections. Teachers can also introduce real or homemade versions of instruments that are typical of children's cultures.

Memory and sequencing are required to coordinate music and movement, and both require children to follow directions. The skills and knowledge that children gain from participating in music and dance include these (Head Start, 2003; Isenberg & Jalongo, 2013):

- Listening, as when children try to identify the words in a lyric or sounds made by different instruments
- Responding by clapping to the beat or marching around the room
- Creating music, by exploring the sounds made by different instruments and making up a new song or a verse for a familiar song

▶ **Classroom Connection**

Watch this video to see the many ways music and movement benefit children and how children can learn language, literacy, and other content from active participation.

https://www.youtube.com/watch?v=-sYxMKCFmAU

- Understanding, such as whether a piece of music has a slow or fast beat
- Playing music, such as when they use bells or rhythm sticks to accompany a song
- Moving and dancing with or without music—swinging, rotating, twirling, twisting, or shaking their bodies.

Music and Movement in the Classroom   Exposing children to all kinds of music provides many different opportunities for learning. First-grade teacher Malique is an amateur guitarist and music lover. Even though he doesn't sing very well, he never lets that stop him from singing with the children. He knows that children don't mind if the song is off-key as long as they can sing along, too. Malique introduces a different kind of music each week and provides follow-up activities. To launch this music appreciation curriculum, Malique invites sixth-grade band members to bring their instruments and demonstrate the sounds. The children love seeing the instruments up close and learning how to care for them. Then he plays a recording of portions of *Peter and the Wolf* and asks children to listen to how the instruments sound like animals.

Whatever music Malique uses in his classroom, he involves children in thinking and talking about their experiences. He asks questions such as "What do you like or dislike about it?" "How is it similar to and different from other music you have heard?" "What instruments do you hear in different pieces of music?" In this way, children can become critical thinkers about music as well as music appreciators.

Drama

Pretend play and dramatization involve creative production and demonstration. We have already discussed the benefits of socio-dramatic play for language and early literacy skills. Dramatization, however, is more closely tied to a specific story or script. Children in primary grades are more likely to engage in dramatization than younger children, although preschoolers do act out favorite stories. Children can also dramatize traditional stories from their own cultures.

Teachers can structure a drama session to promote literacy skills in story sequence, character development, and plot. Many dramatizations, both child initiated and teacher guided, involve retelling familiar stories. After reading *Three Billy Goats Gruff* to her class of 4-year-olds, Marissa Reese helps them act it out. First, she encourages their recall and story sequencing skills by asking them to tell what happened: "How did the story start?" "What happened next?" She helps them identify emotions or problems that surface in the dialogue: "How did the little billy goat feel?" As the children practice acting out the different roles, they get an opportunity to play with dialogue, changing their tone of voice and expression to fit the character of each goat or the troll.

Scaffolding dramatization requires providing different kinds and the right amount of support for different children (Davidson, 1996). Providing props of varying realism can meet the needs of inexperienced as well as capable players. Some will need realistic props to get into character, such as a variety of dress-up clothes or the actual props used by characters in a story. For example, after reading *The Little Old Lady Who Was Not Afraid of Anything* (Williams, 1988), a kindergarten teacher gives children props to act out the story—shoes, pants, shirts, and a hat—and create a scarecrow at the end. Other children can take on a creative role with more open-ended objects such as cardboard tubes, unit blocks, or pieces of cloth. Videotaping the production and sharing it on a class website or on YouTube encourages children to do their best work.

Seeing the Arts with New Eyes

Pablo Picasso once said that every child is an artist (cited in Arts Education Partnership, 1998). But given the current emphasis on the basics of reading, writing, and mathematics in early schooling, time and resources for arts education are diminishing. Many children today have less opportunity to experience the arts. However, all forms of art offer new ways in which children can build language and literacy skills, learn about their own and other cultures, and develop cognitive and social skills (Brown et al., 2010). Each of the creative arts can enhance development and learning in other areas. For example, children might count musical beats, draw or construct a model of the earth, analyze the message in a painting, or write dialogue for a drama.

A large body of research on the effects of early arts experiences finds a positive relationship with improved academic performance (Ruppert, 2006). Research in the arts also demonstrates that when creativity is developed at an early age, its results transfer to many intellectual tasks (Isenberg & Jalongo, 2013; Thompson, 2013). Given the power of the creative arts to promote children's learning and enrich their lives, teachers can use all forms of art in their teaching to keep students engaged and excited about learning.

Today, state standards and program goals for early childhood education always include language and literacy. Reading proficiency has become the overarching purpose of primary grades. Teachers who know and love young children, however, never lose sight of the long-term goal: learning to communicate creatively in all forms of the arts.

 Check Your Understanding 12.6: Communicating through the Arts

Revisiting the Case Study

. . . Thurgood Marshall School

At the beginning of this chapter, we visited a primary school where a school-wide art project was occurring. The curriculum at Thurgood Marshall, as at every other school in the United States, is full to the brim. Teachers need to be creative to cover the breadth of the curriculum while helping children gain depth in important subject areas. The art study was an excellent example of how teachers can integrate curriculum in meaningful ways. Teachers didn't miss an opportunity to infuse language and literacy throughout the day in all areas of study.

Having examined how children acquire language and become literate, we can now see how the art project promoted these skills. Children learned new vocabulary words and used language in conversation and analysis. They also used digital media and read books on topics of interest, thus promoting their motivation to read. They produced their own art and learned to appreciate and evaluate the work of other artists. These experiences developed symbolic representation ability and visual literacy. Firsthand experience with art sharpened children's observations and critical-thinking skills. All of these experiences motivated the children to become more competent and confident readers, writers, speakers, and artists.

12 Chapter Summary

- Children gradually learn language over many years from verbal interaction with adults and other children. Language development follows a relatively predictable sequence, but there is a wide range of individual variation that is well within the range of normal.

- Research-based vocabulary-building strategies include one-to-one and extended conversations, listening, decontextualized speech, intentional teaching of new and rare words, interactive book reading, and play.

- The developmental sequence of second language acquisition is similar but not identical to first language learning. To help children acquire English while also maintaining their home language, teachers must work effectively with parents and use proven classroom strategies, including play.

- Literacy is the result of many cumulative, interrelated experiences beginning at birth. Research demonstrates that there is a specific set of early literacy skills and knowledge that predict later success in learning to read and write: phonological awareness, alphabet knowledge, print awareness, and vocabulary. Other important skills that contribute to later reading ability include early writing, listening comprehension, motivation to read, and background knowledge.

- Conventional reading is the ability to gain meaning from unfamiliar text. The most effective reading instruction helps children master the alphabetic principle *and* acquire meaning from text in what is called a balanced approach. Components of an evidence-based reading program include phonemic awareness, phonics, fluency, vocabulary, and comprehension. Motivation is key to reading achievement.

- Common Core English Language Arts Standards emphasize students' developing higher-order thinking skills by reading complex texts with academic vocabulary, analyzing evidence, and gaining content knowledge from information books.

- Children learn to communicate through the creative arts: visual arts, music, movement, dance, drama, and media arts. The arts promote the development of symbolic representation, creativity, and visual literacy. Children's enjoyment and accomplishment in the creative arts depends on teachers providing adequate materials, time, and instruction in specific artistic skills.

Key Terms

- academic discourse
- alliteration
- alphabetic principle
- babble
- background knowledge
- balanced approach
- code switch
- completion prompt
- comprehension
- concepts of print
- conventional reading
- cooing
- decode

- decontextualized speech
- dialogic reading
- digital literacy
- distancing questions
- dual language learning
- early literacy
- encode
- expressive language
- extended discourse
- fluency
- invented spelling
- listening
- narrative

- open-ended questions
- parentese
- phonemes
- phonemic awareness
- phonics
- phonological awareness
- play-by-play language
- predictable books
- predictors
- print awareness
- rare words
- recall questions
- receptive language

- rhyme
- script language
- sequential language learning
- simultaneous acquisition
- symbolic representation
- syntax
- telegraphic speech
- visual arts
- visual literacy
- vocabulary
- *Wh-* questions
- word identification

 Demonstrate Your Learning

Click here to assess how well you've learned the content in this chapter.

Readings and Websites

Isenberg, J. P., & Jalongo, M. R. (2013). *Creative thinking and arts-based learning: Preschool through fourth grade*, 6th ed. Upper Saddle River, NJ: Pearson.

Neuman, S. B., & Wright, T. S. (2013). *All about words: Increasing vocabulary in the Common Core classroom, PreK–2.* New York: Teachers College Press.

Schickedanz, J. A., & Collins, M. F., (2013). *So much more than the ABCs: The early phases of reading and writing.* Washington, DC: National Association for the Education of Young Children.

Shanahan, T., Callison, K., Carriere, C., Duke, N. K., Pearson, P. D., Schatschneider, C., & Torgeson, J. (2010). *Improving reading comprehension in kindergarten through 3rd grade: A practice guide.* Available online at U.S. Department of Education's What Works Clearinghouse.

FPG Child Development Institute CONNECT Module 6—Dialogic Reading Practices

This website provides a step-by-step teacher's guide and series of 11 how-to videos demonstrating dialogic reading, one of the most effective language and literacy teaching strategies.

International Literacy Association (ILA)

Previously the International Reading Association, this organization's website offers a wealth of resources for teaching language and literacy from pre-K through third grade.

National Core Arts Standards

On this website you will find the most recent, comprehensive set of national learning standards for dance, music, theatre, visual arts, and media arts.

The Hanen Centre—Helping You Help Children Communicate

The Hanen Centre offers practical resources for early educators and parents to support young children's language, social, and early literacy development as well as information for working with children with autism or language delays.

Tap, Click, Read

Visit this new website for the most up-to-date information and resources to appropriately and effectively use digital tools to build children's literacy.

13

Teaching Children to Investigate and Solve Problems: Mathematics, Science, and Technology

Learning Outcomes

After studying this chapter, you should be able to:

13.1 Explain why learning mathematics and science is important in the early years.

13.2 Describe the continuum of cognitive development and how it relates to learning mathematics and science.

13.3 Apply effective teaching strategies and curricula that help children learn mathematics.

13.4 Apply effective teaching strategies and curricula that help children learn science.

13.5 Describe what children need to know about technology and how it can be used to teach effectively.

arrell Burns and Sofia Moreno co-teach in a state-funded prekindergarten program that is operated in a local child care center. The school district has just introduced a new preschool curriculum to align with the K–3 math curriculum. At first, Darrell and Sofia are skeptical about their children's ability to learn the content, and they feel somewhat anxious about tackling mathematics education themselves. "Math was always my worst subject," Darrell admits. "I majored in early childhood education rather than elementary because I didn't want to teach math." Sofia nods. "I know how you feel. I kind of memorized stuff for the test and never really understood it."

After several weeks, however, the teachers' attitudes change. The curriculum plan helps them understand the number and geometry concepts they are teaching as well as the important sequences of mathematics learning. Much to their surprise, the children are capable of learning sophisticated math concepts and truly enjoy the activities in which they participate.

Darrell and Sofia find that opportunities for learning math abound in their classroom. During center time, Sofia works with a small group of children on basic counting principles, using 1-inch cubes. Four-year-old Tori points at the blocks as she says, "One, two, three, five, seven, eight." "No, no," says her friend Parker, "You skipped four! I'll show you." Parker proceeds to say all the numbers in the correct order, but touches some blocks twice. Instead of counting six blocks, he comes up with eight. Sofia notes that Tori has yet to master the number word list, so she'll engage Tori in verbal counting more often. As for Parker, Sofia simply says, "Slow down a little, and touch each block as you say the word." After two more tries, Parker successfully counts six blocks.

Darrell oversees four children playing a board game with a number on each square. Two girls are working on a digital tablet, moving shapes to complete puzzles. Several children are building with unit blocks on the floor. Darrell observes them and adds math words to their play: "Dante, you've made a rectangle space with these cylinder blocks. Can someone else figure out how to make a rectangle?"

As the children become more interested in math, they start counting everything in sight and looking for shapes in the classroom and on the playground. They figure out ways to create new shapes, such as putting six triangle blocks together to form a hexagon. The children especially like taking digital photos of three-dimensional shapes such as spheres and cones, which they use to make a book on shapes. Sofia and Darrell help them make connections between what they are learning about math and their physical science study of the characteristics of light. The children look forward every day to measuring and comparing their shadows on the playground. ■

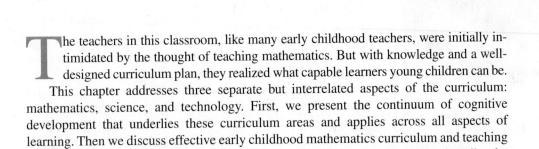

he teachers in this classroom, like many early childhood teachers, were initially intimidated by the thought of teaching mathematics. But with knowledge and a well-designed curriculum plan, they realized what capable learners young children can be. This chapter addresses three separate but interrelated aspects of the curriculum: mathematics, science, and technology. First, we present the continuum of cognitive development that underlies these curriculum areas and applies across all aspects of learning. Then we discuss effective early childhood mathematics curriculum and teaching strategies that lay the foundation for later school mathematics. Next, we describe the science curriculum and how teachers can engage children in the scientific process. Throughout the chapter, we describe ways to use technology in teaching and learning math and science. A key goal is to raise awareness of the importance of math and science for *all* children. We particularly focus on the need to narrow the persistent achievement gap in mathematics between children from low-income families and their more affluent peers.

The Importance of Mathematics and Science

In recent years, mathematics and science education have generated considerable interest for several reasons. The first is widespread concern about the nation's ability to produce a workforce qualified to compete in the global economy. Second is the issue of equal educational and economic opportunity for all citizens.

With so many competing goals in early childhood programs, why is mathematics important? Preschool math matters because it is highly related to later math achievement and because effective curriculum and teaching can narrow the knowledge gap early on (Duncan et al., 2007; Sammons et al., 2008). Research demonstrates that young children are capable of learning important mathematics and science concepts, but they are usually not given the opportunity to do so (National Research Council [NRC], 2009).

The Need for an Educated Workforce

Mathematics knowledge in preschool is a strong predictor of later success in learning both math and reading. Although an achievement gap exists as early as preschool, research shows that good teaching and math experiences can narrow the gap early on.

In today's global economy, a large number of jobs require mastery of what is called STEM—science, technology, engineering, and mathematics (American Association for the Advancement of Science, 2009). However, in international comparisons of mathematics and science achievement, children in other nations regularly outperform American children (Fleischman, Hopstock, Pelczar, & Shelley, 2010). Moreover, these

© Jules Selmes/Pearson Education

differences in mathematics knowledge are apparent as early as age 4 or 5 (Starkey & Klein, 2008; Starkey et al., 1999).

Although achievement in science and technology is important, understanding mathematics is strongly connected to both of these areas. As a result, more emphasis is being placed on children developing a firm foundation in mathematics during the early years of school. In 2009, the NRC issued a major report on early childhood mathematics that outlined recommendations for improving mathematics teaching and learning for all children ages 3 to 6.

The Mathematics Achievement Gap

Significant gaps exist not just between our country and others, but within our country. As in reading, a mathematics achievement gap of as much as three years exists between children growing up in more affluent communities and those living in poverty (NRC, 2009).

Mathematics Predicts School Success Although reading has received much more attention, research now demonstrates that math skills at kindergarten entry are the *strongest* predictor of later school achievement and executive function (Duncan et al., 2007). In an analysis of six large-scale longitudinal studies in the United States, Great Britain, and Canada, researchers found that early math skills predicted not only later math ability but also success in reading (Duncan et al.,

2007). By contrast, early literacy skills were related only to later reading. Apparently, the cognitive abilities employed in mastering mathematics apply broadly to other curriculum content areas.

Children who struggle with math are much less likely to graduate from high school and attend college (Szekely, 2014). Mathematics is a cumulative topic of study. Later understanding not only builds on earlier concepts but *depends* on them. Many adults who disliked math in school did not have a firm foundation on which to build. As a result, in later grades, more complex math didn't make sense and they began to feel less competent. Early education can narrow the gap. Research in the United States and other countries demonstrates that using a math-focused curriculum can significantly improve math achievement for all children (Clements & Sarama, 2007a, 2008; Griffin, 2004; Preschool Curriculum Evaluation Research Consortium [PCERC], 2008; Starkey, Klein, & Wakeley, 2004).

International Research Can Inform U.S. Instruction One international study compared mathematics learning among preschoolers of high and low socioeconomic status (SES) in China and the United States (Starkey, 2007). Two findings were noteworthy. First, Chinese 3-year-olds started out knowing more about math than their American counterparts regardless of their SES status. In fact, the low-SES Chinese group knew more math than the high-SES Americans. Nevertheless, a knowledge gap between socioeconomic groups existed in both countries at age 3. But by the end of preschool, the gap between the two groups had narrowed considerably for the Chinese youngsters but had actually widened for the Americans. What accounts for these differences? There are two feasible explanations:

1. Teaching mathematics in preschool and promoting mathematics at home is a higher priority in countries like China and Japan than in the United States (Starkey & Klein, 2008). The studies demonstrate that when young children, even those growing up in poverty, are taught more focused math, they learn it and carry it into later schooling.
2. A fundamental cultural difference seems to exist in the value these countries place on mathematics and their beliefs about what it takes to succeed. In the United States, we tend to assume that mathematics achievement results from having talent or innate ability; by contrast, in Eastern countries, the assumption is that students can achieve in mathematics if they work hard enough (NRC, 2001).

In the previous sections, we presented the case for teaching and learning mathematics in the early years. To truly understand the learning process, it is important to be aware of the cognitive foundations that underlie mathematics and science learning.

✓ **Check Your Understanding 13.1:** The Importance of Mathematics and Science

The Cognitive Foundations of Early Learning

The word *cognition* generally means "to know." In education, *cognitive development* refers to mental processes such as attention, remembering, language, and problem solving. These processes are essential for all learning to take place. However, in discussing one domain such as cognition, it is important to remember that children's development cannot be separated neatly into compartments. Cognitive, social, and emotional development are highly connected.

In this section, we delve into the domain of cognitive development. We begin by describing the continuum of cognitive development and then discuss several mental processes that are the foundations of all early learning, especially children's understanding of mathematics and science. These processes include executive function, concrete and abstract thinking, and language (Diamond & Lee, 2011; Ginsburg, Lee, & Boyd, 2008).

The Continuum of Cognitive Development

Children's cognitive abilities such as their attention, memory, thinking, reasoning, and problem solving develop over time as their experience increases and becomes more complex and their brains mature. For a description of these processes in children from birth through age 8, read the *Developmental Continuum: Cognitive Development* feature.

Executive Function

executive function The processes that control cognitive functioning such as thinking before acting, cognitive flexibility, and memory.

Perhaps the most significant cognitive achievement of childhood and adolescence is the development of executive function. **Executive function** has been called the brain's "air traffic control system" (Center on the Developing Child at Harvard University, 2011). Imagine the coordination it takes to ensure that hundreds of airplanes fly to the right places at the right times and don't collide with one another during takeoff and landing. Similar to the job of the air traffic controller, executive function coordinates essential abilities that make all other learning possible (Diamond, 2012). These include at least three key abilities: working memory, cognitive self-control, and cognitive flexibility (Center on the Developing Child at Harvard University, 2011).

working memory The ability to retain information for a short period of time, which enables transfer to long-term memory.

inhibitory control or **cognitive self-control** The ability to think before we act and to focus attention on what is necessary.

cognitive (mental) flexibility The ability to find new solutions or revise plans in response to changing circumstances.

These executive functions are vital for all learning. Memory is essential for new learning to take place and for previous learning to be retrieved when it is needed. **Working memory** is the ability to hold information in our heads for a short period of time, such as a phone number or where we laid down a sock. Working memory is necessary for children to follow multistep directions such as "go to the writing center, choose paper and markers, and draw a picture of yourself." **Inhibitory control** (also called **cognitive self-control**) is the ability to think before we act, which is very difficult for young children to do. In school, many tasks require mental self-control, such as waiting to be called on. Self-control requires focusing attention on what is necessary, such as the reading lesson, and ignoring irrelevant information, such as the fly on the wall. **Cognitive (mental) flexibility** involves finding new solutions or revising plans in response to changing circumstances.

Consider how children practice these executive functions when they engage in an activity such as socio-dramatic play. If a group of preschoolers play airport, they have to remember their role (pilot, passenger, or flight attendant), inhibit their actions (not jump out of the seat while the plane is flying), and think flexibly (adapt to the twists and turns of the plot, such as the plane being delayed).

Just as the air traffic control system integrates many complex parts working simultaneously, executive functions are interrelated. These abilities, which develop over time, are particularly important for reasoning and problem solving in mathematics and experimenting in science (Klahr, Zimmerman, & Jirout, 2011).

Children's Thinking

Three-year-old Levi was walking with his mother when he asked why she wasn't talking to him (N. Karp, 2011, personal communication). His mom, Gail, replied, "I'm thinking about the work I have to do." Levi got all excited and replied, "I'm thinking, too! I'm thinking about numbers. I love numbers. I love the way they look, I like the shapes, I like the names, and I love to count. I just like to think about numbers!" Like Levi, most young children have a natural interest in mathematical and scientific ideas, spontaneously count, and love big numbers (Ginsburg et al., 2008; Greenes, Ginsburg, & Balfanz, 2004).

In the past, educators assumed that young children had little capacity to learn mathematics or think scientifically; therefore, teachers often considered it developmentally inappropriate to teach math (Ginsburg et al., 2008). Researchers today believe children are more competent than previously thought and capable of learning sophisticated math ideas (Gelman & Gallistel, 1978; NRC, 2009).

Developmental Continuum
Cognitive Development

Approximate Age	Widely Held Expectations
Birth to about 9 months	• Learn through their senses (especially taste, touch) • Gain increasing control over their bodies • Increasingly able to remember people, objects, and favorite toys • Focus attention for short time • Gradually learn about cause and effect (3-month-old turns to noise; 6-month-old bangs toy to make noise) • Intentionally act on objects (kicks to move the mobile) • Enjoy solving simple problems, such as taking objects in and out of containers, and discovering consequences of actions • Develop object permanence (remembers that out-of-sight objects are still there)
About 9 to 18 months	• Increasing memory for games, toys, and people from previous days • Enjoy doing things over and over such as carrying and dumping • Use trial and error to solve problems • Observe and imitate others' actions • Begin to understand symbols (*M* for McDonald's) • Play with objects
About 18 to 36 months	• Begin to solve problems mentally (think before acting) • Develop memory and problem solving • Understand basic cause and effect • Begin to sort by categories (blue or red), compare size and shape • Complete simple puzzles accurately • Follow two-step directions • Pretend with objects
3- to 6-year-olds	• Experiment with and begin to understand cause and effect • Increasingly able to plan ahead, predict, and carry out an activity • Engage in socio-dramatic play with other children • Can generate more than one solution to simple problems • Can reason, but logic may be flawed ("The food goes into your legs and makes them grow.") • Increasingly able to focus attention, persist at tasks, self-regulate behavior and emotions • Able to compare and contrast, quantify (find out how many), put objects and events in order or sequence, understand spatial relationships • Has basic sense of present, past, and future
6- to 9-year-olds	• Can symbolically represent thoughts and ideas in many ways (drawing, writing, speaking, modeling) • Memory capacity increases considerably • Can take multiple perspectives (teachers, book authors) • Aware of patterns and part-whole relationships • Can make accurate predictions • Thinking and problem solving become more flexible • Can categorize and think conceptually • Play more complex games with rules, understand fairness • Solve concrete problems easier than abstract problems

© Lord and Leverett/Pearson Education

Young children are more capable of learning sophisticated math concepts than previously thought. Preschoolers are interested in and enjoy learning about mathematics.

subitizing The ability to look at a small set of objects (four or fewer) and know how many there are without counting.

Both Competent and Incompetent Children's minds are not simple, however. Compared to adults, children are *both* competent *and* incompetent; they are *both* concrete *and* abstract thinkers (Ginsburg et al., 2008). On the one hand, from an early age, they spontaneously demonstrate math interest and ability well before entering school. At the same time, children display certain kinds of mathematical incompetence, as when they struggle with *conservation* problems (Piaget, 1952). Conservation is the understanding that the quantity of objects stays the same regardless of changes in appearance. For example, Noah and Martina each have four graham crackers. Martina lines her crackers up with spaces in between, looks over at Noah and declares, "I gots more than you." Typically, children of this age cannot reverse the operation in their minds to realize that no more crackers were added. In certain situations, however, children can perform conservation tasks, depending on how an adult asks the question or alerts children to events they might not have focused on.

Both Concrete and Abstract Even 3-year-olds can look at a small set of objects (four or fewer) and know how many there are without counting, a skill called **subitizing**, a necessary precursor to later math competence (Clements & Sarama, 2007a). They can see that a set of three toy bears is smaller than a set of five.

In other ways, however, young children's thinking is abstract. Consider 4-year-old Francine counting her stuffed animals. She touches each one as she says, "One, two, three, four, five." Her teacher asks, "How many animals do you have?" Francine answers "Five," which seems like a very simple thing to do. However, this little girl had to know and say the counting words in the right order; connect each word to one and only one bear; and know that the last word said in the sequence not only stood for the last bear but also represented the total number of bears. That is, she had to remember that she had counted five bears in order to answer that she had five altogether—she had to hold two thoughts in her head at once. And she had to think about a very abstract concept—what *five* is. Five is still five whether it refers to five bears, five chairs, five children, or five fingers. She also sees, reads, and has to interpret an abstract symbol—the numeral 5—in different places. The numeral 5 is posted near the climbing loft because only five children are allowed at a time.

Conceptions and Misconceptions Children are actively thinking all the time as they try to make sense of their world. Some of these conceptions are accurate, such as Francine's computation of the five bears, while others are not. For example, a common "mistake" young children make is to assume that a "skinny," elongated triangle cannot be a triangle; they think that true triangles can only be equilateral triangles—ones with three equal sides (Clements & Sarama, 2007a). Children also form their own hypotheses about events, some of which seem like magical thinking. They may assume that the sun goes to bed because they do, not the other way around. Even primary-grade children think that a coat provides its own warmth rather than heat coming from inside their bodies.

Most misconceptions are actually partial hypotheses, or early theories, about how the world works. For example, 5- to 7-year-olds can readily state that the earth is round because they have been taught this fact. However, when asked to draw a picture of the earth and where the people live, their representations reveal their understanding (Hannust & Kikas, 2007). They may actually think the earth is a flattened sphere with the people living on top or that the earth is hollow and the people live inside. These partial hypotheses are gradually replaced by more accurate ones because, as children get older, their thinking becomes more abstract, and experience challenges their earlier ideas.

Some misconceptions can be prevented by broadening children's experiences. For example, unless children are helped to understand the common properties that make a shape a triangle, they will persist in thinking that "skinny" versions are not really triangles. It is normal for preschool children to make "errors" as they learn counting and other math and science concepts. Therefore, teachers should be cautious about correcting "errors"; they should encourage children's enthusiasm instead of making them hesitant to voice their own ideas (NRC, 2009).

Language and Cognition

Language plays a key role in cognitive development and, therefore, in learning mathematics and science. By age 2, children begin learning the language of counting. The first 10 or so number words are essentially meaningless—children memorize these words by rote (NRC, 2009). Even though this skill is learned before it has true meaning, knowing the number sequence is not the same thing as being drilled on it. Children memorize the sequence by playfully repeating it over and over, the same way they learn the alphabet sequence by singing the alphabet song long before the letters are fully meaningful. Knowing the alphabet sequence, however, is useful only for *alphabetizing*, a skill that preschoolers do not yet need; by contrast, learning the number sequence is absolutely essential.

The Language of Mathematics Beyond the first 10 numbers, language reflects the underlying structure of the number system. For example, in English, after the child learns "twenty," all she has to do is repeat "twenty" and add on the numbers one to nine up to "twenty-nine." Thus, saying the number words goes beyond simple memory to reflect the organization of the **base ten place value system**. The base ten system is a highly efficient way of using just 10 symbols—0, 1, 2, 3, 4, 5, 6, 7, 8, 9—to write any counting number, no matter how large (NRC, 2009). To do so, we use place value in which the meaning of a numeral depends on where it is placed within the number—that is, the numeral 1 can stand for 1 or 1 trillion.

Children also learn other kinds of mathematical language, such as the names of shapes and words for quantity (*more*, *less*), position (*under*, *inside*), and relationship (*bigger*, *smaller*, *first*) (Ginsburg et al., 2008). These words are so commonly used that we don't even think of them as mathematical or scientific terms. Most important, language is necessary to express and explain mathematical thinking. Consider this example:

> Mr. Blaine's kindergarten class needs to divide into four groups. He explains that there will be four chaperones to accompany children to different sections of the zoo, and he asks for suggestions:
>
> *Naomi suggests:* Let's just pick the group we want.
> *Darius notes:* But what if we all pick the same one? It will be too crowded and we won't learn different things to tell the other kids about.
> *Flair:* There are twenty kids. How can we divide up? We could line up in four lines.
> *Mr. Blaine asks:* How would that help?
> *Flair:* We need four groups and four lines are four groups.
> *Doug jumps in:* That would work. But it would be easier if we just drew four lines on the chart paper and wrote our names where we want to go.
> *Darius is still skeptical:* But what if we all put our name in the same box?
>
> After each suggestion, Mr. Blaine asks each child to explain why her or his idea would work. The explanations reveal and extend their ideas about how to compose equal-size groups.

The Language of Science Science, too, has its own vocabulary and exposes children to a vast array of words—both nouns and verbs—that they might not otherwise encounter. Children are eager to and capable of learning "big" words, such as *hypothesis, prediction, experiment, observe, reflect,* and *decide.* They also learn the vocabulary attached to scientific information—words like *incline, magnifier,* or *telescope.*

base ten place value system
Highly efficient system of using just 10 numerals to write any counting number no matter how large, in which the meaning of a numeral depends on where it is placed within the number.

Young children's play is rich in "everyday mathematics." This informal knowledge provides a foundation for later mathematics learning when intentional teachers introduce the language of math—words that describe quantity and relationships.

everyday mathematics
Informal, intuitive knowledge about math, including basic ideas about quantity (more and less), size, shape, and pattern.

mathematize To understand and think about everyday problems and experiences in explicitly mathematical terms.

Science information books are rich sources of language along with hands-on experiences. Language is such an important part of children's cognitive development, as well as science and mathematics learning, that teachers should take every opportunity to introduce and reinforce this rich vocabulary (Gelman & Brenneman, 2004).

Mathematical Language and the Achievement Gap

Evidence suggests that the mathematics achievement gap exists because low-income children do not have sufficient opportunity to learn the language of mathematics (Ginsburg, 2006; Ginsburg & Pappas, 2004). How do we know this? Observations of lower- and middle-income preschoolers find little difference in the everyday mathematics they spontaneously demonstrate during free play (Ginsburg, 2006). Both groups exhibit a good deal of mathematical competence on which to build.

Informal, Everyday Mathematics One of the first words babies utter is *more*—evidence of their intuitive understanding of quantity. As they grow, they pay considerable attention to who is bigger and when something is "All gone." Well before school entry, children of all socioeconomic groups demonstrate considerable informal math knowledge.

Informal knowledge about math, including basic ideas about quantity (more and less), size, shape, and pattern, is also called **everyday mathematics** (Ginsburg et al., 2008). Research demonstrates that by age 5, everyday mathematical knowledge is a universal aspect of cognitive development (NRC, 2009). Even babies and toddlers demonstrate basic understandings about some math and science concepts. When they reach out to make a toy move or repeat a sound, they begin to understand the idea of cause and effect (Gelman & Brenneman, 2004). These intuitive ideas about mathematics and science are prior knowledge on which teachers can build.

Children's play is full of mathematical and scientific ideas. They order blocks by size, create and extend interesting patterns, and conduct their own experiments, such as seeing if a ball rolls faster down a steeper incline (Seefeldt, Galper, & Stevenson-Garcia, 2012; Seo & Ginsburg, 2004). The main difference is that children living in poverty are generally provided less support and opportunity to learn the language that connects their informal, basic math knowledge to later, more abstract school mathematics. To do so, teachers must help children *mathematize* their everyday experiences, a critically important process described next.

Learning to Mathematize Experience To **mathematize** means to understand and think about everyday problems and experiences in explicitly mathematical terms (NRC, 2009). When children mathematize, they focus on the mathematics aspect of a situation, they learn to represent and think about its quantitative or spatial aspects, and they create a mathematical model of the situation to solve problems (NRC, 2009).

Mathematical models can be created with objects (such as beads or paper), actions (such as counting), or through solving real-life problems mathematically. For example, children building a house create a model of mathematics learning when they figure out how many more blocks they need to make the house twice as tall.

To link the concrete world to the abstract world of math, teachers need to help children learn to mathematize, to connect the informal experiences they have to mathematical ideas and symbols (Ginsburg et al., 2008). Consider the following situation. Children are often asked to share toys. Teachers tend to think of sharing as a social skill, but it can also be considered mathematically—as addition, subtraction, and division. When 4½-year-old Corky wants more toy cars than Eugene has, the situation is actually a math problem. If he takes two cars from Eugene, he is adding, while Eugene experiences subtraction (take away). If Corky gets two more cars from the shelf, Eugene's pile stays the same. Corky then has to figure out whether either solution gives him more than Eugene has. Unless he knows how many they both started with, he can't be sure whether either of his solutions worked. His teacher could step in and simply prevent a squabble by dividing the cars herself or telling Corky he has to share. Or she could engage them in a conversation about how to create two equal sets of cars or one set that is two cars larger.

✓ **Check Your Understanding 13.2:** The Cognitive Foundations of Early Learning

Effective Mathematics Curriculum and Teaching

Teaching mathematics involves several key elements. First, teachers must know the math concepts and skills or operations themselves. This should go without saying, but many early childhood teachers like Darrell and Sofia, whom we met at the beginning of this chapter, do not fully understand the mathematics concepts they are expected to teach (Ginsburg et al., 2008). In fact, college-level math courses are often not helpful or relevant to early childhood mathematics. For this reason, the 2009 NRC report includes a chapter, "Foundational Mathematics Content," that explains the fundamentals of beginning mathematics for teachers.

The other elements of teaching mathematics are interrelated. Teachers need to know (1) the math content and processes that children need to learn and when they are most effectively taught, and (2) how to plan and implement effective curriculum and teaching strategies.

Mathematics Curriculum Content

A broad consensus exists about the early childhood mathematics curriculum based on standards developed by the National Council of Teachers of Mathematics (NCTM) (2000). In 2009, NCTM published *Curriculum Focal Points*, which identifies the math content to focus on at each grade level to ensure that children gain deep understanding of the key concepts and skills needed for later learning. The K–12 Common Core Mathematics standards now serve this function in many states and further raise the bar on expectations for children (Common Core State Standards [CCSS] Initiative, 2011b).

The Common Core calls for three key changes in how mathematics should be taught (CCSS Initiative, 2015b). First, there should be more focus on deep understanding of fewer topics. In the past, the math curriculum has been described as a "mile wide and an inch deep," with students exposed to many different skills but failing to understand and apply them. Another emphasis is on enhancing curriculum coherence by linking topics across grade levels. Finally, a key change is that the standards are more rigorous, requiring equal emphasis on understanding, skills, and real-world problem-solving. For example, compare these two activities: (1) children compete a worksheet with addition problems such as 6 + 3 and 4 + 5, or (2) teachers present an equation such as 6 + ? = 9 and ask the children to make up word problems that can be represented this way.

These standards identify the *big ideas of mathematics*—the overarching concepts and skills of the early childhood curriculum. From age 3 to grade 3, the content goals focus on number and operations and geometry, spatial relations, and measurement.

Mathematics Learning Trajectories The NRC (2009) report on early childhood mathematics specifies the learning trajectories for children age 2 to first grade (which they called teaching–learning paths). These describe the goals or significant steps, with each new step building on the earlier step. **Learning trajectories** (Clements & Sarama, 2013) are also called *developmental* or *learning continua*, and they are a key part of curriculum planning.

learning trajectory Sequence of teaching and learning knowledge or skills in a content area. Also called *developmental* or *learning continua*.

Mathematics is abstract. Even the seemingly simple act of finger counting involves understanding and applying several different mathematical principles.

enumeration The act of counting.

stable order principle The concept that number words need to be said in the same order every time.

one-to-one correspondence Attaching one and only one number word to each object being counted.

cardinality The concept that the last number said stands for the total number in the set.

abstraction The concept that anything can be counted.

order irrelevance principle The concept that counting can begin with any object in the set as long as each is counted only once.

operations Working with and solving problems about relationships such as *more than* or *less than*.

▶ Classroom Connection

In this classic and very funny *Sesame Street* video, Ernie and the Muppets demonstrate the basic principles of how the number system works and its importance for understanding and communication.

https://www.youtube.com/watch?v=hgZwSRpfouQ

Learning trajectories have two sources:

1. The content of the discipline—that is, the mathematics skills and knowledge that provide the foundation for later learning
2. What is achievable and understandable for children at a certain age.

Learning trajectories are linked to age/grade levels and are valuable because they can guide curriculum planning and help teachers use formative assessments to scaffold children's learning along the path (Clements & Sarama, 2013). For an example, read the feature *Learning Trajectory: Mathematics*, which is based on the NRC report and the Common Core Standards for K–3 mathematics.

One important recommendation in planning math curriculum is that equal attention should not be given to all topics (CCSS Initiative, 2011b; NRC, 2009). There is always limited time in the school day, and decisions need to be made about priorities. In preschool, more focused time should be devoted to number competence (NRC, 2009). The K–2 curriculum should emphasize concepts, skills, and problem solving related to addition and subtraction (CCSS Initiative, 2011b). This does not mean that number is taught in isolation, nor does it mean that geometry and measurement are unimportant. In fact, learning in these areas can promote learning number concepts. Nevertheless, the goal is that children achieve the foundational number and operations goals necessary for their continued progress in later grades.

Number and Operations Understanding number, even the seemingly simple act of counting—called **enumeration**—involves several key concepts (Gelman & Gallistel, 1978). Children need to know that number words should be said in the same order every time—the **stable order principle**. They need to know **one-to-one correspondence**—that one and only one number word should be attached to each object. They also need to learn **cardinality**, the concept that the last number said stands for the total number in the set. Another key idea, called **abstraction**, is that anything can be counted, whether bears, toes, or people. Finally, counting involves the **order irrelevance principle**, the idea that counting can begin with any object in the set as long as each is counted only once.

The term **operations** refers to working with and solving problems about relationships, such as *more than* or *less than,* and addition and subtraction. Teaching operations should involve real objects and word problems. For example, in meeting with her kindergartners, Ms. Guiffre raises a real-world math problem:

Ms. Guiffre: There are four people absent today, and we usually have twenty-two people in our class. We need to send our lunch count to the cafeteria staff. How can we figure out the number of lunches we need?

The children offer several suggestions and then try out some of them:

Melissa: We can count out twenty-two little blocks and take away four, and then count out how many we have left.

Tyrone: I know. Let's count our coat hooks. But not the ones for the kids who aren't here.

Learning trajectories help teachers scaffold children's progress (Clements & Sarama, 2013; NRC, 2009). For example, teachers use strategies to help children learn to count accurately and efficiently, such as slowly touching each object as each number name is said. Teachers should also encourage children to use their fingers to count and explore part/whole relationships (a concept that underlies addition and subtraction). The teacher might say, "Brianna is showing us how old her brother is by holding up five [fingers] and two. What's another way to show seven with your fingers?"

Learning Trajectory: Mathematics

Approximate Age Group	Widely Held Expectations
2-year-olds	• Use subitizing to recognize 1, 2, or 3 objects • Rote count, may skip some numbers ("1, 2, 3, 5") • Identify basic shapes • Count 1 to 3 objects
3-year olds	• Know number names and count 1 to 10 in sequence • Count objects with one-to-one correspondence • Know relationships such as more than, less than, equal • Do simple put-together/take-apart problems (2 apples and 2 more is 4)
4-year-olds	• Understand cardinality—the last number said represents the total number of objects • Write numbers 1 to 10 (not always legibly) • Count objects accurately to 10 and beyond (about 30) • Solve simple number word problems • Count backwards • Use mental subitizing of up to 5 objects to solve problems up to 10 (automatically know that adding 2 crackers to 4 is 6) • Recognize and describe attributes of 2- and 3-dimensional shapes
5-year-olds	• Compare numbers • Understand addition as putting together and adding to, and subtraction as taking apart and taking from • Work with numbers 11–19 to gain foundations for place value • Describe and compare measurable attributes (length, weight) • Classify objects and count the number of objects in categories • Analyze, compare, create, and compose shapes
6-year-olds	• Count to 100 from any number • Represent and solve problems involving addition and subtraction • Extend the counting sequence (count on from any number) • Begin to understand base ten number system and place value concept (pattern of ones, tens, hundreds) • Tell and write time • Reason with shapes and attributes
7-year-olds	• Consistently conserve number (i.e., knows quantity remains the same despite rearrangement of objects) • Skip count forward and backward, with meaning • Represent and solve problems involving addition and subtraction (i.e., measuring length) • Understand and use place value to add and subtract • Work with equal groups of objects to gain foundations for multiplication • Work with time and money
8-year-olds	• Represent and solve problems involving multiplication and division • Understand the relationship between multiplication and division • Use place value understanding to perform multi-digit arithmetic • Multiply and divide within 100 • Develop understanding of fractions as numbers

Sources: Based on *Common Core Standards for Mathematics*, by Common Core State Standards Initiative, 2011, Washington, DC: Council for Chief State School Officers and National Governor's Association; *Mathematics Learning in Early Childhood: Paths toward Excellence and Equity*, by National Research Council, 2009, Washington, DC: National Academies Press; *Learning and Teaching Early Math*, by D. Clements and J. Sarama, 2009, New York: Routledge.

Culture Lens

Finger Counting in Cultural Context

Finger counting plays an important role in young children's early mathematics learning. Some people even speculate that the base ten number system evolved because humans have 10 fingers. But like every other aspect of development and learning, finger counting has a cultural element, as we see in the following example.

Located in a downtown office building in a large city, West Street Early Learning Center is an employer-sponsored child care center that serves a diverse group of children and families from all over the world. Today is the first day of class for the 3-year-olds. Ella, a new teacher, is just getting to know the children. To draw out one of the shy little boys, she stoops down in front of him and asks, "How old are you, Kenny?" "Free," he replies, and counts off his middle three fingers. Turning to Mizuki, whose family is Japanese, Ella asks the same question. Mizuki doesn't say anything and appears to wave her fingers. Ella is confused. Certainly, she thinks, Mizuki knows how old she is.

Just like most 3-year-olds, Mizuki does know her age. However, her way of communicating this knowledge to Ella reflects her cultural background. Most countries around the world actually use one of three ways of raising fingers to show numbers. In early childhood programs that serve children from different parts of world, teachers are likely to see these different methods.

The most common way—used frequently in Latin American countries—is to raise the thumb first and then the fingers across to the smallest one. In the United States, the most common method is to raise the index finger first, then the other fingers in order (holding down unused fingers with the thumb), and then lastly the thumb—as Kenny did. Another way, also used in some Latin American countries, is to begin with the little finger and move across to the thumb.

Other methods are less frequently used, such as Mizuki's, where fingers are raised and then lowered. Mizuki wasn't just waving her fingers, she was raising and lowering three fingers to show her age. In India, children may count by touching the lines of the fingers with the thumb.

Given that many programs in the United States serve children from throughout the world, teachers may encounter some of these different finger-counting methods. Fingers are a very important tool for young children to solve numerical problems, not just to show their age. Therefore, teachers should recognize that there are different ways of counting on fingers and not try to change what's working for a child.

Source: Based on *Mathematics Learning in Early Childhood: Paths toward Excellence and Equity*, by National Research Council Committee on Early Childhood Mathematics, 2009, Washington, DC: National Academies Press.

Counting on your fingers is an important part of learning about number. Teachers may not realize, however, that there are cultural differences in how children count on their fingers. To broaden your view of finger counting, read the *Culture Lens: Finger Counting in Cultural Context* feature.

Geometry, Spatial Relations, and Measurement
In addition to number and operations, a second area of focus for the early childhood math curriculum is geometry, spatial relations, and measurement (NRC, 2009).

geometry The study of shapes and space, including flat, two-dimensional space and three-dimensional space.

Geometry Children are naturally motivated to engage with **geometry**, the study of shapes and space, including flat, two-dimensional space and three-dimensional space (Clements & Sarama, 2007b). Geometry involves size, position, direction, and movement, and describes and organizes the physical world in which we live. Children can learn about angles, shapes, and solids by observing and manipulating objects in the physical world and in the virtual one via technology (Clements & Sarama, 2007b).

Research finds that most curricula severely underestimate children's ability to learn geometry (Clements & Sarama, 2013). Teachers continue to focus only on naming basic shapes (circle, triangle, square) long after children have mastered these concepts. Geometry is far more complex and involves the ability to put together and take apart shapes (composing and decomposing), as well as talk about the properties of shapes (number of angles, sides, orientation).

spatial relations Spatial sense and familiarity with shape, structure, and location.

Spatial Relations Learning about **spatial relations** gives children an awareness of themselves in relation to the people and objects around them. Spatial sense and familiarity with shape, structure, and location help children understand both their spatial world and also other mathematics topics (NRC, 2009). For instance, as Carmel examines a three-dimensional pyramid, her teacher encourages her to explore number concepts as well. For example, the teacher asks: "How many sides does a pyramid have? Why is it hard to figure out?"

Measurement Measurement is the process of determining size, length, area, or volume using a standard unit (inch, gallon). Children look for and analyze relationships in the real world using measurement. Measurement is a learning goal in itself, but it also plays a useful role in building children's understanding of number and spatial relations. When children measure and compare the length, height, and weight of objects, they use *units* such as inches, feet, or pounds. When measuring, children focus on how big, little, long, or short things are and how to figure that out.

measurement The process of determining size, length, area, or volume using a standard unit.

Children will sometimes explore measurement by using parts of their body or toys in the classroom—what are called *nonstandard units*. For example, Damien and Issata use their own feet to measure the length of the boat they've built and discover that they get two different answers. Because children naturally use and can learn from nonstandard measurement, many state math standards call for children to use nonstandard and standard units of measurement. Such a standard has sometimes been misinterpreted to mean that teachers should withhold standard measurement tools such as rulers. But this is not the case. Children enjoy and can learn about standard units using rulers and scales, and doing so can prevent the development of misconceptions about measurement (NRC, 2009).

For example, Mina puts out rulers for her kindergartners to explore during center time. At first, they play with the rulers, pretending that they are objects such as magic wands or pirate swords. But when the children become interested in earthworms on the playground, Mina brings out the rulers and the children begin to pay attention to the numbers on the rulers and what they mean. They get excited about measuring and comparing the length of the worms, and begin to use the rulers for other purposes as well.

Measuring Time: A Word of Caution Many teachers spend time every morning "doing" the calendar because they think it is a good way to teach math. In fact, more than 90% of kindergarten teachers teach the calendar every day (NRC, 2009). Although the calendar can be used to plan and anticipate future events, it has limited value as a math teaching tool (Beneke, Ostrosky, & Katz, 2008; NRC, 2009).

The calendar's organization—7-day weeks—bears no resemblance to the base ten number system that children need to master (NRC, 2009). Most of the time, children simply recite the numbers in order while someone points to blocks on the calendar. This task is repeated long after the children have mastered the number list and long before they can fully understand the concept of time (Beneke et al., 2008). In addition, pointing to the spaces on the calendar is not as effective for teaching number as counting real objects. The amount of time spent on the calendar each day could be better spent helping children make progress on the mathematics learning paths. More valuable experiences that help children begin to develop understanding of time concepts include the following:

A relatively simple, enjoyable activity such as measuring a table or comparing strips of paper helps children learn spatial relationships and basic geometry concepts.

- Children compare one activity with another in terms of which takes more time: "Who can stand on one foot longer?"
- Teachers point out the time schedule and the passing of time, with ideas like *after lunch* or *before story time,* or using more abstract notions like *yesterday, today,* and *tomorrow*, although they don't expect children to fully comprehend.
- Teachers use a calendar in much the same way people use one in their homes—to note, plan for, anticipate, and remember significant events such as birthdays, trips, and visitors. They place calendars in the house or office center, where it is used in the real world. They introduce names of days of the week and months of the year, but don't drill children on these ideas.

© Lord and Leverett/Pearson Education

Mathematics Process Skills

Math experts consistently identify five general cognitive process goals that cut across content areas and that should be interwoven throughout the teaching and learning of mathematics for all age groups (NCTM, 2006; NRC, 2009). These processes are problem solving, reasoning, communicating, making connections, and designing and analyzing representations. Any mathematics learning experience might involve all of these processes. These processes are also relevant for other areas of the curriculum, especially science. Perhaps most important, these learning processes build children's curiosity, creativity, and willingness to take risks, all of which may be the most long-lasting and important goals of mathematics education.

Problem Solving and Reasoning

Mathematics is about thinking. It is not simply manipulating objects, but constructing mathematical meaning from the experience (CCSS Initiative, 2011b). To become mathematical thinkers, children need to solve problems and reason about number and operations, geometry, spatial relations, and measurement. They need to understand that there are different ways to solve a problem and that more than one answer is often possible. Even in situations where one correct answer exists ("We need fifteen chairs for fifteen children"), there are usually a number of ways to arrive at that solution ("We can give each person his or her own chair" or "We can count fifteen chairs").

reasoning Thinking logically to come to a conclusion or find a result.

Reasoning is thinking logically to come to a conclusion or find a result. As children tackle problems, teachers should encourage them to talk about—mathematize—their thinking. This brings their reasoning to a conscious level, where other children or the teacher can expand on it. Teachers need to create a learning environment in which children feel free to take risks and search for solutions.

Communicating

To promote children's mathematical thinking, one of the most important things teachers can do is to talk with them about problems, relationships, and mathematical connections. It is equally if not more important to listen to what they say. When children discuss their thinking and describe what they are doing, their own thoughts become clearer (NCTM, 2000).

In addition, when children and teachers describe and debate their reasoning, they use the language of math. Then teachers can introduce and reinforce math vocabulary. Open-ended questions such as "How do these blocks compare to each other?" and "How do you know that a square is a rectangle?" increase the amount of math talk. Gradually children internalize these questions (ask them of themselves) and are more likely to understand the world from a mathematical perspective.

connections Refers to understanding links between different areas of math and connecting math concepts to real-world problems.

Making Connections

In mathematical terms, making **connections** refers to understanding links between different areas of math as well as connecting math concepts to real-world problems. For example, measurement can be connected to number because it involves counting units of measurement (i.e., inches), or it could be used to figure out if a shoe fits.

representing Expressing mathematical ideas with words, diagrams, pictures, and/or symbols.

Designing and Analyzing Representations

Exploring ways of expressing mathematical ideas with words, diagrams, pictures, and/or symbols, called **representing**, is an essential part of mathematizing. Imagine a group of kindergartners singing the song "Five Little Monkeys Jumping on the Bed." The teacher first uses her fingers to represent the monkeys as the children sing "One fell off and bumped his head." Soon the children follow her lead with their own fingers. From these concrete representations, the children begin to picture the monkeys in their heads—they form a mental image. Other ways they can represent the monkeys include scribbling circles or drawing pictures of them. Their representations gradually become more abstract. They may make marks on the page to represent the monkeys as the number goes from 11111 to 1111 down to 1. Eventually, children will represent these subtraction problems in symbols: $5 - 1 = 4$.

There are many ways to involve children in designing and analyzing representations of math concepts and problems as well as talking about them. Figure 13.1 graphically depicts a first grader's collection and analysis of data about her classmates' breakfast choices. Note how her analysis of results represents her understanding of quantity as well as her creative invented spelling—*cerel* for cereal and *choies* for choices.

In addition to these general processes, some specific mathematical processes are used across content areas, such as identifying patterns, solving problems that involve putting together/taking apart, and unitizing, which we discuss next.

Identifying Patterns In recent years, math standards have included learning about patterns. The ability to identify patterns, however, is a process skill that cuts across all math content areas (NRC, 2009). For instance, geometry and spatial relations involve composing and analyzing patterns. The number list is a pattern in which each new number is one more than the last; counting can be done in patterns (by twos, fives, or tens). Classifying objects by some attribute such as size or shape also involves seeing patterns. Following are strategies for building children's awareness of patterns (Head Start, 2003):

- Help children find patterns (*ab*, *ab* or *abc*, *abc*) in designs and pictures, as well as in movement and in recurring events such as the daily schedule.
- Sing songs with patterns—"If You're Happy and You Know It"; march or move to a rhythm; and clap patterns.
- Play detective and spy patterns in the classroom, on the playground, or in children's clothes.
- Engage children in creating and noticing patterns as they string beads, place shapes or blocks into arrays, and arrange other materials. Over time children can reproduce and create more complex patterns.

Putting Together and Taking Apart Mathematics at all levels involves putting groups together and taking them apart—the processes of **composing** and **decomposing** (NRC, 2009). These processes are the basic components of addition, subtraction, multiplication, and division. Measurements are composed of larger units (feet) that can be decomposed to smaller units (inches).

Understanding these concepts begins with early experiences. From age 2 through primary grades, children create collections of objects. Toddlers love stacking toys and filling and dumping containers. Preschoolers will repeatedly compose and decompose puzzles, challenging themselves to do it faster each time. Children can sing a song like "B-I-N-G-O" in which the word starts out composed (with all the letters), and then is decomposed as each letter of the word is no longer articulated. Primary-grade children learn about fractions by dividing a pizza.

Unitizing Finding or creating a mathematical unit, **unitizing**, is important in learning number, geometry, and spatial relations (Sophian, 2013). When children count, they have to use or create a unit of what they are going to count. For example, they can count people, or couples, or people's hands. When they measure length, they use a unit, whether it is their feet, their body, or a yardstick. When they count by 2s, 5s, or 10s, the units are 2, 5, and 10.

Mathematics is based on understanding and applying the concept of a unit. For example, to understand the base ten place value system, children must be able to recognize that 10 ones can form a single unit of 10. For this reason, the concept of unit should be a core idea in the early childhood math curriculum (Sophian, 2013). Of course, children learn this abstract idea through many meaningful, concrete experiences such as making patterns or counting.

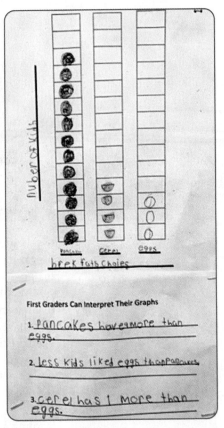

FIGURE 13.1 First Grader's Mathematical Representation and Analysis This first-grader is learning how to represent and compare quantity by creating a graph, and then interpreting what the graph means.

composing/decomposing Mathematical processes of putting together and taking apart (for example, addition and subtraction).

unitizing Finding or creating a mathematical unit.

As you can see, even very young children experiment with basic mathematics and science concepts—such as sorting and classifying.

© Jules Selmes/Pearson Education

In the previous sections, we described the important mathematics content and processes that children are learning in progressively more complex and sophisticated form from infancy through the primary grades. Next we describe mathematics curriculum and teaching strategies.

Effective Mathematics Curriculum

Responding to children's natural interest in math and problem solving and taking advantage of the teachable moments during children's play and routines are valuable ways to promote math learning, but they are not enough (Schoenfeld & Stipek, 2011). An effective curriculum is more than a collection of activities; it must be coherent, focused on important mathematics, and well articulated across the grades (CCSS Initiative, 2015b).

Very little time is devoted to mathematics in early childhood classrooms despite the fact that the amount of focused time on math instruction strongly predicts children's outcomes (Farran, Lipsey, & Wilson, 2011). Most programs do not include experiences in which mathematics is the primary goal. Instead, they address math as part of an integrated curriculum in which mathematics is a secondary goal; as a result, math teaching occurs only occasionally and rarely in depth (PCERC, 2008). In one study, researchers observed only 58 seconds of math teaching during an entire preschool day (Farran, Lipsey, Watson, & Hurley, 2007). In general, studies have found that integrated math instruction is less effective than learning activities in which mathematics is the primary goal (NRC, 2009; PCERC, 2008).

A focused mathematics curriculum not only improves children's math skills but also increases their interest in math (Arnold, Fischer, Doctoroff, & Dobbs, 2002). Teachers, too, report that they increase their knowledge and enjoyment in implementing math activities. Studies on the effects of mathematics curricula indicate that more intentional teaching of math leads to better math outcomes for children, especially dual language learners and children from low-income families (Schoenfeld & Stipek, 2011).

An effective curriculum involves children actively in "doing mathematics." With a coherent curriculum, such as *Building Blocks—Foundations for Mathematical Thinking* (Clements & Sarama, 2007b), children encounter math experiences in small and large groups, and in everyday experiences with blocks, art, puzzles, dramatic play, and music. They learn math by using specially designed software that makes the most of digital media's capacities for supporting learning. *Building Blocks* has been found to significantly improve not only children's math outcomes but also their oral language and general reasoning (Sarama, Lange, Clements, & Wolfe, 2012).

Technology is an essential component. For example, young children are limited in their ability to mentally manipulate shapes—to imagine the shapes turned or flipped. Once children accumulate experiences in sliding, rotating, and flipping objects—whether with physical objects or a computer tool—they will be able to develop skills of mental imagery and understand the possibilities for manipulating shapes. Digital environments, in which children need to think abstractly and give concrete and precise commands, can be particularly helpful in getting a feel for such transformations and for other aspects of mathematical thinking.

Other focused mathematics curricula include *Number Worlds* (Griffin, 2004), *Big Math for Little Kids* (Greenes et al., 2004), and *Numbers Plus © Preschool Mathematics Curriculum* (HighScope, 2007).

Effective Mathematics Teaching

In this section, we present research-based ways of intentionally teaching mathematics. They include specific teacher behaviors that relate to positive outcomes, math talk, and grouping. We then discuss the role of play when teaching math.

Teacher Behaviors Research demonstrates the effectiveness of specific teaching behaviors that are related to positive learning outcomes for children (Clements & Sarama, 2008). Clements and Sarama (2007b) developed the *Classroom Observation of Early Mathematics—Environment and Teaching* (COEMET), a useful observation instrument to evaluate the quality of mathematics instruction. Some specific teacher behaviors on the COEMET are listed next that relate to children's improved math knowledge (Clements & Sarama, 2007b, 2008; Sarama & Clements, 2007):

1. How much time the teacher is actively engaged in math activities
2. Whether the teacher builds on and elaborates children's mathematical ideas and strategies
3. How much the teacher facilitates children's responding to math questions and situations

The COEMET describes both high-quality and poor-quality teaching, some examples of which appear in Figure 13.2. Other teacher behaviors that strongly relate to children's math learning include (Clements & Sarama, 2007b, 2008; Sarama & Clements, 2007):

- Teachers' curiosity about and enthusiasm for mathematics
- Teachers' ability to set high but realistic expectations
- Teachers' observations of children, note taking to record their observations, and use of learning trajectories to individualize instruction

Math Talk Tamara's kindergarten is well stocked with board games that the children enjoy playing. But Tamara observes that some children rarely use them. One day, she invites four of the reluctant players to join her. Tamara introduces the activity: "For this game, we need to roll the dice. Look carefully at this cube. What do you observe about the dots?" As the children examine the dice and count the dots on each side, Tamara extends the math talk: "What's the largest number you can get when you roll one die?" After turning the dice around, the children agree on "six." As the conversation continues, Tamara introduces math talk such as "What do you observe about the number of dots on each side of the cube? How are they different? Do you see a pattern? The dice is shaped like a cube. What do the dots tell you about cubes?" After the children have mastered the game using one die, Tamara brings out a second one and further extends the math learning, "You rolled a four and a five, so how many spaces can you move?"

This scene from Tamara's classroom demonstrates how even a simple board game provides a great opportunity for **math talk**. Given the critical role of language in learning math, it is not surprising that one of the most effective teaching strategies is what is simply called *math talk*. Teachers should also point out that in these situations children are "doing" math.

The amount of math-related talk children experience is positively related to their mathematical knowledge (Klibanoff, Levine, Huttenlocher, Vasilyeva, & Hedges, 2006). However, there is an enormous amount of variation in the amount of math talk that children experience. One study found that in a 1-hour observation of 26 preschool classrooms, teachers' math talk ranged from 1 to 104 math-related words (Klibanoff et al., 2006). An even greater difference occurs in parent-child interactions. A longitudinal study that recorded math talk between parents and their children, between the ages of 14 and 30 months, found that over 7½ hours of observation, some parents spoke as few as 4 math words with their children while others produced 287 (Levine, Suriyakham, Roe, Huttenlocher, & Gunderson, 2010). The researchers interpreted this finding to mean that over the first 2½ years of life, some children heard 600 times as many number words as other children.

Given the importance of math talk to children's mathematical understanding, the question arises, what if the children don't speak the same language as their teachers? Teaching math to dual language learners requires adapting curriculum and individualizing instruction.

math talk Using the language and vocabulary of mathematics.

EXAMPLE 1: The teacher showed curiosity about and enthusiasm for math ideas and connections to other ideas or real-world situations.

• commented on or discussed mathematical ideas in reading a story
• showed interest in the mathematics that emerged in children's play, construction, or discussions

Situation

The children are building with blocks. The teacher says, "What are you making?"
Children respond that it's a skyscraper.

Low-Quality Instruction	High-Quality Instruction
• The teacher says, "Nice. Be careful it doesn't fall on you."	• The teacher says, "It looks the same on this side [gesturing] as it does on this side [gesturing]. It's symmetrical! Are you going to keep building a symmetric building?"
	• The teacher asks, "I wonder how tall it is?"
	• The teacher says, "I see you put the long blocks at the bottom and the smaller ones on top. Could you tell me how that helped you make your building?" "What might happen if you put the long ones on the top?"
	• The teacher asks, "If you put these curved ones here, can you build more on top of them or not? What would happen if you did?"

EXAMPLE 2: The teacher facilitated children's responding.

• elicited many solution methods for one problem
• encouraged elaboration of children's responses
• waited for and listened attentively to individual children
• responded to errors as learning opportunities

Situation

The teacher asks one child to figure out how many 1 more than 3 is.

Low-Quality Instruction	High-Quality Instruction
• When a child has difficulty, the teacher says, "Someone else can answer."	• When a child has difficulty, the teacher says, "Can you show me 3 to get started?"
• When another child gives the correct answer, the teacher moves to the next task.	• The child says, "Four." The teacher asks, "Can you teach us how you did that?"
	• The teacher asks, "Did anybody do it a different way?"

FIGURE 13.2 Examples of High- and Low-Quality Mathematics Teaching This figure compares and contrasts examples of high-quality effective math teaching strategies with ineffective practices. *Source:* From *Manual for Classroom Observation of Early Mathematics—Environment & Teaching (COEMET)* version 3. J. Sarama, Author: D. H. Clements, © 2007 Reprinted with permission.

Grouping for Instruction Alice's preschool children love it when she brings out the plastic attribute blocks, which vary by color, shape, size, and thickness. She introduces the activity by saying, "There are so many ways these blocks are the same, but they are also different. Yesterday, we sorted them into groups by two attributes: color and shape.

Today, let's see if we can sort them another way. Does anybody have an idea?"

Alfredo says, "Some are big and some are little."

"That's boring," counters Bernadette.

"Okay, you want a challenge," Alice responds. "We'll play a game. I'll give clues and you try to find the shape. Alfredo, can you find the big, fat, blue pentagon?"

Small-group activities for four to six children are especially useful for teaching mathematics, and the skills children acquire during small-group instruction can transfer to knowledge and abilities that have not been taught (Clements & Sarama, 2007).

Although whole-group time can also be used to teach mathematics, to be effective, it should be only one component of instruction, along with small groups, individual activity, and technology (Clements & Sarama, 2007b, 2008). The most effective whole-group interactions include a combination of teacher-led brief discussions, problem solving with a partner (another child or an adult), and physical activities such as marching while counting or doing a shape hunt (Clements & Sarama, 2007b, 2008).

Effective teachers use various ways of grouping for instruction, including individual activity, whole group, small groups, and technology.

The Role of Play in Teaching and Learning Mathematics

Opportunities for mathematics learning abound in different types of play: block building, socio-dramatic play, exploration and practice during play, playing games, using table toys (manipulatives, puzzles, etc.), and book reading.

Block Building As we have seen, block play provides valuable opportunities for children to explore and engage in mathematical activity on their own (Pollman, 2010). Children enjoy building with blocks and they naturally engage in mathematical play with them (Seo & Ginsburg, 2004).

However, block building during free play alone doesn't automatically result in math learning. When teachers discuss mathematical ideas with children during block play, their learning is enhanced (Tepylo, Moss, & Stephenson, 2015). Teachers can introduce new words such as *unit* or *equal*, and raise problems, such as "How can you make your bridge high enough for the biggest boat to go under?" When teachers provide this kind of support, it enhances children's learning at the time, but is also valuable because children incorporate these new ideas when they play on their own. Block building contributes to children's knowledge of geometry and spatial relations, especially three-dimensional shapes.

Socio-Dramatic Play Sociodramatic play contributes to the development of self-regulation and executive function in children (Bodrova & Leong, 2007). Because these two basic cognitive abilities are essential for mathematics understanding, socio-dramatic play is an important opportunity to promote math and science learning.

Socio-dramatic play provides a context for children to use their developing math skills. For example, while playing restaurant, children write and read the prices on a menu, count their "money," and use one-to-one correspondence as they set the table. Pretend play also provides many opportunities for children to practice their developing math skills, as we describe next.

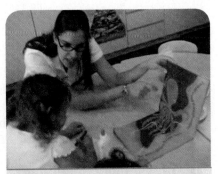

▶ Classroom Connection

The children in this video are looking at a book that shows an octopus, and the pictures they draw reflect what they've learned. As you watch, consider the variety of teaching strategies the teacher uses to help the girls learn not just about an octopus but also number and geometry concepts.

© Corbis Super RF/Alamy

Small group experiences like playing board or card games are very effective for teaching mathematics. What other kinds of games might be fun ways of learning mathematics?

Exploration and Practice during Play

Many mathematics competencies such as counting require a lot of practice as well as demonstration, modeling, or scaffolding from adults (Fuson, 1988). Children need practice to master these skills, but such practice should be meaningful and motivating for children—and play is an excellent context for it.

During play, children will often initiate their own practice. For example, 2-year-olds will repeat a drumbeat until adults get tired. Three- and 4-year-old children will repeatedly string a set of beads in a pattern until they have mastered the skill to their personal satisfaction. While swinging, several girls take turns pushing each other and count the pushes as they go along. When they get to 20, they switch places. Seven-year-old Garrett repeatedly asks his mom to try to stump him with two-digit addition and subtraction problems as she puts him to bed each night.

Games

Board games in which children count spaces along a number list (numbered squares) are an effective way to develop children's numerical knowledge. The power of such games is demonstrated in an experiment conducted in a Head Start program (Siegler & Ramani, 2008). Children who played a board game similar to Chutes and Ladders (that used a linear rather than a circular pattern) became more skilled at counting, comparing, naming, and estimating numbers. This study showed how something as basic as playing a board game with numbered squares can significantly improve the number knowledge of children from low-income families, many of whom don't have the opportunity to play such games at home. Games such as cards and dominoes are also fun as long as they don't become too competitive.

Further research on number board games finds that the most effective strategy is to engage children in "counting on" rather than counting from 1 every time. For example, if a child's marker is on the square marked 18 and she rolls a 3, instead of counting 1, 2, 3, she counts 19, 20, 21 (Laski & Siegler, 2014). Children need prompting by adults to successfully play the game but it can greatly expand their knowledge of the number system.

Table Toys

manipulatives Small-sized blocks, cubes, pattern blocks, beads, pegs, and the like that are designed for children's play and learning.

One of the most effective ways for children to learn math is to use concrete materials such as puzzles, matching games, and manipulatives. **Manipulatives** are small-sized blocks, cubes, pattern blocks, beads, pegs, and the like that are designed for children's play and learning.

Puzzles and manipulatives can enhance math knowledge, especially geometric and spatial thinking, in preschool as well as elementary-age children (Clements & Sarama, 2007a, 2007b). Up to about age 5½, children need concrete objects to learn counting and to solve larger number problems using addition and subtraction (Levine, Jordan, & Huttenlocher, 1992). Manipulatives make abstract tasks meaningful.

However, simply providing manipulatives and concrete materials does not ensure learning. Rather, teachers need to scaffold children's use of manipulatives if they get stuck using the materials in the same way over and over. Six-year-old Martha loves to play with Unifix cubes, and for several days she creates one row of 10 cubes. Her teacher says, "Martha, you seem to like counting to ten. What if we make two rows of ten? How many cubes do you think we'll need altogether?"

▶ Classroom Connection

As you watch this video of preschool children playing shoe store, reflect on the mathematics content that they are learning. Observe how the teacher uses effective strategies and math talk in the context of play.

http://www.youtube.com/watch?v=DekMNAFpsqs

Book Reading

Books have great potential for teaching mathematics and are often used to integrate math into other areas of the curriculum, especially literacy (B. Casey, 2004; M. B. Casey, Erkut, Ceder, & Young, 2008;

Schickedanz, 2008). Math concepts can be found in an enormous number of storybooks. In some stories, such as *The Three Bears*, math concepts are readily apparent. In other stories, the math is more implicit, such as in *Rosie's Walk* (Hutchins, 1968), which uses spatial vocabulary to describe a fox following a hen on her winding way (Schickedanz, 2008). In such books, math learning is secondary to another goal, usually language and literacy. Numerous children's books are also published each year for the explicit purpose of teaching math and science.

The use of books is especially powerful, however, when the primary goal is teaching math. The work of Beth Casey and her colleagues (2008) provides strong evidence that presenting math content (such as spatial and number skills) as part of a meaningful story is more effective than teaching the content alone. They developed *Storytelling Sagas*, a series of specially written math storybooks for children in preschool through grade 2 that have proven to be very effective—especially with girls—in teaching math.

In previous sections, we described the importance of building a firm foundation in mathematics understanding for all young children. Next we turn to the topic of science, which is often integrated with mathematics curriculum in the early years.

 Check Your Understanding 13.3: Effective Mathematics Curriculum and Teaching

Effective Science Curriculum and Teaching

Young children tend to be curious and inquisitive. They constantly ask questions such as "What's that?" "Why?" "How come?" They also are inclined to actively explore and observe their environment. They want to know "What would happen if . . . ?" To find answers, they readily dig in the mud, dump and splash water, or move their bodies in every way imaginable. At the same time, they try to make sense of these experiences, so they develop and test their own theories about how the world works. As a result, children are often called "natural scientists" (Worth & Grollman, 2003).

In the following sections, we describe the early childhood science curriculum—the content and processes that children from infancy through third grade can and should be learning. Then, we describe effective teaching strategies to promote children's scientific knowledge and understanding. We begin with the role of science and technology in an integrated curriculum.

Science and Technology in the Early Childhood Curriculum

The purpose of **science** is to study and understand the physical and natural world, especially by observing and experimenting. Science plays two important roles in the early childhood curriculum. The primary role is to lay a foundation of conceptual understanding and knowledge that will deepen and broaden as children move through school. Second, science exploration is an excellent way of integrating learning across the curriculum, as the following example illustrates:

science Study of the physical and natural world, especially by observing and experimenting.

> Rose Grindel's first graders are studying life science and exploring concepts such as living and nonliving things and growth and change. As part of their study, they visit a nearby apple orchard. Before their visit, Rose brings in types of apples for tasting (Macintosh, Granny Smith) and the children graph their preferences. A lively debate ensues about why apples look and taste different. Theo comes to the wise conclusion that apples must be kind of like people: They are the same in most ways, but they look different.
>
> Rose continues, "I guess we need to find out the kind of apples that grow at the orchard. Are there other things you want to find out? Do you think apples are

alive?" This last question draws laughs, but then some other queries. Grason says, "Well, trees are alive and apples grow on trees. So they could be alive, too." Grason's comment sparks a debate about what the word *living* means. This topic will be further explored throughout the month as children explore the characteristics of living and nonliving things.

At the orchard, children write down the farmer's answers to their questions and take photos to document their visit. Hunter wants his picture taken next to a tree as a way to measure it. Later in the year, the class will return and compare their photos of the fruit-bearing trees to the flowering trees in spring. Their documentation will pique memories. Hunter thinks his photo will show how much the tree grows.

At the farm, each child picks 10 apples (counting by ones), and back at school they group the apples by tens. The children come up with several ways to figure out that the total number they picked is 210! They also organize the apples by size, and choose the smallest to cook and the larger ones to eat. Because they picked so many apples, Ebony suggests that they donate some to the food bank. When the children cut the apples, they work with halves and quarters. They also bake apples and make applesauce, all the while predicting and observing the changes that take place.

In the previous example, life science is the main curriculum focus. Children learn science facts and concepts while *doing* science—asking questions, predicting, observing, and drawing conclusions. But other curriculum areas are well integrated. Children represent their learning in many ways—drawing pictures, taking photos, and writing about the apple orchard. Mathematics learning includes number and operations (counting, adding, using the base ten system, and dividing); classifying; creating and analyzing data (graphing); and measurement. Language and literacy are also involved, with children reading information books and learning new vocabulary (Gelman, Brenneman, MacDonald, & Román, 2010).

Science Content

A coalition of scientists and science educators agree on the goals of the K–12 science curriculum, which are articulated in the *Next Generation Science Standards* (Achieve, Inc., 2013). The content of early childhood science is directly related to young children's natural interest and curiosity about how the world works, living things, their bodies, the earth, insects and animals, and other topics they find fascinating (Seefeldt, Galper, & Jones, 2012).

As in mathematics, both content and process are not only essential, but also integrally connected. Children can't do a science experiment that isn't connected to science knowledge and concepts, nor can they make sense of discrete facts and concepts presented apart from meaningful context. In short, children can't learn science from a book alone; they have to *do* science.

Scientific Knowledge Goals
As important as it is to foster children's interest and active engagement in doing science, equally important is to expand their content knowledge. The curriculum includes physical, life, and earth and space science. Following are definitions of these science topics and some related goals (Achieve, Inc., 2013).

Physical Science   In the area of physical science, children learn basic ideas about the properties of liquids and solid materials and objects (size and shape). They learn how things move and change position. They show increasing understanding of cause-and-effect relationships—for instance, how force affects the distance a ball rolls. They also explore characteristics of sound and light—how shadows are produced and change, or how sound results from vibrations.

From infancy, children gain knowledge of the physical world by acting on objects to see what happens; babies love to throw their bottle out of a high chair over and over to see

physical science Basic ideas about the properties of liquids and solid materials, how things move and change position, and cause-and-effect relationships.

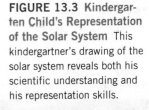

what happens. At times they act to get a desired effect—rolling, pushing, and dropping objects. To extend learning, teachers can ask children what will happen if they squeeze an object or challenge them to blow on a spool to make it move. Often children explore and manipulate effects without knowing how they achieved the results; when teachers ask children how or why they think something happened, an everyday experience is turned into a scientific event (Seefeldt, Galper, & Jones, 2012).

Life Science Life science is the study of the characteristics, life cycles, and environments of organisms. Children identify features of plants and animals, their habitats, and needs (food and water). They learn about living and nonliving things, and how living things grow and change. They also learn parts of the human body, how they function, what people need to stay healthy, and how human beings are alike and different.

life science The study of the characteristics, life cycles, and environments of organisms.

Earth and Space Science This topic involves studying properties of earth materials, changes on the earth, and patterns of movement and changes of the sun and moon. Once thought to be a topic beyond their understanding, many young children today are fascinated and knowledgeable about space as demonstrated by the kindergartner's drawing in Figure 13.3. The learning goals of earth and space science include:

- Recognizing repeating patterns in nature (day and night; seasons)
- Observing weather changes
- Understanding the effect of people on the environment
- Learning about geographic features of the earth (mountains, oceans) and the movement of objects in the sky

earth and space science Studying properties of earth materials, changes on the earth, patterns of movement, and changes of the sun and moon.

Key Scientific Concepts Across the three content areas of science are several key concepts or big ideas that create a strong foundation for later science learning. These concepts include *understanding change* and *cause-and-effect relationships*. Another concept that is revisited through school is the idea of a *system*—that a whole is composed of related parts that affect each other. For example, the human body is a system; there are weather systems and, of course, there is the vast solar system.

These complex concepts are vital to the work of all scientists. Preschoolers can grasp such concepts at a basic level when teachers draw attention to them in planned and spontaneous learning experiences. For example, when Jonah asks why insects and birds fly but fish that also have wings don't fly, his teacher poses the question to the class. A lively discussion ensues about the differences between wings and fins and how some birds, like ducks, both swim and fly.

Children's conceptual understanding deepens when they have a variety of experiences related to the same concept (French & Woodring, 2013). For example, children deepen their understanding of the concept of life cycles by planting and tending a garden, observing a class pet, and studying how humans grow.

FIGURE 13.3 Kindergarten Child's Representation of the Solar System This kindergartner's drawing of the solar system reveals both his scientific understanding and his representation skills.

Change can be continually observed in the natural world. Some changes occur too rapidly to be observed without special tools such as microscopes, whereas others occur too slowly for children to fully comprehend, such as the changing seasons. On the other hand, some changes can be readily observed and investigated by any age child. Teachers can encourage children to look for all sorts of changes:

- What happens to the plant when it is left in the dark?
- What happens to your shadow at different times of the day? Is your shadow there every day?
- What changes can be reversed? Can water be turned into ice and back into water?

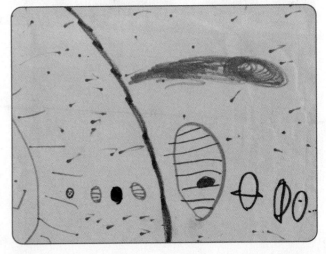

▶ **Classroom Connection**

The teacher in this video interacts with the children as they observe a tadpole. Note the scientific concepts the children are learning and the strategies the teacher uses to engage children in the scientific process. Also observe the documentation on the wall of the classroom project.

Effective Science Teaching

The fact that most young children are naturally curious and inclined to explore and investigate does not mean that they "naturally" or automatically learn science concepts and processes. To understand concepts and acquire skills, children need intentional teachers who plan and implement a coherent science curriculum. Science learning is too important to be left to chance. Intentional teachers promote science learning by carefully organizing the environment, providing focused learning experiences and information, and integrating science into children's play and everyday routines, but most of all, engaging children in the scientific process.

Organize the Environment   Science requires a planned environment, materials, and tools, such as cups, containers, trays, and jars to help children observe, collect, organize, and display evidence. Children need tools for investigation, including a variety of magnifying glasses, binoculars, mirrors, flashlights, magnets, levers, pulleys, and scales. Information books and access to the Internet are also essential resources for studying science.

Recording and representing evidence and conclusions requires tools as simple as notebooks, writing implements, and chart and graph paper, and as technologically sophisticated as digital and video cameras, tablets, computers, and whiteboards. For example, an Eyeclops™ is a computerized magnifier that can project onto a wall or screen. Children can aim it at all kinds of objects—their skin, the inside of a seed, or a butterfly in a jar.

Provide Focused Experiences   An effective science curriculum should reflect a coherent progression of science skills and content (French & Woodring, 2013). Learning goals and topics should build on one another so that children develop progressively more complex understandings. Content should align with state or national science standards.

Teachers can plan in-depth projects or topics of study related to science knowledge that build on and expand children's interests. Sufficient time should be devoted to topics for children to go into some depth. For instance, in a class study of animals, small groups of children or individuals might study one animal and report their findings to the others in the group.

Curriculum should focus on knowledge that is familiar and meaningful to children, such as concepts of temperature based on their experiences with weather. Although children are more capable of abstract learning than previously thought, it is usually easier to begin with more concrete, accessible experiences such as scientific phenomena that can be directly seen, touched, tasted, or heard (French & Woodring, 2013). In addition, teachers shouldn't impose scientifically accurate explanations for phenomena before children are able to grasp their meaning (Worth & Grollman, 2003).

scientific inquiry Involving children in observing, predicting, and investigating.

Children learn by doing science. They need to use the methods of scientists—questioning, predicting, investigating, experimenting, and drawing conclusions.

Engage Children in the Scientific Process
An overarching aspect of the curriculum is the process of doing science, or **scientific inquiry**. Scientific inquiry involves children in several processes such as questioning, predicting, observing, investigating, experimenting, recording, and documenting (National Center on Quality Teaching and Learning, 2013). In Table 13.1, we list these processes and illustrate them with a physical science example—children studying shadows to learn the properties and characteristics of light.

TABLE 13.1 Scientific Inquiry Processes in Children

Children engaging in a shadow study, as described here, use the same inquiry processes as professional scientists.

Process of Scientific Inquiry	Example: Properties of Light
Noticing, wondering, exploring, and asking questions out of curiosity or to further existing knowledge	On a bright, sunny day outdoors, preschoolers notice and play with their shadows, exploring how to make the shadows longer or shorter and wondering whether they can "get away" from them. The teacher asks, "Where do you think a shadow comes from?"
Formulating preliminary predictions, explanations, or hypotheses to answer questions	Children offer their theories about shadows: People make shadows; shadows follow you; shadows are skinny; only the sun makes shadows. Some think shadows go away at night and some disagree.
Gathering evidence by actively observing, investigating, and/or experimenting	The children observe and gather evidence about shadows: They trace their shadows at different times of the day outdoors; they play with a shadow theater indoors (a sheet in front of a large window), guessing the objects creating the shadows.
Recording, reporting, explaining, discussing, and reflecting on evidence	The children refine their ideas about shadows: Other sources of light make shadows, not just the sun; people need light to make shadows; shadows change shape.
Refining questions, refocusing observations, and engaging in more focused explorations	The teacher sets up an overhead projector for children to focus on what more can be learned about shadows. The teacher sends home a letter to families encouraging them to help children observe shadows at night.
Sharing and discussing ideas, listening to other perspectives, and asking new questions	Children share their observations from home, such as street lights can make shadows, and they ask new questions: "Can the moon make shadows?" The study continues with new questions and interests.

Source: Based on *Worms, Shadows, and Whirlpools: Science in the Early Childhood Classroom*, by K. Worth and S. Grollman, 2003, Portsmouth, NH: Heinemann.

Intentionally Teach Science Providing a scientifically engaging learning environment and opportunities to explore are essential, but children do not learn science from manipulating materials alone. Research shows that when teachers explicitly introduce children to science concepts, vocabulary, and processes during brief circle time lessons, children spend more time and are more engaged in science, and their scientific knowledge increases (Hong & Diamond, 2012; Nayfeld, Brenneman, & Gelman, 2009). Children need intentional teachers to connect their experiences to scientific concepts and vocabulary, as described in the feature titled *Becoming an Intentional Teacher: Science in Block Building*.

Table 13.2 lists key strategies that teachers can use to promote children's enthusiasm and understanding of science knowledge, concepts, and methods. These strategies are also effective for teaching mathematics.

Adapt for Individual and Cultural Diversity Science is engaging, interesting, and fun for many children. But every child is different. Teachers need to pay particular attention to adapting learning experiences for dual language learners and children with special needs. They also need to be mindful of providing girls with equal opportunities to learn science and mathematics.

Children with Special Needs Providing access to science experiences for children with disabilities is an especially important task for teachers. To widen your view of effective science teaching, read the *Including All Children: Science Exploration* feature on page 448.

Dual Language Learners Science presents an opportunity as well as a challenge for children who are learning English. Because science involves real things and events, it can help children learn vocabulary words, especially names of objects, living things, and tools. On the other hand, specific scientific terms such as *inquiry* or *evidence* can be especially difficult for

► **Classroom Connection**

This video shows an effective science curriculum in action. What science content are these children learning? In what ways are they "doing" science? What effective strategies are the teachers using?

Becoming an Intentional Teacher

Integrating Physical Science in Block Building

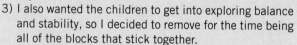

Here's What Happened The block area was running smoothly, but I wanted to take my preschoolers' block building experiences to a new level and extend their awareness of physical science in construction. My goal was to get them thinking about some basic principles of physics: how solid objects move and change position, and how slope affects the distance a ball rolls. I took the following actions:

1) Added various materials for the children to create ramps including open molding and plastic tubing plus spheres of various sizes (marbles, plastic and rubber balls) and small cars.

2) Put away the blocks that stick together, such as Legos and Duplos.

3) Began observing in the block area and talking with children about construction.

Here's What I Was Thinking Physics principles are at the heart of block construction, but I felt that in my classroom we weren't using the full potential of blocks for exploring these ideas. Here is the thinking behind my actions:

1) I added photos to the block area of various types of ramps, such as an off-ramp and overpass of a highway and a skateboard park. The children and I talked about the images in the block area in order to increase their awareness of different types of ramps and encourage them to branch out in their construction. Such pictures were handy, too, for children to refer to as they grappled with creating and experimenting with various kinds and angles of ramps.

2) Because I wanted the children to hypothesize, observe, and think about the effect of the slope of the ramps

on the motion of objects, I added various types of material to construct ramps as well as different size and weight of objects that roll.

3) I also wanted the children to get into exploring balance and stability, so I decided to remove for the time being all of the blocks that stick together.

4) I observed in the block area to get a feel for the kinds of things the children were doing there. I noted that they were very interested in creating ramps and shooting objects down the slope as fast they could go but that this behavior became repetitive. If I asked questions related to the slope of the ramps and the motion of the objects ("What could you do to make the marbles roll slower?"), they became intrigued and focused more attention on the activity. I wanted to extend their thinking without interfering with their play.

I also found that using large- or small-group time worked well for introducing new materials or a new challenge. I found that the children incorporated such elements in their block play and discussed them—with me and with one another—yet the construction and play were under their control.

Reflection What do you think about this teacher's approach to integrating science content in play? Why did she intervene? In what other ways could she intentionally teach physical science concepts?

Source: Based on *Ramps and Pathways: A Constructivist Approach to Physics with Young Children*, by R. DeVries and C. Sales, 2011, Washington, DC: National Association for the Education of Young Children.

dual language learners (Albert Shanker Institute, 2009). These children will need lots of cues, gestures, and repetition to learn these words in meaningful context. Read the feature *What Works: Teaching STEM to Dual Language Learners* to learn more on page 449.

Gender Differences During a visit to the nature center, first-grade teacher Trula Mann is startled when the naturalist brings out a snake for the children's inspection. She hates snakes and cringes at the thought of touching it. She sees that the boys eagerly gather around the snake while most of the girls look frightened and withdraw. Trula swallows her anxiety and reaches out to touch the snake. She is surprised to find that it is not at all slimy. The naturalist asks, "How can a snake find food or defend itself since it doesn't have arms or legs?" At the end of the discussion, the children conclude that they would bite, too, if they were a snake who was threatened.

In overcoming her trepidation, Trula served as a valuable model for the children, especially some of the girls. Such modeling behavior is important for girls in both science and mathematics. One study found that first- and second-grade girls whose female teachers had math anxiety were likely to be anxious about math themselves (Beiland, Gunderson, Ramirez, & Levine, 2010). By the end of the school year, the girls came to believe that boys are good at math and girls are good at reading. Most important, the young girls' anxiety negatively affected their math achievement.

TABLE 13.2 Effective Science Teaching Strategies

The strategies listed and described here are not only effective in teaching scientific knowledge, concepts, and methods but also motivate children's interest in and enthusiasm for science.

Science Teaching Strategy	Explanation
Model and welcome curiosity, openness, and flexibility to questioning without needing to know all the answers. Teachers are sometimes intimidated by science because they don't have enough knowledge themselves.	While teachers don't need vast knowledge before tackling a topic, they do need to prepare and learn as much as possible. When they don't know an answer to a child's question, the best response is, "I don't know. What do you imagine?" or "I'm curious about . . ."
Be open to and appreciate creativity and beauty in science. Sometimes science is erroneously thought to be only about cold, hard facts.	Examine NASA-produced photos of sunrise on Mars or the rings around Saturn. Watch a butterfly emerge from its cocoon. Such experiences can inspire children to produce their own creative representations of the natural and physical world.
Encourage children to reflect on their experiences and share their ideas with others. Direct experience with materials is important to their science learning, but it is not enough.	Engage children in thinking about, representing, and discussing their experiences and observations. Discussion among teachers and children, informally and in planned groups, gives children the chance to hear others' thinking and perspectives and to develop skills communicating about science.
Teach children observation skills.	Encourage children to go beyond just looking. Have children describe, draw, discuss, redraw, and describe again to refine observation skills and build vocabulary. Ask, "What did we learn about . . . ?"
Provide a variety of ways for children to document and represent their work.	Give children journals, writing tools, and digital cameras to record their observations, gather data, and communicate their findings to others.
Listen to children and ask about what they are seeing and doing.	When children talk about what they see, hear, and think, they do more noticing, wondering, and reflecting. They make connections, think about causes, and learn new, often rare words.
Build on and extend children's interests in the natural world and living things.	Use information books, field trips, technology, and visitors, to open up the classroom.
Engage children in formulating their own questions (*What do you want to know?*), designing experiments (*How can we find out?*), and making predictions (*What do you think will happen if . . . ?*).	Children attend more closely to what they see, hear, smell, and feel when they have put forth their own prediction or question or have considered how to go about investigating something. They are more likely to think about what their observations mean.
Don't bombard children with talk as they explore and investigate. Instead, watch closely and use a well-timed question or comment.	Prompt children to: • Make a prediction (*What will it look like if . . . ?*). • Think aloud (*What are you doing now? What next?*). • Reflect on their actions (*What did you do before that happened? How do you know? How did you figure that out?*).
Integrate science in play and routines	Science is everywhere. Children learn science when they play in the water table, ride down a slope on a tricycle, or observe ants on a sidewalk. Rich science opportunities occur in blocks, sand, clay, cooking, art, music, movement, stories, and outdoors.

Sources: Based on *Benchmarks for Science Literacy*, American Association for the Advancement of Science, 2009, Washington, DC: Author, retrieved September 15, 2009, from http://www.project2061.org/publications/bsl/default.htm; *Using the Scientific Method* by National Center on Quality Teaching and Learning, 2013, Washington, DC: U.S. Department of Health and Human Services, Office of Head Start.

Such gender differences are apparent as early as preschool. For example, one study found that boys demonstrated more curiosity, spontaneity, and extensive knowledge about nature and vertebrate and invertebrate (worms, snakes) animals than did girls (Desouza & Czerniak, 2002). On the other hand, girls, although more fearful, were also more concerned about the welfare of animals. Boys and girls also differed in their play preferences, with boys more active and more likely than girls to bring into their play the science concepts that were introduced at group time the day before.

Because the science and engineering professions have been traditionally dominated by white males, particular efforts need to be made to address stereotypes and open the

Including All Children

Science Exploration

Most children are naturally interested in science topics and motivated to engage in investigations using all of their senses. However, children with sensory disabilities may lose out on such learning unless teachers make appropriate accommodations.

Sheila Kohn loves science, and so do the children in her first-grade class. Currently, the curriculum topic is earth science. The children have formulated questions and are exploring a wooded area near the school. They want to know what lives under the ground and how it survives. They have brought little shovels, collection containers, and magnifying glasses for observation. Their questions include these: How does the earth smell? How does it feel? What lives in a small amount of earth? How do they breathe? What do they eat? What happens if it rains?

Most of the children are very excited and eagerly approach the investigation. Delores, however, has a vision impairment. The trek outside intimidates her, and all the talk of observing and using the magnifying glass makes her feel left out. Sheila discusses the situation with Delores and they agree on a plan. Together they will visit the outdoors in a small group, and Delores will use her other senses to investigate the earth. Delores will be in charge of the questions that she is most able to address: What does the earth feel like and how does it smell? Delores is an especially astute listener as well, so she will also report on what she hears outside. Because the other children focus on what they see, they usually miss a great deal of information that can be obtained through their other senses.

Ira has a different special need—sensory integration disorder—which requires an altogether different accommodation. Children who have sensory integration disorders have difficulty processing and connecting sensory information. Each of the five senses obtains information from the environment in different ways. In the course of typical development, the senses work together to sort out and make sense of the input. Children with sensory integration disorders, however, may be overly sensitive to one or more of the senses—touch or sound, for example. Or they may fixate on one sense such as sight or smell.

In Ira's case, the busyness of the classroom overwhelms him at times. He is especially disturbed by confusing experiences like science study that seem to come at him from all directions. To ensure Ira's successful participation, Sheila includes him in the small group with Delores on the walk. Unlike Delores, however, who is encouraged to use as many senses as possible, Sheila helps Ira limit his sensory input. She gives him earplugs to lessen the noise and sunglasses to minimize the light. Under such conditions, Ira is an astute observer and spends a long time carefully watching a worm wiggling through his pile of earth.

As we see from Delores's and Ira's situations, successful inclusion of all children requires knowledge of each child's needs and strengths and individually planned accommodations and modifications.

fields early on to girls and to children from diverse linguistic and cultural groups. Given that gender, racial, and cultural differences in STEM begin early and persist, it is never too early to introduce powerful role models such as female, African American, and Latino astronauts, inventors, or architects via real-life examples, books, toys, and materials.

 Check Your Understanding 13.4: Effective Science Curriculum and Teaching

⬆ Teaching about and with Technology

technology Tools used to change or modify the natural world to meet human needs.

Whereas science is the study of the natural world, the goal of **technology** is to change or modify the natural world to meet human needs (NRC, 2012). Technology, in its many forms, is a tool for all kinds of learning throughout life. It can be as simple as a handheld magnifying glass or as complex as the Hubble space telescope exploring the origins of the universe. Both of these tools make it possible for people to see things beyond the capability of the human eye.

Technology in itself is neither good nor bad; the same tool—such as a computer—can be used productively or destructively. Today, a major curriculum goal is to improve

What Works
Teaching STEM to Dual Language Learners

Considerable attention is paid to research on how dual language learners acquire English and learn to read. At times, there is an assumption that because mathematics is about numbers and quantity, language is less of a barrier. However, mathematics itself is a language, and as we have seen, math talk is what makes its abstract concepts comprehensible for children. Other areas of STEM have their own vocabulary and involve academic language that children do not encounter in everyday interactions. In short, STEM learning presents unique challenges for dual language learners.

Many of the same strategies for teaching dual language learners in general are effective in teaching STEM. For example, gestures such as a circling motion are useful in helping young children understand basic concepts such as the whole amount or putting together and taking apart. Children readily count or form shapes with their fingers. Teachers can set up an obstacle course for children to use their whole bodies to learn position words such as *above*, *below*, *between*, and *through*. A strategy for older children is to create a math, science, or technology dictionary of relevant terms. Such a resource engages children in using different ways of representing a concept—in this case, words that can be referred to later.

Another effective strategy is having children talk to one another in pairs or small groups. When children are learning a new language, it is important not to put them on the spot. They shouldn't be expected to respond in front of the whole class. In a small group, it is easier to practice concepts and "errors" are more likely to be viewed as part of the learning process. This is especially important with a topic like math that may have only one correct answer.

Introducing a math or science concept to the whole class can be done effectively using an interactive whiteboard. Then children can be prompted to respond to questions chorally as a whole group. Not every child will answer correctly, and no one child's response will be singled out.

Another proven strategy when introducing a math or science concept is to explicitly teach it by modeling, supplying the specific name, and having children repeat the word. Also helpful is introducing and using a consistent sentence such as the one first

graders used to interpret their graphs in Figure 13.1.

Problem solving is playing a larger role in today's curriculum due to the Common Core standards, but word problems complicate the challenge of math instruction for dual language learners. Teachers should avoid tricky word problems that create confusion, such as: "Jonas has 2 cars and 3 trucks; how many vehicles does he have?" Such a question poses a language test rather than a math problem. A related challenge presented by word problems is the culturally implicit knowledge they often require. Solving a problem usually requires that a child understand the situation in which it occurs, whether it's purchasing groceries or driving a car at a certain speed.

Manipulatives are hailed as an excellent tool to teach STEM, and yet many children cannot relate to these toys. Few such toys reflect the racial, cultural, and gender diversity of our classrooms. For example, Lego® has introduced some plastic figures portraying people of color as doctors, scientists, architects, and other STEM occupations. However, most STEM toys still promote stereotypes of only white males in these roles.

What works most effectively are the practices that are developmentally appropriate for all children—hands-on, meaningful experiences coupled with teacher scaffolding, as opposed to worksheets that test what children should have already learned. Dual language learners need to actively "do" science, technology, and engineering tasks—as teachers and other children supply the words. And most important of all, teachers need to have high expectations that all children can learn challenging STEM content.

Sources: Based on "6 Tips When Discussing Math with the English Language Learner," by B. Austin, 2014, Chicago, Erikson Early Math Collaborative, retrieved March 17, 2015, from http://earlymath.erikson.edu/6-tips-discussing-math-english-language-learner; "It's Time for More Racial Diversity in STEM Toys" by M. Weinstock, 2015, *Scientific American*, Voices: Exploring and Celebrating Diversity in Science, retrieved March 8, 2015, from http://blogs.scientificamerican.com/voices/2015/02/23/its-time-for-more-racial-diversity-in-stem-toys/?WT.mc_id=SA_sharetool_Twitter.

STEM skills and understanding, with *T* standing for technology. In other words, children need to think critically about how technology is used to solve problems as well as learn how to use technological tools in intentional and creative ways.

A Developmentally and Technologically Appropriate Classroom

A preschool teacher creates a class website that is updated regularly. The children create a slide show about their class pet using Kid Pix software to share with families. For an integrated science study on the properties of water, kindergartners produce information books on the computer using digital photos of their water experiments.

Children today need to learn with and about technology. How can teachers use interactive digital media to promote mathematics and science in learning?

First graders work together using an interactive whiteboard, a large digital touchscreen with a computer, and the Internet. They explore pictures and information about birds in different parts of the world. They e-mail their questions to a first-grade class in Australia.

These are some examples of how creative teachers use technology to expand children's worlds beyond the classroom. In some cases, a relatively inexpensive form of media such as a digital camera is used, whereas an interactive whiteboard constitutes a much larger investment. Given the costs, educators must make informed decisions and be taught to use the tools effectively. For example, teacher may use digital tablets with individual children or pairs to differentiate reading instruction. A handheld device allows teachers to match apps, games, or other instructional tools to a child's learning level and needs. An interactive whiteboard, on the other hand, is most effective for larger groups or even whole-class instruction in which children actively participate (Linder, 2012). Teachers can introduce a new concept via the whiteboard and then children can solve problems in small groups or individually.

Use Interactive Media Effectively Hundreds of children's media products flood the marketplace every year, for both home and school use. Given limited budgets and the vital importance of choosing developmentally and culturally appropriate tools, early educators need help making decisions. Warren Buckleitner, an authority on interactive media for children, provides an online service for this purpose: *Children's Technology Review* (http://www.childrenstech.com), which is the world's largest online collection of educational reviews of children's interactive media. In addition, the NAEYC Technology and Young Children Interest Forum provides an interactive support group for teachers through its website.

Decisions about technology should be based on how well the particular tool serves the purposes of the classroom and the teaching and learning goals for children. "Technology does not drive purposeful learning; teachers' intentional instructional planning does" (NAEYC Technology and Young Children Interest Forum, 2008, p. 50).

Technology has many uses, from complex problem solving to practice on individual skills, managed at the children's level of thinking (Donohue, 2015). Working with appropriate software builds collaboration, creativity, and language. In fact, preschoolers actually talk almost twice as much at the computer than during any other activity, including blocks and art (Clements & Sarama, 2003).

Digital media allow children to break free of the physical world and manipulate objects and space in ways that are otherwise impossible, using virtual manipulatives (Linder, 2012). For example, when children put together a wooden puzzle, there are strict limits on how pieces can be placed. Similarly, trying to correct or change marks formed on paper can be difficult and frustrating. By contrast, with Kid Pix drawing software and many other programs like it, a child can take actions that are impossible in the real world—change the shape of a design or instantly change colors—and easily alter their creations. In this way, digital media helps children become explicitly aware of and intentional about what they are doing (Clements & Sarama, 2007a).

Choosing appropriate apps is an important responsibility for teachers. The best apps have some of the same benefits as traditional play (Gray, 2015), as described in the feature *Promoting Play: Digital Play and Traditional Play.*

Ensure Access for All Children Technology raises the issue of equity because some children have considerable access to technology at home while others do not. In addition, when digital media devices are available, boys tend to choose them more often than girls and to work on them longer.

Promoting Play

Digital Play and Traditional Play

Young children learn through play in all kinds of ways. Every type of play—building blocks, playing games, manipulating table toys, pretending with other children, physically engaging their whole bodies outdoors—has its own intrinsic rewards as well as benefits. Children also play with digital tablets and smart phones virtually every day. Early childhood educators often ask themselves, "Is this a good or bad thing?"

Like the answer to most questions about developmentally appropriate practice, "It depends." An important consideration is how much time children spend engaged with digital devices, but the more important criterion is the quality of the experience. If the game or app is not high quality, then it deserves no time. On the other hand, if children's minds are truly engaged, their own initiative and curiosity may be the best guide.

In making decisions about using technology, teachers may be wise to consider what the experience has in common with traditional play. One reason children love to play is because they are in control. When playing, children will often stay engaged for long periods of time, until they have mastered a task to their own satisfaction, repeating an activity such as putting together a puzzle or playing a matching game. These facts about play have important implications for choosing appropriate software for digital tools. Many apps emphasize extrinsic rewards like bells, gold stars, or flashing lights; but apps that engage children's intrinsic motivation to create, invent, think, and solve problems are more likely to promote imaginative play and its benefits.

Traditional play also provides a vital context for children to develop social skills as they interact with other children. One frequent criticism of digital tools is that they interfere with this opportunity. However, some popular apps are designed to promote social interaction in several ways. For example, *Toca Boca* provides a large selection of apps that promote play and creativity on a range of topics such as nature, construction, and transportation, and in settings such as hair salon or pet doctor. *Toca Tea Party* enables a child to create an imaginary tea table and serve a meal to a favorite stuffed animal or toy figure. Research shows that children often share a tablet, taking turns touching the screen, and talking. With *Toca Tea Party* or the other *Toca* apps, a child can also pretend with another child or an adult. Some shared apps enable children to interact with one another via the Internet. Or they can interact with the animated characters on the screen, an application that will be enhanced as speech recognition technology improves.

None of these examples of digital play should replace traditional play. But digital media have the advantage of being portable and almost endless in the variety of social situations they can present. Engaging children who don't nap with playful, creative media is a far better alternative than requiring them to be quiet so their peers can sleep. Having touch tablets available as one option during choice time can promote imaginative play in children whose prior experience with pretend play is limited. The app can model how to play with real objects, props, and other children. In the end, teachers determine whether digital play is a good or bad for children.

Source: Based on "Digital Play and Traditional Play Have More in Common Than You May Think" by J. Gray, 2015, *Sparking Kids' Imagination with Digital Toys*, retrieved from http://tocaboca.com/magazine/sparking-imagination/.

For interactive media to be effective, teachers need to encourage experimentation with open-ended problems. They also need to use a wide range of teaching strategies to encourage, question, prompt, model, demonstrate, and give children choices without taking over or limiting children's opportunities to explore. Developmentally appropriate interactive media allows children to be in control, to function independently, and to create and invent their own activities; it also needs to be flexible and allow for more than one correct response (NAEYC and Fred Rogers Center for Early Learning and Children's Media, 2012).

In this chapter, we explored the importance of providing developmentally appropriate, effective curriculum and intentional teaching in the related areas of mathematics, science, and technology. We described how teachers can help children become effective problem solvers and investigators. With this knowledge in mind, we return to Darrell and Sofia's classroom.

 Check Your Understanding 13.5: Teaching about and with Technology

Revisiting the Case Study

. . . Mr. Burns and Ms. Moreno's Classroom

At the beginning of this chapter, we met Darrell and Sofia who, like many Americans, feel math anxiety. Using a well-planned, focused curriculum, they found that young children are not only capable of learning significant mathematics but also enjoy and are interested in learning it. They incorporated mathematics learning goals and introduced mathematics language into children's play. The teachers worked with children in small groups using math manipulatives and games. They also individualized their teaching to help each child make progress along the learning trajectories that lay the essential foundation for later math understanding.

These teachers also integrated part of the curriculum around a science topic that was motivating for children and created a meaningful way for them to apply math concepts in context—a shadow study that included measurement. They used technology—digital cameras, computers—as a tool to build on and expand children's interest and extend their experiences beyond the classroom. ■

13 Chapter Summary

- A math achievement gap among lower-SES and higher-SES groups of children is present at the time of kindergarten entry and tends to widen as children progress through school. This knowledge gap exists to some extent because children living in poverty do not have sufficient opportunity to learn the language of mathematics that connects their informal, basic math knowledge to later, more abstract school mathematics.

- Children's cognitive development and abilities, such as their thinking, reasoning, and problem solving, develop over time as their experience increases and becomes more complex, and their brains mature. Executive function, which includes working memory, cognitive flexibility, and mental self-control, is strongly related to how children learn mathematics and science.

- Young children are capable of learning sophisticated mathematics, and they are interested in learning it. Teachers can contribute to narrowing the achievement gap and improving the math learning of all children by helping children mathematize their play and

everyday experiences as well as by planning specific, math-focused curriculum.

- Broad consensus exists among mathematics experts that from age 3 to grade 3, content goals should focus on these topics: number and operations and geometry, spatial relations, and measurement. Mathematics process goals include problem solving, reasoning, communicating, connecting, and designing and analyzing representations.

- Early childhood science curriculum includes knowledge and concepts of life science, physical science, earth and space science, and the process of scientific inquiry—questioning, predicting, observing, investigating, and documenting.

- Intentional teachers promote science learning by organizing the environment, providing focused experiences, intentional teaching, and integrating science in play and routines.

- Interactive digital media are effective tools for teaching young children curriculum content and for expanding their thinking and communication skills.

Key Terms

- abstraction
- base ten place value system
- cardinality
- cognitive (mental) flexibility
- composing/decomposing
- connections
- earth and space science
- enumeration

- everyday mathematics
- executive function
- geometry
- inhibitory control (cognitive self-control)
- learning trajectory
- life science
- manipulatives
- math talk
- mathematize

- measurement
- one-to-one correspondence
- operations
- order irrelevance principle
- physical science
- reasoning
- representing
- science

- scientific inquiry
- spatial relations
- stable order principle
- subitizing
- technology
- unitizing
- working memory

 ## Demonstrate Your Learning

Click here to assess how well you've learned the content in this chapter.

Readings and Websites

Copple, C. (Ed.). (2012). *Growing minds: Building strong cognitive foundations in early childhood.* Washington, DC: National Association for the Education of Young Children.

Early Childhood Math Collaborative, Erikson Institute. (2014). *Big ideas of early mathematics: What teachers of young children need to know.* Upper Saddle River, NJ: Pearson.

Shillady, A. (Ed.). (2013). *Spotlight on young children: Exploring science.* Washington, DC: National Association for the Education of Young Children.

TEC (Technology in Early Childhood) Center

This website is the work of a cutting-edge technology center at Erikson Institute in Chicago.
Here you'll find all the latest research and applications for using digital media with children in developmentally appropriate ways.

Erikson Early Math Collaborative

The Erikson Early Math Collaborative website provides a wealth of practical resources for pre-K to third-grade teachers to help children learn foundational mathematics through effective, developmentally appropriate approaches to teaching and learning.

National Council of Teachers of Mathematics

Search this site to find *NCTM Curriculum Focal Points, PreK to Grade 3* and other resources for teaching early childhood mathematics.

National Science Teachers Association

On this website, you will find an interactive version of the *Next Generation Science Standards* and many resources for planning science curriculum to help children in kindergarten through 3rd grade meet the standards.

14

Teaching Children to Live in a Democratic Society: Social-Emotional Learning and Social Studies

Learning Outcomes

After studying this chapter, you should be able to:

14.1 Define social-emotional development and discuss the social and emotional foundations of early learning.

14.2 Describe ways in which teachers use the continuum of social and emotional development to foster children's learning.

14.3 Explain the role of play in children's social and emotional development and learning.

14.4 Identify effective curriculum and teaching strategies to promote children's social and emotional competence.

14.5 Formulate the content of the social studies curriculum in early childhood and elaborate on effective and developmentally appropriate strategies for teaching social studies.

© iofoto/Shutterstock

t is Waylon's birthday and he gets to be the "Big Cheese" in his kindergarten class at Jefferson Elementary School. He bounds in the door with his "About Me, My Family, and My Community" poster, featuring a collage of photos including his grandparents' wedding, his first birthday, his first haircut, and his pet dog. His mom will visit at circle time to share the story of how they picked his name and what it means. Waylon gets to deliver the attendance sheet to the office and select a friend to accompany him. Later, Waylon's teacher, Ms. Hans, asks the class to vote for which of Waylon's two favorite books to read. A few more votes are cast for *Leonardo the Terrible Monster*, and the children know that the majority rules. The children excitedly gather on the rug looking for spots with their names, sometimes stumbling over each other. Ms. Hans says in a soothing voice, "Close your eyes. Now pretend to smell a flower." Each child takes a deep breath and holds it. Then she says very calmly, "Now pretend to slowly blow out some candles." Ms. Hans begins reading, and the children visibly relax while listening to the story about friendship.

Down the hall, Mr. Bell is working with a small group of third graders on their maps of the Gulf Coast, which has recently been hit by a damaging hurricane followed by a massive oil spill. Four children are working on a report about severe weather and its effects on geography, the economy, and people's lives. One group is working on a report about oil: what it is used for, how much we use in America, and how much we get from foreign sources. The group is huddled around a tablet, searching the Internet for some of these answers. Another group is brainstorming ways to support the children whose homes or schools have been destroyed. They decide on a stuffed toy drive for the younger children, a "letter buddy" system, and a school supply collection. The group excitedly tells Mr. Bell about the buddy project. Eight-year-old Tasha explains, "Well, you see, third graders—like us—will work with kindergarten and first graders to help write e-mails and letters to our neighbors and businesses around here to get them to donate."

Mr. Bell tells the children that he likes the idea and that they need to figure out how much it will cost and what materials they will need. Mr. Bell's class has been working on this project for several weeks. He incorporates reading, writing, and mathematics into the social studies unit. ■

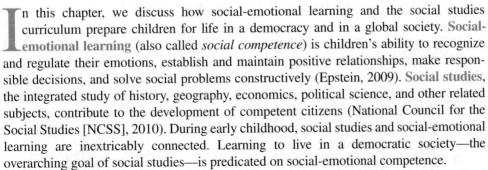

In this chapter, we discuss how social-emotional learning and the social studies curriculum prepare children for life in a democracy and in a global society. **Social-emotional learning** (also called *social competence*) is children's ability to recognize and regulate their emotions, establish and maintain positive relationships, make responsible decisions, and solve social problems constructively (Epstein, 2009). **Social studies**, the integrated study of history, geography, economics, political science, and other related subjects, contribute to the development of competent citizens (National Council for the Social Studies [NCSS], 2010). During early childhood, social studies and social-emotional learning are inextricably connected. Learning to live in a democratic society—the overarching goal of social studies—is predicated on social-emotional competence.

In this chapter, we focus on how the social studies prepare children to be **engaged citizens**—change agents in their schools, communities, and eventually the world. As we saw in Mr. Bell's class, he extends his class's learning beyond the local community and helps children learn economics and geography while working to make the world a better

social-emotional learning Children's ability to recognize and regulate their emotions, establish and maintain positive relationships, make responsible decisions, and solve social problems constructively. Also called *social competence*.

social studies The integrated study of the history, geography, economics, political science, and other related aspects of societies of the past, present, and future.

engaged citizens Children as change agents in schools, communities, and eventually in the world.

place. In Ms. Hans' kindergarten, she lays the foundation for engaged citizenry by focusing on social-emotional learning and beginning democracy through voting.

We begin with a discussion of how social-emotional development lays the foundation for all learning. Next, we present an overview of the continuum of social and emotional development from birth through age 8 and ways teachers can foster children's social-emotional learning. Then we discuss social studies content and effective teaching strategies and curriculum approaches.

Social-Emotional Foundations of Early Learning

Research demonstrates the critical importance of social-emotional learning for success in school and life (Landy, 2009; Thompson & Goodman, 2009). Development in the social and emotional domains is inextricably linked; consequently, they are often referred to as one concept, *social-emotional development*. When children establish warm and responsive relationships with adults—the foundation of social development—they are more likely to develop important emotional skills such as identifying feelings and learning to regulate their emotions and express them appropriately. In turn, these emotional skills pave the way for the development of interpersonal problem solving, an essential social skill. The following example illustrates the interaction of social and emotional development.

> Louise was overjoyed the day her daughter Kate was born. Louise's friends tease her that she never puts Kate down for a moment. Indeed, Louise often holds and gazes at her baby. She imitates her expressions and, at first, picks her up whenever she cries. As a newborn baby, Kate is beginning to trust Louise to meet her needs. Kate generalizes this trust to other adults in her life. In the context of these relationships, Kate is also learning key emotion words that eventually will help her to regulate her emotions and, in turn, to solve interpersonal problems. Ever since Kate was a tiny baby, her parents have labeled her various states with feeling words, "You are sad. . . . Katie is frustrated. . . . Katie loves her mommy. . . . Katie is happy to see her grandma. . . ." When Kate begins to talk, her sentences are often peppered with feeling words that help her parents, teachers, and peers understand what she needs and how to help.

This snapshot of Kate's daily life reveals how early interactions contribute to the development of essential social-emotional foundations of learning. These include the ability to express feelings, establish positive relationships, and the overarching construct called self-regulation.

Emotional Development

emotional development Acquisition of important emotional skills such as identifying feelings and learning to regulate emotions and express them appropriately.

emotional literacy Children's ability to identify their own and others' emotions, having words to express emotions in a healthy way, and to self-regulate their feelings.

Emotional development begins at birth, and continues through the lifespan. Over time, children's emotional development is shown in their ability to identify their own and others' emotions, to express emotions in a healthy way, and to regulate their feelings (Epstein, 2009). **Emotional literacy** refers to recognizing emotions in self and others, having words to express feelings, and knowing how emotional expression affects others. Emotional literacy helps children express their emotions appropriately, in personal situations, such as when they become frustrated or discouraged, and in social contexts, such as when their feelings are hurt.

Teachers must understand that emotions play a significant role in early learning. For example, some children are especially sensitive to criticism. Working on a dropout prevention project for African American and Latino boys in pre-K through third grade, Ritchie (2011) found that if teachers ignored or embarrassed them in any way, the boys were likely to disengage mentally or physically from the task at hand and not re-engage for up to an hour. Over the course of a school year, consider how much learning time these children will lose.

Self-Regulation

When kindergarten teachers are asked to define school readiness, they rarely mention letters and numbers. Instead they inevitably say that children entering school need to be able to "follow directions, pay attention, delay gratification, and get along with others." These abilities are aspects of what developmental psychologists now call *self-regulation* (Diamond, 2012).

Experienced teachers understand that self-regulation is the underlying ability that makes learning possible in all areas from reading to science. When children are self-regulated, they control their impulses and pay attention when the teacher gives directions. They are more likely to think before they speak or act, and not behave impulsively (Diamond, 2012). Of course, these abilities do not emerge automatically even in the most self-regulated of children. They develop over time and with experience and support from parents and teachers.

When children use **self-regulation**, they manage their thoughts and emotions in order to control their behavior and impulses and use constructive problem-solving to achieve their goals (Murray, Rosanbalm, Christopoulos, & Hamoudi, 2014). In fact, a study of 1,000 children born in the same city in the same year found that children with less self-control (i.e., less persistent, more impulsive, and poorer attention regulation) had worse health, earned less, and committed more crimes as adults *30 years later* than did those with more self-control as young children, regardless of IQ, gender, social class, and family circumstances (Moffitt et al., 2011). Self-regulation in preschool predicts children's academic success in the early grades, in both literacy and math, over and above their intelligence or family backgrounds (Blair & Razza, 2007; McClelland, Acock, & Morrison, 2006).

Studies such as these provide important guidance for educators. Problems in self-regulation are strongly related to learning difficulties. Many efforts are underway to close the achievement gap in schools, but most of them focus on directly teaching academic skills without attention to the underlying issue of self-regulation. Academic skills are important but should not be taught in ways that undermine children's self-regulation and social-emotional development.

Individual differences in self-regulation are apparent almost at birth (Calkins & Williford, 2009). Some babies quickly fall into regular patterns of sleep and wakefulness and almost entertain themselves; others struggle mightily to adjust as their parents become more frustrated and feel more inadequate. Over time, these differences can be worsened by poor parenting, environmental conditions such as community violence, or negative school experiences and peer relationships. But on a positive note, these problems can also be lessened by providing experiences in preschool and early grades that promote the development of self-regulation.

Social Development

Social development refers to the process by which children learn to form and sustain positive relationships with adults and other children. Like other domains, social learning occurs along a developmental continuum, which we describe later in this chapter. Skills become more complex as children are placed in more demanding social situations such as early childhood programs, schools, after-school programs, and special interest clubs and classes.

Self-regulation in preschool has been found to predict children's academic success in the early grades, in both literacy and math, over and above their intelligence or family background.

self-regulation The act of managing thoughts and emotions in order to control behavior and impulses, use constructive problem-solving, and achieve goals.

social development Young children's ability to form and sustain positive relationships with adults and other children.

One of the greatest joys of childhood is making friends. Having friends contributes to social-emotional development and later success in school and life.

As children grow, their ability to establish friendships with peers becomes more important and influences how they view themselves and the world (Gallagher, 2013; Gallagher & Sylvester, 2009). Within the context of these relationships, children learn and practice cooperation, the ability to form and sustain friendships, and the ability to solve problems in positive ways. Cooperation with peers requires that children understand other people's rights and perspectives, empathize, and balance their own needs and desires with those of others. For example, when Mimmo, Bart, and Chelsea want to play restaurant, they can't all be the waiters; they have to figure out who will do what. Similarly, when Sasha tries to join the group, further cooperation is required to see how she will fit in.

Stress in Children's Lives

Young children today experience considerable stress in their lives, which can negatively impact their social-emotional development and success in school. About 10% of kindergarten children demonstrate some symptoms of emotional behavior problems, and among low-income children the number approaches 20% (Thompson, 2010). Head Start teachers report that increasing numbers of children show signs of depression, aggression, and other emotional difficulties. Brain research reveals that stress causes many of these problems (Center on the Developing Child at Harvard University, 2007, 2010).

Some childhood stress is actually positive and necessary. Exposure to the typical moderate stresses of childhood such as starting school or visiting the dentist is a normal and essential part of healthy development and helps children learn coping skills (Thompson, 2010). At times, children are exposed to unique but relatively tolerable stressors such as an illness in the family or an injury to themselves. Although difficult, these situations can be weathered if they are short-lived and children have the support of loving relationships with parents and teachers.

toxic stress Extreme, prolonged, unrelenting stress without the protection of caring adults.

However, increasing numbers of children experience what is now called **toxic stress**—extreme, prolonged, unrelenting stress without the protection of caring adults (Center on the Developing Child at Harvard University, 2010). Toxic stress can result from single events of trauma such as abuse, neglect, natural disaster, or injury. It can also result from ongoing patterns of trauma and stress such as parental mental illness, dangerous neighborhoods, or domestic violence (Zero to Six Collaborative Group, 2010). Childhood trauma is not so rare. Research has shown that two-thirds of all adults experienced at least one traumatic event during their childhood (Felitti et al., 1998). Early trauma has potential to cause the most harm, as young children often do not have the cognitive and emotional skills to process and express how the trauma has affected them.

In circumstances in which the traumatic stress is ongoing, it can become toxic. Trauma or toxic stress cause a child to feel unsafe and includes physiological responses of racing heart, fast breathing, and the release of stress hormones, such as cortisol, into the body (http://nctsn.org). This constant activation of the stress system can impair brain development, leading to lifelong problems in behavior, health, and learning (Zero to Six Collaborative Group, 2010). Infants and toddlers who experience trauma may be developmentally delayed, display frequent tantrums, and become easily frustrated. They may have difficulty attaching to caregivers. School-age children who experience trauma may have difficulty with school skills and peer relationships, sleep problems, and trouble focusing and organizing their learning—and appear to have ADD/ADHD (American Academy of Pediatrics, n.d.).

When teachers learn that children in their care have experienced trauma, they need to draw on all the tools in their strategy toolbox as well as consult with early intervention and mental health professionals. The National Child Traumatic Stress Network (NCTSN Core Curriculum on Childhood Trauma Task Force, 2012) has resources for teachers and schools to help understand and support children and families who experience traumatic stress. Given the prevalence of stress in the lives of children and the power of early experiences to mitigate it, positive relationships between teachers and children become more important than ever. Next we turn to a description of the continuum of typical social-emotional development and how teachers can support children's social and emotional competence.

✓ **Check Your Understanding 14.1:** Social-Emotional Foundations of Early Learning

🔺 Continuum of Social and Emotional Development

In this section, we describe some of the typical social and emotional accomplishments that occur for children from birth through age 8. These descriptions are followed by examples of how teachers can support children's progress. Social-emotional learning is to a large extent the product of development—relatively predictable, age-related changes in children. At the same time, social and emotional skills are learned and, therefore, can be taught.

Infants and Toddlers

The major social-emotional task for babies is the development of a warm and responsive relationship with primary caregivers (Shonkoff & Phillips, 2000). Between birth and 12 months, an indicator of emotional development is the ability to quiet when comforted. Babies also begin to show preferences for primary caregivers and work to maintain interactions with caregivers. For example, babies imitate caregivers' gestures and sounds and also initiate interaction by patting the caregiver or through eye gaze and smiles.

Toward the first birthday, babies show a preference for familiar people. This time period may also be marked by **separation anxiety**, in which a child cries when the caregiver is not in sight or clings to a caregiver in the presence of strangers; such anxiety diminishes over time. In the second year, toddlers continue to demonstrate a strong attachment to caregivers and initiate interactions with familiar adults.

Emotional Development in Infants and Toddlers During their first year, infants experience a range of emotions, starting with expressions of comfort and discomfort, and emerging into a wide variety of emotions including fear, joy, and frustration. In the second and third year of life, toddlers begin to name their own and other's emotions, and they demonstrate empathy by noticing how adults or peers feel and trying to comfort them. For example, Lonnie brings a stuffed animal to Francie, who is sad because her mommy just left. His teacher quickly reinforces Lonnie's behavior: "What a caring friend you are, Lonnie."

These first years are also marked by tremendous growth in self-awareness and awareness of others. Infants will observe themselves in mirrors and notice other's physical characteristics and when a member of the group is missing. For example, a toddler may pat a child's head to feel her curly hair. They explore their own body, observing their hands or reaching for their toes; they may explore the face and body parts of others.

Toddlers begin to identify gender and other basic similarities and differences, although they

separation anxiety Feeling a baby experiences when the caregiver is not in sight; the baby may cry or cling to a caregiver in the presence of strangers; usually occurs around 8 months of age.

Separation anxiety is a natural part of social-emotional development at about 8 to 10 months of age, but it can make parents anxious as well. What can teachers do to help ease this experience for babies and families?

© Studio 8/Pearson Education

▶ **Classroom Connection**

As you watch this video illustrating the social and emotional development of infants and toddlers, reflect on the competence they demonstrate. How is their behavior different from what you might expect from children of this young age?

parallel play Children play next to each other, but not with each other; they may speak, but don't really converse.

may think that changing clothes changes their gender. They also begin to test limits and strive for independence. They notice when others are looking at them, and they often exaggerate movements or act silly when they are being watched.

Social Development in Infants and Toddlers During the first year, babies show interest in other children, particularly siblings, by watching them and tracking their behavior. They smile spontaneously and show enjoyment in interactions with peers, as expressed in gestures, facial expressions, and vocalizations. They may reach out to touch other children or grab their toys. Infants begin to take turns with teachers during play, as in peek-a-boo, laying a foundation for turn taking with other children, which develops during the second and third years of life.

Toddlers and 2-year-olds often engage in **parallel play**, playing next to each other but not interacting. They observe and imitate another child's behavior or activity and, by age 3, they initiate social interactions with peers. They may approach another child and ask to play, but will also be quick to assert ownership of toys by saying "Mine." Between 2 and 3 years of age, children start to show preferences for familiar playmates.

The *Developmental Continuum* feature describes social-emotional development in infants and toddlers and ways that teachers can help promote these competencies.

Preschool and Kindergarten

During preschool and kindergarten, children develop the ability to regulate their emotions more competently, allowing them to become increasingly adept at building relationships. Preschoolers begin to try to please adults and use adults for assistance in solving problems, for getting their needs met, and for emotional support.

Emotional Development in 3- through 5-Year-Olds During these years, most children become increasingly capable of regulating their own emotions. Most preschoolers can wait for a turn and sometimes, though not always, show patience during group activities, a skill that improves in kindergarten. With guidance from teachers, most preschoolers can calm themselves after feeling strong emotions, going to a quiet corner or requesting a favorite book to be read when upset. At this age, children can associate emotions with words and facial expressions and use pretend play to understand and respond to emotions, such as when pretending to be a fierce animal to express negative emotions.

Preschool and kindergarten children also demonstrate growth in self-concept and self-esteem. They describe themselves as a person with a mind, body, and feelings, and they often exert their will and have strong preferences for certain foods, toys, or activities. They also tend to overestimate their own competence, and experiment with their own abilities, try new activities, and test limits such as "skipping bars" on the monkey bars at the playground.

All of the social-emotional skills described here require teachers to provide more or less assistance, depending on individual children's needs and abilities.

Social Development in 3- through 5-Year-Olds Enhanced emotional development and increased self-understanding allow children to develop stronger peer relationships. In fact the preschool and kindergarten years are marked by tremendous growth in interactions with peers. Children initiate interactions with other children and will make and maintain a friendship with at least one other child. These relationships contribute to cognitive and language development and to overall well-being (Buysse, Goldman, West, & Hollingsworth, 2007). With occasional assistance from teachers, children can share toys and materials during play and use simple strategies to solve social problems appropriately, as discussed later in this chapter.

Developmental Continuum
Social-Emotional Development in Infants and Toddlers

Widely Held Expectations	How Teachers Can Help
Bonds and forms attachment with parents and other special people in life	Encourage and support parent-child relationships (such as enabling mothers' breast-feeding),
Enjoys when familiar adult cuddles and talks with them.	Hold, cuddle, hug, smile, and laugh with the child.
Exhibits separation anxiety by crying when familiar caregiver leaves.	Provide environment with consistent, small number of trustworthy adults.
Establishes an attachment with a consistent adult other than the primary caregiver.	Respond to child's emotional and physical needs, verbal and nonverbal communications.
Explores the environment, but checks in with caregiver.	Encourage exploration, and reassure child that you are still present. Reassure child when you leave the setting, "I'll be back," and when you return, "See, I'm back."
Smiles spontaneously at other children and shows interest in other children by watching them and tracking their behavior.	Provide opportunities for children to play and interact with other children; carefully supervise so that children don't hurt each other.
Seeks adult assistance with challenges.	Respond positively to child's questions and calls for assistance.
Plays side by side with other children at times.	Provide enough toys of the same kind so children can play side by side but don't have to share.
With adult support, waits for turns during play (usually 2-year-olds).	Play turn-taking games like pat-a-cake with babies. Help children learning turn-taking skills: "It's Curtis's turn to sit on my lap. You're next, Cassie."
May frustrate easily when unable to achieve a desired goal (e.g., building tower of blocks).	Observe child for emerging frustration, and offer support when needed (but not too soon).
Toddlers follow social routines with reminders (e.g., put your coat in your cubby).	Encourage independence and reinforce learning of social routines ("Thank you for putting your coat away!").

Sources: Based on *North Carolina Foundations for Early Learning and Development*, by North Carolina Foundations Task Force, 2013, Raleigh, NC: Author; *Washington State Early Learning and Development Benchmarks*, by State of Washington, 2012, retrieved February 22, 2015, from http://www.del.wa.gov/publications/development/docs/guidelines.pdf.

Preschoolers can give reasons for a position, such as "I don't want to play right now because I am tired." By the end of preschool, children can understand the effects of their actions on others, as in "I took the marker away from her and now she is crying." This accomplishment is essential to interpersonal problem-solving. Read the *Developmental Continuum* feature for a description of social-emotional learning in 3- through 5-year-old children and effective teaching strategies to promote it.

Developmental Continuum
Social-Emotional Learning in
3- through 5-Year-Olds

Widely Held Expectations	How Teachers Can Help
Demonstrates affection and comfort with significant adults.	Warmly welcome and return appropriate affection.
Begins to self-regulate attention, feelings, and behavior, and sometimes needs adult support.	Model calmness and patience. Teach children words to use to express emotions, and help them practice these skills in real-life situations.
Seeks adult support for emotional, physical and social support, including solving problems and approval.	Support and validate child's feelings and efforts at cooperation, and reinforce the child's positive problem-solving skills.
Enjoys learning and enthusiastically plays with other children.	Provide opportunities for child to engage in a variety of play activities with other children (e.g., dramatic play, art projects, free play outside, and dance and movement).
Makes and maintains a friendship with one or more children.	Provide opportunities for children to choose activities that interest them, the time to pursue these activities, and the freedom to interact with preferred playmates who share similar interests. Give ample time for children to be silly and enjoy each other's company. Read stories about friendship and discuss the behaviors that made the character in the story a good friend.
Demonstrates understanding of social rules in interactions with children; shares materials and toys during play, increasingly cooperative.	Acknowledge cooperation when child plays with other children and provide opportunities for children to share materials.
Demonstrates awareness that their behavior can affect others' feelings.	Provide opportunities for dramatic play so that child can practice taking another's role or perspective ("Pretend you're Gera and can't have a turn. How do you feel?").
Describes reasons for feelings, and uses strategies for managing strong emotions.	Name and discuss feelings throughout the day (e.g., "You're disappointed because . . . ").
Uses social skills such as sharing, taking turns, and resolving conflicts in interactions with other children.	When there is a conflict between two children, demonstrate empathy for both children.
Demonstrates awareness of group membership ("I'm a boy") and acknowledges own abilities ("I'm good at soccer").	Provide opportunities for children to describe and see positive images of their own cultural and physical characteristics.

Sources: Based on *North Carolina Foundations for Early Learning and Development*, by North Carolina Foundations Task Force, 2013; *Washington State Early Learning and Development Benchmarks*, State of Washington, 2012, retrieved February 22, 2015, from http://www.del.wa.gov/publications/development/docs/guidelines.pdf.

Primary Grades

During the primary grades, peer relationships become increasingly important. Most primary-grade children show loyalty to friends. They sustain friendships by cooperating, helping, sharing, and suggesting new ideas for play. At this age, most children prefer friends of the same gender.

Interpersonal problem solving becomes more complex during the primary grades. Children attempt to settle disputes or solve problems with another child through negotiation, addressing their own rights as well as the other child's needs, sometimes needing assistance from teachers. Children in primary grades can participate in cooperative groups and take different roles at times—sometimes leader, sometimes follower. Primary-grade children become excessively concerned about fairness and can recognize stereotypes and culturally or linguistically unfair or biased behavior.

In terms of self-esteem, a major development during the primary years is that children gain the ability to realistically judge and compare their own academic, physical, and social abilities to those of other children. Unlike preschoolers, who overestimate their competence, primary-grade children may judge themselves too harshly; for example, "I'm not smart like Natalie" or "I can't play baseball." Read the *Developmental Continuum* feature for a description of social-emotional development and learning during the primary grades and effective ways teachers can support this learning.

Teachers need to understand the continua of social-emotional development to have realistic expectations for children's behavior and to provide effective amounts and kinds of assistance. For example, willful behavior on the part of 2-year-olds is typical, as is strong insistence on fairness among third and fourth graders. Knowledge of the social-emotional continua can also help teachers to assess where individual children are on the trajectory and to decide how to intervene when they are not making expected progress. Although we offer these descriptions of "typical" social and emotional learning, teachers need to remember that there is no such thing as a typical child, as we discuss next.

> ▶ **Classroom Connection**
>
> Listen to the primary grade children in this video as they cleverly describe the essential attributes of friendship in an imaginary scenario of creating a recipe for friendship soup.
>
> http://www.youtube.com/watch?v=H7w7yXkJTuO

Diversity and Social-Emotional Development

Individual and cultural differences play significant roles in how children express their emotions and how they behave in groups. Individual differences are present even at birth, and children's experiences at home, in child care, and at school make a big difference in how and when they develop these abilities. Because children's social and emotional development are linked to the contexts, cultures, and relationships in which they grow and learn, adults play a critical role in shaping children's positive social and emotional development.

Cultural Diversity The values and practices of each child's family and community shape the feelings, knowledge, and expectations that influence social and emotional development (Hanson & SooHoo, 2007). For example, in China, where children are encouraged to "fit in" socially, shy behavior is seen as desirable, whereas in the United States, where "standing out" is acceptable, shyness is often associated with negative qualities such as anxiety or social isolation. Similarly, Waylon's enthusiasm for being the "Big Cheese" might not be shared by a child from another cultural group.

Children need to develop respect for people with ideas and experiences that are both similar to and different from their own. Lulu's best friend in preschool is Bethel. When Lulu invites Bethel to her birthday party and Bethel doesn't come, Lulu's feelings are hurt. Angela, the girls' teacher, notices that Lulu doesn't want to play with Bethel anymore. Angela explains to Lulu that Bethel's family does not celebrate birthdays or holidays. Her not attending Lulu's party doesn't mean that Bethel doesn't like Lulu. Angela draws a parallel to Lulu's family being vegetarian. When this is explained to Lulu, she understands and readily seeks out Bethel as a playmate again.

Developmental Continuum
Social-Emotional Learning in the Primary Grades

Widely Held Expectations	How Teachers Can Help
Describes their emotions and the situations that cause them and demonstrates constructive ways to deal with emotions.	Have children discuss situations that trigger strong emotions and role-play strategies to cope with them.
Identifies own likes and dislikes. Describes things they do well and not well.	Help children to make accurate, realistic assessments of their own competence ("It's true that this math lesson is hard, but I can see how hard you're working and how much you've learned since last week.").
Understands expectations and responsibility to promote a safe and productive environment. Demonstrates understanding of when to bring issues to adult attention.	Help children feel comfortable in coming to you with questions and assistance, but also encourage them to try to solve problems independently. Model cross-cultural communication and provide strategies for child to address bias. Actively address bullying or children's attempts to exclude others.
Shows loyalty to friends; prefers same-sex peers.	Provide opportunities for children to play and work with friends in self-selected groups. At times, organize mixed-gender or other diverse groups to ensure that children do not limit their interactions or consistently exclude others.
Follows suggestions given by a friend about how to proceed in their play.	Provide opportunities for children to be part of group activities (e.g., games, cultural events).
Works with other children to overcome challenges.	Discuss and demonstrate how different things can be achieved when children work together (dramatizing a story or building a model). Children can read (or be read to) and write stories about actual people who have overcome challenges, such as Jackie Robinson. Model and promote respect for diversity in all its forms.
Uses multiple strategies to resolve social conflicts.	Guide children through conflict resolution. Support children's attempts to solve social problems.
Feels empathy for other people and describes how own actions make others feel and behave. Recognizes that others may have different perspectives or feelings than own. Recognize words and actions that hurt others.	Read or help children read chapter books, such as *Charlotte's Web*, that depict emotionally challenging events or social situations. Demonstrate and provide opportunities for children to take another's perspective before making decisions (e.g., "What would Ella think if you gave her your book?").
Participates cooperatively in large- and small-group activities, play, and games.	Provide opportunities for small-group projects (creating a map, planning and carrying out an experiment). Encourage participation in group games, allowing children to make or modify rules.
Communicates about others' feelings.	Provide opportunities for children to share and discuss feelings. Discuss why a character reacts as he or she did in a story, taking cultural differences into consideration.

Source: Based on *Assessing and Guiding Young Children's Development and Learning,* Enhanced e-text, 6th edition, by O. McAfee, D. J. Leong, and E. Bodrova, 2015, Upper Saddle River, NJ: Pearson.

Healthy social-emotional development is influenced by the match between children's feelings and expressive behaviors and the expectations of the social situation in which they find themselves. Teachers need to provide a respectful atmosphere in which cultural, religious, racial, linguistic, age, gender, and ability differences are valued.

Children with Disabilities Children who have disabilities, developmental delays, or who are at risk for developmental delays may require special attention and support to promote their social-emotional development. Many children with disabilities face particular challenges in developing successful peer relationships. Children with even mild delays tend to participate less in sustained play, spend more time alone when other children are playing, express more sadness when playing with other children, get angry more, and use less effective conflict resolution strategies (Strain & Joseph, 2006).

Successful inclusion requires that children with disabilities actively participate and that their needs are met. Among those important needs is the need for positive social relationships with other children. Indeed, early friendships are the most powerful single predictor of long-term adjustment for children with disabilities (Strain & Schwartz, 2001). To consider social-emotional development through the wider lens of special education, read the *Including All Children: Fostering Friendships in the Inclusive Classroom* feature.

Successful inclusion requires that children with disabilities fully participate in the classroom community. Making friends is especially important to their healthy development.

Including All Children
Fostering Friendships in the Inclusive Classroom

Children from ages 3 to 5, especially those with disabilities, may not naturally acquire the skills to function socially with their peers, which can be a barrier to developing friendships. They need teachers to help them. Young children's social relationships involve three main concepts, which occur along a continuum in inclusive settings: friendships, social acceptance, and social rejection. More passive than friendship, social acceptance occurs when a child is treated as a member of the group; other children play, smile, and sit beside the child throughout the day. By contrast, social rejection occurs when peers do not choose to play with a child or outwardly refuse the child's requests to join in their play.

Not only are friendships a critical component and predictor of positive mental health, but children develop and learn important social and communication skills in the context of social relationships. Therefore, it is critically important that teachers use proven strategies to promote friendships among children with disabilities and their typically developing classmates. Following are effective strategies teachers can use to facilitate social relationships in inclusive settings:

- Teachers and peers model specific behaviors for children with disabilities.
- Pair two children to complete classroom jobs or during transitions (walk outside together, do errands).

- Compose small groups in order to provide peer models for children with disabilities.
- Read books and have class discussions about friendship, coping with difficult feelings, expressing anger and disappointment, problem solving, and conflict resolution.
- Use puppets to model problem solving and friendship skills during whole-group discussions.
- Set up a "buddy" center during choice time where children use toys and games that require two children to play.
- Arrange "buddy" days where teachers pair children with disabilities and typically developing peers.
- Use materials that require social interaction (for example, a wagon or board game).
- Prompt children to play together (for example, suggest reversing roles—"You have been the patient, how about being the doctor now.").
- Support children to rehearse and practice in advance (for example, before choice time ask children what they are going to do, who they are going to play with).

Source: Based on "Social Skills Interventions for Young Children with Disabilities," by S. Vaughn et al., 2003, *Remedial and Special Education, 24*(1), 2–15.

Check Your Understanding 14.2: Continuum of Social and Emotional Development

The Role of Play in Social-Emotional Learning

The importance of play is very apparent in the previous descriptions of the continuum of social-emotional learning. Because peer relationships are such a critical component of social-emotional development, play is an especially important context for children to acquire and practice self-regulation and social skills.

Emotional Development and Play

Play has long been linked with emotional development and helps children in several ways (Hyson, 2004). Play provides a context for children to address their fears, develop coping skills and resilience, and feel in control of their environment.

Play and Fears   During the preschool years and as children's cognitive development progresses, they acquire a well-developed imagination. Along with this new flexibility in thinking comes an increase in their fears. Three-, 4-, and 5-year-olds may be afraid of animals, the dark, monsters, or whatever they can conjure up. Given the dangers in today's world—strangers, violence, and abuse—their fears may be real as well as imaginary. Consider this example:

> Four-year-old Taylor is afraid of dogs, especially the big boxer that just moved in next door. He cries every time he leaves home and doesn't want to go to school anymore. After talking to Taylor's mother, Ms. Jerome purchases a set of plastic dogs for the classroom and sets up a pretend dog training school. Taylor gradually begins to play with the plastic dogs and Ms. Jerome overhears him saying to the boxer, "Bad dog. Don't jump. Stay in your yard. No barking." After a few days, Taylor takes over the dog training school, and tells the stuffed dogs that they better be good or he will tell their mommies. Taylor's mother also talks to the neighbor about controlling the dog, but his play experiences at school help Taylor work through his fear.

In play, children like Taylor can pretend to be mighty and strong and conquer their fears. They fantasize that they are the giant animal or the monster, thus giving themselves power over the feared creature.

Building Coping Skills and Resilience   As we described earlier, young children experience all kinds of stresses in their everyday lives: going to child care when they want to stay home, moving to a new house, going to the doctor, and so forth. At times, extraordinary stressors occur—serious illness or injury in the family, homelessness, observing or being a victim of violence. Play helps children develop the ability to cope with life's traumas and acquire resilience (Honig, 2010).

Play can serve as a cathartic activity for children to express the negative emotions that life events precipitate. When children are angry, they can take out their feelings by pounding playdough or hammering nails. When they are tense, they can pretend to be a rag doll or curl up like a kitten. Three-year-old Grace has a new baby brother, Miles. Her mother assures her teacher that Grace just loves the baby and isn't jealous at all. But during playtime, her teacher observes Grace shaking a baby doll and saying in a harsh voice, "Get in your bed and stop crying." Obviously, Grace knows she can't treat baby Miles this way. By playing out her resentment and jealousy at school, however, she can cope more effectively with this major change in her life.

Gaining Control through Play In general, young children's lives are not in their control. Grown-ups and older children make them do things that they don't want to do: eat what is served, pick up their toys, get dressed, go outside, take a nap. Sometimes they resist even when they want to do something simply because it wasn't their idea.

Children love to play (and it is so emotionally supportive) because it is *child initiated* and controlled (Johnson, Christie, & Wardle, 2005; Wiltz & Klein, 2001). They decide when to start and stop, what to do, and whom to do it with. If teachers intrude on children's play—try to take over or direct the play to their own ends—children will usually stop playing. It's no longer fun. Child-initiated play affords children power in a safe environment and also helps them learn to make choices and live with the consequences of their choices. If Chloe chooses to build with blocks, she may not have time to do puzzles or paint at the easel.

Social Development and Play

Children's play has been a topic of study for centuries. Early in the 20th century, researchers began to systematically observe and record how young children's social interactions during play changed over time. Now-classic studies conducted by Parten (1933) identified four developmental levels of social play and approximate ages when each type of play dominates, as presented in Table 14.1. Parten also identified unoccupied and onlooker behavior as two situations in which children do not engage in play.

Social development begins in play. As you can see, these toddlers are parallel playing, a first step in learning to play with other children.

© Studio 8/Pearson Education

TABLE 14.1 Levels of Social Play

Based on systematic observation of children over time, this chart identifies and describes four developmental levels of social play.

Type of Social Play	Approximate Age	Example
Solitary play—children play alone, usually with toys or objects.	2 to 2-1/2 years old (according to Parten) All ages (as understood today)	Two-year-old Jeannette pounds her plastic hammer on her workbench or tucks her baby doll into bed. Five-year-old Imelda pretends to be a doctor, dresses up in a lab coat with a stethoscope, and starts treating the dolls and stuffed animals.
Parallel play—children play next to but not with each other. They may speak but don't really converse.	2-1/2 to 3-1/2 years old	Three-year-olds Nina and Dora sit next to each other with their dolls. Nina says, "My baby is sick." Dora says, "I'm going to grandma's house."
Associative play—children play and share with each other, usually one other child.	3-1/2 to 4-1/2 years old	Four-year-olds Chris and Cory are each building a tower with blocks. Cory says, "You need a pointy one on top. Here's one."
Cooperative play—children assume different roles and share a purpose for the play.	4-1/2 years and older	Four preschoolers build a bus with the hollow blocks. Sasha says, "I'm the driver, but I need a ticket taker. You take the tickets, Rinaldo." Toya states, "Me and Isaac will be passengers. Take us to the circus. Then I get to drive."

Source: Based on "Social Participation among Preschool Children," by M. Parten, 1933, *Journal of Abnormal and Social Psychology, 27*, 243–269.

solitary play Children play alone, usually with toys or objects.

associative play Children play and share with each other, usually one other child.

cooperative play Children assume different roles and share a purpose for the play.

▶ **Classroom Connection**

The children in this video are working together to build a house. As you watch, consider the ways in which play can enhance young children's social-emotional skills. What could an effective teacher do to help the boys who don't actively participate?

Although most play researchers still agree that children engage in these different types of social play, they do not agree about the order or the ages at which children progress in their play (Johnson et al., 2005). For example, parallel play, where children play side by side but do not interact, is now considered the least mature form of play, rather than solitary play. Older children continue to engage in solitary play and, at times, switch back and forth between cooperative and solitary play. Solitary play can involve toys/objects or make-believe. For example, Toya enjoys the cooperative scenario of taking the trip, but afterward she sits by herself and pretends to drive the bus. Even after children develop more socially complex play abilities, they will use all types of play at times. Imelda may share her stethoscope with Lora, who also wants a turn—associative play—without cooperating in the shared goal of running a hospital.

In fact, solitary play may be evidence of a personality trait; some people are just more social than others. But if children never play with others, they miss the valuable learning opportunities that play affords. Additionally, if children do not move beyond solitary play, this may signal a difficulty in children's social development (Johnson et al., 2005). Children with disabilities, such as autism, can also benefit from teachers' support in developing play skills (Wong, 2013). Teachers need to be aware of children's play patterns and intervene if necessary; for example, if children watch others play and appear to want to join in but don't know how or are rejected by their peers, teachers need to model the words to say or suggest other strategies to use.

✓ **Check Your Understanding 14.3:** The Role of Play in Social-Emotional Learning

Effective Social-Emotional Curriculum and Teaching

Teachers and children interact constantly in early childhood programs, so social-emotional development is naturally and almost invisibly interwoven into the day. Because of this, some people don't think it necessary to include social and emotional development in a planned curriculum. However, the increase in challenging behaviors and emotional difficulties among very young children has led to the need for a more intentional approach to social-emotional curriculum.

Intentional teachers help children learn many alternative strategies to solve social problems among themselves.

© 2xSamara.com/Shutterstock

Social and Emotional Curriculum Goals

As discussed earlier, the main goal of a social-emotional curriculum is to promote children's social competence and self-regulation. Widely-used comprehensive curriculum models such as *HighScope* (Epstein & Hohmann, 2012) and *Tools of the Mind* (Bodrova & Leong, 2007) integrate these goals throughout. In recent years, more focused evidence-based curricula have been developed that include whole- and small-group teacher-guided lessons designed to be incorporated in a larger curriculum framework. Among these curricula are *The Incredible Years* (Webster-Stratton, 1999); *I Can Problem Solve* (Shure, n.d.), and *Preschool PATHS* (Domitrovich, Greenberg, Cortes, & Kusche,

2005). Research finds that these curricula are effective in improving children's knowledge and understanding about emotions, their social problem-solving skills, and their social behavior (Morris et al., 2014).

Social Problem Solving Children's problem-solving skills are a key feature in the development of social competence (Webster-Stratton, 1999). The power of problem solving lies in three areas. First, these skills travel well with children; they can be used in any social situation to resolve any number of social dilemmas. Second, these skills prevent challenging behavior. Finally, problem-solving skills allow children to quickly repair breaches in their relationships with peers, such as typical squabbles over toys, taking turns, or competition among friends.

Problem solving is a highly effective deterrent to aggression and antisocial behavior. Consequently, every validated curriculum designed to teach social competence includes instruction in these skills (Joseph & Strain, 2004). Teachers can help children learn the following problem-solving steps that are common to most evidence-based curricula (see the Readings and Websites section at the end of this chapter):

1. What is my problem?
2. What are some solutions?
3. What would happen next?
4. Give the solution a try!

Step 1: *What is my problem?* As a first step in problem solving, children should be taught to pay attention to their feelings. When they are experiencing a negative emotion such as anger or frustration, that is their cue that they have a problem.

After children recognize they have a problem, they need to describe it. This is why teaching young children an emotional vocabulary is essential for effective problem solving (Joseph & Strain, 2003a; Webster-Stratton, 1999). Adults and/or puppets can model the process of describing a problem for children. Initially, children will need guidance to reframe the situation from the other person's problem to their own. For example, instead of "They won't let me play," the problem becomes "I want to play with them." This reframing, although subtle, helps children generate more appropriate solutions.

Step 2: *What are some solutions?* Young children need help generating several alternative solutions to interpersonal problems. Children who engage in aggression and antisocial behavior have fewer solutions than their typically developing peers (Joseph, 2002). These children may in fact have a positive solution in their repertoire, but tend to have only one, such as saying "please." Their other solution is aggression, which in the short run is often more effective and efficient at getting their needs met.

Children who have more solutions to choose from usually solve the problem before resorting to aggression. For these reasons, teachers need to teach children alternative solutions to common problems and have children generate their own solutions. Because no one solution is always effective, the key is to teach children to generate as many different solutions as possible, as illustrated in the following example:

> Preschool teacher Ms. Trina brings hypothetical as well as real problems to the group and challenges the class to come up with multiple solutions to the problem. Yesterday, Ms. Trina asked the class what they would do if they were feeling lonely and wanted to join a group of children playing on the Big Toy structure.
>
> *Tobias:* You could ask them.
>
> *Ms. Trina:* Yes, you could ask them. That is a solution. What else could you try?
>
> *Savannah:* If they said no, you could find another friend to play.
>
> *Ms. Trina:* Yes, that is another solution. So far we have two solutions. Let's try to think of five more.

Step 3: *What would happen next?* After children generate many alternative solutions to problems, they can begin to evaluate consequences. Teachers ask, "What would happen next?" Three questions can guide a child's decision to determine if the consequences would be good or bad (Webster-Stratton, 1999):

- Will this solution keep our bodies, feelings, and things safe?
- Is the solution fair?
- How will everyone feel?

Once again, teachers can use role-play to help children learn these strategies. Feeling satisfied with the number of diverse solutions the children generated, Miss Trina helps them evaluate the consequences of solutions, using a puppet to introduce the three criteria for evaluating solutions. For example, the puppet demonstrates their solution of taking turns, and then asks the children, "Is it safe?" Aaron and Javier shout, "Yes!" The puppet congratulates them on good thinking and then demonstrates another solution, grabbing toys. The puppet asks, "Is it safe?" When the children respond, "No," the puppet asks, "Why not?"

Step 4: *Give the solution a try!* At this step, children are taught to act on the best solution that they generated and what to do if a solution does not work. When a prosocial solution does not work, children can draw on the other solutions they generated in Step 2 that might have positive consequences. When teachers focus on building problem-solving skills, children are likely to begin supporting and encouraging each other's efforts.

▶ Classroom Connection

In this video, you observe a well-established, research-based social-emotional curriculum, *The Incredible Years*, in action. What do you think are the benefits of using a focused curriculum such as this in addition to promoting skills through play and other daily interactions?

https://www.youtube.com/watch?v=Y3LwBiXWmIQ

Solve Problems in the Moment Many unanticipated social-emotional problems occur throughout each day. Teachers need to assist children with problem solving on a moment-to-moment basis. At times, it's enough for teachers to anticipate a problem and be nearby to prompt a child through the problem-solving steps. For example, 6-year-old Oralie got off the bus this morning with a scowl on her face. Her teacher keeps an eye on her, and when Oralie squabbles with Clancy over the computer, her teacher is there to encourage them to think of and try various solutions.

Children need support from teachers to remember the problem-solving steps and to stay in the situation. Those who are not skilled problem solvers may be prone to flee. Others may lose control of their temper and have an emotional meltdown. Teachers need to be equipped with strategies to support children through these difficult moments. Recent research suggests that mindfulness-based practices are one such strategy that can be used in classrooms. **Mindfulness** refers to noticing one's sensations, thoughts, and feelings in the present moment, without judgment. When children are taught to notice their breathing and bodily sensations and emotions—in the present moment—they may develop better self-regulation (Zelazo & Lyons, 2012). They may even develop better cognitive and social skills (Flook, Goldberg, Pinger, & Davidson, 2015). Another research-based strategy that helps children respond to stressful situations, the Turtle Technique, is described in the *What Works* feature.

mindfulness Noticing one's sensations, thoughts, and feelings in the present moment, without judgment.

Relationships with Peers Mr. Wilson's kindergarten class meeting begins with a question: "Do you know how to make a new friend?" Hands shoot up immediately and children chant, "I do, I do." Almost whispering, Mr. Wilson says, "We don't need hands yet. Now stop and think for a second." The children know this routine by now. After a few seconds, Mr. Wilson calls on children in turn and most of them say some variation of "play with them." So Mr. Wilson asks, "How would you invite a friend to play?" and he writes down their ideas to post on the wall: What can we play? Want to go to the park? Do you like Clay Boy? Want to play frog? and on and on as their ideas become more creative and detailed.

Mr. Wilson's planned lesson is to help the children practice self-regulation and friendship skills in advance. By asking the children to think before they answer, he encourages impulse control. By posting their ideas, he provides a scaffold to revisit when children need to work on friendship skills later.

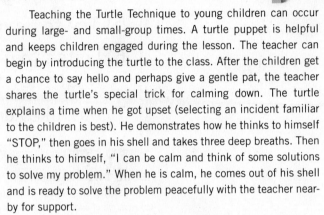

What Works

The Turtle Technique

Four-year-old Maxim has been in preschool for only a few weeks. It is his first group experience and, as an only child, he has not been around other children very often and has never had to share his toys. Maxim tends to play alone and will spend 20 minutes or more with playdough, which is his favorite activity. One day, Nate sits down beside Maxim and reaches for some playdough and plastic molds. Maxim immediately pulls the toys out of Nate's hands and pushes him away. When Nate resists, Maxim loses control entirely; he falls on the floor and wails that he wants to go home. He is inconsolable until snack time distracts him from his anger.

When Maxim's mother comes to pick him up at the end of the day, the teacher, Ms. Gallo, tells her about the incident and his mother worries that Maxim is too immature for preschool. Ms. Gallo, who has taught preschool for many years, reassures her that preschool is where Maxim needs to be to learn to regulate his emotions and express them more constructively. She explains that in the future she will use a research-based strategy, the Turtle Technique.

When a teacher notices a child getting agitated and upset she can cue the child to "calm down" by remembering the Turtle Technique. The Turtle Technique was originally developed to teach adults anger management skills, and then was successfully adapted and integrated into social skills curricula for school-age and preschool children. The basic steps of the Turtle Technique are as follows:

1. Recognize that you feel angry.
2. Think "STOP."
3. Go into your "shell" and take three deep breaths and think calming, coping thoughts: "It was an accident. I can calm down and think of good solutions. I am a good problem solver."
4. Come out of your "shell" when calm and think of some solutions to the problem.

Teaching the Turtle Technique to young children can occur during large- and small-group times. A turtle puppet is helpful and keeps children engaged during the lesson. The teacher can begin by introducing the turtle to the class. After the children get a chance to say hello and perhaps give a gentle pat, the teacher shares the turtle's special trick for calming down. The turtle explains a time when he got upset (selecting an incident familiar to the children is best). He demonstrates how he thinks to himself "STOP," then goes in his shell and takes three deep breaths. Then he thinks to himself, "I can be calm and think of some solutions to solve my problem." When he is calm, he comes out of his shell and is ready to solve the problem peacefully with the teacher nearby for support.

Rather than singling out Maxim for instruction, the next day, Ms. Gallo uses the turtle puppet to teach the technique to all of the children. During center time, she reminds children to practice the technique when they feel frustrated or angry. It takes several weeks for Maxim to successfully use the technique to calm himself. But in the meantime, Nate is more successful in playing near him, and soon they are best friends.

Source: Based on "The Turtle Technique: An Extended Case Study of Self-Control in the Classroom," by A. Robin, M. Schneider, & M. Dolnick, 1976, *Psychology in the Schools, 13*, 449–453.

Social-Emotional Competence in the Whole Group On the wall in Ms. Colello's inclusive preschool classroom is the list of rules depicted in Figure 14.1. It is easy to see that these rules were generated by the children and that Ms. Colello respected their exact words. By establishing the rules together, children gain a sense of ownership and are more likely to remember and abide by them. Thinking and articulating them in advance promotes self-regulation and commitment to caring about each other and their school.

A major goal of the Far Hills Elementary School is to create a school-wide community of learners. The principal and teachers have high expectations for academic achievement but they also know that learning is founded on social-emotional development. They have created a school culture of caring and compassion. At every grade level, children are expected to practice three acts of kindness every day—whether holding the door for someone, saying you're sorry for interrupting, or just smiling at a new student. The primary-grade children keep a running list of acts of kindness and are striving to reach 100.

The foundation of active citizenship is the ability to establish positive relationships with other people and solve social problems. In the *Promoting Play* feature, learn how a teacher used play with board games to support the social-emotional learning for her

1) There are no bad guys in our school.

2) Always tell the truth.

3) Keep the toys and books safe.

4) Destroying your friends' is not ok.

5) Try to be helpful.

6) Listen to all the teachers and always do what they tell you to do.

7) Mistakes are ok.

FIGURE 14.1 Classroom Rules Generated by Preschoolers
When children themselves generate the classroom rules, as these preschoolers did, they are more likely to feel a sense of ownership and abide by them.

energetic second graders. We now turn to the related area of the curriculum in which children see these skills in action in themselves and other people—social studies.

 Check Your Understanding 14.4: Effective Social-Emotional Curriculum and Teaching

Effective Social Studies Curriculum and Teaching

Positive social-emotional development is integrally connected to other areas of development, such as language, and to learning curriculum content, particularly in social studies. In Chapter 10, we described a model for curriculum planning that draws on content knowledge from the disciplines as well as knowledge of child development. Social studies content comes from the subject matter disciplines of history, geography, political science, and economics. These provide the key concepts—the "big ideas"— and processes that children need to learn. Understanding typical patterns and sequences of child development determines which of these concepts to include in the curriculum for different ages. In addition, knowing children's predictable interests and capabilities makes it possible to teach relatively complex concepts in ways that are meaningful and accessible for children.

For example, one big idea in social studies is that institutions such as the family, community, and government play key roles in individuals' lives. At the college level, these concepts are part of courses in sociology and political science. By contrast, in preschool, teachers tap into children's natural interest in their families as a theme for organizing curriculum and teaching how people depend on and help each other. This same topic can be explored in greater complexity as children get older. First graders might study how their community supports families by investigating if the park is accessible for persons with disabilities and, if not, contacting town council members to call for change.

Promoting Play

Learning to Get Along Using Board Games

Elena loves her class of 25 urban, diverse second graders. They are curious and energetic, and really enjoy problem solving. They become particularly engaged within math problems, board games, and passionate discussions. Recently, several of the children had disagreements on the school bus that ended in fights, and brought their disagreements into the classroom. Their disagreements focused on fairness—who was first in line and who "budged"—and power—who was the strongest and should be the "leader." Their disagreements became louder and more passionate, and Elena realizes that she needs to intervene. While she knows social studies is the perfect context for some structured social-emotional learning, she also knows that she would not be successful just telling this group of children rules about how others should be treated. She decides to combine this group's love of board games and discussion to create a playful social learning game.

Elena takes an old board game and repurposes it, creating a game to support discussions and problem solving around social challenges. Children can choose a "challenge" card that introduces a social problem, such as, "Another kid gets in front of you in the bus line. You tell him he should go to the back, and not budge, but he ignores you, and stays in front of you. What might you do?" Children think of solutions, and then pitch them to the cardholder. The cardholder considers the answers and may choose

from among them, or choose some alternative answers provided on "solution" cards. For an answer to be considered, it has to (1) be nonviolent, (2) respect all parties, and (3) be one that all can "live with."

Elena introduces and explains the game during social studies, and puts it out for center time. She makes sure that it is available while children play. She ensures that everyone has a chance to play the first week and holds a class discussion to name the game, adjust the rules, and add to the social problems. She is a bit surprised to see how excited the children are about the game, and how enthusiastically they add new cards to the social challenges. Every Friday, they discuss the "Do Right" game, and often add new skills to the solution cards. For example, one Friday session leads to discussion of "I statements," phrases used to help express how situations make people feel. During the next week, she hears children using I statements in their game play ("When you _____, I feel _____."). Over the remainder of the school year, the children enjoy playing the game, and share many heated discussions over "right" ways to act toward others, and to protect themselves. And their "play" practices begin to show up in real-life social situations. The bus driver reports fewer conflicts, and playground disagreements are more often solved without help from adults. Elena reflects happily on one more example of how play is an excellent context for learning.

What Is Social Studies?

Social studies is not a single topic or field of study. According to the National Council for the Social Studies (NCSS), social studies is the "integrated study of the social sciences and humanities to promote civic competence. . . . The primary purpose of social studies is to help young people make informed and reasoned decisions for the public good as citizens of a culturally diverse, democratic society in an interdependent world" (NCSS, 2010, p. 1).

Social studies includes the political, economic, cultural, and environmental aspects of societies of the past, present, and future. Children learn about their community and the world as well as developing skills in problem solving, decision making, collaboration, collecting and analyzing information, and making informed judgments. Above all, the social studies help children become responsible, participating citizens, whether in their play group, the school, the community, or the world. As we see, there is considerable overlap between the goals inherent in teaching social-emotional learning and in social studies.

© Alice McBroom/Pearson Education

Social-emotional learning and social studies during early childhood lay the foundation for children to become engaged citizens in their community and the world.

identity Characteristics that individuals recognize as constituting their sense of self and belonging to a group.

equity pedagogy The idea that teaching about differences needs to include teaching about oppression and equity.

widening horizons approach Approach to social studies curriculum planning designed to begin "where children are" and then expand outward.

Social Studies Content Goals

Although social studies includes a vast amount of content, a relatively small share of curriculum time is allotted to it, especially in primary grades (McGuire, 2007). So what can and should children learn about social studies in the early years? The NCSS (2010) suggests thematic strands that serve as the basis for social studies standards in many states. Each theme includes concepts that are most easily understood as well as relevant and engaging for young learners. Table 14.2 lists nine social studies themes and key concepts for young learners.

In the sections that follow, we briefly describe many of the themes and ways teachers can help children learn key social studies concepts.

Foster Children's Sense of Identity A major goal of the social studies for young children is to help them develop a positive **identity**. Children need to understand that they are unique, but that they also have some commonalities with other children. General principles for helping young children develop a sense of identity include:

- Have children share information about their interests and families.
- Provide opportunities for children to make appropriate and varied decisions.
- Delight in children's accomplishments and explorations.
- Ensure that children can see themselves in books, pictures, and play materials.
- Help children distinguish people and relationships.

Value Diversity An overarching goal of social studies is to create an engaged citizenry in which democratic values are an essential element of early education. James Banks (2008), director of the Center for Multicultural Education at the University of Washington, coined the term **equity pedagogy**, the idea that teaching about differences needs to include teaching about oppression, equity, and the rights of diverse people, as this example illustrates:

Gail and Jim co-teach in a preschool classroom and decide to read some classic fairy tales. Fully aware that fairy tales often convey racism, sexism, and ageism, the two decide to incorporate the goal of teaching about equity. After reading versions of *Sleeping Beauty* and *Cinderella*, Jim asks the children why they think the princesses always have blonde hair and light skin. The children decide that this was because the author chose to draw only white people. The class collectively decides to "rewrite" and illustrate the fairy tales, featuring characters of color. The children also reenact the stories with princesses saving princes. In this example, Jim and Gail are teaching children to value diversity and also to think critically about books, movies, television, and other media.

Learning about diversity often focuses on differences; however, children need to understand that people are similar as well as different. The Milestones Project, described in the *Culture Lens* feature, is designed to accomplish this important goal.

Understand Families and Communities Helping young children develop a sense of self and a positive identity begins with learning about the important people in their environment. A wide variety of activities help children think about who is in their family—immediate and extended—and community. These themes date back to the **widening horizons approach** to social studies curriculum developed by Lucy Sprague Mitchell and incorporated in the Bank Street approach (Mitchell & David, 1992). This approach to curriculum planning is designed to begin where "children are" and then expand outward.

TABLE 14.2 Social Studies Themes and Concepts

Social studies in early childhood integrates several traditional subject matter disciplines and translates them into developmentally appropriate, key concepts for children to learn.

Theme and Traditional Discipline(s)	Big Ideas from the Discipline	Key Concepts for Young Learners
Individual Development and Identity (Psychology)	Personal identity is shaped by one's culture, by groups, and by institutional influences.	Developing a positive self-concept and feelings of self-efficacy; making and keeping friends.
Individuals, Groups, and Institutions (Sociology, Political Science)	Institutions such as families, schools, government agencies, and the courts play a role in people's lives.	Different kinds of families, making group decisions, living in a democracy.
Culture (Anthropology)	Aspects of human cultures—art, language, history, and geography—exhibit both similarities and differences.	Concepts such as alike and different, appreciation and respect for diversity in all of its forms.
Time, Continuity, and Change (History)	Children come to understand themselves in terms of the passage of time and develop the skills of the historian.	Routines that teach time sequencing; projects that teach how things change over time.
People, Places, and Environment (Geography, Archeology, Ecology)	Children learn to locate themselves in space, become familiar with landforms in their environment, and develop an understanding of the human-environment interaction.	Mapping for young children, beginning with picture maps of their classroom and extending to their community; caring for and protecting the environment.
Production, Distribution, and Consumption (Economics)	Projects address questions such as "What is to be produced?" and "How is production to be organized?"	Understanding that everyone has wants and needs and how these can be fulfilled.
Science, Technology, and Society (Mathematics, Science, and Technology)	The modern world is greatly affected by technology and the sciences that support it.	Becoming familiar with, evaluating, and using various technologies.
Global Connections (Political Science, Ecology, Economics)	We have connections and tensions with the rest of the world.	Being stewards of the environment; human rights; economic competition.
Civic Ideals and Practices (Political Science, Civics)	Children need an understanding of civic ideals and the practices of citizenship.	Involving children in developing the rules and holding class meetings to resolve conflicts.
Power, Authority, and Governance (Political Science, History, Civics)	People work together to bring about change in democratic societies.	Helping children understand the basic ideas of fairness, rights, and responsibilities in various contexts.

Source: Based on *National Curriculum Standards for Social Studies: A Framework for Teaching, Learning, and Assessment,* by National Council for the Social Studies, 2010, Silver Spring, MD: Author.

Although the basic concept of widening horizons is still relevant, social studies should not be limited to immediate, firsthand experiences. Children's horizons are and can be much wider today. Consider how the widening horizons approach is used in the following example:

Lily Nguyen teaches in an inclusive preschool classroom. For a study about families, she plans a project that families can work on together. Lily sends home colorful construction paper, child-sized scissors, glue sticks, crayons, stickers, and directions to trace one hand from each person in the family, decorate it, and then glue it to the large piece of construction paper. When the hand pages come back, Lily is delighted. The families are very creative and many note that they had great fun. After laminating the pages and compiling them into a book, Lily shares the completed project with the children, stopping after each page to count and discuss the members of each family. The children then help graph the number of family members each child has.

Culture Lens

Learning about Cross-Cultural Similarities through the Milestones Project

When teachers think about culture, the focus is almost always on differences. However, human beings from diverse cultural backgrounds are not only different, they also share many similarities. The Milestones Project is designed to focus more attention on the ways people across cultures are alike.

Deeply concerned over divisive world events such as ethnic cleansing, religious hatred, and racism, Richard and Michele Stickel launched the Milestones Project in 1998. They believe that if more people could see how all humans are alike, people would be more accepting, understanding, and respectful of each other. To achieve this goal, the Stickels travel the world, photographing children of various nationalities, races, religions, and cultures. They document the same milestones in development at about the same points in time. Milestones include such significant achievements and events as first step, first tooth, first day of school, and best friend. Photos depict faces, hats, tongues, and other shared aspects of the human experience. Subjects also write or dictate stories about these life experiences. The Milestones website makes the photos and stories available for anyone in the world to see. They have also published books, including an interactive workbook in English and Spanish coauthored with the Great Kids Head Start program in Denver, Colorado.

Inspired by the Milestones Project, first-grade teacher Kay Isaacs decided to do a similar project in her classroom. Her school is located near a large city in a neighborhood that is sometimes called a mini-United Nations. A local store contributed digital cameras to the school and the project was launched.

Kay began by having the children visit the Milestones website in pairs. She asked them to record their responses to what they saw. The children's notes included statements like "Kids everywhere like to have friends." "Boys always like boys best." "Most kids lose a tooth when they are in first grade." "Everybody smiles the same."

The children became so excited looking at the photos and reading other children's stories that they wanted to produce their own Milestones Project. Kay organized them into small groups to decide which milestones each group wanted to study. Some groups simply picked the same ones they saw on the web. Others were more creative. One group picked older people (their grandparents or great-grandparents), choosing to document what they look like when their grandchildren visit or when they get a present. Each group identified people—either their own families or neighbors—representing various races, ethnicities, religions, and cultures. Then they used digital cameras to capture faces and tape-recorded stories or reactions from the participants.

As a culminating event, Kay's class prepared a PowerPoint presentation and section of the school website featuring quotes from the participants and beautiful color photos, which they shared with their families at a parent meeting. The other first-grade classrooms in the school also viewed the show and decided to do their own Milestones Projects.

The Milestones Project is one example of how early childhood teachers can support children's identity and build respect for cultural diversity at the same time. For a complete description of the project and to view the wonderful photographs, visit http://www.milestonesproject.com.

In this project, Lily has many opportunities to talk about and demonstrate respect for diverse families. The children come from a variety of family structures, such as single parents, gay and lesbian families, extended families, and foster families. An additional subject emerges as Lily's class discusses families. Some children talk about relatives who are no longer living. This topic leads into another social studies theme and related concepts—history and how people change over time.

Learn about the Past and the Concept of Time   Social studies can equip young children with knowledge and understanding of the past and how things, people, and places change over time. Preschoolers begin learning concepts of time by experiencing a predictable schedule. As children get older, they are increasingly able to mark the passage of time and how things change over days, weeks, months, and seasons.

Children can also learn to use the methods used by historians, such as identifying problems and questions, collecting information and artifacts, and observing and reaching conclusions about the past. Elementary-age children learn about the past by engaging in

Becoming an Intentional Teacher

Integrating Social Studies Content to Meet Standards

Here's What Happened I teach second grade in a rural public school. Seven-year-old Amy's great-grandmother, whom she calls Gigi, recently came to live with the family. Prior to this move, Gigi lived in the same farmhouse where she grew up. Amy tells me that Gigi isn't happy. Amy tries to cheer Gigi up by asking her to tell stories, which sometimes works.

With Amy's agreement, I invite Gigi to visit our class to talk about what life was like in our community when she was a little girl. At first Gigi is hesitant, but with much encouragement, Gigi agrees to come. To prepare for her visit, the children generate a list of questions to ask her: "What was your school like?" "How did you get there?" "How did you talk to people far away?" "How did you get food?" The list goes on and on. Carl suggests that it would be neat if we could videotape Gigi's interview, and she grants permission.

On the day of Gigi's visit, Amy proudly introduces her great-grandmother, who says that she is 89 years old. The children do the math to figure out what year she was born and how much older she is than they are. The interview lasts 30 minutes. The children can hardly imagine what it must have been like not to have e-mail or cell phones, much less not to have phones at all! They also can't believe that Gigi's father was a blacksmith and that, in earlier days, people used horses to travel. A few people had cars, but they were very expensive and there weren't many paved roads. Gigi has brought some black-and-white photos that show her family and farm and the buildings in the small town back then.

Gigi's visit generates a great deal of interest among the children. She returns for several more interviews, and the children produce a documentary video as the culmination of their living history project. The children seek out other elders in the community to learn about their lives when they were young, their jobs, and how the area looked at the time.

Here's What I Was Thinking Our school curriculum reflects the state learning standards. For second grade, the history, geography, and economics standards require children to learn key concepts and processes for studying the discipline. One such history concept—continuity and change—is related to the standard "Children understand that basic human needs remain the same but how they are met changes with technology."

I find it difficult to teach abstract concepts such as this. And there isn't time in the day to address all of these standards, especially because in second grade we need to focus so much on reading and math. In my experience, however, children learn best when their interests are piqued and they actively inquire about a meaningful problem or question.

I saw an opportunity for integrating many key social studies concepts into the living history project. After the children generated their list of questions and decided how they would get answers, I went through the state standards and noted which ones related to this study. I also planned for children to use the actual processes and tools of historians. For example, they interviewed subjects, recorded data, examined old photos and documents, read books about the period, and came to conclusions based on the evidence. Thus, children practiced their reading and writing skills during the living history project as well.

A serendipitous outcome of the project was that Gigi became an honorary member of our second-grade class. Children frequently consult her when they have questions about past and even current events. And since Amy taught her to use e-mail and Skype, communication with her became even easier.

Reflection People often think that history is developmentally inappropriate for young children because they cannot experience it concretely and they will not develop an accurate sense of time until they are 11 or 12 years old. But all children and their families share stories about the past. What are some other project ideas for teaching history to preschool and primary grades?

"living history" projects in which they interview older members of their family or community. The *Becoming an Intentional Teacher* feature illustrates how one teacher engaged children in a living history project to integrate social studies and other curriculum areas.

Learn about Where We Live: Geography and Mapping Geography is an important part of our daily lives and of the early childhood curriculum. Children learn geographic concepts through active experiences and engaging in geographic thinking. For example, preschoolers and kindergartners can take a walk around the school or neighborhood, collect objects or take pictures along the way, and then create a map of their surroundings. Primary-grade children's geography understanding can go well beyond their immediate experience as in the following example, illustrated in Figure 14.2.

Maps		
K What I Know	**W** What I Want to Know	**L** What I Learned
Atlas are on maps. the COMPASS rose is on maps.	what is washington states capital. does Denver capitol have rocky moutains	that the Maps have rivers. that Maps have moutains. that the Map has capitol

FIGURE 14.2 Second-Grade Geography Study
As part of a geography study on mapping, second graders identified what they already know, the questions they want to answer, and what they learned at the conclusion of the study.

Second-grade teacher Ms. Polan introduces a unit on maps and globes designed to meet the state geography standards. First, each child prepares their own K-W-L chart identifying their current knowledge and questions. Then with the whole group, the teacher uses the smartboard and the website, Brainpop Jr., to help children learn how to read a map, view videos of various land forms, and play related games. Other activities include using Google Earth to tour the world's continents and oceans. The children create a map of the United States, identify rivers and mountains, and locate their own state and its geographic characteristics. During the 2-week study, they explore interactive maps such as the Rand McNally website and also learn mapping terminology such as *birds-eye view* and *legend* by examining a school map.

The *Geography for Life* national standards (Heffron, 2012) identify big ideas to be used in geographic inquiry. One basic concept is location, where in the world something is and why things are located in certain places. A related concept is how the characteristics of any given place tell a lot about where people live, why they settle there, and how they use natural resources. By asking questions with this geography concept in mind, teachers can help children develop an understanding of places and their distinctive characteristics (Seefeldt, Castle, & Falconer, 2013). A related idea is movement, which focuses on how people, things, ideas, products, and information move from one place to another. The most common movement children see and think about is people traveling every day to school or work. Some children will have traveled much farther afield or have family members around the globe.

Children can also learn about relationships within places. This concept, which has been getting more attention because of issues such as climate change, explores how humans impact the environment as well as how the environment influences human behavior (Seefeldt et al., 2013). Another big idea is geographic regions—how they are united by similar physical conditions and common cultural traits. Related questions include how human actions modify the physical environment, how physical systems affect human systems, and the changes that occur in the meaning, use, distribution, and importance of resources.

The national geography standards, *Geography for Life* (Heffron, 2012) are designed for older children; however, they identify skills that children begin developing during their preschool and primary years. These are listed in Table 14.3 with suggestions for how teachers can help children learn these skills.

Learn about Wants and Needs: Early Economics Economic concepts are basic to children's lives. Teachers sometimes avoid the topic of economics, however, because it raises sensitive issues around social class (Derman-Sparks & Edwards, 2010). However, the recent economic downtown in the world has raised this topic in everyone's consciousness. At one end of the economic spectrum, increasing numbers of children are falling into poverty and their basic needs are not being met. At the other end, many children get everything they ask for and more.

Teachers need to be sensitive to families' economic situations. They can help children take pride in how their family cares for them regardless of their work or home situation (Derman-Sparks & Edwards, 2010). Constantly drawing attention to children's possessions such as new clothes or toys can be painful for some children. More appropriate ideas to introduce early economics include helping children learn not to waste resources or to think critically about television advertisements.

All young children have wants and needs that act as powerful motivation to begin understanding economic systems. This topic can be an opportunity to raise awareness about commercialism in society. Table 14.4 presents six key early economics concepts young children can learn, along with examples of teaching strategies.

TABLE 14.3 Geography Education Standards

Geography can be a topic of great interest to children if teachers use strategies such as those described here.

Geographic Skill	Teaching Strategies
Asking geographic questions	Acknowledge and encourage geographic questions. Join children in their sense of wonder about the natural world and how it formed (e.g., "Where does rain come from?" "How do mountains grow?"). Model asking geographic questions ("Which way do you come to school?").
Acquiring geographic information	Provide children with resources such as maps, globes, map puzzles, relief maps, and books depicting other lands and people.
Organizing geographic information	Provide children with materials and inspiration to draw maps, construct graphs, and tell and write stories about places they have been or want to go.
Analyzing geographic information	Show children how to locate themselves on maps and globes. Locate the places of origin of children's families, especially immigrant families.
Answering geographic questions	Have children present their maps, stories, buildings, drawings, and findings of other places to their peers. Teachers and peers can ask questions about the child's work.

Source: Based on *Geography for Life: National Geography Standards,* 2nd edition, edited by S. Heffron, 2012, Washington, DC: National Council for Geographic Education.

Learn to Live in a Democracy: Making Choices and Voting

John Dewey strongly believed that an essential purpose of education is to empower an engaged citizenry. In a democracy, people have the power to make a variety of meaningful choices pertaining to their daily lives—to become agents of change. In early childhood programs, children are not just preparing to become members of a democratic society; they actually are citizens of a democracy (Dewey, 1916). Therefore, teachers need to engage them in group decision-making and discussion of differing opinions during class

TABLE 14.4 Teaching Early Economics

Economics may seem too advanced a topic for young children, but developmentally appropriate strategies such as these can make it highly accessible and engaging.

Economics Concept	Teaching Strategies
Scarcity means that there is always a conflict between never-ending wants and limited resources.	Comment on the scarcity of materials when children engage in conflict over them. Explain that there are limited numbers of toys, and more children want them than there are toys to go around.
Because resources are limited, people must choose some things and give up others.	Building on the example above, this is a time to talk about other solutions to problems involving scarce materials. Ideas include sharing, getting another toy to play with, or waiting for a turn.
People produce and consume. When they produce, they make goods. When they consume, they use goods and services.	Ask family members to share their work with the class, and (if possible) to share active experiences with the children (cooking, making art, writing). Create a "market day" where children produce and sell things. The class can vote on how the profits will be spent.
Money and trade or barter are used to obtain goods and services.	Create a store in the classroom. Include merchandise, a cash register, play money and food stamps, pads for receipts, and props for workers and consumers.
People work in a variety of jobs.	Take field trips to local businesses and organizations or invite parents to visit the class and discuss what they do.
Helping others who do not have their basic needs met is socially desirable.	Host a class clothing drive. Children can make signs about the drive, collect and organize clothing, and count and graph the types and sizes of clothing collected.

Source: Based on *Active Experiences for Active Children: Social Studies,* 2nd edition, by C. Seefeldt and A. Galper, 2006, Upper Saddle River, NJ: Pearson.

meetings and help them understand the concepts of voting and majority. As children get older, their understanding of history and current events expands and they engage more with American democratic experiences.

In previous sections, we presented some of the social studies curriculum themes recommended by the National Council for the Social Studies, the key concepts for children to learn, and examples of teaching strategies. Next we discuss effective approaches for planning and implementing social studies curriculum.

Effective Strategies for Teaching Social Studies

One of the biggest challenges in teaching social studies is deciding what content and topics are developmentally appropriate for young children; that is, which learning goals are achievable for children and when? These decisions are particularly difficult in social studies because subjects such as history and geography involve highly abstract ideas. For example, comprehending history requires understanding chronological time—an ability that is not fully developed until age 11 or later (Seefeldt et al., 2013). Similarly, geography requires an understanding of complex concepts such as location and direction, and that maps and globes are abstract representations of reality (Seefeldt et al., 2013).

Using the NCSS themes to plan early childhood social studies curriculum is a good way to make such abstract concepts more understandable for young children and, therefore, more developmentally appropriate. It is also important to use teaching strategies that build on what children already know, help them make sense of new experiences, and connect facts to larger concepts and ideas. Three commonly used, developmentally appropriate approaches to social studies curriculum meet those criteria: (1) engaging children in play and active learning, (2) using a project approach to integrate social studies, and (3) using technology to expand children's firsthand experiences and worldview.

Play and Active Learning Experiences "Children are born into social studies. From birth, they begin exploring their world" (Mindes, 2006, p. 4). In good schools for young children, social studies take place naturally (Seefeldt et al., 2013). Such schools allow children to experience the curriculum firsthand through child-guided exploration and play within a carefully planned environment. Children learn social studies when they interact to solve problems such as how to produce a guidebook for school visitors.

Teachers can extend this learning by inviting guest speakers for children to meet and interview. However, teachers should prepare guests in advance; people who have not had experience with young children may have inappropriate expectations for their behavior, such as expecting them to remain quiet for a lecture. A more successful approach is for guests to bring hands-on materials such as antique tools from the history museum for the children to see, touch, and talk about.

Field work is another active way to extend social studies learning, whether in the form of an exploration of the school building, a visit to the florist, or a trip to the planetarium. However, like all early childhood experiences, field trips must be planned and structured carefully to be safe and support active student learning (Seefeldt et al., 2013). It is important to have a clear purpose for a field trip that identifies specific learning goals. In addition to following school procedures and policies related to field trips, teachers should visit the field trip site in advance, noting parking facilities and safe walking paths, and how children with disabilities might be accommodated. It is also important to prepare the adults at the field trip site with information about the children in your group and their learning goals for the trip.

Children should also be prepared for the field trip experience. In addition to preparing the children regarding safety and expected behavior, it is helpful to provide background content for the experience. This does not mean that field trips should necessarily come at the end of learning units, and in fact, it is often useful to have a field trip at the beginning of a unit to ground the children's learning in real experiences. Either way, children should learn about the field trip schedule and activities and have an opportunity to see photos or videos and ask questions. Teachers should plan for children to document their experiences in some way. They can use a tablet, recorder, camera or other technology to record photos and videos and interviews. Older children can take notes.

Children should be helped to document their experiences when they return to school. They can discuss and record their memories in writing, drawing, painting, or through other forms of creative expression. They can work their experiences into their play with appropriate props; for example, they might create a pretend flower shop after a visit to the florist. They also can extend learning by reading books and through technology such as looking on the NASA website following a planetarium trip.

Field trips have the potential to expand children's horizons in many ways. However, trips can also be missed opportunities for learning if the experience is just a whirlwind of unfocused activity. When asked what they remember from a trip to the nature center, children might say "Tasha got sick" or "I jumped in the puddle of water." While these reports are undoubtedly factual, they should not be all the children bring back from the experience.

An Integrated Approach to Teaching Social Studies There is a limited amount of time in the school day and year to address all of the content that comprises the social studies. Fortunately, the various strands of social studies lend themselves to project work and integrated curriculum, as the following example illustrates:

> One winter day, Gabriella Johnson notices that someone put several unkempt duffle bags and a sleeping bag on the back porch of the child care center. Gabriella sees a note that reads: "I am homeless right now. Please do not remove my things. If I need to move them, let me know."
>
> At circle time, Gabriella reads the note to the children and describes the possessions. The children have many questions. Lani asks why the person is homeless. Leo asks if it is a man or a woman. Jeremiah wants to know where the person is right now. Helen wonders if he is going to sleep there. A rich discussion ensues, and Gabriella explains that she doesn't have the answers to the questions.
>
> The children take a vote and decide the things can stay. Alexa wants to write the person a note. Gabriella helps the children write notes explaining that the stuff can stay and asking some of their questions. The next day, the notes are gone, but the person leaves one for the children that says "Thanks." The children are disappointed that the person didn't answer their questions and think of reasons why, but also are glad the belongings are still there. Leo worries that the person might not have enough to eat, so he asks if they could put the leftovers from lunch on the back porch.
>
> The discussions, note writing, and caretaking continue for several weeks, until the person removes the bags. The children make up stories about where he went. Jackson wonders aloud if the person moved into the shelter he and his mom stayed in at the beginning of the year. Gabriella decides to invite one of the soup kitchen volunteers to visit and talk about her work. This inspires the children, and Gabriella arranges for a service learning opportunity for them to organize a food drive. Tanya suggests that the food drive include pet food, too. The children make signs, set goals, write letters, and graph the amount and types of food they collect.

Gabriella takes an opportunity to build a powerful social studies project from this event. Throughout the project, the children learn concepts of culture, wants and needs, power and privilege, fairness, similarities and differences, and the importance and value of service learning—all while building language, literacy, and math skills.

Technology and Social Studies Children can also use global positioning system (GPS) devices during field trips to learn about newer technologies related to geography. To learn more about the world at large, children can explore other cultures and places with Internet searches and electronic pen pals. Many schools, for example, Skype with or send e-mails and photos of their drawings to children in other schools, particularly ones in the hometowns or countries of children in the class.

Children can also produce and disseminate projects on the web. For example, young elementary-age children might put together a web page about the topics they are studying. Children could also prioritize a "wish list" that includes items to be used in the class; this allows the class to explore economics learning.

virtual field trip Trip taken via the Internet in which children can go anywhere in the world.

Travel costs and supervision concerns often limit opportunities to take field trips. However, **virtual field trips** allow children to use the Internet to go anywhere in the world. In this way, children can explore another community, state, or even country. They also can interview experts online via e-mail or participate in live chats with other children or workers in various jobs. The possibilities of using technology to teach social studies are limited only by the technology available to children.

 Check Your Understanding 14.5: Effective Social Studies Curriculum and Teaching

Revisiting the Case Study

. . . Jefferson Elementary School

At the beginning of this chapter, we visited the kindergarten and third-grade classrooms at Jefferson Elementary School. Having discussed social-emotional development and learning as well as social studies curriculum and teaching, we can now revisit the school and see more clearly what and how children are learning about social studies.

It is evident from Waylon's experiences in kindergarten that his teacher focuses on both social-emotional development and social studies in her curriculum. Each child has an opportunity to develop a strong sense of identity, while all the children learn about each other, their family history, and the community in which they live. Ms. Hans, his teacher, operates her classroom as a mini-democracy in which children make choices, accept responsibility, and learn how voting functions to make group decisions.

The in-depth study of the Gulf Coast in Mr. Bell's third grade is an example of integrated social studies curriculum. Current events in the news motivate the children to learn more and get actively involved as citizens in helping others. They express empathy and concern for other people. They also learn about global connections between products developed and used in different places. The topic is rich with opportunities to learn geography, economics, and the environment while also developing skills in reading, writing, and researching. ■

14 Chapter Summary

- Social-emotional learning (also called social competence) is children's ability to recognize and regulate emotions, establish and maintain positive relationships, make responsible decisions, and solve social problems constructively.

- Teachers need to understand the developmental continuum of significant social-emotional accomplishments across the period from birth to third grade to have appropriate and realistic expectations for children's

behavior, and to know how and when to effectively promote social-emotional learning.

- Play is a vital context for children to develop positive peer relationships and practice social skills. Play is equally important for emotional development, providing a context for children to address their fears, develop coping skills and resilience, and feel in control of their environment.

- Effective social-emotional curricula include specific strategies for teaching social problem-solving skills, friendship skills, and self-regulation.

- Social studies—the integrated study of history, geography, economics, political science, and other related subjects—contribute to the development of competent citizens. During early childhood, social studies topics and social-emotional learning are inextricably connected. Learning to live in a democratic society—the overarching goal of social studies—is predicated on social-emotional learning.

- Developmentally appropriate, effective approaches to teaching the social studies in early childhood programs include engaging children in play and active learning experiences, using an integrated approach to link social studies learning and other curriculum areas, and using technology to expand children's worldviews.

Key Terms

- associative play
- cooperative play
- emotional development
- emotional literacy
- engaged citizens
- equity pedagogy
- identity
- mindfulness
- parallel play
- self-regulation
- separation anxiety
- social development
- social-emotional learning
- social studies
- solitary play
- toxic stress
- virtual field trip
- widening horizons approach

 Demonstrate Your Learning

Click here to assess how well you've learned the content in this chapter.

Readings and Websites

Bohart, H., Charner, K., & Koralek, D. (Eds.). (2015). *Spotlight on exploring play*. Washington, DC: National Association for the Education of Young Children.

Kersey, K., & Masterson, M. (2012). *101 Principles for positive guidance with young children: Creating responsive teachers*. Upper Saddle River, NJ: Pearson.

Mindes, G. (2013). *Social studies for young children: Preschool and primary curriculum anchor* (2nd ed.). Lanham, MD: Rowman & Littlefield Education.

Center for Social Emotional Foundations of Early Learning

This website, sponsored by Vanderbilt University, offers numerous resources for supporting children's social and emotional learning, including emotional literacy and self-regulation activities.

Center for Early Childhood Mental Health Consultation

Developed for Head Start programs, go to this website to find resources for supporting children's social and emotional development, and addressing challenging behavior.

National Childhood Traumatic Stress Network

This website offers resources for teachers, designed to support children and families who have experienced traumatic events and toxic stress.

Collaborative for Academic, Social, and Emotional Learning

This website offers resources to support primary-grade children's social and emotional learning, and documents the benefits of social-emotional competence for academic achievement.

National Council for the Social Studies

This website offers social studies resources for teachers, including textbooks, lesson plans, and assessment and curriculum ideas.

15 Teaching Children to Be Healthy and Fit: Physical Development and Health

Learning Outcomes

After studying this chapter, you should be able to:

15.1 Identify the benefits of physical fitness and health and explain its importance for children's development and learning.

15.2 Outline the sequences of gross motor, fine motor, and perceptual motor development in young children.

15.3 Examine the role of indoor and outdoor play in children's physical development, fitness, and health.

15.4 Describe the teacher's role in meeting health and safety standards in early childhood programs.

15.5 Synthesize teaching strategies and effective curricula that promote physical development, fitness, and health.

Ms. Perez's class of 3- to 5-year-olds joyfully bounds out the door for their favorite part of the day—outdoor play. A well-planned environment greets the children on the playground. In addition to choosing from the permanent options of a climbing structure and tricycle path, today they can paint on a long piece of paper attached to the fence, water the class garden, or play with the ball collection in the large grassy area.

In less than a minute, all of the children except Allison choose an activity and are busy playing. She is standing by the balls, but hasn't picked one up. Ms. Perez asks, "Allison, do you want to play catch?"

Allison replies, "No, I want to kick the ball but I can't do it."

Ms. Perez smiles and says, "I can help you learn." The teacher sets the balls up in a straight line, positions Allison in front of one ball, stands next to her, and demonstrates how to kick the ball. Allison tries and the ball rolls slowly away to the side without much motion. Ms. Perez says, "You kicked it! Let's see what happens to the next kick. I bet it goes farther." Allison is excited about this possibility. Ms. Perez demonstrates again, commenting on the position of her foot in relation to the ball. Allison kicks the ball again—a longer way this time. Ms. Perez steps back and says, "That was a big kick."

Allison continues to kick the balls until they are all over the playground. Drew arrives and says, "I want a turn." Ms. Perez suggests that Drew ask Allison if he can play. He does, and Allison says, "Yes, but I go first." Drew agrees and together Allison and Drew collect the balls, line them up, and kick each one. They run off to collect the balls to repeat the game and play together until it is time to go inside.

After 45 minutes outside, Ms. Perez calls the children inside. They wind down by doing quieter activities. JaNaye and her two friends continue working on the collages they began this morning, using objects such as buttons, foam cutouts, scraps of ribbon, and lace. Mitchell and Carletta write notes to friends. Another teacher, Ms. Aliote, assists four children as they string beads and use small pegboards to create patterns. Seth and Asia use a computer program to draw pictures, changing colors and line width by clicking the mouse; Amos, whose fine-motor development is less well-developed, works on a touchscreen tablet. As lunch arrives, Regina and Alexei help set the table, and the children take turns at the sink next to a child-sized poster reminding them how to properly wash their hands. Their meal is served family style, with children maneuvering serving spoons and passing dishes to each other. Brooks exclaims, "Look, Ms. Perez, I poured my milk and no spills." ■

As in any high-quality early childhood program, movement is an essential part of living and learning in Ms. Perez's classroom. From tiny babies to active second graders, young children take on and embrace the world with their whole bodies. Healthy children of all ages love physical activity and play, but more than fun is involved. With the help of parents and teachers, children master critically important physical skills and also establish habits related to fitness and health that can last a lifetime.

In this chapter, we address the critical health and fitness issues facing our nation's children today. We discuss the continuum of children's motor development from birth through age 8, and how intentional teachers promote optimal development through play and focused teaching of physical skills. We also discuss curriculum and teaching practices that promote children's fitness, health, and nutrition, and those that prevent illness and injury.

The Importance of Physical Fitness and Health

physical fitness Children's overall physical condition: growth, strength, stamina, and flexibility.

Physical fitness refers to children's overall physical condition: growth, strength, stamina, and flexibility. Children's physical fitness depends on a number of factors, including heredity, access to good nutrition and health care, and participation in fitness-enhancing activities. Most physically active children grow up to be physically active adults. On the other hand, only 2% of adults who were inactive as children become active in adulthood (National Association for Sports and Physical Education [NASPE], 2004).

Benefits of Physical Fitness

When they feel strong and fit, children are more confident; they are likely to gain self-esteem, enjoy playing and learning with others, and eagerly take on new challenges (Sanders, 2002). Healthy physical development is closely and consistently linked to children's subsequent academic success (Centers for Disease Control and Prevention [CDC], 2010). In addition, ample evidence (CDC, 2014c) confirms that regular physical activity helps children by:

- Building and maintaining healthy bones, muscles, and joints
- Controlling weight
- Building lean muscle and reducing fat
- Preventing or delaying high blood pressure and cholesterol and type 2 diabetes
- Reducing feelings of depression, stress, and anxiety
- Improving physical fitness
- Increasing capacity for learning

health-related fitness Any aspect of health that can be improved by physical exercise and activity.

cardiorespiratory (aerobic) system Body system made up of the heart, lungs, and blood; provides the stamina needed to be active for a long period of time.

muscular strength and endurance The ability to keep moving without stopping because of fatigue.

flexibility The ability to bend and stretch easily.

body composition Weight and body fat.

Health-related fitness is the aspect of health that can be improved by exercise and activity. It consists of the following four components (Goodway, Ozmun, & Gallahue, 2013):

1. The **cardiorespiratory**, or **aerobic**, **system** includes the heart, lungs, and blood. When working well, this system provides the stamina needed to actively participate for a long period of time.
2. **Muscular strength and endurance** allow for effective use of muscles. *Strength* allows children to use force to perform a task such as kicking a ball or hammering a nail. *Endurance* is the ability to keep moving without stopping because of fatigue.
3. **Flexibility** is the ability to bend and stretch easily, which helps prevent muscle and tendon injuries.
4. **Body composition** refers to weight and body fat. Excess fat puts stress on ligaments, tendons, bones, and tissues that support the body's weight.

All of these components are important parts of children's fitness and health. Each should be considered in planning effective early childhood programs. In recent years, however, children's health-related fitness has become an urgent concern as the rate of childhood obesity in America has increased significantly (Ogden, Carroll, Kit, & Flegal, 2014).

Childhood Obesity Crisis

Since children's physical development is so variable, their weight status is defined as their body-mass index (BMI) in relation to what is typical for their age and sex. Children are considered overweight when their BMI is above the 85th percentile for their age and sex, and obese when their BMI is above the 95th percentile (CDC, 2012b). The CDC reported dramatic increases in childhood obesity during the past 30 years. While obesity rates among preschoolers have declined recently (Ogden et al., 2014), 23% of 2- to 5-year-olds are overweight or obese. These rates are higher for preschoolers who live in low-income families, and among African American, Latino, Native American, and Alaskan Native children (CDC, 2012b). Over a third of 6- to 11-year-olds are overweight or obese. These problems often continue into adulthood: 70% of severely overweight children become obese adults (CDC, 2014b).

The causes of obesity are complex and involve genetics, lifestyle, and poor nutrition. But the consequences are profound. Overweight children are at greater risk of cardiovascular disease, diabetes, and other serious illnesses, miss four times as much school as normal-weight children, and can suffer from other health consequences such as depression and anxiety disorders (CDC, 2012b). Obese children are also more likely to be socially isolated from their peers and have low self-esteem, which negatively affects their academic performance (CDC, 2010). A higher percentage of children from low-income families have poor nutrition and are also more likely to be overweight or obese (CDC, 2012b), which becomes another risk factor associated with poverty. Children whose parents are obese are at greatest risk (Whitaker, Wright, Pepe, & Seidel, 1997). So while it is difficult to predict if overweight/obese children will grow to be obese adults, it makes sense to make physical health a central aspect of the early childhood curriculum for all children.

Physical development is largely controlled by biological growth, but children do not acquire physical skills automatically. Intentional teachers help children gain more control over their bodies and teach them motor skills.

Implications for Early Childhood Programs

Early childhood programs have a responsibility to counter the obesity crisis and improve physical fitness in all children by complying with the following recommendations for children's physical activity (CDC, 2015; SHAPE America, 2014):

- Children should engage in 60 minutes or more of moderate to vigorous physical activity every day. When children engage in moderate aerobic activity, their heart beats faster and they breathe faster than normal; during vigorous exercise, heart and respiration rates are much faster.
- Preschoolers need between 60 minutes and several hours of daily, unstructured free play every day. **Unstructured free play** is chosen and initiated by children, such as that which occurs on a playground.
- Physical activity for preschoolers should include at least 60 minutes of **structured physical activity** (in short, 15-minute segments), which is adult-guided play designed for a purpose such as increasing endurance or flexibility, such as when a teacher leads a game of Simon Says). Toddlers need 30 minutes of this type of play.
- Children should not sit for more than 60 minutes in any activity. Television viewing should be limited to less than 2 hours per day.
- Children's diets need to be improved with decreased intake of fast food and increased intake of fruits, vegetables, and whole grains.

unstructured free play Play that is chosen and initiated by children, such as that which occurs on a playground.

structured physical activity Adult-guided play that is designed for a purpose such as increasing endurance or flexibility.

These recommendations have direct implications for early childhood programs and schools, especially considering a program's hours of operation. For example, in a full-day child care center where children might spend 8 to 10 hours a day, it is essential to provide significant amounts of time for structured and unstructured physical activity. The children may have limited time for active play once they leave the center. If children spend 3 or 4 hours in a program, teachers should plan at least 30, and preferably 45 minutes, of gross-motor play, in one or two time periods. Family child care may provide greater flexibility.

We know from research, however, that preschool children are not engaging in sufficient amounts of physical activity. For example, one study (Brown et al., 2009) of 24 preschools found that children spent less than 4% of the day engaged in moderate to vigorous physical activity, mostly outdoors. Indoor activity was essentially sedentary, except for rarely occurring teacher-initiated music and movement experiences. Given the benefits of physical activity for young children, as well as the risks of poor levels of fitness, teachers need to ensure that promoting physical development and health are core curriculum goals and not simply add-ons. Movement is fun, and most children love it, but the many benefits of physical activity for children's health and well-being are a serious justification for including it in the early childhood curriculum.

How Physical Development Occurs

Physical development during early childhood may seem a little magical; it begins at the moment of conception and continues throughout the life span. Yet physical development is anything but effortless. Individual children's physical growth and development vary considerably, depending on heredity, environmental factors, nutrition, gender, and access to health care. Over time, the interplay brings on dramatic, noticeable changes in children.

Changes in physical development are rapid, with later abilities, skills, and knowledge building on already acquired skills. Although children's development follows a relatively predictable sequence, variation exists—most notably in the pace of development. For example, although most children jump first with both feet and then learn to balance on one foot, Kinisha begins to balance at age 3; Jarrod acquires this skill at age 4.

Children's ways of perfecting physical skills are also different. Brent tries hopping, but falls when he loses his balance. Amalie hops while holding hands with a friend or while holding onto a railing. Li watches others hop, learning from their successes and failures before trying the skill. Another aspect of individuality is the sporadic and uneven nature of development. Physical growth in children sometimes occurs in spurts; at other times development is steady and incremental.

gross-motor development
Physical skills related to moving the whole body or major parts of the body.

fine-motor development
Physical skills related to the small muscles found in individual body parts, especially those in the hands and feet.

perceptual-motor development
Occurs when children use their senses to take in information about objects in the environment and use this information to coordinate their movements.

Types of Physical Development   There are three types of physical development:

1. **Gross-motor development** refers to physical skills related to moving the whole body or major parts of the body. For babies, one of these skills is gaining control of the head, neck, and torso to enable sitting and, later, standing. In preschoolers, gross-motor skills are walking, running, and jumping.

2. **Fine-motor development** involves changes in skills related to the small muscles found in individual body parts, especially those in the hands and feet. As children increasingly direct the movements of their fingers, hands, and wrists, they learn to perform more complex fine-motor tasks such as tying shoes and drawing or writing.

3. **Perceptual-motor development** involves children using their senses to take in information about objects in the environment and then using this information to coordinate their movements. Information collected by the senses helps determine how the muscles of the body respond.

Characteristics of Physical Development   Although individual differences exist, three general principles of muscle development apply:

1. In general, the *direction* of muscle development is from top of the head to the tips of the toes. Babies learn to lift their heads before they can raise their torsos and use their arms before they can stand with, and then without, support.

2. The *sequence* of muscle development begins with those closest to the center of the body and progresses to those in the extremities—the hands and feet. Most children learn to crawl before they can pick up objects using the thumb and forefinger, called the **pincer grasp**. Thus, children refine their gross-motor movements, such as those used to walk or throw a ball, before they can control the fine-motor skills used to zip a jacket or turn the pages of a book.

pincer grasp Grasp used to pick up objects with the thumb and forefinger.

3. The *process* of physical development is a result of experience—the opportunities children have to explore, practice, refine, and increasingly coordinate those motor movements that drive physical development.

As children learn to roll over, sit, stand, walk, and run, the impact of exploration and practice is clear in gross-motor skill acquisition. In addition, adult guidance and, sometimes, direct teaching stimulate physical development, as when children learn to swim, balance on a beam, or throw a basketball through the hoop. The direction, sequence, and process of physical development are not the same for all children, especially for those with disabilities. However, relatively predictable, though not rigid, sequences exist in each of these areas of motor development, as we see in the next section.

✓ **Check Your Understanding 15.1:** The Importance of Physical Fitness and Health

 # The Continuum of Physical Development

During the first 3 years of life, the pace of physical development is staggering: children go from newborn helplessness to competence in controlling their own bodies in space and coordinating their arm, hand, and finger movements. The pace slows down somewhat during the preschool years as children gain greater control over these skills. During the primary years, children develop increasing coordination of their arms and legs as well as better control and refinement of skills.

locomotor movements Movements that allow the body to proceed in a horizontal or vertical direction from one place to another, such as walking, running, leaping, or jumping.

Phases of Motor Development

The four broad phases of motor development from infancy to age 8 (Gallahue, Ozmun, & Goodway, 2012) are presented in Table 15.1. Although the sequence of motor skill acquisition is similar in typically developing children, the age range varies considerably. For example, children learn to skip between 5 and 7 years of age (Gallahue et al., 2012). As children get older, individual differences increase because children

When children's motor skills develop optimally, they are more likely to enjoy and engage in physical activity. Fun outdoor play and physical activity can build children's health and fitness and fight today's childhood obesity crisis.

have such widely varying opportunities to participate in physical activities—for instance, while one child constantly watches television, another child may ski and swim regularly.

These phases and related skills constitute the goals of the physical education curriculum. From ages 2 to 7, the goal is for children to develop and refine the following fundamental movement skills (Goodway, Ozmun, & Gallahue, 2013):

- **Locomotor movements**, through which the body proceeds in a horizontal or vertical direction from one place to another, such as walking, running, leaping, or jumping.

© stefanolunardi/Shutterstock

TABLE 15.1 Phases of Motor Development

Motor skill development follows a predictable sequence, as described in this table, but a wide range of variation exists in the ages when individual children acquire these skills.

Typical Age	Movement Phase	Movement Characteristics
Infants—birth to age 1	Reflexive movement phase	Babies gradually replace inborn reflexive movements such as sucking with more voluntary movements.
Toddlers–to age 2	Rudimentary movement phase	As infants become toddlers, they gain more control over their bodies as characterized by grasping, sitting, standing, and walking.
From ages 2 to 7	Fundamental movement phase	During this phase, children master most of the locomotor skills of walking, running, jumping, hopping, galloping, and skipping.
Begins about age 7 and continues to adolescence	Specialized movement phase	Children combine fundamental movements with other skills to develop coordinated, specialized skills such as running and kicking a soccer ball.

Source: Based on "Motor Development in Young Children," by J. D. Goodway, J. C. Ozmun, and D. L. Gallahue, 2013, in *Handbook of research on the education of young children*, 3rd edition, edited by O. N. Saracho and B. Spodek, pp. 80–101, New York: Routledge.

gross-motor manipulative movements Large muscle movements involving giving or receiving force from objects such as throwing, catching, or kicking.

stability movements Movements in which the body remains in place but moves around its horizontal or vertical axis; examples include balancing, dodging, starting, and stopping.

- **Gross-motor manipulative movements**, through which the body gives or receives force from objects such as throwing, catching, or kicking.
- **Stability movements**, in which the body remains in place but moves around its horizontal or vertical axis, such as balancing, dodging, starting, and stopping.

In the sections that follow, we present the typical expectations for gross-, fine-, and perceptual-motor development and explain how teachers can foster development in each area.

Gross-Motor Development

Even though physical development is strongly influenced by biological growth, teachers need to be intentional in promoting children's physical development. The *Developmental Continuum* feature describes gross-motor skill acquisition for children from birth through age 8.

Gross-Motor Development from Birth to Age 3 Remarkable physical change happens to babies during the first year or so of life. During infancy, babies learn to control and lift their heads and turn from side to side. Next, they roll from back to side, then front to side, and then completely over. This ability to change position is followed fairly rapidly by scooting, sitting, crawling, pulling to a stand, and walking with support.

Between 14 months and the second birthday, toddlers typically perfect walking without support and learn to squat down and stand back up, carry large objects, and sweep things off of tables and shelves. Twos are quite good at dumping out containers of toys and materials, propelling riding toys with their feet, walking tentatively up stairs one foot at a time, and carrying large objects from one place to another.

As toddlers continue to explore the world and begin to mimic the gross-motor behaviors of older children and adults, their actions become more purposeful. Two-year-old Chad is helped out of his car seat by his mother and stands by the car as she hands him his diaper bag. He puts it on his shoulder, bending his body sideways and raising his arm high in the air to keep it on his shoulder. This awkward position barely keeps the bag from dragging on the ground as he takes his mother's hand and walks toward his child care center. When his mother offers to carry it, he says emphatically, "No, my bag!" and toddles off.

Fostering gross-motor development during this stage is often about getting out of the way! During this period, most children have a built-in drive to master and move on.

Developmental Continuum
Gross-Motor Skills from Birth through Age 8

Approximate Age	Widely Held Expectations
Infants (Birth to 12 months)	• Gradually gain control over reflexes • Excitedly wave arms and legs • Lift head when on tummy • Sit with support • Roll over • Sit without support • Move around by crawling, scooting, or creeping. • Stand with help • Cruise by holding furniture • By 1st birthday, stand without support and may start to walk
Toddlers (About 12 to 36 months)	• Walk on their own • Like to pull and carry toys while walking • Run awkwardly • Climb stairs one at a time by about 18 months • Eager to explore world • Delight in jumping, marching, walking backward, propelling a riding toy with their feet • Love to run but can't control stopping and turning • Throw a ball a short way • By age 3, run and jump with control • Pedal a tricycle
Preschoolers and Kindergartners (Age 3 to 6)	• Gradually increase control and refinement of fundamental motor skills • Walk up and down stairs alternating feet without support • Balance on one foot for several seconds, walk on a balance beam • Master fundamental motor skills including walking, running, hopping, galloping • Increasingly able to coordinate hands and arms to roll, throw, catch (traps object against body), and kick a ball
Primary Grades (Ages 6 to 9)	• By age 7, skip easily • Coordinate fundamental motor skills into skills needed to play organized games and sports • Jump and catch a ball, kick a ball while running • Jump rope • Perform motor skills in adult-like manner

Sources: Based on *Assessing and Guiding Young Children's Development and Learning*, by O. McAfee and D. J. Leong, 2011, Upper Saddle River, NJ: Pearson; *Basics of Developmentally Appropriate Practice: An Introduction for Teachers of Infants and Toddlers*, by C. Copple and S. Bredekamp, with J. Gonzalez-Mena, 2011, Washington, DC: NAEYC.

Creating safe and well-supervised opportunities to continue gross-motor practice is the primary task for teachers of babies and toddlers.

It is also important to remember that cultural groups differ in their views of appropriate child-rearing practices; therefore, infants' and toddlers' gross-motor experiences will vary among diverse cultures. For examples of diverse cultural practices that impact gross-motor development, read the *Culture Lens: Cultural Influences on Gross Motor Movement and Development* feature.

Gross-Motor Development in Preschoolers and Kindergartners

Gross-motor play continues to be important during the preschool and kindergarten years. Children during this period need physical activity throughout the day to maintain their focus and on-task behavior during the more structured parts of the school day. By age 3, children learn to climb stairs, walking up and down, as well as how to alternate feet as they climb. Preschoolers get better at running, pedaling a tricycle, and jumping up and down on both feet. Endurance increases, although younger children still fatigue easily.

Culture Lens

Cultural Influences on Gross-Motor Movement and Development

Children's physical development is strongly influenced by biology, and yet cultural experience plays a key role. Consider two very different approaches to infant caregiving and their effects on babies' motor development.

The Pikler Institute is a residential nursery (previously called an orphanage) located in Budapest, Hungary, that was founded after World War II to serve children left without families. Dr. Emmi Pikler created a program for children from birth through age 3 that focuses on freedom of movement, which means that babies are never put in positions that they cannot get into on their own. For example, they aren't placed in restrictive devices such as infant seats, high chairs, jumpers, or walkers. They lie on their backs, awake or asleep, until they are able to roll over by themselves and move into different positions. The rule is "No adult interference with children's movement."

Allowing infants to move freely results in remarkable competence, balance, coordination, and calculated risk-taking. Visitors to the Pikler Institute are impressed with the ease and confidence with which very young children move their bodies. The children know how to handle their bodies, have impressive equilibrium, and their body awareness is far above average. In addition, there is a very low accident rate at the Institute.

Another example of Dr. Pikler's philosophy in action is how babies were put down to sleep. Sixty years ago, no one was talking about "Back to Sleep," placing babies on their backs to prevent sudden infant death syndrome (SIDS). However, Pikler was doing it—back to sleep and back to play as well, without one SIDS incident ever. American advocates for "tummy time" fear that too much time on their backs will compromise infant development

and misshape heads. Neither of these problems is evident at the Pikler Institute, even though babies are never on their tummies until they can turn over by themselves. Freedom of movement promotes gross-motor development as well as a strong sense of competence within babies who find out that they can move and learn on their own without the assistance of an adult.

Contrast the Pikler approach to the child-rearing practice of the Au people of Papua, New Guinea. Anthropologist David Tracer has documented that during the first 12 months of life, Au babies are carried by their mothers or siblings 86% of the time. When they are put down, they are usually placed in a sitting position, not on their stomachs. Instead of crawling, Au babies go through a "scooting" phase—pushing themselves along with their hands and scooting on their backsides. Au parents discourage crawling to reduce the risk of their babies contracting disease. Their babies do not crawl; they learn to walk, although a few months later than children in the United States and Europe.

These examples and countless others demonstrate how cultural practices influence children's development—even their physical development—which is so dependent on biology and maturation. Consider how these approaches compare to the expectations for babies' freedom of movement in your own cultural group.

Sources: "The Pikler Institute: A Unique Approach to Caring for Children," by J. Gonzalez-Mena, E. Chahin, and L. Briley, 2005, *Exchange, 166,* 49–51, retrieved from http://www.pikler.org; *Will Baby Crawl?,* by National Science Foundation Discoveries, 2005, retrieved September 18, 2009, from http://www.nsf.gov/discoveries/disc_summ.jsp?cntn_id=103153&org=NSF.

Coordination and balance improve as kindergartners learn to jump rope, hop on one foot, and skip. An increasing awareness of their own skills and abilities leads to better understanding of unsafe behaviors; however, children can still lose control and become overexcited or unable to manage during large-group activities.

The ability of the brain to conceive, organize, and carry out a series of unfamiliar actions is called **motor planning** and takes center stage as children work to gain control over their growing bodies. For example, 2½-year-old Lena tries to catch a ball by extending her arms. She knows what should happen, yet ends up with the ball bouncing off. By contrast, 4-year-old Derek moves his body so he can enclose the ball in his arms. Finally, kindergartner Julianne moves her body around so she can catch the ball between her hands with no assistance from her forearms.

motor planning The ability of the brain to conceive, organize, and carry out a series of unfamiliar actions.

The primary goal of the curriculum for preschoolers and kindergartners is to help them make progress on fundamental motor skills. In acquiring physical skills, competence leads to confidence and further persistence, so success matters. Therefore, it is important for teachers to intentionally teach fundamental motor skills, just as Ms. Perez did with Allison at the beginning of this chapter. Intentional teachers provide encouragement, coaching, and modification of the toys and materials to increase the chances of successful skill learning. They offer cues about how to perform specific skills, such as suggesting that children widen their stance to increase stability while bending forward. They also challenge children to extend, hold, or repeat skills as they practice, or they may add a challenge such as "Recite a poem while balancing on one foot." Table 15.2 describes effective strategies and examples of how teachers can promote gross-motor development in children from birth to kindergarten.

▶ **Classroom Connection**
The two children in this video have been friends for a long time. As you watch them play together, note the ways in which their motor development is typical for children of this age.

Inclusion of children with disabilities requires that they participate as fully as possible in all activities. Embedding interventions in the regular classroom day is an excellent way to meet the needs of all children during one activity. For example, Caden, a 2-year-old with severe disabilities, cannot roll over on his own. His physical therapist works with him on the floor, gently rolling his body from side to side. To the other children in the class, this looks like great fun, and soon five other children are rolling on the floor and laughing along with Caden.

Gross-Motor Development in the Primary Grades During the primary grades, children practice and perfect a wide range of gross-motor skills, often connected to their interests. They have high energy levels and rarely show physical fatigue. Interest in group games increases as children are able to coordinate more than one gross-motor activity at a time, such as hitting a pitched ball. They can coordinate the movements required for dancing, skating, bike riding, swimming, and playing games such as soccer, basketball, and volleyball. As they practice using motor, balancing, and manipulative skills, they become increasingly competent and coordinated, often perfecting the skills needed to participate successfully in a wide range of games and sports. Table 15.3 lists strategies and examples of how teachers can promote gross motor development in the primary grades.

Because the primary-grade day is so full, one of the best strategies is to integrate physical education with other subject areas. For example, one elementary school has periodic field days during which children move from station to station using different muscles and skills such as rope climbing or bike riding that are fun but challenging. To link to the broader curriculum, the children take photos and write about the experience. As is evident in Figure 15.1, one second grader had a great time.

Importance of Recess Because motor skill development is closely tied to opportunity, recess is not a luxury for children in the primary grades (American Academy of Pediatrics, 2013). As the pressure to improve scores on standardized tests has increased, as many as 40% of elementary schools have severely limited or eliminated recess

TABLE 15.2 Effective Strategies: Gross-Motor Skills from Birth through Age 5

Intentional teachers use effective strategies such as these to support children's gross-motor development, which is not an automatic process.

Teaching Strategy	Examples
Respond to babies and take delight in their motor skills.	Smile and laugh as babies kick their legs over and over. Provide constant supervision and a safe environment (e.g., no objects that might be swallowed).
Give babies opportunities to control their own bodies without restraint or external support.	Avoid the use of infant seats, swings, playpens, and other equipment that restricts movements or limits explorations and repetition.
Give babies places and spaces to explore in a safe environment.	Provide floor time ("tummy time" for non-crawlers) with a clean carpet or blanket on the floor.
For toddlers, provide sufficient space and low indoor climbing equipment for them to practice new skills.	Pay particular attention to children's safety as they explore and take risks.
Include periods of time for uninterrupted gross-motor play.	Organize the classroom to provide sufficient indoor space so that children can move without getting in each other's way.
Provide active outdoor play.	Provide space and time for children to freely engage in unstructured play and physical activity such as running, climbing, digging, and tricycle riding.
Plan structured opportunities to build and practice gross-motor skills indoors.	Act out the movements to songs, rhymes, chants, and finger plays.
Provide gross-motor opportunities that use a range of different skills and combine skills in novel and interesting ways.	Set up an obstacle course or play a game such as having children move to music and freeze their bodies in place when the music stops.
Use a variety of developmentally appropriate toys and materials.	Supply balance beams, ladders, large wooden and plastic blocks, jump ropes, balls, floor puzzles, push carts, tumbling mats, scooter boards, and so forth.
Provide structured play experiences that help children build and practice fundamental motor skills.	Engage children in activities such as rolling balls, bowling, tossing bean bags into baskets, climbing stairs, or tumbling on mats. Have children play games using hula hoops, streamers, parachutes, or beach balls. Have them participate in music activities such as marching to the beat of a musical selection.
Use motor movements during routines and transitions.	Have children waddle like a duck or jump like a frog to get from the classroom to the cafeteria.
Integrate movement with other curriculum topics such as literacy or music.	Select action-oriented books to read to children and then add movements to the stories (e.g., *Dinosaur Roar!*).
Consciously choose, adapt, and use materials to ensure maximum participation by all children, including children with disabilities.	Provide equal encouragement to boys and girls. If children have difficulty with materials, adapt them by adding handles, buttons, or knobs; prevent slipping with Velcro or mats. Simplify the task by limiting the range of difficulty; by adding sensory cues such as color, sound, textures, or scents; or by encouraging cooperation among children who can do the gross-motor activities and those who cannot.

Sources: Based on *Innovations: The Comprehensive Preschool Curriculum*, by K. Albrecht and L. G. Miller, 2004, Beltsville, MD: Gryphon House; "Developmentally Appropriate Practice in the Kindergarten Year—Ages 5–6: An Overview," by H. B. Tomlinson, 2009a, 187–216, and "Developmentally Appropriate Practice in the Preschool Years–Ages 3–5: An Overview," by H. B. Tomlinson and M. Hyson, 2009, 111–148, both in *Developmentally Appropriate Practice in Early Childhood Programs Serving Children from Birth through Age 8*, revised edition, edited by C. Copple and S. Bredekamp, Washington, DC: NAEYC.

(Robert Wood Johnson Foundation, 2010). This trend is troubling and potentially damaging to children's academic achievement—opposite of the desired effect (Goodway, Ozmun, Derringer, & Lee, 2013).

A large body of research demonstrates the educational, social, and physical benefits of recess (American Academy of Pediatrics, 2013). Playful breaks maximize children's ability to perform higher-level cognitive tasks and improve social competence, adjustment

TABLE 15.3 Effective Strategies: Gross-Motor Skills in the Primary Grades

The structure of elementary schools may make it difficult to support children's gross-motor development so teachers must use multiple strategies such as those illustrated here.

Teaching Strategy	Examples
Arrange the classroom to allow for movement activities.	Arrange desks or tables to provide room for calisthenics and movement accompanied by music.
Plan breaks throughout the day for physical exercise and stress relief.	Have children stand, stretch, do motor mirroring (pairs of children mirror each other's movements), or move from place to place.
Integrate motor skill learning and practice into other areas of the curriculum.	Have children act out rhymes and stories, dance, repeat rhythms, express emotions with the entire body, play charades, and pantomime stories.
Offer opportunities for children to create, modify, and play group games and child-initiated team sports.	Encourage children to choose and participate in noncompetitive games such as hopscotch, jump rope, parachute games, hula hooping, and playing tag and games such as Red Light/Green Light.
Plan activities in which everyone has a chance to participate as opposed to organized sports where only the best players make the team and get to play.	Because of primary-grade children's growing inclination to compare themselves with others, avoid pushing competitive activities. Instead, help children compete with their own prior performances rather than those of other children ("Last time you hit the target only once. Today you hit it three times").
Collaborate with physical education, music, and fine arts specialists to make sure that children have opportunities for motor-skill learning every day.	At the elementary level, teachers are not likely to be in control of physical education activities, but they can work with other professionals to ensure that children have many rich opportunities to learn and practice motor skills throughout the school day.

Source: Based on "Developmentally Appropriate Practice in the Primary Grades—Ages 6–8: An Overview," by H. B. Tomlinson, 2009b, pp. 257–288, in *Developmentally Appropriate Practice in Early Childhood Programs Serving Children from Birth through Age 8,* revised edition, edited by C. Copple and S. Bredekamp, Washington, DC: NAEYC.

to school, and physical health. In a study of almost 11,000 third graders, children who had at least 15 minutes of daily recess behaved more positively than those who didn't (Barros, Silver, & Stein, 2009). And children of color from low-income families in urban areas were less likely to have recess—the very children who may need it most. Ironically, eliminating recess is the strategy schools often use to try to close the achievement gap for this same group of children (Goodway, Ozmun, Derringer, & Lee, 2013).

FIGURE 15.1 Second Grader's Field Day Story This second grader's documentation of her field day experience illustrates how gross-motor experiences can be incorporated into the school day and link to other areas of the curriculum such as literacy.

Promoting Play

Teaching Sports Skills in Primary Grades

While observing children on the playground in fall, second-grade teachers Alex and Mel noticed that children were beginning to put teams together and play "sports." They watched as children put together a soccer game, which rapidly devolved into arguments about rules and all abandoning the game. Alex and Mel recognized that primary-school children enjoy games with rules, and that the gross-motor play during recess would help their learning and development. But they also realized that the children needed support with playing more complex games. At class meeting the next Monday, they surveyed children about their interest in sports, asking which ones children liked most and would like to learn to play. The children voted for soccer, and agreed they would like to learn to play baseball (whiffle ball) in spring.

Using visuals and clips of soccer from YouTube, Alex and Mel introduced soccer during large-group time—especially for children who were not familiar with the game from family and friends. They were sure to explain that these professional soccer players were so skilled because of years of practice. Focusing on the skills used in soccer, Mel and Alex developed a series of games around kicking balls, kicking while running, and aiming at a target. They

provided many balls and used cones to mark places on the playground to run around and kick through. For the last 10–15 minutes of every 45-minute lunch recess, they helped the children play a short game of soccer. They organized the children's teams daily, making sure to mix up the team membership. Mel and Alex emphasized teamwork with the children—assists in scoring were celebrated as much as the scoring.

The children's skills grew, and Mel and Alex began to teach the children more of the rules, and higher-level skills, such as passing the ball. In addition to their growing gross-motor skills, the teachers noticed that children began to develop more confidence in their interactions. They negotiated in their other areas of play, and got along better with children in general. Over the course of the fall, Mel and Alex were less needed during the soccer games, and were available to support disputes and made certain that all children had equal opportunities to play. Not all children played soccer every day—some children preferred sports more than others. But children who did play benefited in important ways. They looked forward to the spring, when they would teach whiffle ball, which would help children with different skills and rules.

Some think that recess interferes with children's attention spans, but the opposite is true; research finds that in kindergarten and primary grades, children are more inattentive before than after recess (American Academy of Pediatrics, 2013). Recess increases the amount of time children stay on task and reduces fidgeting (Jarrett et al., 1998). Furthermore, since children in the primary grades have more advanced gross-motor skills and can play games with rules, many enjoy learning how to play sports with their classmates. Read the *Promoting Play* feature to learn how one teaching team introduced sports to their second grade class.

Fine-Motor Development

fine-motor manipulative movements Control, precision, and accuracy of small muscle movement.

The term **fine-motor manipulative movement** refers to control, precision, and accuracy of small muscle movement, such as those inherent in picking up objects with the thumb and forefinger, tying shoes, cutting with scissors, or using a keyboard. Fine-motor skills allow children to explore how things work, get dressed, use writing tools, put puzzles together, prepare snacks and meals, and engage in many more activities that require hand, finger, and wrist movements. Strength, control, and coordination of hand, finger, and wrist movements are part of fine-motor development. Strength is needed to cut with scissors; control allows for buttoning and zipping; coordination is used to put together puzzles and thread beads on laces.

Fine-motor skills are connected to healthy brain development. When the small muscles of the body move, brain circuitry is stimulated and strengthened, and the coordination between neurons and between the parts of the brain improves (Levitt, 2008). As children repeat fine-motor skills, such as stringing beads, working with clay, and putting pegs in

Children need a lot of practice to master fine-motor skills and eye-hand coordination.

pegboards, they not only refine these skills but also improve brain connections. In fact, a study of thousands of children from birth to kindergarten found that fine-motor skills in preschool are a strong predictor of later achievement (Grissmer, Grimm, Aiyer, Murrah, & Steele, 2010).

Fine-motor development progresses slowly as individual children experience different degrees of difficulty in performing fine-motor tasks. Children often encounter failure and become frustrated as they try to master these difficult skills; consequently, they need adequate time and adult support to keep them interested enough to practice. Read the *Developmental Continuum* feature for a description of fine-motor skill acquisition in children from birth through the primary grades.

Fine-Motor Development from Birth to Age 3 Babies spend the first year of life working on grasping objects and tracking movements with their eyes and heads. They perfect picking up objects with their whole hand, pointing, putting objects into containers, and drinking from a cup.

Toddlers begin to use a spoon to eat, turn pages, stack blocks, scribble with crayons or markers, hold drinking cups, and remove clothing. By age 2, they are able to remove shoes and some clothing, hold a cup or glass in one hand, unbutton large buttons, turn doorknobs, stack small blocks, fit large pegs in pegboards, pour and fill containers at a sensory table, unzip large zippers, and begin to show a preference for one hand. Toward the end of toddlerhood, children tackle toileting, which involves many motor skills such as pulling underwear down and up and controlling the small muscles that hold and release bodily functions. Table 15.4 provides examples of ways teachers can promote fine-motor skills in very young children.

Fine-Motor Development in Preschoolers and Kindergartners By age 3, children usually exhibit a preference for one hand (although they don't know left from right) and can complete puzzles, string beads, put pegs in pegboards, easily turn the pages of a book, grasp a pencil or marker (though not always with an adult-like grip), and draw and write with crayons and markers. Four- and five-year-olds complete board and floor puzzles; draw recognizable images; copy shapes, letters, and numbers; cut with scissors; button their clothes; and pour from a pitcher into a glass.

Many preschoolers and most kindergartners print letters recognizably, disassemble and reassemble manipulative constructions, use scissors to accomplish desired tasks, hit nails with a hammer head, and use a keyboard and mouse with age-appropriate computer programs. By age 5, children's drawings are more detailed and they may be able to tie

Developmental Continuum
Fine-Motor Skills from Birth through Age 8

Approximate Age	Widely Held Expectations
Birth to about 9 months	Small muscles respond reflexively in newborns (automatically grasp object) Reach for and grab objects with hands, hold rattle Gradually gain control in grasping and explore objects (often mouths them)
About 9 to 18 months	May use pincer grasp (thumb and forefinger) to pick up objects Gain control in exploring and manipulating objects Use both hands, may show preference for one hand May undress self, untie shoes, begin to feed self Scribbles with crayons
About 18 to 36 months	Can hold utensils and feed self (with spills) Dress self with loose clothing, except for buttons and shoelaces Does three- to five-piece puzzle Scribble, paint, and draw making recognizable lines and shapes
3- and 4-year-olds	Gain more control over fine muscles Build complex patterns and structures using interlocking pieces such as Lego blocks, pegboards, puzzles, beads Increasingly able to take care of own needs including hand washing, toileting, feeding, and dressing (may unbutton and unzip) Can use scissors, glue, collage materials
5- and 6-year-olds	Increasingly skilled in drawing and writing Hold pencil with fingertips Demonstrate handedness Eye-hand coordination increases Dress independently, tie shoes Use a fork and knife
7- and 8-year-olds	Independently use fine-motor skills to accomplish tasks and goals Control handwriting, begin cursive writing Use keyboard easily Use tools such as saw, hammer, and nails successfully

Sources: Based on *Basics of Developmentally Appropriate Practice: An Introduction for Teachers of Infants & Toddlers*, edited by C. Copple and S. Bredekamp, with Janet Gonzalez-Mena, 2011, Washington, DC: NAEYC; *Basics of Developmentally Appropriate Practice: An Introduction for Teachers of Children 3 to 6*, edited by C. Copple and S. Bredekamp, 2006, Washington, DC: NAEYC.

their own shoes. When children's fine-motor skills are well developed and practiced, their creativity can take off. Five-year-old Sandi loves creating things using items from her family's recycling box and a non-hot glue gun. Figure 15.2 is Sandi's robot mommy with a baby in her tummy. By contrast, her twin sister Ella has little interest in doing the same kind of projects.

TABLE 15.4 Effective Strategies: Fine-Motor Skills in Infants and Toddlers

Providing developmentally appropriate materials and lots of supervised play, as exemplified here, are excellent ways to promote fine-motor development in infants and toddlers.

Teaching Strategy	Examples
Give babies and toddlers many opportunities to explore objects, people, and things using the muscles necessary for reaching, grasping, pulling, picking up, chewing, holding, and letting go.	Play interactive games like peek-a-boo; look at picture books, particularly books with textures, sounds, and actions to imitate; display images that are interesting from a baby's or toddler's perspective, taking into account that very young infants are usually looking up from their backs at the world.
Provide developmentally appropriate toys such as action/reaction toys that help children connect cause and effect as well as stimulate fine-motor skills.	Provide appropriate toys that make noise and respond to the child's manipulation in interesting ways such as rattles, teethers, toys to stack and sort, pull toys, soft blocks, and toys that pop up or roll away. Children who aren't mobile like play mats with objects to kick or reach for; toddlers can do puzzles with a few separate pieces, stack blocks, and roll wheeled toys.
Provide developmentally appropriate equipment.	Provide eating utensils for children in graduated sizes and complexity to provide incremental motor practice using the small muscles of the fingers and the hand, e.g., spoons, then forks; bowls, then plates.
Provide age-appropriate materials. Ensure that most fine-motor toys and materials are easy to clean and sanitize and large enough that they do not present a choking hazard.	Babies put almost everything into their mouths—as they use the sense of touch, taste, and smell to gather information about the object with which they are playing. Toddlers like to tear paper, pull things off of shelves, dump toys out of containers, and play with miniatures such as interconnecting blocks. Banging and clapping are great fun, as is playing with sand, water, and playdough.
Provide art materials such as large crayons, watercolor markers, and a variety of sizes and types of paper.	Let children explore materials. Be realistic about the amount of mess.

Sources: Based on *Innovations: The Comprehensive Infant Curriculum,* by K. Albrecht and L. G. Miller, 2000a, Beltsville, MD: Gryphon House; *Innovations: The Comprehensive Toddler Curriculum,* by K. Albrecht & L. G. Miller, 2000b, Beltsville, MD: Gryphon House; *Innovations: Infant and Toddler Development,* by K. Albrecht & L. G. Miller, 2001, Beltsville, MD: Gryphon House.

(a)   (b)

FIGURE 15.2a & 15.2b Five-Year-Old's Robot Mommy with Baby in the Tummy Using "found" materials, tape, and glue, this 5-year-old constructed a robot mommy that opens up to see the baby inside, demonstrating both her fine-motor skills and her creativity.

TABLE 15.5 Effective Strategies: Fine-Motor Skills in Preschool and Kindergarten

During preschool and kindergarten, children's fine-motor skills become more refined if teachers provide developmentally appropriate materials and experiences such as these.

Teaching Strategy	Examples
Provide a range of materials and activities for children.	Use materials and activities in which children with different levels of fine-motor skills can participate with success, such as puzzles with different numbers of pieces and more or less complexity.
Provide appropriate toys and materials.	Supply objects to sort, count, and put into patterns; pegboards and beads to string; clothing and other items that zip and button for dress-up play; a variety of drawing and writing tools and paper; scissors, paint, and clay.
Offer opportunities to practice functional skills.	Allow children to pour milk, hammer nails, and use other tools. These activities may require accommodation or modification for all children to use them successfully or when materials cause frustration or fatigue.
Provide open-ended activities that allow children to practice fine-motor skills. Choose activities that fit their current level of competence as well as those that are more challenging yet within reach.	Arrange for open-ended experiences such as drawing and painting, working with playdough or clay, building with blocks, and constructing with Duplos and Legos and other interconnecting blocks.

Sources: Based on *Innovations: The Comprehensive Preschool Curriculum*, by K. Albrecht and L. G. Miller, 2004, Beltsville, MD: Gryphon House; *Basics of Developmentally Appropriate Practice: An Introduction for Teachers of Children 3 to 6*, edited by C. Copple and S. Bredekamp, 2006, Washington, DC: NAEYC.

Gender differences in motor skills are evident in this period. In general, girls tend to be more advanced than boys in fine-motor skills and in gross-motor skills that require precision, whereas boys tend to do better with skills that require force and power (Berk, 2008). Table 15.5 presents ways to help preschoolers and kindergartners master fine-motor skills.

When fine-motor experiences lead to frustration and fatigue or when children prefer gross-motor activities, they need encouragement and support and sometimes instruction in skills or models of what to try next. Teachers need to carefully observe children to be sure they are ready to tackle the next challenge. Here again, intentional teaching is important, as described in the feature *Becoming an Intentional Teacher.*

Fine-Motor Development in the Primary Grades Fine-motor development in primary-grade children is all about refinement. Writing, drawing, and keyboard skills are more precise. By second grade, wrist, hand, and finger muscles are more coordinated, writing becomes more uniform, and drawing skills include detail and display early attempts at perspective. Primary-age children master the ability to coordinate movements: they can cut with scissors while turning the paper to make arches, angles, borders, and other cutouts. They enjoy working on projects or crafts over time and, rather than finish an activity in one session, they will return repeatedly to it if it interests them.

In general, during this time, girls are ahead of boys in fine-motor development (Haywood & Gretchell, 2005). However, gender differences are at least partially the result of differences in practice opportunities, with boys and girls developing at a similar pace given similar opportunities (Craig & Baucum, 2002). This research highlights the importance of providing equal opportunities to all children to develop physical skills.

Children in the primary grades like to use real things such as hammers and nails and scrap lumber rather than toys. They need instruction about how to use the tools but will often resist the offer of support until they have tried their own ideas. Teachers can draw on their interests, arranging for them to create friendship bracelets or birdhouses. Six- to eight-year-olds will work for extended periods of time on projects, particularly if they result in "real" products.

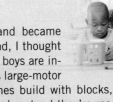

Becoming an Intentional Teacher
Teaching Fine-Motor Skills

Here's What Happened In my kindergarten class I have three boys whose lack of fine-motor skills is holding them back in writing. They're all very physical and love to run, jump, and climb. They aren't attracted to puzzles, working with playdough, or stringing beads, although they do build with blocks at times. I brought in some mini-Legos and small cars, and they began building garages and race tracks for the cars. I've given them writing tools and various kinds of paper and encouraged them to make signs for their race track. Also, I have begun pairing the three boys with other kids at the computer and on the iPad using software I think will get their interest.

Here's What I Was Thinking Boys are sometimes behind girls in their fine-motor development, and this seems especially likely when they don't spend much time in activities that involve the small hand muscles. Some of my fellow teachers told me that I should just make the boys practice writing more. But I observed that they fatigued while trying to write and became easily frustrated. Instead, I thought about what these three boys are interested in. A lot of it is large-motor play, but they sometimes build with blocks, and outside they ride their trikes and pretend they're race car drivers. These interests hadn't gotten them involved with much fine-motor activity when they worked with the usual materials. But I thought if I brought in small-scale materials for them to build and pretend with, there might be a change. And the computer will allow the boys to do some writing without the difficulty of forming the letters slowing them down so much. And at the same time they'll be working with the mouse and keyboard, which are good tasks for promoting fine-motor skills.

Reflection What other ways could this teacher promote the boys' fine motor skills and writing ability?

Perceptual-Motor Development from Birth through Age 8 Perceptual-motor development plays an important role in learning fundamental movement skills. Perceptual-motor skills include auditory, visual, and tactile-kinesthetic skills as well as body awareness. Children develop these skills while using their senses to collect, monitor, interpret, and respond to information from the environment. As their ability to collect and use information improves, motor skills grow and develop, as we see in the following example.

> Fourteen-month-old Tara sits on her teacher's lap with her finger in the air. Her teacher, Miss Laura, begins the finger play she knows Tara is asking her to say. She points to Tara's facial features gently as she repeats the rhyme: "Eye winker (touches one eyelid), tom tinker (then the other eyelid), nose smeller (touches the tip of her nose), mouth eater (points to her mouth), chin chopper (touches her chin), gully, gully, gully (gently tickles her neck)." Tara is already showing her teacher how she perceives input from her senses (the words she hears, the touch she feels) and combines them with her memory of previous times when the teacher played this game to anticipate what will happen next. Tara closes her eyes before they are touched, sticks her nose in the air as Laura says "nose smeller," and lowers her chin and laughs heartily in anticipation of the gentle tickle on her neck.

Perceptual-motor development is maturational—as attention to and perception of sensory information improves, subsequent motor coordination improves. This growth is largely dependent on the development of the brain and central nervous system, although the timing of such maturity varies. Perceptions of where the body is (**spatial awareness**), speeding up or slowing down a movement (**temporal awareness**), anticipating which way to go (**directional awareness**), and listening to verbal input or distinguishing between different sounds (**auditory awareness**) are all part of perceptual-motor development.

Perceptual-Motor Development in Babies and Toddlers Babies and toddlers learn through movement. As they move their arms, legs, and bodies, they encounter the world by touching it and being touched by it. They explore using all of the senses,

spatial awareness Perceptions of where the body is.

temporal awareness Speeding up or slowing down a movement.

directional awareness Anticipating which way to go.

auditory awareness Listening to verbal input or distinguishing between different sounds.

Name: __EVIE__

Date: __11-9-11__

SIGHT

With my sense of sight I _saw a shadow_
with my sister.

FIGURE 15.3 Page from Evie's *My Five Senses* Book This page from Evie's *My Five Senses* book is an example of how a preschool teacher can use an interesting curriculum topic to promote children's perceptual-motor development.

particularly touch and taste. Babies begin processing sensory information and trying to make sense of it, anticipating, for example, that pushing a button on a toy will produce a sound. They manipulate tools, such as spoons or a cup, and demonstrate a basic understanding of quantities of more or less.

Toddlers continue the exploration, now from an upright vantage point. They increasingly manipulate objects with a purpose, such as stacking blocks or lining up cars. They gather sensory data from watching others and imitate other children and adults.

Perceptual-Motor Development in Preschoolers and Kindergartners

During the preschool and kindergarten years, the senses of sight, smell, touch, taste, and hearing are all well developed. Young children delight in exploring the world and preschool teachers often use the senses as an engaging curriculum topic, as we see in a page from 4½-year-old Evie's *My Five Senses* book (see Figure 15.3).

However, in spite of their physical capacities for excellent sensation and perception, this age group's processing of the incoming information is not complete; children have yet to develop some of the cognitive strategies and language needed to make sense of all the information coming in through their senses. Children's ability to perceive patterns and discriminate various forms improves during the preschool years. Visually, preschool children are farsighted; they have trouble switching focus between close and distant targets and are still developing binocular vision (the ability of the eyes to work together), which necessitates larger print. Their depth perception is still developing and they tend to run into things and each other (Pica, 2006).

Preschoolers and kindergartners may make letter reversals (confusing the letters *q* and *p* or *d* and *b*), but this is not a perceptual problem. It is a natural confusion based on experience with objects in the physical world that have the same function regardless of their directional orientation—a chair is still a chair whether it is facing left or right.

Hearing is also well developed; this age group loves listening to music, stories, and conversations. They recognize rhyming words and play with the sounds of language. They perceive when two words sound the same or begin with the same sound (Schickedanz & Collins, 2013). If children do not participate or respond during these activities, it may be a sign of hearing problems due to chronic middle ear infections or other causes that should be evaluated by a physician.

Perceptual-Motor Development in the Primary Grades

Children in the primary grades have learned to use all of the senses to influence their motor movements. As their ability to simultaneously take in sensory input and make modifications to their motor movements improves, so does motor coordination, balance, and timing. Increasingly, children are able to integrate previously acquired skills into more complex actions, particularly if they have had considerable practice.

Environments filled with interesting things to touch, smell, see, listen to, and manipulate provide sensory input for children to perceive and interpret. From birth to age 8, similar types of experiences promote perceptual-motor development, as listed in Table 15.6.

As children gain perceptual-motor skills and their body awareness increases, teachers can increase the level of difficulty and challenge of the tasks to help them refine these skills further. In the next section, we turn to the all-important contribution of play to children's physical fitness and health.

TABLE 15.6 Effective Strategies: Perceptual-Motor Development from Birth to Age 8

Intentional teachers use effective strategies such as these to promote perceptual-motor development in children from birth to age 8.

Teaching Strategy	Examples
Provide a variety of interesting sounds and rhythms to hear.	Use songs, rhymes, finger plays, and chants to provide interesting sounds and rhythms. Finger plays (such as "The Itsy, Bitsy Spider"), which require the coordination of the spoken word with hand or body movements, are good perceptual motor experiences for children ages 5 and under. Primary-age children often add hand and body movements to familiar songs, rhymes, and chants. Build auditory awareness by adding novel input such as the sounds of orchestra instruments or nature.
Stimulate visual acuity for all ages by providing interesting pictures and displays at children's eye level in the environment.	Provide visual stimulation for young children. Babies spend long periods of time gazing at things that interest them; toddlers and twos will explore photographs and pictures. Have preschoolers, kindergartners, and primary-grade children examine pictures from a variety of sources, including the Internet and magazines, and use digital and video cameras to enhance visual awareness.
Offer a variety of textures and objects to feel, see, smell, and manipulate to provide sensory input for children to perceive and interpret.	Provide experiences that require children to use the senses independently, such as having them identify hidden objects by touch or various odors by smell. Also have them use the senses together to figure things out: they might smell the results of a cooking project and see food change form as it is cooked.
Help children explore space to build awareness of their body to learn about the parts of their bodies, to become aware of how much space their bodies take up, and to learn how to control their body as they move from one place to another.	Support perceptual-motor skills by giving children freedom to explore under tables and chairs and inside of cozy spaces. Balance the familiar perspective of not being as tall as adults with the unfamiliar perspective of being taller by encouraging children to visit the loft or use the climber.
Give children a variety of points of view within and beyond the classroom.	Provide multiple levels with raised platforms or use foam structures or pits. Peek-a-boo hideouts and windows into the next classroom are sources of visual and auditory stimuli, as are low windows that provide a view of the world beyond the classroom.
Provide experiences that promote visual, body, and directional awareness.	Use obstacle courses to build understanding of directions in space such as *under*, *over*, *around*, and *through*. Ask children to imitate body movements: move like an animal, insect, or amphibian. Have children use their body to make letters or numbers

Sources: Based on *Innovations: The Comprehensive Preschool Curriculum*, by K. Albrecht and L. G. Miller, 2004, Beltsville, MD: Gryphon House; "Developmentally Appropriate Practice in the Kindergarten Year—Ages 5–6: An Overview," by H. B. Tomlinson, pp. 187–216, and "Developmentally Appropriate Practice in the Preschool Years—Ages 3–5: An Overview," by H. B. Tomlinson and M. Hyson, pp. 111–148, both in *Developmentally Appropriate Practice in Early Childhood Programs Serving Children from Birth Through Age 8*, revised edition, edited by C. Copple and S. Bredekamp, 2009, Washington, DC: NAEYC.

 Check Your Understanding 15.2: The Continuum of Physical Development

 # The Role of Play in Physical Development

From our previous discussion of types of motor skill learning, we have seen that play is an essential context in which children acquire and practice physical abilities. Different types of play have different benefits and are developmentally appropriate for children at different age levels (Milteer, Ginsburg, & Council on Communications and Media Committee on Psychosocial Aspects of Child and Family Health, 2012). Here, we focus on the critical roles of outdoor play and, particularly, **rough-and-tumble** or **"big body" play**, the

rough-and-tumble play or **big body play** The boisterous, large-motor, physical activity children seem to crave.

"boisterous, large motor, physical activity children seem to crave" (Carlson, 2011, 2015). The outdoors is one of the most stimulating, engaging contexts for children's development and learning and for this type of play. However, current changes in children's lives threaten their exposure to nature, as described next.

Childhood Experiences with the Natural Environment

Richard Louv, in his book *Last Child in the Woods* (2005), chronicles changes in children's exposure, contact, and experience with the natural world and concludes that something important has been lost as children's time in natural environments has diminished. This concern is shared by many early childhood educators (Honig, 2015; Rivkin, 2014; Shillady, 2011). As the late Jim Greenman, author of *Caring Spaces, Learning Places* (2005a), states: "Children are losing habitat—the real world of people and nature and machines and an opportunity to explore that world (directly, not just electronically) and be a part of it" (Greenman, 2005b, p. 2).

nature-deficit disorder Hypothetical disorder related to lack of exposure and experience outdoors and in the natural world.

Address Nature Deficit Louv (2005) proposes that children, families, and communities are experiencing "**nature-deficit disorder.**" The hypothetical disorder describes the human costs of alienation from nature that include "diminished use of the senses, attention difficulties, and higher rates of physical and emotional illnesses" (Louv, 2005, p. 34). These concerns led to an examination of how outdoor environments are designed and constructed and to a movement toward more natural outdoor playgrounds (Rivkin, 2014).

A growing trend among playground planners rejects the idea of playgrounds full of commercially purchased plastic, metal, or wood structures surrounded by safety zones filled with wood chips. Instead, these planners favor environments that make creative use of natural features and objects while still meeting the health and safety standards required for children's outdoor playgrounds (see American Academy of Pediatrics, American Public Health Association, & National Resource Center for Health and Safety in Child Care and Early Education, 2011). They believe that playgrounds should have areas with trees, grass, shrubs, planters, pots, and paths to show children what the world is made of—the real stuff, not a plastic or simulated version (Rivkin, 2014).

> ▶ **Classroom Connection**
>
> Watch this video to see how one community created a high-quality outdoor play environment using all natural materials.
>
> https://www.youtube.com/watch?v=DhZNX3y60ds

Benefits of Natural Environments Contact with nature has restorative powers for children. Nature buffers the impact of life stresses and lowers the incidence of behavior disorders, anxiety, and depression; children who play outside are sick less often and have a higher measure of self-worth (Rivkin, 2014). Exposure to nature has a calming effect that helps children focus attention. For example, children who play in natural environments show fewer symptoms of attention deficit/hyperactivity disorder (ADHD) than do children who play mostly with manufactured playground equipment (Torquati, Gabriel, Jones-Branch, & Miller, 2011). Even a walk in the park can reduce symptoms of ADHD and improve concentration (Faber Taylor & Kuo, 2009).

The quality of children's experience is different when they play in natural environments; it is more diverse, imaginative, and creative. Such play fosters language and collaborative skills and stimulates social interaction between children (American Academy of Pediatrics, 2013). Children who play regularly in natural environments show more advanced motor fitness, including coordination, balance, and agility, and are better able to concentrate after contact with nature (Goodway, Ozmun, Derringer, & Lee, 2013).

Natural environments also build an understanding of science concepts and engage them in scientific inquiry (Meier & Sisk-Hilton, 2013). For those children experiencing developmental, psychological, or relational disorders, research suggests that their symptoms are relieved after contact with nature (Kuo, 2010; Taylor, Kuo, & Sullivan,

2001) and that bullying behavior is reduced by frequent play in natural environments (Malone & Tranter, 2003).

Outdoor Play Environments

Good outdoor environments have similar characteristics (Rivkin, 2014). Space is typically divided into defined areas for different kinds of activities. Areas are dedicated to motor activities such as:

- Climbing, sliding, and crawling
- Riding wheeled toys and transporting things
- Building and construction
- Gross-motor activities such as running, jumping, throwing, kicking, bouncing, and balancing
- A messy play area for sand and water play
- Places to pretend and for creative expression
- A gardening or digging area
- A place for swings and other dynamic equipment
- An area for art activities
- Places to watch, get away from it all, or slow down

On playgrounds, climbing structures for children need to be sturdy and well anchored. But children also need equipment and materials that they can arrange in a variety of ways—providing experience with controlling the environment. Children like to rearrange crates, planks, boxes, blocks, and toys. They like tents, fabric scraps, and beach umbrellas to create places to climb into, under, or around.

Spacious settings equipped with age-appropriate toys, materials, and apparatus are also important for primary-grade children. Outdoor settings with hills, obstacle courses, softball diamonds, mazes, basketball hoops, tunnels, four-square and hopscotch grids, and volleyball nets are likely to interest children. Walking and running tracks, tetherball poles, and plenty of movable parts such as planks, large blocks, and tree trunks and branches help children sustain gross-motor play. Additional materials, such as balls of all types (large and small playground balls, softballs, basketballs, soccer balls, sensory balls), parachutes, jump ropes, hoops, cones, and beanbags add variety and give children opportunities to practice a variety of physical skills.

Schools should have outdoor equipment such as balance beams that are low to the ground to encourage children to practice skills at their own level. Such equipment limits spills to tumbles instead of serious falls. Digging in the sand or soil is another great outdoor motor activity for children. Water added to dry sand and soil or placed in a water table adds interest as children explore these components of the natural world.

Creating outdoor play environments and supporting participation in natural environments for children with disabilities can be complicated. Depending on their particular developmental challenges, children with disabilities often have motor delays and may have difficulty with balance and visual-motor tasks. Furthermore, they may need extra support in following directions and understanding and following safety guidelines. Teachers should plan carefully for accommodating the outdoor play needs of all children, and programs must ensure inclusive outdoor play spaces. Universal design—creating materials and environments that are accessible to all—is one way programs can accommodate all children. For example, many programs use play surfaces such as wood chips or tire

Children today are more likely to spend time watching television or playing video games than experiencing nature firsthand, leading to "nature-deficit disorder." Natural play environments address this problem and also provide laboratories for science investigation.

© Jules Selmes/Pearson Education

pieces. However, these surfaces are very difficult for children who move with a walker or wheelchair to navigate. Teachers must observe how children with and without disabilities access their current outdoor play space, and introduce materials and structures that allow children to participate more fully, including interacting with peers while playing.

When children are given ample time to play outdoors, they can practice and perfect many physical skills; they feel powerful and successful. For this reason, most children love the outdoors—it is a "can do" place. Yet the fast-paced activity of the outdoors can also be overstimulating and overwhelming for some. Children need quiet places to cool off, calm down, or rest; they also need water available to quench their thirst. A blanket in the shade can provide a place for children to spend some time with the teacher, refueling and recharging before heading back out to explore the world again. Time outdoors provides a change of pace, freedom from being close to other children, and a constant source of interesting stimuli.

Many people worry that technology interferes with children's outdoor experiences. However, teachers can integrate technology goals and activities outdoors (Blagojevic & Thomes, 2014). While exploring the natural environment, children can use tablets to photograph and document nature-based art, and can research their discoveries online. They can document aspects of nature they find exciting or beautiful, and integrate these into their writing projects back in the classroom.

The Value of Rough-and-Tumble Play

With childhood obesity hitting epidemic proportions, and academic pressure and technology leading to more sedentary lifestyles, early childhood educators call for greater awareness of the importance of "big body" play, where children literally use their whole bodies to run, jump, roll, climb, fall, tumble, somersault, and generally engage in vigorous, playful activity (Carlson, 2011). When such activity involves contact with another child, such as chasing, wrestling, tickling, rolling on top of each other, or play-fighting, it is usually called rough-and-tumble play.

Perhaps because there is so much emphasis today on protecting children, rough-and-tumble play has gotten a bad name. Some people interpret it as aggression or misbehavior and actually forbid it. However, there are important differences between fighting and other intentionally harmful acts and roughhousing—the goal of which is to have fun. I clearly remember rolling on the ground with my best friend in the yard one day and my mother calling from the front porch, "Are you playing or fighting?" "Playing!" we both hollered back immediately. The distinction, which children are well aware of and is easily observable, is that they are smiling, and they not only want to participate but they want to extend the play (Carlson, 2011). By contrast, fighting is something that most children obviously do not enjoy, would prefer to avoid, and want to stop.

As we've seen from discussing the research on active play, there are developmental benefits to rough-and-tumble play. Children practice and learn to control their bodies in space. They also learn self-regulation, social, and cognitive skills; to sustain the play, they have to take another person's point of view (a difficult cognitive skill) and read their friend's nonverbal cues. As long as Susie is smiling and giggling with her eyes shut, it's fine to continue, but as soon as she starts to frown, stare, and pull away, it's time to stop (Carlson, 2011).

Individual and cultural differences also exist in rough-and-tumble play. On average, boys are rougher and more physical in their play than girls are, and boys are more often disciplined by teachers (Goodway, Ozmun, & Gallahue, 2013). But girls need active play, too, and teachers could help by modeling actions such as hopping, jumping, skipping, and twirling games like ring around the rosie. Individual children may hold back from rough-and-tumble for many reasons, such as fear, shyness, or aversion to being touched. Cultural groups also play with children differently—some more gently than others. Teachers need to consider all of these factors in planning for and supporting rough-and-tumble play.

Given the benefits of rough-and-tumble play, however, teachers need to facilitate it in several ways. The class can establish a few clear rules such as: keep hands below the neck, no pinching, no hitting, and stop when the other person says, "Stop!" (Carlson, 2011). Because big body play can easily turn into real fighting, supervision is critical (Carlson,

2015). Teachers need to make sure the environment where children play is safe and stay close by to supervise at all times, key elements of health and safety standards in early childhood programs, which we discuss in the next section.

 Check Your Understanding 15.3: The Role of Play in Physical Development

 # Health and Safety Standards

Children's success in school and life is integrally connected to their health. To protect young children, early childhood programs must comply with legally mandated health and safety regulations. In addition, teachers have a responsibility to keep children safe and prevent disease. In the sections that follow, we discuss ways of supporting children's health and wellness, and teaching practices that prevent illness and injury.

The Teacher's Role in Health and Safety

Adults must be vigilant to protect young children's health and safety. The American Academy of Pediatrics, American Public Health Association, and the National Resource Center for Health and Safety in Child Care and Early Education (2011) has established national model standards for programs. Keeping children safe requires adequate and attentive supervision during all activities and experiences, and providing safe, appropriate furniture, toys, and materials and systematic monitoring to keep them that way (Aronson, 2012).

By nature, children are messy beings. In the early childhood setting, this translates into the need to keep everything clean and sanitized so as to prevent the spread of germs. Adults who model keeping the environment clean teach children how to clean up after themselves. Disease prevention starts with pre-enrollment requirements such as immunization and physical checkups, and continues with instilling habits that will lead children to eat well, get adequate rest, and participate in plenty of vigorous exercise.

Emergency preparedness is another dimension of health and wellness. In schools, sheltering-in-place strategies and evacuation procedures and drills need to be understood by all and practiced until they become routine for adults as well as children (Head Start, 2015b). Natural disasters such as hurricanes, tornadoes, or earthquakes are prevalent in certain geographic areas and require specific disaster preparedness plans. In addition to natural disasters, our world today is threatened by terrorism and criminal behavior, and emergency preparedness must address these possibilities as well (Greenman, 2001).

Prevent Illness Preventing the spread of germs is an essential disease-prevention strategy for young children to learn. Most experts agree that the single most effective practice that prevents the spread of germs is proper hand washing by adults and children. Teachers can stop the spread of germs by washing their hands and teaching children correct hand-washing practices. NAEYC accreditation standards as well as state licensing standards require regular, systematic hand washing at specific times for adults and children, such as before and after eating, using the toilet, or diapering. Despite the critical importance of these procedures, these standards are among the least frequently met in early childhood programs. Hand washing that actually prevents the transfer of germs is a process with specific steps, as described in Figure 15.4.

Prevent Injury When children are involved in active play, the role of the teacher is to provide constant attention and supervision. Teachers need to observe zones of the outdoor area and pay close attention to what children are doing so that they can intervene quickly, remind children of safety considerations, and be close enough to step in and stop risky behavior when it occurs.

▶ **Classroom Connection**

Observe this video to learn about teaching children proper hand washing and the role in preventing the spread of illness in group programs.

- Always use warm, running water and a mild, preferably liquid, soap. Antibacterial soaps may be used, but are not required.

- Wet the hands and apply a small amount (dime to quarter size) of liquid soap.

- Rub hands together vigorously until a soapy lather appears and continue for at least 15 seconds. Be sure to scrub between fingers, under fingernails, and around the tops and palms of the hands.

- Rinse hands under warm running water. Leave the water running while drying hands.

- Dry hands with a clean, disposable (or single use) towel, being careful to avoid touching the faucet handles or towel holder with clean hands.

- Turn the faucet off using the towel as a barrier between your hands and the faucet handle.

- Discard the used towel in a trash can, lined with a fluid-resistant (plastic) bag. Trash cans with foot-pedal operated lids are preferable.

- Consider using hand lotion to prevent chapping of hands. If using lotions, use liquids or tubes that can be squirted so that the hands do not have direct contact with container spout to avoid contaminating the lotion inside the container.

- When assisting a child in handwashing, either hold the child (if an infant) or have the child stand on a safety step at a height at which the child's hands can hang freely under the running water. Assist the child in performing all of the above steps and then wash your own hands.

FIGURE 15.4 Proper Hand-Washing Procedures The most effective way to prevent illness is for both adults and children to always use these proper hand-washing procedures.
Source: Reprinted from *Handwashing Procedure*, by Centers for Disease Control and Prevention, retrieved March 20, 2012, from http://www.cdc.gov/handwashing/.

Teachers also need to teach children about accident prevention, tricycle and bicycle safety, walking in traffic, and preparedness for emergencies. The majority of injuries that occur at school happen on the playground (CDC, 2012a). Nonfatal playground injuries are most often caused by falls. Children under age 4 are more likely to suffer head and face injuries, whereas children ages 5 to 14 are more likely to suffer injuries to the arms and hands (Mack, Hudson, & Thompson, 1997).

Balance Risk and Challenge In striving to protect children's safety and health, however, early childhood educators need to understand the impact of the amount of risk and challenge in the environment, what is called the **risk vs. challenge continuum** (Greenman, 2005a). The concept is that extremes of either risk or challenge—too much or too little— are not in the best interest of children (Curtis, 2010; Gramling, 2010). Too little risk, and children may withdraw or try harder to make something happen by using inappropriate or dangerous behaviors. Too much risk will certainly result in accidents and injuries.

Concern for children's safety is absolutely necessary, and environments should be designed to minimize risks and eliminate hazards as much as possible. A **hazard** is a serious danger that must be avoided; a **risk** is a possibility of harm that can be minimized with planning and supervision (Carlson, 2011). An attempt to eliminate all risk can lead to eliminating all challenge. Children not only need to be safe, they also need to be challenged if they are to advance their skills and learn how to keep themselves safe.

From infancy on, children try out challenging activities that might put them at risk for injury, most of them as a part of normal exploration. Consider the concept of

risk vs. challenge continuum Concept that children not only need to be safe but they also need to be challenged if they are to advance their skills and learn how to keep themselves safe.

hazard A danger that must be avoided.

risk A possibility of harm that can be minimized with planning and supervision.

risk vs. challenge in deciding whether children should be allowed to climb trees. One teacher might consider the risk of injury is too high and, therefore, that tree limbs on playgrounds should be trimmed to prevent tree climbing. However, from the perspective of a veteran child care center director, tree climbing is a learnable skill that can be safely taught to children and practiced with careful supervision (Curtis, 2010).

 Check Your Understanding 15.4: Health and Safety Standards

Effective Curriculum and Teaching to Promote Physical Fitness and Health

The purpose of developmentally appropriate physical education is to help children learn to move and learn through movement (Gallahue, 1995). In the sections that follow, we first describe curriculum and teaching strategies to promote physical development. We then address how to plan a health education curriculum.

Curriculum for Physical Development

You will recall from Chapter 10 that curriculum planning draws on both the content of the disciplines and knowledge of child development. In planning curriculum for physical development, the disciplines of physical education, nutrition, and health provide the learning goals for children. To make these goals meaningful and accessible to young children, teachers need to translate them into topics of interest. The teachers then plan the learning experiences keeping in mind what they know about the continuum of physical development so they can set achievable goals for children's gross-motor and fine-motor skills. Then, based on their observation and assessment, teachers set goals for individual children, as the following example illustrates:

> The 4-year-olds in Betty Bartock and Jake Springer's child care class eagerly anticipate the arrival of the circus in their town. Betty and Jake decide to make the circus the big idea for planning curriculum to address their goals for children's physical development and health. The group has read books about the circus and learned circus songs and games. When they discuss the topic with the children in a group meeting, many ideas are generated. "I'll be the tightrope walker," says Durrell, who is proud of his skill on the high balance beam. "We can have a parade. We can pretend we're different animals and walk like them," suggests Deretha. "Let's dress up like clowns." "I'm going to be the animal tamer. I'll use the stuffed animals," states Maggie.
>
> The circus project becomes one of the highlights of the year. Betty and Jake use it to motivate several of the reluctant children to try out new physical skills like balancing on one foot. They observe that Barton's eye-hand coordination is exceptional for his age. Although Barton is often disruptive in class, the circus tasks focus his attention, and he becomes the "juggler"—perfecting his ability to toss a small ball hand to hand.
>
> After a few weeks of circus-inspired physical activity, Betty and Jake decide to share the fun with families. The children write invitations to their circus, plan costumes, and paint advertising signs. For the big day, they need refreshments. This generates a lengthy discussion of what kinds of "circus" foods are healthy. The children settle on unbuttered popcorn and Rice Krispies treats, which they prepare. Many family members attend the circus, watching the parade and enjoying the children's performances of songs and skills. Then they visit the various "acts" arranged in sections of the room or stop to pay a penny for a treat at the food booth.

The circus project was a big hit with children, families, and teachers. But it also provided a framework for Betty and Jake to help children make progress in the areas of physical development, motor skill acquisition, and health. They were able to use children's

Playing is one of the greatest joys of childhood and also essential for children's physical fitness and health.

interests to help them achieve goals such as building Barton's fine-motor skill or getting a less-skilled child to try out the balance beam.

The context of a meaningful curriculum topic such as the circus provides numerous opportunities for children to learn and practice physical skills. Just growing up is not enough to ensure that all children develop the fundamental motor skills they need. They require more than an appropriate environment and supportive adults; children also need instruction (Goodway, Ozmun, & Gallahue, 2013). Effective teaching strategies to build physical skills include movement exploration, explicit teaching, and teacher-supported practice (Goodway, Ozmun, & Gallahue, 2013).

Movement Exploration Movement exploration gives children a role in learning the skills being taught and allows for wider experimentation as the learning unfolds (Pica, 2006). Tina Sabuco, the founder of *Arts Alive!* in Houston, Texas, asks preschool and kindergarten children during her movement classes to find a way to connect with each other without touching. As children explore this idea, they discover ways to encircle each other's legs or arms, straddle another person's reclined body, crawl through spread legs, or mirror another child's hand or foot movements—all appropriate though different solutions to the challenge. As children discover their own motor solutions, they develop self-confidence and independence, and their fear of failure lessens. In the current educational milieu of high-stakes testing, where there is often only one right answer to any question, movement exploration is invaluable for solidifying children's view of themselves as able to make things happen and to figure out solutions.

Explicit Teaching Some children benefit from a more direct approach. Teachers using a direct approach describe, model, and demonstrate the necessary components of the physical skill being taught. A benefit of the direct approach is that it is immediately clear if children can or cannot perform the skills.

An additional benefit of explicit teaching is that it is efficient. It takes less time to show children how to do movements than to let them figure them out on their own. Children also learn to do the skills correctly, which can prevent injuries. On the other hand, the direct approach leaves little room for creativity and individuality. During early childhood, the direct approach should be used infrequently and in an individualized way rather than as a primary teaching strategy (Pica, 2014).

Teacher-Supported Practice Young children are usually highly motivated to master new skills. But even when teachers use appropriate teaching strategies, children still need plenty of practice to master physical skills. In one research-proven, child-centered strategy called "mastery motivational climate," teachers provide materials and plan lesson components, but children initiate and participate according to their preferences (Goodway, Ozmun, Derringer, & Lee, 2013).

Without opportunities to practice and perfect what they are learning to do, children may never achieve proficient levels of skill, particularly children living in poverty who are often found to be significantly delayed in motor skills development (Goodway, Robinson, & Crowe, 2010). When children are learning new skills, and even while they are practicing, children need verbal prompts and reminders, feedback on performance, and encouragement to keep trying (Goodway, Ozmun, Derringer, & Lee, 2013). Read the *What Works* feature for examples of effective ways to teach physical skills to all children.

Teachers' attitudes are extremely important. When adults are not enthusiastic about motor play and do not engage with children, children are unlikely to be enthusiastic and

What Works

Teaching Physical Skills

Children don't automatically develop the skills of throwing, catching, kicking, skipping, climbing, balancing, and the like; they require instruction and practice. To acquire foundational skills, children need the guidance of involved adults within an environment that has developmentally appropriate equipment. They learn both through free play and exploration and through adult-guided instruction. Young children are most likely to learn physical skills and develop enjoyment and confidence in physical activity when teachers use these strategies:

- *Design tasks for gradual and sequential learning.* Keep in mind that tasks should be more general than specific. You could say, "Show me that you can throw the ball at the wall," rather than "See if you can hit the bull's-eye."

- *Break down motor skills into small, "do-able" actions.* The goal is for everyone to participate, even if this means partial participation for some. For instance, if a child cannot grip a racket to strike a balloon, encourage her to strike the balloon with her hand.

- *Provide cues that help children refine specific skills.* Observe their movements and make helpful, concrete suggestions. The best cues provide children with little steps that help them learn a skill more quickly and correctly and, at the same time, keep them from forming bad habits. When children are learning to catch, for example, some will benefit from the tip "Keep your eye on the ball."

- *Embed skills in playful experiences.* Suggest that children who are learning to hop can pretend to be rabbits. When they're practicing long jumps, place mats in a row to be the river they are trying to jump across. Give them fun challenges, such as "Let's see how many ways we can think of to get across the room besides walking."

- *Individualize.* Simplify or add complexity to fit the child's skill level. For example, if a child is having trouble throwing a ball into the air and catching it, try giving him a larger rubber ball and asking him to bounce and catch it.

- *Show skills in action.* Many children have difficulty learning physical actions from verbal instruction alone; they may do better when they can watch someone modeling the skill.

- *Offer a variety of tasks, materials, and learning centers.* Help children practice specific skills and learn to use different types and sizes of equipment by offering them variety. For example, provide balls of all sizes, shapes, and weights in the form of beanbags, yarn balls, sock balls, and rubber and plastic balls. Then set up centers to allow children to practice throwing, bouncing, and rolling the balls in different ways.

Source: Excerpted and adapted from "Physical Education in Kindergarten," by S. W. Sanders, 2006, pp. 135–137, in *K Today: Teaching and Learning in the Kindergarten Year*, edited by D. F. Gullo, Washington, DC: NAEYC. Reprinted with permission from the National Association for the Education of Young Children (NAEYC). www.naeyc.org.

persist. The first step to effective teaching is for teachers themselves to be physically active and interested in meaningful physical activity.

Effective Health Curriculum and Teaching

Teaching children healthy and safe practices is the best way to support health and wellness. Nutrition education is also an essential part of the curriculum.

Learning Safety An important curriculum goal is educating children about accident prevention, particularly on the playground. Accidents are actually preventable. Teachers need to teach children safe ways to play and interact in indoor as well as outdoor environments to prevent injuries. Safety should be considered from the perspectives of adults as well as children.

Learning how to use wheeled toys safely is an important curriculum goal. Universal use of helmets by children ages 4 to 15 when riding tricycles or bicycles could prevent deaths, head injuries, and scalp and face injuries (CDC, 2013). Children need to understand how to operate wheeled toys without injuring themselves or others—in other words, they need to learn the rules of the road.

Learning Wellness The curriculum goal of disease prevention is a natural extension of children's interest in their own bodies (Hendricks & Smith, 1995). Children's

FIGURE 15.5 Choose MyPlate Helps Children Learn Healthy Eating Habits The U.S. Department of Agriculture uses the image MyPlate to teach children to make healthy food choices. *Source:* Reprinted from MyPlate, U.S. Department of Agriculture, no date, retrieved April 5, 2015, from http://www.choosemyplate.gov.

▶ **Classroom Connection**

Watch this video and observe how this teacher encourages healthy eating and incorporates playful experience and physical activity into the nutrition lesson.

shared experiences of visiting the doctor and dentist and getting regular immunizations are conceptual organizers for this topic. They can also learn about germs and how germs are spread from one person to another. Many children's books treat the topic of visiting the physician and other health and wellness topics. Examples include *Corduroy Goes to the Doctor* (Freeman, 2001), *Wash Your Hands!* (Ross, 2000), and *Germs Are Not for Sharing* (Verdick, 2006).

Nutrition Education Good nutrition in early childhood is related to children's readiness for school and academic success (Pascoe, Shaikh, Forbis, & Etzel, 2007). Children who eat a nutritionally poor diet, such as fast food, score lower on tests of reading and math achievement (Tobin, 2013). Even skipping breakfast is associated with poorer cognitive performance (Liu, Hwang, Dickerman, & Compher, 2013), and eating breakfast cereal improves mood and alertness (Smith, 2010). However, attention and memory are improved with breakfast cereal that is lower in sugar content (Ingwersen, Defeyter, Kennedy, Wesnes, & Scholey, 2007).

The goals of nutrition education are teaching children about healthy eating, introducing children to different types of foods, and promoting exploration of and interest in a well-balanced diet (Kalich, Bauer, & McPartlin, 2014). The U.S. Department of Agriculture's MyPlate symbol, depicted in Figure 15.5, is a good vehicle for helping children to learn about the kinds and amounts of food to eat each day. The message of MyPlate is that half of children's daily diet should be fruits and vegetables. They also should eat more whole grains and, after age 2, they should drink 1% or nonfat milk.

One effective strategy to help children make better nutritional choices is to teach them about *anytime* foods and *sometime* foods. This idea is part of the Healthy Habits for Life curriculum developed by Sesame Workshop, Nemours Health and Prevention Services, and KidHealth.org (2007). One of children's favorite characters, Cookie Monster, makes it clear that cookies are a "sometime" food, like potato chips or ice cream; whereas bananas or carrots can be eaten anytime. Research shows that children's eating habits can be powerfully influenced by role models. For example, in one study, when children watched Elmo promote eating broccoli rather than chocolate, their interest in eating broccoli increased 127% (Cohen & Kotler, 2005).

Nutrition education has the potential to affect children's health behaviors for a lifetime, particularly when the family is included in the education process. Educating children begins by offering them a variety of foods as part of a balanced diet. Nutrition education continues by interesting children in where food comes from, how it is prepared, and the wide variety of food that is available for inclusion in a balanced diet to help children grow up healthy. Serving meals family style also controls portion size because children tend to choose the amount they will eat and not more.

For babies and toddlers, teachers can start by offering food on demand and at regular intervals. Then, as toddlers begin to eat table food, teachers give them repeated opportunities to try new foods. Color, texture, and temperature of food may be as important as taste during initial offerings.

Preschool and kindergarten children often have a reputation as picky eaters. This suggests a go-slow approach to introducing new food choices and refraining from too much external pressure to try new things. Children need repeated opportunities to try new foods; they may need to see a new food many times before they are willing to taste it. One strategy is to set up a self-serve snack center, similar to the other learning centers in the classroom (Bernath & Masi, 2006). Food is presented in small store-bought packages or preproportioned in cups with napkins, plates, and utensils for children to serve themselves.

While children should be exposed to new foods and encouraged to try them, they should not be coerced to try foods, using "one bite" rules. When adults control children's eating

practices in this way, children can develop un-
healthy relationships with food and mealtimes
(McBride & Dev, 2014). Some children are reluctant eaters due to their developmental disabilities. It is particularly important in this situation
to work with children's parents to support children's nutrition while also supporting healthy
eating behaviors. In the feature, *Including All
Children*, read how one teacher supported a
child with autism in his nutrition and eating.

Cooking with Children Cooking is
an excellent way to introduce and encourage
children to try new foods. Classroom cooking
offers many learning opportunities including
seeing foods change state as they cook (sci-
ence), measuring and mixing ingredients (mathematics), introducing new vocabulary and
reading recipes (language and literacy), and predicting outcomes (science) and preferences. Many resources such as children's books and simple recipes are available to help
early childhood teachers cook with children in the classroom (Colker, 2005). Also, cooking can be a way to reinforce understandings about food allergies and why some foods
such as peanuts may not be allowed in the classroom.

Young children can be picky
eaters. Cooking is one of the
most effective ways to get them
to try new, more healthy foods.

Routines That Promote Health and Wellness Young children need adult
support to remember and practice what they have learned about health and wellness.
Without including healthy practices in the daily, weekly, and monthly routines, children
aren't likely to integrate them into their lives and apply them at home and in other spheres.

Children's health is also affected by their growing independence in carrying out personal routines, their awareness of health and safety concerns, and their ability to follow

Including All Children
Nutrition and Children with Developmental Disabilities

Snack time is busy in Mara's preschool classroom. After washing their hands, 14 children gather for snack
at two tables. They talk about the food, ask questions,
and pass dishes family style. One child, Henry, passes
the snack dishes, but does not take food. Mara puts
out an additional dish of crackers, and Henry, a child
with autism, takes some of these and passes to his
classmates. Henry eats only crackers at school. When
Henry first started in her class, he would not sit at the
snack table. He would take a cracker and run around
the room, and would scream and cry when encouraged
to take tastes of the snack food. Mara was concerned
that Henry was not able to join the class at snack time,
and that he might not be getting sufficient nutrition.

Working with Henry's parents and a nutrition therapist,
Mara learned about Henry's sensory sensitivity and his
difficulty joining in meals. She learned that Henry was
not just a "picky eater," but that he was very afraid of
trying new foods and was anxious when around new

foods. She also learned that Henry drank a fortified
drink several times a day to meet his nutritional needs
while he was learning to eat a variety of foods.

Mara, Henry's parents, and the nutrition therapist developed a set of goals around mealtimes, including
washing hands, sitting at the table for initially short
and increasing periods of time, and using a spoon to
serve a small amount of crackers that his parents provided. Mara asked if his parents would provide crackers for all the children, so that Henry could experience
sharing the food with others. At first, Henry sat only a
few seconds at the table, but after a while he was able
to stay at the snack table for almost the entire time
with his classmates. Last week, Henry even tried a
piece of toast that was offered at snack time. Henry's
parents were thrilled that he was making progress, and
Mara was very happy that she had found a way for
Henry to join the other children during this very special time of the preschool day.

rules and take steps to keep themselves safe and healthy. Teachers can use different strategies with different children to teach health and wellness practices, such as hand washing or sanitizing table tops before lunchtime, offering specific feedback (such as washing the front, back, and in between the fingers), creating or adding a challenge such as washing for as long as the child sings "Happy Birthday," or modeling appropriate hand washing for a child who skips steps.

We began this chapter with alarming statistics about the health and fitness of our nation's children and the disturbing childhood obesity crisis. Having explored the continuum of motor development and effective curriculum and teaching strategies for promoting health and fitness, we return to Ms. Perez and Ms. Aliote's classroom to see how they implement these practices.

   Check Your Understanding 15.5: Effective Curriculum and Teaching to Promote Physical Fitness and Health

Revisiting the Case Study

. . . Ms. Perez and Ms. Aliote's Classroom

At the beginning of this chapter, we visited the classroom of Ms. Perez and Ms. Aliote. These teachers plan indoor and outdoor environments that foster children's physical development and learning. They encourage gross-motor and fine-motor skills with a wide variety of materials and experiences in the classroom and on the playground.

Outdoors, children engage in unstructured play, such as tricycle riding, climbing, and running, as well as structured physical activities—learning how to kick a ball at a higher level of proficiency and playing kickball with a friend. These teachers use a variety of effective teaching strategies and adapt for individual children's needs. Ms. Perez intentionally taught Allison the skills she needed for kicking the ball. At the same time, she helped Drew build his social-emotional and language skills as she encouraged him to ask Allison if he could play, and they began to play cooperatively.

The teachers incorporate health education in their day by offering healthy food choices and prompting children to wash their hands before eating. Children's physical fitness and health are priorities in this classroom. Their teachers integrate these topics in fun and meaningful ways throughout the day. The end result is that these children are more likely to remain active and healthy throughout their lives. ■

15 Chapter Summary

- Given the benefits of physical activity for young children as well as the risks of poor levels of fitness, teachers need to ensure that promoting physical development and health are core curriculum goals and not simply add-ons. Children's physical fitness and health have become urgent concerns as the rate of childhood obesity in America has increased significantly.

- Physical development—gross-motor, fine-motor, and perceptual-motor development—follows a relatively predictable sequence that is influenced by both maturation and experience.

- Teachers foster children's physical development by providing age-appropriate materials and learning environments, supporting play and movement exploration, and explicitly teaching motor skills.

- Children need opportunities for unstructured and structured play, including rough-and-tumble play, throughout the day to promote physical activity and develop skills. Outdoor play is a particularly valuable context for promoting physical activity. Some children today do not get enough exposure to nature and its many benefits.

- Physical fitness and health and wellness habits are formed early in life. Children benefit from teachers who intentionally plan engaging curriculum to promote physical development and fitness.

- Health education curriculum goals include teaching children health and safety procedures such as emergency preparedness, practices for preventing illness and injury, and good nutrition.

Key Terms

- auditory awareness
- body composition
- cardiorespiratory (aerobic) system
- directional awareness
- fine-motor development
- fine-motor manipulative movements
- flexibility
- gross-motor development
- gross-motor manipulative movements
- hazard
- health-related fitness
- locomotor movements
- motor planning
- muscular strength and endurance
- nature-deficit disorder
- perceptual motor development
- physical fitness
- pincer grasp
- risk
- risk vs. challenge continuum
- rough-and-tumble play or big body play
- spatial awareness
- stability movements
- structured physical activity
- temporal awareness
- unstructured free play

 Demonstrate Your Learning

Click here to assess how well you've learned the content in this chapter.

Readings and Websites

Administration for Children and Families, U.S. Department of Health and Human Services (2015). *Caring for our children basics: Health and safety foundations for early care and education.* Retrieved from http://www.acf.hhs.gov/sites/default/files/ecd/caring_for_our_children_basics.pdf.

Aronson, S. S. (2012). *Healthy young children: A manual for programs* (5th ed.). Washington, DC: National Association for the Education of Young Children.

Honig, A. S. (2015). *Experiencing nature with young children: Awakening delight, curiosity, and a sense of stewardship.* Washington, DC: NAEYC.

Rivkin, M. S. (2014). *The great outdoors: Advocating for natural spaces for young children* (Rev. ed.). Washington, DC: National Association for the Education of Young Children.

Be Active Kids

On this website, you'll find resources to help adults support children's healthy play based physical activity and nutrition, in child care programs, school, and at home.

Playground Professionals

This website has many resources for planning outdoor play environments for young children.

Nature Action Collaborative for Children (NACC)

Visit this website to find out about developmentally appropriate educational resources designed to enhance children's connection with nature.

Natural Learning Initiative

This website highlights how the environment can act as a third teacher, including "Preventing Obesity by Design," using landscape architecture, natural materials, and developmentally appropriate play settings to create natural playgrounds.

16 Putting It All Together in Practice: Making a Difference for Children

Learning Outcomes

After studying this chapter, you should be able to:

16.1 Describe what it is like to be a teacher of infants and toddlers, preschoolers, kindergartners or primary-grade children; and analyze some factors to consider in deciding which age group you want to teach.

16.2 Apply the NAEYC Code of Ethical Conduct, describe the role of early childhood professionals as advocates, and analyze the obligations and commitments to children that early childhood professionals must understand and embrace.

© Kathryn Tunstal

Students are gathering on the first day of class in a college course titled *Foundations of Early Childhood Education*. Each individual contemplates the next semester from his or her own experience. Consider how their diverse paths have led them to this shared place. Aisha has always wanted to be a teacher. Her mother and grandmother were teachers before her, and education is strongly valued in her family. When she was a little girl, her favorite thing to do was to "play" school. She is excited that this class will begin her journey toward that lifelong dream. Laron is a little surprised to find himself here. He never thought of education as a career goal. But the last two summers, he worked as a lifeguard and discovered that giving swimming lessons to preschool-aged children was the most fun he'd ever had in a job. He felt so good every time a 4-year-old gave him a giant smile after overcoming that initial fear of the water. Now he's considering early childhood education as a major. Julienne is certain about why she is here. She has decided to get a dual major in early childhood education and early intervention in order to be certified as an early childhood special educator. Her twin brother has cerebral palsy, and she is committed to serving children with disabilities in inclusive settings.

Compared to Aisha, Laron, and Julienne, Rita is feeling nervous. She is a 32-year-old single mother of three who is starting college now that her children are all in school. She can't help feeling a little out of place with all these younger people. But raising her own children and taking care of nieces and nephews made her want to become a teacher herself. Oralie has a similar story. She volunteered in her children's Head Start program, obtained a CDA Credential, was employed as an assistant teacher, and now is pursuing her college degree with support from her supervisors.

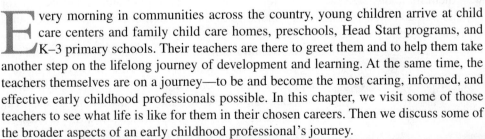

The other students in the class have their own stories—all different. Some will learn that they have little interest or aptitude for becoming teachers. If so, it is wise for them to pursue another field. Others will be amazed at all there is to learn about young children. They assumed that teaching young children would be simple compared to older children, but they will come to understand the complexity as well as the challenge of this work. Eventually a number of them will be better parents for having taken this course of study. Most important, many of them will become the effective teachers that every child needs and deserves. ■

Every morning in communities across the country, young children arrive at child care centers and family child care homes, preschools, Head Start programs, and K–3 primary schools. Their teachers are there to greet them and to help them take another step on the lifelong journey of development and learning. At the same time, the teachers themselves are on a journey—to be and become the most caring, informed, and effective early childhood professionals possible. In this chapter, we visit some of those teachers to see what life is like for them in their chosen careers. Then we discuss some of the broader aspects of an early childhood professional's journey.

Throughout this book, we describe ways that effective teachers help build strong foundations of development and learning for young children. This work has three interconnected dimensions. Effective teachers must:

- Know children—*who* they teach.
- Understand *how* to teach—the complex roles of the teacher, which include building caring relationships with children, working with families, planning and implementing curriculum, assessing children, and adapting teaching strategies.
- Know *what* to teach—the goals and content for children's learning and development.

Experienced teachers know that these dimensions of their work cannot be separated. They teach the whole child. And they do not work in isolation; they are connected to colleagues, families, and communities. One of the biggest challenges for teachers is putting it all together.

Life as an Early Childhood Educator

Among the major questions early childhood educators face is which age group they would most like to work with and why. Many teachers change jobs, settings, and/or age levels over the course of a career; however, most early childhood teachers gravitate toward one age group and stay there.

The following sections describe things to consider as you weigh your career options. After reading about a "day in the life" of teachers in diverse settings, you will see some ways in which teachers engage in effective practices. In reality, there is no such thing as a typical day in any program for children. There should be a predictable schedule and routine, a prepared age-appropriate environment, and a planned curriculum. But children themselves are unpredictable. They change from day to day, in wonderful and challenging ways, and they come up with great ideas that lead in new directions. In addition, conditions impinge that are beyond a teacher's control—for example, an emergency or a serendipitous event. Teachers need to be prepared to handle any and all situations.

In many ways, it is the unpredictable nature of teaching young children that makes it such fascinating work. A career in early childhood education is filled with never-ending rewards and challenges. It is a field like no other, as we see from brief visits to classrooms in the following sections.

Caring for and Educating Infants and Young Toddlers

Some people do not consider those who work with babies and toddlers to be teachers. Because much physical care is required for this age group, the term *caregiver* is often used for this role. Nevertheless, babies are always learning in the context of loving care (Copple, Bredekamp, Koralek, & Charner, 2013a). We choose to call all professional caregivers *teachers.*

A Day in the Life of an Infant/Toddler Teacher   Victoria Thomas and Luisa Franco co-teach a group of eight babies and young toddlers. Their children stay with them for about 2½ years to provide continuity of care and secure relationships for the children and their families. Each morning as the children arrive, Victoria and Luisa greet them warmly and casually chat with the family member who drops them off. They learn vital information about the baby's sleeping and eating patterns, as well as who is feeling fussy or especially happy. Luisa positions the three nonmobile babies where they can watch the action and hear her talking as she picks up little Ella, who is clearly in need of a diaper change. Throughout the day, the teachers will engage in feeding, diapering, and hand-washing routines as the children eat and rest on their own schedules.

After meeting Ella's immediate needs, Luisa puts Sam down for his midmorning nap and then positions Foster and Lydia on the rug for some tummy time. She gets down and plays with them at their eye level with a ball that makes music as it rolls. The babies love swatting the ball to produce the sounds.

High-quality early childhood programs provide a joyous experience for both children and teachers.

© Jules Selmes/Pearson Education

Meanwhile, across the room, Victoria calmly plays on the rug with the mobile toddlers, who are just beginning to talk. They are enchanted by a set of large, plastic, colored blocks that they can pick up and place together, forming a big pattern on the floor. Victoria describes what they are doing as it happens: "Alan has a red peg. He put it next to the green one." Alan starts to fuss when Wanda pushes against him. "Wanda, you are in Alan's space. Can you move just a little?" asks Victoria in a soft voice. Alan calms and Wanda smacks a kiss on his cheek. Victoria smiles, "You're a good friend, Wanda."

As the play time comes to an end, Victoria says, "Let's see who is big and strong and can help me pick up the pegs." As Victoria places the full bin onto the shelf, Gary holds on, too. Victoria says, "It's heavy. We have to lift it up high." Gary responds, "Up," and Victoria says, "Yes, let's put it *up* on the shelf. Now, let's go outside. It's warm and we can play on the ride-on toys or go for a walk in the stroller."

In this brief scene, we see effective practices in action. Victoria and Luisa create a calm and warm climate for these young children, focusing on building a relationship with each child. They model kindness and social skills, which even these very young children are starting to emulate. They weave into play ways to support all areas of development and learning. The teachers help the children develop physical skills (rolling the ball, placing the pegs) and knowledge about the world while building language skills. They model rich vocabulary such as spatial relation words like *next to* and *up* and explain the phrase "You're in his space." And they are keen to create new experiences to stimulate children's senses and interests, such as being outside in nature, the beginning of science learning.

▶ **Classroom Connection**

This video takes you inside a high-quality infant and toddler program. Observe the interactions between the teachers and children. How do the teachers feel about their work? What do you think are the most gratifying aspects of working with this age group?

Throughout the day, Victoria and Luisa keep careful records about each baby—what they eat and drink, bowel movements, their moods, and any special accomplishments—to share with parents at the end of the day. Observing and recording is an effective way of assessing children and communicating what families want and need to know. These exchanges help build close relationships with the families, who then feel more secure about leaving their precious infants in the care of others.

Considerations for Working with Infants and Toddlers Some people would never consider working with babies and toddlers; others can think of nothing more rewarding. Teachers of infants and toddlers usually work in child care centers, Early Head Start programs, or family child care homes. Table 16.1 lists some considerations in deciding whether to work with these very young children.

Teaching the Whole Child in the Preschool

Three- to five-year-olds are some of the most interesting people in the world. They are miniature navigators, explorers, writers, artists, acrobats, linguists, and comedians (although much of their humor can be silly or of the bathroom variety). At this age, their potential seems boundless.

Teachers who are drawn to preschoolers have many choices of work site or employer. They may choose Head Start, a child care center, family child care, or a public or private preschool. The length of time the children spend in the program will make some difference in what a teacher's day is like. Although preschoolers are more capable of taking care of their own needs, they continue to need vigilant supervision and a lot of physical care and attention. They also need experiences that engage their minds and actively involve them in the world around them (Copple, Bredekamp, Koralek, & Charner, 2013b). Most of all, they need intentional teachers to help them achieve their full potential (Epstein, 2014).

A Day in the Life of a Preschool Teacher As a white van pulls up at Small Steps Learning Center, Masami and his assistant teacher, Ana, greet the children—some

TABLE 16.1 Considerations for Infant/Toddler Teachers

Working with infants and toddlers can be difficult but also delightful as described in this table.

IF YOU ARE THINKING OF TEACHING INFANTS AND TODDLERS, YOU MIGHT CONSIDER THAT:

On the One Hand	On the Other Hand
A great deal of physical care is required—diapering, feeding, dressing, frequent hand washing, and constant supervision.	Caregiving routines provide time to connect and talk one-on-one with babies and to build loving relationships.
Babies' actions are repetitive and can be frustrating—they drop the cup off the high chair again and again to see what happens.	Babies' actions are obvious evidence of their development and opportunities to share in their joy of discovery.
Babies and toddlers grow and develop so rapidly that just when you think you know what to expect, they change.	From the earliest moments of life, young children demonstrate that they are unique, so life with them is always challenging and never boring.
Caring for babies requires close, constant communication with families. Relationships can be difficult due to competition, differences of opinion, or diverse cultural values.	Relationships with families can be close and rewarding, marked by shared power and responsibility as teachers and parents learn from each other and work toward common goals.
Babies and toddlers are so vulnerable and dependent on adults to protect their health, safety, and emotional security that the responsibility can feel overwhelming.	Protecting very young children from harm as they discover and rediscover the world every day is immensely rewarding.
Babies and toddlers can't tell you what they want and need. They cry and fuss and can make adults feel helpless or inadequate.	Babies and toddlers communicate their needs and wants through cries, expressions, and gestures. Nothing compares with a baby's or a toddler's smile and belly laugh.

in English and some in Spanish. The children head off to wash their hands and settle in for breakfast. Ana helps them serve oatmeal and orange slices and pour their own milk, while Masami sits and begins a conversation about the bus ride.

The sixteen 3- and 4-year-olds live in an economically disadvantaged community. Some have been exposed to violence and a few have serious emotional problems. Masami and Ana's program places a strong emphasis on building social skills and emotional self-regulation. They use a comprehensive curriculum that promotes language and thinking

Intentional preschool teachers work with small groups of children at times during the day to assess their current levels of ability and scaffold their learning.

through interesting projects that build science, math, and literacy skills. It also includes lots of art and music. To achieve the curriculum goals and build secure, continuous relationships, Masami and Ana each work with a group of eight children at times during the school day, which lasts from 8:30 A.M. to 3:30 P.M.. For instance, half the group will go outside with Ana while the rest stay in with Masami, and then they switch.

After breakfast, Masami leads the children in singing and then reads a book about a new baby. The group is involved in a long-term science project about how people grow and change. Then they discuss the choices for center time. Learning centers include dramatic play (set up as a hospital with props and dress-up materials), creative art, math/manipulatives, writing center, library area, and blocks. Masami talks with the children about where they plan to play and what they'd like to do, which helps them regulate their behavior and thinking. The children are becoming better listeners. As they describe their plans, Ana helps them leave the group and transition to the next activity. Sharde calls out, "I got room at my table for Keyona's wheelchair."

During center time, Masami works with a small group in the art center. They examine their own baby pictures, look in the mirror, and use different media including digital cameras to represent how they look. The discussion centers on how big they can make their drawings. They get excited at the idea of projecting their faces on the large interactive whiteboard. Some children write recognizable letters on their pictures, while others dictate their thoughts for Masami to write. In the dramatic play area, Assata dresses as the doctor while Ben and Rhonda bring their new baby for a checkup. Ayah goes to the writing center, makes marks on a piece of paper, and hands it to Assata, "Here's a letter."

Mia, who has just turned 3, heads toward the restroom. Ana congratulates her on listening to her body and getting to the toilet in time. Mia beams in response. Ana helps her get her pants buttoned (she pulls them up all by herself) and then they wash their hands. In the library area, Arturo studies an information book about baby animals. Ana talks with him about how some look like their mothers, and some do not. Their conversation continues as Arturo, who was adopted from Costa Rica, explains that he doesn't look like his mom, either.

After cleanup, the children join Masami on the carpet and tell him about what they did during activity time. Mia proudly says she went to the toilet (although that is not exactly what she said!). Arturo says he read a book; others talk about how they observed each other's drawings of themselves—"Marco has brown eyes and he made them blue."

On the playground, Arturo and Kiesha ride on the wheeled toys. Mia starts climbing to the loft of the playhouse. Jorge calls to her to join him in the sandbox. Masami asks Mia if she heard Jorge's invitation. She nods. He coaches her to tell Jorge she wants to climb, so he will know what her answer is.

After lunch, the children settle in for naps. Ana and Masami play soft music, pat a few backs and soon the children sleep. After naptime, the children find several activity areas, including a self-service snack area. Children write their names or make a mark by their photo when they wash their hands and serve themselves a snack.

At the end of the day, Masami and Ana meet to review the day and record their observations of the children's progress. Masami plans to inform Mia's mother about her toileting success, and Arturo's mother about his reflections on adoption. They also plan ways to build vocabulary through children's interests in babies and their growing bodies.

 Classroom Connection

In this video, you will hear experienced teachers describe the joys and rewards of teaching in a high-quality preschool. Note the children's and parent's evaluations of the preschools and also children's growing competence as young learners.

https://www.youtube.com/watch?v=6LNAmFROxjA&app=desktop

Considerations for Working with Preschoolers Ana and Masami's day is far busier than this general portrait can communicate. As we saw in the brief interactions with Mia, they must know each child and how to support her or his progress. They plan ahead but are constantly thinking on their feet as they interact with individuals and groups. Table 16.2 lists some things to consider in contemplating becoming a preschool teacher.

TABLE 16.2 Considerations for Preschool Teachers	
Preschoolers are usually enchanting and enthusiastic explorers, which makes preschool teaching a fun and rewarding career.	
IF YOU ARE THINKING OF TEACHING PRESCHOOL, YOU MIGHT CONSIDER THAT:	
On the One Hand	On the Other Hand
Preschoolers become increasingly capable of taking care of their own physical needs, but still need help with skills like toileting, feeding, and dressing (zipping, tying). Messiness and spills are normal.	Routine caregiving and meals provide times to interact one-on-one or in small groups and enjoy children as individuals. They also provide learning opportunities.
Many preschoolers have difficulty regulating their emotions and behavior and can be aggressive. Teachers can feel like they spend all their time guiding behavior.	Effective teachers help children make great strides in social-emotional learning and development. Behavior is less of a problem when children have interesting things to do and learn.
Preschool children are active and curious and can be loud and boisterous. Teaching them requires patience and can be exhausting.	Preschoolers are competent, active learners both physically and mentally. They try to make sense of the world and take on new challenges. Preschool teachers are constantly learning with and about them, and taking on new challenges, too.
Preschool children are all different in so many ways, making it hard to teach a large group. Working with diverse cultural groups and languages can be daunting. Successful inclusion of children with special needs can be difficult.	Individual differences in children are what make preschoolers so interesting and enjoyable. Cultural backgrounds and language are fascinating aspects of everyone's identity. Inclusion, with appropriate support, benefits all children.
Preschool programs must meet standards for operation that can seem onerous. Some preschools measure child outcomes and stress teachers' accountability for children's learning.	Standards are designed to protect children and support their healthy development. Meeting them also protects teachers. Professional educators care about children achieving developmentally appropriate goals and are willing to be accountable for children's progress and learning.
Preschools are usually staffed with a teacher and an assistant, requiring skills for working with and perhaps supervising another adult, as well as working with children.	Having two teachers provides better teacher-child ratios, creating more opportunity for individual attention and small-group interaction. Different teachers have different interests and abilities to bring to the class. Collaborating, they can be more creative and effective than alone.
Working with preschoolers requires frequent, almost daily communication with families. Some families are demanding, whereas others are uninvolved.	Partnering with families makes teachers more effective. Children sense when their parents are respected and feel more comfortable and connected to teachers.

Teaching the Whole Child in the Kindergarten

Kindergarten holds a special place in children's lives. Even if a child has been in child care for the previous 5 years, entering kindergarten marks the major transition to formal school. Given this momentous event, kindergarten teachers are very important to children. They help children negotiate a significant life change and build the foundation for their future educational career.

A Day in the Life of a Kindergarten Teacher The morning bell rings as Hope Millner greets her 21 kindergartners at the classroom door. Toting backpacks and displaying mostly grins, these 5- and 6-year-olds feel very grown up as they navigate the corridors and expectations of "real" school. After a brief settling-in period, the group gathers on the rug for a morning meeting.

"Let's review what happened yesterday, and think ahead to today's plans," Hope suggests. The children wave their hands in the air for a turn to talk about the visit to the aquarium. Although the sharks made the biggest impression, some children were enthralled by the stingrays. "I hear from your descriptions that you were observing very carefully," Hope says. "I know that most of you used your clipboards, made some drawings. During choice time this morning, I'd like you to refer to those and write in your journals about what you saw and learned. We also have digital photos that we'll put on the computer and project on the wall to help you remember details. Now, I'm going to read parts of an information book about sea life that you can look at later in the library area."

During the morning activity period, two children feed the fish in the classroom aquarium and write a brief note: "Fsh et." Hope assists the children in their journal writing, helping them with letters and words, but emphasizes communicating their ideas rather than correct spelling. She also works with a small group who are still struggling with recognizing letters. An inviting library area is stocked with a variety of diverse, high-quality books at varying reading levels, including multiple copies of kindergarten-level texts. Storybooks and information books reflect the cultural and linguistic diversity of the group. Some children listen to audio books and follow along in the printed book.

Following the midmorning snack, children independently browse or read self-selected familiar books, especially ones that Hope has previously read aloud, such as the fish book. The field trip, books, and ongoing science study of sea life broaden the children's background knowledge and vocabulary. To build reading comprehension, Hope guides discussions about what is being read or listened to. She asks the children to predict events, retell or act out stories, and notice when a text does not make sense.

The kindergartners also have physical education classes three times a week. Working with Hope, the PE teacher plans related movement activities—How would you move like you're swimming? What if you were a fish and there was no water? In the classroom, Hope has a creative art center where some children make representations of their favorite fish and underwater environments; others create simply from their imaginations. After lunch and outdoor play, the children have another 60-minute choice period before dismissal. This is a favorite time for many because they especially like dramatic play, block building, and board games. During this time, Hope works with small groups on the mathematics curriculum goals. Today, a group spontaneously decides to replicate the aquarium with unit blocks. This leads to lengthy debates about how to re-create the water because a flat piece of blue paper wouldn't really hold up the fish. At the end of the day, the group meets to reflect on their day and look forward to tomorrow.

 Classroom Connection

In this video, you'll hear about a day in the life of a kindergarten teacher. Observe how she interacts with the children, teaches literacy and math, and describes the rewards of teaching this age group.

https://www.youtube.com/watch?v=AsHCK1LLGhc

Considerations for Teaching Kindergarten

Hope Millner has taught kindergarten in a suburban school district for 15 years. In that time, she has seen changes in the curriculum, especially recently with the Common Core standards on English language arts and mathematics, and less administrative support for play. She has also observed that a higher proportion of her students now attend preschool and enter school with more basic knowledge about how the written language system works. At the same time, Hope knows that, developmentally, 5- and 6-year-olds haven't fundamentally changed and that they benefit from both "learningful play and playful learning" (Graue, 2006). Her task is to make the curriculum meaningful and engaging and to use play and other effective teaching strategies to intentionally promote each child's continuing progress. Most of all Hope is committed to a building positive, warm relationship with every child. One of the children's drawings reminds Hope of how important her job is; she literally "looms large" in the lives of her kindergartners (see Figure 16.1).

Most public school kindergartens today set high expectations for children's reading progress. How can kindergarten teachers use developmentally appropriate practices to help children build early literacy skills?

FIGURE 16.1 Kindergarten Child's Image of Her Teacher
As is clear from this kindergarten child's drawing, teachers play an enormously important role in children's lives.

One of the biggest challenges for kindergarten teachers is to provide developmentally appropriate practice, while also implementing an increasingly rigorous curriculum (Copple, Bredekamp, Koralek, & Charner, 2014b). Teaching kindergarten today involves balancing some potentially conflicting needs and goals, as demonstrated in Table 16.3.

Teaching the Whole Child in the Primary Grades

A great deal of growth and change takes place from ages 6 through 8. Similarly, the curriculum and, therefore, teachers' experiences will vary if they are teaching in the first, second, or third grade (Copple, Bredekamp, Koralek, & Charner, 2014a). Here we visit a first-grade classroom, but the considerations for teaching in the primary grades generally apply across the age span.

A Day in the Life of a First-Grade Teacher Lina Truesdale's 22 first graders have very different backgrounds and abilities. Early in the school year, Lina spent time getting to know the children and assessing their abilities. She found that five of them were reading at the second-grade level or above, and four did not know all the letters and sounds.

TABLE 16.3 Considerations for Kindergarten Teachers

With the increased academic demands of kindergarten, committed teachers must strive to engage in developmentally appropriate, effective practices that meet the needs of the whole child.

IF YOU ARE THINKING OF TEACHING KINDERGARTEN, YOU MIGHT CONSIDER THAT:

On the One Hand	On the Other Hand
Kindergarten is part of the formal school system, often more structured and with more challenging learning standards and curriculum expectations than in the past.	Teachers are still the most important influence on the quality and appropriateness of children's experiences in school. The school system tends to offer higher salaries, better benefits, and more job security than do child care or preschool programs.
Kindergartners vary widely in their prior learning opportunities both at home or in preschool. Teachers face the challenge of teaching a general curriculum to diverse learners.	Effective teachers don't expect all the children to achieve the same thing, at the same time, in the same way. By individualizing teaching and working with small groups, teachers experience the rewards of seeing children who are initially behind their peers make great strides.
Kindergartners don't think and learn exactly like adults and older children—there are limits to their understanding of complex concepts.	Kindergartners are more competent learners and thinkers than many people assume. They strive to make sense of the world, solve problems, and are fascinated by learning about topics that interest them.
Kindergarten classes are usually larger than those in preschool and teachers do not always have the benefit of an assistant, making it more difficult for teachers to individualize their teaching.	Most schools have multiple kindergarten classrooms, and teachers can collaborate with colleagues within grade level and across grades. Specialists in music, art, physical education, and special education may also be available to offer support.
Kindergartners can function independently in self-help skills and need less adult support than preschoolers.	Kindergartners are still young children who rely on teachers for emotional as well as physical support and usually want to please their teachers.
The kindergarten curriculum tends to focus on literacy and math, raising concerns that there is insufficient attention to social-emotional development.	Good kindergarten teachers know that both children's cognition and social development are essential. Their teaching integrates academic skills and concepts with positive social-emotional development and warm, responsive relationships.
Kindergarten may be included in school district accountability requirements. Children are sometimes tested inappropriately.	Effective teachers use ongoing assessment of children's learning to adapt curriculum and teaching. They don't place undue emphasis on formal tests but do hold themselves accountable to children and families.

The district curriculum is designed for children somewhere in the middle. But like every good first-grade teacher, Lina knows that she teaches children first and curriculum second.

The school district requires that there be a 90-minute language arts block each morning in first grade. Lina knows that the children are more likely to stay energetic and focused if she varies the activities during this time, and makes sure that the children are as active as possible, both mentally and physically. She begins the morning with whole-group instruction and discussion of new concepts, introducing and explaining new vocabulary words in everyday language. Then the class divides into smaller groups. Each day, Lina works with small groups on guided reading, during which she assesses their reading comprehension and ability to monitor themselves for understanding. She coaches them to ask questions such as "Does that make sense?" "What does that mean?" and "How you know?"

A major portion of the day in primary grades is devoted to reading and writing instruction. What are some ways that intentional teachers can integrate other areas of the curriculum such as science and social studies with reading and writing?

At the same time, others read independently or in pairs. Then, children continue with individual work, such as writing in journals, while Lina observes and offers individual help as needed. She ends the language arts period with a whole-group read-aloud, which the children love. At this point in their reading journey, the books the children can decode on their own have limited vocabulary and are not as interesting as the stories that Lina reads to them. Lina keeps careful records of children's reading progress. She takes great pride in their achievements while also focusing on ways to adapt her teaching for those who are behind.

Some days the class has physical education before lunch, and other days they have music. After lunch, they play outside for 20 minutes and then return for focused math time. Again, Lina varies the teaching context. She may introduce a new math concept, such as a put-together/take-apart problem, to the whole group. Then she gives them a problem to discuss with their neighbors: "Sixteen plus what number equals 21?" The children report their solutions and reasoning to the whole group. Seven-year-old Nancy explains, "We got 5. We started with 16 and counted 17, 18, 19, 20, 21, and that's five numbers." Lina says, "That's one way to solve the problem. Is there another way?"

Lina observes children's grasp of the problem. Then, she follows the whole-group time with small-group work, during which she focuses on those who haven't grasped the new concept, or gives more difficult problems to those who need challenge. Science or social studies projects follow that integrate literacy, language, and mathematics goals.

At the end of her day, Lina meets with the other first-grade teachers to talk about effective ways of helping struggling readers and children who are having trouble grasping basic math concepts. She also seeks their advice on ways to assist Irina and Carlos, who are learning English. She plans to communicate with their families as well.

Considerations for Teaching in the Primary Grades Do you remember your first-grade teacher? What experiences come to mind? Of all your teachers between kindergarten and third grade, which ones do you remember best, and for what reasons?

The primary grades—first through third—are prime time for learning. They set the stage for much that comes after. Primary-grade teachers have a significant, measurable impact on children's educational careers and, hence, their lives. They have the opportunity to make lasting contributions to the world; their work is both demanding and stimulating, as described in Table 16.4.

▶ **Classroom Connection**

In this video, primary-grade teachers talk about the rewards of their work. As you watch, reflect on your own goals for a career in early education. What challenges and rewards do you expect?

TABLE 16.4 Considerations for Primary Grade Teachers

During the primary grades, children need to acquire the fundamentals of literacy and mathematics, which increases the emphasis on accountability but also the rewards of teaching.

IF YOU ARE THINKING OF TEACHING IN THE PRIMARY GRADES, YOU MIGHT CONSIDER THAT:

On the One Hand	On the Other Hand
Primary-grade children have longer attention spans and are increasingly capable of independent work.	Primary-grade children are still in their early childhood. They become more inattentive and exhausted from sitting and listening for long periods than from movement. Good teachers respect their need to be physically and mentally active.
By third grade, children's self-concepts, academic ability, and social skills are well established and become more difficult to change.	Teachers have the power to really make a difference to children's self-concept and academic and social success through positive relationships and intentional teaching.
The primary-grade curriculum tends to be so focused on reading that little time is left over for other subject areas.	Teaching a child to read, which for some children is a relatively easy task but for others is a seemingly overwhelming hurdle, is one of the most satisfying experiences of a teacher's life.
The primary-school curriculum is usually dictated by the district or state and can be overly prescriptive with little room for flexibility on the part of teachers.	Teachers know that children cannot be scripted. They take their cues from children and follow their lead more than they follow the prescribed lesson plan.
Primary-grade children tend to develop focused interests such as collecting, sports, music, or art.	Children's interests can be the vehicles for teaching them important skills and content. They can read and write about sports or practice number problems with a collection of their favorite objects.
Schoolwork gets harder during the primary grades, requiring greater attention and sustained effort. This discourages some learners.	Throughout the primary grades, if they have engaged and talented teachers, most children are motivated to learn and, therefore, like school.
Standardized achievement testing in third grade (and sometimes earlier) can place considerable stress on children and teachers. Test scores may be used as the sole measure of accountability.	Teachers can work across grade levels and with families to focus on helping every child learn and succeed, resisting the pressure to narrow the curriculum to what is tested. Good teachers have high expectations for every child and do not assign blame when children are behind or need extra help.

In this section, we used broad strokes to paint images of life in classrooms for teachers of children from birth through age 8. However, teachers lead important professional lives beyond the classroom, as discussed in the next section.

 Check Your Understanding 16.1: Life as an Early Childhood Educator

Beginning Your Journey as an Early Childhood Professional

Becoming a professional early childhood educator involves commitments in addition to working with children and families. In its *Standards for Early Childhood Professional Preparation*, NAEYC (Lutton, 2012) describes the following aspects of becoming a professional:

- Identifying and involving oneself with the early childhood field
- Knowing about and upholding ethical standards and other professional guidelines
- Engaging in continuous, collaborative learning to inform practice
- Integrating knowledgeable, reflective, and critical perspectives on early education
- Engaging in informed advocacy for children and the profession.

Become a Professional

A **profession** is an occupation that requires extensive education and/or specialized training, such as the legal or medical professions. Professionals draw on this specialized body of knowledge and expertise to guide their decisions and behavior, but not prescribe it (Feeney & Freeman, 2012). Professions also mandate requirements for entry and standards for practice by their members. They tend to be exclusive in that only those individuals who meet the requirements can call themselves members of the profession (Goffin, 2013).

profession An occupation that requires extensive education and/or specialized training.

Although some positions in the early childhood field abide by this strict definition of a professional, others do not. In general, teachers at the elementary level are considered professionals because they are required to have baccalaureate degrees and licenses and to participate in continuing professional development to stay current in the field. By contrast, there are no uniform educational requirements for teachers of children from birth to age 5. Nevertheless, early childhood education is evolving and can boast several key characteristics of a profession, such as a commitment to a greater good—the welfare of children, a body of knowledge to guide practice, professional associations, and a code of ethics (Feeney & Freeman, 2012; Lutton, 2012).

Become Involved in the Early Childhood Field One of the most valuable steps in becoming a professional is joining an organization that offers resources and services to its members, such as conferences and publications. These affiliations provide a sense of identity, the opportunity to establish relationships with like-minded people, and access to the most current research and information about the field. Professional associations, such as the American Medical Association, restrict membership to qualified individuals. Early childhood education, on the other hand, has several professional associations, but membership in them is open to all.

The National Association for the Education of Young Children (NAEYC) is the largest association of individuals who work with and for children from birth through age 8. Other organizations also strengthen individuals' ties to their chosen field and advocate on behalf of children, including the National Black Child Development Institute, National Council of La Raza, National Head Start Association, and the National Association for Family Child Care. Most national associations such as these also have state and/or local affiliate groups through which new and experienced teachers can find support from colleagues and mentors.

Most elementary school teachers belong to one of the two teacher unions: the National Education Association or the American Federation of Teachers. Increasingly, child care professionals are joining unions as well in order to band together for improved wages and working conditions. Many primary-grade teachers belong to a content specialty organization such as the International Literacy Association or the National Council of Teachers of Mathematics.

Uphold Professional Standards Because young children are at such a critical point in their development and learning, and because they are vulnerable and cannot articulate their own rights and needs, early childhood professionals must know about and uphold professional and ethical standards (Lutton, 2012).

Standards and guidelines vary depending on the type of program or school, but they may include those for program accreditation (NAEYC, 2007) and for developmentally appropriate practice (NAEYC, 2009). Other relevant professional standards may include:

- Child care licensing requirements
- National, state, or local standards for curriculum content and child outcomes.
- Requirements for reporting and preventing child abuse, which we discuss in detail later in this chapter.

code of ethics Defines the core values of a profession and provides guidance for what professionals should do when they encounter difficult or conflicting obligations or responsibilities in their work.

Uphold the NAEYC Code of Ethical Conduct One of the hallmarks of a profession is the existence of a **code of ethics**, which defines the core values of the field and provides guidance for what professionals should do when they encounter difficult or conflicting obligations or responsibilities in their work. The *NAEYC Code of Ethical Conduct* (NAEYC, 2011a) guides early childhood educators in their relationships with children, families, colleagues, and the broader society. Supplements to the code also exist for program administrators, principals, teacher educators, and others involved in professional development.

Individual people have their own personal views about **morality**—what they think is right and wrong and how they should behave. **Ethics** involves critical thinking about morality and the ability to make choices about one's own values. In contrast to individual morality, **professional ethics** are "the kinds of actions that are right or wrong in the workplace and are a public matter" (Feeney & Freeman, 2012, p. 6). They help individuals resolve moral dilemmas they encounter in their work.

Understanding Ethical Responsibilities Ethical responsibilities refer to the obligations that every teacher agrees to uphold with honesty, integrity, and respect. In fulfilling these responsibilities, early childhood educators should adhere to principles articulated in NAEYC's Code of Ethical Conduct. For example, the first principle is the most important and takes precedence over all others:

> Above all, we shall not harm children. We shall not participate in practices that are emotionally damaging, physically harmful, disrespectful, degrading, dangerous, exploitative, or intimidating to children. (NAEYC, 2011a, p. 3)

Other examples of teachers' ethical responsibilities include never sharing confidential information about a child or family with a person who has no legitimate need for knowing, obeying relevant laws (especially those regarding child abuse), and respecting the rights of children with disabilities. In difficult situations, teachers should consult the code for guidance about their ethical responsibilities, as illustrated in the following situation:

> Daniel is a child in Kiera Blaine's kindergarten class. His parents are divorcing and involved in a nasty custody battle. Kiera has had several conferences with Daniel's father because he is concerned about the effect of the divorce on his son. Daniel's mother hasn't said anything to Kiera. After several months, Daniel's father asks Kiera to testify on his behalf in the custody case. Kiera feels bad for Daniel's father and wants to help him, but isn't sure if she should.

Here is a case in which consulting the code can ease Kiera's mind and help her do the right thing. The code clearly states: "In cases where family members are in conflict with one another, we shall work openly, sharing our observations of the child, to help all parties involved make informed decisions. We shall refrain from becoming an advocate for one party" (NAEYC, 2011a, p. 4).

Resolving Ethical Dilemmas Sometimes the right answer in a difficult situation is not clear. An **ethical dilemma** involves deciding the right thing to do when two or more values conflict, as in the following case:

> Little Achievers is a well-respected child care center in a relatively affluent community with a long waiting list for admission. Beverly Stanos is excited to get a job there as an infant/toddler teacher that pays more than any other position she has had. Soon she begins to feel bewildered and conflicted. The center moves the babies and toddlers to a new group every 6 months; the director explains that they do this so that the babies don't get attached to the teachers.
>
> Beverly is upset; this practice goes against everything she has learned in her teacher education program about the importance of early attachments for babies' development. She checks the licensing standards and

morality Personal views about what is right and wrong and how to behave.

ethics Critical thinking about morality and people's ability to make choices about their own values.

professional ethics The kinds of actions that are right or wrong in the workplace and are a public matter.

ethical responsibilities The obligations that every teacher agrees to uphold with honesty, integrity, and respect.

ethical dilemma Deciding the right thing to do when two or more values conflict.

Over the course of your teaching career, you are likely to encounter difficult situations when you aren't sure about the right decision. In these cases, NAEYC's Code of Ethical Conduct will help you resolve ethical dilemmas.

finds nothing to prohibit the practice. Finally, she meets with the director to try to get her to change the policy based on research about child development. The director dismisses Beverly's ideas because she says the policy is a good selling point with parents who don't want their babies to become attached to anyone but them. On the one hand, Beverly thinks she should quit this job, but she knows that if she just quits nothing will change. On the other hand, she feels an obligation to tell the parents that the policy is wrong.

Although many early childhood professionals choose their jobs based on the philosophy of the school or program, many find that at some point in their career, they may encounter an ethical dilemma, as Beverly does, in which values conflict. In Beverly's case, several principles in the code apply and she should weigh them as she attempts to resolve the dilemma:

- The code states that early childhood professionals should be familiar with the knowledge base of the profession and appreciate the vulnerability of children and their dependence on adults, which Beverly clearly does in this case.
- The code also guides her to acknowledge families' child-rearing values and their right to make decisions for their children.
- The code directs early childhood educators "to do nothing that diminishes the reputation of the program in which we work unless it is violating laws and regulations designed to protect children or is violating the provisions of this Code" (NAEYC, 2011a, p. 5).

Beverly's dilemma causes her to feel stress and discomfort and forces her to consider:

- Who she is most obligated to in this situation
- What she should do to address her dilemma
- Examining the code for additional guidance

As an early childhood professional, you will most likely encounter ethical dilemmas of your own. Knowing the resources and tools to refer to is a first step in resolving the conflict. It is also important to understand the philosophy of any place where you are considering taking a position. If Beverly had known from the start what the program's practice was for moving children from one group to the next, she very well might have continued her job search. Read the *Promoting Play: Resolving an Ethical Dilemma about Play* feature and consider how you would use the Code of Ethical Conduct to address this dilemma.

Engage in Continuous, Collaborative Learning to Inform Practice

Knowledge about child development and learning and about effective curriculum and teaching is always changing and expanding. Early childhood educators have an obligation to keep up to date with the latest research developments in the field (Institute of Medicine [IOM] & National Research Council [NRC], 2015). Professional education doesn't end with completion of a degree or initial licensure. Rather, teachers commit themselves to lifelong professional learning. Technology greatly facilitates collaborative practice and continuous learning.

Teachers can learn a great deal directly from children and from other teachers. For this reason, NAEYC (Lutton, 2012) calls for teachers to collaborate with colleagues on their own classroom-based research, investigate ways to improve their

Professionals reflect on their decisions and discuss, debate, and analyze their practices with their colleagues. Becoming a professional teacher means committing to becoming a lifelong learner.

© Paul Jenkins/Pearson Education

Promoting Play

Resolving an Ethical Dilemma about Play

You teach 3- and 4-year-olds in a large, diverse child care agency. Your personal teaching philosophy is that children learn a great deal through play, especially socio-dramatic play. Your classroom environment includes a large housekeeping area. You regularly provide specific props related to children's interests or the current topic of study to encourage and extend their pretend play. Many of the families, however, are members of cultural groups that object to the children taking on pretend roles that they do not consider culturally appropriate. For example, some of the Latino parents are upset to see boys playing in the housekeeping area. Some of the Arabic families do not want boys and girls playing together at all. You personally are opposed to gender stereotyping and try to counteract it in your classroom whenever possible.

You are faced with an ethical dilemma. To resolve it, you consult the NAEYC Code of Ethical Conduct, which leads you to first consider the knowledge base about child development and learning. You are already convinced that socio-dramatic play is valuable. Research informs you that preschool children often show preference for playmates of their own gender. At the same time, research indicates that young children become aware of and often react negatively to differences among people, which requires straightforward anti-bias teaching and learning experiences to counteract.

Next, you consult the code of ethics, which includes an important, applicable principle that early childhood environments must support each child's culture, language, ethnicity, and family structure. A similar principle requires that professionals respect the dignity and preferences of families to ensure a culturally consistent environment for children. And that families must be listened to and involved in program decisions.

No simple resolution to the situation exists. However, applying both the code of ethics and what you know about child development, here are some appropriate actions:

- Meet with families to listen to their specific concerns and desires for their children.
- Provide interesting socio-dramatic play themes that do not involve housekeeping.
- Encourage but don't force friendships between children or across genders.
- Foster positive relationships among all children and teach anti-bias approaches to diversity.
- Respect children's choice of playmates but prohibit expressions of bias toward other children for any reason.
- Provide toys and play experiences that appeal to both genders.
- Explain to families, through a translator if necessary, how you are working to accommodate their concerns, respect their cultural values and preferences, and also provide a developmentally appropriate program for their children.

own practices, participate in conferences, and stay current by reading and discussing publications and Internet sites. For example, a group of kindergarten teachers might figure out how to share a limited set of materials across classrooms to enhance the complexity of children's play. A team of preschool teachers might meet regularly to compare observations of children's interests and thinking. The staff of a child care center might read an article on biting and agree on ways to handle the problem with toddlers and families.

Integrate Knowledgeable, Reflective, and Critical Perspectives on Early Education Even relatively routine decisions about which book to read, how to help children settle a dispute, or how to organize a safe, educational field trip require teachers to draw on professional knowledge and values. Developmentally appropriate practice is a decision-making process that requires teachers to be knowledge-able about the latest research findings in the field.

However, none of the professional guidelines or standards, including the Code of Ethical Conduct, contains one simple, true answer to any of the myriad questions teachers confront. In fact, early childhood professionals who share the same core values do not agree on the answers to some of the most central questions such as the name of the field, the proper balance of teacher-guided and child-guided experience, or what *developmentally appropriate* really means (Bredekamp, 1997a; Goffin, 2013; NAEYC, 2009). Therefore, professionals need to be reflective and critical, analyzing and evaluating the effectiveness of their own practices to improve their work with young children. They also must be open to views that differ from their own. To learn more about the value of critical, reflective practice, read the feature *Becoming an Intentional Teacher: Advocating for Effective Inclusion of Children with Disabilities*.

Become an Informed Advocate for Children and the Profession Early childhood education is an imperfect field. The quality of services for children is uneven and, in many cases, inadequate. High-quality programs are expensive, and many families cannot afford them. Early childhood teachers, whose jobs require a high level of professional knowledge and responsibility, are grossly undercompensated.

To make a real difference in children's lives, early childhood professionals have the additional obligation of becoming informed advocates for children and the profession (Lutton, 2012). **Advocacy** is aiding a cause that you believe in. It can be as personal as referring a family for counseling or as political as lobbying your representative for an increase in Head Start funding.

advocacy Aiding a cause that you believe in.

The key word is *informed*. Effective advocates present valid information and draw on their knowledge of research and real-world experience. Representatives are more likely to vote for increased funding if they are convinced that such programs work. Successful

> ▶ **Classroom Connection**
>
> Intentional teachers stay up to date about new knowledge and continue to grow as professionals. In this video, you will see a high-quality preschool program in action and hear the teachers discuss the importance of continuing their education.
>
> http://www.youtube.com/watch?v=cffwyDahq80

Becoming an Intentional Teacher

Advocating for Effective Inclusion of Children with Disabilities

Here's What Happened Two children with disabilities and IEPs are in my first-grade class. April has Tourette's syndrome and Willis has autism. I learned about inclusion in my college classes, but until now I haven't encountered children with disabilities as severe as theirs. In searching the Internet for help, I found the joint position statement on Early Childhood Inclusion by the Division for Early Childhood and NAEYC, which says that the defining features of inclusion are *access, participation,* and *systemic supports.* The next time that I attended each child's IEP team meeting, I spoke up. I confessed that in each case, the child was present in the classroom but not really participating. I asked for resources to read and the opportunity to attend some workshops to help me learn more effective strategies. My biggest concern is that neither the children nor I are getting the systemic supports we need to be successful. As a result, I spoke with the principal and April's and Willis's parents. We arranged meetings with the school district special education coordinator to advocate for changes in how the children are served, such as having therapists work with them in the regular classroom rather than pulling them out.

Here's What I Was Thinking After reading and reflecting on the position statement, I realized that April and Willis weren't really included in the class because although they had access, they weren't fully participating and they needed more support to achieve their IEP goals and the goals of the regular curriculum. Reflecting on and thinking critically about my own behavior, I admitted to myself that I wasn't fully participating in team meetings and was unsure about how best to teach Willis and April. I also realized that both of these children and I were not getting the supports we needed from the school system. This led me to exercise my professional responsibility to work with families and colleagues to advocate on their behalf.

Reflection What else might this teacher have done to help children succeed in her inclusive classroom?

- Write letters or e-mails to support better child care licensing standards or legislation to support funding for child care assistance.

- Join a child advocacy group such as NAEYC, NBCDI, or NHSA, and stay informed about policy issues through their websites and e-mail alerts.

- Provide information for parents to help them advocate for their children.

- Get to know and collaborate with colleagues across the full age spectrum of birth through 8. Avoid pitting the needs of one age group or sector against those of another.

- Participate in efforts to improve compensation and benefits for early childhood professionals.

- Advocate for sufficient funding and effective services for all children, including children with disabilities.

- Build your knowledge and understanding of cultural and linguistic diversity by reading and joining diverse civic, community, volunteer and/or faith-based groups.

- Attend school board meetings and voice your opinion on educational issues such as developmentally appropriate practice, or appropriate curriculum and assessment.

- Share your critical views with manufacturers of children's products such as violent video games or advertisers of junk food aimed at children.

- Vote in every election, help register parents to vote, and/or run for public office.

FIGURE 16.2 Becoming an Informed Advocate   Effective teachers not only focus on the children in their classrooms, but also advocate for high-quality programs for all children and families, and better work environments for professionals.

Sources: Based on *Advocates in Action: Making a Difference for Young Children*, revised edition, by A. Robinson and D. R. Stark, 2005, Washington, DC: NAEYC; *Essentials for Child Development Associates Working with Young Children*, revised edition, edited by C. B. Day, 2005, Washington, DC: Council for Professional Recognition.

advocates present research on program effectiveness, but they also share the stories of children and families whose life experience is represented by the data.

Informed advocacy requires that early childhood professionals be familiar with the central policy issues affecting the field, including compensation for teachers, financing of the early education system, standards for curriculum, and appropriate methods of assessment. They also need to understand how public policies are developed and demonstrate essential advocacy skills, such as clear verbal and written communication skills and the ability to work effectively with others toward a common goal (Kieff, 2009). Figure 16.2 lists ways in which informed advocates act on behalf of children and the profession.

Protect Children from Abuse and Neglect

Early childhood educators tend to focus on the positive and want only the best for young children. But our responsibility goes beyond providing excellent care and education for children to protecting them from harm to the extent possible. For this reason, reporting suspected cases of child abuse and neglect is not only one of our most difficult professional responsibilities but also the most sacred. To meet this responsibility, teachers need to know the signs and symptoms of child abuse and also the legal requirements surrounding it. The federal government's Child Welfare Information Gateway website (http://www.childwelfare.gov) provides up-to-date resources to help professionals fulfill these obligations.

Signs and Symptoms of Child Abuse and Neglect There are several types of child abuse, including physical abuse, neglect, sexual abuse, and emotional abuse. In most cases, however, children experience these abuses in combination—a sexually abused child is also harmed physically and mentally. Teachers need to be alert to general warning signs for abuse. If a teacher suspects a parent or other adult of abusing a child, it is important to observe both the child's and adult's behavior individually and also to observe the interaction between them. For example, a child might be always watching as though waiting for something bad to happen, a parent may show little concern for the child, and when together they may avoid looking at or touching each other (Child Welfare Information Gateway, 2007). Teachers also need to know the typical warning signs of specific types of abuse, which are listed in Table 16.5.

Reporting Requirements Almost every day the media report tragic incidents of child abuse that could have been alleviated if someone had reported their suspicions to the proper authorities. Too many people feel that it is none of their business or they are afraid

TABLE 16.5 Recognizing Potential Signs of Child Abuse

Knowing these potential warning signs is essential for teachers to fulfil their legal and moral responsibility to report suspected incidents of child abuse and neglect.

Type of Abuse	Consider the Possibility of Abuse When the Child:	Consider the Possibility of Abuse When the Parent or Adult Caregiver:
Physical Abuse	• Has unexplained burns, bites, bruises, broken bones, or black eyes • Has fading bruises or other marks noticeable after an absence from school • Seems frightened of the parents and protests or cries when it is time to go home • Shrinks at the approach of adults • Reports injury by a parent or another adult caregiver	• Offers conflicting, unconvincing, or no explanation for the child's injury • Describes the child as "evil," or in some other very negative way • Uses harsh physical discipline with the child • Has a history of abuse as a child
Neglect	• Is frequently absent from school • Begs or steals food or money • Lacks needed medical or dental care, immunizations, or glasses • Is consistently dirty and has severe body odor • Lacks sufficient clothing for the weather • States that there is no one at home to provide care	• Appears to be indifferent to the child • Seems apathetic or depressed • Behaves irrationally or in a bizarre manner • Is abusing alcohol or other drugs
Sexual Abuse	• Has difficulty walking or sitting • Suddenly refuses to change clothes or to participate in physical activities • Reports nightmares or bedwetting • Experiences a sudden change in appetite • Demonstrates bizarre, sophisticated, or unusual sexual knowledge or behavior	• Is unduly protective of the child or severely limits the child's contact with other children, especially of the opposite sex • Is secretive and isolated
Emotional Abuse	• Shows extremes in behavior, such as overly compliant or demanding behavior, extreme passivity, or aggression • Is either inappropriately adult (parenting other children, for example) or inappropriately infantile (frequently rocking or head-banging, for example) • Is delayed in physical or emotional development	• Constantly blames, belittles, or berates the child • Is unconcerned about the child and refuses to consider offers of help for the child's problems • Overtly rejects the child

Source: Child Welfare Information Gateway, retrieved from https://www.childwelfare.gov/pubs/factsheets/ques.cfm.

of offending parents or colleagues. Although anyone can and should report suspected abuse, teachers, child care workers, and school officials are *mandatory* reporters. They are required by law to report maltreatment of children. Every state has child abuse reporting procedures, but the specific regulations regarding confidentiality and how to report vary from state to state. The Child Welfare Information Gateway provides links to each state's requirements.

Teachers are not only legally mandated to report suspected child abuse but also have an ethical responsibility to do so. The NAEYC Code of Ethical Conduct (NAEYC, 2011a) states that even when another person tells us of their suspicion, we should assist them in taking action, and if a child protective service agency fails in its responsibilities, we should advocate for improved services. Being the one person in a child's life who intervenes to stop the horror of abuse is probably the most difficult task of any teacher's career but would also make the biggest difference in an individual child's life.

Join a Profession That Makes a Difference

Teaching young children is a career that brings great personal fulfillment. Every hour, your small charges burst into laughter, need comforting, figure something out, and learn new words. Each day has its small rewards—a wilting dandelion, a shared joke, an "Ah-ha!" expression of understanding, or a whispered "I love you, Teacher." Looking back at the end of every year, teachers can't believe how far most of their children have come, and they regret that some have not come further. Over time, teachers learn more *about* children but mostly *from* children, and they are humbled by the job. They realize how much they don't know and that there are no simple answers to complex questions. They are awed by the trust that children and parents place in them and they use their power wisely. Most of all, they know that the lives they touch will be changed, as will their own. They are committed to making a positive difference in children's lives. Read the feature *What Works: Having an Effective Teacher* to find out just how important high-quality teachers can be.

We end with a succinct statement of the early childhood professional's commitment to children. The *Statement of Commitment* (NAEYC, 2011a) in Figure 16.3 is not an official part of the NAEYC's Code of Ethical Conduct, but rather a personal acknowledgment

What Works

Having an Effective Teacher

Most people intuitively know that good teachers make a difference in how well children learn. In fact, some studies show that the most effective teachers can contribute as much as an extra year's growth in academic achievement for the fortunate children in their classes. But conducting such research is difficult because it is hard to know whether the differences were caused more by the children's inborn abilities or their environmental circumstances than by the teacher's practice.

A well-designed study addressed the question of cause and effect directly by measuring the reading achievement of identical and fraternal twins who had more- or less-effective teachers. Using twins enabled the researchers to control for genetics because identical twins share 100% of their genes, and fraternal twins share 50%. In the study of more than 800 first and second graders,

teacher effectiveness was measured by how much the twins' classmates' reading ability improved over the course of the year. What the researchers found was that among identical twins with different teachers, the twin with the more effective teacher had better reading skills. Looking at fraternal and identical twins, the researchers concluded that if teachers are equally excellent, genetics plays a larger role in reading achievement, but that poor-quality, ineffective teaching inhibits children's ability to reach their full potential.

Source: Based on "Teacher Quality Moderates the Genetic Effects on Early Reading," by J. Taylor, A. D. Roehrig, B. S. Hensler, C. M. Connor, & C. Schatschneider, 2010, *Science, 328*(5977), 512–514.

As an individual who works with young children, I commit myself to furthering the values of early childhood education as they are reflected in the ideals and principles of the NAEYC Code of Ethical Conduct. To the best of my ability I will:

- Never harm children.

- Ensure that programs for young children are based on current knowledge and research of child development and early childhood education.

- Respect and support families in their task of nurturing children.

- Respect colleagues in early childhood care and education and support them in maintaining the NAEYC Code of Ethical Conduct.

- Serve as an advocate for children, their families, and their teachers in community and society.

- Stay informed of and maintain high standards of professional conduct.

- Engage in an ongoing process of self-reflection, realizing that personal characteristics, biases, and beliefs have an impact on children and families.

- Be open to new ideas and be willing to learn from the suggestions of others.

- Continue to learn, grow, and contribute as a professional.

- Honor the ideals and principles of the NAEYC Code of Ethical Conduct.

FIGURE 16.3 NAEYC Statement of Commitment The NAEYC Code of Ethical Conduct and all the organization's work is based on this foundational statement of commitment to children and families.

Source: From *Code of Ethical Conduct and Statement of Commitment*, revised edition, 2011a, Washington, DC: NAEYC. Reprinted with permission from the National Association for the Education of Young Children.

of the individual's willingness to embrace the values and moral obligations that lead to becoming part of the early childhood profession.

 Check Your Understanding 16.2: Beginning Your Journey as an Early Childhood Educator

Revisiting the Case Study

. . . the College Classroom

At the outset of this chapter we saw into the thoughts and motivations of several college students as they embarked on an early childhood education class. Those brief descriptions reveal only some of the diverse paths that individuals take into the field. Undoubtedly, their paths will diverge again as they make decisions about which of the many career options, settings, and age groups they wish to pursue. We've shined a light on what future days might be like, and some of what they need to consider in their choices.

We began this journey by looking back at the beginnings of early childhood education and the contributions of dauntless women and men who provided the foundations on which it stands today. While those foundations are firm, they are not limiting. The future of children and of early childhood education continues to be built as we learn more about effective practices and our country commits more resources to improving schools for young children. Early childhood education is indeed a field on the rise. If you join this profession, you will discover that you have the power to shape that future for the better. ■

16 Chapter Summary

- A career in early childhood education is filled with never-ending rewards and challenges. Among the major questions early childhood educators face is which age group(s) they would most like to work with and why. For each age group/position, there are interesting points to consider.

- The NAEYC Code of Ethical Conduct guides early childhood educators in making decisions about their professional responsibilities and resolving ethical dilemmas that arise in their relationships with children, families, colleagues, and society.

- Early childhood educators are also effective advocates for children and the profession. They know about the central policy issues in the field, including professional compensation, financing of the early education system, and standards for curriculum and assessment.

- Teachers and child care providers must know the warning signs of child abuse and neglect, and are required by law to report suspected abuse to the proper authorities.

- Early childhood teachers have the opportunity to make lasting, positive contributions to the lives of children and to make a significant difference in the world.

Key Terms

- advocacy
- code of ethics
- ethical dilemma
- ethical responsibilities
- ethics
- morality
- profession
- professional ethics

Demonstrate Your Learning

Click here to assess how well you've learned the content in this chapter.

Readings and Websites

Institute of Medicine (IOM) & National Research Council (NRC) (2015). *Transforming the workforce for children birth through age 9: A unifying foundation.* Washington, DC: National Academies Press.

Chenfeld, M. B. (2014). *Still teaching in the key of life: Joyful stories for early childhood settings.* Washington, DC: National Association for the Education of Young Children.

Feeney, S., & Freeman, N. K. (2012). *Ethics and the early childhood educator: Using the NAEYC code* (2nd ed.). Washington, DC: National Association for the Education of Young Children.

Lutton, A. (Ed.). (2012). *Advancing the early childhood profession: NAEYC standards and guidelines for professional development.* Washington, DC: National Association for the Education of Young Children.

Child Welfare Information Gateway

On this government website, you will find information on identifying signs of child abuse and neglect, reporting requirements, and effective ways to prevent child abuse.

MenTeach

MenTeach is a clearinghouse for both men and women seeking information and resources about men teaching. This website provides information on careers and resources for recruiting men into early education.

National Black Child Development Institute

The National Black Child Development Institute works with policy makers, professionals, and parents on critical issues that directly impact African American children and their families. This website provides culturally relevant resources on early childhood education, health, child welfare, literacy, and family engagement, addressing the unique strengths and needs of Black children.

National Head Start Association

The National Head Start Association is a nonpartisan, not-for-profit organization that advocates on behalf of more than 1 million children, 200,000 staff, and 1,600 Head Start grantees in the United States. Their website provides resources to assist advocates, and professional development information and services for Head Start staff members.

Glossary

absorbent mind—Maria Montessori's image of the child as actively learning from sensory experiences.

abstraction—The concept that anything can be counted.

academic discourse—The language of school, which is important for school success.

accommodation—When new information or experience doesn't fit within an existing concept (scheme), the child must modify it or construct a new scheme.

accommodations—Changes in assessment procedures, materials, or setting to eliminate barriers related to the child's disability that might keep children from demonstrating their full capabilities.

accountability—The process of holding teachers, schools, or programs responsible for meeting a required level of performance.

accreditation system—NAEYC's voluntary system for identifying high-quality early childhood centers and schools serving children from birth through kindergarten.

acculturation—The process whereby children learn expected rules of behavior.

achievement tests—Tests designed to measure what children have learned in general or in a content area such as reading or mathematics.

acknowledging—Giving positive verbal or nonverbal attention that promotes the child's persistence and effort.

adaptation—The mental process of altering concepts (schemes) in response to experience, which occurs in two ways: through assimilation and accommodation.

advance organizers—Ways of introducing new information that serve as a bridge between what the student already knows and the new learning.

advocacy—Aiding a cause that you believe in.

age appropriate—Age-related human characteristics that allow teachers to make general predictions within an age range about what materials, interactions, and experiences will be safe, interesting, challenging, and within reach for children and, thus, likely to best promote their learning and development.

aggressive communication—Speaking the truth in a hurtful way.

alignment—Coordination of the curriculum from one level of education to the next in order to build on what children have already learned and to ease transitions for students between schools and school levels.

alliteration—Two words beginning with the same sound.

alphabetic principle—The understanding that there is a systematic relationship between letters and sounds, and that all spoken sounds and words can be represented by a limited set of agreed-on symbols called *letters*.

alternative assessments—Assessments that call for a child to produce a response rather than select from a list of possible responses.

anecdotal records—Short descriptions written by teachers and based on observations of incidents, or anecdotes, involving one or more children.

anti-bias education—Learning experiences and teaching strategies that are specifically designed not only to prepare all children for life in a culturally rich society, but also to counter the stereotyping of diverse groups, and to guard against expressions of bias

apprenticeship—The process of children learning by observing adults and more accomplished peers performing tasks and by practicing the skills themselves with adult guidance and support.

approaches to learning—Behaviors, tendencies, or typical patterns that children use in learning situations that include both how they feel about learning—their level of enthusiasm, interest, and motivation—and how they engage with learning.

aptitude tests—Tests designed to measure children's potential for learning in the future.

assertive communication—Telling the truth in a thoughtful and considerate way; considered the most effective form of communication.

assessment—The ongoing process of gathering evidence of children's learning and development, and then organizing and interpreting the information to make informed decisions about instructional practice.

assimilation—When new information or experience is understood in connection with existing knowledge (schemes).

assistive technology—A piece of equipment or product that is used to increase, maintain, or improve the functional capabilities of individuals with disabilities.

associative play—Children play and share with each other, usually one other child.

attachment theory—The theory that children's ability to learn depends on their developing trusting relationships with caregivers.

auditory awareness—Listening to verbal input or distinguishing between different sounds.

autism spectrum disorder (ASD)—Complex developmental disabilities that impact the normal development of the brain processes related to social interaction and communication skills.

babble—Produce consonant/vowel sounds such as "ba ba."

background knowledge—Concepts and basic information about how the world works that is essential for reading comprehension.

balanced approach—Effective reading instruction that helps children master the alphabetic principle *and* acquire meaning from text.

Bank Street approach—Originating with Lucy Sprague Mitchell at Bank Street College and later called the Developmental-Interaction approach, a curriculum framework based on individual children's development, emphasizing that learning begins in children's experiences in the immediate environment (here and now).

base ten place value system—Highly efficient system of using just 10 numerals to write any counting number no matter how large, in which the meaning of a numeral depends on where it is placed within the number.

behavior intervention plan—Describes the strategies adults will use to prevent a child's negative behavior and to teach more acceptable behavior.

behaviorism or behavioral learning—Theory that learning is a change in behavior that is controlled by the consequences, either positive or negative, that follow the behavior.

bias—Negative feelings and expressions toward groups or individuals.

bicultural—Capable of operating successfully in both the home environment and the dominant culture of the larger world.

body composition—Weight and body fat.

bullying—Occurs when a person repeatedly commits aggressive acts that intend to harm, and an imbalance of power makes it hard for the victim to defend himself or herself.

cardinality—The concept that the last number said stands for the total number in the set.

cardiorespiratory (aerobic) system—Body system made up of the heart, lungs, and blood; provides the stamina needed to be active for a long period of time.

caring community of learners—A group or classroom in which children and adults engage in warm, positive relationships, treat each other with respect, and learn from and with each other.

challenging behavior—Any behavior that interferes with children's learning, development, and success at play; is harmful to the child, other children, or adults; or puts a child at high risk for later social problems or school failure.

charter schools—Independently operated, publicly funded schools that have greater flexibility than regular schools in meeting regulations and achieving goals.

checklists—Practical and versatile tools for gathering assessment information about children's behavior, skills, or attitudes.

Child Care and Development Block Grants (CCDBG)—Federal funds allocated to states for low-income working families to purchase child care.

child care center—Group program that provides care and education for young children during the hours that their parents are employed.

child care licensing standards—Minimum requirements, legally established by each state, for a child care program to operate.

Child Development Associate (CDA) credential—National competency-based credential for entry-level early childhood educators.

child study movement—Early 20th-century effort to scientifically observe and systematically document children's individual development under the leadership of G. Stanley Hall and Arnold Gesell.

child-centered curriculum—John Dewey's idea that curriculum should reflect the concepts and topics that the child is interested in and capable of learning.

child-initiated experiences—Experiences that allow children to gain knowledge and skills through their own exploration and interactions with objects and other children.

children with disabilities—Children who have been identified as having a specific category of disability, such as autism or cerebral palsy.

children with special needs—A broad term used to describe children who may have multiple risk factors, specialized health care needs, mental or emotional health concerns, severe allergies, or physical and/or cognitive disabilities.

chronosystem—System that refers to effects of circumstances over time.

classification systems—Systems teachers use to help children build concepts by identifying similarities and differences or by comparing and contrasting objects and ideas.

Classroom Assessment Scoring System (CLASS)—Preschool and elementary classroom observational instrument that assesses the quality of teachers' relationships and interactions with children and the instructional strategies used to support children's learning.

closed questions—Lower-level questions that have one right answer and usually require children to recall information or facts.

co-construction—Children learning by solving problems collaboratively with the teacher's support or by working with peers; also called *social construction of knowledge*.

code of ethics—Defines the core values of a profession and provides guidance for what professionals should do when they encounter difficult or conflicting obligations or responsibilities in their work.

code switch—The ability to understand and use both the mainstream version of English and the home dialect or language.

cognitive (mental) flexibility—The ability to find new solutions or revise plans in response to changing circumstances.

cognitive development—Thinking, intelligence, and language abilities.

Common Core State Standards—Rigorous national standards in English language arts and mathematics for kindergarten through grade 12 developed by the Council of Chief State Officers (CCSSO) and the National Governor's Association (NGA).

competent child—The image of children as active players in their own development and learning.

completion prompt—A prompt that requires the child to verbally complete the end of a sentence.

composing/decomposing—Mathematical processes of putting together and taking apart (for example, addition and subtraction).

comprehension—The ability to understand what is read and to interpret and analyze the author's meaning; the ability to make sense of what is read.

concepts of print—Beginning understandings about the forms and functions of written language, such as that words carry messages.

conceptual frameworks—Mental models that connect new learning to prior knowledge, enhance memory, and deepen understanding.

conceptual organizer—Ways of organizing curriculum, such as the project approach, that make content knowledge more meaningful, interesting, and understandable for children.

connections—Refers to understanding links between different areas of math and connecting math concepts to real-world problems.

consequences—Principle of operant conditioning that behavior changes as a result of what occurs immediately afterward.

conservation—The understanding that the quantity of objects stays the same regardless of changes in appearance.

constructivism—Learning theory derived from the work of Jean Piaget, which assumes that children actively build their knowledge from firsthand experiences in stimulating environments.

content standards—Describe what students should know and/or be able to do within a particular discipline such as math or science.

conventional reading—Reading in which the reader gains meaning from unfamiliar text.

cooing—Vocalizing vowel sounds.

cooperative play—Children assume different roles and share a purpose for the play.

co-player—Teachers actually join in and take an active role in children's play.

Council for Exceptional Children (CEC)—The national professional association for special educators.

criterion-referenced tests—Tests that compare a person's score to a predetermined level of performance.

cultural competence—The ability to work effectively across cultural groups.

culturally appropriate—Applying knowledge of the social and cultural contexts in which children live, which helps teachers build on children's prior knowledge and make experiences meaningful and responsive.

culture—The explicit and implicit values, beliefs, rules, and expectations for behavior of members of a group that are passed on from one generation to the next. These rules determine to a large extent what group members regard as important and what values shape their actions and judgments.

curriculum—A written plan that describes the goals for children's learning and development, and the learning experiences, materials, and teaching strategies that are used to help children achieve those goals.

curriculum approach—Describes the main elements or direction of a program; is less detailed than a curriculum model.

curriculum framework—A guide for designing or choosing a curriculum.

curriculum model—A research-based, idealized version of what and how teaching and learning should occur.

curriculum-embedded assessment—Formative assessment that is integrated into the curriculum; this assessment does not occur as a separate procedure.

day nurseries—Programs designed to serve working families in the late 19th and early 20th centuries; the forerunner of present-day child care centers.

decode—The ability to figure out what written symbols—letters of the alphabet—represent.

decontextualized speech—Talk about events, experiences, or people that are beyond the here and now or that inhabit children's imaginations.

demonstrating—Showing the correct way to perform a skill or procedure while children observe the outcome.

development—Age-related change that results from an interaction between biological maturation and physical and/or social experience; development occurs as children grow, adapt, and change in response to various experiences.

developmental continuum—A predictable, but not rigid, sequence of typical accomplishments within age ranges that is used to plan curriculum; also an effective assessment tool used to focus teacher attention on what is important to assess—what children can do—and to identify goals for continued progress.

developmental domain—An area of development such as fine- and gross-motor skills, cognitive abilities, self-help capabilities, and social and communication skills.

developmentally appropriate practice (DAP)—Ways of teaching that engage children's interests and adapt for their age, experience, and ability to help them meet challenging and achievable learning goals.

diagnostic tests—Tests designed to identify the specific learning or developmental problems a child has and to plan interventions; must be administered by specially trained professionals.

dialogic reading—Interactive, shared picture book reading during which the adult and the child gradually switch roles so that the child learns to become the storyteller with the assistance of the adult, who plays the role of active listener and questioner.

differentiated instruction—The creation of multiple paths so that children of different abilities, interests, and learning needs experience equally appropriate ways to achieve important learning goals.

digital literacy—The ability to obtain, use, interpret, and evaluate information available through multimedia, digital sources.

direct instruction—Explicitly giving directions for completing a task; providing facts, verbal labels, or other specific information; or providing instructions for a child's action or behavior.

directional awareness—Anticipating which way to go.

disequilibrium—An imbalance in thinking that occurs when new information or physical experience cannot be understood in terms of what is already known (cannot be assimilated).

disorganized/disoriented attachment—Seen in children who lack secure attachments with adults due to having experienced neglect, abuse, or violence in the home, who have not developed useful strategies for seeking comfort or attention or handling difficulties.

distancing questions—Questions that relate pictures and words in the book to children's own experiences beyond the book.

Division for Early Childhood (DEC)—Subdivision of the Council for Exceptional Children that is the national professional organization for early childhood special educators and early intervention specialists.

domain-general processes—Broad abilities that cut across traditionally defined developmental domains.

domains of development—Areas of human development and functioning that include cognitive, social, emotional, and physical.

dual language learners—Children who are learning to speak two languages at the same time—usually their home language and English.

dual language learning—Simultaneously learning two languages: the home or first language as well as English or another second language.

dynamic assessment—Analyzes a child's performance not just in terms of what the child can do independently, but what the child can do with the assistance of a teacher or peer.

early childhood education—Education and child care services provided for children from birth through age 8.

Early Childhood Environment Rating Scale (ECERS-3)—Observational instrument used to rate program quality on a 7-point scale from inadequate to excellent.

early childhood special education—Services for children with disabilities or special needs who meet eligibility guidelines that are determined on a state-by-state basis according to the Individuals with Disabilities Education Act.

Early Head Start—Federally funded program serving low-income pregnant mothers, infants, and toddlers that promotes healthy family functioning.

early intervention—Services for infants and toddlers who are at risk of developmental delay and their families.

early learning standards—Describe what children should know and be able to do before entering kindergarten.

early literacy—Skills and knowledge that come before and lead up to (forerunners) conventional reading and writing.

earth and space science—Studying properties of earth materials, changes on the earth, patterns of movement, and changes of the sun and moon.

ecological systems theory—Bronfenbrenner's theory that describes the diverse, interactive contexts that influence children's development over time.

effective teaching—The use of approaches that are proven to be successful based on scientific evidence and that have a high probability of enhancing children's learning and development.

efficacy—Children's belief in their own ability to accomplish what they set out to do.

egocentrism—The process whereby very young children tend to see everything from their own intellectual and emotional point of view.

Elementary and Secondary Education Act (ESEA)—Law governing how the federal government distributes education funds to states and holds public schools accountable for the use of funding.

eligibility guidelines—Guidelines established on a state-by-state basis according to IDEA that determine whether children may receive special education services.

emergent curriculum—Curriculum that develops in an educational environment in response to children's interests and needs rather than according to predeveloped plans.

emotional development—Acquisition of important emotional skills such as identifying feelings and learning to regulate emotions and express them appropriately.

emotional literacy—Children's ability to identify their own and others' emotions, to express emotions in a healthy way, and to self-regulate their feelings.

encode—Translating speech sounds into symbols—the letters of the alphabet—to create writing.

encouragement—Verbal comments or non-verbal signs such as pats or high fives that promote the child's persistence and effort.

engaged citizens—Children as change agents in schools, communities, and eventually in the world.

enumeration—The act of counting.

equilibration—The process whereby humans try to make sense of new experiences by creating new concepts (schemes) or adapting existing ones.

equity pedagogy—The idea that teaching about differences needs to include teaching about oppression and equity.

ethical dilemma—Deciding the right thing to do when two or more values conflict.

ethical responsibilities—The obligations that every teacher agrees to uphold with honesty, integrity, and respect.

ethics—Critical thinking about morality and people's ability to make choices about their own values.

ethnicity—The shared characteristics and experiences of a group of people, such as nationality, race, history, religion, and language.

evaluation—The process of making a judgment about assessment results; frequently considered the last step in assessment.

everyday mathematics—Informal, intuitive knowledge about math, including basic ideas about quantity (more and less), size, shape, and pattern.

evidence—An outward sign or indication of children's learning, such as their response to a question or their solution to a problem.

exceptional children—An all-encompassing term used to communicate inclusion of gifted and talented children as well as children whose development is below the expected range.

executive function—The ability to control emotions, focus attention, plan and think ahead, and monitor cognitive processes.

exosystem—Systems that affect the child's microsystems, but that the child doesn't directly participate in, including economic, media, education, health, legal and political entities that directly affect a person or circumstance in the child's microsystem.

expressive language—The ability to communicate; use and knowledge of spoken language.

extended discourse—Talking with children in ways that build on and expand what they say.

extinction—The process whereby a conditioned behavior diminishes and eventually disappears when reinforcers are removed.

facilitating—Providing short-term, temporary assistance to help a child achieve the next level of functioning.

family-centered practice—Providing resources and supports to families that promote children's development and learning and, at the same time, strengthen the competency of families in their role.

family child care home—Child care in which caregivers provide care in their own homes for a small group of children, often multi-age groups.

family systems theory—Views family members as interconnected parts, with each member influencing the others in predictable and recurring ways.

feedback loop—Back-and-forth communication between a teacher and a child or small group of children in an effort to reach deeper understanding.

fidelity—Faithful implementation of a curriculum model.

fine-motor development—Physical skills related to the small muscles found in individual body parts, especially those in the hands and feet.

fine-motor manipulative movements—Control, precision, and accuracy of small muscle movement.

5- to 7-year shift—Major transition in cognitive abilities that gradually occurs between 5 and 7 years of age, resulting in increased ability to think logically, self-regulate, and solve problems.

flexibility—The ability to bend and stretch easily.

fluency—Rapid, efficient, and accurate word recognition skills that permit the reader to comprehend the meaning of text.

formal assessment—Assessment that follows a specific procedure and uses a specially designed instrument or tool.

formative assessment—The process of gathering information about children and using it to plan effective and individualized instruction.

free appropriate public education (FAPE)—Education for children with disabilities that is required by IDEA, so that children with disabilities are not denied the same opportunities offered to everyone else.

frequency counts—Method used by teachers to keep track of how often a behavior occurs.

Froebel's occupations and gifts—Invented by Froebel for kindergartners, occupations were planned experiences designed to train children's eye-hand coordination and mental activity, and gifts were concrete materials, many of which influenced later toy development.

functional assessment or functional analysis—The process of determining why a child is behaving a certain way, based on the principle that all behavior serves a function or purpose.

functional skills—The essential abilities needed to fulfill goals parents have for their children, such as communicating, making friends, and learning self-help skills.

funds of knowledge—Experiences, traditions, goals, resources, and rich culture that families bring to their roles.

generative skills—Skills that can be used across settings, people, events, and objects.

geometry—The study of shapes and space, including flat, two-dimensional space and three-dimensional space.

graphic representation—The process of depicting thoughts and ideas through drawing, modeling, or other media.

gross-motor development—Physical skills related to moving the whole body or major parts of the body.

gross-motor manipulative movements—Large muscle movements involving giving or receiving force from objects such as throwing, catching, or kicking.

guidance—The process of teaching children the life skills they need to function productively with other children.

hazard—A danger that must be avoided.

Head Start—Federally funded, national program that promotes school readiness by enhancing the social and cognitive development of children ages 3, 4, and 5 through providing educational, health, nutritional, social, and other services to the nation's poorest children and families.

Head Start Program Performance Standards—National standards that establish the level of quality of services provided by every Head Start program.

health-related fitness—Any aspect of health that can be improved by physical exercise and activity.

high-context culture—Culture in which communication relies less on words and more on contextual cues, such as facial expressions, gestures, or other physical clues, to convey meaning.

high-stakes testing—Using standardized test scores to make decisions about individual children, teachers, or schools that have potential long-term consequences.

home-based programs—Programs based on visits to families designed to support parents in the parenting role, involve them in their children's education, and help them achieve their own life goals.

home visiting—Visits made by a teacher to the child's home on a regular basis to get to know children and their families.

hypothesis—An assumption about or tentative explanation of a phenomenon.

hypothesis generating and testing—Applying previously acquired knowledge to a new situation by making a prediction and then observing and reflecting on the outcome.

identity—The collection of characteristics that individuals recognize as constituting their sense of self and belonging to a group.

inclusion—Participation and services for children with disabilities and special needs in programs and settings where their typically developing peers are served.

individualistic cultural groups—Cultural groups that focus on the needs of the individual, independence, self-expression, and personal property and choice.

individualized education program (IEP)—A written plan designed to meet the unique needs of a child with a disability or special need; it is developed, reviewed, and revised by an IEP team during meetings for each child who is eligible for special education services.

individualized family service plan (IFSP)—Documents and guides the early intervention process for children with disabilities from birth to age 3 and their families; contains information about the services necessary to facilitate a child's development and enhance the family's capacity to facilitate the child's development.

individualized intervention—A systematically planned and implemented set of actions designed to alter the course of a child's development or learning.

individually appropriate—Information about the strengths, interests, abilities, and needs of each individual child in the group that enables teachers to adapt to and be responsive to individual variation.

Individuals with Disabilities Education Act (IDEA)—Federal law governing provision of services for children with disabilities and special needs.

informal assessment—Gathering information for teacher's use to make everyday classroom decisions or adjustments to teaching.

inhibitory control or cognitive self-control—The ability to think before we act and to focus attention on what is necessary.

insecure-ambivalent/resistant attachment—Children's inability to trust adults to keep them safe due to neglect, abuse, or other difficult circumstances that results in a lack of social competence.

insecure-avoidant attachment—Rejection and insensitivity from adult caregivers that causes children to turn away from or avoid adults and not seek their comfort.

integrated curriculum—Learning plan that addresses goals across multiple areas of the curriculum at the same time.

intentional teachers—Teachers who have a purpose for the decisions they make and can explain that purpose to others.

interdependent cultural groups—Cultural groups that focus on the needs of the group rather than those of the individual, also called collectivist.

interviews—Teacher-created, predetermined questions that are designed to reveal what children understand.

invented spelling—Developmental or phonetic spelling that represents children's initial attempts to associate sounds with letters.

kindergarten—Typically considered the first year of formal schooling; serves 5- and 6-year-olds.

K-W-L—An advance organizer strategy in which teachers ask children what they already know (K) about the topic of study, what they want (W) to know, and then what they learned (L).

laboratory school—School operated by colleges and universities that usually serves children of students and faculty and also acts as a model of excellent education for student teachers.

Lanham Act—Federal legislation to provide emergency child care and other services for families employed in the war effort during World War II.

learning—A change in knowledge or skill that results from experience or instruction.

learning centers—Defined areas of the classroom that have a particular purpose and that contain relevant furnishings and materials.

learning continuum, learning trajectory, or learning path—Similar to a developmental continuum, but focuses on sequences of knowledge or skill in a content area.

learning standards—Expectations for student learning.

learning strategy—How children construct meaning in any context or situation.

learning trajectory—Sequence of teaching and learning knowledge or skills in a content area. Also called *developmental* or *learning continuum*.

life science—The study of the characteristics, life cycles, and environments of organisms.

listening—The process of taking in information through the sense of hearing and making meaning from what is heard.

locomotor movements—Movements that allow the body to proceed in a horizontal or vertical direction from one place to another, such as walking, running, leaping, or jumping.

logico-mathematical knowledge—The relationships that are constructed in our minds between objects or concepts.

low-context culture—Culture that focuses on direct, logical, precise verbal communication.

macrosystem—System that includes the overarching cultural context of the values, beliefs, laws, and policies of a society

manipulatives—Small-sized blocks, cubes, pattern blocks, beads, pegs, and the like that are designed for children's play and learning.

mathematize—To understand and think about everyday problems and experiences in explicitly mathematical terms.

math talk—Using the language and vocabulary of mathematics.

maturationist—Theory of development that assumes that the sequence of changes in abilities and behavior is largely predetermined by children's biological growth processes rather than by their experiences or learning.

measurement—The process of determining size, length, area, or volume using a standard unit.

mesosystem—Interaction of different microsystems in a child's life.

metacognitive activities—Activities that engage children in thinking and reflecting about their own learning.

microsystem—System in which the child directly participates on a regular basis and include the family, child care, school and faith-based settings.

mindfulness—The practice of purposefully and nonjudgmentally noticing sensations (bodily, mentally, emotionally) in the present moment.

mistaken behavior—Alternative term for children's misbehavior, recognizing the fact that young children are still learning acceptable behavior and that they are bound to make mistakes.

modeling—Teacher showing children a skill or desirable way of behaving or speaking; also children imitating the behavior of others.

modifications—Changes in an assessment that alter what the assessment measures or what the results mean.

morality—Personal views about what is right and wrong and how to behave.

motor planning—The ability of the brain to conceive, organize, and carry out a series of unfamiliar actions.

multi-language learners—Children who are learning more than two languages.

muscular strength and endurance—The ability to keep moving without stopping because of fatigue.

narrative—A story with a beginning, middle, and end; characters; dialogue; and a plot with a problem to solve or a dilemma to be resolved.

narrative records—Teachers' attempts to record detailed descriptions of children in a situation or event that is the focus of the observation.

National Association for the Education of Young Children (NAEYC)—The world's largest organization of early childhood educators, whose mission is to act on behalf of the needs and interests of children from birth through age 8. NAEYC establishes standards for teacher preparation and accreditation of early childhood programs.

natural learning environments—Settings that are natural or normal for the child's same-age peers without disabilities such as child care centers, parks, a neighbor's house, or the zoo, as opposed to hospitals, clinics, and therapy offices.

naturally occurring reinforcers—Consequences that are likely to occur *whenever* the child performs the skill and are, therefore, highly effective.

nature—The hereditary or genetic contributions to human development.

nature-deficit disorder—Hypothetical disorder related to lack of exposure and experience outdoors and in the natural world.

negative reinforcement—An unpleasant consequence that is avoided if the person performs a desired behavior more frequently.

neurons—Nerve cells in the brain that receive information through the senses or from other neurons, and then communicate information back to other parts of the body.

normal curve—A distribution of scores that looks like a bell shape, with most people scoring at the midrange and fewer scoring at the higher and lower ends.

norm-referenced tests—Tests that compare an individual's score to that of other test takers.

nursery schools—Schools serving children younger than kindergarten age; out-of-date term for preschool or prekindergarten.

nurture—Environmental factors and experiences that influence human development and behavior.

object permanence—A concept that babies lack early in the period of sensorimotor development, so that when an object is no longer in their sight, it ceases to exist for them.

one-to-one correspondence—Attaching one and only one number word to each object being counted.

onlooker—Teachers act as the audience for children's play.

open-ended questions—Questions that require children to analyze information in some way and that have many possible answers.

operant conditioning—The process of using pleasant or unpleasant consequences to control behavior.

operations—Working with and solving problems about relationships such as *more than* or *less than*.

order irrelevance principle—The concept that counting can begin with any object in the set as long as each is counted only once.

parallel play—Children play next to each other, but not with each other; they may speak, but don't really converse.

parent cooperative—Preschool program owned, operated, and partially staffed by parents.

parentese—The high-pitched tone of voice adults and even children tend to use naturally with babies; also called *motherese*.

passive communication—Speaking in a way that is sensitive to the listener's feelings, but so vague that the message is easily misunderstood.

pedagogy—What a teacher says or does that engages children and contributes to their learning and development.

perceptual-motor development—Occurs when children use their senses to take in information about objects in the environment and use this information to coordinate their movements.

performance assessment or authentic assessment—Determines what children know and can do from their demonstration of a skill or their creation of a product.

performance standards—Describe the knowledge or skill that students should acquire by a particular point in their schooling, usually tied to grade or age level; also known as *benchmarks*.

person-first language—Language that recognizes that a child is a child first, whether or not he or she has a disability (e.g., saying "child with special needs" as opposed to "special needs child").

phonemes—The individual sounds of spoken language; changing one in a word changes the meaning of the word.

phonemic awareness—Recognizing that spoken words are made up of individual sounds that can be manipulated.

phonics—A system of teaching the correspondences between letters or groups of letters and the sounds they represent.

phonological awareness—Consciousness that the stream of spoken language is made up of smaller units or chunks of sound.

physical development—Biological growth and acquisition of fine-motor and gross-motor skills.

physical fitness—Children's overall physical condition: growth, strength, stamina, and flexibility.

physical knowledge—Understanding how objects move and function in space and how the physical world works.

physical science—Basic ideas about the properties of liquids and solid materials, how things move and change position, and cause-and-effect relationships.

pincer grasp—Grasp used to pick up objects with the thumb and forefinger.

planning—Requires children to make intentional choices and encourages them to identify their goals, consider the options for achieving them, make predictions, and anticipate consequences; helps build children's higher-level thinking and problem solving.

plasticity—The brain's ability to develop and change in response to experiences.

play-based assessment—Similar to curriculum-embedded assessment, but the context for observing and interacting with children is the children's play.

play-by-play language—Language that describes what is happening during routines and social interactions with babies and toddlers; also called *running commentary*.

play leader—Teachers participate in children's play; includes making deliberate attempts to enrich and extend the play episode.

portfolios—Systematic and organized collections of children's work and demonstrations of their progress relevant to the goals of the curriculum.

position statement—A document that articulates a stance, usually research based, that an organization is taking in response to an issue or a problem.

positive behavior support (PBS)—A method of identifying the causes and functions of problem behaviors in order to develop support strategies that prevent challenging behaviors and teach new, more appropriate skills.

positive reinforcement—A reward or pleasant consequence that follows a behavior, causing that behavior to be repeated.

predictable books—Books with controlled vocabulary using parallel text structures that become familiar to children.

predictors—Set of early literacy skills and knowledge that increase the likelihood of later success in learning to read and write.

prekindergarten (pre-K)—Educational program serving 3- and 4-year-olds, usually in public schools.

preschool—Educational programs serving 3- and 4-year-olds delivered under various sponsorships.

primary grades—First, second, and third grade; sometimes includes kindergarten.

print awareness—Beginning knowledge about written language.

private speech—The process whereby interpersonal understanding or socially constructed knowledge is turned into intrapersonal knowledge (thinking aloud becomes thinking to oneself).

process quality—The quality of the relationships and interactions among teachers and children, and the appropriateness of the materials, learning experiences, and teaching strategies occurring in an early childhood program.

profession—An occupation that requires extensive education and/or specialized training.

professional ethics—The kinds of actions that are right or wrong in the workplace and are a public matter.

professionals—Members of an occupational group that make decisions based on a specialized body of knowledge, continue to learn throughout their careers, and are committed to meeting the needs of others.

program evaluation—The process of gathering information about a program's quality and effectiveness.

progressive education movement—Major effort to reform schooling in the early 20th century to make it more democratic and responsive to children's needs. This movement was highly influential on early childhood education and later ideas about developmentally appropriate practice.

project—An in-depth investigation of a topic worth learning more about, usually involving a small group, but occasionally the whole class.

project approach—Strategy for conceptually organizing curriculum by engaging children in in-depth investigation of a topic, focused on finding answers to questions posed by the children, the teacher, or the teacher working with the children.

prompts—Gestural, model, physical, pictorial, or verbal clues that elicit responses from children to assist them in using a specific skill.

protective factors—Mechanisms, both inherited and experiential, that may minimize the potentially negative effects for children living in identified high-risk situations.

proximal processes—Interactions in the context of daily living that have the most impact on a child's development, due to their frequent, ongoing nature, often over extended periods of time.

pruning—The process whereby the brain eliminates unnecessary or unused synapses, which contributes to efficient brain operation, aids learning and memory, and increases the brain's flexibility.

punishment—An unpleasant consequence that stops or decreases the frequency of a behavior.

push-down curriculum—Content previously taught in a higher grade in school being expected to be learned in an earlier grade.

quality rating and improvement systems (QRIS)—State-operated tiered systems that evaluate and rate the quality of child care programs according to achievement of benchmarks beyond those required for minimal licensing, such as having more highly qualified teachers or better ratios.

questioning—Eliciting different types of responses and promoting different types of thinking.

rare words—Multisyllable words that are not typically part of a young child's vocabulary.

rating scales—Method of recording teacher's judgments about how a child's performance compares to that of peers or to a predetermined standard.

readiness tests—Achievement tests administered to children at entry to kindergarten.

reasoning—Thinking logically to come to a conclusion or find a result.

recall questions—Questions asked by the teacher about a book to see what children remember.

receptive language—The ability to understand what is being said.

reciprocal relationship—A two-way relationship in which information and power are shared evenly.

reciprocal teaching—A strategy that promotes children's reading comprehension and higher-order thinking by engaging them in summarizing, questioning, clarifying, and predicting.

redirection—Drawing a child's attention or behavior toward a more desirable alternative than the one on which the child is currently focusing.

reflection—Teaching strategy in which teachers help children go beyond remembering what they did to becoming aware of what they learned, what was interesting, how they felt about the experience, and what they can do to build on and extend the experience.

reinforcer—Consequence—either positive or negative—that increases or strengthens a behavior.

reliability—The extent to which the results obtained from a test are accurate and consistent over time.

replacement behaviors—Desirable prosocial behaviors that replace problem behaviors.

representing—Expressing mathematical ideas with words, diagrams, pictures, and/or symbols.

resilience—A child's ability to overcome, adapt to, or minimize the damaging effects of adversity.

Response to Intervention (RTI)—A three-tiered framework intended to prevent learning delays in primary grades from becoming learning disabilities.

rhymes—Two words ending with the same sound.

risk—A possibility of harm that can be minimized with planning and supervision.

risk factors—Inherited or experiential conditions that potentially contribute to poor developmental outcomes for children, such as peer rejection, academic failure, juvenile delinquency, and school expulsion.

risk vs. challenge continuum—Concept that children not only need to be safe but they also need to be challenged if they are to advance their skills and learn how to keep themselves safe.

rough-and-tumble play or big body play—The boisterous, large-motor, physical activity children seem to crave.

rubrics—Descriptive rating scales that detail the qualities related to each rank on the scale; includes clear descriptions of each point on the scale or guidelines for making judgments about a rating.

running record—A chronological record, like a diary, of an individual child's behavior that helps teachers better understand that behavior.

scaffolding—The assistance, guidance, and direction teachers provide children to help them accomplish a task or learn a skill (within their ZPD) that they could not achieve on their own.

scheme or schema—The organization of mental structures people use to think or guide behavior; the structures develop and change with experience.

school readiness—Children's competencies related to success in kindergarten, including physical development, health, and well-being; social-emotional development and learning; cognitive development and general knowledge such as mathematics and science; positive approaches to learning such as curiosity and motivation; and language development and early literacy skills.

science—Study of the physical and natural world, especially by observing and experimenting.

scientifically based curriculum—Derives from research evidence about what kinds of learning outcomes relate to later achievement, and what types of teaching and learning experiences help children acquire those outcomes. Such a curriculum has been evaluated and its effectiveness demonstrated.

scientifically based instructional practices—Curriculum and instructional practices that research has demonstrated improve learning outcomes.

scientific inquiry—Involving children in observing, predicting, and investigating.

scientific method—Method of beginning with a hypothesis, testing it with an experiment, making observations and gathering data, and then confirming or disconfirming the initial hypothesis.

scope—The particular focus of the curriculum at a given point in time; that is, how much of a larger content area will be taught.

screening tests—Tests administered to all children, usually in preschool or kindergarten, as the first step in a process to determine which children are at risk of a possible disability or learning problem; also called *developmental screening*.

script language—The typical ways that people communicate in different contexts or settings.

secure attachment relationship—A responsive and sensitive relationship with caregivers that allows children to venture forth and comfortably explore and learn about the world.

secure base—An attachment figure (mother or caregiver) who serves as an anchor for children to rely on and from which children can safely venture out and explore.

self-actualization theory—Maslow's view that behavior and learning are motivated by a hierarchy of needs.

self-concept—Children's stable perceptions about themselves despite variations in their behavior.

self-esteem—Children's perception of their own worth.

self-regulated learning—Bandura's theory that people not only learn by modeling the behavior of others, but by observing and evaluating their own.

self-regulation—The ability to adapt or control behavior, emotions, and thinking according to the demands of the situation.

separation anxiety—Feeling a baby experiences when the caregiver is not in sight; the baby may cry or cling to a caregiver in the presence of strangers; usually occurs around 8 months of age.

sequence—The order in which knowledge and skills will be taught.

sequential language learning—Learning a second language *after* the first language is relatively well established.

shaping—Teaching a new skill or behavior by rewarding each step or successive approximation toward the goal.

simultaneous acquisition—Learning two languages at the same time during the earliest years of life.

slippery egg messages—Communications that are difficult to "toss" (send) and "catch" (receive), and must be expressed gently to be sure that the "catcher" receives the communication as intended.

social cognitive theory—Bandura's theory that people can learn efficiently from observing the consequences of another person's behavior.

social development—The ability to establish positive relationships with adults and peers, make friends, cooperate, and resolve conflicts.

social studies—The integrated study of the history, geography, economics, political science, and other related aspects of societies of the past, present, and future.

social-conventional knowledge—The culturally agreed-on names and symbols that need to be transmitted to the learner directly.

social-emotional learning—Children's ability to recognize and regulate their emotions, establish and maintain positive relationships, make responsible decisions, and solve social problems constructively. Also called *social competence*.

sociocultural theory—Vygotsky's theory that children learn from social interaction within a cultural context.

socioeconomic status (SES)—Family income level.

solitary play—Children play alone, usually with toys or objects.

spatial awareness—Perceptions of where the body is.

spatial relations—Spatial sense and familiarity with shape, structure, and location.

specialized instruction—Involves teachers matching an individual child's goals and objectives with appropriate teaching methods and materials, deciding what amount of assistance each child with special needs requires, providing the assistance, and then determining whether the instruction was effective.

stability movements—Movements in which the body remains in place but moves around its horizontal or vertical axis; examples include balancing, dodging, starting, and stopping.

stable order principle—The concept that number words need to be said in the same order every time.

stage manager—Teachers set the stage for children's play by providing the props and theme and being available to respond to children's requests.

standardized assessment—Assessment of all children using the same procedures and performing the same task under the same conditions.

standardized testing—Uses prescribed methods for administering and scoring.

structural quality—Features of an early childhood program, such as maximum group sizes, teacher/child ratios, and teacher qualifications, that are relatively easy to quantify and measure.

structured physical activity—Adult-guided play that is designed for a purpose such as increasing endurance or flexibility.

subitizing—The ability to look at a small set of objects (four or fewer) and know how many there are without counting.

successive approximations—Behaviors that are reinforced (shaped) that are not the actual desired behaviors, but each approximate behavior that is closer to the goal.

summative assessment—Assessing student learning at the end of an educational experience to evaluate the effectiveness of the experience.

supporting—Providing assistance that helps the child to accomplish a difficult task by making it easier.

symbolic representation—The process of mentally using one thing to stand for something else.

synapses—Connections in the brain that carry information between neurons.

syntax—Grammar and sentence structure.

teacher-initiated experiences—Learning experiences in which teachers take the lead by providing explicit information and modeling or demonstrating a skill, as determined by the teacher's goals and direction.

teaching strategy—A behavior or activity that a teacher deliberately selects and flexibly applies to help students construct meaning.

technology—Tools used to change or modify the natural world to meet human needs.

telegraphic speech—Combining words into two-word utterances.

temperament—The pattern of arousal and emotionality that is characteristic of an individual.

temporal awareness—Speeding up or slowing down a movement.

Temporary Assistance for Needy Families (TANF)—Federally funded program, more commonly known as Welfare to Work, that provides temporary financial aid but requires recipients to move into the labor force or schooling.

tennis ball messages—Communications that are easily "tossed" and easily received and that help form the foundation of a relationship; they constitute the everyday chitchat between teachers and parents.

testing—A systematic procedure for evaluating a child's behavior and knowledge that is then assigned a score.

thematic curriculum—Way of integrating curriculum in which a broad topic of interest or a "big idea" provides the basis for making connections across learning goals.

theory—An explanation of how information and observations are organized and relate to one another.

theory of multiple intelligences—Theory developed by Howard Gardner that identifies eight different intelligences as opposed to a single score on an intelligence test; this theory is useful for thinking about variation among children and teaching to their strengths.

time-out—Removing a child to a specified chair or area of the room for a period of time following an unacceptable behavior.

tourist curriculum—An approach in which a culture is visited as though it were an exotic destination where people dress, talk, dance, and eat differently before returning to the "normal" place where we all live.

toxic stress—Children's experience of intense, frequent, and/or prolonged anxiety such as abuse, neglect, violence, or economic deprivation without adult support to help them cope.

transactional theory of development—Theory that development is the result of both biology and experience and how they influence each other.

transitions—Changes from one activity or place to another.

unitizing—Finding or creating a mathematical unit.

universal design—The concept that materials and environments need to be usable by everyone, including those with disabilities, to the greatest extent possible.

universal voluntary prekindergarten—Publicly funded preschool, usually for 4-year-olds but sometimes 3-year-olds; available to any family that chooses to use it.

unstructured free play—Play that is chosen and initiated by children, such as that which occurs on a playground.

utility—Used to benefit children.

validated curriculum—Curriculum that has been evaluated and its effectiveness demonstrated.

validity—The degree to which an instrument measures what it purports to measure.

vicarious learning—Learning by observing the effects of other people's behavior, rather than experiencing rewards or punishments directly.

virtual field trip—Trip taken via the Internet in which children can go anywhere in the world.

visual arts—Creative processes and products that involve drawing, painting, sculpting with clay, or making models of objects using a variety of materials.

visual literacy—Ability to create visual messages and to interpret messages contained in visual communications.

vocabulary—A combination of receptive and expressive language; the number of words a person knows and uses when listening or speaking.

wait time—The length of time that a teacher waits for a response after asking a question or responding to a comment.

webbing—A planning tool that teachers and children create together to organize curriculum content.

Wh- questions—Questions that begin with "Why" or "What" to get children thinking about characters' motives or feelings.

widening horizons approach—Approach to social studies curriculum planning designed to begin "where children are" and then expand outward.

windows of opportunity—Periods of time during which human brains are particularly susceptible and responsive to certain types of experience.

word identification—The process of decoding unfamiliar words and recognizing high-frequency (both regularly and irregularly spelled) words by sight.

working memory—The ability to retain information for a short period of time, which enables transfer to long-term memory.

WPA nurseries—Federal emergency relief nursery schools, funded by the Works Progress Administration (WPA) during the Great Depression, designed to support the economy by providing jobs for those who worked on the site and child care services to families seeking work.

zone of proximal development (ZPD)—The distance between the actual developmental level an individual has achieved (her independent level of problem solving) and the level of potential development she could achieve with adult guidance or through collaboration with other children.

References

Chapter 1

Almon, J., & Miller, E. (2011). *The crisis in early education: The case for more play and less pressure.* College Park, MD: Alliance for Childhood. Retrieved from http://www.allianceforchildhood.org/sites/allianceforchildhood.org/files/file/crisis_in_early_ed.pdf

Annie E. Casey Foundation. (2014). *2014 Kids Count data book: State trends in child well-being.* Baltimore: Author. Retrieved November 16, 2014, from http://www.aecf.org/2014db

Aud, S., Fox, M., & KewalRamani, A. (2010). *Status and trends in the education of racial and ethnic groups* (NCES 2010-015). U.S. Department of Education, National Center for Education Statistics. Washington, DC: U.S. Government Printing Office.

Barnett, W. S. (2008). *Preschool education and its lasting effects: Research and policy implications.* Boulder, CO, and Tempe, AZ: Education and the Public Interest Center & Education Policy Research Unit. Retrieved February 23, 2009, from http://epicpolicy.org/publication/preschooleducation

Barnett, W. S. (2013a). *Expanding access to quality pre-K is sound public policy.* New Brunswick, NJ: National Institute for Early Education Research.

Barnett, W. S. (2013b). *Getting the facts right on pre-K and the president's pre-K proposal: Policy report.* New Brunswick, NJ: National Institute for Early Education Research.

Barnett, W. S., & Carolan, M. E. (2014). *Facts about fadeout: The research base on long-term impacts of high quality pre-K* (CEELO FastFact). New Brunswick, NJ: Center on Enhancing Early Learning Outcomes.

Barnett, W. S., Carolan, M. E., Fitzgerald, J., & Squires, J. H. (2011). *The state of preschool 2011: State preschool yearbook.* New Brunswick, NJ: National Institute for Early Education Research.

Barnett, W. S., Carolan, M. E., Squires, J. H., & Brown, K. C. (2013). *The state of preschool 2013: State preschool yearbook.* New Brunswick, NJ: National Institute for Early Education Research, Rutgers Graduate School of Education.

Barnett, W. S., & Frede, E. (2010). The promise of preschool: Why we need early education for all. *American Educator, 34*(1), 21–29, 40.

Barnett, W. S., & Yarosz, D. J. (2007, November). *Who goes to preschool and why does it matter?* (Preschool Policy Brief, Issue 15). New Brunswick, NJ: National Institute for Early Education Research. Retrieved October 9, 2009, from http://nieer.org/resources/policybriefs/15.pdf

Berrueta-Clement, J. R., Schweinhart, L. J., Barnett, W. S., Epstein, A. S., & Weikart, D. P. (1984). *Changed lives: The effects of the Perry preschool program on youths through age 19.* Ypsilanti, MI: High/Scope Press.

Bornfreund, L., McCann, C., Williams, C., & Guernsey, L. (2014). *Beyond subprime learning: Accelerating progress in early education.* Washington, DC: New America Foundation.

Bureau of Labor Statistics. (2014). *Employment characteristics of families.* Washington, DC: U.S. Department of Labor. Retrieved November 24, 2014, from http://www.bls.gov/news.release/famee.nr0.htm

Burger, K. (2010). How does early childhood care and education affect cognitive development? An international review of the effects of early interventions for children from different social backgrounds. *Early Childhood Research Quarterly, 25*(2), 140–165.

Campbell, F. A., Wasik, B. H., Pungello, E. P., Burchinal, M., Barbarin, O., Kainz, K., et al. (2008). Young adult outcomes from the Abecedarian and CARE early childhood educational interventions. *Early Childhood Research Quarterly, 23*(4), 452–466.

Center for Law and Social Policy (CLASP). (2011). *CLASP DataFinder.* Retrieved September 8, 2011, from http://www.clasp.org/data

Child Care Aware® of America. (2013). *We can do better: Ranking of state child care center regulations and oversight 2013 update.* Arlington, VA: Author.

Children's Defense Fund (CDF). (2011). *State of America's children 2011.* Washington, DC: Author.

Children's Defense Fund (CDF). (2014). *The state of America's children 2014.* Washington, DC: Author. Retrieved June 29, 2015, from http://www.childrensdefense.org/library/state-of-americas-children/2014-soac.pdf

Colasanti, M. (2007). *Kindergarten entrance age: A 30 year trend analysis.* Denver, CO: Education Commission of the States. Retrieved November 24, 2014, from http://inpathways.net/kindergarten_trend_analyses.pdf

Colker, L. (2008). Twelve characteristics of effective early childhood teachers. *Young Children, 63*(2), 68–73. Retrieved from https://www.naeyc.org/files/yc/file/200803/BTJ_Colker.pdf

Collins, M. F. (2012). Sagacious, sophisticated, and sedulous: The importance of discussing 50-cent words with preschoolers. *Young Children, 67*(5), 66–72.

Committee for Economic Development. (2012). *Unfinished business: Continued investment in child care and early education is critical to business and America's future.* Washington, DC: Author. Retrieved from http://www.ced.org

Copeland, K. A., Sherman, S. N., Kendeigh, C. A., Kalkwarf, H. J., & Saelens, B. E. (2012). Societal values and policies may curtail preschool children's physical activity in child care centers. Retrieved from http://pediatrics.aappublications.org/content/early/2012/01/02/peds.2011-2102.full.pdf+html

Copple, C., & Bredekamp, S. (Eds.). (2009). *Developmentally appropriate practice in early childhood programs serving children from birth through age 8* (Rev. ed.). Washington, DC: National Association for the Education of Young Children.

Cost, Quality, and Child Care Outcomes Study Team. (1995). *Cost, quality, and child outcomes in child care centers* (2nd ed.). Denver: University of Colorado at Denver, Economics Department.

Curby, T. W., Brock, L., & Hamre, B. (2013). Teachers' emotional support consistency predicts children's achievement gains and social skills. *Early Education and Development, 24,* 292–309.

De Bellis, M. D., Keshaven, M. S., Clark, D. B., Casey, B. J., Giedd, J. B., Boring, A. M., et al. (1999). Developmental traumatology. Part 2: Brain development. *Biological Psychiatry, 45,* 1271–1284.

Division for Early Childhood & National Association for the Education of Young Children. (2009). *Early childhood inclusion: A joint position statement of the Division for Early Childhood (DEC) and the National Association for the Education of Young Children (NAEYC).* Chapel Hill: The University of North Carolina, FPG Child Development Institute. Retrieved from http://npdci.fpg.unc.edu/sites/npdci.fpg.unc.edu/files/resources/EarlyChildhoodInclusion_0.pdf

Downer, J. T., Lopez, M. L., Grimm, K. J., Hamagami, A., Pianta, R. C., & Howes, C. (2012). Observations of teacher-child interactions in classroom serving Latinos and dual language learners: Applicability of the Classroom Assessment Scoring System in diverse settings. *Early Childhood Research Quarterly, 27*(1), 21–32.

Education Commission of the States. (2013). *Kindergarten entrance age: 50 state analysis.* Denver, CO: Author.

Ennis, S. R., Ríos-Vargas, M., & Albert, N. G. (2011). *The Hispanic population: 2010. 2010 Census Briefs.* U.S. Census Bureau. (2011). Retrieved from http://www.census.gov/prod/cen2010/briefs/c2010br-04.pdf

Epstein, A. S. (2007). *The intentional teacher: Choosing the best strategies for young children's learning.* Washington, DC: National Association for the Education of Young Children.

Espinosa, L. M. (2013). *Pre-K–3rd: Challenging common myths about dual language learners, an update to the seminal 2008 report.* New York: Foundation for Child Development.

Fernald, A., Marchman, V. A., & Weislader, A. (2013). SES differences in language processing skill and vocabulary are evident at 18 months. *Developmental Science, 16*(2), 234–248.

Fight Crime: Invest in Kids. (2014). *I'm the guy you pay later: Sheriffs, chiefs, and prosecutors urge America to cut crime by investing now in high-quality early education and care.* Washington, DC: Author. Retrieved November 22, 2014, from http://www.fightcrime.org/wp-content/uploads/NE-Im-the-Guy-Report-1.pdf

First Five Years Fund. (2014) *America speaks: New poll shows investing in early childhood education is a national priority.* Retrieved June 29, 2015, from http://ffyf.org/wp-content/uploads/2014/07/F_FFYF_ResearchSummaryHandout_071414.pdf

Foundation for Child Development. (2008). *America's vanishing potential: The case for preK–3rd education.* New York: Author.

FPG Child Development Institute. (2008). How is pre-K quality measured? Findings from NCEDL suggest new directions. *Early Developments, 12*(1), 5–9.

Fuller, B. F. (2007). *Standardized childhood: The political and cultural struggle over early education.* Palo Alto, CA: Stanford University Press.

Goffin, S. G., & Washington, V. (2007). *Ready or not? Leadership choices in early care and education.* New York: Teachers College Press.

Gormley, W. T. (2008). *The effects of Oklahoma's universal pre-kindergarten program on Hispanic children,* Washington, DC: Center for Research on Children in the U.S. (CROCUS), Georgetown University, retrieved July 28, 2009, from http://www.crocus.georgetown.edu

Graue, M. E. (2009). Reimagining kindergarten: Restoring a developmental approach when accountability demands are pushing formal instruction on the youngest learners. *The School Administrator, 66*(10), 10–15.

Hamre, B., La Paro, K., Pianta, R., & Locasale-Crouch, J. (2014). *Classroom Assessment Scoring System (CLASS) manual, infant*. Baltimore: Paul H. Brookes.

Harms, T., Clifford, R. M., & Cryer, D. (2014). *Early Childhood Environment Rating Scale (ECERS-3)* (3rd ed.). New York: Teachers College Press.

Head Start. (2011a). *About Head Start*. Retrieved June 16, 2015, from http://eclkc.ohs.hhs.acf.gov/hslc/about%20Head%20Start

Head Start. (2013). *Head Start program facts, fiscal year 2013*. Retrieved November 24, 2014, from http://eclkc.ohs.acf.hhs.gov/hslc/data/factsheets/docs/hs-program-fact-sheet-2013.pdf

Head Start. (2014a). *Early Head Start Program Facts for Fiscal Year 2012*. Retrieved November 24, 2014, from http://eclkc.ohs.acf.hhs.gov/hslc/tta-system/ehsnrc/about-ehs

Head Start. (2014b). Head Start Program Facts Fiscal Year 2014. Retrieved June 26, 2015, from http://eclkc.ohs.acf.hhs.gov/hslc/data/factsheets/docs/hs-program-fact-sheet-2014.pdf

Head Start. (2014c). *Office of Head Start—Services snapshot: National all programs 2013–2014*. Retrieved November 24, 2014, from http://eclkc.ohs.acf.hhs.gov/hslc/data/psr/2014/NATIONAL_SNAPSHOT_ALL_PROGRAMS.pdf

Head Start. (2015a). *Head Start early learning outcomes framework 2015*. Retrieved June 29, 2015, from http://eclkc.ohs.acf.hhs.gov/hslc/hs/sr/approach/cdelf

Head Start. (2015c). *Head Start program performance standards*. Washington, DC: U.S. Department of Health and Human Services.

Heckman, J. (2013, December 7). *Invest in early childhood development: Reduce deficits, strengthen the economy*. Retrieved November 24, 2014, from http://heckmanequation.org/content/resource/invest-early-childhood-development-reduce-deficits-strengthen-economy

Hemphill, F. C., & Vanneman, A. (2011). *Achievement gaps: How Hispanic and white students in public schools perform in mathematics and reading on the National Assessment of Educational Progress* (NCES 2011-459). Washington, DC: National Center for Education Statistics, Institute of Education Sciences, U.S. Department of Education. Washington, DC.

Hernandez, D. J. (2011). *Double jeopardy: How third grade reading scores and poverty influence high school graduation*. Baltimore: Annie E. Casey Foundation. Retrieved August 29, 2011, from http://gradelevelreading.net/wp-content/uploads/2012/01/Double-Jeopardy-Report-030812-for-web1.pdf

Huang, F. L., Invernizzi, M. A., & Drake, E. A. (2012). The differential effects of preschool: Evidence from Virginia. *Early Childhood Research Quarterly, 27*(1), 33–45.

Institute of Medicine (IOM) & National Research Council (NRC). (2015). *Transforming the workforce for children birth through age 9: A unifying foundation*. Washington, DC: National Academies Press.

Jacobson Chernoff, J., Flanagan, K. D., McPhee, C., & Park, J. (2007). *Preschool: First findings from the preschool follow-up of the Early Childhood Longitudinal Study, Birth Cohort (ECLS-B)* (NCES 2008-025). Washington, DC: U.S. Department of Education, Institute of Education Sciences, National Center for Education Statistics.

Jones, J. (2014, September 8). *In U.S., 70% Favor Federal Funds to Expand Pre-K Education*. Washington, DC: Gallup. Retrieved November 24, 2014, from http://www.gallup.com/poll/175646/favor-federal-funds-expand-pre-education.aspx

Kauerz, K., & Coffman, J. (2013). *Framework for planning, implementing, and evaluating pre-K–3rd grade approaches*. Seattle, WA: College of Education, University of Washington. Retrieved November 28, 2014, from http://depts.washington.edu/pthru3/PreK-3rd_Framework_Legal%20paper.pdf

La Paro, K., Hamre, B., & Pianta, R. (2012). *Classroom Assessment Scoring System (CLASS) manual, toddler*. Baltimore: Paul H. Brookes.

Lipsey, M., Farran, D., Hofer, K., Bilbrey, C., & Dong, N. (2011). *The effects of the Tennessee Voluntary Pre-Kindergarten Program: Initial results*. Peabody Research Institute, Vanderbilt University.

McLoyd, V. C., & Purtell, K. M. (2008). How childhood poverty and income affect children's cognitive functioning and school achievement. In S. Neuman (Ed), *Educating the other America: Top experts tackle poverty, literacy, and achievement in our schools* (pp. 53–72). Baltimore: Paul H. Brookes.

Minervino, J. (2013). Quality in center-based early learning: High-level findings and trends. In *Lessons from research and the classroom: Implementing high-quality pre-K that makes a difference for young children* (September 2014, pp. 3–7). Seattle, WA: Bill and Melinda Gates Foundation. Retrieved from https://docs.gatesfoundation.org/documents/Lessons%20from%20Research%20and%20the%20Classroom_September%202014.pdf

Minervino, J. (2014, January). The essential elements of high-quality pre-K: An analysis of four exemplar programs. In *Lessons from research and the classroom: Implementing high-quality pre-K that makes a difference for young children* (September 2014, pp. 21–29). Seattle, WA: Bill and Melinda Gates Foundation. Retrieved from https://docs.gatesfoundation.org/documents/Lessons%20from%20Research%20and%20the%20Classroom_September%202014.pdf

Mitchell, A. (2012). *Considerations for an effective, inclusive, and implementable Quality Rating and Improvement System*. BUILD Initiative, QRIS National Learning Network. Retrieved from http://qrisnetwork.org/sites/all/files/resources/gscobb/2012-08-03%2016:42/Considerations%20for%20QRIS%20Standards.pdf

National Association for the Education of Young Children (NAEYC). (2008b). *Overview of the NAEYC Early Childhood Program Standards*. Washington, DC: Author. Retrieved November 22, 2014, from http://www.naeyc.org/files/academy/file/OverviewStandards.pdf

National Association for the Education of Young Children (NAEYC). (2009). *Developmentally appropriate practice in early childhood programs serving children from birth through age 8: Position statement*. Washington, DC: Author.

National Association for the Education of Young Children (NAEYC). (2011a). *Code of ethical conduct and statement of commitment* (Reaffirmed and updated May 2011). Retrieved September 9, 2011, from http://www.naeyc.org/files/naeyc/file/positions/PSETH05.pdf

National Association for the Education of Young Children (NAEYC). (2011b). *2010 NAEYC Standards for Initial & Advanced Early Childhood Professional Preparation Programs: For use by Associate, Baccalaureate and Graduate Degree Programs*. Washington, DC: Author.

National Association for the Education of Young Children (NAEYC) & the Fred Rogers Center for Early Learning and Children's Media. (2012). *Technology in early childhood programs serving children from birth through age 8. Joint Position Statement*. Washington, DC: Authors.

National Association of Child Care Resource and Referral Agencies (NACCRRA). (2011). *We can do better: 2011 Update: NACCRRA's ranking of state child care center regulation and oversight*. Arlington, VA: Author.

National Center for Children in Poverty (NCCP). (2014). *Child poverty*. Retrieved November 13, 2014, from http://www.nccp.org/topics/childpoverty.html

National Center for Education Statistics. (2013). *The nation's report card: A first look: 2013 mathematics and reading*. Washington, DC: Institute of Education Sciences, U.S. Department of Education.

National Center for Education Statistics. (2014a). *The condition of education: Charter school enrollment*. Washington, DC: U.S. Department of Education. Retrieved November 24, 2014, from http://nces.ed.gov/programs/coe/indicator_cgb.asp.

National Center for Education Statistics. (2014b). *The condition of education: Preprimary enrollment*. Washington, DC: U.S. Department of Education. Retrieved November 24, 2014, from http://nces.ed.gov/programs/coe/indicator_cfa.asp

National Center on Family Homelessness at American Institutes for Research. (2014). *America's youngest outcasts: A report card on child homelessness*. Waltham, MA: Author.

National Institute of Child Health and Human Development (NICHD) Early Child Care Research Network. (2002). The relation of first grade classroom environment to structural classroom features, teacher, and student behaviors. *The Elementary School Journal, 102*, 367–387.

Neugebauer, R. (2011, March/April). *The proud story of military child care*. Redmond, WA: Exchange Magazine.

Neuman, S. B. (Ed.). (2008). *Educating the other America: Top experts tackle poverty, literacy, and achievement in our schools*. Baltimore: Paul H. Brookes.

Office of Early Learning. (2014). *Early learning: America's middle class promise begins early: The plan*. Washington, DC: U.S. Department of Education. Retrieved from http://www.ed.gov/early-learning

Parkinson, J., & Rowan, B. (2008). Poverty, early literacy achievement, and education reform. In S. Neuman, (Ed.), *Educating the other America: Top experts tackle poverty, literacy, and achievement in our schools* (pp. 73–90). Baltimore: Paul H. Brookes.

Peisner-Feinberg, E. S., Burchinal, M. R., Clifford, R. M., Culkin, M. L., Howes, C., Kagan, S. L., et al. (1999). *The children of the Cost, Quality, and Child Outcomes Study go to school*. Chapel Hill: University of North Carolina.

Pianta, R. C., La Paro, K. M., & Hamre, B. K. (2008). *Classroom assessment scoring system (CLASS)*. Baltimore: Paul H. Brookes.

Puma, M., Bell, S., Cook, R., Heid, C., Lopez, M., Zill, N., et al. (2005). *Head Start impact study: First year findings*. Washington, DC: U.S. Department of Health and Human Services, Administration for Children and Families.

Ravitch, D. (2013, February 26). Why I cannot support the Common Core standards. *Diane Ravitch's Blog*. Retrieved July 2, 2014, from http://dianeravitch.net/2013/02/26/why-i-cannot-support-the-common-core-standards

Reynolds, A. J., Temple, J. A., Robertson, D. L., White, B. A. B., & Ou, S. R. (2011). Age 26 cost–benefit analysis of the child-parent center early education program. *Child Development, 82*(1).

Schechter, C., & Bye, B. (2007). Preliminary evidence for the impact of mixed-income preschools on low-income children's language growth. *Early Childhood Research Quarterly, 22*(1), 137–146.

Schweinhart, L. J., Barnes, H. V., & Weikart, D. P. (1993). *Significant benefits: The High/Scope Perry Preschool study through age 27*. Ypsilanti, MI: High/Scope Press.

Schweinhart, L. J., Montie, J., Xiang, Z., Barnett, W. S., Belfield, C. R., & Nores, M. (2005). *Lifetime effects: The High/Scope Perry Preschool study through age 40* (Monographs of the High/Scope Educational Research Foundation, 14). Ypsilanti, MI: High/Scope Press.

Schweinhart, L. J., Xiang, Z., Daniel-Echols, M., Browning, K., & Wakabayashi, T. (2012). *Michigan Great Start Readiness Program evaluation: High school graduation and grade retention findings*. Ypsilanti, MI: HighScope Educational Research Foundation.

Scott-Little, C. (2011). *Aligning state standards, the Head Start Child Development and Early Learning Framework, and our work with children and families*. Baltimore: Paper presented at the Office of Head Start, February 2011, Retrieved from http://eclkc.ohs.acf.hhs.gov

Shonkoff, J. P. (2011). Protecting brains, not simply stimulating minds. *Science, 333*(6045), 982–983.

Shonkoff, J. P., Garner, A. S., & the Committee on Psychosocial Effects of Child and Family Health. (2012). *Pediatrics, 129*(1), e232–e246. Retrieved from http://pediatrics.aappublications.org/content/129/1/e232.full.pdf+html

Shuler, C. (2009). *Pockets of potential: Using mobile technologies to promote children's learning*, New York: The Joan Ganz Cooney Center at Sesame Workshop.

Thai, A., Lowenstein, D., Ching, D., & Rejeski, D. (2009). *Game changer: Investing in digital play to advance children's learning and health*. New York: The Joan Ganz Cooney Center at Sesame Workshop.

Vogel, C. A., Yange, Y., Moiduddun, E. M., Kisker, E. E., & Carlson, B. W. (2010). *Early Head Start children in grade 5: Long-term follow-up of the Early Head Start Research and Evaluation Study sample*. OPRE Report #2011-8. Washington, DC: Office of Planning, Research, and Evaluation, Administration for Children and Families, U.S. Department of Health and Human Services.

Walters, C. (2014, October). *Inputs in the production of early childhood human capital: Evidence from Head Start*. Berkeley, CA: National Bureau of Economic Research. Retrieved November 25, 2014, from http://www.nber.org/papers/w20639

Whitebook, M. (2014). *Building a skilled teacher workforce: Shared and divergent challenges in early care and education and in grades K–12*. Bill and Melinda Gates Foundation. Retrieved November 24, 2014, from http://www.irle.berkeley.edu/cscce/wp-content/uploads/2014/09/Building-a-Skilled-Teacher-Workforce_September-2014_9-25.pdf

Whitebook, M., Phillips, D., & Howes, C. (2014). *Worthy work, STILL unliveable wages: The early childhood workforce 25 years after the National Child Care Staffing Study*. Berkeley, CA: Center for the Study of Child Care Employment, University of California, Berkeley.

Yoshikawa, H., Weiland, C., Brooks-Gunn, J., Burchinal, M. R., Espinosa, L. M., Gormley, W. T., et al. (2013). *Investing in our future: The evidence base on preschool education*. New York: Foundation for Child Development. Retrieved from http://fcd-us.org/sites/default/files/Evidence%20Base%20on%20Preschool%20Education%20FINAL.pdf

Chapter 2

Anderson, C. J. (2013). Child champion, professionals' mentor, hothead: Substance of "A Giant in the Field." In B. F. Hinitz (Ed.), *The hidden history of early childhood education* (pp. 215–237). New York: Routledge.

Ansari, A., & Winsler, A. (2014). Montessori public school pre-K programs and the school readiness of low-income Black and Latino children. *Journal of Educational Psychology, 106*(4), 1066–1079.

Aries, P. (1962). *Centuries of childhood: A social history of family life*. New York: Vintage Books.

Biber, B. (1977). A developmental-interaction approach: Bank Street College of Education. In M. C. Day &

R. K. Parker (Eds,), *The preschool in action: Exploring early childhood programs* (2nd ed., pp. 421–460). Boston: Allyn and Bacon.

Bredekamp, S. (2001). Improving professional practice: A letter to Patty Smith Hill. In *NAEYC at 75: Reflections on the Past, Challenges for the Future* (pp. 89–124). Washington, DC: National Association for the Education of Young Children.

Bredekamp, S., & Copple, C. (Eds.). (1997). *Developmentally appropriate practice in early childhood programs* (Rev. ed.). Washington, DC: National Association for the Education of Young Children.

Bredekamp, S., & Glowacki, S. (1996). The first decade of NAEYC accreditation: Growth and impact on the field. In S. Bredekamp & B. A. Willer (Eds.), *NAEYC accreditation: A decade of learning and the years ahead* (pp. 1–10). Washington, DC: National Association for the Education of Young Children.

Bunseki Fu-Kiai, K. K., & Lukondo-Wamba, A. M. (1988). *Kindezi: The Kongo art of babysitting*. New York: Vantage Press.

Cantor, P. (2013, May). Elizabeth Peabody: America's kindergarten pioneer. *Young Children, 68*, 92–93. Retrieved September 10, 2014, from http://www.naeyc.org/yc/files/yc/file/201305/0513_OPH_Elizabeth_Peabody.pdf

Cerda, N., & Hernandez, C. M. (2006). *History of bilingual education*. Cervantes, A., & Callanan, M. (1998). Labels and explanations in mother-child emotion talk: Age and gender differentiation. *Developmental Psychology, 34*(1), 88–98.

Copple, C., & Bredekamp, S. (Eds.). (2009). *Developmentally appropriate practice in early childhood programs serving children from birth through age 8* (Rev. ed.). Washington, DC: National Association for the Education of Young Children.

Cunningham, C. E., & Osborn, D. K. (1979). A historical examination of blacks in early childhood education. *Young Children, 34*(3), 20–29.

Dewey, J. (1900). *The school and society*. Chicago: University of Chicago Press.

Dewey, J. (1916). *Democracy and education*. New York: Free Press.

Dewey, J. (1929). *My pedagogic creed*. Washington, DC: Progressive Education Association.

Elkind, D. (2007). *The hurried child: Growing up too fast, too soon* (25th Anniversary ed.). Cambridge, MA: Da Capo Press.

Elkind, D. (2015). *Giants in the nursery: A biographical history of developmentally appropriate practice*. St. Paul, MN: Redleaf Press.

Field, S. L., & Baumi, M. (2014). Lucy Sprague Mitchell: Champion for experiential learning. *Young Children, 69*(4), 94–99.

Giardiello, P. (2014). *Pioneers in early childhood education*. New York: Routledge.

Greenberg, P. (1987). Lucy Sprague Mitchell: A major missing link between early childhood education in the 1980s and progressive education in the 1890s–1930s. *Young Children, 42*(5), 70–83. Hall, E. L., & Rudkin, J. K. (2011). *Seen and heard: Children's rights in early childhood education*. New York: Teachers College Press.

Hewes, D. W. (1976). Patty Smith Hill: Pioneer for young children. *Young Children, 31*(4), 297–306.

Hewes, D. W., & the NAEYC Organizational History and Archives Committee. (2001). NAEYC's first half-century: 1926–1976. In *National Association for the Education of Young Children (NAEYC), NAEYC at 75: 1926–2001* (pp. 35–52). Washington, DC: Author.

Hill, P. S. (1926/1987). The function of the kindergarten. *Young Children, 42*(5), 12–19.

Hinitz, B. S. F. (2014, May). Head Start: A bridge from past to future. *Young Children,69*, 94–97. Retrieved September 10, 2014, from http://www.naeyc.org/yc/files/yc/file/201405/YC0514_OPH_Hinitz.pdf

Hoberman, M. A. (2004). *Whose garden is it?* Boston: Houghton Mifflin Harcourt.

Krauss, R. (1945). *The carrot seed*. New York: HarperCollins.

Lascarides, V. C., & Hinitz, B. F. (2000). *History of early childhood education*. New York: Routledge.

Levin, D., & Kilbourne, J. (2008). *So sexy, so soon: The new sexualized childhood and what parents can do to protect kids*. New York: Ballantine Books.

Lillard, A. S. (2005). *Montessori: The science behind the genius*. New York: Oxford University Press.

Lillard, A. S., & Else-Quest, N. M. (2006). An evaluation of Montessori education. *Science, 313*, 1893–1894.

MacKenzie, B. (2011). Caring for Rosie the Riveter's children. *Young Children, 66*(6), 68–70.

Marks, E. L., & Graham, E. T. (2004). *Establishing a research agenda for American Indian and Alaska Native Head Start programs*. Washington, DC: U.S. Department of Health and Human Services, Head Start Bureau.

Mbiti, J. (1992). *African religions and philosophy* (2nd ed.). Portsmouth, NH: Heinemann.

Mitchell, A., & David, J. (1992). *Explorations with young children: A curriculum guide from the Bank Street College of Education*. Mt. Rainier, MD: Gryphon House.

Montessori, M. (1909/1964). *The Montessori method*. New York: Schocken.

Montessori, M. (1912/1964). *The Montessori method*. Translated by A. E. George. New York: Schocken.

Neugebauer, B. (1995, January/February). Meet cover advocate Winona Elliott Sample, Santa Clara, California. *Child Care Information Exchange*, 57–58.

Nourot, P. M. (2005). Historical perspectives on early childhood education. In J. L. Roopnarine & J. E. Johnson (Eds.), *Approaches to early childhood education* (5th ed., pp. 3–43). Upper Saddle River, NJ: Pearson.

Osborn, D. K. (1991). *Early childhood education in historical perspective* (3rd ed.). Athens, GA: Daye Press.

Pratt, C. (1948). *I learn from children*. New York: Simon & Schuster.

Reagan, T. (2005). *Non-Western educational traditions: Indigenous approaches to education thought and practice* (3rd ed.). Mahwah, NJ: Lawrence Erlbaum Associates.

Rumbaut, R. G. (2006). The making of a people. In M. Tienda & F. Mitchell (Eds.), *Hispanics and the future of America* (pp. 16–65). Washington, DC: National Academies Press.

Shapiro, E. K., & Nager, N. (1999). *The developmental-interaction approach to education: Retrospect and prospect*. New York: Bank Street College of Education. Retrieved from https://s3.amazonaws.com/bankstreet_web/media/filer_public/filer_public/2013/02/12/occasional-papers-1.pdf

Simpson, J. (2012, November). Oneida Cockrell: Pioneer in the field of early childhood education. *Young Children, 67*, 58–60. Retrieved September 10, 2014, from http://www.naeyc.org/yc/files/yc/file/201211/Heritage1112.pdf

Simpson, J. W., & McConnell-Farmer, J. L. (2013). Selected African-American pioneers of early childhood education. In B. F. Hinitz (Ed.), *The hidden history of early childhood education*, 143–158. New York: Routledge.

Simpson, W. J. (n.d.). A biographical study of black educators in early childhood education. Unpublished dissertation, Fielding Institute.

Snyder, A. (1972). *Dauntless women in early childhood education, 1856–1931*. Washington, DC: Association for Childhood Education International.

Some, S. (1999). *Welcoming spirit home: Ancient African teachings to celebrate children and community*. Novato, CA: New World Library.

Stoltz, L. M. H. (1977). *An American child development pioneer: Lois Meek Stoltz* (Interview by R. Takanishi, typescript). Washington, DC: National Archives.

Strauss, V. (2014, July 19). Mom: My kindergartner was "work-sheeted to death." *Washington Post.* Retrieved July 19, 2014, from http://www.washingtonpost.com/blogs/answer-sheet/wp/2014/07/19/mom-my-kindergartner-was-work-sheeted-to-death/

Wolfe, J. (2000). *Learning from the past: Historical voices in early childhood education.* Mayerthorpe, Alberta: Piney Branch Press.

Wortham, S. C. (2002). *Childhood: 1892–2002.* Wheaton, MD: Association for Childhood Education International.

Zellizer, V. (1981). The price and value of children: The case of children's insurance. *American Journal of Sociology, 86*(5), 1036–1056.

Chapter 3

Alliance for Childhood. (2010). *The loss of children's play: A public health issue.* College Park, MD: Author. Retrieved from http://www.allianceforchildhood.org

Almon, J., & Miller, E. (2011). *The crisis in early education: The case for more play and less pressure.* College Park, MD: Alliance for Childhood. Retrieved from http://www.allianceforchildhood.org/sites/allianceforchildhood.org/files/file/crisis_in_early_ed.pdf

Barbarin, O. A., & Wasik, B. H. (Eds.). (2009). *Handbook of child development and early education: Research to practice.* New York: Guilford Press.

Barker, K. (2005, November 30). Paparazzi get an audience with the panda. *Washington Post,* p. B5.

Barnett, W. S., Jung, K., Youn, M.-J., & Frede, E. C. (2013). *APPLES, Abbott Preschool Program longitudinal effects study: Fifth grade follow-up.* New Brunswick, NJ: National Institute for Early Education Research, Rutgers University. Retrieved from http://nieer.org/sites/nieer/files/APPLES%205th%20Grade.pdf

Bassok, D., & Reardon, S. F. (2013). "Academic redshirting" in kindergarten: Prevalence, patterns and implications. *Educational Evaluation and Policy Analysis, 35*(3), 293–297.

Bassok, D., & Rorem, A. (2014). *Is kindergarten the new first grade? The changing nature of kindergarten in the age of accountability.* EdPolicy Works Working Paper Series No. 20. Retrieved from http://curry.virginia.edu/uploads/resourceLibrary/20_Bassok_Is_Kindergarten_The_New_First_Grade.pdf

Berk, L. E. (2012). *Child Development* (9th ed.). Upper Saddle River, NJ: Pearson.

Bierman, K. L., Domitrovich, C. E., Nix, R. L., Gest, S. D., Welsh, J. A., Greenberg, M. T., et al. (2008). Promoting academic and social–emotional school readiness: The Head Start REDI program. *Child Development, 79*(6), 1802–1817.

Bishop-Josef, S. J., & Zigler, E. (2011). The cognitive/academic emphasis versus the whole child approach: The 50-year debate. In E. Zigler, W. S. Gilliam, & W. S. Barnett (Eds.), *The pre-k debates: Current controversies and issues* (pp. 83–88). Baltimore: Brookes.

Bowman, B. T., Donovan, M. S., & Burns, S. (Eds.). (2001). *Eager to learn: Educating our preschoolers* (National Research Council, Committee on Early Childhood Pedagogy Report). Washington, DC: National Academies Press.

Bredekamp, S. (Ed.). (1987). *Developmentally appropriate practice in early childhood programs serving children from birth through age 8* (Expanded ed.). Washington, DC: National Association for the Education of Young Children.

Bredekamp, S. (1997a). Developmentally appropriate practice: The early childhood teacher as decision maker. In S. Bredekamp & C. Copple (Eds.), *Developmentally appropriate practice in early childhood programs* (Rev. ed., pp. 33–52). Washington, DC: National Association for the Education of Young Children.

Bredekamp, S. (1997b). NAEYC issues revised position statement on developmentally appropriate practice in early childhood programs. *Young Children,52*(2), 34–40.

Bredekamp, S., & Copple, C. (Eds.). (1997). *Developmentally appropriate practice in early childhood programs* (Rev. ed.). Washington, DC: National Association for the Education of Young Children.

Bronfenbrenner, U. (Ed.). (2004). *Making human beings human: Bioecological perspectives on human development.* Thousand Oaks, CA: Sage.

Bryant, D. (2010). *Observational measures of quality in center-based early care and education programs,* OPRE Research-to-Policy, Research-to-Practice Brief OPRE 2011-10c. Washington, DC: Office of Planning, Research, and Evaluation, Administration for Children and Families, U.S. Department of Health and Human Services.

Campaign for Commercial-Free Childhood & Alliance for Childhood. (2012, October). *Facing the screen dilemma: Young children, technology, and early education.* Boston: Campaign for Commercial-Free Childhood; New York: Alliance for Childhood.

Carle, E. (1969). *The very hungry caterpillar.* New York: Philomel, Penguin Group.

Common Core State Standards Initiative. (2011a). *Common core standards for English language arts.* Washington, DC: Council for Chief State School Officers and National Governor's Association. Retrieved February 17, 2012, from www.corestandards.org

Common Core State Standards Initiative. (2011b). *Common core standards for mathematics.* Washington, DC: Council for Chief State School Officers and National Governor's Association. Retrieved February 17, 2012, from http://www.corestandards.org

Common Sense Media. (2013, Fall). *Zero to eight: Children' media use in America 2013. A Common Sense Media research study.* Retrieved September 3, 2014, from https://www.commonsensemedia.org/file/zero-to-eight-2013pdf-0/download

Copple, C., & Bredekamp, S. (2006). *Basics of developmentally appropriate practice: An introduction for teachers of children 3 to 6.* Washington, DC: National Association for the Education of Young Children.

Copple, C., & Bredekamp, S. (Eds.). (2009). *Developmentally appropriate practice in early childhood programs serving children from birth through age 8* (Rev. ed.). Washington, DC: National Association for the Education of Young Children.

Copple, C., Bredekamp, S., Koralek, D., & Charner, K. (Eds.). (2013a). *Developmentally appropriate practice: Focus on infants and toddlers.* Washington, DC: National Association for the Education of Young Children.

Copple, C., Bredekamp, S., Koralek, D., & Charner, K. (Eds.). (2013b). *Developmentally appropriate practice: Focus on preschoolers.* Washington, DC: National Association for the Education of Young Children.

Copple, C., Bredekamp, S., Koralek, D., & Charner, K. (Eds.). (2014a). *Developmentally appropriate practice: Focus on children in first, second, and third grades.* Washington, DC: National Association for the Education of Young Children.

Copple, C., Bredekamp, S., Koralek, D., & Charner, K. (Eds.). (2014b). *Developmentally appropriate practice: Focus on kindergartners.* Washington, DC: National Association for the Education of Young Children.

Dahlberg, G., Moss, P., & Pence, A. R. (2007). *Beyond quality in early childhood education: Languages of evaluation* (2nd ed.). New York: Routledge.

Defending the Early Years. (2014). *Six reasons to reject the Common Core standards for K–grade 3.* Jamaica Plain, MA: Author. Retrieved from http://deyproject.org/2014/05/01/6-reasons-to-reject-the-common-core-state-standards-for-k-grade-3/

Diamond, K. E., Justice, L. M., Siegler, R. S., & Snyder, P. A. (2013). *Synthesis of IES research on early intervention and early childhood education.* (NCSER 2013-3001). Washington, DC: National Center for Special Education Research, Institute of Education Sciences, U.S. Department of Education. Retrieved from http://ies.ed.gov/

Donohue, C. (Ed.). (2015). *Technology and digital media in the early years.* New York: Routledge Taylor & Francis Group.

Epstein, A. S. (2014). *The intentional teacher: Choosing the best strategies for young children's learning* (Rev. ed.). Washington, DC: National Association for the Education of Young Children.

Fuligni, A. S., Howes, C., Huang, Y., Hong, S. S., & Lara-Cinisomo, S. (2012). Activity settings and daily routines in preschool classrooms: Diverse experiences in early learning settings for low-income children. *Early Childhood Research Quarterly, 27*(2), 198–209.

Graue, M. E. (2009). Reimagining kindergarten: Restoring a developmental approach when accountability demands are pushing formal instruction on the youngest learners. *The School Administrator, 66*(10), 10–15.

Graue, M. E., & Delaney, K. (2011, November 4). *Being developmentally and culturally responsive.* Paper presented at the annual meeting of the National Association for the Education of Young Children, Atlanta, GA.

Graue, M. E., Kroeger, J., & Brown, C. (2003, Spring). The gift of time: Enactments of developmental thought in early childhood practice (online). *Early Childhood Research & Practice.* Retrieved June 21, 2015, from http://ecrp.uiuc.edu/v5n1/graue.html

Guernsey, L. (2014). *Envisioning a digital age architecture for early education.* Washington, DC: New America Foundation. Retrieved from http://www.newamerica.net/sites/newamerica.net/files/policy-docs/DigitalArchitecture-20140326.pdf

Hamre, B. K., & Pianta, R. C. (2005). Can instructional and emotional support in the first-grade classroom make a difference for children at risk of school failure? *Child Development, 76*(5), 949–967.

Hamre, B. K., & Pianta, R. C. (2007). Learning opportunities in preschool and early elementary classrooms. In R. C. Pianta, M. J. Cox, & K. Snow (Eds.), *School readiness, early learning, and the transition to kindergarten* (pp. 49–83). Baltimore: Paul H. Brookes.

Hamre, B. K., & Pianta, R. C. (2010). Classroom environments and developmental processes: Conceptualization and measurement. In J. L. Meece & J. S. Eccles (Eds.), *Handbook of research on schools, schooling, and human development* (pp. 25–41). New York: Routledge.

Hill, C. J., Gormley, W. T., Adelstein, S., & Willemin, C. (2012). *The effects of Oklahoma's pre-kindergarten program on 3rd grade test scores.* Washington, DC: The Center for Research on Children in the U.S. (CROCUS) at Georgetown University. Retrieved from http://fcd-us.org/sites/default/files/Long-term%20Policy%20Brief_05-22-2012%20(2).pdf

Honig, A. S. (2010). *Little kids, big worries: Stress-busting tips for early childhood classrooms.* Baltimore: Paul H. Brookes.

Kostelnik, M. J., Soderman, A. K., Whiren, A. P., & Rupiper, M. Q. (2014). *Developmentally appropriate curriculum: Best practices in early childhood education* (6th ed.). Upper Saddle River, NJ: Merrill/Pearson.

Martin, B. (1996). *Brown bear, brown bear, what do you see?* New York: Henry Holt.

Mashburn, A. J., Pianta, R., Hamre, B. K., Downer, J. T., Barbarin, O., Bryant, D., et al. (2008). Measures of classroom quality in pre-kindergarten and children's development of academic, language and social skills. *Child Development, 79*(3), 732–749.

Matychuk, P. (2005). The role of child-directed speech in language acquisition: A case study. *Language Sciences, 27*, 301–379.

Miller, E., & Almon, J. (2009). *Crisis in the kindergarten: Why children need to play in school.* College Park, MD: Alliance for Childhood.

Miller, E., & Carlsson-Paige, N. (2013, January 29). A tough critique of the Common Core on early childhood education. *Washington Post.* Retrieved July 2, 2014, from http://www.washingtonpost.com/blogs/answer-sheet/wp/2013/01/29/a-tough-critique-of-common-core-on-early-childhood-education/

National Association for the Education of Young Children (NAEYC). (2009). *Developmentally appropriate practice in early childhood programs serving children from birth through age 8: Position statement.* Washington, DC: Author.

National Association for the Education of Young Children (NAEYC). (2012). *The Common Core State Standards: Caution and opportunity for early childhood education.* Washington, DC: Author.

National Association for the Education of Young Children (NAEYC) & the Fred Rogers Center for Early Learning and Children's Media. (2012). *Technology in early childhood programs serving children from birth through age 8. Joint Position Statement.* Washington, DC: Authors.

National Association for the Education of Young Children (NAEYC) & National Association of Early Childhood Specialists in State Departments of Education (NAECS/SDE). (2003). *Early childhood curriculum, assessment, and program evaluation: Building an effective, accountable system in programs for children birth through age 8. Joint position statement.* Washington, DC: National Association for the Education of Young Children.

National Institute of Child Health and Human Development (NICHD) Early Child Care Research Network. (2003). Social functioning in first grade: Prediction from home, child care, and concurrent school experience. *Child Development, 74,* 1639–1662.

Pianta, R. C., Barnett, W. S., Burchinal, M., & Thornburg, K. R. (2009). The effects of preschool education: What we know, how public policy is or is not aligned with the evidence base, and what we need to know. *Psychological Science in the Public Interest, 10*(2) 49–88.

Pianta, R. C., Barnett, W. S., Justice, L. M., & Sheridan, S. M. (Eds.). (2012). *Handbook of early childhood education.* New York: Guilford Press.

Rimm-Kaufman, S. E., La Paro, K. M., Downer, J. T., & Pianta, R. C. (2005). The contribution of classroom setting and quality of instruction to children's behavior in kindergarten classrooms. *Elementary School Journal, 105*(4), 377–394.

Rogow, F. (2015). Media literacy in early childhood education: Inquiry-based technology integration. In C. Donohue (Ed.), *Technology and digital media in the early years* (pp. 303–340). New York: Routledge, Taylor and Francis Group.

Sammons, P., Sylva, K., Melhuish, E., Siraj-Blatchford, I., Taggart, B., Hunt, S., et al. (2008). *Effective preschool and primary education 3–11 project (EPPE 3–11): Influences on children's cognitive and social development in year 6* (Department of Children, Schools and Families Research Brief). London: Institute of Education, University of London. Retrieved October 14, 2009, from http://eppe.ioe.ac.uk

Schweinhart, L. J., & Weikart D. P. (1997). The High/Scope preschool curriculum comparison study through age 23. *Childhood: A Global Journal of Child Research, 143*(1997), 117–143.

Schweinhart, L., Weikart, D., & Larner, M. (1986). Consequences of three preschool curriculum models through age 15. *Early Childhood Research Quarterly, 1*(1), 15–46.

Shanker, S. (2012). *Calm, alert, and learning: Classroom strategies for self-regulation.* Pearson Education Canada, Toronto, Ontario, Canada.

Shonkoff, J., & Phillips, D. A. (2000). *From neurons to neighborhoods: The science of early childhood development.* Washington, DC: National Academies Press.

Squires, J. (2014). "First you work, and then it's play." *Preschool Matters Today: A blog of the National Institute for Early Education Research.* Retrieved from http://preschoolmatters.org/2014/06/19/first-you-work-and-then-its-play/

Stipek, D. (2011). Classroom practices and children's motivation to learn. In E. Zigler, W. S. Gilliam, & W. S., Barnett, W. S. (Eds.), *The pre-k debates: Current controversies and issues* (pp. 98–103). Baltimore: Brookes.

Strauss, V. (2014, July 19). Mom: My kindergartner was "work-sheeted to death." *Washington Post.* Retrieved July 19, 2014, from http://www.washingtonpost.com/blogs/answer-sheet/wp/2014/07/19/mom-my-kindergartner-was-work-sheeted-to-death/

Sylva, K., Melhuish, E., Sammons, P., Siraj-Blatchford, I., & Taggart, B. (2004). *The effective provision of pre-school education (EPPE) project: Final report.* London: Institute of Education, University of London.

Weiland, C., & Yoshikawa, H. (2013). Impacts of a prekindergarten program on children's mathematics, language, literacy, executive function, and emotional skills. *Child Development,* p. 11.

Woodhead, M. (2006). Changing perspectives on early childhood: Theory, research and policy. *International Journal of Equity and Innovation in Early Childhood, 4*(2), 5-48.

Yoshikawa, H., Weiland, C., Brooks-Gunn, J., Burchinal, M. R., Espinosa, L. M., Gormley, W. T., et al. (2013). *Investing in our future: The evidence base on preschool education.* New York: Foundation for Child Development. Retrieved from http://fcd-us.org/sites/default/files/Evidence%20Base%20on%20Preschool%20Education%20FINAL.pdf

Zigler, E., Gilliam, W. S., & Barnett, W. S. (Eds.) (2011). *The pre-k debates: Current controversies and issues.* Baltimore: Paul H. Brookes.

Chapter 4

Alliance for Childhood. (2010). *The loss of children's play: A public health issue.* College Park, MD: Author. Retrieved from http://www.allianceforchildhood.org

Ames, L. B., & Ilg, F. (1979). *The Gesell Institute's child from one to six.* New York: Harper & Row.

Bandura, A. (1973). *Aggression: A social learning analysis.* Upper Saddle River, NJ: Prentice Hall.

Bandura, A. (1986). *Social foundations of thought and action: A social-cognitive theory.* Upper Saddle River, NJ: Prentice Hall.

Bandura, A. (1997). *Self-efficacy: The exercise of control.* New York: Freeman.

Bauer, P. J. (2009). Neurodevelopmental changes in infancy and beyond: Implications for learning and memory. In O. A. Barbarin & B. H. Wasik (Eds.), *Handbook of child development and early education: Research to practice* (pp. 78–102). New York: Guilford Press.

Baumrind, D. (1971). Current patterns of parental authority. *Developmental Psychology, 4,* 1–103.

Berk, L. E. (2006). Looking at the kindergarten child. In D. F. Gullo (Ed.), *K today: Teaching and learning in the kindergarten year* (pp. 11–25). Washington, DC: National Association for the Education of Young Children.

Berk, L. E., Mann, T. D., & Ogan, A. T. (2006). Make-believe play: Wellspring for development of self-regulation. In D. G. Singer, R. M. Golinkoff, & K. Hirsh-Pasek (Eds.), *Play = learning: How play motivates and enhances children's cognitive and social-emotional growth* (pp. 74–100). New York: Oxford University Press.

Blair, C., & Razza, R. C. (2007). Relating effortful control, executive function and false belief understanding to emerging math and literacy ability in kindergarten. *Child Development, 78*(2), 647–663.

Bodrova, E., & Leong, D. J. (2007). *Tools of the mind: The Vygotskian approach to early childhood education.* Upper Saddle River, NJ: Pearson.

Bodrova, E., & Leong, D. J. (2012a). Developing self-regulation in kindergarten: Can we keep all the crickets in the basket? In C. Copple (Ed.), *Growing minds: Building strong cognitive foundations in early childhood* (pp. 119–122). Washington, DC: National Association for the Education of Young Children.

Bodrova, E., & Leong, D. J. (2012b). Scaffolding self-regulated learning in young children: Lessons from Tools of the Mind. In R. C. Pianta, W. S. Barnett, L. M. Justice, & S. M. Sheridan (Eds.), *Handbook of early childhood education* (pp. 352–369). New York: Guilford Press.

Boyd, J., Barnett, W. S., Bodrova, E., Leong, D. J., & Gomby, D. (2005, March). *Promoting children's social emotional development through preschool* (Preschool Policy Report). New Brunswick, NJ: National Institute for Early Education Research.

Bredekamp, S. (2004). Play and school readiness. In E. F. Zigler, D. G. Singer, & S. J. Bishop-Josef (Eds.), *Children's play: The roots of reading* (pp. 159–174). Washington, DC: ZERO to THREE Press.

Bronfenbrenner, U. (1979). *The ecology of human development: Experiments by nature and design.* Cambridge, MA: Harvard University Press.

Bronfenbrenner, U. (Ed.). (2004). *Making human beings human: Bioecological perspectives on human development.* Thousand Oaks, CA: Sage.

Bronfenbrenner, U., & Morris, P. A. (2006). The bioecological model of human development. In R. M. Lerner & W. Damon (Eds.), *Handbook of child psychology* (6th ed.), *Vol. 1, Theoretical models of human development* (pp. 793–828). Hoboken, NJ: John Wiley & Sons.

Calkins, S. D., & Williford, A. P. (2009). Taming the terrible twos: Self-regulation and school readiness. In O. A. Barbarin & B. H. Wasik (Eds.), *Handbook of child development and early education: Research to practice* (pp. 172–198). New York: Guilford Press.

Case, R., & Okamoto, Y. (1996). *The role of central conceptual structures in the development of children's thought* (Monographs of the Society of Research in Child Development, Vol. 61, No. 2, Serial no. 246). Chicago: University of Chicago Press.

Center on the Developing Child at Harvard University. (2010). *Early experiences can alter gene expression and affect long-term development: Working paper #10.* Retrieved October 28, 2011 from http://www.developingchild.harvard.edu

Erikson, E. (1950/1963). *Childhood and society* (2nd ed.). New York: Norton.

Clements, D. H., & Sarama, J. (2009). *Learning and teaching early math: The learning trajectories approach.* New York: Routledge.

Copple, C., & Bredekamp, S. (Eds.). (2009). *Developmentally appropriate practice in early childhood programs serving children from birth through age 8* (Rev. ed.). Washington, DC: National Association for the Education of Young Children.

Diamond, A., & Lee, K. (2011, August 19). Interventions shown to aid executive function development in children 4 to 12 years old. *Science, 333*(6045), 959–964. doi:10.1126/science.1204529

Division for Early Childhood of the Council for Exceptional Children. (2014). *DEC recommended practices in early intervention/early childhood special education*. Los Angeles, CA: Author. Retrieved February 1, 2015, from http://www.dec-sped.org/recommendedpractices

Elkind, D. (2008). *The power of play: Learning what comes naturally*. Cambridge, MA: Da Capo Press.

Frost, J. L., Wortham, S. C., & Reifel, S. (2012). *Play and child development* (4th ed.). Upper Saddle River, NJ: Pearson.

Fusaro, M., & Nelson, C. A., III. (2009). Developmental cognitive neuroscience and education practice. In O. A. Barbarin & B. H. Wasik (Eds.), *Handbook of child development and early education: Research to practice* (pp. 57–77). New York: Guilford Press.

Galinsky, E. (2010). *Mind in the making: The seven essential life skills every child needs*. New York: Harper.

Gapin, J., & Etnier, J. L. (2010). The relationship between physical activity and executive function performance in children with Attention Deficit Hyperactivity Disorder. *Journal of Sport & Exercise Psychology, 32*(6), 753–763.

Gelman, R. (2000). Domain specificity and variability in cognitive development. *Child Development, 71,* 854–856.

Gelman, R., & Baillargeon, R. (1983). A review of some Piagetian concepts. In P. M. Mussen (Ed.), *Handbook of child psychology* (Vol. 3, pp. 167–230). New York: Wiley.

Gesell, A. (1940). *The first five years of life*. New York: Harper & Row.

Gilpin, A., Boxmeyer, C., DeCaro, J., & Lochman, J. (2014), *Power PATH universal preschool intervention effects on executive function*. Paper presented, July 7, 2014, at Head Start's 12th National Research Conference on Early Childhood, Washington, DC.

Ginsburg, H. P. (2006). Mathematical play and playful mathematics: A guide for early education. In D. G. Singer, R. M. Golinkoff, & K. Hirsh-Pasek (Eds.), *Play = learning: How play motivates and enhances children's cognitive and social-emotional growth* (pp. 145–165). New York: Oxford University Press.

Gopnik, A., Meltzoff, A. N., & Kuhl, P. K. (1999). *The scientist in the crib: Minds, brains, and how children learn*. New York: William Morrow.

Hirsh-Pasek, K., Golinkoff, R. M., Berk, L. E., & Singer, D. (Eds.). (2009). *A mandate for playful learning in preschool: Applying the scientific evidence*. New York: Oxford University Press.

Hyson, M. (2012). Becoming enthusiastic and engaged. In C. Copple (Ed.), *Growing minds: Building strong cognitive foundations in early childhood* (pp. 41–61). Washington, DC: National Association for the Education of Young Children.

Johnson, J. E., Christie, J. F., & Wardle, F. (2005). *Play, development, and early education*. Upper Saddle River, NJ: Pearson.

Jones, S., & Bailey, R. (2014). *Mapping executive function: Technical and applied definitions and their implications for the classroom*. Paper presented July 7, 2014, at Head Start's 12th National Research Conference on Early Childhood, Washington, DC.

Kohn, A. (2014). *The myth of the spoiled child: Challenging the conventional wisdom about children and parenting*. Boston: Da Capo.

Levitt, P. (2008). Building brain architecture and chemistry: A primer for policymakers. In A. Tarlov & M. P. Debbink (Eds.), *Investing in early childhood development: Evidence to support a movement*

for educational change. New York: Palgrave Macmillan.

Lieberman, D. A. (2006). What can we learn from playing interactive games? In P. Vorderer & J. Bryant (Eds.), *Playing video games: Motives, responses, and consequences*. Mahwah, NJ: Lawrence Erlbaum Associates.

Maslow, A. H. (1954). *Towards a psychology of being*. New York: Van Nostrand.

McClelland, M. M., Acock, A. C., & Morrison, F. J. (2006). The impact of kindergarten learning-related skills on academic trajectories at the end of elementary school. *Early Childhood Research Quarterly, 21*(4), 471–490.

McWayne, C. M., Owsianik, M., Green, L. E., & Fantuzzo, J. W. (2008). Parenting behaviors and preschool children's social and emotional skills: A question of the consequential validity of traditional parenting constructs for low-income African Americans. *Early Childhood Research Quarterly, 23,* 173–192.

Mix, K. S., Huttenlocher, J., & Levine, S. C. (2002). *Quantitative development in infancy and early childhood*. New York: Oxford University Press.

Murphy, S. (2014). Finding the right fit: Inclusive strategies for students with characteristics of ADHD. *Young Children, 60*(3), 66–71.

National Association for the Education of Young Children (NAEYC). (2009). *Developmentally appropriate practice in early childhood programs serving children from birth through age 8: Position statement*. Washington, DC: Author.

Obradović, J., Portilla, X. A., & Boyce, W. T. (2012). Executive functioning and developmental neuroscience: Current progress and implications for early childhood education. In R. C. Pianta, W. S. Barnett, L. M. Justice, & S. M. Sheridan (Eds.), *Handbook of early childhood education* (pp. 324–351). New York: Guilford Press.

Ornstein, P. A., Coffman, J. L., & Grammer, J. K. (2009). Learning to remember. In O. A. Barbarin (Ed.), *Handbook of child development and early education: Research to practice* (pp. 103–122). New York: Guilford Press.

Palmer, K., Miller, M., & Robinson, L. (2013). Acute exercise enhances preschoolers' ability to sustain attention. *Journal of Sport & Exercise Psychology, 35*(4), 433–437.

Papert, S. (1999, March 29). Time 100: Piaget. *Time* magazine. Retrieved October 9, 2009, from http://www.time.com/time/time100/scientist/profile/piaget.html

Piaget, J. (1930). *The child's conception of physical causality*. Harcourt Brace & Co.

Piaget, J. (1952). *The origins of intelligence in children*. New York: International Universities Press.

Piaget, J. (1962). *Play, dreams, and imitation in childhood*. New York: Norton.

Reineke, J., Sonsteng, K., & Gartrell, D. (2008). Nurturing mastery motivation: No need for rewards? *Young Children, 63*(6), 89.

Rogoff, B. (2012). Learning without lessons: Opportunities to expand knowledge. *Infancia Y Aprendizaje /Journal for the Study of Education and Development, 35*(2), 233–252. doi:10.1174/021037012800217970.

Sameroff, A. J. (Ed.) (2009). *The transactional model of development: How children and contexts shape each other*. Washington, DC: American Psychological Association.

Sameroff, A., & McDonough, S. (1994). Educational implications of developmental transitions: Revisiting the 5- to 7-year shift. *Phi Delta Kappan, 76*(3), 188–193.

Shonkoff, J. P., Garner, A. S., & the Committee on Psychosocial Effects of Family and Child Health.

(2012). *Pediatrics, 129*(1), e232–e246. Retrieved from http://pediatrics.aappublications.org/content/129/1/e232.full.pdf+html

Smilansky, S. (1968). *The effects of sociodramatic play on disadvantaged preschool children*. New York: Wiley.

Smilansky, S., & Shefatya, L. (1990). *Facilitating play: A medium for promoting cognitive, socioemotional, and academic development in young children*. Gaithersburg, MD: Psychological and Educational Publications.

Stetsenko, A., & Vianna, E. (2009). Bridging developmental theory and educational practice: Lessons from the Vygotskian project. In O. A. Barbarin (Ed.), *Handbook of child development and early education: Research to practice* (pp. 38–54). New York: Guilford Press.

Tierney, A. L., & Nelson, C. A., III. (2009). Brain development and the role of experience in the early years. *Zero to Three, 30*(2), 9–13.

Vygotsky, L. S. (1962). *Thought and language*. Cambridge, MA: MIT Press.

Vygotsky, L. S. (1977). Play and its role in the mental development of the child. In M. Cole (Ed.), *Soviet developmental psychology* (pp. 76–99). Armonk, NY: M. E. Sharpe.

Vygotsky, L. S. (1978). *Mind in society*. Cambridge, MA: Harvard University Press.

Wiltz, N. W., & Klein, E. L. (2001). "What do you do in child care?" Children's perceptions of high and low quality classrooms. *Early Childhood Research Quarterly, 16*(2), 209–236.

Wong, C., Odom, S. L., Hume, K. Cox, A. W., Fettig, A., Kucharczyk, S., et al. (2014). *Evidence-based practices for children, youth, and young adults with Autism Spectrum Disorder*. Chapel Hill, NC: The University of North Carolina, Frank Porter Graham Child Development Institute.

Zigler, E. F., & Bishop-Josef, S. J. (2004). Play under siege: A historical overview. In E. F. Zigler, D. G. Singer, & S. J. Bishop-Josef (Eds.). *Children's play: The roots of reading.* (pp. 1–13). Washington, DC: ZERO to THREE Press.

Zigler, E. F., Singer, D. G., & Bishop-Josef, S. J. (Eds.) (2004). *Children's play: The roots of reading*. Washington, DC: ZERO to THREE Press.

Chapter 5

Allington, R. L. (2009). *What really matters in response to intervention: Research-based designs*. Upper Saddle River, NJ: Pearson.

American Psychiatric Association. (2013). *Diagnostic and statistical manual of mental disorders* (5th ed.). Arlington, VA: American Psychiatric Publishing.

Bates, J. E. (2012). Temperament as a tool in promoting early childhood development. In S. L. Odom, E. P. Pungello & N. Gardner-Neblett (Eds.), *Infants, toddlers, and families in poverty: Research implications for early child care* (pp. 153–177). New York: Guilford Press.

Bowman, B. T., Donovan, M. S., & Burns, S. (Eds.). (2001). *Eager to learn: Educating our preschoolers* (National Research Council, Committee on Early Childhood Pedagogy Report). Washington, DC: National Academies Press.

Bruder, M. B. (2001). *The individual family service plan (IFSP)* (ERIC Digest). Retrieved November 27, 2007, from http://www.ericdigests.org/2001-4/ifsp.html

Bukatko, D., & Daehler, M. W. (2003). *Child development: A thematic approach* (4th ed.). Boston: Houghton Mifflin.

Burchinal, M., & Willoughby, M. (2013). The Family Life Project: An epidemiological and developmental study of young children living in poor rural communities: IV. Poverty and associated social risks: Toward a cumulative risk framework. *Monographs of the Society for Research in Child Development, 78*(5), 53–65.

Burr, J. E., Ostrov, J. M., Jansen, E. A., Cullerton-Sen, C., & Crick, N. R. (2005). Relational aggression and friendship during early childhood: "I won't be your friend!" *Early Education and Development, 16*(2), 161–183.

Casey, M. B., Erkut, S., Ceder, I., & Young, J. M. (2008). Use of a storytelling context to improve girls' and boys' geometry skills in kindergarten. *Journal of Applied Developmental Psychology, 29*, 29–48.

Center on the Developing Child at Harvard University. (2010). *Early experiences can alter gene expression and affect long-term development: Working paper #10.* Retrieved October 28, 2011 from http://www.developingchild.harvard.edu

Centers for Disease Control and Prevention (CDC). (2014a). *Autism spectrum disorder: Data and statistics.* Retrieved August 14, 2014, from http://www.cdc.gov/ncbddd/autism/data.html

Cervantes, A., & Callanan, M. (1998). Labels and explanations in mother-child emotion talk: Age and gender differentiation. *Developmental Psychology, 34(1)*, 88–98.

Clements, D. H., & Sarama, J. (2008). Experimental evaluation of the effects of a research-based preschool mathematics curriculum. *American Educational Research Journal, 45*, 443–494.

Coleman, M. R., & Johnsen, S. K. (2011). *RtI for gifted students: A CEC-TAG educational resource.* Waco, TX: Prufrock Press.

Coleman, M. R., Roth, F. P., & West, T. (2009). *Roadmap to Pre-K RTI: Applying Response to Intervention in preschool settings.* New York: National Center for Learning Disabilities. Retrieved October 9, 2009, from http://www.rtinetwork.org/images/roadmaptoprekrti.pdf

Colker, L. (2005). *The cooking book: Fostering young children's learning and delight.* Washington, DC: National Association for the Education of Young Children.

Crick, N., Casas, J. F., & Mosher, M. (1997). Relational and overt aggression in preschool. *Developmental Psychology, 33*(4), 579–588.

Dawson, G., Rogers, S., Munson, J., Smith, M., Winter, J., Greenspan, J., et al., (2010). Randomized, controlled trial of an intervention for toddlers with autism: The Early Denver Model. *Pediatrics, 125*(1), 17–23.

Division for Early Childhood & National Association for the Education of Young Children. (2009). *Early childhood inclusion: A joint position statement of the Division for Early Childhood (DEC) and the National Association for the Education of Young Children (NAEYC).* Chapel Hill: The University of North Carolina, FPG Child Development Institute. Retrieved from http://npdci.fpg.unc.edu/sites/npdci.fpg.unc.edu/files/resources/EarlyChildhoodInclusion_0.pdf

Division for Early Childhood of the Council for Exceptional Children. (2014). *DEC recommended practices in early intervention/early childhood special education.* Los Angeles, CA: Author. Retrieved February 1, 2015, from http://www.dec-sped.org/recommendedpractices

Dolgin, K., & Kim, S. (1994). Adolescents' disclosure to best and good friends: The effects of gender and topic intimacy. *Social Development, 3(2)*, 146–157.

Dunst, C. J. (2011). *Family-centered practices, parent engagement, and parent and family functioning.* Paper presented at the June 7, 2011, meeting of the Head Start Advisory Committee on Research and Evaluation, Washington, DC. Retrieved from http://www.acf.hhs.gov/programs/opre/hs/advisory_com/index.html.

Dunst, C. J., Hamby, D., Trivette, C. M., Raab, M., & Bruder, M. B. (2000). Everyday family and community life and children's naturally occurring learning opportunities. *Journal of Early Intervention, 23*, 151–164.

Eliot, L. (2009). *Pink brain, blue brain: How small differences grow into troublesome gaps—and what we can do about it.* Boston: Houghton Mifflin Harcourt.

Erwin, P. (1998). *Friendship in childhood and adolescence.* New York: Routledge.

Espinosa, L. M. (2010a). Assessment of young English language learners. In E. E. Garcia & E. C. Frede, (Eds.), *Young English language learners: Current research and emerging directions for practice and policy* (pp. 119–142). New York: Teachers College Press.

Gallagher, K. C. (2013). Guiding children's friendship development: An essential part of the early childhood curriculum. *Young Children, 68*, 5.

Gardner, H. (2004). *Frames of mind: The theory of multiple intelligences* (20th Anniversary ed.). New York: Basic Books.

Gardner, H. (2006). *Multiple intelligences: New horizons in theory and practice.* New York: Basic Books.

Gartstein, M. A., Putnam, S. P., & Rothbart, M. K. (2012). Etiology of preschool behavior problems: Contributions of temperament attributes in early childhood. *Infant Mental Health Journal, 33*(2), 197–211.

Gest, S. D., & Davidson, A. J. (2011). A developmental perspective on risk, resilience, and prevention. In M. K. Underwood & L. H. Rosen (Eds.), *Social development: Relationships in infancy, childhood, and adolescence.* (pp. 427–454). New York: Guilford Press.

Hamre, B. K., & Pianta, R. C. (2010). Classroom environments and developmental processes: Conceptualization and measurement. In J. L. Meece & J. S. Eccles (Eds.), *Handbook of research on schools, schooling, and human development* (pp. 25–41). New York: Routledge.

Hart, B., & Risley, T. R. (1999). *The social world of learning to talk.* Baltimore: Paul H. Brookes.

Hart, B., & Risley, T. R. (2003, Spring). The early catastrophe: The 30 million word gap by age 3. *American Educator, 27*(1), 4–9. Retrieved January 25, 2015, from http://www.aft.org/pdfs/american-educator/spring2003/TheEarlyCatastrophe.pdf

Heward, W. L. (2014). *Exceptional children: An introduction to special education* (10th ed., Pearson new international edition). Upper Saddle River, NJ: Pearson.

Howes, C., & Ritchie, S. (2002). *A matter of trust: Connecting teachers and learners in the early childhood curriculum.* New York: Teachers College Press.

Huffman, L. C., Mehlinger, S. L., Kerivan, A. S., Cavanugh, D. A., Lippitt, J., & Moyo, O. (2001). *Off to a good start: Research on the risk factors for early school problems and selected federal policies affecting children's social and emotional development and their readiness for school.* Washington, DC: Foundations and Agencies Workgroup.

Hyson, M. (2008). *Enthusiastic and engaged learners: Approaches to learning in the early childhood classroom.* New York: Teachers College Press.

Jacklin, C. M. (1989). Female and male: Issues of gender. *American Psychologist, 44*, 127–133.

Jensen, A. R. (1980). *Bias in mental testing.* New York: Free Press.

Krinzinger, H., Wood, G., & Willmes, K. (2012). What accounts for individual and gender differences in the multi-digit number processing of primary

school children? *Zeitschrift für Psychologie, 220*(2), 78–89. http://dx.doi.org/10.1027/2151-2604/a000099

Maccoby, E. (2002). Gender and group process: A developmental perspective. *Current Directions in Psychological Science, 11*(2), 54–58.

Masten, A. S., & Powell, J. L. (2003). A resilience framework for research, policy, and practice. In S. Luthar (Ed.), *Resilience and vulnerability: Adaptation in the context of childhood adversities.* Cambridge: Cambridge University Press.

McDermott, P. A., Rikoon, S. H., & Fantuzzo, J. W. (2014). Tracing children's approaches to learning through Head Start, kindergarten, and first grade: Different pathways to different outcomes. *Journal of Educational Psychology, 106*(1), 200–213.

McWilliam, R. A. (2010). *Routines-based early intervention: Supporting young children and their families.* Baltimore: Brookes.

Moore, K. A. (2006). *Defining the term "at risk"* (Research to Results Briefs). Washington, DC: Child Trends.

National Association for the Education of Young Children (NAEYC). (2009). *Developmentally appropriate practice in early childhood programs serving children from birth through age 8: Position statement.* Washington, DC: Author.

National Association for Gifted Children. (2008). *Pre-K–Grade 12 gifted education programming standards.* Retrieved December 2, 2011, from http://www.nagc.org/index.aspx?id=960

National Association for Gifted Children. (2010). *Redefining giftedness for a new century: Shifting the paradigm.* Retrieved August 1, 2014, from http://nagc.org

National Center on Response to Intervention. (2010). *Essential components of RTI—A closer look at Response to Intervention.* Retrieved January 16, 2011, from http://www.rti4success.org.

National Professional Development Center on Inclusion (NPDCI). (2012). *Response to intervention (RTI) in early childhood: Building consensus on defining features.* Chapel Hill: The University of North Carolina, FPG Child Development Institute, Author.

National Professional Development Center on Inclusion (NPDCI). (2007). *Research synthesis points on early childhood inclusion.* Chapel Hill: The University of North Carolina, FPG Child Development Institute.

National Professional Development Center on Inclusion (NPDCI). (2009). Research synthesis points on early childhood inclusion. Retrieved August 1, 2014 from http://npdci.fpg.unc.edu

Neitzel, J., & Wolery, M. (2009). *Overview of prompting.* Chapel Hill, NC: The National Professional Development Center on Autism Spectrum Disorders, Frank Porter Graham Child Development Institute, The University of North Carolina. Retrieved September 10, 2014, from http://csesa.fpg.unc.edu/sites/csesa.fpg.unc.edu/files/ebpbriefs/Prompting_Overview.pdf

Rothbart, M. K. (2011). *Becoming who we are: Temperament and personality in development.* New York: Guilford Press.

Rudasill, K. M., Gallagher, K. C., & White, J. M. (2010). Temperamental attention and activity, classroom emotional support, and academic achievement in third grade. *Journal of School Psychology, 48*, 113–134.

Sabol, T. J., & Pianta, R. C. (2013). Relationships between teachers and children. In W. M. Reynolds, G. E. Miller & I. B. Weiner (Eds.), *Handbook of psychology, Vol. 7: Educational psychology* (2nd ed., pp. 199–211). Hoboken, NJ: John Wiley & Sons.

Sameroff, A. J. (Ed.) (2009). *The transactional model of development: How children and contexts shape each other*. Washington, DC: American Psychological Association.

Sandall, S. R., & Schwartz, I. S. (2008). *Building blocks for teaching preschoolers with special needs* (2nd ed.). Baltimore: Paul H. Brookes.

Shonkoff, J., & Phillips, D. A. (2000). *From neurons to neighborhoods: The science of early childhood development*. Washington, DC: National Academies Press.

Skinner, B. F. (1953). *Science and human behavior*. New York: Macmillan.

Skinner, B. F. (1968). *The technology of teaching*. New York: Appleton-Century-Crofts.

Stright, A. D., Gallagher, K. C., & Kelley, K. (2008). Infant temperament moderates relationships between maternal parenting and children's adjustment in first grade. *Child Development, 79*(1), 186–200.

Tarullo, L., Aikens, N., Moiduddin, E., & West, J. (2010). *A second year in Head Start: Characteristics and outcomes of children who entered the program at age three*. Washington, DC: U.S. Department of Health and Human Services, Administration for Children and Families, Office of Planning, Research and Evaluation.

Thompson, R. A., & Goodman, M. (2009). Development of self, relationships, and socioemotional competence: Foundations for early school success. In O. A. Barbarin & B. H. Wasik (Eds.), *Handbook of child development and early education: Research to practice* (pp. 147–171). New York: Guilford Press.

Tomlinson, C. A. (2014). *The differentiated classroom: Responding to the needs of all learners* (2nd ed.). Alexandria, VA: Association for Supervision & Curriculum Development.

Werner, E. E., & Smith, R. S. (2001). *Journeys from childhood to midlife: Risk, resilience, and recovery*. Ithaca, NY: Cornell University Press.

West, J., Denton, K., & Germino-Hausken, E. (2000). *America's kindergartners: Findings from the Early Childhood Longitudinal Study, kindergarten class of 1998–99, Fall 1998*. Washington, DC: U.S. Department of Education, National Center for Education Statistics.

Wolery, M., & Wilbers, J. (1994). *Including children with special needs in early childhood programs*. Washington DC: National Association for the Education of Young Children.

Wolery, M., Strain, P. S., & Bailey, D. (1992). Reaching potentials of children with special needs. In S. Bredekamp & T. Rosegrant (Eds.), *Reaching potentials: Appropriate curriculum and assessment for young children* (Vol. 1, pp. 92–111). Washington, DC: National Association for the Education of Young Children.

Wong, C., Odom, S. L., Hume, K. Cox, A. W., Fettig, A., Kucharczyk, S., et al. (2014). *Evidence-based practices for children, youth, and young adults with Autism Spectrum Disorder*. Chapel Hill, NC: The University of North Carolina, Frank Porter Graham Child Development Institute. Woolfolk, A., & Perry, N. E. (2015). *Child and adolescent development* (2nd ed.). Upper Saddle River, NJ: Pearson.

Zakriski, A., Wright, J., & Underwood, M. (2005). Gender similarities and differences in children's social behavior: Finding personality in contextualized patterns of adaptation. *Journal of Personality and Social Psychology, 88*(5), 844–855.

Chapter 6

Alanis, I. (2013). Where's your partner? Pairing bilingual learners in preschool and primary grade dual language classrooms. *Young Children, 68*(1), 42–46.

Banks, J. A. (2012). *An introduction to multicultural education* (5th ed.). Boston: Allyn & Bacon.

Barbarin, O. (2011). *Imagining auspicious environments for the development of African American boys*. Paper presented at the ETS Addressing Achievement Gaps Symposium co-sponsored with Children's Defense Fund, June 14, 2011, Washington, DC: Educational Testing Service. Retrieved August 11, 2011, from http://www.ets.org/s/sponsored_events/achievement_gap/pdf/2011_conference/oscar_barbarin_presentation.pdf

Barrueco, S., Lopez, M., Ong, C., & Lozano, P. (2012). *Assessing Spanish-English bilingual preschoolers: A guide to better approaches and measures*. Baltimore: Brookes.

Bowman, B. T., Donovan, M. S., & Burns, S. (Eds.). (2001). *Eager to learn: Educating our preschoolers* (National Research Council, Committee on Early Childhood Pedagogy Report). Washington, DC: National Academies Press.

Bredekamp, S. (1997a). Developmentally appropriate practice: The early childhood teacher as decision maker. In S. Bredekamp & C. Copple (Eds.), *Developmentally appropriate practice in early childhood programs* (Rev. ed., pp. 33–52). Washington, DC: National Association for the Education of Young Children.

Bredekamp, S., & Copple, C. (Eds.). (1997). *Developmentally appropriate practice in early childhood programs* (Rev. ed.). Washington, DC: National Association for the Education of Young Children.

Bronfenbrenner, U. (1979). *The ecology of human development: Experiments by nature and design*. Cambridge, MA: Harvard University Press.

Bronfenbrenner, U. (Ed.). (2004). *Making human beings human: Bioecological perspectives on human development*. Thousand Oaks, CA: Sage.

California Department of Education Child Development Division. (2008). *California preschool learning foundations* (Vol. 1). Sacramento, CA: Author. Retrieved July 1, 2015, from http://www.cde.ca.gov/sp/cd/re/documents/preschoollf.pdf

Church, V. (1997). *Colors around me*. Chicago: African American Images.

Dahlberg, G., Moss, P., & Pence, A. R. (2007). *Beyond quality in early childhood education: Languages of evaluation* (2nd ed.). New York: Routledge.

Day, C. B. (2006). Every child is a cultural being. In J. R. Lally, P. L. Mangione, & D. Greenwald (Eds.), *Concepts for care: Essays on infant/toddler development and learning* (pp. 97–99). San Francisco: WestEd.

Delpit, L. (2006). *Other people's children: Cultural conflict in the classroom* (Updated ed.). New York: New Press.

Derman-Sparks, L., & Edwards, J. O. (2010). *Anti-bias education for young children and ourselves*. Washington, DC: National Association for the Education of Young Children.

Derman-Sparks, L., & Ramsey, P. G., with Edwards, J. O. (2011). *What if all the kids are white? Anti-bias, multicultural education with young children and families* (2nd ed.). New York: Teachers College Press.

Espinosa, L. M. (2010a). Assessment of young English language learners. In E. E. Garcia & E. C. Frede, (Eds.), *Young English language learners: Current research and emerging directions for practice and policy* (pp. 119–142). New York: Teachers College Press.

Espinosa, L. M. (2010b). Classroom teaching and instruction "best practices" for young English language learners. In E. E. Garcia & E. C. Frede, (Eds.), *Young English language learners: Current research and emerging directions for practice and policy* (pp. 143–164). New York: Teachers College Press.

Espinosa, L. M. (2010c). *Getting it right for young children from diverse backgrounds: Applying research to improve practice*. Upper Saddle River, NJ: Pearson.

Gonzalez-Mena, J. (2008). *Diversity in early care and education: Honoring differences* (5th ed.). New York: McGraw-Hill.

Graue, M. E., & Delaney, K. (2011, November 4). *Being developmentally and culturally responsive*. Paper presented at the annual meeting of the National Association for the Education of Young Children, Atlanta, GA.

Hale, J. E. (1994). *Unbank the fire: Visions for the education of African American children*. Baltimore: Johns Hopkins University Press.

Hamayan, E., Genesee, F., & Cloud, N. (2013). *Dual language instruction from A to Z: Practical guidance for teachers and administrators*. Portsmouth, NH: Heinemann.

Hanson, M. J. (2011). Diversity in service settings. In E. W. Lynch & M. J. Hanson (Eds.), *Developing cross-cultural competence: A guide for working with children and their families* (4th ed., pp. 2–19). Baltimore: Paul H. Brookes.

Hanson, M. J., & Lynch, E. W. (2004). *Understanding families: Approaches to diversity, disability, and risk*. Baltimore: Paul H. Brookes.

Harms, T., Clifford, R. M., & Cryer, D. (2005). *Early Childhood Environment Rating Scale (ECERS-R)* (Rev. ed.). New York: Teachers College Press.

Head Start. (2010b). *Revisiting and updating the multicultural principles for Head Start programs serving children ages birth to five: Addressing culture and home language in Head Start program systems and services*. Retrieved from http://eclkc.ohs.acf.hhs.gov/hslc/tta-system/cultural-linguistic

Heath, S. B. (1983). *Ways with words: Language, life, and work in communities and classrooms*. Cambridge: Cambridge University Press.

Heath, S. B. (1989). Oral and literate traditions among Black Americans living in poverty. *American Psychologist, 44*, 367–373.

Killen, M. (2012). *Kids on race: The hidden picture*. Report for CNN *AC360°*. Retrieved August 28, 2013, from http://www.cnn.com/2012/04/02/us/ac360-race-study/

Li, K., Hu, B. Y., Pan, Y., Qin, J., & Fan, X. (2013). Chinese Early Childhood Environment Rating Scale (trial) (CECERS): A validity study. *Early Childhood Research Quarterly, 29*(3), 268–282.

Lynch, E. W. (2011). Developing cross-cultural competence. In E. W. Lynch & M. J. Hanson (Eds.), *Developing cross-cultural competence: A guide for working with children and their families* (4th ed., pp. 41–77). Baltimore: Paul H. Brookes.

Lynch, E. W., & Hanson, M. J. (Eds.). (2011). *Developing cross-cultural competence: A guide for working with children and their families* (4th ed.). Baltimore: Paul H. Brookes.

Magruder, E. S., Hayslip, W. W., Espinosa, L. M., & Matera, C. (2013). Many languages, one teacher: Supporting language and literacy development for preschool dual language learners. *Young Children, 68*(1), 8–15.

Mallory, B. L., & New, R. S. (Eds.). (1994). *Diversity and developmentally appropriate practices: Challenges for early childhood education*. New York: Teachers College Press.

National Association for the Education of Young Children (NAEYC). (2007). *NAEYC Early childhood program standards and accreditation criteria: The mark of quality in early childhood education*. Washington, DC: Author.

National Association for the Education of Young Children (NAEYC). (2009). *Developmentally appropriate practice in early childhood programs serving children from birth through age 8: Position statement*. Washington, DC: Author.

National Association for the Education of Young Children (NAEYC). (2008a). *Families and community relationships: A guide to the NAEYC early childhood program standards and related accreditation criteria.* Washington, DC: Author.

National Center for Education Statistics. (2014c). *The condition of education 2014.* Washington, DC: U.S. Department of Education. Retrieved August 22, 2014, from http://nces.ed.gov/pubs2014/2014083_highlights.pdf

Oertwig, S., Gillanders, C., & Ritchie, S. (2014). The promise of curricula. In S. Ritchie & L. Gumann (Eds.), *First school: Transforming pre-K–3rd grade for African American, Latino, and low-income children.* New York: Teachers College Press.

Olsen, L., Bhattacharya, J., & Scharf, A. (2007). *Cultural competency: What it is and why it matters.* Sacramento: California Tomorrow.

Paradis, J., Genesee, F., & Crago, M. G. (2011). *Dual language development and disorders: A handbook on bilingualism and second language learning* (2nd ed.). Baltimore: Paul H. Brookes.

Ramsey, P. G. (2004). *Teaching and learning in a diverse world: Multicultural education for young children* (3rd ed.). New York: Teachers College Press.

Ritchie, S., & Gutmann, L. (Eds.). (2014). *First school: Transforming pre-K–3rd grade for African American, Latino, and low-income children.* New York: Teachers College Press.

Rogoff, B. (2003). *The cultural nature of human development.* New York: Oxford University Press.

Rotner, S., & Kelly, S. M. (2010). *Shades of people.* New York: Holiday House.

Sandall, S. R., & Schwartz, I. S. (2008). *Building blocks for teaching preschoolers with special needs* (2nd ed.). Baltimore: Paul H. Brookes.

Sanders, K. E., Diehl, A., & Kyler, A. (2007). DAP in the 'hood: Perceptions of child care practices by African American child care directors caring for children of color. *Early Childhood Research Quarterly, 22*(3), 394–406.

Slavin, R. E., & Cheung, A. (2005). A synthesis of research on language of reading instruction for English language learners. *Review of Educational Research, 75*(2), 247–281.

Sparrow, J. (2011). *Culture, community, and complex systems: Touchpoints in intervention, adaptation, and co-construction.* Paper presented at the September 21, 2011, meeting of the Head Start Advisory Committee on Research and Evaluation, Washington, DC. Retrieved from http://www.acf.hhs.gov/programs/opre/hs/advisory_com/index.html

Tabors, P. O. (2008). *One child, two languages: A guide for early childhood educators of children learning English as a second language,* 2nd ed. Baltimore: Paul H. Brookes.

Teaching Tolerance. (2012). *Teaching tolerance anti-bias framework.* Montgomery, AL: Teaching Tolerance, a Project of the Southern Poverty Law Center. Retrieved August 27, 2014, from http://www.tolerance.org/anti-bias-framework

Trawick-Smith, J. (2013). *Early childhood development: A multicultural perspective* (6th ed.). Upper Saddle River, NJ: Pearson.

U.S. Department of Education. (2014, March 21). *Expansive survey of America's public schools reveals troubling racial disparities: Lack of access to preschool, greater suspensions cited.* Retrieved August 26, 2014, from http://www.ed.gov/news/press-releases/expansive-survey-americas-public-schools-reveals-troubling-racial-disparities

Wardle, F. (2008a, February 10). *Multicultural and multilingual education in early childhood (infants to age 8) programs.* Denver, CO: Center for the Study of Biracial Children.

Wardle, F. (2008b). *Responding to racial and ethnic diversity in schools and early childhood programs. Does race matter?* Denver, CO: Center for the Study of Biracial Children.

Wardle, F. (2014, August 14). *Do mixed-race (Black/White) people have an ethical obligation to identify as Black?* Center for the Study of Biracial Children. Retrieved August 27, 2014, from http://csbchome.org/?p=57

Wong Filmore, L. (1991). When learning a second language means losing the first. *Early Childhood Research Quarterly, 6*(3), 323–347.

Woolfolk, A., & Perry, N. E. (2012). *Child and adolescent development.* Upper Saddle River, NJ: Pearson.

Zepeda, M., Rothstein-Fisch, C., Gonzalez-Mena, J., & Trumbull, E. (2006). *Bridging cultures in early care and education: A training module.* Mahwah, NJ: Lawrence Erlbaum Associates.

Chapter 7

Baker, A. C., & Manfredi-Petitt, L. A. (2004). *Relationships, the heart of quality care: Creating community among adults in early care settings.* Washington, DC: National Association for the Education of Young Children.

Bandy, T., & Moore, K. A. (2008). *The parent-child relationship: A family strength.* Washington, DC: Child Trends.

Brazelton, T. B., & Greenspan, S. I. (2000). *The irreducible needs of children: What every child must have to grow, learn, and flourish.* New York: Perseus.

Bredekamp, S. (1997a). Developmentally appropriate practice: The early childhood teacher as decision maker. In S. Bredekamp & C. Copple (Eds.), *Developmentally appropriate practice in early childhood programs* (Rev. ed., pp. 33–52). Washington, DC: National Association for the Education of Young Children.

Bredekamp, S. (1997b). NAEYC issues revised position statement on developmentally appropriate practice in early childhood programs. *Young Children, 52*(2), 34–40.

Bronfenbrenner, U., & Morris, P. A. (2006). The bioecological model of human development. In R. M. Lerner & W. Damon (Eds.), *Handbook of child psychology* (6th ed.), *Vol. 1, Theoretical models of human development* (pp. 793–828). Hoboken, NJ: John Wiley & Sons.

Bryant, D., Maxwell, K. L., & Burchinal, M. (1999). Effects of a community initiative on the quality of childcare. *Early Childhood Research Quarterly, 14*(4), 449–464.

Cabrera, N. (2013). Minority children and their families: A positive look. In National Black Child Development Institute, *Being Black is not a risk factor: A strengths-based look at the state of the Black child.* Washington, DC: National Black Child Development Institute. Retrieved October 27, 2014, from http://www.nbcdi.org/resource

Child Trends. (2007). *Early childhood program enrollment.* Child Trends Data Bank. http://www.childtrends.org.

Child Trends. (2014a). *Family structure.* Child Trends Data Bank. Retrieved November 10, 2014, from http://www.childtrends.org

Child Welfare Information Gateway. (2014). *Philosophy and key elements of family-centered practice.* Washington, DC: Administration for Children and Families. Retrieved November 13, 2014, from https://www.childwelfare.gov/famcentered/philosophy.cfm

Children's Defense Fund (CDF). (2011). *State of America's children 2011.* Washington, DC: Author.

Children's Defense Fund (CDF). (2014). *The state of America's children 2014.* Washington, DC: Author. Retrieved June 29, 2015, from http://www.childrensdefense.org/library/state-of-americas-children/2014-soac.pdf

Christian, L. G. (2006). Understanding families: Applying family systems theory to early childhood practice. *Young Children, 61*(1), 12–20.

Cohen, R. C., Vogel, C., & the Baby FACES Team. (2011). *Reaching families in Early Head Start: Data from Baby FACES.* Paper presented at the June 7, 2011, meeting of the Head Start Advisory Committee on Research and Evaluation, Washington, DC. Retrieved from http://www.acf.hhs.gov/programs/opre/hs/advisory_com/index.html.

Council for Professional Recognition. (2012). *Child Development Associate assessment system and competency standards for home visitors* (2nd ed.). Washington, DC: Author.

Cowan, P. A., Cowan, C. P., Pruett, M. K., Pruett, K. D., & Wong, J. (2009). Promoting fathers' engagement with children: Preventive interventions for low-income families. *Journal of Marriage and the Family, 71*, 663–679.

Dearing, E., Kreider, H., Simpkins, S., & Weiss, H. (2007). *Family involvement in school and low-income children's literacy performance* (Family Involvement Research Digest). Cambridge, MA: Harvard Family Research Project. Retrieved January 18, 2012, from http://www.gse.harvard.edu/hfrp/publications-resources/publications_series/family_involvement research_digests/family-involvement-in-school-and-low-income-children's-literacy-performance.

Driscoll, K. C., Wang, L., Mashburn, A. J., & Pianta, R. C. (2011). Fostering supportive teacher-child relationships: Intervention implementation in a state-funded preschool program. *Early Education and Development, 22*(4), 593–619.

Dunst, C. J. (2011). *Family-centered practices, parent engagement, and parent and family functioning.* Paper presented at the June 7, 2011, meeting of the Head Start Advisory Committee on Research and Evaluation, Washington, DC. Retrieved from http://www.acf.hhs.gov/programs/opre/hs/advisory_com/index.html.

Early, D. M., & Winton, P. (2001). Preparing the workforce: Early childhood teacher preparation at 2- and 4-year institutions of higher education. *Early Childhood Research Quarterly, 16*(3), 285–306.

Ellis, R. R. & Simmons, T. (2014). *Co-resident grandparents and their grandchildren: 2012.* Retrieved November 10, 2014, from http://www.census.gov/content/dam/Census/library/publications/2014/demo/p20-576.pdf

Epstein, J. L., Sanders, M. G., Sheldon, S. B., Simon, B. S., Clark Salinas, K., Rodriquez Jansorn, N., et al. (2009). *School, family, and community partnerships: Your handbook for action* (3rd ed.). Thousand Oaks, CA: Corwin Press.

Fisher, R., Ury, W., & Patton, B. (2011). *Getting to yes: Negotiating agreement without giving in* (Rev. ed.). Penguin.

Gonzalez, N., Moll, L. C., & Amanti, C. (Eds.). (2005). *Funds of knowledge: Theorizing practices in households and classrooms.* Hillsdale, NJ: Lawrence Erlbaum Associates.

Halgunseth, L. C., Peterson, A., Stark, D. R., & Moodie, S. (2009). *Family engagement, diverse families, and early childhood programs: An integrated review of the literature.* Washington, DC: National Association for the Education of Young Children and The Pew Charitable Trusts.

Hanhan, S. F., & Kartoshkina, Y. (2012). Parent-teacher communication: Who's talking? In G. Olsen & M. L. Fuller (Eds.), *Home and school relations: Teachers and parents working together* (4th ed., pp. 101–129). Upper Saddle River, NJ: Pearson.

Iruka, I. U. (2013). *The Black family: Re-Imagining family support and engagement for children.* In National Black Child Development Institute, *Being Black is not a risk factor: A strengths-based look at the state of the Black child.* Washington, DC: National Black Child Development Institute. Retrieved from http://www.nbcdi.org/resource

Kaldor, T. (2015). Technology as a tool to strengthen the home-school connection. In C. Donohue (Ed.), *Technology and digital media in the early years: Tools for teaching and learning* (pp. 201–217). New York: Routledge.

Keyser, J. (2006). *From parents to partners: Building a family-centered early childhood program.* St. Paul, MN: Redleaf Press.

Kreider, R. M., & Ellis, R. (2011, June). *Living arrangements of children: 2009.* Washington, DC: United States Census Bureau.

Lerner, C., & Barr, R. (2014). *Screen sense: Setting the record straight. Research-based guidelines for screen use for children under three years old.* Washington, DC: ZERO to THREE.

Lim, S. (2012). Family involvement in education. In G. Olsen & M. L. Fuller (Eds.), *Home and school relations: Teachers and parents working together* (4th ed., pp. 130–155). Upper Saddle River, NJ: Pearson.

Minnesota Fathers and Families Network. (2013). *Linking fathers: Father involvement in early childhood programs.* Plymouth, MN: Author. Retrieved from http://www.mnfathers.org/wp-content/uploads/2013/06/Early-Childhood-Sector-Analysis.pdf

Mitchell, S. M., Foulger, T. S., & Wetzel, K. (2009). Ten tips for involving families through Internet-based communication. *Young Children, 64*(5), 46–49.

Moore, K. A. (2006). *Defining the term "at risk"* (Research to Results Briefs). Washington, DC: Child Trends.

Moore, K. A., Chalk, R., Scarpa, J., & Vandivere, S. (2002). *Family strengths: Often overlooked, but real* (Research Brief). Washington, DC: Child Trends.

National Association for the Education of Young Children (NAEYC). (2014). *NAEYC early childhood program standards and accreditation criteria and guidance for assessment.* Washington, DC: Author. Retrieved November 13, 2014, from http://www.naeyc.org/academy/files/academy/file/AllCriteriaDocument.pdf

National Association for the Education of Young Children (NAEYC). (1998). *The leading edge workbook.* Washington, DC: Author.

National Association for the Education of Young Children (NAEYC). (2008c). *Relationships: A guide to the NAEYC early childhood program standard and related accreditation criteria.* Washington, DC: Author.

National Center for Children in Poverty (NCCP). (2014). *Child poverty.* Retrieved November 13, 2014, from http://www.nccp.org/topics/childpoverty.html

National Research Council (NRC). (2014). *New directions in child abuse and neglect research.* Washington, DC: Author.

Nemeth, K. N. (2015). Technology to support dual language learners. In C. Donohue (Ed.), *Technology and digital media in the early years: Tools for teaching and learning* (pp. 115–128). New York: Routledge.

Olsen, G., & Fuller, M. L. (2012). *Home and school relations: Teachers and parents working together* (4th ed.). Upper Saddle River, NJ: Pearson.

Pew Center on the States. (2010a). *Home visiting fact sheet.* Retrieved January 3, 2012, from http://www.pewcenteronthestates.org

Pew Center on the States. (2010b). *The case for home visiting: Strong families start with a solid foundation.* Retrieved January 2, 2012, from http://www.pewcenteronthestates.org

Powell, D. R. (2013). Involving parents and community members: Coming together for children. In D. R. Reutzel (Ed.), *Handbook of research-based practice in early education* (pp. 46–61). New York: Guilford Press.

Powell, D. R., & Gerde, H. K. (2006). Considering kindergarten families. In D. F. Gullo (Ed.), *K today: Teaching and learning in the kindergarten year* (pp. 26–35). Washington, DC: National Association for the Education of Young Children.

Powell, D. R., & O'Leary, P. M. (2009). Strengthening relations between parents and early childhood programs. In E. L. Essa & M. M. Burnham (Eds.), *Informing our practice: Useful research on young children's development* (pp. 193–202). Washington, DC: National Association for the Education of Young Children.

Roggman, L. (2011). *Parent engagement in Early Head Start home visits: Home visiting strategies and training.* Paper presented at the June 7, 2011, meeting of the Head Start Advisory Committee on Research and Evaluation, Washington, DC. Retrieved from http://www.acf.hhs.gov/programs/opre/hs/advisory_com/index.html

Sheldon, S. B. (2009). Improving student outcomes with school, family, and community partnerships: A research review. In J. L. Epstein & Associates, *School, family, and community partnerships: Your handbook for action* (3rd ed., pp. 40–56). Thousand Oaks, CA: Corwin Press.

Swick, D. C., Head-Reeves, D., & Barbarin, O. (2006). Building relationships between diverse families and school personnel. In C. Franklin, M. B. Franklin, & P. Allen-Meares (Eds.), *The school services sourcebook: A guide for school-based professionals* (pp. 793–801). New York: Oxford University Press.

Trivette, C. M., Dunst, C. J., & Hamby, D. W. (2010). Influences of family-systems intervention practices on parent-child interactions and child development. *Topics in Early Childhood Special Education, 30*(1), 3–19.

U.S. Department of Health and Human Services. (n.d.) *Risk and protective factors for mental, emotional, and behavioral disorders across the life cycle.* Retrieved July 31, 2015, from http://www.crpcorp.com/Mandatory_Capacity_Building_Initiative_(Cohort_10)/Matrix_ReportBrief.pdf

Welch, K. J. (2011). *Family life now: Census update* (2nd ed.). Upper Saddle River, NJ: Pearson.

Chapter 8

Ainsworth, M. D. S., Blehar, M. C., Waters, E., & Wall, S. (1978). *Patterns of attachment.* Hillsdale, NJ: Lawrence Erlbaum Associates.

Barbarin, O. (2011). *Imagining auspicious environments for the development of African American boys.* Paper presented at the ETS Addressing Achievement Gaps Symposium co-sponsored with Children's Defense Fund, June 14, 2011, Washington, DC: Educational Testing Service. Retrieved August 11, 2011, from http://www.ets.org/s/sponsored_events/achievement_gap/pdf/2011_conference/oscar_barbarin_presentation.pdf

Barbarin, O. (2013). A longitudinal examination of socioemotional learning in African American and Latino boys across the transition from pre-K to kindergarten. *American Journal of Orthopsychiatry, 83*, 156–164. doi:10.1111/ajop.12024

Barbarin, O., Iruka, I. U., Harradine, C., Winn, D. C., McKinney, M. K., & Taylor, L. C. (2013). Development of social-emotional competence in boys of color: A cross-sectional cohort analysis from pre-k to second grade. *American Journal of Orthopsychiatry, 83*, 145–155. doi:10.1111/ajop.12023

Bowlby, J. (1969/2000). *Attachment and loss: Volume I: Attachment.* New York: Basic.

Center on the Social and Emotional Foundations for Early Learning. (n.d.). *Pyramid model for supporting social and emotional competence in infants and young children.* Retrieved February 2, 2012 from http://csefel.vanderbilt.edu.

Curby, T. W., Brock, L., & Hamre, B. (2013). Teachers' emotional support consistency predicts children's achievement gains and social skills. *Early Education and Development, 24*, 292–309.

DeVries, R., & Zan, B. (2012). *Moral classrooms, moral children: Creating a constructivist atmosphere in early education* (2nd ed.). New York: Teachers College Press.

Diamond, A. (2012, January 20). *What nurtures the human spirit may also be best for executive functions and school success.* Presentation at the Maryland State Department of Education Early Care and Education Research Forum, Towson, MD.

Driscoll, K. C., & Pianta, R. C. (2010). Banking time in Head Start: Early efficacy of an intervention designed to promote teacher-child relationships. *Early Education and Development, 21*, 38–64.

Durlak, J. A., Weissberg, R. P., Dymnicki, A. B., Taylor, R. D., & Schellinger, K. B. (2011). The impact of enhancing students' social and emotional learning: A meta-analysis of school-based universal interventions. *Child Development, 82*(1), 405–432.

Early, D. M., Iruka, I., Ritchie, S., Barbarin, O., Winn, D., Crawford, G., et al. (2010). How do pre-kindergarteners spend their time? Gender, ethnicity, and income as predictors of experiences in pre-kindergarten classrooms. *Early Childhood Research Quarterly, 25*(2).

Fox, L., & Lentini, R. H. (2006, November). "You got it!" Teaching social and emotional skills. *Young Children, 61*(6), 36–42.

Fox, L., Carta, J., Strain, P., Dunlap, G., & Hemmeter, M. L. (2009). Response to Intervention and the Pyramid Model. Tampa, FL: University of South Florida, Technical Assistance Center on Social Emotional Intervention for Young Children. Retrieved from http://www.challengingbehavior.org

Fox, L., Dunlap, G., Hemmeter, M. L., Joseph, G. E., & Strain, P. S. (2003). The teaching pyramid: A model for supporting social competence and preventing challenging behavior in young children. *Young Children, 58*(4), 48–52.

Galinsky, E. (2010). *Mind in the making: The seven essential life skills every child needs.* New York: Harper.

Gallagher, K. C. (2013). Guiding children's friendship development: An essential part of the early childhood curriculum. *Young Children, 68*, 5.

Gallagher, K. C., & Sylvester, P. (2009). Supporting peer relationships in early education. In O. Barbarin & B. H. Wasik (Eds.), *Handbook of child development and early education: Research to practice* (pp. 223–246). New York: Guilford Press.

Gallagher, K. C., Kainz, K., White, K. M., & Vernon-Feagans, L. (2013). Development of student-teacher relationships in early education. *Early Childhood Research Quarterly, 28*, 520–528.

Gartrell, D. (2006, March). Guidance matters. In *Beyond the journal: Young children on the web.* Retrieved December 14, 2014, from https://www.naeyc.org/files/yc/file/200603/GuidanceBTJ.pdf

Gartrell, D. (2011). A guidance approach for the encouraging classroom. Clifton Park, NY: Wadsworth Cengage Learning.

Gilliam, W. S. (2008). *Implementing policies to reduce the likelihood of preschool expulsion.* New York: Foundation for Child Development. Retrieved December 10, 2014, from http://medicine.yale.edu/childstudy/zigler/350_34772_PreKExpulsionBrief2.pdf

Greenman, J. (2005a). *Caring spaces, learning places.* Redmond, WA: Exchange Press.

Greenman, J., Stonehouse, A., & Schweikert, G. (2007). *Prime times: A handbook for excellence in infant and toddler programs* (2nd ed.). St. Paul, MN: Redleaf Press.

Hamre, B. K. (2014). Teachers' daily interactions with children: An essential ingredient in effective early childhood programs. *Child Development Perspectives, 8*(4), 223–230. doi:10.1111/cdep.12090

Hamre, B. K. (2014). Teachers' daily interactions with children: An essential ingredient in effective early childhood programs. *Child Development Perspectives, 8*(4), 223–230. doi:10.1111/cdep.12090

Hamre, B. K., & Pianta, R. C. (2005). Can instructional and emotional support in the first-grade classroom make a difference for children at risk of school failure? *Child Development, 76*(5), 949–967.

Hemmeter, M. L., Snyder, P., Fox, L., & Algina, J. (2011). *Professional development related to the Teaching Pyramid Model for addressing the social emotional development and challenging behavior of young children.* Presentation at the 2011 International Society on Early Intervention Conference, May 5, 2011, New York, NY.

Howes, C., & Ritchie, S. (2002). *A matter of trust: Connecting teachers and learners in the early childhood curriculum.* New York: Teachers College Press.

Janson, G. R., & King, M. A. (2010). Creating emotionally healthy learning environments: Eliminating emotional maltreatment from your school. *Focus on Elementary, 23*(1), 1–7. Silver Spring, MD: Association for Childhood Education International.

Jennings, P. A. (2014). Early childhood teachers' well-being, mindfulness, and self-compassion in relation to classroom quality and attitudes towards challenging students. *Mindfulness.* Published online. doi:10.1007/s12671-014-0312-4

Johnson, S. R., Seidenfeld, A. M., Izard, C. E., & Kobak, R. (2013). Can classroom emotional support enhance prosocial development among children with depressed caregivers? *Early Childhood Research Quarterly, 28*, 282–290. doi:10.1016/j.ecresq.2012.07.003

Joseph, G. E., & Strain, P. S. (2003a). Enhancing emotional vocabulary in young children. *Young Exceptional Children, 6*(4), 18–27.

Joseph, G. E., Webster-Stratton, C., & Reid, J. (2006). *Fostering social and emotional competence: Implementing Dina Dinosaur's social skills and problem solving curriculum in inclusive early childhood programs.* Retrieved from http://www.incredibleyears.com/Library/items/fostering-social-emotional-curriculum_06.pdf

Joseph, G., Strain, P. S., & Ostrosky, M. M. (2006). *Fostering emotional literacy in young children: Labeling emotions* (What Works Brief No. 21). Champaign, IL: Center on the Social and Emotional Foundations for Early Learning. Retrieved October 14, 2009, from http://www.vanderbilt.edu/csefel/briefs/wwb21.html

Kaiser, B., & Rasminsky, J. S. (2017). *Challenging behavior in young children: Understanding, preventing, and responding effectively* (4th ed.). Upper Saddle River, NJ: Pearson.

King, M., & Janson, G. R. (2010). The special needs of boys. In B. Erford (Ed.), *Professional school counseling: A handbook of theories, programs and practices* (2nd ed.). Austin, TX: Pro-Ed.

King, M., with Gartrell, D. (2004). Guidance with boys. In D. Gartrell (Ed.), *The power of guidance: Teaching social-emotional skills in early childhood classrooms.* Clifton Park, NY: Delmar Learning.

Kusché, C. A., & Greenberg, M. T. (2012). The PATHS Curriculum: Promoting emotional literacy, prosocial behavior, and caring classrooms. In S. R. Jimerson, A. B. Nickerson, M. J. Mayer, & M. J. Furlong (Eds.), *Handbook of school violence and school safety: International research and practice* (2nd ed., pp. 435–446). New York: Routledge/Taylor & Francis Group.

Ladd, G. W., Herald, S. L., & Andrews, R. K. (2006). Young children's peer relations and social competence. In B. Spodek & O. N. Saracho (Eds.),

Handbook of research on the education of young children (2nd ed., pp. 23–54). Mahwah, NJ: Lawrence Erlbaum Associates.

Lawner, E. K., & Terzian, M. A. (2013). *What works for bullying programs: Lessons from experimental evaluations of programs and interventions.* Bethesda, MD: Child Trends. Retrieved December 2, 2014, from http://www.childtrends.org/wp-content/uploads/2013/10/briefing_bullying5_anm1.pdf

Lieber, J. (2009). Social and emotional development. In S. R. Hooper & W. Umansky (Eds.), *Young children with special needs* (5th ed., pp. 345–379). Upper Saddle River, NJ: Merrill/Pearson.

Main, M., & Solomon, J. (1990). Procedures for identifying infants as disorganized-disoriented during the Ainsworth strange situation. In M. Greenberg, D. Cicchetti, & E. M. Cummings (Eds.), *Attachment in the preschool years: Theory, research, and intervention* (pp. 161–184). Chicago: University of Chicago Press.

Malone, L., Hulsey, L., Aikens, N., West, J., & Tarullo, L. (2010). *ACF-OPRE Report: Data Tables for FACES 2006 Head Start Children Go to Kindergarten Report.* Washington, DC: U.S. Department of Health and Human Services, Administration for Children and Families, Office of Planning, Research and Evaluation.

MenTeach. (2012). *Data about men teachers.* Minneapolis, MN: Author. Retrieved December 14, 2014, from http://www.menteach.org/resources/data_about_men_teachers

Moffitt, T. E., Arseneault, L., Belsky, D., Dickson, N., Hancox, R. J., Harrington, H. L., et al. (2011). A gradient of childhood self-control predicts health, wealth, and public safety. *Proceedings of the National Academy of Sciences, 108*(7), 2693–2698.

Morhard, R. H. (2013). *Wired to move: Facts and strategies for nurturing boys in an early childhood setting.* Lewisville, NC: Gryphon House.

National Association for the Education of Young Children (NAEYC). (2008c). *Relationships: A guide to the NAEYC early childhood program standard and related accreditation criteria.* Washington, DC: Author.

National Association for the Education of Young Children (NAEYC). (2009). *Developmentally appropriate practice in early childhood programs serving children from birth through age 8: Position statement.* Washington, DC: Author.

Neilsen, S. L., Olive, M. L., Donovan, A., & McEvoy, M. (1999). Challenging behaviors in your classroom? Don't react—teach instead! In S. Sandall & M. Ostrosky (Eds.), *Practical ideas for addressing challenging behaviors* (pp. 5–15). Denver, CO: Division for Early Childhood of the Council for Exceptional Children.

Paley, V. (1992). *You can't say you can't play.* Cambridge, MA: Harvard University Press.

Pianta, R. C., La Paro, K. M., & Hamre, B. K. (2008). *Classroom assessment scoring system (CLASS).* Baltimore: Paul H. Brookes.

Raikes, H. H., & Edwards, C. P. (2009). *Extending the dance in infant and toddler caregiving: Enhancing attachment and relationships.* Baltimore: Paul H. Brookes.

Ramming, P., Kyger, C. S., & Thompson, S. D. (2006). A new bit on toddler biting: The influence of food, oral motor development, and sensory activities. *Young Children, 61*(2), 17–23.

Raver, C. C., Garner, P. W., & Smith-Donald, R. (2007). The roles of emotion regulation and emotion knowledge for children's academic readiness. In R. C. Pianta, M. J. Cox, & K. L. Snow (Eds.), *School readiness and the transition to kindergarten in the era of accountability* (pp. 121–147). Baltimore: Paul H. Brookes.

Riley, D., San Juan, R. R., Klinkner, J., & Ramminger, A. (2008). *Social and emotional development:*

Connecting science and practice in early childhood settings. St. Paul, MN: Redleaf Press.

Scroufe, L. A. (1996). *Emotional development: The organization of emotional life in the early years.* New York: Cambridge University Press.

Sprung, B., Froschl, M., & Gropper, N. (2010). *Supporting boys' learning: Strategies for teacher practice, pre-K–grade 3.* New York: Teachers College Press.

Strain, P. S., & Hemmeter, M. L. (1999). Keys to being successful when confronted with challenging behaviors. In S. Sandall & M. Ostrosky (Eds.), *Practical ideas for addressing challenging behaviors* (pp. 17–25). Denver, CO: Division for Early Childhood of the Council for Exceptional Children.

Temkin, D. (2014). *Five things to know about bullying.* Bethesda, MD: Child Trends. Retrieved December 2, 2014, from http://www.childtrends.org/wp-content/uploads/2014/10/2014-51CT5Bullying.pdf

U.S. Department of Education Office of Civil Rights. (2014, March 21). *Civil rights data collection: Data snapshot: Early childhood education.* Retrieved December 14, 2014, from http://www2.ed.gov/about/offices/list/ocr/docs/crdc-early-learning-snapshot.pdf

Vance, E. (2013). *Class meetings: Young children solving problems together* (Rev. ed.). Washington, DC: NAEYC.

Watson, M. (2003). Attachment theory and challenging behaviors: Reconstructing the nature of relationships. *Young Children, 58*(4), 12–20.

Wheeler, E. J. (2004). *Conflict resolution in early childhood: Helping children understand and resolve conflicts.* Upper Saddle River, NJ: Pearson.

Whitaker, R. C., Dearth-Wesley, T., Gooze, R. A., Becker, B. D., Gallagher, K. C., & McEwen, B. S. (2014). Adverse childhood experiences, dispositional mindfulness, and adult health. *Preventive Medicine, 67*, 147–153. doi:10.1016/j.ypmed.2014.07.029

Williford, A. P., Vick Whittaker, J. E., Vitiello, V. E., & Downer, J. T. (2013). Children's engagement within the preschool classroom and their development of self-regulation. *Early Education & Development, 24*, 162–187. doi:10.1080/10409289.2011.628270

Zins, J. E., Bloodworth, M. R., Weissberg, R. P., & Walberg, H. J., (2007). The scientific base linking social and emotional learning to school success. *Journal of Educational and Psychological Consultation, 17*(2–3), 191–210.

Chapter 9

Abou-Sayed, Y. (2011). Using small groups and workstations: From chaotic to constructive. *Texas Child Care Quarterly, 35*(3). Retrieved October 30, 2014, from http://www.childcarequarterly.com/winter11_story2.html

Ausubel, D. P. (1978). *Educational psychology: A cognitive view* (2nd ed.). Boston: Holt McDougal.

Bailey, M., & Blagojevic, B. (2015). Innovate, educate, and empower: New opportunities with new technologies. In C. Donohue (Ed.), *Technology and digital media in the early years: Tools for teaching and learning* (pp. 162–182). New York: Routledge.

Barnett, W. S., Jung, K., Yarosz, D. J., Thomas, J., Hornbeck, A., Stechuk, R., & Burns, S. (2008). Educational effects of the Tools of the Mind Curriculum: A randomized trial. *Early Childhood Research Quarterly, 23*(3), 299–313.

Bates, C. C. (2013). Flexible grouping during literacy centers: A model for differentiating instruction. *Young Children, 68*(2), 30–33.

Beck, I. L., McKeown, M. G., & Kucan, L. (2013). *Bringing words to life: Robust vocabulary—instruction* (2nd ed.). New York: Guilford Press.

Beneke, S. J., & Ostrosky, M. M. (2013). The potential of the project approach to support diverse young learners. *Young Children, 68*(2), 22–28.

Bodrova, E., & Leong, D. J. (2007). *Tools of the mind: The Vygotskian approach to early childhood education.* Upper Saddle River, NJ: Pearson.

Bowman, B. T., Donovan, M. S., & Burns, S. (Eds.). (2001). *Eager to learn: Educating our preschoolers* (National Research Council, Committee on Early Childhood Pedagogy Report). Washington, DC: National Academies Press.

Bransford, J. D., Brown, A. L., & Cocking, R. R. (Eds.). (2000). *How people learn: Brain, mind, experience and school* (Expanded ed.). Washington, DC: National Academies Press.

Buysse, V., & Wesley, P. (Eds.). (2006). *Evidence-based practice in the early childhood field.* Washington, DC: ZERO to THREE Press.

Cameron, C. E., & Morrison, F. J. (2011). Teacher activity orienting predicts preschoolers' academic and self-regulatory skills. *Early Education and Development, 22*(4), 620–648.

Clark, K. F., & Graves, M. F. (2005). Scaffolding students' comprehension of text. *The Reading Teacher, 58*(6), 570–580.

Cohen Group. (2011). *Young children, apps, and iPads.* U.S. Department of Education Ready to Learn Program. Retrieved February 7, 2011, from http://www.mcgrc.com.

Cohrssen, C., Church, A., & Tayler, C. (2014). Purposeful pauses: Teacher talk during early childhood mathematics activities. *International Journal of Early Years Education, 22*(2), 169–183.

Common Core State Standards Initiative. (2011a). *Common core standards for English language arts.* Washington, DC: Council for Chief State School Officers and National Governor's Association. Retrieved February 17, 2012, from www.corestandards.org

Common Sense Media. (2013, Fall). *Zero to eight: Children' media use in America 2013. A Common Sense Media research study.* Retrieved September 3, 2014, from https://www.commonsensemedia.org/file/zero-to-eight-2013pdf-0/download

Copple, C., & Bredekamp, S. (Eds.). (2009). *Developmentally appropriate practice in early childhood programs serving children from birth through age 8* (Rev. ed.). Washington, DC: National Association for the Education of Young Children.

Copple, C., Sigel, I. E., & Saunders, R. (1984). *Educating the young thinker: Classroom strategies for cognitive growth.* Hillsdale, NJ: Lawrence Erlbaum Associates.

Daugherty, L., Dossani, R., Johnson, E.-E., & Wright, C. (2014). *Moving beyond screen time: Redefining developmentally appropriate technology use in early childhood education.* Santa Monica, CA: RAND Corporation. Retrieved October 16, 2014, from http://www.rand.org/content/dam/rand/pubs/research_reports/RR600/RR673z2/RAND_RR673z2.pdf

Dean, C. B., Hubbell, E. R., Pitler, H., & Stone, B. J. (2012). *Classroom strategies that work: Research-based strategies for increasing student achievement* (2nd ed.). Alexandria, VA: ASCD; & Denver, CO: McREL.

Diamond, A. (2012, January 20). *What nurtures the human spirit may also be best for executive functions and school success.* Presentation at the Maryland State Department of Education Early Care and Education Research Forum, Towson, MD.

Diamond, A., & Lee, K. (2011, August 19). Interventions shown to aid executive function development in children 4 to 12 years old. *Science, 333*(6045), 959–964. doi:10.1126/science.1204529

Dickinson, D. (2001). Large-group and free-play times: Conversational settings supporting language and literacy development. In D. Dickinson & P. Tabors (Eds.), *Beginning literacy with language: Young children learning at home and school* (pp. 223–256). Baltimore: Paul H. Brookes.

Dickinson, D. K. (2011, August 19). Teachers' language practices and academic outcomes of preschool children. *Science, 333*(6045), 964–967. doi:10.1126/science.1204526

Dickinson, D. K., & Smith, M. W. (1993). Long-term effects of preschool teachers' book readings on low-income children's vocabulary and story comprehension. *Reading Research Quarterly, 29*(2), 104–122.

Division for Early Childhood & National Association for the Education of Young Children. (2009). *Early childhood inclusion: A joint position statement of the Division for Early Childhood (DEC) and the National Association for the Education of Young Children (NAEYC).* Chapel Hill: The University of North Carolina, FPG Child Development Institute. Retrieved from http://npdci.fpg.unc.edu/sites/npdci.fpg.unc.edu/files/resources/EarlyChildhoodInclusion_0.pdf

Donohue, C. (Ed.). (2015). *Technology and digital media in the early years.* New York: Routledge Taylor & Francis Group.

Early, D. M., Barbarin, O., Bryant, D., Burchinal, M., Chang, F., Clifford, R., et al. (2005). *Prekindergarten in 11 states: NCEDL's multi-state study of pre-kindergarten and study of state-wide early education programs (SWEEP).* Chapel Hill, NC. Retrieved August 8, 2008, from http://www.fpg.unc.edu/NCEDL/pdfs/SWEEP_MS_summary_final.pdf

Early, D. M., Iruka, I., Ritchie, S., Barbarin, O., Winn, D., Crawford, G., et al. (2010). How do pre-kindergarteners spend their time? Gender, ethnicity, and income as predictors of experiences in pre-kindergarten classrooms. *Early Childhood Research Quarterly, 25*(2).

Edwards, C., Gandini, L., & Forman, G. (Eds.). (2012). *The hundred languages of children: The Reggio Emilia experience in transformation* (3rd ed.). Santa Barbara, CA: Praeger.

Elias, C. L., & Berk, L. E. (2002). Self-regulation in young children: Is there a role for sociodramatic play? *Early Childhood Research Quarterly, 17*(2), 216–238.

Epstein, A. S. (2012). How planning and reflection develop young children's thinking skills. In C. Copple (Ed.), *Growing minds: Building strong cognitive foundations in early childhood* (pp. 111–118). Washington, DC: National Association for the Education of Young Children.

Epstein, A. S. (2013). *Essentials of active learning in preschool: Getting to know the High/Scope curriculum* (2nd ed.) Ypsilanti, MI: High/Scope Press.

Epstein, A. S. (2014). *The intentional teacher: Choosing the best strategies for young children's learning* (Rev. ed.). Washington, DC: National Association for the Education of Young Children.

Espinosa, L. M. (2010c). *Getting it right for young children from diverse backgrounds: Applying research to improve practice.* Upper Saddle River, NJ: Pearson.

Forman, G. (1994). Different media, different languages. In L. G. Katz & B. Cesarone (Eds.), *Reflections on the Reggio Emilia approach.* Urbana, IL: ERIC Clearinghouse on Elementary and Early Childhood Education.

Gadzikowski, A. (2013b). Differentiation strategies for exceptionally bright children. *Young Children, 68*(2), 8–14.

Gonzalez, J. E., Pollard-Durodola, S. Simmons, D. C., Taylor, A. B., David, M. J., Fogarty, M., & Simmons, L. (2014). Enhancing preschool children's vocabulary: Effects of teacher talk before, during and after shred reading. *Early Childhood Research Quarterly, 29*(2), 214–226.

Graue, E., Clements, M. A., Reynolds, A. J., & Niles, M. D. (2004). More than teacher directed or child initiated: Preschool curriculum type, parent involvement, and children's outcomes in the child-parent centers. *Education Policy Analysis Archives, 12.* Retrieved from http://epaa.asu.edu/ojs/article/viewFile/227/353

Hamre, B. K., & Pianta, R. C. (2001). Early teacher-child relationships and the trajectory of children's school outcomes through eighth grade. *Child Development, 72,* 625–638.

Hamre, B. K., & Pianta, R. C. (2005). Can instructional and emotional support in the first-grade classroom make a difference for children at risk of school failure? *Child Development, 76*(5), 949–967.

Hamre, B. K., & Pianta, R. C. (2007). Learning opportunities in preschool and early elementary classrooms. In R. C. Pianta, M. J. Cox, & K. Snow (Eds.), *School readiness, early learning, and the transition to kindergarten* (pp. 49–83). Baltimore: Paul H. Brookes.

Hamre, B. K., & Pianta, R. C. (2010). Classroom environments and developmental processes: Conceptualization and measurement. In J. L. Meece & J. S. Eccles (Eds.), *Handbook of research on schools, schooling, and human development* (pp. 25–41). New York: Routledge.

Hamre, B., Hatfield, B., Pianta, R., & Jamil, F. (2014). Evidence for general and domain-specific elements of teacher-child interactions: Associations with preschool children's development. *Child Development, 85,* 1257–1274.

Heward, W. L. (2013). *Exceptional children: An introduction to special education* (10th ed.). Upper Saddle River, NJ: Pearson.

Hohmann, M., & Weikart, D. P. (2002). *Educating young children: Active learning practices for preschool and child care programs* (2nd ed.). Ypsilanti, MI: High/Scope Press.

Hong, S.-Y., & Diamond, K. E. (2012). Two approaches to teaching young children science concepts, vocabulary, and scientific problem-solving skills. *Early Childhood Research Quarterly, 27*(2), 295–305.

Hooper, S. R., & Umansky, W. (Eds.). (2010). *Young children with special needs* (5th ed.). Upper Saddle River, NJ: Pearson.

Howes, C., Burchinal, M., Pianta, R., Bryant, D., Early, D., Clifford, R., et al. (2008). Ready to learn? Children's pre-academic achievement in pre-kindergarten programs. *Early Childhood Research Quarterly, 23*(1), 27–50.

Johnson, J. E., Christie, J. F., & Wardle, F. (2005). *Play, development, and early education.* Upper Saddle River, NJ: Pearson.

Jones, E., & Reynolds, G. (2011). *The play's the thing: Teachers' roles in children's play* (2nd ed.). New York: Teachers College Press.

Justice, L. M., Mashburn, A. J., Hamre, B. K., & Pianta, R. C. (2008). Quality of language and literacy instruction in preschool classrooms serving at-risk pupils. *Early Childhood Research Quarterly, 2,* 51–68.

Kleeman, D. (2010). "A screen is a screen is a screen" is a meme. *Huffington Post,* December, 8, 2010. Retrieved November 26, 2012, from http://www.huffingtonpost.com/david-kleeman/a-screen-is-a-screen-is-a_b_792742.html

Landry, C. E., & Forman, G. (1999). Research on early science education. In C. Seefeldt (Ed.), *The early childhood curriculum: Current findings in theory and practice* (pp. 133–158). New York: Teachers College Press.

Lerner, C., & Barr, R. (2014). *Screen sense: Setting the record straight. Research-based guidelines for screen use for children under three years old.* Washington, DC: ZERO to THREE.

Levin, D. E. (2013). *Beyond remote-controlled childhood: Teaching young children in the media age.* Washington, DC: National Association for the Education of Young Children.

Linebarger, D. L., McMenamin, K., & Wainwright, D. K., (n.d.). *Summative evaluation of Super Why!: Outcomes, dose, and appeal.* Philadelphia: Annenberg School of Communications, Children's Media Lab.

Malaguzzi, L. (1998). History, ideas, and basic philosophy: An interview with Lella Gandini. In C. Edwards, L. Gandini, & G. Forman (Eds.), *The hundred languages of children: The Reggio Emilia approach—Advanced reflections* (2nd ed., 49–97). Greenwich, CT: Ablex.

Marzano, R. J., Pickering, D. J., & Pollock, J. E. (2001). *Classroom instruction that works: Research-based strategies for increasing student achievement.* Alexandria, VA: Association for Supervision and Curriculum Development.

McCardle, P., & Chhabra, V. (Eds.). (2004). *The voice of evidence in reading research.* Baltimore: Paul H. Brookes.

McDermott, M. J. (2012, June/July). Using graphic organizers in preschool. *Teaching Young Children, 5*(5). Washington, DC: National Association for the Education of Young Children. Retrieved October 13, 2014, from http://www.naeyc.org/tyc/article/using_graphic_organizers_in_preschool

Meacham, S., Vukelich, C., Han, M., & Buell, M. (2014). Preschool teachers' questioning in sociodramatic play. *Early Childhood Research Quarterly, 29*(4), 562–573.

Mehigan, K. R. (2005). The strategy toolbox: A ladder to strategic teaching. *The Reading Teacher, 58*(6), 552–566.

Montie, J. E., Xiang, X., & Schweinhart, L. J. (2006). Preschool experience in 10 countries: Cognitive and language performance at age 7. *Early Childhood Research Quarterly, 21*(3), 313–331.

Morrow, L. M., & Smith, J. K. (1990). The effects of group size on storybook reading. *Reading Research Quarterly, 25*, 213–231.

National Association for the Education of Young Children (NAEYC) & the Fred Rogers Center for Early Learning and Children's Media. (2012). *Technology in early childhood programs serving children from birth through age 8.* Joint Position Statement. Washington, DC: Authors.

National Association for the Education of Young Children (NAEYC). (2009). *Developmentally appropriate practice in early childhood programs serving children from birth through age 8: Position statement.* Washington, DC: Author.

National Early Literacy Panel (NELP). (2008). *Developing early literacy: Report of the National Early Literacy Panel. A scientific synthesis of early literacy development and implications for intervention.* Washington, DC: Author. Retrieved from http://lincs.ed.gov/publications/pdf/NELPReport09.pdf

National Institute of Child Health and Human Development (NICHD) Early Child Care Research Network. (2002). The relation of first grade classroom environment to structural classroom features, teacher, and student behaviors. *The Elementary School Journal, 102*, 367–387.

National Institute of Child Health and Human Development (NICHD) Early Child Care Research Network. (2003). Social functioning in first grade: Prediction from home, child care, and concurrent school experience. *Child Development, 74*, 1639–1662.

National Institute of Child Health and Human Development (NICHD). (2000). *Report of the National Reading Panel. Teaching children to read: An evidence-based assessment of the scientific research literature on reading and its implications for reading instruction.* Washington, DC: Author.

National Research Council (NRC). (2000). *How people learn: Brain, mind, experience, and school* (exp. ed.). Washington, DC: National Academies Press.

National Research Council (NRC). (2009). *Mathematics learning in early childhood: Paths toward excellence and equity.* Washington, DC: National Academies Press.

Neuman, S. B., & Wright, T. S. (2013). *All about words: Increasing vocabulary in the common core classroom, PreK–2.* New York: Teachers College Press.

Oczkus, L. D. (2010). *Reciprocal teaching at work: Powerful strategies and lessons for improving reading comprehension* (2nd ed.). Newark, DE: International Reading Association.

Oertwig, S., & Holland, A. L. (2014). Improving instruction. In S. Ritchie & L. Gutmann (Eds.), *First school: Transforming pre-K–3rd grade for African American, Latino, and low-income children.* New York: Teachers College Press.

Ogle, D. M. (1986). KWL: A teaching method that develops active reading of expository text. *The Reading Teacher, 39*(6), 564–570.

Palincsar, A. S., & Brown, A. L. (1984). Reciprocal teaching of comprehension: Fostering and comprehension-monitoring activities. *Cognition and Instruction, 1*(2), 117–175.

Pianta, R. C., La Paro, K. M., & Hamre, B. K. (2008). *Classroom assessment scoring system (CLASS).* Baltimore: Paul H. Brookes.

Reutzel, R. (Ed.). (2013). *Handbook of research-based practice in early education.* New York: Guilford Press.

Ritchie, S., & Willer, B. (2008b). *Relationships: A guide to the NAEYC early childhood program standard and related accreditation criteria.* Washington, DC: National Association for the Education of Young Children.

Ritchie, S., & Willer, B. (2008c). *Teaching: A guide to the NAEYC early childhood program standard and related accreditation criteria* (Updated ed.). Washington, DC: National Association for the Education of Young Children.

Rogoff, B. (1990). *Apprenticeship in thinking.* New York: Oxford University Press.

Rogoff, B. (2003). *The cultural nature of human development.* New York: Oxford University Press.

Sammons, P., Sylva, K., Melhuish, E., Siraj-Blatchford, I., Taggart, B., Hunt, S., et al. (2008). *Effective preschool and primary education 3–11 project (EPPE 3–11): Influences on children's cognitive and social development in year 6* (Department of Children, Schools and Families Research Brief). London: Institute of Education, University of London. Retrieved October 14, 2009, from http://eppe.ioe.ac.uk

Sarama, J., & Clements, D. H. (2002). Learning and teaching with computers in early childhood education. In O. N. Saracho and B. Spodek (Eds.), *Contemporary perspectives on science and technology in early childhood education* (pp. 171–219). Greenwich, CT: Information Age Publishing.

Sarama, J., & Clements, D. H. (2004). Building blocks for early childhood mathematics. *Early Childhood Research Quarterly, 19*(1), 181–189.

Shuler, C. (2012). *iLearn II: An analysis of the education category of the iTunes app store.* New York: The Joan Ganz Cooney Center at Sesame Workshop.

Singer, D. G., Golinkoff, R. M., & Hirsh-Pasek, K. (Eds.). (2006). *Play = learning: How play motivates and enhances children's cognitive and social-emotional growth.* New York: Oxford University Press.

Smilansky, S., & Shefatya, L. (1990). *Facilitating play: A medium for promoting cognitive, socio-emotional, and academic development in young children.* Gaithersburg, MD: Psychological and Educational Publications.

Sutton-Smith, B. (1980). Children's play: Some sources of theorizing. In K. Rubin (Ed.), *Children's play* (pp. 1–16). San Francisco: Jossey-Bass.

Tharp, R., & Entz, S. (2012). From high chair to high school: Research-based principles for teaching complex thinking. In C. Copple (Ed.), *Growing minds: Building strong cognitive foundations in early childhood* (pp. 131–136). Washington, DC: National Association for the Education of Young Children.

Vygotsky, L. S. (1978). *Mind in society.* Cambridge, MA: Harvard University Press.

Wainwright, D. K. (2006). *Ready to learn literature review. Part 1: Elements of effective TV.* Philadelphia: Annenberg School of Communication. Children's Media Center.

Wasik, B. (2008). When fewer is more: Small groups in early childhood classrooms. *Early Childhood Education Journal, 35*, 515–521.

Whitehurst, G. J., & Lonigan, C. J. (1998). Child development and emergent literacy. *Child Development, 69*(3), 848–872.

Wiltz, N. W., & Klein, E. L. (2001). "What do you do in child care?" Children's perceptions of high and low quality classrooms. *Early Childhood Research Quarterly, 16*(2), 209–236.

Wood, D., Bruner, J. S., & Ross, G. (1976). The role of tutoring in problem solving. *Journal of Child Psychology and Psychiatry, 17*, 89–100.

Zigler, E. F., Singer, D. G., & Bishop-Josef, S. J. (Eds.) (2004). *Children's play: The roots of reading.* Washington, DC: ZERO to THREE Press.

Chapter 10

Baldini, R., Cavallini, I., Moss, P., & Vecchi, V. (Eds.). (2012). *One city, many children: Reggio Emilia, a history of the present.* Reggio Emilia, Italy: Reggio Children.

Barnett, W. S. (2010). Universal and targeted approaches to preschool education in the United States. *International Journal of Child Care and Education Policy, 4*(1), 1–12.

Biddle, J. K., & White, B. (Eds.). (2010). *The power of we: The Ohio study group experience.* Charlotte, NC: Information Age Publishing.

Bierman, K. (2011, April 13). *Thinking across broad domains: Integrating curricula and instruction.* Paper presented at the meeting of the Advisory Committee on Head Start Research and Evaluation. Washington, DC.

Blair, C., & Raver, C. C. (2014). Closing the achievement gap through modification of neurocognitive and neuroendocrine function: Results from a cluster randomized controlled trial of an innovative approach to the education of children in kindergarten. *PLoS ONE, 9*(11), e112393. doi:10.1371/journal.pone.0112393

Bodrova, E., & Leong, D. J. (2007). *Tools of the mind: The Vygotskian approach to early childhood education.* Upper Saddle River, NJ: Pearson.

Bowman, B. T., Donovan, M. S., & Burns, S. (Eds.). (2001). *Eager to learn: Educating our preschoolers* (National Research Council, Committee on Early Childhood Pedagogy Report). Washington, DC: National Academies Press.

Bransford, J. D., Brown, A. L., & Cocking, R. R. (Eds.). (2000). *How people learn: Brain, mind, experience and school* (Expanded ed.). Washington, DC: National Academies Press.

Bredekamp, S. (2008). Malaguzzi's metaphors: The power of imagery to transform educational practice and policy. In L. Gandini, S. Etheredge, & L. Hill (Eds.), *Insights and inspirations from Reggio Emilia: Stories of teachers and children from North America* (pp. 48–49). Worcester, MA: Davis Publications.

Bredekamp, S. (2009). Early learning standards and developmentally appropriate practice: Contradictory or compatible? In S. Feeney, A. Galper, & C. Seefeldt (Eds.), *Continuing issues in early childhood education* (pp. 258–271). Upper Saddle River, NJ: Pearson.

Bredekamp, S., & Rosegrant, T. (Eds.). (1992). *Reaching potentials: Appropriate curriculum and assessment for young children* (Vol. 1). Washington, DC: National Association for the Education of Young Children.

Bredekamp, S., & Rosegrant, T. (Eds.). (1995). Reaching potentials through transforming curriculum, assessment, and teaching. In S. Bredekamp & T. Rosegrant (Eds.), *Reaching potentials: Transforming early childhood curriculum and assessment* (pp. 15–22). Washington, DC: National Association for the Education of Young Children.

Bronfenbrenner, U., & Morris, P. A. (2006). The bioecological model of human development. In R. M. Lerner & W. Damon (Eds.), *Handbook of child psychology* (6th ed.), *Vol. 1, Theoretical models of human development* (pp. 793–828). Hoboken, NJ: John Wiley & Sons.

Chalfour, I., & Worth, K. (2004). *Building structures with young children* (The Young Scientist Series). St. Paul, MN: Redleaf Press.

Christodoulou, D. (2014, Spring). Minding the knowledge gap: The importance of content in student learning. *American Educator.* Retrieved January 9, 2015, from http://www.aft.org/sites/default/files/periodicals/Christodoulou.pdf

Clements, D. H., & Sarama, J. (2007a). Early childhood mathematics learning. In F. K. Lester, Jr. (Ed.), *Second handbook of research on mathematics teaching and learning* (pp. 461–555). New York: Information Age Publishing.

Clements, D. H., & Sarama, J. (2009). *Learning and teaching early math: The learning trajectories approach.* New York: Routledge.

Commeyras, M. (2007). Scripted reading instruction? What's a teacher educator to do? *Phi Delta Kappan, 88*(5), 404–407.

Common Core State Standards Initiative. (2011a). *Common core standards for English language arts.* Washington, DC: Council for Chief State School Officers and National Governor's Association. Retrieved February 17, 2012, from www.corestandards.org

Common Core State Standards Initiative. (2011b). *Common core standards for mathematics.* Washington, DC: Council for Chief State School Officers and National Governor's Association. Retrieved February 17, 2012, from http://www.corestandards.org

Copple, C., Bredekamp, S., Koralek, D., & Charner, K. (Eds.). (2013a). *Developmentally appropriate practice: Focus on infants and toddlers.* Washington, DC: National Association for the Education of Young Children.

Core Knowledge Foundation. (2013). Core knowledge sequence: Content and skill guidelines for preschool. Retrieved January 13, 2015, from http://www.coreknowledge.org/mimik/mimik_uploads/documents/494/CKFSequence_PreK_Rev.pdf

Cunningham, A. E., & Davidson, M. (2007). *Professional development in preschool literacy curricula: Developing a framework for increasing teacher knowledge and skills.* Paper presented at the biennial meeting of the Society for Research in Child Development, Boston, MA.

David, J. L. (2008). What research says about … project-based learning. *Educational Leadership, 65*(5), 80–82.

Diamond, A., & Lee, K. (2011, August 19). Interventions shown to aid executive function development in children 4 to 12 years old. *Science, 333*(6045), 959–964. doi:10.1126/science.1204529

Dodge, D. T., Colker, L. J., & Heroman, C. (2010). *The creative curriculum system for preschool* (5th ed.). Washington, DC: Teaching Strategies.

Edwards, C., Gandini, L., & Forman, G. (Eds.). (2012). *The hundred languages of children: The Reggio Emilia experience in transformation* (3rd ed.). Santa Barbara, CA: Praeger.

Epstein, A. S., & Hohmann, M. (2012). *The HighScope preschool curriculum* (4th ed.). Ypsilanti, MI: High/Scope Press.

Epstein, A. S., Marshall, B., & Gainsley, S. (2014). *COR Advantage.* Ypsilanti, MI: HighScope Press.

Espinosa, L. M. (2013). *Pre-K–3rd: Challenging common myths about dual language learners, an update to the seminal 2008 report.* New York: Foundation for Child Development.

Fantuzzo, J. W., Gadsden, V. L., & McDermott, P. A. (2010). An integrated curriculum to improve mathematics, language, and literacy for Head Start children. *American Educational Research Journal, 48,* 763–793.

Fleming, D. (2006). *Alphabet under construction.* New York: Square Fish.

Fountas, I. C., & Pinnell, G. S. (1996). *Guided reading: Good first teaching for all children.* Portsmouth, NH: Heinemann.

Frede, E., & Ackerman, D. J. (2006). Curriculum decision-making: Dimensions to consider. New Brunswick, NJ: National Institute for Early Education Research.

Gandini, L. (2008). Introduction to the schools of Reggio Emilia. In L. Gandini, S. Etheredge, & L. Hill (Eds.), *Insights and inspirations from Reggio Emilia: Stories of teachers and children from North America* (pp. 24–27). Worcester, MA: Davis Publications.

Gewertz, C. (2014, September 3). Big year looms for Common Core testing. Bethesda, MD: *Education Week.* Retrieved January 13, 2015, from http://www.edweek.org/ew/articles/2014/09/03/03assessment.h34.html

Goffin, S. G., & Washington, V. (2007). *Ready or not? Leadership choices in early care and education.* New York: Teachers College Press.

Gonzalez-Mena, J., & Eyer, D. W. (2014). *Infants, toddlers and caregivers: A curriculum of respectful, responsive, relationship-based care and education.* New York: McGraw-Hill.

Grissmer, D. W., Grimm, K. J., Aiyer, S. M., Murrah, W. M., & Steele, J. S. (2010). Fine motor skills and early comprehension of the world: Two new school readiness indicators. *Developmental Psychology, 46*(5), 1008–1017.

Head Start. (2010a). *Head Start child development and early learning framework: Promoting positive outcomes in early childhood programs serving children 3–5 years old.* Washington, DC: U.S. Department of Health and Human Services.

Heckman, J., Pinto, R., & Savelyev, P. (2013). Understanding the mechanisms through which an influential early childhood program boosted adult outcomes. *American Economic Review, 103*(6), 2052–2086.

Helm, J. H. (2014). *Becoming young thinkers: Deep project work in the classroom.* New York: Teachers College Press.

Helm, J. H., & Katz, L. G. (2010). *Young investigators: The project approach in the early years* (2nd ed.). New York: Teachers College Press.

Helm, J. H., Beneke, S., & Steinheimer, K. (2007). *Windows on learning: Documenting young children's work* (2nd ed.). New York: Teachers College Press.

Henry, G. T., Ponder, B. D., Rickman, D. K., Mashburn, A. J., Henderson, L. W., & Gordon, C. S. (2004). *An evaluation of the implementation of Georgia's pre-K program: Report of the findings from the Georgia early childhood study (2002–03).* Atlanta, GA: Georgia State University, Andrew Young School of Policy Studies. Retrieved from: http://www.issuelab.org/click/download1/evaluation_of_the_implementation_of_georgias_pre_k_program_report_of_the_findings_from_the_georgia_early_childhood_study_2002_03

Hirsch, E. D., & Wiggins, A. K. (Eds.). (2009). *Preschool sequence and teacher handbook.* Charlottesville, VA: Core Knowledge Foundation.

Institute of Education Sciences. (2009). *What Works Clearinghouse.* Washington, DC: U.S. Department of Education. Retrieved from http://ies.ed.gov/ncee/wwc/reports

Jones, E., & Nimmo, J. (1994). *Emergent curriculum.* Washington, DC: National Association for the Education of Young Children.

Jones, E., & Nimmo, J. (1994). *Emergent curriculum.* Washington, DC: National Association for the Education of Young Children.

Katz, L. G., & Chard, S. C. (2000). *Engaging children's minds: The project approach.* Norwood, NJ: Ablex.

Kauerz, K., & Coffman, J. (2013). *Framework for planning, implementing, and evaluating pre-K—3rd grade approaches.* Seattle, WA: College of Education, University of Washington. Retrieved November 28, 2014, from http://depts.washington.edu/pthru3/PreK-3rd_Framework_Legal%20paper.pdf

Kauffman, D., Johnson, S. M., Kardos, S. M., Liu, E., & Peske, H. G. (2002). "Lost at sea": New teachers' experiences with curriculum and assessment. *Teachers College Record, 104*(2), 273–300.

Lally, J. R., Mangione, P. L., & Greenwald, D. (Eds.). (2006). *Concepts for care: Essays on infant/toddler development and learning.* San Francisco: WestEd.

Landry, S. H. (2005). *Effective early childhood programs: Turning knowledge into action.* Houston: University of Texas–Houston, Health Science Center.

Malaguzzi, L. (1993). For an education based on relationships. *Young Children, 49*(1), 9–12.

McAfee, O., & Leong, D. J. (2011). *Assessing and guiding young children's development and learning* (5th ed.). Upper Saddle River, NJ: Pearson.

National Association for the Education of Young Children (NAEYC) & National Association of Early Childhood Specialists in State Departments of Education (NAECS/SDE). (2003). *Early childhood curriculum, assessment, and program evaluation: Building an effective, accountable system in programs for children birth through age 8. Joint position statement.* Washington, DC: National Association for the Education of Young Children.

National Association for the Education of Young Children (NAEYC). (2009). *Developmentally appropriate practice in early childhood programs serving children from birth through age 8: Position statement.* Washington, DC: Author.

National Center for Children in Poverty (NCCP). (2007). *Promoting effective early learning: What every policymaker and educator should know.* New York: Columbia University, Mailman School of Public Health.

National Center on Quality Teaching and Learning. (2011). *Choosing a preschool curriculum.* Office of Head Start. Retrieved from http://www.eclkc.acf.hhs.gov

National Center on Quality Teaching and Learning. (2014). *Preschool curriculum consumer report.* Washington, DC: U.S. Department of Health and Human Services, Office of Head Start. Retrieved January 8, 2015, from http://eclkc.ohs.acf.hhs.gov/hslc/tta-system/teaching/practice/docs/curriculum-consumer-report.pdf

National Council of Teachers of Mathematics. (2000). *Principles and standards for school mathematics.* Reston, VA: Author. Retrieved from http://standards.nctm.org

National Council of Teachers of Mathematics. (2006). *Curriculum focal points.* Reston, VA: Author.

National Early Literacy Panel (NELP). (2008). *Developing early literacy: Report of the National Early*

Literacy Panel. A scientific synthesis of early literacy development and implications for intervention. Washington, DC: Author. Retrieved from http://lincs.ed.gov/publications/pdf/NELPReport09.pdf

National Institute of Child Health and Human Development (NICHD). (2000). *Report of the National Reading Panel. Teaching children to read: An evidence-based assessment of the scientific research literature on reading and its implications for reading instruction.* Washington, DC: Author.

National Research Council (NRC). (2009). *Mathematics learning in early childhood: Paths toward excellence and equity.* Washington, DC: National Academies Press.

Nayfeld, I., Brenneman, K., & Gelman, R. (2009). *Science in the classroom: Finding a balance between autonomous exploration and teacher-led instruction in preschool settings.* Paper presented at the biannual meeting of the Society for Research in Child Development.

Neuman, S. B., & Roskos, K. (2005). The state of state pre-kindergarten standards. *Early Childhood Research Quarterly, 20,* 125–145.

Post, J., Hohmann, M., & Epstein, A. S. (2011). *Tender care and early learning: Supporting infants and toddlers in child care settings* (2nd ed.). Ypsilanti, MI: HighScope Educational Research Foundation.

Preschool Curriculum Evaluation Research Consortium (PCERC). (2008, July). *Effects of preschool curriculum programs on school readiness.* Washington, DC: U.S. Department of Education, Institute of Education Sciences, National Center for Education Research.

Reardon, S. F. (2011). The widening academic achievement gap between the rich and the poor: New evidence and possible explanations. In G. Duncan & R. Murnane (Eds.), *Whither opportunity? Rising inequality, schools, and children's life chances* (pp. 91–116). New York: Russell Sage Foundation

Reggio Children & Project Zero. (2001). *Making learning visible: Children as individual and group learners.* Reggio Emilia, Italy: Reggio Children.

Rinaldi, C. (2006). *In dialogue with Reggio Emilia: Listening, researching and learning.* New York: Routledge.

Roopnarine, J., & J. E. Johnson (Eds.). (2013). *Approaches to early childhood education* (6th ed.). Upper Saddle River, NJ: Pearson.

Rose, M. (2010). Standards, teaching, and learning. *Phi Delta Kappan, 91*(4), 21–27.

Sarama, J., & Clements, D. H. (2009). *Early childhood mathematics education research: Learning trajectories for young children.* New York: Routledge.

Scheinfeld, D. R., Haigh, K. M., & Scheinfeld, J. P. (2008). *We are all explorers: Learning and teaching with Reggio principles in urban settings.* New York: Teachers College Press.

Schweinhart, L. J., Barnes, H. V., & Weikart, D. P. (1993). *Significant benefits: The High/Scope Perry Preschool study through age 27.* Ypsilanti, MI: High/Scope Press.

Schweinhart, L. J., Montie, J., Xiang, Z., Barnett, W. S., Belfield, C. R., & Nores, M. (2005). *Lifetime effects: The High/Scope Perry Preschool study through age 40* (Monographs of the High/Scope Educational Research Foundation, 14). Ypsilanti, MI: High/Scope Press.

Schweinhart, L., Weikart, D., & Larner, M. (1986). Consequences of three preschool curriculum models through age 15. *Early Childhood Research Quarterly, 1*(1), 15–46.

Scott-Little, C. (2011). *Aligning state standards, the Head Start Child Development and Early Learning Framework, and our work with children and families.* Baltimore: Paper presented at the Office of Head Start, February 2011, Retrieved from http://eclkc.ohs.acf.hhs.gov

Shanahan, T. (2006, August/September). Shanahan responds. *Reading Today, 24*(1), 16.

Siraj-Blatchford, I., Muttock, S., Sylva, K., Gilden, R., & Bell, D. (2003, January). *Researching effective pedagogy in the early years: Report of the effective provision of preschool project* (Research Report RR356). London: Institute of Education, University of London. Retrieved August 28, 2009, from http://www.dcsf.gov.uk/research/data/uploadfiles/RR356.pdf

Vecchi, V. (2002). *Theater curtain: The ring of transformations.* Reggio Emilia, Italy: Reggio Children.

Vecchi, V. (2010). *Art and creativity in Reggio Emilia: Exploring the role and potential of ateliers in early childhood education.* New York: Routledge.

Weiland, C., & Yoshikawa, H. (2011, March). *The impact of an urban universal pre-kindergarten program on children's early numeracy, language, literacy, and executive function outcomes.* Paper presented at the Society for Educational Effectiveness Conference, Washington, DC. Retrieved from: http://www.eric.ed.gov.novacat.nova.edu/PDFS/ED519342.pdf

Wilson, S. J., Dickinson, D. K., & Rowe, D. W. (2013). Impact of an Early Reading First program on the language and literacy achievement of children from diverse language backgrounds. *Early Childhood Research Quarterly, 28*(3), 578–592.

Yoshikawa, H., Weiland, C., Brooks-Gunn, J., Burchinal, M. R., Espinosa, L. M., Gormley, W. T., et al. (2013). *Investing in our future: The evidence base on preschool education.* New York: Foundation for Child Development. Retrieved from http://fcd-us.org/sites/default/files/Evidence%20Base%20on%20Preschool%20Education%20FINAL.pdf

Zill, N., Sorongon, A., Kim, K., Clark, C., & Woolverton, M. (2006). *Children's outcomes and program quality in Head Start (FACES 2003 Research Brief).* Washington, DC: Head Start Bureau.

Chapter 11

American Educational Research Association (AERA), American Psychology Association, & National Council on Measurement in Education. (2014). *Standards for educational and psychological testing.* Washington, DC: AERA.

Atkins Burnett, S., Bandel, E., & Aikens, N. (2012). *Research brief #9: Assessment tools for the language and literacy development of young dual language learners (DLLs).* Chapel Hill: The University of North Carolina, FPG Child Development Institute. CECER-DLL.

Au, W. (2007). High-stakes testing and curricular control: A qualitative metasynthesis. *Educational Researcher, 36*(5), 258–267.

Copple, C., & Bredekamp, S. (Eds.). (2009). *Developmentally appropriate practice in early childhood programs serving children from birth through age 8* (Rev. ed.). Washington, DC: National Association for the Education of Young Children.

Division for Early Childhood of the Council for Exceptional Children. (2014). *DEC recommended practices in early intervention/early childhood special education.* Los Angeles, CA: Author. Retrieved February 1, 2015, from http://www.dec-sped.org/recommendedpractices

Edwards, C., Gandini, L., & Forman, G. (Eds.). (2012). *The hundred languages of children: The Reggio Emilia experience in transformation* (3rd ed.). Santa Barbara, CA: Praeger.

Epstein, A. S., Marshall, B., & Gainsley, S. (2014). *COR Advantage.* Ypsilanti, MI: HighScope Press.

Espinosa, L. M. (2010a). Assessment of young English language learners. In E. E. Garcia & E. C. Frede, (Eds.), *Young English language learners: Current research and emerging directions for practice and*

policy (pp. 119–142). New York: Teachers College Press.

Espinosa, L. M. & Garcia, E. (2012). *Developmental assessment of young dual language learners with a focus on kindergarten entry assessments: Implications for state policies.* Working paper #1. Center for Early Care and Education Research-Dual Language Learners (CECER-DLL). Chapel Hill: The University of North Carolina, FPG Child Development Institute.

FairTest. (2006). *What's wrong with standardized tests?* Boston: National Center for Fair and Open Testing. Retrieved October 9, 2009, from http://www.fairtest.org/facts/whatwron.htm

FairTest. (2007). *Criterion- and standards-referenced tests.* Boston: National Center for Fair and Open Testing. Retrieved August 31, 2009, from http://fairtest.org/facts/csrtests.html

Garcia, E. E. (2005). *Teaching and learning in two languages: Bilingualism and schooling in the United States.* New York: Teachers College Press.

Gullo, D. F. (2006). Alternative means of assessing children's learning in early childhood classrooms. In B. Spodek & O. N. Saracho (Eds.), *Handbook of research on the education of young children* (2nd ed., pp. 443–455). Mahwah, NJ: Lawrence Erlbaum Associates.

Harms, T., Clifford, R. M., & Cryer, D. (2014). *Early Childhood Environment Rating Scale (ECERS-3)* (3rd ed.). New York: Teachers College Press.

Helm, J. H., Beneke, S., & Steinheimer, K. (2007). *Windows on learning: Documenting young children's work* (2nd ed.). New York: Teachers College Press.

Hills, T. W. (1992). Reaching potentials through appropriate assessment. In S. Bredekamp & T. Rosegrant (Eds.), *Reaching potentials: Appropriate curriculum and assessment for young children* (Vol. 1, pp. 43–63). Washington, DC: National Association for the Education of Young Children.

Horton, C., & Bowman, B. T. (2002). *Child assessment at the preprimary level: Expert opinion and state trends.* Chicago: Erikson Institute.

Macy, M., & Bagnato, S. J. (2010). Keeping it "R-E-A-L" with authentic assessment. *NHSA Dialog, 13*(1), 1–20.

McAfee, O., Leong, D. J., & Bodrova, E. (2015). *Assessing and guiding young children's development and learning* (Enhanced e-text, 6th ed.). Upper Saddle River, NJ: Pearson.

McDevitt, T. M., & Ormrod, J. E. (2013). *Child development and education* (5th ed.). Upper Saddle River, NJ: Pearson.

Meisels, S. (2007). Accountability in early childhood: No easy answers. In C. Pianta, M. J. Cox, & K. Snows (Eds.), *School readiness and the transition to kindergarten in the era of accountability* (pp. 31–47). Baltimore: Paul H. Brookes.

Meisels, S. J., Marsden, D. B., Dombro, A. L., Weston, D. R., & Jewkes, A. M. (2003). *The Ounce Scale.* Upper Saddle River, NJ: Pearson Education.

Meisels, S. J., Marsden, D. B., Jablon, J. R., & Dichtelmiller, M. (2013). *The Work Sampling System* (5th ed.). New York: Pearson Education.

Mindes, G., & Jung, L. A. (2015). *Assessing young children* (5th ed.). Upper Saddle River, NJ: Pearson.

National Association for the Education of Young Children (NAEYC) & National Association of Early Childhood Specialists in State Departments of Education (NAECS/SDE). (2003). *Early childhood curriculum, assessment, and program evaluation: Building an effective, accountable system in programs for children birth through age 8. Joint position statement.* Washington, DC: National Association for the Education of Young Children.

National Center on Response to Intervention. (2010). *Essential components of RTI—A closer look at Response to Intervention.* Retrieved January 16, 2011, from http://www.rti4success.org.

National Research Council (NRC). (2008). *Early childhood assessment: Why, what, and how*. Washington, DC: National Academies Press.

Pianta, R. C., La Paro, K. M., & Hamre, B. K. (2008). *Classroom assessment scoring system (CLASS)*. Baltimore: Paul H. Brookes.

Pretzel, R. E., Hiemenz, J., & Kahng, R. (2009). Assessment of young children: Standards, stages, and approaches, In S. R. Hooper & W. Umansky (Eds.), *Young children with special needs* (5th ed., pp. 382–417). Upper Saddle River, NJ: Pearson.

Ravitch, D. (2010). *The death and life of the great American school system: How testing and choice are undermining education*. New York: Basic Books.

Reggio Children & Project Zero. (2001). *Making learning visible: Children as individual and group learners*. Reggio Emilia, Italy: Reggio Children.

Reifel, S. (2011). Observation and early childhood teaching: Evolving fundamentals. *Young Children, 66*(2), 62–65.

Riley-Ayers, S. (2014). *Formative assessment: Guidance for early childhood policymakers* (CEELO Policy Report). New Brunswick, NJ: Center on Enhancing Early Learning Outcomes.

Ritchie, S., & Willer, B. (2008a). *Assessment of child progress: A guide to the NAEYC early childhood program standard and related accreditation criteria*. Washington, DC: National Association for the Education of Young Children.

Santos, R. M. (2004). Ensuring culturally and linguistically appropriate assessment of young children. *Young Children, 59*(1), 48–50.

Scott-Little, C., Bruner, C., Schultz, T., & Maxwell, K. (2013). *Kindergarten entry assessment discussion guide*. Retrieved from http://www.buildinitiative.org/WhatsNew/ViewArticle/tabid/96/ArticleId/662/Kindergarten-Entry-Assessment-Discussion-Guide-2013.aspx

Snow, K. (2011). *Kindergarten readiness and other large-scale assessment systems: Necessary considerations in the assessment of young children*. Washington, DC: National Association for the Education of Young Children.

Vagh, S. B., Pan, B. A., & Mancilla-Martinez, J. (2009). Measuring growth in bilingual and monolingual children's English productive vocabulary development: The utility of combining parent and teacher report. *Child Development, 80*(5), 1545–1563.

Valencia, S. W., & Buly, M. R. (2004). Behind test scores: What struggling readers *really* need. *The Reading Teacher, 57*(6), 520–531.

Wortham, S. C. & Hardin, B. J. (2015). *Assessment in early childhood education* (7th ed.). Upper Saddle River, NJ: Pearson

Chapter 12

Adams, M. (1990). *Beginning to read: Thinking and learning about print*. Cambridge, MA: MIT Press.

Arts Education Partnership. (1998). *Position paper for Task Force on Children's Learning and the Arts: Birth to age 8*. Washington, DC: Council of Chief State School Officers.

Bates, C. C. (2013). Flexible grouping during literacy centers: A model for differentiating instruction. *Young Children, 68*(2), 30–33.

Beck, I. L., McKeown, M. G., & Kucan, L. (2013). *Bringing words to life: Robust vocabulary—instruction* (2nd ed.). New York: Guilford Press.

Bredekamp, S. (2002). Language and early childhood programs. In C. T. Adger, C. E. Snow, & D. Christian (Eds.), *What teachers need to know about language*. Washington, DC: Center for Applied Linguistics.

Brown, E. D., Benedett, B., & Armistead, M. E. (2010). Arts enrichment and school readiness for children

at risk. *Early Childhood Research Quarterly, 25*(1), 112–124.

Carlson-Paige, N., McLaughlin, G. B., & Almon, J. W. (2014). *Reading instruction in kindergarten: Little to gain and much to lose*. Jamaica Plain, MA: Defending the Early Years and the Alliance for Childhood. Retrieved from https://deyproject.files.wordpress.com/2015/01/readinginkindergarten_on-line-1.pdf

Chall, J. (1967). *Learning to read: The great debate*. New York: McGraw Hill.

Cheung, A. C. K., & Slavin, R. E. (2012). Effective reading programs for Spanish-dominant English language learners (ELLs) in the elementary grades: A synthesis of research. *Review of Educational Research, 82*, 351–395.

Collins, M. F. (2012). Sagacious, sophisticated, and sedulous: The importance of discussing 50-cent words with preschoolers. *Young Children, 67*(5), 66–72.

Common Core State Standards Initiative. (2011a). *Common core standards for English language arts*. Washington, DC: Council for Chief State School Officers and National Governor's Association. Retrieved February 17, 2012, from www.corestandards.org

Common Core State Standards Initiative. (2015a). *Key shifts in English language arts*. Washington, DC: Council for Chief State School Officers and National Governor's Association. Retrieved January 13, 2015, from http://www.corestandards.org/other-resources/key-shifts-in-english-language-arts/

Davidson, J. (1996). *Emergent literacy and dramatic play in early education*. Albany, NY: Delmar.

Dickinson, D. K. (2011, August 19). Teachers' language practices and academic outcomes of preschool children. *Science, 333*(6045), 964–967. doi:10.1126/science.1204526

Dickinson, D. K., & Tabors, P. O. (Eds.). (2001). *Beginning literacy with language: Young children learning at home and school*. Baltimore: Paul H. Brookes.

Duke, N. K. (2014). *Inside information: Developing powerful readers and writers of informational text through project-based instruction*. New York: Scholastic.

Epstein, A. S. (2007). *The intentional teacher: Choosing the best strategies for young children's learning*. Washington, DC: National Association for the Education of Young Children.

Espinosa, L. M. (2013). *Pre-K–3rd: Challenging common myths about dual language learners, an update to the seminal 2008 report*. New York: Foundation for Child Development.

Fernald, A., Marchman, V. A., & Weisleder, A. (2013). SES differences in language processing skill and vocabulary are evident at 18 months. *Developmental Science, 16*(2), 234–248.

Garcia, E. E. (2005). *Teaching and learning in two languages: Bilingualism and schooling in the United States*. New York: Teachers College Press.

Gonzalez, J. E., Pollard-Durodola, S. Simmons, D. C., Taylor, A. B., David, M. J., Fogarty, M., & Simmons, L. (2014). Enhancing preschool children's vocabulary: Effects of teacher talk before, during and after shred reading. *Early Childhood Research Quarterly, 29*(2), 214–226.

Graham, S., & Harris, K. R. (2013). How do you write? Writing for young children. In D. R. Reutzel (Ed.), *Handbook of research-based practice in early education* (pp. 380–394). New York: Guilford Press.

Greenberg, J., & Weitzman, E. (2014). *I'm ready! How to prepare your child for reading success*. Toronto: The Hanen Centre.

Grissmer, D. W., Grimm, K. J., Aiyer, S. M., Murrah, W. M., & Steele, J. S. (2010). Fine motor skills and early comprehension of the world: Two new school readiness indicators. *Developmental Psychology, 46*(5), 1008–1017.

Guernsey, L., Levine, M., Chiong, C., & Severns, M. (2012). *Pioneering literacy in the digital wild west: Empowering parents and educators*. New York: Campaign for Grade-Level Reading, New America Foundation, and Joan Ganz Cooney Center. Retrieved from http://gradelevelreading.net/wp-content/uploads/2012/12/GLR_Technology-Guide_final.pdf

Hart, B., & Risley, T. R. (1995). *Meaningful differences in the everyday experience of young American children*. Baltimore: Paul H. Brookes.

Hart, B., & Risley, T. R. (1999). *The social world of learning to talk*. Baltimore: Paul H. Brookes.

Hart, B., & Risley, T. R. (2003, Spring). The early catastrophe: The 30 million word gap by age 3. *American Educator, 27*(1), 4–9. Retrieved January 25, 2015, from http://www.aft.org/pdfs/american-educator/spring2003/TheEarlyCatastrophe.pdf

Head Start. (2003). *The Head Start leaders guide to positive child outcomes: Strategies to support positive child outcomes*. Washington, DC: U.S. Department of Health and Human Services.

Hirsch, E. D. (2007). *The knowledge deficit: Closing the shocking education gap for American children*. Boston: Mariner Books.

Huntsinger, C. S., Jose, P. E., Krieg, D. B., & Luo, Z. (2011). Cultural differences in Chinese American and European American children's drawing skills over time. *Early Childhood Research Quarterly, 26*(1), 134–145.

International Reading Association (IRA) & National Association for the Education of Young Children (NAEYC). (1998). *Learning to read and write: Developmentally appropriate practices for young children: A joint position statement, adopted May, 1998*. Retrieved October 14, 2009, from http://208.118.177.216/about/positions/pdf/PSREAD98.PDF

Isenberg, J. P., & Jalongo, M. R. (2013). *Creative thinking and arts-based learning: Preschool through fourth grade* (6th ed.). Upper Saddle River, NJ: Pearson.

Jalongo, M. R. (2008). *Learning to listen, listening to learn: Building essential skills in young children*. Washington, DC: National Association for the Education of Young Children.

Johnson, M. H. (2008). Developing verbal and visual literacy through experiences in the visual arts: 25 tips for teachers. *Young Children, 63*(1), 74–79.

Jones, C. D., Clark, S. K., & Reutzel, D. R. (2012). Enhancing alphabet knowledge instruction: Research implications and practical strategies for early childhood educators. *TEaL Faculty Publications*, Paper 404. Retrieved from http://digitalcommons.usu.edu/teal_facpub/404

Karweit, N., & Wasik, B. (1996). The effects of story reading programs on literacy and language development of disadvantaged pre-schoolers. *Journal of Education for Students Placed At-Risk, 4*, 319–348.

Kim, J. S. (2008). Research and the reading wars. *Phi Delta Kappan, 89*(5), 372–375.

Labbo, L. D., & Nogueron-Liu, S. (2013). Digital reading and writing: Pedagogy for the digital child. In D. R. Reutzel (Ed.), *Handbook of research-based practice in early education* (pp. 193–204). New York: Guilford Press.

McAfee, O., Leong, D. J., & Bodrova, E. (2015). *Assessing and guiding young children's development and learning* (Enhanced e-text, 6th ed.). Upper Saddle River, NJ: Pearson.

McGee, L. M. (2013). Read me a story: Reaping the benefits of reading for children. In D. R. Reutzel (Ed.), *Handbook of research-based practice in early education* (pp. 364–379). New York: Guilford Press.

Morrow, L. M. (1988). Young children's responses to one-to-one reading in school settings. *Reading Research Quarterly, 23*, 89–107.

Munsen, S. (2013). No fine art left behind: Creative and expressive education. In D. R. Reutzel (Ed.), *Handbook of research-based practice in early education* (pp. 309–325). New York: Guilford Press.

National Coalition for Core Arts Standards. (2014). *National core arts standards: Dance, media arts, music, theatre, and visual arts.* Retrieved January 24, 2015, from http://nationalartsstandards.org/

National Early Literacy Panel (NELP). (2008). *Developing early literacy: Report of the National Early Literacy Panel. A scientific synthesis of early literacy development and implications for intervention.* Washington, DC: Author. Retrieved from http://lincs.ed.gov/publications/pdf/NELPReport09.pdf

National Institute of Child Health and Human Development (NICHD). (2000). *Report of the National Reading Panel. Teaching children to read: An evidence-based assessment of the scientific research literature on reading and its implications for reading instruction.* Washington, DC: Author.

Neuman, S. B., & Celano, D. (2002). Access to print in middle- and low-income communities: An ecological study of four neighborhoods. *Reading Research Quarterly, 36,* 8–26.

Neuman, S. B., & Wright, T. S. (2013). *All about words: Increasing vocabulary in the common core classroom, PreK–2.* New York: Teachers College Press.

Neuman, S. B., Copple, C., & Bredekamp, S. (Eds.). (2000). *Learning to read and write: Developmentally appropriate practices for young children.* Washington, DC: National Association for the Education of Young Children.

Neuman, S. B., Roskos, K., Wright, T., & Lenhart, L. (2007). *Nurturing knowledge: Linking literacy to science math, social studies, and much more.* New York: Scholastic.

Pelatti, C. Y., Piasta, S. B., Justice, L. M., & O'Connell, A. (2014). Language- and literacy-learning opportunities in early childhood classrooms: Children's typical experiences and within-classroom variability. *Early Childhood Research Quarterly, 29*(4), 445–456.

Pikulski, J. J., & Chard, D. J. (2005). Fluency: Bridge between decoding and reading comprehension. *The Reading Teacher, 58*(6), 510–519.

Price, L. H., Bradley, B. A., & Smith, J. M. (2012). A comparison of preschool teachers' talk during storybook and information book read-alouds. *Early Childhood Research Quarterly, 27*(3), 426–440.

Puranik, C. S., & Lonigan, C. J. (2012). Name-writing proficiency, not length of name, is associated with preschool children's emergent literacy skills. *Early Childhood Research Quarterly, 27*(2), 284–294.

Quenqua, D. (2014, October 16). Quality of words, not quantity, is crucial to language skills, study finds. *New York Times.* Retrieved February 5, 2015, from http://www.nytimes.com/2014/10/17/us/quality-of-words-not-quantity-is-crucial-to-language-skills-study-finds.html?emc=eta1&_r=0

Rasinski, T. (Ed.). (2009). *Essential readings on fluency.* Newark, DE: International Reading Association.

Rivera-Gaxiola, M., Silva-Pereyra, J., & Kuhl, P. K. (2008). Brain potentials to native and non-native speech contrasts in 7- and 11-month-old American infants. *Developmental Science, 8*(2), 162–172.

Rodriguez, D., Carrasquillo, A., & Lee, K. S. (2014). *The bilingual advantage: Promoting academic development, biliteracy, and native language in the classroom.* New York: Teachers College Press.

Roskos, K. A., Tabors, P. O., & Lenhart, L. A. (2009). *Oral language and early literacy in preschool: Talking, reading, and writing* (2nd ed.). Newark, DE: International Reading Association.

Roskos, K., & Neuman, S. B. (2011). The classroom environment: First, last, and always. *The Reading Teacher, 65*(2), 110–114.

Ruppert, S. S. (2006). *Critical evidence: How the arts benefit student achievement.* National Assembly of State Arts Agencies & Arts Education Partnership. Retrieved January 29, 2015, from http://www.nasaa-arts.org/Publications/critical-evidence.pdf

Schickedanz, J. A., & Collins, M. F. (2013). *So much more than the ABCs: The early phases of reading and writing.* Washington, DC: National Association for the Education of Young Children.

Shanahan, T., & Lonigan, C. J. (2013). *Early childhood literacy: The National Early Literacy Panel and beyond.* Baltimore: Brookes.

Snow, C. E., Burns, M. S., & Griffin, P. (Eds.). (1998). *Preventing reading difficulties in young children.* Washington, DC: National Academies Press.

Stahl, K. A. D. (2014). Research into practice: New insights about letter learning. *The Reading Teacher, 68*(4), 261–265.

Stanovich, K. E. (1986). Matthew effects in early reading: Some consequences of individual differences in the acquisition of literacy. *Reading Research Quarterly, 24,* 402–433.

Strickland, D. S. (2011). *Teaching phonics today: Word study strategies through the grades* (2nd ed.). Newark, DE: International Reading Association.

Strickland, D. S., & Schickedanz, J. A. (2009). *Learning about print in preschool: Working with letters, words, and beginning links with phonemic awareness* (2nd ed.). Newark, DE: International Reading Association.

Thomas, W. P., & Collier, V. P. (n.d.). *A national study of school effectiveness for language minority students' long-term academic achievement.* Center for Research on Education, Diversity, and Excellence. Retrieved from http://www.usc.edu/dept/education/CMMR/CollierThomasExReport.pdf

Thompson, C. M. (2013). Reposition the visual arts in early childhood education: Continuing reconsideration. In O. N. Saracho & B. Spdek (Eds.), *Handbook of research on the education of young children* (3rd ed., pp. 219–240). New York: Routledge.

Williams, L. (1988). *The little old lady who was not afraid of anything.* New York: HarperCollins.

Yopp, H. K., & Yopp, R. H. (2009). Phonological awareness is child's play. *Young Children, 64*(1), 12–17.

Chapter 13

Achieve, Inc. (2013). *Next Generation Science Standards, for states, by states.* Retrieved from http://www.nextgenscience.org/search-standards-dci

Albert Shanker Institute. (2009). *Preschool curriculum: What's in it for children and teachers.* Washington, DC: Author.

American Association for the Advancement of Science. (2009). *Benchmarks for science literacy.* Washington, DC: Author. Retrieved September 15, 2009, from http://www.project2061.org/publications/bsl/default.htm

Arnold, D. H., Fischer, P. H., Doctoroff, G. L., & Dobbs, J. (2002). Accelerating math development in Head Start classrooms. *Journal of Educational Psychology, 94*(4), 762–770.

Beiland, S. L., Gunderson, E. A., Ramirez, G., & Levine, S. C. (2010). Female teachers' math anxiety affects girls' math achievement. *Proceedings of the National Academy of Sciences, 107*(5), 1860–1863.

Beneke, S. J., Ostrosky, M. M., & Katz, L. G. (2008). Calendar time for young children: Good intentions gone awry. *Young Children, 63*(3), 12–16.

Bodrova, E., & Leong, D. J. (2007). *Tools of the mind: The Vygotskian approach to early childhood education.* Upper Saddle River, NJ: Pearson.

Casey, B. (2004). Mathematics problem-solving adventures: A language-arts-based supplementary series for early childhood that focuses on spatial sense.

In D. H. Clements, J. Sarama, & A.-M. DiBiase (Eds.), *Engaging young children in mathematics: Standards for early childhood mathematics education* (pp. 377–389). Mahwah, NJ: Lawrence Erlbaum Associates.

Casey, M. B., Erkut, S., Ceder, I., & Young, J. M. (2008). Use of a storytelling context to improve girls' and boys' geometry skills in kindergarten. *Journal of Applied Developmental Psychology, 29,* 29–48.

Center on the Developing Child at Harvard University. (2011). *Building the brain's "air traffic control" system: How early experiences shape the development of executive function: Working Paper #11.* Retrieved from http://www.developingchild.harvard.edu

Clements, D. H., & Sarama, J. (2007a). Early childhood mathematics learning. In F. K. Lester, Jr. (Ed.), *Second handbook of research on mathematics teaching and learning* (pp. 461–555). New York: Information Age Publishing.

Clements, D. H., & Sarama, J. (2007b). Effects of a preschool mathematics curriculum: Summative research on the Building Blocks project. *Journal for Research in Mathematics Education, 38*(2), 136–163.

Clements, D. H., & Sarama, J. (2008). Experimental evaluation of the effects of a research-based preschool mathematics curriculum. *American Educational Research Journal, 45,* 443–494.

Clements, D. H., & Sarama, J. (2013). Solving problems: Mathematics for young children. In D. R. Reutzel (Ed.), *Handbook of research-based practice in early education* (pp. 348–363). New York: Guilford Press.

Common Core State Standards Initiative. (2011b). *Common core standards for mathematics.* Washington, DC: Council for Chief State School Officers and National Governor's Association. Retrieved February 17, 2012, from http://www.corestandards.org

Common Core State Standards Initiative. (2015b). *Key shifts in mathematics.* Washington, DC: Council for Chief State School Officers and National Governor's Association. Retrieved January 13, 2015, from http://www.corestandards.org/other-resources/key-shifts-in-mathematics/

Desouza, J. M. S., & Czerniak, C. M. (2002, Summer/Spring). Social behaviors and gender differences among preschoolers: Implications for science activities, *Journal of Research in Childhood Education, 16*(2), 175–188.

Diamond, A. (2012, January 20). *What nurtures the human spirit may also be best for executive functions and school success.* Presentation at the Maryland State Department of Education Early Care and Education Research Forum, Towson, MD.

Diamond, A., & Lee, K. (2011, August 19). Interventions shown to aid executive function development in children 4 to 12 years old. *Science, 333*(6045), 959–964. doi:10.1126/science.1204529

Donohue, C. (Ed.). (2015). *Technology and digital media in the early years.* New York: Routledge Taylor & Francis Group.

Duncan, G. J., Dowsett, C. J., Claessens, A., Magnuson, K., Huston, A. C., Klebanov, P., et al. (2007). School readiness and later achievement. *Developmental Psychology, 43,* 1428–1446.

Farran, D., Lipsey, M., & Wilson, S. (2011). *Experimental evaluation of the Tools of the Mind Pre-K Curriculum* [Working paper]. Retrieved from https://my.vanderbilt.edu/toolsofthemindevaluation/files/2011/12/Tools-Report-8-10-11-Appendices-Removed1.pdf

Farran, D. C., Lipsey, M. W., Watson, B., & Hurley, S. (2007). *Balance of content emphasis and child content engagement in an Early Reading First program.* Paper presented at the American Educational Research Association, Chicago, IL.

Fleischman, H. L., Hopstock, P. J., Pelczar, M. P., & Shelley, B. E. (2010). *Highlights from PISA 2009: Performance of U.S. 15-year-olds in reading, mathematics, and science literacy in an international context.* Washington, DC: U.S. Department of Education, National Center for Education Statistics.

French, L. A., & Woodring, S. D. (2013). Science education in the early years. In O. N. Saracho & B. Spodek (Eds.), *Handbook of research on the education of young children* (3rd ed., pp. 179–196). New York: Routledge.

Fuson, K. C. (1988). *Children's counting and concept of number.* New York: Springer-Verlag.

Gelman, R., & Brenneman, K. (2004). Science learning pathways for young children. *Early Childhood Research Quarterly, 19*(1), 150–158.

Gelman, R., & Gallistel, C. R. (1978). *The child's understanding of number.* Cambridge, MA: Harvard University Press.

Gelman, R., Brenneman, K., MacDonald, G., & Román, M. (2010). *Preschool pathways to science: Facilitating scientific ways of thinking, talking, doing, and understanding.* Baltimore: Paul H. Brookes.

Ginsburg, H. P. (2006). Mathematical play and playful mathematics: A guide for early education. In D. G. Singer, R. M. Golinkoff, & K. Hirsh-Pasek (Eds.), *Play = learning: How play motivates and enhances children's cognitive and social-emotional growth* (pp. 145–165). New York: Oxford University Press.

Ginsburg, H. P., & Pappas, S. (2004). SES, ethnic, and gender differences in young children's informal addition and subtraction: A clinical interview investigation. *Journal of Applied Developmental Psychology, 25,* 171–192.

Ginsburg, H. P., Lee, J. S., & Boyd, J. S. (2008). Mathematics education for young children: What it is and how to promote it. *Social Policy Report, 22*(1), 3–23.

Gray, J. (2015). Digital play and traditional play have more in common than you may think. *Sparking Kids' Imagination with Digital Toys.* Retrieved from http://tocaboca.com/magazine/sparking-imagination/

Greenes, C., Ginsburg, H. P., & Balfanz, R. (2004). Big math for little kids. *Early Childhood Research Quarterly, 19*(1), 159–166.

Griffin, S. (2004). Number worlds: A research-based mathematical program for young children. In D. H. Clements & A.-M. DiBiase (Eds.), *Engaging young children in mathematics: Standards for early childhood mathematics education* (pp. 325–342). Mahwah, NJ: Lawrence Erlbaum Associates.

Hannust, T., & Kikas, E. (2007). Children's knowledge of astronomy and its change in the course of learning. *Early Childhood Research Quarterly, 22*(1), 89–104.

Head Start. (2003). *The Head Start leaders guide to positive child outcomes: Strategies to support positive child outcomes.* Washington, DC: U.S. Department of Health and Human Services.

HighScope. (2007). Numbers Plus Preschool Mathematics Curriculum. Ypsilanti, MI: Author.

Hong, S.-Y., & Diamond, K. E. (2012). Two approaches to teaching young children science concepts, vocabulary, and scientific problem-solving skills. *Early Childhood Research Quarterly, 27*(2), 295–305.

Hutchins, P. (1968). *Rosie's walk.* New York: Simon & Schuster.

Klahr, D., Zimmerman, C., & Jirout, J. (2011). Educational interventions to advance children's scientific thinking. *Science, 333*(6045), 971–975.

Klibanoff, R. S., Levine, S. C., Huttenlocher, J., Vasilyeva, M., & Hedges, L. V. (2006). Preschool children's mathematical knowledge: The effect of teacher "math talk." *Developmental Psychology, 42*(1), 59–69.

Levine, S. C., Jordan, N. C., & Huttenlocher, J. (1992). Development of calculation abilities in young children. *Journal of Experimental Child Psychology, 53,* 72–103.

Levine, S. C., Suriyakham, L. W., Roe, M. L., Huttenlocher, J., & Gunderson, E. A. (2010). What counts in the development of young children's number knowledge? *Developmental Psychology, 46*(5), 1309–1319.

Linder, S. M. (2012). Interactive whiteboards in early childhood mathematics: Strategies for effective implementation in pre-K–grade 3. *Young Children, 67*(3), 26–35.

National Association for the Education of Young Children (NAEYC) Technology and Young Children Interest Forum. (2008). Meaningful technology integration in early learning environments. *Young Children, 63*(5), 48–50.

National Association for the Education of Young Children (NAEYC) & the Fred Rogers Center for Early Learning and Children's Media. (2012). *Technology in early childhood programs serving children from birth through age 8.* Joint Position Statement. Washington, DC: Authors.

National Center on Quality Teaching and Learning. (2013). *Using the scientific method.* Washington, DC: U.S. Department of Health and Human Services, Office of Head Start. Retrieved March 8, 2015, from http://eclkc.ohs.acf.hhs.gov/hslc/tta-system/teaching/eecd/Domains%20of%20Child%20Development/Science/using-scientific-method-poster-1.pdf

National Council of Teachers of Mathematics. (2000). *Principles and standards for school mathematics.* Reston, VA: Author. Retrieved from http://standards.nctm.org

National Council of Teachers of Mathematics. (2006). *Curriculum focal points.* Reston, VA: Author.

National Research Council (NRC). (2001). *Adding it up: Helping children learn mathematics.* Washington, DC: National Academies Press.

National Research Council (NRC). (2009). *Mathematics learning in early childhood: Paths toward excellence and equity.* Washington, DC: National Academies Press.

National Research Council (NRC). (2012). *A framework for K–12 science: Practices, crosscutting concepts, and core ideas.* Washington, DC: National Academies Press.

Nayfeld, I., Brenneman, K., & Gelman, R. (2009). *Science in the classroom: Finding a balance between autonomous exploration and teacher-led instruction in preschool settings.* Paper presented at the biannual meeting of the Society for Research in Child Development.

Piaget, J. (1952). *The origins of intelligence in children.* New York: International Universities Press.

Pollman, M. J. (2010). *Blocks and beyond: Strengthening early math and science skills through spatial learning.* Baltimore: Brookes.

Preschool Curriculum Evaluation Research Consortium (PCERC). (2008, July). *Effects of preschool curriculum programs on school readiness.* Washington, DC: U.S. Department of Education, Institute of Education Sciences, National Center for Education Research.

Sammons, P., Sylva, K., Melhuish, E., Siraj-Blatchford, I., Taggart, B., Hunt, S., et al. (2008). *Effective pre-school and primary education 3–11 project (EPPE 3–11): Influences on children's cognitive and social development in year 6* (Department of Children, Schools and Families Research Brief). London: Institute of Education, University of London. Retrieved October 14, 2009, from http://eppe.ioe.ac.uk

Sarama, J., & Clements, D. H. (2007, March 12). *Manual for classroom observation of early mathematics—Environment and teaching (CO-EMET), Version 3.* Retrieved from http://www.UBTRIAD.org

Sarama, J., Lange, A. A., Clements, D. H., & Wolfe, C. B. (2012). The impacts of an early mathematics curriculum on oral language and literacy. *Early Childhood Research Quarterly, 27*(3), 489–502.

Schickedanz, J. A. (2008). *Increasing the power of instruction: Integration of language, literacy, and math across the preschool day.* Washington, DC: National Association for the Education of Young Children.

Schoenfeld, A. H., & Stipek, D. (2011). *Math matters: Children's mathematical journeys start early.* Berkeley, CA: Heising-Simons Foundation. Retrieved February 28, 2015, from http://earlymath.org/earlymath/wp-content/uploads/2014/09/Math-Matters-Report_2ndEd1.pdf

Seefeldt, C., Galper, A., & Jones, I. (2012). *Active experiences for active children: Science* (3rd Ed.). Upper Saddle River, NJ: Pearson.

Seo, K.-H., & Ginsburg, H. P. (2004). What is developmentally appropriate in early childhood mathematics education? Lessons from new research. In D. H. Clements, J. Sarama, & A.-M. DiBiase (Eds.), *Engaging young children in mathematics: Standards for early childhood mathematics education* (pp. 91–104). Hillsdale, NJ: Lawrence Erlbaum Associates.

Siegler, R. S., & Ramani, G. B. (2008). Playing board games promotes low-income children's numerical development. *Developmental Science, 11*(5), 655–661.

Sophian, C. (2013). Mathematics for early childhood education. In O. N. Saracho & B. Spdek (Eds.), *Handbook of research on the education of young children* (3rd ed., pp. 169–178). New York: Routledge.

Starkey, P. (2007, December 1). Presentation to the National Research Council Committee on Early Childhood Mathematics, Washington, DC.

Starkey, P., & Klein, A. (2008). Sociocultural influences on young children's mathematical knowledge. In O. N. Saracho & B. Spodek (Eds.), *Contemporary perspectives on mathematics in early childhood education* (pp. 253–276). Charlotte, NC: Information Age Publishing.

Starkey, P., Klein, A., & Wakeley, A. (2004). Enhancing young children's mathematical knowledge through a pre-kindergarten mathematics intervention. *Early Childhood Research Quarterly, 19*(1), 99–120.

Starkey, P., Klein, A., Chang, I., Qi, D., Lijuan, P., & Yang, Z. (1999). *Environmental supports for young children's mathematical development in China and the United States.* Albuquerque, NM: Society for Research in Child Development.

Szekely, A. (2014). *Unlocking young children's potential: Governors' role in strengthening early mathematics learning.* Washington, DC: National Governors Association center for Best Practices. Retrieved from http://www.nga.org/files/live/sites/NGA/files/pdf/2014/1410UnlockingYoungChildrensPotential.pdf

Tepylo, D. H., Moss, J., & Stephenson, C. (2015). A developmental look at a rigorous block play program. *Young Children, 70*(1), 18–25.

Worth, K., & Grollman, S. (2003). *Worms, shadows, and whirlpools: Science in the early childhood classroom.* Portsmouth, NH: Heinemann.

Chapter 14

American Academy of Pediatrics. (n.d.). *Trauma guide.* Retrieved March 1, 2015, from https://www.aap.org/traumaguide

Blair, C., & Razza, R. C. (2007). Relating effortful control, executive function and false belief understanding to emerging math and literacy ability in kindergarten. *Child Development, 78*(2), 647–663.

Bodrova, E., & Leong, D. J. (2007). *Tools of the mind: The Vygotskian approach to early childhood education.* Upper Saddle River, NJ: Pearson.

Buysse, V., Goldman, B. D., West, T., & Hollingsworth, H. (2007). Friendships in early childhood: Implications for early education and intervention. In W. H. Brown, S. L. Odom, & S. R. McConnell (Eds.), *Social competence of young children: Risk, disability, and evidence-based practices* (2nd ed.). Baltimore: Paul H. Brookes.

Calkins, S. D., & Williford, A. P. (2009). Taming the terrible twos: Self-regulation and school readiness. In O. A. Barbarin & B. H. Wasik (Eds.), *Handbook of child development and early education: Research to practice* (pp. 172–198). New York: Guilford Press.

Center on the Developing Child at Harvard University. (2007b). *The timing and quality of early experiences combine to shape brain architecture: Working paper #5.* Retrieved from http://www.developing-child.harvard.edu

Center on the Developing Child at Harvard University. (2010). *Early experiences can alter gene expression and affect long-term development: Working paper #10.* Retrieved October 28, 2011 from http://www.developingchild.harvard.edu

Derman-Sparks, L., & Edwards, J. O. (2010). *Anti-bias education for young children and ourselves.* Washington, DC: National Association for the Education of Young Children.

Dewey, J. (1916). *Democracy and education.* New York: Free Press.

Diamond, A. (2012, January 20). *What nurtures the human spirit may also be best for executive functions and school success.* Presentation at the Maryland State Department of Education Early Care and Education Research Forum, Towson, MD.

Domitrovich, C. E., Greenberg, M. T., Cortes, R., & Kusche, C. A. (2005). *The Preschool PATHS Curriculum.* Deerfield, MA: Channing-Bete Publishers.

Epstein, A. S. (2009). *Me, you, us: Social-emotional learning in preschool.* Ypsilanti, MI: HighScope Educational Research Foundation.

Epstein, A. S., & Hohmann, M. (2012). *The HighScope preschool curriculum* (4th ed.). Ypsilanti, MI: High/Scope Press.

Felitti, V. J., Anda, R. F., Nordenberg, D., Williamson, D. F., Spitz, A. M., Edwards, V., & Koss, M. P. (1998). The relationship of adult health status to childhood abuse and household dysfunction. *American Journal of Preventive Medicine, 14,* 245–258.

Flook, L., Goldberg, S. B., Pinger, L., & Davidson, R. J. (2015). Promoting prosocial behavior and self-regulatory skills in preschool children through a mindfulness-based kindness curriculum. *Developmental Psychology, 51*(1), 44–51.

Gallagher, K. C. (2013). Guiding children's friendship development: An essential part of the early childhood curriculum. *Young Children, 68,* 5.

Gallagher, K. C., & Sylvester, P. (2009). Supporting peer relationships in early education. In O. Barbarin & B. H. Wasik (Eds.), *Handbook of child development and early education: Research to practice* (pp. 223–246). New York: Guilford Press.

Hanson, M. J., & SooHoo, T. (2007). Cultural influences on young children's social competence. In W. Brown, S. Odom, & S. McConnell (Eds.), *Social competence of young children: Risk, disability, and intervention.* Baltimore: Paul H. Brookes.

Heffron, S. (Ed.). (2012). *Geography for life: National geography standards* (2nd ed.). Washington, DC: National Council for Geographic Education.

Honig, A. S. (2010). *Little kids, big worries: Stress-busting tips for early childhood classrooms.* Baltimore: Paul H. Brookes.

Hyson, M. (2004). *The emotional development of young children: Building an emotion-centered curriculum.* New York: Teachers College Press.

Johnson, J. E., Christie, J. F., & Wardle, F. (2005). *Play, development, and early education.* Upper Saddle River, NJ: Pearson.

Joseph, G. E. (2002). *If you're happy and you know it: The emotional literacy and social information processing scripts of young, high-risk children.* Paper presented at Conference on Research Innovations in Early Intervention, San Diego, CA.

Joseph, G. E., & Strain, P. S. (2004). Building positive relationships with young children. *Young Exceptional Children, 7*(4), 21–29.

Landy, S. (2009). *Pathways to competence: Encouraging healthy social and emotional development in young children.* Baltimore: Brookes.

McClelland, M. M., Acock, A. C., & Morrison, F. J. (2006). The impact of kindergarten learning-related skills on academic trajectories at the end of elementary school. *Early Childhood Research Quarterly, 21*(4), 471–490.

McGuire, M. (2007). What happened to social studies? The disappearing curriculum. *Phi Delta Kappan, 88*(8), 620–624.

Mindes, G. (2006). Social studies in today's early childhood curricula. In D. Koralek & G. Mindes (Eds.), *Spotlight on young children and social studies* (pp. 4–10). Washington, DC: National Association for the Education of Young Children.

Mitchell, A., & David, J. (1992). *Explorations with young children: A curriculum guide from the Bank Street College of Education.* Mt. Rainier, MD: Gryphon House.

Moffitt, T. E., Arseneault, L., Belsky, D., Dickson, N., Hancox, R. J., Harrington, H. L., et al. (2011). A gradient of childhood self-control predicts health, wealth, and public safety. *Proceedings of the National Academy of Sciences, 108*(7), 2693–2698.

Morris, P., Mattera, S. K., Castells, N., Bangser, K., Bierman, K., & Raver, C. (2014). *Impacts findings from the CARES Demonstration: National evaluation of three approaches to improving preschoolers' social and emotional competence.* OPRE Report 2014-44. Washington, DC: Office of Planning, Research and Evaluation, Administration for Children and Families, U.S. Department of Education.

Murray, D. W., Rosanbalm, K., Christopoulos, C., & Hamoudi, A. (2014). *Self-regulation and toxic stress: Foundations for understanding self-regulation from an applied developmental perspective.* OPRE Report #2015-21, Washington, DC: Office of Planning, Research and Evaluation, Administration for Children and Families, U.S. Department of Health and Human Services.

National Child Traumatic Stress Network (NCTSN) Core Curriculum on Childhood Trauma Task Force (2012). *The 12 core concepts: Concepts for understanding traumatic stress responses in children and families.* Core Curriculum on Childhood Trauma. Los Angeles, CA, and Durham, NC: UCLA-Duke

National Council for the Social Studies. (2010). *National curriculum standards for social studies: A framework for teaching, learning, and assessment.* Silver Spring, MD: Author. Retrieved from http://www.socialstudies.org/standards/execsummary

Parten, M. (1933). Social participation among preschool children. *Journal of Abnormal and Social Psychology, 27,* 243–269.

Ritchie, S. (2011, November). *FirstSchool: Improving the preK–3rd grade experience of African-American, Latino, and low income children.* Paper presented at the annual meeting of the National Association for the Education of Young Children, Orlando, FL.

Seefeldt, C., Castle, S., & Falconer, R. C. (2013). *Social studies for the preschool/primary child* (9th ed.). Upper Saddle River, NJ: Pearson.

Shonkoff, J., & Phillips, D. A. (2000). *From neurons to neighborhoods: The science of early childhood development.* Washington, DC: National Academies Press.

Shure, M. B. (n.d.). *ICPS: I can problem solve.* Retrieved from https://www.researchpress.com/sites/default/files/books/addContent/ICPS-research.pdf

Strain, P. S., & Joseph, G. E. (2006). *You've got to have friends* (Young Exceptional Children Monograph Series 8: Social Emotional Development). Longmont, CO: Sopris West.

Strain, P. S., & Schwartz, I. S. (2001). Applied behavior analysis and the development of meaningful social relations for young children with autism. *Focus on Autism and Developmental Disabilities, 16,* 120–128.

Thompson, R. A. (2010). *Social and emotional development: Foundations for learning in preschool.* Presentation to California Community College Early Childhood Educators, April 9, Long Beach, CA.

Thompson, R. A., & Goodman, M. (2009). Development of self, relationships, and socioemotional competence: Foundations for early school success. In O. A. Barbarin & B. H. Wasik (Eds.), *Handbook of child development and early education: Research to practice* (pp. 147–171). New York: Guilford Press.

Webster-Stratton, C. (1999). *How to promote children's social and emotional competence.* London: Paul Chapman Publishing.

Wiltz, N. W., & Klein, E. L. (2001). "What do you do in child care?" Children's perceptions of high and low quality classrooms. *Early Childhood Research Quarterly, 16*(2), 209–236.

Wong, C. S. (2013). A play and joint attention intervention for teachers of young children with autism: A randomized controlled pilot study. *Autism, 3,* 340–357.

Zelazo, P. D., & Lyons, K. E. (2012). *The potential benefits of mindfulness training in early childhood: A developmental social cognitive neuroscience perspective.* University of Minnesota. Retrieved March 3, 2015, from http://research.familylife.com.au/wp-content/uploads/2012/05/the-potential-benefits-of-mindfulness-training-in-early-childhood.pdf

Zero to Six Collaborative Group, National Child Traumatic Stress Network. (2010). *Early childhood trauma.* Los Angeles, CA, & Durham, NC: National Center for Child Traumatic Stress.

Chapter 15

American Academy of Pediatrics. (2013). The crucial role of recess: Policy statement. *Pediatrics, 131*(1), 183–188. doi:10.1542/peds.2012-2993

American Academy of Pediatrics, American Public Health Association, & National Resource Center for Health and Safety in Child Care and Early Education. (2011). *Caring for our children: National health and safety performance standards: Guidelines for early care and early education programs* (3rd ed.). Elk Grove Village, IL: American Academy of Pediatrics; Washington, DC: American Public Health Association.

Aronson, S. S. (2012). *Healthy young children: A manual for programs* (5th ed.). Washington, DC: National Association for the Education of Young Children.

Barros, R. M., Silver, E. J., & Stein, R. E. K. (2009). School recess and classroom behavior. *Pediatrics, 123*(2), 431–436.

Berk, L. E. (2008). *Infants and children: Prenatal through middle childhood* (6th ed.). Upper Saddle River, NJ: Pearson/Allyn & Bacon.

Bernath, P., & Masi, W. (2006). Smart school snacks: A comprehensive preschool nutrition education program. *Young Children, 61*(3), 20–24.

Blagojevic, B., & Thomes, K. (2014). Preschoolers take tech outdoors. *Teaching Young Children, 7*(2), 30–31.

Brown, W. H., Pheiffer, K. A., McKiver, K. L., Dowda, M., Addy, C. L., & Pate, R. R. (2009). Social and environmental factors associated with preschoolers' nonsedentary physical activity. *Child Development, 80*(1), 45–58.

Carlson, F. M. (2011). *Big body play: Why boisterous, vigorous, and very physical play is essential to children's development and learning.* Washington, DC: National Association for the Education of Young Children.

Carlson, F. M. (2015). Infants through third grade—big body play: Understanding and supporting it. In H. B. Bohart, K. Charner, & D. Koralek (Eds.), *Spotlight on young children: Exploring play* (pp. 107–117). Washington, DC: National Association for the Education of Young Children.

Centers for Disease Control and Prevention (CDC). (2012a). *Playground injuries: Fact sheet.* Retrieved April 5, 2015, from http://www.cdc.gov/HomeandRecreationalSafety/Playground-Injuries/playgroundinjuries-factsheet.htm

Centers for Disease Control and Prevention (CDC). (2012b). Trends in the prevalence of extreme obesity among U.S. preschool-aged children living in low-income families, 1998–2010. *Journal of the American Medical Association, 308*(24), 2563–2565.

Centers for Disease Control and Prevention (CDC). (2013). *Bicycle-related injuries.* Retrieved April 5, 2015, from http://www.cdc.gov/HomeandRecreationalSafety/Bicycle/

Centers for Disease Control and Prevention (CDC). (2014b). *Childhood obesity facts.* Retrieved April 5, 2015, from http://www.cdc.gov/healthyyouth/obesity/facts.htm

Centers for Disease Control and Prevention (CDC). (2014c). *Physical activity facts.* Retrieved April 5, 2015, from http://www.cdc.gov/healthyyouth/physicalactivity/facts.htm

Centers for Disease Control and Prevention (CDC). (2015). *How much physical activity do children need?* Retrieved March 15, 2015, from http://www.cdc.gov/physicalactivity/everyone/guidelines/children.html

Cohen, D., & Kotler, J. (2005). *Preschoolers' perception of healthy food.* Paper presented at the Biennial Meeting of the Society for Research in Child Development, Atlanta, GA.

Colker, L. (2005). *The cooking book: Fostering young children's learning and delight.* Washington, DC: National Association for the Education of Young Children.

Craig, G. J., & Baucum, D. (2002). *Human development* (9th ed.). Upper Saddle River, NJ: Prentice Hall.

Curtis, D. (2010). What's the risk of no risk? *Exchange, 32*(1), 52–60.

Faber Taylor, A., & Kuo, F. E. (2009). Children with attention deficits concentrate better after walk in the park. *Journal of Attention Disorders, 12*(5), 402–409.

Freeman, D. (2001). *Corduroy goes to the doctor.* New York: Penguin Putnam.

Gallahue, D. L. (1995). Transforming physical education curriculum. In S. Bredekamp & T. Rosegrant (Eds.), *Reaching potentials: Transforming early childhood curriculum* (Vol. 2, pp. 125–144). Washington, DC: National Association for the Education of Young Children.

Gallahue, D. L., Ozmun, J. C., & Goodway, J. D. (2012). *Understanding motor development: Infants, children, adolescent, adults* (7th ed.). Boston: McGraw-Hill.

Goodway, J. D., Ozmun, J. C., Derringer, S. T., & Lee. J. (2013). Promoting physical literacy and activity in young children. In D. R. Reutzel (Ed.),

Handbook of research-based practice in early education (pp. 293–308). New York: Guilford Press.

Goodway, J. D., Ozmun, J. C., & Gallahue, D. L. (2013). Motor development in young children. In O. N. Saracho & B. Spodek (Eds.), *Handbook of research on the education of young children* (3rd ed., pp. 80–101). New York: Routledge.

Goodway, J. D., Robinson, M. A., & Crowe, H. (2010). Developmental delays in fundamental motor skill development of ethnically diverse and disadvantaged preschoolers. *Research Quarterly for Exercise & Sport, 81*, 17–25.

Gramling, M. (2010). Zero risk, zero gain: Tom Sawyer, won't you please come home? *Exchange, 32*(1), 50–51.

Greenman, J. (2001). *What happened to my world? Helping children cope in turbulent times.* Cambridge, MA: Bright Horizons Family Solutions. Retrieved October 14, 2009, from http://www.brighthorizons.com/resources/pdf/talktochildren/docs/what_happened_to_my_world.pdf

Greenman, J. (2005a). *Caring spaces, learning places.* Redmond, WA: Exchange Press.

Greenman, J. (2005b). Places for childhood in the 21st century. *Beyond the Journal, Young Children on the Web.* Retrieved July 26, 2008, from http://journal.naeyc.org/btj/200505/01Greenman.pdf

Grissmer, D. W., Grimm, K. J., Aiyer, S. M., Murrah, W. M., & Steele, J. S. (2010). Fine motor skills and early comprehension of the world: Two new school readiness indicators. *Developmental Psychology, 46*(5), 1008–1017.

Haywood, K. M., & Gretchell, N. (2005). *Life span motor development* (4th ed.). Champaign, IL: Human Kinetics.

Head Start. (2015b). *Head Start emergency preparedness manual: 2015 edition.* Retrieved July 8, 2015, from http://eclkc.ohs.acf.hhs.gov/hslc/tta-system/health/docs/head-start-emergency-prep-manual-2015.pdf

Hendricks, C., & Smith, C. J. (1995). Transforming health curriculum. In S. Bredekamp & T. Rosegrant (Eds.), *Reaching potentials: Transforming early childhood curriculum and assessment* (Vol. 2, pp. 65–79). Washington, DC: National Association for the Education of Young Children.

Honig, A. S. (2015). *Experiencing nature with young children: Awakening delight, curiosity, and a sense of stewardship.* Washington, DC: NAEYC.

Ingwersen, J., Defeyter, M. A., Kennedy, D. O., Wesnes, K. A., & Scholey, A. B. (2007). A low glycaemic index breakfast cereal preferentially prevents children's cognitive performance from declining throughout the morning. *Appetite, 49*(1), 240–244. doi:10.1016/j.appet.2006.06.009

Jarrett, O. S., Maxwell, D. M., Dickerson, C., Hoge, P., Davies, G., & Yetley, A. (1998). The impact of recess on classroom behavior: Group effects and individual differences. *Journal of Educational Research, 92*(2), 121–126.

Kalich, K., Bauer, D., & McPartlin, D. (2014). Creating the nutritionally purposeful classroom. *Young Children, 69*(5), 8–13.

Kuo, F. E. (Ming). (2010). *Parks and other green environments: Essential components of a healthy human habitat.* Ashburn, VA: National Recreation and Park Association. Retrieved April 5, 2015, from http://www.nrpa.org/uploadedFiles/nrpa.org/Publications_and_Research/Research/Papers/MingKuo-Research-Paper.pdf

Levitt, P. (2008). Building brain architecture and chemistry: A primer for policymakers. In A. Tarlov & M. P. Debbink (Eds.), *Investing in early childhood development: Evidence to support a movement for educational change.* New York: Palgrave Macmillan.

Liu, J., Hwang, W., Dickerman, B., & Compher, C. (2013). Regular breakfast consumption is associated with increased IQ in kindergarten children.

Early Human Development, 89(4), 257–262. doi:10.1016/j.earlhumdev.2013.01.006

Louv, R. (2005). *Last child in the woods.* Chapel Hill, NC: Algonquin.

Mack, M. G., Hudson, S., & Thompson, D. (1997). A descriptive analysis of children's playground injuries in the United States 1990–2004. *Injury Prevention, 3*, 100–103.

Malone, K., & Tranter, P. (2003). School grounds as sites for learning: Making the most of environmental opportunities. *Environmental Education Research, 9*, 282–303.

McBride, B. A., & Dev, D. A. (2014). Preventing childhood obesity: Strategies to help preschoolers develop healthy eating habits. *Young Children, 69*(5), 36–42.

Meier, D. R., & Sisk-Hilton, S. (Eds.). (2013). *Nature education with young children: Integrating inquiry and practice.* New York: Routledge.

Milteer, R. M., Ginsburg, K. R., & Council on Communications and Media Committee on Psychological Aspects of Child and Family Health. (2012). The importance of play in promoting healthy child development and maintaining strong parent-child bonds: Focus on children in poverty. *Pediatrics, 129*(1), e204–e213. Retrieved from http://www.pediatrics.aappublications.org

National Association for Sports and Physical Education (NASPE). (2004). *Physical activity for children: A statement of guidelines for children ages 5–12* (2nd ed.) Reston, VA: Author.

Ogden, C. L., Carroll, M. D., Kit, B. K., & Flegal, K. M. (2014). Prevalence of childhood and adult obesity in the United States, 2011–2012. *Journal of the American Medical Association, 311*(8), 806–814. doi:10.1001/jama.2014.732

Pascoe, J. M., Shaikh, U., Forbis, S. G., & Etzel, R. A. (2007). Health and nutrition as a foundation for success in school. In R. C. Pianta, M. J. Cox, & K. L. Snow (Eds.), *School readiness and the transition to kindergarten in the era of accountability* (pp. 99–120). Baltimore: Brookes.

Pica, R. (2006). Physical fitness and the early childhood curriculum. *Young Children, 61*(3), 12–19.

Pica, R. (2014). *Preschoolers and kindergartners moving and learning: A physical education curriculum.* St. Paul, MN: Redleaf Press.

Rivkin, M. S. (2014). *The great outdoors: Advocating for natural spaces for young children* (Rev. ed.). Washington, DC: National Association for the Education of Young Children.

Robert Wood Johnson Foundation. (2010). *State of play: Gallup survey of principals on school recess.* Princeton, NJ: Author. Retrieved March 20, 2012, from http://www.playworks.org/sites/default/files/d6/StateOfPlayFeb2010.pdf

Ross, T. (2000). *Wash your hands.* San Diego, CA: Kane/Miller Book Publishers.

Sanders, S. W. (2002). *Active for life.* Washington, DC: National Association for the Education of Young Children.

Schickedanz, J. A., & Collins, M. F. (2013). *So much more than the ABCs: The early phases of reading and writing.* Washington, DC: National Association for the Education of Young Children.

Sesame Workshop, Nemours Health and Prevention Services, & KidHealth.org. (2007). *Healthy habits for life child care resource kit.* New York: Sesame Workshop. Retrieved March 20, 2012 from http://sesamestreet.org

SHAPE America. (2014). *National standards and grade-level outcomes for K–12 physical education.* Reston, VA: Author.

Shillady, A. (Ed.). (2011). *Spotlight on young children and nature.* Washington, DC: National Association for the Education of Young Children.

Smith, A. P. (2010). An investigation of the effects of breakfast cereals on alertness, cognitive function and other aspects of the reported well-being of children. *Nutritional Neuroscience, 13*(5), 230–236. doi:10.1179/147683010X12611460764642

Taylor, A. F., Kuo, F. E., & Sullivan, W. C. (2001). Coping with ADD: The surprising connection to green play settings. *Environments and Behavior, 33*(1), 54–77.

Tobin, K. J. (2013). Fast-food consumption and educational test scores in the USA. *Child: Care, Health & Development, 39*(1), 118–124. doi:10.1111/j.1365-2214.2011.01349.x

Torquati, J., with Gabriel, M. M., Jones-Branch, J., & Miller, J. L. (2011). Environmental education: A natural way to nurture children's development and learning. In A. Shillady (Ed.), *Spotlight on young children and nature* (pp. 8–14). Washington, DC: National Association for the Education of Young Children.

Verdick, E. (2006). *Germs are not for sharing.* Minneapolis, MN: Free Spirit Publishing.

Whitaker, R. C., Wright, J. A., Pepe, M. S., & Seidel, K. D. (1997). Predicting obesity in young adulthood from childhood and parental obesity. *The New England Journal of Medicine, 13*, 337.

Chapter 16

Bredekamp, S. (1997a). Developmentally appropriate practice: The early childhood teacher as decision maker. In S. Bredekamp & C. Copple (Eds.), *Developmentally appropriate practice in early childhood programs* (Rev. ed., pp. 33–52). Washington, DC: National Association for the Education of Young Children.

Child Welfare Information Gateway. (2007). *Recognizing child abuse and neglect: Signs and symptoms.* Retrieved March 20, 2012, from http://www.childwelfare.gov/can

Copple, C., Bredekamp, S., Koralek, D., & Charner, K. (Eds.). (2013a). *Developmentally appropriate practice: Focus on infants and toddlers.* Washington, DC: National Association for the Education of Young Children.

Copple, C., Bredekamp, S., Koralek, D., & Charner, K. (Eds.). (2013b). *Developmentally appropriate practice: Focus on preschoolers.* Washington, DC: National Association for the Education of Young Children.

Copple, C., Bredekamp, S., Koralek, D., & Charner, K. (Eds.). (2014a). *Developmentally appropriate practice: Focus on children in first, second, and third grades.* Washington, DC: National Association for the Education of Young Children.

Copple, C., Bredekamp, S., Koralek, D., & Charner, K. (Eds.). (2014b). *Developmentally appropriate practice: Focus on kindergartners.* Washington, DC: National Association for the Education of Young Children.

Epstein, A. S. (2014). *The intentional teacher: Choosing the best strategies for young children's learning* (Rev. ed.). Washington, DC: National Association for the Education of Young Children.

Feeney, S., & Freeman, N. K. (2012). *Ethics and the early childhood educator: Using the NAEYC code* (2nd ed.). Washington, DC: National Association for the Education of Young Children.

Goffin, S. G. (2013). *Early childhood education for a new era: Leading our profession.* New York: Teachers College Press.

Graue, M. E. (2006). This thing called kindergarten. In D. F. Gullo (Ed.), *K today: Teaching and learning in the kindergarten year* (pp. 3–10). Washington, DC: National Association for the Education of Young Children.

Institute of Medicine (IOM) & National Research Council (NRC). (2015). *Transforming the workforce for children birth through age 9: A unifying foundation.* Washington, DC: National Academies Press.

Kieff, J. (2009). *Informed advocacy in early childhood care and education: Making a difference for young children and families.* Upper Saddle River, NJ: Pearson Education.

Lutton, A. (Ed.). (2012). *Advancing the early childhood profession: NAEYC standards and guidelines for professional development.* Washington, DC: National Association for the Education of Young Children.

National Association for the Education of Young Children (NAEYC). (2007). *NAEYC Early childhood program standards and accreditation criteria: The mark of quality in early childhood education.* Washington, DC: Author.

National Association for the Education of Young Children (NAEYC). (2009). *Developmentally appropriate practice in early childhood programs serving children from birth through age 8: Position statement.* Washington, DC: Author.

National Association for the Education of Young Children (NAEYC). (2011a). *Code of ethical conduct and statement of commitment* (Reaffirmed and updated May 2011). Retrieved September 9, 2011, from http://www.naeyc.org/files/naeyc/file/positions/PSETH05.pdf

Name Index

Subject Index

Suggested Correlation of Sue Bredekamp's *Effective Practices in Early Childhood Education*, 3e with NAEYC® Standards for Early Childhood Professional Preparation Programs

STANDARD	KEY ELEMENTS OF THE STANDARD	CHAPTER AND TOPIC
		11: Culturally and Linguistically Responsive Assessment
		11: Language Lens: Involving Parents in Assessment of Dual Language Learners (F)
		11: Including All Children: Individually Appropriate Assessment Practices (F)
		11: Observation and Recording to Improve Learning
		11: Observing and Gathering Evidence
		11: Promoting Play: Play as an Assessment Context (F)
		11: Table 11.3, Learning to Observe
		11: Recording What Children Know and Can Do
		11: Becoming an Intentional Teacher: Using Assessment to Inform Teaching (F)
		11: Interpreting and Using Evidence to Improve Teaching and Learning
		11: What Works: Using Technology to Assess Learning (F)
		11: Standardized Testing of Young Children
		11: Assessment and the Common Core
		11: Kindergarten Entry Assessment
4: Using Developmentally Effective Approaches to Connect with Children and Families	4a. Understanding positive relationships and supportive interactions as the foundation of their work with children 4b. Knowing and understanding effective strategies and tools for early education 4c. Using a broad repertoire of developmentally appropriate teaching/learning approaches 4d. Reflecting on their own practice to promote positive outcomes for each child	1: Resolving Contradictions between Enduring Values and Current Trends
		1: Embracing Both/And Thinking
		3: Ch. 3, Understanding and Applying Developmentally Appropriate Practice
		3: What Is Developmentally Appropriate Practice?
		3: Promoting Play: Does Developmentally Appropriate Practice = Play? (F)
		3: Intentional Teaching
		3: Developmentally Appropriate Decision-Making
		3: Including All Children: Developmentally Appropriate Practice and Children with Disabilities (F)
		3: The Complex Role of the Teacher
		4: Becoming an Intentional Teacher: Teaching in the "Zone" (F)5: Figure 5.1 Model of Differentiated Instruction
		5: Responsive Education for All Learners
		5: Figure 5.2, Response to Intervention (RTI) in Early Childhood
		5: Individualized Education Programs
		5: Promoting Play: Supporting Pretend Play for Children with Disabilities (F)
		5: Effective Practices for Children with Diverse Abilities
		5: Becoming an Intentional Teacher: Individualizing Group Time (F)
		6: Understanding Your Own Cultural Perspective
		6: Teaching in a Culturally and Linguistically Diverse World
		6: Including All Children: Cultural Diversity and Diverse Ability (F)
		6: Promoting Play: African American Children and Play (F)
		6: Effective Practices for Diverse Learners
		6: What Works: Making Education Culturally Compatible (F)
		6: Linguistically Responsive Teaching
		6: Language Lens: Using Technology to Teach Dual Language Learners (F)
		6: Culturally Responsive Teaching
		6: Developmentally Appropriate and Culturally Responsive Practices
		6: Becoming an Intentional Teacher: Responding to Cultural Differences (F)
		8: Ch. 8, Creating a Caring Community of Learners: Guiding Young Children
		8: A Caring Community of Learners: The Teaching Pyramid Model
		8: Figure 8.1, Teaching Pyramid Model for Promoting Children's Social and Emotional Competence
		8: Positive Relationships with Children
		8: Promoting Play: All Can Play (F)
		8: Table 8.1, What a Caring Community Looks Like
		8: Personal, Family, and Cultural Views of Children's Behavior
		8: Examine Your Own Attitudes toward Challenging Behavior
		8: High-Quality Supportive Environments
		8: Teaching Social-Emotional Competence and Guiding Behavior
		8: What Works: Teaching Emotional Literacy (F)
		8: Table 8.2, Strategies for Teaching Conflict Resolution
		8: Intensive Individualized Interventions
		9: Ch. 9, Teaching to Enhance Learning and Development
		9: A Repertoire of Effective Teaching Strategies
		9: Table 9.1, Effective Teaching Strategies
		9: The Power of Scaffolding: An Integrated Approach
		9: Figure 9.1, Scaffolding in Action
		9: Including All Children: Project DATA: A High-Quality Comprehensive Early Intervention Program for Children with Autism Spectrum Disorders (F)
		9: Connecting Teaching Strategies and Learning Goals
		9: What Works: Reciprocal Teaching (F)
		9: Grouping as an Instructional Approach
		9: Becoming an Intentional Teacher: Working in Small Groups (F)
		9: Language Lens: Teachable Moments with Dual Language Learners (F)
		9: Play as a Context for Learning
		9: Teachers' Involvement during Play
		9: Figure 9.3, Continuum of Teacher Roles in Play
		9: Teaching with Digital Media
		9: Promoting Play: Teaching and Learning through Transmedia Play (F)
		9: Assistive Technology for Children with Diverse Abilities
		12: Scaffolding Children's Language Development
		12: Table 12.1, Improving Teacher-Child Conversations
		12: What Works: Dialogic Reading (F)
		12: Culture Lens: Understanding and Responding to Code Switching (F)
		12: Language Lens: Teaching Dual Language Learners (F)
		12: Developmental Continuum: Early Literacy (F)
		12: Literacy-Rich Environments
		12: Becoming an Intentional Teacher: Teaching the Alphabet and Phonological Awareness (F)
		12: Promoting Play: How Play Supports Language and Literacy Development
		12: Literacy in the Primary Grades
		12: Developmental Continuum: Literacy in Kindergarten and Primary Grades (F)
		12: Digital Literacy
		12: Impact of the Common Core State Standards
		12: Scaffold Artistic Development and Learning
		13: Effective Mathematics Teaching
		13: Figure 13.2, Examples of High- and Low-Quality Mathematics Teaching
		13: The Role of Play in Teaching and Learning Mathematics
		13: Effective Science Teaching
		13: Table 13.2, Effective Science Teaching Strategies
		13: Including All Children: Science Exploration (F)
		13: What Works: Teaching STEM to Dual Language Learners (F)
		13: Teaching about and with Technology
		13: Promoting Play: Digital Play and Traditional Play (F)
		14: Including All Children: Fostering Friendships in the Inclusive Classroom (F)